MICROSOFT® PROFESSIONAL

Microsoft® Office 97 Resource Kit

Microsoft Press

PUBLISHED BY
Microsoft Press
A Division of Microsoft Corporation
One Microsoft Way
Redmond, Washington 98052-6399

Copyright © 1997 by Microsoft Corporation

Images© 1996 PhotoDisc, Inc.

All rights reserved. No part of the contents of this book may be reproduced or transmitted in any form or by any means without the written permission of the publisher.

Library of Congress Cataloging-in-Publication Data pending.

ISBN 1-57231-329-3

Printed and bound in the United States of America.

1 2 3 4 5 6 7 8 9   QMQM   2 1 0 9 8 7

Distributed to the book trade in Canada by Macmillan of Canada, a division of Canada Publishing Corporation.

A CIP catalogue record for this book is available from the British Library.

Microsoft Press books are available through booksellers and distributors worldwide. For further information about international editions, contact your local Microsoft Corporation office. Or contact Microsoft Press International directly at fax (206) 936-7329.

Apple, Macintosh, QuickTime, and TrueType are registered trademarks and Ballon Help and QuickDraw are trademarks of Apple Computer, Inc. MathType is a trademark of Design Science, Inc. Kodak is a registered trademark of Eastman Kodak Company. Bookshelf, DriveSpace, FoxPro, Microsoft, Microsoft Press, MS-DOS, Multiplan, PivotTable, PowerPoint, TipWizard, Visual Basic, Visual C++, Win32, Win32s, Windows, Windows NT, and Wingdings are registered trademarks and ActiveMovie, ActiveX, FrontPage, IntelliMouse, IntelliSense, JScript, Microsoft At Work, MSN, Office logo, Outlook, QuickShelf, Rushmore, Visual FoxPro, and Visual SourceSafe are trademarks of Microsoft Corporation. Crystal Reports is a trademark of Seagate Software, Inc. Java is a trademark of Sun Microsystems, Inc. Other product and company names mentioned herein may be the trademarks of their respective owners.

Acquisitions Editor: Casey D. Doyle
Project Editor: Maureen Williams Zimmerman

This book and its online version on the World Wide Web were produced by members of the Office Product Unit of Microsoft Corporation.

Project Lead
Carl Chatfield

Tools and Utilities Program Manager
Ann McCurdy

Writers
Carl Chatfield, Gary Ericson, Roxanne Kenison, Mark Roberts

Editing Lead
Jennifer Morison Hendrix

Editors
Donna Johnston, Roxanne Kenison

Copy Editors
Ramona Gault, Donna Johnston

Designers
Kristin Lynn Bergsma, Lesley Jacobs, Daniela Lammers

Indexer
Jeffrey Gilbert

Production
Kristin Lynn Bergsma, Lori Fields, Bart McKeirnan, Erik Olson

Additional Contributors
Amy Blair, Pamela Bradbury, Cheryl Channing, Bryna Hebert, Mark Huentelman, Linda Johnson, Bonnie Speer McGrath, Rob Sandelin, Mary Sobczyk

Vinod Anantharaman, Andy Arluk, Brian Bakke, Chris Caile, Brian Capson, Bart Chellis, Robert Davidson, Scott Gode, Sunni Goeller, David Gonzalez, David Goodhand, Bill Hunter, Carol Jacobson, Heikki Kanerva, Jeff Larsson, Dave LeFevre, Eric LeVine, Marlene Matt, Jennifer Mead, Dean O'Neill, Gurpreet Pall, Ronna Pinkerton, David Switzer, Scott Thurlow, Laura Tillet, Mandira Virmani

Contents at a Glance

Part 1 Welcome to Microsoft Office 97 1
Chapter 1 How to Use the Microsoft Office 97 Resource Kit 3
Chapter 2 What's New in Microsoft Office 97 9

Part 2 Deploying Microsoft Office 47
Chapter 3 Deployment Guide for Microsoft Office 49
Chapter 4 Installing Microsoft Office 71
Chapter 5 System Requirements for Microsoft Office 99
Chapter 6 Customizing Client Installations 105
Chapter 7 Customizing and Optimizing Microsoft Office 137
Chapter 8 Training and Support Programs for Microsoft Office 185
Chapter 9 Troubleshooting Installation 201

Part 3 Upgrading to Microsoft Office 223
Chapter 10 Upgrading from Previous Versions of Microsoft Office 225
Chapter 11 Upgrading from Previous Versions of Microsoft Access 253
Chapter 12 Upgrading from Previous Versions of Microsoft Excel 301
Chapter 13 Upgrading to Microsoft Outlook 333
Chapter 14 Upgrading from Previous Versions of Microsoft PowerPoint 361
Chapter 15 Upgrading from Previous Versions of Microsoft Word 399

Part 4 Switching from Other Applications 437
Chapter 16 Switching to Microsoft Office 439
Chapter 17 Switching to Microsoft Access 451
Chapter 18 Switching to Microsoft Excel 491
Chapter 19 Switching to Microsoft Outlook 545
Chapter 20 Switching to Microsoft PowerPoint 561
Chapter 21 Switching to Microsoft Word 573

Contents at a Glance

Part 5 Using Microsoft Office Throughout Your Organization 619

Chapter 22 Supporting Multiple Versions of Microsoft Office 621
Chapter 23 Tracking Collaboration with Document Properties 637
Chapter 24 Integrating Microsoft Office with Your Intranet 645
Chapter 25 Web Support in Microsoft Office Applications 665
Chapter 26 Finding Microsoft Office Documents on the Network 717
Chapter 27 Sharing Information with Microsoft Office Applications 745
Chapter 28 Working with Messaging Systems and Connectivity Software 793
Chapter 29 Workgroup Features in Microsoft Access 803
Chapter 30 Workgroup Features in Microsoft Excel 855
Chapter 31 Workgroup Features in Microsoft Outlook 865
Chapter 32 Workgroup Features in Microsoft PowerPoint 877
Chapter 33 Workgroup Features in Microsoft Word 891

Part 6 Microsoft Office Architecture 903

Chapter 34 Microsoft Office Architecture 905
Chapter 35 Microsoft Access Architecture 915
Chapter 36 Microsoft Excel Architecture 939
Chapter 37 Microsoft Outlook Architecture 959
Chapter 38 Microsoft PowerPoint Architecture 967
Chapter 39 Microsoft Word Architecture 991

Appendixes 1009

Appendix A Microsoft Office 97 Resource Kit Tools and Utilities 1011
Appendix B Setup Command-Line Options and File Formats 1045
Appendix C Registry Keys and Values 1053
Appendix D List of Installed Components 1081
Appendix E Other Support Resources 1091

Contents

Part 1 Welcome to Microsoft Office 97 1

Chapter 1 How to Use the Microsoft Office 97 Resource Kit 3
Welcome 3
Updated Information on the World Wide Web 4
Contents of the Office Resource Kit 5
   Using the Printed or Online Book 5
   Using the Tools and Utilities CD 6
Conventions Used in This Book 7
Tell Us What You Think 7

Chapter 2 What's New in Microsoft Office 97 9
Improved Software Administration 9
   Office 97 Setup 9
   System Policy Templates 10
   Network Installation Wizard 10
   Microsoft Systems Management Server 11
   Office 97 Upgrade Wizard 11
   File Format Compatibility 11
Intelligent Applications 12
   Intelligent Applications in Office 97 12
   Intelligent Applications in Microsoft Access 97 14
   Intelligent Applications in Microsoft Excel 97 16
   Intelligent Applications in Microsoft Outlook 97 20
   Intelligent Applications in PowerPoint 97 26
   Intelligent Applications in Word 97 28
Intranet and Workgroup Solutions 29
   Intranet and Workgroup Solutions in Office 97 29
   Intranet and Workgroup Solutions in Microsoft Access 97 33
   Intranet and Workgroup Solutions in Microsoft Excel 97 36
   Intranet and Workgroup Solutions in Microsoft Outlook 97 39
   Intranet and Workgroup Solutions in PowerPoint 97 41
   Intranet Solutions in Word 97 42

Part 2 Deploying Microsoft Office 47

Chapter 3 Deployment Guide for Microsoft Office 49

Overview 50
   Deploying Microsoft Windows 50
   Deploying Office 97 50
Evaluating and Installing Windows 51
   Choosing Windows Features 51
   Installing Windows 52
Evaluating Office 97 53
Assembling the Planning Team and Tools 54
Specifying the Test Client Configuration 56
Conducting the Lab Test 59
Planning the Pilot Rollout 62
Conducting the Pilot Rollout 65
Finalizing the Rollout Plan 66
Rolling Out Office 68
Maintaining and Supporting Office 69

Chapter 4 Installing Microsoft Office 71

Choosing Configuration and Installation Options 71
   Decide Where to Install Office Files 72
   Select the Type of Installation 74
   Select the Installation Media 74
   Select the Installation Method 75
   Determine Application-Specific Requirements 75
Rolling Out Office 97 77
   Installing Office from the Network 77
   Installing Office from the Office CD 86
   Installing Office from Floppy Disks 88
Licensing and Distributing Office in Your Organization 90
   Product Identification 90
   Compliance Checking 91
   Licensing 94
Installing New Releases of Office 94
   Updating Office with the Same Configuration 94
   Updating Office with a New Configuration 96

Chapter 5 System Requirements for Microsoft Office 99
Microsoft Office Products for Windows 99
   Microsoft Office 97, Standard Edition 99
   Microsoft Office 97, Professional Edition 101
   Microsoft Office 97, Professional Edition with Bookshelf Basics 102
   Microsoft Office 97, Professional Edition with Bookshelf Basics and Microsoft IntelliMouse 103
Microsoft Office Products for the Macintosh 104

Chapter 6 Customizing Client Installations 105
Understanding the Office Setup Program 105
   Customizing a Network Installation 106
   Customizing Installations from Physical Media 107
Modifying Client Setup with the Network Installation Wizard 108
   Start the Network Installation Wizard 109
   Specify the STF and INF Files 110
   Select a Primary Location for the Office Application Files 110
   Select a Default Folder for Office Documents 112
   Select a Location for Shared Office Applications 113
   Specify an Installation Log 115
   Choose the Type of Installation 116
   Configure the Installation Environment 121
   Select Items for Program Manager 123
   Select Items for the Start Menu 124
   Add Additional Files to the Office Installation 125
   Add Registry Entries 127
   Update the INF File 129
   Save the Modified STF File 130
Running Client Setup with the Modified STF File 130
   Installing Office over the Network 131
   Using Microsoft Systems Management Server to Install Office 132

Chapter 7 Customizing and Optimizing Microsoft Office 137
Using Windows System Policies to Customize Office 137
   Windows System Policies 138
   The System Policy Editor 138
   Client Computer Requirements for System Policies 144

Customizing Office Connections to the World Wide Web   146
   Disabling Commands on the Microsoft on the Web Submenu   148
   Adding Your Own Commands to the Microsoft on the Web Submenu   149
Optimizing Individual Office Applications   152
   Optimizing Microsoft Access   152
   Optimizing Microsoft Excel   179
   Optimizing Microsoft PowerPoint   180
   Optimizing Microsoft Word   184

Chapter 8   Training and Support Programs for Microsoft Office   185

Overview   186
   Budgeting for Training and Support   186
   Designing a Migration Training Program   186
Implementing Office Training Tasks   187
   Assemble the Training and Support Teams   188
   Prepare the Training and Support Teams   189
   Develop the Training Plan   190
   Prepare the Documentation   195
   Schedule the Pilot Training   196
   Promote Office 97 and the Training Plan   196
   Test the Training Plan During the Pilot Rollout   197
   Measure Your Success   198
   Implement the Training Plan During the Office 97 Rollout   198

Chapter 9   Troubleshooting Installation   201

Removing Previous Versions of Office   201
   Using the Office 97 Upgrade Wizard   202
   Running the Clean-up Process   207
   Customizing the Office 97 Upgrade Wizard   208
Solving Common Setup Problems   219
   Problems Related to Running Setup   219
   Problems Caused by Previously Installed Files   220

Part 3   Upgrading to Microsoft Office   223

Chapter 10   Upgrading from Previous Versions of Microsoft Office   225

Overview   225
Upgrading from Microsoft Office 95 for Windows   226
   Upgrading Microsoft Access 95   226
   Upgrading Microsoft Excel 95   227

Upgrading PowerPoint 95   227
Upgrading Word 95   227
Upgrading Your Office 95 Electronic Mail Client   228
Upgrading Your Office 95 Scheduling Application   228
Upgrading Office 95 Binders   229
Upgrading from Microsoft Office 4.x   230
Upgrading Microsoft Access 2.0   231
Upgrading Microsoft Excel 5.0   231
Upgrading PowerPoint 4.0   231
Upgrading Word 6.0   232
Upgrading Your Office 4.x Electronic Mail Client   232
Upgrading Microsoft Office Manager for Windows   232
Upgrading from Microsoft Office 3.x for Windows   235
Upgrading Microsoft Access 1.x   235
Upgrading Microsoft Excel 4.0   236
Upgrading PowerPoint 3.0   236
Upgrading Word 2.0   236
Porting Your 16-bit Office-Based Solutions to 32-bit Office   236
How This Section Is Organized   238
Which API Should Your Solution Code Call?   238
Calling the Win32 API   239
Writing a Single Code Base for 16-bit and 32-bit Office Applications   244
Determining Whether a 32-bit Application Is Running   246
Recompiling DLLs   249
Thunking   249
Advanced Programming Topics   250

Chapter 11   Upgrading from Previous Versions of Microsoft Access   253

Overview   254
Converting Databases   254
Converting Unbound Object Frame Controls to Image Controls   256
Converting a Database Secured with a Database Password   256
Converting a Database Secured with User-level Security   256
Converting a Replicated Database   259
Working with Microsoft Access 1.x and 2.0 Databases with Attached ODBC Tables   261

Upgrading from Microsoft Access 95   262
   Menu Changes   263
   File Format Changes   268
   Template Changes   268
   Macro Changes   269
   Visual Basic Code Changes   270
   New Toolbars, Menus, and Shortcut Menus   270
Upgrading from Microsoft Access 2.0   271
   Menu Changes   271
   File Format Changes   278
   Template Changes   279
   Macro Changes   279
   Access Basic Code Changes   281
   New Toolbars, Menu Bars, and Shortcut Menus   294
Upgrading from Microsoft Access 1.x   294
   Access Basic Code Changes   295
Sharing Databases with Microsoft Access 1.x, 2.0, or 95   297
   Enabling a Database   297
   Creating a Front-end Database Linked to Table Data in a Previous Version Back-end Database   298

Chapter 12   Upgrading from Previous Versions of Microsoft Excel   301

Overview   301
Upgrading from Microsoft Excel 95   302
   Menu Changes   303
   File Format Changes   306
   Template Changes   306
Upgrading from Microsoft Excel 5.0   307
   Menu Changes   307
   File Format Changes   312
   Template Changes   312
   Chart Format Changes   313
   Macro Changes   313
Sharing Workbooks with Microsoft Excel 5.0 or 95   314
   Saving Workbooks in Microsoft Excel 97 and 5.0/95 Format   314
   Saving Workbooks in Microsoft Excel 5.0 or 95 Format   317

Upgrading from Microsoft Excel 4.0   320
   Menu Changes   321
   Upgrading XLM Macros to Visual Basic for Applications   327
Sharing Workbooks with Microsoft Excel 4.0   328

Chapter 13 Upgrading to Microsoft Outlook   333

Overview   334
   Items   335
   Folders   335
   Views   336
Upgrading from Microsoft Exchange Client   336
   Upgrading Microsoft Exchange Client Folders and Views   337
   Upgrading Microsoft Exchange Client Forms   338
   Upgrading Microsoft Exchange Client Extensions   338
Sharing Information with Microsoft Exchange Client   339
   Exchanging Forms   339
   Sharing Public Folders   342
Upgrading from Microsoft Mail 3.x for Windows   343
   Importing Microsoft Mail Files   345
   Using Microsoft Mail Custom Commands, Menus, and Messages   347
   Upgrading Remote Users and Offices   349
   Migrating to Microsoft Exchange Server   350
Sharing Information with Microsoft Mail 3.x   350
   Exchanging Messages   351
   Sharing Public Folders   352
Upgrading from Microsoft Schedule+ 95   352
   Importing the Schedule+ 95 Data File   353
Sharing Information with Microsoft Schedule+ 95   355
   Managing Group Scheduling   355
   Sharing Other Information   355
   Using Schedule+ 95 as the Primary Calendar   356
Upgrading from Microsoft Schedule+ 1.0   357
   Importing the Schedule+ 1.0 Data File   357
Sharing Information with Microsoft Schedule+ 1.0   359
   Managing Group Scheduling   360

Chapter 14 Upgrading from Previous Versions of Microsoft PowerPoint 361

Overview 361
Upgrading from PowerPoint 95 362
   Menu Changes 363
   File Format Changes 368
   Template Changes 368
Sharing Presentations with PowerPoint 95 369
   Saving Presentations in PowerPoint 95 & 97 Format 369
   Saving Presentations in PowerPoint 95 Format 370
Upgrading from PowerPoint 4.0 374
   Menu Changes 374
   File Format Changes 381
   Template Changes 381
Sharing Presentations with PowerPoint 4.0 382
   Saving PowerPoint 97 Presentations in PowerPoint 4.0 Format 382
Upgrading from PowerPoint 3.0 386
   Menu Changes 386
   File Format Changes 395
   Template Changes 395
Sharing Presentations with PowerPoint 3.0 396

Chapter 15 Upgrading from Previous Versions of Microsoft Word 399

Overview 399
Upgrading from Word 6.0 or 95 400
   Menu Changes 401
   Upgrading WordBasic Macros to Visual Basic 406
Sharing Documents with Word 6.0 or 95 407
   Saving Word 97 Documents in Word 6.0/95 Format 408
   Opening Word 97 Documents in Word 6.0 or 95 411
Upgrading from Word 2.0 414
   Menu Changes 415
Sharing Documents with Word 2.0 421
   Saving Word 97 Documents in Word 2.0 Format 421
Upgrading from Word 5.x or 6.0 for MS-DOS 426
   Word 97 Terms and Features for Word for MS-DOS Users 426
   Opening Word 5.x and 6.0 for MS-DOS Documents in Word 97 427

Using Word for MS-DOS Styles in Word 97   428
Converting Graphics to Word 97   428
Sharing Documents with Word 5.x or 6.0 for MS-DOS   429
Saving Word 97 Documents in Word 5.x or 6.0 for MS-DOS Format   429
Using Word 97 Styles in Word 5.x or 6.0 for MS-DOS   432
Upgrading from Word 5.x for the Macintosh   432
Opening Word 5.x for the Macintosh Documents in Word 97   433
Sharing Documents with Word 5.x for the Macintosh   433

Part 4   Switching from Other Applications   437

Chapter 16   Switching to Microsoft Office   439

Overview   439
Switching Your Organization to Office   441
Plan Your Migration to Office   441
Test the New Applications   444
Train New Users   444
Convert Existing Files to Office Formats   446
Distribute Office Throughout Your Organization   447
Take Advantage of the New Office Features   449

Chapter 17   Switching to Microsoft Access   451

Using Database Features in Microsoft Access 97   452
Single File Architecture   452
Database Objects   452
More About Microsoft Access   458
Converting Your Data to Microsoft Access   460
Using External Data in Microsoft Access   460
Developing Your Application   465
Setting Keyboard Options   467
Switching from dBASE   468
Microsoft Access 97 Terms for dBASE Users   469
Using dBASE Files in Microsoft Access   469
Creating Queries   472
Creating Forms   473
Creating Reports   475
Converting Catalogs   475

Exporting a Table to a dBASE File   475
Microsoft Access Registry Settings for dBASE   476
Switching from FoxPro   476
Using FoxPro Files in Microsoft Access   477
Using FoxPro 2.5 Files in Microsoft Access   479
Exporting a Table to a FoxPro File   479
Microsoft Access Registry Settings for FoxPro   480
Switching from Paradox   480
Microsoft Access 97 Terms for dBASE Users   481
Using Paradox Tables in Microsoft Access   481
Using Paradox Databases in Microsoft Access   483
Exporting a Table to a Paradox File   486
Microsoft Access Registry Settings for Paradox   487
Running Multiple Data Access Applications   487
Using Built-in Drivers and ODBC Drivers   488
Built-in Drivers   489
ODBC Drivers   489

Chapter 18   Switching to Microsoft Excel   491

Converting File Formats in Microsoft Excel   492
Opening Other File Formats in Microsoft Excel   492
Converting Documents from Other File Formats   492
Importing Text Files   494
Saving Microsoft Excel Workbooks in Other File Formats   494
Switching from Lotus 1-2-3   496
Using Microsoft Excel Tools for Lotus 1-2-3 Users   497
Converting Lotus 1-2-3 Worksheets to Microsoft Excel   506
Sharing Documents with Lotus 1-2-3   529
Using Lotus 1-2-3 Help   533
Switching from Quattro Pro for MS-DOS   535
Converting Quattro Pro for MS-DOS Worksheets to Microsoft Excel   535
Sharing Documents with Quattro Pro for MS-DOS   536
Running Quattro Pro for MS-DOS Macros in Microsoft Excel   536
Switching from Quattro Pro for Windows   536
Switching from Multiplan   538
Converting Multiplan Files to Microsoft Excel   538
Sharing Documents with Multiplan   538
Using Multiplan Command Equivalents   539

Switching from Microsoft Works   542
    Converting Microsoft Works Files to Microsoft Excel   542
    Sharing Documents with Microsoft Works   543

Chapter 19   Switching to Microsoft Outlook   545

Overview   546
Importing and Exporting File Types   546
Using E-mail Information Services Provided with Outlook   547
Switching from Lotus cc:Mail   548
    Using cc:Mail Bulletin Boards with Outlook   549
    Importing cc:Mail Folders into Outlook   549
    Using cc:Mail Private Lists and Address Book with Outlook   550
Switching from Symantec ACT! 2.0   550
    Mapping Fields from ACT! 2.0 to Outlook   551
Switching from NetManage ECCO Pro 3.0, 3.01, or 3.02   552
    Mapping Fields from ECCO Pro to Outlook   553
Switching from Starfish Sidekick Deluxe 95   555
    Mapping Fields from Sidekick to Outlook   555
Switching from Lotus Organizer 1.0, 1.1, or 2.1   557
    Mapping Fields from Lotus Organizer to Outlook   558
Switching from Other Client/Server Messaging Systems   560

Chapter 20   Switching to Microsoft PowerPoint   561

Converting File Formats in PowerPoint 97   562
    Using Converters and Graphics Filters   562
    Converting Presentations from Other File Formats   566
    Saving PowerPoint Presentations in Other File Formats   567
    Opening and Saving Text Files   568
    Opening and Saving Graphics Files   569
Switching from Harvard Graphics   570
Switching from Lotus Freelance   571

Chapter 21   Switching to Microsoft Word   573

Converting File Formats in Word 97   574
    Using Text Converters and Graphics Filters   574
    Converting Documents from Other File Formats   580
    Specifying Fonts for Converted Documents   584
    Opening and Saving Plain-Text Files   587
    Saving Word Documents in Other File Formats   588

Switching from WordPerfect   589
   Word 97 Concepts for WordPerfect Users   589
   Word 97 Tools for WordPerfect Users   593
   Converting WordPerfect Documents to Word 97   594
   Converting Documents from WordPerfect 6.*x*   596
   Sharing Documents with WordPerfect 6.*x*   599
   Converting Documents from WordPerfect 5.*x*   599
   Sharing Documents with WordPerfect 5.*x*   601
   Using WordPerfect Help   604
Switching from Microsoft Works 3.0 or 4.0 for Windows   608
   Sharing Documents with Works for Windows   609
Switching from Text with Layout   612
   Sharing Documents with Applications That Read Text with Layout Format   612
Switching from Lotus Ami Pro   616
Switching from DisplayWrite   616
Switching from Microsoft Windows Write 3.0 or 3.1   616
Switching from RFT-DCA Format Files   616
Switching from MultiMate   616
Switching from WordStar   617

Part 5 Using Microsoft Office Throughout Your Organization 619

Chapter 22 Supporting Multiple Versions of Microsoft Office   621
Specifying the Default Format in Which to Save Office Documents   621
Running Multiple Versions of Microsoft Access   623
   Sharing Databases Across Operating Systems and Versions   623
   Running Multiple Versions of Microsoft Access on a Single Computer   624
Running Multiple Versions of Microsoft Excel   626
   Sharing Workbooks Across Operating Systems and Versions   626
   Running Multiple Versions of Microsoft Excel on a Single Computer   627
Running Multiple Versions of Electronic Mail and Scheduling Applications   628
   Sharing Information with Microsoft Exchange Client   629
   Sharing Information with Microsoft Mail 3.x for Windows   629
   Sharing Information with Microsoft Schedule+ 95   629
   Sharing Information with Microsoft Schedule+ 1.0   630

Running Multiple Versions of PowerPoint   630
   Sharing Presentations Across Operating Systems and Versions   631
   Running Multiple Versions of PowerPoint on a Single Computer   633
Running Multiple Versions of Microsoft Word   634
   Sharing Documents Across Operating Systems and Versions   635
   Running Multiple Versions of Word on a Single Computer   635

Chapter 23   Tracking Collaboration with Document Properties   637

Overview   637
Viewing Document Properties   638
Entering Document Properties   638
Creating Custom Document Properties   639
Using Document Properties in Office 97   641

Chapter 24   Integrating Microsoft Office with Your Intranet   645

Using Office with an Intranet   645
   Intranets and the Internet   646
   Security Issues with Intranets   646
   Tools for Intranet Creation and Administration   646
   Netscape Web Server Support   648
Combining Web and Office Tools on Intranets   649
   Integrating Office Documents with Web Browsers   650
   Creating Hyperlinks in Office Documents   651
   Creating Content for Intranets   653
   Analyzing Data on an Intranet   653
   Collaborating on Documents in a Workgroup   654
   Sharing Information Throughout Your Organization   656
   Managing Your Communications with Microsoft Outlook   656
   Searching for Office Documents on an Intranet   657
   Using Office Viewers   657
Opening and Saving Documents on the Internet   658
Publishing to the Web or an Intranet   659
Setting Up a Personal Web Server   660
   Installation Requirements   661
   Publication Requirements   661
   Installing the Personal Web Server   662
   Installing Peer Web Services   663
   More Information About the Personal Web Server or Peer Web Services   663

Chapter 25 Web Support in Microsoft Office Applications 665

Web Support in Microsoft Access 97 665
   Using Hyperlinks in Microsoft Access Applications 669
   Making Microsoft Access Data Available on the Internet 676
   Importing, Linking, and Exporting Data to the Internet 688
   Displaying Web Pages and Other Documents in Microsoft Access Forms 691

Web Support in Microsoft Excel 97 693
   Converting Microsoft Excel Data and Charts to HTML 693
   Using Microsoft Excel Web Queries 695
   Collecting Database Input with Web Forms 696

Web Support in Microsoft Outlook 97 704
   Working with Internet Mail 704
   Using Hyperlinks in Messages 705
   Using Outlook as a Web Browser 705

Web Support in Microsoft PowerPoint 97 707
   Using Action Settings as Hyperlinks 707
   Creating Web Documents 710
   Saving Presentations as HTML Documents 710
   Using Microsoft PowerPoint Animation Player for ActiveX 711
   Using PowerPoint Central 712

Web Support in Microsoft Word 97 713
   Using the Web Page Wizard 714
   Using the Blank Web Page Template 714
   Saving Existing Documents in HTML 714

Chapter 26 Finding Microsoft Office Documents on the Network 717

Overview 717
   Differences Between Find Fast and Web Find Fast 718
   What Types of Documents Can Be Indexed 724
   Security Issues 727
   The Find Fast Indexer Log 728
   What Happens to Office 95 Indexes in Office 97 728

Supporting Find Fast 729
   Installing Find Fast 729
   Creating and Maintaining Indexes with Find Fast 729
   Finding Documents with Find Fast 732

Supporting Web Find Fast   733
  Installing Web Find Fast   735
  Creating and Maintaining Indexes with Web Find Fast   736
  Finding Documents with Web Find Fast   742

Chapter 27   Sharing Information with Microsoft Office Applications   745
Overview   745
Sharing Information with Microsoft Access 97   746
  Using External Data with Microsoft Access   746
  Using Microsoft Access with ODBC and Client/Server Operations   759
Sharing Information with Microsoft Excel 97   768
  Sharing Data Between Microsoft Excel and SQL Server   768
  Using Microsoft Excel and Microsoft Query   769
  Exporting Microsoft Excel Data to Lotus Notes   769
Sharing Information with Outlook 97   769
  Recording Office Items in the Outlook Journal   770
  Creating Tasks from Office Applications   770
  Importing and Exporting Items   770
  Using Outlook with PowerPoint   777
Sharing Information with PowerPoint 97   781
  Importing Outlines from Word   781
  Exporting Presentations to Word   783
Sharing Information with Word 97   786
  Importing Worksheets from Microsoft Excel   787
  Importing Worksheets from Lotus 1-2-3   788
  Exporting Word Outlines to PowerPoint   790
  Exporting Word Documents to Lotus Notes   790
Using Microsoft Bookshelf in a Workgroup   790
  Bookshelf Integration with Microsoft Excel   791
  Bookshelf Integration with PowerPoint and Word   791
  Office Integration with Bookshelf   791
Using Microsoft Camcorder in a Workgroup   792

Chapter 28   Working with Messaging Systems and Connectivity Software   793
Interoperability with Electronic Mail   793
  Integrating Electronic Mail with Office   794
  Supporting Mailing, Routing, and Posting   798

Interoperability with Microsoft Exchange Server   798
   Posting Documents to Public Folders   799
   Creating Custom Properties and Views in Public Folders   799
Interoperability with Microsoft Mail 3.*x*   799
Interoperability with Lotus Notes Mail and cc:Mail   800
Interoperability with Lotus Notes/FX   800
Interoperability with Other Electronic Mail Systems   801

Chapter 29   Workgroup Features in Microsoft Access   803

Security Features in Microsoft Access   803
   Restricting User Access with Startup Options   804
   Protecting File Open with a Database Password   805
   Protecting Source Code with an MDE File   806
   Encrypting a Database   810
   Setting User-Level Security   810
Multiuser Applications and Locking   825
   Controlling How a Database Opens   825
   Setting the Refresh Interval   825
   Using Locking Options   826
   Choosing a Locking Strategy   828
   Using the Locking Information File   830
   Forcing Microsoft Access to Lock Individual Records   830
   Splitting a Database into a Front-end/Back-end Application   832
   Troubleshooting Other Multiuser Issues   833
Database Replication   834
   Implementing Database Replication   837
   Replicating a Database   839
   Tracking Changes When a Database Is Replicated   840
   Making Additional Replicas   843
   Replicating Part of a Database   844
   Synchronizing Replicas   845
   Handling Replication Conflicts and Errors   846
   Compacting a Replicated Database   850
   Setting Security for Replicated Databases   850
   Designating a New Design Master   851
   Making a Replicated Database into a Regular Database   852
Visual SourceSafe   852

Chapter 30   Workgroup Features in Microsoft Excel   855
Security Features in Microsoft Excel   855
Shared Workbooks   858
Workbook Merging and Data Consolidation   860
    Merging Workbooks   861
    Consolidating Data   861
Workgroup Review of Workbooks   862
    Tracking Changes and Comments   862
    Routing Workbooks with Electronic Mail   863

Chapter 31   Workgroup Features in Microsoft Outlook   865
Group Scheduling   865
    Viewing Free/Busy Information in a Workgroup   866
    Scheduling Resources   867
Microsoft Exchange Public Folders   868
    Setting Up Public Folders   869
    Distributing Public Folder Shortcuts to Users   870
    Making Public Folders Secure   871
Extended Task Management Capabilities with Microsoft Team Manager   873
    Setting Up Team Manager   874
    Switching from Schedule+ to Outlook to View Team Tasks   874

Chapter 32   Workgroup Features in Microsoft PowerPoint   877
Security Features in PowerPoint   877
Presentation Conferencing   878
    System Requirements   879
    Understanding the Conferencing Process   879
    Understanding the Presenter's Role   882
    Understanding the Audience's Role   884
    Troubleshooting   885
Workgroup Review of Presentations   886
The Pack and Go Wizard   888
    Packing the Viewer   888
    Unpacking the Presentation   889

Chapter 33 Workgroup Features in Microsoft Word 891
Security Features in Word 891
Workgroup Review of Documents 893
   Creating a Document with Many Authors 894
   Tracking Changes 895
   Commenting on a Document 896
   Saving and Comparing Different Versions of Documents 898
   Routing Documents with Electronic Mail 901

Part 6 Microsoft Office Architecture 903

Chapter 34 Microsoft Office Architecture 905
Overview 905
Office Support for Object Linking and Embedding 905
Office Support for ActiveX 906
   ActiveX Controls 907
   ActiveX Documents 908
Security Features in Office 908
Shared Office Components 909
   Coordination of Applications 909
   Shared Application Tools 909
   Office Art 911
   Spelling Checker Dictionary 911
   Microsoft Clip Gallery 912
   Visual Basic for Applications 913

Chapter 35 Microsoft Access Architecture 915
How Microsoft Access Is Structured 915
   Tables 916
   Queries 918
   Forms 921
   Reports 921
   Macros 922
   Modules 922
   Controls 923
   Form and Report Templates 923
   Library Databases 924
   Add-ins 925

Workgroup Information Files   930
  Microsoft Access and the Microsoft Jet Database Engine   931
How You Can Customize Microsoft Access   934
  User-Defined Options   935
  Custom Toolbar, Menu Bar, and Shortcut Menu Settings   935
How Microsoft Access Resolves Conflicts   936
  Replication Conflicts   936
  Locking Conflicts   937

Chapter 36   Microsoft Excel Architecture   939

How Microsoft Excel Is Structured   939
  Workbooks   940
  Templates   947
  Add-ins   949
How You Can Customize Microsoft Excel   951
  User-Defined Options   952
  Startup and Alternate Startup Folders   952
  Autotemplates   953
  Workspace Files   954
  Custom Toolbar Settings and Lists   955
How Microsoft Excel Resolves Conflicts   956
  Startup and Alternate Startup Folders   956
  Custom Toolbars   956
  Custom Add-ins   956

Chapter 37   Microsoft Outlook Architecture   959

How Outlook Is Structured   959
  Items   961
  Folders   962
  Views   963
How You Can Customize Outlook   965

Chapter 38   Microsoft PowerPoint Architecture   967

How PowerPoint Is Structured   967
  Presentations   968
  Templates   975
How You Can Customize PowerPoint   977
  User-Defined Options   977
  Macros   978

        Add-ins   978
        Custom Templates   980
        Custom Toolbar Settings   984
        Custom Export Formats   985
        AutoClipArt   985
        Custom AutoContent Wizard Interface   986
    How PowerPoint Resolves Conflicts   989

    ### Chapter 39   Microsoft Word Architecture   991
    How Word Is Structured   991
        Understanding Templates   992
        Locating Word Components   997
        Managing Wizards   1006
        Creating Add-ins   1006
    How You Can Customize Word   1006
    How Word Resolves Conflicts   1008

Appendixes   1009

   ### Appendix A   Microsoft Office 97 Resource Kit Tools and Utilities   1011
   Client Installation Tools   1011
        Network Installation Wizard   1012
        Package Definition Files   1012
        System Policy Editor and Office 97 Policy Templates   1013
    Conversion Utilities   1014
        PowerPoint Converters   1014
        PowerPoint Viewers   1015
        Word Converters   1017
    Documentation   1019
        Advanced Documentation   1020
        Find Fast Stop Word List   1021
        Informational Worksheets   1021
        Microsoft Technical Support Documents   1022
        Microsoft Technical Support Help File   1023
        Office Upgrade Wizard File List   1023
        Outlook Extension Configuration File Document   1024
        PowerPoint AutoClipArt Concept List   1024
        Setup Simulator   1024
        Ultimate Printer Manual   1025

Word 97 How-to Documents   1026
Visual Basic Win32 API Declarations   1026
General Tools   1027
Gallery Location Tools   1027
Microsoft Excel 97 File Recovery Macro   1027
Outlook 97 Profiles   1028
Outlook 97 Sample Forms   1030
Office 97 Deployment Planner   1031
Office 97 Unbind Utilities   1032
Office Upgrade Wizard   1033
SwitchForms for Outlook   1033
Wipename for Outlook   1035
Crystal Reports for Microsoft Outlook 97   1035
RegClean Utility   1036
Tools for Extracting and Copying Files from Office Floppy Disks   1037
CopyAll and CopyDisk   1038
Extract Utility   1039
Wextract Utility   1041
World Wide Web and Intranet Tools   1041
Microsoft Excel 97 Web Connectivity Kit   1041
Office MIME Type Information for Netscape Web Servers   1042
PowerPoint Animation Player   1043
PowerPoint 95 Animation Publisher   1043
PowerPoint 95 Internet Assistant   1044

Appendix B   Setup Command-Line Options and File Formats   1045

Setup File Formats   1045
   The INF Files   1046
   The STF File   1046
Setup Command-Line Options   1047
   Command-Line Option Descriptions   1048
   ERRORLEVEL Values   1050
Setup Process   1051
   Determining Maintenance Mode Installation   1052

Appendix C   Registry Keys and Values   1053

Installing the System Policy Editor   1053

Using Office 97 System Policies   1055
    Computer Settings   1055
    User Settings   1058
List of Office 97 System Policies   1068
    Policies in the Off97w95.adm Template   1069
    Policies in the Access97.adm Template   1075
    Policies in the Outlk97.adm Template   1077
    Policies in the Query97.adm Template   1079

Appendix D   List of Installed Components   1081

Custom and Typical Installations   1081
Run from Network Server Installation   1082
Run from CD Installation   1085

Appendix E   Other Support Resources   1091

Getting Support from Microsoft   1091
    Primary Support   1092
    Priority Support   1092
    Other Support Options   1093
    Text Telephone   1093
    Microsoft FastTips   1093
    Microsoft Sales   1093
Microsoft on the World Wide Web   1094
Other Microsoft Support Programs   1094
    Microsoft Through Online Services   1094
    The Microsoft Knowledge Base   1095
    Microsoft Download Service   1095
    Microsoft Software Library   1096
    Microsoft TechNet   1096
    Microsoft Developer Network   1097
    Microsoft Solution Providers   1097
    Microsoft Authorized Support Centers   1098
    Microsoft Consulting Services   1098
Training and Reference Resources   1099
    Microsoft Certified Professional Program   1099
    Microsoft Technical Education   1099
    Microsoft Press Titles   1100
    Microsoft White Papers   1102

Foreword

Today more than 40 million people around the world use Office applications. If you are responsible for rolling out the newest version of Office to some of these 40 million people, or if you administer the networks to which they connect, or if you provide them with technical support or training, then you've found the right book. The *Microsoft Office 97 Resource Kit* contains information and tools to help you install, configure, and support Office 97 in your workgroup. It's written for the administrator in a large organization, but any Office 97 power user will find it useful.

I've been involved with Office from the beginning, and this is the most significant release of Office since we created the product more than six years ago. The first version of Office, released in 1990, was little more than an easy way to purchase the individual applications: Microsoft Word, Microsoft Excel, and Microsoft PowerPoint. In 1993, the Office product came into its own with the release of Office 4.0. In Office 4.0 we saw the beginnings of the integration and user interface consistency that we've taken much farther in Office 97.

In Office 97 you'll find major updates to Microsoft Access (Office Pro only), Word, Microsoft Excel, PowerPoint, and a brand new member of the Office for Windows family, Microsoft Outlook. Outlook is an integrated application that manages e-mail, calendars, contacts, files, and tasks all in one place. If you work with Office in a workgroup, I think you'll be very interested in Outlook.

We took three years to develop Office 97. In that time we visited more than 500 customer sites and did more research and usability testing than for any previous version of Office. We evaluated hundreds of ideas from users like you who gave us feedback. We learned a great deal about the issues and costs that large organizations face in setting up, configuring and supporting Office. We learned, for example, that large organizations often spend as much money rolling out new desktop applications as they do purchasing those applications. So for Office 97 we focused on making installation and customization easier and more flexible.

The Network Installation Wizard, which is included on the Tools and Utilities CD that comes with this book, is one of the tools we developed to make your Office installation easier. Use the wizard to select the installation options you want for your workgroup—the wizard creates the required installation scripts. In this book you'll find several chapters that describe your options for rolling out Office 97 to your workgroup.

During our Office 97 research we also learned that almost half of our users in large organizations run Office from a server. So we improved Office 97 for server-based use. Office 97 can now run more than 90 percent of its code from a server, reducing the hard disk footprint significantly. Not only that, Office 97 applications share more than 50 percent of their code and have the same hardware requirements as Office 95.

Simultaneous with the evolution of Office, we've seen the growth of LANs, workgroup collaboration, and the World Wide Web. Today most computers in your organization probably have high-bandwidth network connections to other computers in the organization, and perhaps to intranet servers and the Web. Maybe you're planning for intranet or Web connectivity now. With Office 97, your workgroup can take advantage of today's level of connectivity as users publish information and coordinate their work.

As you make the move to Office 97, you'll find the *Office Resource Kit* useful in several ways. Use it to help you plan your Office 97 deployment—including which components to install, and where and how to install them. If you're upgrading from a previous version of Office or switching from other applications, use this book to help you convert file formats and understand the differences between your old and new applications. Use the *Office Resource Kit* to take advantage of the considerable workgroup and intranet support available in the Office 97 applications, and to increase your knowledge of how the Office applications work individually and together.

I hope you'll find the *Office Resource Kit* a valuable tool. Our goal was to create nothing less than the ultimate shop manual for Office administrators and support professionals. Good luck with Office 97!

Jon DeVaan, Vice President, Office Product Unit
Microsoft Corporation
November, 1996

PART 1

Welcome to Microsoft Office 97

Contents
Chapter 1 How to Use the Microsoft Office 97 Resource Kit   3
Chapter 2 What's New in Microsoft Office 97   9

CHAPTER 1

How to Use the Microsoft Office 97 Resource Kit

This chapter introduces you to the contents and conventions of the *Microsoft Office 97 Resource Kit*, and points you to the Office Resource Kit site on the World Wide Web for the most up-to-date information. The Office Resource Kit includes this book and the Office Resource Kit Tools and Utilities.

In This Chapter
Welcome 3
Updated Information on the World Wide Web 4
Contents of the Office Resource Kit 5
Conventions Used in This Book 7
Tell Us What You Think 7

Welcome

The *Office Resource Kit* is written for administrators and information systems (IS) professionals. It provides information about rolling out, supporting, and troubleshooting Microsoft® Office 97 on computers running Windows® 95, Windows NT® Server or Window NT Workstation, and the Macintosh®.

In the past several years, IS departments have changed the way they treat desktop applications. Five years ago, for example, local area networks (LANs) were appearing throughout organizations. Individual departments, and even individual users, were deciding which desktop applications they would use based on the set of tasks particular applications could do. Today, however, departments are increasingly interested in how well an application allows people to collaborate and share data within a workgroup or corporate intranet.

Two factors have contributed to this change. First, the use of LANs and wide area networks (WANs) is much more widespread, and IS departments are now managing them centrally rather than departmentally. Many organizations have intranets and provide access to the Internet. Second, in the autumn of 1993 Microsoft Office version 4.0 was launched.

Office 4.0 provided much more consistency and ease of use than was previously available in a group of integrated desktop applications. This encouraged many organizations to standardize on Office. In standardizing on a single, integrated solution, IS organizations came to appreciate the control they had over their departmental desktops; yet they also recognized the importance of supporting and maintaining this software to reap the benefits that standardization provides.

Office 97 is arguably the largest upgrade in the history of Office in terms of new capabilities, workgroup and Internet support, and network installation and support options. The purpose of the *Office Resource Kit* is to provide the information that the IS professional or administrator needs to support Office 97. This includes planning for and deploying Office, deciding which configurations are best for your organization, and understanding what is involved in migrating from earlier versions of Office or from competitive applications.

Updated Information on the World Wide Web

This book was up-to-date at time of publication. However, we are bound to find things to improve, clarify, or fix. To get new information to you as quickly as possible, we maintain a site on the Web that contains all of the text and graphics of the printed *Office Resource Kit*, as well as hyperlinks to the Tools and Utilities CD content. You have full access to this site (provided you have access to the Web). We update the content on the site whenever new information becomes available.

World Wide Web   To view the Office Resource Kit Web site, point your Web browser to the following URL:

http://www.microsoft.com/office/ork/

Contents of the Office Resource Kit

Together, the *Office Resource Kit* and the Tools and Utilities provide you with a wealth of information and utilities for installing and supporting Office in your workgroup. The following sections describe each of these resources in more detail.

Using the Printed or Online Book

The following sections describe the contents of the *Office Resource Kit*. Each part of the book begins with a list of the chapters in that part; the first page of each chapter includes a table of contents for that chapter.

Part 1, Welcome to Microsoft Office 97

In addition to this chapter, Part 1 includes Chapter 2, "What's New in Microsoft Office 97." Use this chapter for a quick glance at the new features in Office 97 and in the individual Office applications. Chapter 2 also explains which features of Office can better support collaboration and sound work practices in your workgroup.

Part 2, Deploying Microsoft Office

The chapters in Part 2 provide you with the details you need to install Office on end-user's computers—including steps for developing an installation strategy, such as assembling a planning team and rolling out a pilot project. You can allow users to install their own software, or you can install Office throughout your organization from an administrative installation point on the network.

Part 2 also describes how to customize client installations with tools such as the Microsoft Systems Management Server and Windows System Policy Editor. (The Office 97 policy templates are also included with the Tools and Utilities.)

Part 3, Upgrading to Microsoft Office

The chapters in Part 3 describe techniques for upgrading users' software to Office 97, whether users are upgrading all of Office or one or more of the individual Office applications. In addition, all Office 97 applications include new capabilities for sharing documents with previous versions of Office. These capabilities are especially useful for workgroups that are upgrading gradually and must share documents between different versions of Office applications.

Part 4, Switching from Other Applications

The chapters in Part 4 provide detailed information about migrating users from other applications to their Office counterparts, such as from WordPerfect to Word, from Lotus 1-2-3 to Microsoft Excel, from Harvard Graphics to PowerPoint®, or from dBASE to Microsoft Access. Part 4 includes information about filters that convert documents to the format of the destination Microsoft application, and it explains how Office applications manage documents and data that were created in other applications.

Part 5, Using Microsoft Office Throughout Your Organization

The chapters in Part 5 describe how to take advantage of the workgroup features built into Office, such as setting up corporate forms and templates and integrating Office applications and electronic mail. Office 97 includes strong support for Internet and intranet protocols; these are also described in Part 5.

Part 6, Microsoft Office Architecture

The chapters in Part 6 provide an overview for IS managers and technical support personnel of the structure of Office and its applications. Use Part 6 as a starting point for troubleshooting problems or unexpected results in Office applications.

Appendixes

The appendixes provide detailed references for items included in the Tools and Utilities, Setup command-line options, registry settings, installed components, and resources for technical support.

Using the Tools and Utilities CD

The Tools and Utilities CD contains all of the software tools and utilities referenced in this book: the Network Installation Wizard, Office 97 policy templates for the Windows System Policy Editor, and many others. For a more detailed description of the Tools and Utilities CD contents, see Appendix A, "Microsoft Office 97 Resource Kit Tools and Utilities."

Conventions Used in This Book

The following terms and text formats are used throughout this book.

Convention	Meaning
Bold	Indicates the actual commands, words, or characters that you type or that you click in the user interface.
Italic	Indicates a placeholder for information or parameters that you must provide. For example, if the procedure asks you to type a *file name*, you type the actual name of a file.
Path\File name	Indicates a Windows file system path or registry key—for example, the file Templates\Normal.dot. Unless otherwise indicated, you can use a mixture of uppercase and lowercase characters when you type paths and file names.
Path:File name	Indicates a Macintosh file system path—for example, the file Template:Normal. Unless otherwise indicated, you can use a mixture of uppercase and lowercase characters when you type paths and file names.
`Monospace`	Represents examples of code text.

Tell Us What You Think

We welcome any feedback that you may have about the Office Resource Kit. We are especially interested in any technical errors or ambiguities you find in the book or in the Office Resource Kit Tools and Utilities.

You can contact us by sending e-mail to the following address:

ork97@microsoft.com

Although we will respond to your feedback as best we can, we cannot provide technical support for the Office 97 applications. For information about obtaining product support for the Office applications, see "Getting Support from Microsoft" in Appendix E, "Other Support Resources."

We hope you find the Office Resource Kit a valuable tool for installing, supporting, and using Office 97 in your workgroup. We appreciate your feedback, and good luck with Office 97!

CHAPTER 2

What's New in Microsoft Office 97

This chapter provides a brief description of the most exciting new features in the Office 97 family of applications. Office 97 combines intelligent applications with the power of intranet solutions to provide significant business advantage to your organization. These new Office 97 features:

- Help users complete tasks in less time and with less effort.
- Create and manage intranet content and work with intranet data.
- Make Office easier to set up, configure, and support.

In This Chapter
Improved Software Administration   9
Intelligent Applications   12
Intranet and Workgroup Solutions   29

Improved Software Administration

For a large organization, the decision to upgrade or switch software is based primarily on what it takes to make the change. Issues that affect this decision include how easy it is to deploy and administer the software, whether existing hardware supports it, and whether users with different versions of the software can work together. Office 97 provides features, tools, and documentation that support the administrator in this transition.

Office 97 Setup

Office 97 Setup gives the network administrator a high degree of control over how Office 97 is deployed. You can install the software on clients' hard disks, on the network, or using a combination of both. A variety of Setup options allow you to determine which Setup script to run and whether users are asked any questions during Setup.

For More Information about running the Office Setup program, see Chapter 4, "Installing Microsoft Office."

System Policy Templates

Both Windows 95 and Windows NT Workstation version 4.0 can use system policies. When a user logs on, these policies—which are set by the administrator—are downloaded to the user's computer. This feature allows a standard set of policies and makes it easier to administer the desktop.

Note Windows NT Workstation version 3.51 and the Macintosh do not support system policies.

Office 97 supports system policies in two ways: first, most of the user settings are stored in the Windows registry; and second, you can determine user settings (such as the default folder or format for saving files) using a set of policy templates that come with the System Policy Editor.

Tools and Utilities The Office Resource Kit Tools and Utilities include Office policy templates for use with the System Policy Editor. For more information, see "System Policy Editor and Office 97 Policy Templates" in Appendix A, "Microsoft Office 97 Resource Kit Tools and Utilities."

For More Information about using system policies, see "Using Windows System Policies to Customize Office" in Chapter 7, "Customizing and Optimizing Microsoft Office."

Network Installation Wizard

Note The Network Installation Wizard runs on the Windows 95 or Windows NT operating system only.

The Network Installation Wizard is used to create custom Setup scripts. It looks and operates like an Office wizard, and prompts you to determine whether the users will run the software from their hard disks or from a network server; what features to include; and how the program items should appear on the **Start** menu or in Program Manager.

Tools and Utilities The Office Resource Kit Tools and Utilities include the Network Installation Wizard. For more information, see "Network Installation Wizard" in Appendix A, "Microsoft Office 97 Resource Kit Tools and Utilities."

For More Information about using the Network Installation Wizard, see "Modifying Client Setup with the Network Installation Wizard" in Chapter 6, "Customizing Client Installations."

Microsoft Systems Management Server

Office 97 for Windows includes support for Systems Management Server to make it easy to deploy Office or individual Office applications in your organization without having to visit each desktop.

The package definition file (PDF) is the set of instructions that Systems Management Server uses to distribute the software. When used with the batch file options for Office Setup, it is possible to perform a customized installation of Office on all desktops in your organization from one central location. When Setup is complete, the message information file (MIF) for Systems Management Server records an entry in your Systems Management Server database about whether the installation was successful or whether errors occurred.

Tools and Utilities The Office Resource Kit Tools and Utilities include PDF files for the Office 97 applications. For more information, see "Package Definition Files" in Appendix A, "Microsoft Office 97 Resource Kit Tools and Utilities."

For More Information about using Systems Management Server, see Using Microsoft Systems Management Server to Install Office" in Chapter 6, "Customizing Client Installations."

Office 97 Upgrade Wizard

Since Office version 4.*x*, Office has installed files and code that are shared not only by the Office applications, but also by applications that meet the Office Compatible program requirements. Because it is difficult to predict whether other applications need old files or code, much of it is left intact when you upgrade to Office 97. The Office 97 Upgrade Wizard allows you to remove all unneeded files, registry entries, INI file entries, and other items during Setup.

Tools and Utilities The Office Resource Kit Tools and Utilities include the Office Upgrade Wizard. For more information, see "Office Upgrade Wizard" in Appendix A, "Microsoft Office 97 Resource Kit Tools and Utilities."

For More Information about using the Office Upgrade Wizard, see "Using the Office 97 Upgrade Wizard" in Chapter 9, "Troubleshooting Installation."

File Format Compatibility

Because some of the file formats for Office 97 have changed since Office 4.*x* and Office 95, Office 97 includes features that make it easier for users to work together when using different versions of Office.

Default Save

Users can determine which file format to use as the default when saving a file. A Microsoft Excel 97 user who shares files with a Microsoft Excel version 5.0 user may choose Microsoft Excel 5.0 format, while another user who does not often share files may choose to stay with Microsoft Excel 97 format. You can also set the default format for all Office applications in your organization using a system policy in Windows 95 or Windows NT Workstation 4.0.

For More Information about the default format to use when saving an Office document, see "Specifying the Default Format in Which to Save Office Documents" in Chapter 22, "Supporting Multiple Versions of Microsoft Office."

New File Converter Architecture

Office 97 implements a new file-converter architecture to make mixed environments easier to work with. This new architecture stores file converters in a network location so new converters can be deployed without having to touch every desktop.

Intelligent Applications

Each new version of Office is aimed at making it easier for users to get their work done, while reducing the strain on your help desk. Built into every Office 97 application is IntelliSense™ technology, which automates repetitive tasks, simplifies complex tasks, personalizes the software, and makes the functionality in the products more accessible.

Intelligent Applications in Office 97

Office 97 includes several enhancements to make Office easier to use. Some of these enhancements are described in this section.

Office Assistant

The role of user assistance in Office has evolved over time. Initially, the goal was to document every feature and its use in a printed manual. However, since many people did not have the time to read that documentation, user assistance was gradually integrated into the product. Previous versions of Office put more information into online Help, making it easier to find particular topics. Added features included Cue Cards, which stay on-screen while you use them, and the TipWizard®, which watches what you do and suggests an easier way to accomplish specific tasks.

While these innovations advanced users' abilities to work with Office, customer feedback and a series of research projects indicated the need for a fresh approach to online assistance. The Office Assistant is based on the familiar figure of the departmental expert; this feature allows you to ask questions in everyday language.

The Assistant serves as the central place to unify all user assistance in all the Office products and is appropriate for all levels of users and for users around the world. The Assistant is shown in the following illustration.

Some of the ways in which the Assistant can help include:

- Natural language assistance

    When you ask the Assistant a question in everyday language—such as "How do I print sideways?"—the Assistant provides the information.

- Tips

    Based on the way you work with Office 97, the Assistant can give tips for methods that are more efficient, or show features you may not have discovered.

- Intelligent Help

    Based on your actions, the Assistant anticipates what you might need assistance with before you ask.

The Assistant is designed to help you work with the existing user interface—not to replace it. It is highly customizable, allowing you to control both its appearance and its behavior. There is an object model so that developers creating custom solutions with Microsoft Office can add their own Help to the Assistant.

For More Information   about creating custom solutions in Microsoft Office, see the *Microsoft Office 97/Visual Basic Programmer's Guide*, published by Microsoft Press® and available wherever computer books are sold. For more information about Microsoft Press, see Appendix E, "Other Support Resources."

Office Art

All of the Office applications now use Office Art, one set of enhanced drawing tools. Using Office Art, you can create three-dimensional objects with shading, formatted fills, or textures that can also be used to enhance charts, Bezier curves, and connectors to create flow charts or diagrams. Special effects include lighting and finishes such as matte or metallic, and there are predefined shapes that you can size to your needs.

Text can be added to any object without creating an additional text box, and any drawing object can have a hyperlink associated with it. This makes it easy for any Office user to create effective navigation buttons or maps within documents or elsewhere.

Toolbars

Toolbars are now implemented as one piece of software across all of the Office applications. This feature is installed only once so it takes up less space on your hard disk, and less random access memory (RAM) when more than one application is in use. In addition, toolbars are now more flexible, allowing you to mix both buttons and menu items on the same toolbar. With more people creating and reading documents online, this flexibility allows you to get the menus and buttons that you use the most on one toolbar, giving you more space for your document.

Office Binder (Windows only)

Office Binder was first introduced in Office 95. It provides a container in which several documents can be brought together—regardless of file type—to create one project file. For example, you may be working on a research project with several Microsoft Excel workbooks in which you do your statistical analysis, a Microsoft Word document where you summarize your findings, another Word document that serves as the survey form, and a Microsoft PowerPoint presentation that you use to present your findings. By assembling these documents in a binder, you can use all of the functionality of the original programs that created the files, but now you have one file that can be more easily distributed.

Improvements have been made to Office Binder for Office 97. It is now possible to print these various file types with consistent headers and footers, including page numbering. In addition, there is now an integrated print preview for the entire binder.

Finally, binders are a great place to work on projects as a group. When an Office binder is used in conjunction with the Windows 95 or Windows NT Workstation 4.0 Briefcase application, the binder is replicated by section. Each user can place a copy of the binder in his or her Briefcase; when the file is updated, only the section that that user was working on is replaced; and the binder is updated with changes to other sections worked on by other users

Intelligent Applications in Microsoft Access 97

Microsoft Access, which is available in Office 97 for Windows, Professional Edition, makes it easier for all levels of users to manage and share information, find answers, and build powerful business solutions.

Database Wizard

Whether you are a novice or an experienced developer, the Database Wizard gets you started quickly. Choose from a list of over 20 types of databases, make some choices about the way you want your database to look, and click **Finish**. The Database Wizard builds a full-featured database and customizes it to your requirements. From there, you can add new elements to your database using the many other time-saving wizards found in Microsoft Access 97.

Import/Export Wizards

You may often need to use data in many different formats. Microsoft Access 97 offers three import/export wizards to help make the process of moving text, spreadsheet, and HTML data easy. When you use the **Import** command (**File** menu, **Get External Data** submenu) to import data, choose **Text Files**, **Microsoft Excel**, or **HTML Documents** in the **Files of type** box; the appropriate wizard takes you step by step through the process. The wizard even gives you a preview of how your data will look in the new format based on the choices you make.

Table Analyzer Wizard

The Table Analyzer Wizard can intelligently identify relationships in unstructured data and recommend the best way to organize that data in a relational database. This helps eliminate the problems associated with flat- file databases, where all information is combined into one table.

Simple Query Wizard

Regardless of the underlying structure of your database, the Simple Query Wizard can intelligently figure out how to bring information together to answer your questions. In the background, the Wizard automatically includes all the tables necessary to bring the desired data together. This process of background joining is found in the Form and Report Wizards as well. The result is that you worry less about how the data is stored, and can focus more on asking the questions.

Filter By Selection and Filter By Form

Often you know only a piece of the information you are trying to find. Filter By Selection allows you to highlight what you are looking for, and then limits your view of the data to only the items that match your selection. Filter By Form lets you use your familiar forms to find data in the same manner. Select an item from the drop-down list generated for a field, and Microsoft Access 97 shows you the records that match your criteria.

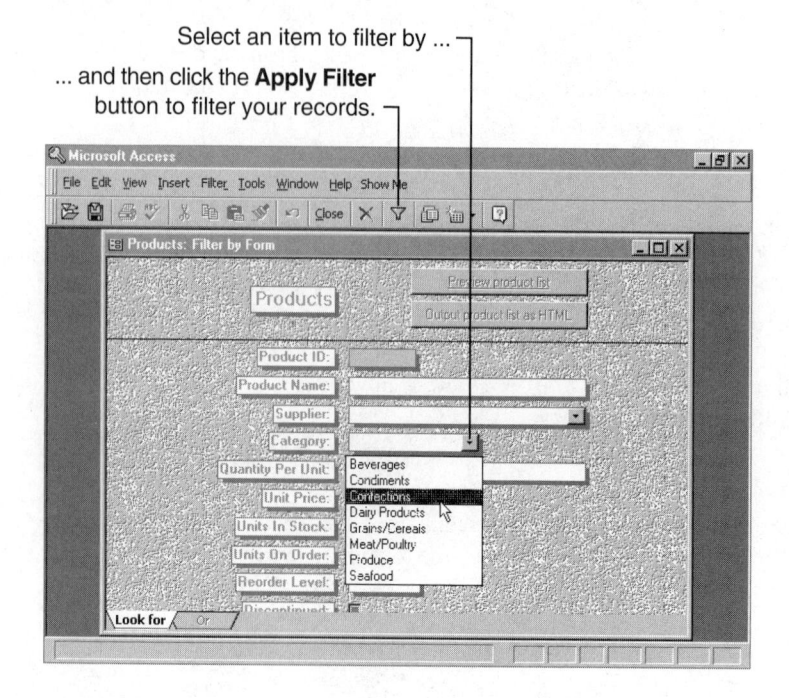

Select an item to filter by ...

... and then click the **Apply Filter** button to filter your records.

Improved Form and Report Wizards

Based on the data on which you want to build a form or report, the Form and Report Wizards now change their behavior to give you appropriate choices for creating forms or reports. For example, if you choose to see information about customers and their orders, the wizard can build a form/subform or grouped report that displays the customer information once and lists the related orders on the same page.

Intelligent Applications in Microsoft Excel 97

Microsoft Excel 97 builds on a long history of simplifying data entry, formatting, and analysis tools. Some of the enhancements in Microsoft Excel 97 are described in this following section.

Natural Language Formulas

Creating formulas using archaic cell references (such as A1+B2) can be difficult for novice users and can make it hard to track down errors. In Microsoft Excel 97, you can use your own terminology—your row and column headings—to create formulas, instead of using cell references.

For example, in the following illustration the formula to find March profit is derived by subtracting March Expenses from March Sales. The value of March Expenses is at the intersection of the column labeled March and the row labeled Expenses.

	January	February	March
Sales	$5,468.00	$4,350.00	$6,550.00
Expenses	$3,459.00	$2,050.00	$4,685.00
Profits	$2,009.00	$2,300.00	=March Sales - March Expenses

Formula AutoCorrect

Microsoft Excel 97 now fixes 15 of the most common mistakes users make when entering formulas. These mistakes are due to common typographical errors, as well as the use of syntax that is different from what Microsoft Excel expects. For example, Microsoft Excel can correct transposed cell references, change the semicolon (;) in a range reference to a colon (:), or add a closing parenthesis to a function's arguments. In the illustration below, Microsoft Excel has corrected the common error of starting a formula with two equal signs.

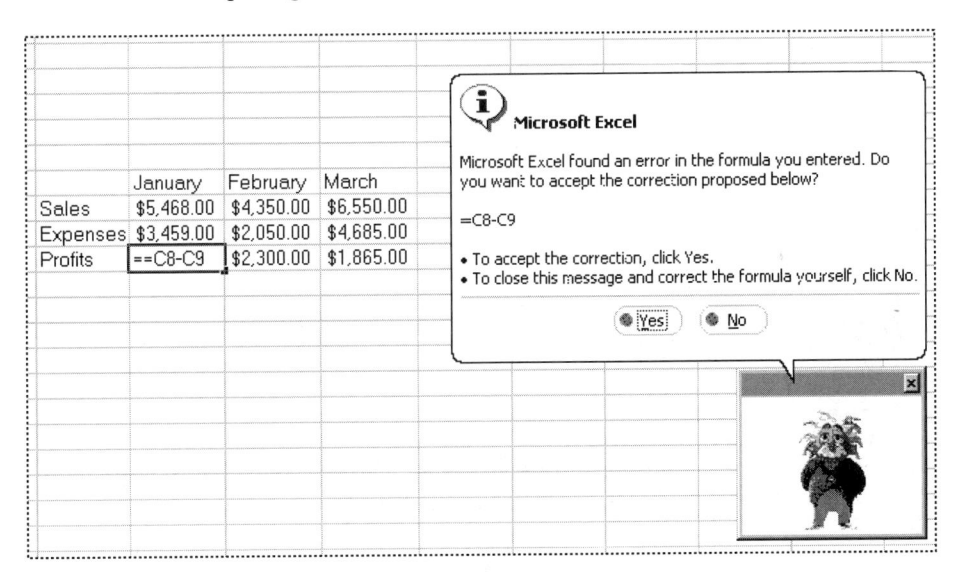

	January	February	March
Sales	$5,468.00	$4,350.00	$6,550.00
Expenses	$3,459.00	$2,050.00	$4,685.00
Profits	==C8-C9	$2,300.00	$1,865.00

Microsoft Excel

Microsoft Excel found an error in the formula you entered. Do you want to accept the correction proposed below?

=C8-C9

- To accept the correction, click Yes.
- To close this message and correct the formula yourself, click No.

● Yes   ● No

Range Finder

Range Finder makes it easy to trace, modify, and understand which figures make up a formula. When you double-click any cell that contains an equation, each part of the equation is highlighted with its own color so you can see the pieces of your formula at a glance. This is implemented throughout Microsoft Excel, including in charts. For example, if you click a data series on a bar chart, the range in your original data is highlighted. Range Finder also allows you to use drag and drop to modify your formula or chart range.

In the following illustration, the cells that are referenced in the PMT formula are color-coded for easy identification.

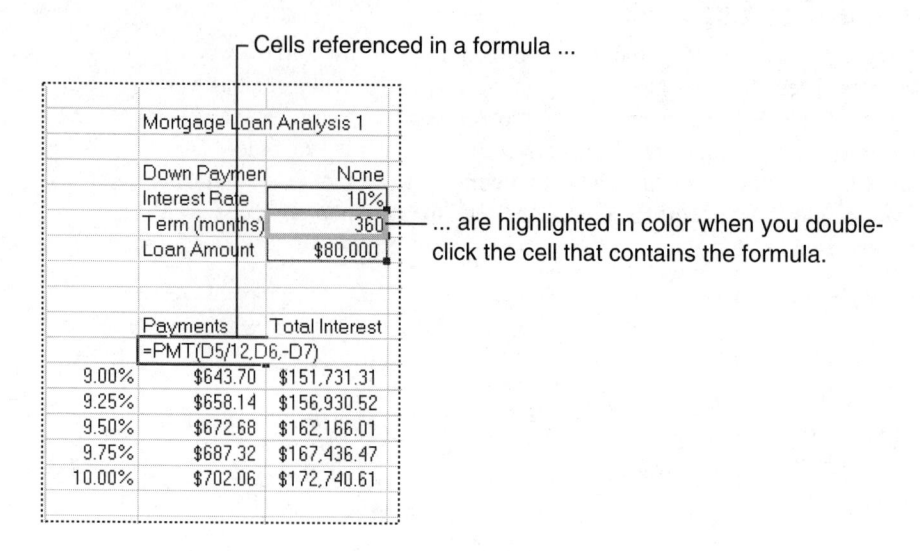

Cells referenced in a formula ...

	Mortgage Loan Analysis 1	
	Down Payment	None
	Interest Rate	10%
	Term (months)	360
	Loan Amount	$80,000
	Payments	Total Interest
	=PMT(D5/12,D6,-D7)	
9.00%	$643.70	$151,731.31
9.25%	$658.14	$156,930.52
9.50%	$672.68	$162,166.01
9.75%	$687.32	$167,436.47
10.00%	$702.06	$172,740.61

... are highlighted in color when you double-click the cell that contains the formula.

Merged Cells

Many users want to add rich formatting to their spreadsheets or forms, but are limited by the gridline layout of a spreadsheet. Microsoft Excel 97 breaks the grid limitation by allowing you to merge multiple cells together to create blocks of large cells, to rotate text to any angle within a cell, and to indent text within a cell. These options are available on the **Alignment** tab in the **Cells** dialog box (**Format** menu).

Updated Charting

The new Chart Wizard makes it easier to get the chart you want the first time by consolidating all the charting tools in one place. There are new chart types (such as pie-of-pie, conical, or bubble charts) and more formatting options (such as shaded or transparent fills) to help make your numbers look more professional. Formatting charts becomes easier as chart tips identify each portion of your graph before you change it, and display the actual value behind each data series.

Visual Printing

Ninety-five percent of Microsoft Excel users print their spreadsheets, and almost all of them have experienced trouble defining exactly which part of their spreadsheet to print. To provide a more intuitive way to set the print area, Microsoft Excel 97 includes the **Page Break Preview** command (**View** menu). Each page displays a watermark showing what information will print on that page. Drag the page break to where you want it, and Microsoft Excel automatically alters the column sizes, row sizes, or font sizes to make it all fit.

Multiple Undo

Microsoft Excel 97 has unlimited undo, similar to Word and PowerPoint, allowing risk-free experimentation with formulas and formatting. To use the multiple undo feature, click the arrow next to the **Undo** button (**Standard** toolbar).

Conditional Formatting

Many users keep large spreadsheets to help track results. For example, it is common to see a spreadsheet displaying a log of sales results, by quarter and then by region, or a large sheet tracking inventory changes. Many users have indicated they would like to be able to track results in a large spreadsheet at a glance, without having to analyze each cell.

The **Conditional Formatting** command (**Format** menu) allows you to apply automatic formatting rules to your spreadsheet—such as color, texture, or pattern—to help you find data you are looking for. For example, under-performing regions might be automatically flagged with a red background, and over-performing regions might be automatically flagged with a green background, so you can analyze a large spreadsheet at a glance.

Intelligent Applications in Microsoft Outlook 97

Microsoft Outlook™ desktop information manager is a new Office for Windows application that builds upon Microsoft Mail for Windows 3.*x*, Microsoft Exchange Client, and Schedule+. Outlook is not only an upgrade for these products, but it also extends and enhances existing features. As an integrated desktop information manager, Outlook combines:

- Electronic mail (e-mail).
- Personal calendar and group scheduling.
- Personal information, such as contacts and tasks.
- Browsing and sharing documents.
- Custom groupware or information-sharing applications.

Outlook Bar

The Outlook Bar is the navigation headquarters for Outlook, housing special shortcuts that allow you to move effortlessly around the product. Using the Outlook Bar, it is easy to switch to:

- Outlook folders (Inbox, Calendar, Tasks, and so forth).
- E-mail folders.
- File folders or network drives.
- Microsoft Exchange public folders.

The Outlook Bar shown in the following illustration comes configured with all of the standard navigation choices; however, you can easily customize this bar to create a personalized desktop organizer.

Chapter 2   What's New in Microsoft Office 97

Click here to switch to e-mail folders

Click here to switch to file folders or network drives

Microsoft Office 97 Resource Kit   21

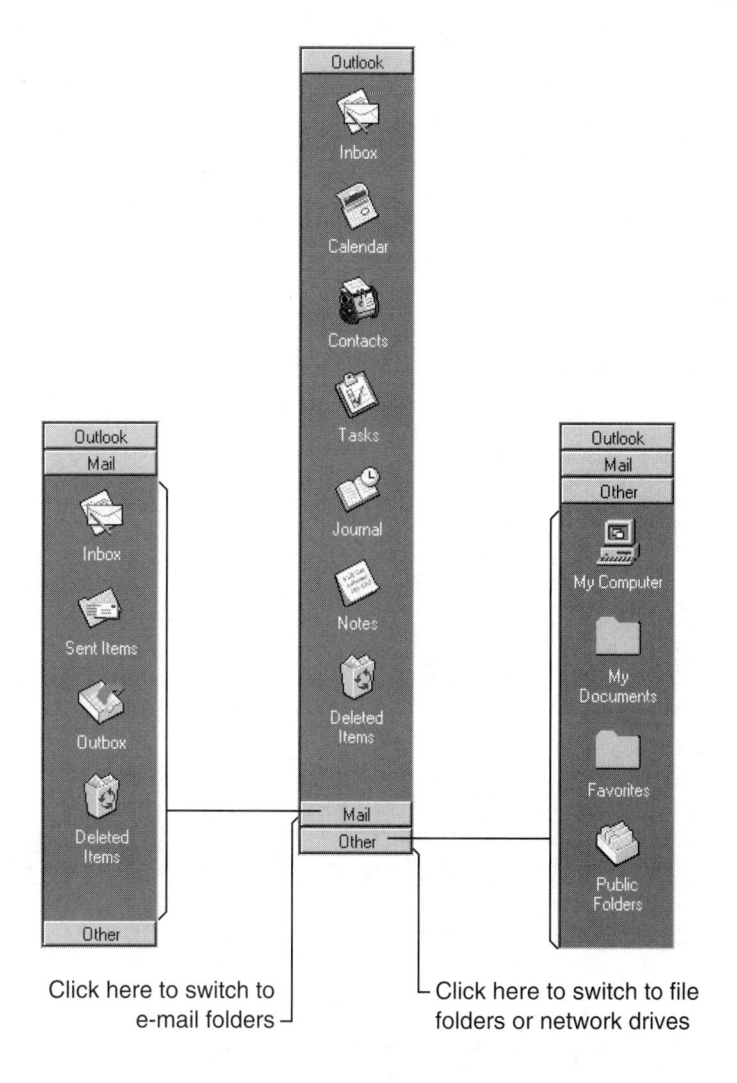

AutoPreview

If you receive numerous e-mail messages in a day, AutoPreview can significantly reduce the time you spend reading these messages. AutoPreview displays the first few lines of the body of each message, so you can quickly process messages without opening them.

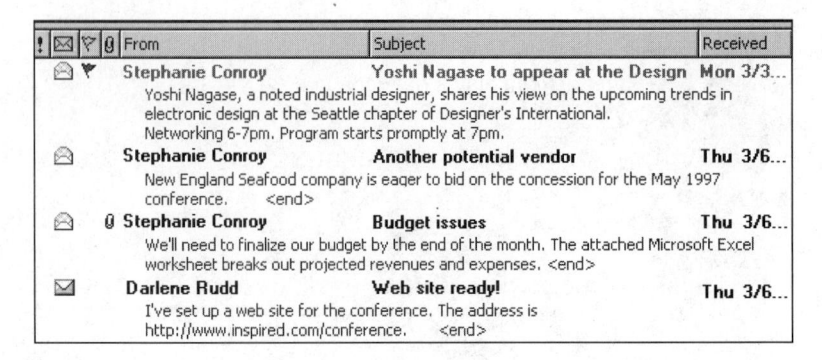

!	✉	▽	📎	From	Subject	Received
	📖	▼		Stephanie Conroy	Yoshi Nagase to appear at the Design	Mon 3/3...
				Yoshi Nagase, a noted industrial designer, shares his view on the upcoming trends in electronic design at the Seattle chapter of Designer's International. Networking 6-7pm. Program starts promptly at 7pm.		
	📖			Stephanie Conroy	Another potential vendor	Thu 3/6...
				New England Seafood company is eager to bid on the concession for the May 1997 conference. <end>		
	📖		📎	Stephanie Conroy	Budget issues	Thu 3/6...
				We'll need to finalize our budget by the end of the month. The attached Microsoft Excel worksheet breaks out projected revenues and expenses. <end>		
	✉			Darlene Rudd	Web site ready!	Thu 3/6...
				I've set up a web site for the conference. The address is http://www.inspired.com/conference. <end>		

AutoNameCheck

AutoNameCheck helps ensure that your e-mail is sent to the intended recipients by quickly and clearly identifying ambiguous e-mail names.

When you compose a message, the Outlook desktop information manager automatically checks the e-mail names. If a name uniquely matches an entry in an address book, Outlook displays the full resolved name. If a name matches more than one address book entry, Outlook marks the ambiguous name with a red underline, similar to a misspelling in Word. You right-click an ambiguous name to choose the correct name from a list of matches. Outlook automatically remembers the ambiguous name as a nickname and proposes the same address book entry the next time you use the nickname.

Finally, Outlook automatically resolves and properly formats Internet e-mail addresses. Outlook removes spaces and changes commas to periods, for example, kylie hansen @ msn,com is resolved as kyliehansen@msn.com.

WordMail

You can use Word 97 as the text editor for your e-mail messages. WordMail seamlessly integrates the familiar editing features of Word with the e-mail functionality of Outlook. Word features such as spelling and grammar checking, AutoText, styles, and templates work with the Outlook features such as AutoNameCheck, digital signatures, message tracking, and message flags.

Message Flags

Message flags are tags and dates you add to messages to remind yourself or a recipient that a message requires a follow-up action. You can flag messages after you receive them or before you send them.

If you work with your Inbox as a to-do list, you can flag specific messages with an action and due date. Actions can include Follow up, Respond, or your own text. Outlook reminds you when flagged messages are overdue and highlights overdue messages with red text. Flagged messages also display a flag icon in the view.

You can flag messages as you send them to indicate to recipients that a response is expected. Recipients see flagged messages with a small flag icon in the Inbox, and when they open the message, they see the text and due date for a response across the top of the message in the InfoBar.

Message is flagged by the sender.

Message Recall

If you inadvertently send a message before you mean to, you can attempt to recall the message from the recipients. Message Recall can either delete or replace the original message. Message Recall works across servers and across the Internet, but it recalls the message only if the recipient has not read it or moved it, and if the recipient is also running Outlook.

Views and View Switching

One of the design innovations introduced with Outlook allows you to quickly and easily adjust the way you look at the information on your screen. A view displays information using preset options for fields, grouping, filtering, and sorting. Each folder has a default view and a set of alternative views. Views do more than just display information—they help you see which information is important, and how information is related.

AutoName and AutoAddress

The full name you enter into a single field is automatically separated into first, middle, and last names. For instance, Outlook knows that Peter Michael Wilson, Jr.'s last name is Wilson, not Jr. If you have ever had to fill in a large database with names, you know how long it takes to separate out the elements of the name into appropriate fields. With the Outlook AutoName feature, this is done automatically. Addresses are handled in a similar manner by AutoAddress.

Journal

The Journal is a new component of personal information management software and is unique to Outlook. The Journal was created to help you keep track of information on your personal computer. This can include e-mail messages, documents you have been working on, a Microsoft Excel spreadsheet someone sent you, or a phone call you made through Outlook.

Any communication or business entry can be recorded in the Journal. You no longer have to remember where a document is located, or under which file you stored a contact's e-mail message. With the Outlook Journal, all you have to remember is when the event occurred. Once you find the entry in the Journal, double-clicking that item opens it. The following illustration shows the Outlook Journal in timeline view.

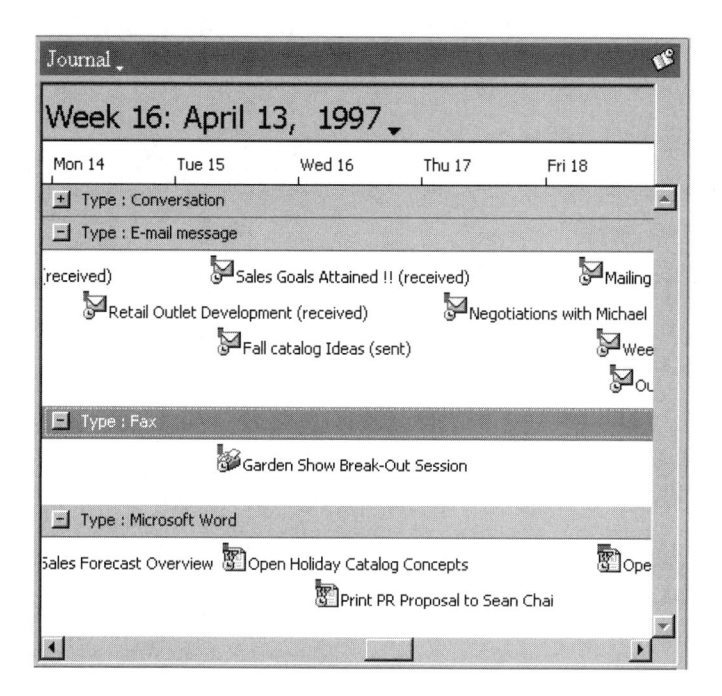

AutoCreate

Software users in all walks of life are continuously burdened by the problem of data entry—there is always some information that needs to be retyped or recopied. With the Outlook AutoCreate feature, it is easy for information to be converted from one format to another without retyping. For example, you can change an e-mail message requesting a meeting into an appointment by dragging the message. Similarly, you can turn an appointment into a task by dragging the meeting from the calendar to the TaskPad. In every case, Outlook also inserts a shortcut in the newly created item, allowing you to move back to the original data.

Intelligent Applications in PowerPoint 97

PowerPoint 97 makes it quicker and easier than ever to create effective, professional-looking presentations. Enhancements to PowerPoint allow you to create presentations quickly and to customize them easily for sharing with your workgroup.

Enhanced AutoContent Wizard

The AutoContent Wizard makes it easy for occasional users to get up and running as quickly as possible by providing predefined formatting and content based on a series of simple questions. In PowerPoint 97, the AutoContent Wizard includes 30 new content templates, including templates for creating online or kiosk presentations.

Slide Finder

When you click **Slides from Files** (**Insert** menu), you can use the Slide Finder to integrate slides from existing presentations into your presentation. Slide Finder allows you to preview and insert only the slides you want from an existing presentation, without having to load the presentation or copy and paste the slides. Best of all, you can add presentations to the Favorites list for immediate access and updating.

Custom Shows

You can use the **Custom Shows** command (**Slide Show** menu) to reuse slides from existing presentations. Many users create multiple versions of a presentation, modifying only a few slides in each version to suit specific audiences. For example, a sales representative might give slightly different versions of the same presentation for two different customers.

The Custom Shows feature allows you to define, save, and print multiple versions of the same presentation in a single presentation file. Not only is it easier to organize these slides, but you save disk space because only one copy of each slide is maintained on your hard disk. When it is time to show your presentation, select the version of the show you want to use.

Expand and Summary Slide

If you have too much content to be easily read on one slide, you can use the new **Expand Slide** command (**Tools** menu) to automatically distribute the information across several slides, based on the bullets on the original slide.

To consolidate content from several slides onto one slide, click the **Summary Slide** button (**Slide Sorter** or **Outlining** toolbar). Summary Slide reads the titles of the slides you indicate and creates a new slide that wraps up your presentation by displaying the titles in a bulleted list.

Animated Templates

PowerPoint 97 includes a number of professionally created presentation designs that include animation effects, making it easy to create presentations that get your audience's attention. These animation effects are stored on the slide master and are automatically added every time you add a new slide to the presentation

New Animation Settings

The new **Custom Animation** dialog box (**Slide Show** menu) provides one place for animating all the objects on a slide, including chart elements. You can easily modify animation effects, rearrange the animation order, and define timing settings for each object.

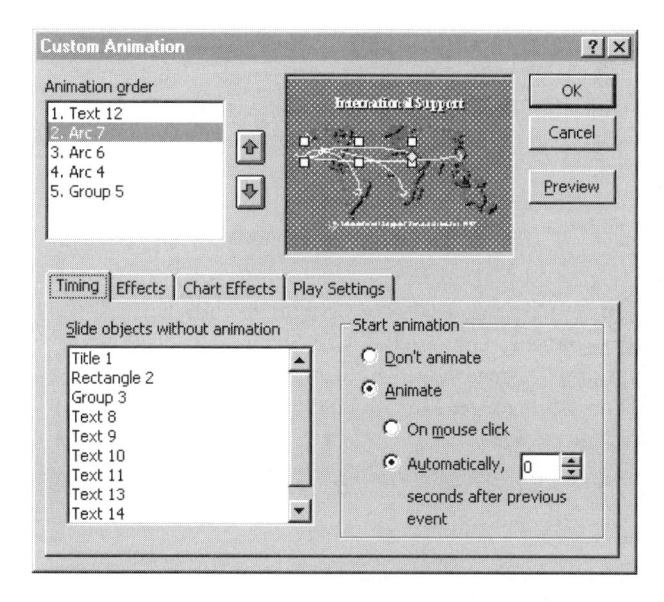

File Size and Loading Improvements

With the new architecture of PowerPoint, you can start working on presentations almost immediately after opening them, and saving files is nearly instantaneous. Built-in support for playing movies allows immediate playback of videos. In addition, file size is smaller because of built-in graphic and sound compression and the option to compress and decompress files on the fly.

Background Spelling Checker

PowerPoint now has background spell-checking that reviews your presentation for errors while you are working, and underlines incorrectly spelled words with a red wavy line. Right-click to see suggestions for the correct spelling of the word, or to select the option to ignore or add the word to your custom dictionary.

Intelligent Applications in Word 97

Word is probably the single largest content-producing application in Office, and possibly on most users' desktops. Word 97 includes several enhancements to make content simpler to produce, more consistent, and better looking.

Letter Wizard

The Assistant in Word works together with the Letter Wizard to offer assistance in creating letters. As soon as the Assistant sees that you are addressing a letter, it offers assistance and starts up the Letter Wizard. The Letter Wizard functions as a central place to choose and edit all letter elements. In addition, the Letter Wizard helps place all the necessary elements with the right punctuation. When you are done with your letter, it offers to guide you through creating an envelope.

You can use the Letter Wizard by double-clicking the Letter Wizard template on the **Letters & Faxes** tab in the **New** dialog box (**File** menu), or you can start typing a letter that begins with a salutation such as Dear or To. Word detects that you are writing a letter, and displays the Assistant.

AutoSummary

Different audiences for your documents often want to see varying levels of detail. Your manager may want all of the details of the project you are working on, but the division vice president may want only a synopsis. Through the **AutoSummarize** command (**Tools** menu), Word 97 helps you automate document summaries by creating them for you. Word analyzes the document statistically and linguistically to generate summaries based on the following choices:

- Choose a percentage of the document or a word-count-based summary
- Condense the document or highlight relevant portions on-screen
- Create an abstract and insert it in the document

Background Grammar Checker

Word 95 introduced the background spelling checker. While you work, Word checks your document and puts a red wavy line underneath misspelled words. Right-click the word to see the suggested corrections.

Background grammar checking is similar to the spelling checker feature in Word. While you work, Word uses its new natural language grammar checker to check your document for grammatical errors. It puts a green wavy line under problem words, phrases, or sentences; and when you right-click the underlined text, it gives you suggested corrections, as shown in the following illustration.

Bring your gardening supplies to there house.
- their
- Ignore Sentence
- Grammar...

By changing the options for the grammar checker on the **Spelling & Grammar** tab in the **Options** dialog box (**Tools** menu), you control what mistakes it looks for.

Table Drawing Tool

What's more intuitive than drawing out a table the way you want it? That's how you do it on paper, and now you can do it that way in Word 97. Click the **Draw Table** button (**Tables and Borders** toolbar) and start drawing. You can draw the rows and columns where you need them, and Word makes sure the lines are straight.

Intranet and Workgroup Solutions

Today, it is often easier to find information on the Internet than to find it within most organizations. Many organizations have their non-database information in Office file formats, and they would like to bring the easy navigation and searching capabilities of the World Wide Web to their internal networks.

For More Information about Office support for intranets, see Chapter 24, "Integrating Microsoft Office With Your Intranet."

Intranet and Workgroup Solutions in Office 97

Office 97 combines the best of the Web with the best desktop productivity tools to provide an easy way for you to create, edit, and analyze information for effective communication. Office 97 also includes features that allow users in a workgroup to work more effectively on projects, and to use Office 97 as a development platform for quick and cost-effective custom solutions.

Hyperlinks

One of the best things about the Web is the ability to create and use hyperlinks. With one click, you can go to another subject. Hyperlinks have now been implemented in all of the Office document types.

Imagine a Word document containing a proposal for a new division. It might contain a high-level overview of the budget needed for starting the division and a hyperlink to the Microsoft Excel spreadsheet that contains all the details. There could be hyperlinks to related projects, presentations to decision makers, research data, or even start-up calendar plans. Hyperlinks within Office documents are critical for a planned intranet, and they are also easy to create, which encourages the ad hoc information sharing that benefits any organization.

Web Toolbar

Word, Microsoft Excel, Microsoft Access, and PowerPoint have the same **Web** toolbar to make it easy to navigate to and use Office documents online. The navigation buttons are the same as those in Microsoft Internet Explorer, and the Office applications use the same list as Microsoft Internet Explorer to track History and Favorites. Wherever you are on your desktop, you can get back to the information you were looking at most recently, regardless of its format.

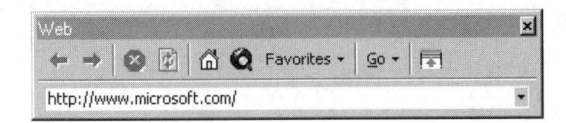

Web Find Fast

Until recently, to find a document on a network you needed to know the server name where the file was stored, the share, where it was nested within the folders, and then the file name the author used. Imagine being able to go to a page on your intranet and asking to see all income statements from 1990 to 1996—and getting a list with hyperlinks to the Microsoft Excel spreadsheet for each year. The Web Find Fast feature in Office 97 makes this possible.

Office first delivered Find Fast full-text searching and indexing in Office 95; this version of Find Fast ran on your hard disk. With Office 97, it is now possible to use Find Fast full-text searching and indexing on both traditional network servers as well as Web servers, indexing HTML files as well as Word, Microsoft Excel, and PowerPoint files. In addition, administrator tools help you set up a search page, create a catalog of all documents, and configure what servers the search should be done on, thereby controlling the network traffic that could be generated.

Not only can Web Find Fast do full-text searching and indexing, it can also search by properties, both standard and custom, that are saved with each Office file such as Title, Author, Create Date, and so forth. This can significantly speed searching performance and dramatically reduce the network bandwidth required for an extensive search.

For More Information   about Web Find Fast, see Chapter 26, "Finding Microsoft Office Documents on the Network."

Viewers

Word, Microsoft Excel, and PowerPoint all provide free viewers. These viewers allow someone who does not have the application to view and print Office documents.

World Wide Web   The Microsoft Excel, PowerPoint, and Word Viewers are available on the Microsoft Web site. For more information, connect to the Office home page at:

http://www.microsoft.com/office/

Browser Integration

Browsing Office documents and HTML documents is seamless in Office 97. A major improvement in this area is integration with browsers such as Microsoft Internet Explorer version 3.0 or higher and Netscape Navigator version 2.0 or higher (with the appropriate plug-in). When you have one of these browsers and you click a hyperlink to an Office document, that document is opened in the browser. You are still in your browser, but all of the tools of the application that created the Office document are available to you.

In the following illustration, a Microsoft Excel 97 file is open within Microsoft Internet Explorer 3.0, which is the initial application running. Most Microsoft Excel and Microsoft Internet Explorer commands and toolbars are available.

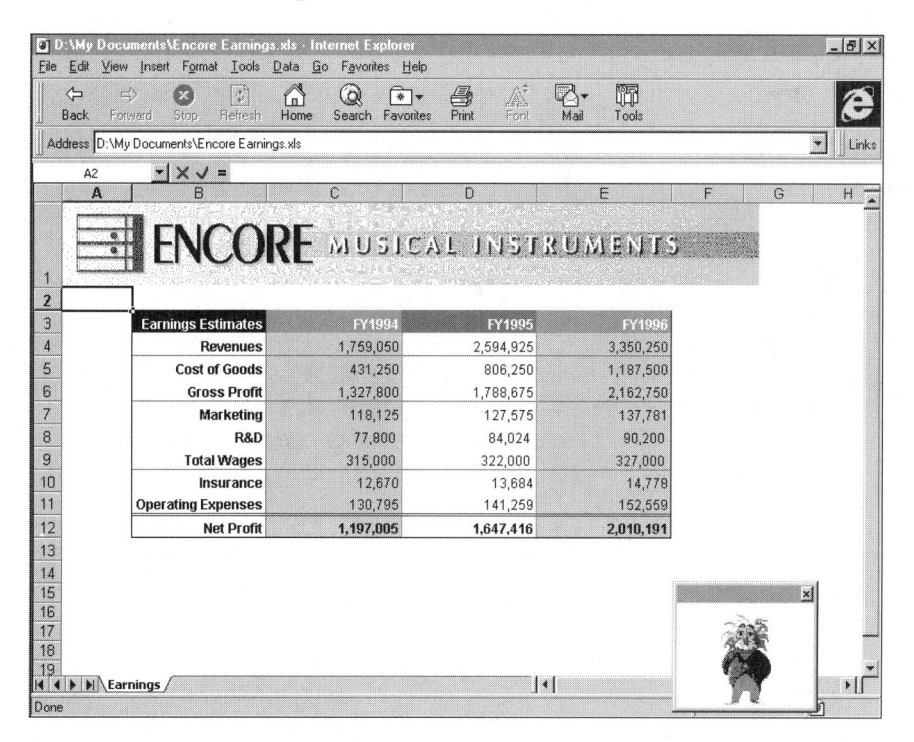

Microsoft FrontPage Support and Integration

Microsoft FrontPage™ is an exciting new product from Microsoft that gives authors the ability to create Web sites and the tools to manage those Web sites. With a graphical view of the structure of your Web site, you can see and edit any of the hyperlinks.

With Office 97, the ability to create intranets with FrontPage is enhanced. FrontPage can track hyperlinks not only to an Office document, but also within an Office document. So if you have your human resources manual on your intranet in Word document form with hyperlinks within it for navigation, FrontPage can now see and manage those hyperlinks.

World Wide Web For the latest information about Microsoft FrontPage, connect to the FrontPage home page at:

http://www.microsoft.com/frontpage/

IntelliMouse

As intranets grow, users are reading more documents online, but navigating in longer documents can be difficult. Microsoft has created a mouse that makes it easier to navigate Office documents. The IntelliMouse™ has a wheel between the two main buttons. Use the wheel to scroll, pan more quickly, or even put Word into a reading mode, in which it scrolls the document for you without your having to click any buttons or keys.

Custom Solutions

Office 97 provides a complete development environment so you can create custom solutions for your intranet quickly, with very little cost. This environment includes the features described in the following sections.

Exposed Functionality

Each Office 97 application has a complete and consistent object model, providing over 600 objects for use in custom development. You gain the benefit of years of developing, testing, and debugging built into Office 97. With this head start, you can quickly create custom solutions using objects from one or more Office applications to solve your business needs.

Visual Basic for Applications

Built on Visual Basic®, the Visual Basic for Applications programming language and the integrated development environment (IDE) built for it, are now included in Microsoft Excel, Word, Microsoft Access, and PowerPoint. Visual Basic is one of the most popular graphical user interface (GUI) programming tools available, with many developers well-versed in its use. The new IDE is also shared among the Office applications, and comes complete with IntelliSense technology that makes programming easier.

Data Access Technologies

Office 97 can serve as the universal client for your desktop computers. With access to legacy and client/server databases through Microsoft Open Database Connectivity (ODBC) databases through Data Access Objects (DAO); to Internet data through support for HTML (Hypertext Markup Language), HTTP (Hypertext Transfer Protocol), and FTP (File Transfer Protocol); and to messaging data through MAPI, it no longer matters where your data resides. You can use the familiar desktop productivity applications to analyze your data.

For More Information   about creating custom programming solutions with Office 97, see the *Microsoft Office 97/Visual Basic Programmer's Guide*, published by Microsoft Press and available wherever computer books are sold. For more information about Microsoft Press books, see Appendix E, "Other Support Resources."

Intranet and Workgroup Solutions in Microsoft Access 97

Microsoft Access provides a number of ways to publish and share data on an intranet, and the Publish to the Web wizard makes it easy. Microsoft Access also provides tools that make it easier to create and optimize the performance of databases shared on a network.

For More Information   about intranet support in Microsoft Access, see "Web Support in Microsoft Access 97" in Chapter 25, "Web Support in Microsoft Office Applications."

Publish to the Web Wizard

Microsoft Access 97 introduces several new features that allow you to share your database information with others over an intranet or the Internet. HTML is a new report output format so you can quickly save your database reports to a Web site. If you prefer to give people a live view of your data, you can use the Publish to the Web

Wizard to quickly set up interactive database pages that let Web browsers query, update, or add information. The following illustration shows the wizard.

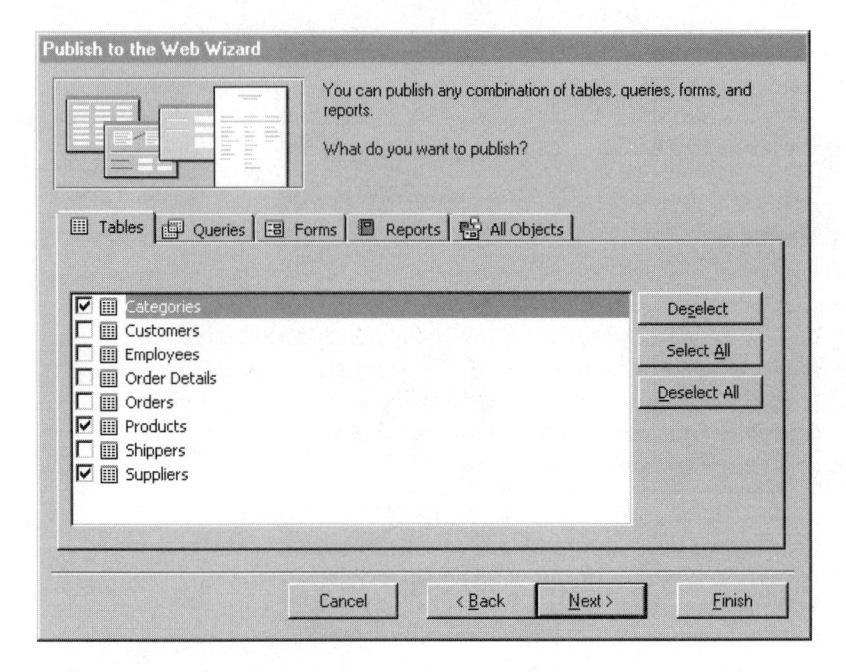

Database Splitter Wizard

The value of a database lies in its ability to have many people working with the same data at the same time. The Database Splitter Wizard in Microsoft Access 97 helps you set up your database so that many people can use it over a network while preserving the best performance. Shared data tables are separated from the rest of the database, which is posted on a file server. Links are then set up to the tables in the new shared file.

Performance Analyzer Wizard

The Performance Analyzer Wizard found in Microsoft Access 97 helps you make your existing database perform more efficiently. The Wizard looks at your database and returns recommendations about how to make it faster. Best of all, the Performance Analyzer Wizard can often make those suggested changes for you.

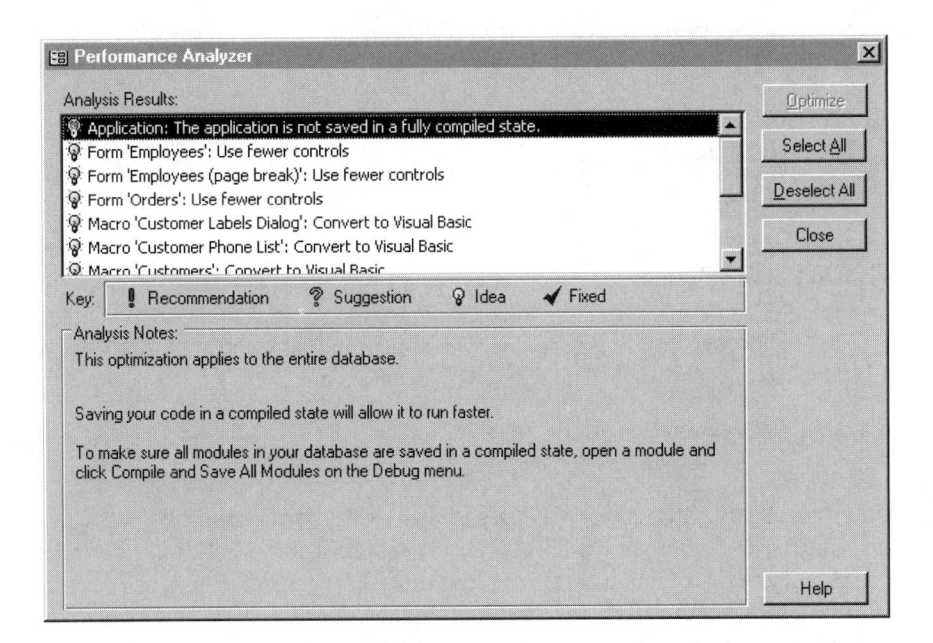

Improved Integrated Development Environment

Microsoft Access 97 uses the programming language Visual Basic, which is shared across all the Office applications. Because Microsoft Access 97 is also an Automation object, Visual Basic can be used both inside and outside Microsoft Access to automate database functions. The IDE in Microsoft Access 97 offers drag-and-drop code, color formatting, an improved debug window, and a new hierarchical object browser.

Programmable Toolbars

Microsoft Access 97 allows solution builders to fully control the user interface of their applications using Visual Basic. Custom toolbars can be created and controlled using the new object model that is shared across Office 97.

Internet Replication

Using Database Replication in Microsoft Access 97, you can now synchronize data from multiple locations using the Internet as your wide-area network (WAN). For example, remote sales people can replicate updates to customer information back to headquarters using an Internet connection from anywhere in the world.

Note Synchronization over the Internet requires the Replication Manager, which is available in Office 97, Developer's Edition.

World Wide Web For the latest information about Office 97, Developer's Edition, connect to the Office Developer Site home page at:

http://www.microsoft.com/officedev/

Removing Source Code

Developers can now remove their source code from the databases they distribute to others, thereby reducing the size of the database and protecting their intellectual property. To remove source code from a database, save a copy of your database as an MDE file.

Web Controls

Microsoft Access 97 includes ActiveX™ controls designed specifically for people developing Web applications. After you install Microsoft Internet Explorer 3.0, you can place the WebBrowser control on Microsoft Access forms. The version of Microsoft Access included in Office 97, Developer's Edition, includes ActiveX controls that support HTTP, FTP, Gopher, and Winsock functionality.

Intranet and Workgroup Solutions in Microsoft Excel 97

Microsoft Excel has a number of tools that allow easy publishing to the Web, such as the Save as HTML Wizard, viewers that allow those without Microsoft Excel to view documents, and the ability to save to an FTP location on the Internet. The greatest value Microsoft Excel provides, however, is the ability to intelligently import data found on the Internet or an intranet for analysis.

For More Information about intranet support in Microsoft Excel, see "Web Support in Microsoft Excel 97" in Chapter 25, "Web Support in Microsoft Office Applications."

Importing from HTML

Microsoft Excel seamlessly imports HTML documents found on a corporate intranet, maintaining the original formatting and turning each cell into live data, which can then be used for further analysis. To import HTML documents, click **Open** on **File** menu, and then select **HTML Documents** in **Files of type** box. Build formulas, charts, or add conditional formatting—all the tools you have in Microsoft Excel can be used with this data.

Web Queries

Although importing from HTML works well with HTML data you encounter when browsing, you might also want to import changing Internet or intranet data regularly into an existing document. For example, you could create a spreadsheet and chart to display your stock portfolio, or a chart that tracks census data. Web queries allow you to set up an automatic hyperlink that brings this HTML data into your spreadsheet from the Web. Once the data is in Microsoft Excel, you can use its powerful analysis tools to analyze the data.

Saving as HTML

With the Internet Assistant Wizard for Microsoft Excel, you can post spreadsheet data for online viewing. This wizard assists in converting spreadsheet data to HTML, either as a separate document or into an existing HTML document. In Microsoft Excel 97, this feature has been enhanced to transform charts into a GIF file.

Using the **Save as HTML** command (**File** menu), you can convert Microsoft Excel spreadsheet data and charts into HTML. If spreadsheet information contains Office hyperlinks (inserted using the **Hyperlink** command on the **Insert** menu), they are automatically converted into HTML hyperlinks.

The **Save as HTML** command allows you to convert all tables and lists into a Web document for the Internet or an intranet, without having to understand the code associated with HTML.

Multiuser Workbooks with Data Tracking

Increasingly, more people are working as teams on projects and sharing information to get their work done. Multiuser workbooks now allow multiple users to work on the same workbook and track changes to that document at the same time. The worksheet can now update changes automatically, and can even track revisions by user in each cell. In addition (similar to Word), you can document your worksheets by leaving comments on the screen for other users.

PivotTable Improvements

PivotTables® have become an essential analysis and presentation tool for many Microsoft Excel users. The enhancements to PivotTables in Microsoft Excel 97 are described in this section.

New PivotTable Wizard

The PivotTable Wizard has been redesigned to make it easier for users of all levels to create dynamic views of their data. It is integrated with the Assistant to give better support to new users, and some of the screens have been redesigned to make them easier to use, while allowing more options from within the wizard.

Persistent Formatting in PivotTable Dynamic Views

The biggest frustration for PivotTable users is that their formatting is erased when they pivot or refresh their data. In Microsoft Excel 97, however, formatting is linked to elements of the worksheet—so it is preserved if you refresh or pivot the table, and it stays with the data it is intended to highlight.

Updated Data Access

Microsoft Excel 97 includes the following enhancements to queries.

Distributable Queries

Distributable queries were designed to solve the problem of distributing predefined queries and reports to users in a corporate environment. Users run the queries when they need them and then complete their analysis in Microsoft Excel.

Parameterized Queries

Parameterized queries are similar to the distributable queries, but parameterized queries also allow per-user customization. For example, one user could choose to see sales for North America, while another might be interested in worldwide sales. By allowing users to define their own parameters within a query, you do not have to design separate reports.

Asynchronous Queries

All queries now execute on a separate thread. This allows you to work on your spreadsheet while a query runs in the background.

Support for URLs

As mentioned previously, it is now possible to create hyperlinks within Microsoft Excel workbooks to files or URL addresses. But there is support for URLs in other places as well. For example, in the **Open** and **Save** dialog boxes (**File** menu) you can use URL addresses instead of network addresses. This makes it easy to open Microsoft Excel files or save files to a server running the HTTP protocol using URL addresses. In addition, you can now create formulas that reference cells in spreadsheets that have URL addresses, as shown in the following illustration.

	January	February	March
Sales	='http://www.mycompany.com/[financials.xls]Jansales'!F29		
Expenses	$3,459.00	$2,050.00	$4,685.00

Intranet and Workgroup Solutions in Microsoft Outlook 97

Microsoft Outlook 97 extends basic workgroup communication functions with advanced e-mail and group scheduling features. In addition, Outlook provides a number of unique features that allow workgroups to work more efficiently and effectively, such as making and tracking task requests, designing custom forms, and automatically tallying votes on an important issue.

For More Information about intranet support in Outlook, see "Web Support in Microsoft Outlook 97" in Chapter 25, "Web Support in Microsoft Office Applications."

Electronic Mail

The simplest workgroup activity that co-workers engage in is e-mail. It's quick, efficient, can be done at any time, and you do not have to play phone tag. For many organizations, it is now the primary means of communication. The best e-mail client for Office 97 users is Outlook. It works like all the other Office applications and has specific integration to make communicating easier.

Outlook IntelliSense features make it easy to communicate within your workgroup. AutoPreview, which shows the first three lines of each message, helps you keep your Inbox under control. The Message Flag feature allows you to add a reminder to an e-mail item to make sure you remember to follow up on it. Use the voting feature to quickly find out what module of a training course your workgroup would like to observe. You can use rich text editing or use Word as your e-mail editor to make your messages more effective.

Outlook works with many back-end mail systems, including Microsoft Mail 3.*x*, Microsoft Exchange Server, POP3, and SMTP.

AutoVoting

When you want others to answer a question, you can use the Outlook voting feature to collect their responses in e-mail. For example, before submitting a bid to a customer, use voting to ensure that the entire team has signed off on it. Outlook automatically tallies the votes as they arrive, so users can look at their copy of the sent message to see the results.

Outlook Forms

Forms Design functionality in Outlook allows you to extend your groupware applications or to customize any of the built-in forms. Outlook includes small, interpretive forms that look and function like many standard paper-based forms. These can be quickly configured, allowing you to switch easily between design and run time. In addition, Outlook also includes a number of preconfigured forms, including the following:

- Expense Reporting

    This form uses Microsoft Excel templates for collecting and reporting employee expenses.

- Vacation and Sick Leave

    These e-mail-based forms synchronize with your calendar for vacation and sick-leave reporting.

- While You Where Out

    Any user can take a message for another employee using a form modeled on the standard pink paper While You Where Out form—and then send the message to the employee's Inbox.

- Timecard

    This e-mail-based form synchronizes with the Outlook Calendar and Journal for timecard reporting.

- Web Site

    This form uses Microsoft Internet Explorer as an ActiveX control and contains a number of fields to categorize information about commonly used Web sites.

Tools and Utilities The Office Resource Kit Tools and Utilities include several additional Outlook sample forms. For more information, see "Outlook 97 Samples Forms" in Appendix A, "Microsoft Office 97 Resource Kit Tools and Utilities."

Group Scheduling

Another common group activity is scheduling meetings. Building on its Schedule+ heritage, Outlook makes it easier for a group of people to find the right time to meet. The Meeting Planner helps you pick required and optional attendees, as well as a conference room or other resources such as audio/visual equipment. AutoPick automatically picks the next available time for all required attendees and resources.

Task Requests and Tracking

Outlook makes it easy for users to send task requests to one another, and for managers to assign tasks to team members. Outlook also automatically tracks the status of task requests and sends updates to the requester. You create task requests in your own task list, and then send them to other users. As the recipient accepts the task, Outlook adds a copy to the recipient's task list. As the recipient updates the task with completion status, Outlook automatically sends an update message back to you and updates your copy of the task.

Outlook task requests are integrated with Microsoft Project and Microsoft Team Manager, allowing users of those products to delegate tasks to Outlook users.

Intranet and Workgroup Solutions in PowerPoint 97

PowerPoint 97 includes enhancements for publishing presentations on the Web. The new AutoContent Wizard includes templates designed for online documents. The ability to convert presentations to HTML is built in to PowerPoint, and the PowerPoint Animation Player works with your Web browser to play multimedia presentations in real time over the Web. Presentation Conferencing, furthermore, allows you to deliver a live presentation over a network or over the Internet.

For More Information about intranet support in Microsoft PowerPoint, see "Web Support in Microsoft PowerPoint 97" in Chapter 25, "Web Support in Microsoft Office Applications."

Save as HTML Wizard

With the **Save as HTML** command (**File** menu), you can build dynamic presentations that can be easily exported as robust HTML pages without having to master HTML. The Save as HTML Wizard asks a series of simple questions:

- Would you like your output to contain frames?
- Would you like your speaker notes displayed as text?
- Would you like to include an outline that allows those viewing your presentation to browse through your slides manually?
- Would you like your presentation to have hyperlinks?
- Would you like your presentation to export as static GIF or JPEG images, or would you like it to export as a full animation?

You can leverage what you know already about PowerPoint to create a dynamic, effective Web page.

PowerPoint Animation Player

You can use PowerPoint 97 to add multimedia elements to a Web page by taking advantage of built-in PowerPoint animation, movies, and sound. Create an animated presentation with the easy-to-use PowerPoint tools, and then click **Save as HTML** (**File** menu) to save the file as a PowerPoint Animation.

Those who want to view the animation can install the PowerPoint Animation Player (a browser extension that works with Netscape Navigator 2.0 or higher and with Microsoft Internet Explorer 3.0 or higher), which allows individuals to view a full-fidelity presentation within a window.

Tools and Utilities   The Office Resource Kit Tools and Utilities include the PowerPoint Animation Player. For more information about the Animation Player, see "PowerPoint Animation Player" in Appendix A, "Microsoft Office 97 Resource Kit Tools and Utilities."

Presentation Conferencing

It is not always possible to collect everyone in the same room for a presentation. The people needed may be scattered around the country or around the world, or perhaps there are not enough conference rooms available when you need to meet. In PowerPoint, you can use the **Presentation Conference** command (**Tools** menu) to hold a virtual meeting and present your information over the network.

Presentation Conferencing allows users to join a conference over the network, and then transmits the presentation to all of those users. It is a live meeting; the presenter advances the slides and controls the presentation on all of the audience members' computers. Presentation Conferencing supports up to 64 users connected through TCP/IP on a LAN, WAN, or an Internet connection.

Intranet Solutions in Word 97

Word has a number of tools that allow easy publishing to the Web, such as the **Save as HTML** command (**File** menu), the ability to save documents to an FTP site, and the Word Viewer that allows those without Word to view documents. Word provides strong support for viewing a document online and quickly moving between parts of a document as well.

For More Information   about saving documents to an FTP site, see "Opening and Saving Documents on the Internet" in Chapter 24, "Integrating Microsoft Office With Your Intranet." For more information about intranet support in Microsoft Word, see "Web Support in Microsoft Word 97" in Chapter 25, "Web Support in Microsoft Office Applications."

AutoHyperlink

There are many new AutoCorrect improvements in Word 97, including AutoHyperlink, which automatically creates a hyperlink from text that appears to be a hyperlink. For example, Word can automatically format the address of a file, a network path, or an Internet address as a hyperlink: The text is formatted in blue with an underline and when the mouse pointer is over it, it turns into a hand to signify that it goes to the destination when clicked.

Document Map

The document map in Word 97 allows you to move around in your document more easily. A split screen displays an outline of your document in the left pane, while the right pane contains the text of your document. Hyperlinks in the outline give you one-click access to points of interest, and serve as a roadmap by highlighting the level at which you are currently located, as shown in the following illustration.

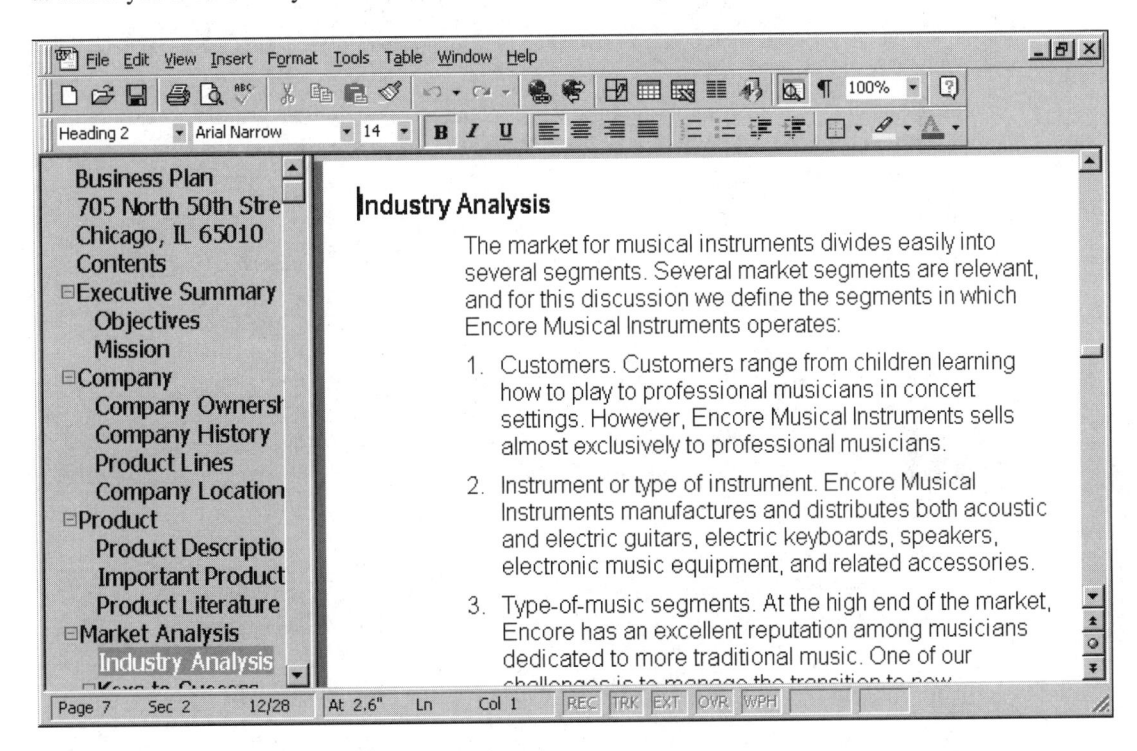

To switch to the document map view, click the **Document Map** command (**View** menu).

Online Reading View

Word 97 makes reading documents online more comfortable. In the past, fonts that were readable in print were not as easy to view online, and it was difficult to move around in long documents. Because the use of intranets will increase the frequency with which people read documents online, Word 97 includes the **Online Layout** command (**View** menu) to make it easier.

In online reading view, the fonts are enlarged slightly and text does not wrap outside of the screen area, which eliminates the need to scroll from side to side. Finally, the Document Map feature is turned on in online reading view, which turns the left-hand section of the screen into an outline with hyperlinks to the full document text. None of these views affect how the document is printed.

Internet Assistant

Using the Internet Assistant for Word 97, you can use the familiar Word features to create Web documents. The Internet Assistant features are available whenever you create or open an HTML document. Word 97 allows you to create sophisticated Web pages without having to learn HTML. Word 97 supports the following HTML tags, which means you can create multimedia pages without having to learn a new program.

- New backgrounds

    Create visually appealing and compelling documents using new background colors and textures. Choose from two dozen built-in textures or create your own custom textures using Office Art.

- Bullets

    Use graphically rich bullets designed specifically for HTML documents.

- Horizontal lines or rules

    Using built-in borders and shading functionality, create colorful and graphical horizontal lines for HTML documents. A new **Horizontal Lines** dialog box (**Insert** menu) allows you to choose from a variety of colorful horizontal line images. For quick access to the last selected line style, click the **Horizontal Line** command (**Insert** menu) when an HTML document is active.

- Pictures

    Insert pictures in a Web page using the same **Picture** command (**Insert** menu) that you use with a standard Word document. Word 97 automatically converts and compresses graphics and OLE objects to JPEG or GIF images. Word 97 also allows graphics to be hyperlinks.

- Video

    Choose the video clip to play, and define when it plays and how often it plays.

- Sound

    Using the background sound control in Word, specify a sound file and the number of times to play it.

- Marquee text

    Create a banner of text that scrolls across your screen. You have control over the animation, direction, speed, background color, and size of text.

- Blinking text

    Apply this popular animation effect to any text in your Web page, just like you can in a standard Word document.

- HTML forms

    Use the same approach to forms design regardless of whether you are creating forms in a standard Word document or an HTML document. Word 97 provides the following form types and buttons:

    - Check box
    - Password control
    - Radio button
    - Text box
    - List box
    - Select drop down
    - Select text area
    - Control submit button
    - Image submit button
    - Reset button

Version Control

The options in the **Versions** dialog box (**File** menu) allow you to save different versions of the same document in the same file. This avoids the extra work and space required for tracking versions in separate files. A version is saved whenever you choose to do so, or you can activate a setting that automatically saves a new version each time you close the file. Save your comments with the version to make it easy to go back to the version you need.

Address Book Integration with Outlook

Outlook contains a contact-management module that can be integrated into the Mail Merge feature in Word. By clicking the **Insert Address** button in the **Envelopes and Labels** dialog box (**Tools** menu), Word users insert names and addresses from Outlook into letters, envelopes, or wherever address information is used.

PART 2

Deploying Microsoft Office

Contents

Chapter 3 Deployment Guide for Microsoft Office 49
Chapter 4 Installing Microsoft Office 71
Chapter 5 System Requirements for Microsoft Office 99
Chapter 6 Customizing Client Installations 105
Chapter 7 Customizing and Optimizing Microsoft Office 137
Chapter 8 Training and Support Programs for Microsoft Office 185
Chapter 9 Troubleshooting Installation 201

CHAPTER 3

Deployment Guide for Microsoft Office

This chapter provides an overview of the significant phases in a typical deployment of Office 97 for Windows. It is written especially for administrators who are responsible for corporate implementation of Office.

In This Chapter

Overview   50

Evaluating and Installing Windows   51

Evaluating Office 97   53

Assembling the Planning Team and Tools   54

Specifying the Test Client Configuration   56

Conducting the Lab Test   59

Planning the Pilot Rollout   62

Conducting the Pilot Rollout   65

Finalizing the Rollout Plan   66

Rolling Out Office   68

Maintaining and Supporting Office   69

See Also

- For a summary of the new features and benefits of Office 97, see Chapter 2, "What's New in Microsoft Office 97."
- For information about installing Office applications, see Chapter 4, "Installing Microsoft Office."
- For information about customizing the client installation process, see Chapter 6, "Customizing Client Installations."

World Wide Web   For the latest information about deploying Office 97, Standard Edition, for the Macintosh, connect to the Office Resource Kit home page at:

http://www.microsoft.com/office/ork/

Overview

Before you can install Office 97 for Windows, you need to install the appropriate operating system: Windows 95 or Windows NT Workstation version 3.51 or later. This section explains how to get started with the Windows deployment and how to use this chapter to plan your Office deployment.

Tools and Utilities The Office Resource Kit Tools and Utilities include the Office 97 Deployment Planner, a Microsoft Project template that outlines the deployment phases described in this chapter. For more information about installing the Deployment Planner (or an equivalent Microsoft Excel spreadsheet), see "Office 97 Deployment Planner" in Appendix A, "Microsoft Office 97 Resource Kit Tools and Utilities."

Deploying Microsoft Windows

Typically, one team upgrades your operating system to Windows 95 or Windows NT, while another team upgrades your applications to Office 97. In this scenario, the Office team can skip those phases that involve the evaluation and installation of Windows.

If you are deploying Windows at the same time as Office, however, you should consider how your Office configuration might affect your planning and deployment of Windows. For more information about Windows features that may assist in your deployment of Office 97, see "Choosing Windows Features" later in this chapter.

For more information about how to deploy Windows 95, see the *Microsoft Windows 95 Resource Kit*, available from Microsoft Press and wherever computer books are sold. For more information about how to deploy the Windows NT operating system, see the *Microsoft Windows NT Server 4.0 Resource Kit* and *Microsoft Windows NT Workstation 4.0 Resource Kit*, also available from Microsoft Press.

Deploying Office 97

Office is designed to make deployment easy in the corporate environment. By understanding how best to plan and automate the installation process, you can reduce the cost of migration.

The deployment process for Office 97 is divided into phases, beginning with an evaluation of the product and ending with a successful installation, usually from a network server. The following are the suggested phases of deployment:

- Evaluating and installing Windows
- Evaluating Office 97
- Assembling the planning team and tools
- Specifying the preferred client configuration

- Conducting the lab test
- Planning the pilot rollout
- Conducting the pilot rollout
- Finalizing the rollout plan
- Conducting the Office 97 rollout
- Maintaining and supporting Office 97

Each phase includes specific tasks that may vary according to your particular organization's structure and needs. For the purpose of this guide, tasks are divided among the following teams, which are made up of employees from your organization.

This deployment team	Includes these individuals
Executive	Project manager or director of information systems; corporate executives
Planning	Project manager; representatives from the support and training teams; representatives form your finance department; installation team members
Installation	Technicians responsible for Office 97 installation; a representative from the Windows deployment team
Support	Help desk or support staff; representatives from the planning team
Training	Staff responsible for employee training

Evaluating and Installing Windows

Before you can deploy Office 97, you need to install Windows on your servers and client systems. As part of the planning process for these installations, you need to consider whether your Office requirements have any effect on the way you configure and install Windows.

Choosing Windows Features

For client systems, several features of Windows may help in the initial Setup of Office, as well as in subsequent maintenance of client systems. These features include:

- System policies
- User profiles

Windows System Policies

In Windows 95 and Windows NT Workstation 4.0, you can use the Windows System Policy Editor to configure client computers from a central location by creating a single system policy file that resides on a server. When users log on to the network, client computers use this file to modify local copies of the Windows registry. The system policy file can be updated at any time.

System policies define the desktop and network functionality on each client computer, including Office features and capabilities. Using system policies, you can perform functions such as disabling peer-sharing services or preventing access to the command prompt for your entire workgroup. Similarly, if you want everyone in your workgroup to save their files in a specific format, such as Word 6.0 for Windows, system policies allow you to set that default file format from a central location.

For More Information about the types of restrictions available and how to implement system policies, see the *Microsoft Windows 95 Resource Kit* or the *Microsoft Windows NT Server 4.0 Resource Kit* and *Microsoft Windows NT Workstation 4.0 Resource Kit*. For more information about customizing Office with system policies, see "Using Windows System Policies to Customize Office" in Chapter 7, "Customizing and Optimizing Microsoft Office."

Windows User Profiles

In Windows 95 and Windows NT Workstation 4.0, user profiles allow individual users or entire workgroups to maintain consistent desktop and environment settings. User profiles display customized desktop settings each time users log on. Multiple users sharing a single computer can customize their individual desktops. Or a single user can move between computers and use the same profile by storing the profile on the server.

An administrator can also take advantage of user profiles to require that a particular desktop configuration be loaded each time a user logs on, or to prevent changes to existing profile settings.

For More Information about how to manage user profiles, see the *Microsoft Windows 95 Resource Kit* or the *Microsoft Windows NT Server 4.0 Resource Kit* and *Microsoft Windows NT Workstation 4.0 Resource Kit*.

Note User profiles are not necessary when only one person uses the computer or when a custom desktop adds no value. Without user profiles, the logon process is shortened slightly; the system does not need to locate and load the profile.

Installing Windows

Before you can install Office 97, you need to install Windows 95 or the Windows NT operating system on your server and client systems. The steps for installing Windows 95 or the Windows NT operating system are listed in the following table and described in the following sections.

Task	Team	Start week	Duration
Acquire the appropriate Windows resource kit.	Executive, Planning	Week 1	1 day
Install Windows 95 or Windows NT operating system	Executive, Planning	Week 1	Varies, depending on the version of Windows. See the appropriate documentation.

Acquire the Windows 95 or the Windows NT Resource Kits

The *Microsoft Windows 95 Resource Kit* and the *Microsoft Windows NT Server 4.0 Resource Kit* and *Microsoft Windows NT Workstation 4.0 Resource Kit* are technical supplements to the Windows product documentation. These manuals are written to assist administrators in installing, supporting, and managing Windows on corporate networks. Both are available from Microsoft Press and wherever computer books are sold.

Install Windows 95 or the Windows NT Operating System

Using the appropriate resource kit, the team responsible for deploying Windows installs Windows on each client and server system that will be running Office 97, or on the system from which you plan to run the Office Setup program.

Evaluating Office 97

The first step in planning the rollout process is to evaluate the new and enhanced features in Office. The steps for evaluating Office 97 resources are listed in the following table and described in the following sections.

Task	Team	Start week	Duration
Review the new features of Office 97.	Executive, Planning	Week 1	3 days
Read the *Office Resource Kit*.	Planning	Week 2	3 days

Review the New Features

For a summary of the many new features of Office 97, read Chapter 2, "What's New in Microsoft Office 97." For more details, you can review the *Microsoft Office 97 Product Enhancements Guide*, which provides an overview of Office features and is a guide to evaluating Office in terms of your company's productivity. For a copy of the *Microsoft Office 97 Product Enhancements Guide*, contact Microsoft Customer Service.

Read the Office Resource Kit

This book, the *Office Resource Kit*, is a technical supplement to other Office product documentation. It is written to assist administrators in installing, supporting, and managing Office on corporate networks. Each planning and installation team member should obtain a copy for use during the deployment process.

Assembling the Planning Team and Tools

After the assigned teams complete their review and have a general understanding of Office features and benefits, you are ready to assemble the people and tools needed to plan the Office implementation.

The tasks for assembling these resources are listed in the following table and described in the following sections.

Task	Team	Start week	Duration
Assign a project manager, and select planning and installation team members.	Planning	Week 1	5 days
Inventory client and server hardware and software configurations.	Planning	Week 2	5 days
Set up a testing lab with equipment and software.	Planning, Installation	Week 2	12 days
If needed, provide team members with additional training.	Installation, Support, Training	Week 3	3 days

Assign a Project Manager and Other Team Members

The deployment project manager participates in the executive team and leads the planning team. This individual is usually the head of your information systems department; however, the executive committee may select another individual, depending on the needs of your organization.

When setting up the planning team, it is important to include representatives from the other groups involved in the deployment process. These include people from corporate support and employee training departments, the corporate standards committee, and selected installation team members. Once the deployment process is underway, individuals from the finance group should also take part in planning and evaluation.

Inventory Client and Server Hardware and Software Configurations

You need to survey a representative sample of your network to compile an inventory of hardware and software used on client and server computers. When this inventory is complete, you can accurately simulate the organizational environment in the lab. Such a simulation helps you make decisions about your organization's computing infrastructure, such as the default desktop configuration.

Software management tools can be used to query computers on the network for their hardware and software configurations. For example, the Microsoft System Information tool (installed with the Office 4.*x* and 95) can run a report describing a computer's hardware and settings and save the output in a text file.

For more detailed information about a large number of computers on a network, you can use system management programs, such as Microsoft Systems Management Server, to conduct the inventory. In addition, Systems Management Server allows you to query the inventory database and quickly get information about which equipment is capable of running Office and which equipment might need upgrading.

For More Information   about Microsoft Systems Management Server, contact Microsoft Customer Service.

Set Up a Testing Lab with Equipment and Software

To effectively evaluate and test the Office installation process, you need to set aside enough physical space and assemble a sufficient number of computers to test everything from server-based Setup to unique options for the local computer. Choose test computer models that are typical of those used in your organization. Then install the appropriate networking software to simulate your network environment.

Before installing Office, make sure that basic operating system functions are working. These functions include:

- Booting
- Connecting to a server
- Printing

It is important that you comprehensively test and implement Office features in the lab with all of your business-specific applications before moving on to the pilot installation. If you have created custom solutions in Office, test those as well.

Note   When upgrading, note that 32-bit applications cannot call 16-bit DLLs or make calls to the 16-bit Windows API. If your applications call DLLs that you created, or if they make Windows 3.*x* API calls, you may need to update these calls. For more information, see "Porting Your 16-bit Office-Based Solutions to 32-bit Office" in Chapter 10, "Upgrading from Previous Versions of Microsoft Office."

Provide Additional Training

Microsoft Authorized Technical Education Centers (ATECs) and Authorized Academic Training Programs (AATPs) offer official Microsoft curriculum delivered by Microsoft-certified trainers. These courses help to educate computer professionals about Microsoft technology, including Office 97.

For More Information   about planning and implementing a training program, see Chapter 8, "Training and Support Programs for Microsoft Office."

Specifying the Test Client Configuration

With the planning team assembled and informed about Office capabilities, the next step is to specify the preferred configuration to use when setting up the test client computers. (For the purpose of this discussion, *client computer* refers to any computer running Office.)

The steps for specifying the client computer configuration are listed in the following table and described in the following sections.

Task	Team	Start week	Duration
Research current server and client configurations.	Planning	Week 3	2 days
Select Office features.	Planning	Week 3	1 day
Choose configuration and installation options.	Planning, Installation	Week 3	1 day

Although you can use other methods to determine the preferred client configuration, Microsoft recommends that you start from the complete configuration—which includes all of the most powerful features of Office—and then work back to the configuration that best fits your organization's needs. The selected configuration and any modifications should be rigorously tested in your lab before you implement them companywide.

Research Server and Client Configurations

To successfully deploy Office 97, you need to catalog your current hardware and software configurations. Your deployment plan is dictated by your current system environments.

Hardware Configuration

Researching the current hardware configurations in your organization helps you make the necessary preparations and choose the best method for deploying Office. Specifically, you need to check the following hardware elements:

- Minimum hardware requirements

  Review current hardware configurations to see if any computers need to be upgraded to meet minimum hardware requirements for Office 97.

- Laptops and desktop computers

  Laptop and desktop users have different configurations, including disk space and access to the network. You must select installation options that work for each type of computer.

- Network access

  Users without network access need to install Office locally from the Office CD. Users with network access can install Office from a network or run Office over the network.

For More Information   about minimum hardware requirements for Office 97, see Chapter 5, "System Requirements for Microsoft Office."

Network Topology

The network can be used in two ways when deploying Office 97: files can be installed on client computers from a network server, or Office applications can be run over the network from a server. You may need different configurations for different levels of network connectivity within your organization. Network considerations include:

- Wide area network (WAN) connections

  For client computers connected over a slow-link network, it may not be practical to install or run Office remotely over the network. In this case, you may need to distribute CDs for these users to install Office.

- Network operating systems

  Consider how your particular network operating system (NOS) affects your plans for deploying Office. NOS issues include server file-sharing methods and client-server permission schemes.

- Network bandwidth

  Consider your network capacity, as well as the performance expectations of your users. Installing Office over the network or executing Office applications over the network places different demands on network bandwidth, both in response time and connection time.

Conversion of Existing Configurations

Whether your current users run Office applications or competitive applications, planning for migrating these users is critical. Determine in advance whether you need to convert existing files, macros, and custom programs, and how you will train new Office 97 users.

Part 2   Deploying Microsoft Office

In many large organizations, users run Office on a variety of operating systems. Microsoft has worked to make this as seamless as possible. Because operating systems are different, however, and because Office 97 includes new features, it is important to understand any differences between operating systems.

For More Information   about using Office in a setting with more than one operating system, see Chapter 22, "Supporting Multiple Versions of Microsoft Office."

Planning the deployment of Windows and Office 97 also provides a good opportunity to review department policies concerning centralized system configuration control and individual user control.

For More Information   about using batch and push installations to standardize client installations, see Chapter 6, "Customizing Client Installations." For more information about using Windows system policies to configure client computers from a central location, see "Using Windows System Policies to Customize Office" in Chapter 7, "Customizing and Optimizing Microsoft Office."

Select Office Features

By reviewing the Office feature set, you can determine how best to configure your client computers for the needs of your users. Because you can choose which components of Office to install, you have flexibility in tailoring client installations to include the best set of features for your users, while reducing use of disk space.

Some Office features affect the productivity of individual users, and you can select these features based on how your users work. These features include such productivity enhancements as the Office Assistant, wizards, and tools such as Microsoft Photo Editor or Microsoft Organization Chart.

Other Office features are designed to enhance the productivity of users in a workgroup, so consider how your users work together and communicate with each other when you are reviewing Office. These workgroup features include communicating through electronic mail, group scheduling, creating an intranet, collaborating on group documents, using presentation conferencing, and managing multiuser databases.

In each case, the features you select may affect how you configure your client installations. For example, the workgroup features you select may require additional software, such as Microsoft Exchange Server.

For More Information   about new Office features, see Chapter 2, "What's New in Microsoft Office 97" or see the *Microsoft Office 97 Product Enhancements Guide*. For more information about Microsoft Exchange Server, see the *Microsoft Windows 95 Resource Kit* or consult your Microsoft Exchange Server documentation.

Choose Configuration and Installation Options

Once you understand the variables in your organization and how they affect your deployment of Office, you can choose the configuration for the test client. You make decisions in the following four areas:

- Where Office program files are located

    You can store Office files on the user's computer or on a network server.

- Which Office Setup installation to choose

    You can install all Office features; you can save disk space by selecting on the features you need; or you can choose to run Office from the network or the Office CD.

- Which media to use to install Office

    You can install Office from a network server or using the Office CD.

- Which method to use to install Office

    You can let users run Setup interactively, provide a Setup batch file, or execute installation from a central location on a network.

For More Information   about installing and customizing Office, see Chapter 4, "Installing Microsoft Office" and Chapter 6, "Customizing Client Installations."

Conducting the Lab Test

Using the client configuration that you have developed on paper, the planning team installs this configuration in the lab for testing and evaluation. You should install Office on your test system in the same way that you plan to install Office on your users' systems. In most cases, this means setting up the network installation location on the server, and then installing Office on the test client system from the server.

Depending on how the test installation proceeds, it may be necessary to modify the configuration by adding or removing selected features. If you are considering more than one configuration, evaluate them side by side to determine which one works best.

The tasks to install and test the client configuration are listed in the following table and described in the following sections.

Task	Team	Start week	Duration
Install Office on the test server.	Installation	Week 4	0.5 day
Prepare the test site.	Installation	Week 4	3 days
Install Office on the test client computers.	Planning, Installation	Week 4	2 days

Task	Team	Start week	Duration
Test the installation	Planning, Installation	Week 4	5 days (longer if required)
Test the uninstall process.	Installation	Week 5	2 days

For More Information about installing Office and selecting features, see Chapter 4, "Installing Microsoft Office," and Chapter 6, "Customizing Client Installations."

Install Office on the Test Server

For client systems to install Office over the network, you must first create a network installation server share by performing an administrative Setup of Office from the Office CD. You can modify the files on this share to customize the client installations, including whether clients run Office locally or from the network. Be sure to document how you customize the installation.

For More Information about creating and customizing a network installation location, see Chapter 4, "Installing Microsoft Office," and Chapter 6, "Customizing Client Installations."

Prepare the Test Site

When you prepare the test site, make sure that all test computers are ready for Office to be installed. Make sure that each computer on which you plan to install Office has enough disk space, random access memory (RAM), and processing speed to run Office.

At the physical site, make sure that you have the appropriate network connection hardware. You may need power supplies and surge protectors for your computers, depending on the number of computers you use for testing. Also, research and eliminate potential problems related to overheating or frequency distortion from the location.

For More Information about hardware the requirements for Office, see Chapter 5, "System Requirements for Microsoft Office."

In addition, run virus detection, disk scanning, and defragmentation programs on each computer to prevent any later problems. Although your machines may appear to be operating properly, software upgrades often uncover hardware or software problems because of the way they read and write data to the hard disk. Checking computers before installing Office helps you stay focused on issues related to the installation process.

Note Be sure to back up critical data and configuration files for the system, in case the installation fails or you need to revert to the old system. If you need to automate the restoration, consider using a commercial backup program instead of copying the files manually.

Finally, when the system hardware is ready, verify that the existing network is fully operational.

Install Office on the Test Client Computers

Install and configure Office, either manually or using an automated installation. Take note of which options you want to predefine in the Setup batch script.

For More Information   about automating the installation process using batch scripts, see Chapter 6, "Customizing Client Installations."

Test the Installation

After you have set up Office on the test computers, you need to verify that it runs correctly and that you can still perform all of your usual tasks. You can run your own set of tests, or you can perform the following recommended tasks:

- Open, run, and close Office applications.
- Test common Office tasks, such as opening, modifying, saving, and printing documents.
- Open existing Office files in the new Office 97 applications.
- Use shared tools, such as the spelling checker, from the network.
- If the client is running Windows from the server, test standard Windows functions, such as printing.
- Shut down completely.

In addition to ensuring that the preferred client configuration works as expected, you may also want to conduct additional testing of optional software features and components. This can help you determine whether you are running Office in the most efficient way. For this kind of testing, conduct side-by-side evaluations on two computers, changing individual features on each one, to determine the following:

- Performance of the hard disk and network
- Ease-of-use for performing common tasks
- Stability of the two computers under stress
- Compatibility with applications and hardware

Test the Uninstall Process

Having thoroughly tested the preferred network client, completely remove Office from one of the test computers to restore the previous client configuration and document the process. Remove Office files by rerunning Setup and clicking the **Remove All** button.

Planning the Pilot Rollout

The goal of the pilot or trial rollout is to create and test your automated installation in everyday use among a limited group of users (for example, between 15 and 50). In the previous phase, you determined the best client configuration for Office. In this phase, appointed teams determine the best methods for automatically installing the specified configuration for a pilot rollout. Planning for this pilot program involves creating the automated installation process, determining the logistics of testing, and preparing a training plan for users.

Automating installation is an important step in reducing the cost of migration. By creating a batch script with answers for installation questions, the installation process can run from start to finish without user intervention. It is also possible to push the installation from the server, so that you can install Office throughout an organization without touching individual computers. This automation work is done in the lab, prior to conducting the pilot rollout.

The steps for the planning process are outlined in the following table and described in the following sections.

Task	Team	Start week	Duration
Install Office on the pilot server.	Planning, Installation	Week 6	2 days
Create and test an automated pilot installation.	Planning, Installation	Week 6	5 days
Plan the pilot installation process.	Planning, Installation	Week 6	7 days
Develop a support plan.	Planning, Support	Week 7	3 days
Develop a user training program.	Planning, Support, Training	Week 5	15 days

Install Office on the Pilot Server

The first step in the pilot rollout is to designate a network server to use as the source for installing Office over the network. Then you run an administrative Setup to install Office source files on the server.

Customize your installation based on your client configuration. For example, decide whether client computers will run Office from the server or locally.

Note Be sure to document any changes you make to the standard installation procedure described in Chapter 4, "Installing Microsoft Office." You may need to duplicate or change your custom installation later.

Create and Test an Automated Pilot Installation

To automate Office installation, write a batch script so that the users do not need to respond to any prompts while Setup is running. You can create a batch script for client installations by modifying the Setup script that is built for you when you run administrative Setup to install Office files on the server. When this script is built, you can specify whether the Office source files on the server are used to set up Office to run locally from a single computer or to run a shared copy from the server.

You can modify the default script to install Office for clients with customized configurations. You can also add other files to the shared folder on the server, such as custom templates or forms, so that client computers are fully configured when Office is installed.

In a *push installation*, the installation process is initiated from the server and runs on a client computer with no intervention by the user. You use a batch installation script to automatically configure the client computer to your specifications.

You can initiate a push installation by modifying user logon scripts to run Setup automatically the next time each user log on to the network. Or, if you use Microsoft Outlook or Microsoft Exchange Client, you can send e-mail to your users with a link to Setup—when the user double-clicks the link, Setup runs with your batch script. You can also use system management software, such as Microsoft Systems Management Server, to start and control installations from a central location.

For More Information about automating the installation process, see Chapter 6, "Customizing Client Installations."

Plan the Pilot Installation Process

Part of the planning for a pilot installation includes determining the timing and the logistics, choosing the pilot user group, and communicating to the group about the pilot rollout.

Even though you are only testing the installation process, the first pilot sets a precedent for the final rollout, so it is important that you are completely prepared for all aspects of the rollout. You need to determine:

- How much time it takes to install Office.
- Which personnel you need for the pilot rollout.
- What tools you need to facilitate the process.
- What the overall schedule should be.
- What your training plan should be.

Estimates for the total installation time are based on the installation time for an individual computer; be sure to schedule the computer downtime for each user. Also, in obtaining tools for the pilot rollout, you may want to include management or debugging software that can help automate the installation.

It is important to choose a pilot user group that is interested in and capable of being the first test case. For example, choosing a pilot group that is not close to a deadline on a project or a group that is traditionally quick to adapt to new technology is likely to increase the chances for a successful pilot installation.

Another step is informing users about the pilot rollout plan. You can use a videotape presentation, an interoffice memo, or a company meeting as the means for communicating with users about the pilot rollout. Regardless of the form used, the message must explain the benefits to users of moving to Office, and describe the overall plan and process by which each group or department will make the move. This makes it easier for your users to plan for and accommodate the migration to Office in their schedules.

Develop a Support Plan

Similar to the training plan, the support plan must be in place the day you begin performing Office installations. The quality of support available during the pilot rollout is an indicator of the quality of the rollout as a whole.

Staff the support team for your pilot rollout with some of your best technicians dedicated solely to the pilot group for the first few weeks. The assigned technicians should carry pagers or be available by phone at all times to give immediate assistance to users.

Track the volume of support calls during the pilot rollout to gauge what effect rolling out Office 97 has on your support staff. You may want to plan for additional staffing during the official rollout, or use this information to determine the rollout schedule.

Develop a User Training Program

With the exception of the new Microsoft Outlook application, the interface for Office 97 applications has not changed appreciably since Office version 4.*x*. In addition, new Office 97 online Help features make it easier for a user to learn the product without formal training. So, depending on the applications and features you install, you may not need to schedule formal training classes for users of Office 4.*x* or Office 95.

For users who do not have experience with Office 4.*x* or Office 95, the first steps in developing a training plan are to acquire a training lab, set up computers in the lab, and appoint a team member as instructor. The instructor is responsible for creating and testing the training program. If in-house resources are not available, use a vendor to develop and conduct the training.

There are numerous ways to approach training and a variety of tools you can use. After creating and testing the program, schedule training sessions to occur immediately before the installation date. This ensures that users retain most of what they learn by putting it to use immediately. It is also important that they are trained before they actually must use the software. You may want to conduct this training while user computers are being upgraded.

For More Information   about planning and implementing a training program, see Chapter 8, "Training and Support Programs for Microsoft Office."

Conducting the Pilot Rollout

The pilot rollout helps you identify problems that may impede or delay the deployment process, and helps you determine what resources you need for the final, company-wide rollout. A successful pilot rollout also helps other installations run smoothly.

The steps for the pilot rollout process are outlined in the following table and described in the following sections.

Task	Team	Start week	Duration
Select and train a pilot user group.	Planning	Week 6	5 days
Install Office on the pilot client computers.	Installation	Week 8	2 days (push installation) or 15 days (manual installation on 50 machines)
Test Office 97 performance and capabilities on pilot computers.	Support	Week 8	10 days
Survey and adjust based on user feedback.	Planning	Week 9	8 days

Select and Train a Pilot User Group

Select a user group that is willing to participate in the pilot Office installation process. They must have the time available and should represent a reasonable cross-section of your total user community.

Install Office on the Pilot Client Computers

Before you begin the pilot installation, back up all computers that have document files. Then perform the installation on the pilot computers in the same manner that you expect to install Office throughout the company.

The schedule for the pilot rollout should simulate—on a smaller scale—the schedule of the final rollout. As you conduct the pilot rollout, you may find that certain tasks take more or less time than expected, that some tasks need to be added, or that some tasks can be eliminated. Modify the pilot rollout schedule to account for such changes, and use the revised pilot schedule for projecting the final rollout timetable.

Test Office 97 Performance and Capabilities on Pilot Computers

In addition to the technicians responsible for conducting the pilot installation, extra technicians should be assigned to measure, observe, and test the installation. By tracking the time per installation, handling problems that arise, and identifying areas for improvement or automation, these individuals help ensure the success of both the pilot and final rollouts.

After Office is installed, these technicians also test system capabilities, such as remote administration, for proper operation. They should monitor the client computers for performance, stability, and functionality, highlighting any inconsistencies with the lab configuration. They should also document areas in which the installation, training, or support can be improved.

Survey and Adjust Based on User Feedback

The final part of the pilot rollout involves surveying users to measure their satisfaction and proficiency with the new installation and to evaluate the level of training and support provided. Test users' proficiency by having them perform a few common tasks or use several of the new features in Office. For example, have these users register their survey comments in a Microsoft Access database on the server.

Based on this initial user feedback, record changes that will increase the satisfaction level and the effectiveness of the installation process. Then continue to monitor the pilot installation for a week or more to ensure that everything runs smoothly.

If the pilot program did not run smoothly or if user feedback was negative, conduct additional pilot installations until the process works well.

Finalizing the Rollout Plan

The results of the pilot installation provide the basis for developing a final plan for rollout. Using the actual time and resource requirements from the smaller-scale pilot rollout, teams make projections for time and resources needed for the company-wide final rollout. If additional resources are required, these should be identified and acquired at this time. In addition, company policies and standards regarding computer and network use should be updated in accordance with the Office implementation.

The steps for the final rollout planning process are outlined in the following table and described in the following sections.

Task	Team	Start week	Duration
Set goals and budget.	Planning, Executive	Week 11	2 days
Obtain approvals and needed resources.	Executive, Planning	Week 11	7 days
Update policies and practices guidelines.	Planning	Week 11	5 days
Create and post the registration template.	Installation	Week 12	2 days

Set Goals and Budget

As you prepare for final rollout, determine your goals for the rollout, including the number of computers on which to install Office and the time expected for completion. Also plan for all tools needed to complete the process within the stated time frame. If necessary, propose a formal budget for the company-wide implementation and present it to management for approval. Your budget should include the costs for personnel and additional resources, such as systems management software.

Obtain Approvals and Resources

After obtaining approval (if necessary), purchase any additional equipment or software you need to facilitate the installation. If you need additional staff, be sure to hire experienced and qualified individuals for the team, and train them completely before starting the project.

Complete your plans for training, communication, and staffing for the final rollout at this time.

Update the Policies and Practices Guidelines

Before beginning the final rollout, update all company policies regarding the use of the network and computers by employees. In addition, update the corporate standards lists for software usage so that you can bring all computers up to compliance during the installation process. Changes in policies should be communicated to employees.

Create and Post the Registration Template

A registration template is used to create a central database for monitoring the progress of the rollout and documenting any areas that require action. As you prepare for the final rollout, create the template using appropriate database management software; include configuration information for every computer and user in the company, and place the template on the server.

As Office is installed during the final rollout, the installation team adds specific information in the template for each computer and user, indicating whether any additional upgrades are needed. The team can then use the template to track open items following the rollout and to measure actual progress against original objectives.

Rolling Out Office

After the extensive research, planning, testing, and analysis performed in the previous phases, the final step in the deployment process is rolling out the Office installation to your entire organization.

The steps for the final rollout process are outlined in the following table and described in the following sections.

Task	Team	Start week	Duration
Prepare installation servers for the final rollout.	Installation	Week 12	5 days
Inform users about the rollout process.	Planning	Week 12	As required
Prepare client computers for the final rollout.	Installation	Week 13	As required
Install Office throughout your organization.	Installation	Week 14	As required

Prepare Installation Servers for the Final Rollout

If you are installing Office from network servers, run an administrative Setup to place Office files on these servers. Customize the installation by modifying the Setup script and by adding or removing files. Create Windows system policy files to define system policies for users.

Inform Users About the Rollout Process

Before the installation process begins, inform users about the process. Distribute preliminary instructions, including preparations users need to make. For those users who need training for Office 97, schedule training sessions to occur before Office is installed.

Prepare Client Computers for the Final Rollout

As needed, upgrade the hardware on client computers and remove any software that does not comply with company policies. Backup critical data and configuration files on the client computers and defragment the client hard disks. Ensure that each client computer is fully operational before proceeding with the Office installation.

Tip Make sure your technicians have proper network access to the client computers so that logon scripts operate correctly.

Chapter 3   Deployment Guide for Microsoft Office

These tasks can be performed manually by your technicians or by the users themselves (with instructions you provide); or they can be completed from a central location with the assistance of system management software, such as Microsoft Systems Management Server.

Install Office Throughout Your Organization

Once the client computers are prepared, install Office using the methods and tools developed during the pilot run. This may involve editing user logon scripts, sending a setup batch file through e-mail, or using system management software. Monitor client computers throughout the process to make sure everything is running smoothly.

For More Information   about the steps involved in installing Office, see Chapter 4, "Installing Microsoft Office."

Maintaining and Supporting Office

Now that you have rolled out Office 97, you must continue to maintain, update, and support your users. For more information about keeping your users productive with Office, see the resources listed in the following tables.

For more information about	See these sections in the Office Resource Kit
Using Windows system policies to configure client computers	"Using Windows System Policies to Customize Office" in Chapter 7, "Customizing and Optimizing Microsoft Office."
Upgrading from previous versions of Office or Office applications	Part 3, "Upgrading to Microsoft Office."
Switching to Office from other applications.	Part 4, "Switching from Other Applications."
Taking full advantage of Office workgroup features	Part 5, "Using Microsoft Office Throughout Your Organization."
Supporting multiple versions of Office	Chapter 22, "Supporting Multiple Versions of Microsoft Office."
Providing training for your users.	Chapter 8, "Training and Support Programs for Microsoft Office."
Obtaining useful resources for continuing support to Office users.	Appendix E, "Other Support Resources."

In addition to the *Office Resource Kit*, the following Microsoft publications may be useful.

For more information about	See these Microsoft publications
Office 97 features	*Microsoft Office 97 Product Enhancements Guide*. Available through Microsoft Customer Service at (800) 426-9400.
How to deploy Windows 95	*Microsoft Windows 95 Resource Kit*. Available from Microsoft Press and wherever computer books are sold.
How to deploy the Windows NT operating system	*Microsoft Windows NT Server 4.0 Resource Kit* and *Microsoft Windows NT Workstation 4.0 Resource Kit*. Available from Microsoft Press and wherever computer books are sold.

CHAPTER 4

Installing Microsoft Office

This chapter describes the basic installation for Microsoft Office 97. Because there is considerable flexibility in the installation process, the chapter begins with the planning phase and installation options, and then describes the specific procedures for installing Office. It concludes with a summary of licensing requirements and instructions for installing Office upgrades.

In This Chapter

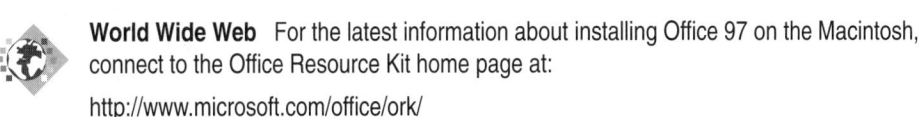

Choosing Configuration and Installation Options   71

Rolling Out Office 97   77

Licensing and Distributing Office in Your Organization   90

Installing New Releases of Office   94

See Also

- For information about preparing for your Office installation, see Chapter 3, "Deployment Guide for Microsoft Office."

- For information about customizing your Office configuration, see Chapter 6, "Customizing Client Installations."

World Wide Web   For the latest information about installing Office 97 on the Macintosh, connect to the Office Resource Kit home page at:

http://www.microsoft.com/office/ork/

Choosing Configuration and Installation Options

Before beginning the process of installing Office in your workgroup, you need to plan the process and review your options. The primary decisions you need to make are described in the following table.

Task	Description
Decide where to install Office files	Locate Office files locally or on a server or use some combination of local and shared installation.
Select the type of installation	Install all Office files or save disk space with other installation types.
Select the installation media	Install Office from the Office CD or over the network.
Select the installation method	Run Setup with or without user intervention.
Determine application-specific requirements	Prepare for any special installation requirements of the Office applications you plan to use.

Some of these decisions affect other decisions. For example, if you choose to install from the Office CD, then all files must be installed on the client computer, and only the interactive Setup method is available.

Decide Where to Install Office Files

When you decide where to install Office files, consider how each client computer is used and evaluate the benefits of each location option, including how the location affects your ability to support the configuration over the long run.

Both Windows and Office can be installed *locally*, where files are installed on the client computer's hard disk. Or they can be *shared*, where files are located on a network server, and users run those files over the network.

Consider the following as you make this decision:

- Performance

  Running Windows and the Office applications locally is generally faster than running them over the network.

- Disk space

  Sharing files on a server reduces the amount of disk space needed on client computers, but it increases the need for disk space on the server.

- Maintenance and support

  Files on a server can be maintained and updated more easily than files on client computers.

- Availability

  Programs installed locally are always available to users, while programs run from a server are not available when the network is offline.

Office program files can also be shared between the server and client computers, or between the hard disk and the Office CD, providing even more options for distributing disk space and managing the files.

Local or Shared Windows Installation

If Windows is installed locally, all Windows files remain on the client hard disk. When Windows is run from a network server, however, you can put most Windows files on the server, leaving only user-specific data files on the hard disk.

Office can be installed in either environment. Some files included with Office are system-level files, and Setup installs them in the Windows folders. If Office is installed in a shared Windows environment, those system-level files are installed on the Windows server, and the space required by Office on the local hard disk is reduced, even if Office itself is installed locally.

Whether Windows is local or shared affects the amount of disk space available for Office, as well as the overall performance of the client computer. It also affects maintenance and support: Windows is easier to manage when it is installed once on a server, rather than separately on each client computer.

For More Information about Windows installation, see the *Microsoft Windows 95 Resource Kit* or the *Microsoft Windows NT Server 4.0 Resource Kit* and *Microsoft Windows NT Workstation 4.0 Resource Kit*.

Tip In Windows 95 and Windows NT Workstation version 4.0, you can use a system policy to configure client computers from a network location, even if Windows is installed locally. For more information, see Chapter 7, "Customizing and Optimizing Microsoft Office."

Local or Shared Office Installation

If you install Office from a network server, you can put some of the files on the hard disk and leave some or all of the Office files on the server. This provides more options for managing local disk space and can be done regardless of whether Windows is local or shared.

If you install Office from the Office CD, you can install some files locally and leave the remaining files on the CD to be opened as needed. This reduces the hard disk space needed for Office. If Office is installed from floppy disks, you must install all files on the client hard disk.

Select the Type of Installation

The following installation types are available in the Office Setup program when you run Setup interactively:

- Typical

    A Typical installation installs a predefined set of the most commonly used Office features.

- Custom

    A Custom installation lets you select from a list of all available Office features and components.

- Run from CD

    When you install Office from the CD, you can choose to leave some Office files on the CD and run them directly from there, rather than copying them to your hard disk.

- Run from Network Server

    When you install Office from a network server, you can choose to leave most Office files on the server, where multiple users can share them.

Tools and Utilities The Office Resource Kit Tools and Utilities include tools for creating a customized Setup script in which you define the features to be installed on the client computer. Setup is run in batch mode using this script, with no interaction by the user, and the components are installed as you define them. For more information, see Chapter 6, "Customizing Client Installations."

Select the Installation Media

Office can be installed on a computer using any of these media:

- Network

    Installing from a network server simplifies the distribution of Office to users, and it provides additional options for sharing files. But it requires a network connection during installation and, if you share Office files over the network, continuous network access while Office is running.

- Office CD

    This media choice requires a CD-ROM drive, and it requires the installer to be physically present at the client computer.

- Floppy disks

    If you are a Select CD customer, you can create Office 97 floppy disks from the Select CD for users who can not use the Office CD and who do not have network access.

Select the Installation Method

After you choose the client configuration, there are three methods that you can use to install Office:

- Install Office interactively

    Users run Setup themselves choosing the installation options they want. If Office is installed from the Office CD or floppy disks, this is the only method that can be used.

- Install Office with minimal interaction

    You create a customized Setup script that predefines all installation options for the user. When Setup is run using the script, installation occurs with minimal user interaction.

- Install Office without user intervention

    A *push installation* is run automatically on a client computer with no user intervention. You can do this by editing the logon script to launch the installation process when the user logs on to the network. Or you can use a tool such as Microsoft Systems Management Server to perform the installation on remote computers.

Note To install or update Office on a Windows NT Workstation client computer using the Windows NT File System (NTFS), you must have administrator privileges on the client computer.

Tip If you use a custom installer program in your organization for installing software and tools on client computers, you may be able to add Office to the installer's list. Using a Setup batch file, you can define a command line for Setup that installs Office with the client options you have chosen. Using Microsoft Exchange Client, you can create a message with a Windows package object that contains a link to the Setup batch script. The script runs when the user double-clicks the object in the mail message.

Determine Application-Specific Requirements

Some Office applications have special installation requirements that you need to consider before completing your Office installation plan. This section helps you understand these special requirements.

You should also read the Ofread8.txt and Netwrk8.txt files included with Office to be sure you understand the latest updates and issues associated with installing and running Office. These files are located on the Office CD; when you install Office, they are copied to the Program Files\Microsoft Office\Office folder on your hard disk.

Electronic Mail-Enabled Applications

Because Office Setup automates the installation of electronic mail (e-mail) support, install any e-mail client software on user systems before installing Office.

If you use The Microsoft Network as an e-mail information service for Outlook, you must use version 4.2.5799 or later. If you use an older version, you cannot send or receive messages.

For More Information about installing and configuring e-mail-enabled applications, including using Word as your e-mail editor, see Chapter 28, "Working with Messaging Systems and Connectivity Software."

Tools and Utilities The Office Resource Kit Tools and Utilities include information about how to use and customize the default messaging profile used by Outlook and e-mail-enabled Office applications. For more information, see "Outlook 97 Profiles" in Appendix A, "Microsoft Office 97 Resource Kit Tools and Utilities."

Microsoft Access 97

If you are using Microsoft Access to link Paradox data on a network while Paradox users are working with the data, you must define a unique Paradox user name in the Windows registry.

The ParadoxUserName entry is in the Windows registry folder **HKEY_LOCAL_MACHINE\SOFTWARE\Microsoft\Jet\3.5\Engines\Paradox**. Setup puts the user name in this registry key when Office is installed. If the user does not specify a user name, or if Setup is run with the **/q** command-line option (to run without user interaction) but without the **/n** option (to specify a user name), then Setup puts the organization name into this registry key.

There cannot be more than one user registered with the same Paradox user name on the same network, so it is important to specify a unique user name during Office Setup.

Microsoft Excel 97

Not all converters are installed with Microsoft Excel when you choose a Typical installation during Setup. To ensure that you get the converters you need, choose the Custom installation and select the converters you want. You can rerun Setup later to add or remove converters as your needs change.

For more information about files installed with each installation type, see Appendix D, "List of Installed Components."

Microsoft PowerPoint 97

Not all converters or graphics filters are installed with PowerPoint when you choose a Typical installation during Setup. For example, PowerPoint uses a separate set of converters to open PowerPoint 97 presentations in PowerPoint version 4.0 or in PowerPoint 95 format. To ensure that you get the graphics filters you need, choose the Custom installation and select the filters you want. You can rerun Setup later to add or remove filters as your needs change.

For more information about files installed with each installation type, see Appendix D, "List of Installed Components."

World Wide Web For the latest information about PowerPoint converters, connect to the Office Resource Kit home page at:

http://www.microsoft.com/office/ork/

Microsoft Word 97

Not all converters are installed with Word when you choose a Typical installation during Setup. To ensure that you get the converters you need, choose the Custom installation and select the converters you want. You can rerun Setup later to add or remove converters as your needs change.

For more information about files installed with each installation type, see Appendix D, "List of Installed Components."

Rolling Out Office 97

Once you have planned your Office installation, the next step is to implement your plan by rolling out Office in your organization. You have selected one of the following options:

- To install Office from the network
- To install Office from the Office CD

These methods of installing Office are described in the following sections.

Installing Office from the Network

To install Office throughout your organization from a network server, you must have an Office 97 user license for each user in your organization. A network installation involves this two-step process:

- First, you create the *administrative installation point*, the set of folders that contains all the Office program files. This folder must be located on a server to which users can connect.
- Second, users run Setup from the administrative installation point to install Office on their computers.

Creating an administrative installation point involves more than copying files from the Office CD to a server. Some or all of the Office program files can be shared from the administrative installation point. Shared Office applications, such as Clip Gallery, can be installed in a separate folder or even on a different server to allow for more flexibility in sharing Office components.

Tip You can modify the administrative installation point to control the way users install Office. For more information about customizing an administrative installation point, see Chapter 6, "Customizing Client Installations."

You use Setup to create the administrative installation point, and your users use the same Setup program to install Office; however, Setup runs in a different way for each of these tasks. In the following sections, these two Setup modes are referred to as follows:

- *Administrative Setup* is run once to create the administrative installation point. Run Setup from the Office CD with the **/a** command-line option
- *Client Setup* is run when a user installs Office on a client computer from the administrative installation point.

Creating the Administrative Installation Point

To create the administrative installation point, first select the server and prepare it, making sure that there is enough disk space and that there are no viruses. Then install the Office program files on the server.

The administrative installation point contains two folders:

- Main Office folder

    This folder contains the Office Setup program (Setup.exe) as well as folders containing all the Office program files. The default folder name is MSOffice.

- Shared applications folder

    This folder contains other program files used by more than one Office application. The default folder name is MSAPPS. The shared applications include: the spelling checker, WordArt, Microsoft Organization Chart, Microsoft Graph 5.0, Microsoft System Information, Microsoft Clip Gallery 3.0, graphics filters, text converters, and Microsoft Excel sheet converters.

World Wide Web For the latest information about installing Office 97 on the Macintosh, including the location of the Office 97 files, connect to the Office Resource Kit home page at: http://www.microsoft.com/office/ork/

When you perform an administrative installation, Setup asks where you want these folders copied. Store them on a server so that users have access to them. You can store them on the same server or on two different servers. Later, when a user installs Office, Setup looks for the shared files at this location on the server.

Chapter 4   Installing Microsoft Office

Server Preparation

The steps required to prepare the administrative installation point on the server are described in the following table.

Task	Description
Make sure that there is sufficient disk space.	Office Standard needs about 280 MB for the administrative installation; Office Professional needs about 325 MB.
Make sure you have access to the folders.	You need read, write, delete, and create permissions to complete the administrative installation.
Make sure that all Office folders are empty.	If a previous version of Office exists, move any custom templates you want to save to another location, and then delete the Office files.
Make sure all users are logged off, and prevent network user access to the folders during the administrative installation.	You must prevent also access by users sharing applications or running shared Windows from this server.
Disable virus detection software.	This prevents erroneous virus detection triggers as Setup writes into various executable files.
Make sure the server is running the correct version of Windows.	To run Setup, you need Windows 95, Windows NT Workstation version 3.51 or later, or Windows NT Server version 3.51 or later.
Share the folders that contain the main Office applications and the shared applications.	Users need read-only access to these folders. You can perform this task before or after running administrative Setup.

Tools and Utilities   The Office Resource Kit Tools and Utilities include the file Top10.doc. This document describes how to prepare the server and client computers for installing Office in more detail. See "Microsoft Technical Support Documents" in Appendix A, "Microsoft Office 97 Resource Kit Tools and Utilities."

Software Installation

After you have the administrative installation point prepared, install the Office program files in those folders.

Tip   If you are installing Office in a server-based Windows environment, Setup copies system files into the shared Windows folders. You need write access to these folders while creating the administrative installation point. After creating the administrative installation point, you also need to perform an initial client Setup with write access to the Windows folders. For more information, see the topic "Installing Office in Shared Windows for the First Time" in the Netwrk8.txt file on the Office CD.

▶ **To create the administrative installation point**

1. Insert the Office CD into the appropriate drive.
2. In Windows 95 or Windows NT Workstation 4.0, click **Run** on the **Start** menu, and then type **setup /a**

   –or–

   In Windows NT Workstation 3.51, click **Run** on the Program Manager or File Manager **File** menu, and then type **setup /a**

   Because you must use the **/a** command-line option to run Setup in administrative mode, you must type the command, rather than double-clicking Setup.

3. In the dialog box that appears, enter the name of your organization.

   During client installation, Setup uses the organization name you type here as the organization name for each user.

4. In the dialog box that appears, enter the product ID printed on the CD package.
5. Enter the name and a path for the folder in which you want to store the main Office application files.
6. Enter the name and a path for the folder in which you want to store the shared application files.
7. In the **Network Server Confirmation** dialog box, under **Network location**, enter the server name and path for the shared applications folder.

   Type the exact path that users must type when they install Office.

8. Under **Connect to server using**, click **Server Name** if you want users to reference the folder with a UNC path.

   –or–

   If you want users to connect to the server using a drive letter, click **Drive Letter** and enter a drive letter in the **Drive** box.

9. In the **Select Paper Form and Language** dialog box, click the paper format for sample documents and language dictionary you want installed.

Note   UNC stands for Universal Naming Convention and refers to the *servername\sharename* syntax used for defining servers and shared areas on the server for LAN Manager-compatible networks.

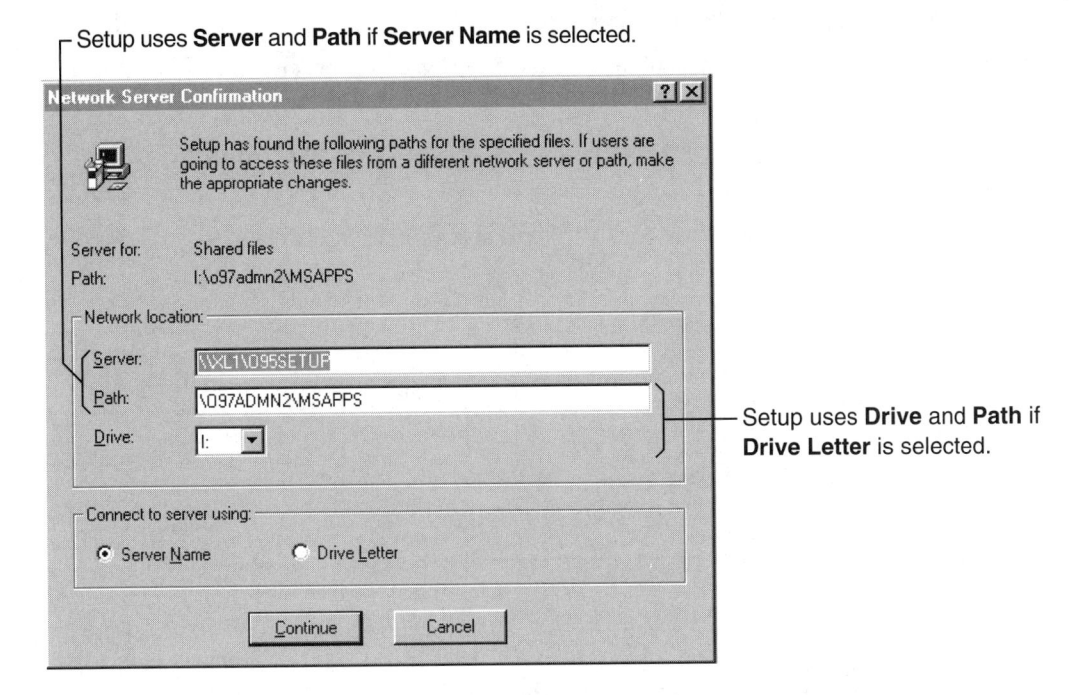

Chapter 4 Installing Microsoft Office

Setup uses **Server** and **Path** if **Server Name** is selected.

[Network Server Confirmation dialog box]

Server for: Shared files
Path: I:\o97admn2\MSAPPS

Network location:
Server: \\XL1\O95SETUP
Path: \O97ADMN2\MSAPPS
Drive: I:

Setup uses **Drive** and **Path** if **Drive Letter** is selected.

Connect to server using:
● Server Name   ○ Drive Letter

[Continue] [Cancel]

Setup verifies the server by connecting to it as specified. If it cannot connect, an error message is displayed. Errors can occur for several reasons. The following table explains what to do to correct the following errors.

If the error is caused by this	Do this
Misspelled server or share name.	Click **Edit** and correct the name.
Share not yet created.	Click **Continue** and create the share before users begin installing Office.
Cannot connect to a local share on the server. (Some networks do not allow you to do this if you run directly from the server.)	Click **Continue**; you can verify the share later from another computer on the network.
Invalid UNC path	Click **Continue**; verify that the share is accessible before users try to install from this server.

After you specify the path for the folders, Setup asks you where users should install their copies of the shared applications.

Microsoft Office 97 Resource Kit   **81**

▶ **To select an installation option for shared applications**

- To have users run shared applications over the network, click **Server**.

  –or–

  To install shared applications on each user's hard disk, click **Local Hard Drive**.

  –or–

  To allow users to choose where to install shared applications during client Setup, click **User's Choice**.

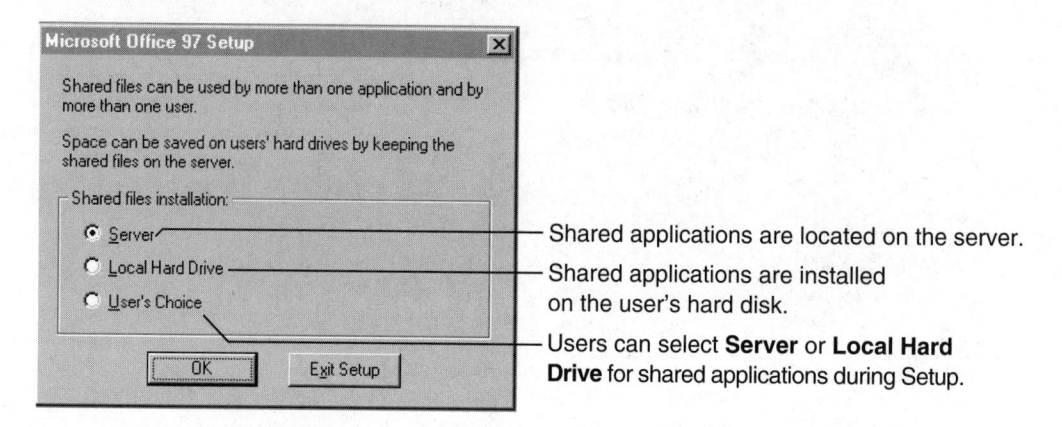

[Microsoft Office 97 Setup dialog box]

- Server — Shared applications are located on the server.
- Local Hard Drive — Shared applications are installed on the user's hard disk.
- User's Choice — Users can select **Server** or **Local Hard Drive** for shared applications during Setup.

Setup checks for available disk space on the server and then copies all the Office files from the Office CD to the administrative installation point. Users can now run client Setup from this administrative installation point and install Office on their computers, based on the options you select while setting up the administrative installation point.

This level of customizing is sufficient for many installations, but there are additional elements of the client installation process that you can customize. For a description of all the ways you can modify the administrative installation point, see Chapter 6, "Customizing Client Installations."

Running Setup on Client Computers

Now that you have created the administrative installation point, users can connect to that location, run client Setup, and install Office. This section describes the client installation process.

Tip If you are installing Office in a server-based Windows environment, you need to perform an initial client Setup with write access to the shared Windows folders. For more information, see the topic, "Installing Office in Shared Windows for the First Time" in the Netwrk8.txt file on the Office CD.

The following procedures describe an interactive client Setup, which means the user selects options presented by Setup. Client Setup can also be run in batch mode, in which Setup options are determined by the client Setup script. For information about customizing the client Setup process, see Chapter 6, "Customizing Client Installations."

▶ **To start Office Setup on a client computer**

1. Connect to the administrative installation point and open the folder containing the main Office application files.
2. Double-click Setup.
3. In the dialog box that appears, enter a user name.

   Setup automatically enters the organization name from the administrative installation point.
4. Click **OK** to verify the product ID.
5. Enter a name for the destination folder for the main Office files.

   This folder can be on your hard disk or it can be a network drive to which you have read, write, create, and delete permissions. If you run Office from the network, Setup still creates a folder on your hard disk with some user-specific files in it.

After you specify a location for the Office folder, Setup may ask for a destination location for shared applications (depending on the selections made during administrative Setup).

▶ **To select a location for shared applications**

- To run shared applications over the network, click **Server**. Setup configures your system to point to the server share.

  –or–

  To install shared applications on your hard disk, click **Local Hard Drive**, and then enter a folder name. Setup copies shared application files to that folder.

Next, Setup asks for the installation to use.

▶ **To select the type of installation**

- To install a predefined set of the commonly used Office components, click **Typical**.

  –or–

  To select from a list of all the available Office features and components, click **Custom**.

  –or–

  To leave the main Office program files on the server and run them from the network, click **Run from Network Server**.

  For More Information about the options included with each installation, see Appendix D, "List of Installed Components."

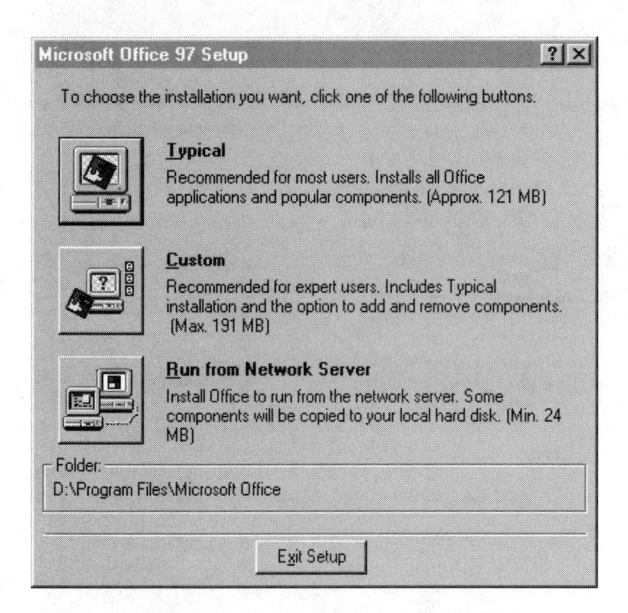

Tools and Utilities The Office Resource Kit Tools and Utilities include the Setup Simulator, a series of HTML pages that guide you through the interactive client Setup process without copying any files or changing any system settings. For more information, see "Setup Simulator" in Appendix A, "Microsoft Office 97 Resource Kit Tools and Utilities."

Custom Installation

If you choose a Custom installation, Setup displays a series of windows with check boxes so you can select which options to install. The first window contains the main Office components:

- Microsoft Office Binder
- Microsoft Excel
- Microsoft Word
- Microsoft PowerPoint
- Microsoft Access (Professional Edition only)
- Microsoft Outlook
- Web Page Authoring (HTML)
- Data Access
- Office Tools
- Converters and Filters
- Getting Results Book

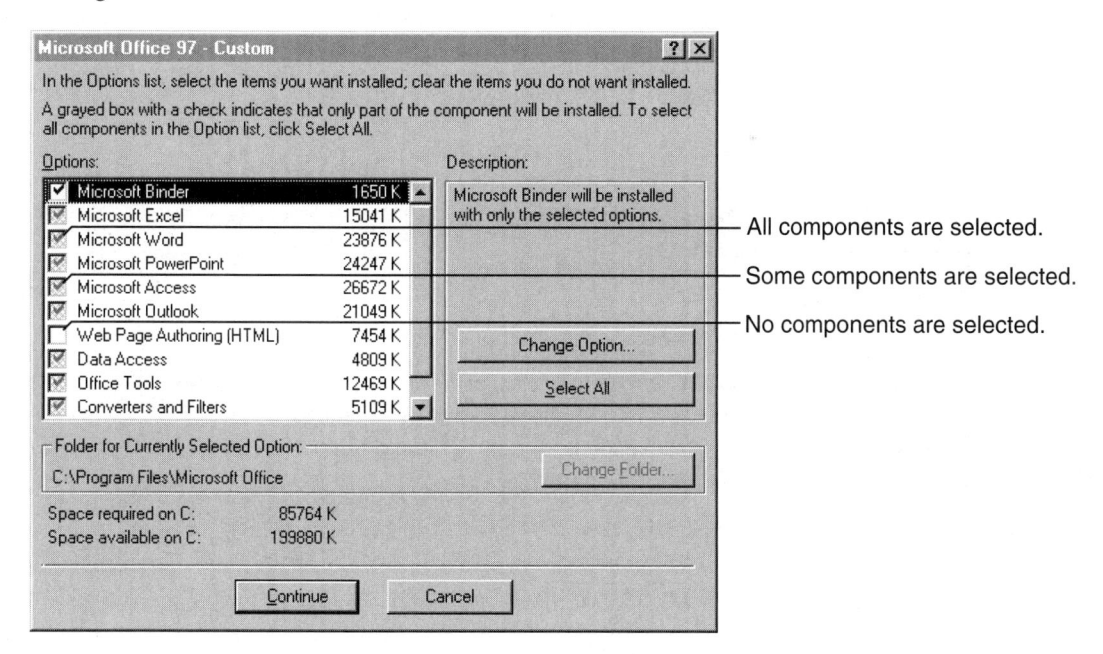

To view a list of additional options for each of these main options, select the one you want, and then click **Change Option**. Another window appears, with another set of check boxes. For example, when you select the **Microsoft Word** option and click **Change Option**, Setup displays the following list of options for Microsoft Word:

- Microsoft Word Program Files
- Help
- Wizards and Templates
- Proofing Tools
- Address Book
- Word Mail in Exchange
- Text Converters

Each of these options may have additional options. If so, the **Change Option** button is available when the option is selected. You can select all or only some of a set of additional components:

- If a check box is selected, all of that option's additional components are selected.
- If a check box is cleared, none of that option's additional components are selected.
- If a check box is grayed, some of that option's additional components are selected. Click **Change Option** to see what those components are.

The **Select All** button allows you to select all the options displayed in the active window, along with all their additional components. For some options, you can also change the folder in which the component is installed. If the folder can be changed, the **Change Folder** button is available.

Note If you are running Windows NT Workstation 3.51, Setup also asks for the Program Group for the program icons after you have finished selecting installation options.

After you select all the installation options you want, Setup checks for available disk space and begins copying files. If Setup determines that there is not enough disk space for all the options you have selected, you can do one of two things:

- You can specify a different destination folder for some components and install them on another hard disk. However, if you change the folder for every component, Setup still installs some files in the original Office folder you specified.
- You can exit and restart Setup, specifying an Office folder on a different hard disk.

Installing Office from the Office CD

To install Office throughout your organization from the Office CD, you must either purchase a copy of Office 97 for each user in your organization; or (if you have multiple licenses) copy the CD to a server and have users run Setup from there. The procedures in this section describe each scenario.

▶ **To install Office from the Office CD**

1 Insert the Office CD into the CD-ROM drive.

2 In Windows 95 or Windows NT Workstation 4.0, double-click Setup in Explorer; or click **Run** on the **Start** menu and type *drive***:\setup** where *drive* is the letter of the CD-ROM drive.

   –or–

   In Windows NT Workstation 3.51, double-click Setup in File Manager; or click **Run** on the Program Manager **File** menu and type *drive***:\setup**

3 Follow the instructions on the screen.

   If needed, give instructions about running Setup to your users before they install Office. Users can also get help while running Setup by pressing F1 or clicking the **Help** button.

4 Choose an installation type by clicking **Typical**, **Custom**, or **Run from CD**.

For a complete description of Office Setup and installation options, see "Running Setup on Client Computers" earlier in this chapter.

If you have a large number of users and multiple licenses, you can share the Office CD with a CD-ROM drive located on a network server, or you can copy the files from the CD to the server. Users can then run Setup from the server, and Setup functions the same as it does when run from the CD (except that users cannot choose the Run from CD installation).

The advantage of sharing the CD on a server, instead of creating an administrative installation point, is that this method takes less server disk space because the shared files are not duplicated. However, it is less flexible and provides less opportunity for customizing. For information about creating an administrative installation point, see "Installing Office from the Network" earlier in this chapter.

▶ **To copy CD contents to a server**

1 Create a folder on the server.

   The server must have enough space for the entire contents of the CD. Office Standard Edition for Windows requires about 330 MB; Office Professional Edition, about 630 MB.

2 Copy all the files from the CD to the folder on the server.

3 Make the server available to users.

Users can now connect to the server, open the folder, and run Setup as if they were installing directly from the Office CD.

Installing Office from Floppy Disks

If you are a Select CD customer, you can create a set of Office 97 floppy disks from the Select CD. For more information, see your Select CD documentation.

If you have multiple licenses, you can install Office throughout your organization from floppy disks by creating multiple sets of disks from your Select CD, or by copying the floppy disks to a server and having users run Setup from there. The procedures in this section describe each scenario.

▶ **To install Office from floppy disks**

1 Insert Disk 1 into the client computer disk drive.

2 In Windows 95 or Windows NT Workstation 4.0, double-click **Setup** in Explorer; or click **Run** on the **Start** menu and type *drive***:\setup**

   –or–

   In Windows NT Workstation 3.51, double-click Setup in File Manager; or click **Run** on the Program Manager File menu and type *drive***:\setup**

3 Follow the instructions on the screen.

   If needed, give instructions about running Setup to your users before they install Office. Users can also get help while running Setup by pressing F1 or clicking the **Help** button.

4 Choose an installation type by clicking **Typical** or **Custom**.

For a complete description of Office Setup and installation options, see "Running Setup on Client Computers" earlier in this chapter.

If you have a large number of users and multiple licenses, you can copy the Office disks to a server. Users can then run Setup from the server, and Setup functions the same as it does when run from the floppy disks, except that it does not prompt users to insert each disk.

The advantage of copying the floppy disks to a server, rather than creating an administrative installation point, is that this method takes less server disk space, because the files are compressed. However, it is much less flexible and provides little opportunity for customizing. For information about creating an administrative installation point, see "Installing Office from the Network" earlier in this chapter.

Because of the special compressed format of the Office floppy disks, you cannot use the Explorer or MS-DOS® **Copy** command to copy the files from the floppy disk to a server. Instead, you must use the Extract program included on the Office Setup disk (Disk 1). For more information about Office floppy disks, see "Office Floppy Disks Use a Compressed Format" later in this chapter.

Tools and Utilities   The Office Resource Kit Tools and Utilities include copies of these files: Extract; Wextra32 (a program similar to Extract that runs on Windows 95 and Windows NT Workstation); and two MS-DOS batch files (CopyAll.bat and CopyDisk.bat) that run Extract to copy the contents of the Office floppy disk set to a server folder. For more information, see "Tools for Extracting and Copying Files from Office Floppy Disks" in Appendix A, "Microsoft Office 97 Resource Kit Tools and Utilities."

Users can now connect to the server, open the folder, and run Setup as if they were running Setup directly from the floppy disk set. Instead of prompting for each floppy disk, Setup goes to each subfolder on the server to find the next set of files.

Office Floppy Disks Use a Compressed Format

With the exception of the Setup disk (Disk 1), Office floppy disks are created in a format that compresses many files into a single cabinet (CAB) file on the disk. By reducing the gap between sectors, Office floppy disks contain up to 1.68 MB of data on a single, high-density 3.5-inch floppy disk. Because the Office floppy disks have a non-standard sector gap, you cannot use standard disk copying and examination utilities, and some low-quality or older disk drives may not read the disk.

Disk 1 of the Office floppy disk set is a 1.44 MB read/write disk, and can be handled using normal disk utilities.

To extract and decompress files from a CAB file, use one of these two programs:

- Wextra32 runs on Windows 95 and Windows NT Workstation.

- Extract runs in MS-DOS and is available on Office Disk 1. Type **Extract /?** to display command-line options. Extract can also be used to copy a complete CAB file from a compressed floppy disk to a local disk or network share.

Note that neither Extract nor Wextra32 can put new or changed files back into a CAB file; they only extract files from the CAB file.

Both Wextra32 and Extract are available in the Office Resource Kit Tools and Utilities. For more information, see "Tools for Extracting and Copying Files from Office Floppy Disks" in Appendix A, "Microsoft Office 97 Resource Kit Tools and Utilities."

Licensing and Distributing Office in Your Organization

This section describes the product identification method used by Microsoft; explains compliance checking, which verifies that the user has an appropriate older version of Office or competitive product installed before upgrading to Office; and covers the licensing options available from Microsoft.

Product Identification

The product ID for Office is a unique identifier for each license of Office. The complete product ID consists of 20 digits and is handled slightly differently depending on the media used to install Office.

Network

Every installation done from the administrative installation point is given a unique, 20-digit product ID with a common root (the first 15 digits). The complete ID is written into the main Office executable files (Winword.exe, Excel.exe, and so forth) on the user's hard disk.

Office CD

For the Office CD, a portion of the product ID is printed on the CD package; the user running Setup is asked to enter that portion manually during the installation process. The complete ID is written into the main Office executable files (Winword.exe, Excel.exe, and so forth) on the user's hard disk.

Select CD

When installing Office from a Select CD (from the Select customer program), the user is not prompted to enter any product ID information. A portion of the ID is stamped on the CD and includes the product code and a Select ID. The remainder of the total product ID is generated at the time the software is installed and is unique for each installation. Multiple client installations of Office from a single Select CD have a common root in the product ID that identifies each installation as coming from the same Select CD.

Floppy Disks

A portion of the product ID is stamped on the floppy disks during manufacturing, and another portion is generated at the time the software is installed. The complete ID is written into the main Office executable files (Winword.exe, Excel.exe, and so forth) on the user's hard disk.

If multiple installations are done from the same set of floppy disks, a different product ID is generated for each installation and is associated with the license for that particular installation. Each product ID consists of a common root (the first 15 digits) that identifies each installation from the same floppy disk set.

When installing from floppy disks, Setup keeps track of the number of installations performed from the same floppy disk set and displays a warning if the legal number is exceeded. Selecting **Remove All** from Setup does not decrement the installation counter. If you hold multiple licenses, you can use a command-line option for Setup to specify the number of licenses you have. For more information about this option, see Appendix B, "Setup Command-Line Options and File Formats."

Compliance Checking

Office 97 is available as an upgrade for those who have a previous version of Office, or for those who are moving to Office from a competitive product. If you purchase Office 97 as an upgrade, client Setup performs a compliance check to verify that the upgrade is being installed in accordance with the upgrade agreement. It verifies that you have an appropriate older version or competitive product installed before it proceeds.

The verification procedure is performed according to a table defined by Microsoft for each upgrade and may vary for each application, each version, and each language depending on international competitive markets. The table consists of a list of products and product versions that satisfy the compliance check, along with a signature for each product that defines how Setup detects that the product is installed.

The signature can consist of one or more of the following items:

- Product files, including a file name, size, and folders to search. The signature can indicate whether to search one or more default folders only, or to search the entire disk.
- INI file entries, including an INI file name, key, and value
- Registry entries key and value

At the beginning of the client installation process, Setup searches the client computer for indications that at least one of the products on the list is installed. The first product it finds satisfies the search, and Setup proceeds with the installation. If the table instructs Setup to search the entire disk, Setup display a message to this effect and lists the products it is looking for.

If no products from the list are found, Setup gives the user a chance to insert the installation floppy disk for a complying product. If the user does not have such a disk, Setup ends and does not install the upgrade. In some cases, the compliance checking table for an upgrade may specify that Setup can continue without finding a compliant product, in which case Setup displays a warning and then continues with the upgrade. This depends on how Microsoft has defined the compliance checking rules for a particular product upgrade.

The following lists the products that Setup searches for when you upgrade to Office 97.

Office Suites
- Microsoft Office for Windows (all versions)
- Microsoft Works for Windows (all versions)
- Borland Office, version 2.0
- Corel WordPerfect Suite 7
- Lotus SmartSuite, version 2.0 or later
- Novell PerfectOffice, version 3.0 or later

Word Processors
- Microsoft Word for MS-DOS, version 2.0 or later
- Microsoft Word for Windows, version 1.0 or later
- Microsoft Word for Windows NT Workstation, version 6.0
- Ami Pro for Windows, version 1.0 or later
- WordPerfect for MS-DOS, version 4.0 or later
- WordPerfect for Windows, version 5.1 or later
- Word Pro 96 Edition for Windows and Windows 95
- WordStar for MS-DOS, version 1.0 or later
- WordStar for Windows, version 1.0 or later
- WordStar 2000 for MS-DOS, version 3.0 or later
- WordStar Pro for MS-DOS, version 1.0 or later

Spreadsheets
- Microsoft Excel for Windows, version 3.0 or later
- Microsoft Excel for Windows NT Workstation, version 5.0
- Microsoft Multiplan®, all versions
- Borland Quattro Pro for MS-DOS, version 1.0 or later
- Borland Quattro Pro for Windows, version 1.0 or later

- Borland Quattro Pro Special Edition, version 1.0
- Lotus 1-2-3 for MS-DOS, release 2.01 or later
- Lotus 1-2-3 for Windows, release 1.0 or later
- SuperCalc for MS-DOS, version 3.1 or later

Presentation Graphics
- Microsoft PowerPoint for Windows, version 2.0 or later
- Aldus Persuasion for Windows, version 2.0 or later
- ASAP, version 1.0 or later
- ASAP WordPower, version 1.0 or later
- Harvard Graphics for MS-DOS, version 2.3 or later
- Harvard Graphics for Windows, version 1.0 or later
- Lotus Freelance for MS-DOS, release 4.0
- Lotus Freelance for Windows, release 1.0 or later
- WordPerfect Presentations for MS-DOS, version 2.0
- WordPerfect Presentations for Windows, version 2.0 or later

Databases
- Microsoft Access, version 1.0 or later
- Microsoft FoxPro® for MS-DOS, version 2.0 or later
- Microsoft FoxPro for Windows, version 2.5 or later
- Microsoft Visual FoxPro™ for Windows, version 3.0
- Borland dBASE 5.0 for MS-DOS
- Borland dBASE 5.0 for Windows
- Borland dBASE IV for MS-DOS, version 1.0 or later
- Borland Paradox for MS-DOS, version 4.5 or later
- Borland Paradox for Windows, version 1.0 or later
- Claris FileMaker Pro for Windows, version 2.0 or later
- DataEase 5.0 for Windows
- Lotus Approach for Windows, version 1.0 or later
- Personal Oracle7 for Windows
- Superbase versions 1.2, 1.3, 2.0, 4.1.3
- Superbase for Windows 95, version 3.0
- Symantec Q&A for MS-DOS, version 4.0
- Symantec Q&A for Windows, version 4.0

Scheduling
- Microsoft Schedule+, version 7.0

Project Management
- Microsoft Project, version 1.0 or later

Contact Microsoft Product Support for additional help with specific upgrading situations.

Licensing

Every user must have a Microsoft Office license, no matter how you install Office in your organization. One license is provided with each retail package of Microsoft Office.

If you do not want to purchase a complete copy of Office for every user, you can purchase a License Pak. Each License Pak allows you to make and use one additional copy of Office. You do not need to store extra copies of Office or the documentation, and it is less expensive than purchasing a retail package. For more information, ask your reseller about licensing options.

Installing New Releases of Office

After the initial release of Office 97, Microsoft may occasionally release software updates. If you decide to install a new version of Office in your organization, you use a process very similar to the one you used to install Office originally.

You can update Office software without modifying the configuration of your client computers, or you can change the way your client systems are configured. For example, you may want to change whether shared applications are installed on the hard disk or shared on the network. The steps you need to follow in either case are described in the following sections.

Updating Office with the Same Configuration

To update Office on client computers without changing client configurations, prepare and install the new version of Office on your client computers.

Important You cannot update an Office installation using the standalone versions of Office applications (Microsoft Access, Microsoft Excel, PowerPoint, Outlook, or Word). To update Office software, you must use an updated version of the Microsoft Office suite of applications.

Installing from the Network

If your users originally installed Office from an administrative installation point on a network server, the process for updating users involves two steps:

- First, you update the Office administrative installation point on the network from which Office was installed originally.
- Second, users run Setup from the administrative installation point to update Office on their computers.

Before you begin the updating process, prepare the server just as you did when you installed Office originally:

- Make sure all users are logged off, and prevent network user access to the folders during the updating process.
- Move any workgroup documents, templates, or other custom files you want to save to another location.
- Delete the existing Office folders on the server. These folders include both the main Office folder (which contains Office program files such Winword.exe and Excel.exe) and the shared applications folder (which contains shared applications such as the spelling checker).

Note If you have customized the Setup.stf (STF) file, do not copy this file into the updated Office folder. Instead, customize the new STF file that is included with the updated version of Office. For more information about STF files, see Chapter 6, "Customizing Client Installations."

▶ **To update the Office administrative installation point with the same configuration**

1. Insert the updated Office CD into the appropriate drive.
2. In Windows 95 or Windows NT Workstation 4.0, click **Run** on the **Start** menu, and then type *drive:*/**setup /a** where *drive* is the letter of the CD-ROM drive.

   –or–

   In Windows NT Workstation 3.51, click **Run** on the Program Manager or File Manager **File** menu, and then type *drive*:**\setup /a** where *drive* is the letter of the CD-ROM.

   This installs the new version of Office into the same folders as the previous version.

3. Enter the name and a path for the folder in which you want to store the shared application files.

   Specify this location the same way you did when you installed Office originally— with the same drive letter or the same UNC path.

After the administrative installation point is updated, users' computers can be updated.

▶ **To update user computers with the same Office configuration**

1. Close all Office applications.
2. Connect to the administrative installation point and open the folder containing the main Office application files.
3. Double-click Setup.
4. Follow the instructions on the screen.

As during the original installation of Office, you can have users run Setup themselves, or you can automate the process using the techniques described in Chapter 6, "Customizing Client Installations."

Note If you purchased the Office 97, Standard Edition, you cannot use the standalone Microsoft Access product to update your Office installation. If you want to add Microsoft Access to your Office installation, you must purchase Office 97, Professional Edition. After you purchase the Professional Edition, follow the steps described earlier in this section for updating Office software.

Installing from CD or Floppy Disks

If your users originally installed Office from the Office CD or floppy disks, they can install the Office update the same way.

▶ **To update Office from CD or floppy disks**

1. Close all Office applications.
2. In Explorer (Windows 95 or Windows NT Workstation 4.0) or Program Manager (Windows NT Workstation 3.51), double-click Setup on the new CD or on Disk 1 of the new floppy disk set.
3. Follow the instructions on the screen.

Updating Office with a New Configuration

When you update Office software, you can change the way Office is configured on your network. With your original installation, user computers may have been configured so that all Office programs are located on the user's hard disk, or some or all of the Office components are shared on a network server. When installing an Office update, you can change this configuration. For example, you may have upgraded your network servers and would now like users to run the shared Office applications from a network server, rather than storing them on their hard disks.

Changing your Office configuration is a two-step process. First, you need to create or update your administrative installation point with updated software and with new configuration options. Second, users must uninstall Office and then reinstall it to get the new version.

If your users originally installed Office from the CD or floppy disks, you need to create an administrative installation point on a network server from which users can install Office. For information about creating an administrative installation point, see "Installing Office from the Network" earlier in this chapter.

Before you begin the updating process, make sure all users are logged off, and prevent network access to the folders during the updating process.

▶ **To create an Office administrative installation point with a new configuration**

1 Prepare a new network server location so that Office Setup can create the new administrative installation point in an empty folder.

   Do not delete the existing Office folder structure; users must use the original Setup program to remove their existing Office installations.

2 Insert the updated Office CD into the appropriate drive.

3 In Windows 95 or Windows NT Workstation 4.0, click **Run** on the **Start** menu, and then type *drive***:\setup /a** where *drive* is the letter of the CD-ROM.

   –or–

   In Windows NT Workstation 3.51, click **Run** on the Program Manager or File Manager **File** menu, and then type *drive***:\setup /a** where *drive* is the letter of the CD-ROM.

4 Enter the name and a path for the folder in which you want to store the main Office files and the shared application files. Also enter any new configuration information—for example, whether users run shared applications from the server.

Once you have created the new administrative installation point, you can use the Network Installation Wizard to further customize the installation. For more information, see Chapter 6, "Customizing Client Installations."

Next, because configuration information is being changed, your users must remove their existing version of Office and then install the new version.

▶ **To update user computers with a new Office configuration**

1 Close all Office applications.

2 Connect to the original administrative installation point and open the folder containing the main Office application files.

3 Double-click Setup.

4 Click **Remove All**.

5 Connect to the new administrative installation point and open the folder containing the main Office application files.

6 Double-click Setup.

7 Follow the instructions on the screen.

As during the original installation of Office, you can have users run Setup themselves, or you can automate the process using the techniques described in Chapter 6, "Customizing Client Installations." To automate the uninstall of Office, use the **/u** command-line option. For more information, see Appendix B, "Setup Command-Line Options and File Formats."

CHAPTER 5

System Requirements for Microsoft Office

This chapter describes system requirements for the various Microsoft Office 97 packages. Note that these system requirements apply to standalone desktop installations. If you install Office over a network, you can substantially customize your Office installation. For example, you can install Office so that shared components, such as clip art and online Help, are stored on network servers, reducing hard disk space requirements on each workstation.

In This Chapter
Microsoft Office Products for Windows   99
Microsoft Office Products for the Macintosh   104

See Also
- For information about network installation options, see Chapter 4, "Installing Microsoft Office."
- For information about customizing your Office configuration, see Chapter 6, "Customizing Client Installations."

Microsoft Office Products for Windows

This section describes Office 97 packages for Windows.

Tip   For the latest information about system requirements and late-breaking news about installing Office, see the Office Readme file, Ofread8.txt. It is copied from the Office CD to your Program Files\Microsoft Office\Office folder when you install Office.

Microsoft Office 97, Standard Edition

Microsoft Office 97, Standard Edition, includes four full-featured programs:
- Microsoft Word 97
- Microsoft Excel 97

- Microsoft PowerPoint 97
- Microsoft Outlook 97

System Requirements

To use Microsoft Office Standard Edition, you need:

- A personal computer with a 486 or higher processor.
- One of the following operating systems:
    - Microsoft Windows 95.

    –or–

    - Microsoft Windows NT Workstation version 3.51 or later with Service Pack 5. (Office 97 does not run on earlier versions of Windows.)

    –or–

    - Microsoft Windows NT Workstation version 4.0 or later with Service Pack 2 (SP2) or later.
- Sufficient memory, as described in the following table. (More memory is required to run additional programs simultaneously.)

To run this Office program	You need this much memory
Any single Office application on Windows 95	8 MB
Any single Office application on Windows NT Workstation	16 MB

- Sufficient hard disk space, as described in the following table.

This Setup installation type	Requires this amount of hard disk space
Typical	102 MB
Custom	67 MB (minimum) to 167 MB (maximum)
Run from CD	51 MB

Note The minimum installation size is derived by installing only the Office applications and the spelling checker.

- One CD-ROM drive. (A coupon for 3.5-inch disks is included in the Office package. However, the disk version of Office does not contain all of the components of the CD-ROM version of Office, such as Microsoft Internet Explorer and clip art.
- VGA or higher-resolution video adapter (SVGA 256 color or higher recommended).
- Microsoft Mouse or compatible pointing device.

Any or all of the following, though not required, can be used with Microsoft Office for Windows:

- Microsoft Mail 3.*x* for Windows, Microsoft Exchange Client, Internet SMTP/POP3, or other MAPI-compliant messaging software for e-mail.
- Microsoft Exchange Server for some advanced workgroup functionality in Outlook.
- 9600-baud or higher modem (14,400-baud or higher modem recommended).
- Audio board with headphones or speakers.

Note Some Internet functionality may require Internet access and payment of a separate fee to an Internet service provider.

Microsoft Office 97, Professional Edition

Microsoft Office 97, Professional Edition, includes all the programs in the Standard Edition plus Microsoft Access 97.

System Requirements

To use Microsoft Office Professional Edition, you need:

- A personal computer with a 486 or higher processor.
- One of the following operating systems:
  - Microsoft Windows 95.

    –or–

  - Microsoft Windows NT Workstation 3.51 or later with Service Pack 5. (Office 97 does not run on earlier versions of Windows.)

    –or–

  - Microsoft Windows NT Workstation 4.0 or later with Service Pack 2 (SP2) or later.

- Sufficient memory, as described in the following table. (More memory is required to run additional programs simultaneously.)

To run this Office program	You need this much memory
Any single Office application on Windows 95	8 MB (12 MB to run Microsoft Access)
Any single Office application on Windows NT Workstation	16 MB

- Sufficient hard disk space, as described in the following table.

This Setup installation type	Requires this amount of hard disk space
Typical	121 MB
Custom	73 MB (minimum) to 191 MB (maximum)
Run from CD	61 MB

Note The minimum installation size is derived by installing only the Office applications and the spelling checker.

- One CD-ROM drive. (A coupon for 3.5-inch disks is included in the Office package. However, the disk version of Office does not contain all of the components of the CD-ROM version of Office, such as Microsoft Internet Explorer and clip art.
- VGA or higher-resolution video adapter (SVGA 256 color recommended).
- Microsoft Mouse or compatible pointing device.

Any or all of the following, though not required, can be used with Microsoft Office for Windows 95:

- Microsoft Mail 3.*x* for Windows, Microsoft Exchange Client, Internet SMTP/POP3, or other MAPI-compliant messaging software for e-mail.
- Microsoft Exchange Server for some advanced workgroup functionality in Outlook.
- 9600-baud or higher modem (14,400-baud or higher modem recommended).
- Audio board with headphones or speakers.

Note Some Internet functionality may require Internet access and payment of a separate fee to an Internet service provider.

Microsoft Office 97, Professional Edition with Bookshelf Basics

Microsoft Office 97, Professional Edition with Bookshelf® Basics, includes everything in the Professional Edition (five programs) plus the following titles from the Microsoft Bookshelf 97 CD-ROM reference library:

- *The American Heritage Dictionary*
- *Roget's Thesaurus*
- *The Columbia Dictionary of Quotations*
- *More About Bookshelf*, which describes additional reference sources available in the full Microsoft Bookshelf product.

For more information about Office integration with Bookshelf Basics, see "Using Microsoft Bookshelf in a Workgroup" in Chapter 27, "Sharing Information with Microsoft Office Applications."

System Requirements

To use Microsoft Office 97, Professional Edition with Bookshelf Basics, you need:

- A multimedia PC with the following:
  - A 486 or higher processor.
  - A CD-ROM drive.
  - An audio board with headphones or speakers.
- All the system requirements for Microsoft Office, Professional Edition.

Microsoft Office 97, Professional Edition with Bookshelf Basics and Microsoft IntelliMouse

Microsoft Office 97 Professional Edition with Bookshelf Basics and Microsoft IntelliMouse includes everything in the Professional Edition with Bookshelf Basics, plus the new Microsoft IntelliMouse.

IntelliMouse puts the power to zoom and scroll at your fingertips with an innovative wheel, so you get more done with less effort. The Microsoft Office 97 applications include unique support for IntelliMouse. Using the IntelliMouse wheel, you can scroll through screens of information and zoom in to view your data while you work—instead of hunting for scrollbars, buttons, and menus on the screen.

System Requirements

The system requirements for this package are the same as those for Microsoft Office 97, Professional Edition with Bookshelf Basics.

Microsoft Office Products for the Macintosh

This section describes Office 97, Standard Edition, for the Macintosh.

Microsoft Office 97, Standard Edition, for the Macintosh includes three full-featured programs:

- Microsoft Word 97
- Microsoft Excel 97
- Microsoft PowerPoint 97

System Requirements

To use Microsoft Office, Standard Edition, for the Macintosh, you need:

- A Mac OS-compatible computer equipped with a PowerPC processor.
- System 7.1.2 operating system or later.
- One 3.5-inch high density disk drive.
- One CD-ROM drive.
- Any Macintosh-compatible monitor and printer (color monitor recommended).

World Wide Web For the latest information about Macintosh system requirements, including memory and hard disk space requirements, connect to the Office Resource Kit home page at: http://www.microsoft.com/office/ork/

CHAPTER 6

Customizing Client Installations

The flexibility available in the standard Setup process is sufficient for many situations. But there are cases in which it is beneficial to customize the client installation process using the tools described in this chapter. For example, if you want to install a uniform configuration of Office on all your Windows client computers, including a specific selection of converters and templates, you can create a customized Setup script using the Network Installation Wizard.

In This Chapter
Understanding the Office Setup Program   105
Modifying Client Setup with the Network Installation Wizard   108
Running Client Setup with the Modified STF File   130

See Also
- For information about installing Office applications, see Chapter 4, "Installing Microsoft Office."
- For information about system requirements for Office 97, see Chapter 5, "System Requirements for Microsoft Office."

Note   The information in the following sections pertains only to the Windows 95 or Windows NT operating system.

Understanding the Office Setup Program

The Office Setup program receives all of its instructions from a set of tables that describe which files are to be installed and how each installation is to occur. There are two primary files used by Setup:

- The tables in the Off97Std.stf or Off97Pro.stf (STF) file specify where and in what order files are copied and what registry entries are created.
- The tables in the Off97Std.inf or Off97Pro.inf (INF) file contain detailed descriptions of all Offices files and are used by the STF file to determine which files to copy during installation.

These files are designed for the standard Office client installation process. By making modifications, however, you can create a customized client installation process.

Caution Do not modify either of these files with a standard text editor. The STF and INF files are tab-delimited files that rely heavily on positional parameters, and they can easily be damaged by modifying them with anything other than the tools described here.

For more information about the contents of the Setup files, see Appendix B, "Setup Command-Line Options and File Formats."

Customizing a Network Installation

Both the STF and the INF file reside in the same folder as Setup.exe. The most common method for creating customized client installations is to create an administrative installation point and modify these Setup files directly on the server. That way, all users who install Office over the network run the custom client installation that you design.

Note The majority of this chapter assumes a network installation. If you want to customize an installation from the Office CD or floppy disks, see "Customizing Installations from Physical Media" later in this chapter. For more information about network installations, see Chapter 4, "Installing Microsoft Office."

There are two ways you can modify the Setup files to customize the client installation. You can change values in the STF file to select the following:

- Type of installation to use during batch mode (Typical, Custom, or Run from Network Server).
- Specific components, such as Microsoft Word or the spelling checker, to install during batch mode.
- Destination folders to use for Office and its components.
- Responses to Yes/No questions, such as "Would you like to remove your previous version of Office?"
- Items to appear on the Windows **Start** menu or Windows NT Workstation version 3.51 program group.
- Default working folder for **Start** menu and Windows NT Workstations 3.51 program group items.

You can also add new entries to the STF or INF file so that Setup performs the following additional tasks during client installation:

- Create additional registry settings.
- Install files other than Office files.

Customizing Installations from Physical Media

You can customize some aspects of client Setup for users installing Office from physical media, although the preparation is more complex. The technique also differs depending on whether you use the Office CD or floppy disks. These techniques are described in the following sections.

Using the Office CD

Because the files on the CD are not compressed, you can modify both the STF and the INF file using the Network Installation Wizard, as described in this chapter. However, because the Office CD is read-only, you cannot write modified files back to the original CD.

If you have the ability to duplicate CDs, and you have multiple user licenses for Office, you can create a new Office installation CD with your modified Setup files and duplicate this CD for users. You can also copy the CD contents to a network server and modify the Setup files on the server. Users installing Office from that location use your customized files. For a description of this latter type of installation, see "Installing Office from the Office CD," in Chapter 4, "Installing Microsoft Office."

Using the Floppy Disks

If you are a Select CD customer, you can create Office 97 floppy disks from the Select CD for users who cannot use the Office CD and do not have network access. Because the STF file on Disk 1 is compressed in a cabinet (CAB) file and cannot be modified, there is no customization you can do for users installing from the floppy disk set. For more information, see "Installing Office from Floppy Disks" in Chapter 4, "Installing Microsoft Office."

Important The Network Installation Wizard application described in the following section cannot be used with the Office floppy disk set because the STF file is inaccessible on the floppy disks.

Part 2 Deploying Microsoft Office

Modifying Client Setup with the Network Installation Wizard

The Network Installation Wizard modifies the STF and INF files for the client Setup used in Office 97. Using this tool, you can change the values for items in the STF file. If the user installs Office in batch mode, Setup uses the default values you specify in the modified STF file. If the user installs Office in interactive mode, the values you set with the Network Installation Wizard appear as default responses during client Setup.

Note The Network Installation Wizard runs on the Windows 95 or Windows NT operating system only.

Tools and Utilities The Office Resource Kit Tools and Utilities include a new version of the Network Installation Wizard. This updated version replaces the Network Installation Wizard in the Microsoft Office for Windows 95 Resource Kit. It works with STF and INF files from both Office 97 and Office 95. For information about installing the updated Network Installation Wizard, see "Network Installation Wizard" in Appendix A, "Microsoft Office 97 Resource Kit Tools and Utilities."

To understand how the Network Installation Wizard modifies Office Setup , first become familiar with the basic client installation process for Office. If you have not already done so, read Chapter 4, "Installing Microsoft Office."

The Network Installation Wizard guides you through the process of creating a customized Setup in the following steps:

1. Start the Network Installation Wizard.
2. Specify the appropriate STF and INF files.
3. Select a destination folder for the Office application files.
4. Select a default folder for Office documents.
5. Select a location for shared Office applications.
6. Specify an installation log.
7. Choose the type of installation.
8. Configure the installation environment.
9. Select items for the **Start** menu or Program Manager.
10. Add additional files to the Office installation (optional).
11. Add Windows registry entries.
12. Update the INF file.
13. Save the modified STF file.

The following sections describe each of these steps in more detail.

World Wide Web For the latest information about the Network Installation Wizard, connect to the Office Resource Kit home page at:

http://www.microsoft.com/office/ork/

Tools and Utilities The Office Resource Kit Tools and Utilities include documents that describe more advanced techniques for customizing your Office installation. For more information, see "Advanced Documentation" in Appendix A, "Microsoft Office 97 Resource Kit Tools and Utilities."

Start the Network Installation Wizard

After you have installed the Network Installation Wizard from the Microsoft Office 97 Resource Kit Tools and Utilities, double-click Niw.exe. Like other Office wizards, the Network Installation Wizard guides you through a series of panels and options. You proceed to the next panel by clicking **Next**, and you can go back to the previous panel by clicking **Back**. The STF file is not modified until you click **Finish**, so you can go back and change any answers before you complete the final panel.

You can quit the Network Installation Wizard at any time by clicking **Cancel**.

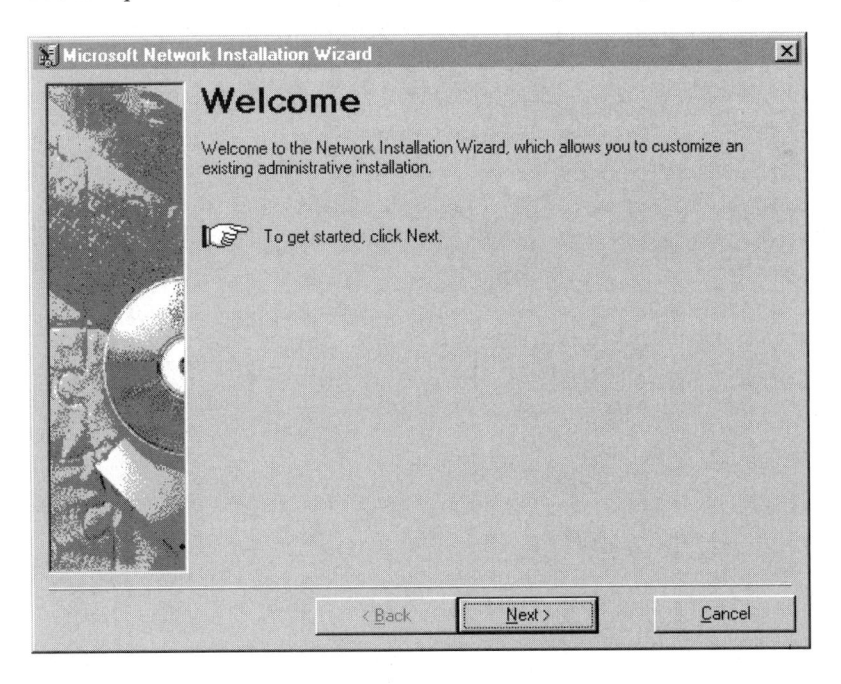

Specify the STF and INF Files

After the initial **Welcome** panel, the Network Installation Wizard asks for the name of the STF file to modify. Enter the name of the STF file from the folder containing the main Office application files. For example, in Office 97, Professional Edition, the file name is Off97Pro.stf.

Tip Save the original Office STF file by making a backup copy before running the Network Installation Wizard.

While the Network Installation Wizard is reading the STF file, which can take a minute or two, it displays a progress bar.

```
Loading table file.
"C:\MSOffice\Off97Pro.STF"

One Moment Please....
```

After opening the STF file, the Network Installation Wizard opens the INF file specified in the STF file. This is in the same folder as the STF file and has the same file name with an INF extension. In Office 97, Professional Edition, the name of the INF file is Off97Pro.inf. If the Network Installation Wizard cannot find the INF file specified in the STF file, it asks you to enter the location and name of the file.

Select a Primary Location for the Office Application Files

The Network Installation Wizard then displays the name of the folder where the main Office application files are installed during client Setup. You can change the default folder by entering a new name, or by clicking **Browse** and selecting a new folder.

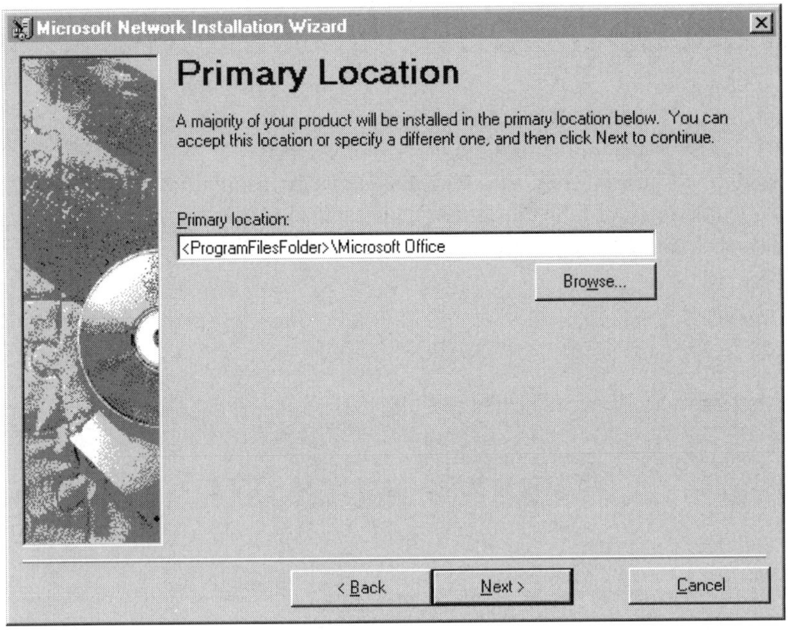
Microsoft Network Installation Wizard
Primary Location
A majority of your product will be installed in the primary location below. You can accept this location or specify a different one, and then click Next to continue.
Primary location:
<ProgramFilesFolder>\Microsoft Office
Browse...
< Back
Next >
Cancel

If you run client Setup in batch mode (using the **/q** command-line option), Setup installs the Office application files in this folder. If a user runs client Setup interactively, this folder appears as the default folder, which the user can change.

Note Remember that the folder name you enter here is used by Setup when users install Office. If you specify a folder on a network server, that folder must be accessible during client Setup. If you specify a local folder, Setup creates a folder with that name on the user's hard disk.

Select a Default Folder for Office Documents

Both Windows 95 and Windows NT Workstation version 4.0 provide a default folder to store all user documents, including Office documents. By default, this folder is named My Documents and is located at the root directory of the C drive. If the default folder has not yet been defined on the user's hard disk, the Network Installation Wizard allows you to specify a name and path for this folder, which is created during client Setup. If the folder has already been defined in the user's hard disk, then setting this option has no effect.

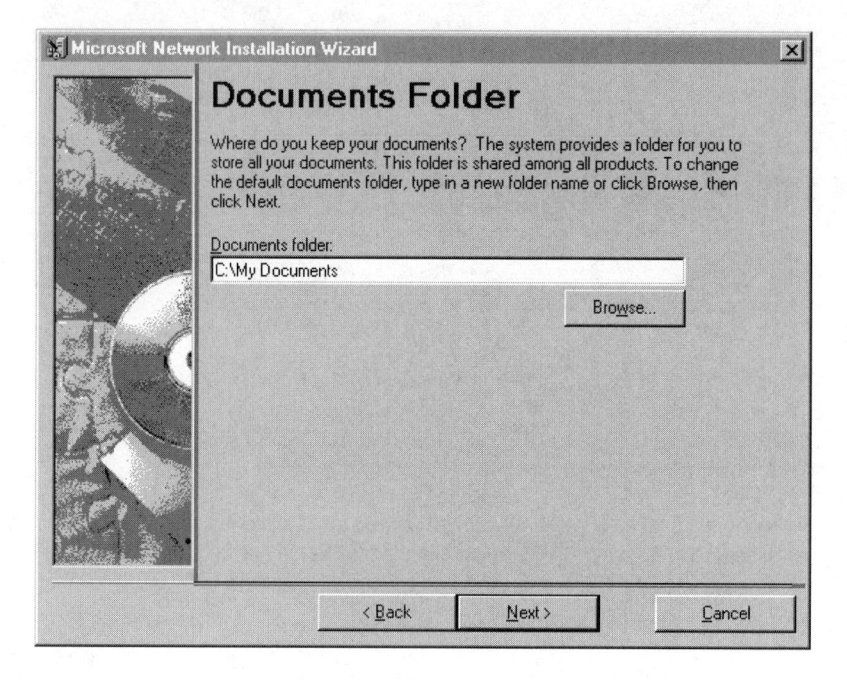

Tip In Windows 95 and Windows NT Workstation 4.0, you can use a system policy to define a default file name and path for the documents folder for all users in your workgroup. In the System Policy Editor, set the following policy:

User\Office\Common\Personal Folder

For more information, see "Using Windows System Policies to Customize Office" in Chapter 7, "Customizing and Optimizing Microsoft Office."

Select a Location for Shared Office Applications

Next, the Network Installation Wizard displays a panel similar to the dialog box that was displayed when you created the administrative installation point. The options in this panel determine whether users choose where to install shared applications, or whether you make that choice for them. The panel contains these options:

- **Server**

    Shared applications are stored on the server, and users run them over the network. Users running client Setup do not make the choice.

- **Local hard drive**

    Shared applications are installed on each user's computer. Users running client Setup do not make the choice.

- **User's choice**

    Users choose where to install shared applications when they run client Setup.

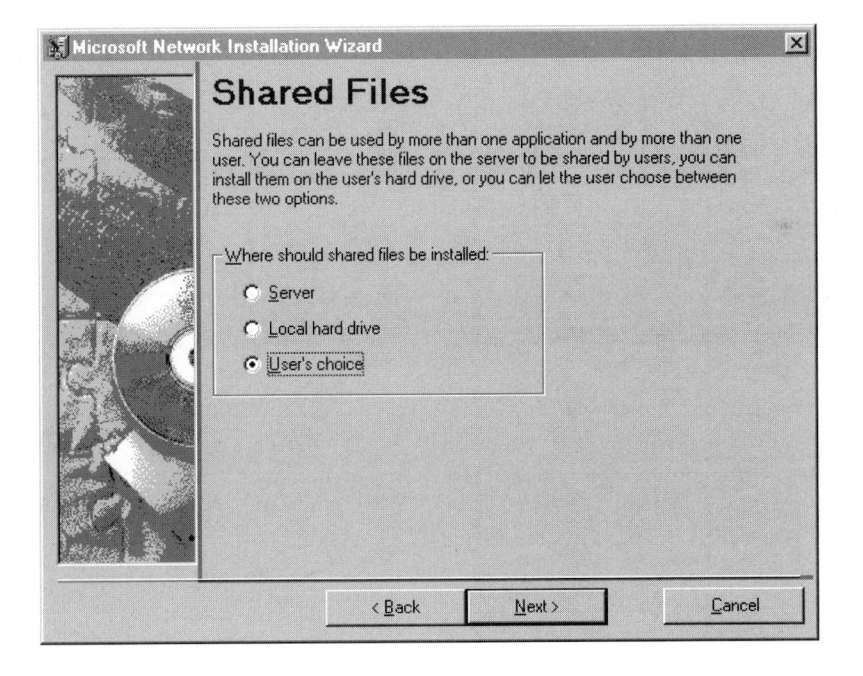

If users install Office in batch mode with no user interaction, you must select either **Server** or **Local hard drive**. If you select **Server**, a second panel is displayed for you to specify a location on the network for the shared applications. (This panel is also displayed if you select **User's choice**, since users in that scenario may choose to store shared applications on the network.)

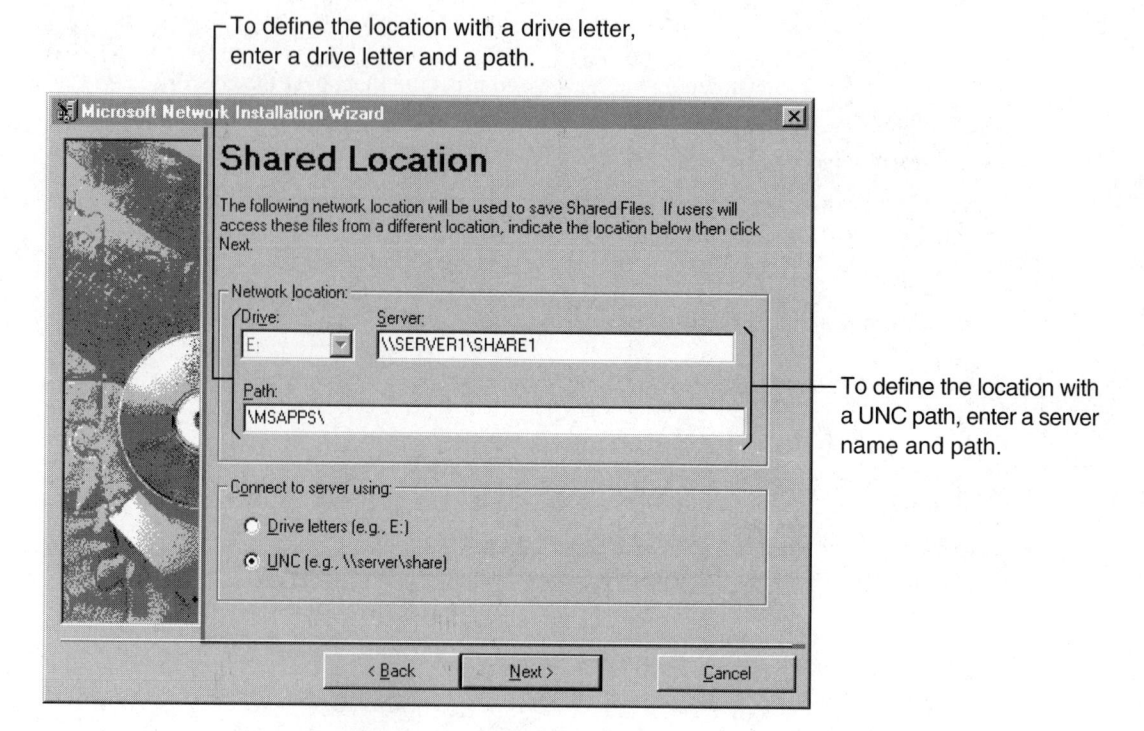

To define the location with a drive letter, enter a drive letter and a path.

To define the location with a UNC path, enter a server name and path.

Under **Connect to server using**, you can specify whether you want the location of the shared applications to be defined with a drive letter or with a UNC path. If you select the **Drive letters** option here, you must enter a drive letter and a path under **Network location**. You do not need to have a valid connection to the drive while running the Network Installation Wizard. However, users must have a valid connection the drive during client Setup. If you select the **UNC** option, you must enter a server name and path under **Network location**.

Note UNC stands for Universal Naming Convention and refers to the *servername\sharename* syntax used for defining servers and shared areas on the server for LAN Manager-compatible networks.

When you click **Next**, the Network Installation Wizard attempts to connect to the server to verify it. If it encounters any errors, the Network Installation Wizard asks whether you want to use the path as specified. To continue and leave the path as it is, click **Yes**; to change the path, click **No**.

The following table shows some reasons why the verification might fail and what you can do to fix the problem.

If the error is caused by this	Do this
Misspelled server or share name.	Click **No** and correct the name.
Share not yet created.	Click **Yes** and create the share before users begin installing Office.
Cannot connect to a share on the server. (Many networks do not allow you to do this if you run directly from the server.)	Click **Yes**; you can verify the share later from another computer on the network.
Invalid UNC path	Click **Yes**; verify that the share is accessible before users try to install from this server

Specify an Installation Log

Office Setup can create a log file containing information about the installation. If you specify a log file in the **Installation Log** panel in the Network Installation Wizard, then each time Office is installed from this administrative installation point, Setup writes one record into the log file. The log file is a text file, and each record contains the following fields:

- Date
- Time
- User name
- Machine name
- Application name—MS Office 97 Standard or MS Office 97 Professional
- Version—a number similar to 97.0.0.1114(1033)
- Operation—for example, Install or RemoveAll

The Network Installation Wizard gives you the opportunity to create a log file by specifying the log file name. If you do not want a log file, click **Next** without entering a file name.

Note The installation log file is a new feature of Setup for Office 97. If you are using the Network Installation Wizard with an Office 95 STF file, the **Installation Log** panel does not appear.

Choose the Type of Installation

Office 97 Setup offers three types of installation: Typical, Custom, and Run from Network Server. If you select **Typical** or **Custom** in the **Installation Type** panel, the Network Installation Wizard displays the **Components** panel so you can select which components you want Setup to install. If you run Setup in batch mode (**/q** command-line option) using the Typical or Custom installation type (**/b** command-line option), Setup installs the components you selected.

Chapter 6 Customizing Client Installations

For example, if you select **Custom** in the **Installation Type** panel and then select a number of text converters in the **Components** panel, you can use the command **setup.exe /q /b2** to install those converters with Office. For more information about Setup command-line options, see Appendix B, "Setup Command-Line Options and File Formats."

If you run Setup interactively, then the components you select with the Network Installation Wizard are displayed as default selections.

Note A fourth installation type, Run from CD, is available when you install Office directly from the Office CD. Because you are modifying the STF file for a network installation, that option is not discussed here.

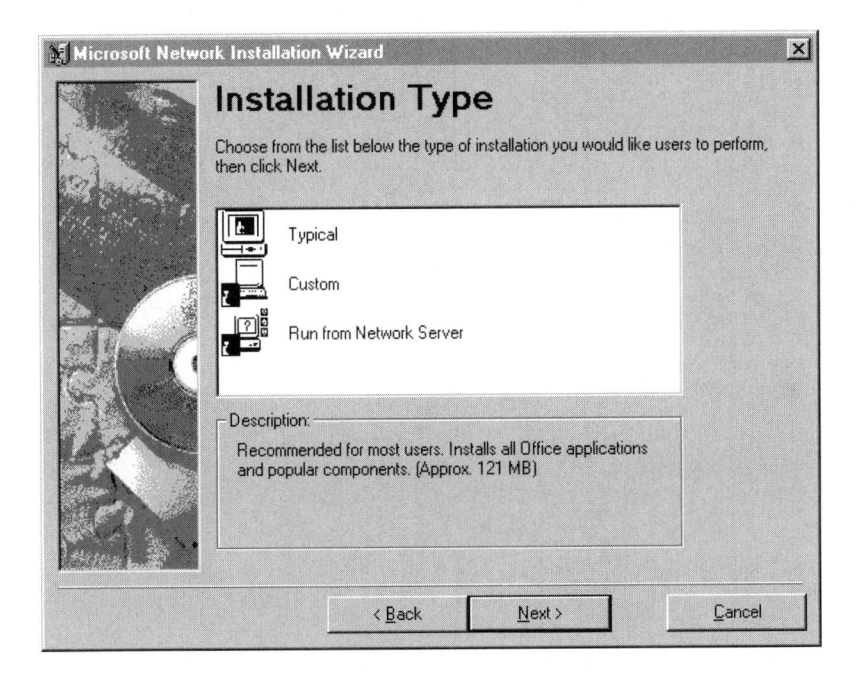

![Microsoft Network Installation Wizard - Installation Type dialog showing options: Typical, Custom, Run from Network Server. Description: "Recommended for most users. Installs all Office applications and popular components. (Approx. 121 MB)"]

Part 2 Deploying Microsoft Office

If you select **Typical** in the **Installation Type** panel, the Network Installation Wizard displays the list of Typical installation options in the **Components** panel in a format similar to the one presented to an end user running client Setup in interactive mode.

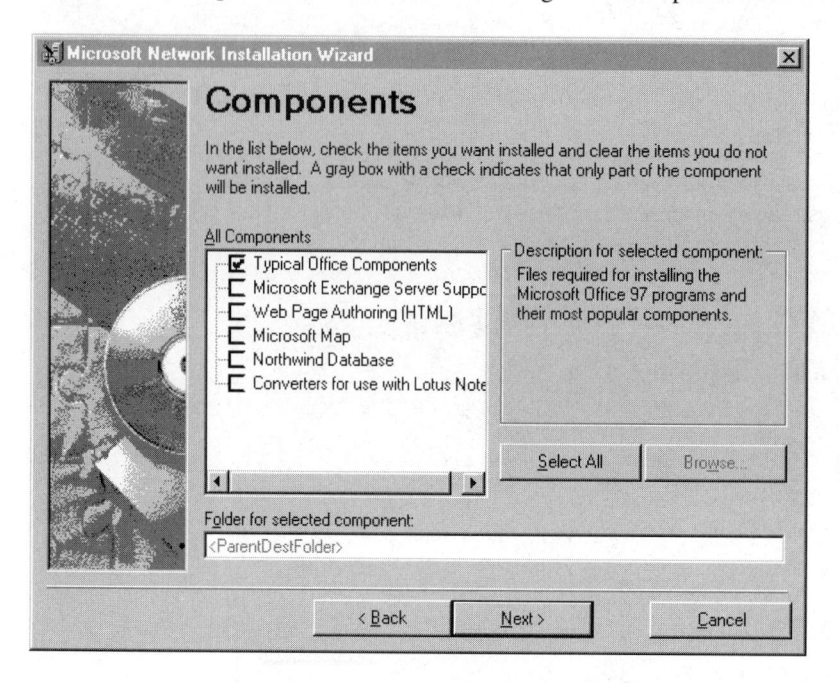

If you select **Custom** in the **Installation Type** panel, the Network Installation Wizard displays the list of Custom options in the **Components** panel.

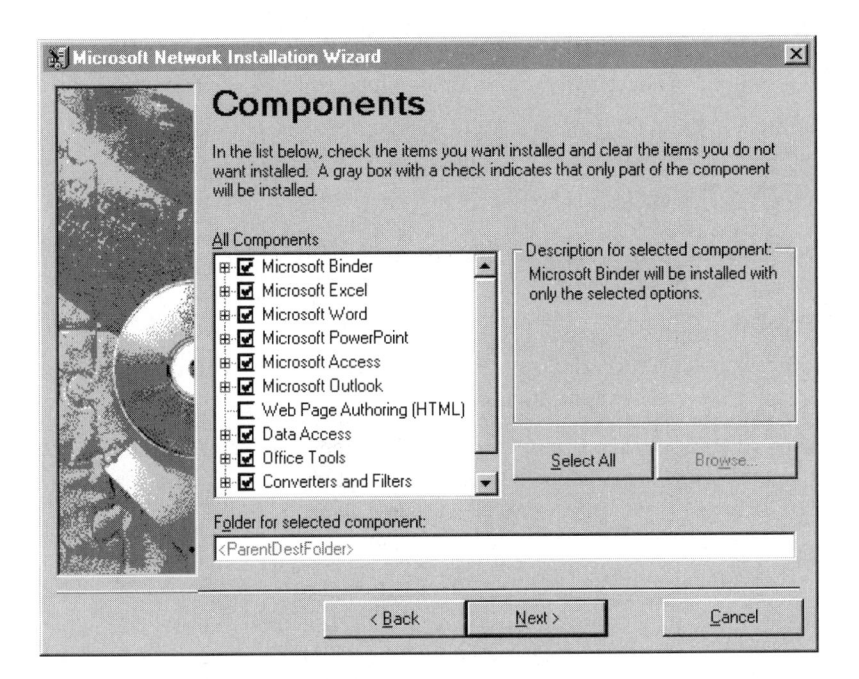

When you select an installation option in the **All Components** box, a description appears under **Description for selected component**, and the folder name appears in the **Folder for selected component** box. Each of these installation options may have additional options—if so, a plus sign (+) appears to the left of the option in the **All Components** box. Clicking the plus sign (+) expands the list, displaying its additional components.

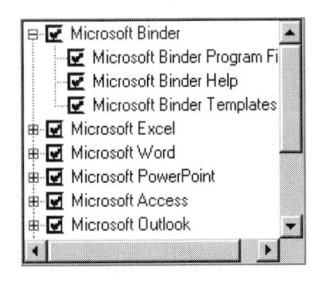

You can select all or only some of a set of additional components:

- If a check box is selected, all of that option's additional components are selected.
- If a check box is cleared, none of that option's additional components are selected.
- If a check box is grayed, some of that option's additional components are selected. Click the plus sign (+) to see what those components are.

The **Select All** button allows you to select all the Office options, along with all their additional components.

If you use the modified STF file in batch mode, the state of a check box for a particular option indicates whether the option is installed when client Setup is run: selected options are installed; cleared options are not.

If you use the modified STF file in interactive mode, the state of the check boxes in the **All Components** box represents the default settings that are presented to the user during client Setup. For example, if you select the **Office Tools** check box, that check box is selected when the user runs client Setup interactively and views the options for a Custom installation.

With the **Browse** button you can modify the default folder for a selected option. Both the long and short names of the folder you select are kept in the STF file. However, the **Return long folder name to previous dialog** check box in the **Browse Folders** dialog box determines which form of the name is displayed in the **Components** panel. This option does not affect the STF file, but only the way you view the folder name in the Network Installation Wizard. (The default is to use long folder names.)

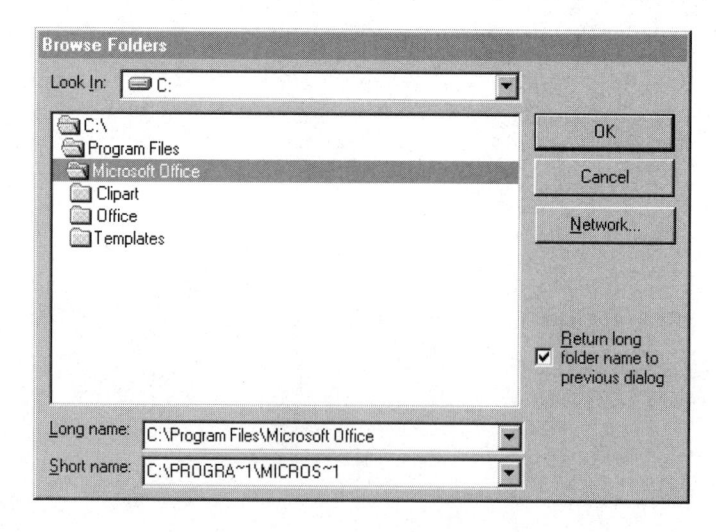

When you are creating a customized network installation, you can use a set of special folder identifiers to specify standard system folders in the **Browse Folders** dialog box. That way, you do not need to know the exact location of these folders on each user's computer.

This folder identifier	Represents this folder
<ParentDestFolder>	The destination folder of the Office component.
<SetupSourceFolder>	The folder from which Setup is run.
<WindowsFolder>	The main Windows folder.
<SystemFolder>	The Windows system folder.
<SharedFilesFolder>	The folder in which shared applications are stored.
<ProgramFilesFolder>	The Program Files folder in Windows 95, or the Windows directory on Windows NT Workstation.

The Network Installation Wizard may also display the identifier <NoneSpecified> for a particular folder. This means that the folder name has not yet been determined, but will be resolved by Setup during installation.

Note You can specify a subfolder for any of these folders by appending a backslash (\) and a subfolder name to the folder identifier—for example, **<WindowsFolder>\Media**.

Configure the Installation Environment

The STF file contains a number of questions that Setup uses to further configure the network installation. The questions Setup displays to the user depend on previous user responses and on the installation environment.

For example, suppose a user is installing Outlook. If Setup finds Microsoft Schedule+ 95 on the hard disk, Setup asks whether to configure Outlook to use Schedule+ as the primary calendar. If Schedule+ 95 is not found, Setup does not display that question. If the same question can be asked in several situations during installation, then the STF file defines that question in multiple locations.

The Network Installation Wizard displays every Yes/No question that may appear during client Setup in the STF file and allows you to determine the default answers. Because a particular question may appear more than once in the STF file, the Network Installation Wizard may repeat the same question several times in the **Yes/No Questions** panel. To ensure that your default answer is used during client Setup, change every occurrence of the question in this panel.

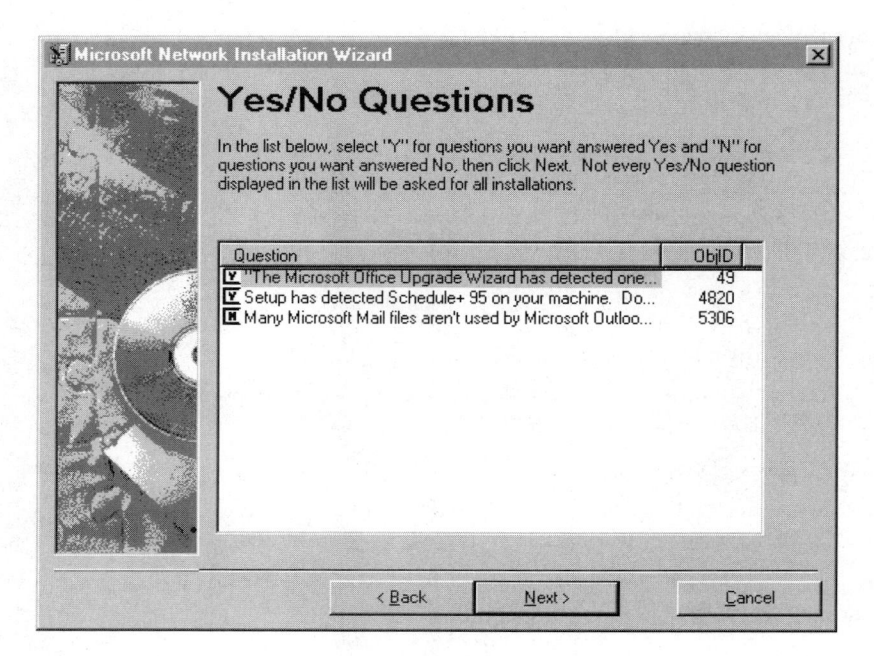

Clicking a question in the **Yes/No Questions** panel switches the answer from **Yes** to **No** and back again.

Why Are There Duplicate Items in the List?

In some of the lists displayed in the Network Installation Wizard, you may see what appear to be duplicate entries. This occurs because there are several execution paths that Setup can take through the STF file, depending on the configuration of the user's computer and whether Setup finds a previous version of Office installed. The same question may appear in more than one path; however, Setup asks each question only once during installation.

Because the Network Installation Wizard does not know what path Setup will take, it displays every instance of a question. If you want to specify a default answer, you must do so for all the duplicate questions in the list, so that Setup uses the same answer in every context.

In these lists, the Network Installation Wizard displays an Object ID column with the heading **ObjID**. The Object ID is a number in the STF file that uniquely identifies each item in the list. This number helps the Network Installation Wizard distinguish between duplicate items in the STF. You do not need to use this number when running the Network Installation Wizard.

For more information about the structure of the STF file, see Appendix B, "Setup Command-Line Options and File Formats."

Select Items for Program Manager

The Network Installation Wizard allows you to specify which application icons you want to install in the Program Manager group when you install Office on a computer running Windows NT Workstation 3.51. In the **Program Manager Items** panel, you can specify the Program Manager group and the default working folder for each item you select. The corresponding Program Manager icons are created when you install Office on a computer running Windows NT Workstation 3.51.

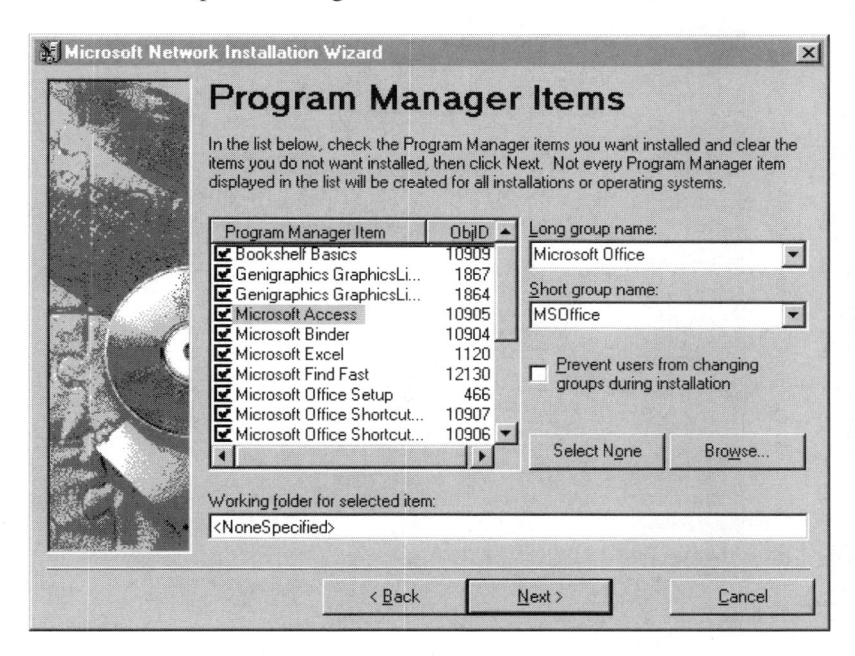

When you click an item in the **Program Manager Item** box, the corresponding Program Manager group appears to the right. You can change the group name, and you can select the **Prevent users from changing groups during installation** check box if you do not want users to modify the location of the selected item.

The working folder for the application appears below the **Program Manager Items** box. This is the default folder used for creating new files or browsing for existing files. Some applications explicitly define the folder to be used for certain types of files (for example, Word defines a specific folder to be used for template files), in which case the working folder is used only for those files that have no other folder explicitly defined for them. You can change this folder by clicking **Browse**.

Clicking **Select None** clears the check boxes for all items in the list.

> ### Which Icons Are Actually Installed?
>
> The items listed in the **Program Manager Items** panel include all the program icons defined in the Office STF file; however, not all of these icons are necessarily installed during client Setup. The icons that are actually installed depend on the options the user selects during Setup, along with other factors that Setup encounters, such as whether a previous version of Office is installed. Clearing a check box in this list, however, guarantees that the corresponding icon is not installed.
>
> If there are duplicates of an item in the list, only one corresponding program icon is actually created in Program Manager during installation. However, you must modify each duplicate item the same way, so that the correct icon is created regardless of the path Setup takes. For an explanation of duplicate items displayed in the **Program Manager Items** or **Shortcuts** panels, see the sidebar "Why Are There Duplicate Items in the List?" earlier in this chapter.

Select Items for the Start Menu

The **Shortcuts** panel in the Network Installation Wizard allows you to select the shortcuts that appear in the Windows\Start Menu folder when you install Office on a computer running Windows 95 or Windows NT Workstation 4.0.

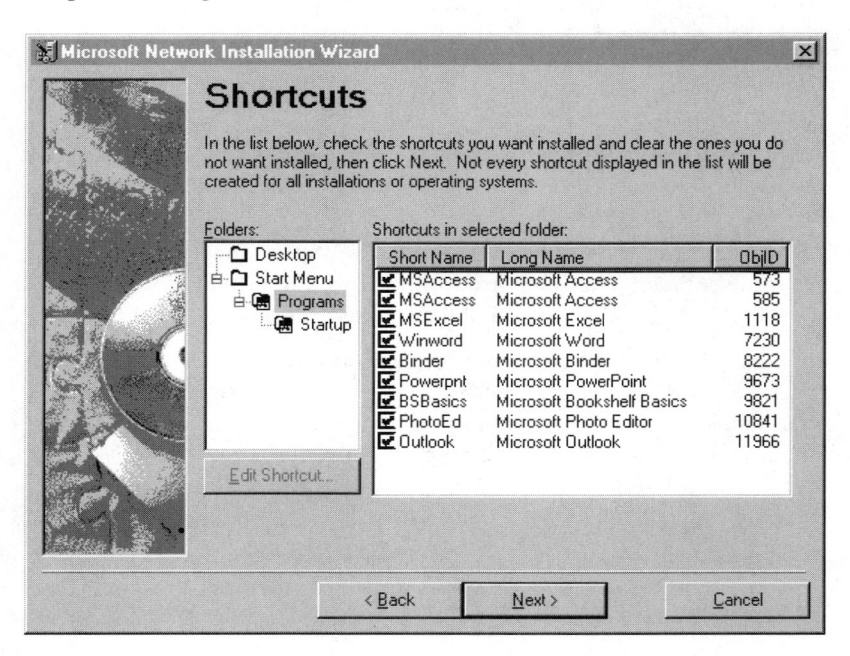

![Microsoft Network Installation Wizard - Shortcuts panel showing folders tree (Desktop, Start Menu, Programs, Startup) and shortcuts list with Short Name, Long Name, and ObjID columns:
MSAccess - Microsoft Access - 573
MSAccess - Microsoft Access - 585
MSExcel - Microsoft Excel - 1118
Winword - Microsoft Word - 7230
Binder - Microsoft Binder - 8222
Powerpnt - Microsoft PowerPoint - 9673
BSBasics - Microsoft Bookshelf Basics - 9821
PhotoEd - Microsoft Photo Editor - 10841
Outlook - Microsoft Outlook - 11966]

To change the properties of a shortcut, select it in the **Shortcuts in selected folder** box, and then click **Edit Shortcut**. In the **Edit Shortcut** dialog box, you can change the folder in which the shortcut is installed, as well as the name and working folder of the shortcut. Click **Browse** to select a new working folder.

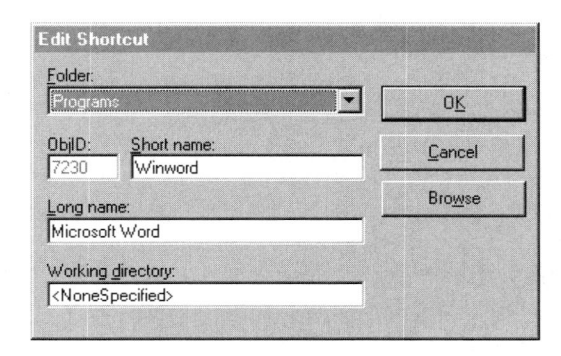

Note The shortcuts listed in the **Shortcuts in selected folder** box include all the program files defined in the Office STF file; however, not all of these items are necessarily installed during client Setup. For more information about which items are installed and about how Setup handles duplicate items, see the sidebar "Why Are There Duplicate Items in the List?" earlier in this chapter.

Add Additional Files to the Office Installation

The Network Installation Wizard allows you to add files to the Office installation process. These are additional files, provided by you, that Setup installs along with the Office files. For example, you could add a Word template file you have created for your workgroup to use.

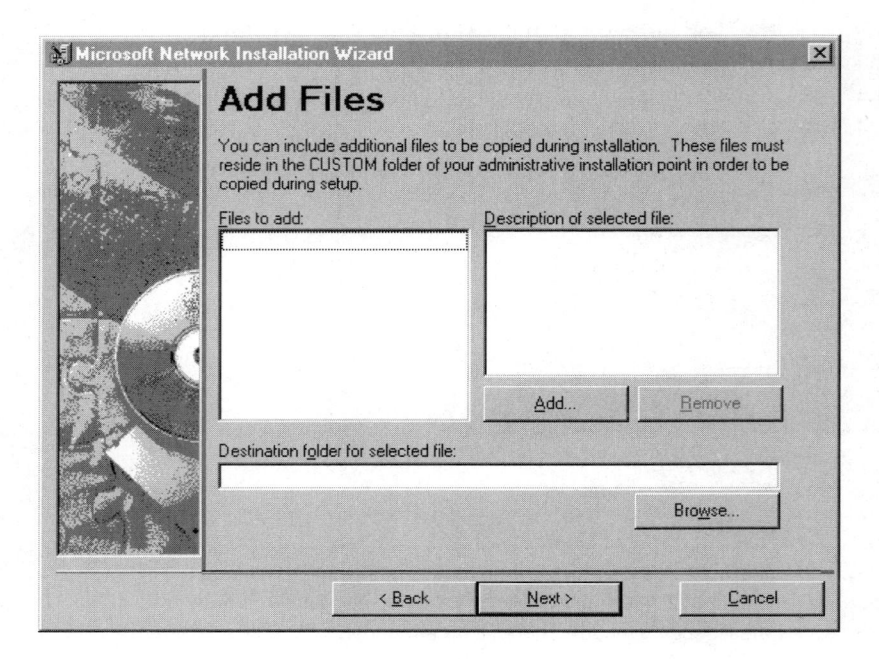

▶ **To add files to the installation process**

1   In the **Add Files** panel, click **Add**.
2   In the **Add** box, select the file you want, and then click **Open**.

    This can be any type of file located anywhere on the network.

3   When the Network Installation Wizard asks if you want to copy the selected file to the Custom folder, click **Yes**.

    In order for added files to be accessible during client Setup, they must reside in the Custom folder. If you click **No**, you must remember to copy the file to the Custom folder yourself.

4   In the **Destination folder for selected file** box, enter a folder name, or click **Browse** to find the folder.

    Setup installs the file in this folder during client Setup. You must specify a folder; entering a description in the **Description for selected file** box is optional.

Add Registry Entries

The Network Installation Wizard allows you to add registry entries to the user's Windows registry during the installation process. This can be useful if, for example, you have written an application that relies on the contents of a particular registry entry. You can add the entry to Office Setup so that your application is ready after the user installs Office.

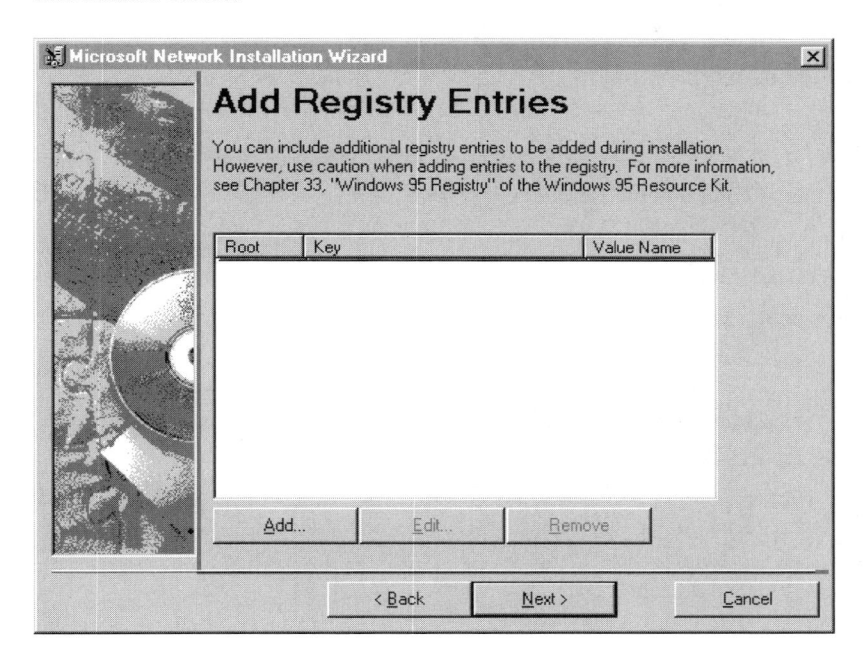

▶ To add a new registry entry

1. In the **Add Registry Entries** panel, click **Add**.

   The **Add** dialog box appears.

2. In the **Root** box, enter the name of the top-level key for the new registry entry.

   Top-level keys include the following: **HKEY_CLASSES_ROOT**; **HKEY_CURRENT_USER**; **HKEY_LOCAL_MACHINE**; and **HKEY_USERS**.

3. In the **Data type** box, click the type of data stored in the new entry—either **DWORD** (double-word integer), or **SZ** (string).

4. In the **Key** box, enter the name of the subkey in which the new entry is stored.

5. In the **Value name** box, enter a name for the new registry entry.

6. In the **Value data** box, enter the data to be stored in the new entry.

   The data must match the data type already specified.

7. In the **Description** box, type a description of the new registry entry.

   This description is stored with the key in the registry and is optional.

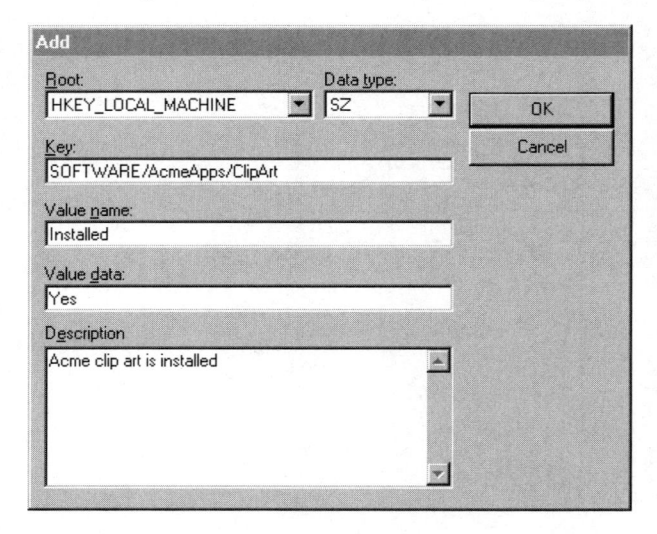

For example, you can enter the new registry key **HKEY_LOCAL_MACHINE \SOFTWARE\AcmeApps\ClipArt\Installed** with a value of **Yes** using the following entries in the **Add** dialog box.

In this box	Select or type this text
Root	HKEY_LOCAL_MACHINE
Data type	SZ
Key	SOFTWARE\AcmeApps\ClipArt
Value name	Installed
Value data	Yes
Description	Acme clip art is installed

Update the INF File

If you add one or more files to the Office installation, the Network Installation Wizard asks you for the name of the INF file so that it can update the file. By default, the INF file name specified in the STF file is used. If you have made a copy of the INF file with a different name (to leave the original Office file unaltered), you can specify that name in the **Save INF File** panel.

Note The name of the INF file is stored in the STF file for Setup to use. If you rename the INF file on the disk, Setup will not be able to find it during installation.

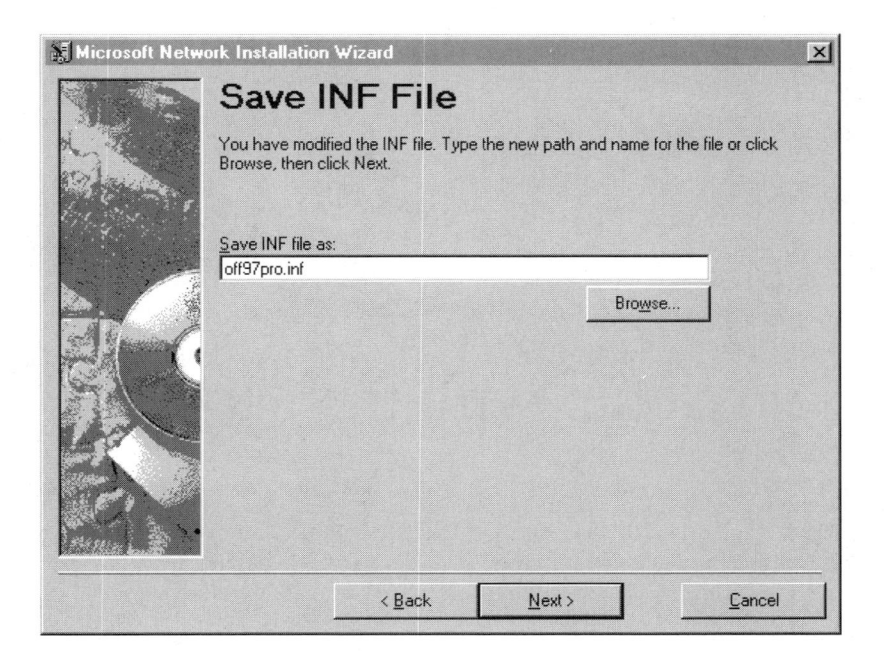

Save the Modified STF File

To complete the customization process, the Network Installation Wizard saves the modified STF file. The original STF file is overwritten, unless you specify a new name in the **Save Table File** panel.

Note You can save the original STF file with a different name as a backup; then you can give your new file the original STF file name. For more information about how to use the modified STF file with Setup, see "Running Client Setup with the Modified STF File" later in this chapter.

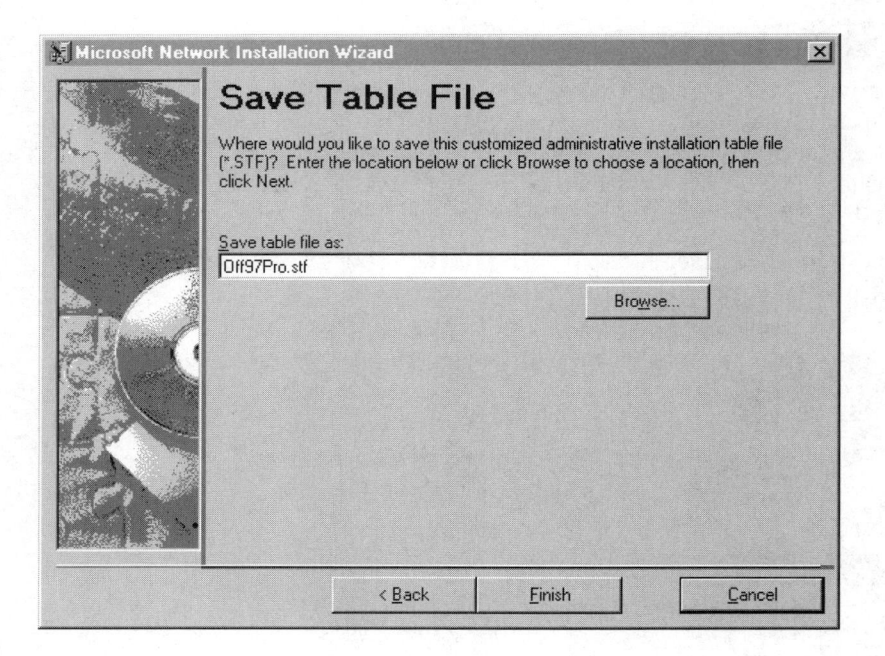

Running Client Setup with the Modified STF File

When you have successfully modified the STF file and INF file, you need to make them available so that users running client Setup use your modified files and not the original ones.

Note Because the name of the INF file is defined in the STF file, you cannot rename the INF file after you create the new STF file with the Network Installation Wizard.

You can set client Setup to use your modified Setup files by renaming the original STF file and giving your modified STF file the original file name: Off97Std.stf (Microsoft Office, Standard Edition) or Off97Pro.stf (Microsoft Office, Professional Edition). When users run Setup to install Office, Setup uses your modified STF file.

For example, if you create a new STF file named Newsetup.stf, you can rename Off97Pro.stf to something else and rename Newsetup.stf to Off97Pro.stf.

Installing Office over the Network

Once you have modified the STF file and INF file, there are three ways to initiate a client installation of Office: interactive, batch, and push.

Interactive Installation

In an *interactive installation*, users connect to the Office server and run Setup using the command-line options you have chosen. Setup prompts the user for installation information. Modifications you have made to the STF file are displayed as default responses to user prompts.

Batch Installation

In a *batch installation*, you create a batch file which runs Setup using your customized STF file with the appropriate command-line options. The user runs the batch file, which in turn installs Office with no additional user interaction. Setup does not prompt the user for information, but uses the responses from the customized STF file instead.

For example, a command line for Setup might be **setup.exe /q1**. The **/q1** option directs Setup to run without further user intervention, displaying only progress indicators to the user. For a description of all the available Setup command-line options, see Appendix B, "Setup Command-Line Options and File Formats."

By placing this command line in a batch file that the user can run, you can create a simple mechanism for users to launch a customized version of Office client Setup.

Push Installation

In a *push installation*, you initiate client Setup automatically with no user intervention. This can be done by putting the customized Setup command line in the user's system logon script, so Office installation is initiated the next time the user logs on to the network.

You can also use a network administration tool, such as Microsoft Systems Management Server, to initiate a push installation. For more information, see the following section, "Using the Microsoft Systems Management Server to Install Office."

Using Microsoft Systems Management Server to Install Office

You can use a network administration tool, such as Microsoft Systems Management Server, to distribute a customized version of Office client Setup to your users.

Microsoft Systems Management Server version 1.2 helps you automate large-scale deployment of Office by performing an automatic installation that requires no intervention from you or the user.

Important This section supplements the Microsoft Systems Management Server documentation; it does not replace it. The procedures that follow provide additional information for using Systems Management Server to install Office, but they do not cover all Systems Management Server options and features. For complete information, see the *Microsoft Systems Management Server Administrator's Guide*.

To use Systems Management Server to distribute Office, perform the following steps:

1. Create a package for Office. A *package* consists of a folder (the *package source folder* that contains all the Office installation files) and a package definition file (PDF). The PDF describes the Setup commands that can be used to install Office on client computers.

2. Create and run a job to distribute the package. A *job* consists of a package and a list of destination client computers. Systems Management Server copies the package to distribution servers servicing the client computers and executes the jobs on the client computers.

Note Before you use Systems Management Server to install Office, you must create an administrative installation point on a server. Systems Management Server uses the administrative installation point as the package source folder. For more information, see "Installing Office from the Network" in Chapter 4, "Installing Microsoft Office."

To install Office on your users' computers, you create a package to run Setup using the standard Typical, Custom, or Run from Network Server installation types, or using a Setup script you have customized. Once the package is created, you create a Run On Workstation job to execute Setup on the user computers that you designate.

Creating a Package for Office

You create a package for Office by using the Systems Management Server Administrator program and importing the Office PDF. The Office PDF is located in the main Office folder in the administrative installation point and is named Off97std.pdf (Standard Edition) or Off97pro.pdf (Professional Edition).

Chapter 6   Customizing Client Installations

Tools and Utilities   The standard Office PDF described in this section supports only local client installations and does not support Run from Network Server installations or sharing Office components over the network. The Office Resource Kit Tools and Utilities include additional PDF files that support Run from Network Server installations. For more information, see "Package Definition Files" in Appendix A, "Microsoft Office 97 Resource Kit Tools and Utilities."

The Office PDF file contains command definitions for the standard installation types: Typical and Custom, as well as the complete installation (a Custom installation with all the Office components selected) and Uninstall options. Each of these command definitions contains a Setup command line that directs Setup to run in batch mode with the specific installation type (except for Custom, which always runs interactively).

For example, the command line for a Typical installation is:

```
CommandLine = setup.exe /q1 /b1
```

The **/q1** command-line option in this example directs Setup to run with no user interaction, and the **/b1** option directs Setup to use the Typical installation type. When this command is run from the Systems Management Server package, Setup automatically installs Office using the predefined options for the Typical installation type. For a description of all the available Setup command-line options, see Appendix B, "Setup Command-Line Options and File Formats."

To use one of the standard Office installation types for installing Office on your client computers, create a package using the unmodified Office PDF.

▶ **To create an Office Setup package**

1   Start the Systems Management Server Administrator program and switch to the Packages window.
2   On the **File** menu, click **New**.
3   In the **Package Properties** dialog box, click **Import**.
4   In the **File Browser** dialog box, select the appropriate PDF file (Off97std.pdf or Off97pro.pdf) and then click **OK**.

    The PDF file is located in the administrative installation point in the folder containing the main Office application files.
5   In the **Package Properties** dialog box, click **Workstations**.
6   In the **Source Directory** box, enter the location of the administrative installation point for Office.
7   In the **Workstation Command Lines** box, click the Office installation type you want, and then click **Close**.

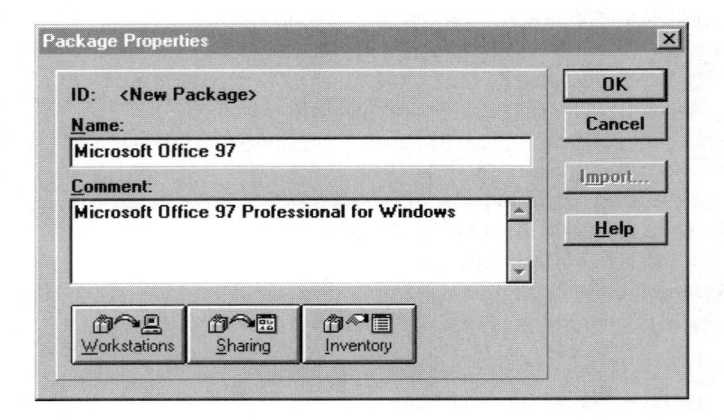

To create a Setup command that differs from those available in the Office PDF, you add a new command to the Office PDF. For example, if you want Setup to generate a log file, then you can add a new command in the PDF that runs Setup using the command-line option **/g**. You do this with the Systems Management Server Administrator program.

▶ **To add a new command to the Office package**

1. Start the Systems Management Server Administrator program, switch to the Packages window, and select the package you created for Office.
2. On the **File** menu, click **Properties**.
3. In the **Package Properties** dialog box, click **Workstations**.
4. In the **Source Directory** box, enter the location of the administrative installation point for Office, and then click **New**.
5. In the **Command Name** box, type a name for the new command.

    For example, type **Install Office**

6. In the **Command Line** box, type the command to run your custom Setup.

    For example, to run a Typical installation of Setup in full quiet mode and generate a log file, type **setup.exe /b1 /qt /g "setup.log"**

7. To indicate that no user input is required to run the package, select the **Automated Command Line** check box.

    If you are installing on Windows NT Workstation, you can also select the **System (Background) Task** check box to indicate that you want the package to run in the background.

8. In the Supported Platforms box, select the appropriate operating systems: Windows 95, Windows NT, or both; and then click OK.
9. In the **Workstation Command Lines** box, select the command you created, and then click **Close**.

Note For more information about creating, modifying, or distributing packages, or for information about other package options available in Systems Management Server, see the *Microsoft Systems Management Server Administrator's Guide*.

Creating a Job for the Office Package

Once you have created the Systems Management Server package for Office, you create a Run On Workstation job to distribute the package.

▶ **To create a Run On Workstation job**

1. Start the Systems Management Server Administrator program, and switch to the Jobs window.
2. On the **File** menu, click **New**.
3. In the **Job Properties** dialog box, click **Details**.
4. In the **Package** box, click the Office package you created.
5. Under **Run Phase**, select the **Run Workstation Command** check box, select one of the Setup commands in the package, and then click **OK**.

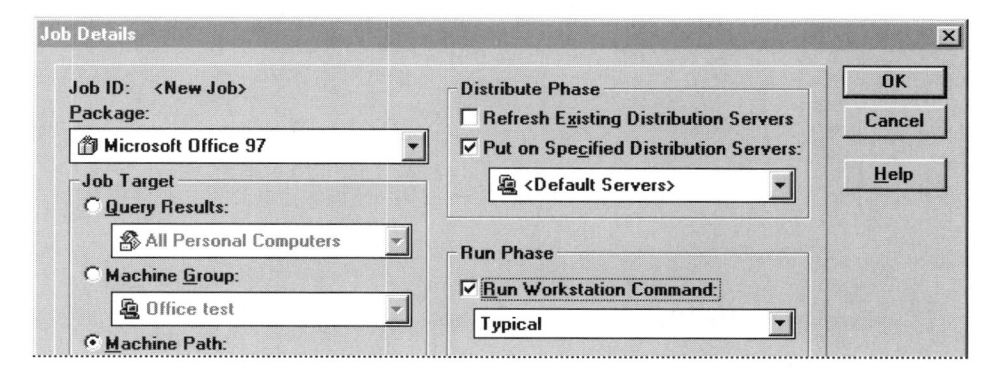

Important The previous procedure describes how to create a simple job for the Office package and how to select the appropriate Office Setup command line. To finish creating the job, you must define *job targets* (user computers) on which to install Office, and you must set the job schedule. For more information about creating and scheduling the job, see the *Microsoft Systems Management Server Administrator's Guide*.

When the job is executed, Systems Management Server copies all the files from the main Office folder on the administrative installation point to a folder on one or more Systems Management Server distribution servers that service the users on your network. When a user runs the package, Setup is run from within this copy of the administrative installation point.

CHAPTER 7

Customizing and Optimizing Microsoft Office

This chapter contains information about customizing user environments in your workgroup and modifying your users' computers for optimum performance of Microsoft Office 97.

In This Chapter
Using Windows System Policies to Customize Office   137
Customizing Office Connections to the World Wide Web   146
Optimizing Individual Office Applications   152

See Also
- For information about installing Office applications, see Chapter 4, "Installing Microsoft Office."
- For information about the system policies available in the Office policy templates, see Appendix C, "Registry Keys and Values."

Using Windows System Policies to Customize Office

Office applications have many options that users can customize to alter the user interface and behavior of the application. As a network administrator, you can set many of these options remotely, for all the users in a workgroup, using Windows system policies. System policies allow you to provide greater consistency among client computers and to centralize support and maintenance efforts.

Note System policies are supported by Windows 95 and Windows NT Workstation version 4.0 only. The Macintosh and Windows NT Workstation version 3.51 operating systems do not support system policies. In this section, Windows refers to Windows 95 and Windows NT Workstation 4.0.

Windows System Policies

The Office applications use keys in the Windows registry to record the values of user-defined options. For example, Microsoft Excel stores the value of the **Save Excel files as** option in a registry key. When a user changes the **Save Excel files as** option on the **Transition** tab in the **Options** dialog box (**Tools** menu), Microsoft Excel records the new value in the registry.

A system policy represents an option corresponds to one or more Windows registry keys. System policies are defined by a system policy template file that associates each policy with the registry keys used by the application for the option that the policy represents. The template also organizes the policies in a hierarchy to make them easier to find.

The Windows System Policy Editor displays system policy values as defined in the policy template file and allows you to change these values. You store the modified policies in a system policy file, which you then place on a network server. When a user logs on to the network, Windows downloads the system policy file from the server and alters the values in the user's Windows registry based on the policies in the file.

For example, you can use the System Policy Editor to set a value for the **Save Excel files as** option described earlier: Set the value in the **Default Save** policy for Microsoft Excel, and then place the system policy file on the network server. When a user logs on, Windows reads the **Default Save** policy value from the policy file and modifies the value entry in the **Save Excel files as** subkey in the user's Windows registry. When the user runs Microsoft Excel, the application uses the new **Save Excel files as** value. Because users logging on to the network all use the same policy file, this same option is set for all users from a central location.

For more information about Windows system policies, see the *Microsoft Windows 95 Resource Kit* or the *Microsoft Windows NT Server 4.0 Resource Kit* and *Microsoft Windows NT Workstation 4.0 Resource Kit*.

The System Policy Editor

To create or modify a system policy file, use the System Policy Editor, which is included in the Office Resource Kit Tools and Utilities. To create a system policy file click the **New Policy** command on the System Policy Editor **File** menu. For more information about how to install the Office policy template files, see "Installing the System Policy Editor," in Appendix C, "Registry Keys and Values."

After you set the policy values you want, place the system policy file in the appropriate folder on the network server.

▶ To store the system policy file on the network server

1. On the System Policy Editor **File** menu, click **Save As**, and save the system policy file as Config.pol.
2. Exit the System Policy Editor.
3. On Windows NT networks, copy Config.pol to the Netlogon folder of the primary domain controller, as defined for your client computers.

   –or–

   On NetWare networks, copy Config.pol to the Public folder of the preferred server, as defined for your client computers.

Tools and Utilities   The Office Resource Kit Tools and Utilities include the latest version of the System Policy Editor. This is the same version that is included with Windows NT Workstation 4.0, and you can use it with both Windows 95 and Windows NT Workstation 4.0. For more information, see "System Policy Editor and Office 97 Policy Templates" in Appendix A, "Microsoft Office 97 Resource Kit Tools and Utilities."

Using Office Policy Template Files

To help you create a policy file for Office, the Office Resource Kit Tools and Utilities include three Office template files that define all the system policies that can be set for Office 97 applications. These template files are described in the following table.

This template file	Defines policies for these applications
Off97w95.adm (Windows 95) or Off97nt4.adm (Windows NT Workstation 4.0)	Microsoft Excel, Microsoft PowerPoint, and Microsoft Word, and general settings for all Office applications
Access97.adm	Microsoft Access
Outlk97.adm	Microsoft Outlook
Query97.adm	Microsoft Query and ODBC

Note   Windows system policy template files have a .adm file extension and are not similar to other Office template files.

The system policies in the Office policy template files are organized by application. Most policies correspond to options that users can set in the **Options** dialog box (**Tools** menu) of each Office application. For example, the **Macro Virus Protection** policy for Word is found under **User\Word 97\Tools_Options\General\Macro Virus Protection**. Some policies do not correspond to settings that users can select; these are organized by application or under the general Office heading.

For a complete index of system policies available in the Office policy templates, see Appendix C, "Registry Keys and Values."

Setting System Policies

Using the System Policy Editor, you can set user policies for all users, for a particular network group, or for a single user. *User policies* are system policies that represent application options relevant to the user currently logged on to Windows, and they are stored in the **HKEY_USERS** portion of the user's Windows registry.

You can also set computer policies for all client computers or for a single computer. *Computer policies* are system policies that represent options relevant to a particular computer, and they are stored in the **HKEY_LOCAL_MACHINE** portion of the Windows registry.

To set system policies for all users, double-click the Default User icon in the main window of the System Policy Editor to display the **Default User Properties** dialog box. This dialog box contains a list of all the system policies you can set for the user. To set system policies for all client computers, double-click Default Computer instead to display the **Default Computer Properties** dialog box.

Note The name of this dialog box changes depending on the name of the icon you double-click in the main window of the System Policy Editor, and is referred to generically in this section as the **Properties** dialog box.

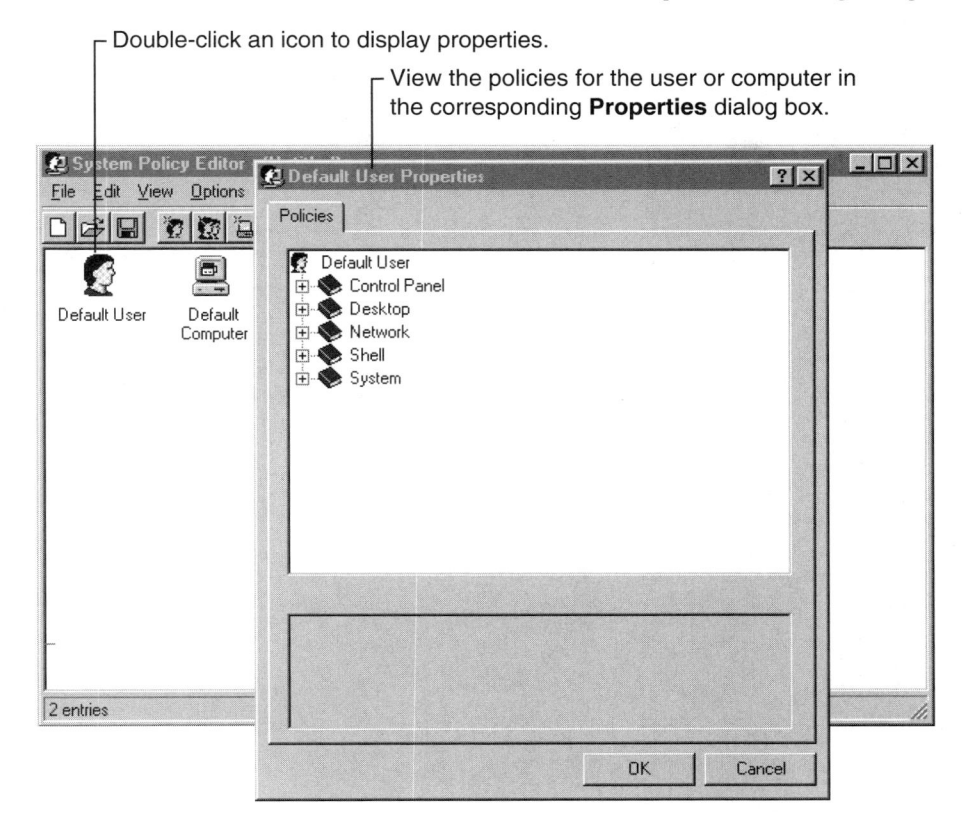

Double-click an icon to display properties.

View the policies for the user or computer in the corresponding **Properties** dialog box.

You can also set system policies for a single user or group of users.

▶ **To set system policies for a specific user or group of users**

1   Start the System Policy Editor.
2   On the **Edit** menu, click **Add User** or **Add Group**.
3   In the **Add User** or **Add Group** box, enter the name of the user or the group.

    The System Policy Editor creates an icon for that user or group in the main window.

4   Double-click the new icon to display the **Properties** dialog box.

Note   The group names you specify in the System Policy Editor must reference user groups that already exist in the network system. You cannot create new groups from within the System Policy Editor.

If you add more than one group, you can set the relative priority for the groups. When a user who is a member of several groups logs on, the policy settings from the highest priority group are processed last so that those settings override the settings from lower priority groups. To set group priorities, click **Group Priority** on the **Options** menu in the System Policy Editor.

In addition to users and user groups, you can set policies for a particular client computer.

▶ **To set system policies for a client computer**

1   Start the System Policy Editor.
2   On the **Edit** menu, click **Add Computer**.
3   In the **Add Computer** box, enter the name of the client computer.

    The System Policy Editor creates an icon for that computer in the main window.

4   Double-click the new icon to open the **Properties** dialog box.

You can expand and collapse groups of policies in the **Properties** dialog box using the plus (+) and minus (−) signs to the left of group headings. Each policy has a check box to the left that indicates its current setting. If a policy requires additional information, an edit control appears at the bottom of the dialog box.

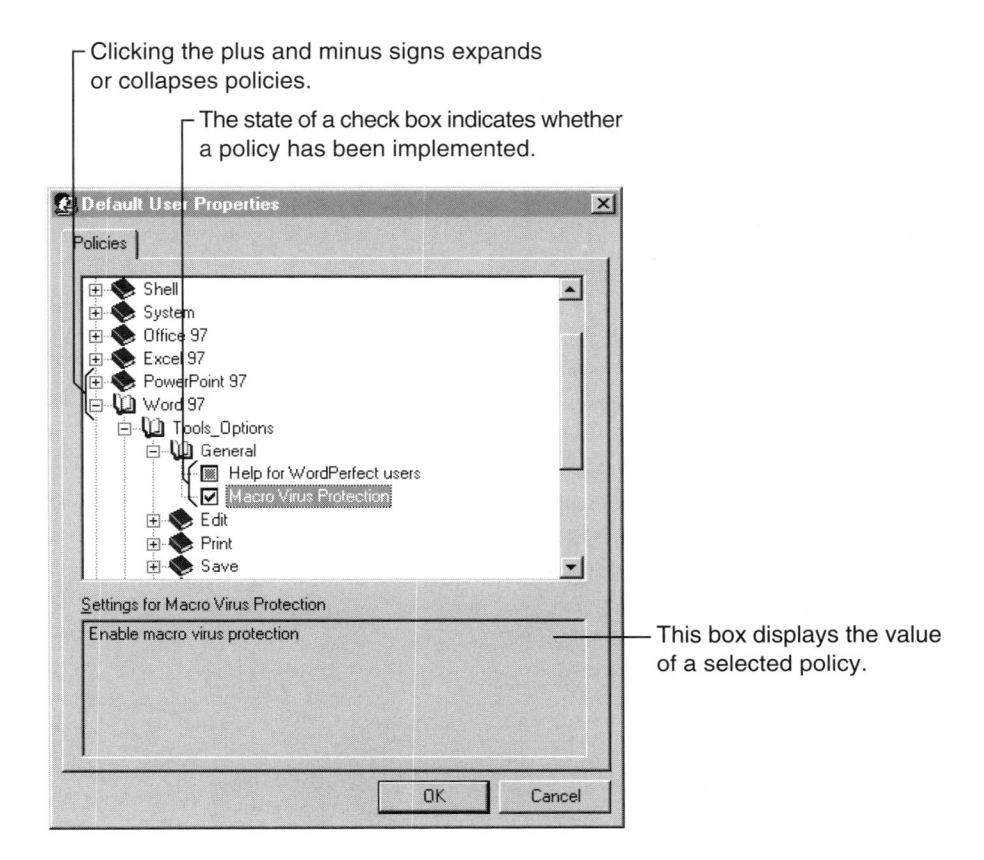

Chapter 7 Customizing and Optimizing Microsoft Office

— Clicking the plus and minus signs expands or collapses policies.

— The state of a check box indicates whether a policy has been implemented.

Default User Properties

Policies

- Shell
- System
- Office 97
- Excel 97
- PowerPoint 97
- Word 97
  - Tools_Options
    - General
      - Help for WordPerfect users
      - **Macro Virus Protection**
    - Edit
    - Print
    - Save

Settings for Macro Virus Protection

Enable macro virus protection

— This box displays the value of a selected policy.

OK   Cancel

A system policy can have one of three settings in the **Properties** dialog box:

- Checked

    The policy has been implemented. When a user logs on, the Windows registry changes to conform to the policy.

- Cleared

    The policy has not been implemented. If it was implemented previously (either through a system policy or the user's configuration settings), the previously specified settings are removed from the registry.

- Grayed

    The setting is unchanged from the last time the user logged on. Windows makes no modifications to the user's configuration settings.

For example, you might select the check box for the policy **Default Save** for Microsoft Excel and assign the value **Microsoft Excel 5.0/95 Workbook**. When a user logs on to the network, the user's registry is modified to set the default file format in which to save Microsoft Excel workbooks to this value. If the user has set this value to another file format, that setting is overwritten. If this check box is cleared in the policy file, then the option in Microsoft Excel is unavailable when the user logs on. If the policy is grayed, then Windows does not modify the user's registry and it retains its previous setting.

Client Computer Requirements for System Policies

Client computers must meet the following requirements to use system policies:

- Windows 95 or Windows NT Workstation 4.0 must be installed.
- If you want to set user policies, client computers must have user profiles enabled.
- If you want to set group policies, the group policy capability must be installed on each client computer.
- For automatic downloading of policies over Windows NT networks, Client for Microsoft Networks must be specified as the primary network logon client, and the domain must be defined on the client computers.

  For automatic downloading of policies over NetWare networks, Microsoft Client for NetWare Networks must be specified as the primary network logon client, and a preferred server must be defined.

Note By default, Windows 95 and Windows NT Workstation 4.0 automatically download system policies you create and place them on the appropriate network server. If you want to change to manual downloading, see the *Microsoft Windows 95 Resource Kit* or the *Microsoft Windows NT Server 4.0 Resource Kit* and *Microsoft Windows NT Workstation 4.0 Resource Kit*. If the client computers are using NETX or VLM, then you must download system policies manually.

How Does Windows Use System Policies?

When the user logs on, Windows checks the user's configuration information for the location of the policy file. Windows then downloads the policies and copies the information in the registry using the following process.

First, if user profiles are enabled, Windows checks for a user policy section that matches the user name and applies the user-specific policy. If Windows does not find a user policy section, it applies the Default User policies. If support for group policies is installed, Windows downloads group policies, starting with the lowest priority group and ending with the highest priority group. Group policies are processed for all groups to which the user belongs. Group policies are not applied if there are user policies defined for the user. These settings are copied into the **USER.DAT** portion of the registry.

Second, Windows applies computer-specific policies to the desktop environment. If a policy section for that computer name does not exist, Windows applies the Default Computer policies. These settings are copied into the **SYSTEM.DAT** portion of the registry.

By default, Windows automatically attempts to download computer and user policies from the file Config.pol in the Netlogon folder on a Windows NT server or the Public folder on a NetWare server. This default location can be overridden in a policy file setting. If no server is present, Windows uses the settings currently on the client computer. For more information about how Windows processes system policies, see the *Microsoft Windows 95 Resource Kit* or the *Microsoft Windows NT Server 4.0 Resource Kit* and *Microsoft Windows NT Workstation 4.0 Resource Kit*.

Part 2 Deploying Microsoft Office

Customizing Office Connections to the World Wide Web

Office 97 allows you to connect your Office applications directly to Microsoft home pages on the World Wide Web through commands on the **Microsoft on the Web** submenu (**Help** menu). You can also modify these commands to include additional Web or intranet sites, or you can hide the commands.

When you start Office, it searches the registry of the computer on which it is installed for a registered Web browser. If it finds one, Office enables the **Microsoft on the Web** submenu commands. These commands are grouped into three sets:

- Commands related to the application
- Commands related to Office
- A **Microsoft Home Page** command

For example, the following illustration shows the **Microsoft on the Web** submenu in Microsoft Excel.

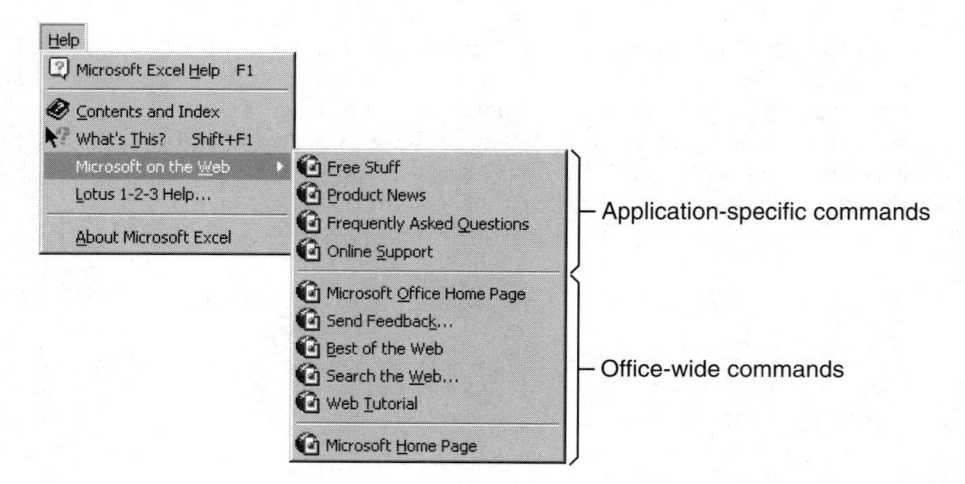

For users who have Web access, these commands provide hyperlinks to a wealth of information about the application and other useful Web resources at the Microsoft Web site. If no registered browser is found, these commands are unavailable. The following tables describes the commands on the **Microsoft on the Web** submenu.

Chapter 7   Customizing and Optimizing Microsoft Office

This command on the Microsoft on the Web submenu	Connects to this page on the Microsoft Web site
Free Stuff	The application's Free Stuff page, from which you can download file converters, add-ons, and other free utilities for the application.
Product News	The application's home page.
Frequently Asked Questions	The application's Frequently Asked Questions (FAQ) page. This page is maintained by Microsoft Support Services.
Online Support	The application's online support page. This page is maintained by Microsoft Support Services.
Microsoft Office Home Page	The Office home page, where you can find Office-wide and application-specific information.
Send Feedback	An Office-wide feedback page, from which you can submit feature requests, bug reports, or product purchasing and licensing information.
Best of the Web	A page that contains hyperlinks to other useful reference sites, such as home, reference, and financial information.
Search the Web	A page that contains hyperlinks to Web search pages.
Web Tutorial	The Microsoft Web tutorial.
Microsoft Home Page	The Microsoft home page at http://www.microsoft.com/.

Note   In the Visual Basic environment of the Office applications, some of the **Microsoft on the Web** commands behave differently. The **Microsoft Office Home Page** command is replaced by the **For Developers Only** command, which connects you to:

http://www.microsoft.com/msdn/

The **Send Feedback** command connects you to:

http://www.microsoft.com/officedev/feedback.htm

Tip   In Windows 95 and Windows NT Workstation 4.0, you can use a system policy to disable or customize commands on the **Microsoft on the Web** submenu for all Office application users in your workgroup. In the System Policy Editor, set the following policy:

User\application\Internet\Help_Microsoft on the Web

For more information, see "Using Windows System Policies to Customize Office" earlier in this chapter.

Disabling Commands on the Microsoft on the Web Submenu

The **Microsoft on the Web** submenu commands are enabled only if an Office application detects a registered Web browser. If these commands are available, but you want to hide or disable them for some or all users in your workgroup, you can do so by modifying Windows registry entries.

You can disable the application-specific commands (commands one through four on the submenu), or the Office-wide commands (commands five through nine on the submenu). If you disable both groups of commands, the **Microsoft Home Page** command is also disabled.

▶ **To disable the application-specific commands on the Microsoft on the Web submenu**

1. Close the Office application you want to customize.

2. To start the Registry Editor in Microsoft Windows 95 or Windows NT Workstation 4.0, click **Run** on the **Start** menu and type **regedit**

   –or–

   In Microsoft Windows NT Workstation 3.51, click **Run** on the **File** menu in Program Manager and type **regedit32**

3. Expand the registry tree to **HKEY_CURRENT_USER\Software\Microsoft \Office\8.0***application***\WebHelp**, where *application* is the name of the Office application (or the Visual Basic environment) you want to customize.

4. If the **WebHelp** key does not already exist, point to **New** on the **Edit** menu, click **Key**, and then type **WebHelp**

5. With the **WebHelp** key selected, point to **New** on the **Edit** menu, and then click **String Value**.

6. To name the new string value, type **Command***x*, where *x* is a numeric value between 1 and 8.

7. Add an alphanumeric data value to the **Command***x* string value; for example **foo**. Make sure that the alphanumeric value you choose does not contain punctuation.

   Adding the alphanumeric string causes the application to hide the application-specific commands on the **Microsoft on the Web** submenu.

When you close the Registry Editor and restart the application you customized, the application-specific commands on the **Microsoft on the Web** submenu appear dimmed.

Chapter 7   Customizing and Optimizing Microsoft Office

▶ **To disable the Office-wide commands on the Microsoft on the Web submenu**

1. Close all Office applications.
2. To start Registry Editor in Microsoft Windows 95 or Windows NT Workstation 4.0, click **Run** on the **Start** menu and type **regedit**

   –or–

   In Microsoft Windows NT Workstation 3.51, click **Run** on the **File** menu in Program Manager and type **regedit32**
3. Expand the registry tree to **HKEY_CURRENT_USER\Software\Microsoft \Office\8.0\Common\WebHelp**
4. If the **WebHelp** key does not already exist, point to **New** on the **Edit** menu, click **Key**, and then type **WebHelp**
5. With the **WebHelp** key selected, point to **New** on the **Edit** menu, and then click **String Value**.
6. To name the new string value, type **Command**x, where x is a numeric value between 1 and 8.
7. Add a alphanumeric data value to the **Command**x string value; for example **foo**. Make sure that the alphanumeric value you choose does not contain punctuation.

   Adding the alphanumeric string causes the application to hide the Office-wide commands on the **Microsoft on the Web** submenu.

When you close the Registry Editor and restart any Office application, the Office-wide commands on the **Microsoft on the Web** submenu appear dimmed.

Adding Your Own Commands to the Microsoft on the Web Submenu

You can replace or add to the default commands on the **Microsoft on the Web** submenu with your own commands. For example, you might have an internal support page on your intranet that you would like users to visit instead of the support pages on the Microsoft Web site. You can add your own commands to the **Microsoft on the Web** submenu by adding registry keys and values for each application you want to customize.

▶ **To replace the default commands on the Microsoft on the Web submenu with your own commands**

1. Close the Office application you want to customize.
2. To start Registry Editor in Microsoft Windows 95 or Windows NT Workstation 4.0, click **Run** on the **Start** menu and type **regedit**

   –or–

In Microsoft Windows NT Workstation 3.51, click **Run** on the **File** menu in Program Manager and type **regedit32**

3 To replace the application-specific commands with your own command, expand the registry tree to **HKEY_CURRENT_USER\Software\Microsoft\Office \8.0***application*, where *application* is the name of the Office application (or the Visual Basic environment) you want to customize.

–or–

To replace the Office-wide commands with your own command, expand the registry tree to **HKEY_CURRENT_USER\Software\Microsoft\Office \8.0\Common**

4 If the **WebHelp** key does not already exist, point to **New** on the **Edit** menu, click **Key**, and then type **WebHelp**

5 With the **WebHelp** key selected, point to **New** on the **Edit** menu, and then click **String Value**.

6 To name the new string value, type **Command***x*, where *x* is a numeric value between 1 and 8.

Tip If you plan to restore some or all of the default commands later, limit your custom command string value names to **Command5** through **Command8** for the application-specific command group, or **Command6** through **Command8** for the Office-wide command group.

7 Double-click the **Command***x* string value.

8 In the **Value data** field, enter the command name and URL using the following syntax. Place the ampersand (&) directly to the left of the character you want to appear underlined on the menu; for example:

&Command name,URL

For example, the following value creates a command named **Corporate Support** that goes to the URL address http://support/default.htm:

&Corporate Support,http://Support/Default.htm

When you close the Registry Editor and restart the application you customized, the new command appears on the **Microsoft on the Web** submenu in place of the default commands. The application hides the application-specific or Office-wide default commands, depending on where in the registry you added the key. If you want to restore some or all of the default commands to the submenu, you must add new registry values for the default commands.

▶ **To display both custom and default commands**

1 Close the Office application you want to customize.

2 To start Registry Editor in Microsoft Windows 95 or Windows NT Workstation 4.0, click **Run** on the **Start** menu and type **regedit**

–or–

Chapter 7   Customizing and Optimizing Microsoft Office

In Microsoft Windows NT Workstation 3.51, click **Run** on the **File** menu in Program Manager and type **regedit32**

3. To restore an application-specific command, expand the registry tree to **HKEY_CURRENT_USER\Software\Microsoft\Office\8.0**application**\WebHelp**, where *application* is the name of the Office application (or the Visual Basic environment) you want to customize.

   –or–

   To restore an Office-wide command, expand the registry tree to **HKEY_CURRENT_USER\Software\Microsoft\Office\8.0\Common\WebHelp**

4. With the **WebHelp** key selected, point to **New** on the **Edit** menu, and then click **String Value**.

5. To name the new string value, type **Command**x, where x is a numeric value between 1 and 4 (to restore a command to the application-specific group) or between 1 and 5 (to restore a command to the Office-wide group).

6. Double-click the **Command**x string value.

7. In the **Value data** field, enter the value data strings shown in the following table, where *application* is the application name **Access**, **Excel**, **Outlook**, **PowerPoint**, **VB**, **VBE**, or **Word**.

To display this command	Enter this value data string in the Value data field
Application-specific commands	
Free Stuff	&Free Stuff,,*application*,,0x0409,8.0,free
Product news	&Product News,, *application*,,0x0409,8.0,news
Frequently Asked Questions	Frequently Asked &Questions,,*application*,,0x0409,8.0,faq
Online Support	Online &Support,, *application*,,0x0409,8.0,support
Office-wide commands	
Microsoft Office Home Page	Microsoft &Office Home Page,,office,,0x0409,8.0,home
Send Feedback	Send Feedbac&k,feedback, , office,,0x0409,8.0,feedback
Best of the Web	&Best of the Web,,msft,,0x0409,,directory,,office8
Search the Web	Search the &Web,,msft,,0x0409,,search,,office8
Web Tutorial	Web &Tutorial,,msft,,0x0409,,tutorial,,office8

When you close the Registry Editor and restart the application you customized, the restored default commands and your custom commands appear on the **Microsoft on the Web** submenu.

Optimizing Individual Office Applications

There are a number of ways that you can customize Office applications to improve the overall performance of Office on client computers. By modifying specific options based on your particular use of Office, you can increase speed or reduce memory or disk usage. The remainder of this chapter discusses how to optimize each of the Office applications.

Optimizing Microsoft Access

Depending on your computer's configuration and your working environment, there may be several things you can do to improve the performance of Microsoft Access or your database. The optimal settings described in the following sections may vary with the type of computer on which you run Microsoft Access.

Using the Performance Analyzer

When you want to optimize the performance of a Microsoft Access database, start with the Performance Analyzer. You can use the Performance Analyzer to analyze a database or selected objects in a database. The Performance Analyzer can make some changes for you automatically.

▶ **To run the Performance Analyzer**

1. Open the Microsoft Access database you want to optimize.
2. On the **Tools** menu, point to **Analyze**, and then click **Performance**.
3. In the **Object Type** box, click the type of database object you want to optimize.

   To view a list of all database objects at once, click **All** in the **Object Type** box.
4. In the **Object Name** box, select the database objects you want to optimize.
5. Repeat Steps 3 and 4 until you have selected all the objects you want to optimize, and then click **OK**.

In the dialog box that appears, the **Analysis Results** box displays three types of optimizations: Recommendations, Suggestions, and Ideas. When you click an item in the **Analysis Results** box, the **Analysis Notes** box displays information about the proposed optimization. Suggestion optimizations have potential tradeoffs to consider. To view a description of the tradeoffs, click a Suggestion optimization in the **Analysis Results** box, and then read the information in the **Analysis Notes** box.

Microsoft Access can perform Recommendation and Suggestion optimizations for you. In the **Analysis Results** box, click each of the Recommendation or Suggestion optimizations you want performed, and then click **Optimize**.

You must perform Idea optimizations yourself. To perform an Idea optimization, click that optimization, and then follow the instructions in the **Analysis Notes** box.

Optimizing a System to Run Microsoft Access

In addition to running the Performance Analyzer, the following suggestions can help you optimize the performance of Microsoft Access and the computer it is running on.

Increase RAM

Because database operations are faster when Microsoft Access can perform them in random-access memory (RAM), the performance of Microsoft Access depends largely on the amount of RAM available. To run as a standalone application, Microsoft Access requires a minimum of 12 MB of RAM for Windows, or 16 MB of RAM for Windows NT Workstation.

The amount of memory Microsoft Access needs to run at top speed depends on a variety of factors, such as how many other applications are running at the same time and what types of operations a Microsoft Access database application performs. When other applications are competing for memory, you can usually improve performance significantly by running with more than the required amount of RAM.

Similarly, if a Microsoft Access database application uses Automation (formerly OLE Automation) to work with another application's objects, you can improve the performance of a Microsoft Access database application by running with more RAM. When running with 32 MB or more of RAM, you may be able to increase performance by adjusting the **MaxBufferSize** setting in the Windows registry. Make sure that you are not using any of your RAM for a RAM drive.

For more information about the **MaxBufferSize** setting, see "MaxBufferSize" later in this chapter.

Optimize Virtual Memory Use

With *virtual memory*, an application sees a large, continuous block of primary memory (RAM) that, in reality, is a much smaller block of primary memory supplemented by secondary memory (such as a hard disk). To temporarily free up space in RAM, blocks of data (called *pages*) are moved between RAM and a *swap file* located on the hard disk.

By default, the Windows 95 swap file is dynamic, so it can shrink or grow based on available disk space and the operations performed on the system. Also, the swap file can occupy a fragmented region of the hard disk with no substantial performance penalty. A dynamic swap file is usually the most efficient use of resources. The simplest way to ensure high virtual memory performance is to make sure that the disk containing the swap file has ample free space so that the swap file size can shrink and grow as needed.

In Windows 3.*x*, enhancing performance by changing virtual memory settings is quite common. Because the Windows 95 swap file is dynamic, the need to change virtual memory settings is less common. However, in some situations adjusting virtual memory settings can improve performance. If you've already tried deleting unnecessary files, and you still have a performance problem, try changing the Windows 95 default virtual memory settings.

If you have more than one drive available, you may get better performance if you specify that Windows locate the swap file on a drive other than the default in the following cases:

- If the default drive does not have much free disk space, and another local drive has space available.
- If another local drive is available that is faster than the current drive (unless that disk is already heavily used).

You also may get better performance if you specify the minimum disk space available for virtual memory to be at least 25 MB minus available RAM. For example, if a computer has 12 MB of RAM, you should specify at least 13 MB of virtual memory. You may want to specify more if you run several large applications at the same time.

For more information about changing Windows 95 virtual memory settings, see Windows 95 online Help.

Compact Databases and Defragment the Hard Disk

Each time users add or update data, a database grows. But when a user deletes data, the database does not automatically get smaller. Microsoft Access makes empty data pages available for reuse after a database is closed, so the next time it is opened, new data pages are available to be filled with new records. If left unused, empty data pages remain in the database until it is compacted.

Compacting the database frees unused disk space, makes all data pages contiguous, and, if a primary key is defined for a table, saves its records in primary key order. For databases in which records are frequently added, deleted, and updated, you should compact frequently.

Note If the database is a replica, you must compact it twice to reclaim all available space. Additionally, if the database is the Design Master in a replicated set, you must take certain precautions when compacting it to prevent it from losing its Design Master status. For more information about replication, see Chapter 29, "Workgroup Features in Microsoft Access."

In addition, you should occasionally use a utility such as the Windows Disk Defragmenter to defragment the hard disk after compacting databases. This increases efficiency by making database files contiguous on the hard disk.

Do Not Use Wallpaper on a Low-Memory Computer

If the Windows desktop has a wallpaper (full-screen background) bitmap and the computer does not have memory to spare, replace the wallpaper with a solid color or pattern bitmap, or no bitmap at all.

> ### Using the System Policy Editor to Change Settings in the Options Dialog Box
>
> You can customize the user environment and achieve some performance optimizations in Microsoft Access by setting options in the **Options** dialog box (**Tools** menu) on individual user's computers. Using the System Policy Editor, however, a network administrator can set these options remotely—for all users, for a particular network group, or for a single user. You can also set options for all client computers or for a single computer.
>
> Instead of making these changes in the **Options** dialog box on individual computers, run the System Policy Editor using the Access97.adm template. For more information about using the System Policy Editor, see "Using Windows System Policies to Customize Office" earlier in this chapter.

Adjusting Microsoft Jet Registry Settings to Improve Performance

In addition to optimizing system memory use, you may want to adjust Microsoft Jet settings in the Windows registry. These settings control how the Microsoft Jet database engine uses memory and performs other aspects of its operations. Microsoft Jet automatically provides default settings that usually give the best performance for most common database operations. However, depending on what kind of operations a database application performs and how much memory is available at any given time, you may be able to improve performance by adjusting Windows registry settings.

Note Keep in mind that the optimum value for a setting in the registry can change from computer to computer, and can change depending on how much memory is available, the kind of operation the user is performing, and the level of activity in the database at any given time. Experiment with these settings to find out what works best.

If you decide to change any of the Microsoft Jet registry settings in the Windows registry, you have three options:

- Change the default values for Microsoft Jet settings in the **HKEY_LOCAL_MACHINE\SOFTWARE\Microsoft\Jet\3.5\Engines\Jet 3.5** key.

    These defaults are written when Microsoft Access 97 is installed. Changes made to settings in this key may affect other applications that use the Microsoft Jet 3.5 database engine, such as Visual Basic version 5.0 or Microsoft Excel 97. Make changes to values in this key only if you want to affect all the applications that use Microsoft Jet 3.5 on a user's computer, or if only Microsoft Access 97 is used to perform operations on Microsoft Jet 3.5 databases on a user's computer.

- Create a **Jet 3.5** subkey below the **KEY_LOCAL_MACHINE\SOFTWARE \Microsoft\Office\8.0\Access\Jet\3.5\Engines** key, and then add values for any default setting you want to override.

   These changes affect only Microsoft Access 97.

- Create a custom set of registry keys, called a *user profile*, that contains settings to override default registry settings.

   These settings affect only a particular database application or session of Microsoft Access. You use the **/profile** command-line option when starting Microsoft Access to specify the user profile you want to use.

For more information about user profiles or changing Microsoft Access registry settings, see Microsoft Access online Help.

Using the SetOption Method to Change Settings in the Windows Registry

You can also change most of the Microsoft Jet registry settings by using the **SetOption** method of the **DBEngine** object in Data Access Objects (DAO) code. Using the **SetOption** method, you can change these settings while a database application is running.

For example, you may want to change the **SharedAsyncDelay** and **PageTimeout** settings to low values to increase performance when an application performs operations on one record at a time or is using controls bound to data; but you may want to increase these values when performing bulk operations, such as update and delete queries or transactions on large numbers of records.

Changing Microsoft Jet settings by using the **SetOption** method does not affect the values stored in the Windows registry. Changes made with the **SetOption** method are in effect only for the current instance of the **DBEngine** object. For more information about the **SetOption** method, see Microsoft Access online Help.

The following sections discuss the Windows registry settings you can adjust to improve performance of Microsoft Access.

Threads

A *thread* is a software process that runs independently on a multitasking operating system such as Windows 95 or Windows NT Workstation. For example, using multiple threads allows you to run a communications software program to download a file at the same time you use your word processor to edit a document.

Microsoft Jet uses threads internally to enhance performance and provide background services such as read-ahead caching, write-behind caching (transaction commit), cache maintenance, and the detection of changes made to shared databases. By default, Microsoft Jet uses up to a maximum of three threads. You may want to try increasing the **Threads** setting if a large number of actions are performed in a database application, or if it contains a large number of linked tables.

MaxBufferSize

Microsoft Jet reads and writes data in 2K pages, placing the data in a temporary holding area called the *buffer* as required by its operations. By default, when performing operations that add, delete, or update records and that are not part of an explicit transaction, Microsoft Jet automatically performs internal transactions that group changes to records and temporarily saves them in the buffer.

After a specified time, or when the size specified by the **MaxBufferSize** setting is exceeded, Microsoft Jet writes the data to the database. This minimizes the time spent reading and writing data to the database. Additionally, Microsoft Jet can minimize the time spent reading data for tables, queries, forms, or reports by reading available data from its buffer.

The **MaxBufferSize** setting specifies a high-water mark for the size of the buffer that Microsoft Jet uses to work with records in memory, measured in kilobytes. Microsoft Jet can temporarily exceed the **MaxBufferSize**. As soon as it does, however, it starts a background thread to write data to the database to bring the buffer's size down to the specified high-water mark.

By default, Microsoft Jet allocates memory for its internal buffer on an as-needed basis up to the **MaxBufferSize**. The default value written in the Windows registry for the **MaxBufferSize** when Microsoft Access is installed is 0, which indicates that Microsoft Jet calculates the setting based on the following formula:

((Total RAM in K − 12,288)/4 + 512K)

For example, on a system with 16 MB of RAM (16,384K), Microsoft Jet uses a setting of 1,536 in **MaxBufferSize**.

You can override the default calculated setting by specifying a different value in **MaxBufferSize**. This sets a new high-water mark. The minimum value that Microsoft Jet uses by default is 512K, but you can specify a value as low as 128K. However, setting the value in **MaxBufferSize** to less than 512K is not recommended for Microsoft Access applications because it can seriously degrade performance.

For computers with 16 MB or less of installed RAM, there is generally no need to override the calculated setting. For computers with 32 MB of RAM, however, you may see some performance improvement when specifying a larger **MaxBufferSize**, as long as no other applications are running at the same time as Microsoft Access. For example, tests have shown performance improvements in applications that perform large transactions when a **MaxBufferSize** as large as 8 MB is specified.

Specifying a **MaxBufferSize** larger than 8 MB has not been found to increase performance. Setting a value too high can degrade performance due to the added CPU overhead needed to manage the cache, and due to the fact that the operating system may start swapping the Microsoft Jet cache to disk as virtual memory.

Important When you specify a **MaxBufferSize** setting larger than the default and you are not using the **FlushTransactionTimeout** setting, increase the **SharedAsyncDelay** setting to increase the time that data is held in the buffer. If you do not increase the value of **SharedAsyncDelay**, Microsoft Jet writes the contents of its buffer to the database before it has had time to utilize the additional memory you specified. For more information, see "SharedAsyncDelay" later in this section.

UserCommitSync

The **UserCommitSync** setting determines whether changes made as part of an explicit transaction (a change made to data using the **BeginTrans**, **CommitTrans**, and **Rollback** methods) are written to the database in synchronous mode or asynchronous mode. In *synchronous* mode, Microsoft Jet does not return control to the application code until the changes made by the **CommitTrans** method are written to the database. In *asynchronous* mode, Microsoft Jet stores the changes in its memory buffer, returns control to the application code immediately, and then writes the changes to the database in a background thread.

Microsoft Jet begins writing the changes either after a specified period of time (determined by the **FlushTransactionTimeout** setting, or by the **SharedAsyncDelay** or **ExclusiveAsyncDelay** settings described later in this section), or when the **MaxBufferSize** is exceeded. The default **UserCommitSync** setting is **Yes**, which specifies synchronous mode. It is not advisable to change this setting, because in asynchronous mode there is no guarantee that information has been written to disk before a database application's code proceeds to the next command.

Note There is no longer a need to use explicit transactions to improve performance of Microsoft Access. In Microsoft Access 95 and Microsoft Access 97, a database application should use explicit transactions only in situations where there may be a need to roll back changes. Microsoft Jet can now automatically perform internal transactions to improve performance whenever it adds, deletes, or changes records.

For more information about transactions, see Chapter 9, "Working with Records and Fields," in *Building Applications with Microsoft Access 97*.

ImplicitCommitSync

By default, when performing operations that add, delete, or update records outside of explicit transactions, Microsoft Jet automatically performs internal transactions that temporarily save data in its memory buffer, and then later write the data to the hard disk. The **ImplicitCommitSync** setting determines whether changes made using these automatic internal transactions are written to the database in synchronous mode or asynchronous mode.

The default **ImplicitCommitSync** setting is **No**, which specifies that changes are written to the database in asynchronous mode; this provides the best performance. If you want internal transactions to be written to the database in synchronous mode, change the **ImplicitCommitSync** setting to **Yes**. This generates behavior similar to Microsoft Jet versions 2.*x* and earlier, when not using explicit transactions in Access Basic code; however, it can also impair performance considerably.

FlushTransactionTimeout

The **FlushTransactionTimeout** setting determines the method Microsoft Jet uses to perform asynchronous writes to a database file. This setting is the number of milliseconds after which Microsoft Jet starts writing database changes to disk from its cache. Changes are written to disk after the specified amount of time has expired and if no new pages have been added to the cache during that interval.

The only exception is if the size of the cache exceeds the **MaxBufferSize** setting, at which point the cache starts asynchronous writes regardless of whether the time has expired. The default setting is 500 milliseconds. The only reason to increase the value of the **FlushTransactionTimeout** setting is if the database is being updated over a slow wide area network (WAN) or local area network (LAN) connection. Increasing this value for databases being updated over fast WAN and typical LAN connections does not improve performance.

The **FlushTransactionTimeout** setting overrides both the **ExclusiveAsyncDelay** and **SharedAsyncDelay** settings, and is the preferred method of determining how Microsoft Jet performs asynchronous writes to a database file. To enable the **ExclusiveAsyncDelay** and **SharedAsyncDelay** settings, you must set the **FlushTransactionTimeout** entry to a value of 0.

ExclusiveAsyncDelay

The **ExclusiveAsyncDelay** setting is the maximum time that can pass before asynchronous mode changes start to be written to a database that is opened exclusively. The default setting is 2,000 milliseconds. Decrease this setting if you want to be sure that changes are written to a database more frequently, but note that this decreases overall performance.

Because the default setting is already quite long, increasing this setting does not improve performance in most cases. However, if a system has 32 MB of RAM or more and you have specified a large **MaxBufferSize**, you may see some performance improvement if you increase this setting. By default, this setting is disabled by the **FlushTransactionTimeout** setting.

SharedAsyncDelay

The **SharedAsyncDelay** setting is the maximum time that can pass before asynchronous mode changes start to be written to a database that is opened in shared mode. The default setting is 50 milliseconds. Note that this produces a small delay before changes are made available to other users. Increasing this value enhances performance in shared databases because there are fewer disk writes. However, it may reduce the overall concurrency because pages are locked while they are in the buffer waiting to be written to the database.

If a database application performs operations that affect many records, increase this setting to give Microsoft Jet additional time to temporarily save additions, deletions, and updates in its buffer before it writes them to the database. This applies whether a database application uses action queries, DAO code, or SQL statements to add, delete, or update records. By default, this setting is disabled by the **FlushTransactionTimeout** setting.

PageTimeout

The **PageTimeout** setting determines how long Microsoft Jet waits before checking to see whether other users have made changes to the database. If changes have been made, Microsoft Jet refreshes the data in its memory buffer.

Note This action is equivalent to pressing F9 while viewing a table or query in Microsoft Access, or using the **Refresh** method in DAO code.

The default **PageTimeout** setting is 5,000 milliseconds. Decreasing this setting increases the amount of time spent reading from the disk, thus impairing performance; but it can also ensure the data available to the user is more current. The **Refresh Interval** setting on the **Advanced** tab in the **Options** dialog box (**Tools** menu) in Microsoft Access overrides the setting in **PageTimeout**.

Tip You can override the **PageTimeout** setting and refresh the cache by using the **dbRefreshCache** argument of the **Idle** method in DAO code. This allows users to see other users' changes immediately. For more information about the **Idle** method, see Microsoft Access online Help.

LockDelay

If Microsoft Access tries to place a lock on a page in a shared database, and a message that locking has failed is returned, the **LockDelay** setting determines how long it waits before it retries. If the time it takes to return the message exceeds the **LockDelay** setting, there is no delay. The default setting is 100 milliseconds.

On systems that do not manage lock retries themselves, such as Windows 95 peer-to-peer networking, the **LockDelay** setting prevents Microsoft Jet from performing repeated retries over a short period of time. If you are using such a system, the default setting is usually sufficient to reduce the number of lock requests sent across the network, which frees up network bandwidth for other purposes.

If a database application or its users frequently lock a large number of records, you may want to try increasing this setting to further reduce the number of lock requests being sent across the network. If you are using a server-based networking system that manages lock retries itself, such as Windows NT Server or Novell NetWare, there is no need to change this setting.

MaxLocksPerFile

The **MaxLocksPerFile** setting determines the maximum number of locks that Microsoft Jet places against a file. The default setting is 9,500 locks. If the number of locks required to perform a transaction exceeds the **MaxLocksPerFile** setting, the transaction commits (writes) the data that has locks associated with it, frees the locks, and then continues processing the transaction.

If the maximum number of locks a server can handle is less than the setting in **MaxLocksPerFile**, the server returns an error message or appears to hang when performing a large transaction. If this occurs, decrease the value of **MaxLocksPerFile**. A NetWare server can be configured to perform a maximum of 10,000 locks per connection. A NetWare server connection can include more than one database, so it is possible to exceed the maximum number of available locks if you are using more than one database at a time.

RecycleLVs

Long value (LV) pages store data in fields with Memo, OLE Object, and Hyperlink data types, as well as the data that defines forms, reports, and modules. When a database is open in shared mode, the size of the database increases when data, forms, reports, and modules are deleted or changed in such a way that the current LV page must be discarded and replaced with a new LV page. Sometimes a new LV page is needed to prevent errors for other users who may still be using the object or data in its original form.

The **RecycleLVs** setting determines when discarded LV pages become available for reuse. The default setting is 0, which specifies that discarded LV pages continue to occupy space in the database and only become available for reuse after the last user closes the database. You can change the default setting to 1 so that discarded LV pages become available for reuse after Microsoft Jet determines that there is only one user in the database in shared mode and that new LV data has been added to the database.

Note that setting **RecycleLVs** to 1 slows performance slightly. Therefore, this is primarily useful during development of a database application, when forms, reports, and modules are being created, because it minimizes the need to compact the database.

When a database is open in exclusive mode, the **RecycleLVs** setting has no effect: discarded LV pages become available for reuse immediately. In both exclusive mode and shared mode, discarded LV pages are reused only when new LV data needs to be written to the database. To remove discarded LV pages before that time, you must compact the database.

Optimizing Table Performance

You can achieve the best performance results by following these guidelines for table design.

Design Tables Without Redundant Data

A well-designed database is a prerequisite for fast data retrieval and updates. If existing tables in your database contain redundant data, you can split the data into related tables so that you can store data more efficiently. This process is called *normalization*.

You can use the Table Analyzer Wizard to normalize your tables manually, or you can have the wizard do this for you automatically. After identifying the data that can be moved to smaller tables, the Table Analyzer Wizard identifies a unique value within each new table to use as a primary key, or if no such value exists, creates an incrementing AutoNumber field to use as the primary key. It creates foreign key fields and uses them with the primary keys to create a relationship between the new tables. Finally, the wizard searches through your data, identifies any values that appear to be inconsistent, and prompts you to choose the correct value.

▶ **To use the Table Analyzer Wizard**

1. On the **Tools** menu, point to **Analyze**, and then click **Table**.

   The first two panels of the wizard contain introductory information about normalization.

2. On the third panel of the wizard, double-click the table that you want to normalize.

3. Follow the instructions in the remaining panels of the wizard.

   In the last panel, you can create a query to view all the information from the split tables in a single datasheet.

For more information about determining which tables, fields, and relationships belong in your database, see Microsoft Access online Help.

Choose Appropriate Data Types for Fields

You can save space in a database and improve join operations by choosing appropriate data types for fields. When defining a field, choose the smallest data type that is appropriate for the data in the field. Also, give fields you use in joins the same or compatible data types.

For more information about data types or the size of data types for fields, see Microsoft Access online Help.

Create Indexes for Fields Used in Joins and When Setting Criteria

An *index* helps Microsoft Access find and sort records faster. You can make dramatic improvements in the speed of queries by indexing fields on both sides of joins, or by creating a relationship between those fields and then indexing any field used to set criteria for the query. Finding records through the **Find** dialog box (**Edit** menu) is also much faster when searching an indexed field. Intelligent indexing of large tables can significantly improve performance when your query uses Rushmore™ query optimization.

For more information about Rushmore query optimization, see Microsoft Access online Help.

Note Microsoft Jet can use a descending index to optimize a query as long as criteria on the indexed field uses an equal sign (=) as the comparison operator. If the index is descending and the comparison operator is something other than an equal sign, the index will not be used. Ascending indexes (the default) can always be used to optimize a query.

Indexes take up disk space and slow down the adding, deleting, and updating of records. In most situations, however, the faster data retrieval outweighs these disadvantages. If a database application updates data frequently or if you have disk space constraints, you may want to limit indexes; otherwise, use them generously. Make sure to create a primary key or unique index if the data in a field or combination of fields uniquely identifies the records in a table.

Use Multiple-Field Indexes When Joining Multiple Fields

If you use *multiple-field indexes*, Microsoft Access can optimize queries that join multiple fields from one table to multiple fields in another table (such as LastName, FirstName in one table to LastName, FirstName in another table) or that search for values in multiple fields.

If you use criteria on a field in a multiple-field index, the criteria must apply to the first field or fields in the index in order for Microsoft Jet to use the index to optimize the query. For example, if you have a multiple-field index on the two fields LastName and FirstName used in a join to the LastName and FirstName fields in another table, Microsoft Jet can use the multiple-field index to optimize the query when you have criteria on LastName only, or on LastName and FirstName, but not if the criteria is on FirstName only. If the criteria is on FirstName only, you must add a single-field index on FirstName to optimize the query.

The simplest approach is to add multiple-field indexes to fields used in multiple-field joins and also add a single-field index to any field on which you use criteria to restrict the values in the field. You can add both a multiple-field index and a single-field index to the same field.

Optimizing the Performance of Linked Tables

Although you can use linked tables as though they were regular Microsoft Access tables, keep in mind that they are not actually in your Microsoft Access database. Each time you view data in a linked table, Microsoft Access has to retrieve records from another file. This can take time, especially if the linked table is on a network or in an SQL database.

If you are using a linked table on a network or in an SQL database, follow these guidelines for the best results:

- Force the linked database to remain open.

  This greatly enhances performance when opening the main database and opening tables and forms. Create an empty table in the linked database and create a link to the table in the main database. Then use the **OpenRecordset** method to open the linked table. This prevents the Microsoft Jet database engine from repeatedly opening and closing the linked database and creating and deleting the associated LDB file.

- View only the data you need.

  Do not page up and down unnecessarily in the datasheet. Avoid going to the last record in a large table. If you want to add new records to a large table, use the **Data Entry** command on the **Records** menu to avoid loading existing records into memory. If you often add records to a linked table, create a form for adding records that has the **DataEntry** property set to **Yes**. When you open the form to enter new data, Microsoft Access does not display any existing records and does not have to retrieve all the records in the linked table.

- Use filters or queries to limit the number of records that you view in a form or datasheet.

  This allows Microsoft Access to transfer less data over the network.

- In queries that involve linked tables, avoid using functions in query criteria.

  In particular, avoid using domain aggregate functions, such as **DSum**, anywhere in your queries. When you use a domain aggregate function, Microsoft Access retrieves all of the data in the linked table to execute the query.

- When a Microsoft Access database is shared on a network, avoid locking records longer than necessary.

Optimizing SQL Database Performance

When you connect to an external SQL database table, you achieve the best performance by using linked tables whenever possible. Linked tables are considerably faster, more powerful, and more efficient than directly opened tables. You can only open tables directly using Visual Basic code, so this is not pertinent if you are accessing SQL server™ data using the Microsoft Access user interface.

Following are additional guidelines for improving performance:

- Retrieve and view only the data you need.

  Use restricted queries to limit the number of records that you retrieve, and select only the columns you need, so Microsoft Access can transfer less data over the network. If you are not updating the data, do not use updatable result sets. You can prevent data from being updated when using a form by setting the form's **RecordSet** property to **Snapshot**.

- If you need to retrieve a large number of records, use a dynaset.

    Dynasets are faster and more efficient than snapshots. For example, when you move to the end of a snapshot, the entire result set must be downloaded to the local computer. With a dynaset, however, only the last screen is downloaded. Also do not page up and down unnecessarily in the data, and avoid going to the last record in a large table—the **Data Entry** command on the **Records** menu is the fastest way to add new records to a table.

- Use cache memory.

    If the data most recently retrieved from the server is requested again while the application is running, it is faster to retrieve many rows from a cache than to fetch many individual rows. Microsoft Access forms and datasheets automatically use a cache. If you are retrieving data using a **Recordset** object created in Visual Basic for Applications, you can use the **CacheStart** and **CacheSize** properties to specify the range you want within the **Recordset** object. Use the **FillCache** method to quickly fill all or part of this range with data from the SQL database server.

- Avoid using queries that cause processing to be done locally.

    When accessing external data, the Jet database engine processes data locally only when the operation cannot be performed by the external database. Query operations (as defined by the SQL commands used to implement them) performed locally include:

    - **JOIN** operations between tables from different remote data sources. (Note that if the join involves a local table or query with few records and a remote table with many more records, and the remote table's join field is indexed, Microsoft Access returns only the records that match the local table or query, thus greatly improving query performance.)
    - **JOIN** operations based on a query with the **DISTINCT** predicate or a **GROUP BY** clause.
    - Outer joins containing syntax not supported by the Open Database Connectivity (ODBC) driver or server.
    - **DISTINCT** predicates containing operations that cannot be processed remotely.
    - The **LIKE** operator used with Text or Memo fields (this may not be supported by some servers).
    - Multiple-level **GROUP BY** arguments and totals, such as those used in reports with multiple grouping levels.
    - **GROUP BY** arguments based on a query with a **DISTINCT** predicate or a **GROUP BY** clause.
    - Cross-tab queries that have more than one aggregate; that have field, row, or column headings that contain aggregates; or that have a user-defined **ORDER BY** clause.

- **TOP***n* or **TOP***n* **PERCENT** predicates.
- User-defined functions, or operators or functions that are not supported by the ODBC driver or server.
- Complex combinations of **INNER JOIN**, **LEFT JOIN**, or **RIGHT JOIN** operations in nested queries.
- For update and delete queries that affect data stored on a server, set the **FailOnError** property to **Yes**.

   This setting tells Microsoft Access to send the query to the server, where all the appropriate records are processed at once instead of one record at a time.

Optimizing Multiuser Performance

This section describes suggestions that can help you optimize the performance of databases that are used in a multiuser environment.

Database performance is faster when only data is sent across the network. Put only the tables on a network server, and keep other database objects on users' computers. You can separate the tables from the other database objects by using the Database Splitter. To split a database, make a backup copy of the database, and then use the **Database Splitter** command (**Tools** menu, **Add-ins** submenu).

Choose the appropriate record locking method. To set the record locking method, use the options on the **Advanced** tab in the **Options** dialog box (**Tools** menu). The options under **Default Record Locking** include the following:

- **No Locks**

   Microsoft Access does not lock the records being edited. When a user tries to save changes to a record that another user has also changed, Microsoft Access gives the option of overwriting the other user's changes, copying the user's version of the record to the Clipboard, or discarding the changes. This strategy ensures that records can always be edited, but it can create editing conflicts between users.

- **Edited Records**

   Microsoft Access locks the record being edited, so no other user can change it. It might also lock other records that are stored nearby on the hard disk. If another user tries to edit a record that is locked, Microsoft Access displays an indicator in the other user's datasheet. This strategy ensures that users can always finish making changes that they have started. It is a good choice if you do not often have editing conflicts.

- **All Records**

   Microsoft Access locks all records in the form or datasheet (and underlying tables) for the entire time it is being edited, so no one else can edit or lock the records. This strategy is very restrictive, so choose it only when you know only one person needs to edit records at any one time.

Note When you edit data in a linked SQL database table using ODBC, Microsoft Access does not lock records; instead, the rules of that SQL database govern locking. In this instance, regardless of the record-locking setting you choose for your database, Microsoft Access always acts as though the **No Locks** setting has been selected.

You can avoid locking conflicts by adjusting the following settings on the **Advanced** tab in the **Options** dialog box (**Tools** menu):

- **Update Retry Interval**

    This sets the number of milliseconds after which Microsoft Access automatically tries to save a changed record that is locked by another user. Valid values are 0 through 1,000 milliseconds. The default setting is 250.

- **Number of Update Retries**

    This sets the number of times Microsoft Access tries to save a changed record that is locked by another user. Valid values are 0 through 10. The default setting is 2.

- **ODBC Refresh Interval**

    This sets the interval after which Microsoft Access automatically refreshes records that are opened using ODBC. Valid values are 1 through 32,766 seconds. The default setting is 1500.

- **Refresh Interval**

    This sets the number of seconds after which Microsoft Access automatically updates records in Datasheet or Form view. Valid values are 1 through 32,766 seconds. The default setting is 60.

Note When Microsoft Access refreshes the current datasheet or form, it does not reorder records, add new records, or remove deleted records. To view these changes, you must requery the underlying records for the datasheet or form.

If a multiuser database uses linked tables, see "Optimizing the Performance of Linked Tables" earlier in this chapter for additional suggestions. If a multiuser database connects to tables in an external SQL database, see "Optimizing SQL Database Performance" earlier in this chapter for additional suggestions.

Optimizing Query Performance

There are several things you can do to make queries run faster. In addition to using the Performance Analyzer to analyze specific queries, consider the following ideas.

- Index fields on both sides of joins, or create a relationship between those fields and index any field used to set criteria for the query.

    Note The Microsoft Jet database engine automatically optimizes queries that join a Microsoft Access table on your hard disk and an ODBC server table (typically an SQL server table) if the Microsoft Access table is small and the joined fields are indexed. In these cases, Microsoft Access improves performance by requesting only the necessary records from the server. Make sure that tables you join from different sources are indexed on the join fields.

- When defining a field in a table, choose the smallest data type or **FieldSize** that is appropriate for the data in the field. Also, give fields you use in joins the same or compatible data types.

- When creating a query, do not add fields that you do not need, and clear the **Show** check box for selection criteria fields whose data you do not want Microsoft Access to display.

- Avoid calculated fields in nested queries. If you add a query that contains a calculated field to another query, the expression in the calculated field slows performance in the top-level query.

    For example, suppose this is Query1:

    ```
    SELECT Format$(Field1)As TempField FROM Table1
    ```

    Query1 is nested in the following query, Query2:

    ```
    SELECT * FROM Query1 Where TempField = 100
    ```

    Nesting Query1 in Query2 causes optimization problems due to the expression `Format$(Field1)` in Query1. For best performance, use calculated fields only in the top-level query of nested queries. If that is not practical, use a calculated control on the form or report based on the query to show the result of the expression, instead of nesting the query.

- When grouping records by the values in a joined field, specify Group By for the field that is in the same table as the field you are totaling (calculating an aggregate on).

    For example, if your query totals the Quantity field in an Order Details table and groups by OrderID, specify Group By for the OrderID field in the Order Details table, not the OrderID field in the Orders table. For greater speed, use Group By on as few fields as possible. As an alternative, use the **First** function where appropriate.

    If a totals query includes a join, consider grouping the records in one query and then adding that query to a separate query that performs the join. This improves performance in some queries.

- Avoid restrictive query criteria on calculated and nonindexed columns whenever possible. For more information, see "Optimizing Criteria Expressions in Queries Using Rushmore Technology" later in this chapter.

- If you use criteria to restrict the values in a field used in a join, test whether the query runs faster with the criteria placed on the *one side* or the *many side* of the join. In some queries, you get faster performance by adding the criteria to the former.

- Use field sorting judiciously, especially with nonindexed fields.
- If your data does not change often, use make-table queries to create tables from your query results. Use the resulting tables rather than queries as the basis for your forms, reports, or other queries.
- Avoid using domain aggregate functions, such as the **DLookup** function, in a query that reads table data. Instead, add the table to the query or create a subquery.
- If you are creating a cross-tab query, use fixed column headings whenever possible. For more information about sorting or limiting column headings in cross-tab queries, see Microsoft Access online Help.
- Use the **Between...And**, **In**, and equal (=) operators on indexed columns to optimize queries. For more information, see "Optimizing Criteria Expressions in Queries Using Rushmore Technology" in the following section.

If a query includes tables in an external SQL database, see "Optimizing SQL Database Performance" earlier in this chapter for additional suggestions.

Optimizing Criteria Expressions in Queries Using Rushmore Technology

Rushmore is a data-access technology that permits sets of records to be queried efficiently. With Rushmore, when you use certain types of expressions in query criteria, your query runs much faster.

Simple Expressions

Microsoft Access can optimize simple expressions in the Criteria row of the query design grid or in a **WHERE** clause in an SQL **SELECT** statement. A simple optimizable expression can form an entire expression or can appear as part of an expression.

A simple optimizable expression takes one of the following forms:

Indexed field Comparison operator Expression
Expression Comparison operator Indexed field

In these expressions, *Indexed field* is a field on which an index is constructed.

Comparison operator is one of the following operators: <, >, =, <=, >=, <>, **Between**, **Like**, or **In**. *Expression* can be any valid expression, including constants, functions, and fields from other tables.

Note For best results, the comparison value in an expression using the **Like** operator must begin with a character, not a wildcard character. For example, you can optimize Like "m*" but not Like "*m*".

Examples of Simple Optimizable Expressions

If you have created indexes for the LastName, Age, and HireDate fields in an Employees table, the following are simple optimizable expressions:

```
[LastName]="Smith"
[Age]>=21
#12/30/90#<[HireDate]
Employees.[LastName]=Customers.[LastName]
[LastName] IN ("Smith", "Johnson", "Jones")
[Age] BETWEEN 18 AND 65
```

If you have a multiple-field index on the LastName, FirstName fields, the following expression is optimizable:

```
((([LastName])="Smith") AND ((([FirstName])="Pat")
```

The SQL **SELECT** statement for the following **COUNT(*)** query is Rushmore optimizable if there are indexes on the LastName and FirstName fields. This query counts the number of employees who are not named Pat Smith:

```
SELECT Count(*)FROM Employees
WHERE (Employees.[LastName] <> "Smith")
AND (Employees.[FirstName] <> "Pat")
```

Complex Expressions

Microsoft Access can also optimize complex expressions made by combining simple expressions with the **AND** or **OR** operators.

A complex optimizable expression takes one of the following forms:

Simple Expression **AND** *Simple Expression*

–or–

Simple Expression **OR** *Simple Expression*

The following rules determine query optimization when combining simple expressions in query criteria.

If you use this operator	To combine this expression	With this expression	The resulting query has these characteristics
AND	Optimizable	Optimizable	Fully optimizable
OR	Optimizable	Optimizable	Fully optimizable
AND	Optimizable	Not optimizable	Partially optimizable
OR	Optimizable	Not optimizable	Not optimizable
AND	Not optimizable	Not optimizable	Not optimizable
OR	Not optimizable	Not optimizable	Not optimizable
NOT	N/A	Optimizable	Not optimizable
NOT	N/A	Not optimizable	Not optimizable

You can use parentheses to group combinations of simple expressions. The preceding rules also apply to combinations of expressions grouped with parentheses.

After you have combined simple optimizable expressions into complex expressions, these complex expressions can, in turn, be combined to form even more complex expressions that are optimizable according to the preceding rules.

Examples of Complex Optimizable Expressions

The following table lists examples of combined simple expressions and the extent to which the result is optimizable.

Note These examples assume that you have created indexes for the LastName and HireDate fields, but not for the MiddleInitial or FirstName fields.

When you combine these expressions	With these expression types and operator	The resulting query has these characteristics
[LastName]="Smith" AND [Hire Date]<#12/30/90#	Optimizable **AND** Optimizable	Fully Optimizable
[LastName]="Smith" OR [Hire Date]<#12/30/90#	Optimizable **OR** Optimizable	Fully Optimizable
[LastName]="Smith" AND [MiddleInitial]="C"	Optimizable **AND** Not Optimizable	Partially Optimizable
[LastName]="Smith" OR [MiddleInitial]="C"	Optimizable **OR** Not Optimizable	Not Optimizable
[FirstName]="Terry" AND [MiddleInitial]="C"	Not Optimizable **AND** Not Optimizable	Not Optimizable
[FirstName]="Terry" OR [MiddleInitial]="C"	Not Optimizable **OR** Not Optimizable	Not Optimizable

Additional Notes on Rushmore Optimization

- The **COUNT(*)** function is highly optimized for queries that use Rushmore.

- If the index is descending and the comparison operator is other than equal (=), the query cannot be optimized.

- Rushmore queries work with Microsoft Access tables, as well as with Microsoft FoxPro and dBASE tables (DBF files). You cannot use Rushmore with ODBC data sources, however, because Microsoft Access sends these queries to the ODBC data source instead of processing them locally.

- You can optimize multiple-field indexes if you query the indexed fields in the order they appear in the Indexes window, beginning with the first indexed field and continuing with adjacent fields (up to and including 10 fields).

    For example, if you have a multiple-field index on LastName, FirstName, you can optimize a query on LastName or on LastName and FirstName, but you cannot optimize a query on FirstName.

Optimizing Filter Performance

If the lists in fields in the Filter By Form window take too long to display or they do not display values from the underlying table, you can set filtering options to change these behaviors. By setting filter options, you can prevent the lists from displaying the underlying table's field values, display field values on the list for certain types of indexed or nonindexed fields only, or change the record limit that determines whether the list displays a field's values.

You can perform this optimization for all tables, queries, and forms in the database, or for specific bound text box controls in forms.

Tip If you use the same nonindexed field repeatedly to filter records, consider indexing it before changing the following settings. This improves filtering and other search operations on the field.

To optimize Filter By Form performance for all tables, queries, and forms, set the options under **Filter By Form Defaults** on the **Edit/Find** tab in the **Options** dialog box (**Tools** menu) according to the performance you want to achieve:

- If the list of values takes too long to display in nonindexed fields only, limit the lists to indexed fields. You can do this by clearing the check boxes for **Local Non-indexed Fields** and **ODBC Fields**.

- If the lists take too long to display in indexed fields because there are too many records in the indexes, also clear the **Local Indexed Fields** check box.

- If lists are not displaying the values from indexed or nonindexed fields, make sure that the appropriate check boxes are selected under **Show list of values in**; or increase the number in the box **Don't display lists where more than this number of records read** so that it is greater than or equal to the maximum number of records in any nonindexed field in the underlying table.

  If the field is indexed, Microsoft Access reads only the unique values, not all the values in a field. If the field is not indexed, Microsoft Access reads all the values in the field. If the number of records it reads is more than the maximum it is allowed to display, Microsoft Access does not display the values for that field on the list.

To optimize a specific bound text box control on a form, display the form in Design view, display the property sheet for the control, and then set the **FilterLookup** property according to the performance you want to achieve:

- If the lists take too long to display in nonindexed fields only, limit the lists to indexed fields. Set the **FilterLookup** property to **Database Defaults**; then, on the **Edit/Find** tab in the **Options** dialog box (**Tools** menu), select the **Local Indexed Fields** check box and clear the **Local Non-Indexed Fields** and **ODBC Fields** check boxes.

- To prevent a list from displaying, regardless of the database defaults, set the **FilterLookup** property to **Never**.

- To force a list to display, regardless of the database defaults, set the **FilterLookup** property to **Always**.
- If lists are not displaying the values from indexed or nonindexed fields, make sure that the **FilterLookup** property for each field is not set to **Never**. If it is not, verify that the options under **Show list of values in** are selected. If they are, increase the number in the **Don't display lists where more than this number of records read** box so that it is greater than or equal to the maximum number of records in any nonindexed field in the underlying table.

Optimizing Find and Replace Performance

For the fastest searches when using the **Find** or **Replace** commands (**Edit** menu), search for whole field values or the first character within a single indexed field. If you search the same nonindexed field repeatedly, index the field.

Optimizing Form and Subform Performance

There are several things you can do to make your forms run faster:

- Avoid overlapping controls.
- Use bitmaps and other graphic objects sparingly.
- Convert unbound object frames that display graphics to image controls.
- Use black-and-white rather than color bitmaps.
- Close forms that are not being used.
- If the underlying record source includes many records and you want to use the form primarily to enter new records, set the **DataEntry** property of the form to **Yes** so that the form opens to a blank record.

    If you open a form with all records showing, Microsoft Access has to read in each record before it can display the blank record at the end of the recordset. If the form is already open, you can click the **Data Entry** command on the **Records** menu to switch to Data Entry mode.

- Do not sort records in an underlying query unless record order is important, especially with multiple-table queries.
- Base subforms on queries rather than tables, and include only fields from the record source that are absolutely necessary. Extra fields can decrease subform performance.
- Index all the fields in the subform that are linked to the main form.
- Index any subform fields used for criteria.
- Set the subform **AllowEdits**, **AllowAdditions**, and **AllowDeletions** properties to **No** if the records in the subform will not be edited. Or set the **RecordsetType** property to **Snapshot**.

- Eliminate code from forms that do not need it by setting the **HasModule** form property to **No**.

  The **HasModule** property specifies whether the form has a form module. A form without a form module loads more quickly and occupies less disk space. If a form or controls on the form do not use event procedures, the form does not require a form module. For example, if your application uses a switchboard form exclusively to navigate to other forms, instead of using command buttons with event procedures, you can use command buttons with macros, or hyperlinks.

  You can still use code with a form that has no form module by calling **Function** procedures from a standard module using an expression. (You cannot use **Sub** procedures, because they cannot be called using an expression.) To do this, define a **Function** procedure in a standard module and then call that function from an event property of the form or a control. For example, to use a command button to call a function to open a form, add an expression like this to the **OnClick** property of the command button: `=OpenDataEntry()`.

  Note If a form currently contains event procedures, and you decide to eliminate all event procedure code from that form, you must set the **HasModule** property to **No** to completely remove the form module.

In addition to these tips, you can use the Performance Analyzer to analyze specific forms in your database. For information about using the Performance Analyzer, see "Using the Performance Analyzer" earlier in this chapter.

Optimizing List Box and Combo Box Performance

There are several things you can do to make list boxes and combo boxes run faster:

- Base the list box or combo box on a saved query instead of an SQL statement.

  If you use a wizard to create the list box or combo box, Microsoft Access automatically sets the **RowSource** property of the control to an SQL statement. To change the **RowSource** property to a saved query, click the **Build** button next to the **RowSource** property. In the SQL Builder window, click **Save** on the **File** menu and enter a name for the query. When you close the SQL Builder window, click **Yes** when Microsoft Access asks if you want to update the property.

- In the query specified in the **RowSource** property, include only fields that are absolutely necessary. Extra fields can decrease performance.

- Index both the first field displayed in the list box or combo box and the bound field (if the fields are different).

- Index any fields used for criteria.

- In combo boxes, set the **AutoExpand** property to **No** if you do not need Microsoft Access to automatically fill in the text box portion of the combo box with a value that matches the characters a user types.

- If the **AutoExpand** property for a combo box is set to **Yes**, the first displayed field should have a **Text** data type instead of a **Number** data type. In order to find a match in the list, Microsoft Access converts a numeric value to text. If the data type is **Text**, Microsoft Access does not have to do this conversion.
- If the bound field in a lookup combo box is not the displayed field:
  - Do not use expressions for the bound field or the displayed field.
  - Do not use restrictions in the row source.
  - Use single-table (or query) row sources rather than multiple-table row sources, if possible.
- Do not create list boxes or combo boxes based on data from linked tables if the data will not change. It is better to import the data into your database, in this case.

For information about optimizing the Filter By Form performance of a list box or combo box, see "Optimizing Filter Performance" earlier in this chapter.

Optimizing Report and Printing Performance

Here are some suggestions for speeding up report and printing performance:

- Avoid overlapping controls.
- Use bitmaps and other graphic objects sparingly.
- Convert unbound object frames that display graphics to image controls.
- Use black-and-white rather than color bitmaps.
- Avoid sorting and grouping on expressions.
- Index fields you sort or group on.
- Base subreports on queries rather than tables, and include only fields from the record source that are absolutely necessary. Extra fields can decrease subreport performance.
- Index all the fields in the subreport that are linked to the main report.
- Index any subreport fields used for criteria.
- Avoid using domain aggregate functions. Include the field in the report's underlying query or use a subreport.
- Make sure the report's underlying query is optimized.
- Use the **HasData** property or **NoData** event to determine whether a report is bound to an empty recordset.

Optimizing Visual Basic Performance

In general, you can do more to improve the speed of your code by choosing more efficient algorithms than by implementing particular coding tricks. However, certain techniques can help make your code run faster.

Compile the code in a database application before distributing it to users
In the Module window, click **Debug**, and then click **Compile And Save All Modules**.

Always explicitly declare variables
You can require that variables be explicitly declared before they are used in a procedure by selecting the **Require Variable Declaration** check box under **Coding Options** on the **Module** tab in the **Options** dialog box (**Tools** menu).

Use the most specific type possible when you declare variables
For example, declare a variable that is used to represent a form as type **Form** rather than as type **Object** or **Variant**. This is especially important if you are working with Automation objects or separate instances of Visual Basic. When working with Automation objects, instead of using a **Variant** data type or the generic **Object** data type, declare objects as they are listed in the **Modules/Classes** box in the Object Browser. This ensures that Visual Basic recognizes the specific type of object you are referencing, allowing the reference to be resolved when you compile.

Use variables to refer to properties, controls, and data access objects
If you refer more than once to the value of a property or control on a form, or to a data access object or its property, create object variables and refer to the variables rather than using full identifiers. This approach is especially effective for speeding up a looping operation on a series of properties, controls, or objects.

Use the Me keyword for form references within an event procedure
When you make form references within an event procedure, use the **Me** object variable to refer to the form. This restricts the search for the form to the local name space.

Use the IIf function judiciously
Avoid using the **IIf** function if either of the return expressions takes a long time to evaluate. Microsoft Access always evaluates both expressions. It is often more efficient to replace the **IIf** function with an **If**...**Then**...**Else** statement block.

Use string functions when appropriate
Some functions have two versions, one that returns a **Variant** data type (for example, the **Str** function) and one that returns a **String** data type (for example, the **Str$** function.) When working with variables declared with the **String** data type or when writing data directly to random-access files, use functions with names that end with **$** if they are available. This makes your operations run faster, because Microsoft Access does not need to perform type conversions. For more information about string functions, see Microsoft Access online Help.

Use the Integer or Long data type for math when the size and type of numbers permit
The **Variant** data type, although more flexible, uses more memory and processor time as it translates between data types. The following table ranks the numeric data types by calculation speed.

Numeric data type	Speed
Integer, **Long**	Fastest
Single, **Double**	Next-to-fastest
Currency	Next-to-slowest
Variant	Slowest

Use dynamic arrays and the Erase or ReDim statement to reclaim memory

Consider using dynamic arrays instead of fixed arrays. When you no longer need the data in a dynamic array, use either the **Erase** statement or the **ReDim** statement with the **Preserve** keyword to discard unneeded data and reclaim the memory used by the array. For example, you can reclaim the space used by a dynamic array with the following code:

```
Erase intArray
```

While the **Erase** statement completely eliminates the array, the **ReDim** statement used with the **Preserve** keyword makes the array smaller without losing its contents.

```
ReDim Preserve intArray(10, conNewUpperBound)
```

Erasing a fixed-size array does not reclaim the memory for the array; it simply clears out the values of each element of the array. If each element was a string, or a **Variant** data type containing a string or an array, then erasing the array would reclaim the memory from those strings or **Variant** data types, but not the memory for the array itself.

Replace procedure calls with inline code

Although using procedures makes your code more modular, performing each procedure call always involves some additional work and time. If you have a loop that calls a procedure many times, you can eliminate this overhead by removing the procedure call and placing the body of the procedure directly inline within the loop. If you place the same code inline in several loops, however, the duplicate code increases the size of your application. It also increases the chance that you will not remember to update each section of duplicate code when you make changes.

Use constants whenever possible to make your application run faster

Constants also make your code more readable and easier to maintain. If your code has strings or numbers that do not change, declare them as constants. Constants are resolved once when your program is compiled, with the appropriate value written into the code. With variables, however, each time the application runs and finds a variable, it needs to get the current value of the variable. Whenever possible, use the intrinsic constants listed in the Object Browser rather than creating your own.

Use bookmarks instead of the FindNext method to return to a particular record

Using the **Bookmark** property, you can write a procedure to find a target record, store its bookmark value in a variable, move to other records, and return to the original record by referring to the bookmark. For more information about the **Bookmark** property, see Microsoft Access online Help.

Use the FindRecord and FindNext methods on indexed fields
When locating records that satisfy a specified criteria, the **FindRecord** and **FindNext** methods are much more efficient than the **Seek** method when used on a field that is indexed

Consider reducing the number of procedures and modules.
While your application runs, each called procedure is placed in its own public block of memory. Microsoft Access incurs some overhead in creating and managing these blocks. You can save some of this overhead by combining short procedures into larger procedures.

Organize the modules in an application
Visual Basic loads modules on demand—that is, it loads a module into memory only when your code calls one of the procedures in that module. If you never call a procedure in a particular module, Visual Basic never loads that module. Placing related procedures in the same module causes Visual Basic to load modules only as needed.

Eliminate dead code and unused variables
As you develop and modify your applications, you may leave behind dead code—entire procedures that are not called from anywhere in your code. You may also have declared variables that are no longer used. Review your code to find and remove unused procedures and variables; for example, `Debug.Print` statements.

To search for references to a particular variable, use the **Find** command on the **Edit** menu. Or, if you have **Option Explicit** statements in each of your modules, you can quickly discover whether a variable is used in your application by removing its declaration and running the application. If the variable is used, Visual Basic generates an error. If you do not see an error, the variable was not used.

If your application has places in which the contents of a string variable or a **Variant** data type containing a string is not needed, assign a zero-length string ("") to that variable. If you no longer need an object variable, set that variable to **Nothing** to reclaim the memory used by the object reference.

You can also use compiler directives and conditional compilation to ignore portions of code based on constant values that you specify. For more information about debugging Visual Basic code, see Chapter 7, "Debugging Visual Basic Code," in *Building Applications with Microsoft Access 97*.

Saving a Database as an MDE File
If the design of forms, reports, and modules is stable, consider saving a database as an MDE file. Saving a database containing code as an MDE file removes the source code from the file and provides some additional optimization of memory use. However, the

design of forms, reports, and all code modules cannot be changed in an MDE file. To modify the design of a database saved as an MDE file, you must open the original copy of the database, make the modification to that database, and then re-save it as an MDE database.

For this reason, saving a database as an MDE file is most appropriate for a database where the design of forms, reports, and modules will not be changed, or for the front-end database in a front-end/back-end database application. A *front-end/back-end database application* consists of two database files. The back-end database contains only the application's tables. The front-end database contains all other database objects (queries, forms, reports, macros, and modules) and links to the tables in the back-end database. Typically, the back-end database is located on a network server, and copies of the front-end database are installed on individual users' computers.

For more information about MDE files, see "Security Features in Microsoft Access" in Chapter 29, "Workgroup Features in Microsoft Access."

Optimizing Microsoft Excel

There are several techniques you can use to optimize Microsoft Excel for size and speed. In general, size optimizations decrease both the amount of memory required and the amount of disk space required. Speed optimizations usually occur when you modify worksheets so that the recalculation engine in Microsoft Excel works more efficiently.

Optimizing for Size

If a worksheet contains links to large ranges on external documents, it may require a large amount of disk space and take a long time to open. To prevent this, clear the **Save external link values** check box on the **Calculation** tab in the **Options** dialog box (**Tools** menu). You do not lose the links to the external data, but clearing this option prevents Microsoft Excel from saving the value with the linked worksheet.

Optimizing for Speed

To optimize Microsoft Excel for speed, use the following guidelines:

- Do not select the **Precision as displayed** check box on the **Calculation** tab in the **Options** dialog box (**Tools** menu) unless you really need it.

    When **Precision as displayed** is off, Microsoft Excel stores the full precision of a number in memory, and displays only the number of digits specified by the formatting. When **Precision as displayed** is on, however, Microsoft Excel performs a math operation on every cell, which rounds the number. The operation forces the precision of the number stored in memory to be equal to the number of decimal places in the cell number format, slowing calculation speed.

- If you use complicated **IF** functions on a worksheet, replace them with **VLOOKUP** or **HLOOKUP** functions.

- Avoid using the functions **AREAS**, **CELL**, **COLUMNS**, **INDEX**, **INDIRECT**, **INFO**, **NOW**, **OFFSET**, **RAND**, **ROWS**, or **TODAY**.

    Formulas that contain these functions, or dependents of those formulas, must be recalculated every time there is a calculation, because their results may change even if their precedent cells have not changed. If you must use these functions, try to avoid having other calculations depend on their results.

- Avoid using user-defined functions and names that are complex expressions, which are recalculated more slowly than the equivalent formula in a cell.

- If your worksheets contain a large number of pictures, you can speed up scrolling by selecting the **Show placeholders** option for objects on the **View** tab in the **Options** dialog box (**Tools** menu).

    If users want to switch quickly between viewing graphics and placeholders, you can assign the following two Visual Basic procedures to custom buttons.

    ```
    Sub ViewObjectPlaceholders()
        ActiveWorkbook.DisplayDrawingObjects = xlPlaceholders
    End Sub

    Sub ViewObjects()
        ActiveWorkbook.DisplayDrawingObjects = xlAll
    End Sub
    ```

- If you have large worksheets that take a long time to recalculate, consider selecting the **Manual** option on the **Calculation** tab in the **Options** dialog box (**Tools** menu).

    Whenever you make a change to the worksheet that necessitates recalculation, Microsoft Excel displays the word Calculate in the status bar. You can continue to change the worksheet, and when you are finished, press F9 to recalculate manually.

- Set your users' monitors to use only 16 or 256 colors.

    For writing reports and working with spreadsheets, users may need only 16 or 256 colors, so they can switch to a video driver that supports a lower resolution and fewer colors. They can always switch back if there is no improvement in performance or if their work requires additional video capabilities.

Optimizing Microsoft PowerPoint

There are several adjustments you can make to help PowerPoint run faster and use less disk space. These adjustments have to do primarily with using less memory or using memory more efficiently. This section explains how to make these adjustments.

Virtual Memory

When you run PowerPoint with virtual memory turned off in Windows 95, you may experience slow performance or receive memory-related messages, such as "You do not have enough memory to perform this function." For optimum performance, run PowerPoint with virtual memory turned on. For more information about using virtual memory consult your Windows documentation

Visual Basic Add-ins

Visual Basic add-ins slow down the launching of PowerPoint if they are loaded automatically. Although PowerPoint add-ins can be created in Visual Basic, consider using DLL add-ins whenever possible for better performance. DLL add-ins load faster than Visual Basic add-ins, and can call Visual Basic add-ins as needed, depending on user input.

A good strategy is to use DLL add-ins for controlling user interface items, and Visual Basic add-ins to carry out the commands added by the DLL. If the DLL add-in is loaded automatically, PowerPoint starts with custom menus, toolbar enhancements, and so forth. When you select one of these customized user interface items, the DLL calls the code in the Visual Basic add-in. This way, PowerPoint loads Visual Basic code and the associated type library on an as-needed basis, which speeds startup considerably.

Image Format and Performance

The amount of time it takes to display an image and the amount of disk space needed to store a graphics file depend on the format of the graphic. There are several adjustments you can make to improve performance where graphics are concerned.

Options for Exporting Pictures

On the **Advanced** tab in the **Options** dialog box (**Tools** menu), you can select the best option for exporting pictures: **Best for printing** or **Best for on-screen viewing**. This selection governs the size of the resulting file when you export slides and presentations to a graphics format. For information about exporting slides and presentations to a graphics format, see Chapter 20, "Switching to Microsoft PowerPoint."

If you are exporting slides as graphics primarily to print them, you should select the **Best for printing** check box. Otherwise, always select **Best for on-screen viewing** for optimum performance. The following table shows the difference in file size depending on which option you select.

Selecting this option	Creates a 24-bit bitmap image of this size
Best for printing	24-bit (16 million colors)
Best for on-screen viewing	8-bit (256 colors)

Tip In Windows 95 and Windows NT Workstation 4.0, you can use a system policy to define the default value for the **Export pictures** option on the **Advanced** tab in the **Options** dialog box (**Tools** menu) for all PowerPoint users in your workgroup. In the System Policy Editor, set the following policy:

User\PowerPoint 97\Tools_Options\Advanced\Picture

For more information, see "Using Windows System Policies to Customize Office" earlier in this chapter.

File Formats for Compressing Graphics

PowerPoint 97 supports two versatile graphics formats: JPEG File Interchange Format (JFIF) and Portable Network Graphics (PNG). Both JFIF and PNG store bitmaps in a compressed format that can greatly improve PowerPoint performance and reduce overhead of system resources.

PowerPoint can read images in these formats directly, without converting them and without using a filter. Images in any other format must be converted to be displayed. Since PowerPoint can read JFIF and PNG formats directly, images stored in these formats load much faster than images stored in any other format.

Note Earlier versions of PowerPoint also included support for JFIF files. However, PowerPoint 97 includes an updated JFIF filter that handles more JPEG formats than did the previous JFIF filters included with PowerPoint.

PowerPoint decompresses the images to display them, but stores them in the compressed format. Storing bitmaps as PNG files typically compresses the size of the file by at least 50 percent; and storing full-color, photographic bitmaps as JFIF files typically compresses the file size by 90 percent or more. Not only do these smaller files require less disk space, they travel faster across the network, reduce network traffic, and reduce the overhead of moving presentations to portable computers.

Did You Know?

The commonly used bitmap format (BMP) actually includes many varieties for storing different types of bitmaps. The PNG format, however, is a superset of all BMP formats, so it is possible to convert any BMP format image to a PNG file with no loss of data. Using the PNG format normally compresses bitmaps as well as the GIF format does, but unlike GIF, PNG supports all BMP formats.

GIF, a common format for images on the Internet, can be safely converted to PNG provided the GIF contains only one image. JPEG, the other common format for images on the Internet, cannot reliably be converted to PNG, so PowerPoint 97 supports the standard JFIF filter for compressing these files.

Sharing Graphics Between Versions of PowerPoint

If you are upgrading gradually from earlier versions of PowerPoint to PowerPoint 97 and a large percentage of users are still running earlier versions, you may want to delay the installation of the PNG and JFIF filters.

At first, when some users are still running an earlier version of PowerPoint, it may be more efficient to store graphics in BMP and JPEG formats. Later, when most users are running PowerPoint 97, consider storing BMPs as PNG files and JPEGs as JFIF files, and installing PNG and JFIF filters on any computers running earlier versions of PowerPoint. Using these filters, earlier versions of PowerPoint can quickly decompress these images, and you can conserve system resources by storing highly compressed graphics files.

Linking Graphics

To centralize storage of images and keep the size of presentations to a minimum, you can store all images separately from presentation files and link, rather than embed, them in presentations. PowerPoint loads the image in order to display it, but stores only a link rather than a copy of the compressed graphics file. Depending on the size of the original image file, the combination of compressing BMP and JPEG files in PNG or JFIF format and then linking these graphics to presentations can result in significant savings of disk space and reduction of network traffic.

Multimedia and Performance

If you use sound and video files in presentations, you can enhance the performance of PowerPoint depending on where you store the files and how you incorporate them into presentations.

To reduce file size, you can link rather than embed sounds and videos. By default, sound files smaller than 100K are embedded in a presentation, and files 100K or larger are linked. You can customize this default on the **Advanced** tab in the **Options** dialog box (**Tools** menu). Sounds attached to animation effects are embedded regardless of file size, so it is best to use small sound files for these.

> **Tip** In Windows 95 and Windows NT Workstation 4.0, you can use a system policy to define the default value for the **Link sounds with file size greater than** option on the **General** tab in the **Options** dialog box (**Tools** menu) for all PowerPoint users in your workgroup. In the System Policy Editor, set the following policy:
>
> **User\PowerPoint 97\Tools_Options\General\Link Sounds File Size**
>
> For more information, see "Using Windows System Policies to Customize Office" earlier in this chapter.

Sound files and video clips linked to a presentation play sooner if they are stored in the same folder as PowerPoint than if they are stored elsewhere. To make it easier for PowerPoint to resolve palette colors, slides containing video clips should have a minimum of colors, including those in special effects such as two-color shaded fills.

Optimizing Microsoft Word

The following issues affect overall Word performance. You can control some of these issues during Setup, but other issues must be addressed on each user's computer.

- Set your users' computers to use the correct video driver for faster screen display.

  Users may not need the highest resolution video driver and the up to 16 million colors their video drivers support. Additional color support in a video driver can dramatically decrease the speed of screen updates when your users scroll or update graphics.

- Consider setting your users' monitors to use only 16 or 256 colors.

  For writing reports and working with spreadsheets, users may need only 16 to 256 colors, so they can switch to a video driver that supports a lower resolution and fewer colors. They can always switch back if there is no improvement in performance or if their work requires additional video capabilities.

To speed up printing, try the following:

- If your users print large documents that take several minutes to print, disable any screen savers during the print job, or switch to a blank screen saver.

  Animated screen savers use computer processor time that you can allocate to a print job. For more information, see your screen saver documentation.

- If your users do not need to continue working while Word is printing, turn off the **Background Printing** option in Word.

  This option allocates processor time to Word during a print job so users can continue working while Word is printing, but this means less processor time is available for printing. To turn off background printing, clear the **Background Printing** check box on the **Print** tab in the **Options** dialog box (**Tools** menu).

Tools and Utilities   The Office Resource Kit Tools and Utilities include *The Ultimate Printer Manual*, a set of HTML documents that describe a large number of printers and other printer-related troubleshooting information. For more information, see "Ultimate Printer Manual" in Appendix A, "Microsoft Office 97 Resource Kit Tools and Utilities."

CHAPTER 8

Training and Support Programs for Microsoft Office

This chapter helps you introduce Microsoft Office 97 to users in your organization. It describes a general plan for implementing training and support programs, preparing documentation, and promoting Office 97 throughout your organization. This information is intended primarily for information systems and training managers who are responsible for preparing users to switch or upgrade to Office 97.

In This Chapter
Overview   186
Implementing Office Training Tasks   187

See Also
- For a summary of new and improved features in Office 97, see Chapter 2, "What's New in Microsoft Office 97."
- For information about rolling out Office 97 in large organizations, see Chapter 3, "Deployment Guide for Microsoft Office."

Speer Software Training, Inc.
This chapter was written by Bonnie Speer McGrath, president of Speer Software Training, a national training company that specializes in helping organizations design and implement instructor-led training programs to support software transition and upgrades to Office. Established in 1986, Speer Software Training today has more than 300 trainers located in many cities around the country, including Atlanta, Chicago, Cleveland, Denver, Los Angeles, Minneapolis, New York, Philadelphia, St. Louis, San Francisco, Seattle, and Washington, D.C. For more information about Speer Software Training, call (612) 996-0015, or point your Web browser to: http://www.speer.com/

Overview

A well-planned training and support program, including promotion of Office 97 and documentation, will help your organization get the most out of Office 97. This is true whether you are switching from a competitive product or upgrading from an earlier version of Office. This chapter focuses on *migration training*, or preparing users for the switch to Office 97.

Budgeting for Training and Support

Consider carefully the cost of migration training, support, promotion, and documentation. Many organizations commit 10 percent to 20 percent of their Office budget to preparing users for the transition, helping them learn the new software, and customizing documentation. Your investment in training helps users master the many features of Office 97 quickly and minimizes disruptions in your organization.

Designing a Migration Training Program

Although deploying Office 97 is a one-time event, learning Office 97 is an ongoing process. The first priority of the migration training program is to prepare users to start using Office 97. However, you may also want to design a migration training program for any or all of the following situations:

- Most people in your organization use Office to some degree, so you have audiences with different learning needs. Scheduling training to coincide with the implementation of Office is a significant task.

- Many users use various electronic mail (e-mail), scheduling, word processing, or spreadsheet applications. Reducing the amount of time that your organization uses dual software systems is helpful.

- Some users may have Office at home. The training program and class groupings must enhance (or correct) existing knowledge.

- Many users have experience with similar software. The training program needs to relate new information to their existing knowledge.

- Some users use two systems for a period of time. They need to understand when and how to convert files to Office 97.

- Some users resist change, especially when you are moving from non-Microsoft products. You need to reduce resistance to Office by providing information about the rollout and training.

- Some users are overwhelmed by new information. To master Office 97, users have many opportunities to learn—opportunities that are geared to how they use Office, such as demonstrations, self-exploration time, computer-guided training, instructor-led training classes, and desk-side support.

- Your organization may want to use customized applications of Office 97. The training program must address these applications.
- Your internal training and support staff knows your current software intimately but has no expertise with the new software. In-depth training prepares your staff to support Office during and after the transition to Office 97.
- During the Office 97 rollout, your training staff must do their current jobs and fulfill their extra rollout responsibilities. You may need to hire a training company to meet the increased need for training and support.
- Demands on the help desk increase significantly as users start using Office 97. Your plans must account for this extra demand on resources.

Implementing Office Training Tasks

The following table lists the critical training tasks for implementing Office 97. Based on the deployment plan in Chapter 3, "Deployment Guide for Microsoft Office," this table assumes that your Office deployment begins in week 14.

Task	Team	Start Week	Average Duration
Assemble the training and support teams	Planning	Week 1–2	10 days
Prepare the training and support teams	Training and support	Week 3–4	Varies depending on software and existing expertise
Develop the training plan	Planning, training, support, and installation	Week 5–6	10 days
Prepare the documentation	Training	Week 7–10	20 days
Schedule training for the pilot rollout group	Training	Week 8	5 days
Promote Office 97 and the training plan	Planning and training	Week 9–13	Varies depending on your plans for promoting Office
Test the training plan during the pilot rollout	Installation, training, and support	Week 14	20 days
Measure your success	Training and support		ongoing process
Implement the training plan during the rollout of Office 97	Installation and training	Usually 4 or more weeks after the pilot rollout	Varies depending on size of organization

Assemble the Training and Support Teams

The training team includes a project manager as well as trainers who deliver training and desk-side support. You may also consider including writers and editors to prepare documentation and manage promotion of Office 97.

The support team includes expert users to deliver telephone support from the help desk. It may also include users who provide informal support, such as word-processing operators or selected power users.

The training and support teams may include internal or external resources. The makeup of the training and support teams depends on the services you plan to offer, the rollout schedule, and the strength and size of your internal staff.

Identifying Internal Training and Support Resources

Use your internal training staff and help desk staff as much as possible during the rollout of Office 97. These groups are your best long-term providers of information, training, and support for Office. If their current jobs prevent them from participating directly in the rollout, keep them up to date about the project and make sure that they are prepared to support Office after the transition to Office 97. Your training staff and support staff have direct contact with users; they can also help you promote Office and the training plan.

Identifying External Training and Support Resources

Many organizations work with an outside training company—a *training partner*—to shorten the rollout process or provide services that are not available internally. Finding the right training partner can be time consuming, but it is worth the effort to find the company that best fits your needs.

Look for these characteristics in a training partner:

- Experience with Microsoft software (for example, a Microsoft Solution Provider)
- Experience in software transition or in upgrade planning, training, documentation, promotion of Office, and support
- Creativity in problem solving
- Flexibility in the face of change
- Team-building skills
- Training philosophy that reflects or complements your training philosophy
- Capacity to meet your rollout schedule
- Ability to tailor the curriculum to different audiences
- Ability to adjust documentation to reflect your customization of Office

If you engage an outside training company, make sure that your internal trainers and support staff have a clear understanding of their roles before, during, and after the rollout.

Many training companies support Microsoft products, giving your organization a variety of choices. For information about authorized training companies that support Office, call (800) SOLPROV. For information about other training and support resources, see Appendix E, "Other Support Resources."

Prepare the Training and Support Teams

Before the rollout, your internal training and support teams must learn Office 97. A special training program dedicated to building their Office skills prepares them to contribute from the beginning of the planning phases for the transition to the end of implementation.

To get the training and support teams started, provide access to the software so they can explore on their own. This is an effective way to get started, particularly if your training and support teams are already using an earlier version of Office. If you are not using Windows, however, you should adopt a more structured mode of learning.

When your staff is ready for more structured training, consider self-paced options, such as videos or computer-based training, to build basic skills. Use instructor-led training to build in-depth and job-specific skills.

Microsoft Office 97 Starts Here

Microsoft Press publishes a multimedia, computer-based training product called Microsoft Office 97 Starts Here. Users view a video introduction for each lesson, practice using the actual Office 97 product, and then take a quiz to test their new skills. This course is available wherever computer books are sold. For more information about Microsoft Press, see Appendix E, "Other Support Resources."

After completing training, members of the training and support teams should use Office 97 to do all of their work. You can broaden their appreciation of Office by having them test templates, macros, software integration, file conversion, and cleanup procedures before you release these to the pilot group.

If you hire an external training company, their trainers already know Office 97. However, they need to become familiar with your current software and learn how your organization plans to use Office. Many training companies find an orientation meeting helpful to learn this type of information. An orientation meeting is also a good way to build the critically important rapport between internal and external trainers.

Develop the Training Plan

With the training and support teams educated about the capabilities of Office 97, the next step is for the teams to prepare the training plan. The purpose of this plan is to identify learning needs and to state the methods you will use for training, support, documentation, and promoting Office 97. The plan should also identify who is responsible for each task and the related costs. For more information about collecting information and building consensus, see "Organization-wide Input for the Training Plan," later in this chapter.

The planning, training, and support teams collaborate to prepare the training plan. To ensure consistency, however, the plan is written by one individual. This person is usually the training director or your training partner's project manager. Once the plan is accepted—usually by the planning team—you can use the plan to generate enthusiasm at different levels in your organization.

Contents of the Training Plan

Preparing the training plan requires 40 to 120 hours, depending on its detail and the number of interviews and surveys conducted. The training plan should include the following:

Executive Summary

An executive summary provides an overview of your plans for promoting Office 97, preparing documentation, delivering training, and providing support to key managers, users, and members of the project team. You should include estimates for all associated costs related to project planning, documentation, promotion, training, and support.

Audience Objectives

Your plan should include a description of each audience, organized by department and location. Each description includes audience size, job function, experience level with related software, and experience level with the new software. Specify learning objectives for each audience with each new software application.

Team Member Responsibilities

You plan should include a description of the roles and responsibilities of the training and support teams and of the individual team members in each department.

Include a delineation of responsibilities between your internal and external resources. Roles and responsibilities during the rollout of Office 97 include designing, developing, editing, and piloting your courseware and training programs; training trainers and support staff; scheduling students for classes; duplicating and distributing materials; setting up classrooms; delivering training for end users; delivering desk-side support; delivering help desk support; managing training; and managing support.

Communication Plan

You should develop a plan for communication among all teams before and during the pilot and rollout in each department (for example, assign each team a group e-mail address and schedule weekly status meetings).

Document how help desk and desk-side support calls are recorded and how issues are tracked and handled until they are resolved. List key contacts responsible for hardware, software, and training. Communication among the installation, training, and support teams is critical for a smooth pilot and rollout. The installation team needs to receive suggestions about the system. The training and support teams benefit from information about system updates. The training team needs to know about frequently asked questions so they can be answered in training. Keeping this three-way communication flowing is critical. It can be accomplished through Microsoft Outlook, using e-mail and discussion groups.

Departmental Plans

Design a plan for each department that lists training tasks, resource needs, and key delivery dates.

Be as explicit as possible. You may need resources to schedule training, distribute materials, provide Office demonstrations, prepare newsletters, deliver training, and deliver support. You may also require additional resources to set up equipment, classrooms, telephone lines, and demonstration monitors. This plan is best created in Microsoft Project and integrated into the overall project plan.

Training Programs

Recommend a training program for each audience. Include what you plan to offer in the following areas:

- Promoting Office 97

    Promoting Office 97 is an important process before, during, and after the rollout. It keeps people informed about key benefits, dates, and issues. It also helps you thank people for their cooperation and patience. The training program identifies key messages, such as "Office was chosen to help us better serve our customers" or "There is no magic date for the rollout—we will roll out Office the day after the system is ready." It also lists promotion ideas and implementation plans. For more information about promoting Office 97, see "Promote Office 97 and the Training Plan," later in this chapter.

- Preparing documentation

    The training program describes materials—such as reference guides, road maps to key features, hands-on practice exercises, quick reference cards, instructor notes, third-party books, and online help—that you plan to create or use. The documentation reflects your unique installation of Office 97 and job-specific needs. It may include references to templates, toolbars, integration with third-party products, samples of your organization's files, file conversion procedures, and other items unique to your organization. For more information about documentation, see "Prepare the Documentation," later in this chapter.

- Delivering training

    The training program explains the training that you will use to introduce users to Office 97. Include the type of training, length of training, and targeted audiences. If self-paced training is offered, formalize a process to ensure that students complete the training. Also include information about ongoing training programs.

- Providing support

    The training program documents your support during and after the rollout. Anticipate increased resource demands as use of the help desk grows. Desk-side support—support that is delivered face-to-face at a person's desk—following training is critical for minimizing the disruption in your organization. Offering desk-side support shows that you recognize that learning is an ongoing process. It is best delivered by skilled trainers who know when to educate and when to answer the question and move on. It is recommended that trainers rotate delivering training and desk-side support throughout the transition to Office 97.

    Note For a sample training program, see "Sample Training Program" later in this chapter.

Organization-wide Input for the Training Plan

You can use the process of creating a training plan to generate enthusiasm for Office and build consensus for the project. To collect information for the plan, conduct surveys and interviews with key personnel in management, information systems, and training, and with typical end users. Listed below are sample questions you might ask each of these groups. These questions are not intended to be exhaustive, but to get you started in this process.

Management

Ask managers questions like these:

- What business objectives are associated with the decision to purchase Office? How can training further the business objectives?
- Will this project present opportunities to reengineer any of our business processes? How can training implement any process reengineering?
- What role will managers play in preparing their employees for the training program and rollout?

- What information will managers need prior to the rollout?
- Will all or part of the training be required? How will management communicate the requirements?

Information Systems

Ask information systems personnel questions like these:

- What new hardware and software will be deployed? Will this happen while users are in training?
- Will the software be deployed in phases or all at once? For example, you might deploy Windows 95 or Windows NT Workstation version 4.0 and Outlook in Phase 1, Microsoft Word in Phase 2, Microsoft Excel in Phase 3, and so forth.
- When will the prototype system be ready? Which features do you plan to customize?
- What is the projected rollout schedule for each group?
- Who is the key contact in each department regarding systems issues during the rollout?
- Do you need any assistance in training the IS department on Office?
- Will users have access to the Internet or an intranet? Will this capability be available in the training room? Will this capability be used in managing the project?
- What procedures will end users need to follow prior to the staging of their new hardware and software? How will you communicate these requirements?

Internal Trainers and Help Desk Staff

Ask internal trainers and help desk staff questions like these:

- What would you change from your last software transition?
- What different audiences have you identified in the organization? What type of training do you think each of these audiences prefers in learning new software?
- What features in your current software are difficult to master? What features in the new software do you anticipate being difficult to master?
- What type of training do you offer to new employees?
- What type of ongoing training do you offer to support your current environment? What do you plan to offer to support Office?
- Do you log help desk calls? What are the 10 most frequently asked questions?
- What do you currently know about the project? What would you like to know?

Typical End Users

Ask end users questions like these:

- What type of training do you prefer: self-guided, instructor-guided, or a combination of the two?
- What do you want to be able to do with Office? Is this similar to how you use your current software tools?
- What tools in Office are of most interest to you? (You will need to demonstrate the tools that you think are most useful in order to get feedback.)
- When do you prefer to learn Office (for example, weekdays, half days, evenings, weekends, or early mornings)?
- What type of documentation do you find most useful (for example, reference guides, online help, quick reference cards, or third-party books)?
- What do you currently know about the rollout?
- What do you want to know before the rollout?
- Are your needs representative of the needs of your peers?

Sample Training Program

Having identified the learning objectives for each audience, you are ready to design the training programs. Each audience-specific training program documents each audience's needs for training, support, documentation, and promotion of Office 97.

The remainder of this section shows what might be included in the training program for secretaries who are upgrading from an earlier version of Office.

Several Weeks Before the Rollout

Several weeks before the secretaries' rollout, the training program focuses on promoting Office 97 organization-wide. For example, it could specify the following activities:

- Periodically produce and distribute a newsletter to all personnel announcing news relevant to the rollout of Office. Include the best new features of Office, plans for training, names of team members, answers to frequently asked questions, relevant dates, and so forth.
- Have managers take the opportunity in staff meetings to discuss Office and their expectations for how Office will be used in their departments.

First Week of Secretaries' Rollout

In the first week of the Office rollout for the secretaries, the training program includes promoting Office 97and providing documentation and training. For example, it could specify the following activities:

- Give a short demonstration of what is new in Office 97 and how it benefits the secretaries; provide lunch with the presentation.

- Hand out a road map during the demonstration that documents the new features. This road map can be used later during self-paced practice sessions.
- Schedule a two-hour session for the secretaries to explore the new software and use a computer-based tutorial on new features in Word, Microsoft Excel, and Outlook.

Second and Third Weeks of Secretaries' Rollout

In the second week of the Office rollout for the secretaries, the training program focuses on training and documentation, but also includes promoting Office 97 and providing support. For example, it could specify the following activities:

- Schedule three hours of small-group, instructor-led training on Word, using a customized reference guide and hands-on practice exercises that reflect the needs of the secretaries.
- Schedule three hours of small-group, instructor-led training on Microsoft Excel, using a customized reference guide and hands-on practice exercises that reflect the needs of the secretaries.
- Schedule three hours of small-group, instructor-led training on Outlook, using a customized reference guide and hands-on practice exercises that reflect the needs of the secretaries.
- Distribute a letter that welcomes back the secretaries from the first class and explains what to expect over the next few weeks.
- Make sure that desk-side support is available when the secretaries return from training.

After the Rollout

After the Office rollout for the secretaries, the training program emphasizes support, but also includes training and documentation. For example, it could specify the following activities:

- Make sure that help desk support is available on an ongoing basis.
- Offer lunch-and-learn sessions or monthly classes on specific topics such as tables, outlining, tables of contents, linking Word and Microsoft Excel documents, and so forth. Documentation includes short handouts.

Prepare the Documentation

The training plan describes the type of documentation needed for promoting Office 97 and training. Documentation may be different for each audience. It may be purchased from a third party, used as is, modified, or written from scratch. Documentation that reflects your software, policies, and procedures is relevant to users and helps them learn more quickly.

Preparing training and reference documentation—such as reference guides, hands-on practice, quick reference cards, and instructor notes—can require days, weeks, or months. The phases involved include design, development, writing, editing, testing during the pilot rollout, and revisions after the pilot. Documentation-related tasks are performed by your training partner or your internal trainers.

If you decide to use a training partner, be aware that courseware is a collaborative effort that requires internal resources. If you opt to create materials in-house, it is useful to license existing materials and then modify them for your organization. Many types of Office courseware are available, and some companies offer industry-specific courseware. Speer Software Training, for example, offers Office courseware specific to the legal industry.

To make documentation relevant to users, you can customize it by including information about your system, templates, macros, software integration, e-mail etiquette, and offline procedures. Also include hands-on practice exercises and policies and procedures that are specific to your organization, such as converting files.

Schedule the Pilot Training

Select the participants for the pilot rollout based on their willingness and ability to use Office 97 immediately following training. Also look for people who are positive, open to change, and persuasive in your organization.

Scheduling classroom time and self-paced training can complex. Schedule all training six or more weeks in advance, so that users can plan ahead. Also schedule any self-paced training so that users complete all requirements in a timely fashion. Classes of six similarly-skilled students are ideal for instructor-led classes.

Promote Office 97 and the Training Plan

Promoting Office 97 prepares users for the rollout. It helps them understand why Office was selected and lets them know how they will benefit. It addresses concerns such as "How long it will take me to learn, and how will my files convert?"

How creative you want to be with promoting Office 97 depends on the culture of your organization and your budget. Promoting Office usually starts soon after selecting Office and continues before and during the transition to Office 97. Usually the planning team or the training team is responsible for promoting Office, but it can be done by other groups.

Here are some ideas for promoting Office 97 and the training plan:

- Write a section in your newsletters about the change to Office 97. Include benefits that the software offers, why it was selected, who is involved in the teams, tips from users, and answers to frequently asked questions.

- Develop Microsoft PowerPoint presentations about Office 97 and the training plan to use at demonstrations and staff meetings and to post on your intranet.

- Provide road maps highlighting key features of Office 97. Install Office 97 on computers in the classroom so people can experiment and use computer-based training.
- Produce video demonstrations of the benefits of Office 97 for remote sites.
- Deliver one-hour briefings to large groups to demonstrate Office 97 and how it will be customized for your organization. Use a PowerPoint presentation to discuss the rollout date, file conversion, training and support that will be available, who covers users' desks during training, why the organization is making the change, how long it takes to master the new software, and so forth. Such a presentation would typically be delivered a week before a group's rollout. To encourage high attendance, include lunch.
- Produce certificates to distribute after training. Include different colored emblems for each software product that is learned.
- Host a departmental lunch with the senior manager a few weeks after training so the manager can reinforce expectations, encourage people to share their best practice ideas, and thank them for their cooperation and patience.
- Prepare and distribute welcome letters and survival bags to users as they return from their first training session. A survival bag could include a T-shirt, a mug, computer-oriented novelty items or candy, monitor cleaner, a pen, and so forth.
- Allow casual dress during training sessions.
- Distribute tips through e-mail to users who have completed the training.
- Encourage discussion groups to use Outlook to share their best practice examples.
- Give raffle tickets to people who attend training. Prizes could include a home computer with Office 97 installed, Microsoft hats, T-shirts, gift certificates, and an extra vacation day.
- Encourage managers to share their expectations with their staffs for how Office 97 should be used on the job.

Test the Training Plan During the Pilot Rollout

When you are ready to test the training plan, have pilot rollout participants test every aspect of it, including promotion of Office 97, training, documentation, and support. They should also test the plans for communication among the installation, training, and support teams.

Prepare questions to be answered during the pilot rollout, such as:

- Are we providing the right amount of information to prepare users for the rollout and training?
- Does the training help users learn what they need to know?
- Are the content, timing, and sequence of topics in the training materials appropriate?

- Is the documentation useful during and after training?
- Do we provide enough desk-side and help desk support?
- Are any of the questions that users ask during or after training surprising?
- Is the customization of the software well received, functional, without error?
- Do related procedures, such as procedures for offline users, work?

Select a pilot rollout group that is enthusiastic about Office 97, willing to provide constructive feedback, and able to start using Office 97 immediately after their training. Inform the pilot group that you expect feedback in the areas of promotion of Office 97, documentation, training, and support. Consider techniques for encouraging feedback, such as giving free entertainment software for home use and a vacation day to the three people who provide the most suggestions used in the rollout.

Measure Your Success

The best way to gauge success in your transition to Office 97 is to observe people in your organization. Are employees using Office 97 effectively in their jobs? Are they asking thoughtful questions? Are they finding answers by using resources you have provided?

Based on the feedback from your trainers, support staff, and pilot rollout participants, adjust the documentation and promotion of Office 97 and the training and support plans. Review communication among all teams involved in the pilot rollout, and make adjustments for the rollout. Finally, update all members of the training and support teams, so they are ready for the rollout.

Implement the Training Plan During the Office 97 Rollout

Four or more weeks after you run the pilot rollout, the rollout of Office 97 begins. The rollout may take weeks, months, or years, depending on the size of your organization. Ease into the rollout by starting gradually with the training and support programs.

For example, if you plan to use four classrooms during the rollout, start with one classroom and gradually increase to four classrooms over the next eight weeks. This gradual ramp-up period allows the installation, training, and support teams to further prepare to support many new users of Office 97. Ramping up gradually also allows you time to respond and to modify the system and training plan as needed. If the rollout is longer than three months, schedule two-week breaks between groups, so that the installation, training, and support teams remain fresh.

If your organization is undertaking a big change, such as a transition from WordPerfect or Lotus SmartSuite, be prepared for resistance among users. The training and support teams need to keep morale high and help users build confidence in mastering the new tools. They also must help users and managers develop realistic expectations regarding the learning curve during the transition.

It is a good idea to review all migration training plans four weeks into the rollout and to finalize the training plans in light of what you learn along the way. Be flexible and recognize that new developments may require revising the training plan as well as notifying those users who have already been trained. Such modifications, although not desirable, are in the best interest of a successful transition to Office 97.

After your organization gets started using Office 97, you can begin planning the ongoing training program. It is likely that your internal resources can create and manage this program, based on their experiences during the transition. The migration training program, combined with the ongoing training program, is the best means for getting the most out of your investment in Office.

CHAPTER 9
Troubleshooting Installation

For administrators who want to completely remove previous versions of Office from the computers in their organization, this chapter describes the Microsoft Office 97 Upgrade Wizard. This chapter also addresses some of the issues that you may encounter when installing Office 97, or that may arise after Office has been installed.

In This Chapter
Removing Previous Versions of Office   201
Solving Common Setup Problems   219

See Also
- For information about installing Office applications, see Chapter 4, "Installing Microsoft Office."
- For information about customizing the Office installation process, see Chapter 6, "Customizing Client Installations."
- For information about available support resources, see Appendix E, "Other Support Resources."

Removing Previous Versions of Office

When you install Office 97, Setup allows you to remove files from previous versions of Office or Office applications from your hard disk. Because some shared files installed with previous versions of Office might be used by other applications, however, Setup may leave some files on your computer.

The Office 97 Upgrade Wizard allows you to find and remove all files left behind by previous installations of Office. This section describes how to use the Upgrade Wizard and how you can customize its operation.

Tools and Utilities The Office Resource Kit Tools and Utilities include the Office 97 Upgrade Wizard. For more information about how to install the Upgrade Wizard, see "Network Installation Wizard" in Appendix A, "Microsoft Office 97 Resource Kit Tools and Utilities."

Using the Office 97 Upgrade Wizard

The Upgrade Wizard helps you find and remove old Office files, registry entries, INI file entries, and **Start** menu items or Program Manager items that you no longer need on your computer. The Upgrade Wizard recognizes components of the following versions of Office and Office-related products:

- Microsoft Office, versions 4.*x* and 95
- Microsoft Project, versions 4.0 and 95
- Microsoft Publisher, versions 2.0, 3.0, and 4.0
- Microsoft Team Manager 97

Note The Office 97 Upgrade Wizard runs on Windows 95 and the Windows NT operating system only.

Start the Upgrade Wizard

To start the Upgrade Wizard, double-click Offcln97.exe. The Upgrade Wizard displays a **Welcome** panel.

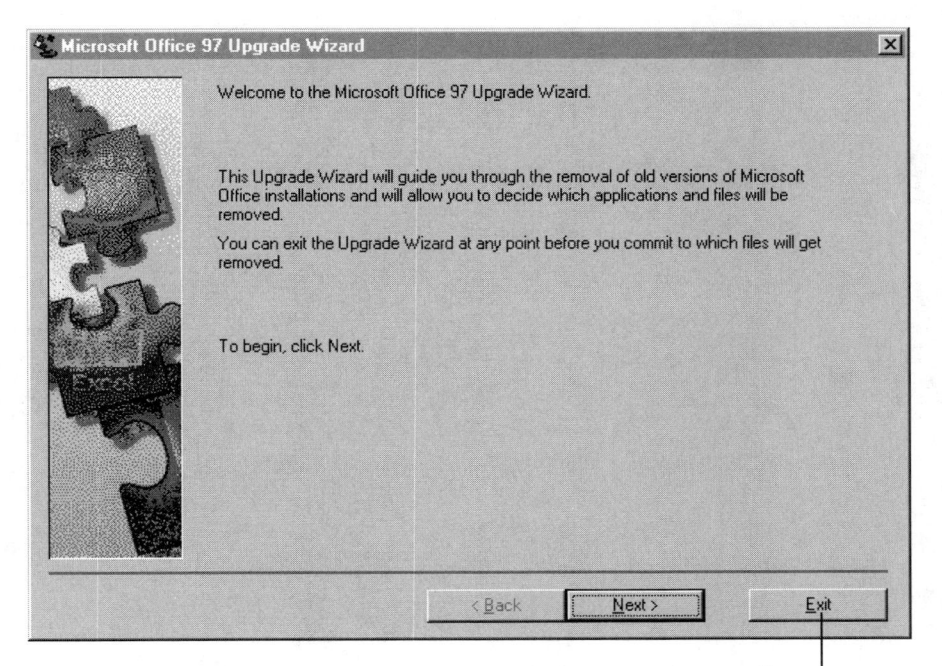

Click **Exit** to quit the Upgrade Wizard before removing any files.

Note No files are removed by the Upgrade Wizard until you click **Finish** in the last panel. Until that time, you can click **Exit** to quit without removing any files, or you can click **Back** to change the option or files you have selected.

Select the Type of Cleanup

After the initial **Welcome** panel, the Upgrade Wizard presents you with three options, so you can control the degree to which the wizard cleans up your system.

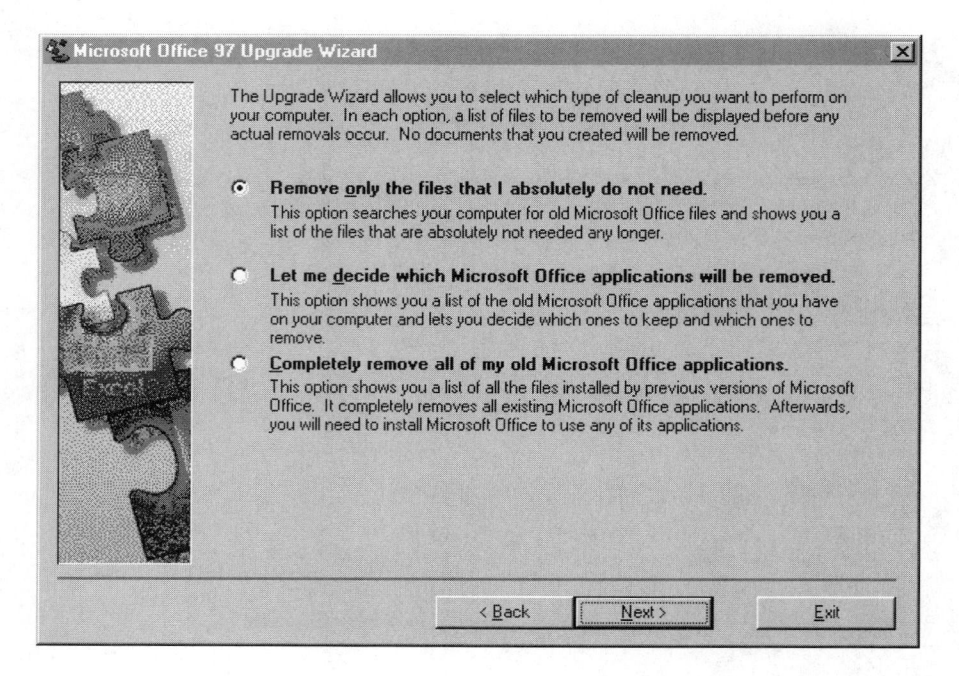

Part 2   Deploying Microsoft Office

[Screenshot of Microsoft Office 97 Upgrade Wizard dialog showing three options: "Remove only the files that I absolutely do not need", "Let me decide which Microsoft Office applications will be removed", and "Completely remove all of my old Microsoft Office applications"]

These options are:

- **Remove only the files that I absolutely do not need**

    The Upgrade Wizard runs in safe mode and looks only for Office files that are not being used by any other application. This typically includes files belonging to versions of Office that are no longer installed on the computer. The Upgrade Wizard does not remove files belonging to currently installed products or files shared among various applications, such as the spelling checker or clip art files.

    When you select this option, the Upgrade Wizard displays the list of files that will be removed and allows you to select files you want to keep.

- **Let me decide which Microsoft Office applications will be removed**

    The Upgrade Wizard runs in safe mode, but first it displays a list of the Office and Office-related applications currently installed on the computer. When you select one or more of these applications, the Upgrade Wizard adds the files from those applications to its list of files to remove, and also allows you to select files you want to keep.

- **Completely remove all of my old Office applications**

    The Upgrade Wizard runs in aggressive mode and looks for files belonging to all previous Office and Office-related applications, as well as all shared files on your computer. In aggressive mode, the Upgrade Wizard performs the most thorough cleaning of your computer. When you select this option, the Upgrade Wizard displays the list of files that will be removed (typically a long list) and allows you to select files you want to keep.

Note If Office 97 is installed on your computer and you select the **Completely remove all of my old Office applications** option, the Upgrade Wizard displays a warning that Office 97 files may be removed. If you continue, you must reinstall Office 97 after the wizard finishes to restore any shared files needed by Office 97.

Select Applications to Remove

If you select the option **Let me decide which Microsoft Office applications will be removed**, the Upgrade Wizard displays a panel with a list of the applications it finds in the **Applications to keep** box. To move an application from this box to the **Applications to remove** box, select the application and then click the appropriate move button. All applications you move to the **Applications to remove** box are removed by the Upgrade Wizard.

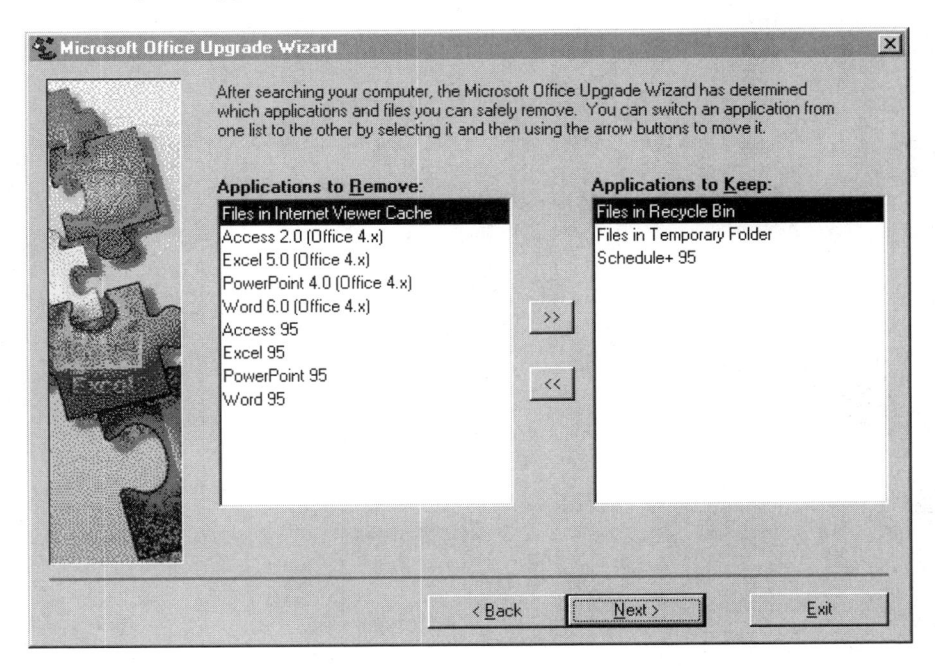

Two special entries in the list of applications are **Files in Temporary Folder** and **Files in Recycle Bin**. If you move **Files in Temporary Folder** to the **Applications to remove** box, then the Upgrade Wizard deletes all files found in the following folders.

Temporary folder	Description
Windows\Temp or Windows\Tmp	The Windows temporary folder.
%TEMP% or %TMP%	The folder identified by the MS-DOS environment variable **%TEMP%** or **%TMP%**.
drive:\Temp or *drive*:\Tmp	The MS-DOS temporary folder; *drive* refers to a hard disk (the Upgrade Wizard looks at every hard disk on the computer).

If you move **Files in Recycle Bin** to the **Applications to remove** box, then the Upgrade Wizard deletes all files currently in the Recycle Bin.

Select Files to Keep

In the next step, the Upgrade Wizard searches the computer for files belonging to the Office and Office-related applications you selected in the previous panels and then displays a list of the files it finds in the **Files to remove** box. All files in this list are removed by the Upgrade Wizard. When you select a file in the **Files to remove** box, a description of the file is displayed below the box, including which applications use the file. To keep a file, select it and then click the appropriate move button to move it to the **Files to keep** box.

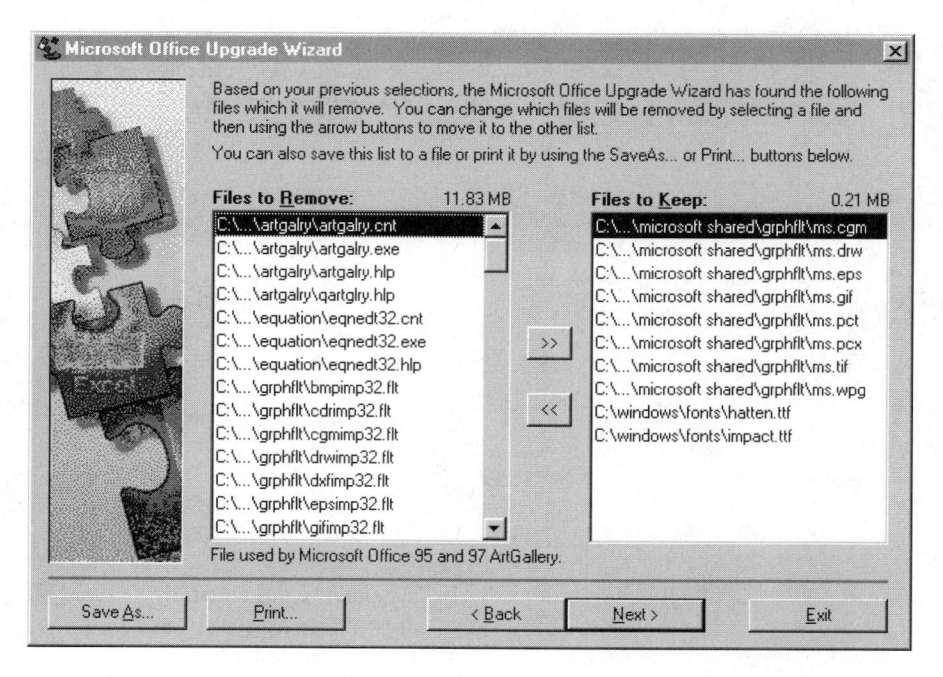

Note Another way to review this list of files is to save the list to a text file by clicking the **Save As** button, or to print the list by clicking the **Print** button.

Start File Removal

In the final panel of the Upgrade Wizard, click **Finish** to remove the selected files from your computer. To return to a previous panel to change options or selected files, click **Back**. Click **Exit** to quit the Upgrade Wizard before any files are removed.

Caution   After you click **Finish**, you cannot stop the Upgrade Wizard as it removes files. Files are removed permanently, and they cannot be retrieved without reinstalling the original applications.

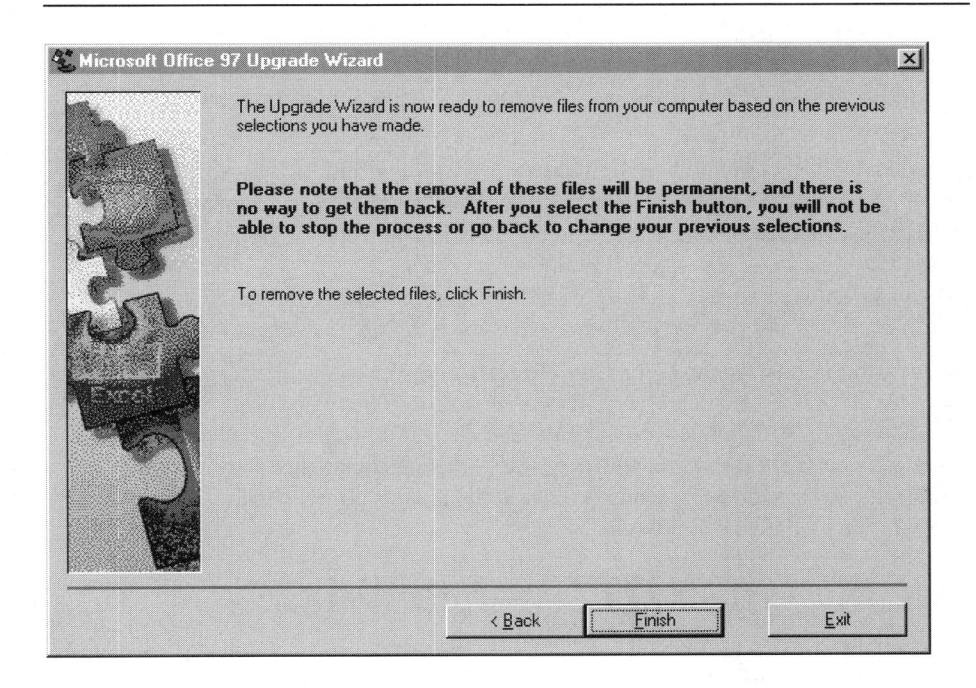

Running the Clean-up Process

The Upgrade Wizard uses a text file (OPC) to identify all files, registry entries, INI entries, or **Start** menu or Program Manager items that were installed or modified by previous versions of Office and Office-related products. The OPC file also contains rules that describe what files or entries to clean up, where they are located, and under what conditions the Upgrade Wizard can delete them. Files that are associated with a single Office application are marked so that they can be deleted in safe mode. Files that are shared by multiple Office applications, or that might be used by other applications, are marked so that they can be deleted only in aggressive mode. The default OPC included in the Office Resource Kit is named Offcln97.opc.

The Upgrade Wizard searches the computer to determine what Office applications have been installed. If you selected **Remove only the files that I absolutely do not need**, then the Upgrade Wizard looks for files belonging to an Office application that is no longer installed on the computer, and it flags only those files for deletion. These are files that may have been left behind due to an incomplete uninstall of the Office application.

In addition, the Upgrade Wizard looks for files belonging to shared components that remain on the system even though a newer version of these components has been installed. For example, if the computer contains files from both Microsoft Graph version 4.0 and Microsoft Graph 95, the Upgrade Wizard flags the Microsoft Graph 4.0 files for deletion because their functionality is replaced by Microsoft Graph 95. However, if the computer has only Microsoft Graph 4.0 files, they are not flagged for deletion.

If you selected **Let me decide which Microsoft Office applications will be removed**, the Upgrade Wizard also gives you the choice of marking for deletion any previous Office applications currently installed on the computer. The Upgrade Wizard does not delete any files that remove functionality from other Office applications. For example, if you select to remove Microsoft Word 95 but not Microsoft Excel 95, then the Upgrade Wizard will not remove any shared files used by Microsoft Excel 95.

If you selected **Completely remove all of my old Office applications**, the Upgrade Wizard looks for all files associated with previous versions of Office applications and marks them for deletion. If you have already installed Office 97, you must reinstall it because there are some files installed by Office 97 that were also installed in previous versions of Office—the Upgrade Wizard removes all these files. To reinstall Office 97, rerun Setup and click **Reinstall**.

Customizing the Office 97 Upgrade Wizard

By specifying command-line options for the Upgrade Wizard, or by creating a copy of the OPC file with a few modifications, you can customize the Upgrade Wizard to perform the operations you need for your users' computers. For example, you can create a batch file that runs the Upgrade Wizard in quiet mode, removing all files from previous versions of Office and emptying the user's temporary folders and Recycle Bin. (For more information, see "Customization Example" later in this chapter.)

Command-Line Options

Using command-line options, you can specify the mode in which the Upgrade Wizard runs, the OPC file it uses, the log file it creates, and so forth. To run the Upgrade Wizard with command-line options, click the **Run** command on the **Start** menu (Windows 95 or Windows NT Workstation version 4.0) or on the **File** menu in Program Manager (Windows NT Workstation version 3.51).

The Upgrade Wizard recognizes the following command-line options:

```
Offcln97.exe [/a|/s [/q[/r]] [/l][!][log file]]] [opc file]
```

Option	Description
/s	Indicates safe mode. This option performs the same function as selecting **Let me decide which Microsoft Office applications will be removed** in the Upgrade Wizard. When you use this command-line option, the Upgrade Wizard does not allow you to select which files to keep.
/a	Indicates aggressive mode. This option performs the same function as selecting **Completely remove all of my old Office applications** in the Upgrade Wizard. When you use this command-line option, the Upgrade Wizard does not allow you to select which files to keep.
/q	Indicates quiet mode. The Upgrade Wizard runs without prompting the user for information or displaying progress indicators. If the system needs to be restarted, the Upgrade Wizard does not do so automatically; the tasks are completed the next time the user restarts the system. This command-line option must be preceded by the **/a** or **/s** option.
/r	Used with the **/q** option to restart the system automatically (without prompting the user) if needed. This command-line option must be preceded by the **/q** option.
/l*logfile*	Generates the log file specified by *logfile*. (There is no space between **/l** and the name of the log file.) If **/l** is specified without a log file name, the default log file created is Pclogout.txt in the current folder of the Upgrade Wizard.
/l!*logfile*	Does the same as **/l**, except the Upgrade Wizard does not delete any files. This option is useful to test what the Upgrade Wizard does before actually deleting files.
Opc file	Indicates the name of the OPC file. The default is Offcln97.opc in the current folder of the Upgrade Wizard.

For example, to run the Upgrade Wizard in aggressive mode without user intervention, restarting the system automatically if needed and creating the default log file, type this:

Offcln97.exe /a /q /r /l

OPC File Syntax

The OPC file consists of two sections: *Definitions* and *Commands*. The Upgrade Wizard uses the Definitions section to help determine which commands in the Commands section to execute. When all the commands in the Commands section have been evaluated and either executed or skipped, the Upgrade Wizard is finished.

By making careful changes to the OPC file, particularly in the Definitions section, you can customize the way in which the Upgrade Wizard works.

Note Throughout the OPC file, comments are identified by a semicolon (;) at the beginning of the line. The Upgrade Wizard ignores all text following a semicolon.

Definitions Section

The Definitions section allows you to change the default value of *dependency variables*. These are special keywords that are used by the Upgrade Wizard in the Commands section to determine which groups of files may be deleted. Dependency variables represent either a specific application, such as Microsoft Word 95, or a special set of files, such as files in the Windows\Temp folder.

The Definitions section consists of one or more lines, formatted as follows:

dependency variable = value

Item	Description
dependency variable	A reserved keyword recognized by the Upgrade Wizard. These may be application names or special purpose keywords used to trigger certain functions.
Value	A dependency variable may have one of three values: • **KEEP** (equivalent terms are **FALSE** or **EXIST**) • **REMOVE** (equivalent terms are **TRUE** or **NOTEXIST**) • **DETECT**

The values of the dependency variables indicate the following:

- **KEEP** indicates that files associated with this variable should not be deleted. The values **FALSE** and **EXIST** are synonymous with the value **KEEP**; these values may be used interchangeably in the OPC file.

- **REMOVE** indicates that files associated with this variable should be deleted. The values **TRUE** and **NOTEXIST** are synonymous with the value **REMOVE**; these values may be used interchangeably in the OPC file.

- **DETECT** is used for dependency variables that represent applications.

    In safe mode, if the dependency variable is assigned the value **DETECT** in the Definitions section, then the Upgrade Wizard examines the computer to determine whether the application is currently installed. If it is, then the Upgrade Wizard reassigns the value **KEEP** to the dependency variable. If the application is not installed, then the Upgrade Wizard reassigns the value **REMOVE** to the dependency variable.

    In aggressive mode, if the dependency variable is assigned the value **DETECT** in the Definitions section, then the Upgrade Wizard reassigns the value **REMOVE** to the dependency variable whether or not the application is currently installed.

After the Upgrade Wizard processes the Definitions section, all dependency variables have either the value **KEEP** or **REMOVE**. For example, suppose Word 95 is currently installed on the computer, and Microsoft Excel 95 is not. The following definitions assign the values shown in safe mode.

This definition	Results in this value
WORD95 = DETECT	**KEEP**
EXCEL95 = DETECT	**REMOVE**

Note The Upgrade Wizard determines whether a particular application is currently installed on the computer by looking for a specific file in a specific folder, or by checking registry or INI entries. The files or entries that the Upgrade Wizard looks for are defined by an internal table in the Upgrade Wizard and cannot be modified by the user. The Upgrade Wizard detects whether an application is installed only if the dependency variable is set to **DETECT**.

The following dependency variable application names are recognized by the Upgrade Wizard.

- Office 4.*x* application and component names
    - **ACCESS94**
    - **ARTGALLERY94**
    - **BOOKS94**
    - **EQUATION94**
    - **EXCEL94**
    - **GRAPH94**
    - **IMAGER94**
    - **MSINFO94**
    - **MSQUERY94**
    - **OFFICEMANAGER94**
    - **ORGCHART94**
    - **POWERPOINT94**
    - **RUNFROMNET94**
    - **SETUP94**
    - **WORD94**
    - **WORDART94**
- Office 95 application and component names
    - **ACCESS95**
    - **ARTGALLERY95**
    - **BINDER95**
    - **BOOKS95**
    - **EQUATION95**
    - **EXCEL95**

- GRAPH95
- IMAGER95
- MSINFO95
- MSQUERY95
- ORGCHART95
- POWERPOINT95
- RUNFROMNETCD95
- SCHEDULE95
- SETUP95
- SHORTCUTBAR95
- WORD95
- WORDART95
- Office 97 application and component names
  - ACCESS97
  - ARTGALLERY97
  - BINDER97
  - BOOKS97
  - DAO97
  - DATAMAP97
  - EQUATION97
  - EXCEL97
  - GRAPH97
  - INFO97
  - OFFICE97
  - ORGCHART97
  - OUTLOOK97
  - PHOTOED97
  - POWERPOINT97
  - QUERY97
  - RUNFROMNETCD97
  - SCHEDULE97
  - SETUP97
  - SHORTCUTBAR97
  - WORD97

- Other application names
  - **PROJECT94**
  - **PROJECT95**
  - **PUBLISHER2**
  - **PUBLISHER3**
  - **PUBLISHER4**
  - **TEAMMANAGER97**

Dependency variables may be special purpose keywords. These have predefined values that may be changed in the Definitions section.

Special purpose keyword	Description
TEMPFOLDERCONTENTS	Used to determine whether to remove files from temporary folders. Defaults to **KEEP**.
TEMPTWIDDLEFILESONLY	Used to determine whether to remove files preceded by a tilde (~) from temporary folders. Defaults to **KEEP**.
RECYCLEBINCONTENTS	Used to determine whether to empty the contents of the Windows Recycle Bin. Defaults to **KEEP**.

The Upgrade Wizard also uses certain special purpose keywords with predefined values that may not be changed in the Definitions section.

Special purpose keyword	Description
RISKY	Set to **REMOVE** in aggressive mode and **KEEP** in safe mode.
SAFE	Always set to **REMOVE**. This keyword is used only to clarify which section in the OPC file might be deleted in safe mode.
AFTER97INSTALL	Defaults to **REMOVE** if **RISKY** has the value **REMOVE** or if **OFFICE97** has the value **KEEP**. Otherwise, it defaults to **KEEP**.

In safe mode, the Upgrade Wizard sets the value of the dependency variable **SAFE** to **REMOVE** and **RISKY** to **KEEP**. The result is that any command that has the dependency variable **RISKY** is not executed in safe mode. In aggressive mode, however, the Upgrade Wizard sets the value of both **SAFE** and **RISKY** to **REMOVE**. The result is that any command that has the dependency variable **RISKY** is executed in aggressive mode, if no other dependency variables have the value **KEEP**.

The OPC file included in the Office Resource Kit uses the **RISKY** dependency variable for commands that include files shared by several applications, such as the spelling checker or clip art files. These files are removed only if the Upgrade Wizard is run in aggressive mode, after which you need to reinstall Office 97 to restore the files.

Commands Section

The Commands section contains one or more commands that consist of a *dependency list* and a set of *actions*. The Upgrade Wizard evaluates the dependency list to determine whether the command should be executed.

The dependency lists contains dependency variables, each of which has the value **KEEP** or **REMOVE**. (The Upgrade Wizard already changed all **DETECT** values to **KEEP** or **REMOVE** when it finished processing the Definitions section.) If all the dependency variables in the dependency list have the value **REMOVE**, then the Upgrade Wizard executes the actions listed in the command. If any dependency variable has the value **KEEP**, then the Upgrade Wizard skips this command and goes to the next one.

Commands are formatted as follows:

[*dependency list*] "*description*"
   action
   action

Item	Description
dependency list	A list of one or more dependency variables separated by commas.
description	A string that describes the files listed under this command. In the Upgrade Wizard, if a user selects a file associated with this command in the **Files to remove** list, the string is displayed. The string may contain any number of characters and spaces, but must not begin with a space, tab character, or quotation mark (").
action	The name and path of a file to delete, a registry entry to remove, an INI file entry to remove, or a special action to execute.

The following sections describe actions that may be associated with commands.

File

This action indicates a file to be removed. The syntax is:

folder\file "*description*"

Item	Description
folder	A fully qualified path, or one of a predefined list of folder keywords; optional
file	The name of the file to be removed
description	An optional string describing the file

A folder name may be an explicit path, such as C:\Users\Tools.dat, or you can use one of the following predefined folder names.

This folder keyword	Represents this folder
WINDIR	Windows root folder
SYSDIR	Windows System folder
ROOTDIR	Root folder of the hard disk containing Office 95
SYSMENUROOTDIR	Windows Start Menu folder
SYSMENUPROGRAMSDIR	Programs folder under Windows Start Menu folder
SYSMENUSTARTUPDIR	Start up folder under Windows Start Menu\Programs folder
SYSPROGRAMFILESDIR	System Program Files folder
OFFICE94DIR	Office 4.3 folder
ACCESS94DIR	Microsoft Access version 2.0 folder
BOOKS94DIR	Bookshelf 4.3 folder
BUTTONS94DIR	MS-Bttns folder under the Office 4.3 folder
CLIPART94DIR	Clip art folder for Office 4.3
EXCEL94DIR	Microsoft Excel version 5.0 folder
MSAPPS94DIR	Shared application files folder for Office 4.3
POWERPOINT94DIR	Microsoft PowerPoint version 4.0 folder
SETUP94DIR	Setup for Office 4.3 folder
STARTMENU94DIR	Office 4.3 folder under Windows Start Menu\Programs folder
WORD94DIR	Word version 6.0 folder
OFFICEROOT95DIR	Office 95 folder
OFFICE95DIR	Office folder under Office 95 folder
ACCESS95DIR	Microsoft Access 95 folder
BINDER95DIR	Office 95 Binders folder
BOOKS95DIR	Bookshelf 95 folder
CLIPART95DIR	Office 95 Clip art folder
EXCEL95DIR	Microsoft Excel 95 folder
EXCEL95VIEWERDIR	Microsoft Excel 95 Viewer folder
IMAGER95DIR	Microsoft Imager 95 folder
MSAPPS95DIR	Shared application files folder for Office 95
POWERPOINT95DIR	PowerPoint 95 folder
POWERPOINT95VIEWERDIR	PowerPoint 95 Viewer folder
SCHEDULE95DIR	Schedule+ 95 folder
SOUNDS95DIR	Shared sound files folder for Office 95
TEMPLATES95DIR	Templates folder for Office 95
WORD95DIR	Word 95 folder
WORD95IADIR	Word 95 Internet Assistant folder
WORD95VIEWERDIR	Word 95 Viewer folder

Registry Entry

This action indicates a registry entry to be removed. The syntax is:

HKxx\key

Item	Description
HKxx	The top-level registry key: • **HKLM** for **HKEY_LOCAL_MACHINE** • **HKCR** for **HKEY_CLASSES_ROOT** • **HKCU** for **HKEY_CURRENT_USER** • **HKUR** for **HKEY_USERS**
key	The registry key or value to remove.

For example:

```
HKCR\MSOfficeSetup
```

Win.ini Entry

This action indicates a section or key to be removed from the Win.ini file. The syntax is:

Win.ini, *section*, *key*

Item	Description
section	Section name in the Win.ini file.
Key	Optional. If present, then only this key is deleted from the Win.ini file. If not present, then the entire section is deleted.

Application INI Entry

This action indicates a section or key to be removed from an application INI file. The syntax is:

INI=*folder\file*, *section*, *key*

Item	Description
folder	A fully qualified path, or one of the predefined folder keywords described earlier in this section.
file	The name of the INI file.
section	The section name in the INI file.
key	Optional. If present, then only this key is deleted from the INI file. If not present, then the entire section is deleted.

Menu Item

This action indicates an item on the **Start** menu (Windows 95 or Windows NT Workstation 4.0) or in a Program Manager group (Windows NT Workstation 3.51) to be removed. The syntax is:

MENU_ITEM=group\item

Item	Description
group	Name of the Program\Start Menu folder or Program Manager group.
tem	Item to be removed.

Special Action

This action includes special functions that are predefined in the Upgrade Wizard. The syntax is:

SPECIAL\function

This function	Removes these files
RemoveTempFiles	All files from any of these folders and subfolders: • Windows\Temp or Windows\Tmp • **%TEMP%** or **%TMP%** (MS-DOS environment variable) • drive:\Temp or drive:\Tmp (all hard disks are checked)
RemoveTwiddleTempFiles	All files that start with a tilde (~) character in the temporary folders listed under **RemoveTempFiles**
RemoveInternetExplorerCacheFiles	All temporary files from the Microsoft Internet Explorer cache folder
RemoveNetscapeCacheFiles	All temporary files from the Netscape Navigator cache folder
EmptyRecycleBinContents	All files except Desktop.ini and Info from the Recycle Bin
RemoveOffice95ShortcutLnksAndTmps	All LMK, TMP, and PIF files in the Office 95 Shortcut Bar folder
RemoveDuplicateWWINTL32DLL	Wwintl32.dll in the Windows\System folder if it is also found in the Word 95 folder

Customization Example

Suppose you want to create a command for your users that does the following:

- Runs the Upgrade Wizard without user intervention
- Removes all files from previous versions of Office
- Empties temporary folders
- Empties the Recycle Bin
- Restarts the computer automatically, if necessary

In addition, suppose you want to remove an internal company tool that is being replaced by Office 97 functionality. The program is called Chart.exe, and it resides in the C:\Program Files\Internal\Chart folder on users' computers, along with support files, Chartsub.dll, Chartprt.dat, and Readme.txt in the same folder.

To do this, use the following procedure:

▶ **To create the customized Upgrade Wizard command**

1. Create a copy of the OPC file and name it Newopc.opc.
2. Open Newopc.opc in a text editor.

   This file is too large for Notepad, but it can be edited in WordPad.

3. Change the following values at the beginning of the file to **REMOVE**, as shown here:

   ```
   RECYCLEBINCONTENTS = REMOVE
   TEMPFOLDERCONTENTS = REMOVE
   TEMPTWIDDLEFILESONLY = REMOVE
   ```

4. To indicate that the listed files will always be deleted, go to the beginning of the Commands section (immediately before the [RECYCLEBINCONTENTS] command) and add the following lines:

   ```
   [SAFE] "Internal charting tool"
   C:\program files\internal\chart\chart.exe
   C:\program files\internal\chart\chartsub.dll
   C:\program files\internal\chart\chartprt.dat
   C:\program files\internal\chart\readme.txt
   ```

5. Save and close Newopc.opc.
6. Test your customized Newopc.opc file on a user's computer using the **/l!***logfile* command-line option to generate a log of the files that would be deleted.

You can distribute your customized OPC file to users, along with the Upgrade Wizard (Offcln97.exe). Instruct users to enter the following command using the **Run** command on the **Start** menu (Windows 95 or Windows NT Workstation 4.0) or on the **File** menu in Program Manager (Windows NT Workstation 3.51):

```
Offcln97.exe /a /q /r Newopc.opc
```

Solving Common Setup Problems

This section addresses some common Setup errors that you may encounter during or after your installation of Office 97. In addition to explaining the possible causes of each error, the following sections also describe steps you can take to resolve the problem. Typically, these Setup errors can be corrected by changing the way you install Office.

Problems Related to Running Setup

The following errors may occur when you run the Office Setup program.

Cannot Open Setup.exe

When you rerun Office Setup to add or remove components after installing Office, and the message "Cannot open Setup.exe" is displayed, Setup is unable to locate the Setup.exe file.

Cause This can occur if you originally installed Office from a network server using a drive letter, but the Setup files have been moved or you are disconnected from the correct network drive.

Solution Connect to the administrative installation point using the same drive letter you used when you installed Office.

Disk Is Full

If you install Office or an Office component on a compressed drive, you may receive a message stating that the disk is full. This can occur even though Setup indicates that you have sufficient disk space for the components when you began the installation process.

Cause When you install to a compressed drive, the amount of available disk space depends on the types of files that are on the compressed drive and how effective the disk compression technology is when you compress different types of data. In some cases, you may need significantly more disk space than the Setup program indicates.

Solution Free some disk space and rerun Setup.

Setup Creates Mscreate.dir in Every Folder

After you run Setup, the file Mscreate.dir appears in every new folder created by the Setup program.

Cause Setup creates Mscreate.dir (a 0-byte hidden file) in each folder to indicate that the folder was created by Setup. When you run Setup in maintenance mode and remove a component or click **Remove All**, Setup uses this file to determine whether an empty folder can be removed. If an empty folder does not contain Mscreate.dir, Setup does not remove the folder.

For example, you might create the folder My Files in the Microsoft Office folder. When you run Microsoft Office Setup in maintenance mode and click **Remove All**, your My Files folder is not removed by Setup, even if it is empty when you run Setup.

Solution No action is needed.

~Mssetup.t\~Msstfqf.t Folder Remains After Setup

After you run Setup, a folder with the name ~Mssetup.t\~Msstfqf.t may be left on your hard disk.

Cause This can occur if you run Setup to add or remove Office components and Setup restarts your computer to complete the installation update. Setup creates these temporary folders during installation, but cannot remove them while the computer is restarting.

Solution After Setup has completed, you can delete these temporary folders manually if they remain on your hard disk after Setup is complete.

Problems Caused by Previously Installed Files

The following errors are caused by previously installed files. Most of these errors can be corrected by manually deleting the old files after you run Setup.

Not All Folders Are Deleted When You Remove Office

After you run Setup and select **Remove All**, the Microsoft Office folder structure (Program Files\Microsoft Office by default or another folder you choose during Setup) remains on your disk.

Cause This behavior is a function of Setup. Setup leaves Office folders intact so that files and INI entries that were not created by Office are not deleted. The Setup program deletes only what it installed.

Solution Once you have removed any user files from the Microsoft Office folder structure, you can delete the folders manually.

Setup Does Not Remove Application Shortcut

When you run Setup and click **Remove All**, the shortcut for the application that you remove may still be available in Windows. (This error occurs only when you install Office 97 in Windows 95 or Windows NT Workstation 4.0.)

Note Shortcuts are added to the Windows\Start Menu\Programs folder and appear on the **Programs** submenu (**Start** menu).

Cause This occurs if you have renamed the shortcut for the application. For example, if you rename the shortcut for Microsoft Word to Word, the shortcut is not removed when you run Setup and click **Remove All**. If Setup cannot locate the shortcut with the original name, it assumes that the shortcut does not exist.

Solution You can delete the shortcut manually after running Setup.

Program Group Cannot Be Displayed

When you run Setup, you may receive the following message: "Program group *groupname* cannot be displayed." The message may appear repeatedly. (This error occurs only when installing Office 97 in Windows NT Workstation 3.51.)

Cause   This occurs when Setup tries to exceed the maximum of 40 program groups that Program Manager allows. If you already have 40 program groups, and you run Setup, you receive this error message if you choose to add a new program group.

Solution   To avoid receiving this error message when you already have 40 program groups in Program Manager, do one of the following:

- Eliminate at least one program group before running Setup.
- When Setup prompts you to add the program icons to a program group, select an existing program group instead of creating a new program group.

Setup Installs Shared Files Locally

When you install Office from an administrative installation point, the Setup program may copy shared files to the hard disk even if you specify that they should be run from the server. You do not receive a message informing you that these files are being installed locally; after Office is installed, the applications function correctly.

Cause   Setup checks the computer to see if a previous version of shared files exists on the hard disk. If so, Setup updates the existing version with Office 97 shared files.

Solution   Rerun Setup and click **Remove All** to uninstall Office 97, remove the previous Office files, and then install Office 97 again. You can remove files from previous versions of Office using the Office 97 Upgrade Wizard. See "Using the Office 97 Upgrade Wizard" earlier in this chapter.

Cannot Install _MSIMP.DLL into Notes Folder

When you run Setup on a workstation on which Lotus Notes is already installed, you may receive the error message: "_MSIMP.DLL can't be installed into Notes directory." _MSIMP.DLL is a converter that allows Lotus Notes to import Word documents.

Cause   If the Lotus Notes program file (Notes.exe) is located on a network server instead of in your local Notes folder and the server location is read-only, Setup cannot write the converter file to the server folder. Lotus Notes requires that the converter be in the same folder as the Lotus Notes program file.

Solution   Change the read-only setting of the Notes folder on the server and run Setup again.

PART 3

Upgrading to Microsoft Office

Contents

Chapter 10   Upgrading from Previous Versions of Microsoft Office   225

Chapter 11   Upgrading from Previous Versions of Microsoft Access   253

Chapter 12   Upgrading from Previous Versions of Microsoft Excel   301

Chapter 13   Upgrading to Microsoft Outlook   333

Chapter 14   Upgrading from Previous Versions of Microsoft PowerPoint   361

Chapter 15   Upgrading from Previous Versions of Microsoft Word   399

CHAPTER 10

Upgrading from Previous Versions of Microsoft Office

This chapter tells you what to expect when you or your workgroup upgrades from a previous version of Microsoft Office.

In This Chapter
Overview   225
Upgrading from Microsoft Office 95 for Windows   226
Upgrading from Microsoft Office 4.x   230
Upgrading from Microsoft Office 3.x for Windows   235
Porting Your 16-bit Office-Based Solutions to 32-bit Office   236

See Also
- For a summary of new and improved features in Office 97, see Chapter 2, "What's New in Microsoft Office 97."
- For information about installing Office applications, see Chapter 4, "Installing Microsoft Office."
- For information about switching to Office from competitive applications, see Chapter 16, "Switching to Microsoft Office."

The remaining chapters in Part 3, "Upgrading to Microsoft Office," provide detailed information about upgrading from individual Office 97 applications.

Overview

Office 97 is designed to make upgrading your workgroup or organization a less painful task than previous upgrades. Office 97 Setup includes new features that preserve user settings and files from previous versions of Office, and remove unneeded files. Office 97 supports a variety of installation strategies for workgroups, including installation through Microsoft Systems Management Server or the Network Installation Wizard. For more information about network installations, see Chapter 4, "Installing Microsoft Office."

After Office 97 is installed, you can take advantage of features that make it easier to share documents between users of different versions of Office and other applications. For example, you can specify that Microsoft Excel 97 and Microsoft Word 97 save documents in Microsoft Excel 95 and Word 95 format. For more information about supporting a gradual upgrade, see the remaining chapters in Part 3, "Upgrading to Microsoft Office."

Note If you install Office 97 on computers running Windows NT Workstation version 3.51, Office 97 automatically enables features that are available with Windows NT Workstation version 4.0 when you upgrade your version of the Windows NT operating system. For example, when you upgrade to Windows NT Workstation 4.0, the Office 97 applications provide the same level of support for your Briefcase application that they do under Windows 95.

Upgrading from Microsoft Office 95 for Windows

All of the desktop applications—Microsoft Access, Microsoft Excel, Microsoft PowerPoint, and Word—change file formats between Office 95 and Office 97. Office 97 also introduces a new electronic mail (e-mail) client and desktop information manager, Microsoft Outlook.

Note Office 95 applications are identified as version 7.0 in some technical documentation. In the *Office Resource Kit*, they are referred to as Microsoft Access 95, Microsoft Excel 95, PowerPoint 95, Schedule+ 95, and Word 95, respectively.

Tip In Windows 95 and Windows NT Workstation version 4.0, you can use a system policy to define the default value for the **Save as type** option in the **Save As** dialog box (**File** menu) for all Office 97 users in your workgroup (except for users of Microsoft Access and Outlook, which do not support this option). In the Windows System Policy Editor, set the following policies:

User\Excel\Tools_Options\Transition\Default Save

User\PowerPoint\Tools_Options\Save\Default Save

User\Word\Tools_Options\Save\Default Save

For more information, see "Using Windows System Policies to Customize Office" in Chapter 7, "Customizing and Optimizing Microsoft Office."

Upgrading Microsoft Access 95

Microsoft Access 97 can read databases saved in Microsoft Access 95 format using a process called enabling. After a Microsoft Access 95 database is enabled, Microsoft Access 97 can read data and run queries, forms, reports, macros, and Visual Basic for

Applications code in the database. Enabling a Microsoft Access 95 database does not change the format, so Microsoft Access 97 users can share the database with Microsoft Access 95 users.

As an alternative to enabling a database, Microsoft Access 97 can establish links to tables in a Microsoft Access 95 database. All Microsoft Access 95 database objects, including macros and Visual Basic code, can also be converted to Microsoft Access 97 format.

If you need to move Microsoft Access 97 data to a Microsoft Access 95 database, Microsoft Access 97 can export only tables. You cannot export any other database objects to the Microsoft Access 95 database, including queries, macros, forms, reports, and modules.

For more information about upgrading to Microsoft Access 97, see Chapter 11, "Upgrading from Previous Versions of Microsoft Access."

Upgrading Microsoft Excel 95

Microsoft Excel 97 can read documents saved in Microsoft Excel 95 format and run macros created in Microsoft Excel 95. For users who have not yet upgraded, Microsoft Excel 97 can also save workbooks in the dual 97 and 5.0/95 file format so that users of both Microsoft Excel version 5.0 or 95 and Microsoft Excel 97 can open and edit the same workbooks. For more information, see "Sharing Workbooks with Microsoft Excel 5.0 or 95" in Chapter 12, "Upgrading from Previous Versions of Microsoft Excel."

Upgrading PowerPoint 95

PowerPoint 97 can open and save presentations in PowerPoint 95 format. PowerPoint 97 can also save presentations in the dual PowerPoint 95 & 97 file format so that users of both PowerPoint 95 and PowerPoint 97 can open and edit the same presentations. For more information, see "Sharing Presentations with PowerPoint 95" in Chapter 14, "Upgrading from Previous Versions of Microsoft PowerPoint."

Upgrading Word 95

Word 97 can read documents saved in Word 95 format and run macros created in Word 95. For users who have not yet upgraded, Word 95 can also read documents saved in Word 97 format. To open a Word 97 document in Word 95, you must first install the Word 97 text converter for Word 95. For more information, see "Sharing Documents with Word 6.0 or 95" in Chapter 15, "Upgrading from Previous Versions of Microsoft Word."

Upgrading Your Office 95 Electronic Mail Client

Office 95 did not include any new e-mail clients, but Outlook can upgrade both the Microsoft Exchange client included with Windows 95 (Microsoft Mail information service) and the e-mail clients included with Microsoft Exchange Server.

When your Office users upgrade to Outlook, Microsoft Exchange Client users can:

- Send e-mail to Outlook users.
- Open Outlook folders.
- Use the Outlook standard message form.

Note Microsoft Exchange Client users cannot use Outlook views, custom forms, or custom commands.

To continue sharing information with Microsoft Exchange Client users, Outlook users can:

- Send e-mail to Microsoft Exchange Client users.
- Open Microsoft Exchange Client folders.
- Use Microsoft Exchange Client views.
- Save views in Microsoft Exchange Client format.
- Use the Microsoft Exchange Client standard message form.
- Use Microsoft Exchange Client custom forms and custom commands.

For more information about using Outlook as your e-mail client, see Chapter 13, "Upgrading to Microsoft Outlook."

Upgrading Your Office 95 Scheduling Application

Outlook can also replace Schedule+ 95, the scheduling application included with Office 95. When your workgroup upgrades to Outlook, Schedule+ 95 users can continue to:

- Send meeting requests to Outlook users.
- Read Outlook free/busy status.

Note Schedule+ 95 users cannot open or read an Outlook calendar file and they cannot view an Outlook user's free/busy details.

To continue sharing information with Schedule+ 95 users, Outlook users can:

- Send meeting requests to Schedule+ 95 users.
- Read Schedule+ 95 free/busy status and details.
- Open a Schedule+ 95 calendar.

For more information about using Outlook as your scheduling application, see Chapter 13, "Upgrading to Microsoft Outlook."

Upgrading Office 95 Binders

The Office Binder application included in Office 97 can open Office 95 binders, but it cannot save in Office 95 Binder format. Nor can Office 97 binder sections be moved to Office 95 binders.

Office 97 binder documents are not supported by previous versions of Microsoft Office for Windows. If you want to work with binder documents on a computer running a previous version of Office for Windows, you must first unbind the binder into its component sections.

▶ **To unbind sections in a binder (Windows 95 or Windows NT Workstation 4.0 only)**

1. In Windows Explorer or on the desktop, right-click the binder document you want to disassemble.
2. On the shortcut menu, click **Unbind**.

   The sections in the binder document are saved as separate files in the folder that contains the binder. The original binder remains intact.

Note The **Unbind** command is not available in Windows NT Workstation 3.51 or Windows 3.*x*.

▶ **To unbind sections in a binder (Windows NT Workstation 3.51 only)**

1. Open the binder document you want to disassemble.
2. Select the section that you want to unbind.
3. On the **Section** menu, click **Save As File**.
4. Repeat Steps 2 and 3 for other sections you wish to unbind.

   The sections in the binder document are saved as separate files in the folder that contains the binder. The original binder remains intact.

Tools and Utilities The Office Resource Kit Tools and Utilities include the Unbind utility for Windows 3.*x*. For more information about installing this utility, see "Office 97 Unbind Utilities" in Appendix A, "Microsoft Office 97 Resource Kit Tools and Utilities."

▶ **To unbind sections in a binder (Windows version 3.*x* only)**

1. Copy the binder document you want to disassemble to a computer running Windows 3.*x*.
2. Double-click Unbind.exe.

3. In the **Open** dialog box, select the binder and click **Open**.

   The sections in the binder document are saved as separate files in the folder that contains the binder. The original binder remains intact.

4. Repeat Step 3 for each binder you want to disassemble.

Note When you disassemble a binder document, the unbound sections must be in a format that Office version 4.*x* or earlier applications can read. For more information about sharing documents between different versions of a particular application, see the relevant chapter in Part 3, "Upgrading to Microsoft Office."

Using Office 95 Binders with Office 97 for the Macintosh

Office 97 binder documents are not supported by Microsoft Office for the Macintosh. To work with binder contents on a Macintosh computer, you must first unbind the binder into its component sections.

Follow these steps for each binder you want to disassemble:

- Copy the binder document to a Macintosh computer.
- Double-click Microsoft Office Unbind, and then click **Open binder** on the **File** menu.
- In the dialog box, select the binder and click **Open**.

The sections in the binder document are saved as separate files in the folder that contains the binder. The original binder remains intact.

Tools and Utilities The Office Resource Kit Tools and Utilities include the Unbind utility for the Macintosh. For more information about installing this utility, see "Office 97 Unbind Utilities" in Appendix A, "Microsoft Office 97 Resource Kit Tools and Utilities."

Upgrading from Microsoft Office 4.x

All of the desktop applications—Microsoft Access (Windows only), Microsoft Excel, PowerPoint, and Word—change file formats between Office 4.*x* and Office 97. Office 97 also introduces a new e-mail client and desktop information manager, Outlook (Windows only).

Tip In Windows 95 and Windows NT Workstation 4.0, you can use a system policy to define the default value for the **Save as type** option in the **Save As** dialog box (**File** menu) for all Office 97 users in your workgroup (except for users of Microsoft Access and Outlook, which do not support this option). In the Windows System Policy Editor, set the following policies:

User\Excel\Tools_Options\Transition\Default Save

User\PowerPoint\Tools_Options\Save\Default Save

User\Word\Tools_Options\Save\Default Save

For more information, see "Using Windows System Policies to Customize Office" in Chapter 7, "Customizing and Optimizing Microsoft Office."

Upgrading Microsoft Access 2.0

Using a process called enabling, Microsoft Access 97 can read data and run queries, forms, reports, macros, and Access Basic code in a Microsoft Access version 2.0 database without changing the format. This allows Microsoft Access 97 users to share data with Microsoft Access 2.0 users. As an alternative to enabling, Microsoft Access 97 can establish links from a Microsoft Access 97 database to tables in a Microsoft Access 2.0 database.

All Microsoft Access 2.0 database objects, including macros and Access Basic code, can also be converted to Microsoft Access 97 format. However, Access Basic code that relies on 16-bit DLLs and API calls must be modified to run in a 32-bit application. For more information, see "Porting Your 16-bit Office-Based Solutions to 32-bit Office" later in this chapter.

If you need to move Microsoft Access 97 data to a Microsoft Access 2.0 database, Microsoft Access 97 can export only tables. You cannot export any other database objects to the Microsoft Access 2.0 database, including queries, macros, forms, reports, and modules.

For more information about upgrading to Microsoft Access 97, see Chapter 11, "Upgrading from Previous Versions of Microsoft Access."

Upgrading Microsoft Excel 5.0

Microsoft Excel 97 can read documents saved in Microsoft Excel 5.0 format, and save documents in Microsoft Excel 5.0 format. Microsoft Excel 97 can also run macros created in Microsoft Excel 5.0; however, macros that make 16-bit DLL or API calls may require changes before they can be run in a 32-bit application. For more information, see "Porting Your 16-bit Office-Based Solutions to 32-bit Office" later in this chapter.

For users who have not yet upgraded, Microsoft Excel 97 can also save workbooks in the dual 97 and 5.0/95 file format so that users of both Microsoft Excel 5.0 or 95 and Microsoft Excel 97 can open and edit the same workbooks. For more information, see "Sharing Workbooks with Microsoft Excel 5.0 or 95" in Chapter 12, "Upgrading from Previous Versions of Microsoft Excel."

Upgrading PowerPoint 4.0

PowerPoint 97 can open and save presentations in PowerPoint 4.0 format. For more information about upgrading to PowerPoint 97, see "Upgrading from PowerPoint 4.0" in Chapter 14, "Upgrading from Previous Versions of Microsoft PowerPoint."

Upgrading Word 6.0

Word 97 can read documents saved in Word version 6.0 format and save documents in Word 6.0 format. Word 97 can also run macros created in Word 6.0; however, macros that make 16-bit DLL or API calls may require changes before they can be run in a 32-bit application. For more information, see "Porting Your 16-bit Office-Based Solutions to 32-bit Office" later in this chapter.

For users who have not yet upgraded, Word 6.0 can also read documents saved in Word 97 format. To open a Word 97 document in Word 6.0, you must first install the Word 97 text converter for Word 6.0. For more information, see "Sharing Documents with Word 6.0 or 95" in Chapter 15, "Upgrading from Previous Versions of Microsoft Word."

Upgrading Your Office 4.x Electronic Mail Client

Outlook can replace Microsoft Mail version 3.*x* for Windows, the e-mail application included in Office 4.*x*. When your workgroup upgrades to Outlook, Microsoft Mail 3.*x* users can continue to send e-mail to Outlook users.

Note Microsoft Mail 3.*x* for Windows users cannot use the Outlook standard message form. Nor can they open Outlook folders or take advantage of Outlook views, custom forms, or custom commands.

To continue sharing information with Microsoft Mail 3.*x* for Windows users, Outlook users can:

- Send e-mail to Microsoft Mail 3.*x* for Windows users.
- Open Microsoft Mail 3.*x* for Windows folders.
- Use the Microsoft Mail 3.*x* for Windows standard message form.
- Use Microsoft Mail 3.*x* for Windows custom commands.

For more information about using Outlook as your e-mail client, see Chapter 13, "Upgrading to Microsoft Outlook."

Upgrading Microsoft Office Manager for Windows

In Office 95 for Windows, the Office Shortcut Bar replaced the Microsoft Office Manager from Office 4.*x*. Office 97 includes an updated Office Shortcut Bar.

When you upgrade from Office 4.*x* to Office 97, Setup creates an Old Office toolbar based on the existing Office 4.*x* Office Manager settings in the Msoffice.ini file. Your existing button arrangement is preserved, and Setup creates shortcuts for each button, preserving the path and working folder information. Setup does not preserve the placement of the old Office Manager.

Setup transfers buttons, menu items, and settings from the Office 4.*x* Microsoft Office Manager, as described in the following table.

Office 4.x item	Upgraded to Windows 95	Upgraded to Windows NT Workstation
Button size	Not transferred	Not transferred
Buttons in each Office application	Microsoft Access, Microsoft Excel, PowerPoint, and Word buttons transferred using paths to the new Office installation	Microsoft Access, Microsoft Excel, PowerPoint, and Word buttons transferred using paths to the new Office installation
Control Panel	Transferred as a shortcut to Control Panel	Transferred as is
File Manager	Transferred as a shortcut to Windows Explorer	Transferred as a shortcut to Windows Explorer (Windows NT 4.0)
		Transferred as is (Windows NT 3.51)
Find File	Transferred as a shortcut to the Office **Open** dialog box (**File** menu)	Transferred as a shortcut to the Office **Open** dialog box. (**File** menu)
All menu items	Not transferred.	Not transferred
Print Manager	Transferred as a shortcut to the Printers folder	Transferred as a shortcut to the Printers folder (Windows NT 4.0)
		Transferred as is (Windows NT 3.51)
Program Manager	Not transferred	Transferred as is
Run	Not transferred	Not transferred
Screen Saver	Transferred as a shortcut to the Office 97 version of Screen Saver	Transferred as a shortcut to the Office 97 version of Screen Saver
Show Title Screen at Startup	Not transferred	Not transferred
Task Manager	Not transferred	Transferred as is

Toolbars on the Office Shortcut Bar

In Office 97, you can create and modify toolbars either by working directly with the Office Shortcut Bar or by adding folders to the Shortcut Bar. By storing shortcuts in the toolbar folders, you can rely on Windows to track changes in the location of files. Folders for blank toolbars and some default toolbars are stored in the Microsoft Office\Office\Shortcut Bar folder. By default, this folder has an Office subfolder with the default items for the Office toolbar. Other toolbars may represent folders elsewhere in the system.

Using the **Toolbars** tab in the **Customize** dialog box (**Tools** menu), you can add the following toolbars to the Office Shortcut Bar, or you can create your own. To see a list of available toolbars, right-click the background of any toolbar.

This toolbar	Contains buttons for these applications or accessories	And is located in this source folder path
Office	Office 97 applications	Microsoft Office\Office\Shortcut Bar
QuickShelf™	Bookshelf QuickShelf	Microsoft Office\Office\QuickShelf
Favorites	Favorites folder	Windows\Favorites
Desktop	Windows 95 desktop	Windows\Desktop
Programs	Windows 95 Start menu	Windows\Start Menu\Programs
Accessories	Windows 95 accessories, such as Paint and Calculator	Windows\Start Menu\Programs\Accessories
Old Office	Applications on the user's Office 4.*x* toolbar	Microsoft Office\Office\Old Office
MSN	MSN forums	Microsoft Office\Office\MSN

Default Configurations for the Office Shortcut Bar

Setup configures the Office Shortcut Bar based on platform or computer speed. The default options for various platforms and speeds are listed in the following table.

Option	Windows 640x480	Windows 800x600+
Always on top	On	On
Auto Fit (title bar)	On	Off
Auto Hide	Off	Off
Docked location	Top	Right (Windows 95); Top (Windows NT Workstation)
Large buttons	Off	Off
Show title screen	On	On
Show ToolTips	On	On
Smooth fill	Off	Off
Standard color	Off	Off

Note On VGA (640x480) systems and in all Windows NT operating environments, the Office Shortcut Bar docks at the top of the screen. For higher resolutions, it docks to the right.

Upgrading from Microsoft Office 3.x for Windows

All of the Office version 3.x for Windows desktop applications—Microsoft Access, Microsoft Excel, PowerPoint, and Word—change file formats between Office 3.x and Office 97. Office 97 also introduces a new e-mail client and desktop information manager, Outlook.

Tip In Windows 95 and Windows NT Workstation 4.0, you can use a system policy to define the default value for the **Save as type** option in the **Save As** dialog box (**File** menu) for all Office 97 users in your workgroup (except for users of Microsoft Access and Outlook, which do not support this option). In the Windows System Policy Editor, set the following policies:

User\Excel\Tools_Options\Transition\Default Save

User\PowerPoint\Tools_Options\Save\Default Save

User\Word\Tools_Options\Save\Default Save

For more information, see "Using Windows System Policies to Customize Office" in Chapter 7, "Customizing and Optimizing Microsoft Office."

Upgrading Microsoft Access 1.x

Using a process called enabling, Microsoft Access 97 can read data and run queries, forms, reports, macros, and Access Basic code in a Microsoft Access version 1.x database without changing the format. This allows Microsoft Access 97 users to share data with Microsoft Access 1.x users. As an alternative to enabling, Microsoft Access 97 can establish links to tables in a Microsoft Access 1.x database.

All Microsoft Access 1.x database objects, including macros and Access Basic code, can also be converted to 97 format. However, Access Basic code that relies on 16-bit DLLs and API calls must be modified to run in a 32-bit application. For more information, see "Porting Your 16-bit Office-Based Solutions to 32-bit Office" later in this chapter.

If you need to move Microsoft Access 97 data to a Microsoft Access 1.x database, Microsoft Access 97 can export only tables. You cannot export any other database objects to the Microsoft Access 1.x database, including queries, macros, forms, reports, and modules.

For more information about upgrading to Microsoft Access 97, see Chapter 11, "Upgrading from Previous Versions of Microsoft Access."

Upgrading Microsoft Excel 4.0

Microsoft Excel 97 can read documents saved in Microsoft Excel version 4.0 format and save documents in Microsoft Excel 4.0 format. Microsoft Excel 97 can also run macros created in the Microsoft Excel 4.0 XLM macro language; however, macros that make 16-bit DLL or API calls may require changes before they can be run in a 32-bit application. For more information, see "Porting Your 16-bit Office-Based Solutions to 32-bit Office" later in this chapter.

For more information about upgrading to Microsoft Excel 97, see Chapter 12, "Upgrading from Previous Versions of Microsoft Excel."

Upgrading PowerPoint 3.0

PowerPoint 97 can open and save presentations in PowerPoint version 3.0 format. For more information about upgrading to PowerPoint 97, see "Upgrading from PowerPoint 3.0" in Chapter 14, "Upgrading from Previous Versions of Microsoft PowerPoint."

Upgrading Word 2.0

Word 97 can read documents saved in Word version 2.0 format, and save documents in Word 2.0 format. Word 97 can also run macros created in the Word 2.0 WordBasic language; however, macros that make 16-bit DLL or API calls may require changes before they can be run in a 32-bit application. For more information, see "Porting Your 16-bit Office-Based Solutions to 32-bit Office" later in this chapter.

For more information about upgrading to Word 97, see Chapter 15, "Upgrading from Previous Versions of Microsoft Word."

Porting Your 16-bit Office-Based Solutions to 32-bit Office

The introduction of 32-bit Windows 95 and Windows NT operating systems brings 32-bit Office applications into common use. Many users are upgrading their Office files, macros, and solutions to the 32-bit versions. This section assists you in porting solution code—that is, code written in the Microsoft Excel macro language (XLM), WordBasic, Visual Basic for Applications, or Access Basic—to 32-bit versions of Office running on 32-bit operating systems.

Changes to your existing code are required if your 16-bit Office solutions (including those created for Microsoft Access or Microsoft Project) calls a 16-bit Windows application programming interface (API) or 16-bit Windows dynamic-link library (DLL), and you are porting that code to a 32-bit Office application (including Microsoft Access 97 or Microsoft Project 97).

Porting your solution code is necessary because 16-bit API calls and 16-bit DLL calls (referred to in this section as API calls) do not execute correctly when the solution code containing those calls is run in a 32-bit Office application. This section applies to solution code that uses APIs in the following products: Microsoft Access, Microsoft Excel, Microsoft Project, and Word.

Note If your 16-bit solutions continue to reside inside a 16-bit application, then they are not affected when you port them to 32-bit Windows. For example, existing 16-bit Office solutions, 16-bit Visual Basic, and 16-bit Microsoft FoxPro applications, even if they call 16-bit APIs, run just fine on Windows 95 or Windows NT operating systems. It is only when users want to run solutions code that includes 16-bit API calls on a 32-bit application that porting is required.

To ensure that Office-based solutions run successfully under the Windows 95 and Windows NT operating systems, solution providers and developers must follow this rule: neither a 32-bit compiled application nor solution code called from a 32-bit Office application can make direct 16-bit API or DLL calls. In addition, neither a 16-bit compiled application nor solution code called from a 16-bit application can make direct 32-bit API or DLL calls. This inability to make calls back and forth between 16-bit and 32-bit layers occurs in both the Windows 95 and Windows NT operating systems because of their advanced flat-memory-model management systems, as well as the way in which they load DLLs.

To prepare for Office 97, you must change your solution code to make Win32® API calls when the solution code is executed from 32-bit Office applications. If this is not possible (for example, you don't have access to the source code of the DLL), you must change the solution code to *thunk* through an intermediate DLL to make the 16-bit API call.

Updating solution code to support Win32 API calls is a relatively simple mechanical process. A more significant task is to write code that is operating-system-independent (that is, so the solution code runs on both 16-bit and 32-bit Office applications). This section discusses both of these tasks, as well as other 16-to-32-bit API issues you may need to handle.

Note Although you must update API calls when porting solution code to 32-bit operating systems, you do not need to change code that uses OLE Automation or dynamic data exchange (DDE). All OLE and DDE code continues to work regardless of whether the applications are 16-bit or 32-bit. OLE and DDE insulate automation calls, so all combinations of containers (clients) and servers (16/16, 16/32, 32/16, and 32/32) work under Windows 95 and Windows NT operating systems.

How This Section Is Organized

The remainder of this section is organized in terms of complexity, from the simplest upgrading scenarios to the most complex.

- "Which API Should Your Solution Code Call?" is a quick overview of which API you should be using, according to your application needs.
- "Calling the Win32 API" describes what an API is and discusses the issues involved in converting existing 16-bit API calls to Win32 API calls, finding **Declaration** statements, and testing the **Declare** statements.
- "Writing a Single Code Base for 16-bit and 32-bit Office Applications" supplies code samples for writing solution code that runs on both a 16-bit and a 32-bit Office applications.
- "Determining Whether a 32-bit Application Is Running" describes how to determine whether your Office application is 16-bit or 32-bit and how to select the appropriate 16-bit or 32-bit API call.
- "Recompiling DLLs" tells you what to do to make the DLL and solution code work on Windows 95 and Windows NT operating systems if your solution code calls a custom DLL.
- "Thunking" tells you how, if you cannot recompile your DLLs, you can add an intermediate DLL.
- "Advanced Programming Topics" explains translating C-API declarations to Visual Basic or Visual Basic for Applications.

Which API Should Your Solution Code Call?

When you write solution code for your own use, you write it for the version of the Office application you have and for your operating system. Distributing this solution to others, however, means that you have to make it also work on their computers, which may use different versions of Windows and Office applications.

While the operating system isn't an issue, whether the Office application is 16-bit or 32-bit is important. The application, and not the operating system, determines which API you use in porting your solution code: you must use 16-bit APIs with 16-bit applications, and 32-bit APIs with 32-bit applications.

Note Office (including 32-bit Microsoft Access and 32-bit Microsoft Project) products do not run on Win32s®. Because FoxPro does run on this operating system, however, FoxPro programmers should use the same rules for choosing the API. Also, the Win32s, Windows NT, and Windows 95 operating systems do not have identical sets of API calls. For more information, see the Win32 SDK documentation in the Development Library (in particular, see the Compatibility Tables in the *Win32 Programmer's Reference*, Vol. 5).

Calling the Win32 API

To write calls to the Win32 API, you must do the following:

- Understand what Windows API calls are.
- Understand the differences between 16-bit and 32-bit Windows APIs.
- Use Win32api.txt to find the correct **Declare** statement.
- Test an API **Declare** statement.

What Is an API Call?

An API call in C, Visual Basic, or other languages places a series of values (parameters) at a location in memory (the *stack*) and then requests the operating system or DLL to execute a function (the *procedure call*) using the values provided. The function reads the values (*call stack*) and executes its function code using those values or the data that the values point to.

If a result is returned, it is placed at another location (*return register*) for the calling application to use. This is shown in the following illustration. To ensure accuracy, the number of bytes of data on the stack is verified before and after the procedure is called. The message "Bad DLL calling convention" appears when the wrong number of bytes are in the stack.

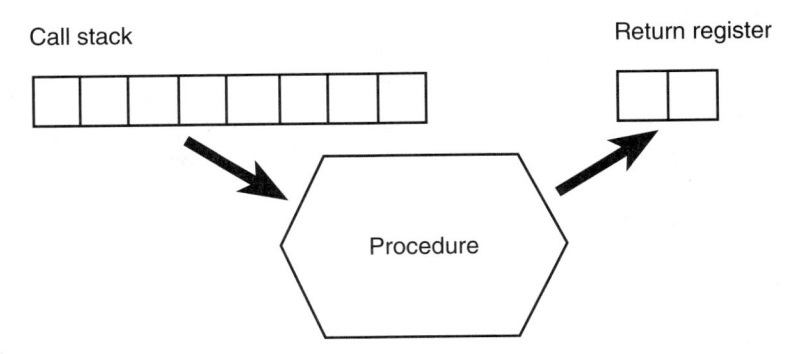

In practical terms, Windows API calls are how applications request services (screen control, printers, memory, and so forth) from the operating system. There are approximately 300 API calls in Windows 3.0, over 700 API calls in Windows 3.1, and over 1,000 API calls in Windows 95. These API calls are packaged in executables and DLLs found in the Windows folder—User.exe, Gdi.exe, and one of the following **KERNEL** files: Krnl286.exe, Krnl386.exe, or Kernel32.dll.

To call an API from your solution code, use these four steps:

1. Identify the file containing the API.
2. Determine the parameters required by the API.

3. Create a **Declare** statement for the API.
4. Call the function with valid parameters.

The following is a simple example for the **GetVersion** API call that obtains the version of Windows that is running. The **GetVersion** API call is located in **KERNEL** under 16-bit Windows and does not use any parameters (so the **Declare** statement has empty parentheses). The following **Declare** statement is written for 16-bit Windows for use by Visual Basic for Applications:

```
Declare Function GetVersion Lib "KERNEL" () As Long
```

By comparison, here is the same function as it would be used by an Office 97 application running on 32-bit Windows:

```
Declare Function GetVersion Lib "KERNEL32" () As Long
```

Although the Windows API name stays the same, the location of the API has changed to **KERNEL32**. Because you are calling from a 32-bit application, you must make a 32-bit API call. The parameter data type, on the other hand, did not change (it remained a **Long**). In general, the function parameters change more and require more attention than the parameters of the return value. Understanding the differences between 16-bit API calls and 32-bit API calls is essential to porting your solution code to Windows 95.

What Are the Differences Between a 16-bit and a 32-bit Windows API?

As shown in the previous example, most 32-bit Windows API calls have the same name or a very similar name to the 16-bit API calls. In fact, the documentation may show the same arguments, with the only apparent difference being the library name change from **KERNEL** to **KERNEL32**. However, the code must handle the following changes in addition to the name change:

- Case-sensitivity
- Unicode or ANSI options
- Change of parameter data type (shown in the previous example)

These items can require subtle changes in the **Declare** statements that are not always easy to identify.

Case Sensitivity

The first issue in moving to 32-bit Windows API calls is case sensitivity in the name of the function. API calls under 16-bit Windows are not case sensitive and work if you enter the function name as **GetVERSION**, **GeTvErSiOn**, or **getversion**. In other words, in 16-bit Windows the following statements are equivalent:

```
Declare Function GetVersion Lib "KERNEL" () As Long
Declare Function GeTvErSiOn Lib "KERNEL" () As Long
```

API calls under 32-bit Windows, however, are case-sensitive for the function call and must be correctly entered in the **Declare** statement. In other words, the following statements are not equivalent in 32-bit Windows:

```
Declare Function GetVersion Lib "KERNEL32" () As Long
Declare Function GeTvErSiOn Lib "KERNEL32" () As Long
```

The easiest way to handle this change is to always use the **Alias** control word. The contents of an **Alias** string map to the actual API call name (which is case sensitive), but the function name used in code, which appears between Function and Lib, is not case sensitive and does not change if you type it different ways in your code or use the same name for variables or procedures. Using the **Alias** control word, the **GetVersion** function (32-bit Windows) would be entered as:

```
Declare Function GetVersion Lib "KERNEL32" Alias "GetVersion" () As Long
```

The case of API names doesn't matter when writing code: as long as you enter the function name correctly in the **Alias** string, and you spell the function name in code the same way as in the **Declare** statement, the function is automatically mapped by Visual Basic or Visual Basic for Applications back to the correct **Declare** function.

Note The **Alias** control word is the single most important thing you can use in preparing to switch to 32-bit operating systems because it means you only have to change the contents of the **Declare** statement and not every instance of the function being called in your code.

Unicode or ANSI Options

Both the Windows NT and Windows 95 operating systems have two API interfaces. One interface is based on the American National Standards Institute (ANSI) character set, where a single byte represents each character. The other interface was created for the Unicode character set, where two bytes represent each character. All 16-bit Windows operating systems and applications use the ANSI character set. All 32-bit versions of Windows add Unicode to allow foreign language characters to be represented. C programmers handle this by setting a flag in their include file (***.h**). The flag causes hundreds of macros throughout the C include files to select the correct Unicode or ANSI functions.

All western language versions of Office products use ANSI for Visual Basic for Applications code. Therefore, programmers using current versions of Visual Basic for Applications or other macro languages should always use the ANSI version of the API call. When using the Win32api.txt file, this choice is made for you. For more information about this file, see "Change of Parameter Data Type," later in this section.

To distinguish the ANSI version from the Unicode version, the ANSI version adds an **A** to the end of the API name, and the Unicode version adds a **W**. (**W** is for wide, as in the width of the bytes provided for characters.) The name of an API call includes either the character **A** or **W** at the end of the API name only if the API requires parameters with string (character) data types.

The Win32 SDK documentation in the Development Library does not record the permutations of the name of the API call. The documentation gives only the name of the root function and its library name. The actual name of the API in the library can be one of the following:

- **MyAPICall**, which uses no character strings in the call.
- **MyAPICallA**, which uses ANSI character strings in the call.
- **MyAPICallW**, which uses Unicode character strings in the call.

To understand the differences, see the following diagram showing the amount of data the API expects to find on possible call stacks for an example function (the 16-bit version is padded because 16-bit Windows always pads the stack to 16 bits).

16-bit API Call	HWND	LPSTR	TCHAR		Integer	
32-bit ANSI API Call	HWND		LPSTR		TCHAR	PADDING
32-bit Unicode API Call	HWND		LPSTR		TCHAR	PADDING

The three possible declarations for **MyAPICall** are shown in the following example, organized to make comparison easier. All of the statements use the **Alias** control word so that the function name used in code (**MyAPICall**) does not have to change even if the name of the function called is appended with an **A** or a **W**:

```
'16 bits
Declare function MyAPICall Lib "MYDLL.DLL" Alias "MyAPICall" (
   ByVal hwndForm As Integer,
   ByVal lpstrCaption$,
   ByVal hAccKey As String,
    ByVal iMagicNumber As Integer
   ) As Integer
'32-bit ANSI
Declare function MyAPICall Lib "MYDLL32.DLL" Alias "MyAPICallA" (
   ByVal hwndForm As Long,
   ByVal lpstrCaption$,
   ByVal hAccKey As String,
   ByVal iMagicNumber As Long
   ) As Long
'32-bit UNICODE * For illustration only.
Declare function MyAPICall Lib "MYDLL32.DLL" Alias "MyAPICallW" (
   ByVal hwndForm As Long,
   ByVal lpstrCaption$,
   ByVal hAccKey As String,
   ByVal iMagicNumber As Long
   ) As Long
```

Chapter 10 Upgrading from Previous Versions of Microsoft Office

Any one of these declarations would add the function **MyAPICall** to your application; you can only have one **MyAPICall** function.

This code sample introduces the **ByVal** keyword, which allows you to pass Visual Basic parameters to a API function by value. **By Value** is the default for functions written in C and is therefore the default for Windows API calls. The reason you must use **ByVal** is that Visual Basic and Visual Basic for Applications default to **ByRef** (**By Reference** passes a pointer to the value rather than the value itself), which is not what API calls expect. **ByVal** can also be used to convert a Visual Basic string to a null-terminated C string. **ByVal** is included in the **Declare** statements in Win32api.txt, so you know when to use it.

Note For more information about **ByVal**, see the Microsoft Developer Network (MSDN) article Q110219 *How to call Windows API from VB*, or published references such as *PC Magazine Visual Basic Programmer's Guide to the Windows API* by Dan Appleman, published by Ziff-Davis Press.

Change of Parameter Data Type

The easiest way to get the new required parameter data types for 32-bit API functions is to copy the appropriate API **Declare** statement from Win32api.txt into your source code.

Tools and Utilities The Office Resource Kit Tools and Utilities include the Visual Basic declaration file called Win32api.txt. For more information about viewing Win32api.txt, see "Visual Basic Win32 API Declarations" in Appendix A, "Microsoft Office 97 Resource Kit Tools and Utilities."

Another source of information is the *Win32 Programmer's Reference* on the MSDN Development Library CD, which is discussed in "Advanced Programming Topics" later in this section. This reference may occasionally be required to resolve questions about the inclusion or exclusion of **ByVal** in the declaration or the need to put parentheses around the actual value passed.

If you use the *Win32 Programmer's Reference*, however, you must be careful to properly convert C to Visual Basic data types. For example, don't mistake a C **int** for a Visual Basic for Applications **Integer**. Many Windows data types and Visual Basic **Integer** data types are no longer the same size, as shown in the following table. It is critical to remember that the sizes of many API parameters have changed, and you must not assume they are the same.

Visual Basic data type	Size of variable	Corresponding 16-bit Windows data types	Corresponding 32-bit Windows data types
Integer	2 bytes	**int**, **short**, **WORD**, **HWND**, **HANDLE**, **WCHAR**	**short**, **WCHAR**
Long	4 bytes	**long**, **LPSTR**	**int**, **long**, **HANDLE**, **HWND**, **LPSTR**

Microsoft Office 97 Resource Kit   **243**

Finally, whether you use Win32api.txt or the *Win32 Programmer's Reference*, judicious use of the **Alias** control word may assist you in changing parameter data types by allowing existing 16-bit code that calls the API to be left unchanged. The **ByVal** control word and automatic type conversion in Visual Basic, Access Basic, WordBasic, and Visual Basic for Applications change the size of parameters for you in many cases (**Integer** to **Long**, for example). Alternatively, type conversion extends integers with a sign (+/−) that may lead to incorrect long parameters and cause overflows on conversion from **Long** to **Integer**. Again, the best solution is to check Win32api.txt or the *Win32 Programmer's Reference* to get the correct functions.

What Types of Errors Can Occur with an API Declare Statement?

After you create a **Declare** statement, it may not work. While there are many mistakes possible in a **Declare** statement, the following are the most common errors:

- Error 453: **Function is not defined in specified DLL**

  Either you misspelled the function name or you have a problem with case in the function name. Functions are case-sensitive in Win32; they are not case-sensitive in 16-bit Windows.

- Error 48: **Error in loading DLL**

  Usually, this error is caused by having the wrong size or arguments, but it may also occur for some of the reasons described under Error 53.

- Error 53: **File Not Found**

  Windows checks the loaded libraries for matches; if the DLL is not loaded, Windows attempts to load the DLL from disk. Many functions available in the 16-bit Windows on Windows (WOW) layer on Windows NT Server are not available directly on Windows NT Workstation.

  Calling the 16-bit Windows and Win32 **GetProfileString** function from a 16-bit and a 32-bit solution gives a confusing set of error messages. The 16-bit application call finds **KERNEL** and fails to find **KERNEL32**, while the 32-bit application finds **KERNEL32** and fails to find **KERNEL**. The general cause of this error is a mismatch of calls and operating systems. The solution is to write code that works in both 16-bit and 32-bit environments.

Writing a Single Code Base for 16-bit and 32-bit Office Applications

If users in your workgroup are running both 16-bit and 32-bit versions of an Office application—Microsoft Excel 5.0 and 97, for example—should you put the 16-bit API call or the 32-bit API call in your solution? Microsoft Excel, for example, is not like Visual Basic version 4.0, which allows conditional compilation of code into executables, but instead runs solution code in workbook files which may be opened in either the 16-bit or the 32-bit version of the application. The solution is to put both the 16-bit API call and the 32-bit API call inside an **If...Then...Else** control structure.

With 32-bit applications using the same solution code as 16-bit applications, you do not know which API to call in the solution code. Your code must determine whether the application is 16-bit or 32-bit in order to make the correct API call. Each application makes this determination using a set of different questions:

- Microsoft Access

    Is the host application 16-bit Microsoft Access 2.0 or earlier, or 32-bit Microsoft Access 95 or 97?

- Microsoft Excel

    Is the host application 16-bit Microsoft Excel 5.0 or earlier, or 32-bit Microsoft Excel 5.0 for Windows NT operating system or 32-bit Microsoft Excel for Windows 95 or 97?

- Microsoft Project
- Is the host application 16-bit Microsoft Project version 3.0, or 32-bit Microsoft Project version 4.0 or later?
- Word
- Is the host application 16-bit Word 6.0 or earlier, or 32-bit Word 6.0 for Windows NT or Word for Windows 95 or 97?

If you make the wrong API call, an error occurs. The solution code must determine whether the application is a 16-bit application or a 32-bit application, so it can make the appropriate call.

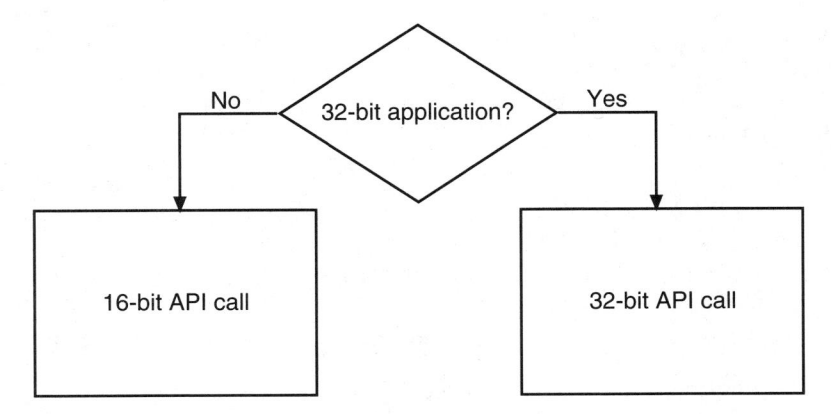

The solution is to put every API call into a wrapper—a Visual Basic procedure or a Microsoft Excel 4.0 macro. This wrapper routinely checks the *bitness* of the application and selects the appropriate API call. Place these wrappers in separate modules so that your code can be easily reused. Some API calls (for example, **GetPrinterDriveDirectory** and **GetWinMetaFileBits**) are not available in all 32-bit operating environments, which means that the structure of an API wrapper can become as complex as this:

```
Function MyAPICall$(ByVal Args)
    If Engine32() Then
        'Select is rarely needed
        Select Case OS32() 'Based on GetVersionEx API
        Case 0 'Win32s
           ....
        Case 1 'NT 3.1
           ....
        Case 2 'NT 3.5
           ....
        Case 3 'Windows 95
           ....
        End Select
    Else '16-bit
        ....
    End If
End Function
```

An API wrapper this complex is the exception, however, and not the rule.

Compiled languages, such as FoxPro and Visual Basic, build 16-bit or 32-bit application executables. The executable targets either 16-bit API calls or 32-bit API calls. You can determine the appropriate API calls while building the application. You can select the calls in one of two ways: either by having all the 16-bit declarations in one file and all the 32-bit declarations in another file and manually switching them in a project; or by using the **#IF... #ELSE...** directives and conditional compilation supported by Visual Basic 4.0.

If you must support Visual Basic version 3.0 and Visual Basic 4.0 applications concurrently, separate files may reduce code maintenance. If you support FoxPro, you have no problem using 16-bit API calls from compiled 32-bit FoxPro solutions because the **RegFN** functions automatically thunk from the 32-bit layer to the 16-bit layer if needed.

Compiled 32-bit languages may require some minor differences in API calls depending on the 32-bit operating system. For example, developers must program context menus differently for Windows 95 than for Windows NT operating systems.

Determining Whether a 32-bit Application Is Running

In the previous section, writing application-independent code is achieved by adding code for both 16-bit and 32-bit scenarios. However, you still need to determine in source code whether the application is a 32-bit application or a 16-bit application.

The code in the following examples determines whether these are 32-bit applications.

- In Microsoft Excel 5.0, Microsoft Excel 95, Microsoft Excel 97, Microsoft Project 4.0, Microsoft Project 95, or Microsoft Project 97:

    ```
    Function Engine32%()
        If instr(Application.OperatingSystem,"32") then Engine32%=True
    End Function
    ```

- In Word 6.0, Word 95, or Word 97:

    ```
    Function Engine32
        If Val(GetSystemInfo$(23)) > 6.3 Or Len(GetSystemInfo$(23)) = 0 _
            Then Engine32 = - 1 Else Engine32 = 0
    End Function
    ```

- In Microsoft Access 1.1 or higher:

    ```
    Function Engine32% ()
    If SysCmd(7) > 2 Then Engine32% = True
    End Function
    ```

Note The **Application.OperatingSystem** property in Microsoft Excel and Microsoft Project does not return the version of Windows you have installed, but the layer of Windows that the application is running on, for example, the 16-bit subsystem in Windows NT Workstation.

Putting It All Together

For examples of code for particular applications, you should consult the MSDN, and find the article entitled *Corporate Developer's Guide to Office 95 API Issues*. For information about connecting to MSDN, see "Microsoft Developer Network" in Appendix E, "Other Support Resources."

The following simple example may help you understand some issues.

```
Declare Function GetTickCount32 Lib "KERNEL32" Alias "GetTickCount" () _
    As Long
Declare Function GetTickCount16 Lib "USER" Alias "GetTickCount" () _
    As Long

Function GetRightTickCount() As Long
If Engine32%() Then
   GetRightTickCount = GetTickCount32()
Else
   GetRightTickCount = GetTickCount16()
End If
End Function
```

In this example, the **GetTickCount** API has the same name for both 16-bit Windows and 32-bit Windows, so you must use an **Alias** control word to change the function name in at least one of the **Declare** statements. In the example, the names in both **Declare** statements are changed to **GetTickCount32** and **GetTickCount16**. Next, depending on the application's bitness, **GetTickCount** is mapped to the correct API function name (**GetTickCount32** or **GetTickCount16**) and its associated API call. In this example, **GetTickCount** in your code is mapped to **GetTickCount32** (in the **GetTickCount** function), which is in turn mapped to **GetTickCount** in **KERNEL32**, when **Engine32%** is **True**.

Word Sample Declare-Method Solution

Word has a different **Declare** format and syntax. The Word solution is more complex because you cannot place both the 16-bit and 32-bit **Declare** statements in the same macro. The solution is to create three macro libraries: **APICALL16** and **APICALL32**, which contain the **Declare** statements for each operating environment; and a 16-bit/32-bit interoperability macro, **APICALLS**.

First, create a macro library called **APICALL16**. This macro contains all the 16-bit API **Declare** statements.

```
'This is APICALL16 -- all 16-bit Declare statements are placed here.
Declare Function GetTickCount16 Lib "USER" Alias "GetTickCount"() _
    As Long
Function GetTickCount
GetTickCount = GetTickCount16
End Function
```

Second, create a macro library called **APICALL32**. This macro contains all the 32-bit API **Declare** statements.

```
'This is APICALL32 -- all 32-bit Declare statements are placed here.
Declare Function GetTickCount32 Lib "KERNEL32" Alias "GetTickCount"() _
    As Long
Function GetTickCount
GetTickCount = GetTickCount32
End Function
```

Third, create a macro library called **APICALLS**. This macro contains **Engine32** and the procedures your solution code calls.

```
'This is APICALLS -- no Declare statements may be in this macro.
Function Engine32
Engine32 = 0
If Val(AppInfo$(2)) > 5 Then
    OS$ = GetSystemInfo$(23)
    If Val(OS$) > 6.3 Or Len(OS$) = 0 Then Engine32 = - 1
End If
End Function

Function GetTickCount
If Engine32 Then
    GetTickCount = APICall32.GetTickCount
Else
    GetTickCount = APICall16.GetTickCount
End If
End Function
'Other API function calls are placed here.
```

You can now call this function from your solution code. You must preface your calls with **APICALLS**. For example:

```
Sub MAIN
MsgBox Str$(APICalls.GetTickCount)
End Sub
```

▶ **To convert Word solutions to run on 16-bit and 32-bit products**

1. Create a new module called **APICALLS**.
2. Create the **Engine32** function in **APICALLS**.
3. Create a new module called **APICALL16**.
4. Locate all the 16-bit **Declare** statements in the solution and move them to **APICALL16**.
5. Create a new module called **APICALL32**.
6. Create the equivalent 32-bit **Declare** statements and put them to **APICALL32**.
7. Using the preceding template, create functions for each API in each of the three macro libraries.
8. Add **APICALLS** before all calls to the API in your solution code.
9. Test each function.

This process allows existing calls in other modules to be left untouched. After the developer defines and tests these macros, the developer can add them to Normal.dot and reuse the macros in other solutions so as to cut conversion time.

Recompiling DLLs

This section has so far focused on the issue of updating Windows API calls—but the issues for solution code that calls 16-bit DLLs that you have bought, developed, or used is exactly the same. The developer must change all 16-bit DLL **Declare** calls in solution code to 32-bit calls. This requires creating a 32-bit version of the DLL (at least) and possibly changing the **Declare** statement (or, in Microsoft Excel 4.0 macros, the **Register** function).

This also means a separate DLL must exist for both the 16-bit application and the 32-bit application. For file management, the name of the 32-bit DLL should include **32** at the end. The developer must recompile the DLL as a 32-bit Ansi.dll. The parameters passed to the DLL must use the stdcall-passing protocol to talk to 32-bit Visual Basic for Applications, instead of the PASCAL-passing protocol used with 16-bit Windows. Place the calls for the 16-bit and 32-bit versions of the DLL in a wrapper similar to the API wrapper described previously.

For more information about recompiling applications, see Chapter 1, "Porting 16-bit Code to 32-bit Windows," in *Programming Techniques* from the Visual C++® 2.1 documentation in the Development Library, or see your C compiler documentation.

Thunking

When you do not have the source code of a DLL, your solution is to use *thunking* to port your solution to Windows 95. Thunking enables direct 16-bit and 32-bit calls but requires much more work than simply changing the Windows API call. If you cannot change or recompile the 16-bit DLL, you must write a new 32-bit DLL wrapper to access the 16-bit DLL. The 32-bit application calls to this 32-bit wrapper DLL, which then calls the original 16-bit DLL.

Thunking allows parameters to be pushed correctly on the stack, enables a DLL of a different bitness to load in your process, and converts memory addresses from **offset** (32-bit) to **segment::offset** (16-bit). Even if you do the thunking work, however, some issues remain. For example, pointers to memory locations require additional work in 16-bit and 32-bit scenarios.

There are several ways to thunk, depending on your operating system: Windows 95 and Windows NT thunk differently. For an overview of thunking across the Windows operation systems, as well as references to more information about thunking, see *Diving into the Requirements for the Windows 95 Logo* in the Development Library.

Advanced Programming Topics

Most developers writing solution code know the C language, and the following information is provided to assist them in using their knowledge of C to create **Declare** statements for Visual Basic and Visual Basic for Applications using the tools they already have.

Working from C Declarations

Apart from the API location changing (from **KERNEL** to **KERNEL32**), the main issue in moving from 16-bit API calls to 32-bit API calls is the change in the size of parameter data types. Some background information may help you understand what has changed and why. Windows 3.*x* was designed for the Intel 80286 CPU, where the hardware handles data two bytes at a time, or in 16-bit words. Windows 95 was designed for later CPUs, where the hardware can handle data four bytes at a time, or in 32-bit words. The following list shows how Visual Basic represents an **Integer** as opposed to how Windows represents an **int**:

- **Integer** and **int** are each two bytes in the 16-bit Windows operating system and in 16-bit Microsoft Excel, Visual Basic, Microsoft Access, Word, and Microsoft Project.

- **Integer** is two bytes in 32-bit Microsoft Excel, Visual Basic, Microsoft Access, Word for Windows, and Microsoft Project.

- **int** is four bytes in the 32-bit Windows operating systems, Windows 95, and Windows NT.

To illustrate how this change in size can affect a call, recall the fictional **MyAPICall** API used earlier. The **MyAPICall** call needs the handle to the application's window (**HWND**), a string, a character, and an integer to be placed on the stack. In C, the function would be:

```
int MyAPICall (HWND hwndForm, LPSTR lpstrCaption, TCHAR tchAccKey, _
    int iMagicNumber)
```

Each parameter has two parts: the data type (**HWND**, **LPSTR**, **TCHAR**, **int**) and the field name (**hwndForm**, **lpstrCaption**, **tchAccKey**, **iMagicNumber**). Each data type requires a specific number of bytes to represent it. Each field name has some odd-looking characters as a prefix—these characters (known as Hungarian notation) indicate the data type, such as **int** or **lpstr**.

Windows has many data types that API calls use as parameters. The following table shows some of the more significant data types used by Windows 95 API calls. Many Windows data types use the C data type of **int**. (When **int** changed from 16-bits to 32-bits, the related Windows data types also changed.)

C data type	Size in Windows 3.x and Windows for Workgroups 3.x (16-bit)	Size in Win32s, Windows NT operating system, and Windows 95 (32-bit)
unsigned int, **UINT**, **int**	2 bytes	4 bytes
short	2 bytes	2 bytes
long	4 bytes	4 bytes
char, **CHAR**	1 byte	1 byte
WORD	2 bytes	2 bytes
Handle (**hWnd**, **hDC**, **hMenu**)	2 bytes	4 bytes
LPSTR	4 bytes	4 bytes
WCHAR	2 bytes	2 bytes
TCHAR (ANSI or Unicode)	1 byte	1 or 2 bytes
POINT	4 bytes	8 bytes

Thus, converting the **MyAPICall** API call from C, the declarations for **MyAPICall** using Visual Basic for Applications, Access Basic, or WordBasic would be as follows (organized to make comparison easier):

```
'16 bits
Declare Function MyAPICall Lib "MYDLL.DLL" Alias "MyAPICall" (
   ByVal hwndForm As Integer,
   ByVal lpstrCaption As String,
   ByVal hAccKey As String,
   ByVal iMagicNumber As Integer
   ) As Integer
'32 bits
Declare Function MyAPICall Lib "MYDLL32.DLL" Alias "MyAPICall" (
   ByVal hwndForm As Long,
   ByVal lpstrCaption As String,
   ByVal hAccKey As String,
   ByVal iMagicNumber As Long
   ) As Long
```

A final tool you may find useful is the following table, which maps C language declaration data types to their Visual Basic equivalents.

C language declaration data type	Visual Basic equivalent	Called with this variable
Boolean	**ByVal B As Boolean**	Any **Integer** or **Variant** variable
Pointer to a string (**LPSTR**)	**By Val S As String**	Any **String** or **Variant** variable
Pointer to an integer (**LPINT**)	**I As Integer**	Any **Integer** or **Variant** variable
Pointer to a long integer (**LPDWORD**)	**L As Long**	Any **Long** or **Variant** variable
Pointer to a structure (for example, **LPRECT**)	**S As Rect**	Any variable of that user-defined type
Integer (**INT, UINT, WORD, BOOL**)	**ByVal I As Integer**	Any **Integer** or **Variant** variable
Handle (**32 bit, HWND**)	**ByVal H As Long**	Any **Long** or **Variant** variable
Long (**DWORD, LONG**)	**ByVal L As Long**	Any **Long** or **Variant** variable
Pointer to an array of integers	**I as Integer**	The first element of the array, such as I(0)
Pointer to a void (**void***)	**V As Any**	Any variable (use **ByVal** when passing a string)
Void (function return value)	**Sub Procedure**	Not applicable
NULL	**As Any**	**ByVal 0&**
Char (**TCHAR**)	**ByVal Ch As String**	Any **String** or **Variant** variable

Using the Win32 Programmer's Reference

The two primary sources for Win32 API information are the *Win32 Programmer's Reference* and a list of Microsoft-supplied Win32 **Declare** statements for Visual Basic, such as Win32api.txt. The Development Library contains a listing with explanations of the entire Win32 API set in the *Win32 Programmer's Reference*. For more information about the Development Library, see "Microsoft Developer Network," in Appendix E, "Other Support Resources."

CHAPTER 11

Upgrading from Previous Versions of Microsoft Access

This chapter tells you what to expect when you or your workgroup upgrades to Microsoft Access 97 from a previous version of Microsoft Access. If you plan a gradual upgrade, users of different versions of Microsoft Access may need to share databases. This chapter describes Microsoft Access 97 features that are not supported in previous versions, which may require you to modify existing macros and application code.

Note Microsoft Access runs on Windows 95 and Windows NT Workstation version 3.51 or later only.

In This Chapter
Overview   254
Converting Databases   254
Upgrading from Microsoft Access 95   262
Upgrading from Microsoft Access 2.0   271
Upgrading from Microsoft Access 1.x   294
Sharing Databases with Microsoft Access 1.x, 2.0, or 95   297

See Also
- For a summary of new and improved features in Microsoft Access 97, see Chapter 2, "What's New in Microsoft Office 97."
- For information about installing Microsoft Access or other Office applications, see Chapter 4, "Installing Microsoft Office."
- For information about switching to Microsoft Access from other database applications, see Chapter 17, "Switching to Microsoft Access."

Overview

The primary questions most Microsoft Access 97 upgraders have are:

- What happens to my old Microsoft Access databases when I convert them to Microsoft Access 97 format?
- Can I share Microsoft Access 97 databases with users of previous versions of Microsoft Access?
- Do my old macros still work in Microsoft Access 97?
- Does my old application code still work in Microsoft Access 97?

If you are upgrading from any of the following versions of Microsoft Access, this chapter answers these questions for you:

- Microsoft Access 95
- Microsoft Access version 2.0
- Microsoft Access version 1.x

Converting Databases

When you convert a database from a previous version of Microsoft Access to Microsoft Access 97, you can use all of the new features available in Microsoft Access 97. After a database is converted, it cannot be opened in previous versions of Microsoft Access, nor can it be converted back to an earlier format. You can, however, export tables from a Microsoft Access 97 database to existing database in a previous version. Before you convert a database to Microsoft Access 97 format, make sure that users who need to use the database have Windows 95 or Windows NT Workstation 3.51 or later and Microsoft Access 97 installed on their computers.

Note If all the users in your workgroup have converted to Microsoft Access 97, or if only Microsoft Access 97 users work with the database, you can convert a Microsoft Access 1.x, 2.0, or 95 database to Microsoft Access 97. If users of previous versions of Microsoft Access use the database, however, do not convert it. For more information about sharing databases across multiple versions, see "Sharing Databases with Microsoft Access 1.x, 2.0, or 95" later in this chapter.

If your database contains Access Basic or Visual Basic for Applications code, you must fully compile your database before you convert it. Depending on the version of Microsoft Access you are converting from, open a module in Microsoft Access and on the **Run** menu, click the command shown in the following table.

If you are running this version of Microsoft Access	Click this command on the Run menu
1.x	**Compile All**
2.0	**Compile Loaded Modules**
95	**Compile All Modules**

Important Before you convert the database, make a backup copy. If you are converting a database with linked (attached) tables, make sure these tables are in the folder referred to by the database you are converting. Finally, close the database before you convert it; if the database is located on a server or in a shared folder, make sure no other user has it open.

▶ **To convert a database**

1   Start Microsoft Access 97, and in the **Startup** dialog box, click **Cancel**.
2   On the **Tools** menu, point to **Database Utilities**, and then click **Convert Database**.
3   In the **Database to Convert From** dialog box, select the database you want to convert, and then click **Convert**.
4   In the **Convert Database Into** dialog box, type a new name (without the MDB extension) for the Microsoft Access 97 database file, or select a different location if you want to keep the same name, and then click **Save**.

If you are converting a secured database, you must take additional steps. For more information, see "Converting a Database Secured with a Database Password" and "Converting a Database Secured with User-level Security" later in this section.

Why won't my database convert?

A Microsoft Access 97 table can contain up to 32 indexes. Very complex tables that are a part of many relationships may exceed the index limit, so you cannot convert the database that contains these tables. Microsoft Access 97 creates indexes on both sides of relationships between tables. If your database does not convert, open it in the version it was created with, delete some relationships, and then try converting the database again.

Under some circumstances, when a database from a previous version of Microsoft Access has a large number of database objects, Microsoft Access 97 may not be able to complete the conversion process. You may be able to resolve this problem by creating a new, blank database in Microsoft Access 97, and then importing the objects from the older version database in groups until all of the objects have been imported.

Additionally, Visual Basic has a limit of 1,082 modules per database. Forms and reports each contain one module. If you receive an "Out of Memory" message when converting a large database, reduce the number of objects in your database or consider dividing your application into multiple databases. If you have modules with a large amount of code, consider using library databases to store the code. For more information about library databases, see Microsoft Access online Help.

Converting Unbound Object Frame Controls to Image Controls

When you convert a database, you have the option to convert unbound object frame controls in forms and reports to image controls. This speeds up the opening of forms and reports, although the object displayed in the image control cannot be edited by double-clicking the control.

▶ **To convert unbound object frame controls to image controls when you convert a database**

1. On the **Database Utilities** menu, click **Convert Databases**.
2. In the **Database to Convert From** dialog box, select the **Convert OLE** check box.

You can also convert an unbound object frame to an image control after converting the database.

▶ **To convert unbound object frame controls to image controls after you convert a database**

- On the **Tools** menu, point to **Analyze**, and then click **Performance** to starts the Performance Analyzer.

  –or–

  Open the form or report in Design view, right-click the control, point to **Change To**, and then click **Image**.

Converting a Database Secured with a Database Password

If a database has been secured by using a database password in Microsoft Access 95, you must supply the password before you can convert the database. If this is the only form of security used with the database, then it is the only requirement to convert the database.

Converting a Database Secured with User-level Security

The *workgroup information file* is a database that stores the user names, passwords, and group accounts for a workgroup. In Microsoft Access 1.*x* and 2.0, this file is called a *workgroup* or *system database*. Users of Microsoft Access 97 can use workgroup information files and secure databases from previous versions of Microsoft Access. However, users of a previous version of Microsoft Access cannot use workgroup information files or databases in Microsoft Access 97 format.

If a member of your workgroup who is not upgrading to Microsoft Access 97 shares databases secured with user-level security, then have all Microsoft Access 97 users in the workgroup join the workgroup information file that was created in the older version. Do not convert any databases shared by all users of the workgroup. For information about how you can share databases across versions, see "Sharing Databases with Microsoft Access 1.x, 2.0, or 95" later in this chapter.

If all members of a secure workgroup defined in a previous version of Microsoft Access are upgrading to Microsoft Access 97, convert all databases used by that workgroup. To convert a database that has been secured in a previous version of Microsoft Access with user-level security, you must do the following:

- Join the workgroup information file that defines the user accounts used to gain access to the database or that was in use when the database was created.
- For the conversion, log on as a member of a user group, such as Admins, with the following permissions:
  - Open/Run and Open Exclusive permissions for the database
  - Modify Design or Administer permissions for all tables in the database, or ownership of all tables in the database
  - Read Design permission for all of the objects in the database

If you are upgrading from Microsoft Access 1.x or 2.0, after you convert a database secured with user-level security, recreate the workgroup information file used with it. For more information, see "Recreating Microsoft Access 1.x or 2.0 Workgroup Information Files" later in this section.

Note If you are upgrading from Microsoft Access 95, use the workgroup information file from Microsoft Access 95, but compact it with Microsoft Access 97 before using it. For information about compacting a workgroup information file, see Microsoft Access online Help.

Joining the Original Workgroup Information File

The Office Setup program creates a new workgroup information file named System.mdw in the System folder (Windows 95) or the System32 folder (Windows NT Workstation 3.51 or later), and specifies that file as your current workgroup information file. If, before upgrading, you are a member of a secure workgroup, you must join your original workgroup information file after upgrading to open or convert secured databases.

▶ **To join a workgroup information file from a previous version of Microsoft Access**

1. In the System folder (Windows 95) or System32 folder (Windows NT Workstation 3.51 or later), double-click Wrkgadm.exe.
2. In the **Workgroup Administrator** dialog box, click **Join**.
3. In the **Database** box, enter the name of the workgroup information file you want to join.

In Windows 95 and Windows NT Workstation 4.0, you can also click **Run** on the Windows **Start** menu, and type **msaccess.exe /wrkgrp** *file name* to join the workgroup information file.

Note You can automatically join a workgroup information file every time you start Microsoft Access 97, using the **/wrkgrp** command-line option. For information about using command-line options, see Microsoft Access online Help.

For more information about the user-level security model, see Chapter 29, "Workgroup Features in Microsoft Access."

Recreating Microsoft Access 1.x and 2.0 Workgroup Information Files

If all members of a secure workgroup from Microsoft Access 1.x or 2.0 are upgrading to Microsoft Access 97, recreate their workgroup information file in Microsoft Access 97 format before they need to use it. Although Microsoft Access 97 can use workgroup information files from a previous version, additional memory is required to do so. Additionally, when users upgrade to the new workgroup information file, they can all view their group memberships.

The following procedures show how to recreate a workgroup information file in Microsoft Access 97 format. To complete this task, you must know the exact, case-sensitive user names, group names, and personal IDs used to create the accounts in the workgroup. You must also know the exact, case-sensitive name, company name, and workgroup ID used to create the original file.

Note If you do not have the information to recreate the workgroup information file, continue to use the previous version; however, only members of the Admins group can view group memberships.

▶ **To create the new workgroup information file in Microsoft Access 97**

1. In Windows Explorer (Windows 95 or Windows NT Workstation 4.0) or File Manager (Windows NT Workstation 3.51), double-click Wrkgadm.exe in the System folder (for Windows 95) or the System32 folder (for Windows NT Workstation 3.51 or later).
2. In the **Workgroup Administrator** dialog box, click **Create**.
3. In the **Workgroup Owner Information** dialog box, enter the exact, case-sensitive name, company name, and workgroup ID used to create the original file.

   If you fail to enter the exact entries used to create the original file, an invalid Admins group is created.

After you have created a new workgroup information file with the original Admins group, you must recreate any user and group accounts.

Chapter 11   Upgrading from Previous Versions of Microsoft Access

▶ **To recreate the user and group accounts for a workgroup information file**

1. On the Microsoft Access **Tools** menu, point to **Security**, and then click **User and Group Accounts**.
2. To recreate any group accounts, click the **Groups** tab, and then click **New**; type the exact, case-sensitive group names and personal IDs and click **OK**.
3. To recreate previous user accounts, click the **Users** tab, and then click **New**; type the exact, case-sensitive user names and personal IDs and click **OK**.
4. In the **User and Group Accounts** dialog box, click **Add** to add users to the appropriate groups, and click **Remove** to remove the Admin user from the Admins group.
5. Click the **Change Logon Password** tab, and define a password for the Admin user.
6. Close the **User and Group Accounts** dialog box and exit Microsoft Access; then restart and log on as a member of the Admins group.
7. On the **Tools** menu, point to **Security**, and then click **User and Group Accounts** to define a password for this account.

When you finish these procedures, the user and group accounts are recreated. The only passwords defined so far are the ones you defined in Steps 5 and 7. You may want to define passwords for other accounts, or users can log on and define their own passwords. As long as you entered the exact, case-sensitive name, company name, and workgroup ID when creating the new file, and the exact, case-sensitive names and personal IDs when setting up the new accounts, all user and group accounts have the same permissions as the accounts in the workgroup information file from the previous version of Microsoft Access.

Note   In Microsoft Access 95 and 97, new workgroup information files have an .mdw extension by default. In previous versions, workgroup information files have an .mda extension. The .mdw extension uniquely identifies workgroup information files and prevents them from appearing in dialog boxes for library database (MDA) files. However, you can use the Workgroup Administrator to join or create workgroup information files with .mda extensions.

Converting a Replicated Database

You cannot convert a replicated database from Microsoft Access directly. Instead, synchronize it with a converted Design Master. A *Design Master* is the first replica in a replica set to which system tables, system fields, and replication properties have been added. You can make changes to the database structure through the Design Master only. In a replica set, any replica can be the Design Master, but only one at a time.

For the conversion to work, all members of the replica set must be accessed from computers with Microsoft Access 97 installed. Also, the Design Master must have been opened in Microsoft Access 95 at least once after it was created before you can convert it. If the Design Master was not opened after it is created, and you try to convert it in Microsoft Access 97, a message displays. In this case, you must open the Design Master in Microsoft Access 95 before you can continue. If you want to use a single computer for the conversion, it must be running both Microsoft Access 95 and 97. For information about running these two versions of Microsoft Access on the same computer, see "Running Multiple Versions of Microsoft Access on a Single Computer" in Chapter 22, "Supporting Multiple Versions of Microsoft Office."

Note You can allow a Microsoft Access 95 replica to run in Microsoft Access 97 without conversion through a process called *enabling*. However, if you open an enabled Microsoft Access 95 replica in Microsoft Access 97 and the replica has not yet been synchronized, Microsoft Access warns you that there is a synchronization pending that cannot occur until the replica is opened and synchronized in Microsoft Access 95. For more information about enabling databases, see "Enabling a Database" later in this chapter.

It is best to take a conservative approach when converting a replica set. The following procedure allows you to test a temporary second replica set before committing your original set to the conversion.

Caution It is important that you do not synchronize the test Design Master and replicas with members of your working replica set. Otherwise, unintended changes to the data or structure of your working replica set may occur.

▶ **To convert a replica set**

1 Make a copy of the current Design Master (created in Microsoft Access 95), and put the copy on a different computer or isolate it completely from any other members of the replica set.

2 In Microsoft Access 95, make the isolated copy the new Design Master by pointing to **Replication** on the **Tools** menu, and then clicking **Recover Design Master**.

3 Create some replicas based on the new Design Master.

4 In Microsoft Access 97, point to **Database Utilities** on the **Tools** menu, and then click **Convert Database** to convert the new Design Master to a Microsoft Access 97 database.

5 On the **Tools** menu, point to **Replication**, and then click **Synchronize Now** to synchronize the new Design Master with the newly created replicas.

6 Run any tests you would like to try.

   If you want to change some objects, you can either make the changes again in the original Design Master after it is converted, or keep the copy and import the changed objects from it.

7 Once you are satisfied that the copy works, delete the new Design Master and all of its replicas. Make sure that all users who open the Design Master and replica databases have installed Microsoft Access 97.

8 Convert the original Design Master to Microsoft Access 97, and then synchronize it with the original replicas.

Important You cannot open synchronized replicas again in Microsoft Access 95. Once you open the replicas in Microsoft Access 97, they are irrevocably converted.

Working with Microsoft Access 1.x and 2.0 Databases with Attached ODBC Tables

Microsoft Access 97 can convert or enable Microsoft Access 1.x and 2.0 databases that have attached (*linked*) tables. However, Microsoft Access 97 cannot open linked tables that refer to Open Database Connectivity (ODBC) sources which use a 16-bit ODBC driver manager and driver. For example, if a Microsoft Access 1.x or 2.0 database refers to an ODBC data source, such as an SQL Server table, the linked table's data source name (DSN) uses the 16-bit version of the ODBC driver manager (Odbc.dll) and the corresponding driver, such as the 16-bit Microsoft SQL Server ODBC driver (Sqlsrvr.dll).

Microsoft Access 97 can open only linked ODBC data sources that use the 32-bit versions of the ODBC driver manager (Odbc32.dll) and the appropriate ODBC driver, such as the 32-bit version of Microsoft SQL Server ODBC driver (Sqlsrv32.dll).

When Microsoft Access 97 converts or enables a Microsoft Access 1.x or 2.0 database with linked ODBC tables, it cannot automatically create new DSNs that use the 32-bit versions of the ODBC driver manager and ODBC driver. When you convert or enable such a database, if you try to open the table or a form that uses the table for its record source, Microsoft Access displays the message, "ODBC connection to *datasourcename* failed." When you close this message, Microsoft Access 97 displays another message indicating that it cannot open the table or form.

To correct this problem, you must first make sure that the 32-bit versions of the ODBC driver manager and the appropriate driver are installed, and then create a new, identically named DSN for each ODBC data source that is linked to the original database.

ODBC drivers are not installed when you choose a Typical installation during Setup. To install the 32-bit version of the Microsoft SQL Server ODBC Driver, rerun the Setup and click **Add/Remove**. Under the **Microsoft Access** option, select **Data Access**, select **Database Drivers**, and then select the **Microsoft SQL Server Driver** option.

Note If the original database does not use the Microsoft SQL Server ODBC Driver, you must contact the vendor of the driver to obtain a 32-bit version of the driver.

After the appropriate driver is installed, create a new, identically named DSN for each ODBC data source that is linked to the original database.

Note In the following procedure, if the 32bit ODBC icon is not available in Control Panel, rerun Setup and install the Microsoft SQL Server ODBC Driver as described earlier. Installing the Microsoft SQL Server ODBC Driver also installs the 32-bit version of the ODBC driver manager and other ODBC support files.

▶ **To create a new, identically named 32-bit DSN**

1. In Control Panel, double-click the 32bit ODBC icon.
2. In the **ODBC Data Source Administrator** dialog box, click the appropriate **DSN** tab.

   For information about using the **User DSN**, **System DSN**, and **File DSN** tabs, click **Help**.
3. Click **Add**.
4. In the **Create New Data Source** panel, select the appropriate driver, and then click **Finish**.
5. In the **ODBC Microsoft Access 97 Setup** dialog box, enter values identical to the original DSN.

   For example, for Microsoft SQL Server you must define the **Data Source Name** and **Server**. You may also need to click **Options** and define additional values, such as the **Database Name**.

If you do not know the original name of the DSN, open the original database in the version of Microsoft Access in which it was created, open the linked table in Design view, and then display the **Table Properties** sheet. The **Description** property contains the definition for the ODBC connection string. The parameter following **DSN=** in the connection string is the name of the DSN. To view the rest of the DSN definition, open Control Panel and double-click the ODBC icon (not the 32bit ODBC icon). In the **Data Source (Driver)** box, click the name of the DSN, and then click **Setup** to view the definition of the DSN.

For more information about enabling a database, see "Enabling a Database" later in this chapter.

Upgrading from Microsoft Access 95

This section describes the differences between Microsoft Access 95 and Microsoft Access 97. Microsoft Access 97 is a major upgrade from previous versions of the application. For more information about the features and benefits of this upgrade, see Chapter 2, "What's New in Microsoft Office 97."

What happens to my old Microsoft Access databases when I convert them to Microsoft Access 97 format? You can open databases created in Microsoft Access 95 directly in Microsoft Access 97, even if you do not convert the database through a process called *enabling*. Once you convert a Microsoft Access 95 database to Microsoft Access 97 format, you cannot open it in Microsoft Access 95, and it cannot be converted back to Microsoft Access 95 format.

Can I share Microsoft Access 97 databases with users of previous versions of Microsoft Access? If your workgroup is using a combination of Microsoft Access 97 and 95, users can share data and databases. However, not all Microsoft Access 97 features are supported in previous versions.

Do my old macros still work in Microsoft Access 97? In most cases, macros created in Microsoft Access 95 run in Microsoft Access 97. If you convert or enable a Microsoft Access 95 database containing macros in Microsoft Access 97, the macros run in Microsoft Access 97.

Does my old Visual Basic application code still work in Microsoft Access 97? In most cases, Visual Basic code created in Microsoft Access 95 runs in Microsoft Access 97. If you convert a Microsoft Access 95 database to Microsoft Access 97, the Visual Basic code is converted to equivalent Visual Basic code that runs in Microsoft Access 97. If you enable a Microsoft Access 95 database in Microsoft Access 97, a copy of the Visual Basic code is converted to equivalent Visual Basic code that runs in Microsoft Access 97; your original code is not altered.

Menu Changes

The following sections summarize the Microsoft Access 95 commands that have changed location or functionality in Microsoft Access 97, as well as commands that are new in Microsoft Access 97.

File Menu

The following table describes changed commands on the **File** menu.

This Microsoft Access 95 command	Changes to this in Microsoft Access 97
Toolbars (when no database is open)	Moved to the **View** menu.
Unhide (when no database is open)	Moved to the **Window** menu.

The following table lists new commands that have been added to the **File** menu.

This Microsoft Access 97 command	Allows you to
Save As HTML	Save tables, queries, forms, and reports so that they can be read by a World Wide Web browser. For more information about Microsoft Access 97 Internet features, see Chapter 25, "Web Support in Microsoft Office Applications."

Edit Menu

The following table lists new commands that have been added to the **Edit** menu.

This Microsoft Access 97 command	Allows you to
Paste As Hyperlink	Paste and format the Clipboard contents as a hyperlink. You must then edit the hyperlink using the **Hyperlink** command (**Insert** menu) to specify a file or URL to which the selected item is to be linked. For more information about Microsoft Access 97 Internet features, see Chapter 25, "Web Support in Microsoft Office Applications."
List Properties/Methods	Display all properties and methods for the statement containing the insertion point in the Module window.
List Constants	Display all constants for the statement containing the insertion point in the Module window.
Quick Info	Display syntax information for the variable, constant, or procedure at the insertion point in the Module window.
Parameter Info	Display all parameters for the statement containing the insertion point in the Module window.
Complete Word	Complete the typing of a property, method, or constant word fragment in the Module window. Use to display all possible choices if a word fragment is not unique.
Bookmarks submenu commands	Add, delete, and move between bookmarks in the Module window. Use bookmarks for designating important lines of code in long modules.

View Menu

The following table describes changed commands on the **View** menu.

This Microsoft Access 95 command	Changes to this in Microsoft Access 97
Toolbars	Replaced by **Toolbars** submenu.
1, 2, 4, 8, 12 (**Pages** submenu in Print Preview)	Renamed **One Page**, **Two Pages**, **Four Pages**, **Eight Pages**, **Twelve Pages**.
Procedure Definition (in the Module window)	Renamed **Definition**.

The following table lists new commands that have been added to the **View** menu.

This Microsoft Access 97 command	Allows you to
Toolbars submenu commands	Display and hide toolbars. Includes the new **Customize** command for creating and customizing toolbars and menu bars.

Insert Menu

The following table describes changed commands on the **Insert** menu.

This Microsoft Access 95 command	Changes to this in Microsoft Access 97
Custom Control (in form and report Design view)	Renamed **ActiveX Control**.
Field (in table Design view)	Renamed **Rows**.
Record (in query Datasheet view)	Renamed **New Record**.
Row (in query and macro Design view)	Renamed **Rows**.
Column (in query Design view)	Renamed **Columns**.

The following table lists new commands that have been added to the **Insert** menu.

This Microsoft Access 97 command	Allows you to
Hyperlink	Insert a Web-style hyperlink to another Office document. In Datasheet and Form views, a hyperlink column must be selected. For more information about hyperlinks, see Chapter 24, "Integrating Microsoft Office with Your Intranet."
Tab Control Page (in form Design view)	Insert a new page to the right of existing pages on a tab control and place it first in the page order sequence.
Hyperlink Column (in table Datasheet view)	Create a new column (field) and set its data type to **Hyperlink**. Use hyperlink columns to store and go to hyperlink addresses.
Class Module (in the Module window)	Insert a class module that is not associated with a form or report into the current database and display its **Declarations** section.

Run Menu

The following table describes changed commands on the **Run** menu.

This Microsoft Access 95 command	Changes to this in Microsoft Access 97
Continue	Renamed **Go/Continue**.
Step Into	Moved to the **Debug** menu.
Step Over	Moved to the **Debug** menu.

This Microsoft Access 95 command	Changes to this in Microsoft Access 97
Step To Cursor	Renamed **Run To Cursor** and moved to the **Debug** menu.
Toggle Breakpoint	Moved to the **Debug** menu.
Clear All Breakpoints	Moved to the **Debug** menu.
Set Next Statement	Moved to the **Debug** menu.
Show Next Statement	Moved to the **Debug** menu.
Compile Loaded Modules	Moved to the **Debug** menu.
Compile All Modules	Moved to the **Debug** menu.

Debug Menu

The **Debug** menu is new in Microsoft Access 97. It contains many commands that were on the **Run** and **Tools** menus in Microsoft Access 95. In addition, the following table lists new commands that have been added to the **Debug** menu.

This Microsoft Access 97 command	Allows you to
Step Out	Run all lines of code and nested procedures in Break mode, beginning with the current executable statement, and then return execution to the preceding procedure in the call tree. Use to avoid stepping through each line of code that calls multiple nested procedures.
Compile and Save All Modules	Compile and save all modules in the database in a single operation.

Tools Menu

The following table describes changed commands on the **Tools** menu.

This Microsoft Access 95 command	Changes to this in Microsoft Access 97
Custom Controls	Renamed **ActiveX Controls**.
Merge It (**Office Links** submenu)	Renamed **Merge It With MS Word**.
Documentor (**Analyze** submenu)	Renamed **Documenter**.
Calls	Renamed **Call Stack** and moved to the **View** menu.
Add Watch	Moved to the **Debug** menu.
Edit Watch	Moved to the **Debug** menu.
Instant Watch	Renamed **Quick Watch** and moved to the **Debug** menu.
Macro	Renamed **Run Macro** and moved to the **Macro** submenu (in the Database window).

The following table lists new commands that have been added to the **Tools** menu.

This Microsoft Access 97 command	Allows you to
Make MDE File (Database Utilities submenu)	Copy a database to an MDE database format. Use to secure Visual Basic source code by removing it, and prevent users from modifying forms, reports, and modules. For more information about MDE databases, see Chapter 29, "Workgroup Features in Microsoft Access."
Macro submenu commands (in the Database window)	Create, run, and manage macros; convert macros to Visual Basic, and create a new Microsoft Access 97-style menu bar, toolbar, or shortcut menu from a macro.

Window Menu

The following table describes changed commands on the **Window** menu.

This Microsoft Access 95 command	Changes to this in Microsoft Access 97
Split Window (in module Design view)	Renamed **Split**.

Help Menu

The following table describes changed commands on the **Help** menu.

This Microsoft Access 95 command	Changes to this in Microsoft Access 97
Microsoft Access Help Topics	Renamed **Microsoft Access Help**. This command displays the Office Assistant, through which you view Help.
Answer Wizard	Removed. Use the Assistant to gain access to the Answer Wizard feature.

The following table lists new commands that have been added to the **Help** menu.

This Microsoft Access 97 command	Allows you to
Contents and Index	Display Microsoft Access Help.
What's This?	Click any area of the screen (such as a toolbar or menu command) to see a brief explanation in a ScreenTip.
Microsoft on the Web submenu commands	Connect to the Microsoft home page on the Web (requires Internet access).

File Format Changes

The format of Microsoft Access tables is the same in Microsoft Access 95 and 97. This means that you can:

- Import a Microsoft Access 97 table into a Microsoft Access 95 database.
- Link a Microsoft Access 97 table to a Microsoft Access 95 database.
- Export a Microsoft Access 97 table to a Microsoft Access 95 database.
- Cut, copy, and paste from a Microsoft Access 97 table to a Microsoft Access 95 table.

Note When you export or import Microsoft 97 tables into Microsoft Access 95, fields with the **Hyperlink** data type are converted to fields with the **Memo** data type and their hyperlink functionality is lost.

The format of database objects other than tables is different in Microsoft Access 97. You cannot import, link, export, cut, copy, or paste these Microsoft Access 97 database objects to Microsoft Access 95.

> **Using the Same Table in Microsoft Access 95 and 97**
> The fact that tables share the same format in Microsoft Access 95 and 97 is useful if you have front-end and back-end databases that must be shared by users of both versions. Users of both Microsoft Access 97 and Microsoft Access 95 can open tables in the back-end database that are in either version. For more information about front-end and back-end databases, see "Creating a Front-end Database Linked to Table Data in a Previous Version Back-end Database" later in this chapter.

If your workgroup is upgrading gradually to Microsoft Access 97, Microsoft Access 97 users may have to share databases with Microsoft Access 95 users. Microsoft Access supports several strategies for sharing databases between different versions. For more information about changes in file format and strategies for sharing databases, see "Sharing Databases with Microsoft Access 1.x, 2.0, or 95" later in this chapter.

Template Changes

The Microsoft Access 97 Report Wizard, Form Wizard, and the **AutoFormat** command (**Format** menu) provide formatting features that are similar to Microsoft Word and Microsoft Excel AutoFormats and templates. The Microsoft Access 97 Database Wizard is similar to a template in that it provides predefined choices that are used to create new databases. Microsoft Access 97 allows users to select from a number of other add-ins and wizards, which also function like templates by providing predefined choices when creating a new table, query, and some properties and controls.

Previous versions of Microsoft Access allow users to customize wizards; however, these customized wizards cannot be converted to Microsoft Access 97 format. Any customization of Microsoft Access 97 wizards must be performed by using the commands available in the Microsoft Access 97 wizards.

To create a form or report without using a wizard, click **Form** or **Report** (**Insert** menu), and then click **Design New**. The template used when you create forms or reports this way is set by using the **Forms/Reports** tab in the **Options** dialog box (**Tools** menu). In order to use a template from previous versions of Microsoft Access, you must convert it to Microsoft Access 97 format.

Macro Changes

In most cases, macros defined in Microsoft Access 95 run in Microsoft Access 97 for both converted and enabled databases. However, changes to menus, commands, and other user interface elements may mean that some of your macros must be rewritten, particularly those that include the **SendKeys** or the **DoMenuItem** action.

SendKeys Action

A macro from a previous version of Microsoft Access that uses the **SendKeys** action does not function properly if the arguments refer to menu commands or dialog box options that have changed. For alternatives to using the **SendKeys** action, see "Using the SendKeys Statement or Action" later in this chapter.

DoMenuItem Action

In Microsoft Access 97, the **RunCommand** action replaces the **DoMenuItem** action, which is included in Microsoft Access 97 only for compatibility with previous versions. When you open and save a macro from a previous version of Microsoft Access that contains a **DoMenuItem** action, the action and its arguments are automatically converted to the equivalent **RunCommand** action. The **DoMenuItem** action no longer appears in the list of actions in the Macro window in Microsoft Access 97.

When you convert a database from a previous version of Microsoft Access, some commands may no longer be available. The command may have been renamed, moved to a different menu, or removed entirely. The **DoMenuItem** actions for such commands are converted to **RunCommand** actions with a blank **Command** argument. You must edit the macro and enter a valid **RunCommand** action, or delete the action.

When you enable a database from a previous version of Microsoft Access, the **DoMenuItem** action continues to work properly. **DoMenuItem** methods used in Visual Basic procedures are unchanged.

Visual Basic Code Changes

Microsoft Access 97 supports some new Visual Basic keywords, so you can no longer use these keywords as identifiers. These keywords are:

- **AddressOf**
- **Assert**
- **Decimal**
- **DefDec**
- **Enum**
- **Event**
- **Friend**
- **Implements**
- **RaiseEvent**
- **WithEvents**

For information about how these new keywords can affect converted or enabled databases, see "Identifiers with the Same Names as Visual Basic Keywords" later in this chapter.

New Toolbars, Menus, and Shortcut Menus

Microsoft Access 97 supports a new style of toolbars, menus, and shortcut menus. When you convert a database from a previous version of Microsoft Access to Microsoft Access 97, any custom toolbars are automatically converted to the new style.

Custom menus and shortcut menus created in a previous version of Microsoft Access are handled differently. Previous versions of Microsoft Access use the Menu Builder to create custom menus and shortcut menus. The Menu Builder generates a macro group containing macros that use the **AddMenu** and **DoMenuItem** actions. In previous versions of Microsoft Access, you can also create custom menus and shortcut menus manually (without the Menu Builder), using these macro actions. Custom menu and shortcut menu macros created using either method still run Microsoft Access 97, but they are not converted to the new style, nor are they available from the new **Customize** dialog box (**View** menu, **Toolbars** submenu).

To save a menu or shortcut menu from a previous version of Microsoft Access in Microsoft Access 97 format, select the macro group used to create the menu or shortcut menu in the Database window, and then click **Create Menu from Macro** or **Create Shortcut Menu from Macro** (**Tools** menu, **Macro** submenu). Unlike new custom menus or shortcut menus created with the **Customize** dialog box, these menus and shortcut menus depend on the macro group from the previous version of

Microsoft Access. If you delete this macro group or any macros it refers to, the menu or shortcut menu no longer works. Alternatively, you can use the **Customize** dialog box (**View** menu, **Toolbars** submenu) to recreate custom toolbars, menu bars, and shortcut menus.

Upgrading from Microsoft Access 2.0

This section describes the changes between Microsoft Access 2.0 and Microsoft Access 97. Microsoft Access 97 is a major upgrade from previous versions of the application. For more information about the features and benefits of this upgrade, see Chapter 2, "What's New in Microsoft Office 97."

What happens to my old Microsoft Access databases when I convert them to Microsoft Access 97 format? You can open databases created in Microsoft Access 2.0 directly in Microsoft Access 97, even if you do not convert the database. To do so, you must perform a process called *enabling*. Once you convert a Microsoft Access 2.0 database to Microsoft Access 97 format, you cannot open it in Microsoft Access 2.0, and it cannot be converted back to Microsoft Access 2.0 format.

Can I share Microsoft Access 97 databases with users of previous versions of Microsoft Access? If your workgroup is using a combination of Microsoft Access 97 and 2.0, users can share data and databases. However, not all Microsoft Access 97 features are supported in previous versions.

Do my old macros still work in Microsoft Access 97? In most cases, macros created in Microsoft Access 2.0 run in Microsoft Access 97. If you convert or enable a Microsoft Access 2.0 database containing macros in Microsoft Access 97, the macros run in Microsoft Access 97.

Does my old Access Basic application code still work in Microsoft Access 97? In most cases, Access Basic application code created in Microsoft Access 2.0 runs in Microsoft Access 97. If you convert a Microsoft Access 2.0 database to Microsoft Access 97, the Access Basic code is converted to equivalent Visual Basic code. If you enable a Microsoft Access 2.0 database in Microsoft Access 97, a copy of the Access Basic code is converted to equivalent Visual Basic code; your original code is not altered.

Menu Changes

The following sections summarize the Microsoft Access 2.0 commands that have changed location or functionality in Microsoft Access 97, as well as commands that are new in Microsoft Access 97.

File Menu

The following table describes changed commands on the **File** menu.

This Microsoft Access 2.0 command	Changes to this in Microsoft Access 97
Compact Database (when no database is open)	Moved to **Tools** menu (**Database Utilities** submenu).
Convert Database (when no database is open)	Moved to **Tools** menu (**Database Utilities** submenu).
Encrypt/Decrypt Database (when no database is open)	Moved to **Tools** menu (**Security** submenu).
Repair Database (when no database is open)	Moved to **Tools** menu (**Database Utilities** submenu).
Toolbars (when no database is open)	Moved to **View** menu.
Unhide (when no database is open)	Moved to **Window** menu.
Run Macro (when no database is open)	Moved to **Tools** menu (**Macro** submenu).
Add-ins (when no database is open)	Moved to **Tools** menu and is available only when a database is open.
Close Database	Renamed **Close**.
New submenu commands	Moved to **Insert** menu.
Rename	Moved to **Edit** menu.
Output To and **Export**	Consolidated in **Save As/Export**.
Import	Moved to **Get External Data** submenu.
Attach Table	Renamed **Link Tables** (**Get External Data** submenu).
Imp/Exp Setup	Removed. Click the **Advanced** button in the Import Text Wizard or Export Text Wizard to work with Import/Export specifications..
Print Setup	Renamed **Page Setup**.
Print Definition	Replaced by **Documenter** (**Tools** menu, **Analyze** submenu).
Save Layout (in the Relationships window)	Renamed **Save**.
Save As and **Output To** (in table and query Design view)	Consolidated in **Save As/Export**.
Save Table (in table Datasheet view)	Renamed **Save**.
Save Query (in query Datasheet view)	Renamed **Save**.
Save Form (in Form view and form Datasheet view)	Renamed **Save**.
Save Query As (in query Datasheet view)	Renamed **Save As/Export**.
Save Form As (in Form view and form Datasheet view)	Renamed **Save As/Export**.
Save Record (in Form and Datasheet view)	Moved to **Records** menu.

This Microsoft Access 2.0 command	Changes to this in Microsoft Access 97
Save As Report (in form Design view)	Removed. Right-click a form in the Database window to save a form as a report.
Sample Preview (in report Design view)	Renamed **Layout Preview** (**View** menu).
Load Text (in the Module window)	Replaced by **Import** (**Get External Data** submenu).
Save Text (in the Module window)	Renamed **Save As Text**.

The following table lists new commands that have been added to the **File** menu.

This Microsoft Access 97 command	Allows you to
Save As HTML	Save tables, queries, forms, and reports so that they can be read by a World Wide Web browser. For more information about Microsoft Access 97 Internet features, see Chapter 25, "Web Support in Microsoft Office Applications."

Edit Menu

The following table describes changed commands on the **Edit** menu.

This Microsoft Access 2.0 command	Changes to this in Microsoft Access 97
Relationships	Moved to **Tools** menu.
Insert Row (in table and query Design view)	Renamed **Rows** (**Insert** menu).
Set Primary Key (in table Design view)	Renamed **Primary Key**.
Undo All (in query Design view)	Removed.
Insert Column (in query Design view)	Renamed **Column** (**Insert** menu).
Undo Current Field (in table, query, and form Datasheet view)	Renamed **Undo Current Field/Record**.
Insert Object (in table, query, and form Datasheet view)	Renamed **Object** (**Insert** menu).
Links (in table, query, and form Datasheet view)	Renamed **OLE/DDE Links**.
Tab Order (in form and report Design view)	Moved to **View** menu.
Find Previous (in the Module window)	Removed. Use **Find** to search backwards.
New Procedure (in the Module window)	Renamed **Procedure** (**Insert** menu).

The following table lists new commands that have been added to the **Edit** menu.

This Microsoft Access 97 command	Allows you to
Create Shortcut	Create a shortcut for the selected object in the Database window so that you can quickly open it by clicking an icon.
Paste As Hyperlink	Paste and format the Clipboard contents as a hyperlink. Edit the hyperlink using the **Hyperlink** command (**Insert** menu) to specify a file or URL. For more information about hyperlinks, see Chapter 24, "Integrating Microsoft Office with Your Intranet."
Indent	Do the equivalent of pressing TAB in the Module window.
Outdent	Do the equivalent of pressing SHIFT+TAB in the Module window.

View Menu

The following table describes changed commands on the **View** menu.

This Microsoft Access 2.0 command	Changes to this in Microsoft Access 97
Tables	Moved to **Database Objects** submenu.
Queries	Moved to **Database Objects** submenu.
Forms	Moved to **Database Objects** submenu.
Reports	Moved to **Database Objects** submenu.
Macros	Moved to **Database Objects** submenu.
Modules	Moved to **Database Objects** submenu.
Table Properties (in table Design view)	Renamed **Properties**.
Palette (in form and report Design view)	Removed. Use the **Formatting** toolbar to perform palette functions.
Control Wizards (in form and report Design view)	Functionality moved to the **Control Wizards** button (**Toolbox** toolbar).
Split Window (in the Module window)	Renamed **Split** (**Window** menu).
Procedures (in the Module window)	Replaced by **Object Browser**.
Next Procedure (in the Module window)	Removed.
Previous Procedure (in the Module window)	Removed.
Immediate Window (in the Module window)	Renamed **Debug Window**.
Calls (in the Module window)	Renamed **Call Stack**.
Toolbars	Moved to the **Toolbars** submenu.

The following table lists new commands that have been added to the **View** menu.

This Microsoft Access 97 command	Allows you to
Pages submenu commands (in layout preview or print preview)	Display 1, 2, 4, 8, or 12 pages in progressively smaller thumbnail views.
Definition	Display the procedure code of the procedure name at the insertion point in the Module window. If the procedure is defined in a DLL, Microsoft Access displays the **Declare** statement used to define the DLL entry point.
Customize (**Toolbars** submenu)	Display and hide toolbars, and create and customize toolbars and menu bars.

Insert Menu

The **Insert** menu is new in Microsoft Access 97. It contains many commands that were on other menus in Microsoft Access 2.0. In addition, the following table lists new commands that have been added to the **Insert** menu.

This Microsoft Access 97 command	Allows you to
ActiveX Control	Add an ActiveX control (formerly a custom control or OLE control) to a form or report. ActiveX controls are stored as separate files and must be entered in the Windows registry.
Hyperlink	Insert a Web-style hyperlink to another Office document. In Datasheet and Form views, a hyperlink column must be selected. For more information about hyperlinks, see Chapter 24, "Integrating Microsoft Office with Your Intranet."
Tab Control Page (in form Design view)	Insert a new page to the right of existing pages on a tab control and place it first in the page order sequence.
Hyperlink Column (in table Datasheet view)	Create a new column (field) and set its data type to **Hyperlink**. Use hyperlink columns to store and go to hyperlink addresses.
Class Module (in the Module window)	Insert a class module that is not associated with a form or report into the current database and display its **Declarations** section.
AutoForm	Automatically create a form for the table or query selected in the Database window.
AutoReport	Automatically create a report for the table or query selected in the Database window.

Tools Menu

The **Tools** menu is new in Microsoft Access 97. It contains many commands that were on other menus in Microsoft Access 2.0. In addition, the following table lists new commands that have been added to the **Tools** menu.

This Microsoft Access 97 command	Allows you to
Make MDE File (**Database Utilities** submenu)	Copy a database to an MDE database format. Use to secure Visual Basic source code by removing it, and prevent users from modifying forms, reports, and modules. For more information about MDE databases, see Chapter 29, "Workgroup Features in Microsoft Access."
Macro submenu commands (in the Database window)	Create, run, and manage macros; convert macros to Visual Basic, and create Microsoft Access 97 style menu bars, toolbars, and shortcut menus from macros.

Relationships Menu

The following table describes changed commands on the **Relationships** menu.

This Microsoft Access 2.0 command	Changes to this in Microsoft Access 97
Add Table	Renamed **Show Table**.
Remove Table	Replaced by **Hide Table**.
Create Relationship	Removed.

Query Menu

The following table describes changed commands on the **Query** menu.

This Microsoft Access 2.0 command	Changes to this in Microsoft Access 97
Add Table	Renamed **Show Table**.
Join Table	Removed.

Format Menu

The following table describes changed commands on the **Format** menu.

This Microsoft Access 2.0 command	Changes to this in Microsoft Access 97
Gridlines (in Datasheet view)	Removed. Use the **Cells** command to format gridlines.
Apply Default (in form Design view)	Replaced by **AutoFormat**.
Change Default	Renamed **Set Control Defaults**.
Page Header/Footer	Moved to **View** menu.
Form Header/Footer	Moved to **View** menu.

Records Menu

The following table describes changed commands on the **Records** menu.

This Microsoft Access 2.0 command	Changes to this in Microsoft Access 97
Go To	Moved to **Edit** menu.
Quick Sort	Renamed **Sort**.
Edit Filter/Sort	Renamed **Filter**.
Allow Editing	Removed.

Macro Menu

The **Macro** menu in module Design view has been renamed the **Run** menu.

Run Menu

The following table describes changed commands on the **Run** menu. (In Microsoft Access 2.0, these commands appear on the **Macro** menu in module Design view.)

This Microsoft Access 2.0 command	Changes to this in Microsoft Access 97
Compile Loaded Modules	Renamed **Compile All Modules** (**Debug** menu).
Continue	Renamed **Go/Continue**.
Step Into	Moved to **Debug** menu.
Step Over	Moved to **Debug** menu.
Set Next Statement	Moved to **Debug** menu.
Show Next Statement	Moved to **Debug** menu.
Toggle Breakpoint	Moved to **Debug** menu.
Clear All Breakpoints	Moved to **Debug** menu.
Modify Command$	Removed.

Debug Menu

The **Debug** menu is new Microsoft Access 97. It contains many commands that were on the **Run** menu in Microsoft Access 2.0. In addition, the following table lists new commands that have been added to the **Debug** menu.

This Microsoft Access 97 command	Allows you to
Step Out	Run all lines of code and nested procedures in Break mode, beginning with the current executable statement, and then return execution to the preceding procedure in the call tree. Use to avoid stepping through each line of code that calls multiple nested procedures.
Compile and Save All Modules	Compile and save all modules in the database in a single operation.

Window Menu

The following table describes changed commands on the **Window** menu.

This Microsoft Access 2.0 command	Changes to this in Microsoft Access 97
Tile	Replaced by **Tile Horizontally** and **Tile Vertically**.

Help Menu

The following table describes changed commands on the **Help** menu.

This Microsoft Access 2.0 command	Changes to this in Microsoft Access 97
Contents	Renamed **Contents and Index**.
Search and Cue Cards	Removed. **Use Microsoft Access Help** to display the Office Assistant, through which you view Help.
Technical Support	Functionality moved to the **Tech Support** button in the **About Microsoft Access** dialog box.

The following table lists new commands that have been added to the **Help** menu.

This Microsoft Access 97 command	Allows you to
Contents and Index	Display the Microsoft Access Help.
What's This?	Click any area of the screen (such as a toolbar or menu command) to see a brief explanation in a ScreenTip.
Microsoft on the Web submenu commands	Connect to the Microsoft home page on the Web (requires Internet access).

File Format Changes

The format of Microsoft Access 97 databases and the database objects within them is different from Microsoft Access 2.0 databases and objects. You cannot import, link (attach), export, cut, copy, or paste from Microsoft Access 97 database objects to Microsoft Access 2.0. However, you can do the following:

- Import Microsoft Access 2.0 database objects into Microsoft Access 97.
- Link (attach) Microsoft Access 2.0 tables in a Microsoft Access 97 database.
- Export a Microsoft Access 97 table to a Microsoft Access 2.0 database.

  Note When you export tables to Microsoft Access 2.0, fields with the **Hyperlink** data type are converted to fields with the **Memo** data type and hyperlink functionality is lost. Functionality of fields with the following property settings is lost:

- **Lookup** property settings
- **AutoNumber** data type with the **FieldSize** property set to **ReplicationID**
- **AutoNumber** data type with the **NewValues** property set to **Random**

If your workgroup is upgrading gradually to Microsoft Access 97, Microsoft Access 97 users may have to share databases with Microsoft Access 2.0 users. Microsoft Access supports several strategies for sharing databases between different versions. For more information about changes in file format and strategies for sharing databases, see "Sharing Databases with Microsoft Access 1.x, 2.0, or 95" later in this chapter.

Template Changes

The Microsoft Access 97 Report Wizard, Form Wizard, and the **AutoFormat** command (**Format** menu) provide formatting features that are similar to Microsoft Word and Microsoft Excel AutoFormats and templates. The Microsoft Access 97 Database Wizard is similar to a template in that it provides predefined choices that are used to create new databases. Microsoft Access 97 allows users to select from a number of other add-ins and wizards, which also function like templates by providing predefined choices when creating a new table, query, and some properties and controls.

Note Previous versions of Microsoft Access allow users to customize wizards; however, these customized wizards cannot be converted to Microsoft Access 97 format.

To create a form or report without using a wizard, click **Form** or **Report** (**Insert** menu), and then click **Design New**. The template used when you create forms or reports this way is set by clicking the **Forms/Reports** tab in the **Options** dialog box (**Tools** menu). In order to use a template from previous versions of Microsoft Access, you must convert it to Microsoft Access 97 format.

Macro Changes

In most cases, macros defined in Microsoft Access 2.0 run in Microsoft Access 97 for both converted and enabled databases. However, changes to menus, commands, and other user interface elements may mean that some of your macros must be rewritten, particularly those that include the **SendKeys** action. In addition, some macro actions work differently in Microsoft Access 97 than in Microsoft Access 1.x and 2.0. This section explains these differences.

Using the SendKeys Statement or Action

If you are converting a Microsoft Access 1.x or 2.0 database to Microsoft Access 97, changes in some dialog boxes and menus may require you to recode the **SendKeys** statement or **SendKeys** action. For example, the **Add-ins** submenu has been moved from the **File** menu to the **Tools** menu, and the previous **Import** and **Attach** commands on the **File** menu have moved to the **Get External Data** submenu. Because changes like this are likely to occur for each new version of Microsoft Access, avoid using the **SendKeys** statement or action to carry out commands or fill in dialog boxes wherever possible.

If you must use the **SendKeys** statement or action, consider the following guidelines:

- Before you use the **SendKeys** statement or action to carry out a menu command, check for an equivalent macro action or Visual Basic method.

  Most commands that are commonly carried out by a menu command or option have an equivalent action or method. For example, you can now use the **Dropdown** method of a combo box rather than the code `SendKeys "{F4}"`.

- If a menu command does not have an equivalent action or method, use the **RunCommand** action rather than the **SendKeys** statement or action.

- Avoid using the **SendKeys** statement or action to set options in the **Options** dialog box.

  New versions of Microsoft Access are likely to have new and changed options, so the code in your **SendKeys** statement or action could easily break. Instead, use the **GetOption** and **SetOption** methods.

- When you use the **SendKeys** statement to carry out an action, consider referencing the built-in key code constants. You can view built-in key code constants by opening the Module window and pressing F2 to display the **Object Browser**. Key code constants are displayed as members of the **Constants** class in the Access type library. Alternatively, you can declare constants for the values in your **SendKeys** statement.

  Defining your keystrokes as constants makes updating your code easier in the future.

- Do not enclose the **Keystroke** argument in quotation marks.

  In Microsoft Access 2.0, you can enclose the **Keystrokes** argument of the **SendKeys** action in quotation marks, but it is not required. If you enclose this argument in quotation marks in subsequent versions of Microsoft Access, however, an error occurs. To use quotation marks in the **Keystrokes** argument, you must type two sets of quotation marks, as in **Michael ""Mick"" Suyama**.

Using the DoCmd Object

To carry out macro actions from code in Microsoft Access 97, use the **DoCmd** object and its methods. This object replaces the **DoCmd** statement that you used in Microsoft Access 1.*x* and 2.0 to carry out a macro action.

When you convert a database, Microsoft Access automatically converts any **DoCmd** statements and the actions that they carry out in your Access Basic code to methods of the **DoCmd** object by replacing the space with the dot (**.**) operator.

Using the TransferSpreadsheet and TransferText Actions

Microsoft Access 97 cannot import Microsoft Excel version 2.0 spreadsheets or Lotus 1-2-3 release 1.0 spreadsheets. If your converted database contains a macro that provides this functionality by using the **TransferSpreadsheet** action in Microsoft Access 1.*x* or 2.0, converting the database changes the **Spreadsheet Type** argument to Microsoft Excel version 3.0 (if you originally specified Microsoft Excel version 2.0) or causes an error if you originally specified Lotus 1-2-3 1.0 format.

To work around this problem, convert the spreadsheets to a later version of Microsoft Excel or Lotus 1-2-3 before importing them into Microsoft Access.

Also, in Microsoft Access 97, you cannot use an SQL statement to specify data to export when you are using the **TransferText** action or the **TransferSpreadsheet** action. Instead of using an SQL statement, you must first create a query and then specify the name of the query in the **Table Name** argument.

Access Basic Code Changes

In Microsoft Access 97, Visual Basic replaces Access Basic. In most respects, Visual Basic is identical to Access Basic, and Microsoft Access automatically makes most of the necessary conversions to your code when you convert your database.

However, the conversion process makes some changes to your code that you need to be aware of, and there are some additional changes that you must make yourself in order for your application to run successfully in Microsoft Access 97.

16-bit DLLs

If your database application calls procedures in other 16-bit DLLs, you must create or obtain 32-bit versions of those DLLs and make any necessary modifications to your code when you convert your database to Microsoft Access 97.

If you cannot obtain a 32-bit version of a DLL, use an intermediary DLL that can convert 32-bit calls to 16-bit calls. For more information, see "Windows Application Programming Interface" later in this chapter.

ActiveX Controls

If your application contains ActiveX controls (formerly OLE control or custom controls) that were set up in Microsoft Access 2.0, you may need to insert the **ByVal** keyword in front of arguments that are passed to event procedures called from ActiveX control events, as in the following example:

```
Sub ChangeMonth_Click(ByVal intCurrentYear As Integer)
```

In order to determine whether an argument needs to be passed by value, click **Compile All Modules** (**Debug** menu) in module Design view. If you receive the following message, you need to insert the **ByVal** keyword in front of the argument: "Event procedure declaration doesn't match description of event having the same name."

Because type checking of arguments is improved in Microsoft Access 97, new event procedures created for ActiveX controls automatically have the **ByVal** keyword inserted when it is needed.

ActiveX Controls on Forms and Reports

When you convert a Microsoft Access 2.0 database for use in Microsoft Access 97, ActiveX controls on forms and reports may not be converted automatically. Microsoft Access 2.0 supports 16-bit OLE controls, while Microsoft Access 97 supports only 32-bit ActiveX controls.

If you are converting a database that contains a form or report that has a 16-bit version of an ActiveX control, and the 32-bit version does not yet exist on your system, Microsoft Access generates an error message. You must obtain a 32-bit version of each ActiveX control that you wish to update and then enter it in the Windows registry. After you register the new ActiveX control, save the form or report in the converted database and then close and reopen the database.

Automation Errors

In Microsoft Access 1.*x* and 2.0, ActiveX components that support Automation (formerly OLE Automation) return a generic error. However, Visual Basic now allows an ActiveX component to return error information specific to the error that has occurred. If your existing databases include code to handle a generic Automation error, you may have to update that code to handle the more specific errors that are now returned.

Category Property

You cannot use an object variable in your code to refer to a **Category** property. The **Category** property is no longer supported for **Form**, **Report**, and **Control** objects.

CurDir Function

The **CurDir** function behaves differently in Microsoft Access 97 than it does in Microsoft Access 1.*x* or 2.0 due to the way that applications interact with Windows 95. Since each application has its own current folder, setting the current folder in Windows 95 by double-clicking an icon does not affect the current folder in Microsoft Access. The **CurDir** function in Microsoft Access 97 always returns the current path.

CurrentDb Function Compared to DBEngine(0)(0)

Use the **CurrentDb** function instead of **DBEngine(0)(0)** to return a Database object variable that points to the current database. The **CurrentDb** function creates another instance of the current database, while **DBEngine(0)(0)** refers to the open copy of the current database. If you use **DBEngine(0)(0)**, it limits your ability to use more than one variable of type **Database** that refers to the current database.

The **DBEngine(0)(0)** syntax is still supported in Microsoft Access 97, so your code does not change during the conversion process. However, it is recommended that you consider making this modification to your code in order to avoid possible conflicts in a multiuser environment.

DAO Object Libraries

Microsoft Access 97 includes Data Access Objects (DAO) objects, methods, and properties that replace those in Microsoft Access 1.*x*, 2.0, and 95. While the code in Microsoft Access 97 is compatible with all previous DAO code, future versions of Microsoft Access may not provide support for some older objects, methods, and properties. The following sections explain how to take advantage of the backward-compatibility features in Microsoft Access 97, as well as how to create new applications and modify current applications to prepare for converting to future versions of Microsoft Access.

Taking Advantage of Backward-Compatibility Features

If you want to continue to use the older versions of DAO objects, methods, and properties in your application, you must first establish a reference to the Microsoft DAO version 2.5/3.5 compatibility library.

▶ **To establish a reference to the Microsoft DAO version 2.5/3.5 compatibility library**

1. Switch to module Design view.
2. On the **Tools** menu, click **References**.
3. In the **Available References** box, click **Microsoft DAO version 2.5/3.5 Compatibility Library**.

   The Microsoft DAO 2.5/3.5 compatibility library provides complete backward compatibility with Microsoft Access 1.*x*, 2.0, and 95. A reference to this version of the library is added to Microsoft Access 1.*x*, 2.0, and 95 applications that you convert to Microsoft Access 97.

The Microsoft DAO 3.5 object library, which does not include the older objects, methods, and properties, is selected by default whenever you create a new database. All new applications created in Microsoft Access 97 should reference only the Microsoft DAO 3.5 object library to ensure the application is not using old methods. Also, if your application references only the Microsoft DAO 3.5 object library, you do not have to distribute the Microsoft DAO 2.5/3.5 compatibility library when you distribute your application to other users.

Tip To verify that your application only uses the objects, methods, and properties in the Microsoft DAO 3.5 object library, clear the **Microsoft DAO 2.5/3.5 Compatibility Library** check box in the **References** dialog box (**Tools** menu). Make sure that **Microsoft DAO 3.5 Object**

Library is selected, and then recompile your application by clicking **Compile All Modules** (**Debug** menu) in module Design view. If your application recompiles without errors, you no longer need to maintain the reference to the Microsoft DAO 2.5/3.5 compatibility library, and your application will work with the next version of DAO.

Preparing for Conversion to Future Versions

The following table lists the objects, methods, and properties that are not included in the Microsoft DAO 3.5 object library, as well as the features that have been provided to replace them. You can use the new items in the second column to modify code written in previous versions of Microsoft Access, so that your application is prepared for conversion to future versions of Microsoft Access, when the items in the first column are no longer available.

Functionality not present in DAO 3.5	Recommended DAO 3.5 replacements
FreeLocks	**Idle** method of the **DBEngine** object (not needed for Microsoft Access 95 and 97 databases)
SetDefaultWorkspace	**DefaultUser/DefaultPassword** properties of the **DBEngine** object
SetDataAccessOption	**IniPath** property of the **DBEngine** object
Database.**BeginTrans**	*Workspace*.**BeginTrans**
Database.**CommitTrans**	*Workspace*.**CommitTrans**
Database.**CreateDynaset**	*Database*.**OpenRecordset** of type **dbOpenDynaset**
Database.**CreateSnapshot**	*Database*.**OpenRecordset** of type **dbOpenSnapshot**
Database.**DeleteQueryDef**	**Delete** method of the **QueryDefs** collection
Database.**ExecuteSQL**	*Database*.**Execute** method and *Database*.**RecordsAffected** property
Database.**ListTables**	*Database*.**TableDefs** collection
Database.**OpenQueryDef**	*Database*.**QueryDefs** collection
Database.**OpenTable**	*Database*.**OpenRecordset** of type **dbOpenTable**
Database.**Rollback**	*Workspace*.**Rollback**
ListFields method of the **Table**, **Dynaset**, and **Snapshot** objects	*Recordset*.**Fields** collection
Table.**ListIndexes**	*TableDef*.**Indexes** collection
QueryDef.**CreateDynaset**	*QueryDef*.**OpenRecordset**
QueryDef.**CreateSnapshot**	*QueryDef*.**OpenRecordset**
QueryDef.**ListParameters**	*QueryDef*.**Parameters** collection
Dynaset object	Dynaset-type **Recordset** object
Snapshot object	Snapshot-type **Recordset** object

Functionality not present in DAO 3.5	Recommended DAO 3.5 replacements
Table object	Table-type **Recordset** object
CreateDynaset method of the **Dynaset** and **QueryDef** objects	*Recordset*.**OpenRecordset** with **dbOpenDynaset** parameter
CreateSnapshot method of the **Dynaset** and **QueryDef** objects	*Recordset*.**OpenRecordset** with **dbOpenSnapshot** parameter

For examples of how to modify your code, see the Microsoft Access online Help.

Database Renaming

When you rename a database, compiled code in the database is decompiled. To recompile code and save all modules in a compiled state, open the database, open a module in Design view, and then click **Compile and Save All Modules** (**Debug** menu).

DDE Channels Declared as Variant or Long

If you use the **DDEInitiate** function to open a dynamic data exchange (DDE) channel, you can declare the variable that stores the channel number, which is a **Long** value, as either a **Variant** or a **Long** value. In Microsoft Access 1.*x* and 2.0, the channel number is an **Integer** value, so you must modify any **Declaration** statements in your code that create variables of type **Integer** to store the channel number.

Error Information

In Microsoft Access 95 and 97, you cannot use the **Error** function to return a description of Microsoft Access errors. For example, the following reference does not work:

```
Error(2450)
```

In Microsoft Access 97, use the properties of the **Err** object to obtain information about errors.

When a Microsoft Access error occurs, you can get the error number and the error description by using the **Number** and **Description** properties of the **Err** object, as in the following example:

```
Debug.Print Err.Number, Err.Description
```

To return information about Microsoft Access, Visual Basic, or DAO errors, use the **AccessError** method. With the **AccessError** method, you can obtain error information regardless of whether the error has actually occurred.

Exclamation Point Compared to Dot Operator

If you used the dot (**.**) operator syntax when referring to a **Field** object of a **Recordset** object in applications created in Microsoft Access 1.*x* or 2.0, you must modify those references to use the exclamation point (**!**) operator syntax. Or, if you want to continue using the dot (**.**) operator syntax, you must establish a reference to the Microsoft DAO 2.5/3.5 compatibility library in the **References** dialog box (**Tools** menu) while in module Design view.

Functions Not Supported in Expressions

The following Visual Basic functions cannot be used in expressions outside a user-defined **Sub** or **Function** procedure:

- EOF
- Loc
- FileAttr
- LOF
- FreeFile
- Seek

If you need to use one of these functions in an expression outside a procedure, call the function from within a user-defined function that you call from the expression.

hWnd Property

If you use the **hWnd** property in your code to pass a window handle of a form or a report to a Windows routine, you can pass the value directly to the routine. You do not need to assign the value of this property to a variable. For example:

```
If Not IsZoomed(Screen.ActiveForm.hWnd) Then
    DoCmd.Maximize
EndIf
```

In Microsoft Access 1.*x* and 2.0, the **hWnd** property of a form or report is an **Integer** value. In Microsoft Access 97, the **hWnd** property is a **Long** value; you must change your code to accept it.

Line Numbers in Visual Basic Procedures

You cannot assign line numbers greater than 65,529 to statements in your Visual Basic procedures. If your converted Microsoft Access 1.*x* or 2.0 application contains line numbers greater than 65,529, you must modify them to fall within the acceptable range.

Microsoft Access Wizards

Code in your Microsoft Access 1.*x* or 2.0 application may call procedures that are located in Microsoft Access wizards. If this is the case, you must, after you convert the application, establish a reference from the application to the wizard database that contains the procedures that you call. For more information about establishing references, see Microsoft Access online Help.

In Microsoft Access 2.0, there is no distinction between wizards and libraries, so their public code is always available to the current database. In Microsoft Access 97, wizards and other add-ins are no longer treated as libraries. In addition, because wizards may change a great deal from one version of Microsoft Access to the next, you may need to rewrite some of your code to adapt to the changes after upgrading to a new version of Microsoft Access.

For code that is no longer provided in the Microsoft Access wizards, such as the AutoDialer, functionality has been added to Utility.mda, a special library database that is provided with Microsoft Access. A reference to this library is automatically added when you convert a database to Microsoft Access 97.

Module Changes

In Microsoft Access 1.*x* and 2.0, modules containing procedures that are not specific to any form or report module are called global modules. In Microsoft Access 97, these are called *standard modules*.

In Microsoft Access 97, form and report modules are now called *class modules*, which means that they can act as templates for a user-defined object. Any public procedures in a form or report module become methods and properties of the new form or report when you create a new instance of it. For more information about class modules, see the Microsoft Access online Help.

Next Procedure and Previous Procedure Buttons

The **Next Procedure** and **Previous Procedure** buttons on the **Module** toolbar in Microsoft Access 1.*x* and 2.0 are not available in Microsoft Access 97. If you convert a Microsoft Access 1.*x* or 2.0 database with a custom toolbar that contains one of these buttons, you do not receive an error, but the buttons have no effect when clicked.

Null Values and Zero-Length Strings

In Microsoft Access 2.0, you can use the **Format** function to return one value for a zero-length string and another for a **Null** value, and you can similarly use the **Format** property to automatically format fields in table Datasheet view or controls on a form or report. For example, you can use a format expression such as the following with the **Format** function to return the appropriate string value from code:

```
Dim var As Variant, strX As String
' Assign some value to strX and pass to Format function.
var = Format(strX, "@;ZLS;Null")
```

In Microsoft Access 97, you must test separately for the **Null** value case and then return the appropriate value based on the result. For example, you could use the **IIf** function in an expression with the **Format** function, such as the following:

```
var = IIf(IsNull(strX),"Null", Format(strX, "@;ZLS"))
```

This change applies only when you use the **Format** function to format a value depending on whether it is a zero-length string or a **Null** value. Other format expressions used with the **Format** function continue to work as they do in previous versions of Microsoft Access.

If you convert a database from Microsoft Access 2.0 to Microsoft Access 97, you must change any code or property settings to use these methods. You cannot use the **Format** property in table Datasheet view to distinguish between **Null** values and zero-length strings.

Objects in the Debug Window

When you are testing and debugging code, you must fully qualify all references to objects that you use in the Debug window, unless you have suspended execution in a form or report module. This means that in the Immediate pane of the Debug window, you must use the code `Forms!Categories!CategoryID` to refer to the CategoryID control on the Categories form in Form view, instead of just CategoryID, even when the Categories form is the current form.

Also, you cannot use the **Me** keyword in the Debug window to refer to an object on a form or report when that form or report is in Design view unless you have suspended the execution of code in the form or report.

OLE Objects Assigned to a Variable

If you manipulate OLE objects or other binary data in your code, use an array of bytes to store binary data. In Microsoft Access 1.*x* and 2.0, you assign OLE objects, or other binary data less than 64K in size, to string variables when you need to manipulate the objects or data in code. You also assign the data returned by the **GetChunk** method to string variables. However, Visual Basic supplies a **Byte** data type and Byte functions such as **LeftB** and **RightB**. In Microsoft Access 97, store binary data in an array of bytes instead of a string variable, and use the **Byte** functions to manipulate that data.

Parent Property

In Microsoft Access 97, if you use the **Parent** property of a control in code or in an expression on a form or report, it typically returns the **Form** or **Report** object that contains the control. For example, if CategoryID is a text box on the Categories form, the code `Forms!Categories!CategoryID.Parent` returns a reference to the Categories form.

There are two exceptions:

- For attached labels, the **Parent** property now returns the control to which the label is attached.

- For controls in an option group, the **Parent** property now returns the option group control.

Percent Sign (%) in Strings

You cannot assign a string containing a percent sign (%) to a variable or a field that has a numeric data type, as in the following example:

```
Dim intX As Double
    intX = "10"            ' This works.
    intX = "10%"           ' This returns an error.
```

Procedures in Form and Report Modules

In Microsoft Access 1.*x* and 2.0, you cannot call a procedure defined in a form or report from anywhere but within that form or report module. In Microsoft Access 97, you can call a public procedure in a form or report module from any procedure in the current database. You must qualify the procedure with the class name of the form or report module. For example, to call a procedure named **DisplayMessage** that is defined in the module of the Orders form, use the following syntax:

```
Form_Orders.DisplayMessage
```

It is better to place procedures that you call from outside a form or report in a standard module if possible, rather than in a form or report module.

Reference to a Microsoft Access Database

You cannot set a reference to a database created with a previous version of Microsoft Access from Microsoft Access 97. You must convert the database to a Microsoft Access 97 database in order to set a reference to it. For information about converting databases, see "Converting Databases" earlier in this chapter.

Time Values in Query Criteria

When you convert a Microsoft Access 1.*x* or 2.0 database to Microsoft Access 97, queries that contain criteria based on specific time values in Date/Time fields may return different results than they do in previous versions. This behavior may also occur if you link tables from a Microsoft Access 1.*x* or 2.0 database to a Microsoft Access 97 database. Only the time portion of Date/Time fields is affected.

Visual Basic Scoping and Object Naming

The following Visual Basic scoping rules affect the names you choose for your objects, modules, and procedures.

Modules and Other Objects with the Same Name

When you name a module, avoid prefacing module names with "Form_" or "Report_". Naming a module in this way could conflict with existing code you have written behind forms and reports.

If you have a module in an application from Microsoft Access 1.x or 2.0 that does not follow these naming rules, Microsoft Access 97 generates an error when you try to convert the application. For example, a module named Form_Orders in a Microsoft Access 1.x or 2.0 database generates an error, and you are asked to rename the module before attempting to convert it.

Modules and Procedures with the Same Name

A procedure can have the same name as a module. However, to call that procedure from an expression anywhere in your application, you must use a fully qualified name for the procedure, including both the module name and the procedure name, as in the following example:

```
IsLoaded.IsLoaded("Orders")
```

Procedures and Controls with the Same Name

If you call a procedure from a form, and that procedure has the same name as a control on the form, you must fully qualify the procedure call with the name of the module in which it resides. For example, if you want to call a procedure named PrintInvoice that resides in a standard module named Utilities, and there is also a button on the same form named PrintInvoice, use the fully qualified name—Utilities.PrintInvoice—when you call the procedure from your form or form module.

Controls with Similar Names

A control's name must not differ from an existing control's name by only a space or a symbol. For example, if you have a control named [Last_Name], you cannot have a control named [Last Name] or [Last+Name].

Modules with the Same Names as Type Libraries

You cannot save a module with the same name as a type library. If you try to save a module with the name DAO, Access, or VBA, a message is generated, stating that the name conflicts with an existing module, project, or object library. Similarly, if you have set a reference to another type library, such as the Microsoft Excel type library, you cannot save a module with the name Excel.

Fields with the Same Names as Methods

If a field in the table has the same name as a DAO method on a **Recordset** object, you cannot refer to the corresponding field in the recordset with the dot (**.**) operator syntax. You must use the exclamation point (**!**) operator syntax, or Microsoft Access generates an error. The following example shows how to refer to a field called AddNew in a recordset opened on a table called Contacts:

```
Dim dbs As Database, rst As Recordset
Set dbs = CurrentDb
Set rst = dbs.OpenRecordset("Contacts")
Debug.Print rst!AddNew
```

Modules with the Same Names as Visual Basic Functions

If you save a module with the same name as an intrinsic Visual Basic function, Microsoft Access generates an error when you try to run that function. For example, if you save a module named MsgBox, and then try to run a procedure that calls the MsgBox function, Microsoft Access generates the error "Expected variable or procedure, not module."

Modules with the Same Names as Objects

If a database created in a previous version of Microsoft Access includes a module that has the same name as a Microsoft Access object or a DAO object, you may encounter compilation errors when you convert your database to Microsoft Access 97. For example, a module named Form or Database may generate a compilation error. To avoid these errors, rename the module.

Fields Used in Expressions or Bound to Controls on Forms and Reports

When you create a field in a table that is bound to a control on a report or used in an expression in the **ControlSource** property of a control or a report, avoid assigning the field a name that is the same as a method of the **Application** object. To see a list of methods of the **Application** object, click **Object Browser** (**View** menu) while in module Design view. Click **Access** in the **Project/Library** box, click **Application** in the **Classes** box, and then view the methods of the **Application** object in the **Members Of** box.

When you create a field in a table that is bound to a control on a form or report, avoid assigning the field any of the following names:

- AddRef
- GetIDsOfNames
- GetTypeInfo
- GetTypeInfoCount
- Invoke
- QueryInterface
- Release

These are the names of methods used internally by Microsoft Access to work with forms and reports. If you use them as names for fields, they could cause conflicts or unexpected behavior when referenced in expressions or Visual Basic code.

Identifiers with the Same Names as Visual Basic Keywords

The version of Visual Basic that is used by Microsoft Access 97 contains some new Visual Basic keywords, so you can no longer use these keywords as identifiers:

- **AddressOf**
- **Assert**
- **Decimal**
- **DefDec**
- **Enum**
- **Event**
- **Friend**
- **Implements**
- **RaiseEvent**
- **WithEvents**

When you convert or enable a database from a previous version of Microsoft Access, existing identifiers that are the same as a new Visual Basic keyword cause Microsoft Access 97 to display the following message: "There were compilation errors during the conversion or enabling of this database." This message is displayed, for example, if you try to enable or convert the Northwind Traders sample database from Microsoft Access 2.0. This is because the **ShowEvent Sub** procedure in the Utility Functions module uses **Event** as a string variable.

To correct this problem, open the module that contains the code that uses one or more of the new keywords as identifiers and rename them. For example, after converting the Northwind Traders database, open the Utility Functions module, and change the **Event** string variable name throughout the procedure to another name, such as **strEvent**.

Windows Application Programming Interface

If your existing Microsoft Access 1.*x* or 2.0 Access Basic code makes calls to the Windows application programming interface (API), you must modify these calls when you convert your database to Microsoft Access 97. Microsoft Access 1.*x* and 2.0 are 16-bit applications and run on 16-bit versions of Windows. Microsoft Access 97 is a 32-bit application and runs on the 32-bit Windows 95 and Windows NT operating systems.

The Windows API consists of a set of DLLs containing system-related procedures that include functions, messages, data structures, data types, and statements you can use in creating applications that run under Windows 95 or Windows NT operating system. To call these procedures from Visual Basic, you must first declare them with a **Declare** statement. You can then call them as you would any other procedure.

The following list provides some tips for converting your code:

- Check any **Declare** statements to ensure that they refer to the correct DLLs.

16-bit Windows DLL	32-bit Windows DLL
User.dll	User32.dll
Kernel.dll	Kernel32.dll
GDI.dll	GDI32.dll

- Check to make sure that you have entered the procedure name and alias name correctly.

    The names of some functions in the 32-bit Windows API have changed. Additionally, functions in the 32-bit Windows API are case-sensitive.

- Consult one of the references listed later in this section to determine the function calls you must update.

    Some functions have new parameter data types in the 32-bit Windows API.

- Check for 16-bit DLLs with the same name as 32-bit DLLs.

    If a 16-bit version of a DLL with the same name as a 32-bit DLL exists on your computer, Microsoft Access may try to call a function in that DLL if your path lists its folder before the folder that contains the new DLL.

- If the function takes string-type arguments, try appending an **a** or **w** to the function name.

    Some 32-bit DLLs contain functions with slightly different versions to accommodate both Unicode and ANSI strings. An **a** at the end of the function name specifies the ANSI version. A **w** at the end of the function name specifies the Unicode version.

For more information about using 32-bit Windows API procedures and about porting your existing database applications to 32-bit Microsoft Access 97, consult the following resources:

- "Porting Your 16-bit Microsoft Office-Based Solutions to 32-bit Office" in Chapter 10, "Upgrading from Previous Versions of Microsoft Office."
- The Win32 API Viewer, available in Microsoft Office 97, Developer Edition. The viewer includes Visual Basic syntax for all 32-bit declarations, data types, and constants.
- The Microsoft Win32 Software Development Kit. This kit provides complete reference information for 32-bit Windows API procedures.

World Wide Web For the latest information about modifying 16-bit calls for 32-bit Office in Microsoft Access, connect to the Microsoft Access Developer Web site at:

http://www.microsoft.com/accessdev/

New Toolbars, Menu Bars, and Shortcut Menus

Microsoft Access 97 supports a new style of toolbars, menus, and shortcut menus. When you convert a database from a previous version of Microsoft Access to Microsoft Access 97, any custom toolbars are automatically converted to the new style.

Custom menus and shortcut menus created in a previous version of Microsoft Access are handled differently. Previous versions of Microsoft Access use the Menu Builder to create custom menus and shortcut menus. The Menu Builder generates a macro group containing macros that use the **AddMenu** and **DoMenuItem** actions. In previous versions of Microsoft Access, you can also create custom menus and shortcut menus manually (without the Menu Builder) using these macro actions. Custom menu and shortcut menu macros created using either method still run Microsoft Access 97, but they are not converted to the new style, nor are they available from the new **Customize** dialog box (**View** menu, **Toolbars** submenu).

To save a menu or shortcut menu from a previous version of Microsoft Access in Microsoft Access 97 format, select the macro group used to create the menu or shortcut menu in the Database window, and then click **Create Menu from Macro** or **Create Shortcut Menu from Macro** (**Tools** menu, **Macro** submenu). Unlike new custom menus or shortcut menus created with the **Customize** dialog box, these menus and shortcut menus depend on the macro group from the previous version of Microsoft Access. If you delete this macro group or any macros it refers to, the menu or shortcut menu no longer works. Alternatively, you can use the **Customize** dialog box (**View** menu, **Toolbars** submenu) to recreate custom toolbars, menu bars, and shortcut menus.

Upgrading from Microsoft Access 1.x

This section describes the differences between Microsoft Access 1.*x* and Microsoft Access 97. Microsoft Access 97 is a major upgrade from previous versions of the application. For more information about the features and benefits of this upgrade, see Chapter 2, "What's New in Microsoft Office 97."

What happens to my old Microsoft Access databases when I convert them to Microsoft Access 97 format? You can open databases created in Microsoft Access 1.*x* directly in Microsoft Access 97, even if you do not convert the database using a process called *enabling*. Once you convert a Microsoft Access 1.*x* database to Microsoft Access 97 format, you cannot open it in Microsoft Access 1.*x*, and it cannot be converted back to Microsoft Access 1.*x* format.

Can I share Microsoft Access 97 databases with users of previous versions of Microsoft Access? If your workgroup is using a combination of Microsoft Access 97 and 1.*x*, users can share data and databases. However, not all Microsoft Access 97 features are supported in previous versions.

Do my old macros still work in Microsoft Access 97? In most cases, macros created in Microsoft Access 1.*x* run in Microsoft Access 97. If you convert or enable a Microsoft Access 1.*x* database containing macros in Microsoft Access 97, the macros run in Microsoft Access 97.

Does my old Access Basic application code still work in Microsoft Access 97? In most cases, Access Basic application code created in Microsoft Access 1.*x* runs in Microsoft Access 97. If you convert a Microsoft Access 1.*x* database to Microsoft Access 97, the Access Basic code is converted to equivalent Visual Basic code. If you enable a Microsoft Access 1.*x* database in Microsoft Access 97, a copy of the Access Basic code is converted to equivalent Visual Basic code; your original code is not altered.

Note All of the conversion issues that apply when you upgrade from Microsoft Access 2.0 also apply to opening and running a Microsoft Access 1.0 or 1.1 database in Microsoft Access 97. The following section addresses issues that apply only to opening and running Microsoft Access 1.*x* databases in Microsoft Access 97.

Access Basic Code Changes

In Microsoft Access 97, Visual Basic for Applications replaces Access Basic. In most respects, Visual Basic is identical to Access Basic, and Microsoft Access automatically makes most of the necessary conversions to your code when you convert your database.

However, the conversion process makes some changes to your code that you need to be aware of, and there are some additional changes that you must make yourself in order for your Microsoft Access 1.0 and 1.1 application to run successfully in Microsoft Access 97.

Backquote Character (`) in Object Names

If an object name in a Microsoft Access 1.*x* database includes a backquote character (`), you cannot open that object using Microsoft Access 97 or convert the database to Microsoft Access 97 format. Rename the object in Microsoft Access 1.*x*, and then change references to that object in your queries, forms, reports, macros, and modules. Use the **Documenter** command (**Tools** menu, **Analyze** submenu) to find occurrences of the old name in your references.

Combo Boxes and List Boxes

For combo boxes and list boxes that have their **RowSource** property set to a table or a query, Microsoft Access 97 displays data in the rows of the combo or list box by using the format defined for the data in the **Format** property of the underlying field. Microsoft Access 1.*x*, by contrast, does not use the **Format** property of the underlying field.

Query Fields

In Microsoft Access 97 your queries and the forms based on them are less restrictive than in Microsoft Access 1.x. Using Microsoft Access 97, you can update the data in some fields in multiple-table queries that you cannot update using Microsoft Access 1.x. For example, in a query that includes fields from a Customers table and an Orders table (where one customer can have more than one order), you cannot update fields from the Customers table using Microsoft Access 1.x. Using Microsoft Access 97, however, you can update fields from the Customers table in most situations. If you do not want users to update such fields in a form, use Microsoft Access 1.x to set the **Locked** property to **Yes** for form controls that are bound to the fields.

Validation Rules for Tables

In Microsoft Access 97, validation rules you set for fields and records in a table protect your data regardless of how it is entered or modified: whether by using a datasheet or form, importing data, using action queries, or carrying out Visual Basic commands. If you have the same validation rule set for both a field in a table and a control on a form that is bound to that field in a Microsoft Access 1.x database, after converting the database, you can delete the rule set for the control.

If your Microsoft Access 1.x database validation rules contain elements not allowed in Microsoft Access 97, the rules are not converted to Microsoft Access 97 format. When Microsoft Access encounters invalid validation rules while converting your Microsoft Access 1.x database, it creates the ConvertErrors table in the converted database with information to help you fix the rules.

Visible Property

In Microsoft Access 1.x, setting the **Visible** property of a control to **No** makes the control invisible in Form view and also hides its column in Datasheet view. In Microsoft Access 97, the **Visible** property does not hide a control's column in Datasheet view. If you want to hide a column in Microsoft Access 97, click the **Hide Columns** command (**Format** menu).

Sharing Databases with Microsoft Access 1.x, 2.0, or 95

If your workgroup is upgrading gradually to Microsoft Access 97, some users may need to share databases with users of Microsoft Access 1.x, 2.0, or 95. There are two strategies for sharing databases between different versions of Microsoft Access:

- Open the database in its existing format, which is called *enabling* the database.
- Create a front-end database in Microsoft Access 97 format that is linked to table data in a back-end database from a previous version of Microsoft Access.

The following table summarizes the advantages and disadvantages of each strategy.

Strategy	Advantages	Disadvantages
Enable previous version databases	All Microsoft Access users can open databases and add, edit, or delete data.	Database file size can increase substantially. Microsoft Access 97 users cannot modify or add new objects, or take advantage of many features unique to Microsoft Access 97.
Create a front-end database in Microsoft Access 97 format linked to table data in a back-end database from a previous version of Microsoft Access	All Microsoft Access users can open databases and add, edit, or delete data. Microsoft Access 97 users can modify or add new objects, (except tables) and can take advantage of features unique to Microsoft Access 97.	Additional development of the front-end databases must be synchronized. Changes made to the front-end database in Microsoft Access 97 must be repeated in the back-end database. Features unique to Microsoft Access 97 are not supported in the older version back-end database.

Enabling a Database

Enabling a database keeps the format intact so it can be shared by users of different versions of Microsoft Access. When a Microsoft Access 97 user enables a Microsoft Access 1.x, 2.0, or 95 database, other users can browse the database and add, delete, or modify records; but they cannot switch to Design view on any objects. To modify the design of existing objects or to add new objects, the database must be opened in the version of Microsoft Access used to create it.

Note Before you enable a database, make sure it is not open in a previous version of Microsoft Access. If the database is located on a server or shared folder, make sure no one else has it open. Finally, if you have a database open in Microsoft Access 97, close it.

▶ **To enable a Microsoft Access 1.x, 2.0, or 95 database**

1. On the **File** menu, click **Open Database**.
2. In the **Open** dialog box, select a database.

   The first time a database from a previous version of Microsoft Access is opened, Microsoft Access 97 displays the **Convert/Open Database** dialog box.
3. Click **Open Database** to open the database without converting it.

If the database contains forms, reports, and modules, Microsoft Access 97 creates separate copies of these objects and their Access Basic (Microsoft Access 1.x or 2.0) or Visual Basic (Microsoft Access 95) code so that they can run under Microsoft Access 97. This information is stored in a hidden table named MSysModules2. Depending on the size of the forms, reports, and modules in the database, the addition of the MSysModules2 table can increase the file size by as much as double. If a Microsoft Access 1.x or 2.0 database has been enabled previously by Microsoft Access 95, it has a similar table named MSysModules, which further increases the size of the database.

Microsoft Access 97 does not display the **Convert/Open Database** dialog box the next time the database is opened unless a change is made to code in modules, forms, or reports in the previous version of Microsoft Access. If a change has been made to the code, you must enable the database again.

You can speed up the process of enabling a large database created with Microsoft Access 1.x or 2.0 by increasing the maximum buffer size beyond the default. To change this setting, modify the Windows registry by setting the **MaxBufferSize** value to 4096, decimal base in the key **HKEY_LOCAL_MACHINE\SOFTWARE \Microsoft\Jet\3.5\Engines\Jet 2.x**. For more information about editing the Windows registry, see Appendix C, "Registry Keys and Values."

Creating a Front-end Database Linked to Table Data in a Previous Version Back-end Database

Enabling a database as described in the previous section places limitations on Microsoft Access 97 users, increases the size of the database, and requires additional memory, particularly when running code. As an alternative, you can split the database into a Microsoft Access 97 front-end database that contains all objects other than tables, and then link this database to a shared back-end database in the older version format. The back-end database contains the tables.

In general, it is good practice for developers to keep application code and objects in a separate database from the tables. This allows administrators to convert a copy of the front-end database to Microsoft Access 97 format while leaving the back-end database containing the tables in the previous version format until all users have upgraded to

Microsoft Access 97. In this way, the converted copy of the front-end database gains all the features and functionality of Microsoft Access 97, yet the back-end database containing the tables is still available to all users.

Many developers who use previous versions of Microsoft Access organize shared databases as front-end/back-end databases. If this is the case for you, convert a copy of the front-end database and distribute it to all Microsoft Access 97 users, and then use the **Linked Table Manager** (**Tools** menu, **Add-ins** submenu) to relink the tables in the back-end database. If the current database has not been split in this fashion, you can do so in the previous version of Microsoft Access, and then convert the front-end database.

You can also use Microsoft Access 97 to split the database and link to the older version tables. In Microsoft Access 97, convert the database, split it using the Database Splitter Wizard, and then use the **Linked Table Manager** (**Tools** menu, **Add-ins** submenu) to relink the original tables in the previous version database.

Note Before you create and link a front-end database, make sure the linked database is not open in a previous version of Microsoft Access. If the database is located on a server or shared folder, make sure no one else has it open. Finally, if you have a database open in Microsoft Access 97, close it.

▶ **To create a Microsoft Access 97 front-end database**

1 In Microsoft Access 97, point to **Database Utilities** on the **Tools** menu, and then click **Convert Database**.

2 In the **Database to Convert From** dialog box, select the database, and then click **Convert**.

3 In the **Convert Database Into** dialog box, type a new name (without the .mdb extension) for the Microsoft Access 97 database.

   –or–

   Select a different location for the Microsoft Access 97 database, and then click **Save**.

Microsoft Access creates a converted copy of the database in Microsoft Access 97 format without altering the original database. Then you can link the copy of the database to the original table data.

▶ **To link a front-end database to table data in a back-end database from a previous version of Microsoft Access**

1 On the **Tools** menu, point to **Add-ins**, and then click **Database Splitter**.

2 Follow the instructions in the Database Splitter Wizard.

3 Delete the back-end database created by the Database Splitter Wizard, and then open the converted front-end database.

4. On the **Tools** menu, point to **Add-ins**, and then click **Linked Table Manager**.
5. Select the **Always prompt for new location** check box.
6. Select the check boxes for all the tables, and then click **OK**.
7. In the **Select New Location of** *table name* dialog box, specify the location of the previous version database, click **Open**, and then click **OK**.

Tip You can also open a new, blank database in Microsoft Access 97. To import all objects except for tables into the new database, point to **Get External Data** on the **File** menu and click **Import**. Then link the tables from the previous version database by clicking **Link Tables** on the **Get External Data** submenu (**File** menu).

CHAPTER 12

Upgrading from Previous Versions of Microsoft Excel

This chapter tells you what to expect when you or your workgroup upgrades to Microsoft Excel 97 from a previous version of Microsoft Excel. If you plan a gradual upgrade, users of different versions of Microsoft Excel may need to share workbooks. This chapter describes Microsoft Excel 97 features that are not supported in previous versions, which may result in loss of data or formatting.

In This Chapter
Overview   301
Upgrading from Microsoft Excel 95   302
Upgrading from Microsoft Excel 5.0   307
Sharing Workbooks with Microsoft Excel 5.0 or 95   314
Upgrading from Microsoft Excel 4.0   320
Sharing Workbooks with Microsoft Excel 4.0   328

See Also
- For a summary of new and improved features in Microsoft Excel 97, see Chapter 2, "What's New in Microsoft Office 97."
- For information about installing Microsoft Excel or other Office applications, see Chapter 4, "Installing Microsoft Office."
- For information about switching to Microsoft Excel from other spreadsheet applications, see Chapter 18, "Switching to Microsoft Excel."

Overview

The primary questions most Microsoft Excel 97 upgraders have are:
- What happens to my old workbooks when I open them in Microsoft Excel 97?
- Can I share Microsoft Excel 97 workbooks with users of previous versions?
- Do my old macros still work in Microsoft Excel 97?

If you are upgrading from Microsoft Excel version 4.0 or 5.0 or Microsoft Excel 95, this chapter answers these questions for you.

As the following illustration shows, some platforms and versions of Microsoft Excel share the same file format.

Common File Formats in Microsoft Excel

Operating System				
Windows	4.0	5.0	95	97
Macintosh	4.0	5.0		97

To convert a workbook from an earlier version of Microsoft Excel to Microsoft Excel 97, simply open the workbook. Microsoft Excel handles the conversion automatically. To complete the conversion, save the workbook in Microsoft Excel 97 format.

Upgrading from Microsoft Excel 95

This section describes the changes between Microsoft Excel 95 for Windows and Microsoft Excel 97. Microsoft Excel 97 is a major upgrade from previous versions of the application. For more information about the features and benefits of this upgrade, see Chapter 2, "What's New in Microsoft Office 97."

What happens to my old workbooks when I open them in Microsoft Excel 97? You can open files created in Microsoft Excel 95 directly in Microsoft Excel 97. All data and formatting created in Microsoft Excel 95 are fully supported by Microsoft Excel 97. However, sound notes created in previous versions of Microsoft Excel are lost.

Can I share Microsoft Excel 97 workbooks with users of previous versions? If your workgroup uses any combination of Microsoft Excel 97, 95, or 5.0, users can exchange workbooks between versions. However, not all Microsoft Excel 97 features are supported in previous versions. For more information, see "Sharing Workbooks with Microsoft Excel 5.0 or 95" later in this chapter.

Do my old macros still work in Microsoft Excel 97? Microsoft Excel 97 fully supports your Microsoft Excel 95 Visual Basic for Applications macros. Because of changes to the Microsoft Excel architecture, you may encounter some problems with macros written in Microsoft Excel 95. For more information, see "Macro Changes" later in this chapter.

Tip To convert several documents at once to Microsoft Excel 97 format, you can use the File Conversion Wizard, which is supplied with Microsoft Excel 97. For more information about this wizard, see "Converting File Formats in Microsoft Excel" in Chapter 18, "Switching to Microsoft Excel."

Menu Changes

The following sections summarize the Microsoft Excel 95 commands that have changed location or functionality in Microsoft Excel 97, as well as commands that are new in Microsoft Excel 97.

File Menu

The following table describes changed commands on the **File** menu.

This Microsoft Excel 95 command	Changes to this in Microsoft Excel 97
Shared Lists	Renamed **Share Workbook** (**Tools** menu). For more information about enhanced multiuser workbook capabilities, see Chapter 30, "Workgroup Features in Microsoft Excel."
Send	Renamed **Mail Recipient** (**Send To** submenu).
Add Routing Slip	Renamed **Routing Recipient** (**Send To** submenu).

The following table lists new commands that have been added to the **File** menu.

This Microsoft Excel 97 command	Allows you to
Send To submenu commands	Send a workbook to others electronically. For more information about working with messaging systems, see Chapter 28, "Working with Messaging Systems and Connectivity Software."

Edit Menu

The following table describes changed commands on the **Edit** menu.

This Microsoft Excel 95 command	Changes to this in Microsoft Excel 97
Notes (**Clear** submenu)	Renamed **Comments** (**Clear** submenu).

View Menu

The following table describes changed commands on the **View** menu.

This Microsoft Excel 95 command	Changes to this in Microsoft Excel 97
View Manager (requires View Manager add-in)	Renamed **Custom Views**. This command no longer requires an add-in.

The following table lists new commands that have been added to the **View** menu.

This Microsoft Excel 97 command	Allows you to
Normal	Switch from other views to normal view.
Page Break Preview	Switch to page break preview, in which you can adjust page breaks and see how the worksheet will print.
Comments	Display or hide all comments on the worksheet. This command also displays the **Reviewing** toolbar, with which you can review existing comments and add new comments to the worksheet.
Custom Views	Create unique settings with which to view your document. Custom views can include print and filter settings and hidden rows or columns.

Insert Menu

The following table describes changed commands on the **Insert** menu.

This Microsoft Excel 95 command	Changes to this in Microsoft Excel 97
Chart submenu commands	Removed. The **Chart** command now starts the Chart Wizard, with which you specify whether the new chart is inserted in a worksheet or in a new chart sheet.
Macro submenu commands	Removed. Macro sheets are no longer visible. Use the **Visual Basic Editor** (**Tools** menu, **Macro** submenu) to view the Visual Basic environment.
Note	Renamed **Comment**. Sound notes are not supported in Microsoft Excel 97.

The following table lists new commands that have been added to the **Insert** menu.

This Microsoft Excel 97 command	Allows you to
Hyperlink	Insert a World Wide Web-style hyperlink to another Office document or to an Internet address. For more information about hyperlinks, see Chapter 24, "Integrating Microsoft Office with Your Intranet."

Format Menu

The following table lists new commands that have been added to the **Format** menu.

This Microsoft Excel 97 command	Allows you to
Conditional Formatting	Apply formatting automatically to a cell if its value meets criteria you specify.

Tools Menu

The following table describes changed commands on the **Tools** menu.

This Microsoft Excel 95 command	Changes to this in Microsoft Excel 97
Macro	Renamed **Macros** (**Macro** submenu).
Record Macro submenu commands	Moved to **Record New Macro** (**Macro** submenu).

The following table lists new commands that have been added to the **Tools** menu.

This Microsoft Excel 97 command	Allows you to
Track Changes submenu commands	Mark or review changes to the active workbook.
Merge Workbooks	Merge changes from one copy of a workbook into another. For more information about workbook collaboration, see Chapter 30, "Workgroup Features in Microsoft Excel."

Data Menu

The following table describes changed commands on the **Data** menu.

This Microsoft Excel 95 command	Changes to this in Microsoft Excel 97
PivotTable	Renamed **PivotTable Report**.
PivotTable Field	Removed. To hide or show PivotTable field items, double-click the field heading.

The following table lists new commands that have been added to the **Data** menu.

This Microsoft Excel 97 command	Allows you to
Validation	Format cells to accept only a specific type or range of data, and to specify the messages users see when working in the range.

Help Menu

The following table describes changed commands on the **Help** menu.

This Microsoft Excel 95 command	Changes to this in Microsoft Excel 97
Microsoft Excel Help Topics	Renamed **Microsoft Excel Help**. This command displays the Office Assistant, through which you view Help.
Answer Wizard	Removed. Gain access to the Answer Wizard feature through the Assistant.

The following table lists new commands that have been added to the **Help** menu.

This Microsoft Excel 97 command	Allows you to
Contents and Index	Display the Help contents.
What's This?	Click any area of the screen (such as a toolbar or menu command) to see a brief explanation in a ScreenTip.
Microsoft on the Web submenu commands	Connect to the Microsoft home page on the Web (requires Internet access). For information about customizing these commands, see "Customizing Office Connections to the World Wide Web" in Chapter 7, "Customizing and Optimizing Microsoft Office."

File Format Changes

The Microsoft Excel 97 file format differs from that of previous versions of Microsoft Excel. If your workgroup is upgrading gradually to Microsoft Excel 97, some users may have to share workbooks with users of Microsoft Excel 95. Microsoft Excel supports several strategies for sharing workbooks among different versions. For more information about changes in file format and strategies for sharing workbooks, see "Sharing Workbooks with Microsoft Excel 5.0 or 95" later in this chapter.

Template Changes

The Spreadsheet Solutions templates introduced in Microsoft Excel 95 have been enhanced to take advantage of the forms capabilities and other new features available in Microsoft Excel 97. For example, the Spreadsheet Solutions templates include support for merged cells, indented and rotated text, and data validation.

Although you can save the new Spreadsheet Solutions templates in Microsoft Excel 95 format, Microsoft Excel 95 may not have all the features required to fully support the templates. However, all Microsoft Excel 95 templates work in Microsoft Excel 97.

Tip In Windows 95 and Windows NT Workstation 4.0, you can use a system policy to define the path to user and workgroup templates on a network server for all Microsoft Excel users in your workgroup. In the System Policy Editor, set the following policies:

User\Office\Common\User Templates

User\Office\Common\Workgroup Templates

For more information, see "Using Windows System Policies to Customize Office" in Chapter 7, "Customizing and Optimizing Microsoft Office."

Upgrading from Microsoft Excel 5.0

This section describes the changes between Microsoft Excel version 5.0 for Windows or the Macintosh and Microsoft Excel 97. Microsoft Excel 97 is a major upgrade from previous versions of the application. For more information about the features and benefits of this upgrade, see Chapter 2, "What's New in Microsoft Office 97."

What happens to my old workbooks when I open them in Microsoft Excel 97? You can open files created in Microsoft Excel 5.0 directly in Microsoft Excel 97. All data and formatting created in Microsoft Excel 5.0 are fully supported in Microsoft Excel 97. However, sound notes created in previous versions of Microsoft Excel are lost.

Can I share Microsoft Excel 97 workbooks with users of previous versions? If your workgroup uses any combination of Microsoft Excel 97, 95, or 5.0, users can exchange workbooks between versions. However, not all Microsoft Excel 97 features are supported in previous versions. For more information, see "Sharing Workbooks with Microsoft Excel 5.0 or 95" later in this chapter.

Do my old macros still work in Microsoft Excel 97? In most cases, your Visual Basic and XLM macros run unmodified in Microsoft Excel 97. For more information about working with XLM code in Microsoft Excel 97, see "Upgrading XLM Macros to Visual Basic for Applications" later in this chapter.

Tip To convert several documents at once to Microsoft Excel 97 format, you can use the File Conversion Wizard, which is supplied with Microsoft Excel 97. For more information about this wizard, see "Converting File Formats in Microsoft Excel" in Chapter 18, "Switching to Microsoft Excel."

Menu Changes

The following sections summarize Microsoft Excel 5.0 commands that have changed location or functionality in Microsoft Excel 97, as well as commands that are new in Microsoft Excel 97.

File Menu

The following table describes changed commands on the **File** menu.

This Microsoft Excel 5.0 command	Changes to this in Microsoft Excel 97
Find File	Removed. Document searching has been moved to the **Open** dialog box (**File** menu). For more information about locating Office documents, see Chapter 26, "Finding Microsoft Office Documents on the Network."
Summary Info	Renamed **Properties**. For more information about using document properties, see Chapter 23, "Tracking Collaboration With Document Properties."
Send	Renamed **Mail Recipient** (**Send To** submenu).
Add Routing Slip	Renamed **Routing Recipient** (**Send To** submenu).

The following table lists new commands that have been added to the **File** menu.

This Microsoft Excel 97 command	Allows you to
Send To submenu commands	Send a workbook to others electronically. For more information about working with messaging systems, see Chapter 28, "Working with Messaging Systems and Connectivity Software."

Edit Menu

The following table describes changed commands on the **Edit** menu.

This Microsoft Excel 5.0 command	Changes to this in Microsoft Excel 97
Notes (**Clear** submenu)	Renamed **Comments** (**Clear** submenu).

View Menu

The following table describes changed commands on the **View** menu.

This Microsoft Excel 5.0 command	Changes to this in Microsoft Excel 97
View Manager (requires View Manager add-in)	Renamed **Custom Views**. This command no longer requires an add-in.

Graphics Formats Native to PowerPoint

PowerPoint can import the following graphics formats directly:

- Windows enhanced metafile (EMF)
- JPEG File Interchange Format
- Portable Network Graphics (PNG)
- Windows bitmap (BMP)
- Windows metafile (WMF)
- Macintosh PICT

Graphics Filters Included with PowerPoint

To import non-native graphics formats, you must install additional graphics filters. If you choose a Typical installation during Setup, several PowerPoint graphics filters are installed automatically. If the graphics filters you need are not installed, rerun the Setup, click **Add/Remove**, and then select the graphics filters you need.

Graphics filters are installed in the following locations.

Operating system	Graphics filters default location
Windows	Program files\Common files\Microsoft shared\Grphflt
Macintosh	Microsoft Shared Apps:Graphic Filters (PPC)

The graphics filters that come with PowerPoint support files in the following formats.

The graphics filter for this application or format	Is located in this file	Comments
AutoCAD (DXF)	Dxfimp32.flt	Supported by PowerPoint for Windows only.
CompuServe GIF (GIF)	Gif32.flt (Windows); GIF import & export (Macintosh)	Included in a Typical installation.
Computer Graphics Metafile (CGM)	Cgmimp32.flt, Cgmimp32.fnt, Cgmimp32.cfg, Cgmimp32.hlp	Supported by PowerPoint for Windows only.
CorelDRAW 3.0, 4.0, 5.0, and 6.0 (CDR)	Cdrimp32.flt	Supported by PowerPoint for Windows only.
Encapsulated PostScript (EPS)	Epsimp32.flt (Windows); EPS import (Macintosh)	Included in a Typical installation.
Kodak® Photo-CD (PCD)	Pcdimp32.flt, Pcdlib32.dll (Windows); PCD import, PCD Library (Macintosh)	None.

File Formats Native to PowerPoint

PowerPoint can import and export the following file formats directly (or with the converters installed when you choose a Typical installation during Setup):

- Outline format (including text formats such as RTF and TXT)
- Windows Metafile (WMF)
- Macintosh PICT
- Presentation for PowerPoint 97
- Presentation Template
- PowerPoint Show
- PowerPoint Add-in
- PowerPoint versions 3.0–95

Note If you choose a Typical installation during Setup, the converters for exporting or importing PowerPoint 97 presentations to or from earlier versions of PowerPoint are installed automatically. For more information about these converters and file formats, see "Running Multiple Versions of PowerPoint" in Chapter 22, "Supporting Multiple Versions of Microsoft Office."

Converters That Import Presentations

To install converters for presentations created by other presentation applications, choose a Custom installation during Setup. Select the **PowerPoint** option and then select the converters you want under the **Presentation Translators** option. These converters only import presentations; they do not export PowerPoint presentations to other file formats.

The applications for which converters are available are listed in the following table.

Application	Converter
Harvard Graphics 2.3 for DOS	Hg23dos.pdi
Harvard Graphics 3.0 for DOS	Hg30dos.pdi
Freelance Graphics 4.0 for DOS	Fl40dos.pdi
Freelance Graphics 1.0-2.1 for Windows	Fl21win.pdi

World Wide Web For the latest information about PowerPoint converters, connect to the PowerPoint home page at:

http://www.microsoft.com/powerpoint/

Converting File Formats in PowerPoint 97

PowerPoint 97 recognizes the file formats of several presentation applications, including Harvard Graphics and Lotus Freelance. When these types of presentations are opened, PowerPoint automatically converts them to PowerPoint format, preserving much of the original content and formatting.

PowerPoint uses converters to work with other file formats. If you need to transfer presentations between PowerPoint and applications for which specific converters are not available, you can export presentations in one of several text formats, as Windows metafiles, or in another format for which an export graphics filter or export module has been installed. For information about using export graphics filters or export modules, see "Custom Export Formats" in Chapter 38, "Microsoft PowerPoint Architecture."

Saving a presentation in a text format preserves only the text of a presentation, which can then be opened in most word processing applications as well as PowerPoint. Saving a presentation in a graphics format saves the slides as graphic images only; you can insert the graphics into a wide variety of applications.

Using Converters and Graphics Filters

Converters change the file format of a presentation. If a presentation includes graphics, PowerPoint uses *graphics filters* to import and export graphics that are embedded in or linked to the presentation. To convert presentations to and from different file formats, you must install the appropriate converters. To import and export graphics contained in presentations, you must install the appropriate graphics filters.

When you use the **From File** command (**Insert** menu, **Picture** submenu) to insert a graphic onto a slide, one of three things happens:

- If the graphic is in a format native to PowerPoint, PowerPoint preserves the graphic in its original format.
- If the graphic is in a non-native format and if a compatible graphics filter has been installed, PowerPoint converts the graphic to a format that is native to PowerPoint.
- If the graphic is in a format PowerPoint does not recognize, PowerPoint displays a message and does not convert the graphic.

Several presentation and graphic formats are *native* to PowerPoint. That is, PowerPoint can read them directly without a converter or filter. For several other presentation and graphic formats, however, converters and graphics filters can be installed when you run the Office Setup program.

CHAPTER 20

Switching to Microsoft PowerPoint

This chapter tells you what to expect when you or your workgroup switches to Microsoft PowerPoint 97 from another presentation application.

The primary questions most new PowerPoint users have are:

- What happens to my old presentations when I open them in PowerPoint 97?
- Can I share PowerPoint 97 presentations with users of my old presentation application?

If you are switching to PowerPoint 97, this chapter answers these questions for you.

In This Chapter
Converting File Formats in PowerPoint 97   562
Switching from Harvard Graphics   570
Switching from Lotus Freelance   571

See Also
- For a summary of new and improved features in PowerPoint 97, see Chapter 2, "What's New in Microsoft Office 97."
- For information about installing PowerPoint or other Office applications, see Chapter 4, "Installing Microsoft Office."
- For information about upgrading to PowerPoint 97 from a previous version of PowerPoint see Chapter 14, "Upgrading from Previous Versions of Microsoft PowerPoint."

Switching from Other Client/Server Messaging Systems

Client/server messaging systems are distinguished from local area network (LAN) or post office e-mail systems in that they provide a server-based message store for users. Examples include Novell GroupWise 5.0, IBM PROFS, HP OpenMail, Lotus Notes, and Microsoft Exchange Server. Microsoft Outlook is a MAPI client application and uses the full MAPI store specification, so drivers that work with the Windows Messaging System Inbox or Microsoft Exchange Client do not necessarily work with Outlook. Driver manufacturers must ensure that their message store drivers are fully MAPI-compliant.

Microsoft is working with several providers to ensure they have all the information they need to do this. Microsoft will publish a list of recommended drivers that pass our testing criteria and that work well with Outlook. Currently, the only client/server MAPI store provider certified to work with Outlook is Microsoft Exchange Server.

World Wide Web For the latest information about MAPI-compliant drivers for Outlook, connect to the Outlook home page at:

http://www.microsoft.com/outlook/

This field name in Lotus Organizer	Maps to this field name in Outlook
Home Fax	Home Fax
Work E-mail	E-mail
Home E-mail	E-mail 2
Position	Job Title
Assistant	Assistant's Name
Children	Children
Spouse	Spouse
Category	Categories Versions 1.0 and 1.1 map the Type field.
Notes	Notes
Company	Company

Mapping Appointment, Anniversary, and Planner Fields

The Lotus Organizer converters maps appointment, anniversary, and planner fields as shown in the following table.

This field name in Lotus Organizer	Maps to this field name in Outlook
Subject	Subject Versions 1.0 and 1.1 map Description field.
Start Date	Start Date
Start Time	Start Time
End Date	End Date
End Time	End Time
Alarm on	Reminder
Alarm Date & Time	Reminder Beforehand
Confidential	Private
Category	Categories

Mapping Task Fields

The Lotus Organizer converter maps task fields as shown in the following table.

This field name in Lotus Organizer	Maps to this field name in Outlook
Description	Subject
Start Date	Start Date
Due Date	Due Date
Alarm on	Reminder
Alarm Date, Alarm Time	Reminder Date/Time
Completion Date	Date Completed
Priority	Priority
Category	Categories

about mapping custom fields, see "Sharing Information with Outlook 97" in Chapter 27, "Sharing Information with Microsoft Office Applications."

Note To switch from Lotus Organizer to Outlook, users must have the appropriate version of Lotus Organizer installed and configured on their computers.

Mapping Fields from Lotus Organizer to Outlook

The following conditions apply when you map fields from Lotus Organizer to Outlook:

- Repeated events are converted as individual events.
- Lotus Organizer 2.1 links to other sections are not converted.
- Lotus Organizer 2.1 planner occurrences that span several days convert as daily repeats for the period.

This remainder of this section describes the automatic mapping that the Lotus Organizer converter performs when a Lotus Organizer file is imported into Outlook.

Mapping Contact Fields

The Lotus Organizer converter maps contact fields as shown in the following table.

This field name in Lotus Organizer	Maps to this field name in Outlook
Name	Full Name
Title	Title
Position	Job Title. This field maps in versions 1.0 and 1.1 only.
First Name	First Name
Last Name	Last Name
Work Address	Business Address Street
Work City	Business Address City
Work State	Business Address State
Work Zip	Business Address Postal Code
Work Country	Business Address Country
Home Address	Home Address Street
Home City	Home Address City
Home State	Home Address State
Home Zip	Home Address Postal Code
Home Country	Home Address Country
Work Fax	Business Fax
Phone + ext	Business Phone
Home Tel 1	Home Phone

This field name in Sidekick	Maps to this field name in Outlook
End Date/Time	End
Alarm on/off	Reminder
Alarm Date/Time	Reminder Date/Time Special Days only

Mapping Task Fields

The Sidekick converter maps task fields as shown in the following table.

This field name in Sidekick	Maps to this field name in Outlook
Task	Subject
Regarding	Notes
Due Date	Due Date Range is 1990–2005; due time is not converted.
Completed	% Completed
Priority	Priority
Category	Categories
Status Complete	Request Status

Switching from Lotus Organizer 1.0, 1.1, or 2.1

Moving your data from Lotus Organizer is a simple process. First install the appropriate converter, and then import the data into Microsoft Outlook using the Import and Export Wizard.

Note The Lotus Organizer converter is not included when you choose a Typical installation during Setup. To install this converter, rerun Office Setup and click **Add/Remove**. Under the **Microsoft Outlook** option, select the **Lotus Organizer Converters** check box.

▶ **To import Lotus Organizer data into Outlook**

1. On the Outlook **File** menu, click **Import and Export**.
2. In the first panel of the wizard, click **Import from Schedule+ or another program or file**.
3. Follow the instructions in the Import and Export Wizard.

The Import and Export Wizard maps the fields in the converted program files to the appropriate fields in Outlook. For a list of fields used in Outlook or for more details

This remainder of this section describes the automatic mapping that the Sidekick converter performs when a Sidekick file is imported into Outlook.

Mapping Contact Fields

The Sidekick converter maps contact fields as shown in the following table.

This field name in Sidekick	Maps to this field name in Outlook
First Name	First Name
Last Name	Last Name
Salutation	Title
Address 1	Business Address Street
City	Business Address City
State	Business Address State
Zip	Business Address Postal Code
Country	Business Address Country
Fax	Business Fax
Office Phone	Business Phone
Home Phone	Home Phone
Mobile Phone	Mobile Phone
Other Phone	Other Phone
Pager	Pager
Internet	E-mail 1
Other E-mail	E-mail 2
Position	Job Title
Anniversary	Anniversary
Birthday	Birthday
Hobby	Hobby
Spouse	Spouse
Notes/Contacts	Notes
Company	Company

Mapping Appointment Fields

The Sidekick converter maps appointment fields as shown in the following table.

This field name in Sidekick	Maps to this field name in Outlook
Task	Subject
Regarding	Description
Start Date/Time	Start

Chapter 19   Switching to Microsoft Outlook

Switching from Starfish Sidekick Deluxe 95

Moving your data from Sidekick is a simple process. First install the appropriate converter and then import the data into Outlook using the Import and Export Wizard.

Note   The Sidekick converter is available in the Office 97 Value Pack. In the ValuPack\Convert\Outlook folder, double-click the file Outcvt.exe (Windows 95 or Windows NT Workstation 4.0) or Outcvtnt.exe (Windows NT Workstation 3.51). For more information about the Value Pack and how to use its contents, see Valupack.hlp in the ValuPack folder on the Office CD. If you have Web access, you can also point to **Microsoft on the Web** (**Help** menu) in any Office application and then click **Free Stuff**.

▶ **To import Sidekick data into Outlook**

1 On the Outlook **File** menu, click **Import and Export**.
2 In the first panel of the wizard, click **Import from Schedule+ or another program or file**.
3 Follow the instructions in the Import and Export Wizard.

The Import and Export Wizard maps the fields in the converted program files to the appropriate fields in Outlook. For a list of fields used in Outlook or for more details about mapping custom fields, see "Sharing Information with Outlook 97" in Chapter 27, "Sharing Information with Microsoft Office Applications."

Mapping Fields from Sidekick to Outlook

Sidekick field definitions may be created or modified by the user. All fields are text and are mapped automatically to the closest reasonable match. The mapping is based on the names in the Business and Personal templates in Sidekick.

The following conditions apply when you map fields from Sidekick to Outlook:

- The Sidekick 95 and 2.0 contact log is treated as an extended Notes field. It is not mapped automatically, but you can map it manually using the **Field Map** dialog box in the Import and Export Wizard.
- Recurring appointments are converted to individual appointments. Sidekick Special Days are converted to annual recurring appointments if they recur—if not, they are translated as individual appointments.
- All Sidekick address fields are converted to Outlook business address fields. To change the Outlook field, map the field manually using the **Field Map** dialog box.
- Sidekick tasks, calls, and goal lists are all converted into tasks. The goal list is converted as a list of undated tasks. Recurring tasks appear as individual tasks.

This field name in ECCO Pro	Maps to this field name in Outlook
Country	Home Address Country
Fax #	Business Fax
Work #	Business Phone
Home #	Home Phone
Cell #	Mobile Phone
Assistant	Assistant's Name
Alt #	Other Phone
Anniversary	Anniversary Translated as an appointment with the All Day Event flag set and repeated yearly.
Birthday	Birthday Translated as an appointment with the All Day Event flag set and repeated yearly.
E-mail	E-mail

Mapping Appointment Fields

The ECCO Pro converter maps appointment fields as shown in the following table.

This field name in ECCO Pro	Maps to this field name in Outlook
Description	Subject
Outline Notes	Notes
Start Date & Start Time	Start
End Date & End Time	End
Alarm	Reminder In ECCO Pro 3.01, only the first alarm prior to the event is converted. Alarms set after the event are not converted.
Alarm Date	Reminder Beforehand

Mapping Task Fields

The ECCO Pro converter maps task fields as shown in the following table.

This field name in ECCO Pro	Maps to this field name in Outlook
Description	Subject
Outline Notes	Notes
Start Date	Start Date
Done	Date Completed
Priority	Priority

▶ **To import ECCO Pro data into Outlook**

1. On the Outlook **File** menu, click **Import and Export**.
2. In the first panel of the wizard, click **Import from Schedule+ or another program or file**.
3. Follow the instructions in the Import and Export Wizard.

The Import and Export Wizard maps the fields in the converted program files to the appropriate fields in Outlook. For a list of fields used in Outlook or for more details about mapping custom fields, see "Sharing Information with Outlook 97" in Chapter 27, "Sharing Information with Microsoft Office Applications."

Mapping Fields from ECCO Pro to Outlook

ECCO Pro must be installed before you can import items into Outlook. ECCO Pro requires user input when opening the file if the file contains alarms, or if the file was created in ECCO Pro 3.0 but is being opened in ECCO Pro 3.01. Outlines, alarms, and recurring events from ECCO Pro 3.0 are not converted. User-defined fields in ECCO Pro are not mapped automatically. Custom priorities in ECCO Pro are all converted to Normal Importance.

This remainder of this section describes the automatic mapping that the ECCO Pro converter performs when an ECCO Pro file is imported into Outlook.

Mapping Contact Fields

The ECCO Pro converter maps contact fields as shown in the following table.

This field name in ECCO Pro	Maps to this field name in Outlook
Name (First, Last)	Full Name
Mr./Mrs.	Title
Company	Company
Job Title	Job Title
Address 1 Business Address 2 Business	Business Address Street
City-Business	Business Address City
State-Business	Business Address State
Zip-Business	Business Address Postal Code
Country-Business	Business Address Country
Address1 Home Address2 Home	Home Address Street
City-Home	Home Address City
State-Home	Home Address State
Zip-Home	Home Address Postal Code

Mapping Appointment Fields

The ACT! 2.0 converter maps appointment fields as shown in the following table.

This field name in ACT! 2.0	Maps to this field name in Outlook
Regarding	Subject
Start Date	Start
End Date	End
Alarm On	Reminder
Alarm Date	Reminder Beforehand
Priority	Importance
Access	Sensitivity

Mapping Task Fields

The ACT! 2.0 converter maps task fields as shown in the following table.

This field name in ACT! 2.0	Maps to this field name in Outlook
Regarding	Subject
Start Date	Start Date
End Date	Due Date
Alarm On	Reminder
Alarm Date	Reminder Time
Access	Sensitivity
Priority	Priority
Contact	Contacts

Switching from NetManage ECCO Pro 3.0, 3.01, or 3.02

Moving your data from ECCO Pro is a simple process. First install the appropriate converter, and then import the data into Outlook using the Import and Export Wizard.

Note The ECCO Pro converter is available in the Office 97 Value Pack. In the ValuPack\Convert\Outlook folder, double-click the file Outcvt.exe (Windows 95 or Windows NT Workstation 4.0) or Outcvtnt.exe (Windows NT Workstation 3.51). For more information about the Value Pack and how to use its contents, see Valupack.hlp in the ValuPack folder on the Office CD. If you have Web access, you can also point to **Microsoft on the Web** (**Help** menu) in any Office application and then click **Free Stuff**.

The Import and Export Wizard maps the fields in the converted program files to the appropriate fields in Outlook. For a list of fields used in Outlook or for more details about mapping custom fields, see "Sharing Information with Outlook 97" in Chapter 27, "Sharing Information with Microsoft Office Applications."

Mapping Fields from ACT! 2.0 to Outlook

This section describes the mapping that the ACT! 2.0 converter performs when an ACT! 2.0 file is imported into Outlook.

Mapping Contact Fields

The ACT! 2.0 converter maps contact fields as shown in the following table.

This field name in ACT! 2.0	Maps to this field name in Outlook
Contact	Full Name ACT! combines the full name into one field. This is mapped to a combined name in Outlook.
Company	Company
Title	Job Title
Address (3 fields)	Business Address Street ACT! maps three street address fields into one.
City	Business Address City
State	Business Address State
Zip	Business Address Postal Code
Address (3 fields)	Home Address Street ACT! maps three street address fields into one.
City	Home Address City
State	Home Address State
Zip	Home Address Postal Code
Business Fax	Business Fax
Business Phone	Business Phone ACT! appends a separate extension field to phone numbers.
Car Phone	Car Phone
Home Phone	Home Phone
Alt Phone 1 & 2	This field is not automatically mapped.
Assistant	Assistant's Name
E-mail ID	E-mail
Notes	Notes
Referred by	Referred By

▶ **To import cc:Mail folders into Outlook**

1. On the Outlook **Tools** menu, point to **cc:Mail Service Tools**, and then click **Import cc:Mail Folders**.
2. Select the folders you want to import, and then click **Begin**.

Using cc:Mail Private Lists and Address Book with Outlook

In Outlook, you can download the cc:Mail post office address book for working offline.

▶ **To download the cc:Mail post office address book**

- On the Outlook **Tools** menu, point to **cc:Mail Service Tools**, and then click **Update Local Copy of cc:Mail Address Book**.

  The cc:Mail directory and mail lists appear in the **Show Names from the** box in the **Address Book** dialog box (**Tools** menu).

You can also import cc:Mail private mail lists into Outlook.

▶ **To import cc:Mail private mail lists**

- On the Outlook **Tools** menu, point to **cc:Mail Service Tools**, and then click **Import cc:Mail Private Lists to Personal Address Book**.

Switching from Symantec ACT! 2.0

Moving your data from ACT! is a simple process. First install the appropriate converter, and then import the data into Outlook using the Import and Export Wizard.

Note The ACT! 2.0 converter is available in the Office 97 Value Pack. In the ValuPack\Convert\Outlook folder, double-click the file Outcvt.exe (Windows 95 or Windows NT Workstation 4.0) or Outcvtnt.exe (Windows NT Workstation 3.51). For more information about the Value Pack and how to use its contents, see Valupack.hlp in the ValuPack folder on the Office CD. If you have Web access, you can also point to **Microsoft on the Web** (**Help** menu) in any Office application and then click **Free Stuff**.

▶ **To import ACT! 2.0 data into Outlook**

1. On the Outlook **File** menu, click **Import and Export**.
2. In the first panel of the wizard, click **Import from Schedule+ or another program or file**.
3. Follow the instructions in the Import and Export Wizard.

Using cc:Mail Bulletin Boards with Outlook

When you add the cc:Mail messaging service to your profile, the **cc:Mail Service Tools** command is added to the Outlook **Tools** menu. Copy information on cc:Mail bulletin boards from the post office to your computer using the **Import cc:Mail Bulletin Boards** or **Update cc:Mail Bulletin Boards** command on the **cc:Mail Service Tools** submenu.

To use cc:Mail bulletin boards with Outlook, you must have the file Export.exe in your path, and you must create an address entry in your Personal Address Book for the bulletin board. Entries to a bulletin board are sent as e-mail messages addressed to the bulletin board.

▶ **To set up cc:Mail bulletin boards using the Outlook client**

1. In the cc:Mail post office, copy Export.exe from the Ccadmin folder to the post office Ccmail folder.

    This places the file in your post office share, which is on your path.

2. On the Outlook **Tools** menu, point to **cc:Mail Service Tools**, and then click **Import cc:Mail Bulletin Boards**.

3. Select the name of the bulletin board from the list, and then click **Begin**.

    –or–

    Add a bulletin board to the list by clicking **Edit List**, clicking **Add**, and typing the name of the bulletin board.

4. In the Address Book, create a new cc:Mail Recipient entry, and then enter the name of the bulletin board in the **Electronic Address** box.

To send a message to the bulletin board, create a new e-mail message and address it using the address for the bulletin board in the Personal Address Book.

The **Update cc:Mail Bulletin Boards** command copies only items posted by other users. To copy the bulletin board and include your entries, you must use the **Import cc:Mail Bulletin Boards** command. This creates a new copy of the bulletin board folder (with a number such as 001) in your Folder List. Each time you import a bulletin board, a new folder is created that includes all the current contents.

The **New Post in This Folder** command (**Compose** menu) posts a new message to your local copy of the bulletin board, not to the post office version. Other users of the bulletin board do not see these posted messages.

Importing cc:Mail Folders into Outlook

If you created personal folders in cc:Mail, you can import them into Outlook. You must have the cc:Mail file Export.exe in the path to complete this procedure.

If your e-mail service provider is not included in the preceding list, you must obtain the appropriate software from your service provider. In the meantime, you can use Outlook without e-mail. For information about how to add an information service to a profile in Outlook, see Outlook online Help.

Switching from Lotus cc:Mail

You can install Microsoft Outlook in your workgroup with the cc:Mail information service, a MAPI service provider that allows you to use Outlook as an e-mail client with a cc:Mail post office. When Outlook users install the cc:Mail service provider and then add the information service to their user profiles, they can exchange mail with other cc:Mail and Outlook users, use cc:Mail bulletin boards, download the post office address book for working offline, and have all the power of Outlook with a cc:Mail e-mail account.

Note Outlook features such as Voting buttons, Message Flags, and AutoPreview are all fully functional using a cc:Mail post office, but they are available only to Outlook users.

For Windows NT Workstation 3.51 or later, you must install the 32-bit version of Vendor-Independent Messaging (VIM), available from Lotus Development Corporation.

Note The cc:Mail transport provider is available in the Office 97 Value Pack. In the ValuPack\Ccmail folder, double-click the file Ccmailsp.exe (Windows 95 or Windows NT Workstation 4.0) or Ccmailnt.exe (Windows NT Workstation 3.51). For more information about the Value Pack and how to use its contents, see Valupack.hlp in the ValuPack folder on the Office CD. If you have Web access, you can also point to **Microsoft on the Web** (**Help** menu) in any Office application and then click **Free Stuff**.

▶ **To add the cc:Mail information service to your user profile**

1   In Control Panel, double-click the Mail and Fax icon.
2   Click the **Services** tab, and then click **Add**.
3   In the **Available information services** box, click **MS Outlook support for Lotus cc:Mail**.

To get the full functionality of Outlook, you must turn on Rich Text Format (RTF).

▶ **To turn on RTF in Outlook**

1   On the Outlook **Tools** menu, click **Services**.
2   On the **Services** tab, select the **MS Outlook support for Lotus cc:Mail** service, and then click **Properties**.
3   Click the **Delivery** tab, and then select the **Send using Microsoft Exchange rich text format** check box.

To import data from or export data to any of the following applications, however, you must use the appropriate converters:

- ACT! 2.0
- ECCO Pro 3.0, 3.01, or 3.02
- Sidekick 1.0-95

With the appropriate converter, you can also directly import or export items in the Outlook Journal or Notes folder.

Note Outlook converters are available in the Office 97 Value Pack. For more information about the Value Pack and how to use its contents, see Valupack.hlp in the ValuPack folder on the Office CD. If you have Web access, you can also point to **Microsoft on the Web** (**Help** menu) in any Office application and then click **Free Stuff**.

Using E-mail Information Services Provided with Outlook

Outlook includes software for the following popular e-mail service providers and for the Internet.

- Microsoft Exchange Server
- Microsoft Mail
- Microsoft At Work™ fax software

  If you already have Microsoft At Work fax software installed on your computer, the software is updated automatically when you install Outlook. Otherwise, install the Microsoft At Work fax software driver from your Windows 95 disks before you install Outlook.

- Internet Mail.

  This service is also known as Simple Mail Transfer Protocol (SMTP) or POP version 3.

- MSN, The Microsoft Network

  You can use the Internet Mail service provider to use this online service.

- cc:Mail

Note The cc:Mail driver is available in the Office 97 Value Pack. For more information about the Value Pack and how to use its contents, see Valupack.hlp in the ValuPack folder on the Office CD. If you have Web access, you can also point to **Microsoft on the Web** (**Help** menu) in any Office application and then click **Free Stuff**.

Overview

When you switch to Outlook, importing data is an easy process. The Microsoft Office 97 Value Pack contains converters so you can import data directly from many of the leading personal information management (PIM) products. Outlook can also import from intermediary formats, such as Tab Separated Values or Comma Separated Values, so any data that can be exported from a program in these formats can be imported into Outlook folders.

Outlook is an e-mail client that can be used with any fully MAPI-compliant e-mail system, including Microsoft Exchange Server, Microsoft Mail 3.*x*, Post Office Protocol (POP), and Lotus cc:Mail.

Note The CD-ROM version of Office includes the Office 97 Value Pack, a collection of application extras such as clip art, maps, sounds, presentation enhancements, and utilities. For more information about the Value Pack and how to use its contents, see Valupack.hlp in the ValuPack folder on the Office CD. If you have World Wide Web access, you can also point to **Microsoft on the Web** (**Help** menu) in any Office application and then click **Free Stuff**.

Importing and Exporting File Types

Using the **Import and Export** command (**File** menu), you can import and export information directly between Outlook and any of the file types listed in following table.

Product	File extension	Import	Export
Comma Separated Values (DOS)	.txt	Yes	Yes
Comma Separated Values (Windows)	.csv	Yes	Yes
dBASE	.dbf	Yes	Yes
Lotus Organizer 1.0, 1.1, 2.1	.org, .or2	Yes	No
Microsoft Access	.mdb	Yes	Yes
Microsoft Excel	.xls	Yes	Yes
Microsoft Exchange Personal Address Book	.pab	Yes	Yes
Microsoft FoxPro	.dbf	Yes	Yes
Microsoft Schedule+ 1.0	.cal	Yes	No
Microsoft Schedule+ 95	.scd	Yes	No
NetManage ECCO Pro 3.0, 3.01, or 3.02	.eco	Yes	No
Starfish Sidekick 1.0/95	.skcard	Yes	No
Symantec ACT! 2.0 for Windows	.dbf	Yes	No
Tab Separated Values (DOS)	.txt	Yes	Yes
Tab Separated Values (Windows)	.txt	Yes	Yes

CHAPTER 19

Switching to Microsoft Outlook

This chapter tells you what to expect when you or your workgroup switches to Microsoft Outlook from other scheduling, calendar, or electronic mail (e-mail) applications.

In This Chapter
Overview   546
Importing and Exporting File Types   546
Using E-mail Information Services Provided with Outlook   547
Switching from Lotus cc:Mail   548
Switching from Symantec ACT! 2.0   550
Switching from NetManage ECCO Pro 3.0, 3.01, or 3.02   552
Switching from Starfish Sidekick Deluxe 95   555
Switching from Lotus Organizer 1.0, 1.1, or 2.1   557
Switching from Other Client/Server Messaging Systems   560

See Also
- For a summary of new features in Outlook, see Chapter 2, "What's New in Microsoft Office 97."
- For information about installing Outlook or other Office applications, see Chapter 4, "Installing Microsoft Office."
- For information about upgrading to Outlook from other Microsoft e-mail and calendar applications, see Chapter 13, "Upgrading to Microsoft Outlook."

Note   Microsoft Outlook runs on Windows 95 and Windows NT Workstation version 3.51 or later only.

▶ **To save a converted Microsoft Works worksheet in Microsoft Excel format**

1 On the **File** menu, click **Save As**.
2 In the **File name** box, enter a new name for the converted worksheet.

   This preserves the original Microsoft Works worksheet as a backup.
3 In the **Save as type** box, click **Microsoft Excel workbook**.

Sharing Documents with Microsoft Works

If your workgroup is upgrading gradually to Microsoft Excel, some users may have to share documents with users of Microsoft Works.

▶ **To save the active sheet of a Microsoft Excel workbook in Microsoft Works format**

1 On the **File** menu, click **Save As**.
2 In the **Save as type** box, click **WKS (1-2-3)**.
3 In the **File name** box, enter a name for the converted worksheet.

   Microsoft Excel saves only the active sheet. To save other sheets in the workbook, repeat this procedure separately for each sheet.

Multiplan Transfer Clear Window Command Equivalents

There is no direct equivalent to the Multiplan **Transfer Clear Window** command in Microsoft Excel. Instead, do one of the following:

- To create a new workbook, choose **New** (**File** menu).
- To close the active workbook, choose **Close** (**File** menu).
- To clear cell contents from the active worksheet, select the cells you want to clear, and then press DELETE. (To select an entire worksheet, click the button located at the intersection of the row headers and column headers.)

Switching from Microsoft Works

Microsoft Excel can open worksheets created in earlier versions of Microsoft Works (version 2.*x* and earlier) for Windows or for the Macintosh. Later versions of Microsoft Works (version 3.*x* and later) can save worksheets in Microsoft Excel format.

Converting Microsoft Works Files to Microsoft Excel

The majority of your Microsoft Works 3.*x* and earlier worksheets can be converted to Microsoft Excel format by opening them and then saving them in Microsoft Excel.

▶ **To open a Microsoft Works worksheet file in Microsoft Excel**

1. On the **File** menu, click **Open**.
2. In the **Files of type** box, click **Microsoft Works 2.0 Files**.
3. Below the **Look in** box, select the name of the worksheet.
4. Click **Open**.

   Microsoft Excel converts the Microsoft Works worksheet and opens it.

Tip To import worksheets from Microsoft Works 4.0 for Windows, first save the worksheets in Microsoft Excel SS format in Microsoft Works. The Microsoft Excel SS format is the same as Microsoft Excel 4.0 format, which Microsoft Excel 97 can open.

Tip To import worksheets from Microsoft Works 4.0 for the Macintosh, first save the worksheets in Microsoft Excel 5.0 format in Microsoft Works.

After you convert a Microsoft Works worksheet to Microsoft Excel, the converted worksheet exists only in your computer's memory; the original worksheet remains unchanged. To complete the conversion, you need to save the converted worksheet in Microsoft Excel format.

Multiplan Print Options Command Equivalents

The following table describes the equivalent Microsoft Excel features or actions for Multiplan options.

This Multiplan option	Corresponds to this Microsoft Excel feature or action
Area	**Set Print Area** (**File** menu, **Print Area** submenu)
Setup (Multiplan version 3.04 and earlier)	**Page Setup** (**File** menu)
Formulas	**View** tab in the **Options** dialog box (**Tools** menu)
Row-col numbers	**Page Setup** (**File** menu)
Printer (Multiplan version 4.0 and earlier)	**Page Setup** (**File** menu)
Model (Multiplan version 4.0 and earlier)	**Page Setup** (**File** menu)
Draft (Multiplan version 4.0 and earlier)	**Page Setup** (**File** menu)
Number of copies (Multiplan version 4.2)	**Print** (**File** menu)

Multiplan Run Command Equivalents

There is no direct equivalent to the Multiplan **Run** command in Microsoft Excel, but you can activate the command prompt from **Start** menu.

▶ **To activate the command prompt in Windows 95 or Windows NT Workstation 4.0**

- Click **Start** menu, point to **Programs**, and then click **MS-DOS Prompt**.

▶ **To activate MS-DOS on the Windows NT 3.51 operating system**

- In the Main program group, double-click the Command Prompt icon.

Multiplan Run Report Command Equivalents

The following table describes the equivalent Microsoft Excel features or actions for Multiplan options.

This Multiplan option	Corresponds to this Microsoft Excel feature or action
Cross-ref	No direct equivalent. You can trace formula precedents and dependents using the **Auditing** submenu commands (**Tools** menu).
Names	To get a list of defined names in a worksheet, select an empty area of the worksheet and click **Name** (**Insert** menu); then click **Paste** and click the **Paste List** button.
Summary	No direct equivalent. To identify conditions in a worksheet that are likely to cause errors, use the **Auditing** submenu commands (**Tools** menu).

Part 4 Switching from Other Applications

Multiplan Cell Editing Command Equivalents

The following table describes the equivalent Microsoft Excel features or actions for Multiplan options.

This Multiplan key	Corresponds to this Microsoft Excel feature or action
SHIFT+F1, SHIFT+F6	On the **Window** menu, select the number of the window you want.
SHIFT+F3, arrow key or @), @, arrow key	**Function** (**Insert** menu).
F3, arrow key or @, arrow key	**Paste** (**Insert** menu, **Name** submenu).
SHIFT+F5 or CTRL+T	**Step Macro** button (**Macro** toolbar).
SHIFT+F9 or SHIFT+F7 or CTRL+R, CTRL+R	**Record New Macro** and **Stop Recording** (**Tools** menu, **Record Macro** submenu).

Multiplan Option Command Equivalents

The following table describes the equivalent Microsoft Excel features or actions for Multiplan options.

This Multiplan option	Corresponds to this Microsoft Excel feature or action
Recalc	**Calculation** tab in the **Options** dialog box (**Tools** menu).
Iteration	**Calculation** tab in the **Options** dialog box (**Tools** menu).
Test at	**Calculation** tab in the **Options** dialog box (**Tools** menu).
Alpha/value	You don't need to specify alpha or value; Microsoft Excel accepts any type of valid data in the selected cell.
Learn	Select all the cells in which you want to enter data. The ENTER, TAB, and arrow keys move the active cell within the selection.
Mute	In the Windows Control Panel, double-click the Sounds icon to manage the system sounds.
Old menus (Multiplan version 4.0 and later)	No equivalent.
Hold Alpha (Multiplan version 4.0 and later)	No direct equivalent; Microsoft Excel is always ready to accept data in the selected cell.

Multiplan Print File Command Equivalents

There is no procedure in Microsoft Excel for the Multiplan **Print File** command. For information about printing to a text file, see your Windows documentation.

▶ **To save the active sheet of a Microsoft Excel workbook as a Microsoft Excel 2.1 worksheet**

1   On the **File** menu, click **Save As**.
2   In the **File name** box, enter a name for the converted workbook.
3   In the **Save as type** box, click **Microsoft Excel 2.1 Worksheet**.

    Microsoft Excel saves only the active sheet. To save other sheets in the workbook, repeat this procedure separately for each sheet.

Using Multiplan Command Equivalents

The following tables list frequently used Multiplan commands and their equivalent commands in Microsoft Excel.

Multiplan Format Options Command Equivalents

The following table describes the equivalent Microsoft Excel features or actions for Multiplan options.

This Multiplan option	Corresponds to this Microsoft Excel feature or action
Commas (Multiplan version 3.04 and earlier)	**Number** tab in the **Cells** dialog box (**Format** menu)
Decimal separator (Multiplan version 4.0 and later)	Changing the decimal separator
Error messages (Multiplan version 4.0 and later)	No equivalent
Formulas	**View** tab in the **Options** dialog box (**Tools** menu)

Multiplan Selection Command Equivalents

The following table describes the equivalent Microsoft Excel features or actions for Multiplan options.

This Multiplan key	Corresponds to this Microsoft Excel feature or action
F1, SEMICOLON (;) or CTRL+W	On the **Window** menu, select the number of the window you want.
F2 or CTRL+F	With worksheet protection turned on, press TAB.
SHIFT+F2 or CTRL+R, CTRL+F	With worksheet protection turned on, press SHIFT+TAB.
F4 or EXCLAMATION point (!)	F9, or the **Calc Now** button on the **Calculation** tab in the **Options** dialog box (**Tools** menu).
F6 or COLON (:)	Extend the selection by dragging with the mouse.
ALT+H or QUESTION MARK (?)	**Help** menu.

Switching from Multiplan

To transfer Multiplan files to Microsoft Excel, you must first save the Multiplan worksheet in SYLK format.

Converting Multiplan Files to Microsoft Excel

Both Multiplan and Microsoft Excel can work with SYLK files. To use your Multiplan files in Microsoft Excel, first save them in SYLK format, and then you can open them in Microsoft Excel.

▶ **To open a SYLK file in Microsoft Excel**

1. On the **File** menu, click **Open**.
2. In the **Files of type** box, click **SYLK (Symbolic Link) Files**.
3. Below the **Look in** box, select the name of the file.
4. Click **Open**.

   Microsoft Excel converts the SYLK file and opens it.

After you convert a Multiplan worksheet to Microsoft Excel, the converted worksheet exists only in your computer's memory; the original worksheet remains unchanged. To complete the conversion, you need to save the converted worksheet in Microsoft Excel format.

▶ **To save a converted Multiplan worksheet in Microsoft Excel format**

1. On the **File** menu, click **Save As**.
2. In the **File name** box, enter a new name for the converted worksheet.

   This preserves the original SYLK file as a backup.
3. In the **Save as type** box, click **Microsoft Excel workbook**.

Sharing Documents with Multiplan

If your workgroup is upgrading gradually to Microsoft Excel, some users may have to share documents with users of Multiplan. Use the SYLK format, with which both Multiplan and Microsoft Excel can work.

▶ **To save the active sheet of a Microsoft Excel workbook in SYLK format**

1. On the **File** menu, click **Save As**.
2. In the **File name** box, enter a name for the converted workbook.
3. In the **Save as type** box, click **SYLK Files**.

   Microsoft Excel saves only the active sheet. To save other sheets in the workbook, repeat this procedure for each sheet.

After you convert a Quattro Pro for Windows notebook to Microsoft Excel, the converted notebook exists only in your computer's memory; the original notebook remains unchanged. To complete the conversion, you need to save the converted notebook in Microsoft Excel workbook format.

▶ **To save a converted Quattro Pro for Windows notebook in Microsoft Excel format**

1 On the **File** menu, click **Save As**.
2 In the **File name** box, enter a new name for the converted notebook.

   This preserves the original Quattro Pro for Windows notebook as a backup.
3 In the **Save as type** box, click **Microsoft Excel workbook**.

The following Quattro Pro for Windows features do not have direct equivalents in Microsoft Excel and are not imported:

- Microsoft Excel cannot open Quattro Pro files that are password protected. Before you open the file in Microsoft Excel, make sure you have removed any password on the file.
- Microsoft Excel cannot run macros created in Quattro Pro for Windows.
- Microsoft Excel cannot directly open a Quattro Pro for Windows 6.0 file. Save Quattro Pro for Windows 6.0 files in an earlier Quattro Pro format or in another format, such as Lotus 1-2-3.
- External links in Quattro Pro for Windows version 6.0 files do not convert when you open the file in Microsoft Excel.
- Quattro Pro for Windows graphs are stored in a different manner than Microsoft Excel stores its charts, and are not imported.
- The Microsoft Excel Scenario Manager is not directly equivalent to the Quattro Pro for Windows Scenario Manager. Therefore, Microsoft Excel imports only the data from the scenario that is currently displayed (the last time the file was saved). You can use the Microsoft Excel Scenario Manager to create, store, and retrieve what-if assumptions for multiple sets of up to 32 changing cells.
- Quattro Pro for Windows Hot Links to external database tables or to the Data Modeling Desktop are not compatible with ODBC, Microsoft Query, or Microsoft Excel PivotTables, so they are not imported.
- Embedded OLE objects are not imported.
- For gradient fills, the object is formatted using the primary color from the fill.

Part 4 Switching from Other Applications

Sharing Documents with Quattro Pro for MS-DOS

If your workgroup is upgrading gradually to Microsoft Excel, some users may have to share documents with users of Quattro Pro for MS-DOS.

▶ **To save a Microsoft Excel document in Quattro Pro for MS-DOS format**

1. On the **File** menu, click **Save As**.
2. In the **File name** box, enter a name for the converted document.
3. In the **Save as type** box, click **WQ1 (Quattro Pro/DOS)**.

Running Quattro Pro for MS-DOS Macros in Microsoft Excel

Microsoft Excel for Windows runs Quattro Pro macros that are compatible with Lotus 1-2-3 Release 2.01. For more information, see "Running Lotus 1-2-3 Macros in Microsoft Excel" earlier in this chapter.

To run a Quattro Pro macro in Microsoft Excel, hold down the CTRL key and press the macro letter name that is normally used with the backslash (\) key in Quattro Pro.

Switching from Quattro Pro for Windows

The majority of your Quattro Pro for Windows 5.*x* and earlier notebooks can be converted to Microsoft Excel format by opening them and then saving them in Microsoft Excel.

Note The Quattro Pro for Windows file converter (Xlqpw.dll) is not installed when you choose a Typical installation during Setup. If **Quattro Pro for Windows** does not appear in the **Open** dialog box (**File** menu), rerun Setup and click **Add/Remove**. Under the **Microsoft Excel** option, select the **Spreadsheet Converters** option, and then select the **Quattro Pro 1.0/5.0 (Win)** option.

▶ **To open a Quattro Pro for Windows notebook in Microsoft Excel**

1. On the **File** menu, click **Open**.
2. In the **Files of type** box, click **Quattro Pro for Windows**.
3. Below the **Look in** box, select the name of the worksheet.
4. Click **Open**.

   Microsoft Excel converts the Quattro Pro for Windows worksheet and opens it.

Note Microsoft Excel cannot open Quattro Pro version 6.0 for Windows files. If you need to convert such a file to Microsoft Excel, first save it to Quattro Pro 5.0 for Windows format.

For commands requiring additional information, such as cell references, you are prompted for the necessary information at the top of the Microsoft Excel window before the demonstration starts.

The **Faster** and **Slower** buttons allow you to choose from among five demonstration speeds, with 5 being the fastest and 1 the slowest. The current speed is displayed in the box to the right of the two buttons.

Switching from Quattro Pro for MS-DOS

Microsoft Excel lets you use your existing Quattro Pro 4.0 for MS-DOS files while taking advantage of the ease and power of Microsoft Excel. You can open Quattro Pro for MS-DOS files in Microsoft Excel and run Quattro Pro macros that are compatible with Lotus 1-2-3 release 2.01.

Note Microsoft Excel cannot open Quattro Pro 5.0 for MS-DOS files. If you need to convert such a file to Microsoft Excel, first save each sheet in the Quattro Pro notebook to Quattro Pro 4.0 for MS-DOS format.

Converting Quattro Pro for MS-DOS Worksheets to Microsoft Excel

The majority of your Quattro Pro for MS-DOS worksheets can be converted to Microsoft Excel format by opening them and then saving them in Microsoft Excel.

▶ **To open a Quattro Pro for MS-DOS worksheet in Microsoft Excel**

1 On the **File** menu, click **Open**.
2 In the **Files of type** box, click **Quattro Pro/DOS**.
3 Below the **Look in** box, select the name of the worksheet.
4 Click **Open**.

   Microsoft Excel converts the Quattro Pro for MS-DOS worksheet and opens it.

After you convert a Quattro Pro for MS-DOS worksheet to Microsoft Excel, the converted worksheet exists only in your computer's memory; the original worksheet remains unchanged. To complete the conversion, you need to save the converted worksheet in Microsoft Excel format.

▶ **To save a converted Quattro Pro for MS-DOS worksheet in Microsoft Excel format**

1 On the **File** menu, click **Save As**.
2 In the **File name** box, enter a new name for the converted worksheet.

   This preserves the original Quattro Pro for MS-DOS worksheet as a backup.

3 In the **Save as type** box, click **Microsoft Excel workbook**.

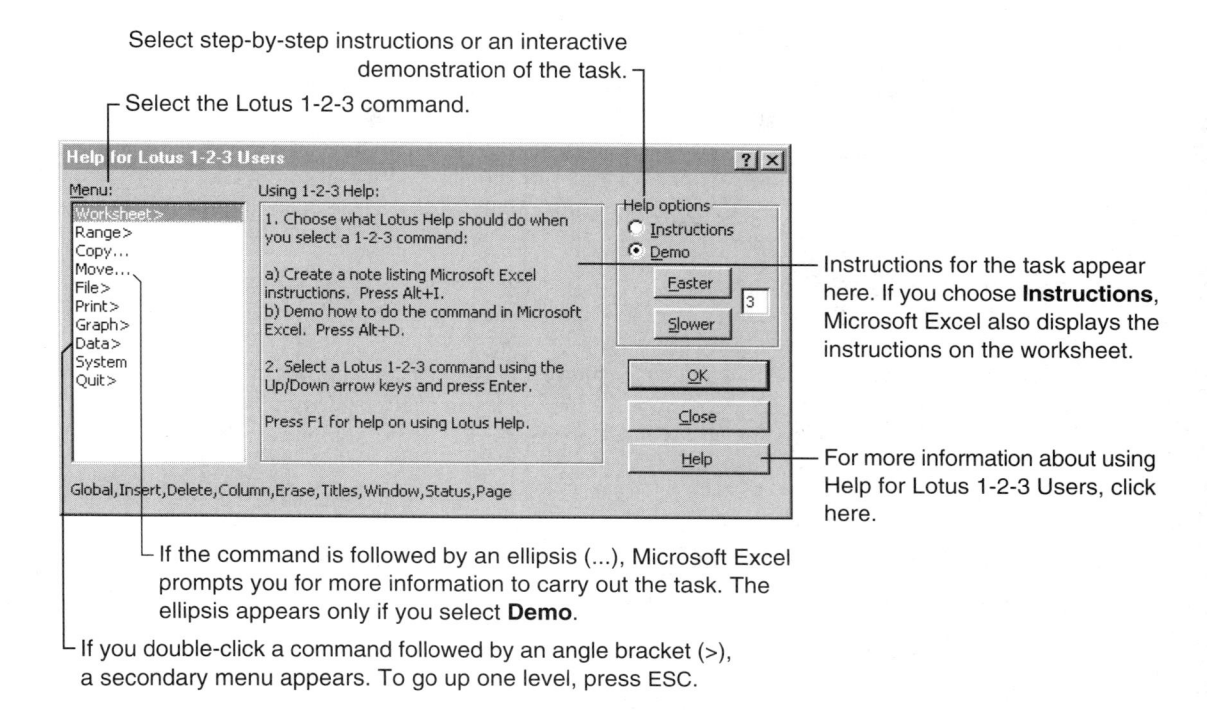

Select step-by-step instructions or an interactive demonstration of the task.

Select the Lotus 1-2-3 command.

```
Help for Lotus 1-2-3 Users                                    ? X
Menu:              Using 1-2-3 Help:                  ┌Help options─
 Worksheet>         1. Choose what Lotus Help should do when    ○ Instructions
 Range>             you select a 1-2-3 command:                 ● Demo
 Copy...
 Move...            a) Create a note listing Microsoft Excel     [Faster]
 File>              instructions. Press Alt+I.                           [3]
 Print>             b) Demo how to do the command in Microsoft   [Slower]
 Graph>             Excel. Press Alt+D.
 Data>
 System             2. Select a Lotus 1-2-3 command using the    [  OK  ]
 Quit>              Up/Down arrow keys and press Enter.
                                                                 [ Close ]
                    Press F1 for help on using Lotus Help.
                                                                 [ Help  ]

Global,Insert,Delete,Column,Erase,Titles,Window,Status,Page
```

Instructions for the task appear here. If you choose **Instructions**, Microsoft Excel also displays the instructions on the worksheet.

For more information about using Help for Lotus 1-2-3 Users, click here.

If the command is followed by an ellipsis (...), Microsoft Excel prompts you for more information to carry out the task. The ellipsis appears only if you select **Demo**.

If you double-click a command followed by an angle bracket (>), a secondary menu appears. To go up one level, press ESC.

The following sections describe options in the **Help for Lotus 1-2-3 Users** dialog box.

Menu

The **Menu** box in the **Help for Lotus 1-2-3 Users** dialog box displays a list of Lotus 1-2-3 menu items. Type the Lotus 1-2-3 keystrokes you would use to choose a command. Depending on the type of help you select under **Help options**, Microsoft Excel either begins a demonstration or displays instructions for carrying out the equivalent actions in Microsoft Excel. For multilevel Lotus 1-2-3 menus, Microsoft Excel displays the submenu at the bottom of the dialog box. To move to the next menu level, select the menu item in the **Menu** box, and then press ENTER or press the first letter of the menu item.

Help Options

In the **Help options** box in the **Help for Lotus 1-2-3 Users** dialog box you can choose either to display a text box containing the Microsoft Excel equivalent procedure for carrying out a Lotus 1-2-3 command (the **Instructions** option), or to watch Microsoft Excel demonstrate the equivalent steps for you (the **Demo** option).

Using Lotus 1-2-3 Help

In Microsoft Excel for Windows, the Lotus 1-2-3 Help feature allows you to use familiar Lotus 1-2-3 keys and commands while you learn how to use Microsoft Excel. For example, you can choose a Lotus 1-2-3 key or command and have Microsoft Excel display step-by-step instructions for the corresponding action in Microsoft Excel. Or Microsoft Excel can demonstrate and actually carry out the corresponding action.

Note The Lotus 1-2-3 Help feature also provides Help topics for users switching from Lotus 1-2-3 for MS-DOS.

You can press a Lotus 1-2-3 key and have Microsoft Excel either automatically demonstrate the corresponding feature or list the steps you need to perform it in Microsoft Excel. If you are not sure which Lotus 1-2-3 key to press, you can choose from a list of Lotus 1-2-3 commands.

▶ **To use Lotus 1-2-3 Help**

1 On the **Tools** menu, click **Options**, and then click the **Transition** tab.
2 Under **Settings**, click **Lotus 1-2-3 Help**.

Next you need to indicate whether you want to see step-by-step instructions or demonstrations when you press Lotus 1-2-3 keys.

▶ **To see step-by-step instructions or demonstrations**

1 On the **Help** menu, click **Lotus 1-2-3 Help**.
2 Under **Help options**, click **Instructions** to see step-by-step instructions.

   –or–

   Click **Demo** to see demonstrations.

When you're working in a Microsoft Excel document and you press the SLASH key (/), or the key you specified on the **Transition** tab in the **Options** dialog box (**Tools** menu), the **Help for Lotus 1-2-3 Users** dialog box appears. Select the Lotus 1-2-3 command you want, and then click either **Instructions** or **Demo**.

Lotus 1-2-3 Releases 1a and 2.01 do not support external references (file linking) to other worksheets, so any Microsoft Excel formulas containing external references are not exported to WKS or WK1 file formats. In these cases, Microsoft Excel substitutes the value of the formula for the formula itself.

Microsoft Excel Functions Without Lotus 1-2-3 Equivalents

Many Microsoft Excel functions have equivalent Lotus 1-2-3 functions. However, the following Microsoft Excel functions have no equivalents in Lotus 1-2-3 Release 3.1 or earlier, or Lotus 1-2-3/W Release 1.0, and generate an error message in Lotus 1-2-3.

Note Microsoft Excel also provides many add-in functions and statistical functions in the Analysis ToolPak that don't have Lotus 1-2-3 equivalents; these are not included in this list.

Microsoft Excel functions without equivalents in Lotus 1-2-3 3.1 or earlier

AREAS	MATCH
DOLLAR	MDETERM
DPRODUCT	MINVERSE
FACT	MIRR
FREQUENCY	MMULT
GROWTH	PPMT
INT	PRODUCT
IPMT	SEARCH
ISBLANK	SUBSTITUTE
ISERROR	TEXT
ISLOGICAL	TRANSPOSE
LINEST	TREND
LOGEST	TYPE
LOOKUP	WEEKDAY

You can use the **Links** command (**Edit** menu) to open the Lotus 1-2-3 worksheet that contains the source data for the Microsoft Excel worksheet you are editing. You can also redirect links to refer to another worksheet.

Consolidating Microsoft Excel and Lotus 1-2-3 Worksheets

When you switch to Microsoft Excel, you might need to include data from Lotus 1-2-3 worksheets in summary reports created in Microsoft Excel. In Microsoft Excel you can include details from Lotus 1-2-3 worksheets. The addresses of these data sources are stored in the worksheet, and you can call them whenever an update is needed using the **Consolidate** command (**Data** menu). You can also construct dynamic links to the source data that update the figures in the consolidation worksheet automatically.

For example, suppose you have a departmental budget that consists of monthly data from several different sources throughout the department. The source sheets can be a variety of Microsoft Excel and Lotus 1-2-3 files. Each source might have a set of daily, weekly, or monthly worksheets itemizing actual and projected budgets. Each source can use consolidation to collect specific data from the set of worksheets in order to create a summary worksheet. The person responsible for the overall budget can use consolidation formulas to collect this summary information from each source across the network and, in turn, create a master departmental summary worksheet.

Using Microsoft Excel References in Lotus 1-2-3

When converting Microsoft Excel files to Lotus 1-2-3 format, the following difficulties arise because Lotus 1-2-3 has no equivalent functionality:

- Microsoft Excel cannot export formulas containing references to nonadjacent selections, unless they are arguments to translatable functions.
- Functions that produce references as a result are not exported to WKS format.
- The Microsoft Excel intersection (blank space) and union (comma) operators are not exported to Lotus 1-2-3.

In these cases, Microsoft Excel substitutes the value of the formula for the formula itself.

When you save a Microsoft Excel worksheet in a Lotus 1-2-3 file format, any references to rows beyond 2048 (for WKS file format) or 8192 (for WK1 and WK3 file formats) wrap around the end of the row. For example, when you save a reference to cell A8193 in WK1 format, the reference changes to A1 in Microsoft Excel.

Linking Lotus 1-2-3 Worksheets and Microsoft Excel Worksheets

By linking cells, you can use values from a Lotus 1-2-3 worksheet without exporting the worksheet to Microsoft Excel. Then, when you change the data in the Lotus 1-2-3 worksheet, the Microsoft Excel worksheet is automatically updated. For example, you can link sales figures from various Lotus 1-2-3 worksheets to a single Microsoft Excel worksheet and then use the formatting and printing features of Microsoft Excel to create a summary report of sales.

▶ **To link a Lotus 1-2-3 worksheet to a Microsoft Excel worksheet**

1. In Microsoft Excel, open both the Lotus 1-2-3 worksheet and the Microsoft Excel worksheet you want to link.
2. Switch to the Lotus 1-2-3 worksheet.
3. Select the cell or range containing the data you want to link to the Microsoft Excel worksheet.
4. On the **Edit** menu, click **Copy**.

    A moving border appears around the selected cell or range.
5. Switch to the Microsoft Excel worksheet.
6. Select the cell or the upper-left corner of the range that you want linked to the Lotus 1-2-3 worksheet.
7. On the **Edit** menu, click **Paste Special**.
8. Click **Paste Link**.

Microsoft Excel enters a formula in each cell that links the worksheets.

Note If the linked data from Lotus 1-2-3 is pasted into more than one cell, Microsoft Excel enters the formula that links the worksheets as an array formula. You cannot clear, delete, or move individual cells that contain an array formula. If you want to be able to edit individual cells, copy and link each cell individually.

You can link Microsoft Excel worksheets to files saved in any of the following Lotus 1-2-3 formats:

- WKS
- WK1
- WK3
- WK4

If you use Lotus 1-2-3 to edit a Lotus 1-2-3 worksheet linked to a Microsoft Excel worksheet, the linked cells are updated when you open the Microsoft Excel workbook.

Sharing Documents with Lotus 1-2-3

If your workgroup is upgrading gradually to Microsoft Excel, some users may have to share documents with users of Lotus 1-2-3.

▶ To save a Microsoft Excel workbook in Lotus 1-2-3 format

1. On the **File** menu, click **Save As**.
2. In the **File name** box, enter the name for the converted workbook.
3. In the **Save as type** box, click the Lotus 1-2-3 version in which you want to save the file.

   If the format you select does not support multisheet workbooks, Microsoft Excel prompts you to save each sheet individually.

Microsoft Excel can save data in the following Lotus 1-2-3 file formats.

In Microsoft Excel, save data in this file format	To share data with this Lotus 1-2-3 release
WKS (saves the active sheet only)	1, 1A
WK1, ALL (saves the active sheet only)	2.0, 2.01, 2.2
WK1, FMT (saves the active sheet only)	2.3, 2.4
WK3	3.0
WK3, FM3	3.1, 3.1+, 1-2-3/W, R1.1
WK4, WT4	4.0, 5.0

Tip End users can specify the default format in which Microsoft Excel saves new documents.

▶ To specify the default format in which to save documents

1. On the **Tools** menu, click **Options**, and then click the **Transition** tab.
2. In the **Default Save as type** box, click the file format you want.

   The next time you save a document that is not already saved in Microsoft Excel format, you are prompted to save it in this format.

For more information about selecting a default format in which to save documents, see "Specifying the Default Format in Which to Save Files" in Chapter 22, "Supporting Multiple Versions of Microsoft Office."

Tip In Windows 95 and Windows NT Workstation 4.0, you can use a system policy to define a default value for the **Save as type** option in the **Save As** dialog box (**File** menu) for all Microsoft Excel users in your workgroup. In the System Policy Editor, set the following policy:

User\Excel\Tools_Options\Transition\Default Save

For more information, see "Using Windows System Policies to Customize Office" in Chapter 7, "Customizing and Optimizing Microsoft Office."

Errors Caused by Special Characters

Because Microsoft Excel does not allow all of the special characters in names that Lotus 1-2-3 does, names that contain different special characters but are otherwise identical are converted to an identical name, resulting in an error.

Besides letters and numbers, Microsoft Excel allows only underscore and backslash (\) characters to be used in names. Microsoft Excel converts any invalid characters in names to the underscore character (_) when reading Lotus 1-2-3 worksheets. Microsoft Excel notifies the user that it cannot read the record if two or more defined names on the worksheet contain special characters that cause them to resolve to the same name.

For example, if you have defined the names TOTAL$ and TOTAL# on a Lotus 1-2-3 worksheet and you open the worksheet in Microsoft Excel, the first defined name TOTAL$ is converted to TOTAL_, and the second defined name TOTAL# is lost. You can work around this by checking for invalid characters in your Lotus 1-2-3 worksheets before converting them to Microsoft Excel.

Lotus 1-2-3 Releases 4 and 5 Features Without Microsoft Excel Equivalents

Lotus 1-2-3 features without direct equivalents in Microsoft Excel are not imported. These include the following:

- Range versions created with the Lotus 1-2-3 Version Manager

    No direct equivalent exists in Microsoft Excel for range versions created with the Lotus 1-2-3 Version Manager. Microsoft Excel imports only the data from the version that is currently displayed (the last time the file was saved). However, you can use the Microsoft Excel Scenario Manager to create, store, and retrieve what-if assumptions for multiple sets of up to 32 changing cells.

- Database records in Lotus 1-2-3 Release 4

    Because these are not compatible with either ODBC or Microsoft Query, they are not imported.

- Embedded OLE objects

    These include the Lotus Maps objects from Release 5.

- Rotated text or drawing

    These objects are imported, but they are displayed with normal horizontal alignment.

- Gradient fills

    The cell or object is formatted using only the primary color from the fill.

This Lotus 1-2-3 printer command	Corresponds to this Microsoft Excel feature or action
Clear	
All	Reset individual settings.
Range	On the **Insert** menu, point to **Name**, and then click **Define** and delete **Print_Area**.
Borders	On the **Insert** menu, click **Name**, and then click **Define** and delete **Print_Titles**.
Format	On the **File** menu, click **Page Setup** to reset margins. Page length and setup string are handled by the printer driver.
Align	None.
Go	**Print** (**File** menu).
Quit	Press ESC key.

WK3 Functions Without Microsoft Excel Equivalents

A number of Lotus 1-2-3 WK3 functions—nonaggregate functions that use three-dimensional references—do not properly convert to Microsoft Excel. A *nonaggregate* function is one that is not commonly used with a range of values. An *aggregate* function is one that is always used with a range of values, such as SUM, AVERAGE, MIN, and MAX.

For example, the nonaggregate function @INDEX does not convert if it uses references that encompass more than one ply of a three-dimensional worksheet. (It converts properly if no three-dimensional reference is used.) WK3 functions are unsupported when they include a three-dimensional argument; if a normal argument is used, they may work. These unsupported functions are shown in the following list.

Nonaggregate functions with three-dimensional references

@CELL	@IRR	@ROWS
@COLS	@ISRANGE	@S
@COORD	@N	@SHEETS
@INDEX	@NPV	@SUMPRODUCT

In addition, Microsoft Excel cannot convert formulas with more than one table argument using @DSUM, @DAVG, @DMIN, @DMAX, @DSTD, @DVAR, @DSTDS, or @DVARS. Other functions that present conversion problems include @DQUERY when using the DataLens add-in, and @CELLPOINTER when using the sheet argument.

This Lotus 1-2-3 global printer command	Corresponds to this Microsoft Excel feature or action
Interface	Setting up a printer and port
Auto-LF	None; handled by printer driver
Left	**Page Setup** (**File** menu)
Right	**Page Setup** (**File** menu)
Top	**Page Setup** (**File** menu)
Bottom	**Page Setup** (**File** menu)
Pg-Length	**Page Setup** (**File** menu)
Wait	None; handled by printer driver
Setup	None; handled by printer driver
Name	**Page Setup** (**File** menu)
Quit	ESC key

Lotus 1-2-3 Line Print Command Equivalents

There is no command in Microsoft Excel that is equivalent to the Lotus 1-2-3 **Line Print** command. Instead, use the LINE.PRINT macro function.

Lotus 1-2-3 Print Printer Command Equivalents

Microsoft Excel has equivalent features for most Lotus 1-2-3 print printer commands.

This Lotus 1-2-3 printer command	Corresponds to this Microsoft Excel feature or action
Range	**Set Print Area** (**File** menu, **Print Area** submenu).
Page	None.
Options	
Header	**Page Setup** (**File** menu).
Footer	**Page Setup** (**File** menu).
Margins	**Page Setup** (**File** menu).
Borders	On the **File** menu click **Page Setup**, and then click the **Sheet** tab. Under **Print titles**, enter the row and column references you want to appear.
Setup	Select the cells; on the **Format** menu, click **Cells**, and then click the **Font** tab.
Pg-Length	On the **File** menu click **Page Setup**, and then click the **Page** tab. In the **Paper size** box, select the page size you want.
Other	Worksheet is printed as displayed. To display values or formulas, click the **View** tab in the **Options** dialog box (**Tools** menu). To add or remove headers and footers, click **Page Setup** (**File** menu). To add or remove page breaks, click **Page Break** or **Remove Page Break** (**Insert** menu).
Quit	ESC key.

▶ **To set an axis scale to automatic in Microsoft Excel**

1 Click the x-axis (category) or y-axis (value).

2 On the **Format** menu, click **Selected Axis**, and then click the **Scale** tab.

Except for xy scatter charts, the options on the **Scale** tab are different for the x-axis and the y-axis.

3 Select the **Auto** check box for any option you want to return to automatic.

Manual, Lower, and Upper
You can control the chart scale manually.

▶ **To control a chart scale manually in Microsoft Excel**

1 Click the x-axis (category) or y-axis (value).

2 On the **Format** menu, click **Axis**, and then click the **Scale** tab.

Except for xy scatter charts, the options on the **Scale** tab are different for the x-axis and the y-axis.

3 Change the options you want.

Format
You can change the number format on the chart scale.

▶ **To change the number format on a chart scale in Microsoft Excel**

1 In the chart, click the y-axis (value).

You can change the x-axis number format only in xy scatter charts.

2 On the **Format** menu, click **Selected Axis**, and then click the **Number** tab.

3 Select the number format you want to use on the chart.

Indicator
You can display chart scale indicators.

▶ **To display or hide chart scale indicators in Microsoft Excel**

1 Select the chart.

2 On the **Chart** menu, click **Chart Options**, and then click the **Axes** tab.

3 Select or clear the **Value (X) Axis** or **Value (Y) Axis** check box.

Working With Printers
This section describes differences in printer setup and printing procedures between Lotus 1-2-3 and Microsoft Excel.

Lotus 1-2-3 Worksheet Global Default Printer Command Equivalents
Microsoft Excel has equivalent features for most Lotus 1-2-3 global printer commands.

Lotus 1-2-3 Graph Options Grid Command Equivalents

The Lotus 1-2-3 Graph Options Grid commands apply to all graph types with axes.

▶ **To add and delete gridlines in a chart in Microsoft Excel**

1. Right-click a blank area of the chart, and then click **Chart Options** on the shortcut menu.
2. Click the **Gridlines** tab, and select the options you want.

Lotus 1-2-3 Graph Type Command Equivalents

In Microsoft Excel, you change the chart type after you create the chart. Click the **Chart Type** command (**Chart** menu) when a chart is active. This command also allows you to select additional chart types, such as three-dimensional charts.

Lotus 1-2-3 Graph View Command Equivalents

After you create a chart in Microsoft Excel, it remains visible on a worksheet as a embedded chart, or as a separate chart sheet in the workbook. Therefore, the procedure for creating a chart in Microsoft Excel is the closest equivalent to the Lotus 1-2-3 **Graph View** command.

Lotus 1-2-3 Graph Options Color Command Equivalents

There is no direct equivalent in Microsoft Excel for the Lotus 1-2-3 **Graph Options Color** command. However, you can change the color of individual chart items.

▶ **To change the color of a chart item in Microsoft Excel**

1. Click the chart item you want to format.
2. On the **Format** menu, point to **Selected** *Chart Item*.
3. In the dialog box that appears, select the options you want.

Note The name of the **Selected** *Chart Item* command on the **Format** menu changes based on the chart item you select. For example, if you select a chart axis, the command **Axis** appears on the **Format** menu.

Lotus 1-2-3 Graph Options Scale Command Equivalents

The following sections describe Microsoft Excel equivalents for Lotus 1-2-3 Scale commands.

Auto

Microsoft Excel creates the scale automatically. If you designate any aspect of the scale as manual, you can return it to automatic.

One use of these commands might be to replace calls to Lotus 1-2-3 add-ins with calls to Microsoft Excel add-ins or Visual Basic procedures. Using XLCALL, you can run a Microsoft Excel procedure, after which control returns to the Lotus 1-2-3 macro. Using XLBRANCH, Microsoft Excel takes over control and does not return to the original Lotus 1-2-3 macro.

With these two commands, you can rebuild part or all of complex Lotus 1-2-3 macro statements with more concise Visual Basic code; it is not necessary to rewrite the entire macro.

Erasing the Active Worksheet and Starting a New One

Microsoft Excel files are called workbooks, and each workbook can contain multiple worksheets. You can have more than one workbook open at once, so you can keep the active workbook open while starting a new one. The following procedure corresponds to the Lotus 1-2-3 **Worksheet Erase** command, which removes the active worksheet from memory but not from your disk, so you can start a new one.

▶ **To remove the active workbook from memory**

1 On the **File** menu, click **Close**.

   If you made unsaved changes to the active worksheet, a dialog box appears asking if you want to save your changes.

2 To close the active workbook without saving changes, click **No**.

3 On the **File** menu, click **New** to open a new workbook.

Using Lotus 1-2-3 Charts in Microsoft Excel

Microsoft Excel and Lotus 1-2-3 format charts differently. This section discusses Microsoft Excel equivalents for Lotus 1-2-3 chart format commands.

Lotus 1-2-3 Graph Options Format Command Equivalents

The Lotus 1-2-3 Graph Options Format commands apply to line and xy (scatter) charts only.

▶ **To format a line or xy (scatter) chart in Microsoft Excel**

1 Select a data series.

2 On the **Format** menu, click **Data Series**, and then click the **Patterns** tab.

3 Under **Line**, select a line style, color, and weight.

   –or–

   If you do not want any lines, click **None**.

4 Under **Marker**, select a marker style, foreground color, and background color.

   –or–

   If you do not want any markers, click **None**.

Removing Lotus 1-2-3 Add-ins

Be sure to remove any occurrence of keystrokes or command names that attach, start, or use a Lotus 1-2-3 add-in, such as the Allways add-in and its menu structure. For example, remove statements such as /a and {app1}.

Altering Lotus 1-2-3 Macros That End in a Menu

When you run a Lotus 1-2-3 macro in Microsoft Excel, the Lotus 1-2-3 macro cannot end in a menu, such as the keystrokes /PP (Print Printer). If a macro does end in a menu, a message appears stating that macros cannot end in a menu. Then the macro terminates. The macro can, however, end in a prompt for more information, such as the keystrokes /PPR (Print Printer Range), so that you can specify the print range.

Getting Help Within Macro Prompts

When you run a Lotus 1-2-3 macro that contains a command for user input, such as /XN, /XL, {GETLABEL}, or {GETNUMBER}, Microsoft Excel displays a dialog box requesting user input. Enter the information, and then click **OK**.

If a Lotus 1-2-3 macro contains custom menu commands, such as /XM, {MENUBRANCH}, or {MENUCALL}, the **Menu** dialog box appears and displays your menu choices.

Tip For online Help with macro prompt dialog boxes, press F1.

Verifying Options Before Running Lotus 1-2-3 Macros

When you run a Lotus 1-2-3 macro, transition formula entry and transition navigation keys are temporarily turned on, and the Move Selection After Enter option is temporarily turned off. However, transition formula evaluation is not automatically turned on when you run a Lotus 1-2-3 macro. For more information, see "Microsoft Excel Transition Options" earlier in this chapter.

Adjusting Screen Size Before Running Lotus 1-2-3 Macros

For best visual results, you should maximize the Microsoft Excel window, as well as the active document window. Note that the {PGUP}, {PGDN}, {BIGRIGHT}, and {BIGLEFT} commands work with the current page size, not with the 20-row page size that is standard in Lotus 1-2-3.

Calling Microsoft Excel Procedures from Lotus 1-2-3 Macros

Two Microsoft Excel macro commands allow you to call or branch to Visual Basic procedures or Microsoft Excel 4.0 XLM macros written in Microsoft Excel from within a Lotus 1-2-3 macro. These functions are {XLCALL} and {XLBRANCH}, and take the following form:

```
{XLCALL xl_name}
{XLBRANCH xl_name}
```

where *xl_name* is the procedure name.

This Lotus 1-2-3 macro action	Corresponds to this Microsoft Excel feature
Request data by line item or build a data entry form on the worksheet	**Form** command (**Data** menu) for data entry and editing that automatically creates a custom data form without macros
Change to commonly used directories using the **File Dir** command. (The **File Dir** command is a separate command from the **File Retrieve**.)	Change folders and open files in the **Open** dialog box (**File** menu)
Split horizontal or vertical windows	Drag window split bar
Insert monthly, quarterly, or weekly headers	Use the AutoFill feature by dragging the fill handle

Running Macros Created in Lotus 1-2-3 Release 2.2

Microsoft Excel can run macros that contain any Lotus 1-2-3 Release 2.2 advanced macro commands, such as {BORDERSON}, {BORDERSOFF}, {FRAMEON}, {FRAMEOFF}, {GRAPHON}, and {GRAPHOFF}. Microsoft Excel also reads linking formulas created by Release 2.2. However, Microsoft Excel cannot run macros that use slash menu commands that are specific to Release 2.2.

Converting Lotus 1-2-3 Release 2.2 Macro Library Files

If you have Lotus 1-2-3 macros in macro libraries (macros in Lotus 1-2-3 Release 2.2 MLB file format), you can convert them to Microsoft Excel.

▶ To convert Lotus 1-2-3 MLB files

1. In Lotus 1-2-3, load the file by attaching the add-in.
2. In the Lotus Macro Library Manager, copy the library commands to a worksheet using the **Edit** command.
3. Save the worksheet in Lotus 1-2-3 WK1 format.
4. Open the Lotus 1-2-3 worksheet in Microsoft Excel.

Running Autoexec Macros

If you have a Lotus 1-2-3 autoexec macro (named \0) on your worksheet, the macro runs automatically when you open the worksheet in Microsoft Excel.

▶ To open a worksheet without running the autoexec macro

1. On the **File** menu, click **Open**.
2. Under the **Look in** box, select the workbook, and then hold down SHIFT and click **OK**.

If you have both a Microsoft Excel macro named Auto_Open that refers to a macro sheet and a Lotus 1-2-3 \0 macro on the same worksheet, the Auto_Open macro runs first, and then the \0 macro runs.

The Macro Interpreter runs all your Lotus 1-2-3 macros with the following exceptions:

- Macros that are not compatible with Lotus 1-2-3 Release 2.01
- Macros that contain keystrokes for menu commands available only in Release 2.2 or later
- Macros that call a Lotus 1-2-3 add-in

When a macro does not run, a dialog box appears that identifies the cell address where the error occurred. It is a good idea to make a note of this cell reference. Also, the dialog box contains a **Help** button that you can click to see more information about possible causes of the error. If you have macros that call Lotus 1-2-3 add-ins, you need to remove these macro statements from your Lotus 1-2-3 macros. You can, however, call Microsoft Excel procedures from Lotus 1-2-3 macros, as described later in this section.

Substituting Standard Microsoft Excel Features for Lotus 1-2-3 Macros

Many Lotus 1-2-3 macros do not need to be converted. These macros, which aid the user with formatting or printing from Lotus 1-2-3, are replaced by standard features in Microsoft Excel. Some of the most common Lotus 1-2-3 macros and the Microsoft Excel features that replace them are described in the following table.

This Lotus 1-2-3 macro action	Corresponds to this Microsoft Excel feature
Input printer setup strings	**Font** tab in the **Cells** dialog box (**Format** menu) and **Page Setup** dialog box (**File** menu)
Accept dates, parse into YY,MM,DD, and then re-enter with @Date and formats	Automatic date acceptance and formatting
Prompt to select ranges for chart data	**Chart Wizard** button (**Standard** toolbar)
Format anything quickly	**Style** command (**Format** menu)
Adjust column width	Drag the right border of the column heading, or double-click for best fit
Adjust multiple-column widths simultaneously	Select multiple columns, and then drag the right border of a column heading or double-click a border column heading for best fit
Sum a column or row	**AutoSum** button (**Standard** toolbar)
Align text with Range Label Align	**Align Left**, **Align Right**, or **Center** buttons (**Formatting** toolbar)
Underline	**Border** and **Font** tabs in the **Cells** dialog box (**Format** menu)
Shift a block of cells	**Insert** and **Delete** commands on the shortcut menu
Enter commonly used formulas	Workbook containing a Microsoft Excel Visual Basic for Applications module with function procedures to share among users
Redefine and update multiple data tables (Lotus 1-2-3 can have only one data table active at a time)	Multiple data tables available in a worksheet without redefinition

Note If the **Data Analysis** command does not appear on the **Tools** menu, you need to install the Analysis ToolPak add-in. To do this, click **Add-Ins** on the **Tools** menu, and then select the **Analysis ToolPak** check box. If the **Analysis ToolPak** option does not appear in the **Add-Ins** dialog box, rerun Setup and click **Add/Remove**. Under the **Microsoft Excel** option, select the **Add-Ins** option, and then select the **Analysis ToolPak** option.

Using Equivalents for Lotus 1-2-3 Data Matrix Commands

The Microsoft Excel equivalents for the Lotus 1-2-3 data matrix commands are array functions, rather than commands.

This Lotus 1-2-3 data matrix command	Corresponds to this Microsoft Excel array function
Invert	MINVERSE
Multiply	MMULT

Using Equivalents for Lotus 1-2-3 Data Regression Commands

The Microsoft Excel equivalents for the Lotus 1-2-3 data regression commands are array functions and do not translate directly. Instead, Microsoft Excel includes the LINEST, TREND, LOGEST, and GROWTH functions for performing regression analysis.

You can also use the **Data Analysis** command (**Tools** menu) to perform regression analysis using the **Regression** analysis tool.

Running Lotus 1-2-3 Macros in Microsoft Excel

Most Lotus 1-2-3 users have invested time over the years building macros. These users are concerned about how Microsoft Excel works with their macros. Microsoft Excel includes the Macro Interpreter for Lotus 1-2-3 Users, which provides strong macro conversion support.

Using the Macro Interpreter for Lotus 1-2-3 Users

Users can run large Lotus 1-2-3 macro applications, including custom menus, without modification in Microsoft Excel using the Macro Interpreter. This utility runs all Lotus 1-2-3 macros that are compatible with Lotus 1-2-3 Release 2.01.

The name assigned to a macro in Lotus 1-2-3, such as \a, is defined in Microsoft Excel as a Lotus 1-2-3 macro name when you open a Lotus 1-2-3 worksheet in Microsoft Excel. You can run any macro that is assigned to a macro name consisting of a backslash (\) followed by a single letter. Microsoft Excel assigns a lowercase letter to each macro name.

To run a Lotus 1-2-3 macro in Microsoft Excel, hold down the CTRL key and press the macro letter name that is normally used with the backslash (\) key in Lotus 1-2-3.

Using Mathematical Operators in Lotus 1-2-3 and Microsoft Excel

The following table shows the mathematical operators used by Microsoft Excel and Lotus 1-2-3, in descending order of evaluation.

Lotus 1-2-3 order of operators	Microsoft Excel order of operators
^	AND, OR, NOT functions
+ or – (unary)	+ or – (unary)
* or /	^
+ or –	* or /
= < > <= >= <>	+ or –
#not# (unary)	&
#and# #or#	= < > <= >= <>
& (Release 2.0 and later)	

In Lotus 1-2-3, the exponentiation operator (^) is evaluated before the negation operator (–); in Microsoft Excel, negation is evaluated first. Thus, the formula

=-2^4

produces the value –16 in Lotus 1-2-3, and 16 in Microsoft Excel. To change this, use parentheses to force the preferred order of evaluation in Microsoft Excel. For example:

=-(2^4)

Using Three-dimensional Formulas in Workbooks

If you store a group of worksheets with identical layouts, such as monthly reports, in the same workbook, you can use three-dimensional formulas to consolidate data into summary worksheets. These three-dimensional formulas allow you to specify sheet ranges in a workbook, which are similar to cell ranges on a worksheet. You can apply a number of different functions, such as SUM and AVERAGE, to the resulting three-dimensional range.

For example, the formula SUM(Sheet1:Sheet4!A1) sums the contents of cell A1 on the contiguous sheets named Sheet1, Sheet2, Sheet3, and Sheet4.

You can also use the **Consolidate** command (**Data** menu) to create summary reports for sheets that have an identical or similar layout.

Using Equivalents for the Lotus 1-2-3 Data Distribution Command

There is no equivalent command in Microsoft Excel for the Lotus 1-2-3 **Data Distribution** command. Instead, Microsoft Excel provides the FREQUENCY function, which calculates a data distribution. You can also choose the **Data Analysis** command (**Tools** menu) and select the **Histogram** analysis tool to calculate frequencies for a range of data.

This Lotus 1-2-3 function	Corresponds to this Microsoft Excel function	Comments
@TIME	TIME	
@TIMEVALUE	TIMEVALUE	
@TODAY	TODAY	
@TRIM	TRIM	
@TRUE	TRUE	
@UPPER	UPPER	
@VALUE	VALUE	
@VAR	VARA	
@VARP	VARPA	
@VARS	VAR or VARA	The @VARS function is available in Lotus 1-2-3 Release 3 and later.
@VDB	VDB	
@VLOOKUP	VLOOKUP	In Microsoft Excel turn on transition formula evaluation to use the Lotus 1-2-3 evaluation rules.
@YEAR	YEAR	

Getting Help with Microsoft Excel Functions

For details about Microsoft Excel functions, click the **Paste Function** button (**Standard** toolbar), select the function you want, and then click the **Question Mark** button. In the Office Assistant, click **Help with this feature**, and then click **Help on selected function**.

Functions are divided into categories in the **Function Wizard** dialog box. For example, the FREQUENCY, LINEST, LOGEST, GROWTH, and TREND functions are located in the **Statistical** category, while the MINVERSE and MMULT functions are located in the **Math & Trig** category. Help for the Analysis ToolPak is available by clicking the **Help** button in any **Analysis ToolPak** dialog box.

Translating Lotus 1-2-3 Pure Functions

Lotus 1-2-3 includes several *pure functions* that are evaluated in the same way as some Microsoft Excel and Multiplan functions. For example, the @PUREAVG function is evaluated in the same way as the Microsoft Excel function AVERAGE: Both functions evaluate only numeric data. When a Lotus 1-2-3 worksheet is opened in Microsoft Excel, all pure functions are automatically converted to their corresponding Microsoft Excel functions, regardless of the setting of the **Transition formula entry** option on the **Transition** tab in the **Options** dialog box (**Tools** menu).

This Lotus 1-2-3 function	Corresponds to this Microsoft Excel function	Comments
@MONTH	MONTH	
@N	N	
@NA	NA	
@NOW	NOW	
@NPV	NPV	
@PI	PI	
@PMT	PMT	The arguments for the PMT function are in different order than they are in @PMT.
@PROPER	PROPER	
@PV	PV	The arguments for the PV function are in different order than they are in @PV.
@RAND	RAND	In Microsoft Excel the RAND function calculates values randomly each time it is recalculated; @RAND calculates the same values in each work session.
@RATE	RATE	The arguments for the RATE function are in different order than they are in @RATE.
@REPEAT	REPT	
@REPLACE	REPLACE	
@RIGHT	RIGHT	
@ROUND	ROUND	
@ROWS	ROWS	
@S	T	
@SECOND	SECOND	
@SIN	SIN	
@SLN	SLN	
@SQRT	SQRT	
@STD	STDEVP or STDEVPA	
@STDEV	STDEV or STDEVA	
@STDEVP	STDEVP	
@STDS	STDEV or STDEVPA	The @STDS function is available Lotus 1-2-3 Release 3 and later.
@STRING	FIXED	
@SUM	SUM	
@SYD	SYD	
@TAN	TAN	
@TERM	NPER	The arguments for the NPER function are in different order than they are in @TERM.

This Lotus 1-2-3 function	Corresponds to this Microsoft Excel function	Comments
@ERR	None	In Microsoft Excel no equivalent is necessary, because Microsoft Excel lets you type error values directly into cells and formulas.
@EXACT	EXACT	
@EXP	EXP	
@FALSE	FALSE	
@FIND	FIND	
@FV	FV	
@HLOOKUP	HLOOKUP	In Microsoft Excel turn on transition formula evaluation to use the Lotus 1-2-3 evaluation rules.
@HOUR	HOUR	
@IF	IF	In Microsoft Excel the last two arguments of the IF function can be any value, not just numbers or strings, as in @IF.
@INDEX	INDEX	In Microsoft Excel the INDEX function also has a form for selecting values from an array.
@INT	TRUNC or INT	
@IRR	IRR	In Microsoft Excel the arguments are given in reverse order.
@ISERR	ISERR	The ISERR function detects any of six Microsoft Excel error values.
@ISNA	ISNA	
@ISNUMBER	ISNONTEXT or ISNUMBER	
@ISRANGE	ISREF	The @ISRANGE function is available in Lotus 1-2-3 Release 3 and later.
@ISSTRING	ISTEXT	
@LEFT	LEFT	
@LENGTH	LEN	
@LN	LN	
@LOWER	LOWER	
@LOG	LOG	
@MAX	MAX or MAXA	
@MID	MID	
@MIN	MIN or MINA	
@MINUTE	MINUTE	
@MOD	MOD	In Microsoft Excel turn on transition formula evaluation to use the Lotus 1-2-3 evaluation rules.

This Lotus 1-2-3 function	Corresponds to this Microsoft Excel function	Comments
@@	INDIRECT	
@ABS	ABS	
@ACOS	ACOS	
@ASIN	ASIN	
@ATAN	ATAN	
@ATAN2	ATAN2	
@AVG	AVERAGE	
@CELL	CELL	
@CELLPOINTER	CELL	In Microsoft Excel, when you use the CELL function without a second argument, it returns information about the current selection.
@CHAR	CHAR	
@CHOOSE	CHOOSE	
@CLEAN	CLEAN	
@CODE	CODE	
@COLS	COLUMNS	
@COS	COS	
@COUNT	COUNTA	
@CTERM	NPER	In Microsoft Excel the NPER function requires periodic payment instead of future value.
@DATE	DATE	
@DATEVALUE	DATEVALUE	
@DAVG	DAVERAGE	
@DAY	DAY	
@D360	DAYS360	The @D360 function is available in Lotus 1-2-3 Release 3 and later.
@DCOUNT	DCOUNTA	
@DDB	DDB	
@DGET	DGET	
@DMAX	DMAX	
@DMIN	DMIN	
@DSTD	DSTDEVP	
@DSTDS	DSTDEV	The @DSTDS function is available in Lotus 1-2-3 Release 3 and later.
@DSUM	DSUM	
@DVAR	DVARP	
@DVARS	DVAR	The @DVARS is available in Lotus 1-2-3 Release 3 and later.

conversion. However, many such nested formulas exist in order to construct elaborate alternative calculations based on a range of current conditions, such as @IF statements. In this case, a better solution is to create a formula using @VLOOKUP and refer to a table elsewhere on the worksheet. Then no nesting is needed, and you end up with a more readable and structured formula.

For example, suppose that in one cell you have the following Lotus 1-2-3 formula that arrives at a value, based on the name of a month from January to September:

```
@IF(a1="Jan",12,@IF(a1="Feb",2,@IF(a1="Mar",4,@IF(a1="Apr",34,
@IF(a1="May",32,@IF(a1="Jun",8,@IF(a1="Jul",43,@IF(a1="Aug",3,
@IF(a1="Sep",67,0)))))))))
```

This formula has nine levels of nesting. To make conversion to Microsoft Excel easier, rewrite the formula like this in Lotus 1-2-3:

```
@VLOOKUP(a1,table,1)
```

where *table* is a range name that refers to the following two-column table, located anywhere on the worksheet.

```
Jan    12
Feb     2
Mar     4
Apr    34
May    32
Jun     8
Jul    43
Aug     3
Sep    67
```

When you then open the file in Microsoft Excel (and transition formula evaluation is automatically turned on), the formula converts without problems, and it works properly. (The offset argument 1 is automatically converted to 2 because Microsoft Excel starts counting at 1, not 0.) Using a table in this way is not only easier to read than the original formula, but it is also easy to modify by changing or adding new values.

Translating Lotus 1-2-3 Functions

Most Lotus 1-2-3 functions have an equivalent in Microsoft Excel. When transition formula entry is activated, you can type most Lotus 1-2-3 functions directly into the formula bar, where they are automatically converted to their Microsoft Excel equivalents. The functions you cannot enter in this way are specific to Lotus 1-2-3 Release 3 and later. For more information about transition formula entry, see "Microsoft Excel Transition Options" earlier in this chapter.

Microsoft Excel also uses different rules than Lotus 1-2-3 when evaluating text in formulas, certain database criteria, and the value of certain logical operators. When transition formula evaluation is activated, some functions are interpreted as they would be in Lotus 1-2-3. These functions are listed alphabetically in the following table, along with their Microsoft Excel equivalents.

Auditing with Cell Tracers

Another auditing feature included with Microsoft Excel is *cell tracers*. Cell tracers are arrows drawn on a worksheet that point to the precedents or dependents of a selected cell, or trace the error path of a cell containing an error value. Use the **Auditing** submenu commands (**Tools** menu) to display tracer arrows. Alternatively, you can point to **Auditing** and then click **Show Auditing Toolbar** to display the **Auditing** toolbar, which you can use to trace the flow of data between cells on your worksheet.

In the following illustration, cell J8 was selected and the **Trace Precedents** button (**Auditing** toolbar) was clicked twice. The first click added arrows pointing to the first level of precedent cells, J5:J7; the second click indicated the second level of precedent cells, C2:C4 and C8:C10.

Using Lotus 1-2-3 Formulas in Microsoft Excel

Most Lotus 1-2-3 formulas and functions convert to their Microsoft Excel equivalents when the worksheet is opened. If Microsoft Excel finds formulas that it cannot convert when you open a Lotus 1-2-3 worksheet, then only the resulting values are preserved; the original formula is lost. Microsoft Excel indicates this in two ways:

- First, when Microsoft Excel encounters a formula that it cannot convert, a message notifies the user that Microsoft Excel cannot read the record.
- Second, a cell comment (along with a cell comment indicator) appears in the cell, containing the message "Formula failed to convert."

Translating Lotus 1-2-3 Nested Formulas

Perhaps the most common reason for the "Cannot read record" message when converting Lotus 1-2-3 formulas to Microsoft Excel occurs when a formula in your Lotus 1-2-3 worksheet uses more than seven levels of nesting. To get around this, you can break the formula into sections of less than seven nested segments before

▶ **To search for cells containing formulas that did not convert correctly**

1. On the **Edit** menu, click **Find**.
2. In the **Look in** box, click **Comments**.
3. In the **Find what** box, type **formula failed to convert**
4. Click **Find Next**.

   The first cell containing the text you entered is selected. A message appears if the text cannot be found.

5. Click the **Find Next** button again to go to the next cell with a comment containing the text.

After you have converted the worksheet, you can select all cells with cell comments.

▶ **To select all cells with cell comments**

1. On the **Edit** menu, click **Go To**.
2. Click **Special**, and then click **Comments**.

This selects all cells with comments, allowing you to see where your formulas did not convert.

You can also print the comments along with the sheet and then use this printed document as a reference for troubleshooting.

▶ **To print cell comments**

1. On the **File** menu, click **Page Setup**, and then click the **Sheet** tab.
2. In the **Comments** box, select the option you want.

Cell comments consist of all comments inserted by Microsoft Excel during the conversion process, as well as all cells converted from WK3 files that contain Lotus 1-2-3-style text notes in their formulas.

The **Special** button in the **Go To** dialog box (**Edit** menu) is a powerful tool for auditing converted worksheets. Using the options in this dialog box, you can find cells that:

- Supply values to the active cell (**Precedents** option)
- Use the value in the active cell (**Dependents** option)
- Contain only values (**Constants** option)
- Contain only formulas (**Formulas** option)
- Contain error values (**Errors** check box under **Formulas** option)
- Contain comments (**Comments** option)
- Contain different reference patterns in a row or column (**Row differences** or **Column differences** option)

columns, are achieved in Microsoft Excel with the text underlining options on the **Font** tab or the cell border options on the **Border** tab in the **Cells** dialog box (**Format** menu).

Replacing the Lotus 1-2-3 System Command (Windows only)

There is no direct equivalent for the Lotus 1-2-3 **System** command in Microsoft Excel, but you can activate the command prompt from the **Start** menu.

▶ **To activate the command prompt in Windows 95 or Windows NT Workstation 4.0**

- Click the **Start** menu, point to **Programs**, and then click **MS-DOS Prompt**.

▶ **To activate the command prompt in Windows NT Workstation 3.51**

- In the Main program group, double-click the Command Prompt icon.

Auditing Converted Worksheets

Audits conducted by the industry on corporate MS-DOS-based worksheets have found that approximately 30 percent of all worksheets contain serious errors. In some cases, major decisions have been made using worksheets that have been incorrect for years.

The only way to catch these errors is with a worksheet audit. You can do the audit while the worksheet is in Lotus 1-2-3 or after it is converted to Microsoft Excel. The best course is a partial audit on both sides, since each audit catches different problems.

Auditing Your Worksheets Before Conversion

Auditing your Lotus 1-2-3 worksheets before conversion catches problems inherent in the original worksheet, such as values that have replaced formulas, circular errors, incorrect results, and bad range names.

Auditing Your Worksheets After Conversion

Auditing after conversion catches problems introduced by the conversion process or by reorganization and linking. Auditing worksheets in Microsoft Excel helps you find formulas that did not convert, links that are incorrect, or unexpected problems for which you might need additional help. The following Microsoft Excel features are particularly useful for auditing:

- **Auditing** submenu commands (**Tools** menu)
- **Find** command (**Edit** menu)
- **Special** button in the **Go To** dialog box (**Edit** menu)

Note If Microsoft Excel encounters formulas that it cannot convert when you open a Lotus 1-2-3 worksheet, only the resulting values are displayed. The original formula is discarded. Microsoft Excel indicates this by displaying a cell comment (and cell comment indicator) in the cell, containing the message "Formula failed to convert." For more information, see "Using Lotus 1-2-3 Formulas in Microsoft Excel" later in this section.

This Lotus 1-2-3 number format	Corresponds to this Microsoft Excel number category	With these Microsoft Excel number formats
Hidden	**Custom**	In the **Type** box, type ;;; Or click **Row** or **Column** on the **Format** menu, and then click **Hide** to hide entire rows or columns.
Reset	**General**	None.

When you convert a Lotus 1-2-3 worksheet to Microsoft Excel, you must also convert the file that contains the formatting. Many Lotus 1-2-3 users have add-ins to help format their worksheets. Lotus 1-2-3 Releases 2.01 and 2.2 use the Allways add-in (which produces an ALL file); Releases 2.3 and later use the WYSIWYG or Impress add-in (which produces an FMT or FM3 file).

Allways Formatting

Microsoft Excel fully supports Allways (ALL) files. When you import a Lotus 1-2-3 worksheet that has a corresponding ALL file (with the same name and in the same folder), Microsoft Excel opens the ALL file automatically. When you save the Lotus 1-2-3 file, Microsoft Excel saves both the WK1 file and a separate ALL file, if one existed originally. You can also create an ALL file when you save a WK1 file, even if none existed originally.

If a Lotus 1-2-3 worksheet has both an FMT or FM3 and ALL file associated with it, Microsoft Excel ignores the ALL file and applies the formatting specified in the FMT or FM3 file.

WYSIWYG and Impress Formatting

When you open a Lotus 1-2-3 WK1 or WK3 worksheet that has a corresponding FMT or FM3 file created with the WYSIWYG or Impress add-in in the same folder, Microsoft Excel opens the WYSIWYG or Impress file automatically and applies the equivalent formatting in Microsoft Excel. Conversely, when you use Microsoft Excel to save a Lotus 1-2-3 worksheet in Lotus 1-2-3 format, an FMT or FM3 file is automatically saved along with it (if one existed originally).

The Lotus 1-2-3 WYSIWYG or Impress add-in creates embedded graphs, and also draws arrows, ovals, and other objects on top of these graphs. In Microsoft Excel, when you import a Lotus 1-2-3 worksheet and its associated WYSIWYG or Impress file, the embedded graph appears, but any overlaid drawings do not. However, after the worksheet and graph are imported, you can use any of the Microsoft Excel drawing tools to enhance them as long as you save the worksheet in Microsoft Excel format.

Underlining

When you open a Lotus 1-2-3 worksheet that contains double underlines, the double underlines are converted to single underlines in Microsoft Excel. Many underlining tasks, such as double underlining or single underlining at the bottom of summed

Translating Lotus 1-2-3 Formatting

When formatting is applied to a Lotus 1-2-3 WK1 or WK3 worksheet, a separate file is created and saved along with the worksheet. In Microsoft Excel, however, formatting information is saved in the workbook file.

This section describes the general procedure used to apply formatting in Microsoft Excel, and describes how formatting in Microsoft Excel corresponds to formatting in Lotus 1-2-3. For example, the following procedure demonstrates how to format numbers in a Microsoft Excel worksheet.

▶ **To format numbers in Microsoft Excel**

1 Select the cells you want to format.
2 On the **Format** menu, click **Cells**, and then click the **Number** tab.
3 Under **Category**, click **Number**, and then select the formats you want.

You use the same general procedure to apply other types of formatting, using the other categories and tabs in the **Cells** dialog box (**Format** menu).

The following table lists the Microsoft Excel equivalents for Lotus 1-2-3 number formats. The second and third columns indicate the category and selected options of the format, as they appear on the **Number** tab in the **Cells** dialog box (**Format** menu) in Microsoft Excel.

This Lotus 1-2-3 number format	Corresponds to this Microsoft Excel number category	With these Microsoft Excel number formats
Fixed	**Number**	Default settings.
Scientific	**Scientific**	Default settings.
Currency	**Currency**	In the **Negative numbers** box, select (**$1,234.10**).
Comma	**Number**	Select the **Use 1000 Separator (,)** check box.
General	**General**	None.
+/-	No equivalent	None.
Percent	**Percentage**	Default settings.
Date	**Date**	Under **Type**, select **04-Mar-97**.
Time	**Time**	Under **Type**, select **1:30:55 PM**.
Text	**Text**	You can display formulas or values for the entire worksheet. On the **Tools** menu, click **Options**, and then click the **View** tab. Under **Window options**, select the **Formulas** check box. You can also see individual formulas in the formula bar.

If you have formulas in cells that cannot be converted, Microsoft Excel notifies you that it cannot read the record, and then displays another dialog box asking you whether to continue alerting you each time a cell does not convert. Formulas that do not convert are discarded, but the result of the formula is preserved and Microsoft Excel attaches a comment to the cell, containing the message "Formula failed to convert."

If the Lotus 1-2-3 worksheet you want to convert has graphs associated with it, Microsoft Excel converts the Lotus 1-2-3 graphs to Microsoft Excel charts, and places them on a separate chart sheet in the workbook. However, if the charts are created using either the Impress or Allways add-in, they are embedded on the corresponding worksheet.

After you convert a Lotus 1-2-3 worksheet to Microsoft Excel, the converted worksheet exists only in your computer's memory; the original worksheet remains unchanged. To complete the conversion, you need to save the converted worksheet in Microsoft Excel format.

▶ **To save a converted Lotus 1-2-3 worksheet in Microsoft Excel format**

1 On the **File** menu, click **Save As**.

2 In the **File name** box, enter a new name for the converted worksheet.

   This preserves the original worksheet in Lotus 1-2-3 format as a backup.

3 In the **Save as type** box, click **Microsoft Excel workbook**.

Keep a copy of the original Lotus 1-2-3 worksheet; when a formula does not convert, you can refer to the original Lotus 1-2-3 formula and rebuild it using the equivalent Microsoft Excel method. The most prevalent conversion problems occur in formulas that have more than seven levels of nesting in one formula, which is common with formulas that use multiple @IF functions. For more information about converting such formulas, see "Using Lotus 1-2-3 Formulas in Microsoft Excel" later in this chapter.

Converting Multiple Lotus 1-2-3 Worksheets

To convert multiple Lotus 1-2-3 worksheets, open several worksheets at the same time in the **Open** dialog box (**File** menu). Microsoft Excel converts each worksheet you select. When you finish editing the worksheets, save each worksheet as described in the previous section.

Tip In Windows, you can open more than one file at a time if all the files are within a single folder. To select a contiguous group of worksheets, click the name of the first worksheet you want to open, and then hold down SHIFT and click the name of the last worksheet you want to open. Or hold down CTRL and click the names of the individual worksheets you want to open.

If you want to convert multiple worksheets to or from Lotus 1-2-3 format, you can also use the File Conversion Wizard add-in. For more information, see "Converting Documents from Other File Formats" earlier in this chapter.

Part 4 Switching from Other Applications

Converting Lotus 1-2-3 Worksheets to Microsoft Excel

You can use Microsoft Excel with your existing Lotus 1-2-3 worksheets by opening your Lotus 1-2-3 worksheet in Microsoft Excel the same way you open any Microsoft Excel workbook. When you finish editing the worksheet, you can save it as a Microsoft Excel workbook or as a Lotus 1-2-3 worksheet.

Note If you open a Lotus 1-2-3 .WK* file in Microsoft Excel, the transition formula evaluation feature is automatically activated, and Microsoft Excel uses Lotus 1-2-3 rules for calculating formulas. For more information about transition formula evaluation, see "Using Microsoft Excel Tools for Lotus 1-2-3 Users" earlier in this chapter.

Microsoft Excel opens and saves the following Lotus 1-2-3 file formats.

This Lotus 1-2-3 release	Saves data in this file format
1, 1A	WKS
2.0, 2.01, 2.2	WK1, ALL
2.3, 2.4	WK1, FMT
3.0	WK3
3.1, 3.1+, 1-2-3/W, R1.1	WK3, FM3
4.0, 5.0	WK4

Note When you open either WK3 or WK4 formats, Microsoft Excel reads and writes both two-dimensional and three-dimensional worksheets.

When you open a Lotus 1-2-3 worksheet, Microsoft Excel automatically opens the corresponding ALL, FMT, or FM3 file. Drop shadows and objects drawn on top of charts are not imported to Microsoft Excel. Also, double underlines and wide underlines appear as single underlines in Microsoft Excel.

When you save a Lotus 1-2-3 worksheet in Microsoft Excel, an FMT or FM3 file is automatically saved. However, because of the limitations of the Impress add-in, you can save only the first eight styles you create and the first eight fonts you use.

Opening and Saving Lotus 1-2-3 Worksheets in Microsoft Excel

The majority of your Lotus 1-2-3 worksheets can be converted to Microsoft Excel format by opening them and then saving them in Microsoft Excel.

▶ **To open a Lotus 1-2-3 worksheet in Microsoft Excel**

1 On the **File** menu, click **Open**.
2 In the **Files of type** box, click **Lotus 1-2-3 Files**.
3 Below the **Look in** box, select the name of the worksheet.
4 Click **Open**.

   Microsoft Excel converts the Lotus 1-2-3 worksheet and opens it.

Note If you select the **Transition navigation keys** option on the **Transition** tab in the **Options** dialog box (**Tools** menu), Lotus 1-2-3 keyboard equivalents are automatically activated, and these Microsoft Excel keyboard equivalents do not apply. For more information, see "Using Microsoft Excel Tools for Lotus 1-2-3 Users" earlier in this chapter.

Function Keys

The following table compares function key assignments in Lotus 1-2-3 and their equivalents in Microsoft Excel.

This Lotus 1-2-3 function key	Corresponds to this Microsoft Excel function key	And has this meaning
F1	F1	Help
F2	F2	Edit
F3	F3	Name
F4	F4	Switches between absolute and relative formula references
F5	F5	Go To
F6	F6	Next pane (if panes are not frozen)
F8	Performed automatically	Table
F9	F9	Calculate
F10	F11 or ALT+F1	Graph

Navigation Keys

The following table compares navigation key assignments in Lotus 1-2-3 and their equivalents in Microsoft Excel.

This Lotus 1-2-3 navigation key	Corresponds to this Microsoft Excel navigation key
UP ARROW, DOWN ARROW	UP ARROW, DOWN ARROW
LEFT ARROW, RIGHT ARROW	LEFT ARROW, RIGHT ARROW
END, UP ARROW	CTRL+UP ARROW or END+UP ARROW
END, DOWN ARROW	CTRL+DOWN ARROW or END+DOWN ARROW
END, LEFT ARROW	CTRL+LEFT ARROW or END+LEFT ARROW
END, RIGHT ARROW	CTRL+RIGHT ARROW or END+RIGHT ARROW
HOME	CTRL+HOME
TAB	ALT+PAGE DOWN
SHIFT+TAB	ALT+PAGE UP
PAGE UP	PAGE UP
PAGE DOWN	PAGE DOWN

Microsoft Excel Equivalents for Lotus 1-2-3 Commands

The following table lists frequently used Lotus 1-2-3 commands and the equivalent commands in Microsoft Excel.

This Lotus 1-2-3 command	Corresponds to this Microsoft Excel command or option
/c	**Copy** and **Paste** (**Edit** menu)
/fd	**Open** (**File** menu)
/few	**Delete** on the document shortcut menu in the **Open** dialog box (**File** menu)
/fr	**Open** (**File** menu)
/fs	**Save As** (**File** menu)
/gv	**Open** (**File** menu, when the chart is in a separate file)
/m	**Cut** and **Paste** (**Edit** menu)
/ppg	**Print** (**File** menu)
/ppr	**Set Print Area** (**File** menu, **Print Area** submenu)
/qy	**Exit** (**File** menu)
/re	**Clear** (**Edit** menu)
/rf	**Number** tab in the **Cells** dialog box (**Format** menu)
/rfc	**Number** tab in the **Cells** dialog box (**Format** menu)
/rfp	**Number** tab in the **Cells** dialog box (**Format** menu)
/rnl	**Create** (**Insert** menu, **Name** submenu)
/rnc	**Define** (**Insert** menu, **Name** submenu)
/wcs	**Width** (**Format** menu, **Column** submenu)
/wdc	**Delete** (**Edit** menu)
/wdr	**Delete** (**Edit** menu)
/wey	**Close** and **New** (**File** menu)
/wic	**Columns** (**Insert** menu)
/wir	**Rows** (**Insert** menu)
/wtc	**Unfreeze Panes** (**Window** menu)
/wth	**Freeze Panes** (**Window** menu)
/wtv	**Freeze Panes** (**Window** menu)

Microsoft Excel Equivalents for Lotus 1-2-3 Keyboard Commands

Microsoft Excel default keyboard equivalents to Lotus 1-2-3 keys are listed in the following tables.

This Lotus 1-2-3 term	Corresponds to this Microsoft Excel term or concept
Graph	Chart
Graph labels	Chart text
Graph titles	Chart titles
Highlight	Select or selection
Indicator	Status bar
Input range	Database range
Label	Text
Label-prefix	Alignment
Label/matching criteria	Comparison criteria
Logical 0	FALSE
Logical 1	TRUE
Menu pointer	Menu selection
Mode indicator	Status bar
Move	Cut and paste
Number/matching criteria	Comparison criteria
Numeric format	Number format
Output range	Extract range
Picture file	Chart document
Pointer movement keys	Arrow keys
Print range	Print area
PrintGraph	Printing a chart
Prompt	Dialog box
Protected cell	Locked/protected cell
Range highlight	Selected range
Repeating label	Fill alignment
Retrieve a file	Open a file
Row numbers	Row headings
Stacked bar graph	Column chart, bar chart
Status indicator, status line	Status bar
String	Text
Target cell	Dependent cell
Target file	Dependent document
Time format	Number format
Titles	Split worksheet window with frozen panes
Translate utility	**Open** and **Save As** (**File** menu)
Value	Number
Window	Multiple windows, pane

Part 4   Switching from Other Applications

Value type	Non-A functions	A functions
Numbers	Treated normally	Treated normally
Text	Text is ignored	Text has a value of **0**
TRUE Logical Value	TRUE is ignored	TRUE has a value of **1**
FALSE Logical Value	FALSE is ignored	FALSE has a value of **0**

Tools and Utilities   The Office Resource Kit Tools and Utilities include the Office 97 Resource Kit Help file, a collection of KnowledgeBase articles about Office 97 written by Microsoft Product Support Services. The article *XL97: New A Functions in Microsoft Excel 97* (ID: Q156445) contains detailed information about the new A functions. For more information, see "Microsoft Technical Support Help File" in Appendix A, "Microsoft Office 97 Resource Kit Tools and Utilities."

Microsoft Excel Terms for Lotus 1-2-3 Users

The following table lists Lotus 1-2-3 terms and their Microsoft Excel counterparts. The Microsoft Excel term is not necessarily an exact equivalent of the Lotus 1-2-3 term, but rather a term you can look up in online Help for more information.

This Lotus 1-2-3 term	Corresponds to this Microsoft Excel term or concept
@Function	Function
Address	Reference
Anchor cell	Selecting a range of cells
Border	Row and column headings
CALC indicator	Status bar
Cell pointer	Active cell
Column labels	Column headings
Command prompt	Dialog box
Control panel	Menu bar, formula bar, status bar
Copy	Copy and paste
Crosshatching	Chart patterns
Current cell	Active cell
Current worksheet	Active worksheet or chart or macro sheet
Data labels	Data marker labels
Data range	Data series
Data table 1	One-input table
Data table 2	Two-input table
Date format	Number format
Erase	Clear
Formula criteria	Computed criteria
Global	Workspace

When you open a Lotus 1-2-3 worksheet in Microsoft Excel, transition formula evaluation is automatically turned on for that sheet. This ensures that the formulas are calculated according to the preceding Lotus 1-2-3 rules.

If you save the Lotus 1-2-3 worksheet as a Microsoft Excel workbook, the transition formula evaluation option remains turned on until you turn it off. For workbooks created in Microsoft Excel, however, transition formula evaluation is not automatically turned on.

Note Avoid turning transition formula evaluation on and off while working with a document in Microsoft Excel; otherwise, the values calculated on your worksheet might change. If you leave transition formula evaluation turned off, your worksheet adheres to Microsoft Excel rules. If you leave the option turned on, your worksheet adheres to Lotus 1-2-3 rules.

New A Functions in Microsoft Excel

Microsoft Excel 97 includes several new functions that are evaluated in the same way as their corresponding Lotus 1-2-3 functions, regardless of whether the transition formula evaluation option described in the previous section is turned on. For example, the Microsoft Excel AVERAGE function evaluates only numeric data. However, the new Microsoft Excel function AVERAGEA evaluates numeric as well as non-numeric data, just as its corresponding Lotus 1-2-3 function @AVG does.

Like the COUNTA function introduced previously in Microsoft Excel, these new functions follow the naming convention of *Name*A and are therefore referred to as *A functions*.

The new A functions and their corresponding Lotus 1-2-3 functions are listed in the following table.

This Microsoft Excel A function	Corresponds to this Lotus 1-2-3 function
AVERAGEA	@AVG
MINA	@MIN
MAXA	@MAX
VARA	@VARS
VARPA	@VARP
STDEVA	@STDS
STDEVPA	@STD

Note When a Lotus 1-2-3 sheet is opened in Microsoft Excel, Lotus 1-2-3 functions that correspond to A functions are automatically converted to A functions.

In general, the A functions treat text and logical values differently than the equivalent non-A functions in Microsoft Excel, as described in the following table.

to use transition formula entry feature before you begin working on a worksheet. After you turn on transition formula entry, it remains in effect for that worksheet until you turn it off, even if you save a Lotus 1-2-3 worksheet as a Microsoft Excel workbook.

Note Transition formula entry affects only range names that are simple and absolute, and does not affect range names that refer to nonadjacent selections. All Lotus 1-2-3 range names that originate in Lotus 1-2-3 are affected by transition formula entry.

Transition Formula Evaluation

Microsoft Excel and Lotus 1-2-3 evaluate certain formulas and expressions differently. *Transition formula evaluation* allows Microsoft Excel to calculate formulas and database criteria according to Lotus 1-2-3 rules.

▶ **To use Lotus 1-2-3 rules to calculate formulas and database criteria**

1 On the **Tools** menu, click **Options**, and then click the **Transition** tab.
2 Under **Sheet Options**, select the **Transition formula evaluation** check box.

The following table compares expressions that are evaluated differently in Microsoft Excel and Lotus 1-2-3.

This expression	Is evaluated this way in Lotus 1-2-3	And this way in Microsoft Excel
Cells that contain text	When the cell is used in a formula, it is given a value of zero (0).	The cell containing text is ignored in the calculation. In Microsoft Excel, you cannot combine text and numeric entries in the same formula.
Boolean expressions	Boolean expressions are evaluated to 0 or 1 and display 0 or 1 in the cell. For example, 2<3 shows a 1 in the cell to represent **True**.	Microsoft Excel also calculates Boolean expressions as 0 and 1, but displays FALSE or TRUE, respectively, in the cell.

Note also the following differences:

- In Microsoft Excel, database criteria ranges are evaluated differently when you are extracting data, finding data, and using database functions.

    For example, computed criteria can use existing field names.

- Certain Lotus 1-2-3 functions, including @MOD, @VLOOKUP, and @HLOOKUP, are evaluated differently than the equivalent Microsoft Excel functions.

    For example, the Lotus 1-2-3 @VLOOKUP function performs literal matches on text, whereas the Microsoft Excel VLOOKUP function returns a lookup value for nonliteral text, using the nearest entry in alphabetic order.

When the **Transition navigation keys** check box is selected, you can use the following text-alignment prefix characters to assign alignment formats as you enter data into cells.

This prefix character	Performs this action in Microsoft Excel
Apostrophe (')	Aligns data in the cell to the left
Quotation mark (")	Aligns data in the cell to the right
Caret (^)	Centers data in the cell
Backslash (\)	Repeats characters across the cell

Transition Formula Entry

Microsoft Excel uses a different syntax than Lotus 1-2-3 in formulas and functions. Using *transition formula entry* to learn the Microsoft Excel syntax, you can enter any formula or function exactly as you would in Lotus 1-2-3, and you are shown how it is entered in Microsoft Excel.

▶ **To enter a formula, function, or range name in Lotus 1-2-3 syntax**

1. On the **Tools** menu, click **Options**, and then click the **Transition** tab.
2. Under **Sheet Options**, select the **Transition formula entry** check box.

Note Microsoft Excel does not automatically turn on transition formula entry for Microsoft Excel workbooks or Lotus 1-2-3 worksheets. You must select the option on the **Transition** tab.

When the **Transition formula entry** check box is selected, you can:

- Enter any formula or function as you would in Lotus 1-2-3.

    Microsoft Excel automatically translates the formula into a Microsoft Excel formula when you click the enter box (the checked box) in the formula bar or press ENTER. For example, if you enter the formula @AVG(A1..A5), Microsoft Excel changes it to =AVERAGE(A1:A5).

- Enter a reference that corresponds to a defined range name.

    The range name appears in the formula after you click the enter box or press ENTER.

- Edit the reference of a range name in the formula bar by clicking the formula bar, which automatically displays the reference.

    The range name reappears when you click the enter box or press ENTER.

- Delete a range name.

    All formulas that contain that range name change to display the reference instead of the range name.

- Use a dollar sign ($) before a range name to make the range name absolute.

When you turn transition formula entry on or off, formulas do not automatically reapply names or revert names to references. So you should decide whether you want

Options dialog callouts

- Enter an activation key.
- Display Help for Lotus 1-2-3 Users when the activation key is pressed.
- Work with Microsoft Excel formulas the way you work with Lotus 1-2-3 formulas.

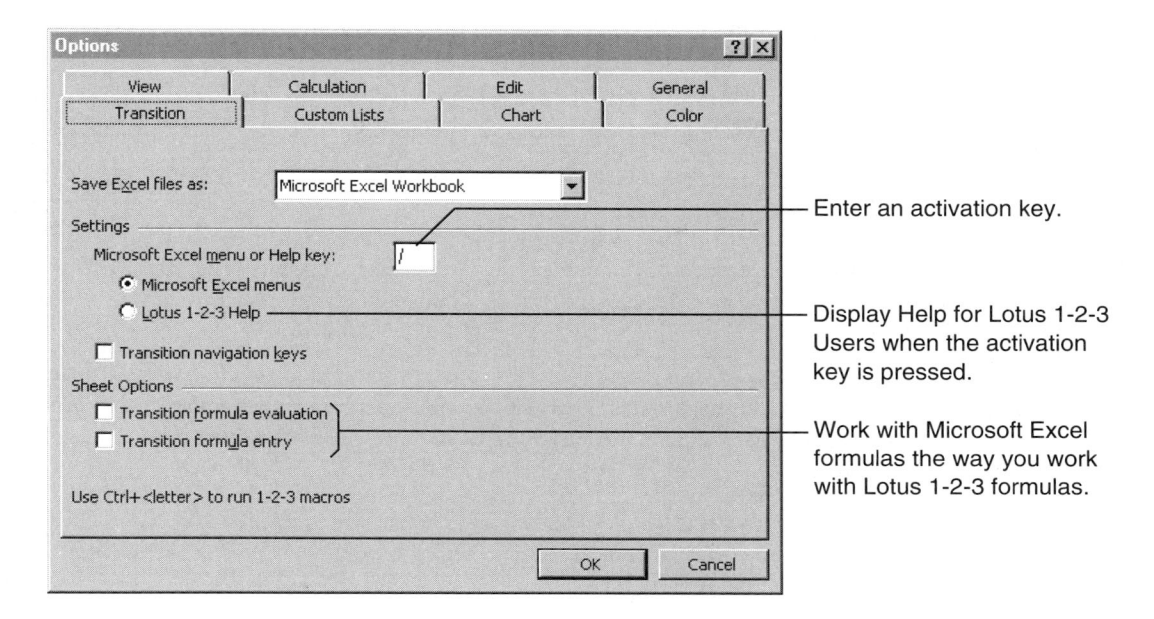

Transition Navigation Keys

Microsoft Excel provides an alternate set of keyboard commands for moving around spreadsheets. For example, in Lotus 1-2-3 pressing HOME moves the active cell highlight to cell A1. In Microsoft Excel, pressing HOME moves the active cell highlight to the first cell in the current row. When you use *transition navigation keys* in Microsoft Excel, however, pressing HOME moves the active cell to cell A1.

▶ **To activate alternate keyboard commands**

1. On the **Tools** menu, click **Options**, and then click the **Transition** tab.
2. Under **Settings**, select the **Transition navigation keys** check box.

The following tables list the keyboard shortcuts that are activated when you select the **Transition navigation keys** check box in Microsoft Excel.

This key combination	Performs this action in Microsoft Excel
CTRL+LEFT ARROW or SHIFT+TAB	Moves left one page
CTRL+RIGHT ARROW or TAB	Moves right one page
CTRL+PAGE UP	Goes to the next sheet in a workbook
CTRL+PAGE DOWN	Goes to the previous sheet in a workbook
HOME	Selects the cell in the upper-left corner of the sheet
F5	Activates the **Go To** command (**Edit** menu)

Do my old macros work in Microsoft Excel? Microsoft Excel includes the Macro Interpreter for Lotus 1-2-3 users, which provides strong macro conversion support. For more information, see "Converting Lotus 1-2-3 Worksheets to Microsoft Excel" later in this section.

Using Microsoft Excel Tools for Lotus 1-2-3 Users

Although the commands and procedures for entering data in Lotus 1-2-3 differ from those of Microsoft Excel, several features built into Microsoft Excel allow you to use what you know about working with Lotus 1-2-3 to learn Microsoft Excel. By using some or all of these options, you can be immediately productive and learn Microsoft Excel at the same time.

Note Unless otherwise noted, the options described in the following table are available only in Microsoft Excel for Windows. Microsoft Excel for the Macintosh includes only two options on the **Transition** tab in the **Options** dialog box (**Tools** menu): **Microsoft Excel menu or Help key** and **Transition formula evaluation**.

If you want to	Do this
Use Lotus 1-2-3 commands to learn equivalent Microsoft Excel commands.	On the **Tools** menu, click **Options**, and then click the **Transition** tab. In the **Microsoft Excel menu or Help key** box, type a menu-activation character (the slash character is entered by default), and then click **Lotus 1-2-3 Help** (Windows and Macintosh).
Move through Microsoft Excel worksheets using an alternate command set.	On the **Tools** menu, click **Options**, and then click the **Transition** tab. Select the **Transition navigation keys** check box.
Learn Microsoft Excel formula syntax by using Lotus 1-2-3 function syntax.	On the **Tools** menu, click **Options**, and then click the **Transition** tab. Select the **Transition formula entry** check box.
Assist file conversion to Microsoft Excel by using Lotus 1-2-3 rules for evaluating text fields and database criteria.	On the **Tools** menu, click **Options**, and then click the **Transition** tab. Select the **Transition formula evaluation** check box (Windows and Macintosh).
Run your Lotus 1-2-3 macros.	Open the Lotus 1-2-3 file containing the macros you want to use, hold down CTRL, and press the macro activation letter.

Microsoft Excel Transition Options

Some Microsoft Excel spreadsheet operations—such as calculating formulas, using the keyboard, and entering dates—work differently from those in other spreadsheet applications. However, Microsoft Excel lets you decide how you want these features to work. You can select either the standard Microsoft Excel operation or the operation that matches Lotus 1-2-3 and other Lotus 1-2-3-compatible spreadsheet applications.

To specify how you want Microsoft Excel to operate, use the options on the **Transition** tab in the **Options** dialog box (**Tools** menu).

File Formats That Save Only the Active Sheet

The following table lists file formats that save only the active sheet.

Windows format	Macintosh format
Formatted Text (space-delimited)	Formatted Text (space-delimited)
Text (tab-delimited)	Text (tab-delimited)
CSV (comma-delimited)	CSV (comma-delimited)
Microsoft Excel 4.0 Worksheet	Microsoft Excel 4.0 Worksheet
Microsoft Excel 3.0 Worksheet	Microsoft Excel 3.0 Worksheet
Microsoft Excel 2.1 Worksheet	Microsoft Excel 2.2 Worksheet
WK1, FMT (Lotus 1-2-3))	WK1, FMT (Lotus 1-2-3)
WK1, ALL (Lotus 1-2-3)	WK1, ALL (Lotus 1-2-3)
WQ1 (Quattro Pro/DOS)	Not supported
DBF 4 (dBASE IV)	DBF 4 (dBASE IV)
DBF 3 (dBASE III)	DBF 3 (dBASE III)
DBF 2 (dBASE II)	DBF 2 (dBASE II)
CSV (Macintosh)	CSV (Windows)
CSV (OS/2 or MS-DOS)	CSV (OS/2 or MS-DOS)
DIF (data interchange format)	DIF (data interchange format)
SYLK (Symbolic Link)	SYLK (Symbolic Link)

Switching from Lotus 1-2-3

This section describes the differences between Lotus 1-2-3 2.x-5.x and Microsoft Excel. Microsoft Excel includes several features that protect the Lotus 1-2-3 user's investment in Lotus 1-2-3 knowledge and experience, as well as strong file and macro conversion support for macros compatible with Lotus 1-2-3 Release 2.01.

What happens to my old Lotus 1-2-3 documents when I open them in Microsoft Excel?
You can open files created in Lotus 1-2-3 2.x-5.x directly in Microsoft Excel. Most data and formatting created in Lotus 1-2-3 are fully supported by Microsoft Excel. For more information, see "Converting Lotus 1-2-3 Worksheets to Microsoft Excel" later in this section.

Can I share Microsoft Excel documents with users of Lotus 1-2-3? If your workgroup is using a combination of Lotus 1-2-3 2.x-5.x and Microsoft Excel, users can exchange documents between versions. However, not all Microsoft Excel features are supported in Lotus 1-2-3. For more information, see "Sharing Documents with Lotus 1-2-3" later in this section.

▶ **To specify the default format in which to save workbooks**

1 On the **Tools** menu, click **Options**, and then click the **Transition** tab.
2 In the **Save Excel file as** box, click the file format you want.

For more information about selecting a default format in which to save workbooks, see "Specifying the Default Format in Which to Save Files" in Chapter 22, "Supporting Multiple Versions of Microsoft Office."

Tip In Windows 95 and Windows NT Workstation 4.0, you can use a system policy to define a default value for the **Save as type** option in the **Save As** dialog box (**File** menu) for all Microsoft Excel users in your workgroup. In the System Policy Editor, set the following policy:

User\Excel\Tools_Options\Transition\Default Save

For more information, see "Using Windows System Policies to Customize Office" in Chapter 7, "Customizing and Optimizing Microsoft Office."

You can save Microsoft Excel workbooks or worksheets in the file formats described in the following sections.

File Formats That Save the Entire Workbook

When you save a Microsoft Excel workbook in any of the following file formats, all sheets in the workbook are saved.

Windows format	Macintosh format
Microsoft Excel Workbook	Microsoft Excel Workbook
Template	Template
Microsoft Excel 5.0/95 Workbook	Microsoft Excel 5.0 Workbook
Microsoft Excel 97 & 5.0/95 Workbook	Microsoft Excel 97 & 5.0/95 Workbook
Microsoft Excel 4.0 Workbook	Microsoft Excel 4.0 Workbook
WK4 (1-2-3)	WK4 (1-2-3)
WK3, FM3 (1-2-3)	WK3, FM3 (1-2-3)

Note Not all Microsoft Excel data and formatting is saved in these formats. For more information about lost data or formatting when saving in previous Microsoft Excel formats, see Chapter 12, "Upgrading from Previous Versions of Microsoft Excel."

found in the **Open** dialog box (**File** menu). After the File Conversion Wizard converts the files you select, it creates a summary report in a new workbook.

Note The File Conversion Wizard is not installed when you choose a Typical installation during Setup. If the File Conversion Wizard does not appear in the **Add-Ins** dialog box (**Tools** menu), rerun Setup and click **Add/Remove**. Under the **Microsoft Excel** option, select the **Add-Ins** option, and then select the **File Conversion Wizard** option.

Importing Text Files

When you open a text file in Microsoft Excel, the Text Import Wizard guides you through the steps to import the text file and parse the text properly across columns.

▶ **To convert a text document to Microsoft Excel format**

1 On the **File** menu, click **Open**.
2 In the **Files of type** box, click the document's original format.
3 Below the **Look in** box, select the text file you want to convert.
4 Click **Open**, and then follow the instructions that appear in the Text Import Wizard.

Microsoft Excel does not list the document in the Open dialog box
Make sure that you selected the correct file type or extension in the **Files of type** box. If the document name you are looking for still does not appear, click **All Files**. Also check to make sure that you have selected the correct drive and folder.

Saving Microsoft Excel Workbooks in Other File Formats

You can save Microsoft Excel workbooks or worksheets in file formats that can be read by other applications or by previous versions of Microsoft Excel.

Tip When you save a Microsoft Excel workbook in another file format, use a different file name so that you can keep a copy of the original workbook as a backup.

▶ **To save a Microsoft Excel document in another file format**

1 On the **File** menu, click **Save As**.
2 In the **File name** box, enter a name for the converted workbook.
3 In the **Save as type** box (Windows) or **Save file as type** box (Macintosh), click the format you want.

Tip You can also specify the default format in which Microsoft Excel saves new workbooks.

Note When you convert a document, Microsoft Excel preserves the original content and formatting as much as possible. However, other applications might have similar features that work differently, so you might not always get the results you expect. Major conversion issues for Lotus 1-2-3 and other applications are described later in this chapter. For more information, see the section that corresponds to the application from which you are switching or converting documents.

> **Microsoft Excel did not convert my document properly**
> The file formats that Microsoft Excel supports are listed in the **Files of type** box in the **Open** dialog box (**File** menu). If your document type is not listed, see whether the application that created your documents can save them in a format that is supported by Microsoft Excel.

After you convert a document to Microsoft Excel, the converted document exists only in your computer's memory; the original document remains unchanged. To complete the conversion, you need to save the converted document in Microsoft Excel format.

▶ **To save a converted document in Microsoft Excel format**

1 On the **File** menu, click **Save As**.
2 In the **File name** box, enter a new name for the converted document.

   This preserves the original document as a backup.

To convert multiple documents, open several documents at the same time in the **Open** dialog box (**File** menu). Microsoft Excel converts each document you select. When you finish editing the documents, save each document as described earlier.

Tip In Windows, you can open more than one file at a time if all the files are within a single folder. To select a contiguous group of documents, click the name of the first document you want to open, and then hold down SHIFT and click the name of the last document you want to open. Or hold down CTRL and click the names of the individual documents you want to open.

To convert several documents at once, you can also use the File Conversion Wizard add-in, which is supplied with Microsoft Excel. The File Conversion Wizard makes it easy to convert a large library of spreadsheet files to Microsoft Excel format. However, it does not convert from Microsoft Excel format to other formats.

▶ **To start the File Conversion Wizard**

1 On the **Tools** menu, point to **Wizard**, and then click **File Conversion**.
2 Follow the instructions on your screen.

The File Conversion Wizard converts all files of the format and in the location you specify. The file types available to the File Conversion Wizard are the same file types

Converting File Formats in Microsoft Excel

File formats determine the way information in a spreadsheet document is stored in a file. Different spreadsheet applications use different file formats. Microsoft Excel allows you to open and save files in many different formats, using the **Open** and **Save As** commands on the **File** menu.

The list of formats that appears in the **Save As** dialog box (**File** menu) varies depending on what kind of sheet is active. Some file formats save the entire workbook; others save only the active worksheet. (When saving the latter file type, you must save each sheet in the workbook individually.) See the following sections for a comprehensive summary of these formats.

Opening Other File Formats in Microsoft Excel

Microsoft Excel can open documents saved in any format listed in the **Files of type** box in the **Open** dialog box (**File** menu). However, Microsoft Excel cannot save documents in every one of these file formats.

The following table lists file formats that Microsoft Excel can open but not save.

This source application	Saves data in this file format
Microsoft Works version 2.0 (MS-DOS and Windows only)	WKS
Lotus 1-2-3 Releases 3.0, 3.1+, and 1-2-3/W PIC format	PIC (when included in an ALL file)
Lotus 1-2-3 Release 5 for Windows Templates	WT4
Quattro Pro for Windows Version 5.0	WB1

Converting Documents from Other File Formats

The majority of your spreadsheet documents can be converted to Microsoft Excel format by opening and then saving them in Microsoft Excel.

▶ To open a document in Microsoft Excel

1. On the **File** menu, click **Open**.
2. In the **Files of type** box, click **All Files**.
3. Below the **Look in** box, select the name of the document.
4. Click **Open**.

   Microsoft Excel converts the document and opens it.

CHAPTER 18

Switching to Microsoft Excel

This chapter tells you what to expect when you or your workgroup switches to Microsoft Excel 97 from another spreadsheet program.

The primary questions most new Microsoft Excel users have are:

- What happens to my old documents when I open them in Microsoft Excel 97?
- Can I share Microsoft Excel 97 documents with users of my old spreadsheet program?
- Do my old macros still work in Microsoft Excel 97?

If you are switching to Microsoft Excel 97, this chapter answers these questions for you.

In This Chapter
Converting File Formats in Microsoft Excel   492
Switching from Lotus 1-2-3   496
Switching from Quattro Pro for MS-DOS   535
Switching from Quattro Pro for Windows   536
Switching from Multiplan   538
Switching from Microsoft Works   542

See Also
- For a summary of new and improved features in Microsoft Excel 97, see Chapter 2, "What's New in Microsoft Office 97."
- For information about installing Microsoft Excel or other Office applications, see Chapter 4, "Installing Microsoft Office."
- For information about upgrading to Microsoft Excel 97 from a previous version of Microsoft Excel, see Chapter 12, "Upgrading from Previous Versions of Microsoft Excel."

The Microsoft SQL Server Driver is not included when you choose a Typical installation during Setup. To install the driver, rerun Setup and click **Add/Remove**. Under the **Data Access** option, select **Database Drivers**, and then select the **Microsoft SQL Server Driver** check box.

After you install the Microsoft SQL Server Driver, use the ODBC Data Source Administrator to add or modify ODBC data sources.

▶ **To set up ODBC data sources by using the ODBC Data Source Administrator**

1. In Control Panel, double-click the 32bit ODBC icon.
2. In the **ODBC Data Source Administrator** dialog box, click the appropriate **DSN** tab.

    For information about using the **User DSN**, **System DSN**, and **File DSN** tabs, click **Help**.

For more information about ODBC and how it works, see "Using Microsoft Access with ODBC and Client/Server Operations" in Chapter 27, "Sharing Information with Microsoft Office Applications."

Built-in Drivers

You can use built-in drivers to import, export, or link the following types of data:

- dBASE III, dBASE III+, dBASE IV, and dBASE 5.0
- FoxPro 2.*x* and 3.0 (import only for 3.0)
- Paradox 3.*x*, 4.*x*, and 5.0
- Microsoft Access databases, and other databases that use the Microsoft Jet database engine, such as those created with Visual Basic, Visual C++, or Microsoft Excel

  This includes databases created in previous versions of Microsoft Access.
- Microsoft Excel 3.0, 4.0, 5.0, 95, and 97
- Lotus 1-2-3 WKS, WK1, WK3, and WK4 formats (import and link only for WKS and WK4)
- Delimited and fixed-width text files
- HTML 1.0 lists, and HTML 2.0 and 3.*x* lists and tables
- Internet Database Connector/HTML Extension (IDC/HTX) files (export only)
- Active Server Pages (ASP) files (export only)
- Microsoft Exchange and Microsoft Outlook data (collectively referred to as Microsoft Windows Messaging Service data). Linking data in this format is read-only.
- Microsoft Word for Windows mail merge data files (export only)

Products from other vendors and other Microsoft products also contain ODBC drivers, including drivers for the applications in the previous list. These drivers may have been installed on your computer. If you want to know whether these drivers have been tested and verified for use with Microsoft Access, contact the driver vendor. Drivers for Paradox, Lotus 1-2-3, and Microsoft Messaging are available in the Office 97 Value Pack.

Note The CD-ROM version of Office 97 includes the Office 97 Value Pack, a collection of application extras such as clip art, maps, sounds, presentation enhancements, and utilities. For more information about the Value Pack and how to use its contents, see Valupack.hlp in the ValuPack folder on the Office CD. You can also point to **Microsoft on the Web** (**Help** menu) in any Office application, and then click **Free Stuff**.

ODBC Drivers

If you want to import, export, or link data from an ODBC data source, you need to install a 32-bit version ODBC driver, such as Microsoft SQL Server Driver. The Microsoft SQL Server Driver is an ODBC driver that has been tested and verified for use with Microsoft Access. This driver is supplied with Office.

- If you have Microsoft Office 97, Developer Edition, use the Setup Wizard to create an installation program for a custom Microsoft Access application that sets up a user profile.

    A *user profile* is an alternative set of registry keys that can contain settings that override the standard Microsoft Access and Microsoft Jet 3.5 settings. A user profile is specified by using the **/profile** command-line option when you start your application. User profiles are analogous to the *appname*.ini files used in previous versions of Microsoft Access.

- Create a user profile by using the Registry Editor, and then specify it by using the **/profile** command-line option when you start your application. For more information about user profiles, see Microsoft Access online Help.

For more information about Microsoft Access registry settings, see Microsoft Access online Help.

Similar considerations apply to database applications developed with Microsoft Access 95, Microsoft Excel 95, Microsoft Visual Basic version 4.0, and Microsoft Visual C++ version 4.0, because they can share the same Microsoft Jet version 3.0 database engine. However, database engine settings in these applications do not affect applications that share use of the Microsoft Jet 3.5 database engine, and are read from a separate set of subkeys under the **HKEY_LOCAL_MACHINE\SOFTWARE \Microsoft\Jet\3.0\Engines** key.

These considerations do not apply to Microsoft Access versions 1.*x* and 2.0 and Visual Basic version 3.0, which use INI files for initialization information. The following table shows where each of these previous version applications looks for its initialization information.

This application	Looks in this INI file
Microsoft Access 1.*x*	Msaccess.ini
Microsoft Access 1.*x* or 2.0 custom application	*appname*.ini
Microsoft Access 2.0	Msacc20.ini
Visual Basic 3.0 .exe application	*appname*.ini
Visual Basic 3.0 at design time	Vb.ini
Visual Basic 3.0 at run time	Vb.ini

Using Built-in Drivers and ODBC Drivers

In Microsoft Access, you can import, export, and link data from a number of different database formats and from spreadsheets and text files. To connect to a particular type of data, Microsoft Access uses either a built-in driver or an ODBC driver. A driver is a dynamic-link library (DLL) used to connect a specific data source with another client application; in this case, Microsoft Access.

When you use Visual Basic to create Paradox tables, text columns default to 255 characters if you do not specify a field width by using the **FieldSize** property. Wide columns such as these make it easy for the new table to exceed the 1,350-character maximum width of a Paradox table with a primary key. If you attempt to append a primary index to a Paradox table wider than 1,350 characters, you receive an error message.

Microsoft Access Registry Settings for Paradox

Microsoft Access 97 uses the Microsoft Jet 3.5 database engine to read and write data, whether it is using its own native tables or linking tables in other data formats. The settings Microsoft Jet version 3.5 uses to initialize the Paradox driver are located in the Windows registry in the **HKEY_LOCAL_MACHINE\SOFTWARE\Microsoft\Jet\3.5\Engines\Paradox** key.

The Setup program automatically creates recommended registry settings. However, you can modify the settings in this key, in the Microsoft Access-specific Jet 3.5 registry key, or by using a user profile. For more information, see the following section, "Running Multiple Data Access Applications." For more information about Microsoft Access registry settings, see Microsoft Access online Help.

Running Multiple Data Access Applications

Custom applications developed with Microsoft Access 97, Microsoft Excel 97, Microsoft Visual Basic version 5.0, and Microsoft Visual C++ version 5.0 can use the Microsoft Jet 3.5 database engine to perform their database-related operations. If you run one or more of these applications on the same computer, they all initialize the Microsoft Jet 3.5 database engine by using the Windows registry settings in the **HKEY_LOCAL_MACHINE\SOFTWARE\Microsoft\Jet\3.5\Engines** key.

If you modify any of these settings, your changes apply to all applications using the Microsoft Jet 3.5 database engine on the same computer. There are three ways you can avoid this:

- Change the settings in the **HKEY_LOCAL_MACHINE\SOFTWARE\Microsoft\Office\8.0\Access\Jet\3.5\Engines** key.

  Any settings defined in the **HKEY_LOCAL_MACHINE\SOFTWARE\Microsoft\Office\8.0\Access\Jet\3.5\Engines** key override settings in the **HKEY_LOCAL_MACHINE\SOFTWARE\Microsoft\Jet\3.5\Engines** key and apply only to Microsoft Access 97.

Linking or Opening Paradox Tables in a Private Folder

Microsoft Access 97 cannot link or open Paradox tables in the private folder of an active Paradox session. While you have a linked Paradox table open in Microsoft Access, records added by other users are not visible to you until you close and reopen the table. However, records added by you in Microsoft Access are visible to Paradox users when their screen is refreshed (if they have Auto Refresh turned on).

Deleting Paradox LCK Files

Occasionally the Paradox LCK file is inadvertently left in a folder. This prevents either Microsoft Access or Paradox from accessing files in that folder. To fix this, delete the LCK file.

Exporting a Table to a Paradox File

If you need to save the data from a table or query that has been created in Microsoft Access so that users who are still working in Paradox can use it, you can export that data.

▶ **To export a Microsoft Access table or query to a Paradox file**

1. Open a Microsoft Access database, or switch to the Database window of the open database.
2. In the Database window, click the table or query you want to export.
3. On the **File** menu, click **Save As/Export**.
4. Click **To an External File or Database**, and then click **OK**.
5. In the **Save as type** box, click the Paradox format you want.
6. In the **File name** box, type a file name for the database file you want to export.
7. In the **Save in** box, select the folder where you want to save the file, and then click **Export**.

If you export a table with table or field names that do not fit the requirements of the destination database, Microsoft Access adjusts the names. For example, if you export data to a Paradox table, any field names longer than 10 characters are truncated.

If you attempt to export a Microsoft Access table containing long field names to Paradox, and the first 25 characters are identical to an existing field name, Microsoft Access generates a unique field name.

When Microsoft Access exports a table with a field name containing a number sign (#), it is converted to a period. An opening or closing parenthesis, curly bracket, or quotation mark is converted to an underscore character (_).

Exporting Microsoft Access Memo fields to Paradox format results in extra carriage return characters.

Windows registry. For more information about changing Microsoft Jet database engine settings in the Windows registry, see "Running Multiple Data Access Applications" later in this chapter.

The following sections describe how to define these settings and discuss some additional issues when sharing Paradox files on a network.

Specifying a User Name with the ParadoxUserName Setting

The **ParadoxUserName** setting in the Windows registry defines the name to be displayed by Paradox if a Paradox table is locked by Microsoft Access and a user accessing the data from Paradox attempts to place an incompatible lock.

To share Paradox tables that use Microsoft Access with other Paradox users, you must modify the Windows registry. In the **HKEY_LOCAL_MACHINE\SOFTWARE \Microsoft\Jet\3.5\Engines\Paradox** key, set the **ParadoxUserName** value to a user name. There cannot be more than one user registered with the same **ParadoxUserName** on the same network. If you specify a **ParadoxUserName**, you must also specify **ParadoxNetPath** and **ParadoxNetStyle** values, or you receive an error message when trying to gain access to external Paradox data.

Specifying Identical ParadoxNetPath Settings

In Microsoft Access, for all users sharing the same Paradox database, a setting in the Windows registry must specify the full path to the folder that contains the Paradox.net file (for Paradox 3.*x*) or the Pdoxusrs.net file (for Paradox 4.*x* and 5.0). In the **HKEY_LOCAL_MACHINE\SOFTWARE\Microsoft\Jet\3.5\Engines\Paradox** key, set the **ParadoxNetPath** value to the full path.

In Paradox 4.*x*, you can modify this setting either by running Nupdate.exe or by using the **-net** command-line option. If you use the **-net** command-line option, be sure to include a backslash (\) at the end of the path (Microsoft Access and the Paradox Nupdate.exe program place the backslash at the end automatically). The **-net** command-line option was not available in Paradox prior to version 4.0. For more information, see the *Paradox Network Administrator's Guide*.

Specifying the Locking Style with the ParadoxNetStyle Setting

Use a setting in the Windows registry to specify the network locking style to use when accessing Paradox data. In the **HKEY_LOCAL_MACHINE\SOFTWARE \Microsoft\Jet\3.5\Engines\Paradox** key, set the **ParadoxNetStyle** to **3.***x* for Paradox 3.*x* or **4.***x* for Paradox 4.*x* and 5.0. You can use the Paradox 4.*x* locking style to gain access to Paradox 3.*x*, 4.*x*, and 5.0 tables. You cannot link Paradox 4.*x* tables while using the Paradox 3.*x* locking style.

If a Paradox version 3.5 user opens a table, you cannot open or import from this table by using the 4.*x* locking style. The table is inaccessible from Microsoft Access until the Paradox 3.5 user closes it.

Note You cannot update a Paradox table if its data (DB) or index (PX) file is set to read-only. To check this, use Windows Explorer to display the folder where the files are located, right-click the file, and then click **Properties** on the shortcut menu. If the **Read-only** check box on the **General** tab is selected, clear it and then click **OK**.

Paradox Tables on a Read-only Drive

You cannot link or import from Paradox tables on read-only drives. This is because Microsoft Access cannot create the necessary lock files.

Encrypted Tables

Microsoft Access does not support auxiliary passwords on Paradox tables. To use the table with Microsoft Access, open the table in Paradox and remove the auxiliary password.

Potential Restructure Problem in Paradox for Windows

Problems occasionally occur when you use the Paradox for Windows table restructure routine. If you are having difficulty getting Microsoft Access to open your Paradox 4.*x* table properly, consider restructuring it in Paradox for MS-DOS version 4.0 or 4.5, and then try again.

Paradox Referential Integrity

Microsoft Access referential integrity does not work with linked Paradox tables. You cannot use linked Paradox tables to trigger cascading deletes or updates, or to prevent orphan records.

Collating Sequences

The *collating sequence* determines the sort order used when working with tables. When working with Paradox tables, the Microsoft Jet database engine supports the following collating sequences: ASCII, International, Norwegian-Danish, and Swedish-Finnish.

To import or link Paradox tables, the **CollatingSequence** setting in the Windows registry must match the collating sequence used when the Paradox table was built. The default is setting is ASCII. If necessary, you can change this value in the Windows registry in the **HKEY_LOCAL_MACHINE\SOFTWARE\Microsoft \Jet\3.5\Engines\Paradox** key, in the Microsoft Access-specific Jet 3.5 registry key, or by using a user profile. For more information, see "Running Multiple Data Access Applications" later in this chapter.

Paradox Tables on a Network

If you are using Microsoft Access to link Paradox data on a network while Paradox users are working with the data, you must be sure to define all three **ParadoxUserName**, **ParadoxNetPath**, and **ParadoxNetStyle** settings in the

For information about how to define relationships in Microsoft Access, see "Defining Relationships in Microsoft Access" earlier in this chapter. For additional tips on using imported or linked tables, see "Importing and Linking External Tables" earlier in this chapter.

Converting Paradox Data Types

When you import data from a Paradox table, Microsoft Access converts Paradox data types into the corresponding Microsoft Access data types. The following table lists the data type conversions.

This Paradox data type	Corresponds to this Microsoft Access data type
Alphanumeric	Text
Currency	Number (**FieldSize** property set to Double)
Date	Date/Time
Memo	Memo
Number	Number (**FieldSize** property set to Double)
OLE	OLE Object
Short number	Number (**FieldSize** property set to Integer)

Note Although you can import or link Paradox tables that contain OLE fields, the OLE objects cannot be opened in Microsoft Access, due to differences in the way Microsoft Access and Paradox store OLE object header information. If you add a record to a linked Paradox table with OLE fields, those fields are null (blank). Moreover, if you import or link a Paradox 4.*x* table that contains Memo fields with the **Graphic**, **Binary**, or **Formatted** data types, these fields are not included in the table, because Microsoft Access cannot read fields of these formats.

Using Paradox Databases in Microsoft Access

The following tips and instructions help you use Microsoft Access 97 with Paradox databases.

Primary Keys in Paradox Tables

If you link a Paradox table that has a primary key, Microsoft Access needs the associated index (PX) file in order to open the linked table. If you link a Paradox table with a Memo field, Microsoft Access needs the associated memo (MB) file in order to open the linked table. If you delete or move these files, you cannot open the linked table.

If a multiple-field primary key is greater than 255 bytes, the table is opened read-only. If you link an empty Paradox table with no primary key, you can add records the first time you use the table. However, because Microsoft Access cannot update Paradox tables without primary keys, after the table is closed and reopened, it is read-only.

If you have no need to maintain your Paradox data in its original format, you can import your Paradox tables into Microsoft Access. Unlike linking the Paradox table, importing the data creates a copy of the data in Microsoft Access. Importing a table gives you greater flexibility and control over the data, but excludes users who are not running Microsoft Access from updating the data.

Importing or Linking Paradox Files

Paradox stores important information about a table's primary key in an index (PX) file. If you link a Paradox table that has a primary key, Microsoft Access needs the PX file to open the linked table. If you delete or move this file, you cannot open the linked table.

If you link a Paradox table that does not have a primary key, you cannot update data in the table using Microsoft Access. If you want to be able to update the table, define a primary key for the table in Paradox.

For additional considerations and potential problems when importing and linking Paradox files, see "Using Paradox Databases in Microsoft Access" later in this chapter.

▶ **To import or link a Paradox table**

1. Open a database in Microsoft Access, or switch to the Database window of the open database.

2. On the **File** menu, point to **Get External Data**, and then click **Import** or **Link Tables**.

3. In the **Files of Type** box, click **Paradox**.

4. In the **Look in** box, switch to the appropriate folder and select the file you want, and then click **Import** or **Link**.

5. If the Paradox table you select is encrypted, Microsoft Access prompts you for the password. Type the password for the Paradox table, and click **OK**.

    If you are importing the file, Microsoft Access creates a new table named after the file you selected and imports the data from the DB file.

    If you are linking the file, Microsoft Access adds the table name with a linked table icon to the **Tables** tab of the Database window. When you choose a linked table from the list, you open the Paradox database file that contains the table, and the data is available as if it were part of your Microsoft Access database.

6. Repeat Steps 4 and 5 for each Paradox file you want to import or link, and then click **Close**.

After you have imported all the tables, specify a primary key (a unique identifier used to relate tables), and create indexes on all fields you want to search or sort. In addition, check to see whether you want to modify any data types, field properties, or table properties at this time. Then define the relationships between your tables.

Microsoft Access 97 Terms for dBASE Users

The following table matches Microsoft Access terms with the equivalent term or command in Paradox. The Microsoft Access term is not necessarily an exact equivalent of the Paradox term, but rather a term you can look up in Microsoft Access online Help for more information. You do not need to understand all of these terms before you start using Microsoft Access.

This Paradox term	Corresponds to this Microsoft Access term
Alphanumeric data type	Text data type
Edit/Coedit mode	Exclusive/Shared access
Folder of related files	Database
Form	Form
Image PickForm	Open a form
Key field	Primary key
Lookup	List box, combo box
Modify DataEntry	**Data Entry** command (**Records** menu)
Modify Restructure command	Table Design view
Multiple-record section	Subform
Query	Query
Script	Module
Table	Table
Tools QuerySpeed	Index
ValChecks	Validation rule
View command	Datasheet view
Zoom command	**Find** command (**Edit** menu)

Using Paradox Tables in Microsoft Access

You can use data from tables in Paradox or Paradox for Windows version 3.*x*, 4.*x*, or 5.0. format. You cannot use data from tables in Paradox 7 format; however, you can save tables from Paradox 7 to version 5.0 to use the data with Microsoft Access. If you need to leave your data in Paradox format so that Paradox users can continue to use it, you can link the data to your Microsoft Access database. By using Microsoft Access, you can view and edit the data in linked tables even if others are using it in Paradox.

If you want to share Paradox tables with Paradox 7 users by linking tables from Microsoft Access, Paradox 7 can save and use its tables in version 5.0 format. If you provide the correct password, Microsoft Access can open encrypted Paradox tables.

▶ **To export a Microsoft Access table or query to a FoxPro file**

1. Open a Microsoft Access database, or switch to the Database window of the open database.
2. In the Database window, click the table or query you want to export.
3. On the **File** menu, click **Save As/Export**.
4. In the **Save As** dialog box, click **To an External File or Database**, and then click **OK**.
5. In the **Save as type** box, click the FoxPro format you want.
6. In the **File name** box, type a file name for the database file you want to export.
7. In the **Save in** box, select the folder where you want to save the file, and then click **Export**.

If you export a table with table or field names that do not fit the requirements of the destination database, Microsoft Access adjusts the names. For example, if you export data to a FoxPro table, any field names longer than 10 characters are truncated.

Microsoft Access Registry Settings for FoxPro

Microsoft Access uses the Microsoft Jet database engine to read and write data, whether it is using its own native tables or linking tables in other data formats. The settings Microsoft Jet uses to initialize the Xbase driver (the driver for both dBASE and FoxPro files) are located in the Windows registry in the **HKEY_LOCAL_MACHINE\SOFTWARE\Microsoft\Jet\3.5\Engines\Xbase** key.

The Setup program automatically creates recommended registry settings. However, you can modify these settings in this key, in the Microsoft Access-specific Jet 3.5 registry key, or by using a user profile. For more information, see "Running Multiple Data Access Applications" later in this chapter. For more information about how to modify Microsoft Access registry settings, see Microsoft Access online Help.

Switching from Paradox

To switch from Paradox to Microsoft Access, you can either link or import data from Paradox DB files. You can then modify the structure of the tables and create the other database objects you need. This section discusses the similarities and differences between Paradox and Microsoft Access, including terminology and data type conversion.

Note A primary difference between Microsoft Access and MS-DOS-based applications is the use of the Microsoft Windows graphical user interface. If your are currently using an MS-DOS-based version of Paradox and are new to Windows, study your Windows documentation to learn basic techniques.

Converting FoxPro Data Types

When you import data from a FoxPro file, Microsoft Access converts FoxPro data types into the corresponding Microsoft Access data types. The following table lists the data type conversions.

This FoxPro data type	Is converted to this Microsoft Access data type
Character	Text
Date	Date/Time
General	OLE Object
Logical	Yes/No
Memo	Memo
Numeric, Float	Number (**FieldSize** property set to Double)

For information about the differences between these FoxPro data types and their Microsoft Access equivalents, see "Converting dBASE Data Types" earlier in this chapter.

Using FoxPro 2.5 Files in Microsoft Access

Microsoft FoxPro 2.5 does not distinguish between tables created with the MS-DOS version of FoxPro and those created with the Windows version. Data in tables created with FoxPro 2.5 for MS-DOS is stored in OEM format. Data in tables created with FoxPro 2.5 for Windows is stored in ANSI format. Microsoft Access converts all FoxPro 2.5 data from an OEM code page to the ANSI 1252 code page when importing or linking FoxPro 2.5 data, and it converts the ANSI code page to an OEM code page when exporting to FoxPro 2.5 tables. The result is that *extended characters* (characters with ASCII and ANSI codes above 128) in tables created with FoxPro 2.5 for Windows are not converted properly.

If your FoxPro 2.5 for Windows tables contain extended characters, you may want to ensure that the tables are stored in OEM format (that is, created by FoxPro 2.5 for MS-DOS). Releases of FoxPro subsequent to 2.5 (2.5a, 2.5b, and so on) correctly identify the code page format of the data, so Microsoft Access can correctly determine how to convert extended characters.

Exporting a Table to a FoxPro File

If you need to save the data from a table or query that has been created in Microsoft Access so that users who are still working in FoxPro can use it, you can export that data.

▶ **To import or link a FoxPro file**

1. Open a database in Microsoft Access, or switch to the Database window of the open database.

2. On the **File** menu, point to **Get External Data**, and then click **Import** or **Link Tables**.

3. In the **Files of Type** box, click **Microsoft FoxPro** to import or link version 2.0, 2.5, or 2.6, or click **Microsoft FoxPro 3.0** to import version 3.0.

   Note Microsoft FoxPro 3.0 is not available if you click **Link Tables** in Step 2.

4. In the **Look in** box, switch to the appropriate folder and select the file you want, and then click **Import** or **Link**.

   If you are importing the file, Microsoft Access creates a new table named after the file you selected and imports the data from the FoxPro file.

   If you are linking the file, Microsoft Access displays a dialog box in which you can associate FoxPro index files.

5. For each FoxPro index (IDX or CDX) file you want to link, select the file and click **Select**. When you finish associating indexes, click **Close**. If there are no indexes to associate, click **Cancel** to continue.

6. If an index you have chosen uniquely identifies each record in the table so that indexed fields do not contain any duplicate values, select the index and click **OK**.

   Note If you do not select an index that provides a unique identifier, Microsoft Access may not be able to update data in queries with joins to this table, because records cannot be uniquely identified to maintain referential integrity.

   Microsoft Access adds the table name with a linked table icon to the list on the **Tables** tab in the Database window. When you choose a linked table from the list, you open the FoxPro database file that contains the table, and the data is available as if it were part of your Microsoft Access database.

7. Repeat Steps 4 through 6 for each FoxPro file you want to import or link, and then click **Close**.

After you have imported all the tables, specify a primary key (a unique identifier used to relate tables), and create indexes on all fields you want to search or sort. In addition, check to see whether you want to modify any data types, field properties, or table properties at this time. Then define the relationships between your tables.

For information about how to define relationships with Microsoft Access, see "Defining Relationships in Microsoft Access" earlier in this chapter. For additional tips on using imported or linked tables, see "Importing and Linking External Tables" earlier in this chapter.

Using FoxPro Files in Microsoft Access

You can use data from DBF files in FoxPro 2.*x* format and from DBC files in FoxPro 3.0 format. If you need to leave your data in FoxPro 2.0, 2.5, 2.6 DBF format so that FoxPro users can continue to use it, you can link the data to your Microsoft Access database. By using Microsoft Access, you can view and edit the data in linked tables even if others are using it in FoxPro.

If you have no need to maintain your FoxPro 2.*x* DBF data in its original format or if you are using data from DBC files in FoxPro 3.0 format, you can import these files into Microsoft Access. You cannot link DBC files in FoxPro 3.0 format. Importing a table gives you greater flexibility and control over the data, but excludes users who are not running Microsoft Access from updating the data.

Importing or Linking FoxPro Files

If you link a FoxPro file, you can tell Microsoft Access to use one or more FoxPro index (IDX or CDX) files to improve performance. Microsoft Access keeps track of the indexes in a special information (INF) file. When you use Microsoft Access to update the data in your DBF file, Microsoft Access also updates the index files to reflect your changes.

If you link a DBF file and associate an index (IDX or CDX) file, Microsoft Access needs the index file to open the linked table. If you delete or move index files or the information (INF) file, you cannot open the linked table.

If your FoxPro files are stored on a read-only drive or CD-ROM, Microsoft Access cannot create an INF file in the same folder as your DBF or DBC files. To link tables on a read-only drive, you must specify the path to the folder where you want Microsoft Access to create the INF file. To do so, you need to modify the Windows registry. In the **HKEY_LOCAL_MACHINE\SOFTWARE\Microsoft\Jet\3.5 \Engines\Xbase** key, or in the Microsoft Access-specific **Jet\3.5** key, create the **INFPath** value and point it to a read/write location in which the INF file can be written.

Note You can also use a user profile to set the **INFPath**. For more information, see "Running Multiple Data Access Applications" later in this chapter.

▶ **To export a Microsoft Access table or query to a dBASE file**

1. Open a Microsoft Access database, or switch to the Database window of the open database.
2. In the Database window, click the table or query you want to export.
3. On the **File** menu, click **Save As/Export**.
4. In the **Save As** dialog box, click **To an External File or Database**, and then click **OK**.
5. In the **Save as type** box, click the dBASE format you want.
6. In the **File name** box, type a file name for the database file you want to export.
7. In the **Save in** box, select the folder where you want to save the file, and then click **Export**.

If you export a table with table or field names that do not fit the requirements of the destination database, Microsoft Access adjusts the names. For example, if you export data to a dBASE table, any field names longer than 10 characters are truncated.

Microsoft Access Registry Settings for dBASE

Microsoft Access uses the Microsoft Jet database engine to read and write data, whether it is using its own native tables or linking tables in other data formats. The settings Microsoft Jet uses to initialize the Xbase driver (the driver for both dBASE and FoxPro files) are located in the Windows registry in the **HKEY_LOCAL_MACHINE\SOFTWARE\Microsoft\Jet\3.5\Engines\Xbase** key.

The Setup program automatically creates recommended registry settings. However, you can modify these settings in this key, in the Microsoft Access-specific Jet 3.5 registry key, or by using a user profile. For more information, see "Running Multiple Data Access Applications" later in this chapter. For more information about how to modify Microsoft Access registry settings, see Microsoft Access online Help.

Switching from FoxPro

To switch from FoxPro to Microsoft Access, you can either link or import the data from your FoxPro DBF files. You can then modify the structure of the tables and create the other database objects you need. This section discusses the similarities and differences between FoxPro and Microsoft Access, including data type conversion.

- Most Microsoft Access form controls have a **SpecialEffect** property that you can set to make controls on your forms look three-dimensional.
- You can have more than one Microsoft Access form open at a time.

    For example, you may want to link your Inventory form to your Manufacturing Schedule form and display them simultaneously. If having more than one form open at once is confusing or causes a problem, you can set the **Modal** property of the form to **Yes** to force the user to close the current form before opening another.
- The Microsoft Access equivalent to the dBASE Picture Functions field and the Template field is either the **Format** property or the **InputMask** property.

    There is also a Microsoft Access field property equivalent for most of the dBASE field Edit Options. When you click a property on the property sheet, Microsoft Access displays a brief description in the status bar at the bottom of the screen.

Creating Reports

Microsoft Access uses a banded report designer similar to the one in dBASE, but with extensive graphical tools and data windows. The information in a report is divided into sections, or *bands*. Each section has a specific purpose and prints in a particular order. As with queries and forms, you can use a Report Wizard as a quick way to get started creating a report. If you use a Report Wizard, Microsoft Access creates a complete report with an attractive and consistent look that you can apply to all of your reports. For most reports, the Report Wizards are all you need. If you want to customize a report, you can do so in report Design view.

Tip Like dBASE, Microsoft Access supports calculated fields in reports. In addition, Microsoft Access provides a special **RunningSum** property, which does not exist in dBASE.

Converting Catalogs

The Database window displays all of the objects in your database, much as the Control Center does in dBASE IV. In dBASE, a catalog gives you access to all the files that make up the database. However, in Microsoft Access, all of the objects are contained in a single file with an MDB extension, with the exception of linked objects. For linked objects, the links are stored in the MDB file, but the objects themselves are stored in other files.

Exporting a Table to a dBASE File

If you need to save the data from a table or query that has been created in Microsoft Access so that users who are still working in dBASE can use it, you can export that data.

In Microsoft Access, you do not need to write code to create user-friendly forms. You can use the Form Wizard to create attractive forms from your tables or queries. On the **Forms** tab in the Database window, click the **New** button, and then double-click **Form Wizard**. Because Microsoft Access forms take advantage of the Windows graphical environment, it is easy to create controls such as command buttons, check boxes, and drop-down lists. The Office Assistant and the Form Wizard can guide you through adding features to your forms without programming. Microsoft Access forms also use visual controls to work with built-in features, such as the record navigation buttons at the bottom of each form.

There are many things you can do to update the way your current dBASE form works when you convert to Microsoft Access. Here are some tips for updating your forms to take advantage of Microsoft Access features:

- If you are using multiple-choice fields, such as Picture @M, on a dBASE form, consider substituting option buttons, toggle buttons, or a combo box on the Microsoft Access version of the form.
- If you have one or more logical fields on a dBASE form, consider replacing them with check box controls.
- If your dBASE form is programmed to display detail records in a BROWSE window or screen, consider replacing the separate BROWSE interface with an integrated subform on the Microsoft Access form, as shown in the following illustration.

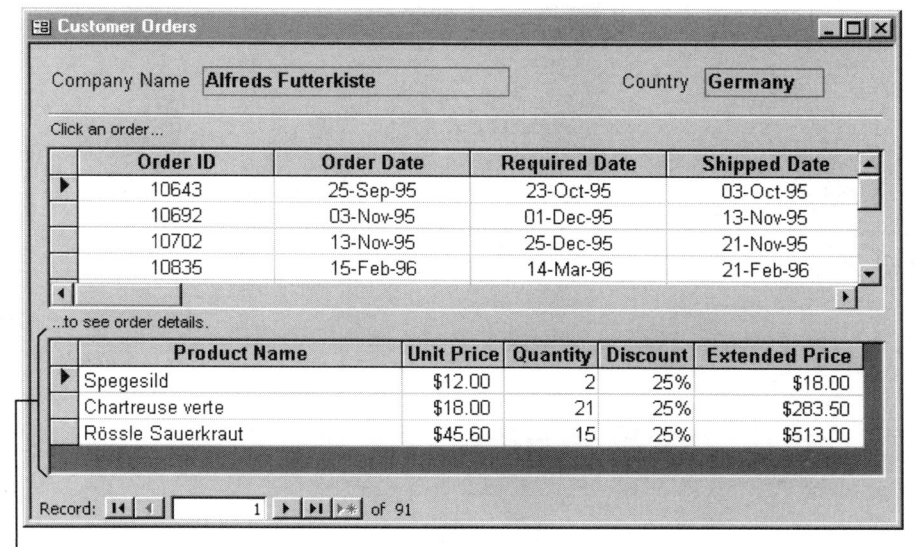

Integrated subform

Chapter 17 Switching to Microsoft Access

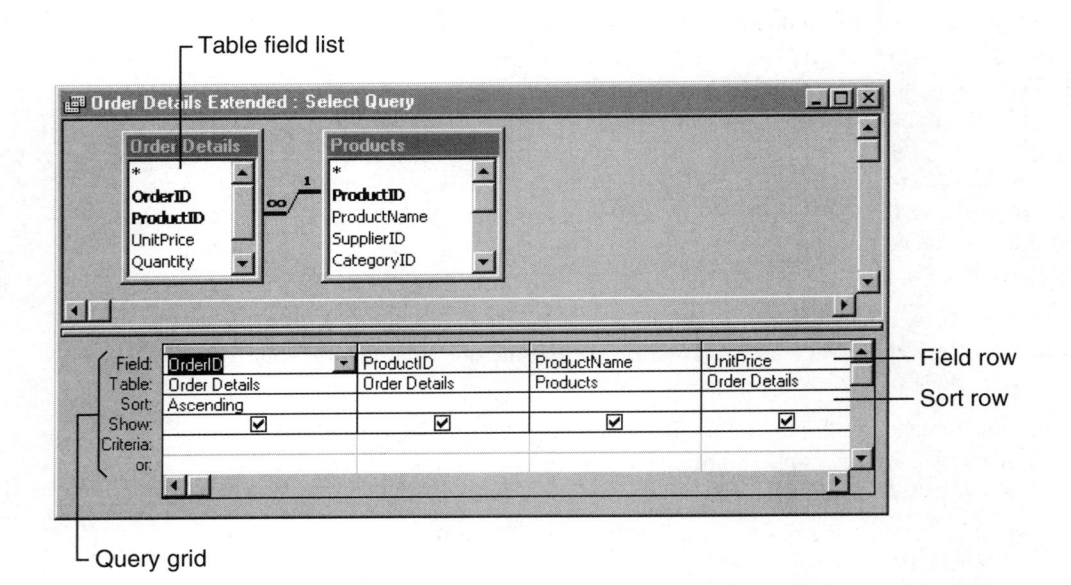

— Table field list
— Field row
— Sort row
— Query grid

To add fields to the query, drag them from the table field list to the query design grid, or select them from the drop-down list in the **Field** row of the design grid. To indicate a sort order for fields, click **Ascending** or **Descending** in the drop-down list in the **Sort** row of the design grid. Enter criteria formulas in the **Criteria** row. Many of the functions and formulas are similar to their dBASE equivalents.

Creating Forms

Microsoft Access forms are equivalent to dBASE screens. The dBASE Form Designer tools limit you to using only fields and text. As a result of this limitation, the traditional dBASE approach to adding features to forms is to set in a program function keys that call procedures related to the form. In dBASE, to make the user aware of these functions, you add text to the form that indicates which function keys to press to invoke certain procedures. You can also write code to create a more user-friendly dBASE form.

Note the following differences between dBASE data types and Microsoft Access data types:

- Numeric data types

    dBASE supports two numeric field types: Numeric and Float. In Microsoft Access, you use the Number data type for most numeric fields and then set the **FieldSize** property to specify the range and kind of numeric values that can be entered into a Number field.

- Additional field data types

    Microsoft Access offers two field data types not provided in dBASE: AutoNumber and Currency. The most common form of AutoNumber field automatically increments a value by one for each succeeding record to generate a unique identifier for each record. This data type is used for primary keys and for creating ID numbers. The Currency data type is tailored to the kind of rounding and calculation typical of currency transactions.

- Fixed-length fields

    As in dBASE, you must specify the length of Text fields. If a record exceeds the specified length, data is truncated. Therefore, set the length of your Text fields to the length of the longest anticipated entry. However, unlike dBASE, Microsoft Access does not actually store all of the unused space characters for fixed-length fields, so that the size of your files is not a consideration.

Creating Queries

After you import or link the data, you can create queries in Microsoft Access—you cannot import your dBASE queries. Microsoft Access has query wizards to help you create many complex queries. Use the query wizards to learn how to build queries in Microsoft Access. Then, as you build more advanced queries, use the wizards as a starting point for your own query designs.

To add a table or query to the query you are creating, you can drag a table from the Database window to the upper portion of the query design grid, or you can click the **Show Table** button on the **Query Design** toolbar. If relationships have been defined between tables, they are reflected in the query automatically. You can double-click the relationship line between two tables to change the relationship. The following illustration shows the query design grid.

6 If an index you have chosen uniquely identifies each record in the table so that indexed fields do not contain any duplicate values, select the index and click **OK**.

Note If you do not select an index that provides a unique identifier, Microsoft Access may not be able to update data in queries with joins to this table, because records cannot be uniquely identified to maintain referential integrity.

Microsoft Access adds the table name with a linked table icon to the list on the **Tables** tab in the Database window. When you choose a linked table from the list, you open the dBASE database file that contains the table, and the data is available as if it were part of your Microsoft Access database.

7 Repeat Steps 4 through 6 for each dBASE file you want to import or link, and then click **Close**.

After you have imported all the tables, specify a primary key (a unique identifier used to relate tables) and create indexes on all fields you want to search or sort. In addition, check to see whether you want to modify any data types, field properties, or table properties at this time. Then define the relationships between your tables.

For information about how to define relationships in Microsoft Access, see "Defining Relationships in Microsoft Access" earlier in this chapter. For additional tips on using imported or linked tables, see "Importing and Linking External Tables" earlier in this chapter.

Converting dBASE Data Types

When you import data from a dBASE file, Microsoft Access converts dBASE data types into the corresponding Microsoft Access data types. The following table lists the data type conversions.

This dBASE data type	Is converted to this Microsoft Access data type
Character	Text
Date	Date/Time
Logical	Yes/No
Memo	Memo
Numeric, Float	Number (**FieldSize** property set to Double)

Importing or Linking dBASE Files

If you link a dBASE file, you can also tell Microsoft Access to use one or more dBASE index (NDX or MDX) files to improve performance. Microsoft Access keeps track of the indexes in a special information (INF) file. When you use Microsoft Access to update the data in your DBF file, Microsoft Access also updates the index files to reflect your changes.

If you link a DBF file and associate an index (NDX or MDX) file, Microsoft Access needs the index file to open the linked table. If you delete or move index files or the information (INF) file, you cannot open the linked table. If you use dBASE to update data, you must update the associated indexes within dBASE as well. Microsoft Access cannot use a linked table unless the indexes you specify are current.

If your dBASE files are stored on a read-only drive or CD-ROM, Microsoft Access cannot create an INF file in the same folder as your DBF files. To link tables on a read-only drive, you must specify the path to the folder where you want Microsoft Access to create the INF file. To do so, you need to modify the Windows registry. In the **HKEY_LOCAL_MACHINE\SOFTWARE\Microsoft\Jet\3.5\Engines\Xbase** key, or in the Microsoft Access-specific **Jet\3.5** key, create the **INFPath** value and point it to a read/write location in which the INF file can be written.

Note You can also use a user profile to set the **INFPath** value. For more information, see "Running Multiple Data Access Applications" later in this chapter.

▶ **To import or link a dBASE file**

1 Open a database in Microsoft Access, or switch to the Database window of the open database.

2 On the **File** menu, point to **Get External Data**, and then click **Import** or **Link Tables**.

3 In the **Files of Type** box, click **dBASE III**, **dBASE IV**, or **dBASE 5**. (The **dBASE III** option works for both dBASE III and III+ files.)

4 In the **Look in** box, switch to the appropriate folder and select the file you want, and then click **Import** or **Link**.

   If you are importing the file, Microsoft Access creates a new table named after the file you selected and imports the data from the dBASE file.

   If you are linking the file, Microsoft Access displays a dialog box in which you can associate dBASE index files.

5 For each dBASE index (NDX or MDX) file you want to link, select the file and click **Select**. When you finish associating indexes, click **Close**. If there are no indexes to associate, click **Cancel** to continue.

   Microsoft Access displays the **Select Unique Record Identifier** dialog box.

Microsoft Access 97 Terms for dBASE Users

The following table matches Microsoft Access terms with the equivalent term or command in dBASE. The Microsoft Access term is not necessarily an exact equivalent of the dBASE term, but rather a term you can look up in Microsoft Access online Help for information. You do not need to understand all of these terms before you start using Microsoft Access.

This dBASE term	Corresponds to this Microsoft Access term
APPEND command	**Data Entry** command (**Records** menu)
BROWSE command	Datasheet view
Catalog	Database
Character data type	Text data type
Database file	Table
Index	Index
LOCATE and SEEK commands	**Find** command (**Edit** menu)
MODIFY STRUCTURE command	Table Design view
Multiple-file screen	Subform
Pick list	List box, combo box
PICTURE/VALID clause	Validation rule
Program file	Module
Query, view	Query
Screen	Form
SET EXCLUSIVE mode	Exclusive/Shared access
SET FORMAT TO; EDIT	Open a form
Unique index	Primary key

Using dBASE Files in Microsoft Access

You can use data from DBF files in dBASE III, dBASE III+, dBASE IV, or dBASE 5.0 format. If you need to leave your data in dBASE DBF format so that dBASE users can continue to use it, you can link the data to your Microsoft Access database. By using Microsoft Access, you can view and edit the data in linked tables even if others are using it in dBASE. You can also create queries, forms, and reports that use the data. You can even combine data from linked tables with the data from any other tables in your Microsoft Access application.

If you have no need to maintain your dBASE data in its original format, you can import your DBF files into Microsoft Access. Unlike linking the dBASE file, importing the data creates a copy of the data in Microsoft Access. Importing a table gives you greater flexibility and control over the data, but excludes users who are not running Microsoft Access from updating the data.

Part 4 Switching from Other Applications

In this option group	Selecting this option	Results in this action in Microsoft Access
Arrow Key Behavior	**Next Field** (default)	Pressing the RIGHT ARROW or LEFT ARROW key moves the selection to the next or previous field. By default, Microsoft Access selects the entire field when you use the arrow keys. To prevent this, select another option under **Behavior Entering Field**.
	Next Character	Pressing the RIGHT ARROW or LEFT ARROW key always moves to the next or previous character, just as in dBASE.
Behavior Entering Field	**Select Entire Field** (default)	Moving from field to field with the ENTER, TAB, and arrow keys selects the entire contents of a field. To activate the insertion point and move it within a field, click the field or press F2.
	Go To Start Of Field	Moving from field to field with the ENTER, TAB, and arrow keys places the insertion point at the start of the field.
	Go To End Of Field	Moving from field to field with the ENTER, TAB, and arrow keys places the insertion point at the end of the field.
Cursor Stops at First/Last Field	Cleared (default)	Pressing the RIGHT ARROW or LEFT ARROW key moves past the first or last field.
	Selected	Pressing the RIGHT ARROW or LEFT ARROW key moves no farther than the first or last field.

Switching from dBASE

To switch from dBASE to Microsoft Access, you can either link or import data from dBASE DBF files. You can then modify the structure of the tables and create the other database objects that you need. This section discusses the similarities and differences between dBASE and Microsoft Access, including terminology and data type conversion.

Note A primary difference between Microsoft Access and MS-DOS-based applications is the use of the Microsoft Windows graphical user interface. If you are currently using an MS-DOS-based version of dBASE and are new to Windows, study your Windows documentation to learn basic techniques.

database objects in Microsoft Access is easy; you can use wizards to create basic database objects and then customize the objects to meet your needs. For more information, see "Creating New Objects" earlier in this chapter.

Programming in Microsoft Access

In many cases, tasks that require programming in most database management systems do not require programming in Microsoft Access. If you need to program in Microsoft Access (for example, to implement error handling or to create your own functions), you use Visual Basic for Applications code.

Visual Basic for Applications is similar to the Microsoft Visual Basic programming language. You write Visual Basic code in blocks called either *procedures* or *functions*. Procedures and functions contain a series of Visual Basic for Applications statements that perform an operation. You store your Visual Basic code in modules. Microsoft Access has standard modules, which contain procedures that can be called by procedures in other modules in the same database or in referenced databases. Microsoft Access also has form and report modules, which contain code that is associated with the form or report. For more information about using Visual Basic with Microsoft Access, see *Building Applications with Microsoft Access 97*.

Setting Keyboard Options

Once you have switched to Microsoft Access, you may notice that the navigation keys work differently in Microsoft Access than in some other database applications. For example, when you are viewing and editing data in a form or datasheet, the arrow keys may behave differently than they did in your former database management system.

For example, in dBASE, pressing the RIGHT ARROW or LEFT ARROW key moves the insertion point one character to the right or left within a field. However, in Microsoft Access, the contents of a field are automatically selected by default, and pressing these keys moves to the next or previous field. If you click in the field or press F2 to activate the insertion point, pressing the RIGHT ARROW or LEFT ARROW key moves the insertion point one character to the right or left within a field.

If you want the navigation keys to work as they do in the application you are used to, you can set keyboard options on the **Keyboard** tab of the **Options** dialog box (**Tools** menu). The following table describes the default keyboard options in Microsoft Access that you may want to change.

In this option group	Selecting this option	Results in this action in Microsoft Access
Move After Enter	**Don't Move**	Pressing ENTER selects the current field but does not move to another field.
	Next Field (default)	Pressing ENTER moves to the next field.
	Next Record	Pressing ENTER moves to the same field in the next record.

Table field list

Relationship line

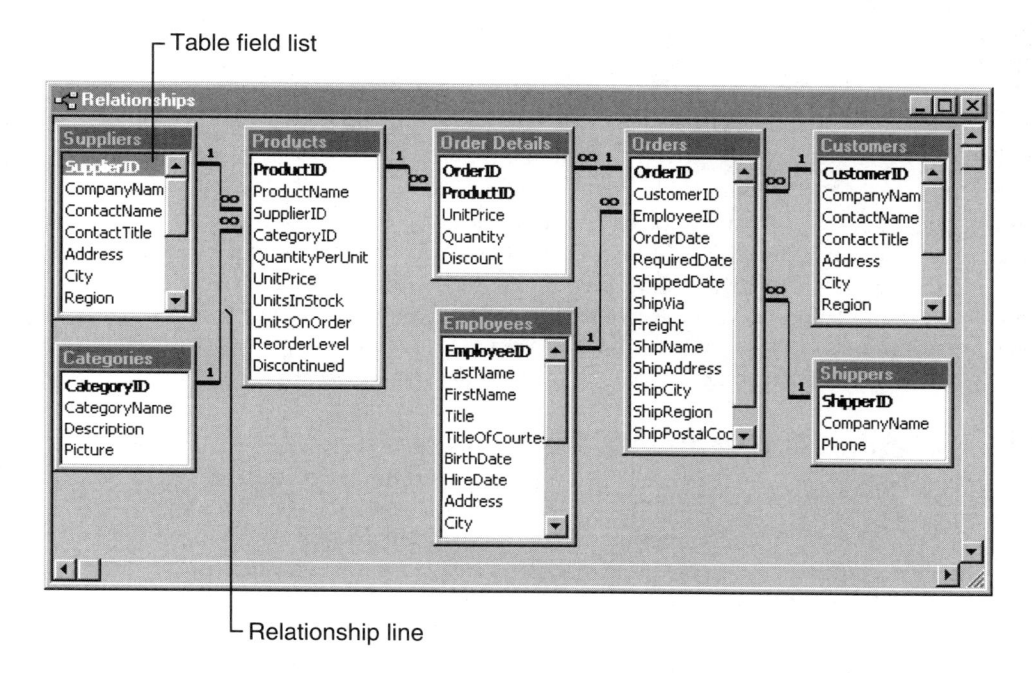

To specify the fields used to create the relationship and the degree of integrity it maintains, double-click the relationship line between the tables to open the **Relationships** dialog box. Microsoft Access saves these relationships and automatically shows them in any query that you build. To delete a relationship, click the relationship line to select it, and then press DELETE.

Defining Table-Level Validation and Referential Integrity

Many other database management systems require you to write validation code for each form and for any other place in your application where data is updated. Some database management systems may also require you to write additional code to maintain referential integrity.

In Microsoft Access, you can define validation rules when you create tables, and referential integrity when you define relationships. These rules then apply to all of your forms and queries. In many cases, table-level validation and referential integrity meet all of your application's validation requirements. If your application requires more sophisticated validation rules, you can use form-level validation and write user-defined functions or procedures in Visual Basic code.

Creating Queries, Forms, and Reports

You cannot import or convert queries, forms, and reports from your old database management system—you must create new ones in Microsoft Access. Creating

- After you import or link an external table, it is a good idea to set table properties in table Design view.

  If you import a table, it is especially important to set a primary key.

Developing Your Application

After you import or link your data, you can build the rest of your Microsoft Access application. First, you need to refine the structure of your tables by specifying a primary key for each table, creating indexes, defining relationships between your tables, entering validation rules, and establishing referential integrity. Then you can create queries, forms, and reports that you use to display and work with your data. To automate tasks and perform complex operations, write macros and Visual Basic code.

Defining Relationships in Microsoft Access

You create and edit relationships between tables in Microsoft Access by using the Relationships window. To display the Relationships window, click the **Relationships** command (**Tools** menu). When you define a relationship in Microsoft Access, you choose the fields you want to use to define the relationship between two tables by dragging a field from one table in the Relationships window to the appropriate field in the other table. Microsoft Access displays the kind of relationship it will create. If only one of the related fields is a primary key or unique index, Microsoft Access creates a one-to-many relationship; if both related fields are primary keys or unique indexes, Microsoft Access creates a one-to-one relationship.

When you define a relationship, you can specify whether to enforce referential integrity and whether to allow cascading updates and cascading deletes. Enforcing referential integrity prevents *orphan records* (a master record is deleted when related detail records still exist in other tables) in your database. For example, if you select the **Enforce Referential Integrity** check box in the **Relationships** dialog box, no one can enter an order for a customer that is not in the Customers table or delete a customer if orders exist for that customer. If you select the **Cascade Update Related Fields** or the **Cascade Delete Related Records** check box, records that have been edited or deleted in the primary table are automatically updated in related tables. You can control how these relationships are maintained through the Relationships window. The following illustration shows the Relationships window.

Access to view or edit this data, you do not want to move it to a Microsoft Access database. In this case, it makes sense to link the Sales table and use Microsoft Access as a front end to your SQL Server database. After you link the table, you can update the data from Microsoft Access and print weekly sales reports.

If your organization and applications are gradually switching to Microsoft Access, first link tables in their current data format, so you can maintain one master set of data during the transition, and then import the data after all users and all applications have switched to Microsoft Access.

Even if all users are using Microsoft Access, you may want to maintain your data in a separate database as linked tables and keep your forms, reports, and other objects in their own database. For more information, see "Splitting a Database into a Front-end/Back-end Application" in Chapter 29, "Workgroup Features in Microsoft Access."

Tips for Importing and Linking Data

When you import or link a table from another database application, keep in mind the following:

- If you import or link a table from a Paradox or an SQL database, you may need to supply a password.

    This password is different from a Microsoft Access user password; it is the password set in the other application.

- If you link a table that requires a password, Microsoft Access stores this password in your database so you can open the table later (this is optional for SQL tables).

    For this reason, you may want to add some form of security to your database to control who can open it. The simplest form of security is requiring a password to open a database, which you can set by using the **Set Database Password** command (**Tools** menu, **Security** submenu). For more information about database passwords, see "Protecting File Open with a Database Password" in Chapter 29, "Workgroup Features in Microsoft Access."

- To link an external table on a network, you must connect to the network and you must have access to the database file.

    If you want Microsoft Access to automatically connect to the appropriate file server each time you open a linked table, specify the fully qualified network path for the file. For example, if you use a Microsoft Windows NT Server network, you can enter the path to connect to a dBASE file by using the following format: *\\server\share\datadir\myfile.dbf*

    This format is called the universal naming convention (UNC) path name and is supported by many networks. When using this format, you do not need to map a drive letter to a file; this prevents problems if the drive letter is changed or the database is moved to a different computer with differently mapped drives.

In Microsoft Access, you can take advantage of the following features with tables you import, but not with tables you link:

- Longer field names

    In Microsoft Access, field names can be up to 64 characters long and can contain spaces. This gives you much more flexibility than dBASE, in which field names are limited to 10 characters. For example, after you import a table from dBASE, you can change the CUSTADDR field name to Customer Address.

- Primary keys

    You can set a primary key that uniquely identifies each record in the table. If you do not have an appropriate primary key in your table, you can add a field with the AutoNumber data type and the **NewValues** property set to **Increment** (this is the default), which automatically assigns a unique sequential number for each record you add.

- Indexes

    To speed up operations in fields that you anticipate searching or sorting often, you can create indexes. Set the **Indexed** property of the field to **Yes**.

- Relationships

    If you import related tables, you can define relationships between them that Microsoft Access uses to relate data in queries, forms, and reports. If you want, Microsoft Access can automatically enforce *referential integrity* when adding or deleting records in related tables. Referential integrity ensures that relationships between records are valid, and that you do not accidentally delete related data.

- More data types

    Microsoft Access provides data types that are not available in some applications but that may be appropriate for your data. For example, the Currency data type is ideal for storing monetary values. After you import a table, you may want to change the data type of such fields from Number to Currency. The AutoNumber data type is a good choice for creating primary keys, indexing, and creating unique relationships if the table does not already contain a unique value for each record.

Deciding Whether to Import or Link an External Table

Whether you import or link a table depends on whether you will continue to use the data with the program that originally produced it. For example, suppose you have a dBASE file that contains a list of products your company sells. You no longer use dBASE, and you would like to have this data handy on your computer. In this case, it makes sense to import the dBASE file into a Microsoft Access table. To improve the appearance and performance of the table, you can set a primary key and perhaps change field names or set other field properties.

In comparison, suppose your company keeps its sales figures in a Microsoft SQL Server database on a network. Because you may use software other than Microsoft

After you link a table from another database, the table icon Microsoft Access displays in the Database window indicates that the data in the table is outside of your database—there is a different icon for tables from each type of data source. Microsoft Access stores all the information you supply when linking the table so it can find the external data whenever you need it. When you open a linked table, Microsoft Access opens the appropriate database file or connection and displays the data. If you delete the icon in the Database window, you delete the link to the table, not the external table itself.

If you plan to use your data only in Microsoft Access, you should import the table. Microsoft Access generally works faster with its own tables, and you can customize Microsoft Access tables to meet your needs.

Whether you plan to import or link tables, start by clicking the **New Database** command (**File** menu) to create your Microsoft Access database. After you have created the new database, use the **Import** or **Link Tables** command (**File** menu, **Get External Data** submenu) to bring your existing data into the new Microsoft Access database.

The following tips can help you get the most from tables you import or link:

- Use long table names

  Microsoft Access table names are not limited to MS-DOS file-naming rules. Table names can include spaces as well as uppercase and lowercase letters. For example, after you import or link a table called SLSDAT96, you can use the **Rename** command (**Edit** menu) to rename the table Sales Data for 1996.

- Adjust column widths

  The first time you open a table in Datasheet view, all the columns have the same width. You can adjust the width of the columns with the mouse and then save the column-width settings by clicking the **Save** command (**File** menu). The next time you open the table, the column layout appears the way you left it.

- Set field properties

  By setting field properties for a table in Design view, you can make data easier to work with. For example, you can specify display formats or validation rules you want Microsoft Access to use in forms and datasheets.

- Change the table structure and set table properties

  When you import your data, you can enhance your tables by opening each one in Design view and changing the structure or properties of the table. It is a good idea to make these changes right away, before you create queries, forms, and reports based on the tables.

- Optimize your application

  For information about optimizing Microsoft Access databases, see "Optimizing Microsoft Access" in Chapter 7, "Customizing and Optimizing Microsoft Office."

- Delimited and fixed-width text files
- HTML version 1.0 lists; HTML versions 2.0 and 3.*x* lists and tables
- Lotus 1-2-3 WKS, WK1, WK3, and WK4 formats
- Microsoft Excel versions 3.0, 4.0, 5.0, 95, and 97
- Microsoft Exchange and Microsoft Outlook data (collectively referred to as Microsoft Windows Messaging Service data).Linked data in this format is read-only.

    Importing and linking Microsoft Windows Messaging Service data is currently available by using Data Access Objects (DAO) code. For more information about importing and linking Microsoft Windows Messaging Service data using DAO, see "Using External Data with Microsoft Access" in Chapter 27, "Sharing Information with Microsoft Office Applications."

World Wide Web A wizard that imports and links data from Microsoft Windows Messaging Service to Microsoft Access will soon be available on the World Wide Web. For the latest information, connect to the Microsoft Access home page at:

http://www.microsoft.com/access/

To gain access to data from external data sources, the Microsoft Jet database engine, which is used by Microsoft Access, uses one of several installable ISAM or ODBC drivers. Before you can gain access to external data, make sure that you have installed the appropriate drivers. For information about how to install drivers, see "Using Built-in Drivers and ODBC Drivers" later in this chapter.

Additionally, for each external data source that you want to connect to using ODBC, you must set up an ODBC data source by using the ODBC Data Source Administrator. To start the ODBC Data Source Administrator, double-click the 32-bit ODBC icon in Control Panel.

Importing and Linking External Tables

If you have data in separate data sources, the first step in converting to Microsoft Access is to make the data available to your Microsoft Access application. You can do this by importing or linking tables. If you want to leave the data in its current format, you can link the tables to a Microsoft Access database. This way, other users can still use the tables in the original application. Conversely, if you plan to use the data only in Microsoft Access, you can import the tables.

If you leave the data in another database or data format and create linked tables, you can use this data just as you use tables stored in a Microsoft Access database. For example, you can edit the data in linked tables, and you can create queries, forms, and reports that use the data. You can even combine data in the linked tables with the data in your Microsoft Access tables. For example, you can design a query based on both Microsoft Access tables and linked tables. Even though some of the data resides on a different computer, Microsoft Access combines the data to answer the query.

World Wide Web For the most up-to-date version of *Building Applications with Microsoft Access 97*, connect to the Building Applications with Microsoft Access 97 Web site at: http://www.microsoft.com/accessdev/buildapp/bapp.htm

Converting Your Data to Microsoft Access

When you convert to Microsoft Access from another database management system, the first step is to bring external data into Microsoft Access by either importing or linking it. Once you have imported or linked the tables that contain the data, you can specify a primary key for each of the tables, create any indexes you want, and define the relationships between the tables. Then you can proceed with creating the other database objects that make up your Microsoft Access application.

The transition to Microsoft Access cannot always be accomplished in one step. Your organization may be so large that you need to convert in phases. This chapter, therefore, describes both the complete transition of organizations to Microsoft Access, and the sharing of database resources between those who have converted to Microsoft Access and those still using another database management system.

This chapter is a starting point in the transition process and offers guidance and information specific to the transition. Many references to other sources are included that can provide further assistance. Foremost among these is the documentation that accompanies Microsoft Access.

Using External Data in Microsoft Access

When you convert to Microsoft Access, you typically want to use existing data from external data sources such as database files, spreadsheets, text files, and Hypertext Markup Language (HTML) files. To use external data in your Microsoft Access application, you can either import or link the data. To successfully import and link data in spreadsheets, text files, or HTML files, the data must be in tabular format.

Microsoft Access can import or link data from the following formats and applications:

- dBASE III, dBASE III+, dBASE IV, and dBASE version 5.0
- Microsoft FoxPro versions 2.*x* and 3.0 (import only for 3.0)
- Paradox versions 3.*x*, 4.*x*, and 5.0
- Applications that supply 32-bit Open Database Connectivity (ODBC) drivers

    For example, SQL databases such as Microsoft SQL Server, Sybase SQL Server, and Oracle Server. (The ODBC driver for Microsoft SQL is available when you install Microsoft Access.)

- Databases that use the Microsoft Jet database engine, such as those created with Visual Basic, Visual C++, or Microsoft Excel

    This includes databases created in previous versions of Microsoft Access.

Microsoft Access Documentation

The documentation provided with Microsoft Access is extensive—you can get assistance while you work from any of the following sources:

- Office Assistant

    Click the **Microsoft Access Help** command (**Help** menu) to display the Office Assistant. Type a search request, and the Assistant returns a list of the Help topics that are most likely to answer your question.

- Contents and Index

    Click the **Contents and Index** command (**Help** menu), and then search for a topic by browsing the table of contents on the **Contents** tab or by entering keywords on the **Index** tab. You can also click the **Find** tab to use a full-text search and look for specific words or phrases.

- Context-Sensitive Help

    Click a text box on a property sheet, a Visual Basic keyword in the Module window, or a keyword in the Object Browser, and then press F1 to display context-sensitive Help.

- ScreenTips

    Click the **What's This?** command (**Help** menu), and then click a menu command, toolbar button, screen region, or dialog box option to display information about that screen element. In addition, you can position your mouse pointer over a toolbar button without clicking it to display a ToolTip that tells you what the button does.

- Direct access to the World Wide Web

    Click the **Microsoft on the Web** command (**Help** menu) to connect to Microsoft Access Web sites directly from Microsoft Access. The Microsoft Access Web sites are a valuable source of information—among other things, they contain technical articles, answers to frequently asked questions, additional sample applications, troubleshooting tips, and free add-ins and tools.

- *Building Applications with Microsoft Access 97*

    Building Applications with Microsoft Access 97 is the developer's guide to creating, managing, and distributing database solutions. A printed version of the book is included with Microsoft Access 97 and Microsoft Office 97, Developer Edition.

    Tip An online version of *Building Applications with Microsoft Access 97* is available in the Office 97 Value Pack. For more information about the Office 97 Value Pack and how to use its contents, see the online Help file Valupack.hlp in the ValuPack folder on the Office CD. If you have Web access, you can also point to **Microsoft on the Web** (**Help** menu) and click **Free Stuff**.

Changing the Design of an Existing Object

To open an object in Design view, select the object name in the Database window and click **Design**. In Design view, you can make changes to the design of tables, queries, and forms. For example, you can change colors and add sound clips, command buttons, subforms, drop-down list boxes, and so on. You can change the design of reports by adding pictures, changing fonts, sizing column widths, and so on. You can also change macros or modules.

Switching Between Views of Objects

To switch between views of objects, click the arrow to the right of the **View** button on the toolbar, and then click the view you want. The following illustration shows the **View** button and the available views.

Using the Object-Specific Menus and Toolbars

The commands available on the menu bar and toolbar vary depending on the database object you are working with and the view in which it is displayed. In Microsoft Access, you can have many objects open at once. The menu bar and toolbar commands that are available correspond to the object that is currently selected. A different set of commands is available when the Database window is selected.

More About Microsoft Access

You can learn more about how to use Microsoft Access by working with the sample applications and by reading the documentation included with Microsoft Access.

Microsoft Access Sample Applications

One of the easiest ways to produce a new database object is to copy one that resembles what you want. The sample databases included with Microsoft Access—which you can find in the Samples folder in the Program Files\Microsoft Office\Office folder—provide examples of typical business databases.

As you browse through the objects in these applications, you can copy any of them by selecting the name in the Database window and clicking **Copy** (**Edit** menu). Then close the sample database, open your own application, click the appropriate tab in the Database window, and click **Paste** (**Edit** menu). If you copy a table, you can modify the field definitions, remove its data, and type or paste your own data into it. If you copy a form or report, you can change the **RecordSource** property to point to the table or query you want to use and change the field references.

- Drag Microsoft Excel worksheet cells to the Database window to create new tables.

You can also copy and paste data between applications by using the **Copy** and **Paste** commands (**Edit** menu).

Creating New Objects

To create a new database object, click the appropriate tab in the Database window (**Tables**, **Queries**, **Forms**, and so on), and then click the **New** button on the right side of the Database window. For example, to create a new query, click the **Queries** tab and then click **New**. Alternatively, you can click the **New Object** button on the **Database** toolbar and then select the type of object you want to create.

When creating new tables, queries, forms, and reports, you can use a wizard or you can create a blank object. Wizards are useful for creating anything from simple to complex objects and for learning about Microsoft Access. As you become more familiar with Microsoft Access and want to customize tables or other objects, you may want to start from scratch or use a wizard, and then make modifications in Design view.

Working with Existing Objects

To work with an existing object, click the appropriate tab in the Database window, click the object, and then choose how you want to work with that object by using the buttons on the right side of the Database window or a button on the toolbar. The following sections describe the most common actions you can perform on database objects.

Working with Data in Tables, Queries, and Forms

To work with the data in a table, query, or form, double-click the name of the object in the Database window, or select the object in the Database window and click **Open**. You can then view, enter, or modify the data. A table or query always appears as a *datasheet*, which displays data in rows and columns much like a spreadsheet. A form opens by default in Form view, but you can switch to Datasheet view if you prefer.

Previewing and Printing Reports

To preview a report, double-click the name of the report in the Database window, or select the report in the Database window and click **Preview**. After the report is displayed, you can print it by clicking the **Print** button on the toolbar. To print a report without opening it, select the report in the Database window, and then click the **Print** button on the toolbar.

Running Macros

Macros are usually linked to a button, linked to a custom menu option, or triggered by an event in a form or report; however, you can also run a macro directly from the Database window. To do this, double-click the name of the macro in the Database window, or select the macro in the Database window and click **Run**.

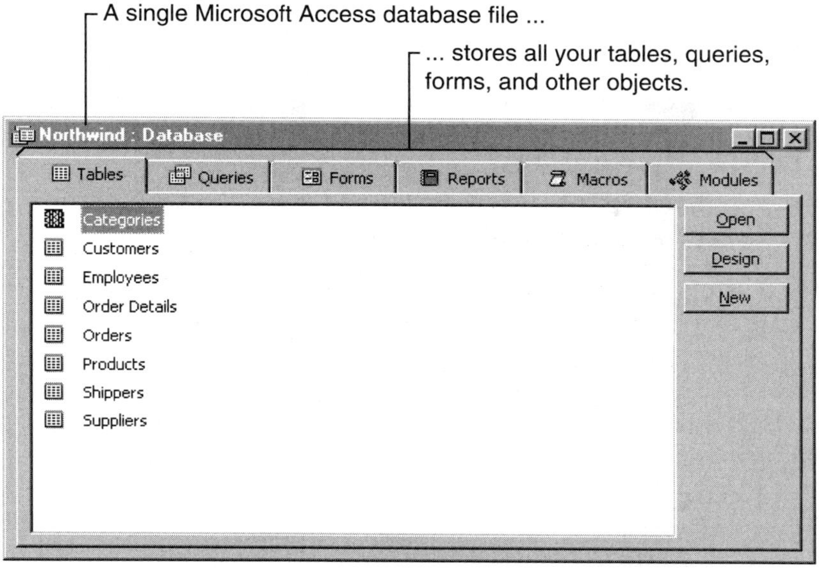
A single Microsoft Access database file ...
... stores all your tables, queries, forms, and other objects.
Northwind : Database
Tables
Queries
Forms
Reports
Macros
Modules
Categories
Customers
Employees
Order Details
Orders
Products
Shippers
Suppliers
Open
Design
New

In Microsoft Access, you can give tables and other objects longer, more descriptive names than those permitted by some other database management systems. For example, you can name a table Order Details instead of ORDERDET, or you can name a field within a table Quarterly Results instead of abbreviating it as required in dBASE and many MS-DOS-based database programs.

If you plan to use Visual Basic to work with data, however, it is easier to refer to the names of objects in the database if their names are relatively short and have no spaces in them. Longer names require more typing, and names with spaces require you to surround them with brackets—for example, `dbs.TableDefs![Quarterly Results]`. As an alternative to longer object names, you can enter a description for an object by right-clicking the object in the Database window and then clicking **Properties**.

By using the **View** menu, you can display large or small icons beside the object names in the Database window. You can also list objects by name and details. The details are the properties of the object: object description, date modified, date created, and object type. Each detail appears in a separate column that you can resize to hide or show more of the information. You can also sort objects to display them in a different order.

The Database window supports a number of drag-and-drop features. You can:

- Drag a table, query, form, report, or macro to the Windows desktop to create a shortcut for opening that object without starting Microsoft Access first.
- Drag tables and queries from the Database window to Microsoft Excel or Microsoft Word to copy that data onto a worksheet or into a document.

Modules

You use modules for advanced programming tasks, such as implementing error handling or creating your own functions. For example, you may want to create a user-defined function that calculates market projections or that masks error messages. Visual Basic for Applications code (procedures, functions, public variables, and so on) resides in modules. Use modules when the actions you want your application to perform cannot be carried out by a simple query or macro.

Which Database Object Should I Use For a Task?

Microsoft Access provides several ways to get information from a database. The type of database object you use depends on the task you want to perform. For example:

- To view all of the products that a particular vendor supplies, or that are out of stock or on order, use a query.
- To view all of the information about a particular product, customer, or supplier at once, use a form.
- To organize and print product sales for a formal presentation, use a report.
- To automate tasks, such as using a button to open a form or to carry out a menu command or series of menu commands each time a database opens, use a macro. You can also create buttons with the Command Button Wizard.
- To write specialized routines that give your application greater functionality, use a module that contains Visual Basic code.

Database Window

You use the Database window to view all of the database objects in MDB files—it is your control center for working with a database. You can use the tabs on the top of the Database window to work with a specific type of Microsoft Access object. The following illustration shows the Microsoft Access Database window.

Forms

Microsoft Access forms are generally based on data from tables or queries. By using forms, you can view, enter, change, and print data. In a Microsoft Access form, you can display data, pictures, graphs, and documents that you are tracking. Using forms to go from one table (for example, Customers) to another (for example, Orders) can be as easy as clicking a button.

You can create forms on your own, or you can have Microsoft Access do it for you by using one of the Form Wizards. The Form Wizards speed up the process of creating forms by doing all the basic work for you. When you use a Form Wizard, Microsoft Access prompts you for information and creates a form based on your answers. You can also create a new default form with one click of your mouse by using the AutoForm Wizard. After you have created a form, you can view it in Form view or Datasheet view. Form view displays all the values for one record; Datasheet view displays multiple records in a tabular format.

Reports

You can use reports to display information from tables and queries in a way that may be more meaningful and readable than just looking at a series of records in a table. Making a quick report is easy in Microsoft Access. You can create most reports by using the Report Wizard. The Report Wizard can automatically create logical groups of data (for example, orders grouped by customer number); totals (for example, the total number of orders for all customers); and subtotals (for example, the total number of orders for each customer). You can add text, data, pictures, lines, boxes, and graphs to your reports.

Macros

You can use macros to automate repetitive tasks and to extend the capabilities of a database. A macro automatically carries out a command or series of commands, called *actions*, for you. To create a macro, you can select from a list of actions. The macro carries out the actions in the order they are listed, by using the objects or data you have specified for the action arguments. This is an easy way to do point-and-click programming. You can link a macro to a button or to an event such as the closing of a form or report. You may find that you can meet all of your application's programming needs by using macros.

Tables

Tables are the basis of any database application. A table is a collection of related data, or *records*. Each table column represents a *field*, and each row represents a *record*. Microsoft Access tables are not stored in separate files but are all included in the Microsoft Access MDB file. You need at least one table in a database. You define relationships between tables in the Relationships window—there is no need for separate index files, such as the NDX files in dBASE.

Queries

A *query* is a question about the data stored in tables. You use queries to select or to perform an action on a subset of data. For example, you could design a query that returns only customers from New York. A query can bring together data from multiple tables—it returns a set of records that is actually a view into the underlying tables. These sets of records can be updatable or read-only. If updatable, the resulting data can be added to, changed, or deleted as with any other table.

For example, you can run a query with a linked table from dBASE, several Microsoft Access tables, and a linked table from Paradox, and then update the results. Microsoft Access makes your changes in all the underlying tables in the query. For information about linked tables, see "Importing and Linking External Tables" later in this chapter.

You can incorporate queries in your application as a substitute for programming. For example, you can use queries to perform any of the following data update tasks:

- Update a field in a specified subset of records to a new value.

    You can specify the value when you design the query, provide the value by using a field on a form, or use a field value from a table or query. This kind of query is called an *update query*.

- Delete a specified subset of records.

    You can determine the scope of records to be deleted by specifying criteria when you design the query, by providing the value of a field on a form, or by using a field value from a table or query. This kind of query is called a *delete query*.

- Add records to a table.

    This kind of query is called an *append query*.

- Create a new table based on another table or a set of related tables.

    This kind of query is called a *make-table query*.

Using Database Features in Microsoft Access 97

Most users in your organization are probably already experienced with database management systems. They understand the basic concepts, the steps used to create tables, and how to create databases for different purposes. For users who are converting their files to Microsoft Access, this section introduces Microsoft Access and some of its basic features—such as single-file architecture, database objects, and documentation.

Single File Architecture

Most database management systems, including dBASE and Paradox, store individual database components, such as database files (tables), reports, and forms, in separate MS-DOS-based files. A complete application may consist of hundreds of individual files.

A Microsoft Access database, by contrast, is a collection of objects (tables, queries, forms, reports, macros, and modules) stored in a single file with the .mdb file name extension. When you open a Microsoft Access database, you also open all the tools that help you use information stored in the database.

Note Although a Microsoft Access database can contain all your objects, you can also work with objects that are stored in separate databases. For example, you can store tables in one database and forms and reports in another database. For more information, see "Splitting a Database into a Front-end/Back-end Application" in Chapter 29, "Workgroup Features in Microsoft Access."

Like other common database management systems, such as dBASE and Paradox, Microsoft Access is a *relational database management system*. To efficiently and accurately provide you with information, a relational database needs facts about different subjects stored in separate tables.

For example, you may have one table that stores only facts about employees, and another that stores only facts about orders. When you define relationships between these tables, Microsoft Access uses the relationships to find associated information stored in your database. Using this example, you might define a relationship between the Employees and Orders tables, so that you can associate an employee with each order. For more information about relationships, see "Defining Relationships in Microsoft Access" later in this chapter.

Database Objects

A Microsoft Access database is made up of different types of objects: tables, queries, forms, reports, macros, and modules.

CHAPTER 17

Switching to Microsoft Access

This chapter tells you what to expect when you or your workgroup switches to Microsoft Access 97 from another database management system.

In This Chapter
Using Database Features in Microsoft Access 97   452
Converting Your Data to Microsoft Access   460
Switching from dBASE   468
Switching from FoxPro   476
Switching from Paradox   480
Running Multiple Data Access Applications   487
Using Built-in Drivers and ODBC Drivers   488

See Also
- For a summary of new and improved features in Microsoft Access 97, see Chapter 2, "What's New in Microsoft Office 97."
- For information about installing Microsoft Access or other Office applications, see Chapter 4, "Installing Microsoft Office."
- For information about upgrading to Microsoft Access 97 from a previous version of Microsoft Access, see Chapter 11, "Upgrading from Previous Versions of Microsoft Access."

Note   Microsoft Access runs on Windows 95 and Windows NT Workstation version 3.51 or later only.

You may also want to investigate other applications that could provide complementary capabilities. For example, Microsoft Office Compatible products have been developed by Microsoft and other software companies to work with (and work like) the programs in Office.

World Wide Web   For more information about Microsoft Office Compatible products, connect to the Office Compatible home page at:

http://www.microsoft.com/office/ofccomp/

- Providing access to experts.

    If you have in-house experts, or people you think can become experts, designate them as a resource available to others. Sometimes people appreciate the recognition and overlook the fact that they now have more work to do! Other options are to hire an expert (sometimes a college intern works out well) or to subscribe to one of Microsoft's telephone support services.

- Establish and communicate an end date.

    Set a finite amount of time for users to get through the transition period. Limit training to a reasonable period of time.

For More Information   about Microsoft support services, see Appendix E, "Other Support Resources."

Take Advantage of the New Office Features

After completing the previous five steps, your organization should be well on its way to greater productivity and efficiency. To fully realize your investment, however, you should tap into the new power available with Office. Here are some ideas to consider:

- Make sure you are using the right tool for each task.

    For example, many people know only word processing. Heavy statistical typing may be better accomplished in Microsoft Excel.

- Encourage employees to generate new ideas about how to use the new applications to work even more effectively.

    If you have an e-mail system or public folders, communicate best practices as they emerge within your organization.

- Develop some custom applications.

    Turn some paper-based forms into Word templates or Outlook forms. Develop some Microsoft Excel macros to automate tasks.

For More Information   about new features in Office 97, see Chapter 2, "What's New in Microsoft Office 97."

If you do not know enough yet to be able to dream up new ways that Office can help your organization, consultants can be very useful in giving you some new ideas. Low-cost sources of new ideas include local user group meetings, as well as Microsoft electronic forums on CompuServe; MSN, The Microsoft Network; or the World Wide Web.

World Wide Web   For more information about using Microsoft Office more effectively, connect to the Office home page at:

http://www.microsoft.com/office/

Running Applications Over the Network

If there is a LAN already in place in your organization, you may want to consider running the Office applications from the network instead of running them on individual computers. The following table lists the advantages and disadvantages of running applications from of a network.

Advantages	Disadvantages
Uses less hard disk space. Although some network applications require certain files to be located on individual computers, much less disk space is required on the hard disk.	May be less reliable. If the network is offline, applications are unavailable.
Saves time. Less time is needed to install or update the software in the future.	Can slow performance. Running off a network is slower than running locally. If the network is slow, applications are even slower.

You can also choose a mixed environment: Furnish individual copies of Office applications to those who use them most, and provide access over the network to more casual users.

Using the Network to Install Software

Even if you decide to run your applications locally, you can use the network to install the software on individual computers. There are several significant benefits of using the network to install software:

- A network installation may be faster, since several users can install applications at the same time.

- A network installation is easier to maintain. If there are any upgrades to the software, you can place a copy of the new software in the shared folder, and all users can be certain they are installing the most current version.

For More Information about network installation options, see Chapter 4, "Installing Microsoft Office."

Getting Back to Business as Usual

Once software is installed, files are converted, and people are trained, the next major goal is to get past the transition phase and return to business as usual. Some tips for quickly restoring order include:

- Encouraging people to use their Office applications to do their daily work.

    Practice makes perfect, and it is always easier to learn by doing.

- Encouraging people to help and support each other.

    Working together and sharing experiences are great way for employees to raise their comfort level.

Distribute Office Throughout Your Organization

At this point in the move, you should have a good understanding of your organization's environment and have made plans for dealing with important files and applications. Some files are already converted as a result of the test. Your people are trained and ready. It is now time to get the entire business running on the new Office software.

Evaluating Your Purchasing Options

If you have not already purchased the software for your organization, you should examine the options available to you through Microsoft's various licensing programs.

Scheduling Installations

It is useful to centralize the installation process by assigning someone to be responsible for performing all of the individual installations in your organization. This technique ensures that everyone receives the new software as planned. Some tips for this approach are:

- Schedule a specific day and time for each installation

   This eliminates surprises and ensures access to the desk and computer at a specified time.

- Avoid surprising people

   People returning from vacation or illness may not react favorably to an unexpected installation of new software.

- Be flexible within reason

   Reschedule as necessary to accommodate busy users, but do not let anyone put off upgrading for too long.

Installing the Applications

During Office Setup, you can choose a Typical installation of the most commonly used Office features and components, or a Custom installation that lets you select exactly which features and components you need. You should perform a test installation so you can evaluate these options rather than experimenting at someone's desk. You may also want to record the installation options you select so you can refer to them during subsequent installations.

Using a Local Area Network

If your organization has a local area network (LAN), you have some additional installation options.

Convert Existing Files to Office Formats

The last step before you move your organization to Office is to prepare your files for the move. Convert the files that you use on a regular basis to the new software format. Use the following sequence as a guide:

1. Determine which files you will need immediately after the move to Office.
2. Back up these files. This prevents permanent losses if you accidentally save over or change files during the conversion process.
3. Convert the files to Office application formats. Office applications include built-in file converters for most popular software.
4. Check the converted files to make sure they contain the information you expected.

During the conversion process, pay special attention to important business applications. Make sure that critical business files, such as a payroll spreadsheet or sales proposal template, are available and working in the new environment. Test the old applications you plan to keep using, and convert or develop alternatives for the rest.

Test the conversion of files that get updated daily. These are files that cannot be out of service for any length of time (a daily telephone log, a daily sales order worksheet, and so forth). Because these files may be updated while you are in the process of converting them, test the conversion process ahead of time and identify any problems that occur. Then convert the most recent version of the file when you are ready.

If you have large libraries of files to convert to Microsoft Excel or Word format, you can use the batch conversion tools included in both programs. If you are converting files for Microsoft Excel format, use the File Conversion Wizard. If you are converting documents to Word format, use the Conversion Wizard.

For More Information   about converting to Microsoft Excel format, see Chapter 18, "Switching to Microsoft Excel." For more information about converting to Word format, see Chapter 21, "Switching to Microsoft Word."

Most remaining files can and should be converted by the file owners themselves. Usually this requires little more than opening them in the new Office application and then saving them in the new format.

Finally, record the conversion process. Think about how to best use what you have learned and pass it on to others. You may want to write up some tip sheets or hold an informal breakfast or lunch meeting after people are up and running to discuss your findings.

If you are constrained by a budget and cannot afford classroom training for everyone, you have other options. You can:

- Educate users about the general differences between their old applications and the new Office 97 applications.
- Give your most communicative people formal training and have them teach everyone else.
- Strongly encourage people to use the online Help included in each Office application.
- Purchase videos or other ready-made training programs and make them available for people to use.

Successful Training

Whether you hire a professional to train your employees, train them with your own resources, or let them learn on their own, you should consider the following:

- Provide training that meets the specific needs of your people.

    Most professional trainers are willing to customize a course for your needs. For example, if your customer service or marketing people send out a lot of mailings using mail merge (form letters), ask the trainer to include a mail merge topic in the Word class.

- Provide uninterrupted training and learning time.

    This is especially important if you are asking people to learn on their own. It is difficult to absorb new material when constantly interrupted with day-to-day responsibilities. If your organization cannot afford to lose people to training during working hours, schedule training before work, after work, or even on weekends. You can also make equipment available off-hours for people to learn on their own.

- Encourage people to use the new Office software.

    The best way to learn how to use a new application is to have real work to do. For example, using Word to type an actual letter to an important client can be a great learning experience.

- Encourage on-going training and learning.

    Offer a monthly refresher course or casual meeting where users can share quick tips and experiences.

When looking for training help, you should consider using one of Microsoft's many nationwide training centers. These Authorized Technical Education Centers (ATECs) are certified by Microsoft to train users on Office applications and Windows. For more information, see Appendix E, "Other Support Resources."

Test the New Applications

For a better idea of what to expect, test the Office applications before you install them. In small companies, a test can be as informal as having someone work with the new software first. In larger companies, you may want to choose a group of users and perform a more structured test. A useful test includes converting important files and applications, training users, and, most importantly, evaluating the process so you can adjust your plan for the final installation of Office.

Conducting a test is a great way to put your implementation plan into practice. It is important to choose a test situation that allows you to build on success and gives you a tangible demonstration of the benefits of Office. Some groups or individuals are better initial testers than others. Use these tips when selecting the test group:

- Select willing participants.
- Keep the scope of the test small and manageable; three people is a good number for a test group. If your organization is very small, one or two users is sufficient.
- Do not attempt the hardest scenario first. Pick a situation of average complexity for solid proof that the plan works for your organization.

Once you have completed your test, be sure to solicit feedback from the test group to determine what went well and what could be improved. This information helps you modify your plan to be better prepared when you proceed with the companywide Office installation.

Train New Users

The next step is to train people to use the Office applications. Fortunately, users of the most common competitive word processing and spreadsheet software can use much of their existing knowledge in Office.

Although the choices and options that each Office application provides may seem overwhelming at first, most things you learn for one Office application are applicable to any other Office application. Shortcut keys, navigational key sequences, buttons you click and other mouse actions, as well as application menus and toolbars are all consistent between the Office applications. Therefore, the time you spend learning one Office application can be leveraged while learning the next one.

Training Classes

Formal training classes can be a very effective way to get people up and running quickly on the new software. You can send your employees to classes held at a professional training center or find someone to come to your office or even right to your desk.

For More Information about setting up a formal training program for Office 97, see Chapter 8, "Training and Support Programs for Microsoft Office."

- Budget

    If your budget is limited, you may want to look for lower-priced training options, such as purchasing the *Step by Step* series of training materials from Microsoft Press. For more information, see Appendix E, "Other Support Resources."

- Peak busy periods

    Holiday sales, tax-filing deadlines, or audits can keep your organization busy enough.

- Other project deadlines

    Do not expect people to cooperate with a move to new software if they are already working unusually long hours on another special project.

- Available resources

    If you have very few people within your organization who can help you with the moving process, you can go to an outside source. For example, find external consultants and trainers to help you, or try spending a little extra on training so that people can better help themselves.

World Wide Web   The Microsoft Solution Provider program can help you locate qualified Microsoft product experts in your area. For more information, connect to the Solution Provider home page at:

http://www.microsoft.com/msp/

For best results, be sensitive to these constraints and work around them. Schedule the switch to Office after major holidays, a new business pitch, or the annual trade show. Avoid overburdening people whose schedules are already overflowing with other important commitments.

Developing a Plan for Your Move

Once you thoroughly understand your current situation, you can plan for the move. Whether you have 3 people or 300, a plan helps ensure that the process runs as smoothly as possible. A plan helps you accomplish what needs to be done, identify how it is going to get done, determine how long it will take, and make sure that you do not overlook any details.

Your plan should:

- Identify specific tasks to be completed.
- Assign responsibility and an expected start date and end date for each task.
- Set realistic dates and assign a manageable number of tasks to each person.
- Adjust over time as needed.

Department	Typical critical applications
Accounting	A/P; A/R; payroll; tax preparation, reporting, and compliance
Sales	Order entry, order confirmation, customer service, proposal creation, inventory
Legal	Contract preparation
Human Resources	Resume tracking

Even if you determine that these files and systems are not affected, the examination process may provide an excellent opportunity to rethink your existing processes in order to take advantage of the enhanced capabilities of Office.

Users' Needs and Abilities

What are the computer abilities and expectations of the people affected by the move to Office? How do people work together and share information on a day-to-day basis?

In planning your move to Office, you should:

- Count the number of people moving to Office.
- Map out groups of people who work together and share files.
- Identify people with good computer skills who can be enlisted to help.
- Identify people who may need special assistance.

It is very important to understand the computing abilities and needs of the people in your organization. First, it helps you determine how big an effort the move represents. Second, you can take advantage of existing knowledge in your organization by identifying people who already know about Office applications from previous experience—and use these people to train and assist others in your organization. Third, you can begin to develop a plan to help beginners who may lack computer experience or who are afraid of change.

It is also useful to identify how people in your organization work together and share files and information. Think about how to keep them working together during the move to Office, although switching to Office ultimately reduces incompatibility problems and allows users to help each other through the transition. Moving small, manageable groups, instead of all employees at once, also helps you use your resources more effectively.

Work Environment

What special circumstances exist within your organization that could affect your move to Office?

Every organization has a unique set of constraints. It is important to identify these in the beginning stages of the move, so that you can plan around them as necessary. Some examples of these constraints include:

Switching Your Organization to Office

This section focuses on the specifics of each step in your migration to Office 97, and identifies issues to consider as you go along.

Plan Your Migration to Office

You probably know from experience that transitions are easier when you have a plan. That is why it is important to assess your situation and determine a plan of action before you make your move.

Assessing Your Current Configuration

The first step in building a solid migration plan is to assess your current environment so you can better plan the actual implementation.

Hardware

Is your current operating system suitable for the new Office applications?

Inventory your existing equipment so you can develop a purchasing plan if necessary. The inventory should address the following questions:

- What kinds of computers are currently installed?
- How much memory is available on each computer?
- How much disk space is available on each computer?
- Is there a network in place?

For More Information about hardware requirements, see Chapter 5, "System Requirements for Microsoft Office."

Existing Applications and Systems

What important files and programs currently exist in your organization and how will the move to Office affect them?

Many of your existing computer files and programs are important to the day-to-day operations of your organization. A payroll spreadsheet, an online order form, the sales proposal creation process, or time and billing tracking are examples of critical business applications. It is important to identify the impact that the new software will have on these tasks so that the transition to Office is a smooth one.

To identify the files, systems, and tasks important to your organization, think about the various activities and functions that keep your organization running. Make sure that you consider all areas of the company. The following table lists some typical examples.

Note Some of the information in this chapter is similar to that in Chapter 3, "Deployment Guide for Microsoft Office." Chapter 3 is a comprehensive description of migration issues for a large organization. This chapter is written for a smaller organization with a less formal deployment process. Look at both chapters, and then decide which information best suits your organization.

The process of moving your organization from other applications to the Microsoft Office suite of desktop applications begins with the planning phase and ends with a successful implementation of Office. Each step in this process is described in the following table.

Task	Description
Plan your migration to Office	Before installing Office, assess your existing hardware and software configurations, as well as the needs and skills of your users; then develop a step-by-step plan for the move.
Test the new applications	Have a representative group of users try out the new Office applications and provide feedback.
Train new users	Educate users about Office 97 before they need to begin using the new applications.
Convert existing files to Office formats	Determine which files you need to convert; then back up your originals and convert files to Office application formats.
Distribute Office throughout your organization	Determine the best way to obtain Office 97 for all your users, and then install Office.
Take advantage of new Office features	Look for additional ways to use Office to improve efficiency, productivity, and your competitive edge; solicit new ideas from users.

CHAPTER 16

Switching to Microsoft Office

This chapter tells you what to expect when you or your workgroup switches from competitive applications to Microsoft Office 97.

In This Chapter
Overview   439
Switching Your Organization to Office   441

See Also
- For a summary of new and improved features in Office 97, see Chapter 2, "What's New in Microsoft Office 97."
- For information about migration issues in a large organization, see Chapter 3, "Deployment Guide for Microsoft Office."
- For information about installing Office applications, see Chapter 4, "Installing Microsoft Office."
- For information about setting up a formal training program for Office 97, see Chapter 8, "Training and Support Programs for Microsoft Office."
- For information about upgrading to Office 97 from previous versions of Office, see Chapter 10, "Upgrading from Previous Versions of Microsoft Office."

The remaining chapters in Part 4, "Switching from Other Applications," provide detailed information about switching to the individual Office applications.

Overview

This chapter describes how to migrate from other applications, such as WordPerfect and Lotus 1-2-3, to Microsoft Office. As an administrator, you probably want to take full advantage of your investment in Office with minimal disruption to your organization. This chapter helps to prepare your organization for Office, and helps you install the new software with as little disruption as possible.

PART 4

Switching from Other Applications

Contents

Chapter 16   Switching to Microsoft Office   439
Chapter 17   Switching to Microsoft Access   451
Chapter 18   Switching to Microsoft Excel   491
Chapter 19   Switching to Microsoft Outlook   545
Chapter 20   Switching to Microsoft PowerPoint   561
Chapter 21   Switching to Microsoft Word   573

When this Word 97 feature	Is saved in Word 5.x for the Macintosh format
Styles	Style definitions numbered greater than 355 are lost, along with any references to them; however, all formatting is preserved.
Subdocuments (INCLUDE field)	If the **RetainInclude** flag is set to **Yes** in the registry, then the INCLUDE field is converted; however, any path information in the field is lost. Otherwise the latest result is inserted in the Word 5.*x* document and the INCLUDE field is lost.
Word 97 macros, and toolbar, menu, and keyboard customizations	Macros and customized elements are lost.
Versions (**File** menu)	Version settings are lost. If you display an older version of a document and then save it in an older format, however, Word 97 suggests a different file name. This makes it difficult to overwrite the Word 97 document and lose data in later versions.

When this Word 97 feature	Is saved in Word 5.x for the Macintosh format
Bullets and numbering	Automatic bullets and numbers are converted to plain text.
Cell borders and shading	Cell borders and shading are converted to the closest Word 5.*x* value.
Character styles	Character style definitions are lost. All formatting is retained.
Comments	Comments are retained in Word 5.1; otherwise, annotations are converted to footnotes.
Cross-references	The latest result appears in the Word 5.*x* document, but the field is lost.
Endnotes	All footnotes and endnotes are retained, but they are merged into one continuous stream.
Extended characters	Some ANSI extended characters have no Macintosh character set equivalent, and vice versa. If the equivalent character is not available, it is replaced by the underscore (_) character. Equivalent characters available in fonts such as Symbol or Wingdings® can be used to replace lost characters following conversion. Characters available in the unique symbol sets of Microsoft TrueType fonts are retained, provided that the same font is available on both Windows and Macintosh operating systems.
Fields (FILENAME)	The latest result appears in the Word 5.*x* document, but the field is lost.
Fields (form and bar code fields)	Results of text form fields are retained. Fields with no results that can be displayed are lost.
Language	Language formatting is lost.
Master Documents	Master documents lose the contents of the subdocuments and the references, but all the subdocuments are converted at the same time as the master document into separate documents.
Object linking and embedding	OLE objects may be edited after conversion, providing their server application is available.
Page numbering	Page numbering is converted to the closest alternative.
Revision marks	Character formatting indicating revised text is retained.

Formatting Features

The following table describes new Word 97 features that may affect your data or formatting in Word 5.x for the Macintosh format.

When this Word 97 feature	Is saved in Word 5.x for the Macintosh format
Character formatting	
Expand/condense	This value is rounded to the closest value that Word 5.x supports.
Outline	Outline text is converted to normal text.
Shadow	Shadow text is converted to normal text.
Superscript/subscript	Superscript/subscript characters are emulated using raised/lowered character formatting.
Paragraph formatting	
Borders and shading	Borders and shading are converted to the closest Word 5.x value.
Column formatting	
Columns	The line between columns is not converted.
Variable-width columns	Variable-width columns are converted to equal-width columns.
Page formatting	
Page orientation	Page orientation is lost.
Page size	Page size is lost.
Paper source	Paper source is lost.
Section formatting	
Line numbering (Start At #)	Line numbering is lost.
Vertical alignment (top, centered, justified)	Vertical alignment is lost.

Graphics Features

The following table describes new features in Word 97 that may affect your data or formatting in previous versions.

When this Word 97 feature	Is saved in Word 5.x for the Macintosh format
Graphics	Graphics are converted to PICT format.
Office Art objects	Office Art objects are lost.

Other Features

The following table describes new Word 97 features that may affect your data or formatting in Word 5.x for the Macintosh format.

Can I share Word 97 documents with users of previous versions of Word? If your workgroup uses a combination of Word 97 and Word 5.x for the Macintosh, users can exchange documents and templates between versions. However, not all Word 97 features are supported in previous versions. For more information, see "Sharing Documents with Word 5.x for the Macintosh" later in this chapter.

Tip To convert several documents at once to Word 97 format, or to customize document conversion, you can use the Conversion Wizard, which is supplied with Word. For more information about this wizard, see "Converting File Formats in Word 97" in Chapter 21, "Switching to Microsoft Word."

Opening Word 5.x for the Macintosh Documents in Word 97

When you upgrade to Word 97, you can still open your old Word 5.x for the Macintosh documents. If the Word 5.x for the Macintosh text converter is installed properly, Word 97 automatically converts Word 5.x for the Macintosh documents to Word 97 file format.

What if Word 5.x for the Macintosh isn't listed?

If you attempt to open a Word 5.x for the Macintosh document, but Word cannot open it properly, Word may prompt you to select the file format from which to convert the document. If **Microsoft Word 4.0–5.1 for the Macintosh** does not appear in the **Convert File** dialog box, you need to install the converter. To install the Word 5.x for the Macintosh converter, rerun Setup and click **Add/Remove**; under the **Converters and Filters** option, select the **Text Converters** check box.

Sharing Documents with Word 5.x for the Macintosh

If your workgroup is upgrading gradually to Word 97, some users may have to share documents with users of Word 5.x for the Macintosh. Word 97 users can save their documents in Word 5.0 for the Macintosh or Word 5.1 for the Macintosh format.

Since not all Word 97 features are supported in Word 5.x for the Macintosh, saving in 5.x format may result in loss of data or formatting. The following sections describe the Word 97 features that are not fully supported in Word 5.x for the Macintosh.

When this Word 97 feature	Is saved in Word 5.x or 6.0 for MS-DOS format
Versions (**File** menu)	Version settings are lost. If you display an older version of a document and then save it in an older format, however, Word 97 suggests a different file name. This makes it difficult to overwrite the Word 97 document and lose data in later versions.

Using Word 97 Styles in Word 5.x or 6.0 for MS-DOS

To convert user-defined style formatting in a Word 97 document into a Word for MS-DOS style sheet, save the file in Word for MS-DOS format. When you save the document in Word for MS-DOS, you are asked if you want to attach a style sheet to the document. You can do one of the following:

- Create a new Word for MS-DOS style sheet to contain the styles from the Word 97 document template.

- Ignore all styles.

    The style formatting in the original Word 97 document is converted to direct formatting in the Word for MS-DOS document.

- Attach an existing Word for MS-DOS style sheet.

    Text formatted with a standard style in Word 97 converts to a Word for MS-DOS style with the same name. If there is no corresponding Word for MS-DOS style name, standard styles are converted to character formatting. Or, if the Word 97 style does not exist in the Word for MS-DOS document, the converter adds the style to the Word for MS-DOS document.

If your Word 97 document contains no user-defined styles, no style prompt appears when you save in Word for MS-DOS format.

Upgrading from Word 5.x for the Macintosh

This section describes the changes between Word version 5.x for the Macintosh and Word 97. Word 97 is a major upgrade from previous versions of the application. For more information about the features and benefits of this upgrade, see Chapter 2, "What's New in Microsoft Office 97."

What happens to my old Word documents when I convert them to Word 97? You can open files created in Word 5.x for the Macintosh directly in Word 97. All data and formatting created in Word 5.x for the Macintosh are fully supported by Word 97.

Graphics Features

The following table describes new features in Word 97 that may affect your data or formatting in previous versions.

When this Word 97 feature	Is saved in Word 5.x or 6.0 for MS-DOS format
Graphics (scaling, cropping)	Links to graphics are preserved if the graphic format is supported in Word for MS-DOS.
Office Art objects	Office Art objects are lost.

Table Features

The following table describes new Word 97 features that may affect your data or formatting in Word 5.x or 6.0 for MS-DOS format.

When this Word 97 feature	Is saved in Word 5.x or 6.0 for MS-DOS format
Tables	Tables are converted to side-by-side paragraphs in Word 5.5 and earlier for MS-DOS. Multiple conversions of the document may result in changes to the left and right indents.

Other Features

The following table describes new Word 97 features that may affect your data or formatting in Word 5.x or 6.0 for MS-DOS format.

When this Word 97 feature	Is saved in Word 5.x or 6.0 for MS-DOS format
Bookmarks	Bookmark names longer than 20 characters are lost.
Fields (DATE, TIME, FILENAME)	Word 97 supports more date and time formats than Word for MS-DOS. The DATE field is converted to (dateprint); the TIME field is converted to (timeprint); The FILENAME field retains the last value of the field.
Footnotes (separators, continuation notices)	Footnote separators are retained but cannot be modified. Continuation notices are lost.
Superscript/Subscript	Superscript and subscript are automatically offset by 6 points above or below the character baseline.
Word 97 macros, and toolbar, menu, and keyboard customizations	Macros and customized elements are lost.

For more information about selecting a default format in which to save documents, see "Specifying the Default Format in Which to Save Office Documents" in Chapter 22, "Supporting Multiple Versions of Microsoft Office."

Tip In Windows 95 and Windows NT Workstation 4.0, you can use a system policy to define the default value for the **Save Word files as** option on the **Save** tab in the **Options** dialog box (**Tools** menu) for all Word users in your workgroup. In the System Policy Editor, set the following policy:

User\Word 97\Tools_Options\Save\Default Save

For more information, see "Using Windows System Policies to Customize Office" in Chapter 7, "Customizing and Optimizing Microsoft Office."

Since not all Word 97 features are supported in Word for MS-DOS, saving in Word 5.*x* or 6.0 for MS-DOS format may result in loss of data or formatting. The following sections describe the Word 97 features that are not fully supported in Word 5.*x* or 6.0 for MS-DOS.

Formatting Features

The following table describes new Word 97 features that may affect your data or formatting in Word 5.*x* or 6.0 for MS-DOS format.

When this Word 97 feature	Is saved in Word 5.x or 6.0 for MS-DOS format
Document properties	New document properties, such as SUBJECT, are lost in Word for MS-DOS.
Footnote position	Footnotes beneath text are converted to end-of-page footnotes. Endnotes become footnotes.
Line between columns	The line between the columns is lost.
Line numbering (Start At #)	Line numbers always start at 1.
Page break before	This formatting is converted to manual page breaks.
Page numbers	Page numbers are put in a header or footer.
Page orientation	Word for MS-DOS supports portrait and landscape orientation in the same document only for printers that support auto-rotation.
Spacing (condensed, expanded)	Condensed and expanded characters are converted to normal characters.
Underline (word)	Word underlining and dotted underlining are converted to single underlining.
Uneven columns	Uneven columns are converted to even columns.

Chapter 15 Upgrading from Previous Versions of Microsoft Word

Sharing Documents with Word 5.x or 6.0 for MS-DOS

If your workgroup is upgrading gradually to Word 97, some users may have to share documents with users of Word 5.x or 6.0 for MS-DOS. Strategies for sharing Word 97 documents with Word for MS-DOS users are described in the following sections.

Tools and Utilities   The Office Resource Kit Tools and Utilities include the Word 5.x and 6.0 for MS-DOS text converter and other tools for Word for MS-DOS upgraders. You must install this text converter to work with documents in Word 5.x or 6.0 for MS-DOS format. For information about installing the text converter, see "Word Converters" in Appendix A, "Microsoft Office 97 Resource Kit Tools and Utilities."

Saving Word 97 Documents in Word 5.x or 6.0 for MS-DOS Format

Users of Word 97 can save documents in Word 5.x or 6.0 for MS-DOS format.

▶ **To save a document in Word 5.x or 6.0 for MS-DOS format (Windows only)**

1   On the **File** menu, click **Save As**.

2   In the **Save as type** box, click either **Word 3.x - 5.x for MS-DOS** or **Word 6.0 for MS-DOS**.

What if Word for MS-DOS isn't listed?

If you attempt to save a Word for MS-DOS document, but **Word 3.x-5.x for MS-DOS** or **Word 6.0 for MS-DOS** does not appear in the **Save as type** box, you need to install the Word for MS-DOS text converter from the Office Resource Kit Tools and Utilities. For information about installing this converter, see "Word Converters" in Appendix A, "Microsoft Office 97 Resource Kit Tools and Utilities."

Tip   End users can specify the default format in which Word saves new documents.

▶ **To specify the default format in which to save documents**

1   On the **Tools** menu, click **Options**, and then click the **Save** tab.

2   In the **Save Word files as** box, click the file format you want.

The next time you save a document that is not already saved in Word 97 format, you are prompted to save it in this format.

Using Word for MS-DOS Styles in Word 97

In Word for MS-DOS, styles are stored in a style sheet file attached to the Word file. When you convert a document from Word for MS-DOS to Word 97 format, the Word for MS-DOS text converter looks for the style sheet file and stores the paragraph and character styles from the original document in the Word 97 document. The Word for MS-DOS Style ID becomes the Word 97 style name.

If the style sheet file is not found, the converter prompts you for the location. If you click **Cancel**, Word 97 converts all the Word for MS-DOS styles to direct formatting.

You can add the styles in the converted document to a Word 97 template and use the template to create other Word 97 documents. If a style with the same name already exists in the active Word 97 template, the Word for MS-DOS style overrides it.

Converting Graphics to Word 97

Word 97 and Word for MS-DOS both support TIFF, EPS, and PCX graphic file formats. Links to any of these graphics contained in a Word for MS-DOS document are automatically converted to Word 97 INCLUDEPICTURE fields. For information about graphics filters included with Word, see Chapter 21, "Switching to Microsoft Word."

Word for MS-DOS includes graphics by specifying a tag that consists of the path and file name of the graphics file to be included in the document. For example, a tag like this:

```
.G.C:\WINWORD\FILENAME.PCX;6";1.158";PCX
```

is converted to the following Word 97 graphics fields:

```
{includepicture C:\\WINWORD\\FILENAME.PCX \* mergeformat}
```

For a graphic to appear in a converted document, the appropriate graphics filter must be installed in Word 97, and the original graphic file must remain in the path specified in the converted document's INCLUDEPICTURE field.

Note Word 97 may not recognize graphics created using the Word for MS-DOS Capture.com utility. These files have a .scr file name extension by default. (Capture.com also creates ASCII text files which have a .lst extension by default.) Linked graphics in PageView file format become bitmaps. These files have a file name extension such as .po1, .po2, .po3, and so on.

Chapter 15   Upgrading from Previous Versions of Microsoft Word

This Word 5.x or 6.0 for MS-DOS term	Corresponds to this Word 97 feature
Character formatting	**Font** command (**Format** menu).
Command fields (5.0)	Dialog boxes with controls and options, which are similar to MS-DOS command fields.
Division (5.0)	Section.
Gallery (5.0)	Styles, which are applied with the **Style** command (**Format** menu).
Outline edit and outline organize modes (5.0, 5.5)	Outline view (**View** menu).
Queued printing	**Background printing** option on the **Print** tab in the **Options** dialog box (**Tools** menu). To control your computer's connection to a network printer, double-click the Printers icon on the Control Panel.
Scrap	The Clipboard, which is a temporary storage location that you can use for moving and copying text and graphics between Word 97 documents and other applications.
Side-by-side paragraphs (5.0, 5.5)	**Table** menu commands.
Style sheet	Styles are part of the active document or the template in Word 97.
Table (5.0, 5.5)	**Insert Table** and **Table AutoFormat** (**Table** menu).
Usage-variant label (5.0)	Not used. Styles are identified by style names. The style defines the format of the paragraphs to which it is applied and the character formatting of the text within the paragraphs.

Opening Word 5.*x* and 6.0 for MS-DOS Documents in Word 97

When you upgrade to Word 97, you can still open your old Word for MS-DOS documents. If the Word for MS-DOS text converter is installed properly, Word 97 automatically converts Word for MS-DOS documents to the Word 97 file format.

Tools and Utilities   The Office Resource Kit Tools and Utilities include the Word 3.*x*, 4.*x*, 5.*x*, and 6.0 for MS-DOS text converter. For information about installing this converter, see "Word Converters" in Appendix A, "Microsoft Office 97 Resource Kit Tools and Utilities."

Upgrading from Word 5.x or 6.0 for MS-DOS

This section describes the changes between Word versions 5.*x* and 6.0 for MS-DOS and Word 97. Word 97 is a major upgrade from previous versions of the application. For more information about the features and benefits of this upgrade, see Chapter 2, "What's New in Microsoft Office 97."

What happens to my old Word documents when I convert them to Word 97 format? If the correct text converter is installed, you can open files created in Word 5.*x* or 6.0 for MS-DOS directly in Word 97. All data and formatting created in Word 5.*x* or 6.0 for MS-DOS are fully supported by Word 97.

Can I share Word 97 documents with users of previous versions of Word? If your workgroup uses any combination of Word 97 and Word 5.*x* or 6.0 for MS-DOS, users can exchange documents and templates between versions. However, not all Word 97 features are supported in previous versions. For more information, see "Sharing Documents with Word 5.x or 6.0 for MS-DOS" later in this chapter.

Do my old macros still work in Word 97? Word for MS-DOS macros are not supported in Word 97, nor can they be automatically converted to Visual Basic. You must recreate your Word for MS-DOS macros in Word 97.

Tools and Utilities The Office Resource Kit Tools and Utilities include the Word 5.*x* and 6.0 for MS-DOS converter and other tools for Word for MS-DOS upgraders. You must install this converter to work with documents in Word 5.*x* or 6.0 for MS-DOS format. For information about installing the converter, see "Word Converters" in Appendix A, "Microsoft Office 97 Resource Kit Tools and Utilities."

Tip To convert several documents at once to Word 97 format, or to customize document conversion, you can use the Conversion Wizard, which is supplied with Word. For more information about this wizard, see "Converting File Formats in Word 97" in Chapter 21, "Switching to Microsoft Word."

Word 97 Terms and Features for Word for MS-DOS Users

This section includes a glossary of Word for MS-DOS terms and the corresponding Word 97 terms or features. Version numbers in parentheses refer to the version of Word for MS-DOS in which the term is used. No version number is given if the term is used in version 5.0 and all later versions.

Tip For more information about a Word 97 term or feature, look it up using **Microsoft Word Help** (**Help** menu).

When this Word 97 feature	Is saved in Word 2.0 format
Tracked changes to properties, paragraph numbers, and display fields (**Tools** menu)	Revision marks for properties, paragraph numbers, and display fields are lost, but other revision marks are retained.
Versions (**File** menu)	Version settings are lost. If you display an older version of a document and then save it in an older format, however, Word 97 suggests a different file name. This makes it difficult to overwrite the Word 97 document and lose data in later versions.

Other Features

The following table describes new features in Word 97 that may affect your data or formatting in previous versions.

When this Word 97 feature	Is saved in Word 2.0 format
Bookmarks and references	These are converted to the closest value available in Word 2.0.
DOCPROPERTY field	The DOCPROPERTY field value is converted.
Endnotes and footnotes	All endnotes and footnotes are retained, but they are merged into one continuous stream.
Form fields	Results of text fields are displayed. Other form fields and bar code fields are lost.
Forms controls	Form controls can be displayed, but not modified.
Page numbering	Page numbers are converted to the closest value available in Word 2.0.
Unicode characters (two bytes per character)	Unicode characters are mapped to corresponding ANSI, or are converted to question marks (?) if no equivalent character is available. Foreign language characters are most likely to be affected.
Variable-width columns	Variable-width columns are converted to equal-width columns.
Word 97 macros, and toolbar, menu, and keyboard customizations	Macros and customized elements are lost.

Table Features

The following table describes new features in Word 97 that may affect your data or formatting in previous versions.

When this Word 97 feature	Is saved in Word 2.0 format
Cell borders and shading	These are converted to the closest value available in Word 2.0.
Vertical text in table cells	Vertical text is reformatted as horizontal text.
Vertically aligned text in table cells	Vertically aligned text is reformatted to align at the top of the cell.
Vertically merged table cells	Merged table cells are unmerged.

Graphics Features

The following table describes new features in Word 97 that may affect your data or formatting in previous versions.

When this Word 97 feature	Is saved in Word 2.0 format
EMF, PNG, and JPEG graphics	Graphics in these formats are converted to WMF (Windows) or PICT (Macintosh) format.
Office Art objects	All Office Art objects are lost.

Workgroup and Internet Features

The following table describes new features in Word 97 that may affect your data or formatting in previous versions.

When this Word 97 feature	Is saved in Word 2.0 format
Document properties (**File** menu)	New document properties are lost.
HYPERLINK field (**Insert** menu)	The result of the HYPERLINK field is retained, but the field cannot be updated.
Password protection options in the **Save As** dialog box (**File** menu)	Word 2.0 users cannot open password-protected Word 97 documents.
Protect Document settings (**Tools** menu)	Document protection is lost.
Revision marks	Multiple author and color revision marks are converted to a single color.

Formatting Features

The following table describes new features in Word 97 that may affect your data or formatting in previous versions.

When this Word 97 feature	Is saved in Word 2.0 format
Font dialog box (**Format** menu)	
Animated text (**Animation** tab)	Animated text formatting is lost.
Embossed and engraved characters (**Font** tab)	Embossed and engraved character formatting is lost.
Shadow and outline effects (**Font** tab)	These effects are lost.
Superscript and subscript characters (**Font** tab)	This property is emulated with raised or lowered character formatting
Underlining (**Font** tab)	New Word 97 underline formats are lost.
Expand and condense effects (**Character Spacing** tab)	Word 97 supports finer control of this property. The value is rounded to the closest value Word 2.0 supports.
Kerning (**Character Spacing** tab)	Kerning is lost.
Borders and Shading dialog box (**Format** menu)	
Page borders (**Page Border** tab)	Page borders are not converted.
Character shading (**Shading** tab)	Character shading is lost.
Character borders (**Borders** tab)	Character borders are lost.
Paragraph borders (**Borders** tab)	Paragraph borders are converted to the closest value available in Word 2.0. Paragraph borders introduced in Word 97 are lost.
Bar tabs	Bar tabs are lost.
Bullets and numbering	All automatic bullets and numbering are converted to plain text.
Multilevel and heading numbering	Lists are converted to plain text.
Floating OLE objects	Floating OLE objects are converted as in-line OLE objects.
Floating pictures surrounded by wrapped text	Floating pictures are converted as in-line pictures in WMF format.
Highlighting applied with the **Highlight** button (**Formatting** toolbar)	Highlighting is lost.
Styles	Style definitions numbered greater than 223 are lost, along with any references to them; however, all formatting is preserved.
Character styles	Style definitions are lost; however the formatting is preserved.

> **What if Word 2.0 isn't listed?**
> If you attempt to save a Word 2.0 document, but **Word 2.x for Windows** does not appear in the **Save as type** box, you need to install the Word 2.0 for Windows converter. To install the converter, rerun Setup and click **Add/Remove**; under the **Converters and Filters** option, select the **Text Converters** check box.

Tip   End users can specify the default format in which Word saves new documents.

▶ **To specify the default format in which to save documents**

1   On the **Tools** menu, click **Options**, and then click the **Save** tab.
2   In the **Save Word files as** box, click the file format you want.

   The next time you save a document that is not already saved in Word 97 format, you are prompted to save it in this format.

For more information about selecting a default format in which to save documents, see "Specifying the Default Format in Which to Save Office Documents" in Chapter 22, "Supporting Multiple Versions of Microsoft Office."

Tip   In Windows 95 and Windows NT Workstation 4.0, you can use a system policy to define the default value for the **Save Word files as** option on the **Save** tab in the **Options** dialog box (**Tools** menu) for all Word users in your workgroup. In the System Policy Editor, set the following policy:

User\Word 97\Tools_Options\Save\Default Save

For more information, see "Using Windows System Policies to Customize Office" in Chapter 7, "Customizing and Optimizing Microsoft Office."

Since not all Word 97 features are supported in Word 2.0, saving in Word 2.0 format may result in loss of data or formatting. The following sections describe the Word 97 features that are not fully supported in Word 2.0.

Basic Use Features

The following table describes new features in Word 97 that may affect your data or formatting in previous versions.

When this Word 97 feature	Is saved in Word 2.0 format
Embedded fonts	The embedded fonts are lost, and Word 2.0 assigns the closest font available.

Help Menu

The following table describes changed commands on the **Help** menu.

This Word 2.0 command	Changes to this in Word 97
Help Index	Renamed **Microsoft Word Help**. Displays the Office Assistant through which you view Help.
Getting Started and **Learning Word**	Removed.
Product Support	Functionality moved to the **Tech Support** button in the **About Microsoft Word** dialog box (**Help** menu).

The following table lists new commands that have been added to the **Help** menu.

This Word 97 command	Allows you to
Contents and Index	Display Word Help.
What's This?	Click any area of the screen (such as a toolbar or menu command) to see a brief explanation in a ScreenTip.
Microsoft on the Web submenu commands	Connect to the Microsoft home page on the World Wide Web (requires Internet access). For information about customizing these commands, see "Customizing Office Connections to the World Wide Web" in Chapter 7, "Customizing and Optimizing Microsoft Office."

Sharing Documents with Word 2.0

If your workgroup is upgrading gradually to Word 97, some users may have to share documents with users of Word 2.0.

Saving Word 97 Documents in Word 2.0 Format

Users of Word 97 can save documents in Word 2.0 format.

▶ **To save a document in Word 2.0 format (Windows only)**

1 On the **File** menu, click **Save As**.
2 In the **Save as type** box, click **Word 2.x for Windows**.

This Word 97 command	Allows you to
Templates and Add-Ins	Update document styles, attach a different template to the document, and use macros and other items stored in another template. You also use this command to load add-in programs.
Customize	Customize toolbar buttons, menu commands, and shortcut key assignments.

Table Menu

The following table describes changed commands on the **Table** menu.

This Word 2.0 command	Changes to this in Word 97
Delete Columns	Renamed **Delete Cells**.
Row Height and **Column Width**	Renamed **Cell Height and Width**.
Gridlines	Renamed **Hide Gridlines**.

The following table lists new commands that have been added to the **Table** menu.

This Word 97 command	Allows you to
Draw Table	Draw tables and cells using a pencil-like mouse pointer.
Split Cells	Split a cell horizontally into multiple cells.
Table AutoFormat	Automatically apply formats, including predefined borders and shading, to a table.
Headings	Designate selected rows as a table heading that is repeated on subsequent pages if the table spans more than one page. This command is available only if the selected rows include the top row of a table.
Sort	Arrange the information in selected rows or lists alphabetically, numerically, or by date.
Formula	Perform mathematical calculations on numbers.

Window Menu

The following table lists new commands that have been added to the **Window** menu.

This Word 97 command	Allows you to
Split	Split the active window into panes, or remove the split from the active window.

Chapter 15   Upgrading from Previous Versions of Microsoft Word

This Word 2.0 command	Changes to this in Word 97
Compare Versions	Renamed **Compare Documents** (**Track Changes** submenu).
Sorting	Renamed **Sort** (**Table** menu).
Calculate	Removed. To calculate values, use **Formula** (**Table** menu).
Repaginate Now	Repagination is automatic in Word 97, unless you clear **Background repagination** on the **General** tab in the **Options** dialog box (**Tools** menu).
Record Macro	Moved to **Record New Macro** (**Macro** submenu).
Macro	Renamed **Macros** (**Macro** submenu).

The following table lists new commands that have been added to the **Tools** menu.

This Word 97 command	Allows you to
AutoSummarize	Create a summary of the document automatically.
AutoCorrect	Correct text automatically as you type. You can also use **AutoCorrect** to store and reuse text and other items you use frequently.
Look Up Reference	Find a selected word or phrase in Bookshelf 97. (This command is available only if Bookshelf is installed.) For more information, see in Chapter 27, "Sharing Information with Microsoft Office Applications."
Merge Documents	Insert another document into the active document.
Protect Document	Prevent changes to all or part of an online form or document except as specified. You can also assign a password so that other users can mark comments or changes, or fill in parts of an online form.
Mail Merge	Produce form letters, mailing labels, envelopes, catalogs, and other types of merged documents.
Letter Wizard	Start the Letter Wizard, with which you can format a letter.

This Word 2.0 command	Changes to this in Word 97
Frame	Removed. Use the **Text Box** tab in the **Format Text Box** dialog box (**Format** menu) to format text boxes.
Picture	Removed. Use the **Picture** tab in the **Format Picture** dialog box (**Format** menu) to format pictures.

The following table lists new commands that have been added to the **Format** menu.

This Word 97 command	Allows you to
Bullets and Numbering	Add bullets or numbers to selected paragraphs, or change the bullet or number format. This command was moved from the **Tools** menu.
Drop Cap	Format selected text with a large initial. Drop caps are used for decoration at the beginning of a paragraph.
Text Direction	Change the orientation of text within table cells. Results are visible only in page layout view.
Change Case	Change the capitalization of selected text.
AutoFormat	Automatically analyze a Word document to identify specific elements, and then format the text by applying styles from the attached template.
Style Gallery	Customize the look of your document using styles from other templates.
Background	Format the background color or image (for example, a watermark) of the document.
Object	Specify the line, color, fill color and pattern, size, and position of the selected object.

Tools Menu

The following table describes changed commands on the **Tools** menu.

This Word 2.0 command	Changes to this in Word 97
Spelling and **Grammar**	Consolidated in **Spelling and Grammar**.
Thesaurus and **Hyphenation**	Moved to **Language** submenu.
Bullets and Numbering	Moved to **Bullets and Numbering** (**Format** menu).
Create Envelope	Renamed **Envelopes and Labels**.
Revision Marks	Renamed **Highlight Changes** (**Track Changes** submenu).

This Word 97 command	Allows you to
Document Map	Display a document outline pane for easier navigation within a large, structured document.
Full Screen	Hide toolbars and other screen elements to see more of your document.

Insert Menu

The following table describes changed commands on the **Insert** menu.

This Word 2.0 command	Changes to this in Word 97
Annotation	Renamed **Comments** (**View** menu).
Index Entry, Index, and Table of Contents	Functionality moved to **Index and Tables**.
Frame	Removed. To insert text boxes, use **Text Box**. To insert pictures, use the commands on the **Picture** submenu.

The following table lists new commands that have been added to the **Insert** menu.

This Word 97 command	Allows you to
AutoText	Create or insert an AutoText entry of boilerplate text or graphics.
Caption	Insert captions for tables, figures, equations and other items.
Cross-reference	Insert a cross-reference to an item in the document.
Hyperlink	Insert a Web-style hyperlink to another Office document. For more information about hyperlinks, see Chapter 24, "Integrating Microsoft Office With Your Intranet."

Format Menu

The following table describes changed commands on the **Format** menu.

This Word 2.0 command	Changes to this in Word 97
Character	Renamed **Font**.
Border	Renamed **Borders and Shading**.
Language	Moved to **Set Language** (**Tools** menu, **Language** submenu).
Page Setup	Moved to **Page Setup** (**File** menu).
Section Layout	Moved to options under **Section Breaks** in the **Break** dialog box (**Insert** menu).

Edit Menu

The following table describes changed commands on the **Edit** menu.

This Word 2.0 command	Changes to this in Word 97
Glossary	Glossary functionality has been moved to **AutoText** (**Insert** menu). You can also use **AutoCorrect** (**Tools** menu) for short glossary entries.

The following table lists new commands that have been added to the **Edit** menu.

This Word 97 command	Allows you to
Paste as Hyperlink	Paste and format the Clipboard contents as a hyperlink. You must then edit the hyperlink using the **Hyperlink** command (**Insert** menu) to specify a file or URL to which the selected text is to be linked. For more information about Word 97 Internet features, see Chapter 25, "Web Support in Microsoft Office Applications."

View Menu

The following table describes changed commands on the **View** menu.

This Word 2.0 command	Changes to this in Word 97
Draft	Removed. Word 97 does not support draft view.
Ribbon	Removed. The ribbon buttons have been moved to the **Formatting** toolbar and the ruler.
Annotations	Renamed **Comments**.
Field Codes	Removed. To show or hide field codes for a specific field, click the field or the field results, and then press SHIFT+F9. To show or hide field codes for all fields in the document, press ALT+F9.

The following table lists new commands that have been added to the **View** menu.

This Word 97 command	Allows you to
Online Layout	Switch to online reading view, which displays your document in a format optimized for navigating and reading on the screen.
Master Document	Organize a long document by dividing it into several subdocuments.

Menu Changes

The following sections summarize the Word 2.0 commands that have changed location or functionality in Word 97, as well as commands that are new in Word 97.

File Menu

The following table describes changed commands on the **File** menu.

This Word 2.0 command	Changes to this in Word 97
Save All	Removed. To save all open documents, hold down SHIFT and click **Save All** (**File** menu).
Find File	Removed. Document searching has been moved to the **Open** dialog box (**File** menu). For information about locating Office documents, see Chapter 26, "Finding Microsoft Office Documents on the Network."
Summary Info	Renamed **Properties**. For information about using document properties, see Chapter 23, "Tracking Collaboration With Document Properties."
Template	Renamed **Templates and Add-Ins** (**Tools** menu).
Print Merge	Print merge functionality has been moved to **Mail Merge** (**Tools** menu)
Print Setup	Print setup functionality has been moved to the **Paper Source** tab in the **Page Setup** dialog box (**File** menu) and the **Properties** button in the **Print** dialog box (**File** menu).
Send	Renamed **Mail Recipient** (**Send To** submenu). For information about using Word 97 with e-mail, see Chapter 28, "Working with Messaging Systems and Connectivity Software."

The following table lists new commands that have been added to the **File** menu.

This Word 97 command	Allows you to
Versions	Display a version summary for the active document. For information about versions, see Chapter 33, "Workgroup Features in Microsoft Word."
Page Setup	Changes margins, paper source, paper size, and page orientation.

Other Features

The following table describes new features in Word 97 that may affect your data or formatting in previous versions.

When this Word 97 feature	Is opened in Word 6.0 or 95 using the converter
DOCPROPERTY field	The DOCPROPERTY field is retained in Word 95, but only the most recent result of the field is retained in Word 6.0.
Forms controls	Forms controls can be displayed, but not modified.
Unicode characters (two bytes per character)	Unicode characters are mapped to corresponding ANSI (Windows) or one byte per character (Macintosh), or are converted to question marks (?) if no equivalent character is available. Foreign language characters are most likely to be affected.

Upgrading from Word 2.0

This section describes the changes between Word version 2.0 for Windows and Word 97. Word 97 is a major upgrade from previous versions of the application. For more information about the features and benefits of this upgrade, see Chapter 2, "What's New in Microsoft Office 97."

What happens to my old Word documents when I convert them to Word 97 format? You can open files created in Word 2.0 directly in Word 97. All data and formatting created in Word 2.0 are fully supported by Word 97.

Can I share Word 97 documents with users of previous versions of Word? If your workgroup uses a combination of Word 97 and Word 2.0, users can exchange documents and templates between versions. However, not all Word 97 features are supported in previous versions. For more information, see "Sharing Documents with Word 2.0" later in this chapter.

Do my old macros still work in Word 97? In most cases, your WordBasic macros run in Word 97. If you open a Word 2.0 template containing WordBasic macros in Word 97, the WordBasic code is converted to equivalent Visual Basic code. For more information about working with WordBasic code in Word 97, see "Upgrading WordBasic Macros to Visual Basic" earlier in this chapter.

Tip To convert several documents at once to Word 97 format, or to customize document conversion, you can use the Conversion Wizard, which is supplied with Word. For more information about this wizard, see "Converting File Formats in Word 97" in Chapter 21, "Switching to Microsoft Word."

Table Features

The following table describes new features in Word 97 that may affect your data or formatting in previous versions.

When this Word 97 feature	Is opened in Word 6.0 or 95 using the converter
Vertical text in table cells	Vertical text is reformatted as horizontal text.
Vertically aligned text in table cells	Vertically aligned text is reformatted to align at the top of the cell.
Vertically merged table cells	Merged table cells are unmerged.

Graphics Features

The following table describes new features in Word 97 that may affect your data or formatting in previous versions.

When this Word 97 feature	Is opened in Word 6.0 or 95 using the converter
EMF, PNG, and JPEG graphics	Graphics in these formats are saved in the document, but Word 97 also creates WMF (Windows) or PICT (Macintosh) format versions. Word 6.0 or 95 displays the WMF or PICT version of the graphics; the original formats are preserved in the document for better fidelity if the document is reopened in Word 97.

Workgroup and Internet Features

The following table describes new features in Word 97 that may affect your data or formatting in previous versions.

When this Word 97 feature	Is opened in Word 6.0 or 95 using the converter
Document properties (**File** menu)	New document properties are preserved in Word 95, but are lost in Word 6.0.
HYPERLINK field (**Insert** menu)	The result of the HYPERLINK field is retained, but the field cannot be updated.
Password protection options in the **Save As** dialog box (**File** menu)	Word 6.0 and 95 users cannot open password-protected Word 97 documents.
Protect Document settings (**Tools** menu)	Document protection is lost.
Tracked changes to properties, paragraph numbers, and display fields (**Tools** menu)	Revision marks for properties, paragraph numbers, and display fields are lost, but other revision marks are retained.

Basic Use Features

The following table describes new features in Word 97 that may affect your data or formatting in previous versions.

When this Word 97 feature	Is opened in Word 6.0 or 95 using the converter
Embedded fonts	The embedded fonts are lost, and Word 6.0 or 95 assigns the closest font available.

Formatting Features

The following table describes new features in Word 97 that may affect your data or formatting in previous versions.

When this Word 97 feature	Is opened in Word 6.0 or 95 using the converter
Font dialog box (**Format** menu)	
Animated text (**Animation** tab)	Animated text formatting is lost.
Embossed and engraved characters (**Font** tab)	Embossed and engraved character formatting is lost.
Shadow and outline effects (**Font** tab)	These effects are lost in Word for Windows, but are preserved in Word for the Macintosh.
Borders and Shading dialog box (**Format** menu)	
Page borders (**Page Border** tab)	Page borders are lost.
Character shading (**Shading** tab)	Character shading is lost.
Character borders (**Borders** tab)	Character borders are lost.
Paragraph borders (**Borders** tab)	Paragraph borders are converted to Word 6.0-95 border styles.
Floating OLE objects	Floating OLE objects are converted in a frame.
Floating pictures surrounded by wrapped text	Floating pictures are converted in a frame to WMF (Windows) or PICT (Macintosh) format.
Highlighting applied with the **Highlight** button (**Formatting** toolbar)	Highlighting is preserved in Word 95, but is lost in Word 6.0.
Multilevel and heading numbering	Lists are converted to plain text, and the numbering property is lost.

When this Word 97 feature	Is saved in Word 6.0/95 format
Password protection options in the **Save As** dialog box (**File** menu)	Because saving in Word 6.0/95 format actually saves in RTF format, password protection is not supported.
Protect Document settings (**Tools** menu)	Document protection is lost.
Tracked changes to properties, paragraph numbers, and display fields (**Tools** menu)	Revision marks for properties, paragraph numbers, and display fields are lost, but other revision marks are retained.
Versions (**File** menu)	Version settings are lost. If you display an older version of a document and then save it in an older format, however, Word 97 suggests a different file name. This makes it difficult to overwrite the Word 97 document and lose data in later versions.

Other Features

The following table describes new features in Word 97 that may affect your data or formatting in previous versions.

When this Word 97 feature	Is saved in Word 6.0/95 format
DOCPROPERTY field	The DOCPROPERTY field is retained in Word 95, but only the most recent result of the field is retained in Word 6.0.
Forms controls	Forms controls can be displayed, but not modified.
Unicode characters (two bytes per character)	Unicode characters are mapped to corresponding ANSI (Windows) or one byte per character (Macintosh), or are converted to question marks (?) if no equivalent character is available. Foreign language characters are most likely to be affected.
Word 97 macros, and toolbar, menu, and keyboard customizations	Macros and customized elements are lost.

Opening Word 97 Documents in Word 6.0 or 95

Users of Word 6.0 for Windows or the Macintosh and users of Word 95 for Windows can open Word 97 documents directly if they install the converter for Word 6.0 or 95.

Tools and Utilities The Office Resource Kit Tools and Utilities include the converter for Word 6.0 or 95. For information about installing the converter, see "Word Converters" in Appendix A, "Microsoft Office 97 Resource Kit Tools and Utilities."

Not all Word 97 features are fully supported by Word 6.0 or 95. The following sections describe data or formatting that may not be converted correctly.

When this Word 97 feature	Is saved in Word 6.0/95 format
Floating pictures surrounded by wrapped text	Floating pictures are converted in a frame to WMF (Windows) or PICT (Macintosh) format.
Floating OLE objects	Floating OLE objects are converted in a frame.
Highlighting applied with the **Highlight** button (**Formatting** toolbar)	Highlighting is preserved in Word 95, but is lost in Word 6.0.

Table Features

The following table describes new features in Word 97 that may affect your data or formatting in previous versions.

When this Word 97 feature	Is saved in Word 6.0/95 format
Vertical text in table cells	Vertical text is reformatted as horizontal text.
Vertically aligned text in table cells	Vertically aligned text is reformatted to align at the top of the cell.
Vertically merged table cells	Merged table cells are unmerged.

Graphics Features

The following table describes new features in Word 97 that may affect your data or formatting in previous versions.

When this Word 97 feature	Is saved in Word 6.0/95 format
EMF, PNG, and JPEG graphics	Graphics in these formats are converted to WMF (Windows) or PICT (Macintosh) format.
Office Art objects	Office Art objects are lost.

Workgroup and Internet Features

The following table describes new features in Word 97 that may affect your data or formatting in previous versions.

When this Word 97 feature	Is saved in Word 6.0/95 format
Document properties (**File** menu)	If the document is edited in Word 95, all document properties are preserved. If the document is edited in Word 6.0, all custom properties and the following built-in properties are lost: Type, Accessed, Attributes, Manager, Company, Category, Bytes, and Document Contents.
HYPERLINK field (**Insert** menu)	The result of the HYPERLINK field is retained.

Since not all Word 97 features are supported in Word 6.0-95, saving in Word 6.0/95 format may result in loss of data or formatting. The following sections describe the Word 97 features that are not fully supported in Word 6.0-95.

Basic Use Features

The following table describes new features in Word 97 that may affect your data or formatting in previous versions.

When this Word 97 feature	Is saved in Word 6.0/95 format
Embedded fonts	The embedded fonts are lost, and Word 6.0 or 95 assigns the closest font available.

Formatting Features

The following table describes new features in Word 97 that may affect your data or formatting in previous versions.

When this Word 97 feature	Is saved in Word 6.0/95 format
Font dialog box (**Format** menu)	
Animated text (**Animation** tab)	Animated text formatting is lost.
Embossed and engraved characters (**Font** tab)	Embossed and engraved character formatting is lost.
Shadow and outline effects (**Font** tab)	These effects are lost in Word for Windows, but are preserved in Word for the Macintosh.
Bullets and Numbering dialog box (**Format** menu)	
Outline numbered list (**Outline Numbered** tab)	Outline numbered lists are converted to regular text, but retain their existing numbering and indentation.
Heading numbered list (**Outline Numbered** tab)	Heading numbered lists are converted to regular text, but retain their existing numbering and indentation.
Multilevel bullets (**Outline Numbered** tab)	Multilevel bullets are converted to regular text, but retain their existing numbering and indentation.
Borders and Shading dialog box (**Format** menu)	
Page borders (**Page Border** tab)	Page borders are not converted.
Character shading (**Shading** tab)	Character shading is lost.
Character borders (**Borders** tab)	Character borders are lost.
Paragraph borders (**Borders** tab)	New Word 97 paragraph borders are lost.

Saving Word 97 Documents in Word 6.0/95 Format

Users of Word 97 can save documents in Word 6.0/95 format.

▶ **To save a document in Word 6.0/95 format**

1   On the **File** menu, click **Save As**.
2   In the **Save as type** box, click **Word 6.0/95**.

Tip   End users can specify the default format in which Word saves new documents.

▶ **To specify the default format in which to save documents**

1   On the **Tools** menu, click **Options**, and then click the **Save** tab.
2   In the **Save Word files as** box, click the file format you want.

The next time you save a document that is not already saved in Word 97 format, you are prompted to save it in this format.

For more information about selecting a default format in which to save documents, see "Specifying the Default Format in Which to Save Office Documents" in Chapter 22, "Supporting Multiple Versions of Microsoft Office."

Tip   In Windows 95 and Windows NT Workstation version 4.0, you can use a system policy to define the default value for the **Save Word files as** option on the **Save** tab in the **Options** dialog box (**Tools** menu) for all Word users in your workgroup. In the System Policy Editor, set the following policy:

User\Word 97\Tools_Options\Save\Default Save

For more information, see "Using Windows System Policies to Customize Office" in Chapter 7, "Customizing and Optimizing Microsoft Office."

Saving in Word 6.0/95 format actually saves in RTF

When you save a Word 97 document in Word 6.0/95 format, the document is actually saved in Rich Text Format (RTF). However, the extension or file type indicates that the saved document is a Word document.

Normally, you do not notice this difference unless you have selected the **Confirm conversion at Open** check box, which is located on the **General** tab in the **Options** dialog box (**Tools** menu). If this option is selected, you see **Rich Text Format (RTF)** in the **Convert File** dialog box when you open the document. Click **OK** to continue.

Products from independent software vendors, such as batch conversion tools that work with Word 6.0/95 format but not RTF format, may not be able to properly open such files.

- For macros that make calls to 16-bit Windows 3.*x* application programming interface (API) functions or subroutines, you must edit the application code to replace the calls with appropriate calls to the Win32 API (Windows only).

For more information about converting WordBasic macros to Visual Basic, see the following:

- Chapter 7, "Customizing and Optimizing Microsoft Office."
- Visual Basic online Help.
- The *Microsoft Office 97/Visual Basic Programmer's Guide*, available from Microsoft Press. For information about Microsoft Press books, see Appendix E, "Other Support Resources."

Sharing Documents with Word 6.0 or 95

If your workgroup is upgrading gradually to Word 97, some users may have to share documents with users of Word 6.0 for Windows or the Macintosh or Word 95 for Windows. There are two strategies for sharing documents among these versions of Word:

- Save Word 97 documents in the dual Word 6.0/95 format.
- Open Word 97 documents directly in Word 6.0 or 95 using the converter for Word 6.0 or 95.

Tools and Utilities The Office Resource Kit Tools and Utilities include the converter for Word 6.0 or 95. For information about installing the converter, see "Word Converters" in Appendix A, "Microsoft Office 97 Resource Kit Tools and Utilities."

The following table shows the advantages and disadvantages of each strategy.

Strategy	Advantages	Disadvantages
Save Word 97 documents in Word 6.0/95 format.	All Word users can open, edit, and save documents.	If a Word 6.0 or 95 user saves the document, features unique to Word 97 are lost.
Open Word 97 documents in Word 6.0 or 95 using the converter for Word 6.0 or 95.	All Word users can open, edit, and save documents.	Word 6.0 and 95 users must install the converter for Word 6.0 or 95 and cannot save documents in Word 97 format; not all Word 97 features are converted in Word 6.0 or 95.

Note Because the file formats between Word 6.0 and Word 95 are very similar, these two versions are considered together in the following sections.

The following table lists new commands that have been added to the **Apple Help** menu.

This Word 97 command	Allows you to
Microsoft Word Help	Display the Assistant through which you view Help.
What's This?	Click any area of the screen (such as a toolbar or menu command) to see a brief explanation in Balloon Help.
Microsoft on the Web submenu commands	Connect to the Microsoft home page on the World Wide Web (requires Internet access). For information about customizing these commands, see "Customizing Office Connections to the World Wide Web" in Chapter 7, "Customizing and Optimizing Microsoft Office."

Upgrading WordBasic Macros to Visual Basic

When you open a Word 6.0 or 95. template containing WordBasic macros, all of the macro code is modified to work with Visual Basic. The modified WordBasic code is functionally equivalent, but not identical, to the Visual Basic code.

For example, a macro that looks like this in WordBasic:

```
Sub Main
Insert "Hello World"
End Sub
```

is converted to this in Word 97:

```
Public Sub Main()
WordBasic.Insert "Hello World"
End Sub
```

which is equivalent to this Visual Basic code:

```
Public Sub Main()
Selection.TypeText Text:="Hello World"
End Sub
```

All WordBasic statements and functions are exposed through the WordBasic object in the Word 97 Visual Basic object model.

When converting to Word 97, you must modify your WordBasic macro code under the following conditions:

- For macros that make calls to custom 16-bit DLLs, you must provide a 32-bit compatibility layer (a *thunking* layer) for the 16-bit DLL, or the DLL source code must be recompiled into a 32-bit version of the DLL.

Table Menu

The following table lists new commands that have been added to the **Table** menu.

This Word 97 command	Allows you to
Draw Table	Draw tables and cells using a pencil-like mouse pointer.

Help Menu (Windows only)

The following table describes changed commands on the **Help** menu.

This Word 6.0 or 95 command	Changes to this in Word 97
Microsoft Word Help Topics	Renamed **Microsoft Word Help**. Displays the Office Assistant through which you view Help.
Answer Wizard	Removed. Gain access to the Answer Wizard feature through the Assistant.

The following table lists new commands that have been added to the **Help** menu.

This Word 97 command	Allows you to
Contents and Index	Display Word Help.
What's This?	Click any area of the screen (such as a toolbar or menu command) to see a brief explanation in a ScreenTip.
Microsoft on the Web submenu commands	Connect to the Microsoft home page on the World Wide Web (requires Internet access). For information about customizing these commands, see "Customizing Office Connections to the World Wide Web" in Chapter 7, "Customizing and Optimizing Microsoft Office."

Apple Help Menu (Macintosh only)

The following table describes changed commands on the **Apple Help** menu.

This Word 6.0 or 95 command	Changes to this in Word 97
Microsoft Word Help, **Search for Help on**, and **Index**	Replaced by **Microsoft Word Help**. This command displays the Assistant, through which you view Help.

Format Menu

The following table describes changed commands on the **Format** menu.

This Word 6.0 or 95 command	Changes to this in Word 97
Heading Numbering	Moved to the **Outline Numbered** tab in the **Bullets and Numbering** dialog box (**Format** menu).
Frame	Removed. Use the **Text Box** tab in the **Text Box** dialog box (**Format** menu) to format text boxes

The following table lists new commands that have been added to the **Format** menu.

This Word 97 command	Allows you to
Text Direction	Change the orientation of text within table cells. Results are visible only in page layout view.

Tools Menu

The following table describes changed commands on the **Tools** menu.

This Word 6.0 or 95 command	Changes to this in Word 97
Spelling and **Grammar**	Consolidated in **Spelling and Grammar**.
Thesaurus and **Hyphenation**	Moved to **Language** submenu.

The following table lists new commands that have been added to the **Tools** menu.

This Word 97 command	Allows you to
Language submenu commands	Change thesaurus, hyphenation, and language settings.
AutoSummarize	Create a summary of the document automatically.
Look Up Reference	Find a selected word or phrase in Bookshelf 97. (This command is available only if Bookshelf is installed.) For more information, see Chapter 27, "Sharing Information with Microsoft Office Applications."
Merge Documents	Insert another document into the active document.
Letter Wizard	Start the Letter Wizard to format a letter.
Macro submenu commands	Create, run, and manage macros; edit Visual Basic for Applications code.

The following table lists new commands that have been added to the **View** menu.

This Word 97 command	Allows you to
Online Layout	Switch to online reading view, which displays your document in a format optimized for navigating and reading on the screen.
Document Map	Display a document outline pane for easier navigation within a large, structured document.

Insert Menu

The following table describes changed commands on the **Insert** menu.

This Word 6.0 or 95 command	Changes to this in Word 97
Annotation	Renamed **Comment**.
Frame	Removed. To insert text boxes, use **Text Box**. To insert pictures, use the commands on the **Picture** submenu.
Form Field	Removed. Use the **Forms** toolbar (**View** menu, **Toolbars** submenu) to insert form fields.

The following table lists new commands that have been added to the **Insert** menu.

This Word 97 command	Allows you to
AutoText	Create or insert an AutoText entry. This command was moved from the **Edit** menu.
Picture submenu commands	Insert new or existing pictures or other objects into the document.
Bookmark	Mark selected text or other items as a bookmark. This command was moved from the **Edit** menu.
Hyperlink	Insert a Web-style hyperlink to another Office document. For more information about hyperlinks, see Chapter 24, "Integrating Microsoft Office With Your Intranet."

The following table lists new commands that have been added to the **File** menu.

This Word 97 command	Allows you to
Versions	Display a version summary for the active document. For more information about versions, see Chapter 33, "Workgroup Features in Microsoft Word."
Send To submenu commands	Send a document to others electronically. For more information about working with messaging systems, see Chapter 28, "Working with Messaging Systems and Connectivity Software."

Edit Menu

The following table describes changed commands on the **Edit** menu.

This Word 6.0 or 95 command	Changes to this in Word 97
AutoText	Moved to **Insert** menu.
Bookmark	Moved to **Insert** menu.

The following table lists new commands that have been added to the **Edit** menu.

This Word 97 command	Allows you to
Paste as Hyperlink	Paste and format the Clipboard contents as a hyperlink. You must then edit the hyperlink using the **Hyperlink** command (**Insert** menu) to specify a file or URL to which the selected text is to be linked. For more information about Word 97 Internet features, see Chapter 25, "Web Support in Microsoft Office Applications."

View Menu

The following table describes changed commands on the **View** menu.

This Word 6.0 or 95 command	Changes to this in Word 97
Annotations	Renamed **Comments**. Use this command to insert a comment marker at the insertion point and display a comments pane in which you can enter a comment or annotation.

Can I share Word 97 documents with users of previous versions of Word? If your workgroup is using any combination of Word 97, 95, or 6.0, users can exchange documents and templates between versions. However, not all Word 97 features are supported in previous versions. For more information, see "Sharing Documents with Word 6.0 or 95" later in this chapter.

Do my old macros still work in Word 97? In most cases, your WordBasic macros run in Word 97. If you open a Word 6.0 or 95 template containing WordBasic macros in Word 97, the WordBasic code is converted to equivalent Visual Basic for Applications code. For more information about working with WordBasic code in Word 97, see "Upgrading WordBasic Macros to Visual Basic" later in this chapter.

Tip To convert several documents at once to Word 97 format, or to customize document conversion, you can use the Conversion Wizard, which is supplied with Word. For more information about this wizard, see "Converting File Formats in Word 97" in Chapter 21, "Switching to Microsoft Word."

Menu Changes

The following sections summarize the Word 6.0 and 95 commands that have changed location or functionality in Word 97, as well as commands that are new in Word 97.

File Menu

The following table describes changed commands on the **File** menu.

This Word 6.0 or 95 command	Changes to this in Word 97
Send	Renamed **Mail Recipient** (**Send To** submenu).
Add Routing Slip	Renamed **Routing Recipient** (**Send To** submenu).
Find File (Word 6.0 only)	Removed. Document searching has been moved to the **Open** dialog box (**File** menu). For information about locating Office documents, see Chapter 26, "Finding Microsoft Office Documents on the Network."
Summary Info (Word 6.0 only)	Renamed **Properties**. For information about using document properties, see Chapter 23, "Tracking Collaboration With Document Properties."

Part 3   Upgrading to Microsoft Office

- Can I share Word 97 documents with users of previous versions of Word?
- Do my old macros still work in Word 97?

If you are upgrading from any of the following versions of Word, this chapter answers these questions for you.

Operating System	Word version
Windows 3.*x*, Windows NT, or Windows 95	2.0, 6.0, 95
MS-DOS	5.*x*, 6.0
Macintosh	5.*x*, 6.0

As the following illustration shows, some platforms and versions of Word share the same file format. You can exchange documents directly within these common file formats; you do not need to install special converters.

Common File Formats in Word

Operating System					
Windows		2.0	6.0	95	97
Macintosh	4.0	5.x	6.0		97
MS-DOS	4.0	5.x	6.0		

Before you can exchange documents between different file formats, however, you might need to install the text converters included with Word or with the Office Resource Kit Tools and Utilities. Some text converters are installed automatically with Word; however, you must install others manually. For more information, see the section later in this chapter that describes the version from which you are upgrading.

To convert a document from an earlier version of Word to Word 97, simply open the document. To complete the conversion, save the document in Word 97 format.

Upgrading from Word 6.0 or 95

This section describes the differences between Word version 6.0 for Windows or the Macintosh, Word 95 for Windows, and Word 97. Word 97 is a major upgrade from previous versions of the application. For more information about the features and benefits of this upgrade, see Chapter 2, "What's New in Microsoft Office 97."

Note   Because the file formats for Word 6.0 and Word 95 are very similar, these versions are considered together in this section.

What happens to my old Word documents when I convert them to Word 97 format?   You can open files created in Word 6.0 or 95 directly in Word 97. All data and formatting created in Word 6.0 or 95 are fully supported by Word 97.

CHAPTER 15

Upgrading from Previous Versions of Microsoft Word

This chapter tells you what to expect when you or your workgroup upgrades to Microsoft Word 97 from a previous version of Word. If you plan a gradual upgrade, users of different versions of Word may need to share documents. This chapter describes Word 97 features that are not supported in previous versions, which may result in loss of data or formatting.

In This Chapter
Overview   399
Upgrading from Word 6.0 or 95   400
Sharing Documents with Word 6.0 or 95   407
Upgrading from Word 2.0   414
Sharing Documents with Word 2.0   421
Upgrading from Word 5.x or 6.0 for MS-DOS   426
Sharing Documents with Word 5.x or 6.0 for MS-DOS   429
Upgrading from Word 5.x for the Macintosh   432
Sharing Documents with Word 5.x for the Macintosh   433

See Also
- For a summary of new and improved features in Word 97, see Chapter 2, "What's New in Microsoft Office 97."
- For information about installing Word or other Office applications, see Chapter 4, "Installing Microsoft Office."
- For information about switching to Word from other word processor applications, see Chapter 21, "Switching to Microsoft Word."

Overview

The primary questions most Word 97 upgraders have are:

- What happens to my old Word documents when I convert them to Word 97 format?

When this PowerPoint 97 feature	Is saved in PowerPoint 3.0 format
Action settings	Action settings are lost.
Animation effects	The effects are applied only to bulleted lists. All other animation effects are lost.
Custom properties	Custom properties are lost.
Embedded fonts	The embedded fonts are lost, and PowerPoint 3.0 assigns the closest font available.
Hyperlinks	Hyperlinks are lost.
Presentation properties	Presentation properties are lost.

Sharing Presentations with PowerPoint 3.0

If your workgroup is upgrading gradually to PowerPoint 97, some users may have to share presentations with users of PowerPoint 3.0 for Windows or the Macintosh. These PowerPoint 97 users must save their presentations in PowerPoint3.0 format. PowerPoint 97 users can save presentations in PowerPoint 3.0 if they have the necessary converters. If you choose the Typical installation during Setup, these converters are installed automatically.

Operating system	Converters
Windows	Pp7x32.dll, Pp7trans.dll, Pptview.dll
Macintosh	Pp8x32, Pptview (PPC)

▶ **To save a presentation in PowerPoint 3.0 format**

1 On the **File** menu, click **Save As**.
2 In the **Save as type** box, click **PowerPoint 3.0**.

Tip End users can specify the default format in which PowerPoint saves new presentations.

▶ **To specify the default format in which to save presentations**

1 On the **Tools** menu, click **Options**, and then click the **Save** tab.
2 In the **Save PowerPoint files as** box, click the file format you want.

For more information about selecting a default format in which to save presentations, see "Specifying the Default Format in Which to Save Office Documents" in Chapter 22, "Supporting Multiple Versions of Microsoft Office."

Tip In Windows 95 and Windows NT Workstation 4.0, you can use a system policy to define the default value for the **Save as type** option in the **Save As** dialog box (**File** menu) for all PowerPoint users in your workgroup. In the System Policy Editor, set the following policy:

User\PowerPoint\Tools_Options\Save\Default Save

For more information, see "Using Windows System Policies to Customize Office" in Chapter 7, "Customizing and Optimizing Microsoft Office."

Because of changes to the PowerPoint file format, saving a PowerPoint 97 presentation in PowerPoint 3.0 can result in lost or changed data or formatting that cannot be recovered in its original form.

All of the limitations that apply when PowerPoint 97 presentations are saved in PowerPoint 4.0 format also apply to presentations saved in PowerPoint 3.0 format. For more information, see "Saving PowerPoint 97 Presentations in PowerPoint 4.0 Format" earlier in this chapter. The following table describes additional PowerPoint 97 features that are not fully supported in PowerPoint 3.0.

Balloon Help Menu (Macintosh Only)

The **Balloon Help** menu has been removed. Help commands relating to PowerPoint have been moved to the **Apple Help** menu in PowerPoint 97. The following table describes changed commands on the **Balloon Help** menu.

This PowerPoint 3.0 command	Changes to this in PowerPoint 97
PowerPoint Help	Removed. Use **Microsoft PowerPoint Help** (**Apple Help** menu) to display the Assistant, through which you view Help.
PowerPoint Shortcuts	Removed. Use **Contents and Index** (**Apple Help** menu) to look up keyboard shortcuts.

Apple Help Menu (Macintosh Only)

The **Apple Help** menu is new in PowerPoint 97. The following table lists new commands that have been added to the **Apple Help** menu.

This PowerPoint 97 command	Allows you to
Microsoft PowerPoint Help	Display the Assistant, through which you view Help.
Contents and Index	Display PowerPoint Help.
What's This?	Click any area of the screen (such as a toolbar or menu command) to see a brief explanation in Balloon Help.
Microsoft on the Web	Connect to the Microsoft home page on the Web (requires Internet access).

File Format Changes

The PowerPoint 97 file format differs from that of PowerPoint 3.0. If your workgroup is upgrading gradually to PowerPoint 97, some users may have to share workbooks with users of PowerPoint 97. PowerPoint 97 users should save their presentations in PowerPoint 3.0 format. For more information about saving presentations in 3.0 format, see "Sharing Presentations with PowerPoint 3.0" later in this chapter.

Template Changes

The presentation templates included with PowerPoint 97 take advantage of the enhanced animation capabilities of PowerPoint 97, which allow users to apply animation effects to objects on the title master and slide master. Although the file format for PowerPoint 97 differs from that of PowerPoint 3.0, PowerPoint 97 and 3.0 users can exchange templates; however, animated features in a PowerPoint 97 template are lost when the template is converted to PowerPoint 3.0 format.

This PowerPoint 97 command	Allows you to
Set Up Show	Define the type of show, a range of slides, advance method, and pen color.
View On Two Screens	Show a presentation from one computer on another through a serial connection.
Action Buttons	Place a button with interactive settings on a slide.
Action Settings	Define an action for the object, such as playing a sound when the object is clicked during a slide show.
Preset Animation	Apply animation effects to the currently selected object.
Custom Animation	Define animation, sound effects, and timing for objects on a slide.
Animation Preview	View the current slide in miniature, including all animation associated with the slide.
Slide Transition	Define special effects when progressing from one slide to the next in a slide show.
Hide Slide	Skip a selected slide during a slide show.
Custom Shows	Create sections within presentations, making it easier to tailor presentations for specific audiences.

Action Menu (Windows Only)

The **Action** menu appears only when Lotus **NotesFlow** commands are associated with the active presentation. PowerPoint displays the custom actions that have been defined for the active presentation on the **Action** menu. For more information about how Office integrates Lotus Notes, see "Interoperability with Lotus Notes/FX" in Chapter 28, "Working with Messaging Systems and Connectivity Software."

Help Menu (Windows Only)

The following table lists new commands that have been added to the **Help** menu.

This PowerPoint 97 command	Allows you to
Microsoft PowerPoint Help	Display the Office Assistant, through which you view Help.
Contents and Index	Browse and search Help topics.
What's This?	Click any area of the screen (such as a toolbar or menu command) to see a brief explanation in a ScreenTip.
Microsoft on the Web	Connect to the Microsoft home page on the Web (requires Internet access).

Chapter 14 Upgrading from Previous Versions of Microsoft PowerPoint

This PowerPoint 97 command	Allows you to
AutoCorrect	Automatically correct errors, using a customizable list of text substitutions and rules.
Look Up Reference	Find a selected word or phrase in Bookshelf 97. (This command is available only if Bookshelf is installed.) For more information, see Chapter 27, "Sharing Information with Microsoft Office Applications."
AutoClipArt	Select clip art that matches concepts in your presentation.
PowerPoint Central	Open a file on the Office CD or connect to a Web site to download clip art, photos, sound files, templates, or other PowerPoint resources.
Presentation Conference	Show or view a presentation with other members of your workgroup.
Meeting Minder	Display notes pages, meeting minutes, and action items.
Expand Slide	Generate a new slide based on the body text of the active slide.
Macro submenu commands	Create, run, and manage macros; edit Visual Basic code.
Add-Ins	Load a Visual Basic procedure or a DLL into the current session of PowerPoint.
Customize	Customize PowerPoint toolbars.
Options	Set preferences for viewing, editing, saving, and printing PowerPoint presentations.

Slide Show Menu

The **Slide Show** menu is new in PowerPoint 97. It contains many commands that were on the **Slide** menu in PowerPoint 3.0. The **Slide Show** menu also includes the following new commands.

This PowerPoint 97 command	Allows you to
View Show	Launch your slide show in full screen view.
Rehearse Timings	Capture timings as you rehearse the presentation.
Record Narration	Make an audio recording to narrate the slide show.

Format Menu

The **Format** menu is new in PowerPoint 97. It contains many commands that were on the **Text** and **Object** menus in PowerPoint 3.0. The **Format** menu also includes the following new commands.

This PowerPoint 97 command	Allows you to
Font	Change font size or style of text.
Bullet	Change the bullet character for the selected paragraphs.
Alignment	Align text left, right, center, or justified.
Line Spacing	Change the spacing between lines and paragraphs.
Change Case	Change the case of the selected text.
Replace Fonts	Replace one font with another throughout a presentation.
Slide Layout	Pick a different layout for the active slide.
Slide Color Scheme	Pick eight coordinated colors for the active slide or for the entire presentation.
Background	Change the background elements for the active slide or for the entire presentation.
Apply Design	Apply the format from an existing presentation to the active presentation.
Colors and Lines	Change line and fill attributes of the selected object.
Object	Choose settings for the active object.

Note The **Object** command changes based on the object selected on the slide. If nothing is selected, or if more than one kind of object is selected, the command is **Object**. If a picture is selected, the command is **Picture**; if a text box is selected, the command is **Text Box**. If anything else is selected, the command is **AutoShape**.

Tools Menu

The **Tools** menu is new in PowerPoint 97. It contains commands that were on other menus in PowerPoint 3.0. The **Tools** menu also includes the following new commands.

This PowerPoint 97 command	Allows you to
Spelling	Check the spelling in the active presentation.
Style Checker	Check for consistency in spelling, visual clarity, and case and end punctuation.
Language	Format the selected characters as foreign language characters.

This PowerPoint 3.0 command	Changes to this in PowerPoint 97
Follow Master submenu commands	
Color Scheme	Use the **Apply** button in the **Color Scheme** dialog box (**Format** menu) to vary from the master.
Background Items	Select the **Omit background graphics from master** option in the **Background** dialog box (**Format** menu) to hide or display background items.
Title Style and Body Style	Removed. Select text on a slide to edit it.

Insert Menu

The **Insert** menu is new in PowerPoint 97. It contains many commands that were on the **Insert** submenu (**Edit** menu) in PowerPoint 3.0. The **Insert** menu also includes the following new commands.

This PowerPoint 97 command	Allows you to
New Slide	Insert a new slide after the current slide.
Duplicate Slide	Duplicate a slide in slide view.
Slide Number	Insert a sequential number on each slide.
Date and Time	Insert the current date or time into the active text object.
Tab	Create a tab stop.
Symbol	Place a symbol character on a slide.
Comment	Add comments to a slide.
Slides from Files	Insert slides from an existing presentation into the active presentation.
Slides from Outline	Insert slides by creating them from a text outline file.
Picture submenu commands	Insert a picture.
Movies and Sounds submenu commands	Insert a movie or sound clip.
Chart	Insert an editable chart for representing numeric data.
Object	Insert an equation, chart, drawing, or some other object.
Hyperlink	Insert a Web-style hyperlink to another Office document. For more information about hyperlinks, see Chapter 24, "Integrating Microsoft Office With Your Intranet."

This PowerPoint 3.0 command	Changes to this in PowerPoint 97
Change Shape	Renamed **Change AutoShape** (**Draw** menu).
Scale	Functionality moved to the **Size** tab in the **Format** *Object* dialog box (**Format** menu).
Rotate/Flip	Moved to **Draw** menu.

Arrange Menu

The **Arrange** menu has been removed. Most commands that appeared on the **Arrange** menu in PowerPoint 3.0 have been moved to the **Draw** menu, which is on the **Drawing** toolbar in PowerPoint 97. The following table describes **Arrange** menu commands that have additionally changed in function or location.

This PowerPoint 3.0 command	Changes to this in PowerPoint 97
Align	Renamed **Align or Distribute** (**Draw** menu).
Bring to Front, Send to Back, Bring Forward, and Send Backward	Moved to **Order** submenu (**Draw** menu).
Group, Ungroup, and Regroup	Moved to **Group**, **Ungroup**, and **Regroup** (**Draw** menu).
Snap to Grid	Moved to **Snap** submenu (**Draw** menu).
Show Guides	Renamed **Guides** (**View** menu).
Show Edges	Removed.

Slide Menu

The **Slide** menu has been removed in PowerPoint 97. The following table describes the new location or functionality of **Slide** menu commands.

This PowerPoint 3.0 command	Changes to this in PowerPoint 97
New Slide	Moved to **Insert** menu.
Delete Slide	Moved to **Edit** menu.
Color Scheme	Renamed **Slide Color Scheme** (**Format** menu).
Transition	Renamed **Slide Transition** (**Slide Show** menu).
Build	Renamed **Preset Animation** (**Slide Show** menu).
Reapply Master	Removed. Use the **Reapply** button in the **Slide Layout** dialog box (**Format** menu) to return a customized slide to its master settings.
Add Title and Add Body	Removed. Use the **Slide Layout** dialog box (**Format** menu) to add title or body text objects.

Text Menu

The **Text** menu has been removed. Most commands that appeared on the **Text** menu in PowerPoint 3.0 have been moved to the **Format** menu in PowerPoint 97. The following table describes the new location or functionality of **Text** menu commands.

This PowerPoint 3.0 command	Changes to this in PowerPoint 97
Font, Size, Style, Color, and Base Line	Moved to the **Font** dialog box (**Format** menu).
Alignment	Moved to **Format** menu.
Bullet	Moved to **Format** menu.
Line Spacing	Moved to **Format** menu.
Show Ruler	Renamed **Ruler** (**View** menu).
Fit Text	Functionality moved to the **Resize autoshape to fit text** check box on the **Text Box** tab in the **Format Text Box** dialog box (**Format** menu). The **Text Box** command is available only when a text box is selected.
Find/Replace	Moved to **Find** and **Replace** (**Edit** menu).
Spelling	Moved to **Tools** menu.
Replace Fonts	Moved to **Format** menu.
Smart Quotes	Functionality moved to the **Replace straight quotes with smart quotes** check box on the **Edit** tab in the **Options** dialog box (**Tools** menu).

Object Menu

The **Object** menu has been removed. Most commands that appeared on the **Object** menu in PowerPoint 3.0 have been moved to the **Format** menu in PowerPoint 97. The following table describes **Option** menu commands that have additionally changed in function or location.

This PowerPoint 3.0 command	Changes to this in PowerPoint 97
Fill, **Line**, **Line Style**, and **Arrowheads**	Functionality moved to the **Colors and Lines** tab in the **Format** *Object* dialog box (**Format** menu).
Shadow and **Shadow Offset**	Removed. Use the **Shadow** button (**Drawing** toolbar) to create and modify shadows.
Recolor	Moved to the **Picture** tab in the **Format Picture** dialog box (**Format** menu). The **Picture** command is available only when a picture is selected.
Crop	Removed. Use the **Crop** button (**Picture** toolbar) to crop pictures.

The following table lists new commands that have been added to the **Edit** menu.

This PowerPoint 97 command	Allows you to
Repeat or **Redo**	Repeat or redo your last action.
Paste as Hyperlink	Paste and format the Clipboard contents as a hyperlink. Edit the hyperlink using the **Hyperlink** command (**Insert** menu) to specify a file or URL to which the selected text is connected.
Delete Slide	Delete the current slide or group of selected slides.
Find	Search the active presentation for specified text.
Replace	Substitute a string of text for specified text throughout the active presentation.
Go to Property	Go to the assigned custom property fields.

View Menu

The following table describes changed commands on the **View** menu.

This PowerPoint 3.0 command	Changes to this in PowerPoint 97
Zoom setting commands (50%, 100%, etc.)	Moved to **Zoom** dialog box (**View** menu).
Notes	Renamed **Notes Page**.
Slide Master, **Notes Master**, and **Handout Master**	Moved to **Master** submenu.
Outline Master	Removed. Use **Handout Master** (**Master** submenu) to adjust the layout of outlines.

The following table lists new commands that have been added to the **View** menu.

This PowerPoint 97 command	Allows you to
Master submenu commands	Change the current view to edit a master.
Black and White	View color slides in black and white.
Slide Miniature	View a color thumbnail of the current slide.
Speaker Notes	Create and view notes for each slide in your presentation.
Toolbars	Display or hide toolbars.
Ruler	Show or hide rulers.
Guides	Display or hide the drawing guide lines.
Header and Footer	Create headers and footers that appear on every slide in a presentation.
Comments	Display or hide comments on a slide.

This PowerPoint 3.0 command	Changes to this in PowerPoint 97
Page Setup (Macintosh only)	Moved to the **Print** dialog box (**File** menu).
Send	Renamed **Mail Recipient** (**Send To** submenu).
Slide Show	Functionality moved to the **Slide Show** menu.

The following table lists new commands that have been added to the **File** menu.

This PowerPoint 97 command	Allows you to
Save as HTML	Convert a presentation so that it can be read by a Web browser.
Pack and Go	Package your presentation to deliver on another computer.
Send To submenu commands	Send a presentation to others electronically. For more information about sending presentations through e-mail, see Chapter 28, "Working with Messaging Systems and Connectivity Software."

Edit Menu

The following table describes changed commands on the **Edit** menu.

This PowerPoint 3.0 command	Changes to this in PowerPoint 97
Edit Text (Windows only)	Renamed **Object**. This command is available only when a text object is selected.
Edit (Macintosh only)	Renamed **Object**. This command is available only when a text object is selected.
Insert submenu commands	Moved to the **Insert** menu.
Pick Up Style	Removed. Use the **Format Painter** button (**Standard** toolbar) to copy the attributes of the selection.
Apply Style	Removed. Use the **Format Painter** button (**Standard** toolbar) to apply copied attributes to the selection.
Create Publisher (Macintosh only)	Removed.
Subscribe to (Macintosh only)	Removed. Select the **Link to file** check box in the **Object** dialog box (**Insert** menu) to insert an object that is updated automatically.
Subscriber Options (Macintosh only)	Removed.

When this PowerPoint 97 feature	Is saved in PowerPoint 4.0 format
Headers and footers	Headers and footers appear on the slides, but cannot be edited.
PowerPoint macros	PowerPoint macros are not converted; there is no macro language in PowerPoint 4.0.
Unicode characters (two bytes per character)	Unicode characters are mapped to corresponding ANSI (Windows) or one byte per character (Macintosh). Foreign language characters are most likely to be affected.

Upgrading from PowerPoint 3.0

This section describes the differences between PowerPoint version 3.0 for Windows or the Macintosh and PowerPoint 97. PowerPoint 97 is a major upgrade, with significant changes in the user interface and file format. For more information about the features and benefits of this upgrade, see Chapter 2, "What's New in Microsoft Office 97."

What happens to my old presentations when I convert them to PowerPoint 97? You can open presentations created in PowerPoint 3.0 directly in PowerPoint 97. All data and formatting created in PowerPoint 3.0 are fully supported by PowerPoint 97.

Can I share PowerPoint 97 presentations with users of previous versions of PowerPoint? If your workgroup uses a combination of PowerPoint 97 and 3.0, users can exchange presentations between versions. However, not all PowerPoint 97 features are supported in PowerPoint 3.0. For more information, see "Sharing Presentations with PowerPoint 3.0" later in this chapter.

Menu Changes

The following sections summarize the PowerPoint 3.0 commands that have changed location or functionality in PowerPoint 97, as well as commands that are new to PowerPoint 97.

File Menu

The following table describes changed commands on the **File** menu.

This PowerPoint 3.0 command	Changes to this in PowerPoint 97
Open Clip Art	Functionality moved to the **Clip Art** tab (**Insert** menu, **Picture** submenu).
Apply Template	Renamed **Apply Design** (**Format** menu).
Slide Setup	Renamed **Page Setup**.
Print Setup (Windows only)	Moved to the **Print** dialog box (**File** menu).

When this PowerPoint 97 feature	Is saved in PowerPoint 4.0 format
Shadows, engraved	Engraved shadows take on embossed shadow effects.
Shadows, perspective	Perspective shadows are converted as shapes and grouped with the shape casting the shadow.
Shapes or arcs with attached text that are new in PowerPoint 97	These are converted to PowerPoint 4.0 freeform shapes or arcs and text boxes.
Text box margins	Margins are averaged to center the text block in the box.
Text effects	Text effects are converted as pictures.
Textured fills	The shaded fill in the object is displayed. If there is no shaded fill, PowerPoint maps to the default fill color.
Thick compound line	Thick compound lines are converted as picture objects.
Two-color shaded fills	The color defined as Color 1 in PowerPoint 97 is displayed. If Color 1 is black, Color 2 is displayed instead.

Workgroup and Internet Features

The following table describes new features in PowerPoint 97 that may affect your data or formatting in previous versions.

When this PowerPoint 97 feature	Is saved in PowerPoint 4.0 format
Comments	Comments are converted to rich text format; hidden comments are displayed.
Hyperlinks that combine Play Sound with other interactive settings	The Play Sound settings are lost.
Hyperlinks within an object	The hyperlinks are lost.
Action settings embedded within an object.	The action settings are lost.

Other Features

The following table describes new features in PowerPoint 97 that may affect your data or formatting in previous versions.

When this PowerPoint 97 feature	Is saved in PowerPoint 4.0 format
Chart	Users cannot edit charts unless they have Microsoft Graph.
Clip Gallery	The clip art is rendered as a picture object; double-clicking clip art does not launch ClipArt Gallery in PowerPoint 4.0.

Graphics Features

The following table describes new features in PowerPoint 97 that may affect your data or formatting in previous versions.

When this PowerPoint 97 feature	Is saved in PowerPoint 4.0 format
3-D effects	3-D effects are converted as pictures.
Arrowheads	Arrowheads are matched to the nearest PowerPoint 4.0 style.
Automatic fills	The default fill color is displayed.
Automatic line colors	The default line color is displayed.
AutoShapes	AutoShapes are matched to the nearest PowerPoint 4.0 shape; if there is no matching shape, they are converted to freeform shapes.
Background patterns on slides	No pattern is applied.
Background pictures on slides	A corresponding picture object is displayed and sized to the fill the slide.
Background textures on slides	No texture is applied.
Black and white view	Slides are rendered in color.
Composite shapes	Composite shapes are converted to separate shapes and lines, which are grouped together.
Connectors	Connectors are converted as freeform lines, and lose their automatic connecting behavior.
Curves	Curves are approximated with connected line segments.
Dashed line style	Dashed lines are matched to the nearest PowerPoint 4.0 style.
Gradient fills	Semi-transparency is lost on gradient fills.
Joins and endcaps of lines	On AutoShapes, these become mitered joins and round endcaps. On freeform shapes, they become round joins and round endcaps.
Object patterns	Object patterns are matched to the nearest PowerPoint 4.0 pattern.
Objects that are linked or embedded	Brightness, contrast, and color transformation settings are lost.
Picture brightness, contrast, and color transformation	These are rendered at current PowerPoint 97 settings.
Picture fills	Picture fills are converted to picture objects.
Picture fills on shapes	The shape is given a solid fill with the last applied foreground color.
Preset shaded fills	No fill is applied.
Semi-transparent object fills	The closest solid color is displayed.

Because of changes to the PowerPoint file format, saving a PowerPoint 97 presentation in PowerPoint 4.0 can result in converted data or formatting that cannot be recovered in its original form. The following sections describe PowerPoint 97 features that are not fully supported in PowerPoint 4.0.

Basic Use Features

The following table describes new features in PowerPoint 97 that may affect your data or formatting in previous versions.

When this PowerPoint 97 feature	Is saved in PowerPoint 4.0 format
Animated chart elements	Animated chart elements are displayed as static chart objects. PowerPoint 4.0 users must have Microsoft Graph to edit charts.
Custom properties	Custom properties are lost.
Custom shows	Slides appear in the presentation, but they are not designated as a group.
Elevator effects	Elevator effects are converted to Wipe Up effects.
Embedded fonts	The embedded fonts are lost, and PowerPoint 4.0 assigns the closest font available.
Native format movies and sounds	Movies and sounds are converted to Media Player and Sound Recorder objects.
Play options for CD tracking and movie looping	Play options are ignored.
Presentation properties	The following presentation properties are preserved: Title, Subject, Author, Keywords, Comments, File Name (MS-DOS name), Directory, Template, and Slides. All other presentation properties are lost.
Preset animation settings	The settings are applied only to bulleted lists. All other effects are lost.

What happened to the TrueType fonts in my PowerPoint 97 presentation?

PowerPoint 4.0 does not support embedded TrueType® fonts. Therefore, when PowerPoint 97 users share presentations with 4.0 users, the **Embed TrueType** option in the **Save** dialog box (**File** menu) has no effect. Instead, PowerPoint 97 users must make sure that the fonts in the presentation are available on the 4.0 user's computer.

Sharing Presentations with PowerPoint 4.0

If your workgroup is upgrading gradually to PowerPoint 97, some users may have to share presentations with users of PowerPoint 4.0 for Windows or the Macintosh. These PowerPoint 97 users must save their presentations in PowerPoint 4.0 format.

World Wide Web For the latest information about converters that allow PowerPoint 4.0 users to open PowerPoint 97 presentations, connect to the PowerPoint home page at:

http://www.microsoft.com/powerpoint/

Saving PowerPoint 97 Presentations in PowerPoint 4.0 Format

PowerPoint 97 users can save presentations in PowerPoint 4.0 if they have the necessary converters. If you choose the Typical installation during Setup, the following converters are installed automatically.

Operating system	Converters
Windows	Pp7x32.dll, Pp7trans.dll, Pptview.dll.
Macintosh	Pp8x32, Pptview (PPC)

▶ **To save a presentation in PowerPoint 4.0 format**

1 On the **File** menu, click **Save As**.

2 In the **Save as type** box, click **PowerPoint 4.0**.

Tip End users can specify the default format in which PowerPoint saves new presentations.

▶ **To specify the default format in which to save presentations**

1 On the **Tools** menu, click **Options**, and then click the **Save** tab.

2 In the **Save PowerPoint files as** box, click the file format you want.

For more information about selecting a default format in which to save presentations, see "Specifying the Default Format in Which to Save Office Documents" in Chapter 22, "Supporting Multiple Versions of Microsoft Office."

Tip In Windows 95 and Windows NT Workstation 4.0, you can use a system policy to define the default value for the **Save as type** option in the **Save As** dialog box (**File** menu) for all PowerPoint users in your workgroup. In the System Policy Editor, set the following policy:

User\PowerPoint\Tools_Options\Save\Default Save

For more information, see "Using Windows System Policies to Customize Office" in Chapter 7, "Customizing and Optimizing Microsoft Office."

Apple Help Menu (Macintosh Only)

The following table describes changed commands on the **Apple Help** menu.

This PowerPoint 4.0 command	Changes to this in PowerPoint 97
PowerPoint Contents and **PowerPoint Index**	Consolidated in **Contents and Index**.
PowerPoint Search For Help On, **PowerPoint Tip of the Day**, and **PowerPoint Cue Cards**	Removed. Use **Microsoft PowerPoint Help** to display the Assistant, through which you view Help.
PowerPoint Quick Preview	Removed.
PowerPoint Technical Support	Functionality moved to the **Tech Support** button on the **About Microsoft PowerPoint** dialog box (**Apple Help** menu).

The following table lists new commands that have been added to the **Apple Help** menu.

This PowerPoint 97 command	Allows you to
Contents and Index	Display PowerPoint Help.
What's This?	Click any area of the screen (such as a toolbar or menu command) to see a brief explanation in Balloon Help.
Microsoft on the Web	Connect to the Microsoft home page on the Web (requires Internet access).

File Format Changes

The PowerPoint 97 file format differs from that of PowerPoint 4.0. If your workgroup is upgrading gradually to PowerPoint 97, some users may have to share workbooks with users of PowerPoint 97. PowerPoint supports several strategies for sharing presentations among different versions. For more information about changes in file format and strategies for sharing presentations, see "Sharing Presentations with PowerPoint 4.0" later in this chapter.

Template Changes

The presentation templates included with PowerPoint 97 take advantage of the enhanced animation capabilities of PowerPoint 97, which allow users to apply animation effects to objects on the title master and slide master. Although the file format for PowerPoint 97 differs from that of PowerPoint 4.0, PowerPoint 97 and 4.0 users can exchange templates; however, animated features in a PowerPoint 97 template are lost when the template is converted to PowerPoint 4.0 format.

This PowerPoint 97 command	Allows you to
Custom Animation	Define animation, sound effects, and timing for objects on a slide.
Animation Preview	View the current slide in miniature, including all animation associated with the slide.
Slide Transition	Define special effects for progressing from one slide to the next in a slide show.
Hide Slide	Skip a selected slide during a slide show.
Custom Shows	Create sections within presentations, making it easier to tailor presentations for specific audiences.

Action Menu (Windows Only)

The **Action** menu appears only when Lotus **NotesFlow** commands are associated with the active presentation. PowerPoint displays the custom actions that have been defined for the active presentation on the **Action** menu. For more information about how Office integrates Lotus Notes, see "Interoperability with Lotus Notes/FX" in Chapter 28, "Working with Messaging Systems and Connectivity Software."

Help Menu (Windows Only)

The following table describes changed commands on the **Help** menu.

This PowerPoint 4.0 command	Changes to this in PowerPoint 97
Contents and **Index**	Consolidated in **Contents and Index**.
Search For Help On, **Tip of the Day**, and **Cue Cards**	Removed. Use **Microsoft PowerPoint Help** to display the Office Assistant, through which you view Help.
Quick Preview	Removed.
Technical Support	Functionality moved to the **Tech Support** button in the **About Microsoft PowerPoint** dialog box (**Help** menu).

The following table lists new commands that have been added to the **Help** menu.

This PowerPoint 97 command	Allows you to
Contents and Index	Display PowerPoint Help.
What's This?	Click any area of the screen (such as a toolbar or menu command) to see a brief explanation in a ScreenTip.
Microsoft on the Web	Connect to the Microsoft home page on the Web (requires Internet access).

This PowerPoint 97 command	Allows you to
Expand Slide	Generate a new slide based on the body text of the active slide.
Macro submenu commands	Create, run, and manage macros; edit Visual Basic code.
Add-Ins	Load a Visual Basic procedure or a DLL into the current session of PowerPoint.

Draw Menu

The **Draw** menu, along with most of its commands, has been moved to the **Drawing** toolbar in PowerPoint 97. The following table describes **Draw** menu commands that have additionally changed location or functionality in PowerPoint 4.0.

This PowerPoint 4.0 command	Changes to this in PowerPoint 97
Bring to Front, **Send to Back**, **Bring Forward**, and **Send Backward**	Moved to the **Order** submenu.
Snap to Grid	Moved to the **Snap** submenu.
Scale	Functionality moved to the **Size** tab in the **Format** *Object* dialog box (**Format** menu).

Slide Show Menu

The **Slide Show** menu is new in PowerPoint 97. It contains many commands that were on the **Tools** menu in PowerPoint 4.0. In addition, the following table lists new commands that have been added to the **Slide Show** menu.

This PowerPoint 97 command	Allows you to
View Show	Launch your slide show in full screen view.
Rehearse Timings	Capture timings as you rehearse the presentation.
Record Narration	Make an audio recording to narrate the slide show.
Set Up Show	Define the type of show, a range of slides, advance method, and pen color.
View On Two Screens	Show a presentation from one computer on another through a serial connection.
Action Buttons	Place a button with interactive settings on a slide.
Action Settings	Define an action for the object, such as playing a sound when the object is clicked during a slide show.
Preset Animation	Apply animation effects to the selected object.

Tools Menu

The following table describes changed commands on the **Tools** menu.

This PowerPoint 4.0 command	Changes to this in PowerPoint 97
Replace Fonts	Moved to **Format** menu.
Transition	Renamed **Slide Transition** (**Slide Show** menu).
Build	Renamed **Preset Animation** (**Slide Show** menu).
Hide Slide	Moved to **Slide Show** menu.
Play Settings	Renamed **Custom Animation** (**Slide Show** menu).
Recolor	Moved to the **Picture** tab in the **Format Picture** dialog box (**Format** menu). The **Picture** command is available only when a picture is selected.
Crop Picture	Removed. Use the **Crop** button (**Picture** toolbar) to crop pictures.

The following table lists new commands that have been added to the **Tools** menu.

This PowerPoint 97 command	Allows you to
Style Checker	Check for consistency in spelling, visual clarity, and case and end punctuation.
Language	Format the selected characters as foreign language characters.
AutoCorrect	Automatically correct errors, using a customizable list of text substitutions and rules.
Look Up Reference	Find a selected word or phrase in Bookshelf 97. (This command is available only if Bookshelf is installed.) For more information, see Chapter 27, "Sharing Information with Microsoft Office Applications."
AutoClipArt	Select clip art that matches concepts in your presentation.
PowerPoint Central	Open a file on the Office CD or connect to a Web site to download clip art, photos, sound files, templates, or other PowerPoint resources.
Presentation Conference	Show or view a presentation with other members of your workgroup.
Meeting Minder	Display notes pages, meeting minutes, and action items.

Format Menu

The following table describes changed commands on the **Format** menu.

This PowerPoint 4.0 command	Changes to this in PowerPoint 97
Periods	Removed. Use the **Periods** button to add or remove periods. (For information about adding buttons to toolbars, see PowerPoint online Help.)
Text Anchor	Functionality moved to the **Text Box** tab in the Format AutoShape dialog box (**Format** menu). The AutoShape command is available on when an AutoShape is selected.
Shadow	Removed. Use the **Shadow** button (**Drawing** toolbar) to create shadows.
Pick Up Object/Text Style	Removed. Use the **Format Painter** button (**Standard** toolbar) to copy the attributes of the selection.
Apply Object/Text Style	Removed. Use the **Format Painter** button (**Standard** toolbar) to apply copied attributes to the selection.
Presentation Template	Renamed **Apply Design** (**Format** menu).
Pick A Look Wizard	Removed. Use the AutoContent Wizard on the **Presentations** tab in the **New Presentations** dialog box (**File** menu) to choose an overall style for your presentation.
Slide Background	Renamed **Background**.

The following table lists new commands that have been added to the **Format** menu.

This PowerPoint 97 command	Allows you to
Replace Fonts	Replace one font with another throughout a presentation. This command was moved from the **Tools** menu.
Object	Choose settings for the active object.

Note The **Object** command changes based on the object selected on the slide. If nothing is selected, or if more than one type of object is selected, the command is **Object**. If a picture is selected, the command is **Picture**; if a text box is selected, the command is **Text Box**. If anything else is selected, the command is **AutoShape**.

View Menu

The following table describes changed commands on the **View** menu.

This PowerPoint 4.0 command	Changes to this in PowerPoint 97
Outline Master	Removed. Use **Handout Master** (**Master** submenu) to adjust the layout of handouts and outlines.

The following table lists new commands that have been added to the **View** menu.

This PowerPoint 97 command	Allows you to
Black and White	View color slides in black and white.
Slide Miniature	View a color thumbnail of the current slide.
Speaker Notes	Create and view notes for each slide in your presentation.
Header and Footer	Create headers and footers that appear on every slide in a presentation.
Comments	Display or hide comments on a slide.

Insert Menu

The following table describes changed commands on the **Insert** menu.

This PowerPoint 4.0 command	Changes to this in PowerPoint 97
Date and **Time**	Consolidated in **Date and Time**.
Page Number	Renamed **Slide Number**.
Clip Art	Moved to **Picture** submenu.
Microsoft Word Table	Moved to **Picture** submenu.
Microsoft Graph	Renamed **Chart**.

The following table lists new commands that have been added to the **Insert** menu.

This PowerPoint 97 command	Allows you to
Duplicate Slide	Duplicate a slide in slide view.
Tab	Create a tab stop.
Symbol	Place a symbol character on a slide.
Comment	Add comments to a slide.
Picture submenu commands	Insert a picture.
Movies and Sounds submenu commands	Insert a movie or sound clip.
Hyperlink	Insert a Web-style hyperlink to another Office document. For more information about hyperlinks, see Chapter 24, "Integrating Microsoft Office With Your Intranet."

This PowerPoint 4.0 command	Changes to this in PowerPoint 97
Find File	Removed. Use the **New Presentation** dialog box (**File** menu) to locate presentations.
Summary Info	Renamed **Properties**.
Slide Setup	Renamed **Page Setup**.
Send	Renamed **Mail Recipient** (**Send To** submenu).
Add Routing Slip	Renamed **Routing Recipient** (**Send To** submenu).

The following table lists new commands that have been added to the **File** menu.

This PowerPoint 97 command	Allows you to
Save as HTML	Convert a presentation so that it can be read by a Web browser.
Pack and Go	Package your presentation to deliver on another computer.
Send To submenu commands	Send a presentation to others electronically. For more information about sending presentations through e-mail, see Chapter 28, "Working with Messaging Systems and Connectivity Software."

Edit Menu

The following table describes changed commands on the **Edit** menu.

This PowerPoint 4.0 command	Changes to this in PowerPoint 97
Create Publisher (Macintosh only)	Removed.
Subscribe to (Macintosh only)	Removed. Click **From File** in the **Object** dialog box (**Insert** menu), and then select the **Link to file** check box to insert an object that is updated automatically.
Subscriber Options (Macintosh only)	Removed.

The following table lists new commands that have been added to the **Edit** menu.

This PowerPoint 97 command	Allows you to
Repeat or **Redo**	Repeat or redo your last action.
Paste as Hyperlink	Paste and format the Clipboard contents as a hyperlink. You must then edit the hyperlink using the **Hyperlink** command (**Insert** menu) to specify a file or URL to which the selected text is to be linked.
Go to Property	Go to the assigned custom property fields.

Other Features

The following table describes new features in PowerPoint 97 that may affect your data or formatting in previous versions.

When this PowerPoint 97 feature	Is saved in PowerPoint 95 format
Charts	Users cannot edit charts unless they have Microsoft Graph.
Clip Gallery	The clip art is rendered as a picture object; double-clicking clip art does not launch ClipArt Gallery in PowerPoint 95.
PowerPoint macros	PowerPoint macros are not converted; there is no macro language in PowerPoint 95.
Unicode characters (two bytes per character)	Unicode characters are mapped to corresponding ANSI. Foreign language characters are most likely to be affected.

Upgrading from PowerPoint 4.0

This section describes the differences between PowerPoint version 4.0 for Windows or the Macintosh and PowerPoint 97. PowerPoint 97 is a major upgrade with significant changes in the user interface and file format. For more information about the features and benefits of this upgrade, see Chapter 2, "What's New in Microsoft Office 97."

What happens to my old presentations when I convert them to PowerPoint 97? You can open presentations created in PowerPoint 4.0 directly in PowerPoint 97. All data and formatting created in PowerPoint 4.0 are fully supported by PowerPoint 97.

Can I share PowerPoint 97 presentations with users of previous versions of PowerPoint? If your workgroup uses a combination of PowerPoint 97, 95, and 4.0, users can exchange presentations between versions. However, not all PowerPoint 97 features are supported in PowerPoint 4.0. For more information, see "Sharing Presentations with PowerPoint 4.0" later in this chapter.

Menu Changes

The following sections summarize the PowerPoint 4.0 commands that have changed location or functionality in PowerPoint 97, as well as commands that are new in PowerPoint 97.

File Menu

The following table describes changed commands on the **File** menu.

Why is my AutoShape a different size?

When PowerPoint 97 converts a PowerPoint 95 AutoShape to PowerPoint 97 format, the AutoShape changes from an inset pen outline to a centered pen outline. Likewise, when a PowerPoint 97 AutoShape is saved in PowerPoint 95 format, it is rendered with an inset, rather than centered, pen.

It is easiest to see the difference between inset and centered pen by outlining an AutoShape with a dashed line. The fill color of the AutoShape allows you to see the difference in pen position through the gaps of the dashed line, as shown in the following illustration.

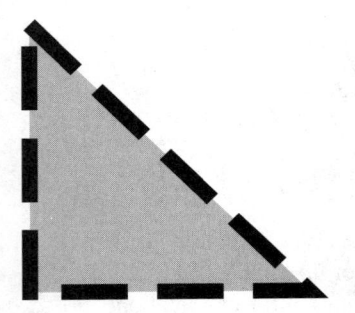

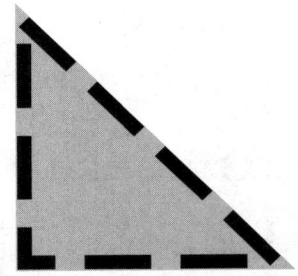

PowerPoint 97 AutoShape: Centered pen

PowerPoint 95 AutoShape: Inset pen

Because the size of shapes drawn with a centered pen may be slightly larger than the same shape drawn with an inset pen, users may need to reduce the size of AutoShapes drawn in PowerPoint 95 to make them look exactly the same in PowerPoint 97.

Workgroup and Internet Features

The following table describes new features in PowerPoint 97 that may affect your data or formatting in previous versions.

When this PowerPoint 97 feature	Is saved in PowerPoint 95 format
Comments	Comments are converted to rich text format; hidden comments are displayed.
Hyperlinks that combine Play Sound with other action settings	Play Sound settings are lost.
Hyperlinks embedded within an object	The hyperlinks are lost.
Action settings embedded within an object.	The action settings are lost.

When this PowerPoint 97 feature	Is saved in PowerPoint 95 format
Composite shapes	Composite shapes are converted to separate shapes and lines, which are grouped together.
Connectors	Connectors are converted as freeform lines, and lose their automatic connecting behavior.
Curves	Curves are approximated with connected line segments.
Gradient fills	Semi-transparency is lost on gradient fills.
Joins and endcaps of lines	On AutoShapes, these become mitered joins and round endcaps. On freeform shapes, they become round joins and round endcaps.
Objects that are linked or embedded	Brightness, contrast, and color transformation settings are lost.
Picture brightness, contrast, and color transformation	These are rendered at current PowerPoint 97 settings.
Picture fills	Picture fills are converted to picture objects.
Picture fills on shapes	The shape is converted as a picture object and is given a solid fill with the last applied foreground color.
Shadows, engraved	Engraved shadows take on embossed shadow effects.
Shadows, perspective	Perspective shadows are converted as shapes and grouped with the shape casting the shadow.
Shapes or arcs with attached text that are new in PowerPoint 97	These are converted to PowerPoint 95 freeform shapes or arcs and text boxes.
Text box margins	Margins are averaged to center the text block in the box.
Text effects	Text effects are converted as pictures.
Thick compound lines	Thick compound lines are converted as picture objects.

For more information about selecting a default format in which to save presentations, see "Specifying the Default Format in Which to Save Office Documents" in Chapter 22, "Supporting Multiple Versions of Microsoft Office."

Tip In Windows 95 and Windows NT Workstation 4.0, you can use a system policy to define the default value for the **Save as type** option in the **Save As** dialog box (**File** menu) for all PowerPoint users in your workgroup. In the System Policy Editor, set the following policy:

User\PowerPoint\Tools_Options\Save\Default Save

For more information, see "Using Windows System Policies to Customize Office" in Chapter 7, "Customizing and Optimizing Microsoft Office."

Because of changes to the PowerPoint file format, saving a PowerPoint 97 presentation in PowerPoint 95 format can result in converted data or formatting that cannot be recovered in its original form. The following sections describe PowerPoint 97 features that are not fully supported in PowerPoint 95.

Basic Use Features

The following table describes new features in PowerPoint 97 that may affect your data or formatting in previous versions.

When this PowerPoint 97 feature	Is saved in PowerPoint 95 format
Animated chart elements	Animated chart elements are displayed as static chart objects. PowerPoint 95 users must have Microsoft Graph to edit charts.
Custom shows	Slides appear in the presentation, but they are not designated as a group.
Elevator effects	Elevator effects are converted to Wipe Up effects.
Native format movies and sounds	Movies and sounds are converted to Media Player and Sound Recorder objects.
Play options for CD tracking and movie looping	Play options are ignored.

Graphics Features

The following table describes new features in PowerPoint 97 that may affect your data or formatting in previous versions. In general, graphics features in PowerPoint 97 are converted to their closest equivalent in PowerPoint 95.

When this PowerPoint 97 feature	Is saved in PowerPoint 95 format
3-D effects	3-D effects are converted as pictures.
AutoShapes	If there is no matching shape, AutoShapes are converted to freeform shapes.

Part 3   Upgrading to Microsoft Office

▶ **To save a presentation in PowerPoint 95 & 97 format**

1   On the **File** menu, click **Save As**.
2   In the **Save as type** box, click **PowerPoint 95 & 97 Presentation**.

Tip   End users can specify the default format in which PowerPoint 97 saves new presentations.

▶ **To specify the default format in which to save presentations**

1   On the **Tools** menu, click **Options**, and then click the **Save** tab.
2   In the **Save PowerPoint files as** box, click the file format you want.

For more information about selecting a default format in which to save presentations, see "Specifying the Default Format in Which to Save Office Documents" in Chapter 22, "Supporting Multiple Versions of Microsoft Office."

Tip   In Windows 95 and Windows NT Workstation 4.0, you can use a system policy to define the default value for the **Save as type** option in the **Save As** dialog box (**File** menu) for all PowerPoint users in your workgroup. In the System Policy Editor, set the following policy:

User\PowerPoint\Tools_Options\Save\Default Save

For more information, see "Using Windows System Policies to Customize Office" in Chapter 7, "Customizing and Optimizing Microsoft Office."

Because the 95 & 97 format stores both PowerPoint 97 and 95 data streams in a single file, the file is up to one and a half times as large as it would be if saved in PowerPoint 97 format. Although file open time is not affected, file save time in PowerPoint 97 increases. Otherwise the 95 & 97 format has no effect on performance.

Saving Presentations in PowerPoint 95 Format

PowerPoint 97 users can save presentations in PowerPoint 95 format if they have the necessary converter. If you choose the Typical installation during Setup, this converter (Pp8x32.dll) is installed automatically.

▶ **To save a presentation in PowerPoint 95 format**

1   On the **File** menu, click **Save As**.
2   In the **Save as type** box, click **PowerPoint 95**.

Tip   End users can specify the default format in which PowerPoint saves new presentations.

▶ **To specify the default format in which to save presentations**

1   On the **Tools** menu, click **Options**, and then click the **Save** tab.
2   In the **Save PowerPoint files as** box, click the file format you want.

Chapter 14 Upgrading from Previous Versions of Microsoft PowerPoint

Sharing Presentations with PowerPoint 95

If your workgroup is upgrading gradually to PowerPoint 97, some users may have to share presentations with users of PowerPoint 95. There are two strategies for sharing presentations between these versions of PowerPoint:

- Save presentations in the dual PowerPoint 95 & 97 format.
- Save PowerPoint 97 presentations in PowerPoint 95 format.

The following table summarizes the advantages and disadvantages of each strategy.

Strategy	Advantages	Disadvantages
Save PowerPoint 97 presentations in dual PowerPoint 95 & 97 format.	All PowerPoint users can open presentations. PowerPoint 97 users can edit and save presentations.	Presentation file size and save time increase.
Save PowerPoint 97 presentations in PowerPoint 95 format.	All PowerPoint users can open, edit, and save presentations. Graphic fidelity is preserved in the conversion.	If a PowerPoint 95 user saves the presentation, features unique to PowerPoint 97 are lost.

World Wide Web For the latest information about converters that allow PowerPoint 95 users to open PowerPoint 97 presentations, connect to the PowerPoint home page at:

http://www.microsoft.com/powerpoint/

Saving Presentations in PowerPoint 95 & 97 Format

The new PowerPoint 95 & 97 file format is designed for workgroups upgrading gradually to PowerPoint 97. You can standardize your workgroup on this format until your PowerPoint 95 users have upgraded to PowerPoint 97. This ensures that all of your PowerPoint users have a common file format with which to collaborate on presentations.

When a PowerPoint 97 user saves a presentation in the 95 & 97 format, PowerPoint creates two data streams in the presentation file: one for PowerPoint 97, and another for PowerPoint 95. When writing the 95 data stream, PowerPoint has the same conversion limitations described in "Saving Presentations in PowerPoint 95 Format" later in this chapter.

When PowerPoint 95 users open a presentation saved in 95 & 97 format, they must open the presentation read-only. PowerPoint 95 reads only the 95 data stream in the file. When it encounters the end of the 95 data stream, it disregards the remainder of the file (that is, the 97 data stream). Consequently, if a PowerPoint 95 user saves the presentation with a new name, the 97 data stream is permanently lost. Similarly, if a PowerPoint 97 user opens a presentation saved in 95 & 97 format and then saves the file in 97 format only, the 95 data stream is lost.

The following table lists new commands that have been added to the **Help** menu.

This PowerPoint 97 command	Allows you to
Contents and Index	Display PowerPoint Help.
What's This?	Click any area of the screen (such as a toolbar or menu command) to see a brief explanation in a ScreenTip.
Microsoft on the Web	Connect to the Microsoft home page on the Web (requires Internet access).

File Format Changes

The PowerPoint 97 file format differs from that of PowerPoint 95. If your workgroup is upgrading gradually to PowerPoint 97, some users may have to share workbooks with users of PowerPoint 97. PowerPoint supports several strategies for sharing presentations among different versions. For more information about changes in file format and strategies for sharing presentations, see "Sharing Presentations with PowerPoint 95" later in this chapter.

Template Changes

The presentation templates included with PowerPoint 97 take advantage of the enhanced animation capabilities of PowerPoint 97, which allow users to apply animation effects to objects on the title master and slide master. Although the file format for PowerPoint 97 differs from that of PowerPoint 95, PowerPoint 97 and 95 users can exchange templates; however, animated features in a PowerPoint 97 template are lost when the template is converted to PowerPoint 95 format.

This PowerPoint 97 command	Allows you to
Record Narration	Make an audio recording to narrate the slide show.
Set Up Show	Define the type of show, a range of slides, advance method, and pen color.
View On Two Screens	Show a presentation from one computer on another through a serial connection.
Action Buttons	Place a button with interactive settings on a slide.
Action Settings	Define an action for the object, such as playing a sound when the object is clicked during a slide show.
Preset Animation	Apply animation effects to the selected object.
Custom Animation	Define animation, sound effects, and timing for objects on a slide.
Animation Preview	View the current slide in miniature, including all animation associated with the slide.
Slide Transition	Define special effects for progressing from one slide to the next in a slide show. This command was moved from the **Tools** menu.
Hide Slide	Skip a selected slide during a slide show. This command was moved from the **Tools** menu.
Custom Shows	Create sections within presentations, making it easier to tailor presentations for specific audiences.

Action Menu (Windows Only)

The **Action** menu appears only when Lotus **NotesFlow** commands are associated with the active presentation. PowerPoint displays the custom actions that have been defined for the active presentation on the **Action** menu. For more information about how Office integrates Lotus Notes, see "Interoperability with Lotus Notes/FX" in Chapter 28, "Working with Messaging Systems and Connectivity Software."

Help Menu (Windows only)

The following table describes changed commands on the **Help** menu.

This PowerPoint 95 command	Changes to this in PowerPoint 97
Microsoft PowerPoint Help Topics	Renamed **Microsoft PowerPoint Help**. This command displays the Office Assistant, through which you view Help.
Answer Wizard	Removed. Gain access to the Answer Wizard feature through the Assistant.
Tip of the Day	Removed. Use **Microsoft PowerPoint Help** to display the Assistant, through which you view tips.

The following table lists new commands that have been added to the **Tools** menu.

This PowerPoint 97 command	Allows you to
Language	Format the selected characters as foreign language characters.
Look Up Reference	Find a selected word or phrase in Bookshelf 97. (This command is available only if Bookshelf is installed). For more information, see Chapter 27, "Sharing Information with Microsoft Office Applications."
PowerPoint Central	Open a file on the Office CD or connect to a Web site to download clip art, photos, sound files, templates, or other PowerPoint resources.
Expand Slide	Generate a new slide based on the body text of the active slide.
Macro submenu commands	Create, run, and manage macros; edit Visual Basic for Applications code.
Add-Ins	Load a Visual Basic procedure or a DLL into the current session of PowerPoint.

Draw Menu

The **Draw** menu, along with most of its commands, has been moved to the **Drawing** toolbar in PowerPoint 97. The following table describes **Draw** menu commands that have additionally changed location or functionality in PowerPoint 97.

This PowerPoint 95 command	Changes to this in PowerPoint 97
Bring to Front, **Send to Back**, **Bring Forward**, and **Send Backward**	Moved to the **Order** submenu.
Snap to Grid	Moved to the **Snap** submenu.
Scale	Functionality moved to the **Size** tab in the **Format** *Object* dialog box (**Format** menu).

Slide Show Menu

The **Slide Show** menu is new in PowerPoint 97. It contains many commands that were on the **Tools** menu in PowerPoint 95. In addition, the following table lists new commands that have been added to the **Slide Show** menu.

This PowerPoint 97 command	Allows you to
View Show	Launch your slide show in full screen view.
Rehearse Timings	Capture timings as you rehearse a presentation.

Chapter 14   Upgrading from Previous Versions of Microsoft PowerPoint

This PowerPoint 95 command	Changes to this in PowerPoint 97
Shadow	Removed. Use the **Shadow** button (**Drawing** toolbar) to create shadows.
Pick Up Object/Text Style	Removed. Use the **Format Painter** button (**Standard** toolbar) to copy the attributes of the selection.
Apply Object/Text Style	Removed. Use the **Format Painter** button (**Standard** toolbar) to apply copied attributes to the selection.
Custom Background	Renamed **Background**.

The following table lists new commands that have been added to the **Format** menu.

This PowerPoint 97 command	Allows you to
Replace Fonts	Replace one font with another throughout a presentation. This command was moved from the **Tools** menu.
Object	Choose settings for the active object.

Note   The **Object** command changes based on the object selected on the slide. If nothing is selected, or if more than one type of object is selected, the command is **Object**. If a picture is selected, the command is **Picture**; if a text box is selected, the command is **Text Box**. If anything else is selected, the command is **AutoShape**.

Tools Menu

The following table describes changed commands on the **Tools** menu.

This PowerPoint 95 command	Changes to this in PowerPoint 97
Replace Fonts	Moved to **Format** menu.
Slide Transition	Moved to **Slide Show** menu.
Hide Slide	Moved to **Slide Show** menu.
Build Slide Text	Renamed **Preset Animation** (**Slide Show** menu).
Animation Settings	Renamed **Custom Animation** (**Slide Show** menu).
Interactive Settings	Renamed **Action Settings** (**Slide Show** menu).
Write-Up	Renamed **Microsoft Word** (**File** menu, **Send To** submenu).
Recolor	Moved to the **Picture** tab in the **Format Picture** dialog box (**Format** menu).
Crop Picture	Removed. Use the **Crop** button (**Picture** toolbar) to crop pictures.

View Menu

The following table lists new commands that have been added to the **View** menu.

This PowerPoint 97 command	Allows you to
Speaker Notes	Create and view notes for each slide in your presentation. This feature was part of Meeting Minder in PowerPoint 95.
Comments	Display or hide comments on a slide.

Insert Menu

The following table describes changed commands on the **Insert** menu.

This PowerPoint 95 command	Changes to this in PowerPoint 97
Clip Art	Moved to **Picture** submenu.
Movie and **Sound**	Consolidated in **Movies and Sounds**.
Microsoft Graph	Renamed **Chart**.
Microsoft Word Table	Moved to **Picture** submenu.

The following table lists new commands that have been added to the **Insert** menu.

This PowerPoint 97 command	Allows you to
Duplicate Slide	Duplicate a slide in slide view.
Symbol	Place a symbol character on a slide.
Comment	Add comments to a slide.
Picture submenu commands	Insert a picture.
Movies and Sounds submenu commands	Insert a movie or sound clip.
Hyperlink	Insert a Web-style hyperlink to another Office document. For more information about hyperlinks, see Chapter 24, "Integrating Microsoft Office With Your Intranet."

Format Menu

The following table describes changed commands on the **Format** menu.

This PowerPoint 95 command	Changes to this in PowerPoint 97
Periods	Removed. Use the **Periods** button to add or remove periods. (For information about adding buttons to toolbars, see PowerPoint online Help.)
Text Anchor	Functionality moved to the **Text Box** tab in the **Format AutoShape** dialog box (**Format** menu). The **AutoShape** command is available only when an AutoShape is selected.

Menu Changes

The following sections summarize the PowerPoint 95 commands that have changed location or functionality in PowerPoint 97, as well as commands that are new in PowerPoint 97.

File Menu

The following table describes changed commands on the **File** menu.

This PowerPoint 95 command	Changes to this in PowerPoint 97
Slide Setup	Renamed **Page Setup**
Send to Genigraphics	Renamed **Genigraphics** (**Send To** submenu).
Send	Renamed **Mail Recipient** (**Send To** submenu).
Add Routing Slip	Renamed **Routing Recipient** (**Send To** submenu).
Post to Exchange Folder	Renamed **Exchange Folder** (**Send To** submenu).

The following table lists new commands that have been added to the **File** menu.

This PowerPoint 97 command	Allows you to
Save as HTML	Convert a presentation so that it can be read by a World Wide Web browser.
Send To submenu commands	Send a presentation to others electronically. For more information about sending presentations through e-mail, see Chapter 28, "Working with Messaging Systems and Connectivity Software."

Edit Menu

The following table lists new commands that have been added to the **Edit** menu.

This PowerPoint 97 command	Allows you to
Paste as Hyperlink	Paste and format the Clipboard contents as a hyperlink. Edit the hyperlink using the **Hyperlink** command (**Insert** menu) to specify a file or URL to which the selected text is connected.

If you are upgrading from PowerPoint 3.0, 4.0, or 95, this chapter answers these questions for you.

As the following illustration shows, several versions of PowerPoint for Windows and for the Macintosh share the same file format. You can exchange presentations directly within these common file formats; you do not need to install special converters.

Common File Formats in PowerPoint

Operating System				
Windows	3.0	4.0	95	97
Macintosh	3.0	4.0		97

Before you can exchange PowerPoint presentations between different file formats, however, you must first install converters that are included with PowerPoint or with the Office Resource Kit Tools and Utilities. For more information, see the section later in this chapter that describes the version from which you are upgrading.

To convert a presentation from an earlier version of PowerPoint to PowerPoint 97, simply open the presentation. The presentation opens as a read-only file. To complete the conversion, save the presentation with a new name in PowerPoint 97 format.

Tools and Utilities The Office Resource Kit Tools and Utilities include a conversion utility you can use to convert several presentations to PowerPoint 97 format at once. For more information about installing the batch converter, see "PowerPoint Converters" in Appendix A, "Microsoft Office 97 Resource Kit Tools and Utilities."

Upgrading from PowerPoint 95

This section describes the differences between PowerPoint 95 and PowerPoint 97. PowerPoint 97 is a major upgrade with changes in the user interface and file format. For more information about the features and benefits of this upgrade, see Chapter 2, "What's New in Microsoft Office 97."

What happens to my old presentations when I convert them to PowerPoint 97? You can open presentations created in PowerPoint 95 directly in PowerPoint 97. All data and formatting created in PowerPoint 95 are fully supported by PowerPoint 97.

Can I share PowerPoint 97 presentations with users of previous versions of PowerPoint? If your workgroup uses a combination of PowerPoint 97and 95, users can exchange presentations between these versions. However, not all PowerPoint 97 features are supported in PowerPoint 95. For more information, see "Sharing Presentations with PowerPoint 95" later in this chapter.

CHAPTER 14

Upgrading from Previous Versions of Microsoft PowerPoint

This chapter tells you what to expect when you or your workgroup upgrades to PowerPoint 97 from a previous version of PowerPoint. If you plan a gradual upgrade, users of different versions of PowerPoint may need to share presentations. This chapter describes PowerPoint 97 features that are not supported in previous versions, which may result in loss of data or formatting.

In This Chapter
Overview   361
Upgrading from PowerPoint 95   362
Sharing Presentations with PowerPoint 95   369
Upgrading from PowerPoint 4.0   374
Sharing Presentations with PowerPoint 4.0   382
Upgrading from PowerPoint 3.0   386
Sharing Presentations with PowerPoint 3.0   396

See Also
- For a summary of new and improved features in PowerPoint 97, see Chapter 2, "What's New in Microsoft Office 97."
- For information about installing PowerPoint or other Office applications, see Chapter 4, "Installing Microsoft Office."
- For information about switching to PowerPoint from other presentation applications, see Chapter 20, "Switching to Microsoft PowerPoint."

Overview

The primary questions most PowerPoint 97 upgraders have are:
- What happens to my old presentations when I open them in PowerPoint 97?
- Can I share PowerPoint 97 presentations with users of previous versions?

Managing Group Scheduling

Outlook and Schedule+ users can freely send and receive meeting requests and responses for group scheduling, although there are some restrictions in how Schedule+ users are able to interact with Outlook. These restrictions are discussed in the following sections.

Sending Meeting Requests and Responses

Outlook and Schedule+ users can freely send and receive meeting requests and responses for group scheduling.

However, advanced features in Outlook meeting requests—such as attachments, meeting locations, and recurring meetings—are not recognized by Schedule+ 1.0. If an Outlook user sends a recurring meeting request to a Schedule+ user, the Schedule+ user receives only the first request.

Viewing Free/Busy Information

Outlook users are able to see whether Schedule+ 1.0 users are free or busy in the **Meeting Planner** tab of an appointment, event, or meeting request item. Schedule+ users can also see whether Outlook users are free or busy in the Schedule+ **Planner** tab.

Viewing Free/Busy Details

Outlook users cannot display the free or busy details of Schedule+ 1.0 users as they can with Schedule+ 95 users. This feature is not available in Schedule+ 1.0.

Viewing or Editing Another User's Calendar

If an Outlook user has been given permission to view or edit another user's calendar, the Outlook user can open the other user's calendar by right-clicking the user's name in the **Meeting Planner** tab of a meeting request, and then clicking **Open Attendee's Calendar**. This capability is available whether the other user is running Outlook or Schedule+.

Note While Schedule+ users can view details or edit calendars of other Schedule+ users, a Schedule+ user cannot open an Outlook user's calendar.

> ### Why do Outlook and Schedule+ synchronize my calendar differently?
>
> Both Outlook and Schedule+ allow you to keep synchronized copies of the calendar folder on the server and on your hard disk. However, the two applications use different methods for keeping offline and server copies of the folder synchronized.
>
> For group scheduling, Schedule+ always maintains a copy of your calendar on the server. Every time you connect to the server, Schedule+ automatically synchronizes the server and the local copies, and continues to keep them synchronized as you make changes to the calendar. Because Schedule+ always keeps a server copy of the calendar when you're working online, you may not be aware that the calendar is being synchronized with the local copy.
>
> Outlook, on the other hand, allows you to keep folders on the server, on a hard disk, or both. If you choose to have both a server and local copy of a folder, you can configure Outlook to synchronize the folder automatically when you exit using options in the **Options** dialog box (**Tools** menu). Or you can synchronize the folder manually using the **Synchronize** command (**Tools** menu).
>
> Synchronization conflicts (for example, an assistant accepts a meeting request while your local copy of the schedule is offline) are handled automatically with Schedule+. In Outlook, however, you may receive a conflict resolution message and must resolve conflicts manually if updates are made to your Calendar folder while you are offline.

Sharing Information with Microsoft Schedule+ 1.0

If your workgroup is upgrading gradually to Outlook, some Outlook users may need to exchange e-mail and share public folders with Schedule+ 1.0 users. Although Outlook and Schedule+ have been designed to make sharing information easy, Outlook uses a different format for storing information.

Important Whenever Outlook and Schedule+ 1.0 share information, Outlook uses Schedule+ 95 to read and interpret Schedule+ 1.0 data. This requires that Schedule+ 95 be installed on your computer. If Schedule+ 95 is not installed, Outlook cannot read any of the Schedule+ 1.0 information.

There are several areas in which Outlook and Schedule+ users can share information, as described in the following sections.

4 To replace duplicate entries in your Outlook folder with Schedule+ entries, click **Replace duplicates with items imported**.

   –or–

   To allow duplicate entries to be imported, click **Allow duplicates to be created**.

   –or–

   To avoid importing duplicate entries, click **Do not import duplicate items**.

5 If requested, enter the password for the schedule file.

6 In **The following actions will be performed** box, select the items you want to import and their destination folders.

   To change the destination folder for an item type, click **Change Destination**. To alter the way Schedule+ fields are imported into Outlook, click **Map Custom Fields**.

By default, Outlook imports Schedule+ information into the following Outlook folders:

- Appointments and events are imported into the Calendar folder.
- Task data is imported into the Tasks folder.

The CAL file is not modified or deleted during the import process. You may import schedule files at any time after Outlook is installed using the **Import and Export** command (**File** menu).

Upgrading from Microsoft Schedule+ 1.0

This section describes the differences between Outlook and Schedule+ 1.0 for Schedule+ 1.0 users who are upgrading to Outlook. Microsoft Outlook includes all the features of Microsoft Schedule+ 1.0, such as appointments, events, contacts, and tasks. Outlook also provides the following features not available in Schedule+ 1.0:

- Integrated e-mail functions, along with contact, journal, and note items
- Additional views for calendar, contact, and task information
- Advanced custom view capabilities
- Task delegation
- Advanced printing options

Can I upgrade to Outlook and maintain my current e-mail and scheduling configuration? Except for changes in the user interface and other features, you can continue working with your calendar and task information just as you did in Schedule+ 1.0.

Can I continue to exchange e-mail, share information, and perform group scheduling tasks with users who have not upgraded to Outlook? You can freely exchange group scheduling information with Schedule+ 1.0 users. However, whenever Outlook and Schedule+ 1.0 share information, Outlook uses Schedule+ 95 to read and interpret Schedule+ 1.0 data.

To upgrade, install Outlook and import the Schedule+ 1.0 data file (CAL); Schedule+ is not removed from your computer. For more information about installing Outlook, see Chapter 4, "Installing Microsoft Office."

Importing the Schedule+ 1.0 Data File

After Outlook is installed, you can import the Schedule+ data file (CAL).

Important Outlook uses the Schedule+ 95 application to import the Schedule+ 1.0 CAL file. If Schedule+ 95 is not installed on your computer, Outlook does not give you the option to import a Schedule+ 1.0 CAL file.

▶ **To import a Schedule+ CAL file**

1. On the Outlook **File** menu, click **Import and Export**, and then click **Import from Schedule+ or another program or file**.
2. In the **Select file type to import from** box, click **Schedule+ 1.0**.
3. In the **File to import** box, enter the CAL file name, or click **Browse** to find the file.

    This dialog box also includes several options for dealing with entries in the CAL file that duplicate entries you already have in your Outlook Calendar, Contacts, or Tasks folders.

Part 3   Upgrading to Microsoft Office

Sender-Side Delegation

When using Microsoft Exchange Server, if a user sends a meeting request to another user who has a delegate defined, then the meeting request is automatically forwarded to the delegate. This works whether the sending or receiving users are using Outlook or Schedule+.

Using Schedule+ 95 as the Primary Calendar

Even though interoperability between Outlook and Schedule+ 95 has been designed to be as seamless as possible, there may be situations in which you may prefer to have everyone in your workgroup using the same scheduling application (for example, to use the Schedule+ direct-booking feature).

For this reason, Outlook allows you to keep Schedule+ 95 as your primary scheduling application.

Note   If multiple users use a single computer through Windows user profiles, then setting this option configures all users on the computer to use Schedule+ as their primary calendar.

▶ **To make Schedule+ 95 your scheduling application**

1   On the Outlook **Tools** menu, click **Options**, and then click the **Calendar** tab.

2   Select the **Use Microsoft Schedule+ 95 as my primary calendar** check box.

When this option is set, Outlook uses Schedule+ for all scheduling functions, and you see the following changes:

- Outlook no longer has a folder shortcut for the Calendar folder on the Outlook Bar.
- Double-clicking meeting requests and responses launches Schedule+ forms instead of the Outlook equivalents.
- The **Schedule+** button appears on the **Outlook** toolbar.
- The **New Meeting Request** command (**Calendar** menu) is unavailable.

If the **Use Microsoft Schedule+ 95 as my primary calendar** check box is subsequently cleared, these changes are reversed, and Outlook manages all scheduling tasks.

Tools and Utilities   This option corresponds to the Windows registry key **HKEY_LOCAL_MACHINE\Software\Microsoft\Office\8.0\Outlook\SchedPlusOption \UseSchedPlus**. A value of 0 means that the check box on the **Calendar** tab is cleared. If you change the value in **\UserCanChange** to 0, the check box is unavailable. In Windows 95 and Windows NT Workstation 4.0, you can use a system policy to define this option for all Outlook users in your workgroup. In the System Policy Editor, set the following policy:

Computer\Outlook 97\ Use Schedule+

For more information, see "Using Windows System Policies to Customize Office" in Chapter 7, "Customizing and Optimizing Microsoft Office."

Sharing Information with Microsoft Schedule+ 95

If your workgroup is upgrading gradually to Outlook, some Outlook users may need to exchange e-mail and share public folders with Schedule+ 95 users. Although Outlook and Schedule+ have been designed to make sharing information easy, Outlook uses a different format for storing information.

There are several areas in which Outlook and Schedule+ users can share information, as is described in the following sections.

Managing Group Scheduling

Outlook and Schedule+ users can freely send and receive meeting requests and responses for group scheduling. Both sets of users can also, with proper permission, view each other's free and busy status. With the proper permission, an Outlook user can open a Schedule+ calendar and view a Schedule+ user's free and busy details; however, a Schedule+ user cannot open an Outlook calendar or view an Outlook user's free and busy details.

Schedule+ recognizes attached files in a meeting request, but not attached Outlook items. If an Outlook user embeds an Outlook item (such as a contact or journal item) into a meeting request and sends it to a Schedule+ user, Schedule+ does not display the item. If the Outlook user attaches a file to the meeting request, however, the Schedule+ user receives the attached file correctly.

Sharing Other Information

Besides sending meeting requests, there are two additional tasks that Outlook and Schedule+ users can perform.

Direct Booking

With the appropriate permissions, a Schedule+ user can directly book a meeting into another Schedule+ calendar without sending a meeting request. An Outlook user can use direct booking to a Schedule+ calendar, but an Outlook user is not able to directly book a meeting into another Outlook calendar, except by opening the other calendar and modifying it.

Tip If an offline Outlook or Schedule+ user sends a meeting request to a Schedule+ user such as a resource account, the request cannot be directly booked into the recipient's calendar. Instead, a normal meeting request is sent to the Schedule+ account. If you are upgrading your Schedule+ users to Outlook, upgrade Schedule+ resource accounts last. This allows Schedule+ users to continue to use these resource accounts.

The SCD file is not modified or deleted during the import process. You may import schedule files at any time after Outlook is installed using the **Import and Export** command (**File** menu).

Note The Covey Seven Habits tool in Schedule+ 95 is not included in Outlook. In addition, because its object model is very different, Outlook does not recognize Automation (formerly OLE Automation) interfaces in Schedule+ 95.

Why do Outlook and Schedule+ synchronize my calendar differently?

Both Outlook and Schedule+ allow you to keep synchronized copies of the calendar folder on the server and on your hard disk. However, the two applications use different methods for keeping offline and server copies of the folder synchronized.

For group scheduling, Schedule+ always maintains a copy of your calendar on the server. Every time you connect to the server, Schedule+ automatically synchronizes the server and the local copies, and continues to keep them synchronized as you make changes to the calendar. Because Schedule+ always keeps a server copy of the calendar when you are working online, you may not be aware that the calendar is being synchronized with the local copy.

Outlook, on the other hand, allows you to keep folders on the server, on a hard disk, or both. If you choose to have both a server and local copy of a folder, you can configure Outlook to synchronize the folder automatically when you exit using options in the **Options** dialog box (**Tools** menu). Or you can synchronize the folder manually using the **Synchronize** command (**Tools** menu).

Synchronization conflicts (for example, an assistant accepts a meeting request while your local copy of the schedule is offline) are handled automatically with Schedule+. In Outlook, however, you may receive a conflict resolution message and must resolve conflicts manually if updates are made to your Calendar folder while you are offline.

Can I continue to exchange e-mail, share information, and perform group scheduling tasks with users who have not upgraded to Outlook? You can freely exchange group scheduling information with Schedule+ 95 users. You also have the option of retaining Schedule+ 95 as your primary calendar and using Outlook for e-mail and other functions.

To upgrade, install Outlook and import the Schedule+ 95 data file; Schedule+ is not removed from your computer. For more information about installing Outlook, see Chapter 4, "Installing Microsoft Office."

Importing the Schedule+ 95 Data File

After Outlook is installed, you can import the Schedule+ data file (SCD).

▶ **To import a Schedule+ SCD file**

1. On the Outlook **File** menu, click **Import and Export**, and then click **Import from Schedule+ or another program or file**.
2. In the **Select file type to import from** box, click **Schedule+ 7.0**.
3. In the **File to import** box, enter the SCD file name, or click **Browse** to find the file.

   This dialog box also includes several options for dealing with entries in the SCD file that duplicate entries you already have in your Outlook Calendar, Contacts, or Tasks folders.

4. To replace duplicate entries in your Outlook folder with Schedule+ entries, click **Replace duplicates with items imported**.

   –or–

   To allow duplicate entries to be imported, click **Allow duplicates to be created**.

   –or–

   To avoid importing duplicate entries, click **Do not import duplicate items**.

5. If requested, enter the password for the schedule file.
6. In **The following actions will be performed** box, select the items you want to import and their destination folders.

   To change the destination folder for an item type, click **Change Destination**. To alter the way Schedule+ fields are imported into Outlook, click **Map Custom Fields**.

By default, Outlook imports Schedule+ information into the following Outlook folders:

- Appointments and events are imported into the Calendar folder.
- Contact data is imported into the Contacts folder.
- Task data is imported into the Tasks folder.

Extended Properties

When a Microsoft Mail 3.x client opens an Outlook message, extended properties (such as the **Sensitivity** property) that are not recognized by the Microsoft Mail 3.x client are ignored. However, all Microsoft Mail 3.x message properties are recognized by Outlook.

Custom Forms

Custom Outlook forms opened by Microsoft Mail 3.x users are displayed using the Microsoft Mail 3.x standard message form. Custom forms sent by Outlook users and opened by Microsoft Mail 3.x users, or vice versa, are displayed using the appropriate custom form handler, provided that the custom form is registered in the receiving user's MSMail.ini or Shared.ini file.

Any custom forms opened by Microsoft Mail 3.x for MS-DOS or Microsoft Mail 3.x for the Macintosh are displayed using the standard message form.

Sharing Public Folders

Outlook users can create, open, read, write, and delete Microsoft Mail 3.x public folders. If an Outlook user stores an Outlook form in a public folder, a Microsoft Mail 3.x user can open the message with the same restrictions and exceptions described in "Exchanging Messages" earlier in this chapter. Similarly, if a Microsoft Mail 3.x user stores a Microsoft Mail 3.x form in a public folder, an Outlook user can open it with the restrictions described previously.

Upgrading from Microsoft Schedule+ 95

This section describes the differences between Outlook and Schedule+ 95 for Schedule+ 95 users who are upgrading to Outlook. Outlook includes all the features of Schedule+ 95, including appointments, events, contacts, and tasks. Outlook also provides the following features not available in Schedule+ 95:

- Integrated e-mail functions, along with journal and note items
- Additional views for calendar, contact, and task information
- Advanced custom view capabilities
- Task delegation
- Advanced printing options

Can I upgrade to Outlook and maintain my current e-mail and scheduling configuration?
Except for changes in the user interface and other features, you can continue working with your calendar, contact, and task information in Outlook just as you did in Schedule+ 95.

Exchanging Messages

When an Outlook user opens a message created by a Microsoft Mail 3.*x* user, Outlook recognizes all of the features of the message. However, when a Microsoft Mail 3.*x* user opens an e-mail message created by an Outlook user, the Microsoft Mail 3.*x* client may not recognize some of the advanced features that the Outlook user is able to include in the message.

Message Size

Outlook can create and read a message of any size (subject to available system resources). However, Microsoft Mail 3.*x* clients have some size restrictions for messages (32K for text and approximately 100 MB for attachments). Although Microsoft Mail 3.*x* users may not be able to open a very large message created by an Outlook user, they can save the message to a file or print it.

Rich Text

Outlook users can format text in a message using rich text attributes such as bold, italic, indent, center, and justify. When an Outlook message with rich text is opened by a Microsoft Mail 3.*x* client, however, all the rich text attributes are replaced by plain text.

Note A Microsoft Mail 3.*x* for MS-DOS user can set some color attributes to characters in a message, but Outlook (as well as other Microsoft Mail 3.*x* clients) does not recognize these attributes and displays the text in the default color.

Attachments and Embedded Objects

The methods Outlook and Microsoft Mail 3.*x* use for attaching files and embedding objects in messages are completely compatible. Outlook users can open attachments or objects within messages created by Microsoft Mail 3.*x*, and vice versa, as long as the appropriate application is installed.

The single exception is that Outlook users can attach a message to another message, but Microsoft Mail 3.*x* does not recognize the attached message.

Embedded Hyperlinks

If an Outlook user clicks a Web-style hyperlink (a URL address of an Internet or intranet Web site) in a message from another Outlook user, Outlook goes to the appropriate Web site using the registered Web browser. If a Microsoft Mail 3.*x* user opens a message with a hyperlink, however, the hyperlink is displayed in the message as plain text only.

Migrating to Microsoft Exchange Server

If you plan to migrate your workgroup from Microsoft Mail 3.*x* to Microsoft Exchange Server, upgrading to Outlook is a good intermediate step. Because Outlook can work with both the Microsoft Mail 3.*x* e-mail system and Microsoft Exchange Server, Microsoft Mail 3.*x* users can be upgraded to Outlook and continue to work with their Microsoft Mail 3.*x* post office.

Later, when you upgrade the post office to Microsoft Exchange Server, these users only need to change their profiles; they can continue to use Outlook. This allows you to manage the upgrade of the user interface and the upgrade of the e-mail system separately.

The process of migrating users from Microsoft Mail 3.*x* post offices to Microsoft Exchange Server involves more than upgrading e-mail client software, and it is beyond the scope of the *Office Resource Kit*. The Microsoft Exchange Server CD contains a document that takes you through all the planning and implementation steps necessary to migrate users from Microsoft Mail 3.*x* to Microsoft Exchange Server. This document is titled "Migrating from Microsoft Mail for PC Networks," and it can be found on the Microsoft Exchange Server CD in Migrate\Docs\Msmailpc.doc.

While this document discusses upgrading Microsoft Mail 3.*x* users to Microsoft Exchange Client, the information also applies to Outlook, because Outlook can be used as a direct replacement for Microsoft Exchange Client. Review this document thoroughly if you plan to move your workgroup to Microsoft Exchange Server.

Sharing Information with Microsoft Mail 3.x

If your workgroup is upgrading gradually to Outlook, some Outlook users may need to exchange e-mail with Microsoft Mail 3.*x* users. While Outlook users are able to exchange e-mail freely with Microsoft Mail 3.*x* users, e-mail messages composed using Outlook may not appear the same when viewed by users of Microsoft Mail 3.*x*.

Outlook users and Microsoft Mail 3.*x* users can share e-mail messages by sending e-mail back and forth, or by making messages available in shared folders. The way Outlook and Microsoft Mail 3.*x* clients work with e-mail messages is the same in either case.

Note If an Outlook user sends e-mail to a Microsoft Mail 3.*x* user who has a delegate account, then Outlook redirects the message to the delegate account. However, if the Outlook user sends the message while offline, then Outlook cannot send the message to the delegate and the message is delivered only to the original Microsoft Mail 3.*x* user.

If Outlook does not find Shared32.ini and MSMail32.ini, it looks for the files Shared.ini and MSMail.ini instead.

Outlook supports an enhancement to the version parameter of the extension registration entry. The version number can be followed by **,16** to indicate a 16-bit-extension DLL or by **,32** to indicate a 32-bit-extension DLL. If the version does not specify either of these settings, Outlook assumes an extension type based on the file in which the extension is found.

If the extension is found in this file	Outlook assumes this extension type
MSMail.ini	16-bit
MSMail32.ini	32-bit
Shared.ini	16-bit
Shared32.ini	32-bit

Note In Microsoft Mail 3.x for either Windows 3.11 or Windows NT Workstation, specifying 16 or 32 bits in the version number results in a syntax error.

Custom Message Types

Microsoft Mail 3.x custom message handlers allow you to use custom forms in place of the standard e-mail message form. Outlook provides complete support for Microsoft Mail 3.x custom message types.

Upgrading Remote Users and Offices

Outlook users running either the Microsoft Mail 3.x information service or the Microsoft Exchange information service can retrieve e-mail remotely using a method that is different from the Microsoft Mail 3.x remote client. Before upgrading the remote client users in your workgroup to Outlook, you need to install, configure, and test this new connection method.

Note Hardware requirements for Outlook are greater than those for Microsoft Mail 3.x remote clients. When planning migration, inventory remote client users to see if any of them need hardware upgrades. For more information, see Chapter 5, "System Requirements for Microsoft Office."

Remote users who upgrade to Outlook can move their MMF files to a personal folder file, as described in "Importing Microsoft Mail Files" earlier in this chapter.

Note If you use Microsoft Mail 3.x for MS-DOS remote client, you cannot migrate your locally stored messages to Outlook personal folders. You must mail them to yourself, save them as text files, or print them.

> **Did You Know?**
>
> In Windows 3.11, Microsoft Mail 3.*x* for Windows uses 16-bit extensions; however, on Windows 95 and Windows NT Workstation, it uses 32-bit extensions. Outlook supports both 16-bit and 32-bit extensions, although 16-bit extensions are given special handling, since Windows 95 and Windows NT Workstation are 32-bit operating systems.
>
> Because Outlook is a 32-bit application, 16-bit extension DLLs cannot be called directly. When a 16-bit extension needs to be called, Outlook launches Ml3Xec16.exe and passes it the parameter block pointer and the name and path of the extension DLL. Ml3Xec16.exe then calls the DLL and passes it the parameter block pointer.
>
> The extensions AppExec.dll and AppXec32.dll are used frequently in Microsoft Mail 3.*x* for Windows to launch an executable file from a custom command with a list of command-line parameters. AppExec.dll (16-bit) is used with Microsoft Mail 3.*x* for Windows 3.11. AppXec32.dll (32-bit) is used with Microsoft Mail 3.*x* for Windows NT Workstation. Outlook supports both DLLs.

Msmail[32].ini and Shared[32].ini Parsing

Outlook supports both 16-bit and 32-bit extensions. Which extensions are used by Outlook depends on where Outlook finds them when it starts up. During startup, Outlook first looks for extensions in the Windows registry under **HKEY_CURRENT_USER\Software\Microsoft\Mail\Microsoft Mail**, where extensions for Microsoft Mail 3.*x* for Windows NT Workstation are installed. This registry key is also used by Outlook with Windows 95.

Outlook then looks for Microsoft Mail 3.*x* extensions defined locally and shared extensions defined for the workgroup. To find these extensions, Outlook retrieves the shared extensions folder location from the Windows registry in the set of value entries **SharedExtsDir**, **SharedExtsServer**, and **SharedExtsPassword** under **HKEY_CURRENT_USER\Software\Microsoft\Exchange\Client\Options**. If these value entries do not exist in the registry, Outlook looks for the value entry **SharedExtensionsDir**, first in MSMail32.ini and then in MSMail.ini, to retrieve the location of the shared extensions folder.

If it finds the shared extensions folder, Outlook opens the Shared32.ini file in that folder and reads the **[Custom Menus]**, **[Custom Commands]**, and **[Custom Messages]** sections to retrieve the shared Microsoft Mail 3.*x* extension definitions. Outlook then reads these same sections from the file MSMail32.ini. If there are any duplicate extensions defined in these two files, Outlook uses those found in MSMail32.ini.

> ### Avoiding Duplicate E-mail Messages
> In Microsoft Mail, you can keep a copy of all the messages in your Inbox in the post office on the server. If you then migrate to Microsoft Exchange Server, these messages may be duplicated: The Inbox in the post office is copied to your Microsoft Exchange Server folders during migration, and you also import the messages from the local MMF using Outlook.
>
> To avoid duplicate messages, click **Options** on the Microsoft Mail 3.*x* for Windows **Mail** menu. In the **Server** dialog box, clear the **Copy Inbox on Postoffice for Dialin Access** check box.

Using Microsoft Mail Custom Commands, Menus, and Messages

Custom menu and command entries in MSMail.ini and Shared.ini are used by Outlook the same way they are in Microsoft Mail 3.*x* for Windows.

Custom Menus

Custom menu add-ins allow you to add top-level menus to Microsoft Mail 3.*x* for Windows. This feature is fully supported in Outlook: Top-level menus specified in the MSMail.ini file are added to the Outlook menu bar.

Note The **Tools** menu is not available by default in Microsoft Mail 3.*x* for Windows, but is commonly added using menu add-ins. Outlook uses its native **Tools** menu in place of creating a second **Tools** menu. Therefore, custom menus with the tag **Tools** in the **[Custom Menus]** section of the INI file are ignored.

Custom Commands

Custom command extensions allow you to add new commands to Microsoft Mail 3.*x* for Windows. Because the menus in Outlook and Microsoft Mail 3.*x* for Windows differ, Outlook handles command add-ins differently than Microsoft Mail 3.x for Windows. When a command add-in is defined for the Microsoft Mail 3.*x* for Windows **Mail** menu, Outlook adds it to its **Compose** menu. If a custom command is added to a Microsoft Mail 3.*x* for Windows **Tools** or **Windows** menu, Outlook adds the custom command to its **Tools** menu.

To move the MMF from the post office to a hard disk

1. On the Microsoft Mail 3.*x* for Windows **Mail** menu, click **Options**.
2. Click **Server**.
3. Click **Local**, and then enter a file name for your MMF.

Once the MMF is on your hard disk or stored on a network server, you can import its contents to an Outlook personal folder.

To import the MMF to a personal folder in Outlook

1. On the Outlook **File** menu, click **Import/Export**.
2. Select **Import from a Microsoft Mail File**, and then click **Next**.
3. In the **File name** box, enter the name of the MMF to import, and then click **Open**.
4. Enter the password (if requested), and select both the **Import messages** and **Import personal address book entries** check boxes.
5. To store messages in existing personal folders, click **Put the messages into existing Personal Folders**, and then click the folder you want.

   –or–

   To create a new personal folders store, click **Put the messages into new Personal Folders** and enter the path name. Click **Display new Personal Folders** to display the new folders in the folder list. Outlook creates the new personal folders and adds them to your profile.

   Outlook imports the messages and personal address book entries from the MMF.

If you have used multiple information services (such as AT&T, MHS, or CompuServe), there may be multiple PABs in the MMF. When importing the MMF with the **Import/Export** command, you can choose which PABs to import.

When importing an MMF, keep the following points in mind:

- If there is a network failure, Outlook retries the network connection 4 times in the next 2 seconds, and then repeats this process every 10 minutes. An error message is displayed during the 10-minute retry period.
- Any errors that occur while importing the MMF are logged to a file in the client directory with the same file name as the MMF and an extension of .log. You can view the log in Notepad or any other text editor.

Note Once you begin using Outlook, there is no easy way to transfer new messages back to an MMF or mailbag file. You can copy the messages to a shared folder and then retrieve them with your old client. However, this does not guarantee privacy.

Note If you install both the Microsoft Mail and the Microsoft Exchange Server information services in the same profile, and you use the **Meeting Planner** in Outlook to check other users' free/busy information, Outlook looks for this information using the Microsoft Exchange Server information service only.

Note Because Outlook runs only on Windows 95 and Windows NT Workstation 3.51 or later, Microsoft Mail 3.*x* for Windows users running on Windows 3.11 or Windows for Workgroups must upgrade to Windows 95 or Windows NT Workstation before upgrading to Outlook. This may require changes in hardware. For more information about hardware requirements for Microsoft Office 97, see Chapter 5, "System Requirements for Microsoft Office."

Upgrading MS-DOS and Macintosh Clients to Outlook

Microsoft Mail 3.*x* for the Macintosh users and Microsoft Mail for MS-DOS users who plan to switch to the Windows operating system and to Outlook must take some extra steps to migrate existing mail messages.

To upgrade MS-DOS or Macintosh clients, install Outlook on a Windows 95 or Windows NT operating system, and then connect to the mailbox on the Microsoft Mail post office. Outlook automatically transfers the Inbox contents to personal folder files.

To read e-mail messages in private folders, MS-DOS and Macintosh users must first install Microsoft Mail 3.*x* for Windows and then migrate these folders into an MMF file, or use their current client to move the folders to the server (if they are stored locally) until they migrate to Microsoft Exchange Server. The migration process moves e-mail stored in private folders onto the server.

The following sections describe how Outlook uses the components of Microsoft Mail 3.*x* for Windows when you install Outlook.

Importing Microsoft Mail Files

After Outlook is installed, you must import the contents of the e-mail message file (MMF). The MMF stores your e-mail messages, attachments, and personal address book (PAB). The MMF can be stored in the post office folder in the MMF directory, or you can move it to your hard disk or a network location.

If the MMF is in the post office, you must first connect to the post office with Microsoft Mail 3.*x* for Windows and then move the MMF to your hard disk (or to an accessible network location) before importing the contents with Outlook.

Because Outlook can be used as a client with the Microsoft Mail 3.x e-mail system, Outlook can serve as a complete replacement for Microsoft Mail 3.x for Windows, and the upgrading process is straightforward: install Outlook.

Can I upgrade to Outlook and maintain my current e-mail configuration? Except for changes in the user interface and other features, you can continue working with e-mail in Outlook just as you did in Microsoft Mail 3.x for Windows. Outlook uses the same MSMail.ini file and other configuration information and can use all Microsoft Mail 3.x for Windows add-ins and custom forms.

Can I continue to exchange e-mail and share information with users who have not upgraded to Outlook? You can share information with Microsoft Mail 3.x for Windows users by sending e-mail back and forth, or by making messages available in shared folders. However, e-mail messages composed using Outlook may not appear the same when viewed by users of Microsoft Mail 3.x for Windows.

Tip To make the user interface of Outlook look more like the user interface of Microsoft Mail 3.x for Windows, you can view the Outlook folder list using the **Folder List** command (**View** menu). Later, you may choose to hide the folder list and use the Outlook Bar exclusively for quick access to Outlook functions, as well as to Windows folders.

Office Setup gives you the option to include support for the Microsoft Mail information service that allows Outlook to use a Microsoft Mail 3.x post office. This service is not installed by default, however, so you must explicitly choose to install it.

▶ **To install the Microsoft Mail 3.x information service**

1   Start the Office Setup program.
2   If you are running Setup for the first time, click **Custom**.

    –or–

    If you are running Setup after Outlook has been installed, click **Add/Remove**.
3   Select the **Microsoft Outlook** option, and then click **Change Option**.
4   Select the **Microsoft Exchange Server Support** check box.

When Setup installs the Microsoft Mail information service, the service is added to your profile. Setup uses information from your MSMail.ini file to configure the service. When Setup is finished, Outlook can use the same post office previously used by Microsoft Mail 3.x for Windows. For more information about installing Outlook, see Chapter 4, "Installing Microsoft Office."

When Outlook is run for the first time, it uses the Microsoft Mail 3.x post office and MMF file defined in MSMail.ini. After Outlook is installed, you work with the same Inbox, Outbox, and Sent Mail folders used by Microsoft Mail 3.x for Windows, as well as any private folders in the MMF file and public folders in the Microsoft Mail 3.x post office.

▶ **To maintain both Outlook and Microsoft Exchange formats for saved table views**

1. On the **File** menu, click **Folder**, and then click **Properties For**.
2. Click the **General** tab, and then select the **Automatically generate Microsoft Exchange views** check box.

With this property set, you can create a new view or modify an existing view (regardless of whether the existing view was originally created by Outlook or Microsoft Exchange Client), and Outlook automatically saves the view in both Outlook and Microsoft Exchange Client format. However, any Outlook-specific view features (such as calculated columns) are not included in the copy saved in Microsoft Exchange Client format.

If the **Automatically generate Microsoft Exchange views** checkbox is not selected, then Outlook saves views only in Outlook format. If a Microsoft Exchange Client user opens a folder, Microsoft Exchange Client displays only the views that have been saved in Microsoft Exchange Client format.

Tip When you design a public folder to be used by both Outlook and Microsoft Exchange Client users, use table views without calculated columns for the main views of the folder. Until all users have upgraded to Outlook, a folder might consist of both table views (which are available to both Outlook and Microsoft Exchange Client users) and more complex views (which are available only to Outlook users).

Note An Outlook user can open a public folder shortcut embedded in a Microsoft Exchange Client message by double-clicking the shortcut icon. However, a Microsoft Exchange Client user cannot open a public folder shortcut embedded in an Outlook message.

Upgrading from Microsoft Mail 3.x for Windows

This section describes the differences between Outlook and Microsoft Mail 3.*x* for Windows for Microsoft Mail users who are upgrading to Outlook. Outlook provides all the features of Microsoft Mail 3.*x* for Windows, but it also provides many new features, such as:

- Integrated calendar functions, along with contact, journal, and task items
- Multiple views of messages
- Custom view capabilities
- Message handling rules
- Custom form creation
- Advanced printing options

public folder that was created using WordMail, then the message is converted to rich text format. For more detailed information about the conversion, see "WordMail Forms" earlier in this chapter.

Other Outlook Forms

Outlook items other than e-mail—appointment, contact, journal, note, and task items—are stored in folders using Outlook forms specific to each item. You can place these items in a public folder or forward them in an e-mail message. If a Microsoft Exchange Client user opens one of these items, however, Microsoft Exchange Client displays an error message and allows the user to open the form with the Microsoft Exchange standard message form.

Outlook Custom Forms

If a Microsoft Exchange Client user attempts to open an Outlook custom form, Microsoft Exchange Client displays an error message and allows the user to open the Outlook custom form using the Microsoft Exchange standard message form, in which case the user sees only those properties that the standard message form displays.

Sharing Public Folders

Outlook and Microsoft Exchange Client users may have access to a common set of public folders. All the limitations described in "Exchanging Forms" earlier in this chapter also apply when you share forms through public folders. There are no special restrictions regarding simultaneous access by both Outlook and Microsoft Exchange Client users; the Microsoft Exchange Server does not distinguish between Outlook and Microsoft Exchange Client when you open public folders.

Note Outlook associates a unique icon with each MAPI folder type (Appointment Items, Mail Items, and so forth), making folders easily identifiable in the Outlook folder list. Microsoft Exchange Client is not able to make this same association, however, so all folders are shown with the standard message folder icon.

The most significant issue in sharing folders is how saved views are handled between the two clients. Outlook supports all the custom view features of Microsoft Exchange Client, but it also supports a number of other features as well. Saved views created by Outlook also have a different format than those created by Microsoft Exchange Client. While Microsoft Exchange Client does not recognize the Outlook format, Outlook recognizes both formats.

Note Only views based on the table view type can be saved by Outlook in Microsoft Exchange Client format. Other views, such as timeline or calendar views, are not recognized by Microsoft Exchange Client.

Outlook can maintain two copies of all saved table views: one in Outlook format, and a copy in Microsoft Exchange Client format.

When this Word format option	Is converted to rich text format
Small caps and all caps	These are converted to normal text.
Hidden	Hidden text is converted to normal text.
Shadow and outline	Hidden text is converted to normal text.
Emboss and engrave	Embossed and engraved characters are displayed with white color
Single underline	Formatting is preserved.
Word-only and double underline	These are converted to single underlines.
Dotted underline	Formatting is preserved.
Thick, dash, dot-dash, and dot-dot-dash underline	Lost in the conversion
Custom character spacing and position, and kerning for fonts	These are converted to normal text.
Paragraph formats	
Custom paragraph spacing	Formatting is preserved.
Left, right, hanging, and first-line indentation	Formatting is preserved.
Left, center, and right paragraph alignment	Formatting is preserved.
Left, right, center, and decimal tabs	Formatting is preserved (tab positions may be slightly different).
Bar tab	Lost in the conversion.
Borders	Lost in the conversion.
Round, diamond, square, and checked bullets	All bullets are converted to round bullets
Highlighting	Formatting is preserved.
Revision marks	Lost in the conversion.
Page formatting, including columns and frames	Lost in the conversion.
WordArt, callouts, and text box objects	Lost in the conversion.

Note If a Word 97 WordMail message is received on a computer that has Word 95 WordMail installed, Word 95 is able to open the body of the message. However, there are some new features in Word 97 that Word 95 may not convert correctly. For more information about how Word 95 opens a Word 97 document, see "Opening Word 97 Documents in Word 6.0 or 95," in Chapter 15, "Upgrading from Previous Versions of Microsoft Word."

Outlook Post Forms

When you post a message to a folder or read a posted message in a folder, Outlook uses the Outlook Post form, which supports WordMail. Microsoft Exchange Client, however, always uses Microsoft Exchange Client Post form, which does not support WordMail. If a Microsoft Exchange Client user opens an Outlook Post form in a

Part 3   Upgrading to Microsoft Office

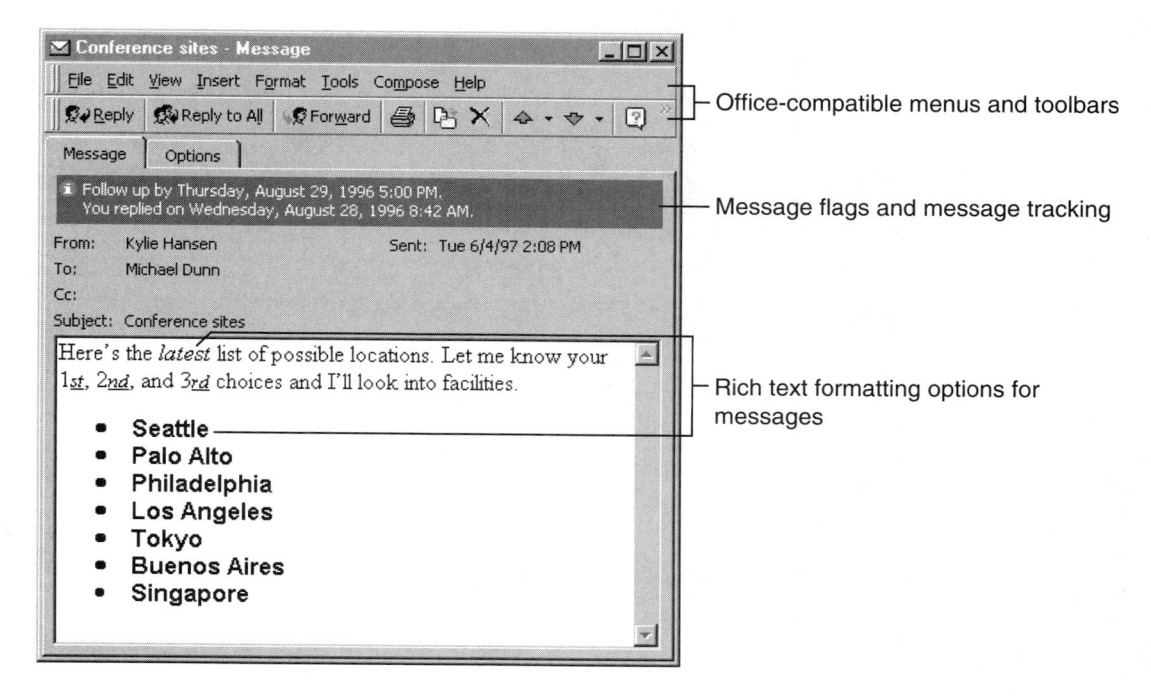

- Office-compatible menus and toolbars
- Message flags and message tracking
- Rich text formatting options for messages

When you send an Outlook standard message form to a Microsoft Exchange Client user, Microsoft Exchange Client looks in the forms registry for instructions about how to open the form. If Microsoft Exchange Client does not find the Outlook standard message form in the forms registry, then it opens your message using Microsoft Exchange Client standard message form.

Note   Microsoft Exchange for MS-DOS and for the Macintosh do not recognize the Outlook standard message form. If either of these clients receives an Outlook form, the standard message form for the MS-DOS or the Macintosh client is used to display the Outlook form.

WordMail Forms

A *WordMail form* is an e-mail message in which Word is used in place of the standard e-mail editor to compose the text. Outlook can use Word 95 or Word 97 as an editor. If a WordMail form is received by a user who does not have WordMail installed, the message text is converted to rich text format. The following table describes how this conversion affects the message text.

When this Word format option	Is converted to rich text format
Character formats	
Font, font style, size, and color	Formatting is preserved.
Strikethrough and double strikethrough	Formatting is preserved.
Superscript and subscript	Formatting is preserved.

All known Microsoft Exchange Client add-ins work without modification in Outlook, although Outlook has expanded the add-in architecture. The administrator or add-in author can provide an optional Extension Configuration File (ECF) file that controls how the add-in is installed (this information is stored in the Windows registry).

Outlook uses the ECF file to delay-load add-ins, to suppress inappropriate add-ins (for example, Outlook suppresses the Schedule+ extension when Outlook is used for group scheduling), and to ensure standard menu and toolbar formats. If there is no ECF file, the add-in still works, but Outlook may not start as quickly.

Tip In Outlook you can turn add-ins on and off by clicking the **Add-in Manager** button on the **General** tab in the **Options** dialog box (**Tools** menu).

Tools and Utilities The Office Resource Kit Tools and Utilities include a document named Ecf.htm, which describes the content and format of ECF files. For more information, see "Outlook Extension Configuration File Document" in Appendix A, "Microsoft Office 97 Resource Kit Tools and Utilities."

Sharing Information with Microsoft Exchange Client

If your workgroup is upgrading gradually to Outlook, some Outlook users may need to exchange e-mail and share public folders with Microsoft Exchange Client users. Outlook and Microsoft Exchange Client have been designed to make this easy; however, there are some features in Outlook that are not recognized by Microsoft Exchange Client.

When your workgroup is using both Outlook and Microsoft Exchange Client, the two primary areas of interest are exchanging forms and sharing public folders.

Exchanging Forms

Outlook can open both standard and custom message forms created by Microsoft Exchange Client, but Microsoft Exchange Client can open only the Outlook standard form. Outlook can create special forms for Outlook items other than e-mail (such as calendar or task items); Microsoft Exchange Client cannot open these forms.

The following sections describe what you can expect when you exchange e-mail messages with Microsoft Exchange Client users.

Standard Message Forms

The Outlook standard message form is similar to Microsoft Exchange Client standard message form, but Outlook includes some additional features, as shown in the following illustration.

While Outlook can create more advanced custom views than Microsoft Exchange Client, Outlook and Microsoft Exchange Client can share public folders where users may exchange custom views. For more information about how Outlook shares folders and views with Microsoft Exchange Client, see "Sharing Information with Microsoft Exchange Client" later in this chapter.

Upgrading Microsoft Exchange Client Forms

MAPI defines a *forms registry* to identify the standard and custom forms available for creating e-mail messages or posting to folders. When you double-click an e-mail message or another item in a folder, the forms registry identifies the appropriate form to display. Outlook continues to use and maintain the forms registry.

Standard Message Form

When you install Outlook in a workgroup, the Outlook standard message form is entered in the forms registry and becomes the default form.

WordMail

With Outlook, you can choose to use Microsoft Word as your e-mail editor in the standard message form. This feature is called *WordMail*. Outlook supports all the standard e-mail features (digital signatures, encryption, tracking, voting, and so forth) in a standard form with WordMail. The Outlook Post form (the form used for posting to a folder) also supports WordMail.

Note Outlook supports WordMail with Word 97 and 95 only.

Custom Forms

If there are Microsoft Exchange Client custom forms in the forms registry, Outlook recognizes them, and you can open and respond to them. You can also create new Outlook custom forms using the **Design Outlook Form** command (**Tools** menu) in a message form. Custom forms you create in Outlook are added to the forms registry.

Microsoft Exchange Client does not recognize Outlook custom forms; if it receives one, Microsoft Exchange Client displays an error message and opens the Outlook custom form using its standard form. For a complete description of how Microsoft Exchange Client handles Outlook forms, see "Sharing Information with Microsoft Exchange Client" later in this chapter.

Upgrading Microsoft Exchange Client Extensions

Some of the features in Microsoft Exchange Client are provided by extensions, or *add-ins*, that have been written using a published application programming interface (API). These add-ins directly modify Microsoft Exchange Client menus and toolbars. Typically, add-ins also add tabs to the **Options** dialog box (**Tools** menu).

Tip To make the new user interface of Outlook look more like the familiar user interface of Microsoft Exchange Client, you can view the Outlook folder list using the **Folder List** command (**View** menu). Later, you may choose to hide the folder list and use the Outlook Bar exclusively for quick access to Outlook functions, as well as to Windows folders.

When you run Outlook the first time, it uses the default mail profile (unless you have explicitly specified another profile) to open your personal address book and personal folders, and it connects to the Microsoft Exchange Server and any other services that are specified in the profile.

Whether the profile is configured to deliver e-mail to the Inbox on the Microsoft Exchange Server or to the Inbox in personal folders on your computer, Outlook continues to expect new e-mail in the same Inbox folder. After Outlook is installed, you work with the same Inbox, Outbox, Sent Items, and Deleted Items folders that were used by Microsoft Exchange Client, as well as any other personal folders defined in the profile.

Outlook starts with the same profile configuration as Microsoft Exchange Client, except that a new information service is added to the default profile. This allows Outlook (and any other MAPI application) to use the Outlook Contacts folder as an e-mail address book. Outlook also recognizes any folder views you have defined and maintains the read or unread status of messages.

Tools and Utilities Outlook is not intended to run on the same computer as the Microsoft Exchange Client; however, your support team may need to support users of both clients, or you may want to test new custom forms or public folder designs on both clients. The Office Resource Kit Tools and Utilities include the Switch Forms utility that allows you to run both Outlook and Microsoft Exchange Client on the same computer. For more information about installing Switch Forms, see "SwitchForms for Outlook" in Appendix A, "Microsoft Office 97 Resource Kit Tools and Utilities."

The following sections describe how Outlook uses e-mail components when you install Outlook on a computer to replace Microsoft Exchange Client.

Upgrading Microsoft Exchange Client Folders and Views

When you install and run Outlook, it opens all the folders defined in the mail profile. All the folders that were created and maintained by Microsoft Exchange Client are e-mail folders, and Outlook recognizes them as such. Outlook also creates the Outlook-specific folders discussed earlier in this chapter: Calendar, Contacts, Journal, Notes, and Tasks.

Any folder views that you specified from within Microsoft Exchange Client, including custom views, are recognized and maintained by Outlook.

Note Outlook uses these folders by default for the corresponding item types listed in the preceding table. However, you can also create additional folders for any of these item types.

Because Outlook performs most of the functions of Explorer in Windows 95 and Windows NT Workstation version 4.0, Outlook can also view folders on your computer and on the network, as well as use additional views to display folder contents.

Views

To display the contents of folders, Outlook provides several types of views. Any of these views can be used with any Outlook folder, providing a great deal of flexibility in displaying folder contents.

This Outlook view type	Contains items in this format
Card	Individual cards, as in a card file
Day/Week/Month	Items arranged as on a calendar, by the day, week, or month
Icon	Items and files represented by individual icons
Table	Grid of rows and columns
Timeline	Horizontal bars indicating chronology and duration

Note The view types in the preceding table are associated with default Outlook folders. For example, mail items appear by default in the Inbox folder in table view. However, you can use any view type with any Outlook folder—for example, you can view mail items in timeline view. You can also use Outlook views with folders on your computer or on the network.

Upgrading from Microsoft Exchange Client

This section describes the differences between Outlook and Microsoft Exchange Client for Microsoft Exchange Client users who are upgrading to Outlook. Because both Outlook and Microsoft Exchange Client are MAPI-compatible applications, Outlook can serve as a complete replacement for Microsoft Exchange Client, and the upgrading process is straightforward: install Outlook.

Can I upgrade to Outlook and maintain my current e-mail configuration? Except for changes in the user interface and other features, you can continue working with e-mail in Outlook just as you did in Microsoft Exchange Client. Outlook uses the same profile and other configuration information and can use all Microsoft Exchange Client extensions and custom forms.

Can I continue to exchange e-mail and share information with users who have not upgraded to Outlook? You can exchange e-mail and share public folders with Microsoft Exchange Client users. Some restrictions are described in the following sections.

Note In addition to replacing front-end e-mail and calendar applications, Outlook can also facilitate a major upgrade from Microsoft Mail 3.*x* to Microsoft Exchange Server. For more information, see "Migrating to Microsoft Exchange Server" later in this chapter.

The following sections briefly describe the basic structure of Outlook to help you understand the upgrading process. For a more thorough discussion of Outlook architecture, see Chapter 37, "Microsoft Outlook Architecture."

Items

Outlook recognizes six Outlook-specific item types, as shown in the following table.

This Outlook item type	Contains this kind of information
Appointment	Appointments, meetings, and events; may be recurring or non-recurring
Contact	Names, street addresses, e-mail addresses, URLs, phone numbers, FAX numbers, and so forth
Journal	Log of phone calls, e-mail, and so on, with associated date and time information
Mail	E-mail messages
Note	Miscellaneous text
Task	To-do items, including information such as owner, due date, priority, and status

Note Outlook also recognizes files. You can use Outlook to display folders on your hard disk, floppy disks, and network drives. Although Outlook is not an upgrade or replacement for the Windows Explorer, it can perform the same file management functions.

Folders

Outlook defines special-purpose folders for containing various Outlook item types. Each folder contains one type of item, as shown in the following table.

This Outlook folder	Contains this item type
Calendar	Appointment Items
Contacts	Contact Items
Journal	Journal Items
Inbox	Mail Items
Outbox	Mail Items
Sent Items	Mail Items
Notes	Note Items
Tasks	Task Items

> **Note** Microsoft Outlook runs on Windows 95 and Windows NT Workstation version 3.51 or later only. Users of Microsoft Exchange Client or Microsoft Mail for the Macintosh or for MS-DOS cannot upgrade directly to Outlook. However, for those users who do migrate to the Windows operating environment, this chapter describes how Outlook can import data from these applications.

Overview

The primary questions most Outlook upgraders have are:

- Can I upgrade to Outlook and maintain my current e-mail and scheduling configuration?
- Can I continue to exchange e-mail, share information, and perform group scheduling tasks with users who have not upgraded to Outlook?

If you are upgrading from any of the following Microsoft e-mail or calendar applications, this chapter answers these questions for you.

Application	Operating system
Microsoft Exchange Client version 4.0	Windows version 3.1, Windows 95, or Windows NT; Macintosh; or MS-DOS
Microsoft Mail version 3.x for Windows	Windows 3.1, Windows 95, or Windows NT
Microsoft Mail version 3.x for MS-DOS	MS-DOS
Microsoft Mail version 3.x for the Macintosh	Macintosh
Microsoft Schedule+ version 1.0 or 95	Windows 3.1, Windows 95, or Windows NT

Outlook combines a number of information management functions into a single application, and it is designed to be a complete upgrade for Microsoft messaging and scheduling applications. The following table shows the functions from several applications that Outlook can replace.

Outlook replaces this function	From this application
Electronic messaging	Microsoft Exchange Client, Microsoft Mail 3.x for Windows
Personal and group scheduling	Schedule+
Managing contact lists	Schedule+
Managing task lists	Schedule+
Viewing and managing folders	Windows Explorer

CHAPTER 13

Upgrading to Microsoft Outlook

This chapter tells you what to expect when you or your workgroup upgrades to Microsoft Outlook from previous Microsoft electronic mail (e-mail) and calendar applications. If you plan a gradual upgrade, Outlook users may need to exchange e-mail and scheduling data with these applications. This chapter describes how Outlook users can interact with users of other applications, highlighting the new features and capabilities of Outlook.

In This Chapter
Overview   334
Upgrading from Microsoft Exchange Client   336
Sharing Information with Microsoft Exchange Client   339
Upgrading from Microsoft Mail 3.x for Windows   343
Sharing Information with Microsoft Mail 3.x   350
Upgrading from Microsoft Schedule+ 95   352
Sharing Information with Microsoft Schedule+ 95   355
Upgrading from Microsoft Schedule+ 1.0   357
Sharing Information with Microsoft Schedule+ 1.0   359

See Also
- For a summary of the new features in Outlook 97, see Chapter 2, "What's New in Microsoft Office 97."
- For information about installing Outlook or other Office applications, see Chapter 4, "Installing Microsoft Office."
- For information about switching to Outlook from other e-mail, scheduling, and information manager applications, see Chapter 19, "Switching to Microsoft Outlook."

Data Access Features

The following table describes new features in Microsoft Excel 97 that may affect your data access in previous versions.

When this Microsoft Excel 97 feature	Is saved in Microsoft Excel 4.0 format
Parameterized queries	Parameterized queries cannot be executed or edited.
Report templates	Lost in the conversion.

Programmability Features

The following table describes new features in Microsoft Excel 97 that may affect your programming in previous versions.

When this Microsoft Excel 97 feature	Is saved in Microsoft Excel 4.0 format
New Microsoft Excel 97 objects, methods, and properties	Not all programming elements are supported. For more information about compatibility, see "Upgrading XLM Macros to Visual Basic for Applications" earlier in this chapter.
ActiveX controls (formerly OLE controls or OCX)	Lost in the conversion.
User forms dialog controls	Lost in the conversion.

Charting Features

The following table describes new features in Microsoft Excel 97 that may affect your data or formatting in previous versions.

When this Microsoft Excel 97 feature	Is saved in Microsoft Excel 4.0 format
Microsoft Excel 97 chart types	Chart types are converted to the nearest chart type available in Microsoft Excel 4.0.
3-D bar shapes (cylinder, pyramid, and cone)	3-D shapes are converted to column charts.
Angled text on axis and data labels	The text is formatted straight (0 degrees).
Combination charts	All series are returned to a primary type.
Data tables on charts	Data tables are lost.
Error bars	Lost in the conversion.
Gradient fills	Gradient fills are converted to the nearest color and pattern.
Office Art objects	Office Art objects are converted to the nearest available shape and tool.
Pie-of-pie and bar-of-pie chart types	These chart types are converted to type 1 pie charts.
Time series axis	Special scaling information is lost, and the axis is converted to a normal category axis.
Trend lines	Lost in the conversion.

PivotTable Features

The following table describes new features in Microsoft Excel 97 that may affect your data or formatting in previous versions.

When this Microsoft Excel 97 feature	Is saved in Microsoft Excel 4.0 format
Microsoft Excel 97 PivotTables	PivotTables are converted to static data; they cannot be converted to a Microsoft Excel 4.0 Crosstab report.

Workgroup and Internet Features

The following table describes new features in Microsoft Excel 97 that may affect your data or formatting in previous versions.

When this Microsoft Excel 97 feature	Is saved in Microsoft Excel 4.0 format
Comments	Comments are converted to notes.
Hyperlink (**Insert** menu)	The HYPERLINK value is lost.
Multiuser workbooks	Sharing is disabled and the change log is lost.
Revision marks and audit trail	Lost in the conversion; the change log is also lost.

When this Microsoft Excel 97 feature	Is saved in Microsoft Excel 4.0 format
Multisheet workbook	In Microsoft Excel 4.0 workbook format, each sheet is converted to a bound sheet in a Microsoft Excel 4.0 workbook. In Microsoft Excel 4.0 worksheet format, only the active sheet is saved.
32,000 characters per cell	Characters beyond 255th character are truncated.
65,536 rows per worksheet	Data in rows below row 16,384 are truncated.

Formatting Features

The following table describes new features in Microsoft Excel 97 that may affect your data or formatting in previous versions.

When this Microsoft Excel 97 feature	Is saved in Microsoft Excel 4.0 format
Angled text	Angled text is reformatted to horizontal orientation.
Conditional formatting	Conditional formatting is lost, and cells are reformatted as normal text.
Data validation	Lost in the conversion.
Indenting within cells	Indentation within a cell is lost, and data remains left-aligned.
Merge cells option on the **Alignment** tab in the **Cells** dialog box (**Format** menu)	Merged cells are unmerged.
New border styles	New border styles are converted to the nearest border style available in Microsoft Excel 4.0.
Partial page breaks	Partial page breaks are converted to full page breaks.
Shrink to fit option on the **Alignment** tab in the **Cells** dialog box (**Format** menu)	Text and data retain the same point size they had before **Shrink to fit** was selected.

Formulas and Functions Features

The following table describes new features in Microsoft Excel 97 that may affect your data or formatting in previous versions.

When this Microsoft Excel 97 feature	Is saved in Microsoft Excel 4.0 format
Defined labels	Lost in the conversion.
English language references in formulas	English language references are converted to A1 reference notations. However, names of named cells and ranges are preserved.

Sharing Workbooks with Microsoft Excel 4.0

If your workgroup is upgrading gradually to Microsoft Excel 97, some users may have to share documents with users of Microsoft Excel 4.0. Microsoft Excel 97 users can save their documents in Microsoft Excel 4.0 format.

▶ **To save a workbook in Microsoft Excel 4.0 format**

1 On the **File** menu, click **Save As**.

2 In the **Save as type** box, click **Microsoft Excel 4.0 Workbook** to save the entire workbook.

–or–

In the **Save as type** box, click **Microsoft Excel 4.0 Worksheet** to save only the active sheet.

Tip End users can specify the default format in which Microsoft Excel 97 saves new workbooks.

▶ **To specify the default format in which to save workbooks**

1 On the **Tools** menu, click **Options**, and then click the **Transition** tab.

2 In the **Save Excel files as** box, click the file format you want.

For more information about selecting a default format in which to save workbooks, see "Specifying the Default Format in Which to Save Office Documents" in Chapter 22, "Supporting Multiple Versions of Microsoft Office."

Tip In Windows 95 or Windows NT Workstation 4.0, you can use a system policy to define the default value for the **Save as type** option in the **Save As** dialog box (**File** menu) for all Microsoft Excel users in your workgroup. In the System Policy Editor, set the following policy:

User\Excel 97\Tools_Options\Transition\Default Save

For more information, see "Using Windows System Policies to Customize Office" in Chapter 7, "Customizing and Optimizing Microsoft Office."

Since not all Microsoft Excel 97 features are supported in Microsoft Excel 4.0, saving in 4.0 format may result in loss of data or formatting. The following sections describe the Microsoft Excel 97 features that are not fully supported in Microsoft Excel 4.0.

Basic Use Features

The following table describes new features in Microsoft Excel 97 that may affect your data or formatting in previous versions.

The following table lists new commands that have been added to the **Help** menu.

This Microsoft Excel 97 command	Allows you to
Contents and Index	Display the Help Contents.
What's This?	Click any area of the screen (such as a toolbar or menu command) to see a brief explanation in a ScreenTip.
Microsoft on the Web submenu commands	Connect to the Microsoft home page on the Web (requires Internet access). For information about customizing these commands, see "Customizing Office Connections to the World Wide Web" in Chapter 7, "Customizing and Optimizing Microsoft Office."

Upgrading XLM Macros to Visual Basic for Applications

In Microsoft Excel 97, you can open and run XLM macros created in Microsoft Excel 4.0 or later. You must modify your macro code under the following conditions:

- For macros that make calls to custom 16-bit DLLs, you must provide a 32-bit compatibility layer (a *thunking* layer) for the 16-bit DLL, or the DLL source code must be recompiled into a 32-bit version of the DLL.

- For macros that make calls to 16-bit Windows 3.*x* API functions or subroutines, you must edit the application code to replace the calls with appropriate calls to the Win32 API (Windows only).

For more information about upgrading XLM macros, see the following:

- "Porting Your 16-bit Office-Based Solutions to 32-bit Office" in Chapter 10, "Upgrading from Previous Versions of Microsoft Office."

- The *Microsoft Office 97/Visual Basic Programmer's Guide*, published by Microsoft Press and available wherever computer books are sold. For more information about Microsoft Press, see Appendix E, "Other Support Resources."

Macro Menu

The **Macro** menu has been removed. The following table describes the new locations and functionality of **Macro** menu commands.

This Microsoft Excel 4.0 command	Changes to this in Microsoft Excel 97
Run	Functionality moved to the **Run** button in the **Macro** dialog box (**Tools** menu, **Macro** submenu).
Record	Moved to **Record New Macro** (**Tools** menu, **Macro** submenu).
Relative Record	Functionality moved to the **Relative Reference** button (**Stop Recording** toolbar). This toolbar is visible only when recording a macro.
Start Recorder, **Set Recorder, Resume**, and **Assign to Object**	Removed.

Window Menu

The following table describes changed commands on the **Window** menu.

This Microsoft Excel 4.0 command	Changes to this in Microsoft Excel 97
View	Renamed **Custom Views** (**View** menu). This command no longer requires an add-in.

Help Menu

The following table describes changed commands on the **Help** menu.

This Microsoft Excel 4.0 command	Changes to this in Microsoft Excel 97
Contents and **Search**	Renamed **Microsoft Excel Help**. This command displays the Office Assistant, through which you view Help.
Product Support	Functionality moved to the **Tech Support** button in the **About Microsoft Excel** dialog box (**Help** menu).
Introducing Microsoft Excel and **Learning Microsoft Excel**	Removed.
Multiplan	Removed. Although Microsoft Excel no longer includes a Multiplan Help feature, you can still exchange documents with Multiplan through the Symbolic Link (SYLK) format. For more information, see Chapter 18, "Switching to Microsoft Excel."

Chapter 12   Upgrading from Previous Versions of Microsoft Excel

This Microsoft Excel 97 command	Allows you to
Access Form (Windows only)	Start AccessLinks, with which you can create a Microsoft Access data entry form for a Microsoft Excel list. Microsoft Access must be installed on the same computer.
Access Report (Windows only)	Start the Access Report Wizard, with which you can create an Access report with Microsoft Excel data. Microsoft Access must be installed on the same computer.
Convert to Access (Windows only)	Convert a Microsoft Excel list to a Microsoft Access database. Microsoft Access must be installed on the same computer.

Options Menu

The **Options** menu has been removed. The following table describes the new locations and functionality of **Options** menu commands.

This Microsoft Excel 4.0 command	Changes to this in Microsoft Excel 97
Set Print Area	Moved to **Print Area** submenu (**File** menu).
Set Print Titles	Moved to the **Sheet** tab in the **Page Setup** dialog box (**File** menu).
Set Page Break	Renamed **Page Break** (**Insert** menu).
Display	Moved to the **View** tab in the **Options** dialog box (**Tools** menu).
Toolbars	Moved to **Toolbars** submenu (**View** menu).
Color Palette	Moved to **Color** tab in the **Options** dialog box (**Tools** menu).
Protect Document	Moved to **Options** button in the **Save As** dialog box (**File** menu).
Calculation	Moved to the **Calculation** tab in the **Options** dialog box (**Tools** menu).
Workspace	Moved to **View** and **Transition** tabs in the **Options** dialog box (**Tools** menu).
Add-ins	Moved to **Add-Ins** (**Tools** menu).
Spelling	Moved to **Spelling** (**Tools** menu).
Group Edit	Removed. To edit a group of worksheets, click the tab for the first sheet, and then hold down SHIFT (if adjacent) or CTRL (if nonadjacent) and click the tab for another sheet.
Analysis Tools	Removed. The analysis tools functionality has been built into Microsoft Excel 97.

Data Menu

The following table describes changed commands on the **Data** menu.

This Microsoft Excel 4.0 command	Changes to this in Microsoft Excel 97
Find, **Extract**, and **Delete**	Removed. Database search functionality has been incorporated into commands on the **Filter** submenu (**Data** menu).
Set Database, **Set Criteria**, and **Set Extract**	Removed. It is not necessary to define a database (by naming a range Database). In Microsoft Excel 97, you can filter, sort, and perform other database activities with any contiguous range.
Series	Functionality incorporated into the AutoFill mouse action (dragging the fill handle). You can create custom AutoFill lists on the **Custom Lists** tab in the **Options** dialog box (**Tools** menu).
Parse	Removed. Parsing functionality has been incorporated into **Text to Columns** (**Data** menu).
Crosstab	Removed. Crosstab functionality has been incorporated into **PivotTable Report** (**Data** menu).

The following table lists new commands that have been added to the **Data** menu.

This Microsoft Excel 97 command	Allows you to
Filter submenu commands	Filter any contiguous range of data.
Subtotals	Add subtotals to any contiguous range of numeric data.
Validation	Format cells to accept only a specific type or range of data, and to specify the messages users see when working in the range.
Text to Columns	Start the Convert Text to Columns Wizard, with which you can parse text strings (such as tab-delimited text) into columns on the worksheet.
Template Wizard	Create a template you can use as a form to enter data in a database.
Group and Outline submenu commands	Create, promote, or demote outline levels.
Get External Data submenu commands	Start Microsoft Query.
Refresh Data	Update data sources specified with **Get External Data** (**Data** menu).

Chapter 12 Upgrading from Previous Versions of Microsoft Excel

This Microsoft Excel 4.0 command	Changes to this in Microsoft Excel 97
Outline	Renamed **Group and Outline** (**Data** menu).
Goal Seek	Moved to **Goal Seek** (**Tools** menu).
Scenario Manager	Renamed **Scenarios** (**Tools** menu).
Solver	Moved to **Solver** (**Tools** menu).

Format Menu

The following table describes changed commands on the **Format** menu.

This Microsoft Excel 4.0 command	Changes to this in Microsoft Excel 97
Number	Moved to the **Number** tab in the **Format Cells** dialog box (**Format** menu).
Alignment	Moved to the **Alignment** tab in the **Format Cells** dialog box (**Format** menu).
Font	Moved to the **Font** tab in the **Format Cells** dialog box (**Format** menu).
Borders	Moved to the **Border** tab in the **Format Cells** dialog box (**Format** menu).
Patterns	Moved to the **Patterns** tab in the **Format Cells** dialog box (**Format** menu).
Cell Protection	Moved to the **Protection** tab in the **Format Cells** dialog box (**Format** menu).
Row Height	Renamed **Height** (**Row** submenu).
Column Width	Renamed **Width** (**Column** submenu).
Justify	Renamed **AutoFit Selection** (**Column** submenu).
Bring to Front and **Send to Back**	Moved to the **Order** submenu on the object's shortcut menu.
Group	Moved to the **Grouping** submenu on the object's shortcut menu.
Object Properties	Moved to the **Properties** tab in the **Format Object** dialog box.

The following table lists new commands that have been added to the **Format** menu.

This Microsoft Excel 97 command	Allows you to
Sheet submenu commands	Rename, hide, or change the background of a sheet within a workbook.
Conditional Formatting	Apply formatting automatically to a cell if its value meets criteria you specify.

The following table lists new commands that have been added to the **Edit** menu.

This Microsoft Excel 97 command	Allows you to
Delete Sheet	Delete the active sheet from the workbook.
Move or Copy Sheet	Move or copy the active sheet in the workbook.
Find	Search the active sheet. This command was moved from the **Formula** menu.
Replace	Replace characters in selected cells or on the active sheet. This command was moved from the **Formula** menu.
Go To	Select a specific cell or named range. This command was moved from the **Formula** menu.
Links	Edit or update links.
Object	Edit, open, or convert an embedded object.

Formula Menu

The **Formula** menu has been removed in Microsoft Excel 97. The following table describes the new locations or functionality of Microsoft Excel 4.0 **Formula** menu commands.

This Microsoft Excel 4.0 command	Changes to this in Microsoft Excel 97
Paste Name	Removed. To paste a name into a formula, select it from the name box on the formula bar.
Paste Function	Renamed **Function** (**Insert** menu).
Define Name	Renamed **Define** (**Insert** menu, **Name** submenu).
Create Names	Renamed **Create** (**Insert** menu, **Name** submenu).
Apply Names	Renamed **Apply** (**Insert** menu, **Name** submenu).
Note	Renamed **Comment** (**Insert** menu).
Goto	Renamed **Go To** (**Edit** menu).
Find	Moved to **Find** (**Edit** menu).
Replace	Moved to **Replace** (**Edit** menu).
Select Special	Removed. Use the **Special** button in the **Go To** dialog box (**Edit** menu).
Show Active Cell	Removed. The active cell reference appears in the name box on the formula bar.

Do my old macros still work in Microsoft Excel 97?   In most cases, your XLM macros run unmodified in Microsoft Excel 97. For more information about working with XLM code in Microsoft Excel 97, see "Upgrading XLM Macros to Visual Basic for Applications" earlier in this chapter.

Tip   To convert several documents at once to Microsoft Excel 97 format, you can use the File Conversion Wizard, which is supplied with Microsoft Excel 97. For more information about this wizard, see "Converting File Formats in Microsoft Excel" in Chapter 18, "Switching to Microsoft Excel."

Menu Changes

The following sections summarize the Microsoft Excel 4.0 commands that have changed location or functionality in Microsoft Excel 97, as well as commands that are new in Microsoft Excel 97.

File Menu

The following table describes changed commands on the **File** menu.

This Microsoft Excel 4.0 command	Changes to this in Microsoft Excel 97
Links	Moved to **Edit** menu.
Save Workbook	Removed. Since the workbook is the Microsoft Excel 97 document type, click **Save** to save a workbook.
Delete	Removed. To delete a workbook, right-click it in the **Open** dialog box (**File** menu), and then click **Delete** on the shortcut menu.
Print Report	Renamed **Report Manager** (**View** menu).
Send Mail	Renamed **Mail Recipient** (**Send To** submenu). For more information about using Microsoft Excel 97 with e-mail, see Chapter 28, "Working with Messaging Systems and Connectivity Software."

Edit Menu

The following table describes changed commands on the **Edit** menu.

This Microsoft Excel 4.0 command	Changes to this in Microsoft Excel 97
Paste Link	**Paste Special**.
Fill Right and Fill Down	Moved to **Fill** submenu.

Data Access Features

The following table describes new features in Microsoft Excel 97 that may affect your data access in previous versions.

When this Microsoft Excel 97 feature	Is saved in Microsoft Excel 5.0 or 95 format
Parameterized queries	Parameterized queries cannot be executed or edited.
Report templates	Lost in the conversion.
Shared queries (connections without a data source name, or DSN)	Files that contain connections without DSN are supported in Microsoft Excel 95 (with ODBC 2.0). In Microsoft Excel 5.0 (with ODBC 1.0) the user is prompted for connection information.

Programmability Features

The following table describes new features in Microsoft Excel 97 that may affect your programming in previous versions.

When this Microsoft Excel 97 feature	Is saved in Microsoft Excel 5.0 or 95 format
New Microsoft Excel 97 objects, methods, and properties	Not all programming elements are supported. For more information about compatibility, see "Macro Changes" earlier in this chapter.
ActiveX controls (formerly OLE controls or OCX)	ActiveX controls appear in the workbook but cannot be used.
User forms dialog controls	Lost in the conversion.

Upgrading from Microsoft Excel 4.0

This section describes the changes between Microsoft Excel version 4.0 for Windows or the Macintosh and Microsoft Excel 97. Microsoft Excel 97 is a major upgrade from previous versions of the application. For more information about the features and benefits of this upgrade, see Chapter 2, "What's New in Microsoft Office 97."

What happens to my old worksheets and workbooks when I open them in Microsoft Excel 97?   You can open files created in Microsoft Excel 4.0 directly in Microsoft Excel 97. All data and formatting created in Microsoft Excel 4.0 are fully supported in Microsoft Excel 97. However, sound notes created in previous versions of Microsoft Excel are lost.

Can I share Microsoft Excel 97 workbooks with users of previous versions?   If your workgroup uses any combination of Microsoft Excel 97, 95, 5.0, or 4.0, users can exchange workbooks between versions. However, not all Microsoft Excel 97 features are supported in previous versions. For more information, see "Sharing Workbooks with Microsoft Excel 4.0" later in this chapter.

When this Microsoft Excel 97 feature	Is saved in Microsoft Excel 5.0 or 95 format
Data tables on charts	Lost in the conversion.
Gradient fills	Gradient fills are converted to the nearest color and pattern.
Office Art objects	Office Art objects are converted to the nearest available shape and tool.
Pie-of-pie and bar-of-pie chart types	These charts are converted to type 1 pie charts.
Time series axis	Special scaling information is lost, and the axis is converted to a normal category axis.

PivotTable Features

The following table describes new features in Microsoft Excel 97 that may affect your data or formatting in previous versions.

When this Microsoft Excel 97 feature	Is saved in Microsoft Excel 5.0 or 95 format
Calculated fields, calculated items, and formatting based on structure	These PivotTable features are preserved until the user makes changes to or refreshes the PivotTable data. Then they are lost.
PivotTable properties sheet	All new properties are lost. These include: • Page field placement across columns or down rows • Alternate strings for NA and error cell display • Server-based page fields • AutoSort and AutoShow on fields • Multiselect on page fields • Persistent grouping and sorting • Data fields displayed as numbers
Preserved formatting	Formatting is saved, but structured behavior is lost as soon a the user makes changes to or refreshes the PivotTable data.

Workgroup and Internet Features

The following table describes new features in Microsoft Excel 97 that may affect your data or formatting in previous versions.

When this Microsoft Excel 97 feature	Is saved in Microsoft Excel 5.0 or 95 format
Comments	Comments are converted to CellTips.
Hyperlink (**Insert** menu)	The HYPERLINK value is lost.
Multiuser workbooks	Sharing is disabled, and the change log is lost.
Revision marks and audit trail	Lost in the conversion; the change log is also lost.

Formatting Features

The following table describes new features in Microsoft Excel 97 that may affect your data or formatting in previous versions.

When this Microsoft Excel 97 feature	Is saved in Microsoft Excel 5.0 or 95 format
Angled text	Angled text is reformatted to horizontal orientation.
Conditional formatting	Conditional formatting is lost, and cells are reformatted as normal text.
Data validation	Lost in the conversion.
Indenting within cells	Indentation within a cell is lost, and data remains left-aligned.
Merge cells option on the **Alignment** tab in the **Cells** dialog box (**Format** menu)	Merged cells are unmerged.
New border styles	New border styles are converted to the nearest border style available in Microsoft Excel 5.0 or 95.
Partial page breaks	Partial page breaks are converted to full page breaks.
Shrink to fit option on the **Alignment** tab in the **Cells** dialog box (**Format** menu)	Text and data retain the same point size they had before **Shrink to fit** was selected.

Formulas and Functions Features

The following table describes new features in Microsoft Excel 97 that may affect your data or formatting in previous versions.

When this Microsoft Excel 97 feature	Is saved in Microsoft Excel 5.0 or 95 format
Defined labels	Lost in the conversion.
English language references in formulas	English language references are converted to A1 reference notations. However, names of named cells and ranges are preserved.

Charting Features

The following table describes new features in Microsoft Excel 97 that may affect your data or formatting in previous versions.

When this Microsoft Excel 97 feature	Is saved in Microsoft Excel 5.0 or 95 format
3-D bar shapes (cylinder, pyramid, and cone)	3-D shapes are converted to 3-D column charts.
Angled text on axis and data labels	The text is formatted straight (0 degrees).
Bubble chart format	Bubble charts are converted to type 1 XY scatter charts.

When to Use the 97 and 5.0/95 Format

The following sample scenarios may help you and your workgroup make the best use of the 97 and 5.0/95 format.

Scenario	Recommendation
A Microsoft Office 95 user receives a compound document from a Microsoft Office 97 user. The compound document includes an embedded object in the 97 and 5.0/95 format. The Microsoft Office 95 user does not want to alter the format of the embedded object, but needs to activate it.	The Microsoft Office 95 user should open the compound document read-only.
A Microsoft Excel 97 user wants to publish a workbook in the 97 and 5.0/95 format to an audience of Microsoft Excel 97 and 95 users. However, the Microsoft Excel 97 user does not want any Microsoft Excel 95 users to alter the workbook.	The Microsoft Excel 97 user should enter a write-reservation password when saving the workbook and distribute the password only to other Microsoft Excel 97 users. This still allows Microsoft Excel 95 users to open the workbook read-only.
A Microsoft Excel 97 user must transmit a workbook to Microsoft Excel 5.0 and 95 users by modem.	The Microsoft Excel 97 user should save the workbook in 5.0 or 95 format, since the resulting file is much smaller and transmits more quickly.

Saving Workbooks in Microsoft Excel 5.0 or 95 Format

Microsoft Excel 97 can save workbooks in previous formats; however, not all Microsoft Excel 97 features are supported in previous versions. Because of changes to the Microsoft Excel file format, saving a Microsoft Excel 97 workbook in a previous version can result in lost data and lost or changed formatting. This section describes features that are not fully supported in Microsoft Excel 5.0 or Microsoft Excel 95.

Tip If you must save a Microsoft Excel 97 workbook in 5.0 or 95 format but you want to copy or link a portion of the workbook into an ActiveX container (for example, a Word document), save the workbook in 5.0 or 95 format before you create the ActiveX object. This ensures that Microsoft Excel creates the proper graphic representation of the object (a Microsoft Excel 5.0 or 95 representation) in the container application.

Basic Use Features

The following table describes new features in Microsoft Excel 97 that may affect your data or formatting in previous versions.

When this Microsoft Excel 97 feature	Is saved in Microsoft Excel 5.0 or 95 format
32,000 characters per cell	Characters beyond the 255th character are truncated.
65,536 rows per worksheet	Data in rows below row 16,384 are truncated.

What happens to Microsoft Excel 97 objects in the 97 and 5.0/95 file format?

When creating or inserting a Microsoft Excel 97 object into a compound document, Microsoft Excel 97 checks the setting in the **Default Save** subkey in the Registry (Windows) or Preferences (Macintosh). If the 97 and 5.0/95 format is set as the default, Microsoft Excel 97 uses 97 and 5.0/95 format for the embedded object.

When not activated, OLE objects are represented in container applications either as an icon or as a portion of a document, such as a worksheet range. This portion of a document is actually a WMF (Windows) or PICT (Macintosh) graphic representation of a portion of the Microsoft Excel 97 data stream from the workbook file.

In most cases, the graphic representation equally represents either the 97 or the 5.0/95 data stream of the object. If the graphic representation includes features unique to Microsoft Excel 97, however, it is possible that users of previous versions of Microsoft Excel may initially see one representation of the object (the graphic image) that differs from the actual embedded object after they activate the object.

For example, if the embedded object includes merged cells (a Microsoft Excel 97 feature) but a Microsoft Excel 5.0 user activates the object, the graphic representation of merged cells disappears and is replaced by corresponding data from the Microsoft Excel 5.0 data stream: unmerged cells. If the user then saves the container document (or the application saves it automatically), Microsoft Excel 5.0 updates only the 5.0/95 data stream. The 97 data stream of the object is permanently lost, and the graphic representation of the object changes to reflect the 5.0/95 data stream.

When Microsoft Excel 5.0 or 95 users open a workbook saved in the new 97 and 5.0/95 format, they are prompted to open the workbook read-only, although they can open the file read/write. Microsoft Excel 5.0 or 95 reads only the 5.0/95 data stream in the file. When it encounters the end of the 5.0/95 data stream, it disregards the remainder of the file (that is, the 97 data stream). Consequently, if a Microsoft Excel 5.0 or 95 user saves the workbook, the 97 data stream is permanently lost.

Tip Microsoft Excel 97 users can save a workbook in the 97 and 5.0/95 format and designate it as read-only. Then Microsoft Excel 5.0 or 95 users must open the workbook read-only. They see only the 5.0/95 data stream, and they cannot edit or remove the 97 data stream.

Because the 97 and 5.0/95 format stores both Microsoft Excel 97 and 5.0/95 data streams in a single file, the file is up to twice as large as it would be if saved in Microsoft Excel 97 format. Although file open time is not affected, file save time in Microsoft Excel 97 increases. Otherwise, the 97 and 5.0/95 format has no effect on performance in either Microsoft Excel 97 or Microsoft Excel 5.0 or 95.

Users of Microsoft Excel 97 can save documents in 97 and 5.0/95 format.

▶ **To save a workbook in Microsoft Excel 97 and 5.0/95 format**

1 On the **File** menu, click **Save As**.

2 In the **Save as type** box, click **Microsoft Excel 97 & 5.0/95 Workbook**.

Tip End users can also specify the default format in which Microsoft Excel 97 saves new workbooks.

▶ **To specify the default format in which to save workbooks**

1 On the **Tools** menu, click **Options**, and then click the **Transition** tab.

2 In the **Save Excel files as** box, click the file format you want.

For more information about selecting a default format in which to save workbooks, see "Specifying the Default Format in Which to Save Office Documents" in Chapter 22, "Supporting Multiple Versions of Microsoft Office."

How to Make 97 and 5.0/95 Format the Default for Your Workgroup

In Windows 95 and Windows NT Workstation version 4.0, you can use a system policy to define the default value for the **Save as type** option in the **Save As** dialog box (**File** menu) for all Microsoft Excel users in your workgroup. In the Windows System Policy Editor, set the following policy:

User\Excel 97\Tools_Options\Transition\Default Save

For more information, see "Using Windows System Policies to Customize Office" in Chapter 7, "Customizing and Optimizing Microsoft Office."

Sharing Workbooks with Microsoft Excel 5.0 or 95

If your workgroup is upgrading gradually to Microsoft Excel 97, some users may have to share workbooks with users of Microsoft Excel 5.0 or 95. There are two strategies for sharing workbooks among different versions of Microsoft Excel:

- Save in the dual Microsoft Excel 97 and 5.0/95 format
- Save in Microsoft Excel 5.0 or Microsoft Excel 95 format

The following table summarizes the advantages and disadvantages of each strategy.

Strategy	Advantages	Disadvantages
Save Microsoft Excel 97 workbooks in Microsoft Excel 97 and 5.0/95 format	All Microsoft Excel users can open and edit workbooks. Microsoft Excel 5.0 or 95 users do not need to install additional software.	Workbook file size and save time increase substantially. Microsoft 5.0 and 95 users may lose data or formatting if they save the workbook.
Save Microsoft Excel 97 workbooks in Microsoft Excel 5.0 or 95 format	All Microsoft Excel users can open, edit, and save workbooks.	Microsoft Excel 97 users cannot take advantage of features unique to Microsoft Excel 97.

Note Because the file formats between Microsoft Excel 5.0 and Microsoft Excel 95 are very similar, these two versions are considered together in the following sections.

Saving Workbooks in Microsoft Excel 97 and 5.0/95 Format

The new Microsoft Excel 97 and 5.0/95 file format is designed for workgroups that are upgrading gradually to Microsoft Excel 97. You can standardize your workgroup on this format until all Microsoft Excel 5.0 and 95 users have upgraded to Microsoft Excel 97. This ensures that all Microsoft Excel users have a common file format with which to collaborate on shared workbooks.

When a Microsoft Excel 97 user saves a workbook in the 97 and 5.0/95 format, Microsoft Excel creates two data streams in the workbook file: one for Microsoft Excel 97, and another for Microsoft Excel 5.0 and 95. Microsoft Excel 97 first writes the 5.0/95 data stream to the file, and then writes the 97 data stream. When writing the 5.0/95 data stream, Microsoft Excel has the same conversion limitations described in "Saving Workbooks in Microsoft Excel 5.0 or 95 Format" later in this chapter.

Chart Format Changes

When you upgrade to Microsoft Excel 97, your custom chart autoformats are updated automatically. Custom autoformats are stored in the file Xl5galry.xls. The Office Setup program copies your existing Xl5galry.xls file to the folder that contains the Microsoft Excel 97 program and renames the file Xlusrgal.xls. Built-in autoformats are stored in the file Xl8galry.xls.

Tip In Windows 95 and Windows NT Workstation 4.0, you can use a system policy to specify the path to a custom chart gallery named Xlusrgal.gra for all Microsoft Excel users in your workgroup. In the System Policy Editor, set the following policy:

User\Excel\Miscellaneous\Chart Gallery

For more information, see "Using Windows System Policies to Customize Office" in Chapter 7, "Customizing and Optimizing Microsoft Office."

Macro Changes

Because of architectural changes in Microsoft Excel 97, some Visual Basic for Applications macros written in Microsoft Excel 95 may not perform as expected in Microsoft Excel 97. The most common macro problems are documented in the Office 97 Resource Kit Help file, which is included with the Tools and Utilities. Of these, the most common problems are described in the following articles:

- *XL97: Problems When Disabling/Enabling Menus in MS Excel 97* (Article ID Q157754)
- *XL97: Text Contained in AutoShapes Does Not Rotate* (Article ID Q156604)
- *XL97: Visual Basic does not Signal an Error has Occurred* (Article ID Q157207)
- *XL97: Run-Time Error Using CreateObject With DAO.DBEngine* (Article ID Q157471)

Tools and Utilities The Office Resource Kit Tools and Utilities include the Office 97 Resource Kit Help file, a collection of KnowledgeBase articles about Office 97 written by Microsoft Product Support Services. For more information, see "Microsoft Technical Support Help File" in Appendix A, "Microsoft Office 97 Resource Kit Tools and Utilities."

World Wide Web For the latest information about Microsoft Excel macro compatibility, connect to the Office Developer Site home page at:

http://www.microsoft.com/officedev/

The following table lists new commands that have been added to the **Apple Help** menu.

This Microsoft Excel 97 command	Allows you to
Microsoft Excel Help	Display the Assistant, through which you view Help.
What's This?	Click any area of the screen (such as a toolbar or menu command) to see a brief explanation in Balloon Help™.
Microsoft on the Web submenu commands	Connect to the Microsoft home page on the Web (requires Internet access). For information about customizing these commands, see "Customizing Office Connections to the World Wide Web" in Chapter 7, "Customizing and Optimizing Microsoft Office."

File Format Changes

The Microsoft Excel 97 file format differs from that of previous versions of Microsoft Excel. If your workgroup is upgrading gradually to Microsoft Excel 97, some users may have to share workbooks with users of Microsoft Excel 95. Microsoft Excel supports several strategies for sharing workbooks among different versions. For more information about changes in file format and strategies for sharing workbooks, see "Sharing Workbooks with Microsoft Excel 5.0 or 95" later in this chapter.

Template Changes

All Microsoft Excel 5.0 templates work in Microsoft Excel 97. In Microsoft Excel 5.0, templates are stored in the following locations.

Operating system	Microsoft Excel 5.0 templates location
Windows	Xlstart folder
Macintosh	Excel Startup Folder (5) folder

In Microsoft Excel 97, built-in templates are stored in the following locations.

Operating system	Microsoft Excel 97 built-in templates location
Windows	Microsoft Office\Templates\Spreadsheet Solutions folder
Macintosh	Microsoft Office:Templates folder

Custom templates in Microsoft Excel 97 are stored in the following locations.

Operating system	Microsoft Excel 97 custom templates location
Windows	Microsoft Office\Templates folder
Macintosh	Microsoft Office:Templates folder

Window Menu

The following table describes changed commands on the **Window** menu.

This Microsoft Excel 5.0 command	Changes to this in Microsoft Excel 97
Show Clipboard (Macintosh only)	Removed.

Help Menu (Windows only)

The following table describes changed commands on the **Help** menu.

This Microsoft Excel 5.0 command	Changes to this in Microsoft Excel 97
Contents	Replaced by **Contents and Index**.
Search for Help On	Replaced by **Microsoft Excel Help**. This command displays the Office Assistant, through which you view Help.
Multiplan	Removed.

The following table lists new commands that have been added to the **Help** menu.

This Microsoft Excel 97 command	Allows you to
Contents and Index	Display the Help contents.
What's This?	Click any area of the screen (such as a toolbar or menu command) to see a brief explanation in a ScreenTip.
Microsoft on the Web submenu commands	Connect to the Microsoft home page on the Web (requires Internet access). For information about customizing these commands, see "Customizing Office Connections to the World Wide Web" in Chapter 7, "Customizing and Optimizing Microsoft Office."

Apple Help Menu (Macintosh only)

The following table describes changed commands on the **Apple® Help** menu.

This Microsoft Excel 5.0 command	Changes to this in Microsoft Excel 97
Quick Preview (**Examples and Demos** submenu)	Replaced by **Microsoft Excel Help**. This command displays the Assistant, through which you view Help.

Format Menu

The following table lists new commands that have been added to the **Format** menu.

This Microsoft Excel 97 command	Allows you to
Conditional Formatting	Apply formatting automatically to a cell if its value meets criteria you specify.

Tools Menu

The following table describes changed commands on the **Tools** menu.

This Microsoft Excel 5.0 command	Changes to this in Microsoft Excel 97
Macro	Functionality moved to the **Run** button in the **Macro** dialog box (**Macro** submenu).
Record Macro submenu commands	Moved to **Record New Macro** (**Macro** submenu).

The following table lists new commands that have been added to the **Tools** menu.

This Microsoft Excel 97 command	Allows you to
Track Changes submenu commands	Mark or review changes to the active workbook.
Merge Workbooks	Merge changes from one copy of a workbook into another. For more information about workbook collaboration, see Chapter 30, "Workgroup Features in Microsoft Excel."

Data Menu

The following table describes changed commands on the **Data** menu.

This Microsoft Excel 5.0 command	Changes to this in Microsoft Excel 97
PivotTable	Renamed **PivotTable Report**.
PivotTable Field	Removed. To hide or show PivotTable field items, double-click the field heading.

The following table lists new commands that have been added to the **Data** menu.

This Microsoft Excel 97 command	Allows you to
Validation	Format cells to accept only a specific type or range of data, and to specify the messages users see when working in the range.

The following table lists new commands that have been added to the **View** menu.

This Microsoft Excel 97 command	Allows you to
Normal	Switch from other views to normal view.
Page Break Preview	Switch to page break preview, in which you can adjust page breaks and see how the worksheet is to be printed.
Comments	Display or hide all comments on the worksheet. This command also displays the **Reviewing** toolbar, with which you can review existing comments and add new comments to the worksheet.
Custom Views	Create unique settings with which to view your document. Custom views can include print and filter settings and hidden rows or columns.

Insert Menu

The following table describes changed commands on the **Insert** menu.

This Microsoft Excel 5.0 command	Changes to this in Microsoft Excel 97
Chart submenu commands	Removed. The **Chart** command now starts the Chart Wizard, with which you specify whether the new chart is inserted in a worksheet or in a new chart sheet.
Macro submenu commands	Removed. Macro sheets are no longer visible. Use the **Visual Basic Editor** (**Tools** menu, **Macro** submenu) to view the Visual Basic environment.
Note	Renamed **Comment**. Sound notes are not supported in Microsoft Excel 97.

The following table lists new commands that have been added to the **Insert** menu.

This Microsoft Excel 97 command	Allows you to
Hyperlink	Insert a Web-style hyperlink to another Office document or to an Internet address. For more information about hyperlinks, see Chapter 24, "Integrating Microsoft Office with Your Intranet."

The graphics filter for this application or format	Is located in this file	Comments
Macintosh PICT (PICT)	Pictim32.flt	Required for PowerPoint for Windows; PICT format is native to PowerPoint for the Macintosh. Included in a Typical installation.
Micrografx Designer/Draw (DRW)	Drwimp32.flt	Supported by PowerPoint for Windows only.
PC Paintbrush (PCX)	Pcximp32.flt	Supported by PowerPoint for Windows only.
Tagged Image File Format (TIFF)	Tiffim32.flt (Windows); TIFF Import (Macintosh)	Included in a Typical installation.
Truevision Targa (TGA)	Tgaimp32.flt	Supported by PowerPoint for Windows only.
Windows Enhanced Metafile (EMF)	Emfimp32_flt (Macintosh)	Required for PowerPoint for the Macintosh; EMF format is native to PowerPoint for Windows. Included in a Typical installation.
Windows Metafile (WMF)	Wmfimp32_flt (Macintosh)	Required for PowerPoint for the Macintosh; WMF format is native to PowerPoint for Windows. Included in a Typical installation.
WordPerfect Graphics/DrawPerfect (WPG)	Wpgimp32.flt, Wpgexp32.flt (Windows); WordPerfect Graphics Import (Macintosh)	Supports import and export in PowerPoint 97 for Windows, and import only in PowerPoint 97 for the Macintosh. Included in a Typical installation.

Note When you install graphics filters, you can save presentations as graphics in formats supported by the filters. For information about saving presentations in a graphics format, see "Opening and Saving Graphics Files" later in this chapter.

Saving PowerPoint 97 presentations in other formats may result in graphics changing formats and some loss of image quality. In all cases, PowerPoint attempts to use the graphics format that is most compatible with the format to which the presentation is being converted.

Moving PowerPoint presentations between Windows and Macintosh computers can also result in changed graphics formats. For example, suppose a presentation created in PowerPoint for Windows contains a graphic image stored in WMF format. When the presentation is moved to PowerPoint for the Macintosh, PowerPoint converts the WMF graphic image to PICT format. The original WMF image is retained in the presentation, but the PICT image is the one that the user sees. In this conversion there may be a slight loss of image quality because Windows and Macintosh computers have similar, but not identical, graphics rendering systems (GDI and QuickDraw™ GX, respectively).

After the presentation is opened in PowerPoint for the Macintosh, one of two things may happen:

- If the Macintosh user disassembles the graphic image to edit it, PowerPoint converts the image to a group of PowerPoint drawing objects, which decreases the image quality. When the presentation is moved back to PowerPoint for Windows, the image is not reassembled, but remains a group of drawing objects.
- If the Macintosh user does not disassemble the graphic image, but modifies its attributes by cropping, recoloring, or changing the brightness or contrast, then PowerPoint converts the WMF graphic to PICT format. However, PowerPoint does not discard the original WMF image. When the presentation is moved back to PowerPoint for Windows, PowerPoint displays the original WMF graphic with no loss of image quality.

If a presentation originates in PowerPoint for the Macintosh and is then moved to PowerPoint for Windows, a similar conversion happens.

Important In presentations that originate in PowerPoint for the Macintosh, PICT images that contain JPEG-compressed QuickTime® data are not converted by the Windows PICT filter, and therefore suffer loss of image quality when opened in PowerPoint for Windows.

Converting Presentations from Other File Formats

To convert presentations in formats other than PowerPoint 97 format, first ensure that the correct converter is installed, and then open the presentation.

▶ **To convert a presentation to PowerPoint 97 format**

1. On the **File** menu, click **Open**.
2. In the **Files of type** box, click the presentation's original format.
3. In the **File name** box, select the file you want to convert.

PowerPoint converts the presentation and opens it.

Note In Windows, the file format does not necessarily correspond to the file name extension. For example, a WordPerfect document may have a .doc or .wpd extension, or no extension at all. When you open a file in another format, PowerPoint looks first at the contents of the file to determine the file format. If PowerPoint does not recognize the file format, it tries to use the converters that correspond to the file name extension. If PowerPoint is still unable to recognize the file format, it displays a message and does not open the presentation.

After you convert a presentation to PowerPoint, the converted presentation exists only in your computer's memory; the original presentation remains unchanged. To complete the conversion, you need to save the converted presentation in PowerPoint format.

▶ **To save a converted presentation in PowerPoint format**

- On the **File** menu, click **Save As**, and give the converted presentation a new name.

  This preserves the original presentation as a backup.

> **PowerPoint didn't convert my presentation properly**
>
> The file formats PowerPoint supports are listed in the **Files of type** box in the **Open** dialog box (**File** menu). If your presentation type is not listed, make sure the converter that supports your file format is installed. If none of the PowerPoint converters support your file format, try saving your presentation in a format that PowerPoint 97 can read, such as RTF or WMF.

To convert multiple presentations, open several presentations at the same time in the **Open** dialog box (**File** menu). PowerPoint converts each presentation you select. When you finish editing the presentations, save each presentation as described earlier.

Tip In Windows, you can open more than one file at a time if all the files are within a single folder. To select a contiguous group of presentations, click the name of the first presentation you want to open, and then hold down SHIFT and click the name of the last presentation you want to open. Or hold down CTRL and click the names of the individual presentations you want to open.

Saving PowerPoint Presentations in Other File Formats

You can save PowerPoint presentations in other formats that can be read by other applications or by earlier versions of PowerPoint.

▶ **To save a PowerPoint presentation in another file format**

1. On the **File** menu, click **Save As**.
2. In the **Save as type** box (Windows) or **Save file as type** box (Macintosh), click the format you want.

Tip When you save a PowerPoint presentation in another format, use a different file name so that you can keep a copy of the original as a backup.

For a list of the available file formats, see "Using Converters and Graphics Filters" earlier in this chapter.

Tip End users can also specify the default format in which PowerPoint saves new presentations.

▶ **To specify the default format in which to save presentations**

1. On the **Tools** menu, click **Options**, and then click the **Save** tab.
2. In the **Save PowerPoint files as** box, click the file format you want.

> **Tip** In Windows 95 and Windows NT Workstation version 4.0, you can use a system policy to define the **Save as type** option in the **Save As** dialog box (**File** menu) for all PowerPoint users in your workgroup. In the System Policy Editor, set the following policy:
>
> **User\PowerPoint\Tools_Options\Save\Default Save**
>
> For more information, see "Using Windows System Policies to Customize Office" in Chapter 7, "Customizing and Optimizing Microsoft Office."

Opening and Saving Text Files

To exchange presentations between PowerPoint and an application for which there is no converter, you can save your presentation in a text file format, which most applications can open. To save your formatting, use rich text format (RTF), which converts the formatting to text instructions that other applications (including compatible Microsoft applications) can read. If you do not want to save text formatting or if your application does not support RTF, you can save your presentation as plain text. RTF and plain-text formats do not save the graphic elements of a presentation, however—only the text.

Note If the graphics in your presentation are more important, you can convert the presentation to a graphics format and then recreate the text. For information about saving presentations in graphics format, see "Opening and Saving Graphics Files" later in this chapter.

▶ To save a PowerPoint presentation in RTF

1. On the **File** menu, click **Save As**.
2. In the **Save as type** box (Windows) or **Save file as type** box (Macintosh), click **Outline/RTF**.

PowerPoint can also import text files. If the application you are importing the text from does not support RTF, save the presentation in a plain-text format, and then import the text into PowerPoint as an outline.

▶ To open a text file as an outline in PowerPoint 97

1. On the **File** menu, click **Open**.
2. In the **Files of type** box, click **All Outlines**.
3. In the **File name** box, select the file you want to convert.

   PowerPoint converts the presentation and opens it.

If the presentation you are importing is in RTF, PowerPoint uses the text formatting instructions to structure the outline. Otherwise, it uses the leading tabs and paragraph marks. For more information about importing outlines as PowerPoint presentations, see "Sharing Information With PowerPoint 97" in Chapter 27, "Sharing Information with Microsoft Office Applications."

Opening and Saving Graphics Files

If you are sharing presentations with an application for which there is no PowerPoint converter, and you want to preserve the graphic design of your presentation, you can save your presentation in a graphics format. Saving presentations in a graphics format saves each slide in the presentation as a separate graphic image. The text is converted to graphics and cannot be edited as text. However, you can move graphical text elements on the slide, or replace them with editable text.

Note If the text in your presentation is more important, you can convert the text of the presentation and then re-create the graphics. For information about saving presentations in text format, see "Opening and Saving Text Files" earlier in this chapter.

PowerPoint can save presentations in any of its native graphics formats or in a graphics format for which a graphics filter is installed.

▶ **To save a PowerPoint presentation in a graphics format**

1. On the **File** menu, click **Save As**.
2. In the **Save as type** box (Windows) or **Save file as type** box (Macintosh), click the graphics format you want
3. In the **File name** box, type a name for the file, and then click **Save**.
4. At the PowerPoint prompt, specify whether you want to export every slide in the presentation or only the current slide.

If you export every slide, PowerPoint saves each slide as a graphics file in a folder with the file name you type. Each slide is named Slide$x$, where x is the slide number, such as 001, 002, and so on. If you export only the active slide, it is saved in the active folder with the file name you type.

For more information about using export graphics filters, see "Custom Export Formats" in Chapter 38, "Microsoft PowerPoint Architecture."

The graphics format I need does not appear in the list

The file types that appear in the **Save as type** (Windows) or **Save file as type** (Macintosh) box in the **Save As** dialog box indicate the file formats for which graphics filters are installed, or which PowerPoint can read directly. If the graphics filters you need are not installed, rerun the Setup, click **Add/Remove**, and then select the graphics filters you want.

In addition to saving presentations in a variety of graphics formats, PowerPoint 97 can also open WMF (Windows) or PICT (Macintosh) graphics files as presentations.

▶ **To open a graphics file in PowerPoint 97**

1. On the **File** menu, click **Open**.
2. In the **Files of type** box, click **All Files**.
3. In the **Name** box, select the WMF or PICT file you want to convert.

   PowerPoint creates a single-slide presentation based on the Blank Presentation template and inserts the graphics file onto that slide.

Note If you are recreating a multislide presentation, create a new slide for each graphics file you want to include, and then click **Picture** (**Insert** menu) to insert the graphics file onto the slide.

You can edit converted slides in slide view by using the **Ungroup** command (**Draw** menu). PowerPoint displays the graphic images as drawing objects so you can edit them.

If the application from which you are importing the presentation does not support WMF or PICT files, save the slides in a graphics format that is native to PowerPoint or for which a graphics import filter is installed. For a list of native graphics formats and graphics filters supported by PowerPoint, see "Using Converters and Graphics Filters" earlier in this chapter.

Switching from Harvard Graphics

This section explains how to convert presentations from Harvard Graphics to PowerPoint 97. PowerPoint includes converters for the following versions of Harvard Graphics:

- Harvard Graphics 2.3 for DOS
- Harvard Graphics 3.0 for DOS

Note PowerPoint 97 does not include converters for later versions of Harvard Graphics. If you want to convert these presentations to PowerPoint 97 format, you must first save the presentations in Harvard Graphics 2.3 or 3.0 for DOS.

What happens to my old presentations when I open them in PowerPoint 97? You can open files created in Harvard Graphics directly in PowerPoint 97. Most data and formatting created in Harvard Graphics are fully supported by PowerPoint 97.

Can I share PowerPoint 97 presentations with users of my old presentation application? If your workgroup is using Harvard Graphics and PowerPoint 97, users cannot exchange presentations directly between these versions. Instead, PowerPoint 97 users must save presentations as text or graphics files that can be opened by Harvard Graphics users. For more information, see "Opening and Saving Text Files" and "Opening and Saving Graphics Files" earlier in this chapter.

To convert a Harvard Graphics presentation to a PowerPoint presentation, open the presentation. PowerPoint handles the conversion automatically. To complete the conversion, save the presentation in PowerPoint 97 format.

▶ **To open a Harvard Graphics presentation in PowerPoint 97**

1 On the **File** menu, click **Open**.
2 In the **Files of type** box, click the appropriate Harvard Graphics format.
3 In the **Name** box, select the name of the presentation.

   PowerPoint converts the Harvard Graphics presentation and opens it.

After you convert a Harvard Graphics presentation to PowerPoint 97, the converted presentation exists only in your computer's memory; the original presentation remains unchanged. To complete the conversion, you need to save the converted presentation in PowerPoint format.

▶ **To save a converted Harvard Graphics presentation in PowerPoint 97 format**

- On the **File** menu, click **Save As**, and give the converted presentation a new name.

  This preserves the original Harvard Graphics presentation as a backup.

To convert multiple Harvard Graphics presentations, open several presentations at the same time in the **Open** dialog box (**File** menu). PowerPoint converts each presentation you select. When you finish editing the presentations, save each presentation as described earlier.

Switching from Lotus Freelance

This section explains how to convert presentations from Lotus Freelance to PowerPoint 97. PowerPoint includes converters for the following versions of Lotus Freelance:

- Lotus Freelance 4.0 for DOS
- Freelance Graphics 1.0–2.1 for Windows

Note PowerPoint 97 does not include converters for later versions of Lotus Freelance. If you want to convert these presentations to PowerPoint 97 format, you must first save the presentations in Lotus Freelance 4.0 for DOS or Freelance Graphics 1.0–2.1 for Windows.

What happens to my old presentations when I open them in PowerPoint 97? You can open files created in Lotus Freelance directly in PowerPoint 97. Most data and formatting created in Lotus Freelance are fully supported by PowerPoint 97.

Can I share PowerPoint 97 presentations with users of my old presentation application? If your workgroup is using Lotus Freelance and PowerPoint 97, users cannot exchange presentations directly between these versions. Instead, PowerPoint 97 users must save presentations as text or graphics files that can be opened by Lotus Freelance users. For more information, see "Opening and Saving Text Files" and "Opening and Saving Graphics Files" earlier in this chapter.

To convert a Lotus Freelance presentation to a PowerPoint presentation, open the presentation. PowerPoint handles the conversion automatically. To complete the conversion, save the presentation in PowerPoint format.

▶ **To open a Lotus Freelance presentation in PowerPoint 97**

1 On the **File** menu, click **Open**.
2 In the **Files of type** box, click the appropriate Lotus Freelance format.
3 In the **Name** box, select the name of the presentation.

   PowerPoint converts the Lotus Freelance presentation and opens it.

After you convert a Lotus Freelance presentation to PowerPoint 97, the converted presentation exists only in your computer's memory; the original presentation remains unchanged. To complete the conversion, you need to save the converted presentation in PowerPoint format.

▶ **To save a converted Lotus Freelance presentation in PowerPoint 97 format**

- On the **File** menu, click **Save As**, and give the converted presentation a new name.

   This preserves the original Lotus Freelance presentation as a backup.

To convert multiple Lotus Freelance presentations, open several presentations at the same time in the **Open** dialog box (**File** menu). PowerPoint converts each presentation you select. When you finish editing the presentations, save each presentation as described in the previous section.

When you convert Lotus Freelance presentations that contain charts or tables, not all of the formatting is preserved in the converted PowerPoint presentation. The following table shows how chart and table features are converted in PowerPoint.

When this Lotus Freelance 4.0 feature	Is converted to PowerPoint 97 format
Automatic summing of data values in a stacked bar chart	Automatic summing is lost in the conversion. You can add the values manually.
Hidden data sets	Hidden sets are displayed.
Size of chart objects	Size is slightly different, affecting word wrapping and alignment of objects that relate to the chart.
Tables	Tables are text objects. You may see a double line around each cell.
Y-axis highest value	Highest value is the nearest full value higher than the highest data value used.
Y-axis lowest value	Lowest value is zero, unless a particular range is specified in the Lotus Freelance file.

CHAPTER 21

Switching to Microsoft Word

This chapter tells you what to expect when you or your workgroup switches to Microsoft Word 97 from another word processor.

The primary questions most new Word users have are:

- What happens to my old documents when I open them in Word 97?
- Can I share Word 97 documents with users of my old word processor?

If you are switching to Word 97, this chapter answers these questions for you.

In This Chapter
Converting File Formats in Word 97   574
Switching from WordPerfect   589
Switching from Microsoft Works 3.0 or 4.0 for Windows   608
Switching from Text with Layout   612
Switching from Lotus Ami Pro   616
Switching from DisplayWrite   616
Switching from Microsoft Windows Write 3.0 or 3.1   616
Switching from RFT-DCA Format Files   616
Switching from MultiMate   616
Switching from WordStar   617

See Also
- For a summary of new and improved features in Word 97, see Chapter 2, "What's New in Microsoft Office 97."
- For information about installing Word or other Office applications, see Chapter 4, "Installing Microsoft Office."
- For information about upgrading to Word 97 from a previous version of Word, see Chapter 15, "Upgrading from Previous Versions of Microsoft Word."

Converting File Formats in Word 97

Word 97 recognizes the file formats of many common word-processing, spreadsheet, and database programs. When these types of documents are opened, Word automatically converts them to Word format, preserving most of the original content and formatting. Users can also save Word documents in other file formats and preserve as much formatting as the other application can support.

Word 97 uses converters to work with other file formats. The Office and Word applications include several converters, such as the WordPerfect 5.*x* converter. Additional converters are included with the Office 97 Resource Kit Tools and Utilities.

Tools and Utilities The Office Resource Kit Tools and Utilities include converters for converting documents between other word processing applications and Word 97. For information about installing these converters, see "Word Converters" in Appendix A, "Microsoft Office 97 Resource Kit Tools and Utilities."

If users need to transfer documents between Word and applications for which specific converters aren't available, they can import and export documents in one of several plain-text formats. Plain-text formats retain the text of a document without saving the formatting. Plain-text formats are also useful for transferring text through electronic mail (e-mail) systems.

Using Text Converters and Graphics Filters

Text converters change the file format of a document. If a document includes graphics, Word uses *graphics filters* to import and export graphics that are within or linked to the document. To successfully convert documents to and from different file formats, you must install the appropriate text converters. To import and export graphics contained in documents, you must install the appropriate graphics filters.

When you use the **Open** command (**File** menu) to open a document that contains graphics, or the **From File** command (**Insert** menu, **Picture** submenu) to insert a graphic into a document, one of three things happens:

- If the graphic is in a format built in, or *native*, to Word, Word preserves the graphic in its original format. For more information, see "Graphics Formats Native to Word" later in this chapter.

- If the graphic is in a non-native format and if a compatible graphics filter has been installed, Word converts the graphic to a format that is native to Word.

- If the graphic is in a format Word does not recognize, Word displays a message and does not convert the graphic.

If you choose the Typical installation during Setup, several text converters and graphics filters are installed. If the text converters and graphics filters you need are not installed, rerun Setup and click **Add/Remove**; select the **Converters and Filters** option, and then select the text converters and graphics filters you need. The Tools and Utilities include additional text converters as well.

Note When you install a text converter for which associated graphics filters are available (for example, the WordPerfect text converters, which are associated with the WPG graphics filters), the Office Setup program also installs the graphics filters.

Text Formats Native to Word

Word can directly import the following text formats:

- MS-DOS Text
- MS-DOS Text with Line Breaks
- Rich Text Format (RTF)
- Text Only
- Text with Line Breaks
- Unicode Text
- Word 4.x–5.1 for the Macintosh
- Word 1.0 for Windows (import only)
- Word 2.0 for Windows
- Word 6.0–95 for Windows

Text Converters Included with Word

In Word, you can install text converters for documents created by the following applications and plain-text file formats.

The text converter for this application or format	Is located in this file	Comments
Hypertext Markup Language (HTML)	Html32.cnv (Windows); HTML Converter (Macintosh)	Supports all HTML level 2.0 extensions and some HTML level 3.0 extensions supported by Microsoft Internet Explorer and Netscape Navigator.
Lotus 1-2-3 2.x–4.0	Lotus32.cnv	Included with Word 97 for Windows only. Supports importing only. For more information about working with Lotus 1-2-3 data in Word, see in Chapter 27, "Sharing Information with Microsoft Office Applications."

The text converter for this application or format	Is located in this file	Comments
Lotus Notes 3.x	Msimp32.dll, Mscthunk.dll, Mswrd632.cnv, Mswrd832.cnv	Included with Word 97 for Windows only. This converter enables Lotus Notes to import Word 6.0, 95, and 97 documents. For more information about working with Lotus Notes, see Chapter 28, "Working with Messaging Systems and Connectivity Software."
Microsoft Excel 2.x–95 and Microsoft Excel 97	Excel32.cnv (Windows); Microsoft Excel 2.x–97 (Macintosh)	Supports importing only. For more information about working with Microsoft Excel data in Word, see in Chapter 27, "Sharing Information with Microsoft Office Applications."
Microsoft FoxPro 2.x/Borland dBASE III, III+, and IV	FoxPro–dBASE	Supports importing only. Included with Word 97 for the Macintosh only; in Windows, use ODBC for conversion. For more information about ODBC, see Chapter 17, "Switching to Microsoft Access."
Microsoft Word 6.0–95	Wrd6ex32.cnv (Windows); Word 6.0–95 Export (Macintosh)	Required only for saving to Word 6.0–95 format; support for opening this format in Word 97 is built in.
Microsoft Word 4.0–5.1 for the Macintosh	Macwrd32.cnv (Windows); Mac Word 4.x–5.x (PPC) (Macintosh)	Required only for saving to Word 4.0–5.1 for the Macintosh format; support for opening this format in Word 97 is built in.
Microsoft Word 2.0 for Windows	Wnwrd232.cnv (Windows); Word 2.x for Windows (Macintosh)	Required only for saving to Word 2.0 for Windows format; support for opening this format in Word 97 is built in.
Microsoft Works 4.x for the Macintosh	Works 4.0 for the Macintosh	Included with Word 97 for the Macintosh only.
Microsoft Works 3.0 for Windows	Works332.cnv	Included with Word 97 for Windows only.
Microsoft Works 4.0 for Windows	Works432.cnv	Included with Word 97 for Windows only.
Text with Layout	Txtlyt32.cnv (Windows); Text with Layout (Macintosh)	Preserves page layout.
WordPerfect 5.x for MS-DOS and Windows	Wpft532.cnv (Windows); WordPerfect 5.x (Macintosh)	None.
WordPerfect 6.x for MS-DOS and Windows	Wpft632.cnv (Windows); WordPerfect 6.x (Macintosh)	Supports importing only.
WordPerfect 2.x–3.1 for the Macintosh	Macintosh WordPerfect 2.x–3.1	Included with Word 97 for the Macintosh only. Supports importing only.
File Recovery	Recovr32.cnv (Windows); Recover Text Converter (Macintosh)	Attempts to recover text from corrupted Word documents.

> **I can't find the converter I need**
> The file types included in the **List files of type** box in the **Open** dialog box (**File** menu) indicate the file formats for which text converters are installed, or which Word can read directly. If the file format you need does not appear in the **List files of type** box, the converter probably is not installed. Not all text converters are included when you choose the Typical installation during Setup. To install the converters you need, rerun Setup and click **Add/Remove**; under the **Converters and Filters** option, select the **Text Converters** check box.

Text converters are stored in the following default locations.

Operating system	Text converters default location
Windows	Program Files\Common Files\Microsoft Shared\Textconv
Macintosh	Microsoft

Text Converters Included with the Office Resource Kit Tools and Utilities

The Office Resource Kit Tools and Utilities include additional text converters for the following file formats:

- Microsoft Windows Write 3.0 or 3.1
- RFT-DCA
- Lotus Ami Pro 3.*x*
- WordStar 3.3–95 for MS-DOS (import only), WordStar 4.0 and 95 for MS-DOS (export only), and WordStar 1.0 and 2.0 for Windows (import only)

These text converters are supported by Word for Windows only. For more information about installing the converters, see the sections for specific applications later in this chapter and "Word Converters" in Appendix A, "Microsoft Office 97 Resource Kit Tools and Utilities."

The Tools and Utilities also include a text converter for Microsoft Word 4.*x*, 5.*x*, and 6.*x* for MS-DOS. For more information, see "Upgrading from Word 5.x or 6.0 for MS-DOS" in Chapter 15, "Upgrading from Previous Versions of Microsoft Word."

Graphics Formats Native to Word

Word can directly import and store the following graphics formats:

- Windows Enhanced Metafile (EMF) (Windows only)
- JPEG File Interchange Format
- Portable Network Graphics (PNG)
- Windows Bitmap (BMP) (Windows only)
- Windows Metafile (WMF) (Windows only)
- PICT (Macintosh only)

To import other graphics formats, you must install additional graphics filters.

> **Installing Graphics Filters for Native Formats**
>
> Although the preceding graphics formats are native to Word, you can install graphics filters for some of these formats during Setup. In this case, the graphics filters are not used by Word, but by other Office applications such as PowerPoint and Microsoft Photo Editor. In addition, some of the Word text converters use the graphics filters.

Graphics Filters Included with Word

The graphics filters that come with Word support files in the following formats. (Unless otherwise noted, these graphics filters support only importing into Word—not exporting to another file format.)

The graphics filter for this application or format	Is located in this file	Comments
AutoCAD (DXF)	Dxfimp32.flt	Supported by Word for Windows only.
CompuServe GIF (GIF)	Gif32.flt (Windows); GIF import & export (Macintosh)	Supports import and export.
Computer Graphics Metafile (CGM)	Cgmimp32.flt, Cgmimp32.fnt, Cgmimp32.cfg, Cgmimp32.hlp	Supported by Word for Windows only.
CorelDRAW 3.0, 4.0, 5.0, and 6.0 (CDR)	Cdrimp32.flt	Supported by Word for Windows only.

The graphics filter for this application or format	Is located in this file	Comments
Encapsulated PostScript (EPS)	Epsimp32.flt (Windows); EPS import (Macintosh)	None.
Kodak Photo-CD (PCD)	Pcdimp32.flt, Pcdlib32.dll (Windows); PCD import, PCD Library (Macintosh)	None.
Macintosh PICT (PICT)	Pictim32.flt	Required for Word for Windows; PICT format is native to Word for the Macintosh.
Micrografx Designer/Draw (DRW)	Drwimp32.flt	Supported by Word for Windows only.
PC Paintbrush (PCX)	Pcximp32.flt	Supported by Word for Windows only.
Tagged Image File Format (TIFF)	Tiffim32.flt (Windows); TIFF Import (Macintosh)	None.
Truevision Targa (TGA)	Tgaimp32.flt	Supported by Word for Windows only.
WordPerfect Graphics/DrawPerfect (WPG)	Wpgimp32.flt, Wpgexp32.flt (Windows); WordPerfect Graphics Import (Macintosh)	Supports import and export in Word 97 for Windows, and import only in Word 97 for the Macintosh.

World Wide Web New releases of Internet Assistant for Word include additional graphics filters. For the latest information, connect to the Microsoft Office home page at:

http://www.microsoft.com/office/

Graphics filters are installed in the following default locations.

Operating system	Graphics filters default location
Windows	Program files\Common files\Microsoft shared\Grphflt
Macintosh	Microsoft Shared Apps:Graphic Filters (PPC)

Under certain circumstances, graphics in Word 97 documents are converted to different formats. This occurs when a Word 97 document is saved in:

- A previous Word format, such as Word 2.0 for Windows format.
- Another text format, such as WordPerfect 5.*x* format.

Under these conditions, Word 97 converts the non-native graphics to WMF (Windows) or PICT (Macintosh) format.

Saving Word 97 documents in other formats may result in graphics changing formats and some loss of image quality. In all cases, Word attempts to use the graphics format that is most compatible with the text format to which the document is being converted. For example, if you save a Word 97 document in WordPerfect format, Word converts the graphics to WordPerfect Graphics format (provided the WordPerfect text converters and graphics filters have been installed).

Moving Word documents between Windows and Macintosh computers can also result in changed graphics formats. For example, suppose a document created in Word for Windows contains a graphic image stored in the document in WMF format. When the document is moved to Word for the Macintosh, Word converts the WMF graphic image to PICT format. The original WMF image is retained in the document, but the PICT image is the one that the user sees. In this conversion there may be a slight loss of image quality because Windows and Macintosh computers have similar, but not identical, graphics rendering systems (GDI and QuickDraw GX, respectively).

After the document is opened in Word for the Macintosh, one of two things may happen:

- If the Word for the Macintosh user edits the graphic image, Word discards the WMF graphic and keeps the changed PICT graphic. When the document is moved back to Word for Windows, Word reconverts the PICT graphic to WMF format, resulting in decreased image quality.
- If the Word for the Macintosh user does not edit the graphic image, Word preserves both the WMF graphic and the PICT graphic in the document. When the document is moved back to Word for Windows, Word displays the original WMF graphic with no loss of image quality.

If a document originates in Word for the Macintosh and is then moved to Word for Windows, a similar conversion happens.

The text of the document was converted correctly, but the graphics disappeared
Either the correct graphics filter is not installed or the graphics are in a format Word cannot import. Not all graphics filters are included when you choose the Typical installation during Setup. To install the graphics filters you need, rerun Setup and click **Add/Remove**; under the **Converters and Filters** option, select the **Graphics Filters** check box.

Converting Documents from Other File Formats

To convert documents in formats other than Word 97 format, first ensure that the correct converter is installed, and then open the document.

▶ **To convert a document to Word 97 format**

1. On the **File** menu, click **Open**.
2. In the **Files of type** box, click the document's original format.
3. In the **File name** box, select the file you want to convert.

   If Word recognizes the file format, it converts the file and displays it in Word. If Word does not recognize the format, it displays the **Convert File** dialog box. Select the appropriate file format; Word converts and opens the file.

> **Word doesn't list the document I'm looking for in the Open dialog box**
> Make sure that you selected the correct file type or extension in the **Files of type** box. If the document name you are looking for still does not appear, select **All Files**. Also check to make sure that you have selected the correct drive and folder.

If a file is not converted correctly, close it without saving the file and then open the file again with a different converter. The original file remains unchanged until you save it in Word or some other format. You can also change the way Word converts some formats. For more information, see "Customizing Conversions and Improving Compatibility" later in this chapter.

Note In Windows, the document format does not necessarily correspond to the file name extension. For example, a WordPerfect document may have a .doc or .wpd extension, or no extension at all. When you open a file in another format, Word looks first at the contents of the file to determine the file format. If Word doesn't recognize the file format, it tries to use the converters that correspond to the file name extension. If Word is still unable to recognize the file format, it asks you to choose a converter and suggests Text Only.

Word can prompt you to select which converter to use every time you open a document in a format other than Word 97 format.

▶ **To set Word to confirm which converter to use**

1. On the **Tools** menu, click **Options**, and then click the **General** tab.
2. Under **General options**, select the **Confirm conversion at Open** check bcx.

Converting Several Documents at Once

To convert several documents at once, you can use the Conversion Wizard, which is supplied with Word. This wizard converts files as described in the preceding section. The appropriate converters and graphics filters must be installed to run the wizard.

Before beginning this procedure, make sure you have installed the Conversion Wizard. The wizard is stored in the following location.

Operating system	Conversion Wizard location
Windows 95	Program Files\Microsoft Office\Office\Macros\Convert8.wiz
Macintosh	Microsoft Word:Macros:Conversion Macros

If the Conversion Wizard is not installed, rerun Setup and click **Add/Remove**; under the **Microsoft Word** option, select **Wizards and Templates**, and then select **Macro Templates** check box.

▶ **To run the Conversion Wizard**

1. On the **File** menu, click **Open**.
2. In the **Look in** box, change to the Program Files/Microsoft Office/Office/Macros folder.
3. In the **Name** box, double-click **Convert8.wiz**.
4. If prompted, click the **Enable Macros** button.
5. Click **A batch conversion of files**, and follow the instructions on the screen.

Customizing Conversions and Improving Compatibility

When you convert a document, Word preserves the document's original content and formatting as much as possible. However, other applications might have similar features that work slightly differently, so you might not always get the results you expect.

For example, the converted document may look different from the original document if text was aligned using spaces instead of tab stops; or line and page breaks may occur in different places due to differences in fonts or printer drivers. You can choose how Word handles some of these differences.

Customizing Conversions

If a document is not converted the way you want, you may be able to change some aspects of the conversion. Depending on the converter you are using, you may be able to specify such things as the preferred line length or how you want certain fields to be converted. For example, when converting documents from Word 97 to Word 5.1 for the Macintosh, you can control how INCLUDETEXT fields are handled.

▶ **To customize the conversion**

1. On the **File** menu, click **Open**.
2. In the **Look in** box, change to the Program Files/Microsoft Office/Office/Macros folder.
3. In the **Name** box, double-click **Convert8.wiz**.
4. If prompted, click the **Enable Macro** button.
5. Click **Edit conversion options**, and follow the instructions on the screen.

Improving Compatibility with Other Word Processors

Word provides special compatibility options that allow you to alter the behavior of Word so that it more closely matches the behavior of another application. These compatibility options change the way Word behaves without changing the document.

For example, in WordPerfect 5.*x*, blank spaces at the end of a line are wrapped to the next line. In Word, the spaces extend beyond the right margin. However, if you select the **Wrap trailing spaces to next line** option on the **Compatibility** tab in the **Options** dialog box (**Tools** menu), Word handles blank spaces at the end of a line the same as WordPerfect 5.*x* would. Using compatibility options in Word is especially useful when you plan to convert a document back and forth between Word and another word processor.

When you convert a document, Word selects the options that are applicable to the original format of the document. You can turn the compatibility options on or off at any time. When you save a converted document, Word saves the compatibility options with it. Keep in mind that these options affect the document only while you are working with it in Word. If you later convert the document back to its original format, it works in the other word processor just as it did before you converted it to Word.

▶ **To specify compatibility options**

1. On the **Tools** menu, click **Options**, and then click the **Compatibility** tab.
2. In the **Recommended options for** box, click the document's original format.

   This selects or clears the appropriate check boxes under **Options**. You can also select or clear check boxes manually.

Tip If you want to use the compatibility options for all new documents that you create based on the active template, click **Default** on the **Compatibility** tab.

> **My line and page breaks are different, or the document I converted increased in length**
>
> There are two reasons why a converted document may have different line breaks and page breaks:
>
> - Various word processors may calculate line spacing, line breaks, and page breaks in slightly different ways.
>
> - Different printer drivers use slightly different fonts and character spacing information when printing to the same printer. You may be able to adjust the line breaks and page breaks by substituting different fonts. Alternatively, you can specify that Word lay out the document based on its fonts and not on printer settings: Select the **Use printer metrics to lay out document** check box on the **Compatibility** tab in the **Options** dialog box (**Tools** menu).

Specifying Fonts for Converted Documents

When you open a converted document on a different computer from the one used to create it, you may find that its line breaks, page breaks, and length don't correspond to the original. This can happen if the two computers have different fonts available. To address this problem, you can specify that fonts available on one computer are converted to the fonts available on the other computer.

Substituting Fonts in Documents Converted to Word 97

If a converted document contains fonts that aren't available on your computer or printer, Word automatically maps these fonts to similar fonts. However, when converting documents between Word 5.*x* or 6.0 for the Macintosh and Word 97, or between Word and certain MS-DOS-based applications, you can specify the fonts that you want Word to substitute.

▶ **To specify fonts for documents converted to Word 97**

1   On the **Tools** menu, click **Options**, and then click the **Compatibility** tab.

2   Click **Font Substitution**.

    The **Missing document font** box lists all fonts used in the document that are not available in Word. The **Substituted font** box lists the Word 97 font used for each missing font.

3   To specify a substitute Word 97 font, click a font in the **Missing document font** box, and then click a corresponding font in the **Substituted font** box.

4   To replace the fonts in the converted document permanently, click **Convert Permanently**.

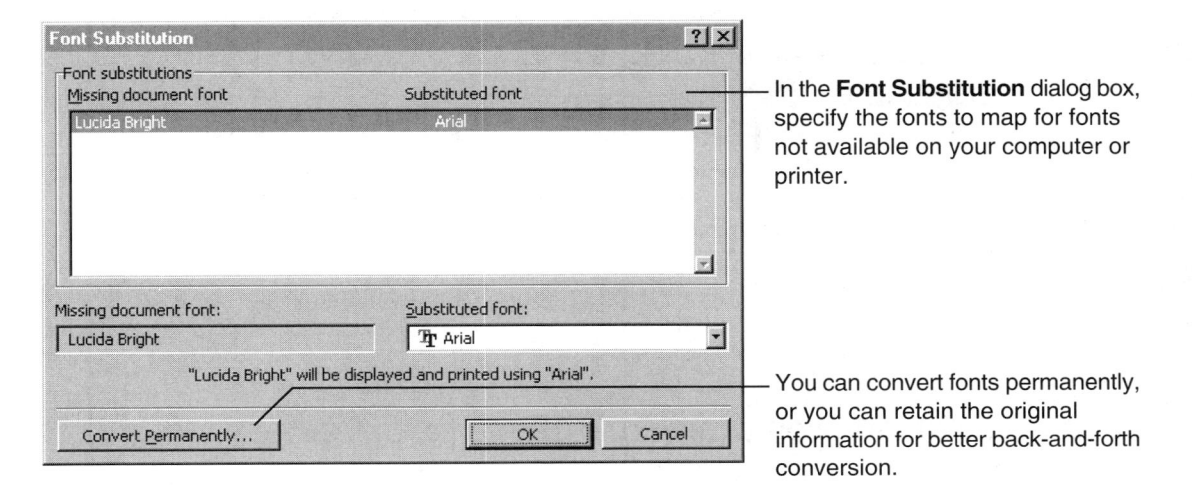

In the **Font Substitution** dialog box, specify the fonts to map for fonts not available on your computer or printer.

You can convert fonts permanently, or you can retain the original information for better back-and-forth conversion.

Note Substituted fonts appear in the document only while you work with it in Word 97. If you convert the document back to its original format, the document retains its original fonts unless you convert them by clicking the **Convert Permanently** button.

Word saves your font substitution settings with the converted document. It also saves these settings in the font substitutions file listed in the following table, so the next time you convert a document from the same file format, Word knows which fonts to substitute.

Operating system	Font substitution file location
Windows	Windows\Msfntmap.ini
Macintosh	System Folder:Preferences:Word Font Substitutions

Sometimes the font substitution settings saved with a document differ from the settings in your font substitution file. For example, if you open a document that was converted on another computer with a different font substitution file, the settings in your font substitution file override the settings in the document.

> **The converted document has symbols and characters in it that I didn't expect**
>
> If Word prompted you to specify which converter to use, you may have chosen the wrong converter. Try choosing a different one. You can also use the **Replace** command (**Edit** menu) to quickly delete unwanted characters from the document.
>
> If the unexpected symbols are few and scattered throughout the document, you may need to specify a different font to substitute for a symbol font used in the original document.

Substituting Fonts in Word 97 Documents Converted to Other Formats

When you convert a Word 97 document to another file format, you can specify the fonts you want to substitute. To do this, you modify the font-mapping files supplied with Word to override the default font mapping performed by the text converters.

The Word 97 font-mapping files are listed in the following table.

For Word 97 documents converted to this format	Modify this font-mapping file
Word for MS-DOS	Rtf_pcw.txt (Windows only)
Word 2.0 for Windows	MS Word for Win FontMap (Macintosh only)
Word 5.*x* for the Macintosh	Rtf_mw5.txt (Windows only)
RFT-DCA	Rtf_dca.txt (Windows only)
WordPerfect 5.*x*	Rtf_wp5.txt (Windows) WordPerfect 5.*x* Export FontMap (Macintosh)

Font-mapping files are stored in the following default locations.

Operating system	Text converters default location
Windows	Program Files\Common Files\Microsoft Shared\Textconv
Macintosh	Microsoft

▶ **To modify a font-mapping file**

1 Open the appropriate font mapping file in Word.

2 Follow the instructions in the font-mapping file.

Tools and Utilities The Office Resource Kit Tools and Utilities include five TrueType fonts to improve conversion of characters from the WordPerfect 5.*x* and 6.*x* character sets. For more information, see "Word Converters" in Appendix A, "Microsoft Office 97 Resource Kit Tools and Utilities."

Opening and Saving Plain-Text Files

To exchange documents between Word and an application for which there is no converter, you can save your document in a plain-text file format. Most applications can open files in plain-text formats.

▶ **To save a Word document in plain-text file format**

1 On the **File** menu, click **Save As**.

2 In the **Save as type** box (Windows) or **Save file as type** box (Macintosh), click the plain-text format you want.

Tip When you save a Word document in plain-text file format, use a different file name so that you can keep a copy of the original document in Word format as a backup.

▶ **To open a plain-text file in Word 97**

1 On the **File** menu, click **Open**.

2 In the **Files of type** box, click the plain-text format in which the document was saved.

Word can open and save plain-text files in several formats, which is described in the following sections. Most plain-text file formats do not include formatting codes, which maintain the layout and appearance of text, so most formatting is lost when you save a document in plain-text format. RTF is an exception to this.

Rich Text Format

Use RTF to convert documents from one Microsoft application to another, or to transfer documents between a Macintosh and an MS-DOS-based system. You can also use RTF to transfer fully formatted documents using communications software that accepts only text files. Saving in RTF saves all formatting. RTF converts formatting to text instructions that other applications (including compatible Microsoft applications) can read.

Text Only

Use Text Only format to share documents between MS-DOS-based, Windows-based, and Macintosh applications. Use this format only if the destination application is unable to read any of the other available file formats. This format saves text without formatting and converts all manual line breaks, section breaks, and page breaks to paragraph marks. This format uses either the ANSI character set (Windows) or the Macintosh character set (both of which include ASCII).

MS-DOS Text

Use MS-DOS Text format to share documents between Word 97 and MS-DOS-based applications not designed for Windows. Saving in this format converts files the same way as the Text Only format described earlier. MS-DOS Text format uses the extended ASCII character set (the standard for MS-DOS-based applications).

Text Only with Line Breaks, MS-DOS Text with Line Breaks

To maintain line breaks—when transferring text to an e-mail system, for example—use either Text Only with Line Breaks or MS-DOS Text with Line Breaks format. These formats save text without formatting and convert all automatic and manual line breaks, section breaks, and page breaks to paragraph marks.

Text with Layout, MS-DOS Text with Layout

To convert a document from a text file format and maintain the page layout, use either Text with Layout or MS-DOS Text with Layout format. You can then reformat the document in Word, using the converted layout as a guide. For more information, see "Switching from Text with Layout" later in this chapter.

These formats preserve the length of lines and insert spaces in the document to approximate indents, tables, spacing between lines, spacing between paragraphs, and tab stops. They also convert section breaks and page breaks to paragraph marks.

Saving Word Documents in Other File Formats

You can save Word documents in file formats that can be read by other applications or by earlier versions of Word.

▶ **To save a Word document in another file format**

1. On the **File** menu, click **Save As**.
2. In the **Save as type** box (Windows) or **Save file as type** box (Macintosh), click the format you want.

Tip When you save a Word document in another file format, use a different file name so that you can keep a copy of the original document in Word format as a backup.

For a list of the available file formats, see "Using Text Converters and Graphics Filters" earlier in this chapter.

Switching from WordPerfect

This section describes the differences between WordPerfect 5.*x* or 6.*x* and Word 97. Word includes several features that protect the WordPerfect user's investment in WordPerfect knowledge and experience, as well as strong file conversion support for WordPerfect.

What happens to my old WordPerfect documents when I open them in Word 97? You can open files created in WordPerfect 5.*x* or 6.*x* directly in Word 97. Most data and formatting created in WordPerfect is fully supported by Word 97. For more information, see "Converting Documents from WordPerfect 5.x" or "Converting Documents from WordPerfect 6.x" later in this chapter.

Can I share Word 97 documents with users of WordPerfect? If your workgroup is using WordPerfect 5.*x* or 6.*x* and Word 97, users can exchange documents between these versions. However, not all Word 97 features are supported in WordPerfect. For more information, see "Sharing Documents with WordPerfect 5.x" or "Sharing Documents with WordPerfect 6.x" later in this chapter.

Word 97 Concepts for WordPerfect Users

Several key concepts help WordPerfect users make the transition to Word 97:

- Selecting text

    In Word, users select an object, such as text or a picture, and then perform an action on that object.

- Editing and formatting text

    Unlike the formatting codes used in WordPerfect, Word applies formatting directly to text, so text in a Word document displays exactly as it prints.

- Correcting mistakes

    Word users can correct formatting errors by using the **Undo** command (**Edit** menu), or troubleshoot problems by displaying a description of the formatting applied to selected text.

Selecting Text

For almost every task in Word, users first select an object and then perform an action on that object. For example, users select text and then delete it.

Viewed this way, selecting in Word 97 is similar to blocking in WordPerfect—for example, blocking text before moving or deleting it. However, many formatting actions in WordPerfect require that users insert codes before and after the text. Word users simply select the text and then format it.

In Word, selected text appears highlighted on the screen.

Atmosphere¶

Besides hydrogen, the atmosphere contains helium, methane, and visible clouds of icy ammonia that blow across the face of the planet. A spot at least twice the diameter of Earth on Jupiter's surface is probably a 13,000-mile-wide storm that has been raging for thousands of years. The spot's dark red color suggests that it may tower thousands of miles above the lighter-colored clouds.¶ — This paragraph is selected.

Moons¶

Jupiter has 16 moons, the largest of which are Europa, Ganymede, Io, and Callisto. Each of these major moons has surface characteristics distinctly different from the others. When Jupiter is nearest the Earth, the moons can be seen clearly through field glasses as they move around the giant planet. ¶

Editing and Formatting Text

WordPerfect treats a document as a stream of text; formatting is applied by inserting codes into the text stream. If a base font code is inserted into the text stream, all the text after the code is formatted in the specified font until another base font code is inserted. If a word from the middle of the text stream is cut and pasted elsewhere, it does not take the formatting with it unless the font codes are correctly duplicated and inserted in the new location.

Word 97, by contrast, follows a paragraph-based formatting model, which associates formatting properties with objects. Formatting is applied directly to the text. If text is cut and pasted in a new location, its attributes move with it. Character formatting, such as bold, italic, and underline, is attached to the text characters to which it is applied. Paragraph formatting, such as indentation and tab stop locations, is stored in a nonprinting paragraph mark (¶) at the end of each paragraph.

Note Many Word formatting commands can also be used in the same way as WordPerfect commands. For example, in Word you can select italic formatting, type a word, and then select italic formatting again to continue typing with normally formatted text.

Working with Paragraphs in Word

In Word, paragraph formats apply to the entire paragraph. This model differs from WordPerfect, which treats paragraphs as multiple lines of text. To center a single line in a paragraph, for example, a WordPerfect user inserts the [Center] code. To accomplish the same task in Word, a user places the line in its own paragraph and then applies the desired formatting using menu commands, toolbar buttons, or Word key combinations.

Tip In Word, users can format a single paragraph by placing the insertion point in the paragraph and applying a style; it isn't necessary to select the entire paragraph before formatting it.

When a user presses ENTER, Word automatically inserts a paragraph mark and applies the current formats to the next paragraph. If a user deletes a paragraph mark, the text merges with the next paragraph in the document and takes on its paragraph formatting.

If a user moves text from one paragraph to another, however, and leaves the paragraph mark behind, the original paragraph formatting is lost. To retain the paragraph formatting when moving or copying text, include the paragraph mark in the selection.

Tip New Word users may benefit from working with paragraph marks displayed. To display paragraph marks, tab stops, and other nonprinting characters, click the **Show/Hide** button (**Standard** toolbar).

Displaying Formatting Information in Word

Word users can find formatting information in the following locations.

To find this Word 97 formatting information	Use this command
Character formatting	**Formatting** toolbar (**View** menu, **Toolbars** submenu) or **Font** dialog box (**Format** menu)
Paragraph formatting	**Formatting** toolbar or **Paragraph** dialog box (**Format** menu)
Nonprinting characters	**Show/Hide** button (**Standard** toolbar)
Page as it appears when printed	**Page Layout** (**View** menu)
All formatting at cursor location	**What's This?** (**Help** menu)

In WordPerfect, users reveal codes to find and correct many errors. There is no need for reveal codes in Word 97. Word is WYSIWYG—what you see is what you get. Users see exactly what a document looks like on the screen. Sometimes, however, it is helpful to see what formatting has been applied to text or a graphic image. The Reveal Formats feature allows this.

Reveal Formats is a graphical way to troubleshoot document formatting, similar to using reveal codes in WordPerfect. In Word, clicking the **What's This?** command (**Help** menu) and then clicking in a document opens a window describing the formatting at the cursor location. The WordPerfect Help feature in Word 97 also displays this information when the user presses ALT+F3, the equivalent WordPerfect Reveal Codes keyboard command.

Part 4 Switching from Other Applications

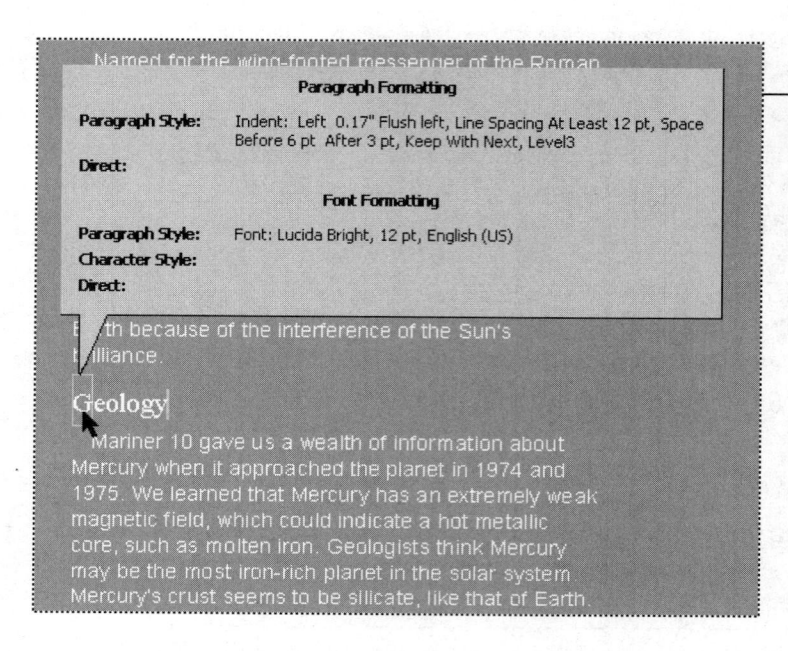

> **Paragraph Formatting**
> **Paragraph Style:** Indent: Left 0.17" Flush left, Line Spacing At Least 12 pt, Space Before 6 pt After 3 pt, Keep With Next, Level3
> **Direct:**
>
> **Font Formatting**
> **Paragraph Style:** Font: Lucida Bright, 12 pt, English (US)
> **Character Style:**
> **Direct:**

This pop-up window shows paragraph and font formatting for the selected text. For graphic images, the window shows picture formatting information, such as size and scale.

Correcting Mistakes

To correct many errors in Word, users can click the **Undo** button (**Standard** toolbar) or use the **Undo** command (**Edit** menu), which is similar to the **Restore** command in WordPerfect. This reverses the effect of formatting commands, as well as restoring deleted text.

The **Undo** command or button reverses the last action performed. By clicking the arrow next to the **Undo** button, users can also select a series of commands to undo.

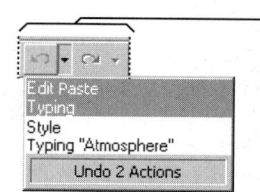

In Word, you can undo and redo up to 100 actions.

Some actions, such as saving a document, cannot be reversed. To indicate that the command is unavailable, **Undo** changes to **Can't Undo** and appears dimmed on the **Edit** menu.

The **Redo** command (**Edit** menu) or **Redo** button (**Standard** toolbar) reapplies the formatting or other action after **Undo** has been applied. In Word 97 you can undo or redo the last 100 actions.

Word 97 Tools for WordPerfect Users

The Word 97 features described in the following table help WordPerfect users make a smooth transition to Word 97.

This Word 97 feature	Allows WordPerfect users to
Blue background, white text (**Tools** menu)	View a Word document in the familiar blue background and white text of a WordPerfect 5.*x* for MS-DOS document.
Full screen view (**View** menu)	Maximize screen space for displaying documents by clearing it of elements such as toolbars, rulers, menu bars, scroll bars, and the status bar. To restore the default Word screen, click the **Full Screen** button or press ESC.
ScreenTips	Display the name of a toolbar button by pausing the mouse pointer over the button.
Undo and **Redo** (**Edit** menu)	View a history of changes to the document and reverse or reapply commands. For more information about **Undo** and **Redo**, see "Correcting Mistakes" earlier in this chapter.

▶ **To display a blue background and white text in a Word document**

1. On the **Tools** menu, click **Options**, and then click the **General** tab.
2. Under **General options**, select the **Blue background, white text** check box.

   When this option is combined with other Word customization options, such as full screen view, a Word document appears similar on the screen to the WordPerfect 5.*x* for MS-DOS environment.

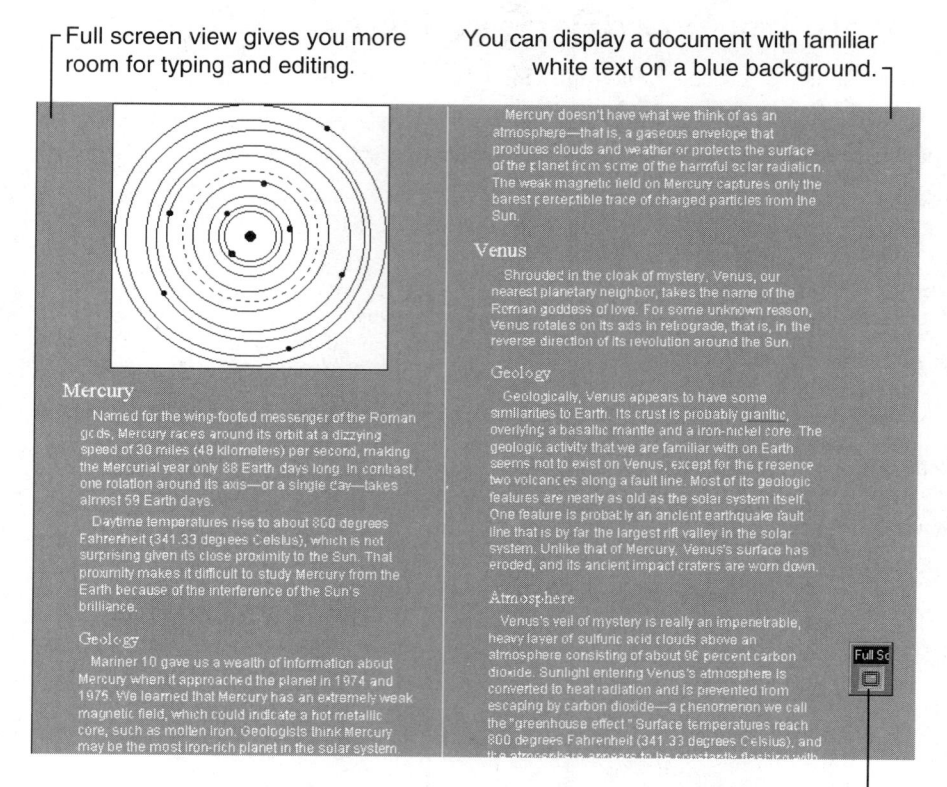

Full screen view gives you more room for typing and editing.

You can display a document with familiar white text on a blue background.

Click the **Full screen** button to return to the previous view.

Converting WordPerfect Documents to Word 97

This section describes how to convert WordPerfect documents to Word 97 format. You can also use a macro to quickly convert multiple WordPerfect documents to Word format. If a document isn't converted the way you want, you can customize the conversion process.

Before you can convert documents, the WordPerfect converter and graphics filters must be installed on your computer. The converter and filters for WordPerfect 5.*x* and 6.*x* for MS-DOS and Windows are installed automatically when you choose the Typical installation during Setup. If the converters and graphics filters you want are not installed, rerun Setup and click **Add/Remove**; then select the **Converters and Filters** option.

Tools and Utilities The Office Resource Kit Tools and Utilities include fonts and templates for better conversions of WordPerfect documents. For more information, see "Word Converters" in Appendix A, "Microsoft Office 97 Resource Kit Tools and Utilities."

To convert a WordPerfect document to a Word document, open the document in Word; Word handles the conversion automatically.

▶ **To open a WordPerfect document in Word 97**

1 On the **File** menu, click **Open**.
2 In the **Files of type** box, click **All Files**.
3 In the **File name** box, select the name of the document.

   Word converts the WordPerfect document and opens it.

After you convert a WordPerfect document to Word 97, the converted document exists only in your computer's memory; the original document remains unchanged. To complete the conversion, you need to save the converted document in Word format.

▶ **To save a converted WordPerfect document in Word 97 format**

1 On the **File** menu, click **Save**, and then (when prompted) click **Yes**.

   –or–

   On the **File** menu, click **Save As**, and give the converted document a new name in Word. This preserves the original WordPerfect document as a backup.

2 When you close the document or quit Word, click **Yes** to save changes to the document.

Converting Multiple WordPerfect Documents

To convert multiple WordPerfect documents, open several documents at the same time in the **Open** dialog box (**File** menu). Word converts each document you've selected. When you finish editing the documents, save each document as described in the previous section.

Tip In Windows, you can open more than one file at a time if all the files are within a single folder. To select a contiguous group of documents, click the name of the first document you want to open, and then hold down SHIFT and click the name of the last document you want to open. Or hold down CTRL and click the names of the individual documents you want to open.

If you want to convert multiple documents to or from WordPerfect format, you can also use the Conversion Wizard. The Conversion Wizard is stored in Convert8.wiz (Windows) or Conversion Macros (Macintosh). For more information about customizing conversions, see "Converting Documents from Other File Formats" earlier in this chapter.

Importing WordPerfect Graphics

When you open a WordPerfect document containing graphics in WordPerfect Graphics (WPG) format in Word 97, the WordPerfect converter uses the WPG graphics filter to convert the graphics embedded in the WordPerfect document. This filter uses the size of the picture frame stored in the WPG file to determine the size of the picture to import. (The picture-frame size of WPG graphics created by DrawPerfect is the size of the screen.)

WPG images often contain a background color that may impair the fidelity of the image when it is imported into Word. By default, the filter removes this background color to improve clarity. To change the actions the filter carries out, edit the Conversion Wizard options. For more information about customizing conversions, see "Converting Documents from Other File Formats" earlier in this chapter.

Converting Documents from WordPerfect 6.x

Word 97 does not handle all data and formatting in the same way that WordPerfect 6.*x* does. Converting WordPerfect 6.*x* documents to Word 97 format may result in changed data or formatting. The following sections describe the WordPerfect 6.*x* features that are handled differently in Word 97.

Character Formatting Features

The following table describes conversion issues that may affect your data or formatting when you save WordPerfect 6.*x* documents in Word 97 format.

When this WordPerfect 6.x feature	Is converted to Word 97 format
Redlining	Redlining is converted to comments.
Strikeout	Strikeout is converted to strikethrough formatting.
Word and letter spacing	Lost in the conversion.

Paragraph Formatting Features

The following table describes conversion issues that may affect your data or formatting when you save WordPerfect 6.x documents in Word 97 format.

When this WordPerfect 6.x feature	Is converted to Word 97 format
Back tabs	Back tabs preceded by text are not converted.
Default tabs	Trailing default tabs are not converted.
Tab leaders	Dot tab leaders, minus sign tab leaders, and underscore tab leaders are converted to the same tab leaders in Word. All other tab leaders become dot leaders.
Center and flush right codes	Center and flush right codes are converted to center-aligned and right-aligned tab stops.
Leading adjustment between lines and baselines	Lost in the conversion.
Paragraph margins	Paragraph margins are converted to left and right paragraph indents.
Spacing between paragraphs	Spacing between paragraphs is converted to Spacing After paragraph format.

Other Features

The following table describes conversion issues that may affect your data or formatting when you save WordPerfect 6.x documents in Word 97 format.

When this WordPerfect 6.x feature	Is converted to Word 97 format
Advance	Advance codes are converted to ADVANCE fields. Advance codes that move text up on a page are not fully emulated in Word. Absolute vertical advance codes in headers are not converted.
Borders and fill (for columns and pages)	Lost in the conversion.
Captions	Lost in the conversion.
Chapter and volume numbers	Lost in the conversion.
Comments	Comments in body text are converted. Comments in headers, footers, footnotes, and endnote text are lost.
Contour wrap for graphics boxes	Contour wrap is converted to square wrap (wrap around property).
Cross-references	Cross-references are converted to hyperlinks.
Drop cap	Lost in the conversion.
Equations	In Windows, equations are converted as editable equation objects. On the Macintosh, only the equation result is retained.

When this WordPerfect 6.x feature	Is converted to Word 97 format
Footnotes	Custom footnote marks are converted to automatic numbered marks. If the numbering format of notes is changed in a document, the notes numbered with the new format are converted to custom notes.
Indexes and lists	Indexes and lists are converted to plain text.
Insert file name	Lost in the conversion.
Labels and bar codes	Label text is preserved, but bar codes are lost in the conversion.
Line numbers	Lost in the conversion.
Macros	Lost in the conversion.
Margins	Margins are adjusted to preserve page layout. Word prompts users to adjust margins manually when necessary on the **Margins** tab in the **Page Setup** dialog box (**File** menu).
Merge codes	Lost in the conversion.
Outlining, paragraph numbers, and counters	These are converted to SEQUENCE fields.
Page features (center page, page binding, and subdivide pages)	Lost in the conversion.
Parallel columns	Parallel columns are converted to tables.
Table vertical cell merge, and cell alignment	Lost in the conversion.
Text boxes, graphics boxes, and lines	Some text boxes and lines are converted to Office Art objects, visible only in page layout view, print preview, and when printing.
	Graphics boxes in tables, parallel columns, and headers/footers that are anchored to a page or paragraph and have wrap-around text in the original document are converted to boxes with wrap-through in Word. In most cases these boxes are converted to Office Art objects.
	All graphics lines are converted to solid lines.
WordPerfect characters	If the WordPerfect fonts containing the characters are available on the computer, all the characters are converted. If one or more of these fonts is not available, some characters may not be converted.

Sharing Documents with WordPerfect 6.x

The WordPerfect 6.x converter included with Word 97 converts documents from WordPerfect 6.0 for MS-DOS and Windows and WordPerfect 6.1 for Windows to Word 97. This converter cannot be used to save Word documents in WordPerfect 6.x format.

You can, however, save Word 97 documents in WordPerfect 5.0 or WordPerfect 5.1 format and then open those documents in WordPerfect 6.x. For more information about conversion issues between Word 97 and WordPerfect 5.x format, see "Sharing Documents with WordPerfect 5.x" later in this chapter.

Converting Documents from WordPerfect 5.x

Word 97 does not handle all data and formatting in the same way that WordPerfect 5.x does. Converting WordPerfect 5.x documents to Word 97 format may result in changed data or formatting. The following sections describe the WordPerfect 5.x features that are handled differently in Word 97.

Character Formatting Features

The following table describes conversion issues that may affect your data or formatting when you save WordPerfect 5.x documents in Word 97 format.

When this WordPerfect 5.x feature	Is converted to Word 97 format
Redlining	Redlining is converted to comments.
Spacing (condensed, expanded)	Lost in the conversion.
Strikeout	Strikeout is converted to strikethrough formatting.
Underlining	Underlining format is preserved, but the type of underlining may be changed.

Paragraph Formatting Features

The following table describes conversion issues that may affect your data or formatting when you save WordPerfect 5.x documents in Word 97 format.

When this WordPerfect 5.x feature	Is converted to Word 97 format
Center and flush right codes	Center and flush right codes are converted to center-aligned and right-aligned tab stops.
Leading/baselines, lines/baselines	Lost in the conversion.
Page break before	Lost in the conversion.
Space before and after paragraphs	Lost in the conversion.
Styles	Paragraph formatting codes are converted to paragraph styles. Character formatting codes are converted to character styles.

Section Formatting Features

The following table describes conversion issues that may affect your data or formatting when you save WordPerfect 5.x documents in Word 97 format.

When this WordPerfect 5.x feature	Is converted to Word 97 format
Margins	Margins are adjusted to preserve page layout. Word prompts users to adjust margins manually, when necessary, on the **Margins** tab in the **Page Setup** dialog box (**File** menu).
Parallel columns	Parallel columns are converted to tables. If a parallel column layout contains a page-anchored box, the entire column is converted to newspaper columns.

Document Formatting Features

The following table describes conversion issues that may affect your data or formatting when you save WordPerfect 5.x documents in Word 97 format.

When this WordPerfect 5.x feature	Is converted to Word 97 format
Mirror even/odd pages	Lost in the conversion.
Widow control	Widow control becomes a paragraph property.

Table Features

The following table describes conversion issues that may affect your data or formatting when you save WordPerfect 5.x documents in Word 97 format.

When this WordPerfect 5.x feature	Is converted to Word 97 format
Decimal table cell alignment	Table cells are right-aligned.
Table formulas and math	Lost in the conversion.

Other Features

The following table describes conversion issues that may affect your data or formatting when you save WordPerfect 5.x documents in Word 97 format.

When this WordPerfect 5.x feature	Is converted to Word 97 format
Equations	Equations are converted as editable equation objects.
Extended characters	Extended characters that are available in both products are converted.

When this WordPerfect 5.x feature	Is converted to Word 97 format
Line draw characters	Line draw characters are converted; however, line spacing in Word leaves gaps between characters on successive lines. To correct this, set line spacing to the exact font size in points using the **Paragraph** command (**Format** menu).
Print merge secondary files	Word automatically converts WordPerfect secondary files to Word data source document format. Conditional print merge constructs and macros are lost.
PRIVATE field codes	PRIVATE fields are inserted to preserve information needed to accurately save the file back to WordPerfect format. These fields should not be edited and have no effect on the document in Word.
Subdocuments (INCLUDE field)	WordPerfect master documents and subdocuments are converted to Word master documents and subdocuments.
Text boxes and lines	Some text boxes and lines are converted to Office Art objects, visible only in page layout view, print preview, and when printing.

Sharing Documents with WordPerfect 5.x

If your workgroup is upgrading gradually to Word 97, some users may have to share documents with users of WordPerfect 5.x. The WordPerfect 5.x converter shipped with Word 97 is designed to take advantage of features and conversion capabilities unique to Word 97.

Note Converting a file from Word format to WordPerfect format and back again may cause the loss of some formatting—for example, fonts, justification, styles, and mail merge—unless you load, paginate, and save the converted file in WordPerfect before converting it back to Word.

▶ **To save a Word document in WordPerfect 5.x format**

1 On the **File** menu, click **Save As**.

2 In the **Save as type** box, click the Word Perfect 5.x version in which you want to save the file.

3 In the **File name** box, enter the name of the converted document.

   If you save the document with a different name, you retain the document in Word format as a backup.

4 When you close the document or quit Word, click **Yes** to save the changes to the document.

Tip End users can specify the default format in which Word saves new documents.

▶ **To specify the default format in which to save documents**

1 On the **Tools** menu, click **Options**, and then click the **Save** tab.
2 In the **Save Word files as** box, click the file format you want.

   The next time you save a document that is not already saved in Word 97 format, you are prompted to save it in this format.

For more information about selecting a default format in which to save documents, see "Specifying the Default Format in Which to Save Files" in Chapter 22, "Supporting Multiple Versions of Microsoft Office."

Tip In Windows 95 and Windows NT Workstation 4.0, you can use a system policy to define the default value for the **Save Word files as** option on the **Save** tab in the **Options** dialog box (**Tools** menu) for all Word users in your workgroup. In the System Policy Editor, set the following policy:

User\Word 97\Tools_Options\Save\Default Save

For more information, see "Using Windows System Policies to Customize Office" in Chapter 7, "Customizing and Optimizing Microsoft Office."

Character Formatting Features

The following table describes conversion issues that may affect your data or formatting when you save Word 97 documents in WordPerfect 5.x format.

When this Word 97 feature	Is saved in WordPerfect 5.x format
All caps	All caps formatting becomes all capital letters.
Hidden text	Hidden text is converted to comment text.
Revision marks	Revision marks are converted to redlining.
Spacing (condensed, expanded)	Lost in the conversion.
Strikethrough	Strikethrough formatting is converted to strikeout.
Underlining	Underlining format is preserved, but the type of underlining may be changed.

Paragraph Formatting Features

The following table describes conversion issues that may affect your data or formatting when you save Word 97 documents in WordPerfect 5.x format.

When this Word 97 feature	Is saved in WordPerfect 5.x format
Leading/baselines, lines/baselines	Lost in the conversion.
Page break before	These are approximated with page breaks.
Space before and after paragraphs	Spaces are approximated with blank lines.
Tab leaders	Tab leaders are converted to dot leaders.

Section Formatting Features

The following table describes conversion issues that may affect your data or formatting when you save Word 97 documents in WordPerfect 5.x format.

When this Word 97 feature	Is saved in WordPerfect 5.x format
Newspaper columns	Lost in the conversion.
Parallel columns	Lost in the conversion.

Document Formatting Features

The following table describes conversion issues that may affect your data or formatting when you save Word documents in WordPerfect 5.x format.

When this Word 97 Feature	Is saved in WordPerfect 5.x format
Default tab stops	Lost in the conversion.
Footnotes	Footnotes placed at the ends of sections are converted to endnotes. Starting numbers and separators are not converted.
Gutter margins, widow control, mirror even/odd pages, and paper size	Lost in the conversion.

Table Features

The following table describes conversion issues that may affect your data or formatting when you save Word 97 documents in WordPerfect 5.x format.

When this Word 97 feature	Is saved in WordPerfect 5.x format
Decimal table cell alignment	Lost in the conversion.
Table formulas and math	Lost in the conversion.
Vertically merged cells in tables	Lost in the conversion.

Other Features

The following table describes conversion issues that may affect your data or formatting when you save Word 97 documents in WordPerfect 5.x format.

When this Word 97 feature	Is saved in WordPerfect 5.x format
Annotations	Annotations are converted to comments.
Date/time stamps	Only default date/time formats are supported.
Equations	Equation objects are converted as editable equation boxes. Equation fields are not converted.
Extended characters	Extended characters that are available in both products are converted.
Outlining, paragraph numbers, and Word 97 lists	Word lists and paragraph numbers in tables and footnotes are converted to SEQUENCE fields.
Data source documents for print merge	Word data source documents must be either tab or comma delimited or in table format to convert to WordPerfect.

Exporting WordPerfect Graphics

When you convert a Word 97 document to WordPerfect 5.x format, a graphics filter converts Windows WMF graphics to WordPerfect Graphic format. The WordPerfect text converter runs this filter for each graphic in the Word document, and then embeds each converted graphic in the WordPerfect document.

Using WordPerfect Help

In Word 97 for Windows, the WordPerfect Help feature allows you to use familiar WordPerfect keys and commands while you learn how to use Word. For example, you can choose a WordPerfect key or command and have Word display step-by-step instructions for the corresponding action in Word. Or Word can demonstrate and actually carry out the corresponding action. You can also set the navigation keys (such as PAGE UP and ESC) to function as they do in WordPerfect.

Note The WordPerfect Help feature in Word 97 provides Help topics for users switching from WordPerfect for MS-DOS.

WordPerfect Help is not installed when you choose the Typical installation during Setup. To install WordPerfect Help, rerun Setup and click **Add/Remove**; under the **Microsoft Word** option, select the **Help** option, and then select the **Help For WordPerfect Users** check box.

Navigation Keys for WordPerfect Users

You can set the navigation keys PAGE UP, PAGE DOWN, HOME, END, and ESC to function in Word 97 as they do in WordPerfect. For example, if you press ESC, you can repeat the previous keystroke as you would in WordPerfect; ESC doesn't cancel a dialog box as it normally does in Word.

▶ **To use WordPerfect navigation keys in Word 97**

1   On the **Help** menu, click **WordPerfect Help**.
2   Click **Options**.
3   Select the **Navigation keys for WordPerfect users** check box.

You can also click **WPH** on the status bar to turn on the WordPerfect navigation keys. When WordPerfect navigation keys are on, **WPH** appears undimmed.

Help for WordPerfect Keys and Commands

You can press a WordPerfect key and have Word either automatically demonstrate the corresponding feature or list the steps you need to perform it in Word. If you're not sure which WordPerfect key to press, you can choose from a list of WordPerfect commands instead.

▶ **To use Help for WordPerfect Keys**

1   On the **Tools** menu, click **Options**, and then click the **General** tab.
2   Under **General options**, select the **Help for WordPerfect users** check box.

    To indicate that Help for WordPerfect keys is on, **WPH** appears undimmed on the status bar. If you've also turned on WordPerfect navigation keys, **WP** appears instead.

Next you need to indicate whether you want to see step-by-step instructions or demonstrations when you press WordPerfect keys.

▶ **To see step-by-step instructions or demonstrations**

1   On the **Help** menu, click **WordPerfect Help**.
2   Click **Options**.
3   Under **Help type**, click **Help text** to see step-by-step instructions.

    –or–

    Click **Demo** to see demonstrations.

When you are working in a Word 97 document and you press a WordPerfect key combination—such as CTRL+F8 to change the point size of selected text—a dialog box appears. Press the number or underlined letter of the command you want, or select a command and then click either the **Help Text** or **Demo** button.

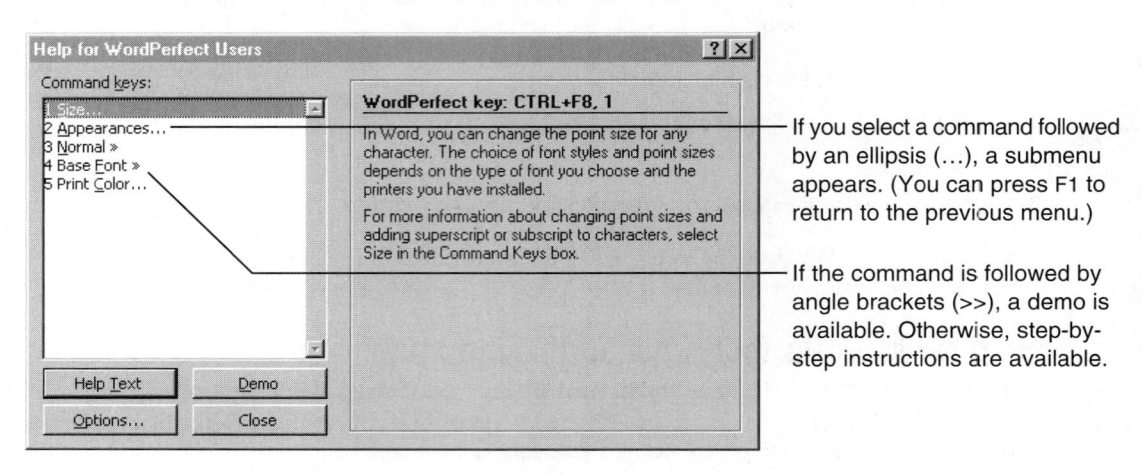

— If you select a command followed by an ellipsis (...), a submenu appears. (You can press F1 to return to the previous menu.)

— If the command is followed by angle brackets (>>), a demo is available. Otherwise, step-by-step instructions are available.

If you choose to display step-by-step instructions, a dialog box appears. The instructions remain on the screen while you work in the document. If the dialog box covers part of the document, you can drag the title bar of the dialog box to move it out of your way.

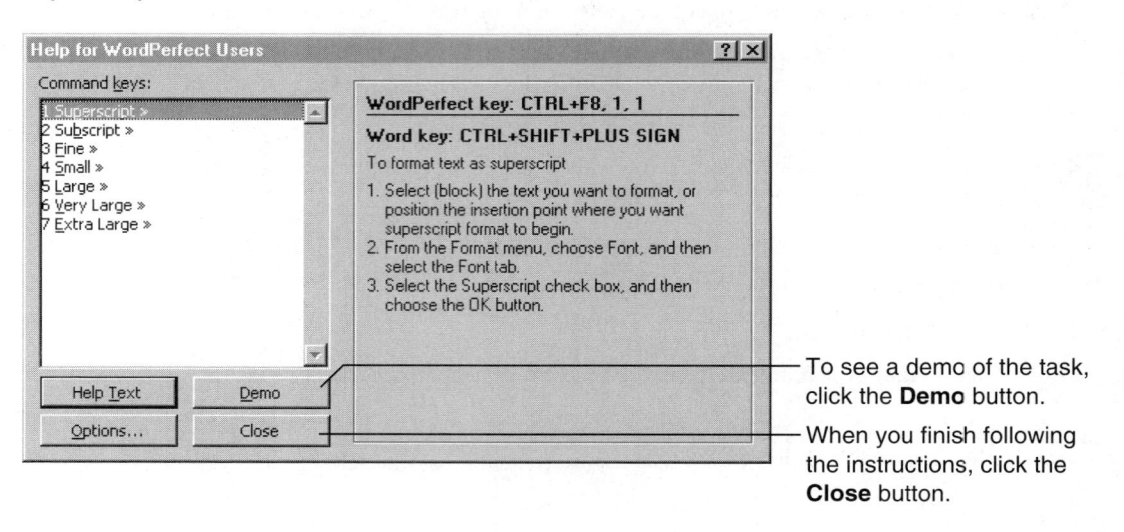

— To see a demo of the task, click the **Demo** button.

— When you finish following the instructions, click the **Close** button.

If you choose to display a demonstration, Word demonstrates the actions necessary to complete the command. If Word needs some input from you, such as a file name, a message tells you what to do.

For example, the following illustration shows WordPerfect Help when a user presses F2, the WordPerfect equivalent for searching forward.

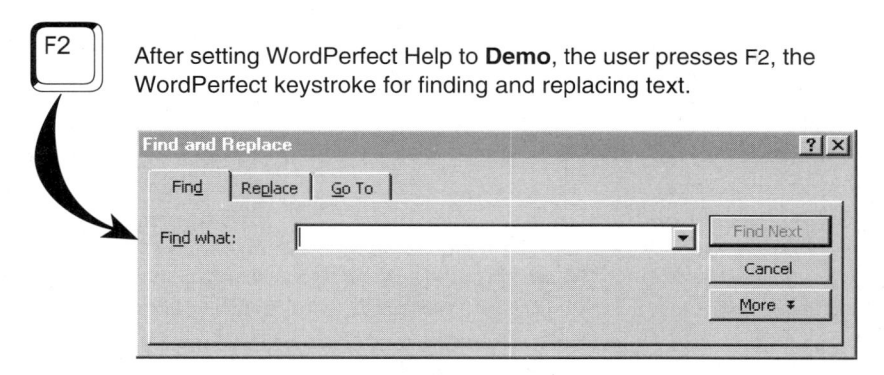

After setting WordPerfect Help to **Demo**, the user presses F2, the WordPerfect keystroke for finding and replacing text.

Word displays the **Find and Replace** dialog box.

To customize the way demonstrations work, you can set the demonstration speed, turn off the mouse simulation, and turn off the display of messages that ask for user input. For more information, see the following section, "Customizing Help for WordPerfect Users."

Customizing Help for WordPerfect Users

You can customize Help for WordPerfect users. For example, you can control the speed of the demonstrations.

Part 4   Switching from Other Applications

▶ **To customize WordPerfect Help**

1   On the **Help** menu, click **WordPerfect Help**.
2   Click **Options**, and then select the options you want.

These Help options are shown in the following illustration.

Select these check boxes to turn on Help for WordPerfect users and WordPerfect navigation keys.

Select the type of help you want displayed when you press a WordPerfect key combination or select a WordPerfect command.

Under **Help Options**, change the demo speed, turn on simulated mouse actions, or turn on the display of messages that ask for user input.

Switching from Microsoft Works 3.0 or 4.0 for Windows

When you upgrade to Word 97 for Windows, you can open your old Works 3.0 or 4.0 for Windows documents in Word 97. If the Works 3.0 for Windows or Works 4.0 for Windows text converter is installed, Word 97 automatically converts the Works document to Word 97 file format.

What if Works for Windows isn't listed?

If you attempt to open a Works for Windows document, but Word cannot open it properly, Word may prompt you to select the file format from which to convert the document. If **Works 3.0 for Windows** or **Works 4.0 for Windows** does not appear in the **Convert File** dialog box, you need to install the Works for Windows text converters. To install the Works 3.0 for Windows or Works 4.0 for Windows converter, rerun Setup and click **Add/Remove**; under the **Converters and Filters** option, select the **Text Converters** option.

Tip For best results when moving documents from Works for MS-DOS to Word, save your Works word processing documents in the following formats.

Save this Works version	In this file format
Works 1.x for MS-DOS	Text Only
Works 2.x or 3.x for MS-DOS	RTF

Sharing Documents with Works for Windows

If your workgroup is upgrading gradually to Word 97, some users may have to share documents with Works for Windows users. Users of Word 97 can save documents in Works for Windows format.

▶ **To save a Word document in Works 3.0 or 4.0 for Windows format**

1 On the **File** menu, click **Save As**.
2 In the **Save as type** box, click **Works 3.0 for Windows** or **Works 4.0 for Windows**.

Tip When you save a Word document in another file format, use a different file name so that you can keep a copy of the original document in Word format as a backup.

What if Works for Windows isn't listed?
If you attempt to save a Word document in Works for Windows format, but **Works for Windows** is not listed in the **Save as type** box, you need to install the Works for Windows text converters. To install the Works 3.0 for Windows or Works 4.0 for Windows converter, rerun Setup and click **Add/Remove**; under the **Converters and Filters** option, select the **Text Converters** option.

Tip End users can specify the default format in which Word saves new documents.

▶ **To specify the default format in which to save documents**

1 On the **Tools** menu, click **Options**, and then click the **Save** tab.
2 In the **Save Word files as** box, click the file format you want.

   The next time you save a document that is not already saved in Word 97 format, you are prompted to save it in this format.

For more information about selecting a default format in which to save documents, see "Specifying the Default Format in Which to Save Files" in Chapter 22, "Supporting Multiple Versions of Microsoft Office."

> **Tip** In Windows 95 and Windows NT Workstation 4.0, you can use a system policy to define the default value for the **Save Word files as** option on the **Save** tab in the **Options** dialog box (**Tools** menu) for all Word users in your workgroup. In the System Policy Editor, set the following policy:
>
> **User\Word 97\Tools_Options\Save\Default Save**
>
> For more information, see "Using Windows System Policies to Customize Office" in Chapter 7, "Customizing and Optimizing Microsoft Office."

Since not all Word 97 features are supported, saving in Works for Windows format may result in loss of data or formatting. The following sections describe the Word 97 features that are not fully supported in Works for Windows format.

Character Formatting

The following table describes conversion issues that may affect your data or formatting when you save Word 97 documents in Works for Windows format.

When this Word 97 feature	Is converted to Works for Windows format
All caps, small caps, hidden text, and color	Lost in the conversion.
Columns	Lost in the conversion.
Outline and shadow	Lost in the conversion.
Spacing (condensed, expanded)	Lost in the conversion.
Underlining (dotted, double, word)	All underlining is converted to single, continuous underlining.

Paragraph Formatting

The following table describes conversion issues that may affect your data or formatting when you save Word 97 documents in Works for Windows format.

When this Word 97 feature	Is converted to Works for Windows format
Background shading and numbering	Lost in the conversion.
Borders	Thin, thick, and double borders are converted properly. Unsupported border styles become thin line borders.
Line numbering	Lost in the conversion.
Negative tabs	Lost in the conversion.
Page break before	These are converted to hard page breaks.
Restart page number at one	Lost in the conversion.
Section breaks (even, odd, continuous, next page)	Section breaks are converted to page breaks.
Section formatting	Lost in the conversion.
Tables	Tables are converted to tab-delimited text.
Vertical alignment (top, centered, justified)	Lost in the conversion.

Page Formatting

The following table describes conversion issues that may affect your data or formatting when you save Word 97 documents in Works for Windows format.

When this Word 97 feature	Is converted to Works for Windows format
Margin (gutter), mirror even/odd pages, page orientation, and paper source	Lost in the conversion.

Document Formatting

The following table describes conversion issues that may affect your data or formatting when you save Word 97 documents in Works for Windows format.

When this Word 97 feature	Is converted to Works for Windows format
Footnotes	Footnotes are placed at the end of the document.
Summary information	Lost in the conversion.

Other Features

The following table describes conversion issues that may affect your data or formatting when you save Word 97 documents in Works for Windows format.

When this Word 97 feature	Is converted to Works for Windows format
ActiveX objects (formerly OLE objects)	Word 97 becomes a client for Works for Windows charts, Microsoft Drawing objects, and Microsoft Excel charts and worksheets.
Annotations	Annotations are converted to footnotes, but retain the page number reference.
Bullets and numbering	Automatic bullets and numbering are converted to plain text.
Cropping of graphics	Lost in the conversion.
Date/time stamps (custom), page number (format, restart), and subdocuments (INCLUDE field)	Lost in the conversion.
Endnotes	Lost in the conversion.
Fields (equations, formulas, links, form fields, bar codes)	Some fields are converted to the text of the most recent result. Check your converted documents for conversion results.
Footnote numbering	Works for Windows counts manual footnote entries in the numbering sequence, whereas Word 97 counts them separately.
Footnote position (end of page, end of document)	All footnotes are converted to endnotes.

When this Word 97 feature	Is converted to Works for Windows format
Footnote starting number, separators, continuation notices, and restart each section	Footnotes are numbered continuously throughout the document, beginning with 1.
Frames	Lost in the conversion.
Office Art objects	Lost in the conversion.
Outlining	Lost in the conversion.
Print merge commands (logic and data files)	Merge fields are converted, but data files are not automatically converted.
Revision marks	Lost in the conversion.
Styles	Styles are converted to direct formatting.
Tables of contents, indexes, and tables of authorities	These tables are converted to the text of the most recent result.

Switching from Text with Layout

If you are switching from an application that can save documents in Text with Layout format, you can open your documents in Word 97. If the Text with Layout text converter is installed, Word 97 automatically converts the Text with Layout document to Word 97 file format.

> **What if Text with Layout isn't listed?**
> If you attempt to open a Text with Layout document, but Word cannot open it properly, Word may prompt you to select the file format from which to convert the document. If **Text with Layout** does not appear in the **Convert File** dialog box, you need to install the Text with Layout converter. To install the converter, rerun Setup and click **Add/Remove**; under the **Microsoft Word** option, select the **Text Converters** option, and then select the **Text with Layout Converter** check box.

Sharing Documents with Applications That Read Text with Layout Format

If you`r workgroup is upgrading gradually to Word 97, some users may have to share documents with users of applications that read Text with Layout format. Users of Word 97 can save documents in Text with Layout format.

▶ **To save a Word document in Text with Layout format**

1. On the **File** menu, click **Save As**.
2. In the **Save as type** box, click **Text with Layout**.

> **What if Text with Layout isn't listed?**
> If you attempt to save a Word document in Text with Layout format, but **Text with Layout** is not listed in the **Save as type** box, you need to install the Text with Layout converter. To install the converter, rerun Setup and click **Add/Remove**; under the **Microsoft Word** option, select the **Text Converters** option, and then select the **Text with Layout Converter** check box.

Tip End users can specify the default format in which Word saves new documents.

▶ **To specify the default format in which to save documents**

1. On the **Tools** menu, click **Options**, and then click the **Save** tab.
2. In the **Save Word files as** box, click the file format you want.

   The next time you save a document that is not already saved in Word 97 format, you are prompted to save it in this format.

For more information about selecting a default format in which to save documents, see "Specifying the Default Format in Which to Save Files" in Chapter 22, "Supporting Multiple Versions of Microsoft Office."

Tip In Windows 95 and Windows NT Workstation 4.0, you can use a system policy to define the default value for the **Save Word files as** option on the **Save** tab in the **Options** dialog box (**Tools** menu) for all Word users in your workgroup. In the System Policy Editor, set the following policy:

User\Word 97\Tools_Options\Save\Default Save

For more information, see "Using Windows System Policies to Customize Office" in Chapter 7, "Customizing and Optimizing Microsoft Office."

Since not all Word 97 features are supported, saving in Text with Layout format may result in loss of data or formatting. The following sections describe the Word 97 features that are not fully supported in Text with Layout format.

Note When saving to or reading from an MS-DOS-based application, use the MS-DOS Text with Layout format.

Character Formatting

The following table describes conversion issues that may affect your data or formatting when you save Word 97 documents in Text with Layout format.

When this Word 97 feature	Is converted to Text with Layout format
Character formatting	Character formatting is not converted. This includes font, font size, color, bold, italic, small caps, hidden, underline, word underline, double underline, subscript, superscript, and expanded and condensed character formats.
Columns	Line Between formatting is not converted.
Page breaks	Lost in the conversion.
Page dimensions	Lost in the conversion.
Widow control	Lost in the conversion.

Paragraph Formatting

The following table describes conversion issues that may affect your data or formatting when you save Word 97 documents in Text with Layout format.

When this Word 97 feature	Is converted to Text with Layout format
Borders, keep lines together, keep with next, and page break before	Lost in the conversion.
Tab leaders	Lost in the conversion.

Section Formatting

The following table describes conversion issues that may affect your data or formatting when you save Word 97 documents in Text with Layout format.

When this Word 97 feature	Is converted to Text with Layout format
Different first page	If a first-page and a subsequent header are defined, the text of the next-page header is placed at the beginning of the document, and the text of the first-page header is lost.
Different odd and even pages	Even-header text is placed at the beginning of the document; odd-header text is lost. If only an odd header is defined, odd-header text is placed at the beginning of the document.
Header/footer	Header/footer text is placed at the beginning of the document.
Header/footer position	Header/footer distance from the page edge is lost. Footers are placed at the beginning of the page.
Line numbering	Lost in the conversion.

When this Word 97 feature	Is converted to Text with Layout format
Page numbering	Lost in the conversion.
Section breaks (even, odd, continuous, next page)	Converted to paragraph marks.

Table Features

The following table describes conversion issues that may affect your data or formatting when you save Word 97 documents in Text with Layout format.

When this Word 97 feature	Is converted to Text with Layout format
Borders, justified text alignment, and minimum row height	Lost in the conversion.
Indents	Right indents and hanging indents applied within table cells are lost.
Table text and structure	Table text and structure are preserved.

Other Features

The following table describes conversion issues that may affect your data or formatting when you save Word 97 documents in Text with Layout format.

When this Word 97 feature	Is converted to Text with Layout format
Annotations	Annotations are inserted at the end of the document in the order in which they appear in the document.
Fields (DATE, TIME)	Fields are converted to the text of the most recent result.
Footnotes	Footnotes are inserted at the end of the document in the order they appear in the document. Footnotes are numbered sequentially throughout the document. Text of custom separators is inserted at the beginning of the document.
Formulas	Lost in the conversion.
Graphics	Lost in the conversion.
Hard space	Hard spaces are converted to normal spaces.
Nonbreaking hyphen	Nonbreaking hyphens are converted to normal hyphens.
Optional hyphen	Lost in the conversion.

Part 4   Switching from Other Applications

Switching from Lotus Ami Pro

Tools and Utilities   The Office Resource Kit Tools and Utilities include 16- and 32-bit Lotus Ami Pro 3.*x* text converters. For more information about installing the converters, see "Word Converters" in Appendix A, "Microsoft Office 97 Resource Kit Tools and Utilities."

Switching from DisplayWrite

Tools and Utilities   The Office Resource Kit Tools and Utilities include an RFT-DCA text converter with which you can open DisplayWrite documents previously saved in RFT-DCA format. For more information about installing the RFT-DCA text converter, see "Word Converters" in Appendix A, "Microsoft Office 97 Resource Kit Tools and Utilities."

Switching from Microsoft Windows Write 3.0 or 3.1

Tools and Utilities   The Office Resource Kit Tools and Utilities include a Windows Write 3.0 or 3.1 text converter. For more information about installing the converter, see "Word Converters" in Appendix A, "Microsoft Office 97 Resource Kit Tools and Utilities."

Tip   After converting a Write 3.*x* document to Word 97 and then back again, it may appear that objects were lost in the conversion. If this happens, repaginate the final document in Write; the objects should reappear.

Switching from RFT-DCA Format Files

Tools and Utilities   The Office Resource Kit Tools and Utilities include an RFT-DCA document converter. For more information about installing the converter, see "Word Converters" in Appendix A, "Microsoft Office 97 Resource Kit Tools and Utilities."

Switching from MultiMate

Tools and Utilities   The Office Resource Kit Tools and Utilities include an RFT-DCA document converter with which you can open MultiMate documents previously saved in RFT-DCA format. For more information about installing the converter, see "Word Converters" in Appendix A, "Microsoft Office 97 Resource Kit Tools and Utilities."

Switching from WordStar

Tools and Utilities The Office Resource Kit Tools and Utilities include a text converter for WordStar 3.3–95 for MS-DOS (import only), WordStar 4.0 and 95 for MS-DOS (export only), and WordStar 1.0 and 2.0 for Windows (import only). For more information about installing the converters, see "Word Converters" in Appendix A, "Microsoft Office 97 Resource Kit Tools and Utilities."

PART 5

Using Microsoft Office Throughout Your Organization

Contents

Chapter 22 Supporting Multiple Versions of Microsoft Office   621
Chapter 23 Tracking Collaboration with Document Properties   637
Chapter 24 Integrating Microsoft Office with Your Intranet   645
Chapter 25 Web Support in Microsoft Office Applications   665
Chapter 26 Finding Microsoft Office Documents on the Network   717
Chapter 27 Sharing Information with Microsoft Office Applications   745
Chapter 28 Working with Messaging Systems and Connectivity Software   793
Chapter 29 Workgroup Features in Microsoft Access   803
Chapter 30 Workgroup Features in Microsoft Excel   855
Chapter 31 Workgroup Features in Microsoft Outlook   865
Chapter 32 Workgroup Features in Microsoft PowerPoint   877
Chapter 33 Workgroup Features in Microsoft Word   891

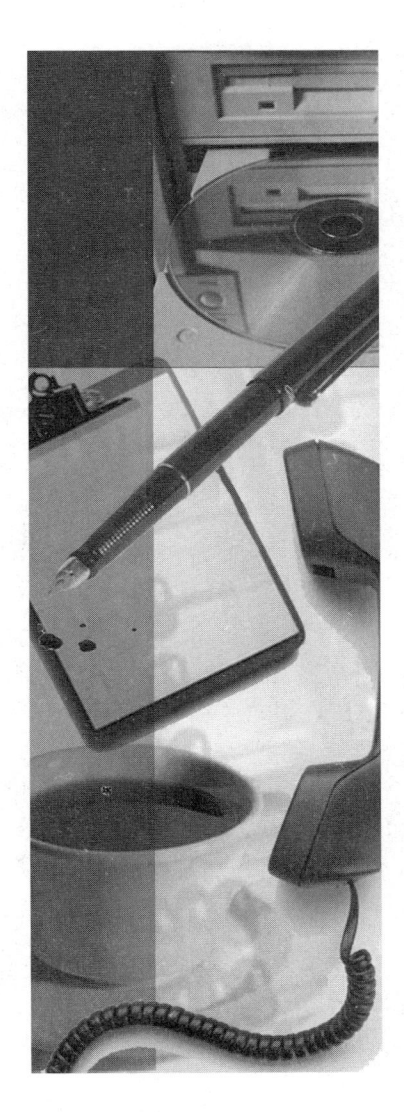

CHAPTER 22

Supporting Multiple Versions of Microsoft Office

This chapter tells you what to expect when you have multiple versions of Microsoft Office installed in your workgroup or on a single computer. It provides an overview of sharing files among different versions of Office applications.

In This Chapter

Specifying the Default Format in Which to Save Office Documents   621

Running Multiple Versions of Microsoft Access   623

Running Multiple Versions of Microsoft Excel   626

Running Multiple Versions of Electronic Mail and Scheduling Applications   628

Running Multiple Versions of PowerPoint   630

Running Multiple Versions of Microsoft Word   634

For information about sharing documents with previous versions of each of the Office applications, see the chapters in Part 3, "Upgrading to Microsoft Office."

Specifying the Default Format in Which to Save Office Documents

If you or your workgroup is upgrading to Office 97 from previous versions of Office applications, you can specify the default file format in which to save new files. By specifying a default format, members of your workgroup can automatically save files in the best format for sharing within the workgroup.

Note   You can specify a default file format in Microsoft Excel, Microsoft PowerPoint, and Microsoft Word.

▶ To specify the default format in which to save files

1. On the **Tools** menu, click **Options**, and then click the **Save** tab (Word and PowerPoint) or **Transition** tab (Microsoft Excel).
2. In the **Save** *Application* **Files as** box, click the file format you want.

Tip In Windows 95 and Windows NT Workstation version 4.0, you can use a system policy to define the default value for the **Save** *Application* **Files as** option in the **Options** dialog box (**Tools** menu) for all Office 97 users in your workgroup. In the System Policy Editor, set the following policies:

User\Excel\Tools_Options\Transition\Default Save

User\PowerPoint\Tools_Options\Save\Default Save

User\Word\Tools_Options\Save\Default Save

For more information, see "Using Windows System Policies to Customize Office" in Chapter 7, "Customizing and Optimizing Microsoft Office."

The next time you save a file that is not already saved in the Office 97 format, you are prompted to save it in this default format. The Office 97 application also gives you the option of saving the file in another format, and warns you if you choose to save in a format that could result in the loss of formatting or data.

Tip In Windows 95 and Windows NT Workstation 4.0, you can use a system policy to define the default-save prompt text for all Office 97 users in your workgroup. In the System Policy Editor, set the following policy:

Computer\Office\Default Save

For more information, see "Using Windows System Policies to Customize Office" in Chapter 7, "Customizing and Optimizing Microsoft Office."

Using Long File Names with Previous Versions of Office

When you save an Office 97 document in Office version 4.*x* format, a user opening the document may be running another operating system, such as Windows version 3.1, that does not support long file names. Such an operating system truncates the file name to eight characters with a three-character extension.

If the document is opened by a user running Office on Windows 95 or Windows NT Workstation 3.51 or 4.0, however, the long file name is preserved.

Although the Macintosh operating system supports long file names, Macintosh file names cannot exceed 32 characters. Names longer than 32 characters are truncated.

Running Multiple Versions of Microsoft Access

This section describes issues relevant to a workgroup or a single computer running any combination of the following versions of Microsoft Access (Windows only):

- Microsoft Access 97
- Microsoft Access 95
- Microsoft Access version 2.0
- Microsoft Access version 1.x

Sharing Databases Across Operating Systems and Versions

While file format differs among different versions of Microsoft Access, Microsoft Access 97 can read databases in previous formats. The following sections explain issues to be aware of when sharing databases among multiple versions of Microsoft Access.

Opening Database Files

To maintain backward compatibility, Microsoft Access 97 can open databases from previous versions without converting them. This process is called *enabling* a database. However, users of previous versions cannot open database files created with Microsoft Access 97. Additionally, Microsoft Access 97 users cannot modify the design of any objects in an enabled Microsoft Access database created in a previous version of Microsoft Access.

As an alternative to enabling databases created in a previous version of Microsoft Access, you can create a database front-end application in Microsoft Access 97 format that is linked to table data from the previous version of Microsoft Access. For more information about both of these ways to share databases, see "Sharing Databases with Microsoft Access 1.x, 2.0, and 95" in Chapter 11, "Upgrading from Previous Versions of Microsoft Access."

Using Secured Databases

To use a secured database from a previous version of Microsoft Access, Microsoft Access 97 users must use a workgroup information file created in the previous version. Use the Workgroup Administrator that comes with Microsoft Access 97 to join the workgroup information file from the previous version.

▶ **To join a workgroup information file from a previous version of Microsoft Access**

1 In the System folder (Windows 95) or System32 folder (Windows NT Workstation 4.0), and double-click Wrkgadm.exe.

   –or–

   In Program Manager, double-click the Workgroup Administrator icon in the Microsoft Office program group (Windows NT Workstation 3.51).

2 In the **Workgroup Administrator** dialog box, click **Join**.

3 In the **Database** box, enter the name of the workgroup information file you want to use.

If all users of a secured database have upgraded to Microsoft Access 97, you can convert the database to Microsoft Access 97 format. For information about converting secured databases, see "Converting a Database Secured with User-level Security" in Chapter 11, "Upgrading from Previous Versions of Microsoft Access."

Modifying Access Basic Code

You may need to make changes to Access Basic code for it to work in Microsoft Access 97. For more information, see "Access Basic Code Changes" in Chapter 11, "Upgrading from Previous Versions of Microsoft Access."

Running Multiple Versions of Microsoft Access on a Single Computer

This section addresses installing and using different versions of Microsoft Access on the same Windows 95 or Windows NT Workstation 3.51 or 4.0 computer. All of the issues noted in the previous section apply to running multiple versions of Microsoft Access on a single system.

> **Why is the wrong version of Microsoft Access trying to open my database?**
>
> When you run multiple versions of Microsoft Access on the same computer, certain actions—such as double-clicking a Microsoft Access database on the desktop or activating an OLE object—start the last version of Microsoft Access that was installed, even if it is not the right version for the database. To avoid this problem, either install Microsoft Access 97 last, or select which version of Microsoft Access to use when you open a database file from the desktop or in Windows Explorer under Windows 95 or Windows NT Workstation 4.0.
>
> For more information about selecting a version of Microsoft Access, see "Choosing the Version That Opens Databases" later in this chapter.

Running Two 32-bit Versions

You can install and run Microsoft Access 95 and 97, both of which are 32-bit versions, on the same computer. If you attempt to remove one version of Microsoft Access, you may lose components shared by both versions, requiring you to reinstall the version you want to keep.

Running 16-bit and 32-bit Versions

You can install and run the 16-bit versions of Microsoft Access (version 1.*x* or 2.0) and Microsoft Access 97 on the same computer, as long as they are installed in different folders. All versions of Microsoft Access can be run at the same time, but only Microsoft Access 97 can open databases created with all other versions.

Choosing the Version That Opens Databases

When you use Windows Explorer (Windows 95 or Windows NT Workstation 4.0) or File Manager (Windows NT Workstation 3.51) to open a database, the database is opened by default in the last version of Microsoft Access you installed. If you install a previous version of Microsoft Access after installing Microsoft Access 97, Microsoft Access cannot open later versions of the files, and displays a message indicating that the file is damaged. However, if you are using Windows 95 or Windows NT Workstation 4.0, you can override the default by selecting which version of Microsoft Access to use.

Note This following procedure works only on Windows 95 and Windows NT Workstation 4.0. It does not work on Windows NT Workstation 3.51.

▶ **To control which version of Microsoft Access opens a database**

1. In Windows Explorer, find a version of Microsoft Access on your computer.
2. Open the Windows\SendTo folder.
3. Using the right mouse button, drag the Microsoft Access application icon to the SendTo folder and click **Create Shortcut(s) Here** on the shortcut menu.
4. Repeat Steps 1 through 3 for every version of Microsoft Access you want to run.
5. In the SendTo folder, rename the Microsoft Access shortcuts so you can easily distinguish them.
6. To specify which version of Microsoft Access to use to open a database, right-click the database in Windows Explorer; and then point to **Send To** on the shortcut menu and click the version you want.

Running Multiple Versions of Microsoft Excel

This section describes issues relevant to a workgroup or a single computer running any combination of the following versions Microsoft Excel:

- Microsoft Excel 97 for Windows or the Macintosh
- Microsoft Excel 95 for Windows
- Microsoft Excel version 5.0 for Windows or the Macintosh
- Microsoft Excel version 4.0 for Windows or the Macintosh

Sharing Workbooks Across Operating Systems and Versions

While the file format differs between Microsoft Excel 97 and previous versions of Microsoft Excel, Microsoft Excel 97 can open workbooks created in previous versions. However, when a Microsoft Excel 97 workbook is saved in a previous version, the workbook is converted to the older file format, and data and formatting may be changed or lost. For information about how workbooks are converted to previous versions of Microsoft Excel, see Chapter 12, "Upgrading from Previous Versions of Microsoft Excel."

In addition to considering the effect on a workbook when it is saved in a previous version of Microsoft Excel, you should be aware of issues relevant to Visual Basic code in workbooks shared among versions of Microsoft Excel or across operating systems.

You can write programs in Visual Basic that run under more than one version of Microsoft Excel. However, some objects, properties, and methods that exist in Microsoft Excel 97 do not exist in Microsoft Excel 95 or previous versions. For a complete list of changes to Visual Basic in Microsoft Excel 97, see Microsoft Visual Basic online Help. See also "Porting Your 16-bit Office-Based Solutions to 32-bit Office" in Chapter 10, "Upgrading from Previous Versions of Microsoft Office."

You can write programs in Visual Basic that run on more than one operating system. Write the Visual Basic code in a workbook and then create an add-in from the source workbook. This add-in can run on both the Windows and Macintosh operating systems. Performance of the add-in may suffer when it runs on an operating system other than the one on which it was created. To ensure best performance of the add-in, move the source workbook to the other operating system and then recreate the add-in.

… Chapter 22 Supporting Multiple Versions of Microsoft Office

Running Multiple Versions of Microsoft Excel on a Single Computer

This section addresses installing and using different versions of Microsoft Excel on the same computer. All of the issues noted in the previous section apply to running multiple versions of Microsoft Excel on a single system.

> **Why is the wrong version of Microsoft Excel trying to open my workbook?**
>
> When you run multiple versions of Microsoft Excel on the same computer, certain actions—such as double-clicking a Microsoft Excel workbook on the desktop or activating an OLE object—start the last version of Microsoft Excel that was installed, even if it is not the right version for the workbook. To avoid this problem, either install Microsoft Excel 97 last, or select which version of Microsoft Excel to use when you open a workbook file on the desktop or in Windows Explorer under Windows 95 or Windows NT Workstation 4.0.
>
> For more information about selecting a version of Microsoft Excel, see "Choosing the Version That Opens Workbooks" later in this chapter.

Running Two 32-bit Versions

You can install and run Microsoft Excel 95 and 97, both of which are 32-bit versions, on the same computer. If you attempt to remove one version of Microsoft Excel, you may lose components shared by both versions, requiring you to reinstall the version you want to keep.

Running 16-bit and 32-bit Versions

You can install and run the 16-bit versions of Microsoft Excel (Microsoft Excel 5.0 or earlier) and Microsoft Excel 97 on the same computer, as long as they are installed in different folders. These versions of Microsoft Excel can be run at the same time, but only Microsoft Excel 97 can open workbooks created in all other versions.

Choosing the Version That Opens Workbooks

When you use Windows Explorer (Windows 95 or Windows NT Workstation 4.0) or File Manager (Windows NT Workstation 3.51) to open a workbook, the workbook is opened by default in the last version of Microsoft Excel you installed. If you install a previous version of Microsoft Excel after installing Microsoft Excel 97, the previous version of Microsoft Excel cannot open later versions of the files. However, if you are using Windows 95 or Windows NT Workstation 4.0, you can override the default by selecting which version of Microsoft Excel to use.

Note The following procedure works only on Windows 95 or Windows NT Workstation 4.0. It does not work on Windows NT Workstation 3.51 or on the Macintosh.

▶ **To control which version of Microsoft Excel opens a workbook**

1. In Windows Explorer, find a version of Microsoft Excel on your computer.
2. Open the Windows\SendTo folder.
3. Using the right mouse button, drag the Microsoft Excel application icon to the SendTo folder and click **Create Shortcut(s) Here** on the shortcut menu.
4. Repeat Steps 1 through 3 for every version of Microsoft Excel you want to run.
5. In the SendTo folder, rename the Microsoft Excel shortcuts so you can easily distinguish them.
6. To specify which version of Microsoft Excel to use to open a workbook, right-click the workbook in Windows Explorer; then point to **Send To** on the shortcut menu and click the version you want.

Tip This strategy works only if the workbook is in a format that can be opened by the version of Microsoft Excel you choose. To ensure that Microsoft Excel 97 saves new workbooks in the proper format, use the **Save Excel files as** option on the **Transition** tab in the **Options** dialog box (**Tools** menu). For more information, see "Specifying the Default Format in Which to Save Office Documents" earlier in this chapter.

Running Multiple Versions of Electronic Mail and Scheduling Applications

This section describes issues relevant to a workgroup running any combination of the following e-mail and scheduling applications:

- Microsoft Outlook
- Microsoft Exchange Client
- Microsoft Mail version 3.x for Windows
- Microsoft Schedule+ 95
- Microsoft Schedule+ 1.0

If your workgroup is upgrading gradually to Outlook, some Outlook users may need to exchange e-mail and meeting requests with users of these applications. Microsoft Outlook has been designed to make sharing information as simple as possible, but there are some issues to consider, especially advanced features of Outlook that are not supported by other e-mail or scheduling applications.

Sharing Information with Microsoft Exchange Client

Outlook can open both standard and custom message forms created by Microsoft Exchange Client. However, Microsoft Exchange Client does not recognize Outlook message forms. When Microsoft Exchange Client receives an Outlook form, it uses a standard Microsoft Exchange Client message form to display the message.

Outlook and Microsoft Exchange Client users can have access to a common set of public folders. Outlook recognizes custom views created with Microsoft Exchange Client, and can create views in Microsoft Exchange Client format. However, Microsoft Exchange Client does not recognize custom views created in Outlook format.

For more information about sharing information between Microsoft Outlook and Microsoft Exchange Client, see "Sharing Information with Microsoft Exchange Client," in Chapter 13, "Upgrading to Microsoft Outlook."

Sharing Information with Microsoft Mail 3.x for Windows

While Microsoft Outlook users are able to exchange e-mail freely with Microsoft Mail 3.x for Windows users, e-mail messages composed using Outlook may not appear the same when viewed by users of Microsoft Mail 3.x for Windows.

When an Outlook user opens a message created by a Microsoft Mail 3.x for Windows user, Outlook recognizes all of the features of the message. However, when a Microsoft Mail 3.x for Windows user opens an e-mail message created by an Outlook user, the Microsoft Mail 3.x client does not recognize some of the advanced features that the Outlook user is able to include in the message. For example, rich text in an Outlook message is not displayed by Microsoft Mail 3.x for Windows.

For more information about sharing information between Microsoft Outlook and Microsoft Mail 3.x for Windows, see "Sharing Information with Microsoft Mail 3.x," in Chapter 13, "Upgrading to Microsoft Outlook."

Sharing Information with Microsoft Schedule+ 95

Outlook and Schedule+ users can freely send and receive meeting requests and responses for group scheduling. Both sets of users can also, with proper permission, view each other's free/busy information. With the proper permission, an Outlook user can open a Schedule+ calendar; however, a Schedule+ user cannot open an Outlook calendar.

If you would prefer to have all your users using the same scheduling application, you can set an option in Outlook to use Schedule+ 95 as the primary scheduling application in your workgroup.

To make Schedule+ 95 your primary scheduling application

1. On the Outlook **Tools** menu, click **Options**, and then click the **Calendar** tab.
2. Select the **Use Microsoft Schedule+ 95 instead of Outlook as my primary calendar** check box.

    This check box is available only if Schedule+ 95 is installed.

Tip In Windows 95 and Windows NT Workstation 4.0, you can use a system policy to set Schedule+ 95 as the scheduling application for all Outlook users in your workgroup. In the System Policy Editor, set the following policy:

Computer\Outlook\Use Schedule+

For more information, see "Using Windows System Policies to Customize Office" in Chapter 7, "Customizing and Optimizing Microsoft Office."

For more information about sharing information between Microsoft Outlook and Schedule+ 95, see "Sharing Information with Microsoft Schedule+ 95," in Chapter 13, "Upgrading to Microsoft Outlook."

Sharing Information with Microsoft Schedule+ 1.0

Outlook and Schedule+ users can freely send and receive meeting requests and responses for group scheduling, and they can view each others' free and busy status. However, Schedule+ 1.0 does not recognize advanced features in Outlook meeting requests—such as attachments, meeting locations, and recurring meetings. In addition, Outlook users cannot view the free/busy details of Schedule+ 1.0 users because that feature is not available in Schedule+ 1.0.

Important In order for Outlook and Schedule+ 1.0 to share information, Schedule+ 95 must be installed on the computer that is running Outlook. Without Schedule+ 95, Outlook cannot read any Schedule+ 1.0 information.

For more information about sharing information between Microsoft Outlook and Schedule+ 1.0, see "Sharing Information with Microsoft Schedule+ 1.0," in Chapter 13, "Upgrading to Microsoft Outlook."

Running Multiple Versions of PowerPoint

This section describes issues relevant to a workgroup or a single computer running any combination of the following versions of PowerPoint:

- PowerPoint 97 for Windows and the Macintosh
- PowerPoint 95 for Windows
- PowerPoint version 4.0 for Windows and the Macintosh
- PowerPoint version 3.0 for Windows and the Macintosh

Note Information about PowerPoint 4.0 and PowerPoint 3.0 applies to both the Windows and Macintosh versions. Issues particular to the Macintosh are noted separately.

Sharing Presentations Across Operating Systems and Versions

While the file format of presentations differs between PowerPoint 97 and previous versions of PowerPoint, PowerPoint 97 can open presentations created in previous versions. However, when a PowerPoint 97 presentation is saved in a previous version of PowerPoint, the presentation is converted to the other format, and data and formatting may change or be lost. For information about how presentations are converted to previous versions of PowerPoint, see Chapter 14, "Upgrading from Previous Versions of Microsoft PowerPoint."

Converters

PowerPoint uses converters to open and save presentations from one file format to another. These converters preserve the data and much of the formatting of the PowerPoint 97 presentation. The converters for saving PowerPoint 97 presentations in a previous format are installed during Setup when you choose a Typical installation.

Tools and Utilities The Office Resource Kit Tools and Utilities include a converter that allows PowerPoint 4.0 users to read PowerPoint 95 presentations. You must use the associated Setup program to install this converter; simply copying the files does not work. For more information about installing the converter, see "PowerPoint Converters" in Appendix A, "Microsoft Office 97 Resource Kit Tools and Utilities."

World Wide Web For the latest information about PowerPoint 97 for the Macintosh converters, connect to the Office Resource Kit home page at:

http://www.microsoft.com/office/ork/

PowerPoint Viewer

If you do not have PowerPoint installed on your computer, you can use the PowerPoint Viewer to read presentations. The PowerPoint Viewer can be freely distributed without any additional license. There are several versions of the PowerPoint Viewer, which correspond to the various releases of PowerPoint.

The 32-bit viewer that comes with PowerPoint 97 is a standalone executable program called Pptview.exe (Windows) or Pptview (Macintosh). This viewer reads presentations created in all versions of PowerPoint. However, if you are saving presentations in 3.0 or 4.0 format, or if the presentations are to be viewed on a computer that does not support 32-bit architecture, you must install the 16-bit viewer, Pptview.dll. Both the 16-bit and 32-bit viewers are installed when you choose the Typical installation during Setup.

Note If you design a custom Setup script to install Office automatically over a network, include the 16-bit PowerPoint Viewer for all users who must be able to save presentations in PowerPoint 4.0 or 3.0 format. Similarly, include the 32-bit PowerPoint Viewer for all users who must be able to save presentations in PowerPoint 95 format.

When you use the Pack and Go Wizard to package a presentation, you can include the 16-bit or 32-bit viewer or both, depending upon the capabilities of the computer used to show the presentation. For more information about the Pack and Go Wizard, see "The Pack and Go Wizard" in Chapter 32, "Workgroup Features in Microsoft PowerPoint."

In addition to allowing non-PowerPoint users to view presentations, PowerPoint 97 and PowerPoint 95 also use the 16-bit viewer, along with converters, to save presentations in 3.0 or 4.0 format when you select that option in the **Save As** dialog box (**File** menu).

PowerPoint 97 for Windows uses the following sequence to save presentations in PowerPoint 3.0 or 4.0 format:

1. PowerPoint 97 creates a temporary file on disk using the converter Pp7x32.dll. The temporary file is in PowerPoint 95 format.
2. PowerPoint 97 starts the 16-bit viewer, Pptview.dll.
3. The 16-bit viewer uses the converter Pp7trans.dll to open the temporary file in PowerPoint 95 format.
4. The 16-bit viewer converts the presentation to 4.0 format, and saves it in PowerPoint 3.0 or 4.0 format.

PowerPoint 97 for the Macintosh uses the following sequence to save presentations in PowerPoint 3.0 or 4.0 format:

1. PowerPoint 97 creates a temporary file on disk. The temporary file is in PowerPoint 97 format.
2. PowerPoint 97 starts the 16-bit viewer.
3. The 16-bit viewer uses its converter to open the temporary file in PowerPoint 97 format.
4. The 16-bit viewer converts the presentation to 4.0 format and saves it in PowerPoint 3.0 or 4.0 format.

PowerPoint 95 for Windows uses the following sequence to save presentations in PowerPoint 4.0 format:

1. PowerPoint 95 creates a temporary file on disk. The temporary file is in PowerPoint 95 format.
2. PowerPoint 95 starts the 16-bit viewer, Pptview.dll.

3. The 16-bit viewer uses the converter Pp7trans.dll to open the temporary file in PowerPoint 95 format.
4. The 16-bit viewer converts the presentation to 4.0 format and saves it in PowerPoint 4.0 format.

Running Multiple Versions of PowerPoint on a Single Computer

This section addresses installing and using different versions of PowerPoint on the same computer. All of the issues noted in the previous section apply to running multiple versions of PowerPoint on a single system.

> **Why is the wrong version of PowerPoint trying to open my presentation?**
>
> When you run multiple versions of PowerPoint on the same computer, certain actions—such as double-clicking a PowerPoint presentation on the desktop or activating an OLE object—start the last version of PowerPoint that was installed, even if it is not the right version for the presentation. To avoid this problem, either install PowerPoint 97 last ,or select which version of PowerPoint to use when you open a presentation file from the desktop or in Windows Explorer under Windows 95 or Windows NT Workstation 4.0.
>
> For more information about selecting a version of PowerPoint, see "Choosing the Version That Opens Presentations" later in this chapter.

Running Two 32-bit Versions

You can install and run PowerPoint 95 and 97, both of which are 32-bit versions, on the same computer. If you attempt to remove one version of PowerPoint, you may lose components shared by both versions, requiring you to reinstall the version you want to keep.

Running 16-bit and 32-bit Versions

You can install and run the 16-bit versions of PowerPoint (PowerPoint 4.0 or earlier) and PowerPoint 97 on the same computer, as long as they are installed in different folders. These versions of PowerPoint can be run at the same time, but only PowerPoint 97 can open presentations created with all other versions.

Choosing the Version That Opens Presentations

When you use Windows Explorer (Windows 95 or Windows NT Workstation 4.0) or File Manager (Windows NT Workstation 3.51) to open a presentation, the presentation is opened by default in the last version of PowerPoint you installed. If you install a previous version of PowerPoint after installing PowerPoint 97, the previous version of PowerPoint cannot open the later versions of the files. However, if you are using Windows 95 or Windows NT Workstation 4.0, you can override the default by selecting which version of PowerPoint to use.

Note The following procedure works only on Windows 95 or Windows NT Workstation 4.0. It does not work on Windows NT Workstation 3.51 or on the Macintosh.

▶ **To control which version of PowerPoint opens a presentation**

1 In Windows Explorer, find a version of PowerPoint on your computer.
2 Open the Windows\SendTo folder.
3 Using the right mouse button, drag the PowerPoint application icon to the SendTo folder and click **Create Shortcut(s) Here** on the shortcut menu.
4 Repeat Steps 1 through 3 for every version of PowerPoint you want to run.
5 In the SendTo folder, rename the PowerPoint shortcuts so you can easily distinguish them.
6 To specify which version of PowerPoint to use to open a presentation, right-click the presentation in Windows Explorer; then point to **Send To** on the shortcut menu and click the PowerPoint version you want.

Tip This strategy works only if the presentation is in a format that can be opened by the version of PowerPoint you choose. To ensure that PowerPoint 97 saves new presentations in the proper format, use the **Save PowerPoint files as** option on the **Save** tab in the **Options** dialog box (**Tools** menu). For more information, see "Specifying the Default Format in Which to Save Office Documents" earlier in this chapter.

Running Multiple Versions of Microsoft Word

This section describes issues relevant to a workgroup or a single computer running any combination of the following versions Word:

- Word 97 for Windows or the Macintosh
- Word 95 for Windows
- Word version 6.0 for Windows or the Macintosh
- Word version 2.0 for Windows
- Word version 5.x for the Macintosh

Sharing Documents Across Operating Systems and Versions

While the file format of documents differs between Word 97 and previous versions of Word, Word 97 can open documents created in previous versions. However, when a Word 97 document is saved in previous versions of Word, the document is converted to the other format, and data and formatting may change or be lost. For information about how documents are converted to previous versions of Word, see Chapter 15, "Upgrading from Previous Versions of Microsoft Word."

Running Multiple Versions of Word on a Single Computer

This section addresses installing and using different versions of Word on the same computer. All of the issues noted in the previous section apply to running multiple versions of Word on a single system.

> **Why is the wrong version of Word trying to open my document?**
> When you run multiple versions of Word on one computer, certain actions—such as double-clicking a Word document on the desktop or activating an OLE object—start the last version of Word that was installed, even if it is not the right version for the document. To avoid this problem, either install Word 97 last, or select which version of Word to use when you open a document file from the desktop or in Windows Explorer under Windows 95 or Windows NT Workstation 4.0.
>
> For more information about selecting a version of Word, see "Choosing the Version That Opens Documents" later in this chapter.

Running Two 32-bit Versions

You can install and run Word 95 and 97, both of which are 32-bit versions, on the same computer. If you attempt to remove one version of Word, you may lose components shared by both versions, requiring you to reinstall the version you want to keep.

Running 16-bit and 32-bit Versions

You can install and run the 16-bit versions of Word (Word 6.0 or earlier) and Word 97 on the same computer, as long as they are installed in different folders. These versions of Word can be run at the same time, but only Word 97 can open documents created with all other versions.

Choosing the Version That Opens Documents

When you use Windows Explorer (Windows 95 or Windows NT Workstation 4.0) or File Manager (Windows NT Workstation 3.51) to open a document, the document is opened by default in the last version of Word you installed. If you install a previous version of Word after installing Word 97, the previous version of Word cannot open later versions of the files. However, if you are using Windows 95 or Windows NT Workstation 4.0, you can override the default by selecting which version of Word to use.

Note The following procedure works only on Windows 95 or Windows NT Workstation 4.0. It does not work on Windows NT Workstation 3.51 or on the Macintosh.

▶ **To control which version of Word opens a document**

1 In Windows Explorer, find a version of Word on your computer.
2 Open the Windows\SendTo folder.
3 Using the right mouse button, drag the Word application icon to the SendTo folder and click **Create Shortcut(s) Here** on the shortcut menu.
4 Repeat Steps 1 through 3 for every version of Word you want to run.
5 In the SendTo folder, rename the Word shortcuts so you can easily distinguish them.
6 To specify which version of Word to use to open a document, right-click the document in Windows Explorer; then point to **Send To** on the shortcut menu and then click the version you want.

Tip This strategy works only if the document is in a format that can be opened by the version of Word you choose. To ensure that Word 97 saves new documents in the proper format, use the **Save Word files as** option on the **Save** tab in the **Options** dialog box (**Tools** menu). For more information, see "Specifying the Default Format in Which to Save Office Documents" earlier in this chapter.

CHAPTER 23

Tracking Collaboration with Document Properties

This chapter describes document properties, which you can use to record information about Office documents such as the author and subject.

In This Chapter
Overview   637
Viewing Document Properties   638
Entering Document Properties   638
Creating Custom Document Properties   639
Using Document Properties in Office 97   641

For more information about searching for document properties, see Chapter 26, "Finding Microsoft Office Documents on the Network."

Overview

In organizations where people collaborate on documents, it is helpful to create a tracking sheet to record who did what work on a document. But the tracking sheet serves its purpose only if it is accessible to everyone who handles the document and if it stays attached to the document. A better solution is to save notes about the status of a document within the document itself. The Office applications include a feature called *document properties* that allows you to do this.

You can record descriptions of Microsoft Access, Microsoft Excel, Microsoft PowerPoint, Microsoft Word, and Microsoft Office Binder documents and save those descriptions, or properties, with the documents. Because the document properties are part of the document, they travel with the document wherever it is stored. Anyone who edits the document can also edit its properties.

Document properties also help you locate documents on the network. Office includes search capabilities built into the **Open** dialog box (**File** menu) and through Web Find

Fast. These search capabilities work with document properties. For example, you can specify the subject of a Word document, and later search for all documents with that subject. Microsoft Outlook can also use document properties cached in a Find Fast index to speed up property displays when displaying Office documents in table views. For more information about searching for Office documents, see Chapter 26, "Finding Microsoft Office Documents on the Network."

Note Unless otherwise noted, information in this chapter applies to Microsoft Access, Microsoft Excel, PowerPoint, and Word, hereafter referred to as the Office applications. The document properties described in this chapter do not apply to Microsoft Outlook. When Office documents are displayed in table view in Outlook, however, you can use the search and filtering options to find the document properties or create custom views of collections of documents based on their properties.

Viewing Document Properties

The Office applications save some document properties automatically. For example, if the Author and Company properties are specified during Setup, the Office applications record these properties when a document is saved.

A user who opens a document can search its document properties through the **Open** and **Advanced Search** dialog boxes (**File** menu).

▶ **To view a document's properties (Windows only)**

1. On the **File** menu, click **Open**.
2. To switch to properties view, click the **Properties** button.
3. In the **Name** box, select the file whose properties you want to view.

   The document properties appear in the box to the right.

You can also view a document's properties after you open it.

▶ **To view an open document's properties**

1. On the **File** menu, click **Properties**.
2. In the **Properties** dialog box, click the tab corresponding to the properties you want to view.

Entering Document Properties

If you enter values in the fields on the **Summary** tab in the **Properties** dialog box (**File** menu), you and other users can search for those values through the **Open** or **Advanced Search** dialog boxes. Since document properties make documents easier to find, recommend to your workgroup that they enter document properties for all their documents. To help ensure that this happens, you can set Microsoft PowerPoint and Word to prompt for summary information whenever a user initially saves a document.

▶ **To always prompt for summary information (Microsoft PowerPoint or Word)**

1 On the **Tools** menu, click **Options**, and then click the **Save** tab.
2 Select the **Prompt For Document Properties** check box.

Similarly, you can set Microsoft Excel to prompt for summary information when a user saves a workbook for the first time.

▶ **To always prompt for summary information (Microsoft Excel)**

1 On the **Tools** menu, click **Options**, and then click the **General** tab.
2 Select the **Prompt For Workbook Properties** check box.

Note This option is not available in Office Binder.

Creating Custom Document Properties

All of the Office applications include the document properties found on the **Summary** tab in the **Properties** dialog box (**File** menu). Microsoft Excel, PowerPoint, Word, and Office Binder also include a **Custom** tab on which you assign values to additional document properties or create new properties. Custom properties allow you to record more detailed information about a document such as the document number, editor, and date completed.

You can also create custom properties that meet the needs of your workgroup. Custom properties can take the following data types:

- Text
- Date
- Number
- Yes/No value

As a document moves through a workgroup, the people who handle the document record information about its history and status on the **Custom** tab in the **Properties** dialog box (**File** menu). Custom properties appear in the **Properties** box in the order they are added with the first property at the top of the list. Since custom properties are saved with the document, they cannot become separated from the document.

▶ **To assign a value to a custom property**

1. On the **File** menu, click **Properties**, and then click the **Custom** tab.
2. In the **Name** box, enter the custom property to which you want to assign a value.
3. In the **Type** box, enter the data type of the custom property.
4. In the **Value** box, type the value you want assigned to the custom property.
5. Click **Add**.

In addition to using the built-in custom properties, you can create your own custom properties.

▶ **To create a new custom property**

1. On the **File** menu, click **Properties**, and then click the **Custom** tab.
2. In the **Name** box, enter the name of the new custom property you want to create.
3. In the **Type** box, enter the data type of the custom property.
4. In the **Value** box, type the value you want assigned to the custom property.
5. Click **Add**.

You can link the value of a custom property to a value in the document. As the value changes, so does the custom property to which it is linked. When the document is closed, the current value to which the custom property is linked is saved as a document property. You can link only certain types of data in each Office application.

This application	Can link a custom property to this value
Microsoft Excel	A named cell or range within the active workbook. If you link a custom property to a named range, Microsoft Excel displays the value in the upper-left corner of the range in the **Properties** dialog box.
PowerPoint	Text on a slide in the active presentation (the text must be selected first).
Word	A bookmark within the active document.

▶ **To link a custom property to a value in the document**

1. Specify the value from the active document you want linked to the custom property.

   The specified value must be a named cell or range in Microsoft Excel, selected text in PowerPoint, or a bookmark in Word.

2. On the **File** menu, click **Properties**, and then click the **Custom** tab.
3. In the **Name** box, enter the name of the custom property.

   –or–

   Type the name of a new custom property.

4 Select the **Link To Content** check box.

5 In the **Source** box, enter the item to which you want the property linked.

Because the custom property is linked to a value in the document, the **Type** box is not available. In the **Properties** box, linked custom properties have a Chain icon next to their name to indicate that they are linked.

Hiding Document Properties for Documents in Public Folders

You can hide properties of documents posted to a Microsoft Exchange public folder by using the underscore character as the first character of the property name. For example, you may want to create a property strictly for selection purposes, such as EmployeesEarningGreaterthan80K, which you would never want to appear.

You can make the property invisible in the Microsoft Exchange viewer by including an underscore character as the first character of the string—for example, _EmployeesEarningGreaterthan80K. The underscore does not cause the **Property** dialog box to hide the property. Rather, it indicates to an application that reads properties, such as the Microsoft Exchange Server, that it should not display the property.

Using Document Properties in Office 97

Office 97 uses a standard set of document properties across all applications. In addition, users can define a wide variety of custom properties. Document properties are stored with the document file.

The properties stored with a document are accessible to any application that supports OLE. For example, when a user drags a Microsoft Excel worksheet into a Word document, the user can manipulate the worksheet properties through Word.

Office applications include the following sets of document properties:

- Summary Information

  These standard properties are familiar to users of Office 4.*x*; they appear in the **Summary Info** dialog box (**File** menu in Office 4.*x*).

- Document Summary Information

  These properties provide an enhanced set of properties, beyond those found in the Summary Information set.

- Custom

  These properties are defined by the user. This allows users to create any property they want with any name they want.

Part 5   Using Microsoft Office Throughout Your Organization

For each of the Office applications, the **Properties** dialog box (**File** menu) includes the following tabs:

- **General**
- **Summary**
- **Statistics**
- **Contents**
- **Custom**

The following sections list the name of each document property by tab.

General Properties

General properties include the following items:

- Icon of application that created document
- File name
- Type
- Location
- Size
- MS-DOS name
- Created
- Modified
- Accessed
- Attributes

Summary Properties

Summary properties include the following items:

- Title
- Subject
- Author
- Manager
- Company
- Category
- Keywords
- Comments
- Hyperlink base (This is a new property in Office 97.)
- Template

Statistics Properties

Statistics properties include the following:

- Created

    The value displayed here is derived from the property ID and not from the operating system, as on the **General** tab. The value on the **General** tab tells when the document was created on the computer and is not necessarily when the document was created absolutely (for example, if it was created on one computer and then copied to another computer).

- Modified
- Accessed
- Printed
- Last saved by
- Revision number
- Total editing time
- Statistics
    - Pages (Word only)
    - Paragraphs
    - Lines (Word only)
    - Words (Word only)
    - Characters (Word only)
    - Characters (with spaces)

        This Word-only property is new in Office 97.
    - Slides (PowerPoint only)
    - Notes (PowerPoint only)
    - Hidden slides (PowerPoint only)
    - Multimedia clips (PowerPoint only)
    - Presentation format (PowerPoint only)

> **Tip** In Windows 95 and Windows NT Workstation 4.0, you can use a system policy to disable the total editing time property for all Microsoft PowerPoint and Word users in your workgroup. In the System Policy Editor, set the following policies:
>
> **User\PowerPoint 97\Miscellaneous\No Edit Time**
>
> **User\Word 97\Miscellaneous\No Edit Time**
>
> For more information, see "Using Windows System Policies to Customize Office" in Chapter 7, "Customizing and Optimizing Microsoft Office."

Contents Properties

The **Contents** tab stores names of the different sections in the document (documents in a binder, sheet names in a workbook, slide titles in a presentation, and so forth).

Custom Properties

The **Custom** tab provides an interface for users to create their own properties, which are either constants stored in the property stream or are linked to some document content, such as PowerPoint text, a Word bookmark, or a Microsoft Excel named range. For more information about creating custom properties, see "Creating Custom Document Properties" earlier in this chapter.

User-defined property names are stored separately from other properties so that users cannot create conflicts by giving a Custom property the same name as a Summary Information or Document Summary Information property. For example, the property Author already exists as a Summary Information property, but a user could also create a custom property named Author. These names are stored separately in the property list and displayed on separate tabs in the **Properties** dialog box.

CHAPTER 24

Integrating Microsoft Office with Your Intranet

This chapter describes the benefits of combining Microsoft Office 97 and intranet tools on your corporate network.

In This Chapter
Using Office with an Intranet   645
Combining Web and Office Tools on Intranets   649
Opening and Saving Documents on the Internet   658
Publishing to the Web or an Intranet   659
Setting Up a Personal Web Server   660

See Also
- For information about searching for Office and Hypertext Markup Language (HTML) documents on a network, see Chapter 26, "Finding Microsoft Office Documents on the Network."
- For information about exchanging data with Office applications, see Chapter 27, "Sharing Information with Microsoft Office Applications."
- For information about integrating Office with messaging systems, see Chapter 28, "Working with Messaging Systems and Connectivity Software."

Using Office with an Intranet

Intranets apply the simple but powerful navigation paradigms of the Internet to corporate networks. Intranets help users share and analyze information, collaborate on projects, and find information.

If your network does not yet have intranet protocols in place, Office still supports some intranet-like features, such as hyperlinks between Office documents. With intranet protocols in place, however, you can integrate Office features and documents smoothly into your existing intranet.

Part 5   Using Microsoft Office Throughout Your Organization

Intranets and the Internet

On the Internet, a relatively small number of people (referred to as *Webmasters*) create content for very large audiences. Internet publishing is their business and content is their product, so they are willing to invest considerable time and effort to learn and use specialized HTML authoring tools. Most intranet users, by contrast, are not Webmasters, but rather business users who need to create, analyze, and share information without too much overhead. Intranet users must be able to create information for an intranet as easily as they do for printing. If it is difficult to publish to an intranet, the average user is not likely to do it.

Office 97 incorporates functionality based on Internet standards into each application. This new functionality allows your workgroup to take full advantage of intranets as content producers and consumers. From an administrator's point of view, one of the best things about combining Office and an intranet is that this combination builds upon the work practices and user experience already in place in many organizations. For example, experienced Office users can immediately integrate Office documents into existing intranets; because all Office applications can import and save HTML documents, Office users can start creating HTML content using the tools they are already familiar with.

Security Issues with Intranets

One issue that concerns many organizations developing intranets is balancing the requirements for security at the enterprise level with the free flow of information and collaboration on the desktop. Often organizations address this issue by separating their companywide and departmental intranets.

Typically, companywide intranet sites are managed by an IS department with a formal security structure that limits most users to read-only access of information. In addition, many organizations institute formal content-publishing procedures that allow only a select group to add or modify content on the intranet. At the workgroup or departmental level, intranet sites are more likely to consist of improvised collections of information and documents with less centralized control. The Office intranet tools described in this chapter integrate well into either scenario.

Tools for Intranet Creation and Administration

This section describes tools and strategies you might want to deploy as an intranet site administrator.

Managing Intranet Content with Microsoft FrontPage

The Microsoft FrontPage Web authoring and management program is designed for nonprogrammers, yet it is robust enough even for experienced Webmasters. Microsoft

FrontPage is a fast, easy way to create and manage professional-quality intranet sites. With easy-to-use tools such as WYSIWYG editing, wizards that guide you through the creation of your intranet site, and integration with Office, it has never been easier to set up an intranet. The capabilities of FrontPage are described in this section.

Authoring Tools
The FrontPage Editor allows users to create and edit pages for the World Wide Web without a detailed knowledge of HTML. Working with graphics is easy with automatic conversion to GIF or JPEG format and easy creation of graphical hyperlinks. Wizards and templates help you generate entire intranet sites or individual pages automatically, and even help you create a standard look and feel throughout your intranet.

Site Management
The FrontPage Explorer gives you intuitive views of your entire Web site. If you move or rename a hyperlink, for example, FrontPage can automatically update all affected links. In addition, multiple team members can work on the site simultaneously.

Integration with Office
You can include Office documents on your Web site and manage them with FrontPage just as you would HTML documents. When you double-click a hyperlink to an Office document in FrontPage, FrontPage starts the appropriate Office application, rather than the FrontPage Editor.

Client/Server Flexibility
Security features—including encryption, assigned Web access rights, and support of proxy servers—encourage collaboration and keep unauthorized visitors from modifying your intranet site. Microsoft FrontPage Server Extensions allow FrontPage to work with leading Web servers, or you can use the FrontPage Personal Web Server to publish and test an intranet site on your own computer.

World Wide Web For the latest information about FrontPage, connect to the FrontPage home page at:

http://www.microsoft.com/frontpage/

Cataloging and Indexing Content with Web Find Fast
The Web Find Fast indexing software performs full content indexing and searching of HTML and Office documents on a network. Web Find Fast runs on most popular network operating systems, such as Windows NT Server and Novell NetWare. It can create a full-content index that spans several servers or shared local drives and folders. Administrators can customize the search page as well as the frequency of index updates. For more information about Web Find Fast, see Chapter 26, "Finding Microsoft Office Documents on the Network."

Creating Office Programming Solutions for Intranets

Office is not only a powerful suite of desktop applications but also a very powerful cross-platform development environment for creating custom solutions. In fact, more than 500,000 developers use the following technologies to create solutions based on Office:

- Rich object models and ActiveX and OLE Controls

    At the core of Office solutions is the functionality provided by the features in each Office application. This functionality is fully exposed to developers through a rich set of object models. In addition, Office provides rich support for ActiveX and OLE Controls. With these prebuilt software components, developers can add rich interactive capabilities to their applications as well as their intranet sites.

- Visual Basic for Applications

    Visual Basic is a shared development environment that programmers can use to create solutions with one or more Microsoft Office applications. Visual Basic includes the Visual Basic language engine (compiler), a powerful editor (syntax checking, color-coded syntax, and so forth), and debugging tools. Every Office application supports Visual Basic.

- Automation (formerly called OLE Automation)

    Automation allows developers to combine and reuse objects from off-the-shelf applications in their custom solutions. This process involves three elements: a series of instructions created in Visual Basic, an application that sends instructions (Automation controller), and an application that responds to those instructions (Automation server).

These technologies work together, allowing the developer to create more powerful applications in less time. In addition, the technologies use software that users are already familiar with, making Office an ideal solutions platform for intranets.

Netscape Web Server Support

When a Web server sends a document to a Web browser, the Web server must send the document in the correct format. In most cases this format is HTML; however, Office 97 also allows for sending documents in Office application formats such as Word DOC format.

Some Web server software programs, such as Microsoft Internet Information Server (IIS), store Multipurpose Internet Mail Extensions (MIME) content type and corresponding file-extension mappings in the Windows registry. Proper MIME type settings in the registry ensure that the Web server sends Office documents in the correct format (rather than as plain text, for example).

Netscape Web servers such as the Netscape Commerce and Fast Track Web servers do not store MIME type settings the in the Windows registry, but instead store them in a file named Mime.types. This may prevent these Netscape Web servers from returning Office documents correctly when requested from a Web browser (through a hyperlink or Web Find Fast query, for example).

To correct this problem, you must add Office MIME type information to the Mime.types files on your Netscape Web server. Note that there may be multiple copies of the file Mimes.types on your Web server; you can find all of them by using the file searching capabilities included with Windows NT Server.

Tools and Utilities   The Office Resource Kit Tools and Utilities include the file Mime.txt, which contains the Office file-extension mappings you need to add to the file Mime.types on your Netscape Web server. For more information, see "Office MIME Type Information for Netscape Web Servers" in Appendix A, "Microsoft Office 97 Resource Kit Tools and Utilities."

Combining Web and Office Tools on Intranets

Most organizations plan intranets that combine HTML and Office documents. With this in mind, Office provides users and organizations with the same easy-to-use tools for creating both HTML and Office documents. For example, you can convert a worksheet range and chart in Microsoft Excel to an HTML table and GIF format graphic image. In fact, all Office 97 applications work directly with HTML.

When you develop an intranet, you select the technology that best addresses your organization's needs. HTML provides an effective solution for broadcasting information across different platforms. For example, many organizations distribute company policy manuals, directories, or product information forms in HTML.

Conversely, native Office document formats are designed for distributing information that is developed collaboratively and changes frequently. For example, a team of individual contributors might develop a business plan with detailed schedules and financial analyses. Features such as comments, revision marks, and version tracking are critical in this context.

Office is a flexible and robust tool for creating content in either Office application formats or in HTML. The following table summarizes common business tasks that you might perform on an intranet and shows whether you would use HTML or Office document formats or both.

Part 5   Using Microsoft Office Throughout Your Organization

To accomplish this task	Use HTML documents	Or use Office documents
Disseminate information to peers, management, and other widespread groups quickly	Yes.	Yes.
Distribute information in several media (on paper, in slide shows, or online)	Not recommended. HTML offers limited options for printing and no capability for slide shows.	Yes.
Search documents for specific content	Yes.	Yes. Office offers more search criteria, such as document properties.
Distribute documents for review by peers or management	No.	Yes. Office includes change tracking and version tracking tools.
Author documents collaboratively	No.	Yes. For example, users can share Microsoft Word documents and Microsoft Excel workbooks.
Analyze data using rich tools	No.	Yes. Microsoft Excel includes tools such as PivotTables, Query Wizard, and charts.
Gain access to enterprise data easily	Not recommended for all users. This requires HTML programming knowledge.	Yes. Office includes data access tools such as Web queries, Microsoft Query, and ODBC.
Create documents with flexible, easy-to-use features	No.	Yes.

Following is a more detailed discussion of Web and Office tools and how they can be used together.

Integrating Office Documents with Web Browsers

Office was designed to integrate seamlessly with the most common Web browsers (Microsoft Internet Explorer, Netscape Navigator, and NCSA Mosaic) using a technology called ActiveX documents. ActiveX documents allow container applications, such as a Web browser, to open native Office files in place.

ActiveX document technology combines the navigation capabilities of the Web browser with the ease and flexibility of Office, complete with toolbars and menu commands. For example, in the following illustration, a Microsoft Internet Explorer user has opened a fully functional Microsoft Excel worksheet. The Microsoft Excel spreadsheet is an *active document* in Microsoft Internet Explorer.

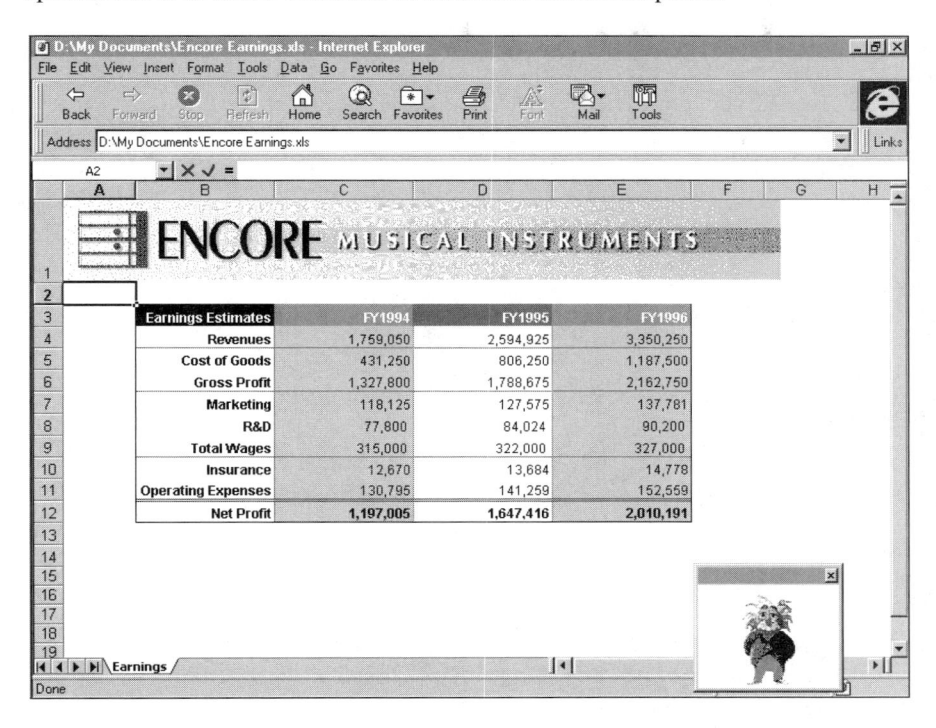

The integration of Office and Microsoft Internet Explorer is particularly tight, which ensures seamless browsing. These products are designed with consistent toolbars, caches, and favorites lists.

Creating Hyperlinks in Office Documents

Many documents are part of a group of related files. Providing hyperlinks between documents gives the reader or author easier access to related information. For example, the specifications for a new bicycle might include hyperlinks to the descriptions of individual parts that make up the bicycle. Or an annual report distributed online as a Microsoft Word document could have hyperlinks to a Microsoft Excel spreadsheet containing the year-end balances, so that users can do their own detailed analyses.

Office includes a simple dialog box that is shared across all Office applications to make it easy for any user to create and edit hyperlinks: the **Insert Hyperlink** dialog box (**Insert** menu).

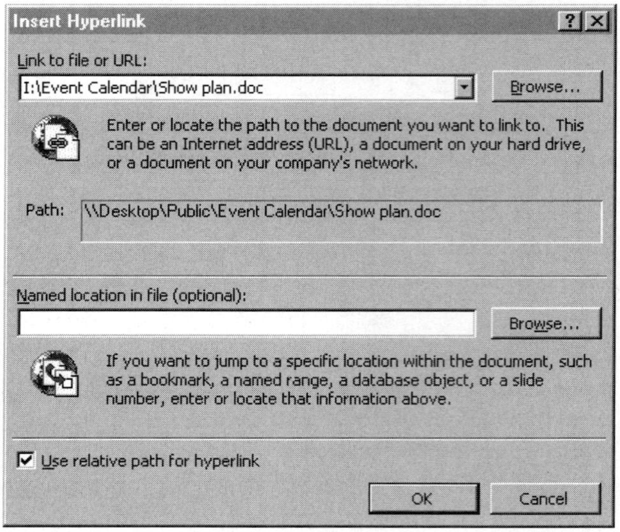
Insert Hyperlink
Link to file or URL:
I:\Event Calendar\Show plan.doc
Browse...
Enter or locate the path to the document you want to link to. This can be an Internet address (URL), a document on your hard drive, or a document on your company's network.
Path:
\\Desktop\Public\Event Calendar\Show plan.doc
Named location in file (optional):
Browse...
If you want to jump to a specific location within the document, such as a bookmark, a named range, a database object, or a slide number, enter or locate that information above.
Use relative path for hyperlink
OK
Cancel

These hyperlinks can go anywhere—to other Office documents, to HTML documents, or to any file with a recognized address through a fully qualified path, Uniform Resource Locator (URL), Universal Naming Convention (UNC), or File Transfer Protocol (FTP) site. Office users can attach hyperlinks to a variety of objects, including text, graphics, tables, presentation slides, spreadsheet cells, and custom database form fields.

From the administrator's perspective, hyperlinks are generally simpler to support than OLE or dynamic data exchange (DDE) links. In the case of OLE or DDE links, Office applications are designed to maintain a connection to the linked source data, and the maintenance of this connection introduces problems such as how to manage the document over a period of time. By contrast, hyperlinks are primarily navigational tools. As such, the interface for creating and navigating hyperlinks is simpler than that of OLE or DDE links.

The hyperlink feature is intended for the corporate or enterprise intranet with high-speed links and direct file access. Hyperlinks work on an enterprise local area network (LAN) or a high-speed wide area network (WAN) without new server functionality. The hyperlink feature does not require HTTP or any special Web server software. Office also supports hyperlinks to documents on the Web, although access time can be much slower.

Using hyperlinks to navigate between Office documents is similar to navigating on the Web. To extend the similarity, Office 97 includes the **Web** toolbar, which is shared across Office applications.

The **Web** toolbar is similar to standard Web browsers, with buttons for navigating forward, backward, and to the home page. With the **Search the Web** button, users can search an intranet or the Web. A user can type a URL or file location in the **Address** box, which even tracks the most recently visited sites. As in the **Open** dialog box (**File** menu) in Office, the **Favorites** menu gives easy access to your most visited sites.

Creating Content for Intranets

All of the Office 97 applications include these features:

- Easy-to-use tools, such as quick conversion between HTML and Office formats

    End users need applications with tools that help them get their work done quickly and efficiently. In addition, these tools must be adept at integrating data from other desktop applications as well as the rest of the enterprise.

- Documents that are easy to update

    Some documents by their nature require frequent revisions and updating. Examples include lists of products and prices, business plans, and design specifications for new products under development. Publishing such content on an intranet helps ensure that all your users see only the most recent version.

Analyzing Data on an Intranet

Once information is created, it is analyzed in many ways. It may be reused in subsequent publications or in making business decisions. For example, a sales report that is published by the finance department may be used by marketing to decide which market to target next. Important information, which is stored in a database in many organizations, has to be easily accessible to users at the desktop level for analysis and effective decision making.

Microsoft Excel, Microsoft Access, and Microsoft Project are the three primary analysis tools in the Office family. Some of their analysis capabilities include the following:

- PivotTable views

    You can create custom reports by dragging the fields in a PivotTable. The data for a PivotTable view can come from a Microsoft Excel workbook or any Open Database Connectivity (ODBC) database, such as SQL Server, Microsoft Access, or a mainframe data source.

Note To use data from an ODBC database, you must have the appropriate driver installed and a Data Source Name (DSN) defined and properly configured. For more information about ODBC, see "Using Microsoft Access with ODBC and Client/Server Operations" in Chapter 27, "Sharing Information with Microsoft Office Applications."

- Web queries

  Not only can you query data from any ODBC database from within your organization, but with Web queries in Microsoft Excel 97, you can also query data on the Web. For example, you can query a database of demographic information and then analyze it in Microsoft Excel to determine whether you are targeting the right market. For more information about Web queries, see "Web Support in Microsoft Excel 97" in Chapter 25, "Web Support in Microsoft Office Applications."

- Relational databases

  Because Microsoft Access is a powerful, easy-to-use database management system, end users can create simple databases, and IS professionals can create full-fledged database applications. For more information about managing databases on an intranet, see "Web Support in Microsoft Access 97" in Chapter 25, "Web Support in Microsoft Office Applications."

- Project management

  You can use Microsoft Project to analyze how long it will take to complete a project, what effect schedule changes will have on the projected completion date, and how your resources are being used.

  Tip If you have Microsoft Project, you can use the Office 97 Deployment Planner to guide you through the process of creating a customized Office 97 installation plan. For more information, see Chapter 3, "Deployment Guide for Microsoft Office."

Collaborating on Documents in a Workgroup

One of the most powerful uses of an intranet is collaboration. Typical examples of collaboration include the following:

- Collaborative authoring

  Often several authors work together to create one document—for example, a budget or extensive specifications for one product.

- Content review

  Peers or managers frequently review a document before the author publishes it in a final version. Office provides a set of tools for collaboration, making it as easy as opening a document and going to work. For example, both Microsoft Excel 97 and Word 97 support comments and change tracking.

- Shared workbooks

    Microsoft Excel 97 makes it easy for two or more users to edit the same workbook simultaneously by using the **Share Workbook** dialog box (**Tools** menu).

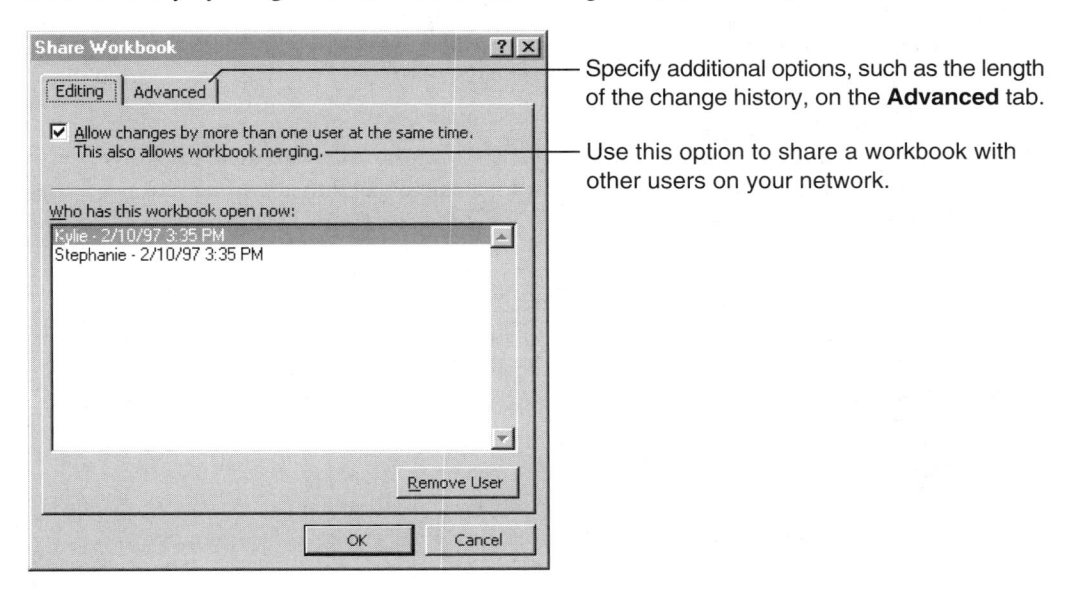

    Specify additional options, such as the length of the change history, on the **Advanced** tab.

    Use this option to share a workbook with other users on your network.

Office also provides the following tools to make it easy to track and review changes in a document, or, if necessary, roll them back to earlier versions:

- Revisions

    Office users can track all changes to a file with revision marks that are color-coded for each user. In Microsoft Excel, a color border appears around a cell, while in Word the modified text appears in a different color or has special formatting such as underlining or strikethrough.

- Conflict resolution

    Multiple changes to the same data are tracked, giving the original author the ability to roll back changes. The **Review** toolbar lets you move through all revisions and comments and decide which changes to accept and which to reject.

- Merged files

    Many people distribute documents through electronic mail (e-mail). With the ability to merge files, you can bring everyone's version of a document together into one file.

For more information about Office tools that support collaboration, see the application-specific chapters in Part 5, beginning with Chapter 29, "Workgroup Features in Microsoft Access."

Part 5   Using Microsoft Office Throughout Your Organization

Sharing Information Throughout Your Organization

Corporate information often needs to be shared throughout an organization. This may include product information, human resources policies, customer relations information, or a company phone book. Some typical situations in which your organization might need to publish or share data include the following:

- Distributing content on an informal or unscheduled basis

   In addition to the traditional publishing methods described earlier, there are many situations in which a user might publish a document on an intranet for review and feedback from other users.

- Publishing in multiple media

   Although many documents are still created for print, many are also being published directly on CD-ROM, on an intranet, or on the Web. Presentations are distributed in an increasing variety of formats, such as 35mm slides, paper, electronic presentations, or HTML documents. Users want one tool to publish in multiple formats.

- Publishing to a widespread audience

   Once documents are published, users may spend a lot of time trying to locate key information or find related documents created by other groups. This effectively limits this size of the audience for the publication—making publication on an intranet a useful alternative.

Managing Your Communications with Microsoft Outlook

New to Office 97 for Windows is Microsoft Outlook, a desktop information manager. Outlook organizes e-mail, calendars, contacts, tasks, documents, and files into a single, integrated environment. Outlook also helps users share information through Microsoft Exchange Server public folders, electronic forms, groupware, and the Internet.

Electronic Mail

Outlook makes it easy for users in your organization to communicate internally or externally using Microsoft Exchange Server or Microsoft Mail. Support for POP3 and SMTP in Outlook also allows users to communicate directly over the Internet. In addition, Outlook automatically creates hyperlinks for any URL or public folder address contained in an e-mail message or any other Outlook item.

Group Scheduling

You can use Outlook to schedule meetings with everyone in your organization or even with external users on the Internet. Outlook users can also assign tasks across the Internet and be notified automatically when any updates to the task occur or when the task is completed. These features extend the ability of users to manage projects and resources beyond their workgroup on an intranet and the Internet.

Public Folders

With Outlook, you can publish in a public folder such items as calendars of company holidays or trade shows, contact lists, and project task lists. Administrators can create custom views of the task, contact, schedule, or journal items in a public folder, and each user can also create personalized views of this shared information.

Workflow Solutions

As with Microsoft Exchange Client, you can create forms in Outlook, but with several important distinctions. ActiveX document technology allows your forms in Outlook to contain Office documents or templates. For example, a Microsoft Excel expense report template can be included in an Outlook form. The user fills out the expense report, and because it is an Outlook form, the report is automatically sent through e-mail to the appropriate person for approval and processing.

Searching for Office Documents on an Intranet

Microsoft Office for Windows 95 introduced Find Fast technology to perform content indexing and searching on Office documents stored on a local hard disk or a network drive. Office 97 extends Find Fast technology with the introduction of Web Find Fast, which performs full-content indexing and searching on both HTML and Office documents across an entire server or group of servers.

The user experience is similar to using an Internet search engine such as Lycos or Alta Vista. The user navigates to a search page, types a keyword or phrase, and clicks **Search**. This triggers the submission of the search to the server, which returns the search results on an HTML page. The search page contains document properties, such as title, author, a brief summary of the document, or other standard document properties. A hyperlink for each document is also provided in the list, so that the document can be opened immediately.

For more information about Web Find Fast, see Chapter 26, "Finding Microsoft Office Documents on the Network."

Using Office Viewers

To make it easy for all users to share Office documents, Microsoft provides freely distributable file viewers for Word, Microsoft Excel, and Microsoft PowerPoint. With these viewers, users can read and print Office documents with the same fidelity as provided by the full applications, without having the applications installed. The viewers also expose certain application features, such as document views in Word or AutoFilter in Microsoft Excel. Office viewers are available for 32-bit Windows and the Macintosh.

World Wide Web   For more information or to download an Office application file viewer, connect to the Free Software area of the Microsoft Office home page at:

http://www.microsoft.com/office/

Opening and Saving Documents on the Internet

In Windows, the **Open** and **Save As** dialog boxes (**File** menu) of the Office 97 applications support logging on to an FTP site and resolving FTP and HTTP addresses. For this reason, Office users can open or save documents on FTP sites just as they can on a local drive.

To enable logging on to an FTP site from within Office applications, the user must have dial-up networking access through an Internet service provider or access through a proxy server on the LAN.

▶ **To connect to an FTP site initially**

1. On the **File** menu, click **Open**.

    –or–

    On the **File** menu, click **Save As**.

2. Click the arrow next to the **Look in** box.

3. Under **Internet Locations (FTP)**, click **Add/Modify FTP Locations**.

4. In the **Add/Modify FTP Locations** dialog box, enter the full FTP path and either an anonymous or a user logon name and a password.

After the initial connection to an FTP site, the Office applications keep track of the FTP address and logon type.

▶ **To connect to an FTP site after the initial connection**

1. On the **File** menu, click **Open**.

    –or–

    On the **File** menu, click **Save As**.

2   Click the arrow next to the **Look in** box.

3   Under **Internet Locations (FTP)**, select the FTP site to which you want to connect.

You can also add, delete, or edit FTP site information.

Tip   When saving Office documents to an FTP site, be sure to include the appropriate file type extension, for example .doc for Word documents.

▶ **To edit FTP site information**

1   On the **File** menu, click **Open**.

   –or–

   On the **File** menu, click **Save As**.

2   Click the **Commands and Settings** button, and then click **Add/Modify FTP Locations**.

3   In the **Add/Modify FTP Locations** dialog box, add, edit, or delete the FTP address and logon information you want.

Tip   In Windows 95 and Windows NT Workstation 4.0, you can use a system policy to add up to 10 FTP sites under the **Look in** box in the **Open** dialog box (**File** menu) for all Office users in your workgroup. In the System Policy Editor, set the following policy:

User\Office\Internet\FTP Sites\Add FTP Sites

For more information, see "Using Windows System Policies to Customize Office" in Chapter 7, "Customizing and Optimizing Microsoft Office."

Publishing to the Web or an Intranet

The Web Publishing Wizard makes it easy to publish Web pages on the Internet (through FTP) or to an intranet. This wizard automates the process of copying files from your computer to a Web server. The Microsoft Web Publishing Wizard is included in the Office Value Pack.

Note   The CD-ROM version of Office 97 includes the Office 97 Value Pack—a collection of application extras such as clip art, maps, sounds, presentation enhancements, and utilities. For more information about the Value Pack and how to use its contents, see Valupack.hlp in the ValuPack folder on the Office CD. You can also point to **Microsoft on the Web** (**Help** menu) in any Office application, and then click **Free Stuff**.

You can use the Web Publishing Wizard to publish Web pages to Internet service providers such as CompuServe, Sprynet, America Online, and GNN and to intranet servers running Microsoft IIS.

Note To use the Web Publishing Wizard, you must be running an English version of Windows 95 or Windows NT Workstation 4.0.

▶ **To install the Web Publishing Wizard**

1. Insert the Office CD into your CD-ROM drive.
2. In the ValuPack\Webpost folder, double-click Webpost.exe.
3. Follow the instructions on your screen.

If you want to publish to an FTP or Web site on the Internet and you have an account with an Internet service provider, you can use the Web Publishing Wizard to copy your Web page to the Internet. The wizard works the same way if you are publishing to your organization's intranet.

▶ **To start the Web Publishing Wizard**

1. On the Windows **Start** menu, point to **Programs**, point to **Accessories**, point to **Internet Tools**, and then click **Web Publishing Wizard**.

   The first time you run the wizard, you must provide information about your Internet service provider or intranet.

2. Follow the instructions on your screen.

   For detailed information about the options in each panel of the wizard, click **Help**.

Setting Up a Personal Web Server

Microsoft provides two server products that make it easy to create a personal Web site on your desktop for low-volume Web publishing: the Microsoft Personal Web Server and Microsoft Peer Web Services. These products are ideal for publishing departmental home pages, personal home pages, and small-scale Web applications on your company's intranet.

Although the Personal Web Server and Peer Web Services are intended for small-scale Web publishing, they provide most of the same services and features as Microsoft IIS, a robust Web server intended for high-volume, dedicated Web publishing. You can use the Personal Web Server or Peer Web Services to develop and test Web applications and scripts and then transfer them to a Web server running Microsoft IIS.

Both the Personal Web Server and Peer Web Services can:

- Publish Web pages on the Internet or over an LAN on an intranet by using the HTTP service.
- Support Microsoft ActiveX controls.
- Transmit or receive files using the FTP service.
- Run Internet Server API (ISAPI) and Common Gateway Interface (CGI) scripts.

- Send queries to ODBC data sources using the Internet Database Connector component (Httpodbc.dll).
- Support the Security Socket Layer.

In addition, Peer Web Services can:

- Use pass-through security to Windows NT Server and Novell NetWare.
- Use local-user security if Microsoft File and Print Sharing is not installed.
- Perform remote administration using a Web-based application.

Installation Requirements

To run the Personal Web Server or Peer Web Services, you must meet the following requirements.

Personal Web Server Requirements

- A computer with Windows 95 installed and with at least the minimum configuration to support Windows 95.
- Windows 95 Setup CD or disks for additional files not supplied by the Personal Web Server Setup program
- Adequate disk space for your information content

Peer Web Services Requirements

- A computer with Windows NT Workstation 4.0 installed and with at least the minimum configuration to support Windows NT Workstation

  Note You can administer a server that is running Peer Web Services from a remote computer running Windows NT Workstation. Install the Peer Web Services Internet Service Manager on that computer, and then connect to the server you want to administer.

- A CD-ROM drive for the installation CD
- Adequate disk space for your information content

  Note It is recommended that all drives used with Peer Web Services be formatted with the Windows NT File System (NTFS).

Publication Requirements

Each computer that will have access to the server must have Transmission Control Protocol/Internet Protocol (TCP/IP) installed. The TCP/IP protocol is included with Windows 95 and Windows NT Workstation 4.0. To install the TCP/IP protocol, click the Network icon in Control Panel to install and configure the TCP/IP protocol and related components.

Each system must meet the following additional requirements, depending on whether you want to use the server on an intranet or the Internet:

Requirements for Publishing on an Intranet
- A network adapter card and LAN connection
- The Windows Internet Name Service (WINS) server or the Domain Name System (DNS) server installed on a computer on your intranet

   WINS and DNS run only on the Windows NT operating system. This optional step allows users to use friendly names instead of Internet Protocol (IP) addresses.

Requirements for Publishing on the Internet
- An Internet connection and IP address from your Internet service provider (ISP)
- A network adapter card suitable for your connection to the Internet
- DNS registration for the IP address

   This optional step allows users to use friendly names instead of IP addresses when connecting to your server. For example, *microsoft.com* is the friendly domain name registered to Microsoft. Within the microsoft.com domain, Microsoft has named its Web server *www.microsoft.com*. Most ISPs can register your domain names for you.

Publishing Active Server Pages

Microsoft Access provides an option to save forms and datasheets as Active Server Pages (ASP) files. To publish ASP files with Personal Web Server or Peer Web Services, additional Active Server Pages components must be installed. These components are not distributed with Personal Web Server or Peer Web Services Setup programs. For more information about saving Microsoft Access forms and datasheets as ASP files, see "Web Support in Microsoft Access 97" in Chapter 25, "Web Support in Microsoft Office Applications."

World Wide Web   For more information about downloading and installing Active Server Pages components, connect to the Microsoft Windows NT Server home page at:

http://www.microsoft.com/ntserver/

Installing the Personal Web Server

The Setup program for the Personal Web Server is available on the Web.

World Wide Web   For more information about downloading Personal Web Server for Windows 95, connect to the Microsoft Personal Web Server home page at:

http://www.microsoft.com/ie/isk/pws.htm

▶ **To install the Personal Web Server**

1 Connect to the Personal Web Server home page on the Web.
2 Download Pws10a.exe.
3 Double-click Pws10a.exe.

   This starts the installation process. You may be required to supply additional files from your Windows 95 Setup program.

4 When installation is finished, click **Yes** to restart your computer.

Note You can install the Personal Web Server if you are running Windows 95 or Windows NT Workstation 4.0. If you are using Windows NT Workstation, however, it is recommended that you install Peer Web Services instead.

Installing Peer Web Services

The Setup program for Peer Web Services is located on the Windows NT Workstation 4.0 CD.

▶ **To install Peer Web Services**

1 In Control Panel, double-click the Network icon.
2 Click the **Services** tab, and then click **Add**.
3 In the **Network Service** box, double-click **Peer Web Services**.

   This starts the installation process. You may be required to supply additional files from your Windows NT Workstation Setup program.

4 In the first **Microsoft Peer Web Services Setup** dialog box, click **OK**.
5 In the second **Microsoft Peer Web Services Setup** dialog box, select the services you want to install, and then click **OK**.
6 In the **Publishing Directories** dialog box, specify the directories you want to use for each service or accept the default names, and then click **OK**.

More Information About the Personal Web Server or Peer Web Services

After you install the Personal Web Server or Peer Web Services, you can refer to the online documentation provided with them for more information.

▶ To view documentation for the Personal Web Server

1. Start your Web browser.

2. In the **Address** box, type **http://*MyServer*/docs/default.htm** where *MyServer* is the name of the computer on which you installed the Personal Web Server.

   To view the name of the computer, open Control Panel, double-click the Network icon, and then click the **Identification** tab.

3. Press ENTER.

▶ To view documentation for Peer Web Services

1. Start your Web browser.

2. In the **Address** box, type **http://*MyServer*/iisadmin/htmldocs/inetdocs.htm** where *MyServer* is the name of the computer on which you installed Peer Web Services.

   To view the name of the computer, open Control Panel, double-click the Network icon, and then click the **Identification** tab.

3. Press ENTER.

CHAPTER 25

Web Support in Microsoft Office Applications

This chapter describes features in each Microsoft Office application that can help you create and manage content on an intranet or on the World Wide Web. It is a companion to Chapter 24, "Integrating Microsoft Office with Your Intranet," which describes Office-wide strategies and features you can implement to integrate Office into your intranet.

In This Chapter
Web Support in Microsoft Access 97   665
Web Support in Microsoft Excel 97   693
Web Support in Microsoft Outlook 97   704
Web Support in Microsoft PowerPoint 97   707
Web Support in Microsoft Word 97   713

See Also
- For information about searching for Office and Hypertext Markup Language (HTML) documents on a network, see Chapter 26, "Finding Microsoft Office Documents on the Network."
- For information about exchanging data with Office applications, see Chapter 27, "Sharing Information with Microsoft Office Applications."
- For information about integrating Office with messaging systems, see Chapter 28, "Working with Messaging Systems and Connectivity Software."

Web Support in Microsoft Access 97

Microsoft Access 97 provides many ways to create applications to display, run, and publish content on the Internet or an intranet. For example, you can use Microsoft Access to publish information from datasheets and reports as Web pages. You can also use Microsoft Access to create files that query a database on a Web server, and then return a Web page to display the results of the query. In addition, you can save a Microsoft Access form as a Web page that emulates many of the features of the form so that users can view, enter, and update information in your database.

You can also use Microsoft Access 97 to create applications that display HTML documents in forms, and create hyperlinks that you click to move between database objects and other Office documents located on a hard disk or a local area network (LAN).

The following table summarizes the features available in Microsoft Access that you can use to work with content on the Internet or an intranet.

To do this	Use these features in Microsoft Access
Connect to content on the Internet or an intranet	Store hyperlinks in fields with the **Hyperlink** data type and follow the hyperlinks to display Internet content.
	Browse the folders of FTP sites in the **Link To File** dialog box when you insert or edit hyperlinks (for example, by clicking the **Insert Hyperlink** command on the **Insert** menu).
	Bind a text box control on a form to a field with the **Hyperlink** data type to enter, display, or follow a hyperlink.
	Bind a text box control on a report to a field with the **Hyperlink** data type to create a hyperlink when you save a report as an HTML document or to print the hyperlink address.
	Reference a hyperlink from a label, image control, or command button on a form or report.
	Use Visual Basic for Applications methods and properties to work with hyperlinks. For example, use the **Follow** method to go to the address referenced in a hyperlink, and use the **AddToFavorites** method to add a hyperlink to the Favorites folder.

To do this	Use these features in Microsoft Access
Connect to other Office documents and files on an intranet	Go to Microsoft Access objects in the current database or other databases by using hyperlinks from the current Microsoft Access database or from another Office application.
	Go to documents from other Office applications by using hyperlinks from Microsoft Access databases.
	Use the **Back** and **Forward** buttons on the **Web** toolbar to move between followed hyperlinks to database objects and other Office documents.
	Locate Microsoft Access databases with Web Find Fast. For information about Web Find Fast, see Chapter 26, "Finding Microsoft Office Documents on the Network."
Publish and share data in a database on the Web	Save the data from table, query, and form datasheets or from reports as static HTML documents.
	Create Internet Database Connector/HTML extension (IDC/HTX) files to query data from a table, query, or form datasheet in a database on an Internet or intranet server and display it in a Web page.
	Save a Microsoft Access form as an Active Server Page (ASP) that emulates many of the features of the form so that users can view, enter, and update information in a database on an Internet or intranet server.
	Create an ASP to query data from a table, query, or form datasheet in a database on an Internet or intranet server and display it in a Web page.
	Use the Publish to the Web Wizard to automate the process of publishing and sharing data, store settings from previous publications, and call the Web Publishing Wizard to copy Web files to your Internet or intranet server.
	Export HTML documents, IDC/HTX files, or ASPs using the **OutputTo** method or action.
	Attach HTML documents, IDC/HTX files, or ASPs to e-mail messages using the **SendObject** method or action.
	Export tables as HTML tables by using the **TransferText** method or action.
Use the Internet with database replication	Synchronize a database replica with a replica or Design Master on an Internet or intranet server.

Part 5   Using Microsoft Office Throughout Your Organization

To do this	Use these features in Microsoft Access
Import, link, and export data located on the Internet or an intranet	Import and link HTML tables and lists by using the Import HTML Wizard and the Link HTML Wizard. When you link HTML tables, the data is read-only.
	Import and link any data on an Internet or intranet server that is supported by a built-in Microsoft Access driver. When you link data on an Internet server, the data is read-only.
	Use the **Import** and **Link** dialog boxes to browse FTP sites when you import or link data (for example, by pointing to **Get External Data** on the **File** menu and then clicking **Import** or **Link table**). You can also use the **Import** and **Link** dialog boxes to enter an HTTP address when you are importing or linking data.
	Import or link HTML tables by using the **TransferText** method or action. When you link HTML tables, the data is read-only.
	Import or link data by using HTTP and FTP addresses, and export data by using FTP addresses in the following Visual Basic properties, methods, and actions:
	Connect property **CreateTableDef** method **OutputTo** method and action **TransferDatabase** method and action **TransferText** method and action **TransferSpreadsheet** method and action
Display Web pages and other documents in Microsoft Access forms	Use the WebBrowser control on your application's forms to browse Web sites, view Web pages and other documents, and download data located on the Internet or an intranet. You can use the WebBrowser control to browse folders on you hard disk and on a network.

Many of these features are described in more detail in the following sections. For more information about Internet features in Microsoft Access, see Chapter 21, "Developing Applications for the Internet and the World Wide Web," in *Building Applications with Microsoft Access 97*.

Using Hyperlinks in Microsoft Access Applications

With Microsoft Access 97, you can create two kinds of hyperlinks in tables, forms, and reports:

- Hyperlinks to display and run standard Internet content, such as HTML documents.
- Hyperlinks that allow you to move between Microsoft Word documents, Microsoft Excel worksheets, Microsoft PowerPoint slides, and Microsoft Access database objects that are stored on a hard disk or on a LAN.

You do not need Internet connections or intranet servers to use Office hyperlinks to move between Office documents or files. You can use both kinds of hyperlinks in the same database application.

There are two ways you can use hyperlinks in Microsoft Access applications:

- Create a field with the **Hyperlink** data type to store hyperlink addresses in a table and then bind that field to a text box on a form.

  Like other bound fields, as the user moves from record to record, the value in the text box changes to display the current record's hyperlink value. For example, you can use hyperlinks in this way to create an application in which users can go to Web pages, or to other content on the Internet or an intranet, from a predefined list of addresses. You can also create an application that displays and manages Office documents.

- Create a label, image control, or command button on a form that references a specified hyperlink address.

  In this case, the hyperlink does not change as you move from record to record. For example, you can use hyperlinks in this way to go to other database objects within the same database, or to open a Web page on an intranet that contains updated information about how to use your application.

Regardless of how a hyperlink is defined in your application, if the hyperlink goes to a database object or opens another Office document, you can use the **Web** toolbar to move between the hyperlinks that you have previously followed. For example, in the following illustration, the Products form has a command button with a hyperlink that opens a report. Once you have clicked the hyperlink, you can use the **Web** toolbar to move between other objects you have opened with hyperlinks.

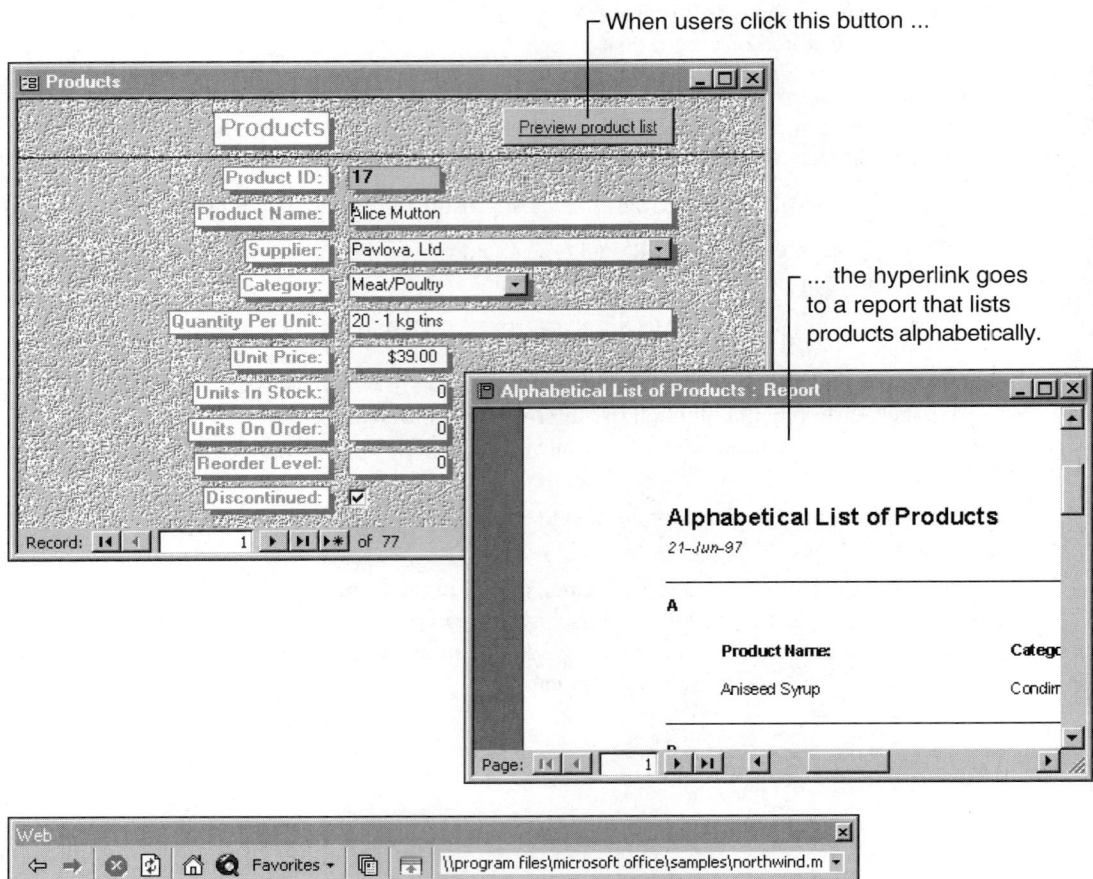

When users click this button ...

... the hyperlink goes to a report that lists products alphabetically.

Once users have visited hyperlinks, they can use **Back** and **Forward** buttons on the **Web** toolbar to move between them.

Similarly, if you follow a hyperlink from a Microsoft Access form to a Word document, you can click the **Back** button on the **Web** toolbar in Word to return to the Microsoft Access form.

Note By default, after a user clicks a hyperlink on a form, Microsoft Access continues to display the **Web** toolbar when the user closes the form. If you want to prevent this, you can use Visual Basic code in the **OnClose** event of the form to hide the toolbar. To see an example of this code, open the Products form in the Northwind sample application in Design view, and then display the event procedure in the **OnClose** event of the form.

Storing Hyperlinks in Tables

In Microsoft Access 97, a field in a table can store hyperlinks as data. To create a Hyperlink field, add a field in table Design view and set its **DataType** property to **Hyperlink**. You can also create a Hyperlink field in table Datasheet view with the **Hyperlink Column** command (**Insert** menu).

You can follow a hyperlink stored in a table by clicking it in the table, but the field is more typically bound to a text box control on a form.

▶ **To add a text box that is bound to a Hyperlink field to a form**

1 Open the form in Design view.
2 Make sure the **RecordSource** property of the form is set to the table that contains the Hyperlink field or to a query that includes the table.
3 Click **Field List** on the toolbar.
4 Drag the Hyperlink field from the field list to the form.

Part 5 Using Microsoft Office Throughout Your Organization

To see an example of how to use a Hyperlink field, open the Suppliers form in the Northwind sample database application. Go to Record 2, New Orleans Cajun Delights. The **Home Page** text box on the form is bound to the HomePage field in the Suppliers table. Clicking the hyperlink in the text box starts your Web browser and displays the supplier's home page.

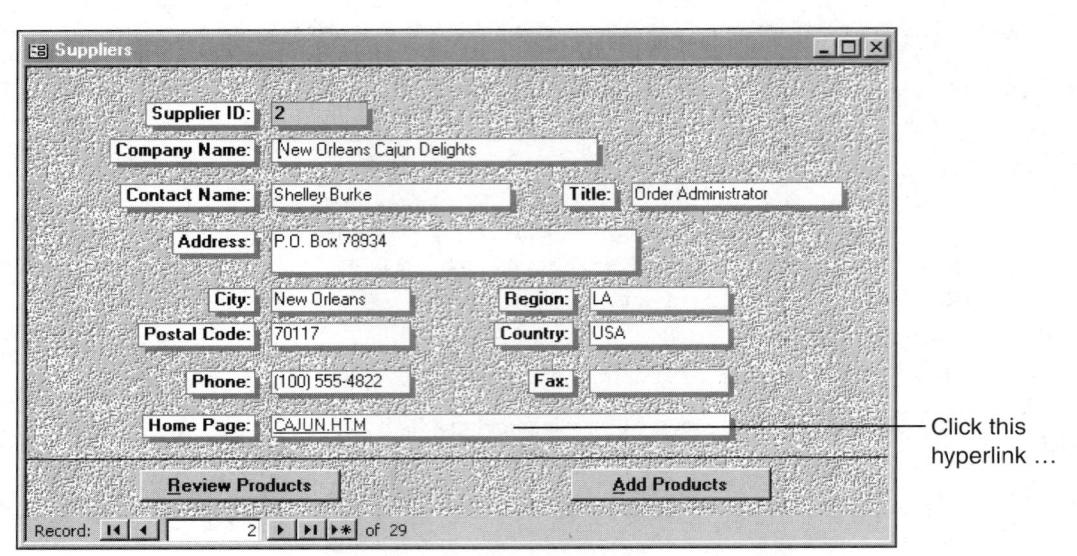

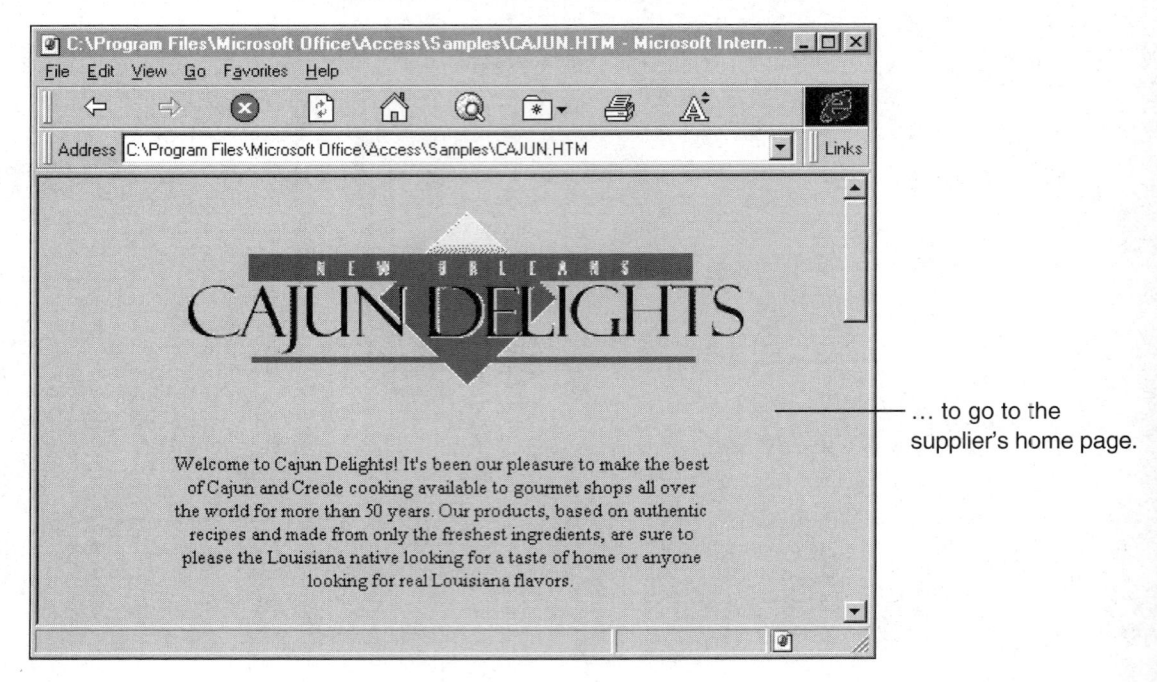

— Click this hyperlink …

… to go to the supplier's home page.

672 Microsoft Office 97 Resource Kit

You can also use hyperlinks in Microsoft Access to go to database objects and other Office documents. For example, you could create a document management application that uses a Hyperlink field to store paths to Word documents on a network. Users of such an application could add records to track new documents or click the hyperlink in a previously added record to open the specified document.

Editing the Hyperlink Field

A Hyperlink field stores up to three pieces of information: the *displaytext*, the *address*, and the *subaddress*. Each piece is separated by the number sign (#), in the following format:

displaytext#*address*#*subaddress*

The following table describes each piece of the Hyperlink field storage format.

Piece	Required?	Description
displaytext	No	The text the user sees in the Hyperlink field in a table or in a text box bound to the Hyperlink field. You can set the display text to any text string. For example, you may want the display text to be a descriptive name for the Web site or object specified by the *address* and *subaddress*. If you do not specify display text, Microsoft Access displays the value of *address* instead.
address	Yes (unless the *subaddress* points to an object in the current database file)	Either a valid URL that points to a page or file on the Internet or an intranet, or the path to a file on a hard disk or LAN. If you enter a path on a LAN, you can omit a mapped drive letter and use the UNC format: *server\share\path\filename*. This prevents the path from becoming invalid if the database is later copied to another hard disk or shared network folder.
Subaddress	No	A specific location within a file or document; for example, a database object, such as a form or report. When referring to a database object, the name of the object should be preceded by its type: Table, Query, Form, Report, Macro, or Module. Other possible values for *subaddress* include a bookmark in a Word document, an anchor in an HTML document, a PowerPoint slide, or a cell in a Microsoft Excel worksheet.

Each piece of the Hyperlink field storage format can be up to 2,000 characters. The maximum length of the entire Hyperlink field value is 6,000 characters. You can display the stored hyperlink format by moving the insertion point into a Hyperlink field using the keyboard and then pressing F2. You can edit the stored hyperlink in this form as long as you enter number signs in the appropriate locations. You can add or edit the *displaytext* part of a hyperlink field by right-clicking a hyperlink in a table, pointing to **Hyperlink** on the shortcut menu, and then typing the display text in the **Display Text** box.

For more information about the Hyperlink field storage format, see Microsoft Access online Help.

Entering a URL as a Hyperlink Address

To create a hyperlink that goes to a Web page or other Internet content, you must enter a valid Uniform Resource Locator (URL) as the hyperlink address. You can enter a URL that points to any Internet file type or resource supported by the browser or to an ActiveX control, such as the WebBrowser control, that is used to display or run it. You enter most URLs in the following format:

*protocol***://***serveraddress***/***path*

Protocol specifies the Internet protocol used to establish the connection to the server, and is generally followed by a colon and two slash marks. *Serveraddress* specifies what is usually called the *domain name* of the Internet server. *Path* specifies the location and name of the page or file on the Internet server. For example, the URL to the home page of the Microsoft Access Developer Forum is:

http://www.microsoft.com/accessdev/

When you type a URL into a Hyperlink field, Microsoft Access automatically recognizes the following Internet protocols.

Internet protocols recognized by Microsoft Access

cid	mailto	pnm
file	mid	prospero
ftp	mms	rlogin
gopher	msn	telnet
http	news	tn3270
https	nntp	wais

If you create a field by importing a column of data and all records in the imported data begin with one of these protocols, Microsoft Access automatically sets the data type of the imported field to **Hyperlink**. Similarly, if you create a new table in Datasheet view and every entry you make in a field begins with one of these protocols, Microsoft Access sets the data type of the new field to **Hyperlink** when you save the table.

Creating Labels, Image Controls, or Command Buttons That Reference a Hyperlink Address

To create a label, image control, or command button on a form that references a specified hyperlink address, set the **HyperlinkAddress** and **HyperlinkSubAddress** properties of the control to point to the content on the Internet or an intranet, or to the Office document or Microsoft Access database object you to which you want to go.

Note The **HyperlinkAddress** and **HyperlinkSubAddress** property settings correspond to the *address* and *subaddress* values entered for a Hyperlink field. For more information about these values, see "Editing the Hyperlink Field" earlier in this chapter.

Additionally, to create the hyperlink display text for a label or command button control, you must set the **Caption** property. Because no text displays for an image control, there is no corresponding display text setting.

You can also create a label that references a hyperlink address by opening the form in Design view, and then clicking the **Hyperlink** command (**Insert** menu). However, this method does not define the display text. To define display text, you must set the **Caption** property of the label.

For more information about creating a label, image control, or command button that references a hyperlink address, see Microsoft Access online Help.

Using Visual Basic Methods and Properties To Work with Hyperlinks

Microsoft Access 97 provides several methods and properties that you can use to work with hyperlinks in Visual Basic code. The following table summarizes these methods and properties.

Method or property name	Description
Follow method	Has the same effect as clicking a hyperlink. When you use the **Follow** method, you do not need to know the address specified by a **HyperlinkAddress** or **HyperlinkSubAddress** property, or by the Hyperlink field that is bound to a text box control. You only need to know the name of the control that contains the hyperlink.
FollowHyperlink method	Goes to a hyperlink specified in code or passed to the method from an unbound text box. For example, you can prompt a user to type a hyperlink address in a dialog box, and then use the **FollowHyperlink** method to go to that address. You can also use the **FollowHyperlink** method to specify a hyperlink for controls other than labels, image controls, and command buttons, or text boxes bound to Hyperlink fields.
AddToFavorites method	Adds the hyperlink address specified in the referenced control to the Favorites folder.
Hyperlink property	Returns a reference to a hyperlink object in code. You can use the **Hyperlink** property to gain access to the hyperlink-specific properties and methods of any control that contains a hyperlink.

Part 5   Using Microsoft Office Throughout Your Organization

Method or property name	Description
HyperlinkAddress property	Specifies or determines the address of a hyperlink for a label, image control, or command button.
HyperlinkSubAddress property	Specifies or determines the location within the Office document or object specified by the **HyperlinkAddress** property.
HyperlinkPart function	Parses the information stored in a Hyperlink field.

For more information about these methods and properties, see Chapter 21, "Developing Applications for the Internet and the World Wide Web," in *Building Applications with Microsoft Access 97*, or see Microsoft Access online Help.

Making Microsoft Access Data Available on the Internet

With Microsoft Access, you can make your data available on the Internet or an intranet by:

- Saving data as HTML documents.
- Synchronizing a database replica with a replica or Design Master on an HTTP or FTP server.

Saving Data as HTML Documents

Microsoft Access provides four ways to save data from your database as HTML documents:

- Save data as static HTML documents

    You can create *static* HTML documents from table, query, and form datasheets and from reports. When you save data as static HTML documents, the resulting pages reflect the state of the data at the time it was saved. If your data changes, you must save the pages again to share the new data.

- Save table, query, and form datasheets as IDC/HTX files

    You can save your table, query, and form datasheets as IDC/HTX files that generate HTML documents by querying a copy of your database located on a Web server for current data.

- Save forms and datasheets as ASPs

    You can save your forms as ASPs that emulate most of the functionality of your forms and display data from a database located on a Web server. You can also save table, query, and form datasheets as ASPs that display current data from a copy of your database located on a Web server.

- Automate the publishing of dynamic and static HTML documents

    You can use the Publish to the Web Wizard to automate the process of saving multiple objects to any combination of all three file types. In the Publish to the Web Wizard, IDC/HTX files and ASP files are referred to as *dynamic* Web pages because these file types display current data to users.

The following sections discuss each of these options in more detail.

Saving Data as Static HTML Documents

With Microsoft Access 97, you can save table, query, and form datasheets and reports as static HTML documents.

▶ **To save a table, query, or form datasheet or a report as a static HTML document**

1   In the Database window, click the table, query, form, or report you want to save.
2   On the **File** menu, click **Save As/Export**.
3   In the **Save As** dialog box, click **To an External File or Database**, and then click **OK**.
4   In the **Save as type** list, click **HTML Documents**.
5   To open the resulting HTML document in your Web browser automatically, select the **Autostart** check box.
6   Specify a file name and location for the HTML file, and then click **Export**.
7   In the **HTML Output Options** dialog box, specify whether you want Microsoft Access to merge an HTML template with the resulting HTML document, and then click **OK**.

    For information about HTML templates, see "Using an HTML Template When You Save Data as HTML Documents" later in this chapter.

You can also save data as static HTML documents by using the Publish to the Web Wizard (available through the **Save As HTML** command on the **File** menu), the **OutputTo** method in code, or the OutputTo action in macros. For more information about saving table, query, or form datasheets and reports as HTML documents, see Microsoft Access online Help.

When saving table, query, and form datasheets, Microsoft Access saves each datasheet to a single HTML file. Microsoft Access saves reports as multiple HTML documents, with one HTML file per printed page. To name each page, Microsoft Access uses the name of the object and appends _Page*nn* to the end of each file name after the first page; for example, ProductList.htm, ProductList_Page2.htm, ProductList_Page3.htm, and so on.

Saving Table, Query, and Form Datasheets as Static HTML Documents

When you save a table, query, or form datasheet as an HTML document, the HTML document generated is based on the table or query associated with the datasheet, including the current setting of the **OrderBy** or **Filter** property of the table or query, which determines how the table, query, or form is sorted or filtered.

The HTML document contains an HTML table that reflects as closely as possible the appearance of the datasheet by using the appropriate HTML tags to specify color, font, and alignment. The HTML document follows as closely as possible the page orientation and margins of the datasheet. Whenever you want to use settings that are different from the default orientation and margins for a datasheet, you must first open the datasheet, and then use the **Page Setup** command (**File** menu) to change settings before you save the datasheet as an HTML document.

If a field has a **Format** or **InputMask** property setting, that setting is reflected in the data in the HTML document. For example, if a **Format** property of the field is set to **Currency**, the data in the HTML document is formatted with a dollar sign, a comma as the thousand separator, and two decimal places; for example, $1,123.45.

Saving Reportsas Static HTML Documents

When you save a report as a series of HTML documents, the HTML documents generated are based on the report's underlying table or query, including the current **OrderBy** or **Filter** property setting of the table or query.

The HTML documents closely approximate the proportions and layout of the actual report and follow as closely as possible the page orientation and margins set for the report. To change the page orientation and margins, open the report in Print Preview, and then click the **Page Setup** command (**File** menu) to change settings before you save the report as HTML documents. These settings are saved from session to session for reports, so if you change them once, they will be used the next time you save the form or report as HTML documents.

If you specify an HTML template that contains placeholders for navigation controls when you save a report as multiple HTML documents, Microsoft Access creates hyperlinks that the user can use to go to the first, previous, next, and last pages in the publication. Where Microsoft Access places the hyperlinks depends on where you locate the placeholders in the HTML template.

For information about HTML templates and placeholders, see "Using an HTML Template When You Save Data as HTML Documents" later in this chapter.

How Microsoft Access Saves Data Types in HTML

When you save data as static HTML documents, Microsoft Access saves values from most data types as strings and formats them as closely as possible to their appearance in the datasheet or report. There are two exceptions:

- OLE Object fields are not saved.
- Hyperlink field values are saved as hyperlinks in the HTML document. The hyperlinks use HTML anchor tags with an **HREF** attribute, as described in the following table.

In this scenario	This anchor tag format is used
The hyperlink does not include a subaddress.	<A HREF="*address*">*displaytext*</A>
The hyperlink includes a subaddress.	<A HREF="*address#subaddress*">*displaytext*</A>
The display text is not specified.	<A HREF="*address*">*address*</A>

Microsoft Access determines the *displaytext*, *address*, and *subaddress* values in the anchor tags by parsing the value stored in the Hyperlink field.

For information about the *displaytext*, *address*, and *subaddress* values, see "Editing the Hyperlink Field" earlier in this chapter.

Saving Table, Query, and Form Datasheets as IDC/HTX Files

With Microsoft Access, you can save a table, query, or form datasheet as IDC/HTX files that generate HTML documents by querying a copy of your database located on a Web server. In contrast to static HTML documents, IDC/HTX files display current data from your database; therefore, the HTML documents that they generate are dynamic.

▶ **To save a table, query, or form datasheet as IDC/HTX files**

1. In the Database window, click the table, query, or form you want to save.
2. On the **File** menu, click **Save As/Export**.
3. In the **Save As** dialog box, click **To an External File or Database**, and then click **OK**.
4. In the **Save as type** list, click **Microsoft IIS 1-2**.
5. Specify a file name and location for the IDC/HTX files, and then click **Export**.
6. In the **HTX/IDC Output Options** dialog box, specify:
   - The data source name to use for a copy of the current database.
   - A user name and password, if required to open the database.
   - An HTML template, if you want Microsoft Access to merge one with the HTML extension (HTX) file.

   Note You can specify any of these items later, except the HTML template, by editing the resulting IDC file in a text editor, such as Notepad.

You can also save a table, query, or form datasheet as IDC/HTX files by using the Publish to the Web Wizard (available through the **Save As HTML** command on the **File** menu), the **OutputTo** method in code, or the OutputTo action in macros.

For more information about saving table, query, or form datasheets as IDC/HTX files, see Microsoft Access online Help

How the Internet Database Connector Works

When you save a table, form, or query datasheet as Internet Connector files, Microsoft Access creates two files: an Internet Database Connector (IDC) file and HTML extension (HTX) file. These files are used to generate a Web page that displays current data from your database.

An IDC file contains the necessary information to connect to a specified Open Database Connectivity (ODBC) data source and to run an SQL statement that queries the database. The information needed to connect to the database includes the data source name and, if user-level security is established for the database, the user name and password required to open the database. For example, if you save the Current Product List query datasheet from the Northwind sample database application as IDC/HTX files, Microsoft Access creates the following IDC file:

```
Datasource:Northwind
Template:Current Product List.htx
SQLStatement:SELECT [Product List].ProductID, [Product List].ProductName
+FROM Products AS [Product List]
+WHERE ((([Product List].Discontinued)=No))
+ORDER BY [Product List].ProductName;

Password:
Username:
```

An IDC file also contains the name and location of an HTML extension (HTX) file. The HTX file is a template for the HTML document; it contains field merge codes that indicate where the values returned by the SQL statement should be inserted. For example, if you save the Current Product List query datasheet from the Northwind sample database application as IDC/HTX files, Microsoft Access creates the following HTX file:

```
<HTML>
<TITLE>Current Product List</TITLE>
<BODY>
<TABLE BORDER=1 BGCOLOR=#ffffff><FONT FACE="Arial" COLOR=#000000>
<CAPTION><B>Current Product List</B></CAPTION>

<THEAD>
<TR>
<TD><FONT SIZE=2 FACE="Arial" COLOR=#000000>Product ID</FONT></TD>
<TD><FONT SIZE=2 FACE="Arial" COLOR=#000000>Product Name</FONT></TD>
</TR>
</THEAD>
<TBODY>
<%BeginDetail%>
<TR VALIGN=TOP>
<TD ALIGN=RIGHT><FONT SIZE=2 FACE="Arial" COLOR=#000000><%ProductID%><BR></FONT></TD>
<TD><FONT SIZE=2 FACE="Arial" COLOR=#000000><%ProductName%><BR></FONT></TD>
</TR>
<%EndDetail%>
</TBODY>
<TFOOT></TFOOT>
</BODY>
</HTML>
```

Microsoft Access saves the HTX file to be used with an IDC file with the same name as the IDC file, but with an .htx extension rather than an .idc extension. After the database information has been merged into the HTML document, the HTML document is returned to the Web browser.

If you open Current Product List.idc from a Microsoft Internet Information Server that has an appropriately defined Northwind data source name (DSN), the Web page shown in the following illustration is generated.

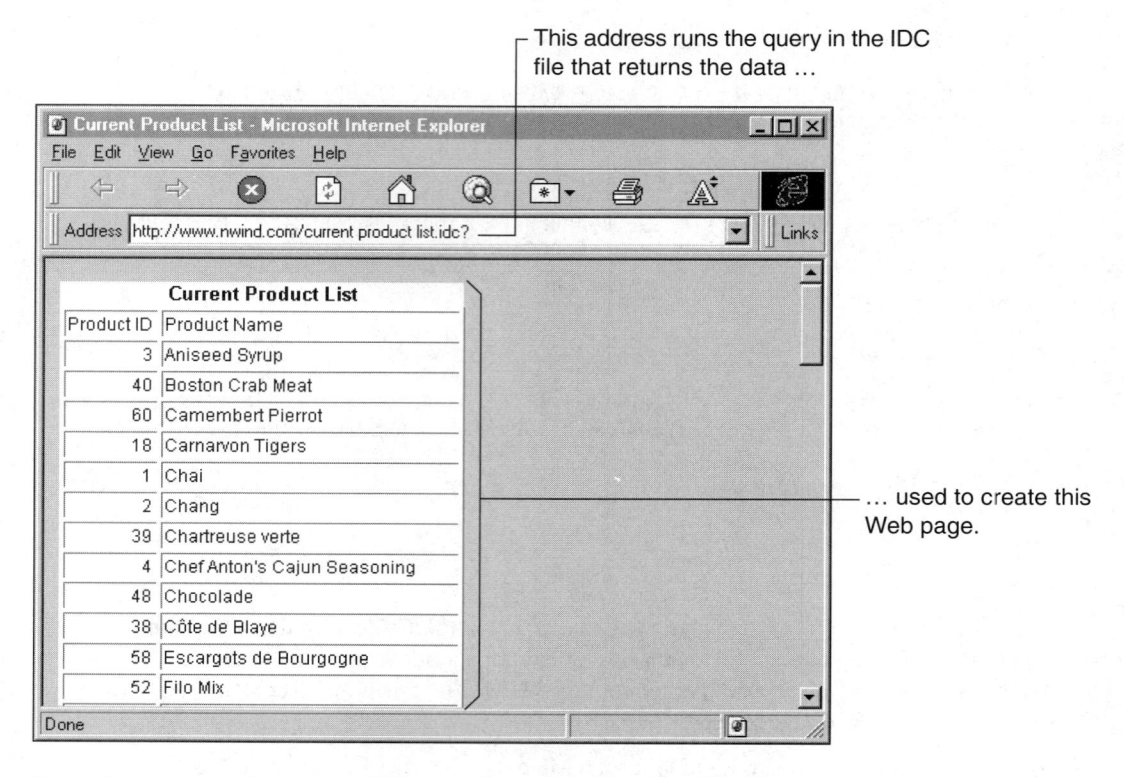

This address runs the query in the IDC file that returns the data ...

... used to create this Web page.

Note You can also reference an HTML template when you create IDC and HTX files. An HTML template contains additional HTML code to enhance the appearance of the resulting pages. If you specify an HTML template, it is merged with the HTX file. For information about the format of an HTML template, see "Using an HTML Template When You Save Data as HTML Documents" later in this chapter.

Requirements for Using IDC/HTX Files

To display and use IDC/HTX files, a copy of your database and the IDC/HTX files must reside on a computer running one of the following operating systems and Internet server environments:

- Windows NT Server version 3.51 or later running Microsoft Internet Information Server (IIS) version 1.0, 2.0, or 3.0.
- Windows NT Workstation version 4.0 with Peer Web Services installed.
- Windows 95 and Personal Web Server installed.

Use Peer Web Services or Personal Web Server only for testing IDC/HTX files or if no more than 10 users use the server simultaneously. Microsoft IIS, Peer Web Services, and Personal Web Server use a component called the Internet Database Connector (Httpodbc.dll) to generate Web pages from IDC/HTX files.

For more information about installing Peer Web Services or Personal Web Server, see "Setting Up a Personal Web Server" in Chapter 24, "Integrating Microsoft Office With Your Intranet."

World Wide Web For more information about Microsoft Internet Information Server, connect to the IIS Web site at:

http://www.microsoft.com/infoserv/iisinfo.htm

The Internet Database Connector component requires ODBC drivers to gain access to a database. To gain access to a Microsoft Access database, the Microsoft Access Desktop driver (Odbcjt32.dll) must be installed on your Web server. This driver is installed when you select the **ODBC Drivers And Administration** check box during IIS Setup.

However, the Microsoft Access Desktop driver is not installed with Peer Web Services or Personal Web Server. If Microsoft Access is installed on the computer you are using to run Personal Web Server, and if you selected the driver when you installed Microsoft Access, the driver is already available. If you do not have Microsoft Access installed on the computer you are using to run Personal Web Server, you must install the Microsoft Access Desktop driver.

▶ **To install the Microsoft Access Desktop driver**

1   Start the Office or Microsoft Access Setup program.

    If you are running Setup for the first time, click **Custom**.

    –or–

    If you are rerunning Setup, click **Add/Remove**.

2   Select the **Data Access** option, and then click **Change Option**.

    Important The **Microsoft Access** option must also be selected or the driver will not be installed.

3   Under the **Database Drivers** option, select the **Microsoft Access Driver** check box.

After the Microsoft Access Desktop driver is installed, you must create either a system DSN or a file DSN that specifies the name and connection information for each database you want to use on the server. You then specify that DSN when you generate the IDC/HTX files.

For information about how to define a system DSN or a file DSN, see Microsoft Access online Help. For more information about using IDC/HTX files, see Microsoft Internet Information Server online Help.

World Wide Web You can learn more about applications that use IDC/HTX files by reading about the Job Forum application. For information about the Job Forum application, connect to the Job Forum white paper at:

http://www.microsoft.com/accessdev/accwhite/jobforpa.htm

Saving Forms and Datasheets as Active Server Pages

With Microsoft Access, you can save a form as an ASP that emulates much of the functionality of your form. When saving a form as an ASP, Microsoft Access saves most but not all controls on the form as ActiveX controls that perform the same or similar functions.

Microsoft Access does not save or run Visual Basic code behind the form or controls. To copy the layout of your form as closely as possible, Microsoft Access uses the Microsoft HTML Layout control to position the controls on an ASP. The resulting page uses a feature of the ASP component of Microsoft Internet Information Server 3.0 called *server-side scripting* to connect to a copy of your database on an Internet server.

World Wide Web For information about the Microsoft HTML Layout control, connect to:

http://www.microsoft.com/workshop/author/layout/layout.htm

Users who open a form saved as an ASP can browse records, update or delete existing records, and add new records.

You can also save table, query, and form datasheets as ASPs. When you open a datasheet saved as an ASP, Microsoft Access displays current data from a copy of your database located on an Internet server, much like IDC/HTX files do. However, unlike IDC/HTX files, ASPs require only one file per datasheet. The ASP file uses scripting to establish a connection to the database on the server and contains information that it uses to format the datasheet. Unlike a form saved as an ASP, users cannot update existing records in or add new records to a datasheet saved as an ASP.

▶ **To save a form or datasheet as an ASP**

1 In the Database window, click the form or datasheet you want to save.
2 On the **File** menu, click **Save As/Export**.
3 In the **Save As** dialog box, click **To an External File or Database**, and then click **OK**.
4 In the **Save as type** list, click **Microsoft Active Server Page**.

5 Specify a file name and location for the ASP file, and then click **Export**.
6 In the **Microsoft Active Server Page Output Options** dialog box, specify:
   - The data source name to use for a copy of the current database.
   - A user name and password, if required to open the database.
   - An HTML template, if you want Microsoft Access to merge one with the ASP.
   - The URL for the server where the ASP will reside.
   - The **Session timeout** setting, which determines how long a connection to the server is maintained after the user stops working with the ASP.

You can also save forms and datasheets as ASPs by using the Publish to the Web Wizard (available through the **Save As HTML** command on the **File** menu), the **OutputTo** method in code, or the OutputTo action in macros.

For more information about saving forms and datasheets as ASPs, see Microsoft Access online Help.

Form Views Supported for APSs

If the form you save as an ASP has its **DefaultView** property set to **Single Form** or **Continuous Forms**, the ASP is displayed as a single form, unless it is opened in Datasheet view with the **Save As/Export** command (**File** menu). If the form has its **DefaultView** property set to **Datasheet**, the ASP is displayed as a datasheet. Subforms are always displayed as datasheets, regardless of their **DefaultView** property setting. All field data types are saved unformatted—that is, the **Format** and **InputMask** property settings are not saved.

Control Types Supported for ASPs

When Microsoft Access saves a form as an ASP, it replaces Microsoft Access controls with ActiveX controls, as described in the following table.

This Microsoft Access control	Is replaced with this ActiveX control
Text box	Text box.
Text box control bound to a Hyperlink field	Text box that displays the hyperlink text, but the hyperlink cannot be followed.
List box	List box (single column only).
Combo box	Combo box.
Label	Label. If the label has **HyperlinkAddress** or **HyperlinkSubAddress** properties set, a hyperlink is created for the label.
Command button	Command button, but any code associated with the button is lost. If the command button has **HyperlinkAddress** or **HyperlinkSubAddress** properties set, a hyperlink is created for the button.

This Microsoft Access control	Is replaced with this ActiveX control
Option group	Option group, but without a group frame.
Option button	Option button.
Check box	Check box.
Toggle button	Toggle button.
ActiveX control	ActiveX control, but any code associated with the control is lost.

Microsoft Access does not support the following when saving a form as an ASP:

- Tab controls
- Rectangles
- Lines
- Page breaks
- Unbound object frames
- Bound object frames
- Image controls
- Background of a form set with the **Picture** property

Requirements for Using ASPs

To display and use an ASP, a copy of your database and ASP components must reside on a computer running one of the following operating systems and Internet server platforms:

- Microsoft Windows NT Server 3.51 or later running IIS 3.0
- Microsoft Windows NT Workstation 4.0 and Peer Web Services with the ASP components installed
- Microsoft Windows 95 and Personal Web Server with the ASP components installed

The Microsoft HTML Layout control must be installed on the computer opening the ASP. If the computer opening an ASP produced by Microsoft Access 97 does not have the HTML Layout control installed, a message is displayed prompting the user to download the control. To display the ASP, the user must click **Yes** to download the control.

World Wide Web The Microsoft HTML Layout control is not included on the Office CD, but you can download it directly from the Web. To download the Microsoft HTML Layout control, connect to:

http://www.microsoft.com/ie/download/ieadd.htm

Chapter 25 Web Support in Microsoft Office Applications

Use Personal Web Server or Peer Web Services only for testing ASPs or if no more than 10 users will be using the server simultaneously. ASPs also require the Microsoft Access Desktop driver and a valid DSN to gain access to a database.

World Wide Web For more information about installing the ASP components for Peer Web Services and Personal Web Server, connect to the Windows NT Server home page at:

http://www.microsoft.com/ntserver/

Using the Publish to the Web Wizard

With the Publish to the Web Wizard, you can publish a set of Microsoft Access database objects to any combination of static HTML documents, IDC/HTX files, or ASPs. Using the wizard, you can:

- Pick any combination of tables, queries, forms, or reports to save.
- Specify an HTML template to use for the selected objects.
- Select any combination of static HTML documents, IDC/HTX files, or ASPs.
- Create a home page to tie together the Web pages you create.
- Specify the folder where you save your files.
- Use the Web Publishing Wizard to move the files created by the Publish to the Web Wizard to a Web server.
- Save the answers you provide the wizard as a Web publication profile and then select that profile the next time you use the wizard. This saves you from having to answer all the questions again.

To run the Publish to the Web Wizard, click **Save As HTML** (**File** menu). For more information about using the Publish to the Web Wizard, see Microsoft Access online Help.

Note The Publish to the Web Wizard and Web Publishing Wizard cannot copy the database itself or create a DSN on your server when publishing IDC/HTX or ASP. You must perform these operations yourself.

Using an HTML Template When You Save Data as HTML Documents

When you save data as HTML documents, you can use an HTML template to give a consistent look to the HTML documents you create. For example, you can include your company logo, name, and address in the page header; use the background that is used throughout your company; or include standard text in the header or footer of the HTML document.

Note You can use an HTML template when you save data as static HTML documents, when you save datasheets as IDC/HTX files, when you save a form or datasheet as an ASP, and when you use the Publish to the Web Wizard.

The HTML template can be any HTML document—that is, a text file that includes HTML tags and user-specified text and references. In addition, the HTML template can include placeholders that tell Microsoft Access where to insert certain pieces of data in the HTML documents. When data is saved as HTML documents, the placeholders are replaced with data. The following table describes each of the placeholders that you can use in an HTML template.

Placeholder	Description	Location
<!--AccessTemplate_Title-->	The name of the object being saved	Between <TITLE> and </TITLE>
<!--AccessTemplate_Body-->	The data or object being saved	Between <BODY> and </BODY>
<!--AccessTemplate_FirstPage-->	An anchor tag to the first page	Between <BODY> and </BODY> or after </BODY>
<!--AccessTemplate_PreviousPage-->	An anchor tag to the previous page	Between <BODY> and </BODY> or after </BODY>
<!--AccessTemplate_NextPage-->	An anchor tag to the next page	Between <BODY> and </BODY> or after </BODY>
<!--AccessTemplate_LastPage-->	An anchor tag to the last page	Between <BODY> and </BODY> or after </BODY>
<!--AccessTemplate_PageNumber-->	The current page number	Between <BODY> and </BODY> or after </BODY>

When you install Microsoft Access, sample HTML template files and graphics files are installed in the Program Files\Microsoft Office\Templates\Access folder.

Synchronizing Database Replicas over the Internet

With Microsoft Access 97, you can synchronize replicas over the Internet. Before you can synchronize over the Internet, you must configure your Internet server for replication. To configure your Internet server, you need Replication Manager, which includes a wizard that guides you through the configuration process.

For more information about Replication Manager, see "Replication Manager" in Chapter 20, "Using Replication in Your Application," in *Building Applications with Microsoft Access 97*.

Importing, Linking, and Exporting Data to the Internet

With Microsoft Access, you can import or link data from HTML tables or other data sources on an Internet server. You can also export data in your database to an Internet server.

Importing and Linking Data from HTML Tables*

You can import or link data formatted as an HTML table to a Microsoft Access database. Before Microsoft Access imports or links the data, it copies the data into the local cache. Whenever you open a linked table, Microsoft Access makes a local copy from the original on the Internet or an intranet before opening it. For this reason, the data in the table is read-only. Similarly, if you export the linked HTML table to an HTML file, Microsoft Access exports from the local copy of the file, not the original file on the Internet.

▶ **To import or link data from HTML tables**

1. On the **File** menu, point to **Get External Data**, and then click either **Import** or **Link tables**.
2. In the **Files of type** list, click **HTML Documents**.
3. To specify the file from which to import or link, use the **Look in** box to browse through the file system on your hard disk or LAN.

   –or–

   In the **File name** box, type a valid HTTP or FTP URL.

   –or–

   In the **Look in** box, click **Internet Locations (FTP)** and select a previously defined FTP site.

   –or–

   In the **Look in** box, click **Add/Modify FTP Locations**, and then specify a new FTP site and browse its files.
4. Click **Import** or **Link**.

For information about linking HTML files using Visual Basic, see "Working with HTML Files" in Chapter 18, "Accessing External Data," in *Building Applications with Microsoft Access 97*.

When you import or link data from an HTML table, Microsoft Access parses the information contained within the HTML tags. The primary HTML tags that define tables are described in the following table.

HTML tag pair	Description
<TABLE>...</TABLE>	Specifies the beginning and end of the table
<TH...>...</TH>	Specifies table header cells
<TR...>...</TR>	Specifies a row in a table
<TD...>...</TD>	Specifies table data cells
<CAPTION...>...</CAPTION>	Specifies the table caption, usually at the beginning or end of the table

Microsoft Access applies the following rules when it interprets the progression of tags and tag pairs within the HTML table it imports or links:

- The <TD> tag pair may be closed with either a </TD> tag or a </TH> tag.
- The <TH> tag pair may be closed with either a </TH> tag or a </TD> tag.
- The <TR> tag is not required to start a new row. If a <TD> tag follows a </TR> tag, Microsoft Access assumes this is the beginning of a new row.
- If a </TABLE> tag is not preceded by a </TR> tag, then Microsoft Access assumes this is the end of the row.

In many cases, a table cell can display something other than text. If a table cell contains an embedded graphic file, there is a <IMG SRC...> tag associated with it. This tag may or may not have additional text that would be displayed. If additional text is present, Microsoft Access imports it, but Microsoft Access does not import the embedded graphic or the tag that defines it. However, this is not true of embedded anchor <A HREF> tags; Microsoft Access imports anchor tags as Hyperlink fields.

HTML tables can contain lists that are embedded within a table cell. Lists in an HTML table cell are formatted with the <LI> and </LI> tags. Microsoft Access inserts a carriage return and line feed (<CR><LF>) after each list item and imports each item in the list as a separate field for that record.

HTML tables can also contain tables that are embedded within a table cell. You can import these as separate tables. To achieve the most predictable results, however, import simple HTML tables with a fixed number of fields per record, without embedded lists or tables.

Exporting, Importing, and Linking Data from Other Data Sources on Internet Servers

You can export any Microsoft Access-compatible external data file to an FTP server. You cannot export files to HTTP servers through the Internet, however, because you cannot write to them using the HTTP protocol.

▶ **To export data from external data sources on Internet servers**

1. On the **File** menu, click **Save As/Export**.
2. In the **Save As** dialog box, click **To an External File or Database**, and then click **OK**.
3. In the **Save as type** list, select the type of file you want to export.

4 To export files on an FTP server, enter a valid FTP URL in the **File name** box.

–or–

In the **Save in** box, click **Internet Locations (FTP)** and select a previously defined FTP site.

–or–

In the **Save in** box, click **Add/Modify FTP Locations**, and then specify a new FTP site and browse its files.

5 Click **Export**.

You can also import and link any Microsoft Access-compatible external data file, except Microsoft Access databases and ODBC data sources, by using an FTP or HTTP connection. An FTP or HTTP connection is only maintained long enough to perform a single transaction. Therefore, when you import or link a file located on an FTP or HTTP server, Microsoft Access copies the data file to the user's local cache. Microsoft Access then imports or links to the data file in the local cache. For this reason, files linked with an FTP or HTTP connection are read-only.

▶ **To import or link data from external data sources on Internet servers**

1 On the **File** menu, point to **Get External Data**, and then click either **Import** or **Link Tables**.

2 In the **Files of type** list, click the type of file you want to import or link.

3 To import or link files on an FTP server, enter a valid FTP URL in the **File name** box.

–or–

In the **Look in** box, click **Internet Locations (FTP)** and select a previously defined FTP site.

–or–

In the **Look in** box, click **Add/Modify FTP Locations**, and then specify a new FTP site and browse its files

4 To import or link files on an HTTP server, enter a valid HTTP URL in the **File name** box.

5 Click **Import** or **Link**.

Displaying Web Pages and Other Documents in Microsoft Access Forms

The Microsoft WebBrowser control is an ActiveX control that you can use on your Microsoft Access database application forms to browse Web sites, view Web pages and other documents, and download data located on the Internet. The WebBrowser control is useful in situations where you do not want to disrupt the work flow in a database application by switching from Microsoft Access to a Web browser or other document-viewing program.

For example, the following illustration shows the Browse Saved Hyperlinks form in the Developer Solutions sample application. (This sample application is installed in the Microsoft Office\Office\Samples folder when you choose a Custom installation during Setup and select the **Sample Databases** option under the **Microsoft Access** option). You can use the Browse Saved Hyperlinks form to browse addresses saved in the Links table.

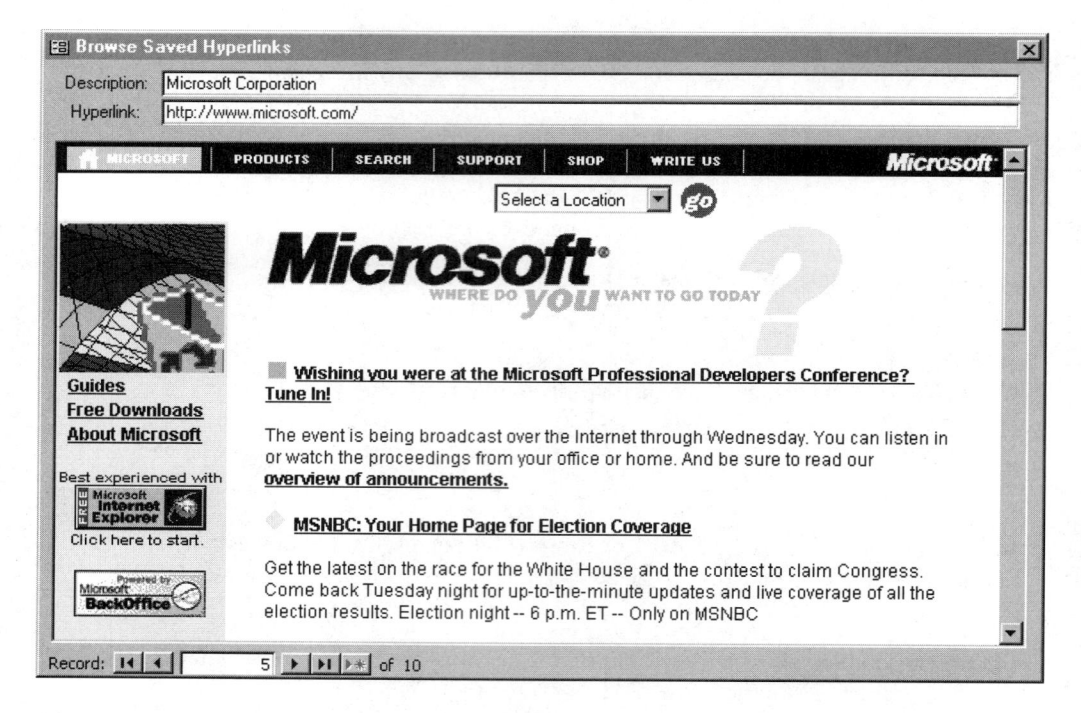

The WebBrowser control can display any Web page that Microsoft Internet Explorer version 3.0 can display. For example, the WebBrowser control can display pages that include any of the following features:

- Standard HTML and most HTML enhancements, such as floating frames and cascading style sheets
- Other ActiveX controls
- Most Netscape plug-ins

- Scripting, such as Microsoft Visual Basic Scripting Edition (VBScript), JScript™, and most JavaScript
- Java™ applets
- Multimedia content, such as video and audio playback
- Three-dimensional virtual worlds created with Virtual Reality Modeling Language (VRML)

In addition to opening Web pages, the WebBrowser control can open any ActiveX document, which includes most Office documents. For example, if Office is installed on a computer, an application that uses the WebBrowser control can open and edit Microsoft Excel spreadsheets, Word documents, and PowerPoint presentations from within the control. Similarly, if Microsoft Excel Viewer, Word Viewer, or PowerPoint Viewer is installed, users can view those documents within the WebBrowser control.

With the WebBrowser control, users of Microsoft database applications can browse sites on the Web, as well as folders on a hard disk or on a LAN. Users can follow hyperlinks by clicking them or by typing a URL into a text box. Also, the WebBrowser control maintains a history list that users can browse to view previously browsed sites, folders, and documents.

Note Additional ActiveX controls that you can use to work with content on the Internet or an intranet are available in Microsoft Office 97, Developer Edition.

For more information about using the WebBrowser control, see "Using the WebBrowser Control" in Chapter 21, "Developing Applications for the Internet and the World Wide Web," in *Building Applications with Microsoft Access 97*.

Web Support in Microsoft Excel 97

Microsoft Excel supports Office-wide Web features, such as hyperlinks and the **Web** toolbar. In addition, Microsoft Excel supports importing and exporting HTML documents, Web queries, and Web forms.

Converting Microsoft Excel Data and Charts to HTML

The Internet Assistant Wizard is an add-in that provides HTML conversion functionality for Microsoft Excel. With the Internet Assistant Wizard, you can:

- Convert worksheet ranges to HTML tables.
- Convert charts to GIF images.

Part 5 Using Microsoft Office Throughout Your Organization

- Create HTML tables or GIF images to be inserted into HTML documents, or create ready-to-view HTML documents that contain the tables or GIF images.

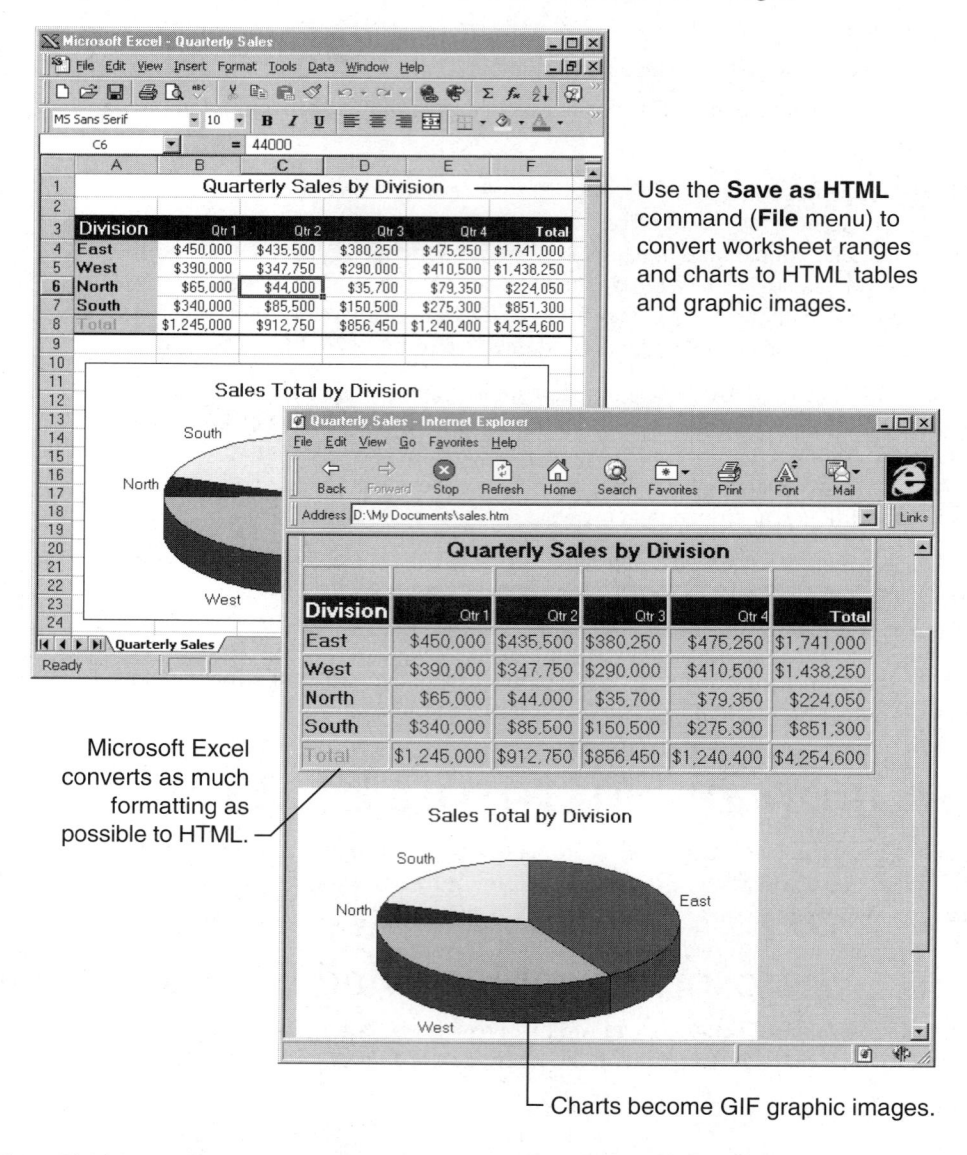

Use the **Save as HTML** command (**File** menu) to convert worksheet ranges and charts to HTML tables and graphic images.

Microsoft Excel converts as much formatting as possible to HTML.

Charts become GIF graphic images.

Note The Internet Assistant Wizard is installed by the HTML add-in; however, the HTML add-in is not installed by default when you choose a Typical installation during Setup. To install the add-in, rerun Setup, click **Add/Remove**, and select the **Web Page Authoring (HTML)** option.

▶ **To convert Microsoft Excel data to HTML**

1 Open the workbook that contains the worksheet ranges or charts you want to convert.
2 On the **File** menu, click **Save As HTML**.
3 Follow the instructions that appear on your screen.

Note If you insert the table based on your Microsoft Excel data into an existing HTML file, you must edit the HTML file before you can insert the table. Open the HTML file in a text editor (such as Notepad) and type **<!--##Table##-->** at the location where you want the table to appear. The Internet Assistant Wizard replaces this string with the table.

HTML Conversion Issues for Worksheet Ranges

When you convert a worksheet range to an HTML table, the following elements are preserved:

- Font size and color
- Font formatting, such as bold or underlined text
- Cell background color
- Merged cells

Note In the conversion, Office hyperlinks are converted to HTML hyperlinks.

GIF Image Conversion Issues for Charts

The Internet Assistant Wizard converts charts to GIF format images with a high degree of fidelity. Because the GIF images are static, however, all links back to the source data on which the chart data series or labels are based are broken.

Using Microsoft Excel Web Queries

To query data from a source on the Internet or your intranet and then import the data into Microsoft Excel, you can use the **Run Web Query** command (**Data** menu, **Get External Data** submenu). Once you import the data, you can manipulate, analyze, and format it. For example, you can create a Web query that retrieves a current product price from a database on your intranet.

Tools and Utilities The Office Resource Kit Tools and Utilities include the Microsoft Excel 97 Web Connectivity Kit. The Connectivity Kit includes detailed instructions for creating Web queries, as well as several sample queries. For more information, see "Microsoft Excel 97 Web Connectivity Kit" in Appendix A, "Microsoft Office 97 Resource Kit Tools and Utilities."

Collecting Database Input with Web Forms

This section describes the Web Form Wizard add-in, which you can use to create data-entry forms on your intranet.

Overview

The Web Form Wizard is a Microsoft Excel add-in that you can use to create data entry forms (called *Web forms*) in Microsoft Excel to capture user input to a database over the Internet or an intranet.

— This is a simple Web form as it appears in Microsoft Excel.

— This is the tab-delimited file (imported into Microsoft Excel) after several records have been submitted with the Web form.

Note The Web Form Wizard is installed by the Web Form add-in; however, the Web Form add-in is not installed by default when you choose a Typical installation during Setup. To install the add-in, rerun Setup, click **Add/Remove**, and select the **Web Page Authoring (HTML)** option.

Web forms have a client/server architecture. On the client side, the user opens a Web form in Microsoft Excel, enters data, and then submits it. On the server side, scripts created by the Web Form Wizard write this data to one of several formats, depending on your server setup and database tools. Following is a description of how a user might complete a Web form.

1. The user requests a Web form by clicking a hyperlink in a Web browser, by opening the Web form on a network server, or by activating an attached document in an e-mail message.
2. The server downloads the Web form to the user's computer. Because the Web form is a Microsoft Excel workbook, Microsoft Excel starts.
3. The user fills out the Web form and then clicks the **Submit Info** button. Microsoft Excel submits the user's information using the HTTP protocol and then closes the Web form without saving changes so that it is ready for future use.
4. On the server side, a script parses the submission into a database record and then sends a submission confirmation to the user's Web browser.

Web forms are best suited for data input. To use Web forms for database queries, you must manually modify the HTML extension (HTX file) created by the Web Form Wizard.

Client Requirements

On the client side, Web forms (which are Microsoft Excel workbooks) require the Microsoft Excel 97 program. If a user opens a Web form from a Web browser (by clicking a hyperlink, for example) and the browser supports Active Documents, Microsoft Excel starts within the Web browser and loads the form.

Because Web forms require Microsoft Excel to handle user input, Web forms are best suited to intranets. Web forms work over the Internet as well, however, because most communication between the client and server is in standard TCP/IP format.

Note Because Microsoft Excel Viewer does not support data input, you cannot use it in place of Microsoft Excel on the client computer.

Server Requirements and Capabilities

Web forms support both the Microsoft Internet Information Server Application Programming Interface (ISAPI) and Common Gateway Interface (CGI) protocols.

Note The Web Form Wizard creates the necessary files to allow the client to insert new records into a database file. To perform more complex actions, however, such as searching a database or retrieving information, you must modify the Internet Database Connector (IDC) file created by the wizard. For more information about modifying an IDC file, see your Web server documentation.

Web Forms and IIS

If you are running IIS on your Web server, you can use Web forms to interact with any Open Database Connectivity (ODBC)-compliant database such as Microsoft SQL Server or Microsoft Access.

With an IIS-based Web server and Web forms you can:

- Create an ODBC-compliant database on the server.
- Insert, delete, or update records in the database based on user input.
- Query the database based on user input.

When you create a Web form for a server running IIS, the Web Form Wizard generates four files:

- The Web form itself, which is a Microsoft Excel workbook.
- A Microsoft Access MDB file to contain the data records generated with the Web form. Each control of the Web form is mapped to a field in the Microsoft Access database. When creating the Web form, you can specify that you want user submissions to be appended to an existing Microsoft Access database instead of creating a new database.
- An IDC file to record information about the user and data source.
- An HTX file that describes the confirmation reply sent to the user's Web browser after the user submits data.

Web Forms and CGI

If you are running CGI on your Web server, you can use Web forms to add records to a tab-delimited database. You can then import this database into Microsoft Access or Microsoft Excel for further manipulation or analysis.

When you create a Web form for a server running CGI, the Web Form Wizard generates three files:

- The Web form itself, which is a Microsoft Excel workbook.
- A Perl script to parse the users' submissions and insert them into a tab-delimited text file.
- A text file that contains the parsed data. The first record of the text file contains the Web form's control names.

Creating a Web Form

Creating a Web form involves the following steps:

1. Design the form in Microsoft Excel, and then start the Web Form Wizard.
2. Specify the controls or cells on the worksheet in which the user will supply data and specify the corresponding labels for each control or cell.
3. If you are running your Web server under Windows NT Server, specify whether your Web server runs IIS or CGI.

4. Specify whether Microsoft Excel should save the Web form as a Microsoft Excel workbook

   –or–

   If you are using FrontPage to administer your Web site, add the Web form to your FrontPage Web and specify the path to which to save the form.

5. Specify the confirmation message and the URL path to the database where the data is to be submitted.

6. If you are running IIS, add an ODBC data source and edit the IDC file created by the Web Form Wizard.

Each of these steps is described in more detail in the following sections.

Design the Web Form and Start the Web Form Wizard

When you design a Web form in Microsoft Excel, use only the **Forms** toolbar (**View** menu, **Toolbars** submenu). The Web Form Wizard only supports forms created with the **Forms** toolbar. It does not support controls created with the **Control Toolbox** or by any other means.

The wizard converts control names to database field names according to the following rules:

- **a** to **z** are accepted without restrictions.
- **A** to **Z** are converted to lowercase.
- **0** to **9** are accepted as long as they do not appear at the beginning of a control name.
- All other symbols are ignored.
- All control names must be unique. If the Web Form Wizard encounters duplicate control names, it numbers them sequentially.

Tip When entering control names in worksheet cells, add a colon to the name—for example **Address:** The Web Form Wizard now adds both the label and the cell reference to the list of available controls. This saves you from having to add the labels and cell references manually to the list.

The Web Form Wizard generates a **Submit Info** button and adds it to the Web form. Do not create a **Submit Info** button yourself.

Tip When using worksheet cells as data input fields, you can use the data input features in Microsoft Excel, such as data validation (**Data** menu), conditional formatting (**Format** menu), and cell and object protection (**Format** menu). For more information about using these data input features, see Microsoft Excel online Help.

To start the Web Form Wizard, click the **Web Form** command (**Tools** menu, **Wizard** submenu). The wizard displays a Welcome panel; click **Next** to continue.

Specify the Data Input Controls and Cells

In Step 2 of the wizard, select the data input controls you want to use. You can remove any of the values that appear in the **Controls and cells** box or add values that do not appear.

For detailed information about these options, click the **Help** button.

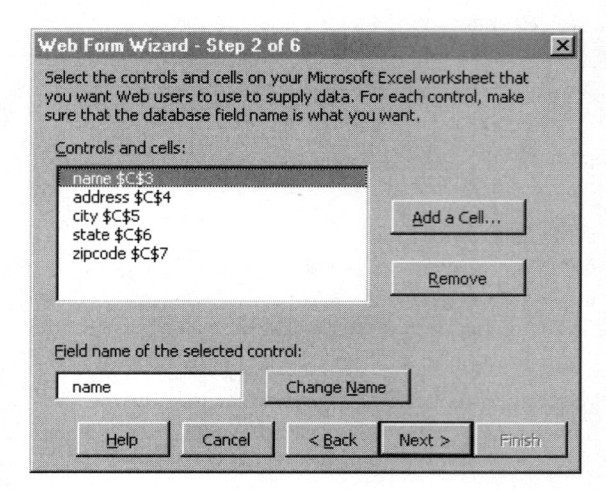

Specify Your Web Server Software (Windows Only)

In Step 3, specify the software running on your Web server: IIS or CGI. Because IIS is not available on Macintosh Web servers, the Web Form Wizard in Microsoft Excel for the Macintosh defaults to CGI and skips Step 3 of the wizard.

You can create or add to a Microsoft Access database only if your Web server is running IIS. For CGI Web servers, the Web Form Wizard creates a tab-delimited file. You can later import this file into Microsoft Access or Microsoft Excel for more analysis.

For detailed information about these options, click the **Help** button.

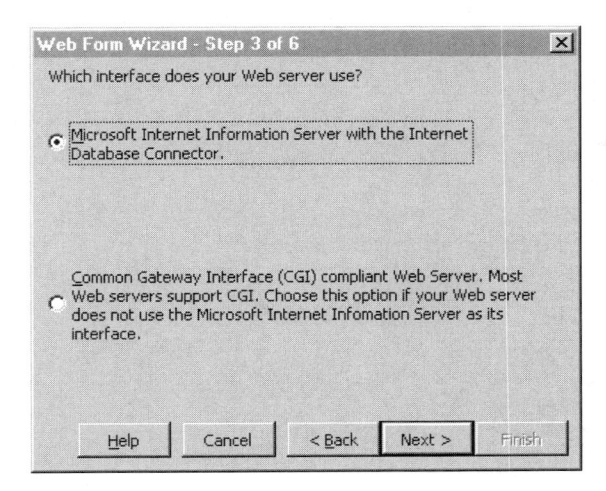

Choose the Results Format and Path

In Step 4, specify whether you want the form to be saved as a Microsoft Excel workbook on your Web server or added to an existing FrontPage server by clicking one of the following options:

- **Save the result as a Microsoft Excel file**

    If you select this option, you must also specify a location in the **File path** box.

- **Add the result to your FrontPage Web**

    If you select this option, you must have a Web site open in the FrontPage Explorer. If FrontPage is not running, the Web Form Wizard starts it, and you must then open a Web site.

    In the **File path** box, specify a location on your Web server where you want the Web form and its related files stored. If the path you specify differs from the path of the workbook in which you initially designed the form, you must also specify a Web form file name. The other files created by the Web Form Wizard are given the same base file name. For example, if you name your Web form Address.xls and specify a CGI interface, the Web Form Wizard creates Address.pl (the Perl script) and Address.txt (the tab-delimited text file) in the same location as Address.xls.

For detailed information about these options, click the **Help** button.

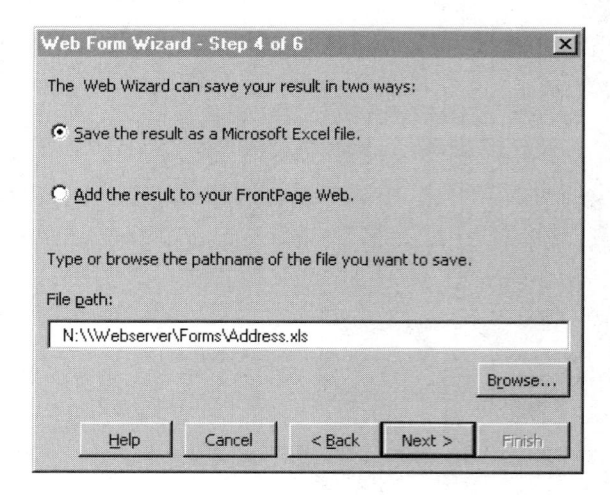

Design the Confirmation Message
In Step 5, design the confirmation message you want returned to the user's Web browser after the user has submitted data.

In the **URL path** box, type the HTTP address of the location of the database file or tab-delimited file you specified in Step 4 of the wizard.

For detailed information about these options, click the **Help** button.

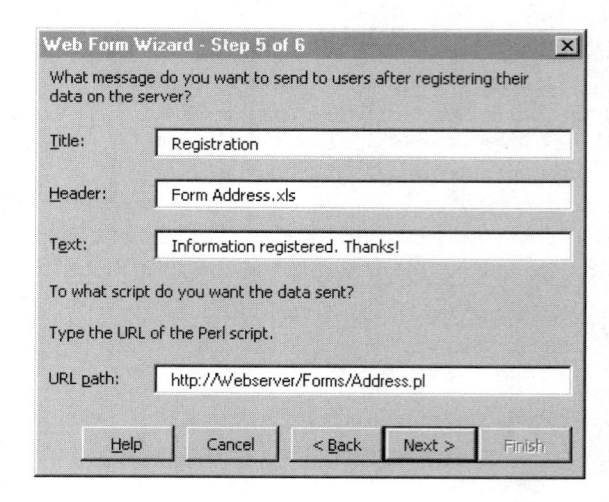

In Step 6 of the Web Form Wizard, click **Finish** to complete your Web form.

Add an ODBC Data Source and Edit the IDC File on Your Web Server (IIS only)

If you selected an IIS Web server in Step 3 of the wizard, you must add a Microsoft Access system data source in the ODBC control panel and then edit the IDC file created by the wizard on your Web server. You may also want to move the files created by the wizard to different folders on your Web server.

Tip For better security you can move the IDC, HTX, and MDB files to a folder on your Web server with execute access but not read access. Set these properties for the folder through IIS Directory Properties. The XLS form itself, however, must remain in a folder with read access.

▶ **To add an ODBC system data source**

1. On the Windows NT Server 4.0 **Start** menu, point to **Settings**, and then click **Control Panel**.

   –or–

   In Microsoft Windows NT Server 3.51, double-click **Control Panel** in the Main group in Program Manager.

2. Double-click **ODBC**.

3. Click the **System DSN** tab, and then click **Add**.

4. In the **Create New Data Source** dialog box, click **Microsoft Access Driver**, and then click **Finish**.

5. In the **Data Source Name** field, enter a descriptive name for your Microsoft Excel Web form; for example, **Commuter Survey Form**.

6. If you want to apply an authorization logon name and password, click **Advanced**.

   This is not required to submit records to the database through the Web form you have created.

7. Click **Select**, and then select your MDB file on your Web server.

   From this point on, do not move your MDB file from this location.

▶ **To edit the IDC file**

1. On your Web server, open the IDC file created by the Web Form Wizard in a text editor.

2. In the IDC file, replace the text `Your data source` with the data source name you specified in the preceding procedure.

3. If you also specified an authorization logon name and password, replace the text `Your username` and `Your password` with the values you specified.

Web Support in Microsoft Outlook 97

Outlook provides a central point from which to communicate with others through the Internet, and provides ways to connect intranets within your organization to the Internet.

This section describes the Internet-related capabilities of Outlook. These include working with Outlook as a client for Internet mail, using hyperlinks in Outlook items, and using Outlook to organize and display Web pages.

Working with Internet Mail

As an administrator, you have many ways to set up your workgroup to send and receive Internet mail with Outlook. If your organization uses Microsoft Exchange Server, Internet mail is handled by the Internet Mail Connector. If your organization does not use Microsoft Exchange Server, e-mail can be sent to and received directly from the Internet using another e-mail service provider that is compatible with the Simple Mail Transfer Protocol (SMTP) or Post Office Protocol (POP) version 3. SMTP and POP3 are MAPI service providers that are installed by default with Outlook.

With an Internet mail connection, your workgroup can use Internet messaging for the following activities in addition to sending and receiving messages:

- Connect to the Internet from a remote location and download messages.

  For example, a traveling salesperson can check for new e-mail while on the road.

- Use rules to process incoming and outgoing e-mail.

  For example, a user can have Outlook file all messages from a particular Internet address in a separate folder.

- Send and receive group scheduling meeting requests.

  For example, a meeting organizer can send a meeting request to offsite clients or suppliers.

- Assign tasks and receive notification when tasks are updated or completed.

  For example, a manager can send a task request to an employee who works at home.

When a user types an Internet e-mail address in the **To** box, Outlook automatically resolves and properly formats the address by removing spaces and changing commas to periods. For example, if a user types **R_King @ NorthWind,com** Outlook formats the address as **R_King@NorthWind.com**

Using Hyperlinks in Messages

Outlook automatically recognizes Internet addresses (URLs) in the body of e-mail messages and converts them to hyperlinks. Internet users can click the hyperlink to view the Web page with Microsoft Internet Explorer (included with Office) or another Web browser.

When you type one of the following Internet protocols in the text box of an e-mail message or other item, Outlook creates a hyperlink from the text. If the Internet address includes spaces, you must enclose the entire address in angle brackets (< >). For example, type **<file://c:\My Documents\MyFile.doc>**

Internet protocols recognized by Outlook

file	https	Outlook
ftp	mailto	prospero
gopher	news	telnet
http	nntp	wais

Using Outlook as a Web Browser

Outlook provides a number of ways to organize and display Web pages. Users can use the Contacts list to keep track of contacts' Web sites, open the Web history folder from within Outlook, or create and share a catalog of Web sites in a public folder.

Keeping Track of Contacts' Web Sites

Outlook provides a way to keep an Internet address for each contact in the Contact list, so you can go directly to a contact's Web page from Outlook. While this feature is useful in individual contact lists, it can also be used by a workgroup. For example, a sales department can maintain a list of customers in a public folder of Outlook contacts. The public folder could include a custom view that shows each customer's name, business phone number, e-mail address, and Web address.

Follow these general steps to create a list of contacts' Web addresses in a public folder.

1. Set up a public folder that can contain contact items.

   For more information about how to set up public folders, see "Microsoft Exchange Public Folders" in Chapter 31, "Workgroup Features in Microsoft Outlook."

2. Create or modify a view to show only the Full Name, Business Phone, E-mail, and Web Page fields.

3. Add or import contacts to the public folder.

Using the Web History Folder in Outlook

The Windows\History folder contains a list of shortcuts to recently visited Web sites in Microsoft Internet Explorer 3.0. Unlike most folders, the History folder cannot be viewed or opened from within Outlook. (Microsoft Internet Explorer 3.0 uses shell extensions that are not compatible with Outlook.) To use the History folder from within Outlook, create a shortcut to the History folder and keep it in the Favorites folder.

▶ **To create a shortcut to the Web History folder**

1. In the Windows folder, right-click the History folder, and then click **Create Shortcut** on the shortcut menu.
2. On the Outlook Bar, click the **Other** group, and then drag the shortcut you just created from Windows Explorer to the Favorites folder in the Outlook Bar.

Tip To use a shortcut in the History folder from within Outlook, click **Favorites** in the **Other** group on the Outlook Bar, double-click the shortcut to the History folder, and then double-click the shortcut you want in Windows Explorer.

Creating a Catalog of Web Sites to Share

If your organization uses the Web as a source of information and also uses Microsoft Exchange Server as a mail server, you can set up a public folder to organize Web site shortcuts for users. Keeping Web site shortcuts in a public folder gives users a way to collect, categorize, sort, and group the Web sites in different ways. When a user double-clicks a shortcut, the Web browser starts up and displays the Web page.

Follow these general steps to create a catalog of Web sites in a public folder:

1. Set up a public folder that can contain mail items.

    For more information about how to set up public folders, see "Microsoft Exchange Public Folders" in Chapter 31, "Workgroup Features in Microsoft Outlook."

2. Create or modify a view to show only the fields you want to use.

3. In your Web browser, locate a Web page you want to include in the catalog and create a shortcut to the Web page.

    In Microsoft Internet Explorer 3.0, you create a shortcut with the **Create Shortcut** command (**File** menu).

4. In Outlook, open the public folder you created and drag the Web page shortcut from your desktop to the public folder.

5. For each Web page you want to add to your catalog, create a shortcut and drag it to the public folder.

> **Customizing the View of a Web Page Catalog**
>
> You can create a custom view to organize a list of Web sites for your organization. For example, you can create a table view that includes custom text fields for owner, audience, address, and page type (such as internal, customer, supplier, and so on). Users can click the field headings to sort Web sites by any of these fields.

Web Support in Microsoft PowerPoint 97

In addition to the Office-wide Web features such as hyperlinks and the **Web** toolbar, PowerPoint includes special features designed for publishing presentations on the Internet or an intranet. This section describes the Web authoring features of PowerPoint.

Performance improvements in PowerPoint 97 have also made PowerPoint presentations more practical for use over a network. When you open a PowerPoint file, PowerPoint now loads only one slide at a time, so you do not wait for an entire presentation to load before you can view it. The text is retrieved first, followed by graphics and linked or embedded objects. These improvements mean that you have quicker access to the presentation online. For more information about ways to improve the performance of PowerPoint, see "Optimizing Microsoft PowerPoint" in Chapter 7, "Customizing and Optimizing Microsoft Office."

Using Action Settings as Hyperlinks

PowerPoint supports Office hyperlinks with the **Hyperlink** command (**Insert** menu) and the **Hyperlink to** option in the **Action Settings** dialog box (**Slide Show** menu). You can make any object on a slide into a hyperlink that goes to another slide in the active presentation, another presentation, another file, or a URL.

▶ **To add a hyperlink to a slide**

1. Select the object or highlight the text that you want to make into a hyperlink.
2. On the **Slide Show** menu, click **Action Settings**, click **Hyperlink to**, and then enter the destination for the hyperlink.

    –or–

    On the **Insert** menu, click **Hyperlink**, and then enter a destination for the hyperlink in the **Link to file or URL** box; if you want to go to a particular location within the destination, enter it in the **Named location in file (optional)** box.

    When a user clicks the object during a slide show, the hyperlink goes to the destination you specify.

Note When you set hyperlinks through the **Action Settings** dialog box, a hyperlink to another presentation opens a particular slide in the presentation, and a hyperlink to another file opens the file. If the other file is an Office Binder document, the hyperlink opens a particular section of the binder.

To standardize the look of interactive buttons, you can also add action buttons to a slide. *Action buttons* are graphic images designed to look like buttons. When you add one to a slide, the **Action Settings** dialog box (**Slide Show** menu) appears automatically so you can specify a destination for the action button.

You can create hyperlinks for objects, such as AutoShapes and text boxes, and you can create hyperlinks for text strings. Because text in PowerPoint exists within a text object, PowerPoint maintains distinct hyperlinks for a text string and for the text object that contains the string. For example, you can have a text box with action settings assigned to it, and you can create a hyperlink within the text box, as shown in the following illustration.

Chapter 25 Web Support in Microsoft Office Applications

Clicking hyperlink display text connects to a URL associated with the text.

The Competition

- **Sales**
  - 8% above Detco
  - 11% above Marsco
- **Costs**
  - 4% below Detco
  - 7% below Marsco
    - Figures based on independe

Clicking anywhere else in the text box activates an action setting, which may be set to another hyperlink.

Action Settings

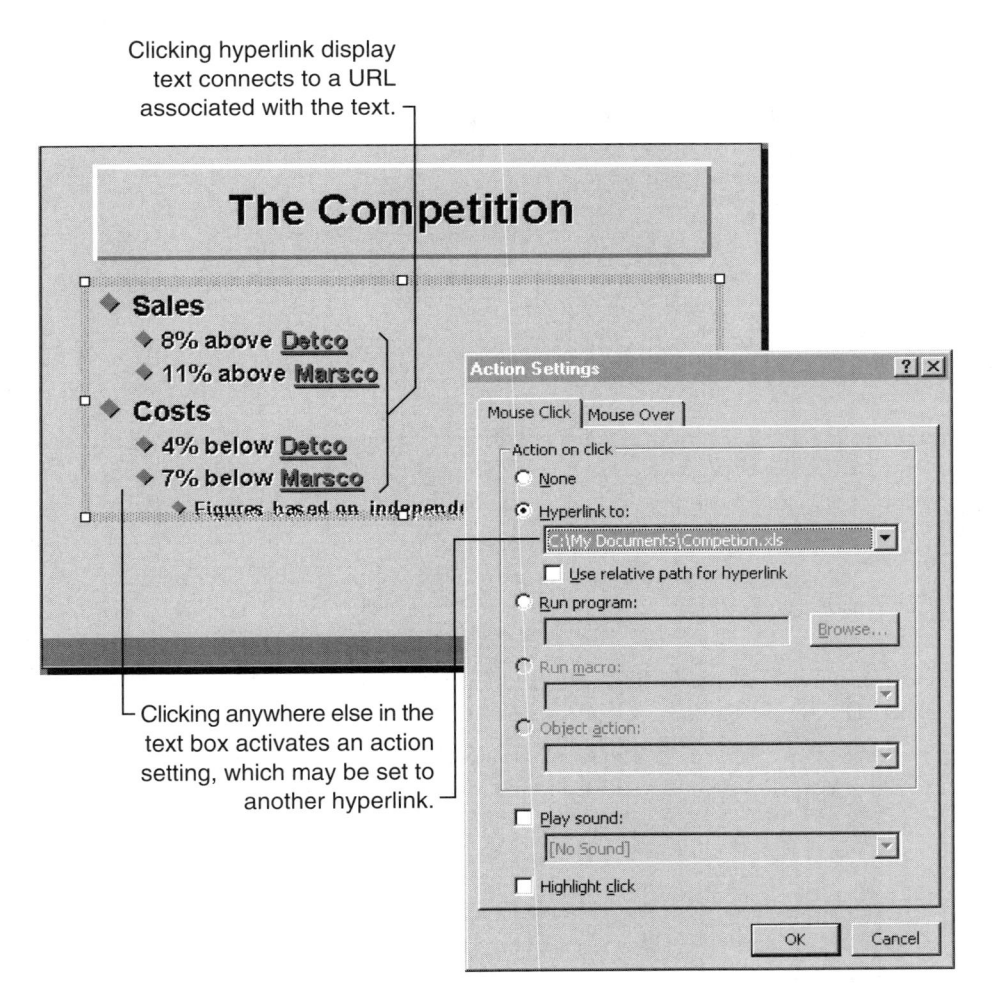

Mouse Click | Mouse Over

Action on click
- None
- Hyperlink to:
  C:\My Documents\Competion.xls
  ☐ Use relative path for hyperlink
- Run program:
  [   ] Browse...
- Run macro:
- Object action:

☐ Play sound:
  [No Sound]
☐ Highlight click

OK   Cancel

Note Although you cannot assign a hyperlink to grouped objects, you can group objects with hyperlinks attached to them.

PowerPoint uses two of the three accent colors in the current color scheme to format hyperlink display text. A hyperlink appears in the first color until you click it; then it appears in the second color. For more information about color schemes, see Chapter 38, "Microsoft PowerPoint Architecture." For more information about hyperlinks, see "Creating Hyperlinks in Office Documents" in Chapter 24, "Integrating Microsoft Office with Your Intranet."

Creating Web Documents

PowerPoint 97 includes new templates and an enhanced AutoContent Wizard to help you create Web documents easily. You can use the online templates to create a home page, an electronic information kiosk, an online personnel directory, and several other kinds of online documents.

To use a template for creating an online document, look for templates with (Online) in their names—for example, Business Plan (Online). The online templates contain graphic elements, such as buttons, bullets and backgrounds, and other objects tailored for using and viewing presentations online.

For information about customizing the templates used by the AutoContent Wizard, see "How You Can Customize PowerPoint" in Chapter 38, "Microsoft PowerPoint Architecture."

Saving Presentations as HTML Documents

By saving your presentation in HTML, you make it possible for anyone with a Web browser to view it. PowerPoint comes with many templates designed for creating Web documents, but you are not restricted to these. You can save any presentation in HTML.

▶ **To save a presentation in HTML**

1 On the **File** menu, click **Save as HTML**.
2 Follow the instructions in the Save as HTML Wizard.

The Save as HTML Wizard prompts you to specify a folder in which to store the HTML files it creates. After the wizard stores the HTML files in this folder, you can move them to your Web site and connect them to existing Web pages.

The Save as HTML Wizard uses a set of templates to build HTML files from your presentation. If you are familiar with HTML tags, you can modify these templates (TPL files) by opening them in a text editor (such as Notepad) and modifying the HTML code created by the wizard.

Note Before you modify the HTML templates, it is a good idea to make backup copies of the original TPL files.

Using Microsoft PowerPoint Animation Player for ActiveX

The Microsoft PowerPoint Animation Player is a PowerPoint add-in that you use with your Web browser to play animated PowerPoint presentations. The Animation Player is similar to the PowerPoint Viewer, which you can use to view a presentation; but unlike the viewer, the PowerPoint Animation Player integrates with your browser to play presentations over the Internet or an intranet in real time.

For users to play a PowerPoint animation over the Internet or an intranet, they must have Microsoft Internet Explorer version 2.0 or later or Netscape Navigator version 1.22 or later installed on their computers, and they must install the Microsoft PowerPoint Animation Player.

Tools and Utilities The Office Resource Kit Tools and Utilities include the Microsoft PowerPoint Animation Player. For information about installing and using the Animation Player, see "PowerPoint Animation Player" in Appendix A, "Microsoft Office 97 Resource Kit Tools and Utilities."

If you want colleagues on the Internet to view your presentation online, you must first save the presentation as a PowerPoint animation.

▶ **To save a presentation as a PowerPoint animation**

1. On the **File** menu, click **Save as HTML**.
2. In the **Graphic type** panel of the Save as HTML Wizard, click the **PowerPoint animation** option.
3. Follow the instructions in the Save as HTML Wizard.

The Save as HTML Wizard prompts you to specify a folder in which to store the PowerPoint animation (PPZ) file and the HTML file it creates. You use the HTML file to gain access to the PowerPoint animation file from a Web browser. If you are familiar with HTML scripting, you can open this file and edit it to get the results you want. To see how your PowerPoint animation looks, open it in your Web browser.

▶ **To view a PowerPoint animation**

- Double-click the HTML file that corresponds to the PowerPoint animation file.

  In Microsoft Internet Explorer 3.0 or Netscape Navigator version 2.0 or later, the PowerPoint animation plays directly in your Web browser.

  In Microsoft Internet Explorer 2.0 or Netscape Navigator 1.22, a hyperlink to the PowerPoint animation is displayed; click the hyperlink to play the animation.

When you are ready to publish the presentation on the Web, copy both the PPZ file and the HTML file to a folder on the server. You must also set up the Web server so that it supports PowerPoint animations.

To add a PowerPoint animation to your Web site

1. Copy the PPZ and HTML files created by the Save as HTML Wizard to a folder on the Web server.
2. Add a hyperlink from an existing Web page to the new HTML file.

Tip You can also use FrontPage to add a PowerPoint animation to your Web site. For information about FrontPage, see "Tools for Intranet Creation and Administration" in Chapter 24, "Integrating Microsoft Office with Your Intranet."

The procedure for setting up the Web server depends on the browser you want to support and the software on the server. If users are viewing Web documents with Netscape Navigator 2.0 or later, configure the Web server to send the PowerPoint animation files as a special type of file to avoid having users receive the message "Netscape was unable to find a plug-in for application/octet-stream." Add the following Multipurpose Internet Mail Extensions (MIME) mapping to the server.

For this PowerPoint file type	Add this MIME mapping
PPT	application/mspowerpoint
PPZ	application/mspowerpoint
PPS	application/mspowerpoint
POT	application/mspowerpoint

If you are using the Microsoft Internet Information Server (IIS), set up the Web server to support PowerPoint animations by modifying the Windows registry. In the registry key **HKEY_LOCAL_MACHINE\System\CurrentControlSet\Services\InetInfo \Parameters\MimeMap**, add the following value entries:

- "application/ms-powerpoint,ppt,,5"=""
- "application/ms-powerpoint,ppz,,5"=""
- "application/ms-powerpoint,pps,,5"=""
- "application/ms-powerpoint,pot,,5"=""

For more information about MIME mapping, consult the documentation for the server you are using. For more information about the PowerPoint Animation Player, point to **Microsoft on the Web** on the PowerPoint **Help** menu, and click **Product News** (requires Internet access).

Using PowerPoint Central

In Windows, you can click **PowerPoint Central** (**Tools** menu) to open a special presentation that contains hyperlinks to Internet sites and the Office 97 Value Pack. PowerPoint Central is included when you choose a Typical installation during Setup.

Note The CD-ROM version of Office includes the Office 97 Value Pack, a collection of application extras such as clip art, maps, sounds, presentation enhancements, and utilities. For more information about the Office 97 Value Pack and how to use its contents, see the Help file Valupack.hlp in the ValuPack folder on the Office CD. If you have Web access, you can also point to **Microsoft on the Web** (**Help** menu) in any Office application and then click **Free Stuff**.

The initial slide in the PowerPoint Central presentation provides a main menu from which you can go to the Internet or the Value Pack for clip art, videos, sound clips, graphic effects, templates, tips and hints, how-to information, and an updated version of the PowerPoint Central presentation itself.

If the PowerPoint Central presentation works well for your organization, you can create your own similar presentation. For example, you could create a PowerPoint presentation that links users to corporate information, files, and other resources on the Internet or an intranet. You could then create a macro or add-in that adds a command to PowerPoint for running the presentation. For information about customizing PowerPoint with macros and add-ins, see "How You Can Customize PowerPoint" in Chapter 38, "Microsoft PowerPoint Architecture."

Web Support in Microsoft Word 97

Word supports the Office-wide Web features, such as hyperlinks and the **Web** toolbar. In addition, Word includes HTML authoring tools for creating Web pages.

The main benefit of using Word as an HTML authoring tool is that you can use your existing knowledge of Word and most of the features in Word immediately, without ever viewing HTML code directly. Detailed information about using the HTML authoring features in Word is included in **Microsoft Word Help** (**Help** menu).

There are several ways to use Word to create Web pages in HTML.

If you want to	Use this method
Create one of several predefined HTML documents such as a form or personal home page	Use the Web Page Wizard
Create an HTML document other than those supported by the Web Page Wizard	Use the Blank Web Page template
Convert one or more existing Word documents to HTML	Save in HTML

Each of these methods is described in the following sections.

Using the Web Page Wizard

Use the Web Page Wizard to create predefined Web pages, such as multicolumn pages, forms, or personal home pages. The Web Page Wizard offers a variety of text formats and graphic images for each type of Web page it supports. After you have created the Web page, use the Word HTML authoring tools to modify it.

Tip In addition to using the Web Page Wizard to create a predefined Web page, you can also use the wizard as a starting point for other Web pages. For example, you can create a multicolumn Web page, and then paste the table portion of the HTML code into another Web page.

▶ **To start the Web Page Wizard**

1 On the **File** menu, click **New**.
2 Click the **Web Pages** tab, and then double-click **Web Page Wizard**.
3 Follow the instructions that appear on your screen.

Note The Web Page Wizard is not installed when you choose the Typical installation during Setup. To install the wizard, rerun Setup, click **Add/Remove**, and select the **Web Page Authoring (HTML)** option.

Using the Blank Web Page Template

When you create a blank Web page, Word attaches the HTML template to a blank document.

▶ **To create a blank Web page**

1 On the **File** menu, click **New**.
2 Click the **Web Pages** tab, and then double-click **Blank Web Page**.

Saving Existing Documents in HTML

If you want to convert an existing Word document to HTML, use the **Save as HTML** command (**File** menu).

▶ **To convert a Word document to HTML**

1 Open the document you want to convert.
2 On the **File** menu, click **Save as HTML**.
3 In the **Save as HTML** dialog box, enter a file name.
4 Make sure **HTML Document** appears in the **Save as type** box, and then click **Save**.

Note Not all Word document elements and formatting are supported in HTML. Some elements and formatting are lost when you save a Word document in HTML. For example, comments inserted with the **Comments** command (**Insert** menu) are lost when you save in HTML. For the complete list of lost or changed elements, see Word online Help.

After you save a Word document in HTML, you can preview it in your Web browser by clicking the **Web Page Preview** button (**Standard** toolbar).

Tip After you convert Office documents to HTML, you can use the Web Publishing Wizard to help you post your content to the Web or to an intranet. For more information about posting to the Web, see "Publishing to the Web or an Intranet" in Chapter 24, "Integrating Microsoft Office with Your Intranet."

CHAPTER 26

Finding Microsoft Office Documents on the Network

This chapter tells you how to use and support the Microsoft Find Fast and Web Find Fast document indexing and searching tools to locate Microsoft Office documents (including HTML documents) on local or network drives, or on your intranet.

In This Chapter
Overview   717
Supporting Find Fast   729
Supporting Web Find Fast   733

Overview

Office 97 includes two tools that help make Office documents on local or network drives easier for your workgroup to find: Find Fast and Web Find Fast. With both of these tools, the Find Fast indexing engine indexes Office documents, as well as other document types such as Hypertext Markup Language (HTML) documents. End users can then search this index file for specific words, phrases, or document properties.

- Use Find Fast to index local or network drives (Windows only). Then users can search the indexes through the **Open** dialog box (**File** menu) of Microsoft Access, Microsoft Excel, Microsoft PowerPoint, Microsoft Word, Office Binder, and Microsoft Project, or through the **Find Items** command (**Tools** menu) of Microsoft Outlook.

- Use Web Find Fast to index shared folders or drives on Windows NT Server or Windows NT Workstation computers configured as Web servers. Then users can search the indexes through Web browsers on Windows or Macintosh client computers on your intranet.

Differences Between Find Fast and Web Find Fast

Depending on your workgroup's network environment, you may find both Find Fast and Web Find Fast to be useful. This section describes the architectural and administrator differences between the two tools.

Note In this section, the term *Find Fast* refers to searching through the **Open** dialog box (**File** menu) of Microsoft Access, Microsoft Excel, PowerPoint, Word, Office Binder, and Microsoft Project, or through the **Find Items** command (**Tools** menu) of Outlook.

System Requirements

From an administrator's perspective, the main difference between Find Fast and Web Find Fast is the computer environment on which they run:

- Indexing and searching with Find Fast work on any computer running the Windows 95 or Windows NT operating system.

- Indexing with Web Find Fast requires a Windows NT Server or Windows NT Workstation computer configured as a Web server with software such as Microsoft Internet Information Server (IIS). Searching requires a Web browser on a Windows or Macintosh client computer. For more information about Web Find Fast system requirements, see "Supporting Web Find Fast" later in this chapter.

Note If you are using Windows NT Workstation, make sure you do not violate the connection license agreement with your HTTP server.

Index Structure

Both Find Fast and Web Find Fast make use of index files created by the Find Fast indexing engine. However, the two searching methods differ in other ways.

When users search for documents with Find Fast, they specify a default start location for the search. For example, in the following illustration, the folder My Documents is the default start location.

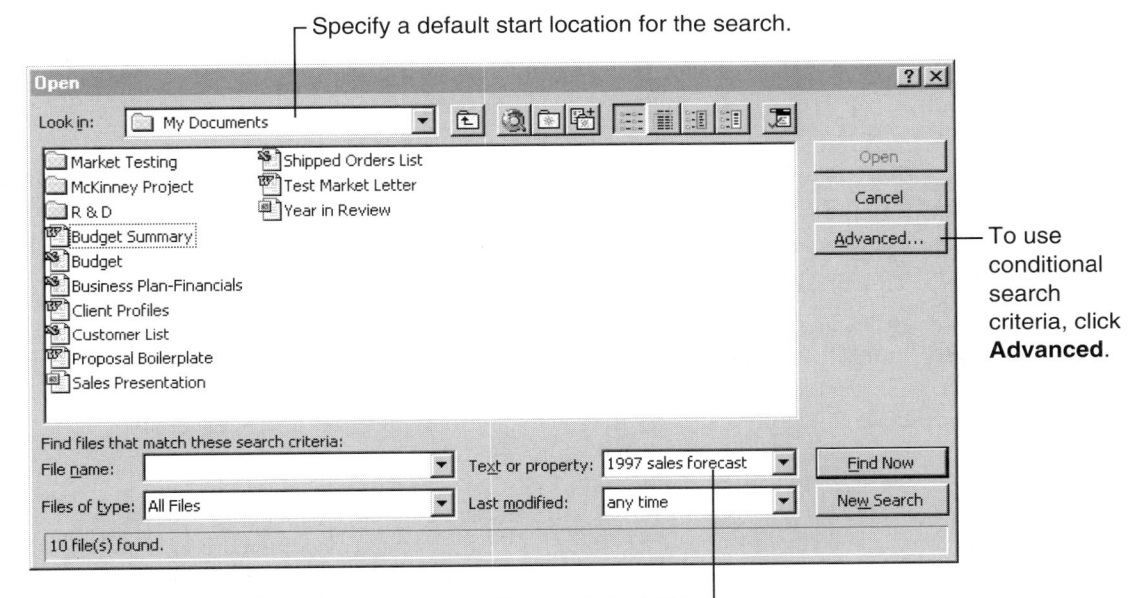

Specify a default start location for the search.

*To use conditional search criteria, click **Advanced**.*

Enter the words or phrases you want to search for here.

Find Fast looks for an index file in the My Documents folder. If it does not find one there, it looks up the folder tree, all the way to the root of the drive. Find Fast uses any index file it finds in or above the default start location in the search.

Tip In the **Advanced Find** dialog box, you can specify more complex search criteria using **AND** and **OR** conditional values. To display the dialog box, click **Open** on the **File** menu of any Office application, and then click **Advanced**. For more information about using search criteria in the **Advanced Find** dialog box, see online Help.

If you select the **Search subfolders** check box in the **Advanced Find** dialog box, Find Fast also looks for index files down the folder tree, below the default start location of the search. In the following example, if the nested subfolder Market Testing had been indexed, Find Fast would use that index to speed up the search for that subfolder.

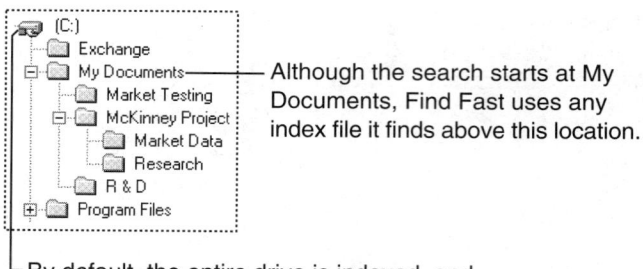

```
(C:)
  Exchange
  My Documents ──────── Although the search starts at My
    Market Testing       Documents, Find Fast uses any
    McKinney Project     index file it finds above this location.
      Market Data
      Research
    R & D
  Program Files
```
By default, the entire drive is indexed, and the index file resides at the root of the drive.

Searching with Web Find Fast uses a different approach. In this case the user submits a search query from an HTML page (Query.htm, for example) in a Web browser on a client computer on the intranet, and Web Find Fast processes the query on a Web server computer. The query page is linked to a specific Find Fast index, and only that index is searched. You must specify the index on the query page by editing its HTML code in a text editor. For more information, see "Supporting Web Find Fast" later in this chapter.

Unlike an index created with Find Fast, a Web Find Fast index can include multiple disjointed folders or drives on the same Web server, plus additional shared folders or network drives on other computers on the network. You can think of a Web Find Fast index as consisting of at least two components: the base index component of the Web server on which the index file resides, and additional index components that cover additional shared folders or drives on the network.

As mentioned earlier, the formats of the index files used by Find Fast and Web Find Fast are identical. If Find Fast encounters an index created by Web Find Fast, Find Fast searches the base index component of that index file.

Accuracy of Index Search Results

Another distinction between Find Fast and Web Find Fast searches is that Find Fast results are potentially more accurate. Find Fast returns search results based on the index files it finds, but then performs an additional accuracy check. Find Fast compares the last modified date of the indexed documents as recorded in the index with the actual last modified dates of the documents. Wherever Find Fast finds differences in those dates, it performs a *brute force* search of the document in question (Find Fast compares the search criteria to the document content directly) and updates the search results if necessary.

Web Find Fast, on the other hand, relies solely on the index to which it is linked. If that index is out of date, the search results are similarly out of date.

User Interface

For the end user, the most obvious difference between Find Fast and Web Find Fast is the interface.

- The user initiates a Find Fast search through the **Open** dialog box (**File** menu) of Microsoft Access, Microsoft Excel, PowerPoint, Word, Office Binder, and Microsoft Project, or through the **Find Items** command (**Tools** menu) of Outlook.

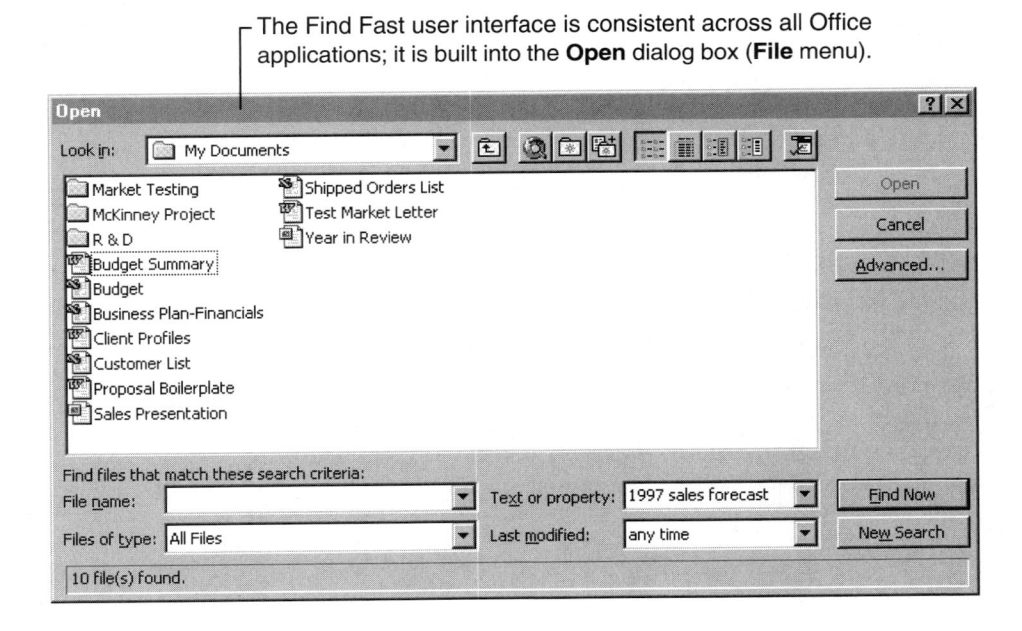

The Find Fast user interface is consistent across all Office applications; it is built into the **Open** dialog box (**File** menu).

- The user initiates a Web Find Fast search through an HTML query page in a Web browser.

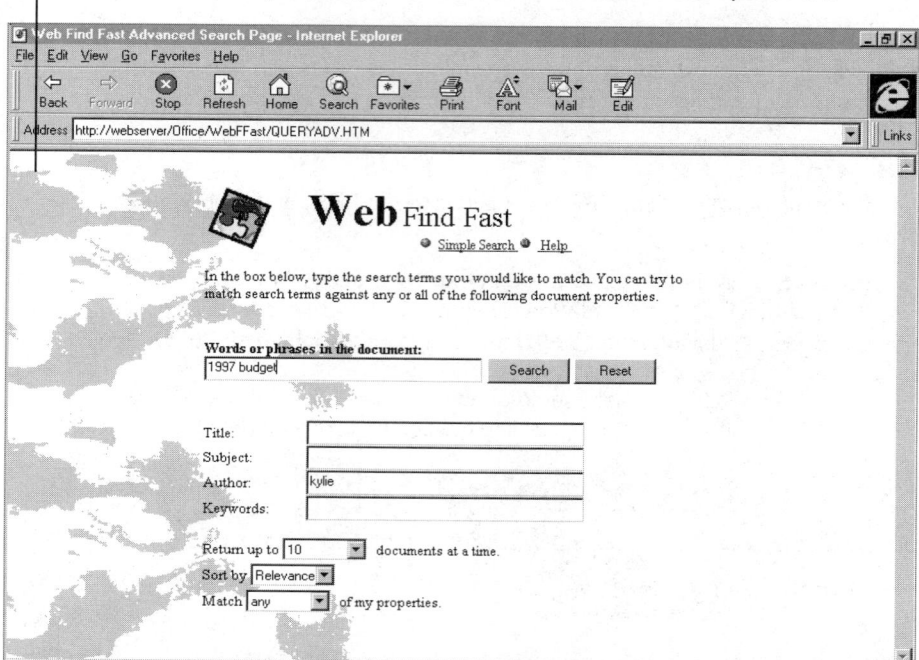

Here the advanced query page is shown in Microsoft Internet Explorer 3.0.

As mentioned earlier, each Web Find Fast query page is connected by HTML code to a specific Web Find Fast index on a Web server. If you index multiple Web servers, you can connect each index to a query page, or you can customize a singe query page so that users can select the index they want searched. For more information, see "Supporting Web Find Fast" later in this chapter.

Summary of Differences

The similarities and differences between these methods of finding documents are summarized in the following table.

Issue	Find Fast	Web Find Fast
Location of index	Local or network drive	Web server running on Windows NT Server or Windows NT Workstation.
Scope of indexing	A single index includes only folders in and below the location at which the index file itself resides on the local or network drive.	A single index includes not only folders in and below the location at which the index file itself resides on the Web server, but also other folders on the Web server or other network drives.
End-user interface	**Open** dialog box (**File** menu) of Microsoft Access, Microsoft Excel, PowerPoint, Word, Office Binder, and Microsoft Project, or the **Find Items** command (**Tools** menu) of Outlook.	Query page in a Web browser.
Administrator interface	Find Fast control panel.	Find Fast NT control panel on the Web server; remote administration page in a Web browser.
Supports phrase searching	Yes.	Yes.
Supports searching by document properties	Yes.	Yes, as specified in the query page HTML code.
Supports relevance ranking	No.	Yes.
Requires Web server software such as Microsoft Internet Information Server (IIS)	No.	Yes; for more information about system requirements, see "Supporting Web Find Fast" later in this chapter.

The remainder of this section describes issues that apply to both Find Fast and Web Find Fast.

What Types of Documents Can Be Indexed

You can specify the file types to be indexed only when you create an index. You cannot change the indexed file types for an existing index; you must delete the index, and then recreate it.

▶ **To specify the file types to be indexed**

1. On the Windows 95 or Windows NT Workstation version 4.0 **Start** menu, point to **Settings**, and then click **Control Panel**.

   –or–

   In Windows NT Workstation version 3.51, double-click Control Panel in the Main group in Program Manager.

2. Double-click **Find Fast**.
3. On the **Index** menu, click **Create Index**.
4. Under **In and Below**, select the drive or folder that contains the documents you want indexed.

   This location is also where the index files are stored.

5. In the **Of type** box, select the file types you want indexed.

When you specify the type of documents to be indexed in the **Create Index** dialog box, Find Fast includes the document types described in the following table.

This document type	Includes documents with these extensions
Office	All the Microsoft Excel, PowerPoint, Microsoft Project, and Word document types listed in this table, plus binders and Microsoft Access .odb, .obt, and .mdb documents (although only document properties in .mdb documents are indexed).
Microsoft Excel	.xl* (workbooks)
PowerPoint	.ppt (presentations), .pot (templates), .pps (auto-running presentations)
Microsoft Project	.mpp, .mpw, .mpt, .mpx, .mpd (Microsoft Project files)
Word	.doc (documents), .dot (templates), .ht* (HTML documents), .txt (text files), .rtf (Rich Text Format files)
All Files	*.*

Note When you select **All Files** in the **Create Index** dialog box, Find Fast does not index file types that do not have textual content, such as BMP, COM or EXE files. For more information about excluded file types, see "File Types That Are Not Indexed" later in this chapter.

In addition to the Office document types listed in the preceding table, Find Fast can index the following document types if their installed conversion filters support minimal RTF mode:

- Lotus 1-2-3 version 2.x–4.0
- RFT-DCA
- Microsoft Works version 3.x for Windows
- Word version 4.x–5.x for the Macintosh
- Works version 4.0 for Windows
- WordPerfect version 5.x
- WordPerfect version 6.x
- WordStar

You can determine whether the filters you have installed support minimal RTF mode by examining the Windows registry. In the registry, view the key **HKEY_LOCAL_MACHINE\SOFTWARE\Microsoft\Shared Tools \Text Converters\Import**

Each filter listed that includes a subkey named **NoDialogs** should support minimal RTF mode and therefore can be used by Find Fast.

Find Fast indexes other document types using its own internal text filters. In all cases, however, words more than 40 characters in length are not indexed.

File Types That Are Not Indexed

Some file types, such as applications (EXE) and pictures (BMP), do not contain meaningful words that Find Fast can index. These file types are referred to as *excluded file types*. Even if you specify to index all files when you create an index, Find Fast ignores files of the types that appear on its excluded file type list to minimize the size of the index files.

The following table lists the excluded file types.

These file types are not indexed by Find Fast

.386	.ffa	.olb
.acl	.ffl	.par
.act	.ffo	.pcs
.ani	.ffx	.pdb
.avi	.flt	.ps
.au	.fon	.pst
.bin	.gid	.scr
.bmp	.gif	.seq

These file types are not indexed by Find Fast

.cab	.hlp	.sys
.cat	.icm	.tar
.cgm	.ico	.tif
.chk	.jpeg	.ttc
.com	.jpg	.ttf
.cnv	.lex	.url
.cpl	.map	.vbx
.cur	.mmf	.vxd
.dll	.mov	.wav
.drv	.nls	.wmf
.dic	.nsf	.xab
.eps	.obj	.z
.exe	.ocx	.zip

Note This list is for reference only; you cannot add to the list to prevent Find Fast from attempting to index additional file types.

> ### Indexing FrontPage Webs
> If you want to index a Web site created by Microsoft FrontPage, you can prevent Find Fast from indexing the configuration folders that contain information about the Web site. These folders have names that begin with **_vti** or **private**. To prevent the indexing of these files, locate this registry path on the computer on which you installed Find Fast:
>
> **HKEY_LOCAL_MACHINE\SOFTWARE\Microsoft\Shared Tools \Find Fast\97**
>
> To this key add the DWORD value **ExcludeFPTemp** and assign it any nonzero value.

Words That Are Not Indexed

Some words, such as *and*, *of*, and *or*, occur frequently in most documents. Because these words are of little value as search words, Find Fast does not index them. Words that are not indexed are referred to as *stop words*.

Stop words have no effect in searches. A search for the phrase **the schedule** is the same as a search for *** and schedule**, so Find Fast looks for any word and **schedule**. A search for **"the schedule"** (enclosed in quotation marks) has the same effect as the search for **"anyword schedule"**: Find Fast looks for any word followed by **schedule**.

Tools and Utilities The Office Resource Kit Tools and Utilities include the complete list of stop words for all languages in the file Stopword.doc. For more information, see "Documentation" in Appendix A, "Microsoft Office 97 Resource Kit Tools and Utilities." Note that this list is for reference only; you cannot add to the list to prevent Find Fast from indexing additional words.

Security Issues

It is usually a more efficient use of disk space, index time, and search time to work with a single large index at the root level of a local or network drive rather than with several smaller indexes. However, large indexes introduce the following access and security concerns:

- When sharing a folder on a local drive where the entire drive is indexed, users who connect to the shared drive do not have access to its index because it resides at a location above the shared folder. Users can still search the shared drive, but the search takes much longer because it does not use an index.

  For example, if you share the folder C:\My Documents\Public as \\Mycomputer\Public, and you have indexed the entire C: drive, users who connect to \\Mycomputer\Public cannot use the index because they do not have access to the root of the C drive. To provide users with an index of \\Mycomputer\Public, remove the index of C: and create an index of C:\My Documents\Public through the Find Fast control panel.

- When you are supporting remote users, make sure that they have read permission for all documents included in the index.

  Potentially, anyone with access to an index can run word association queries and determine that a certain document contains certain words—even if that user does not have read permission for the document itself. For that reason, all users with access to the index should also have read permission for the documents.

Indexing and Password-Protected Documents

Find Fast does not index documents that have been password-protected by Office applications, because they are encrypted and therefore not searchable. Any references to document properties or content in password-protected documents are not included in the index. If Find Fast finds a password-protected document when creating an index, an entry is made in the Find Fast indexer log, Ffastlog.txt.

For more information about Office password protection, see "Security Features in Office" in Chapter 34, "Microsoft Office Architecture."

The Find Fast Indexer Log

The Find Fast indexer log is a text file in which Find Fast enters summaries of indexing tasks. The indexer log is named Ffastlog.txt and is stored in the Windows\System or System32 folder as a hidden file. Indexer log entries include completed or failed index creation and updating, and the names of files that could not be indexed (password-protected documents, for example).

Indexing task entries are ordered so that the most recent events appear at the end of the file. The indexer log is limited in size to 24K. When the file exceeds 24K, the oldest entries are deleted.

▶ **To view the indexer log**

1. On the Windows 95 or Windows NT Workstation 4.0 **Start** menu, point to **Settings**, and then click **Control Panel**.

   –or–

   In Windows NT Workstation 3.51, double-click Control Panel in the Main group in Program Manager.

2. Double-click **Find Fast**.
3. On the **Index** menu, click **Show Indexer Log**.

Tip You can prevent the indexer log from being truncated at 24K. Change the command-line arguments in the shortcut to Find Fast in the Startup folder: Add a **/v** at the end of the line. Or, if you are using Web Find Fast, add a registry value of any type named **verbose** to the key **HKEY_LOCAL_MACHINE\SOFTWARE\Microsoft\Shared Tools\Find Fast\97**. Do not assign any data to the value. When you use this technique, the indexer log is not truncated. You should truncate it manually from time to time, however, to conserve disk space.

What Happens to Office 95 Indexes in Office 97

The file formats for Find Fast 97 and Find Fast 95 differ. An index created by Find Fast 97 cannot be used by Office 95 applications.

When Find Fast is installed with Office 97, it immediately locates all indexes created by Find Fast 95. Those indexes are automatically deleted and replaced by Find Fast 97 indexes with identical index scope and settings. After you upgrade to Office 97, you can create additional indexes as well. If you create a Find Fast 97 index that is above, below, or at the same location as a Find Fast 95 index in a folder hierarchy, Find Fast 97 prompts you to delete the older index and replace it with a new index.

Supporting Find Fast

This section describes how the Find Fast indexing engine and search interface work with local or network drives. Unless otherwise noted, references to Windows include computers running the Windows 95 or Windows NT operating system.

Installing Find Fast

Find Fast is installed during Setup when you choose a Typical installation. When Find Fast is installed, it automatically indexes all Office documents on each local drive in the computer on which it was installed. If you install Find Fast on a network drive, however, you must manually start index creation through the Find Fast control panel.

Creating and Maintaining Indexes with Find Fast

You can open the Find Fast control panel to create additional indexes (for example, on a network drive), delete indexes, and set other options. In general, however, Find Fast indexes Office documents automatically and requires no end-user action.

By default, Find Fast creates a single index on each hard drive on your computer. (Find Fast does not automatically index removable drives.) However, you may want to create multiple indexes on a single drive (especially on shared or network drives). You can do so, although you cannot create indexes that overlap. For example, if you have a Find Fast index of the drive C:, you cannot then create an additional index of the folder C:\My Documents. To create an index of C:\My Documents, you must first delete the index of the drive C: through the Find Fast control panel.

> **Should I index the entire drive or just the folder?**
>
> The following are examples of when you might be better off creating multiple indexes on a single drive, rather than one large index:
>
> - When sharing a folder on a local drive
>
>   If the entire drive is indexed, users who connect to the shared drive do not have access to its index because it resides at a location above the shared folder. By creating an index specifically for the shared folder (and its nested subfolders), you allow users who connect to the shared folder to search its index. For an example of this situation, see "Security Issues" earlier in this chapter.
>
> - When maintaining multiple folders on a network drive
>
>   If your organization's relevant documents are concentrated in a few folders on a network drive, you can index just those folders. For example, if one folder contains documents intended for public viewing, and other folders are intended for private use or storage by individuals, you could index just the folder intended for public viewing.

Locating Index Files

Find Fast index files are located at the topmost level of the hierarchy of the indexed folders. For example, if you index an entire drive, the index file is located at the root of that drive. Find Fast index files are hidden files with the base name of Ffastun and the following extensions.

This index file extension	Indicates this type of file
.ffl	Document list
.ffx	Index
.ffo	Cache of document properties such as Author and Title
.ffa	Status file

Because you create and maintain index files through the Find Fast control panel, you do not normally need to work with these files directly. Do not attempt to copy, move, or change the attributes of these file types. If you need to delete or move a set of indexed folders, delete the index first through the Find Fast control panel, and then recreate the index after you move the folders.

The index files typically require about 7 percent of the space of the text component of the documents they index, or about 1 percent to 3 percent of the total document size.

Using Startup Switches for Find Fast Troubleshooting

In some circumstances you may want to start Find Fast in a special mode. You can do so with the following startup switches. You can use startup switches only when Find Fast is not already running. You can add a switch to the Find Fast shortcut in the Startup folder and then restart your computer, or you can close Find Fast by selecting the **Close and Stop** command (**Index** menu) in the Find Fast control panel and then restart Find Fast with a startup switch.

Note These startup switches are supported by Find Fast only. Do not attempt to use startup switches with Web Find Fast.

▶ **To run Find Fast with a startup switch**

1 In Windows 95 or Windows NT Workstation 4.0, click **Start**, and then click **Run**.

   –or–

   In Windows NT Workstation 3.51, click **Run** on the Program Manager **File** menu.

2 Type the path and name of the Find Fast program, followed by the startup switch you want.

   For example, to run Find Fast in verbose mode, type **"C: \Program Files \Microsoft Office\Office\Findfast /v"** (if the path includes spaces in folder names, you must enclose the entire path in quotation marks, as shown here).

Tip In addition to running these startup switches at the command prompt, you can add them to the Find Fast shortcut in your Startup group, so that Find Fast starts with the switches you specify each time your computer starts.

The startup switches available include the following.

This startup switch	Has this effect
/u *folder name* where *folder name* is the path and name of a folder	Starts Find Fast, updates the index in this folder, and then closes Find Fast. Do not combine this switch with other switches.
/v	Runs the Find Fast log file in verbose mode, so that it is not automatically truncated at 24K.
/showui	Displays the Find Fast user interface.

Finding Documents with Find Fast

Document searching functionality is built into the **Open** dialog box (**File** menu) of Microsoft Access, Microsoft Excel, PowerPoint, Word, Office Binder, and Microsoft Project. The **Text or property** box and all controls in the **Advanced Find** dialog box (viewable by clicking the **Advanced** button in the **Open** dialog box) rely on indexes created by Find Fast.

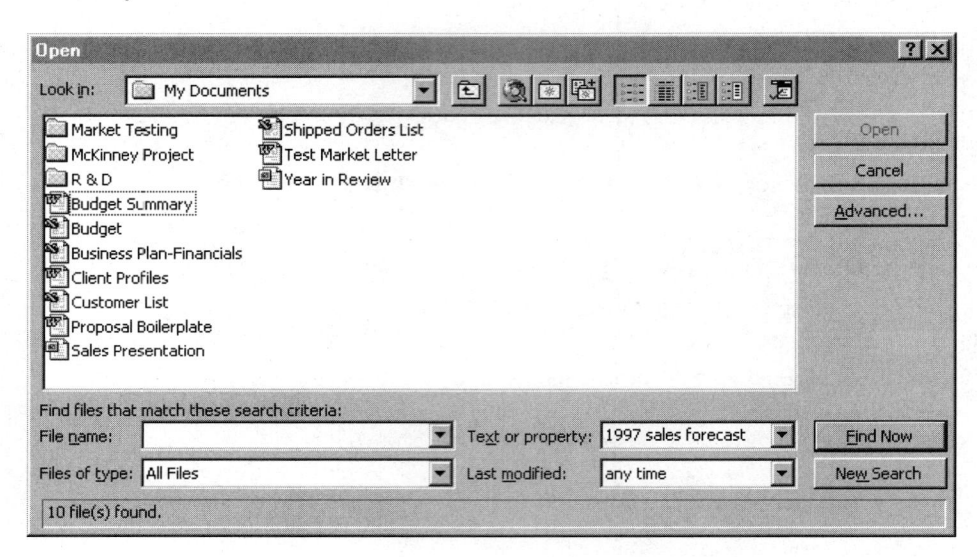

In Outlook, this functionality is viewable by clicking the **Advanced** tab in the **Find** dialog box (**Tools** menu).

If users attempt to search a folder or drive that has not been indexed, they can still enter search criteria into the **Text or property** box or the **Advanced Find** dialog box; however, these searches take much longer to execute because each file needs to be compared against the search criteria individually.

Tip You can search multiple folders or drives simultaneously through the **Advanced Find** dialog box. In the **Look in** box, select the first drive or folder you want searched. Then enter additional drive or folder names separated by a semicolon. For example, if you enter **C:\My Documents;D:\;E:\Public** in the **Look in** box, Find Fast searches the folder My Documents on the C drive, the entire D drive, and the Public folder on the E drive. These drives may be any combination of local or network drives. Note that there are no spaces before or after the semicolons in the string.

Outlook uses the document properties cached in a Find Fast index, if available, when displaying Office documents in table views.

Chapter 26 Finding Microsoft Office Documents on the Network

When you view documents in table view, Outlook uses document properties cached in index files to speed up the display of properties.

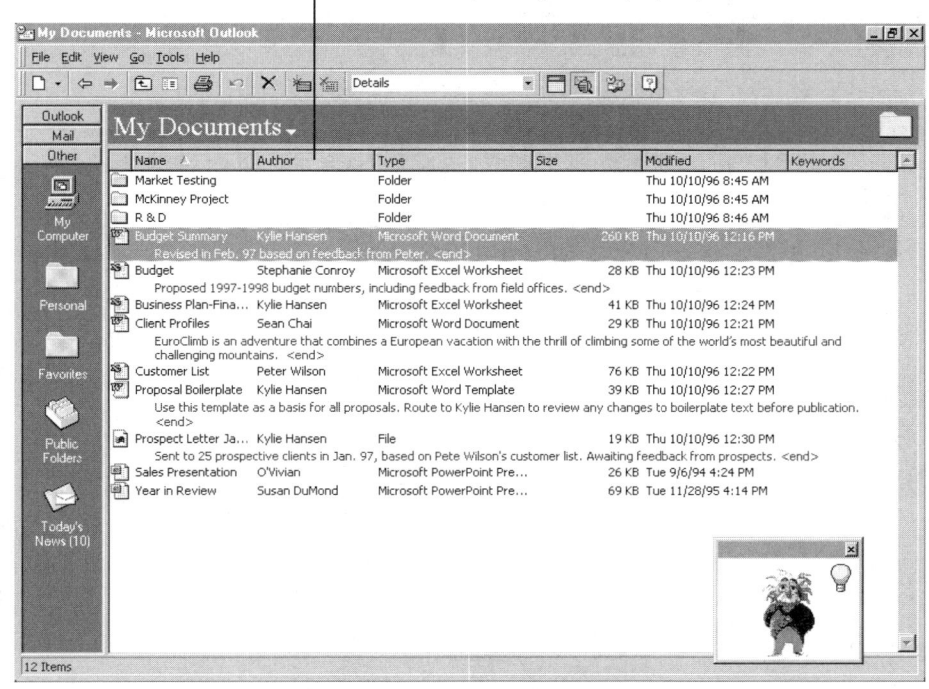

Find Fast caches document properties by default. If document properties caching is turned off, you can turn it on by selecting the **Speed up property display** check box in the **Create Index** dialog box (**Index** menu) of the Find Fast control panel.

Supporting Web Find Fast

This section describes the Web Find Fast tools that are part of the Office Server Pack of utilities.

With Web Find Fast, you can index Office documents on Web servers and network drives or shared folders throughout your intranet. End users can then perform full-text searches of the index for words or phrases, or for specific document properties such as Subject or Author (custom properties are not supported). Users search the index through a Web query page, and the results are returned as a Web page. Clicking the name of a found document opens the document in the appropriate Office application.

There are two ways you can administer Web Find Fast. The first is through the Find Fast NT control panel on your Web server. The second is through the Web Find Fast Administration Tool (a set of HTML files) from any client computer on your intranet.

Microsoft Office 97 Resource Kit   **733**

Web Find Fast without remote administration has the following requirements:

- Windows NT Server 3.51 with Service Pack 5, or Windows NT Server 4.0
- Internet Server API (ISAPI) or CGI-compliant Web server software running on one of the Windows NT operating systems

Note Web Find Fast can be used as an ISAPI DLL under Microsoft Internet Information Server version 1.0 on Windows NT Server 3.51 with Service Pack 5, on Windows NT 4.0 Server or Workstation with Microsoft Internet Information Server version 2.0 or later, or on other Internet servers that support ISAPI.

Web Find Fast with remote administration has the following requirements:

- Windows NT Server 4.0
- An NTFS partition on which to install the Administration Tool files (to enable security)
- Microsoft Internet Information Server 2.0 or later

Web Find Fast includes a CGI wrapper, Webserch.exe, that can be used with several Web servers under the Windows NT operating system. Supported Web servers include the following:

- Microsoft Internet Information Server 1.0 (Windows NT Server 3.51 with Service Pack 5.)
- Microsoft Internet Information Server 2.0 (Windows NT Server 4.0 only).
- Netscape Commerce Server version 1.1 (Windows NT Server 4.0, or Windows NT Server 3.51 with Service Pack 5).
- Netscape Communications Server version 1.1 (Windows NT Server 4.0 and 3.51 with Service Pack 5).
- Netscape Enterprise Server version 2.0 (Windows NT Server 4.0 and 3.51 with Service Pack 5).
- Netscape Fast Track Server (Windows NT Server 4.0 and 3.51 with Service Pack 5).
- IBM Internet Connection Server version 4.1 (Windows NT Server 4.0 and 3.51 with Service Pack 5).
- O'Reilly's Web Site (Windows NT Server 4.0 and 3.51 with Service Pack 5). This server is also ISAPI-compliant and works with Webserch.dll.
- O'Reilly's Web Site Pro (Windows NT Server 4.0 and 3.51 with Service Pack 5). This server is also ISAPI-compliant and works with Webserch.dll.
- Purveyor Encrypt Server version 1.2 (Windows NT Server 4.0 and 3.51 with Service Pack 5).

Note Some Web servers—for example, Netscape Commerce and Netscape Fast Track—do not use the Windows registry to store Multipurpose Internet Mail Extensions (MIME) types but instead store them in other files. This may prevent such Web servers from properly returning Office documents correctly when requested from Web browsers—for example, through a hyperlink or Web Find Fast query. To correct this, you must edit the Mime.types files on your Web server. For more information, see "Netscape Web Server Support" in Chapter 24, "Integrating Microsoft Office with Your Intranet."

Installing Web Find Fast

Web Find Fast must be installed on a Windows NT Server or Windows NT Workstation computer configured as a Web server. If you are installing onto Windows NT Workstation, make sure you do not violate the connection license agreement with your HTTP server.

Tip Before you install Web Find Fast, you should review *drive*:\Srvpack\Readme.txt where *drive* is the letter of the Office Setup CD-ROM drive. The Readme file contains detailed system requirements, installation instructions, and troubleshooting tips.

▶ **To install Web Find Fast**

1   Insert the Office Setup CD into the CD-ROM drive.

2   In Windows NT Server or Windows NT Workstation 4.0, double-click *drive*:\Srvpack\Setup, or click **Run** on the **Start** menu and type *drive***:\Srvpack\Setup.exe** where *drive* is the letter of the CD-ROM drive.

   −or−

   In Windows NT Server or Windows NT Workstation 3.51, double-click *drive*:\Srvpack\Setup, or click **Run** on the Program Manager **File** menu and type *drive***:\Srvpack\Setup.exe** where *drive* is the letter of the CD-ROM drive.

3   When prompted, select the **Web Find Fast** option; do not select **Find Fast, indexer only**.

4   When you are prompted to enter a logon account, select to use the system account if you do not plan to index documents on other servers or shared folders on your network. This option gives the Find Fast service the permissions it needs to create index files on the server on which it is installed and to read all files on the local server (except password-protected documents).

   −or−

   Supply an account that has access permissions for network folders if you plan to add other servers or shared folders on your network to your Web Find Fast index, or if you want to be able to correctly return File URLs in the results set (as opposed to HTTP URLs).

Note When you install Web Find Fast, Find Fast NT does not automatically begin indexing the drive. You must start the Find Fast NT control panel or use the Web Find Fast Administration Tool to create the indexes you want.

Creating and Maintaining Indexes with Web Find Fast

Before users can search a Web Find Fast index, you must create the index and customize the query pages so that they are linked to the index.

▶ **To create a Web Find Fast index**

1. In Control Panel, double-click the Find Fast icon.
2. On the **Index** menu, click **Create Index**.
3. In the **In and Below** box, enter the name of the drive or folder you want to index, or click **Browse** and select a drive or folder. (All of the documents and nested subfolders in the drive or folder are indexed.)

    Tip If you want users to have File access as well as HTTP access to documents on this Web site, enter a universal naming convention (UNC) name in the **Find Fast Browse** dialog box. This UNC must be shared with read access; make sure the account under which you are running the Find Fast NT service has correct logon permissions.

4. In the **Of type** box, select the types of documents you want indexed.

    By default, all Office and HTML documents are indexed.

5. Select or clear any of the following check boxes:
    - **Continue to update automatically**
    - **Speed up property display**
    - **Enable phrase searching**
    - **Include relevance information for Web searching**

    These options are all selected by default. For information about the consequences of disabling any of these options, see "Disabling Index Options" later in this section.

6. Click **Web Options**.
7. In the **Alternate HTTP path** box, enter the HTTP address for the selected path (for example, http://www.company.com/), and then click **Modify**.

    You must be able to reach this HTTP mapping through your browser. If no HTTP URL exists for the selected path, then you must set one up on your Web server.. An HTTP mapping is not necessary if you use the File protocol exclusively.

8 To include HTTP links for returned documents on your results page, click the path for which you want to create an HTTP mapping in the **Index these folders for Web searching** box.

   See your Web server documentation for information about valid HTTP mappings.

9 In the **Friendly Web name for this index** box, enter a unique friendly name for your index.

Note If you want your Web searches to include other Web folders on the same computer or on network shares, you can use the **Web Options** dialog box to add any number of other folders to the index you are creating. Be sure to enter a valid HTTP address that maps to each of these folders, and give the Find Fast NT service an account with permissions to open these folders. Index information for these additional folders is used in Web searching, but not in searching from Outlook or from the **Open** dialog box (**File** menu) in the Office applications.

For more information about creating an index, see *path*\Webadmin\Webadhlp.htm, where *path* is the path to which you installed Web Find Fast on your Web server.

Disabling Index Options

When you create an index, you can choose to disable some of the indexing options supported by Web Find Fast. Doing so may require you to edit the query and results pages, as explained in the following sections.

Speed Up Property Display

If you clear the **Speed up property display** check box, Web Find Fast does not include document properties with search results (although you can still search for document properties).

If you disable this option, you should modify the Query.htm and Queryadv.htm files on your Web server, which by default specify that all properties should be returned. Edit this line:

```
<INPUT TYPE = "hidden" NAME = "Properties" VALUE = "TTTTTTTTTT">
```

Each **T** (TRUE) in this string indicates that a document property should be returned. Change the **T** to an **F** (FALSE) for the property you do not want returned, using this order:

1. GIF icon
2. Title
3. Author
4. Keywords
5. Subject

6. Date Last Modified
7. Comments
8. Category
9. Size
10. Contents
11. URL

Enable Phrase Searching

If you clear the **Enable phrase searching** check box, you can edit the Query.htm and Queryadv.htm files to alert users that phrase searching is disabled. For example, when phrase searching is disabled, searching for the phrase "*annual budget*" (note the quotation marks) does not return the results users might expect. Web Find Fast returns any documents that contain *annual* and *budget* whether or not the two words are adjacent. If you are indexing a large group of documents, disabling phrase searching can have the unexpected consequence of returning more documents than you would like.

Include Relevance Information for Web Searching

If you clear the **Include relevance information for Web searching** check box, you must change the default sort order to something other than relevance. This is determined by the following line in Query.htm or Queryadv.htm:

```
<INPUT TYPE = "hidden" NAME = "SortBy" VALUE = "Relevance">
```

Replace **"Relevance"** in this string with one of the following values:

- **"Author"**
- **"SavedDate"**
- **"FileName"**
- **"Size"**

Note Changing the default sort order slows searches dramatically.

Linking a Query Page to an Index

For each Web Find Fast index you create, you must customize a query page so that the query page is linked to that index. The query pages Query.htm and Queryadv.htm (which provides advanced searching functionality) are located in the folder you selected for Web files during Setup. These are the query pages that use your Web Find Fast index.

You can edit the HTML source page for the query pages using a text editor (such as Notepad); then save the HTML source file back to Query.htm or Queryadv.htm.

▶ **To link the query page to a specific index**

1 Edit the following line in Query.htm:

    < INPUT TYPE = "hidden" NAME = "Index" VALUE = "_">

   Between the quotation marks following **VALUE =**, insert the friendly name you chose for the index when you created it in the Find Fast NT control panel.

2 Save the HTML source file back to Query.htm.

3 Repeat Steps 1 and 2 for Queryadv.htm.

4 Make sure you have created a valid HTTP address for the query page. (See your Web server documentation.) Read and execute permissions are required. Using this address, you can open the query page in any Web browser.

If you create more than one index, give each index a different name. You can copy Query.htm and Queryadv.htm and then customize them to create any number of query pages to search different indexes. Or you can use more advanced HTML tags such as the **Select** tag to let your users choose among different indexes on a single custom query page. For more information, see *path*\Webadmin\Webadhlp.htm, where *path* is the path to which you installed Web Find Fast on your Web server.

A Windows NT Password Change Does Not Propagate to the Find Fast NT Service

The Web Find Fast component of Find Fast NT requires network access to index documents. To get permission for network access, the Find Fast NT service must be logged on under a user account—normally the administrator's account. When an administrator's password is changed or expires on Windows NT Server or Windows NT Workstation, the Find Fast NT service halts indexing and will not restart at the next system restart. To fix this problem, log on to the Find Fast NT service under the new user account or password, and then restart the service. For more information, see "Changing the Find Fast Service Logon Account" later in this section.

Alternatively, you can run the Find Fast service under an account with a password that never expires. For example, if you are indexing documents only on the Web server, you can run the Find Fast service under the LocalSystem account. This account, under which most services run, has no password. The LocalSystem account does not allow access to any network services, however, so it does not support the indexing of content on other computers or using network names (such as UNC names) for folders.

Using the Web Find Fast Administration Tool

As an alternative to using the Find Fast NT control panel, you can use the Web Find Fast Administration Tool to create, modify, and delete indexes and to perform other administrative tasks. The Web Find Fast Administration Tool is a set of HTML documents that you can open with a Web browser from any client computer on your intranet. To allow for proper security, it is recommended that you install the Web Find Fast Administration Tool files on an NTFS partition during Setup.

In addition to working from a remote client computer, you can also perform these tasks directly on your Web server using the Web Find Fast Administration Tool, or you can perform some of these tasks through the Find Fast NT control panel on your Web server.

▶ **To start the Web Find Fast Administration Tool**

1. On any client computer on your intranet or on the Web server itself, open *path*\Webadmin\Adminwiz1.htm, where *path* is the path to which you installed Web Find Fast on your Web server.

2. Follow the instructions on your screen.

For complete instructions about using the Web Find Fast Administration Tool and customizing the query and results pages, open its Help file in *drive*:\Srvpack \Webadmin\Webadhlp.htm, where *drive* is the letter of the Office Setup CD-ROM drive. To view the Help file after installation, open *path*\Webadmin\Webadhlp.htm, where *path* is the path to which you installed Web Find Fast on your Web server.

To become familiar with the search operators and options available to the Web Find Fast user, you should also review the Help file for the query pages. This Help file is located in *path*\Websrch\Queryhlp.htm, where *path* is the path to which you installed Web Find Fast on your Web server.

Understanding the Web Find Fast Index Structure

Unlike the index files used by Find Fast, Web Find Fast has a more monolithic index structure. With Web Find Fast, you can create a base index of your Web server (or a portion of it) and then add additional index components for other Web servers, network drives, or shared folders.

Depending on the organization of the Office documents on your network, this can be a great advantage over Find Fast searching. As the administrator, you can create a single index file that is tied to a single query page. The single index file can cover the exact range of your Web servers and other drives that you want indexed. Because the scope of the index is determined by the administrator, the end user does not think of searching in terms of drives or folders, but in terms of which query page to use.

One disadvantage of this index structure is that for each index file you create, you must customize a query page to search it. You do so by editing HTML code on the query page. For more information, see the Web Find Fast administrator Help file *path*\Webadmin\Webadhlp.htm, where *path* is the path to which you installed Web Find Fast on your Web server.

Web Find Fast relies solely on the accuracy of its index. Unlike Find Fast, Web Find Fast does not perform brute force checks of documents to verify search results. This results in faster performance of Web Find Fast. You can also control the frequency of updating of the indexes Web Find Fast relies on. To change the frequency of index updates, select the **Update Interval** command (**Index** menu) in the Find Fast NT control panel.

Using Web Find Fast for Web Site Administration
Because Web Find Fast can index HTML documents, you may find Web Find Fast to be a useful tool in managing your Web site (either an intranet or Web site). For example, if you want to locate all occurrences of a hyperlink that you need to correct, you can use Web Find Fast to find the documents that contain the hyperlink.

Changing the Find Fast Service Logon Account

After you install Web Find Fast, you can change the account under which the Find Fast NT service is logged on. For example, if you initially logged the service on under an account that has now expired, you can change the service account to a new account.

▶ **To change the Find Fast NT account**

1 On the Windows 95 or Windows NT Server 4.0 **Start** menu, point to **Settings**, and then click **Control Panel**.

   –or–

   In Windows NT Server 3.51, double-click **Control Panel** in the **Main** group in **Program Manager**.

2 Double-click **Services**.

3 In the **Service** box, select **Microsoft Find Fast Service**.

4 If its status is listed as started, click **Stop**.

5 Click **Startup**.

6 To use the LocalSystem account, select **System Account** under **Log On As**.

   –or–

   To use another account, select **This Account** and enter the account name and password.

7 Click **OK**, and then click **Start** to restart the Microsoft Find Fast service.

Part 5 Using Microsoft Office Throughout Your Organization

Finding Documents with Web Find Fast

The user interface for searching with Web Find Fast is an HTML query page viewable in a Web browser. Web Find Fast includes two query pages, Query.htm and Queryadv.htm:

- Query.htm is a simple search page that supports word and phrase searching.
- Queryadv.htm is a more capable search page that supports not only word and phrase searching but also searching for some document properties (such as Title and Subject) and relevance ranking.

Both query pages allow the user to specify the number of documents to be returned at a time. The advanced query page, Queryadv.htm, is shown in the following illustration.

Enter the words or document properties you want to search for and then click **Search**.

After the user submits a Web Find Fast query, Web Find Fast processes the request and returns a list of the found documents in an HTML document, Results.htm.

Web Find Fast returns the document titles and properties of documents that meet your search criteria. To open a document, click its title.

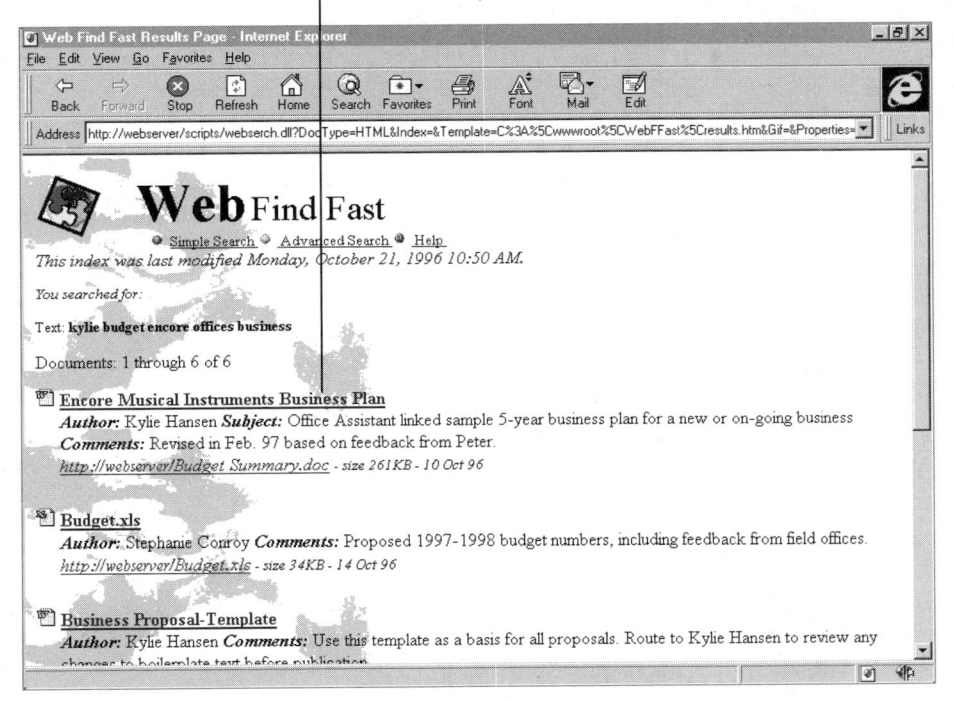

Web Find Fast returns not only the names of the found documents but also other document properties if they are available from the index. Selecting a found document opens it in the appropriate Office application.

The query and results pages are fully customizable. You customize these pages by editing HTML code on the page itself. For more information, see the Web Find Fast administrator Help file *path*\Webadmin\Webadhlp.htm, where *path* is the path to which you installed Web Find Fast on your Web server.

CHAPTER 27

Sharing Information with Microsoft Office Applications

The Office 97 applications support the standard means of exchanging data between applications, such as copying and pasting. In addition, each Office application includes application-specific support for importing and exporting data. This chapter describes these unique features in each Office application.

In This Chapter
Overview   745
Sharing Information with Microsoft Access 97   746
Sharing Information with Microsoft Excel 97   768
Sharing Information with Outlook 97   769
Sharing Information with PowerPoint 97   781
Sharing Information with Word 97   786
Using Microsoft Bookshelf in a Workgroup   790
Using Microsoft Camcorder in a Workgroup   792

See Also
- For information about using Office with an intranet, see Chapter 24, "Integrating Microsoft Office with Your Intranet."
- For information about integrating Office with messaging systems, see Chapter 28, "Working with Messaging Systems and Connectivity Software."

Overview

All Office applications support the following means of copying or linking data:

- Using the **Cut**, **Copy**, and **Paste** commands (**Edit** menu) to paste or link data.
- Using ActiveX and OLE controls based on the Component Object Model (COM).

- Creating hyperlinks between Microsoft Excel, Microsoft PowerPoint, and Microsoft Word documents, as well as hyperlinks to HTML documents.

    For more information about hyperlinks, see "Creating Hyperlinks in Office Documents" in Chapter 24, "Integrating Microsoft Office with Your Intranet."

In addition, each Office application has capabilities for sharing information with other applications. These capabilities are optimized for the purpose of the application and are described in the following sections.

Sharing Information with Microsoft Access 97

Microsoft Access 97 fully supports copying and pasting linked or unlinked data, as described in the "Overview" earlier in this chapter. In addition, Microsoft Access provides a variety of ways to exchange data with other applications and file formats.

Note Microsoft Access is available only with Office 97 for Windows, Professional Edition.

Using External Data with Microsoft Access

Microsoft Access is extremely flexible in its ability to handle data from a variety of sources. External data falls into two categories: Indexed Sequential Access Method (ISAM) and Open Database Connectivity (ODBC). The ISAM data sources are the traditional desktop PC-based database formats. These include Microsoft FoxPro, Paradox, Microsoft Access, and others.

The ODBC data sources are typically Structured Query Language (SQL) server tables, such as Microsoft SQL Server tables; however, Microsoft Access can use other ODBC data sources, as long as a 32-bit Level 1-compliant ODBC driver is installed for that data source.

Importing or Linking Data from External Data Sources

Microsoft Access can either import or link external data. *Importing* reads the external data and creates a new table in the current Microsoft Access database. The original data remains unchanged. *Linking* leaves the external data in its current location and format, and stores a link to that data in the current Microsoft Access database.

When a table from another database is linked, it performs like a native, local table. Users can create queries, forms, and reports that use the external data; combine the external data with the data in Microsoft Access tables; and even view and edit the external data while others are using it in the original application. Use this approach as an alternative to importing if the external data you want to use is also being updated by a database application other than Microsoft Access.

Even if all the data you want to use is in Microsoft Access format, you might find it advantageous to link to external data. By splitting the application (forms, reports, queries, macros, modules, and temporary tables) from the rest of the data, you can ease the support burden of distributing your application. Additionally, network traffic is reduced because forms, reports, and queries are run locally on each workstation instead of across the network.

There are two methods of importing or linking external data:

- Using commands on the **Get External Data** submenu (**File** menu)
- Using Visual Basic for Applications code or macros.

Microsoft Access can import or link data from any of the following external data sources:

- Databases created by applications that use the Microsoft Jet database engine (Microsoft Access, Microsoft Excel, Microsoft Visual Basic, and Microsoft Visual C++)
- ODBC databases such as Microsoft SQL Server version 4.2 or later
- Paradox versions 3.*x*, 4.*x*, and 5.0
- Microsoft FoxPro version 2.*x* (and Microsoft FoxPro version 3.0, import only)
- dBASE III, dBASE III+, dBASE IV, and dBASE 5
- Lotus WKS, WK1, WK3, and WK4 spreadsheets
- Microsoft Excel versions 3.0, 4.0, 5.0, 95, and 97 worksheets
- Delimited text files
- Fixed-width text files
- HTML lists and tables
- Microsoft Exchange Client and Microsoft Outlook data, collectively referred to as Microsoft Windows Messaging Service data. (Linking data in this format is read-only.)

To import or link external data, applications that use the Microsoft Jet database engine use one of several installable ISAM drivers or the Microsoft SQL Server driver. To install most drivers for the external database you want to use, rerun Setup and click **Add/Remove**. Under the **Data Access** option, select the appropriate drivers.

The Paradox, Lotus 1-2-3, and Microsoft Messaging drivers are not installed during Setup. To install these drivers, use the Dataacc.exe program, which is included in the Office 97 Value Pack.

Note The CD-ROM version of Office includes the Office 97 Value Pack, a collection of application extras such as clip art, maps, sounds, presentation enhancements, and utilities. For more information about the Value Pack and how to use its contents, see Valupack.hlp in the ValuPack folder on the Office CD. If you have Web access, you can also point to **Microsoft on the Web** (**Help** menu) in any Office application and then click **Free Stuff**.

The Setup programs for Office 97, Professional Edition, and Microsoft Access supply only one ODBC driver: the Microsoft SQL Server driver. To use ODBC data from another source, you must install a 32-bit version of the appropriate ODBC driver from the vendor of that data format.

Importing and linking Microsoft Windows Messaging Service data are currently possible by using Data Access Objects (DAO) code. For more information about importing and linking Microsoft Windows Messaging Service data using DAO, see "Using Microsoft Windows Messaging Service Data with Microsoft Access" later in this chapter.

Network Access Requirements

To link or directly open an external table on a network, you must be able to connect to the network and have access to the following components:

- The server and share (if applicable) on which the external database is located

    Server and share access are established through network permissions. For information about setting up network permissions, see your network product documentation.

- The external table

    Table access permissions, if they exist, are established using the security features of the external database. Depending on how security has been defined, you might need the appropriate passwords, or you might need to have a network administrator grant you the appropriate permissions to use the external table. For information about setting up access permissions, see your external database product documentation.

When specifying the database name for a database on a network drive, you can do one of the following:

- Specify the network path using the universal naming convention (UNC) format (*server\share\path*), if your network supports it.

- Establish a connection to the network drive first, and then specify the path using the network drive letter.

Performance Guidelines

Although you can use external tables just as you use Microsoft Access tables, it is important to keep in mind that they are not actually in your Microsoft Access database. As a result, each time you view data in an external table, Microsoft Access retrieves records from another file. Performance is optimal if you link tables instead of opening them directly and if you retrieve and view only the data you need. For example, it is a good idea to use restrictive queries to limit the number of returned records, so you do not have to scroll unnecessarily.

For more information about improving performance, see "Optimizing Microsoft Access 97" in Chapter 7, "Customizing and Optimizing Microsoft Office."

Case Sensitivity

Unlike searches on databases that use the Microsoft Jet database engine, searches of external databases may be case-sensitive. However, searches are not case-sensitive in the following instances:

- For Paradox data, if the **CollatingSequence** entry in the **Jet\3.5\Engines\Paradox** key of the Windows registry is set to **International**, **Norwegian-Danish**, or **Swedish-Finnish**
- For FoxPro or dBASE data, if the **CollatingSequence** entry in the **Jet\3.5\Engines\Xbase** key of the Windows registry is set to **International**
- For ODBC data, if the server is configured not to be case-sensitive

In addition, if a search is made across more than one data source type, the case sensitivity depends on the collating sequences of the databases in which the query is stored.

Unsupported Objects and Methods

With the use of Visual Basic code, some DAOs and methods are intended for use only on databases created using the Microsoft Jet database engine, such as databases created by Microsoft Access, Visual Basic, and Microsoft Excel. These DAOs and methods are not supported for use with external databases in other formats.

Unsupported DAOs include:

- **Container**
- **Document**
- **QueryDef**
- **Relation**

Unsupported methods include:

- **CompactDatabase**
- **CreateDatabase**
- **CreateField** (if the table has existing rows)
- **CreateQueryDef**
- **RepairDatabase**

In addition, the following transaction processing methods are supported only if the external database supports transactions:

- **BeginTrans**
- **CommitTrans**
- **Rollback**

Troubleshooting

The following information addresses problems you may encounter when importing from or linking to an external data source.

Connection Problems

If you have trouble connecting to an external data source, check your connection to the network. Make sure you have permission to use:

- The server and share (if applicable) on which the external database is located.
- The external table.

Other things to check include the following:

- Can you connect using another product or a different user account and password?
- Have you exceeded the connection limits on the server?
- Does the server have enough space?
- Does the connection information match the case sensitivity of the server?

If you have checked all these items and you still cannot connect, contact your external database vendor.

Temporary Space

When you query a database, Microsoft Access creates temporary indexes on your hard disk, even if the database is on an external network device. Temporary space requirements can vary from a few thousand bytes to several megabytes, depending on the size of the external tables being queried.

Temporary space is allocated from the folder indicated by the **TEMP** environment variable, typically the Windows\Temp folder. If your system has not defined a **TEMP** environment variable, the current Microsoft Access folder is used. If the **TEMP** environment variable points to an invalid path or if your hard disk does not have sufficient space for these temporary indexes, your application may perform unpredictably if Windows and Microsoft Access run out of resources.

Exporting Data to Other File Formats

Microsoft Access can export data to any of the following file formats:

- ODBC databases such as Microsoft SQL Server 4.2 or later
- Paradox 3.*x*, 4.*x*, and 5.0

- Microsoft FoxPro 2.*x* (and Microsoft FoxPro 3.0, import only)
- dBASE III, dBASE III+, dBASE IV, and dBASE 5
- Lotus WK1 and WK3 spreadsheets
- Microsoft Excel 3.0, 4.0, 5.0, 95, and 97 worksheets
- Delimited text files
- Fixed-width text files
- HTML lists and tables, for table, query, and form datasheets
- HTML documents, for reports
- Internet Database Connector (IDC) files for table, query, and form datasheets
- Active Server Pages (ASP) files for forms and for table, query, and form datasheets
- Word Merge files
- Rich Text Format (RTF) files

Before you can export to some of these formats, you may need to rerun Setup to install one of several ISAM drivers or the Microsoft SQL Server driver. For more information, see "Importing or Linking Data from External Data Sources" earlier in this chapter.

After the appropriate drivers are installed, there are two methods of exporting to other file formats: using the **Save As/Export** command (**File** menu), or using the **OutputTo** method either in Visual Basic code or in macros. For more information about saving in these file formats, see Microsoft Access online Help.

Using Microsoft Access Data in Word

There are four ways you can use Microsoft Access data with Word. You can:

- Export Microsoft Access data to a mail merge data source file that can be used with the mail merge feature of any version of Word.
- Save the output of a datasheet, form, or report as an RTF file. An RTF file preserves formatting, such as fonts and styles, and can be opened in Word and other Windows word-processing or desktop-publishing programs.
- Use the Word Mail Merge Wizard.
- Open the output of a Microsoft Access datasheet, form, or report in Word automatically.

The first two options are available through the **Save As/Export** command (**File** menu). The last two options are described in the following sections.

Using the Word Mail Merge Wizard

If you are using Word 95 or later, you can use the Word Mail Merge Wizard to create a mail merge document in Word using a link to Microsoft Access data. Once the link is established, you can open your document in Word at any time to print a new batch of form letters or labels using the current data in Microsoft Access.

▶ **To merge data from a table or query using the Word Mail Merge Wizard**

1. In the Microsoft Access Database window, click the name of the table or query you want to export.
2. On the **Tools** menu, point to **OfficeLinks** and click **Merge It With MS Word**.
3. Follow the instructions in the **Mail Merge Wizard**.
4. In the Word window, click **Insert Merge Field** to insert the desired fields into the document.

Note You can also begin the operation of merging data into form letters from within Word. For more information, see Word online Help.

Opening Microsoft Access Output in Word Automatically

You can save the output of a datasheet, form, or report as an RTF file and automatically open the file in Word.

▶ **To open the output of a datasheet, form, or report in Word**

1. In the Microsoft Access Database window, click the name of the table, query, form, or report you want to save and open in Word.

   –or–

   To save a portion of a datasheet, open the datasheet and select the portion of the datasheet.

2. On the **Tools** menu, point to **OfficeLinks**, and click **Publish It With MS Word**.

   The output is saved as an RTF file in the folder where Microsoft Access is installed. Word automatically starts and opens the RTF file.

Exchanging Data with Microsoft Excel

Microsoft Access and Microsoft Excel provide five ways of exchanging information. You can:

- Import or link a Microsoft Excel worksheet.
- Format and print Microsoft Excel data in Microsoft Access reports.
- Move Microsoft Excel data into Microsoft Access.
- Create a PivotTable control in a Microsoft Access form.
- Open the output of a Microsoft Access datasheet, form, or report in Microsoft Excel automatically.

For information about importing and linking external data files, see "Importing or Linking Data from External Data Sources" earlier in this chapter. The remaining four methods of exchanging data with Microsoft Excel are described in the following sections.

Formatting and Printing Microsoft Excel Data in Microsoft Access Reports

When you need the grouping and formatting functionality of Microsoft Access reports for data in a Microsoft Excel worksheet, you can use the **Access Report** command on the Microsoft Excel **Data** menu to start the Microsoft Access Report Wizard. For more information, see Microsoft Excel online Help.

Moving Microsoft Excel Data into Microsoft Access

When a Microsoft Excel worksheet is no longer the appropriate tool for your data—for example, if you require more rows than are practical, or if you need to have the data in your worksheet updated by many users—you can create a Microsoft Access database from the worksheet. To do so, use the **Convert To Access** command on the Microsoft Excel **Data** menu. For more information, see Microsoft Excel online Help.

Creating a PivotTable Control in a Microsoft Access Form

If a computer has both Microsoft Access and Microsoft Excel installed, you can create a PivotTable control in a Microsoft Access form. Using the PivotTable Wizard, you can create a control on a form that allows you to summarize large amounts of data using a format and calculation method you choose. A PivotTable is like a crosstab query, but you can switch the row and column headings dynamically to see a different view of the data.

▶ **To create a Microsoft Excel PivotTable on a Microsoft Access form**

1 On the Microsoft Access **Insert** menu, click **Form**.

2 In the **New Form** dialog box, click **PivotTable Wizard**, and then click **OK**.

3 Follow the instructions in the wizard.

Note The source data that the PivotTable uses is not automatically saved with the PivotTable or form. Instead, you must update the PivotTable with the most current data each time you use it, which means that the location where the data is stored must be accessible. If the data source will not be available later, when you want to edit the PivotTable, save a copy of the data with the PivotTable.

Opening Microsoft Access Output in Microsoft Excel Automatically

You can save the output of a datasheet, form, or report as an XLS file and automatically open it in Microsoft Excel. Doing so preserves most formatting, such as fonts and colors. Report group levels are saved as Microsoft Excel outline levels. A form is saved as a table of data.

▶ **To open the output of a datasheet, form, or report in Microsoft Excel**

1 In the Microsoft Access Database window, click the name of the table, query, form, or report you want to save and open in Microsoft Excel.

   –or–

   To save a portion of a datasheet, open the datasheet, and then select the portion of the datasheet.

2 On the **Tools** menu, point to **OfficeLinks**, and then click **Analyze It With MS Excel**.

   The output is saved as a Microsoft Excel XLS file in the folder where Microsoft Access is installed. Microsoft Excel automatically starts and opens it.

Dragging Information Between Microsoft Access and Microsoft Excel or Word

The following drag-and-drop functionality is available in Microsoft Access. You can:

- Drag database objects between open Microsoft Access databases.
- Drag Microsoft Access tables and queries into Word and Microsoft Excel.
- Create a table by dragging a range of cells from a Microsoft Excel worksheet into the Database window.
- Drag OLE objects into an OLE Object field in a form in Form view, or in a form or report in Design view.

Using Microsoft Windows Messaging Service Data with Microsoft Access

If the Microsoft Messaging driver is installed, you can use Microsoft Access to link Microsoft Exchange Client or Outlook data that is stored either on a Microsoft Exchange server or in local Personal Folder (PST) or Personal Address Book (PAB) files. Microsoft Exchange Client and Microsoft Outlook data is collectively referred to as Microsoft Windows Messaging Service data. Currently, linking Microsoft Exchange Client or Outlook data in Microsoft Access is possible only by using DAO code in Visual Basic.

World Wide Web A wizard that links Microsoft Exchange Client and Outlook data through the Microsoft Access user interface will soon be available on the World Wide Web. For the latest information, connect to the Microsoft Access home page at:

http://www.microsoft.com/access/

Installing the Microsoft Messaging Driver

Before you can use DAO to gain access to Microsoft Exchange Client or Outlook data, you must install the Microsoft Messaging driver. The Setup file for the Microsoft Messaging driver is included in the Office 97 Value Pack.

Note The CD-ROM version of Office 97 includes the Office 97 Value Pack, a collection of application extras such as clip art, maps, sounds, presentation enhancements, and utilities. For more information about the Value Pack and how to use its contents, see Valupack.hlp in the ValuPack folder on the Office CD. You can also point to **Microsoft on the Web** (**Help** menu) in any Office application, and then click **Free Stuff**.

▶ **To install the Microsoft Messaging driver**

1. Insert the Office 97 Professional, Professional Edition, or Microsoft Access 97 CD into your CD-ROM drive.
2. In the ValuPack\DataAcc folder, double-click **Dataacc.exe**.
3. In the **Microsoft Data Access Pack** box, click **Yes**.
4. In the **Microsoft Data Access Pack Setup** box, click **Continue**.
5. Specify the destination folder, and then click **OK**.
6. To start installation, click **Complete\Custom Install**.
7. To install all Data Access drivers, select the **Data Access Drivers** option.

   –or–

   To install only the Microsoft Messaging driver, select the **Data Access Drivers** option, click **Change Option**, and select only the **Microsoft Messaging Driver** check box.

Installing the Microsoft Messaging driver with Dataacc.exe does not enter configuration information into the Windows registry. Before you can use the driver, you must manually register the Msexch35.dll file.

▶ **To register the Microsoft Messaging driver**

1. In Windows 95, start the MS-DOS prompt and switch to the Windows\System folder.

   –or–

   In Windows NT Workstation 3.51 or 4.0, start the Command Prompt and switch to the WinNT\System32 folder.

2. Type the following command:

   regsvr32 msexch35.dll

Using DAO with the Microsoft Messaging Driver

The procedures for linking Microsoft Windows Messaging Service data by using DAO are similar to the procedures used for linking the other external data sources. Special considerations and examples are provided in the following sections.

Connection Information

When specifying the connection string for Microsoft Windows Messaging Service data, use the following parameters separated by semicolons.

To specify this element	Use this parameter
Source database type	**Exchange 4.0** (required.)
Table name	**MAPILEVEL=** *path* where *path* is the path to the mail folder or address book (required)
Source table type	**TABLETYPE=0** (for folders) **TABLETYPE=1** (for address books; required)
Database name	**DATABASE=** *path* where *path* is the path to the database in which to store system tables used by the driver (usually the current database; required)
Profile name	PROFILE= *profile* where *profile* is the name of the profile to use. (optional; if not specified, the default profile is used)
Password	**PWD=** *password* where *password* is the logon password. (optional; not required if your network logon password is passed to your Microsoft Exchange server)

To gain access to messages in a Microsoft Exchange Client or Outlook folder, you must specify the path to the parent of the folder you want use. You do this with the **MAPILEVEL=** connection string keyword. For example, to gain access to a folder named Barbara in the Important subfolder in the People folder in the mailbox Mailbox–Dave Jones, first specify the path to the Important folder, using the following connection string:

"Exchange 4.0;MAPILEVEL=Mailbox - Dave Jones|People\Important;"

Then use the **SourceTableName** property in your DAO code to specify the folder named Barbara. You can specify any valid mailbox name to the left of the pipe symbol (|) in the connection string, but the mailbox name must be specified exactly as it appears in the left pane of the Microsoft Exchange Client or Outlook application window. Any spaces and capitalization in the name must be preserved.

In addition to specifying a Microsoft Exchange Server mailbox name to the left of the pipe symbol (|) in the connection string, you can specify the name of a local PST file as it appears in the left pane of the Microsoft Exchange Client or Outlook application window. This name is not necessarily the same name as the PST file itself and does not include the file extension.

To determine how a personal folder name is mapped to the PST file name where its information is stored, click **Services** on the **Tools** menu in the Microsoft Exchange Client or Outlook to display the **Services** dialog box. On the **Services** tab, click the name of a Personal Folder, and then click **Properties**. In the **Personal Folders** dialog box, the information in the **Name** box is the name to specify in your connection string. The information in the **Path** box specifies the path to the PST file where mail data is stored. For example, to gain access to a folder named ToDo in the Inbox folder in the PST named Local Folders, use the following connection string:

```
"Exchange 4.0;MAPILEVEL=Local Folders|Inbox;"
```

And then use the **SourceTableName** property in your DAO code to specify the folder named ToDo.

If you need to supply a profile name and password before gaining access to mailboxes, you can supply the profile name and password with the **PROFILE=** and **PWD=** keywords in the connection string. For example:

```
"Exchange 4.0;MAPILEVEL=Mailbox - Dave Jones|People\Important;PROFILE=DaveJ;PWD=Cisco;"
```

When specifying the connection string to open a folder in a Microsoft Exchange Client or Outlook mailbox, you must supply the path and name of an existing Microsoft Access database using the **DATABASE=** parameter. The Microsoft Messaging driver creates system tables in this database to store information about the structure of the Microsoft Exchange Client or Outlook folders, including any new fields you have appended to these folders. Although it is possible to specify a database other than the current database, it is easiest to specify the current database for this purpose. If you delete the database or system tables used for this purpose, all the information about the structure of the folders is lost and must be recreated.

Linking Microsoft Exchange or Outlook Folders

You can gain access to a folder within a Microsoft Exchange Client or Outlook mailbox by creating a link to the folder within a Microsoft Access database. When you link a folder, the folder is treated as a table. The following DAO code links a Microsoft Exchange or Outlook folder to a Microsoft Access database.

```
Sub LinkExchangeFolder()
   Dim CurrentDatabase As Database
   Dim MyTableDef As TableDef
   Dim str As String

   'Set a reference to the current database.
   Set CurrentDatabase = CurrentDb

   'Build the connection string'
   str = "Exchange 4.0;MAPILEVEL=Mailbox - Dave Jones" _
   & "|People\Important;TABLETYPE=0;" _
   & "DATABASE=c:\ACCESS\DATA\TEST.MDB;" _
   & "PROFILE=DaveJ;PWD=Cisco;"
```

```
'Create a TableDef Object. The name specified for the
'TableDef object is displayed as the name of the link
'in the Database window.
Set MyTableDef = CurrentDatabase.CreateTableDef _
("Linked Exchange Folder")

'Set Connection Information.
MyTableDef.Connect = str
MyTableDef.SourceTableName = "Barbara"

'Append the TableDef Object to create the link.
CurrentDatabase.TableDefs.Append MyTableDef

'Refresh the database window and clear the object variable.
RefreshDatabaseWindow
Set CurrentDatabase = Nothing

End Sub
```

Constraints

In Microsoft Exchange Client or Outlook, some folders may contain only other folders and no messages. You cannot gain access to this type of folder using the Microsoft Messaging driver. It is only possible to gain access to folders that contain messages.

You can only gain access to messages in a Microsoft Exchange Client or Outlook mailbox in read-only mode. You cannot update information in a Microsoft Exchange Client or Outlook message, but you can append new records (messages) to an existing folder. Additionally, you cannot use the **Seek** method, because the Microsoft Messaging driver does not support indexing.

Modifying Windows Registry Settings for External Data Formats

When you install Microsoft Access or external database drivers, Setup writes associated entries to various keys in the Windows registry. Setup writes a set of default values for each installed ISAM engine in a subkey of the **HKEY_LOCAL_MACHINE\SOFTWARE\Microsoft\Jet\3.5\Engines** key. These settings apply to any host application that uses the Jet database engine on the current computer, which can include applications such as Microsoft Excel and Microsoft Visual Basic applications in addition to Microsoft Access.

You can create settings for an ISAM engine that apply only to Microsoft Access by creating a corresponding subkey below the **HKEY_LOCAL_MACHINE \SOFTWARE\Microsoft\Office\8.0\Access\Jet\3.5\Engines** key and then specifying any values you want to override in that subkey. These multiple registrations allow each host application to specify values that apply to its instance of the Microsoft Jet database engine. If a host-specific registration omits particular values, these settings default to the values registered in the **\Microsoft\Jet\3.5\Engines** key.

Although Setup writes logical defaults for the Windows registry entries, your particular environment or preferences might require you to change entries. For information about all registry entries, see Appendix C, "Registry Keys and Values."

Note For the new settings to take effect after you change your initialization settings, you must quit the application and then restart it, using the Microsoft Jet database engine.

Using Microsoft Access with ODBC and Client/Server Operations

In a client/server application, you store your data in remote tables on a database server, such as Microsoft SQL Server, instead of in local tables in your Microsoft Access database. Your Microsoft Access database (the client) sends queries and updates to the server and retrieves the data it needs. A client/server application takes advantage of the processing power available to both the client and the database server components.

By contrast, in a file server application, data simply resides on a network file server, transactions with the data are handled no differently than the reading and writing of any other file on the network, and all processing is performed locally.

Developing, optimizing, and maintaining client/server applications is a complex subject. This section briefly describes what ODBC is and how it allows you to interact with a large variety of SQL data sources. The reasons to adopt a client/server approach are covered, as are the issues involved in converting an existing Microsoft Access application to a client/server application. For more information about developing client/server applications using Microsoft Access, see *Building Applications with Microsoft Access 97*.

Understanding ODBC

Providing data access to the large variety of database applications can be very complex. Applications that use the ODBC standard, such as Microsoft Access and Microsoft Excel, ease this burden by using a vendor-neutral means of working with database management systems (DBMSs). Microsoft has gained very broad support for ODBC, which allows you to use a broad variety of data sources.

ODBC contributes many significant benefits by providing an open, standard way to use data. ODBC allows the following:

- User access to data in more than one data storage location (for example, on more than one server) from within a single application.

- User access to data in more than one type of DBMS (such as DB2, ORACLE, DEC RDB, Apple DAL, dBASE, and Microsoft SQL Server client/server) from within a single application.

- Simpler application development—it is now easier for developers to provide access to data in multiple, concurrent DBMSs.

- A portable application programming interface (API), allowing the same interface and access technology to be a cross-platform tool.

- Applications insulated from changes to underlying network and DBMS versions. Modifications to networking transports, servers, and DBMSs do not create problems for current ODBC applications.

- Use of SQL—the standard language for DBMSs.

- Protection of corporations' investments in existing DBMSs and developers' acquired DBMS skills. ODBC also allows corporations to continue to use existing diverse DBMSs, while developing applications using other systems that are more appropriate to the task at hand.

How ODBC Works

ODBC defines an API. Each ODBC application uses the same code, as defined by the API specification, to exchange information with many types of data sources through DBMS-specific drivers. A driver manager sits between the applications and the drivers. In Windows, the driver manager and the drivers are implemented as dynamic-link libraries (DLLs). The following illustration outlines the process.

ODBC Architecture

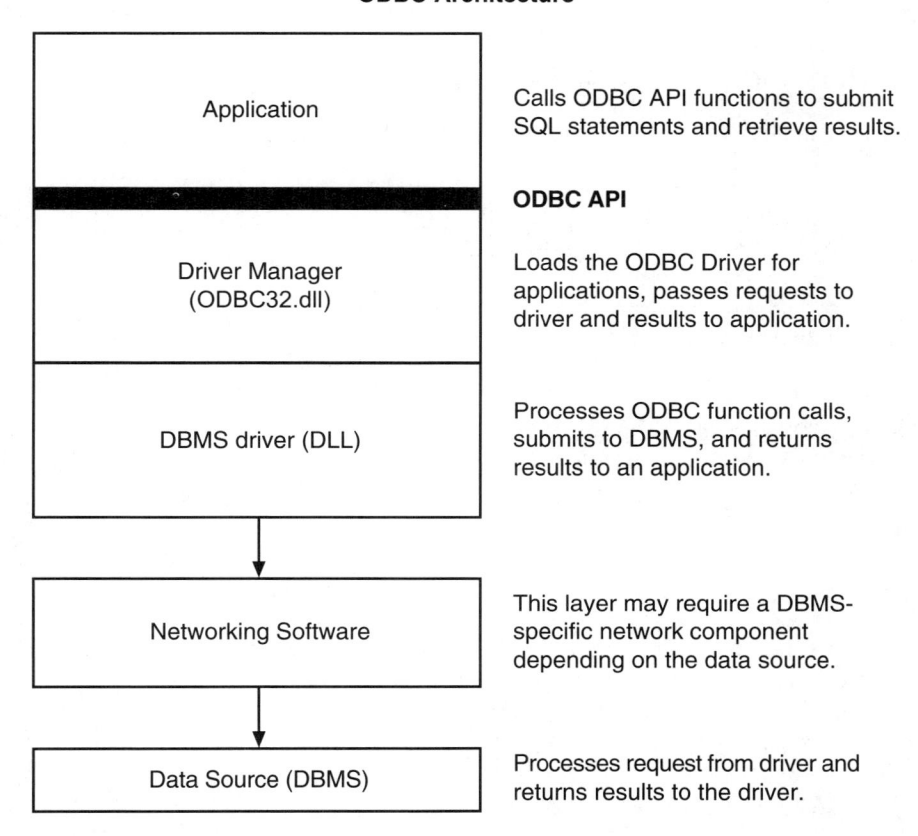

Component	Description
Application	Calls ODBC API functions to submit SQL statements and retrieve results.
	ODBC API
Driver Manager (ODBC32.dll)	Loads the ODBC Driver for applications, passes requests to driver and results to application.
DBMS driver (DLL)	Processes ODBC function calls, submits to DBMS, and returns results to an application.
Networking Software	This layer may require a DBMS-specific network component depending on the data source.
Data Source (DBMS)	Processes request from driver and returns results to the driver.

The application calls ODBC functions to connect to a data source, send and receive data, and disconnect. The driver manager provides an application with information (such as a list of available data sources), loads drivers dynamically as they are needed, and provides argument and state transition checking. The DBMS driver, developed separately from the application, processes ODBC function calls, manages all exchanges between an application and a specific DBMS, and may translate the standard SQL syntax into the native SQL of the target data source. All SQL translations are the responsibility of the driver developer.

Applications are not limited to communicating through one driver. A single application can make multiple connections, each through a different driver, or multiple connections to similar sources through a single driver. To use a new DBMS, a user or an administrator simply installs a driver for the DBMS. The user does not need a different version of the application to use the new DBMS. This is a tremendous benefit for end users, and it also translates into significant savings in support and development costs.

Using ODBC Data in Microsoft Office 97 Applications

ODBC data is available to Microsoft Office applications in the following ways:

- In Microsoft Access 97, by importing from or linking to ODBC data sources using the commands on the **Get External Data** submenu (**File** menu). Microsoft Access can also export to available ODBC data formats using the **Save As/Export** command (**File** menu).

- In Microsoft Excel 97, by using the macro commands and functions available through the ODBC add-in, when building PivotTables using the **Pivot Table** command (**Data** menu); and in Microsoft Query using the **Get External Data** command (**Data** menu).

- When creating custom applications in either Microsoft Access or Microsoft Excel using Visual Basic and DAO code.

The following section describes using Microsoft Access to create a client/server application. For more information about using Microsoft Excel to gain access to ODBC data, see "Sharing Data Between Microsoft Excel and SQL Server" and "Using Microsoft Excel and Microsoft Query" later in this chapter.

Using Client/Server Architecture

The three primary reasons for adopting client/server architecture for database applications are:

- Allowing enterprise-wide access to corporate information

    As computers become smaller, more powerful, and more usable, information is more widely distributed across a corporate enterprise in an increasing number of formats. Client/server technology provides the links to read and manipulate data regardless of its location or storage format.

- Upsizing multiuser file server database applications

    Client/server applications provide improved performance, security, and reliability. Database application solutions can grow and become more complex over time. Client/server architecture provides a way to scale up a database application when it becomes larger and more complex and must support more users and a higher volume of transactions.

- Downsizing mainframe and minicomputer database applications

  The managers and developers of many mainframe database applications move their applications to client/server architecture to take advantage of graphical user interface (GUI) processing. Microsoft Access provides an ideal environment for developing user-driven systems. At the same time, Microsoft Access provides many powerful features for interacting with external data sources. Also motivating this change is the reduced cost of new back-end servers.

  Downsizing, however, is a more difficult and a much slower migration process. As such, the seamless integration from the mainframe world to the client/server world is a priority. When this level of integration is achieved, client/server applications enhance and add value to existing mainframe-based processes.

Upsizing a Microsoft Access File Server Application to a Client/Server Application

A high-level summary of steps involved in migrating from a file server to a client/server environment include:

1. Create the server database.
2. Establish your ODBC data source using the ODBC Administrator.
3. Document your existing Microsoft Access database.
4. Export each table to the server database.
5. Add server-based integrity constraints: validation rules, default values, and referential integrity.
6. Add the indexes to the server tables with the necessary attributes.
7. Link the server tables.

If you want to upsize a Microsoft Access database to Microsoft SQL Server, the simplest way to perform this process is by using the Upsizing Wizard included with the Microsoft Access Upsizing Tools. The Upsizing Wizard preserves your database structure, including data, indexes, field **DefaultValue** property settings, and AutoNumber fields. It also converts your Microsoft Access validation rules and defaults to Microsoft SQL Server equivalents, and maintains your table relationships and referential integrity after upsizing.

World Wide Web   The Microsoft Access Upsizing Tools are available at no cost from the Microsoft Access Developer's Forum. Connect to the Developer's Forum home page at: http://www.microsoft.com/accessdev/

The remainder of this section explains these steps in more detail. For more information about these procedures and about optimizing a client/server application, see *Building Applications with Microsoft Access 97*.

Before You Begin

To ensure that your Microsoft Access applications scale up easily to a client/server database, the following practices are recommended:

- Do not embed spaces in your table names.

   Most servers cannot support embedded spaces. During export, Microsoft Access replaces spaces with underscores in the name, which means that references to those fields in queries, forms, reports, expressions, and Visual Basic code will fail.

- Create a name-mapping query if your application has tables and fields with names containing embedded spaces.

   A name-mapping query is saved as the original table name that includes spaces, but it points to the server table without spaces. If a field name contains embedded spaces, you can map the Microsoft Access field name to the SQL Server column name without spaces using the convention *Field Name*:FIELD_NAME in **Field** row of the query definition.

- Be consistent in the use of the case of your object names.

   Some SQL servers are case-sensitive, but Microsoft Access default behavior is not case-sensitive.

- When using DAO code in Visual Basic, do not use the table-type Recordset to manipulate remote tables; always use the dynaset-type Recordset instead.

   Tables linked using the **Link Tables** command (**File** menu) automatically use dynaset-type Recordsets.

Creating the Server Database

The method for creating a server database depends on the SQL server software you are using. For details, see your SQL server documentation. If you have an existing SQL database that you want to use as the basis for your client/server application, you can export or link tables from Microsoft Access after you have defined this database as an ODBC data source.

Defining Your ODBC Data Source

Use the 32bit ODBC icon in Windows Control Panel to define your ODBC data source. The 32bit ODBC icon is available only when you install the SQL Driver with Office or Microsoft Access. Before you can specify a data source, you must have the appropriate ODBC driver for your database server installed.

You can see which ODBC drivers are available on a computer by double-clicking the 32bit ODBC icon in Control Panel and then clicking the **Drivers** button. Office Setup, as well as the Setup programs for standalone versions of Microsoft Access and Microsoft Excel, include the Microsoft SQL Server driver and support files for the 32bit ODBC Control Panel icon. If the 32bit ODBC icon is not available in Control Panel, rerun Setup and click **Add/Remove**. Under the **Data Access** option, select the **Microsoft SQL Server Driver** check box.

If you are using an SQL database server other than Microsoft SQL Server, contact the vendor of that product to find out about the availability of an ODBC driver. ODBC drivers are also available for data formats other than SQL servers. For example, there is an ODBC driver for Lotus Notes databases. Contact the vendor of the product whose data you want to use for information about the availability of an ODBC driver.

Important Microsoft Office 97 applications can only use 32-bit versions of ODBC drivers. If a previous version of a Microsoft Office application, such as Microsoft Access version 2.0, was installed on a computer, older 16-bit versions of ODBC drivers may still be present. To use the ODBC drivers available with Microsoft Office 97 applications, rerun Setup and install the drivers you need. Similarly, other applications written for Windows 3.*x* may have 16-bit versions of ODBC drivers. Contact the vendor of the product whose data you want to use for information about a current 32-bit ODBC driver.

Documenting Your Existing Microsoft Access Database

Indexes, validation rules (also referred to as business rules, domain integrity rules, or database-specific rules), default values, and referential integrity rules are not created when Microsoft Access exports tables to a client/server database. After exporting, you need to define the indexes, validation rules, and default values on the server tables themselves. If permissions vary for users of the database, you will need this information, too. You can print a comprehensive list of the properties of the tables in your MDB file by opening the database with Microsoft Access and then using the **Documenter** command (**Tools** menu, **Analyze** submenu).

Exporting Microsoft Access Tables to the Server Database

Creating the structure of a complex, multitable, client/server database can be a tedious and time-consuming process. Microsoft Access table export features can speed up this process greatly. Export each table to the server database using the **Export/Save As** command (**File** menu).

There are trade-offs to consider when exporting data. Microsoft Access exports each row one at a time. This ensures that your exported data adheres to all the server-based rules, but it is significantly slower with extremely large tables than using server-based, bulk-copy routines.

If your tables contain a few thousand records or fewer, it is usually faster to export the tables from the Microsoft Access database to the server database than to use bulk-copy programs, such as BCP for SQL Server, with text files. If you do use a batch copy program to load tables on your server, you can test data type and field size consistency before running the batch copy program by exporting at least one record from each table to the server using Microsoft Access.

Most migrations to client/server operation are accomplished in two phases: test and production. To limit the number of records used for the test phase, write a select query in Microsoft Access and then export data from that query.

Adding Server-Based Validation Rules

Validation rules are not exported with a table. You can create triggers or rules on the server table that enforce your rules, or you can define form-level validation rules in your Microsoft Access forms instead. Using form-level rules is easier but not as reliable, because invalid entries are rejected only by the form, not by the server table itself.

A *trigger* is a piece of code residing on the server that executes an SQL statement prior to the occurrence of a specified event, such as **INSERT**, **DELETE**, or **UPDATE**. If you are using a server-based trigger, be aware that many Visual Basic functions, such as the **DatePart** or **Format** function, may have no equivalent on your server.

Adding Default Values and Enforcing Referential Integrity

Most client/server DBMSs provide a default value property. Otherwise, you need to use stored procedures to set default values for fields whose value is not supplied during the append process. If you need to emulate the **Required** property of fields in Microsoft Access tables, you can use the **NOT NULL** command in the definition of your SQL table.

If the server database does not support ANSI SQL reserved words, you need to write stored procedures to enforce referential integrity and perform cascading updates and deletions. None of the rules and stored procedures you create are visible to Microsoft Access; if your application violates the rules, it receives a message from the server.

Adding Indexes

Add the indexes to the server tables with equivalent attributes to those in the Microsoft Access database—for example, PrimaryKey, No Duplicates, or No Nulls. Microsoft Access cannot update a table that does not have a unique index.

In Microsoft Access 2.0 or later, dynaset-type Recordsets support server-based primary key generation from triggers. In earlier versions, as the primary key was generated during an insert, the recordset cursor would act as if the record had been deleted because it was no longer in the same location. Microsoft Access now re-fetches the record, keeping the recordset up-to-date. This is particularly significant because many developers use the convenient AutoNumber field (called a Counter field in previous versions) to generate their primary keys. The equivalent of the Microsoft Access AutoNumber field data type seldom is found in client/server DBMSs, yet it can be critical to your application.

This improvement allows you to create an **INSERT** trigger on the server table that increments the integer value of a field each time a new record is appended to the table. The **Transact-SQL** statement that creates the equivalent of an AutoNumber field is shown in the following example:

```
CREATE TRIGGER add_customer_id ON dbo.customers
FOR INSERT AS
UPDATE dbo.customers
SET inserted.Customer_ID = (SELECT MAX(Customer_ID)
FROM dbo.customers) + 1
WHERE dbo.customers.customer_ID IS NULL
```

When you use a trigger to create the AutoNumber field equivalent, you do not see the generated value in a bound control until you complete the appending process for the record.

Linking Server Tables

Use the **Link Tables** command (**File** menu, **Get External Data** submenu) to link tables in the server database. When you link a table, Microsoft Access stores a copy of the table structure in your Microsoft Access database system tables. This allows you to build queries, forms, and reports as if the linked table were part of your database.

After linking, relationships between tables need to be established in the Relationships window. This establishes the default join conditions and types used when building new queries.

Any operation in Datasheet view that is permissible for a native Microsoft Access table can generally be performed for tables linked by ODBC. In Design view, you can set the values of the **Format**, **InputMask**, and **Caption** properties. All other properties of linked tables are read-only.

Renaming Linked Tables

When Microsoft Access links a remote table, it prefixes the default table owner ID of the SQL Server to each table name. The period separator between the owner ID and the table name is replaced by an underscore because periods in table names are not permitted by Microsoft Access. Thus, the names of linked tables no longer correspond to the original table names in your MDB file. The simplest way to correct this is to rename your tables to their original names after linking.

Sharing Information with Microsoft Excel 97

Microsoft Excel 97 fully supports copying and pasting linked or unlinked data, as described in the "Overview" earlier in this chapter. In addition, Microsoft Excel includes several SQL functions for working with external data. Once the data has been imported, Microsoft Excel offers powerful data analysis and reporting tools such as PivotTables. This section describes the tools available for working with external data in Microsoft Excel.

Sharing Data Between Microsoft Excel and SQL Server

The ODBC add-in for Microsoft Excel, Xlodbc.xla, provides ODBC functions that allow you to connect to SQL Server data sources directly. The following is a list of the functions provided by the ODBC add-in and a description of the arguments for those functions. The arguments for each function are shown here as they are displayed in the **Paste Function** dialog box (**Insert** menu).

- **SQLBind**(*ConnectionNum,Column,Reference*)
- **SQLClose**(*ConnectionNum*)
- **SQLError**( )
- **SQLExecQuery**(*ConnectionNum,QueryText*)
- **SQLGetSchema**(*ConnectionNum,TypeNum,QualifierText*)
- **SQLOpen**(*ConnectionStr,OutputRef,DriverPrompt*)
- *****SQLRequest**(*ConnectionStr,QueryText,OutputRef,DriverPrompt, ColNamesLogical*)
- **SQLRetrieve**(*ConnectionNum,DestinationRef,MaxColumns,MaxRows, ColNamesLogical,RowNumsLogical,NamedRngLogical,FetchFirstLogical*)
- **SQLRetrieveToFile**(*ConnectionNum,Destination,ColNamesLogical, ColumnDelimiter*)

Note The functions **SQLBind**, **SQLClose**, **SQLError**, **SQLExecQuery**, **SQLGetSchema**, **SQLOpen**, **SQLRetrieve**, and **SQLRetrieveToFile** are displayed in the **Paste Function** dialog box (**Insert** menu) when the active sheet is a worksheet. However, these functions can be used only in a macro or module sheet.

For more information about a specific function, see Microsoft Excel online Help. For more information about ODBC, see "Using Microsoft Access with ODBC and Client/Server Operations" earlier in this chapter.

Using Microsoft Excel and Microsoft Query

To use Microsoft Query with Microsoft Excel, you must install the Query application, the Query add-in, the drivers for the types of data you want to retrieve, and the necessary ODBC files. To install these files, rerun Setup and click **Add/Remove**; then select the **Data Access** option. For information about Data Access components, see Appendix D, "List of Installed Components."

When you create a PivotTable that uses an external data source, use Query. In most cases, you can create PivotTables that use data supplied by Query and distribute your PivotTables to other users who can manipulate or refresh the PivotTables. However, if you create a PivotTable that uses either the **Server Based Page Fields** or the **Optimize Memory** options, Microsoft Excel requires that Query be installed on the same computer. If you distribute such a PivotTable to users in your workgroup, they must have Query installed to use these options.

Query is not installed when you choose the Typical installation during Setup. To install Query, choose the Custom installation or rerun Setup and click **Add Remove**; then select the **Microsoft Query** option. For more information about custom installations for a workgroup, see Chapter 6, "Customizing Client Installations."

Exporting Microsoft Excel Data to Lotus Notes

When you install Office, Setup detects whether Lotus Notes version 3.*x* or 4.*x* (16-bit or 32-bit) is installed on the computer. If either of them is installed, Setup automatically installs Lotus Notes converters for Microsoft Excel and Word. With these text converters, you can import Word and Microsoft Excel documents into a Lotus Notes memo. For more information about working with Lotus Notes, see "Interoperability with Lotus Notes/FX" in Chapter 28, "Working with Messaging Systems and Connectivity Software."

Sharing Information with Outlook 97

Outlook 97 fully supports copying and pasting linked or unlinked data, as described in the "Overview" earlier in this chapter. Outlook also has extensive capabilities for importing data from and exporting data to other applications. In addition, Outlook allows other Office applications to track documents automatically in the Outlook Journal folder or to record document-related tasks in the Outlook Tasks folder. Outlook provides PowerPoint with the ability to directly schedule meetings and record action items during presentations.

Recording Office Items in the Outlook Journal

The Outlook Journal folder can automatically track documents created by other Office applications. When Office applications are installed, Setup adds the application names to the **Also record files from** box on the **Journal** tab in the **Options** dialog box (**Tools** menu) in Outlook. When you run Outlook, select the applications whose documents you want to track in this dialog box.

When one of the applications you have selected opens a file, it creates a journal entry with the current time and date and a link to the document. When the application closes the file, Outlook updates the journal entry and records the amount of time you worked on the file in the **Duration** box.

You can also create a journal entry for a document manually by dragging the document (in Windows Explorer or in Outlook) into the Journal folder.

Tip In Windows 95 and Windows NT Workstation 4.0, you can use a system policy to define the applications tracked by the Outlook Journal for all Outlook users in your workgroup. In the System Policy Editor, set the following policies:

User\Outlook\Tools_Options\Journal\Automatically record these items

User\Outlook\Tools_Options\Journal\Also record these files

For more information, see "Using Windows System Policies to Customize Office" in Chapter 7, "Customizing and Optimizing Microsoft Office."

Creating Tasks from Office Applications

As you work in an Office application, you can add a task in the Outlook Tasks folder that corresponds to the work you are doing. For example, while working on a Word document, you can create a task to remind you to have the document reviewed by a certain date. Once the task is created, you can assign the task to others and track its progress.

To create a task from within an Office application, click **Create Microsoft Outlook Task** on the **Reviewing** toolbar. A new task is created in the Outlook Tasks folder containing a shortcut to the document file.

Importing and Exporting Items

You can use the Import and Export Wizard to import data from other applications into Outlook folders or to export data from Outlook folders to other applications. Outlook can import or export data for several applications and in different formats.

If you need to import data to or export data from an application that Outlook does not support directly, you may be able to use one of the intermediary formats that Outlook does support. The following procedures demonstrate how to import a data file from an unsupported application into an Outlook folder.

▶ To save your data in an intermediary file format

1. In your application, save the data in a comma-delimited or tab-delimited text file.

   Be sure to include a heading line in the text file that indicates the names of the data fields in each column, as shown in the example later in this section.

2. Edit the heading line so that column names match Outlook field names, as shown in the example.

Now you can import the data into Outlook.

▶ To import an intermediary data file into an Outlook folder

1. On the Outlook **File** menu, click **Import and Export**.
2. In the **Choose an action to perform** box, select **Import from Schedule+ or another program or file**.
3. In the **Select file type to import from** box, select the appropriate file format, based on the characteristics of your data file.
4. In the **File to import** box, enter the name and path of the text file.
5. In the same panel of the wizard, choose how you want Outlook to deal with items in your text file that duplicate items already in the Outlook folder by selecting one of the following options:

   - **Replace duplicates with items imported**. Outlook overwrites duplicate items with those from your data file.
   - **Allow duplicates to be created**. Outlook adds all of your data, even if there are duplicates.
   - **Do not import duplicate items**. Outlook does not add an item from your file if it is a duplicate of an item that already exists in the Outlook folder.

6. In the **Select destination folder** box, click the Outlook folder into which you want your data imported.

   The folder you select must match the type of data you are importing. For example, if your data consists of names and addresses, you must import it into a folder with contact items, such as the Contacts folder.

7. Click **Map Custom Fields**.

   By default, Outlook maps the data from your file based on the field names you entered in the heading line of the file. If you do not have a heading line in your file, then Outlook imports the fields based on their position in the file. Change or correct these defaults in the **Map Custom Fields** dialog box, and then click **OK**.

8. Click **Finish** to import the data.

You can also export data from Outlook to your application, if your application can read comma-delimited or tab-delimited text files. Outlook exports data by writing every field into the output file in the order shown in the tables later in this section.

Example of a Data File Imported to Outlook

Suppose you have an employee list in an address book program, and you want to import the addresses into the Outlook Contacts folder. The program can save its data in a text file with fields separated by commas.

First, output the data from your application into a text file in the following format. Be sure to include a heading line as the first line of the output file, giving the names of the data fields.

COUNTRY, CITY, LASTNAME, FIRSTNAME, EXTENSION
UK, London, Dalal, Ketan, 452
UK, London, King, Robert, 465
UK, London, Chai, Sean, 428
UK, London, Buchanan, Steven, 3453
USA, Kirkland, Boyd, Shannon, 3355
USA, Redmond, Dunn, Michael, 5176
USA, Seattle, Callahan, Laura, 2344
USA, Seattle, Rudd, Darlene, 5467
USA, Tacoma, Conroy, Stephanie, 3457

Then change the names in the heading line to match the field names for contact items in Outlook, as shown in the following table.

Change this name	To this equivalent Outlook field name
COUNTRY	Business Country
CITY	Business City
LASTNAME	Last Name
FIRSTNAME	First Name
EXTENSION	Business Phone

When you are finished, your heading line should look like this:

Business Country, Business City, Last Name, First Name, Business Phone

Now, run Outlook and import the file. Click **Map Custom Fields** to verify that Outlook has mapped your data correctly.

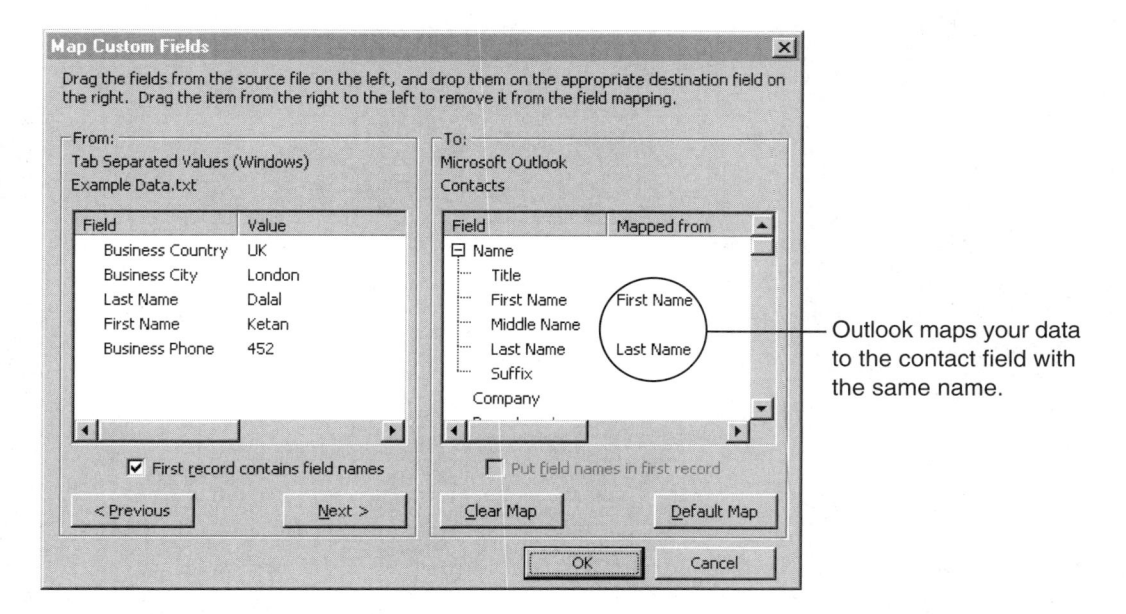

[Screenshot of Map Custom Fields dialog box with annotation: "Outlook maps your data to the contact field with the same name."]

If you do not have a heading line in your data file, you can clear the check box **First record contains field names** in the **Map Custom Fields** dialog box, and Outlook maps your data to Outlook fields in the order in which the data appears in the file. For example, without a heading line, you would type the data in the sample data file as shown here (fields containing no data are left blank):

,,Ketan,,Dalal,,,,,,,,London,,,UK,,,,,,,,,,,,,,,452

How Outlook Maps Field Names from the Data File

The following tables show the field names for each Outlook item type and the order in which they are mapped (if there is no heading line in the data file).

Calendar Item Fields
Subject
Start Date
Start Time
End Date
End Time
All day event
Reminder On/Off
Reminder Date
Reminder Time
Meeting Organizer
Required Attendees
Optional Attendees
Meeting Resources
Billing
Categories
Description
Location
Mileage
Priority
Private
Show Time As

Contact Item Fields
Name
    Title
    First Name
    Middle Name
    Last Name
Suffix
Company
Department
Job Title

Business Address
    Business Street
    Business Street 2
    Business Street 3
    Business City
    Business State
    Business Postal Code
    Business Country
Home Address
    Home Street
    Home Street 2
    Home Street 3
    Home City
    Home State
    Home Postal Code
    Home Country
Other Address
    Other Street
    Other Street 2
    Other Street 3
    Other City
    Other State
    Other Postal Code
    Other Country
Assistant's Phone
Business Fax
Business Phone
Business Phone 2
Callback
Car Phone
Company Main Phone
Home Fax
Home Phone
Home Phone 2

ISDN
Mobile Phone
Other Fax
Other Phone
Pager
Primary Phone
Radio Phone
TTY/TDD Phone
Telex
Account
Anniversary
Assistant's Name
Billing
Birthday
Categories
Children
E-mail 1
    E-mail 1 Address
    E-mail 1 Type
    E-mail 1 Service Code
    E-mail 1 Display Name
E-mail 2
    E-mail 2 Address
    E-mail 2 Type
    E-mail 2 Service Code
    E-mail 2 Display Name
E-mail 3
    E-mail 3 Address
    E-mail 3 Type
    E-mail 3 Service Code
    E-mail 3 Display Name
Gender
Government ID Number
Hobby
Initials

Keywords
Language
Location
Mileage
Notes
Office Location
Organizational ID Number
PO Box
Private
Profession
Referred By
Spouse
User 1
User 2
User 3
User 4
Web Page

Note If you specify a field name with multiple elements in your data file, Outlook attempts to parse the data into its separate parts. For example, if you specify **Name** as the field name in the heading line of your data file, and the data is **Stephanie Conroy**, Outlook places **Stephanie** in the **First Name** field and **Conroy** in the **Last Name** field.

Using Outlook with PowerPoint

PowerPoint includes features designed to work with Outlook. For example, you can use Outlook to schedule a meeting with your colleagues. Then, when the meeting is over, you can use Outlook to send action items to assigned individuals. In both cases, you run Outlook using the **Meeting Minder** command (**Tools** menu) in PowerPoint. If Outlook is not installed on your computer, this command is not available.

Scheduling a PowerPoint Meeting Through Outlook

In PowerPoint, you schedule meetings through Outlook by using the Meeting Minder feature.

▶ **To schedule a PowerPoint meeting through Outlook**

1. On the **Tools** menu, click **Meeting Minder**.

   –or–

   If you are delivering a presentation, right-click in the presentation and point to **Meeting Minder**.

2. Click **Schedule**.

   PowerPoint runs Outlook and opens a blank appointment.

3. On the **Appointment** menu, click **Invite Attendees**.

4. In the **To** box, enter the names of people you want to invite to the meeting.

   –or–

   If you need to find attendees' names in your address book, click **To**.

5. If you want to schedule the meeting based on attendees' availability, click the **Meeting Planner** tab, and select the **Show attendee availability** option.

6. Select start and end times for the meeting in the **Start time** and **End time** boxes on the **Appointment** tab.

   –or–

   Click **AutoPick** on the **Meeting Planner** tab for Outlook to find a block of free time for all required attendees.

7. To invite the attendees, click **Send**.

For more information about scheduling appointments in Outlook, see Outlook online Help. For information about how Outlook reads attendees' free/busy times, see Chapter 31, "Workgroup Features in Microsoft Outlook."

Exporting Action Items to Outlook

If you have been using Meeting Minder to record action items during a presentation, you can export the action items to your task list in Outlook. From your task list, you can mail each action item to the person responsible for completing the item.

▶ **To export action items from PowerPoint to Outlook**

1. In Meeting Minder, click **Export**.

2. Select the **Post action items to Microsoft Outlook** check box, and click **Export Now**.

   PowerPoint starts Outlook and creates a new task for each action item in your task list, as shown in the following illustration.

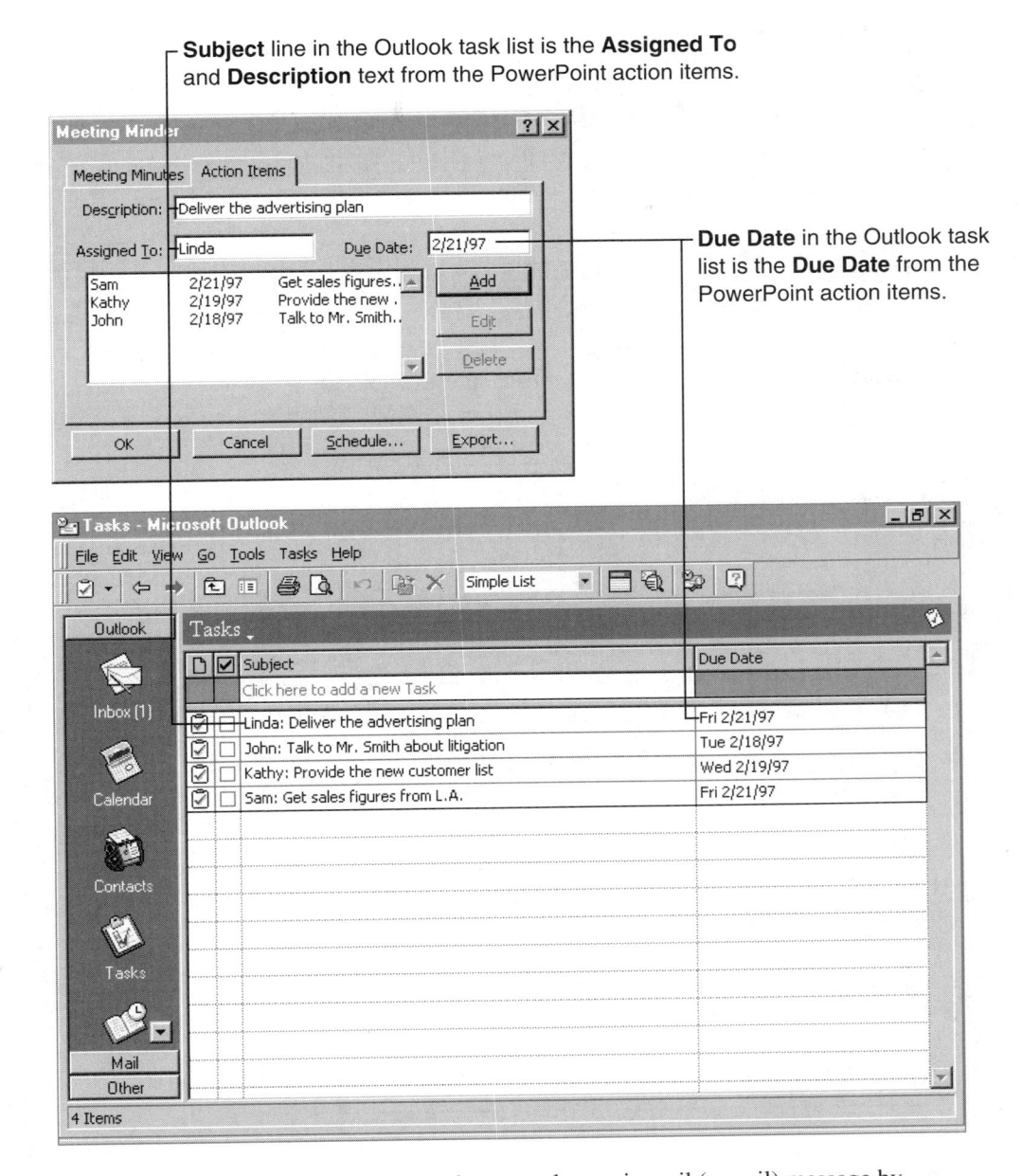

Chapter 27 Sharing Information with Microsoft Office Applications

Subject line in the Outlook task list is the **Assigned To** and **Description** text from the PowerPoint action items.

Due Date in the Outlook task list is the **Due Date** from the PowerPoint action items.

In Outlook, you can send each of these tasks as an electronic mail (e-mail) message by dragging the task to the Outbox.

Microsoft Office 97 Resource Kit **779**

▶ To mail the action items

1. To display the mail icons, click the **Mail** button on the Outlook bar.
2. Click a task in the task list, and drag it to the Outbox icon on the Outlook bar.

   Outlook starts a new message with formatted task information.
3. Enter the recipient's e-mail address on the **To** line, and click **Send**.

   –or–

   If you need help resolving the name of the recipient, click **To** and browse your address book for the name.

The message started by Outlook looks similar to the following illustration. The subject and due date are carried over from the task list, but the recipient name is not generated automatically.

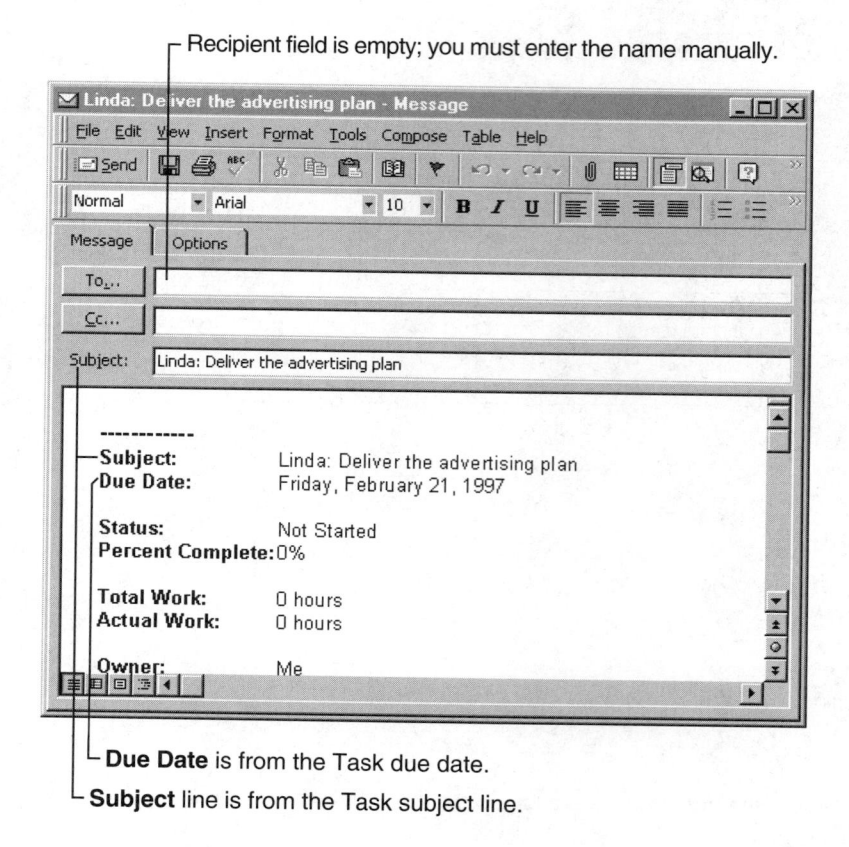

Recipient field is empty; you must enter the name manually.

Due Date is from the Task due date.
Subject line is from the Task subject line.

When recipients receive an action item as a message, they can drag the action item from their Inbox to their task list in Outlook. Storing action items as tasks in Outlook helps attendees keep track of their progress toward completing the action items.

Sharing Information with PowerPoint 97

PowerPoint 97 fully supports copying and pasting linked or unlinked data, as described in the "Overview" earlier in this chapter. In addition, PowerPoint includes special features for importing presentations from and exporting them to Word.

Importing Outlines from Word

PowerPoint determines the outline structure for the presentation based on the paragraph formatting of the imported document, as follows:

- By heading styles

  If the paragraphs are formatted as heading styles in Word, PowerPoint structures the presentation outline according to the headings. Every Heading 1 becomes the title for a new slide, Heading 2 becomes the first level of text, and so forth. Text formatted as anything other than a heading style is not imported to the presentation.

- By indented paragraphs

  If the paragraphs are not styled with heading styles, PowerPoint structures the presentation outline according to how the paragraphs are indented. Every paragraph flush with the left margin becomes the title for a new slide, paragraphs indented once become the first level of text, and so forth.

- By leading tabs

  If the paragraphs are indented with leading tabs—as in a plain text file—PowerPoint uses the number of leading tabs to determine the outline structure. Every paragraph with no leading tab becomes the title for a new slide, paragraphs with one leading tab become the first level of text, and so forth.

Note PowerPoint supports five levels of text. If the imported outline has more than five levels, levels six and beyond are imported as level-five text in PowerPoint.

Part 5 Using Microsoft Office Throughout Your Organization

The following illustration shows a Word outline imported into PowerPoint.

PowerPoint converts heading styles in the Word outline to a presentation structure in outline view.

… Chapter 27 Sharing Information with Microsoft Office Applications

Exporting Presentations to Word

You can export presentations to Word using the Write-Up feature in PowerPoint, and you can export meeting minutes and action items to Word by using the export feature in Meeting Minder. This section describes how these features work.

Using Write-Up

Use the **Write-Up** dialog box to place slides and speaker note text on pages according to options you specify in PowerPoint, as follows. (To display the dialog box, click **Send To** on the **File** menu, then click **Microsoft Word**.)

- **Notes next to slides**

    If you select the **Notes next to slides** option, Word creates a three-column table for the slides and notes. For each slide, Word places the slide number in the first column, the slide in the second column, and the note text in the third column.

- **Notes below slides**

    If you select the **Notes below slides** option, Word places the slides and notes in separate paragraphs. For each slide, Word generates a page with the slide number in the first paragraph, the slide in the second paragraph, and the note text in the third paragraph.

- **Outline only**

    If you select the **Outline only** option, Word creates an outline of the presentation text and does not import slide images. Slide titles are converted to Heading 1 style paragraphs, first-level text is converted to Heading 2 style paragraphs, and so forth.

    Note You can also select the **Blank lines next to slides** or **Blank lines below slides** option to print a series of blank lines in place of speaker notes text, so that audience members can jot down their own notes.

▶ **To export PowerPoint presentations to Word**

1 On the PowerPoint **File** menu, point to **Send To**, and then click **Microsoft Word**.

2 In the **Write-Up** dialog box, select the layout you want.

3 To embed the slides in the Word document, select **Paste**.

   –or–

   To link the slides, select **Paste link**.

Note The option to embed or link slides is available in PowerPoint for Windows only.

Part 5 Using Microsoft Office Throughout Your Organization

PowerPoint starts Word, opens a new document based on the Normal template, and exports the presentation to Word, as shown in the following illustration.

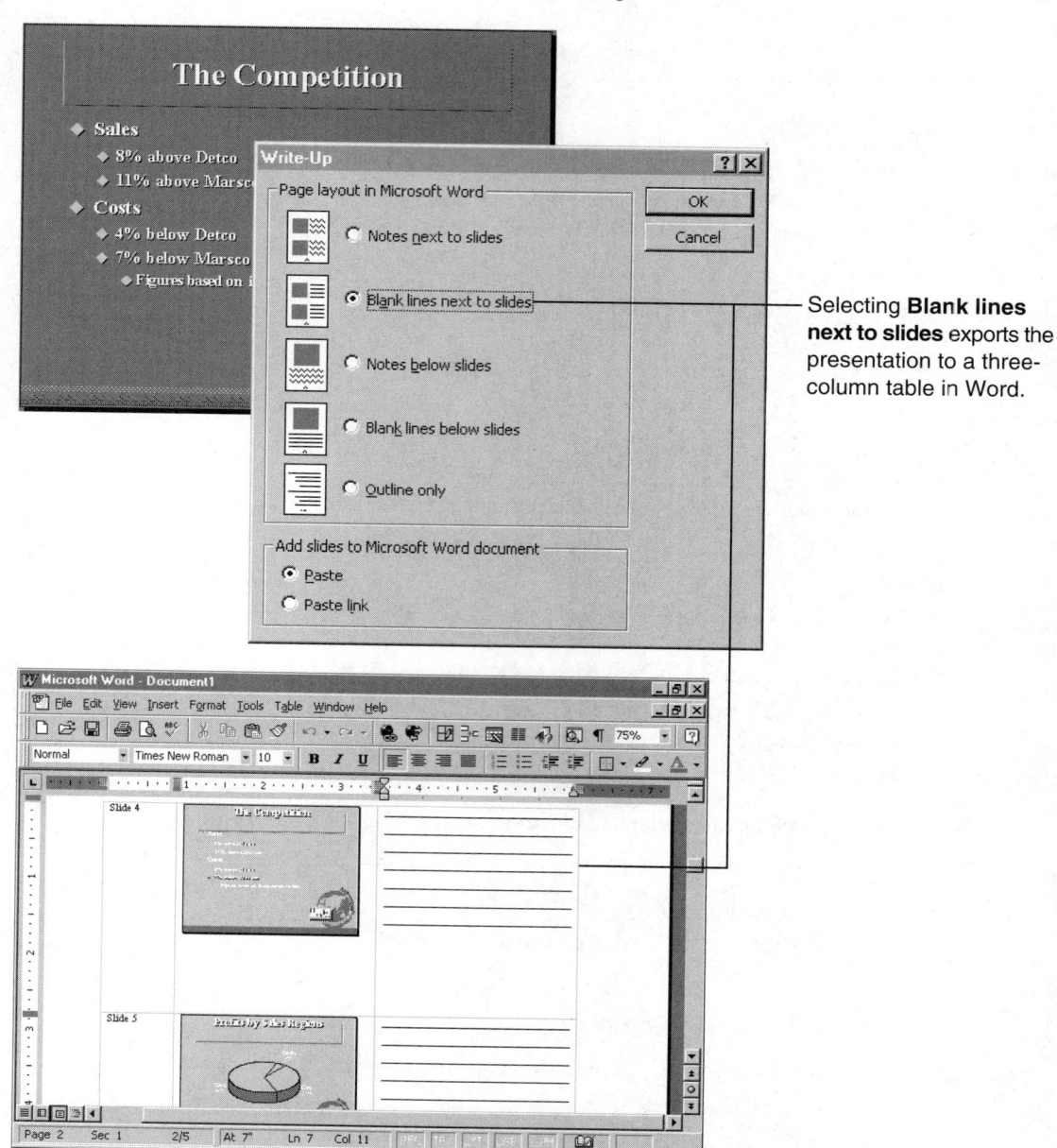

Selecting **Blank lines next to slides** exports the presentation to a three-column table in Word.

Embedding or Linking Slides (Windows only)

You can either embed or link the presentation slides in the Word document, with the following results:

- If you embed PowerPoint slides, the resulting Word document increases substantially in file size and is not updated to reflect changes either to the slides or to the location of the presentation file.
- If you link PowerPoint slides, the resulting Word document remains small and is updated to reflect changes both to the slides and to the location of the presentation file.

Using Meeting Minder

With Meeting Minder, you can format, edit, and print meeting minutes and action items by exporting them to a Word document. Word places all the meeting minutes and action items for the presentation in a single document, where you can edit it before printing or distributing it.

Note You can use Outlook to send action items to the appropriate people. For information about using Outlook with PowerPoint, see Chapter 28, "Working with Messaging Systems and Connectivity Software."

▶ **To export meeting minutes and action items to Word**

1. On the **Tools** menu, click **Meeting Minder**.

    –or–

    If you are running a slide show, right-click in the presentation, and point to **Meeting Minder**.

2. Click **Export**, select the **Send meeting minutes and action items to Microsoft Word** check box, and click **Export Now**.

    PowerPoint starts Word, opens a new document based on the Normal template, and exports the meeting minutes and action items to Word, as shown in the following illustration.

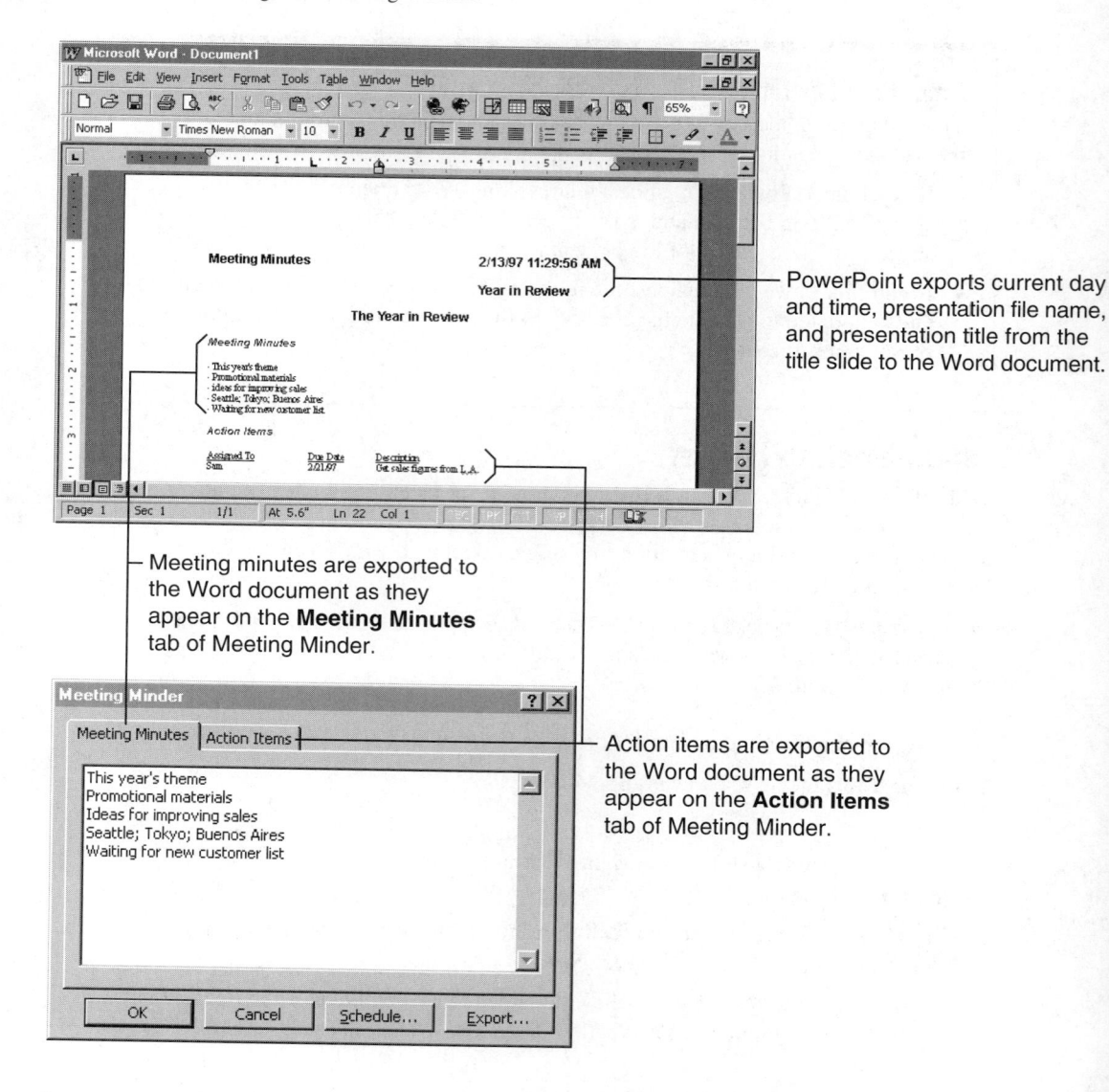

Part 5   Using Microsoft Office Throughout Your Organization

PowerPoint exports current day and time, presentation file name, and presentation title from the title slide to the Word document.

Meeting minutes are exported to the Word document as they appear on the **Meeting Minutes** tab of Meeting Minder.

Action items are exported to the Word document as they appear on the **Action Items** tab of Meeting Minder.

Sharing Information with Word 97

Word 97 fully supports copying and pasting linked or unlinked data, as described in the "Overview" earlier in this chapter. In addition, Word includes text converters for importing Microsoft Excel and Lotus 1-2-3 worksheet data into tables, and for importing Word documents into Lotus Notes.

Note Word also supports the conversion of Word documents to HTML for intranets or the Internet. For more information, see "Web Support in Microsoft Word 97" in Chapter 25, "Web Support in Microsoft Office Applications."

Importing Worksheets from Microsoft Excel

You can open or import Microsoft Excel versions 2.x–97 worksheets or named ranges into Word. In Word, the worksheet is converted to a table in its own document.

▶ **To import a Microsoft Excel worksheet or named range into Word**

1. On the Word **File** menu, click **Open**.

   –or–

   On the **Insert** menu, click **File**.

2. Select the Microsoft Excel workbook that contains the data you want to import, and then click **Open**.
3. If the **Convert File** dialog box appears, select **Microsoft Excel Worksheet**.
4. In the **Open Worksheet** dialog box, select the worksheet that contains the data you want to import. If the data is in a specific named range, select that.

The Microsoft Excel text converter functions in one direction only: Data can be brought into Word from Microsoft Excel worksheets but cannot be saved in Microsoft Excel format.

Formatting Features

The following table describes conversion issues that may affect your data or formatting when you import Microsoft Excel worksheets into Word 97.

When this Microsoft Excel 97 feature	Is imported into Word 97
Fill	Specified fill characters become left-aligned.
Row height	Each row takes on the height of the cell that contains the most text.
Column width	Most columns retain their width. Hidden columns and zero-width columns become a standard width.
Hidden columns	Hidden columns are converted as regular table columns.

Numeric Formatting Features

The following table describes conversion issues that may affect your data or formatting when you import Microsoft Excel worksheets into Word 97.

When this Microsoft Excel 97 feature	Is imported into Word 97
Regular Microsoft Excel formats	Microsoft Excel tries to fit numbers in General format into the current column width. These numbers are brought in at full precision. This may result in more decimal places than are displayed on the worksheet.
User-defined formats	The question mark (?) and asterisk (*) characters are not supported when used to define fractional number formats. For example, if the value of a cell is 0.5 and the user-defined number format is **# ?/?**, Microsoft Excel displays 1/2; Word displays 0.5.

Worksheet Size

The following table describes conversion issues that may affect your data or formatting when you import Microsoft Excel worksheets into Word 97.

When this Microsoft Excel 97 feature	Is imported into Word 97
Fewer than 32 columns	A table is created in Word.
More than 32 columns or wider than 22 inches	The worksheet is imported into Word as tab-delimited text.

Note Microsoft Excel 4.0 allows you to press ALT+ENTER to begin a new line within a text cell. The resulting new-line character is translated to a paragraph mark in a table if the original Microsoft Excel worksheet width is 32 columns or fewer, or to a new-line character in tab-delimited text. These conversions ensure mail-merge compatibility.

Importing Worksheets from Lotus 1-2-3

You can open or import Lotus 1-2-3 2.*x*–4.0 worksheets into Word. Once in Word, the worksheet is converted to a table. The Lotus 1-2-3 text converter functions in one direction only: Data can be brought into Word from Lotus 1-2-3 worksheets but cannot be saved in Microsoft Excel format.

The procedure for importing Lotus 1-2-3 worksheets into Word is the same as the procedure for importing Microsoft Excel worksheets into Word, as described earlier.

Formatting Features

The following table describes conversion issues that may affect your data or formatting when you import Lotus 1-2-3 worksheets into Word 97.

When this Lotus 1-2-3 feature	Is imported into Word 97
Font	All Lotus 1-2-3 data becomes 10-point Courier font.
Numeric formatting	Lotus 1-2-3 tries to fit numbers in General format into the current column width. These numbers are brought in at full precision. This may result in more decimal places than are displayed on the worksheet.

Worksheet Size

The following table describes import issues that may affect your data or formatting when you import Lotus 1-2-3 worksheets into Word 97.

When this Lotus 1-2-3 feature	Is imported into Word 97
Fewer than 32 columns	A table is created in Word.
More than 32 columns or wider than 22 inches	The worksheet is imported into Word as tab-delimited text.

Other Features

The following table describes import issues that may affect your data or formatting when you import Lotus 1-2-3 worksheets into Word 97.

When this Lotus 1-2-3 feature	Is imported into Word 97
Ranges	The converter displays a dialog box asking you to choose from a list of range names. Type a Lotus 1-2-3 range (b2..g43) or choose an existing range name (my_data), or press ENTER to convert the entire worksheet. Note that 3-D range names are supported correctly, but explicit 3-D range definitions (for example, a:a1..c:c5) are not supported.
Password	If the worksheet is password protected, you must enter the password. Note that you may have to reenter the password when beginning a print merge operation. Password-protected files created in Lotus 1-2-3 version 3.*x* cannot be converted.
Empty files	Empty worksheets are imported into Word 97 as a single empty cell.

Note Word can import PIC graphics files created by Lotus 1-2-3 and Borland Quattro Pro. Word cannot import Micrografx PIC or Draw Plus PIC files.

Exporting Word Outlines to PowerPoint

You can export the outline of a Word document to PowerPoint. If the paragraphs are formatted as heading styles in Word, PowerPoint structures the presentation outline according to the heading styles. Every Heading 1 paragraph becomes the title for a new slide, a Heading 2 paragraph becomes the first level of text, and so forth. Text formatted as anything other than a heading style is not imported to the presentation.

If the paragraphs are not styled with heading styles, PowerPoint structures the presentation outline according to the way the paragraphs are indented. For more information about how PowerPoint structures an imported Word document, see "Sharing Information with PowerPoint 97" earlier in this chapter.

▶ **To export a Word outline to PowerPoint**

- On the Word **File** menu, point to **Send to**, and then click **Microsoft PowerPoint**.

    Word exports the heading-level paragraphs to PowerPoint. The Word document opens in PowerPoint as a new presentation in outline view.

After you export the outline, you can add additional text to the presentation in PowerPoint, but there is no link back to the outline in the original Word document.

Exporting Word Documents to Lotus Notes

When you install Office, Setup detects whether Lotus Notes 3.*x* or 4.*x* (16-bit or 32-bit) is installed on the computer. If it is, Setup automatically installs Lotus Notes converters for Microsoft Excel and Word. With these text converters, you can import Word and Microsoft Excel documents into a Notes memo. For more information about working with Lotus Notes, see "Interoperability with Lotus Notes and cc:Mail" in Chapter 28, "Working with Messaging Systems and Connectivity Software."

Using Microsoft Bookshelf in a Workgroup

Microsoft Office 97 for Windows, Professional Edition, and Microsoft Office 97 for the Macintosh include a special edition of Microsoft Bookshelf called Bookshelf Basics. Bookshelf Basics includes the following titles:

- *The American Heritage Dictionary*
- *Roget's Thesaurus*
- *The Columbia Dictionary of Quotations*
- *More About Bookshelf* (This document describes additional reference sources available in the full Microsoft Bookshelf product.)

Setup adds commands to Microsoft Excel, PowerPoint, and Word and to Bookshelf Basics (or to the full Bookshelf product) so that users of these applications can quickly share content between Bookshelf and the Office applications.

Bookshelf Integration with Microsoft Excel

Setup adds the **Look up reference** command to the **Tools** menu in Microsoft Excel. Clicking the **Look up reference** command displays a list of all available reference titles that you can search.

Note   If you are running Office from a CD, this command is not available.

Bookshelf Integration with PowerPoint and Word

Setup adds the **Look up reference** command to the **Tools** menu in Word and in PowerPoint. Clicking the **Look up reference** command displays a list of all available reference titles that you can search.

In addition, right-clicking selected text in Word or PowerPoint displays a shortcut menu. Clicking the **Define** command on the shortcut menu searches *The American Heritage Dictionary* for the definition of the selected word or the word nearest the insertion point.

Note   If you are running Office from a CD, these commands are not available.

Office Integration with Bookshelf

In addition to adding commands to the Office applications, Setup adds functionality to Bookshelf Basics (or to the full Bookshelf product).

Integration with Office for Windows

In Office 97 for Windows, Professional Edition, Setup adds the following commands to the **Edit** menu in Bookshelf Basics (or in the full Bookshelf product).

This command on the Bookshelf Edit menu	Has this effect
Copy to Word	Copies the current Bookshelf topic, and then prompts the user to paste it into the active Word document or into a new document.
Copy to Excel	Copies the current Bookshelf topic, and then prompts the user to paste it into the active Microsoft Excel workbook or into a new workbook.
Copy to PowerPoint	Copies the current Bookshelf topic, and then prompts the user to paste it into the active PowerPoint presentation or into a new presentation.

> **Note** If you are running the full Bookshelf program from a CD, these commands are not available.

Integration with Office for the Macintosh

If you are using Office for the Macintosh, no additional commands are added to the **Edit** menu in Bookshelf. Instead, you can use the **Copy** and **Paste** commands (**Edit** menu) to copy Bookshelf content into Office applications.

Using Microsoft Camcorder in a Workgroup

Microsoft Camcorder is included in the Value Pack in Office 97 for Windows.

> **Note** The CD-ROM version of Office includes the Office 97 Value Pack, a collection of application extras such as clip art, maps, sounds, presentation enhancements, and utilities. For more information about the Office 97 Value Pack and how to use its contents, see Valupack.hlp in the ValuPack folder on the Office CD.

Microsoft Camcorder is a basic screen capture and playback program. With Camcorder, you can capture a sequence of events on your computer screen and save it to an AVI format file, or create a self-running executable that plays back the video clip. If your computer is equipped with sound capabilities, you can also add audio narration as you capture the screen events. Camcorder executables can be played back only on computers running Windows.

Camcorder is a useful tool for workgroup training and support. Because the video clip executables that Camcorder creates are highly compressed, you can easily distribute short video clips throughout your workgroup through e-mail or store them in public folders or on shared network drives.

The following table gives some general indications of the size of Camcorder video clips. A 2-minute sequence of screen events (starting applications, dragging text, and so forth) results in the following approximate video clip sizes.

Video clip format	Without sound	With sound
AVI (requires Camcorder or another playback application)	67K	1.4 MB
EXE (self-running)	54K	240K

As the table shows, Camcorder executables are smaller than AVI files and substantially smaller when sound is included.

CHAPTER 28

Working with Messaging Systems and Connectivity Software

This chapter describes how Microsoft Office 97 applications integrate electronic mail (e-mail) and connectivity software. It addresses how Office applications incorporate e-mail in general, and also explains how Office applications work with specific messaging and connectivity software.

In This Chapter
Interoperability with Electronic Mail   793
Interoperability with Microsoft Exchange Server   798
Interoperability with Microsoft Mail 3.x   799
Interoperability with Lotus Notes Mail and cc:Mail   800
Interoperability with Lotus Notes/FX   800
Interoperability with Other Electronic Mail Systems   801

See Also
- For information about upgrading to Microsoft Outlook from other e-mail applications, see Chapter 13, "Upgrading to Microsoft Outlook."
- For information about how Outlook works with other Office applications, see Chapter 27, "Sharing Information with Microsoft Office Applications."
- For information about using individual Office applications in a workgroup, see the application-specific chapters in Part 5, "Using Microsoft Office Throughout Your Organization."

Interoperability with Electronic Mail

Microsoft Office 97 applications are *mail-enabled*: They can make use of the e-mail application installed on your computer. In addition, Outlook can use Word for composing e-mail messages, a feature known as *WordMail*. This interoperability of

Office applications and e-mail is not dependent on a specific e-mail application, but instead depends on the interface that underlies many e-mail applications.

Most e-mail applications adhere to either the MAPI or Vendor Independent Messaging (VIM). MAPI and VIM provide a common interface that Office applications can use; the details of the specific e-mail application do not matter. This section explains how Office works with MAPI and VIM e-mail applications.

Integrating Electronic Mail with Office

The Office applications include commands to send and route documents through e-mail. These commands work with simple MAPI applications as well as applications that support MAPI 1.0 or later, such as Microsoft Mail 3.*x* for Windows and Microsoft Exchange Client. These commands also work with 16-bit VIM-based mail applications including cc:Mail and Lotus Notes. This section describes how the Office Setup program installs e-mail capability, how to configure Word as your e-mail editor, and how to use e-mail commands in Office applications.

Note 16-bit VIM applications are not supported on Windows NT Workstation version 3.51 or Windows NT Workstation version 4.0.

Installing E-mail Capability

Setup installs e-mail capability automatically when you install Outlook or if you already have an e-mail client (such as Microsoft Exchange Client) installed on the computer. If you have more than one e-mail client, you can designate during Setup which client the Office applications should use.

The following files are installed by Setup for e-mail support.

DLL File	Purpose
Mapi32	Provides 32-bit MAPI support
Mapivi32	Provides 16-bit VIM support
Mapivitk	Communicates with the 16-bit VIM information service

▶ **To install VIM for Office applications**

1. Start the Office Setup program.
2. If you are running Setup for the first time, click **Custom**.

    –or–

    If you are running Setup after Office has been installed, click **Add/Remove**.
3. Select the **Office Tools** option and then click **Change Option**.
4. Select the **Lotus VIM Mail Support** check box.

Using WordMail

Users of Outlook or Microsoft Exchange Client can use Word as their e-mail editor. WordMail allows you to use the editing and formatting capabilities of Word when you compose messages, but maintains compatibility with plain-text e-mail applications.

Installing WordMail

WordMail is installed when you choose the Typical installation during Setup. After running Setup, you can choose whether to use WordMail by making it available or unavailable. If you install Outlook with Office, WordMail is available by default.

▶ **To make WordMail available or unavailable for use with Outlook**

1. On the Outlook **Tools** menu, click **Options**, and then click the **E-mail** tab.
2. Select or clear the **Use Microsoft Word as the e-mail editor** check box.

Note WordMail does not support Microsoft Exchange Client extensions. If you install custom extensions, you must disable WordMail to use the extensions.

Setting Up E-mail Templates

By default WordMail uses the Email.dot template when you compose messages. This template provides styles for message headers and also provides predefined shortcut key functions.

By modifying this template, you can customize the appearance of the message headers, forward and reply headers, fonts, and message text. If you want to create customized WordMail templates, start with a copy of Email.dot to retain the basic e-mail orientation of this template. For example, you can customize the WordMail **Formatting** toolbar by modifying it in Email.dot or in a customized copy of this template.

Composing and Viewing Messages with WordMail

WordMail gives e-mail users access to most of the features of Word, including formatting, AutoCorrect, the spelling checker, and macros. The highlighter pen is particularly useful to mark areas of interest in long messages and replies.

A few Word features are unavailable in WordMail:

- The **New** command (**File** menu)

    Use commands on the **Compose** menu in Outlook to start a new WordMail message.

- The **Save All** command (**File** menu)

    Because each message is in its own window, **Save All** is not needed.

- The **Templates** command (**File** menu)

    To change the template used for WordMail messages, click **Options** on the Outlook **Tools** menu, click the **E-mail** tab, and then click **Template** to change templates. You cannot change the template for a message after you open or start composing a message.

- The **Send To** command (**File** menu)

    Send documents directly from Outlook, or create a document in Word and then route or send it.

- The **Print Preview** command (**File** menu)

    To preview a WordMail message, paste it into a separate Word document and use the Word **Print Preview** command (**File** menu). This gives you a preview of the body of the message only, without the message headers (name, address, and subject lines), which are always included when you print the message in Outlook. To print the Outlook headers on a separate page from the message text, insert a page break at the beginning of the message text in WordMail. This preserves pagination of the body of the message.

- The **MailMerge** and **Envelopes And Labels** commands (**Tools** menu)

    To use WordMail messages in mailings, copy the message into a separate Word document.

- The **Customize** command (**Tools** menu)

    To change the WordMail **Formatting** toolbar, modify it in Email.dot or in a customized copy of the Email.dot template.

- The **Window** menu

    Because each message is in its own window, the **Window** menu commands are not needed. To view the message in a split window, copy the message to a separate Word document.

Sending Messages Between WordMail and Other E-mail Applications

Both Outlook and WordMail save messages in Rich Text Format (RTF). To be compatible with other e-mail clients and editors, WordMail saves messages in both RTF and plain-text formats. Recipients who do not have WordMail, such as users of Microsoft Mail 3.*x* for Windows or cc:Mail, receive the plain-text version.

When converting from RTF to plain text, WordMail converts the RTF items to their nearest plain-text equivalent. If the converted message is returned to WordMail from the plain-text application, all of the RTF items that were converted to plain text remain plain text. WordMail does not reconvert the message to RTF format.

The text editor in Outlook supports some but not all of the RTF features available in WordMail. If you are running Outlook but have not enabled WordMail, you can see most of the rich text in a message created in WordMail. For information about Outlook support of RTF, see "Sharing Information with Microsoft Exchange Client" in Chapter 13, "Upgrading to Microsoft Outlook."

Using E-mail Commands in Office Applications

When Word, Microsoft Excel, and PowerPoint are installed with e-mail capabilities, the **Send To** submenu appears on the **File** menu of each application. Commands on this submenu allow you to send the document as e-mail or to route the document to a number of recipients. The **Mail Recipient** command starts the e-mail client and creates a new message that includes the document as an attachment. The **Routing Recipient** command opens the **Add Routing Slip** dialog box, where you enter a list of recipients, an accompanying message, and routing options.

Unlike the other Office applications, when Microsoft Access is set up to use e-mail, the **Send** command appears on the **File** menu. This command has the same function as the **Mail Recipient** command in the other Office applications. Microsoft Access users who want to route information must export the information to one of the other Office applications.

When Outlook is installed with Office on a computer connected to Microsoft Exchange Server, the **Send To** submenu on the **File** menu in Microsoft Excel, PowerPoint, and Word also includes the **Exchange Folder** command. This command allows you to post a copy of a document in a public folder so that others can open it. For more information about public folders, see your Microsoft Exchange Server documentation.

Using Address Books

Word and WordMail allow you to choose names and addresses from the MAPI personal address book (PAB) or the Outlook or Schedule+ 95 contact list stored on your computer. Click the **Insert Address** button to see a list of the names most recently used, or to browse the address book.

When you insert names and addresses using the **Insert Address** button, their content and layout are determined by the AutoText entries **NameLayout** and **AddressLayout**. You can modify these AutoText entries to conform to the address requirements of your e-mail application.

The default **NameLayout** and **AddressLayout** AutoText entries map to properties in the address book or contact list as follows, where the vertical bar (|) means **OR**, curly brackets ({}) enclose alternatives, and \r indicates a carriage return.

The **NameLayout** entry maps to these properties:

{<PR_GIVEN_NAME> <PR_SURNAME> | <PR_DISPLAY_NAME>}

The **AddressLayout** entry maps to these properties:

{{<PR_GIVEN_NAME> <PR_SURNAME> | <PR_DISPLAY_NAME>}\r}
{{<PR_STREET_ADDRESS>\r}
{{<PR_LOCALITY>}{, <PR_STATE_OR_PROVINCE> <PR_POSTAL_CODE>}\r}
{<PR_COUNTRY>\r}
| <PR_POSTAL_ADDRESS>\r}

The address book capability has the following limitations:

- To have access to the MAPI PAB, MAPI support (such as that provided by Outlook) must be installed on your computer.

  To set up a Contact list, Schedule+ 1.0 users must upgrade to Outlook or Schedule+ 95.

Supporting Mailing, Routing, and Posting

The WordMail and Office Binder features may increase the e-mail traffic on your network. Both Outlook and WordMail messages are larger than plain-text messages. This is true especially if your environment mixes WordMail and plain-text e-mail clients, because plain-text clients receive both plain text and RTF versions of messages from WordMail users. WordMail messages are slightly larger than Outlook messages, but are smaller than a Word document sent as an attachment to an e-mail message. Office Binder files can result in large e-mail messages.

Use the following guidelines to make the best use of network resources:

- When a document can be passed from one recipient to another, encourage users to route the document instead of mailing a separate copy to each recipient.
- Let users know the maximum message size accepted by your e-mail application, and explain what happens when they exceed this size.
- Encourage users to consider alternatives to mailing large documents.
- For example, users can copy large documents to a network server and mail links to the shared file using the Windows Package application. If your site has Microsoft Exchange Server, users can post large documents to public folders. Alternatively, users can share their computer or a folder on their computer over the network.

Interoperability with Microsoft Exchange Server

To post documents to public folders from Office applications, install Microsoft Outlook with Office. When Outlook is installed, the command **Exchange Folder** is added to the **Send To** submenu (**File** menu) in Microsoft Excel, PowerPoint, and Word. Public folders are available only to users who are connected to Microsoft Exchange Server.

Posting Documents to Public Folders

Users can post documents directly from the Office applications to any public folders for which they have permission. To post a document, users must first log on to Microsoft Exchange Server and open the document they want to share with other Microsoft Exchange users.

▶ **To post an Office document to a public folder**

1. On the **File** menu, point to **Send To**, and then click **Exchange Folder**.
2. Select the public folder in which to post the document.

For information about setting up Microsoft Exchange Server and making public folders available to users, see your Microsoft Exchange Server documentation.

Creating Custom Properties and Views in Public Folders

Using Outlook with Microsoft Exchange Server, you can create custom views of the information stored in public folders. Custom views allow you to display details about the stored information and to display them in a particular sequence. When Office documents are posted to a public folder, custom views can make use of the properties stored with each document. You can create highly customized views by basing them on custom properties in documents. For example, a custom view could list information about all documents associated with a particular project using a custom **Project Name** property.

For information about creating custom views see your Microsoft Exchange Server documentation. For information about using document properties in Office applications, see Chapter 23, "Tracking Collaboration with Document Properties."

Interoperability with Microsoft Mail 3.x

Office applications work with Microsoft Mail 3.x clients, but Office users who use a Microsoft Mail 3.x client for e-mail are limited as follows:

- They cannot use WordMail.

  In a mixed e-mail environment, WordMail messages are delivered to Microsoft Mail 3.x clients as plain text.

- They cannot post documents to public folders.

  This capability requires the Microsoft Exchange Server and client software, such as Outlook or Microsoft Exchange Client.

Interoperability with Lotus Notes Mail and cc:Mail

Office applications work with Lotus Notes Mail or cc:Mail clients, but Office users who use a Lotus Notes Mail or cc:Mail client are limited as follows:

- They cannot use WordMail.

    In a mixed e-mail environment, WordMail messages are delivered to Lotus Notes Mail or cc:Mail clients as plain text.

- They cannot post documents to public folders.

    This capability requires the Microsoft Exchange Server and client software, such as Outlook or Microsoft Exchange Client.

For information about installing support for Lotus Notes Mail and cc:Mail, "Integrating Electronic Mail with Office" earlier in this chapter.

Interoperability with Lotus Notes/FX

The Office applications support Lotus Notes/FX versions 1.0 and 1.1 through extensions to OLE. Although Office users cannot post directly to a Lotus Notes database, they can embed documents created by Office applications, including Office Binder, in a Lotus Notes message. Users can open and modify the embedded documents. When you click the **Update** command (**File** menu) from within the document in the Office application, or when you close and save the Lotus Notes message, the changes are written to the Lotus Notes database.

Properties listed on the **General**, **Summary**, and **Statistics** tabs in the **Properties** dialog box (**File** menu) in the Office applications are recognized by Lotus Notes/FX. In addition, any custom properties that you create beginning with **PROP_** are recognized by Lotus Notes/FX.

▶ **To create custom properties for Lotus Notes/FX**

1. On the **File** menu in the Office application, click **Properties**, and then click the **Custom** tab.
2. In the **Name** box, type **PROP_** followed by a name for the custom property.
3. In the **Type** box, select the property type.
4. In the **Value** box, type the text, date, or number, or select **Yes** or **No** for the property, depending on the property type you selected in Step 3.
5. Click **Add**.

Office includes text converters that allow a Lotus Notes user to import text from Microsoft Excel or Word documents. These converters are not installed by default when you choose the Typical installation during Setup. To install the converters, choose the Custom installation or rerun Setup and click **Add/Remove**. Then select the **Converters for use with Lotus Notes** check box under the **Converters** option. The converters allow Lotus Notes versions 3.*x* and 4.*x* to import text from Microsoft Excel versions 2.*x*–7 workbooks, and to import text from Word versions 6.0–97 documents.

Interoperability with Other Electronic Mail Systems

MSN, The Microsoft Network uses Outlook as its message editor. So when you enable WordMail, it replaces the standard MSN editor for reading and composing messages.

In Windows 95, any user with a modem has access to Internet e-mail using MSN. Similarly, because Windows 95 includes CompuServe mail capability for Microsoft Exchange Client, any user who has a CompuServe account can use a Microsoft Exchange client (such as Outlook or Microsoft Exchange Client) and WordMail to read and compose messages.

For information about MSN connectivity and retrieving e-mail on the Internet, see the *Microsoft Windows 95 Resource Kit*, published by Microsoft Press and available wherever computer books are sold.

CHAPTER 29

Workgroup Features in Microsoft Access

This chapter explains how to administer features in Microsoft Access that are designed for sharing database applications developed in Microsoft Access among users in a workgroup. It describes how the various workgroup features of Microsoft Access work and provides information for supporting them.

In This Chapter
Security Features in Microsoft Access   803
Multiuser Applications and Locking   825
Database Replication   834
Visual SourceSafe   852

See Also
- For a summary of new and improved features in Microsoft Access 97, see Chapter 2, "What's New in Microsoft Office 97."
- For information about supporting workgroups that are running more than one version of Microsoft Access, see Chapter 22, "Supporting Multiple Versions of Microsoft Office."
- For information about the structure of Microsoft Access and how its components fit together, see Chapter 35, "Microsoft Access Architecture."

Note Microsoft Access runs only on Windows 95 and Windows NT Workstation version 3.51 or later.

Security Features in Microsoft Access

As a workgroup administrator, you might initiate or oversee workgroup-wide security practices for protecting Microsoft Access database applications. This section describes the options available in Microsoft Access for protecting databases and applications developed in Microsoft Access. These options are independent of any additional security measures at the operating system level.

Microsoft Access supports several levels and methods of file protection:

- User access restriction

    You can use startup options to restrict access to default menus and toolbars, the Database window, and special keys.

- File open protection

    You can set a password to control opening the database.

- Source code protection

    You can save an application as an MDE file to remove Visual Basic for Applications source code and prevent changes to the design of forms, reports, and modules.

- Database encryption

    You can use database encryption to prevent unauthorized users from viewing the objects in an application with a disk editor or other utility program. You can use encryption in conjunction with all other methods of protecting an application.

- User-level security

    You can use user-level security to apply the most powerful and flexible method of protecting an application. However, establishing user-level security is a complex process that may exceed your requirements. If this is the case, use one or more of the other security methods.

The strategy you use depends on the extent of security you need and how the application is used. The following sections explain these options.

Restricting User Access with Startup Options

In a casual environment where strict security is not required, you can use still startup options to restrict access to default menus and toolbars, the Database window, and special keys. To perform the following procedure, the application must have a startup form and a custom menu bar that contains only the commands you want available.

For information about creating a startup form or a custom menu bar, see Microsoft Access online Help.

▶ **To use startup options to protect an application**

1. On the **Tools** menu, click **Startup**.
2. In the **Display Form** box, click the name of the startup form.
3. In the **Menu Bar** box, click the name of the menu bar.
4. Click **Advanced**.

5. Clear the following check boxes: **Allow Full Menus**, **Allow Default Shortcut Menus**, **Display Database Window**, **Allow Built-in Toolbars**, **Allow Toolbar/Menu Changes**, and **Use Access Special Keys**.

6. Use Visual Basic to set the **AllowBypassKey** property to **False**.

   This prevents users from using the SHIFT key to bypass the settings in the **Startup** dialog box. For information about how to set the **AllowBypassKey** property, see Microsoft Access online Help.

A user who knows how to create the appropriate line of Visual Basic code can bypass this method of security by setting the **AllowBypassKey** property of the database back to **True**. If you want a higher level of security, establish user-level security in addition to, or instead of, setting startup options. For information about user-level security, see "Setting User-Level Security" later in this chapter.

Protecting File Open with a Database Password

Assigning a password to a database is an easy way to prevent unauthorized users from opening an application. Use this approach when you want to control which users can open an application, but not whether they can modify or save the application.

Important Before you set the database password, make a backup copy of the database. Also, close the database before you set the password; if the database is located on a server or in a shared folder, make sure no other user has it open.

▶ **To set a database password**

1. On the **File** menu, click **Open Database**.
2. In the **Open** dialog box, select the **Exclusive** check box, and then open the database.
3. On the **Tools** menu, point to **Security**, and then click **Set Database Password**.
4. In the **Password** box, type the password. Passwords are case-sensitive.
5. In the **Verify** box, type the password again to confirm it, and then click **OK**.

Caution If you or a user in your workgroup assigns password protection to a database and then forgets the password, you cannot open the database, gain access to its data in another table through links, remove protection from the database, or recover data from the tables. Keep a list of your passwords and their corresponding database names in a safe place.

Important Do not use a database password if you plan to replicate the database. You cannot synchronize a replicated database if a database password has been set. Defining user-level security permissions does not interfere with replica synchronization. For more information about database replication, see "Database Replication" later in this chapter.

When you set a database password, the **Set Database Password** command changes to **Unset Database Password**. To clear a database password, click **Unset Database Password** on the **Security** submenu (**Tools** menu), type the correct password in the **Password** box, and then confirm it in the **Verify** box.

Anyone who knows the database password and has access to the **Unset Database Password** command can change or clear the password. To prevent users from changing or clearing the password, or from setting an initial password, use user-level security to remove the Administer permission on the database for all users and groups except the database administrator. By default, the Users group, the Admins group, and the creator (owner) of the database all have Administer permission on the database. For more information about permissions, see "Setting User-Level Security" later in this chapter.

If you use a password to protect a database containing tables that are linked to another database, anyone who can open the database that contains the link can open the linked table. When the link is established, Microsoft Access stores the password in an unencrypted form. If this compromises the security of the password-protected database, do not use a database password to protect the database. Instead, establish user-level security to control access to the sensitive data. For more information, see "Setting User-Level Security" later in this chapter.

Note Setting a database password does not prevent someone from using a disk editor or other utility program to read data without opening the database. To prevent this, encrypt the database. For more information about encrypting a database, see "Encrypting a Database" later in this chapter.

Protecting Source Code with an MDE File

Saving a database as an MDE file creates a copy of the database that contains no Visual Basic source code. Saving a database application as an MDE file also reduces the size of the database and makes the application's use of memory more efficient. The code is compiled and functional, but cannot be viewed or edited. In an MDE file, users can view or modify the design of the following objects:

- Macros
- Queries
- Relationships
- Tables

However, users cannot view or modify the design of forms, reports, or modules.

Note Saving a database as an MDE file does not create a run-time version of the database. To use an MDE database, users must have Microsoft Access 97 installed. Alternatively, if you have Microsoft Office 97, Developer Edition, you can save a database as an MDE file and then use the Setup Wizard to create a distributable run-time version of it.

Saving a database as an MDE file prevents a user from:

- Viewing or modifying the design of forms, reports, or modules.
- Creating forms, reports, or modules.
- Adding or deleting references to object libraries or databases by clicking **References** (**Tools** menu).
- Using the Object Browser.
- Changing code by using the properties or methods of the Microsoft Access or Visual Basic object models (because an MDE file contains no source code).
- Importing or exporting forms, reports, or modules.
- Importing forms, reports, or modules from the MDE database into another database.

    However, tables, queries, and macros can be imported from non-MDE databases. Similarly, tables, queries, and macros in an MDE database can be exported to another database.

If you need to modify the design of forms, reports, or modules in a database saved as an MDE file, you must open the original database, modify it, and then save it as an MDE file again.

Caution Be sure to save a backup copy of the original database in a safe place. If you need to modify the design of forms, reports, or modules, you must open the original database to do so. Also, a database saved as an MDE file in Microsoft Access 97 cannot be opened or converted in later versions of Microsoft Access. To convert or open it in later versions of Microsoft Access, you must use the original database.

▶ **To save a database as an MDE file**

1. Close the database. If the database is being shared on a network, make sure no other users have it open.
2. On the **Tools** menu, point to **Database Utilities**, and then click **Make MDE File**.
3. In the **Save As MDE** dialog box, select the database you want to save as an MDE file, and then click **Make MDE**.
4. In the **Save MDE As** dialog box, enter a file name for the database and the location where you want to save it, and then click **Save**.

    The original database is unchanged, and a new copy is saved as an MDE file using the file name and location you specify.

Note The process of saving a database as an MDE file automatically compiles all modules and compacts the destination database, so you do not need to perform these steps.

Because saving a database as an MDE file prevents all users (including database administrators) from modifying the design of forms, reports, and modules, this option may be too restrictive. If you require additional control and flexibility in these areas, do not save a database as an MDE file—establish user-level security instead. For more information, see "Setting User-Level Security" later in this chapter.

> **When should I use an MDE file?**
> Making an MDE file from a database that contains tables creates complications with reconciling different versions of the data if you need to modify the design of the application later. For this reason, saving a database as an MDE file is most appropriate for the front-end of an application that has been split into a back-end database containing only tables and a front-end database containing the remaining objects. For more information about splitting a database, see "Splitting a Database into a Front-end/Back-end Application" later in this chapter.

Using Other Forms of Security with MDE Files

Saving a database as an MDE file is a good way to protect the code and the design of forms and reports in a database application, without requiring users to log on and without having to manage the user accounts and permissions required by user-level security. However, an MDE file does not control how users gain access to tables, queries, and macros.

If you want more control over these database objects, establish user-level security before you save a database as an MDE file. You can use a database password to control who can open an MDE database, and you can use user-level security to control how users gain access to the tables, queries, and macros in the application. To use a database password or establish user-level security for an MDE database, you must implement these features in the original database before you save it as an MDE file. The database password or user-level security is preserved in the new MDE database.

If the database you want to save as an MDE file is secured with user-level security, you must use the Workgroup Administrator before you start Microsoft Access to join the workgroup defined by the workgroup information file that was in use when the database was created. For information about using the Workgroup Administrator, see Microsoft Access online Help.

The workgroup information file defines the user accounts used to gain access to the database. For more information about workgroup information files, see "How Workgroup and Permission Information Is Stored" later in this chapter.

Tip Instead of using the Workgroup Administrator, you can use the **/wrkgrp** command-line option to start Microsoft Access with the workgroup information file you specify. For more information about using startup command-line options, see Microsoft Access online Help.

In addition, make sure your user account has the following permissions:

- Open/Run and Open Exclusive permissions for the database object
- Modify Design or Administer permission for any tables in the database (or you must be the owner of any tables in the database)
- Read Design permission for all objects in the database

For more information about database passwords, see "Protecting File Open with a Database Password" earlier in this chapter. For more information about user-level security, see "Setting User-Level Security" later in this chapter.

Saving a Replicated Database as an MDE File

A replicated database (either a replica or a Design Master) cannot be saved as an MDE file; however, once a database is saved as an MDE file, it can be replicated. For information about replicating databases, see "Database Replication" later in this chapter.

To save a replicated database as an MDE file, you must first remove replication system fields, tables, and properties. For more information about removing replication fields, tables, and properties, see Microsoft Access online Help.

Making an MDE File from a Database That References Another Database

If you try to make an MDE file from a database (MDB) or an add-in database (MDA) that references another database or add-in, Microsoft Access displays an error message and does not complete the operation. To make an MDE file from a database that references another database, you must save all databases in the chain of references as MDE files, starting with the first database referenced. After saving the first database as an MDE file, you must then update the reference in the next database to point to the new MDE file before saving it as an MDE file, and so on.

For example, if Database1.mdb references Database2.mdb, which references Database3.mda, you would proceed as follows:

1. Save Database3.mda as Database3.mde.
2. Open Database 2.mdb and change its reference to point to the new Database3.mde.
3. Save Database2.mdb as Database2.mde.
4. Open Database1.mdb and change its reference to point to the new Database2.mde.
5. Save Database1.mdb as Database1.mde.

For information about referencing another database, see Microsoft Access online Help.

Encrypting a Database

If you want to protect a secured database from unauthorized access by someone using a disk editor or other utility program, you can encrypt it. *Encryption* makes a secured database indecipherable, protecting it from unauthorized viewing or use, particularly during electronic transmission or when it is stored on floppy disk, tape, or compact disc. Encrypting an unsecured database has no effect because anyone can open the database in Microsoft Access or Visual Basic and gain full access to all objects in the database.

The User-Level Security Wizard automatically encrypts a database. You can encrypt or decrypt a database by starting Microsoft Access without opening a database, and then clicking **Encrypt/Decrypt Database** (**Tools** menu, **Security** submenu). When you encrypt a database using the same file name as that of the original database, Microsoft Access deletes the original unencrypted file if the encryption process is successful. If an error occurs, Microsoft Access leaves the original file intact.

Note Encrypting a database slows its performance by up to 15 percent. Also, an encrypted database cannot be compressed by programs such as DriveSpace® or PKZIP. If you try to compress an encrypted database, its size does not change.

Setting User-Level Security

User-level security is the most flexible and secure method of protecting sensitive data, code, and object design in a database application developed in Microsoft Access. In addition, user-level security is the only form of Microsoft Access security that allows you to establish different levels of access to sensitive data and objects.

Before you begin establishing user-level security for an application, make sure you understand how the Microsoft Access user-level security model works. This section explains the significance of a workgroup-based user-level security model; how you can create user and group accounts to create a workgroup and establish permissions; and how you can use the tools that Microsoft Access provides, such as the User-Level Security Wizard, to help secure databases. You can also use Data Access Objects (DAO) in Visual Basic to establish and manage security in ways that are not available in the Microsoft Access user interface.

For information about establishing security using Visual Basic, see "Using Data Access Objects to Establish User-Level Security" in Chapter 14, "Securing Your Application," in *Building Applications with Microsoft Access 97*.

Understanding the Microsoft Access User-Level Security Model

Unlike the security models of most other database systems, the primary form of security in Microsoft Access is *user-level* security rather than *share-level* security. Microsoft Access user-level security is similar to the security used in most network environments, such as Microsoft Windows NT Server versions 3.51 and 4.0. When users start Microsoft Access, they enter a name and password in the **Logon** dialog box. The password confirms user identity by checking the name and password against data in the workgroup information file. Users can change their password at any time without affecting anyone else on the system. When users log on, each user is also identified as a member of one or more groups.

When a user opens a secured database, Microsoft Access determines the user's level of access to an object (including the database itself) by checking the set of permissions assigned to that user for that object. Different users and groups can have different permissions for the same objects. Every time the user tries to perform an action on an object, such as opening a form, running a query, or modifying the data in a table, Microsoft Access checks to see whether the user, or any of the groups to which the user belongs, has the necessary permissions to carry out the operation. If so, the action is performed. If not, Microsoft Access informs the user that he or she does not have permissions to perform the requested action, and the operation fails.

In contrast, database systems that provide share-level security associate passwords with specific objects, and users must supply passwords to gain access to the objects. Users who know the password for a specific object can gain access to it. A user's level of access is determined by the kind of password that user has been given. For example, managers may be given an update password for a table, allowing them to change records, and general staff members may be given a read password, allowing them to view records but not modify them.

Note Microsoft Access does provide a simple form of share-level security: the ability to protect opening a database with a password.

You can create a similar system with Microsoft Access user-level security by creating a Managers group with Update Data permission and a Staff group with only Read Data permission, and then assigning each user to the appropriate group. Users do not supply passwords when accessing the objects, because they are identified as a member of the appropriate group when they log on to Microsoft Access.

How Workgroup and Permission Information Is Stored

Microsoft Access stores information about users and groups in a database called a *workgroup information file*. A workgroup information file stores:

- The name of each user and group.
- The list of users that make up each group.

- The encrypted logon password of each user.
- The *security identifier* (SID) of each user and group.

  The SID is a machine-generated, nonreadable binary string that uniquely identifies the user or group.

Each workgroup information file defines a workgroup and can be used by many Microsoft Access databases. A *workgroup* is a group of users in a multiuser environment who share data and the same workgroup information file. You manage users, their passwords, and the groups they are assigned to in the **User and Group Accounts** dialog box (**Tools** menu, **Security** submenu). For more information about users and groups, see "Users and Groups" later in this chapter.

Permissions that you assign to users and groups for the objects in a database are stored in hidden system tables within the database. Even if a new workgroup information file is created, the permissions associated with the objects in a database do not change. You assign permissions on the **Permissions** and **Change Owner** tabs of the **User and Group Permissions** dialog box; this information affects the objects in the open database, not the workgroup information file.

The following illustration shows how these elements of Microsoft Access user-level security are related.

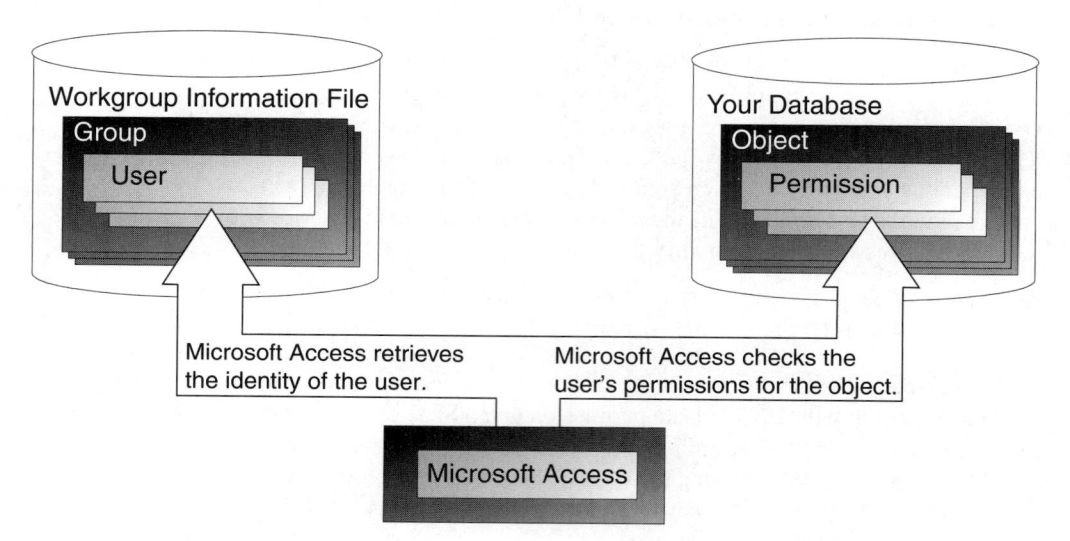

```
Workgroup Information File          Your Database
    Group                              Object
      User                               Permission

Microsoft Access retrieves         Microsoft Access checks the
the identity of the user.          user's permissions for the object.

                    Microsoft Access
```

The location of the workgroup information file in use is specified in the Windows registry. You can create a new workgroup information file or specify which file to use with the Workgroup Administrator.

Tip You can also specify which file to use when starting Microsoft Access with the **/wrkgrp** command-line option. For information about using this command-line option, see Microsoft Access online Help.

For more information about using the Workgroup Administrator or how the workgroup information file is specified in the registry, see Microsoft Access online Help.

Users and Groups

You use the **User and Group Accounts** dialog box (**Tools** menu, **Security** submenu) to create new user and group accounts for your workgroup. When you create a new user or group account, you supply a name and a *personal identifier* (PID). The PID is a case-sensitive alphanumeric string that can be 4 to 20 characters long. Microsoft Access sends the name and the PID to an encryption program to generate the security identifier (SID) for that account. The SID is used internally by Microsoft Access to uniquely identify and validate users and groups. The PID is not a password. It is used only when creating user and group accounts. A user's password can be designated only after an account for that user has been created.

Saving Names and Personal Identifiers (PIDs)

Be sure to write down the exact, case-sensitive names and PIDs that you use to create user and group accounts and keep them in a safe place. If your workgroup information file is damaged or lost and you need to re-create it, you must reenter the exact names and PIDs to re-create identical SIDs for the user and group accounts.

Use the Workgroup Administrator to create an identical workgroup information file to contain these accounts by reentering the name, organization, and workgroup ID (WID) that you used when you created it originally.

A Microsoft Access workgroup information file contains the following default user and group accounts:

- Admin

    Admin is the default user account. Before user-level security is established, all users are automatically logged on using the Admin user account. Therefore, the Admin user owns and has full permissions on all objects created in the database. Because the Admin user's SID is identical across all installations of Microsoft Access and Visual Basic, all objects that the Admin user owns or has permissions on are open to anyone using another copy of Microsoft Access or Visual Basic. When establishing user-level security, it is important to make sure that the Admin user does not own or have any permissions on objects that you want to secure. For assistance in securing objects, run the User-Level Security Wizard provided with Microsoft Access. For more information about running the User-Level Security Wizard, see "Establishing Security with the User-Level Security Wizard" later in this chapter.

- Admins

  Admins is the workgroup administrator's group account. The Admins group must have at least one member at all times. Before user-level security is established, the default Admin user is the only member of the Admins group. Because members of the Admins group have the power to perform actions such as changing permissions, modifying user and group memberships, and clearing users' passwords, be careful when assigning users to this group.

- Users

  Users is the default group account comprising all user accounts. Microsoft Access automatically adds user accounts to the Users group when you create them. Any permissions assigned explicitly to the Users group are available to all users in all installations of Microsoft Access and Visual Basic because, like the SID for the Admin group, the SID for the Users group is identical in all workgroup information files. Likewise, when establishing user-level security, make sure that the Users group does not own or have permissions on objects that you want secure.

How do I create a secure workgroup information file?

The Microsoft Access Setup program uses only the user's name and the company name provided during Setup to create the SID for the Admins group of the default workgroup information file. Because these two values are available from the Microsoft Access Help menu, unauthorized users trying to breach security could re-create an identical Admins account by using the Workgroup Administrator to create a new workgroup information file with these values, and then add themselves to the Admins group.

Before establishing user-level security, use the Workgroup Administrator to create a new workgroup information file, making sure to enter the workgroup ID (WID), which is a value known only to you. This ensures that the new workgroup information file contains a new Admins group with a unique, secure SID. Start the Workgroup Administrator by double-clicking Wrkgadm.exe in the System folder (Windows 95) or the System32 folder (Windows NT Workstation 3.51 or 4.0). For information about using the Workgroup Administrator, see Microsoft Access online Help.

Record the exact, case-sensitive values you type in the **Name**, **Organization**, and **Workgroup ID** boxes, and keep them in a safe place. If the workgroup information file is lost or damaged, you can re-create it with an identical Admins group by reentering these three values. Members of this re-created Admins group can grant themselves permissions on all objects that were created when the old workgroup information file was in effect.

Permissions

Explicit permissions are permissions granted directly to a user; no other users are affected. *Implicit* permissions are permissions granted to a group; all users who are members of a group get the permissions assigned to that group.

The easiest way to administrate a secure workgroup is to create new groups and assign permissions to the groups, rather than to individual users. Then you can change individual users' permissions by adding or removing them from groups. In a simple situation, you may want to use only the default groups to define permissions—assigning administrators to the Admins group and all other users to the Users group. If you do this, keep in mind that because the Users group is identical across all installations of Microsoft Access, any permissions you assign to the Users group are available to all users of Microsoft Access.

For a higher level of security, revoke all permissions for the Users group, create your own groups, and assign permissions to them. There is no need to create an alternative to the Admins group as long as you enter a secure workgroup ID when you create a new workgroup information file. By doing so, you ensure that the Admins group is unique to that file.

When a user tries to perform an operation on an object, the user's security level is determined by the least restrictive of the permissions explicitly granted to the user and the permissions implicitly granted to the groups to which the user belongs. For example, if User1 has no explicit permissions on the Orders table but belongs to the Clerks group, which has Read Data permission on the Orders table, User1 can read the data in the table. If User1 is removed from the Clerks group and does not belong to another group with permissions on the Orders table, User1 is denied access to the Orders table.

Permissions can be changed on an object by:

- Members of the Admins group of the workgroup information file in use when the database was created.
- The owner of the object.
- Any user who has Administer permission on the object.

Permissions for a database can be changed only by the owner of the database or by members of the Admins group.

> **Why can't I revoke Administer permission for the Admins group?**
>
> In the Admins group, the *Administer permission*—the right to change permissions—cannot be revoked using the Microsoft Access user interface. Even if you clear the **Administer** check box on the **Permissions** tab in the **User and Group Permissions** dialog box (**Tools** menu, **Security** submenu) for the Admins group on an object, the permission remains. You can use DAO code to revoke the Administer permission, but this is not recommended because there is no way to grant the permission back again.
>
> Instead, make sure you are using a workgroup information file created with a secure WID, which ensures a unique and secure Admins group, and then make sure only the appropriate users are assigned to the Admins group.

Even though users may not currently be able to perform an action, they may be able to grant themselves permissions to perform the action. This is true if the user is a member of the Admins group of the workgroup information file in use when the database was created, or if the user is the owner of an object.

The following table summarizes the permissions that you can revoke or assign.

This permission	Permits a user to do this	Which applies to these objects
Open/Run	Open a database, form, or report, or run a macro.	Databases, forms, reports, and macros
Open Exclusive	Open a database with exclusive access.	Databases
Read Design	View objects in Design view.	Tables, queries, forms, reports, macros, and modules
Modify Design	View and change the design of objects, or delete the objects.	Tables, queries, forms, reports, macros, and modules
Administer	For databases, set a database password, replicate a database, and change startup properties.	Databases, tables, queries, forms, reports, macros, and modules
	For database objects, have full access to objects and data, including the ability to assign permissions.	
Read Data	View data.	Tables and queries
Update Data	View and modify but not insert or delete data.	Tables and queries
Insert Data	View and insert but not modify or delete data.	Tables and queries
Delete Data	View and delete but not modify or insert data.	Tables and queries

Note Some permissions automatically imply the selection of others. For example, the Update Data permission for a table automatically implies the Read Data and Read Design permissions, because they are needed to modify the data in a table. The Modify Design and Read Data permissions imply the Read Design permission. For macros, the Read Design permission implies the Open/Run permission.

You can set the permissions that users and groups receive by default for all new objects in a database. For example, you can prevent the Users group from getting permission to add tables. This reduces your administrative burden, because you do not need to keep checking to make sure that new objects are properly secured.

Note You can prevent users from creating new tables and queries by using Visual Basic code to remove permissions on the **Container** object, but you cannot prevent users from creating new forms, reports, macros, or modules.

For information about how to assign default permissions for new objects, see Microsoft Access online Help.

Ownership

The user who creates an object is the owner of the object. The owner of an object can always grant permissions on the object, even if a member of the Admins group has revoked his or her explicit permissions on it. One way to change the ownership of an object is to use the **Change Owner** tab in the **User and Group Permissions** dialog box (**Tools** menu, **Security** submenu). In addition to allowing the transfer of ownership to another user, the **Change Owner** tab is the only way to transfer ownership to a group. A group can own any kind of object except the database itself.

Another way to transfer ownership to another user is to log on as that user and re-create the object. To re-create an object, you can make a copy of the object, or you can import it or export it to another database. To re-create an object, you must have Read Design permission for the object and, if the object is a table or query, you must also have Read Data permission.

Note You can change ownership of a query only if you own the query, or if its **RunPermissions** property is set to **User's**. For more information about the **RunPermissions** property, see "Using the RunPermissions Property with User-Level Security" later in this chapter.

The user who creates a database is the owner of the database. Before you establish user-level security, the default Admin user is the owner of the database. The owner of a database can always open the database and create new objects in it and can also grant or revoke the permission to open the database. A database owner's permissions cannot be revoked by using the **Change Owner** tab in the **User and Group Permissions** dialog box (**Tools** menu, **Security** submenu).

Important If you do not transfer database ownership to a secure user account, any user of Microsoft Access or Visual Basic can open the database. The only way to transfer the ownership of all of the objects and the database is to log on as the user whom you want to own the database, create a new blank database, and then import all of the objects. The easiest way to secure your database and transfer ownership of the database and all of its objects to a secure account is by running the User-Level Security Wizard.

Establishing Security with the User-Level Security Wizard

Once you understand how the different pieces of the Microsoft Access user-level security model fit together, you can proceed with the steps to secure a database. Although you can perform individual steps yourself, the User-Level Security Wizard is the easiest and most reliable way to secure a database.

To establish user-level security with the User-Level Security Wizard, you specify the object types that you want secured, and the User-Level Security Wizard revokes permissions on those objects for all users and groups except the user who is currently logged on. The User-Level Security Wizard creates a new, secured copy of the database and leaves the original copy unmodified. The User-Level Security Wizard also re-creates linked tables and table relationships in the new database. After you run the User-Level Security Wizard, you can create new users and groups and assign permissions to control how the objects in the application are used.

Important You must have a secure workgroup information file before you run the User-Level Security Wizard. If you do not have a secure workgroup information file, use the Workgroup Administrator to create one. (For more information, see the sidebar "How do I create a secure workgroup information file?" earlier in this chapter.) When you create a new workgroup information file, it automatically becomes the current file and is used the next time you start Microsoft Access.

▶ **To create a new administrator user for the database**

1. If you have Microsoft Access open, click **File** and then click **Exit**.
2. Use the Workgroup Administrator to join a secure workgroup information file or create a new secure workgroup information file, and then start Microsoft Access.
3. On the **Tools** menu, point to **Security**, and then click **User and Group Accounts**.
4. Click the **Users** tab, and then click **New** to create a new user to be the owner and administrator of the database.
5. In the **Available Groups** box, select **Admins**, and then click **Add** to add the new user to the Admins group.

6   In the **Name** box, select the Admin user, and then click the **Change Logon Password** tab and assign a password to the Admin user.

   This causes the **Logon** dialog box to appear the next time you start Microsoft Access.

7   Click the **Users** tab, select the Admin user in the **Name** box, select **Admins** in the **Member Of** box, and then click **Remove** to remove the Admin user from the Admins group.

Once you have created the new account, or if you already have a secure workgroup information file, use the Workgroup Administrator to make sure it is in use. Then exit Microsoft Access and then restart it, logging on as the administrator user you created (that is, log on as a member of the Admins group).

Important   Before you run the User-Level Security Wizard, you must have a secure workgroup information file in use, and you must be logged on as the administrator user whom you want to be the owner of the secured database.

▶ **To establish security with the User-Level Security Wizard**

1   Open the database you want to secure.

2   On the **Tools** menu, point to **Security**, and then click **User-Level Security Wizard**.

3   Select the check boxes for the object types you want to secure, and then click **OK**.

   The User-Level Security Wizard creates a new database, exports copies of all of the objects from the original database, secures the object types you selected by revoking all permissions of the Users group for those objects in the new database, and then encrypts the new database. The original database is not changed in any way.

4   Create your own users and groups. Assign appropriate permissions to the group accounts, and then add individual users to the appropriate groups.

   Typical permissions may include Read Data and Update Data permissions for tables and queries, and Open/Run permission for forms and reports.

For more information about creating users and groups, see "Users and Groups" earlier in this chapter. For information about how to assign permissions and a list of permissions you can assign, see Microsoft Access online Help.

The new database is now secure. The user whom you logged on as is the owner of all objects as well as the database. The only users who can use the objects in the application are those to whom you gave permissions in Step 4 and members of the Admins group in the workgroup information file you created or specified.

If you choose to secure all object types in the database, the User-Level Security Wizard removes the Users group's Open/Run permission for the database. The only users who can open the new secured database are members of the Admins group of the workgroup information file in use when you ran the wizard and any additional users or groups to whom you gave permissions in Step 4. No other users of Microsoft Access and Visual Basic can open the database or gain access to the secured objects within it.

If you choose to secure only some object types in the database, the User-Level Security Wizard does not remove the Users group's Open/Run permission for the database. In this case, all users of Microsoft Access and Visual Basic can open the new secured database and gain access to unsecured objects, but they cannot gain access to the secured objects within it.

Securing a Front-end/Back-end Application

There are some particular factors to take into account when establishing user-level security for an application that is split into a back-end database containing only tables and a front-end database containing the remaining objects and links to the tables in the back-end database. You may not know the name of the specific network location for the back-end database, or you may want to allow a database administrator to move the back-end database. In either situation, make sure that users can relink the tables in the back-end database.

Follow these general steps to establish user-level security on a front-end/back-end application.

1. Establish security for both databases with the User-Level Security Wizard.
2. Assign permissions to the appropriate groups to read, update, insert, or delete data in the back-end database.

   You can assign permissions directly to the tables in the back-end database, or you can remove all permissions to those tables and create queries in the front-end database that use the tables in the back-end database whose **RunPermissions** property is set to **Owner's**. For more information about the **RunPermissions** property, see "Using the RunPermissions Property with User-Level Security" later in this chapter.

3. Assign Open/Run permission for the back-end database.

   This is required even if you are using queries with the **RunPermissions** property set to **Owner's**.

4. In the front-end database, assign Modify Design permission for the linked tables.

   Granting users Modify Design permission on linked tables in the front-end database does not grant them the same permissions on the tables in the back-end database.

5. By default, after the User-Level Security Wizard is run, users have permission to create new tables and queries in the front-end database. If DAO code has been used to remove this permission, you must use DAO code and the **dbSecCreate** constant to reassign this permission.

   For information about using DAO code to assign permissions, see "Assigning Permissions for Objects" in Chapter 14, "Securing Your Application," in *Building Applications with Microsoft Access 97*.

6. When users first install the application, have them click **Linked Table Manager** (**Tools** menu, **Add-Ins** submenu) in the front-end database to refresh the links to the tables in the back-end database in its new location.

   Tip You can also write code that prompts users during startup to refresh table links. For sample code that does this, see the RelinkTables and RefreshLinks functions in the RefreshTableLinks module of the Orders sample application that comes with Microsoft Access.

Because users have Modify Design permission for the linked tables in the front-end database, they can reset the link to the back-end tables if the location of the back-end database changes. They cannot make any modifications to the design of the tables in the back-end database, however.

Securing a Database Without Requiring Users to Log On

If you want to secure some objects in a database, such as the code modules and the design of objects, but you do not care about establishing different levels of access for different groups of users, you may want to consider securing an application without requiring users to log on.

▶ **To establish user-level security without requiring users to log on**

1. Log on as a member of the Admins group in a secure workgroup information file.
2. Secure the database application using the User-Level Security Wizard.
3. While still logged on as a member of the Admins group, assign permissions to the Admin user account for objects that you want to be available to all users.

   Typical permissions may include Read Data and Update Data permissions for tables and queries, and Open/Run permission for forms and reports. If you have secured the application properly, the Admin user should no longer be a member of the Admins group.
4. Clear the password for the Admin user.

Users can now open the application without logging on. When users start Microsoft Access, they are automatically logged on using the Admin user account. Users have only the permissions you assigned. This works for any workgroup, because the Admin user account is the same in every workgroup information file. Only members of the Admins group of the workgroup information file that was in use when you ran the User-Level Security Wizard have full permissions on the objects in the database.

Important Do not distribute copies of the workgroup information file in use when you secure the database using this procedure. If you need to allow a trusted user to administer the database, give the copy of the workgroup information file only to that user.

To perform administrative functions, you must use the workgroup information file that was in use when you secured the database. There are two ways you can log on as a member of the Admins group of that workgroup information file:

- You can temporarily define a password for the Admin user to reactivate the logon procedure, and log on as a member of the Admins group.

  –or–

- You can use the **/pwd** and **/user** command-line options to specify your password and user name when starting Microsoft Access. If you define a shortcut that uses the **/pwd** and **/user** command-line options to do this, you should physically secure the computer where the shortcut is located to prevent unauthorized users from gaining access to this information.

Removing User-Level Security

If you want to remove user-level security, perform the following procedure.

Important Before you remove user-level security from the database, make a backup copy.

▶ **To remove user-level security**

1 Start Microsoft Access and log on as a workgroup administrator (a member of the Admins group).
2 Open the database.
3 On the **Tools** menu, point to **Security**, then click **User and Group Permissions**.
4 Click the **Permissions** tab, select the **Groups** option, and in the **User/Group Name** box, select **Users**.
5 In the **Object Name** box, select the check boxes to give the Users group full permissions on all objects in the database.

   Tip You can select all of the objects in the **Object Name** box at once by clicking the first item in the list, holding down SHIFT, and then clicking the last item in the list.

6 Exit and restart Microsoft Access, and then log on as the default Admin user.
7 Create a new blank database and leave it open.
8 Import all the objects from the original database into the new database.
9 If users use the current workgroup information file when opening the database, clear the password for the Admin user to turn off the **Logon** dialog box for the current workgroup.

   This is not necessary if users use the default workgroup information file created when installing Microsoft Access.

The new database is now completely unsecured. Anyone who can open the new database has full permissions on all its objects. This works for any workgroup because the Admin user account and Users group account are the same in every workgroup information file, and all users, including the Admin user, are members of the Users group. The workgroup information file in use when the new database is created defines the Admins group for the new database.

Using the RunPermissions Property with User-Level Security

For Microsoft Access to display a table or query, it needs to read the design of the table or query. For example, it needs to read field names and other field properties, such as the **Format** and **InputMask** properties. Therefore, for a user to read and display the data in a table or query, the user must also have permissions to read the design of the table or query. (This is why selecting the **Read Data** permission check box in the **User and Group Permissions** dialog box automatically selects the **Read Design** check box as well.) If you do not want users to see the design of a table or query, you can use the **RunPermissions** property of queries to restrict access to this information.

The **RunPermissions** property determines whether Microsoft Access uses permissions for the query user or the query owner when checking the user-level security permissions for the underlying tables in a query. If the **RunPermissions** property is set to **User's**, then the users of a query have only their own permissions to view data in underlying tables. However, if the owner of a query sets the **RunPermissions** property to **Owner's**, anyone who uses the query has the same level of permissions as the query's owner to view data in the underlying tables.

The **RunPermissions** property allows you to create queries to display data to users who do not have permission to gain access to the underlying tables. Using this feature, you can build different views of the data, resulting in record-level and field-level security for a table.

For example, suppose you have a secure database with an Employees table and a Salary table. By using the **RunPermissions** property, you can build several views of the two tables: one that allows a user or group to view but not update the Salary field; a second that allows a different user or group to view and update the Salary field; and a third that allows another user or group to view the Salary field only if its value is less than a certain amount.

▶ **To prevent users from viewing the design of underlying tables or queries**

1. For the users or groups that you want to restrict, remove all permissions to the underlying tables or queries whose design you want to secure.

2. Build a new query that includes all the fields you want to include from secure tables or queries.

   You can exclude access to a field by omitting it. You can also limit access to a certain range of values by defining criteria for the query.

3. Make sure you or a secure group owns the new query.

4. On the query property sheet, set the **RunPermissions** property of the new query to **Owner's**.

   Note   You can also set the **RunPermissions** property in SQL view of the Query window by using the **WITH OWNERACCESS OPTION** declaration in the SQL statement.

5. Grant appropriate data permissions for the new query to the users and groups whom you want to be able to update data but not view the design of the table or query.

   This typically includes Read Design, Read Data, Update Data, Delete Data, and Insert Data permissions, but you should specify only the permissions you want to allow.

Users can update data in the underlying tables or queries by using the new query or forms based on it. However, if they try to view the design of the tables or the new query, Microsoft Access displays a message that they do not have permissions to view the source tables or queries.

Important   By default, the user who creates a query is its owner, and only the owner of a query can save changes to it if the **RunPermissions** property is set to **Owner's**. Even members of the Admins group or users with Administer permission are prevented from saving changes to a query created by another user if the **RunPermissions** property is set to **Owner's**. However, anyone with Modify Design permission for the query can set the **RunPermissions** property to **User's** and then save changes to the query.

What if more than one user needs to view a query's design?

Because the creator of a query owns it by default, having the **RunPermissions** property set to **Owner's** can create problems if you need to allow more than one user to work with the design of a query. To solve this problem, transfer the ownership of the query to a group. To do this, create a group, change the owner of the query to this group on the **Change Owner** tab in the **User and Group Permissions** dialog box (**Tools** menu, **Security** submenu), and then add the users who need to modify the query to the new group. Any member of the new group can edit the query and save changes.

Multiuser Applications and Locking

Several options and settings in Microsoft Access affect how a Microsoft Access database application functions in a multiuser environment. These settings are described in the following sections.

Controlling How a Database Opens

There are three ways to control how a database is opened in Microsoft Access:

- When you start Microsoft Access, you can include a database name on the command line and either the **/Excl** or **/Ro** parameter to open the database in exclusive or read-only mode, respectively.
- You can select or clear the **Exclusive** check box when using the **Open** dialog box (**File** menu). To open a database as read-only, select the database in the **Open** dialog box, click **Commands and Settings**, and then click **Open Read-Only**.
- You can change the default database open mode by changing the **Default Open Mode** setting on the **Advanced** tab in the **Options** dialog box (**Tools** menu). This setting can be either **Exclusive** for single-user access or **Shared** for multiuser access to the database.

Tip In Microsoft Access versions 1.*x* and 2.0, clicking **Options** (**View** menu) and setting the **Default Open Mode** set only the default behavior, which the user can still override. The same holds true for Microsoft Access 95 and 97, where this setting is available by clicking **Options** (**Tools** menu). You can prevent a user or group from opening a database in exclusive mode by removing the Open Exclusive permission of the database for the user or group. This works only if user-level security has been defined for the workgroup.

Setting the Refresh Interval

Click **Options** (**Tools** menu) to set the refresh interval. Microsoft Access automatically checks the recordsets of open forms and datasheets to determine whether changes have occurred at the frequency set by the refresh interval. The default refresh interval is 60 seconds, which may be too long in some situations. If you set the refresh interval to too small a value, however, you may create excessive network traffic. You may need to experiment to find the proper setting for your situation. In general, the fewer nodes on the network, the smaller you can set the refresh interval without an adverse effect.

You can override the default refresh interval in your applications by using the **Refresh** method, the **Requery** method, or the Requery action. Refreshes of records—either automatic refreshes by Microsoft Access using the refresh interval or manual refreshes using the **Refresh** method—are faster than the **Requery** method or action. However, new records added by other users appear only after a **Requery** method or action. Similarly, records deleted by other users are deleted from your copy only after a

Requery method or action. All the values in the fields of deleted records are replaced with the string "#DELETED" when the record is refreshed.

In most cases, you should use the **Requery** method rather than the almost-equivalent Requery action. The method reruns the query that is already in memory, and the action reloads it from disk. The exception to this rule is when you have used DAO to modify the underlying query definition. When this is the case, you should use the Requery action to reload the **QueryDef** object from disk.

Tip Even if you leave the refresh interval at a very high setting, Microsoft Access automatically refreshes the current record whenever a user attempts to edit it. The benefit of a shorter refresh interval lies chiefly in giving quicker visual feedback when someone else has locked or changed a record while you are viewing it.

Using Locking Options

To provide concurrent access to records by multiple users, Microsoft Access locks records. Unlike some database applications, Microsoft Access does not lock individual records; instead it locks a 2K (2,048 bytes) page of records. The advantage of page locking is that there is less overhead and generally better performance over true record locking when performing operations that affect many records. Unfortunately, this also means that Microsoft Access usually locks more records than you would like. This is especially an issue when you use pessimistic locking, which allows users to keep records locked for long periods of time. For information about pessimistic locking, see "Edited Record" later in this chapter.

In a multiuser environment you can open recordsets in one of three different modes:

- No locks
- Edited record
- All records

This section explains each of these modes.

No Locks

Using no locks is often called *optimistic locking* and is the default setting. When you select the **No Locks** option on the **Advanced** tab in the **Options** dialog box (**Tools** menu), the page of records that contains the currently edited record is locked only during the instant when the record is being saved—not during the editing process. This allows for concurrent editing of records with fewer locking conflicts.

For forms and datasheets, two or more users can edit the same record simultaneously. If two users attempt to save changes to the same record, Microsoft Access displays a message to the second user who tries to save the record. The user can then discard the record, copy it to the Clipboard, or replace the record changed by the other user.

For reports, no records are locked while a user previews or prints a report. However, if a report is printing data from a Memo or OLE Object field, the record is locked until Microsoft Access is finished reading the Memo or OLE Object field data.

For queries, no records are locked while a user runs a query, except for action queries, where all the records are locked until the action query is finished.

Edited Record

When you select the **Edited Record** option on the **Advanced** tab in the **Options** dialog box (**Tools** menu), as soon as a user begins to edit a record, the page containing the currently edited record is locked until the changes are saved. This is known as *pessimistic locking*.

All Records

When you select the **All Records** option on the **Advanced** tab in the **Options** dialog box (**Tools** menu), all the records in the recordset are locked at once, as follows:

- For forms, all records in the underlying table or query are locked while the form is open in Form view or Datasheet view.
- For table and select query datasheets, all records are locked until the datasheet is closed.
- For reports, all records are locked while the report is previewed or printed.
- For action queries, all records are locked while the query is run.

The **All Records** option is really only useful during batch updates or when you are performing administrative maintenance on tables. Although users can read the records, no one can add, delete, or edit any records until the form or datasheet is closed, the report is finished printing or the query is finished running.

Default Record Locking

You can set the default record locking behavior for most objects that access recordsets on the **Advanced** tab in the **Options** dialog box (**Tools** menu). These defaults affect the following objects:

- Table datasheets
- Select query datasheets
- Crosstab query datasheets
- Union query datasheets
- Update queries
- Delete queries
- Make-table queries
- Append queries

- Forms
- Reports

If the default record locking option is set to **No Locks**, it is overridden for update, delete, make-table, and append query operations, because the records must be locked during these operations. Additionally, all records must be locked when you use data-definition queries.

You can set record locking behavior for individual forms, queries, or reports by opening the object in Design view and setting the **RecordLocks** property. This allows you to override the current default setting on the **Advanced** tab in the **Options** dialog box (**Tools** menu).

Note Whether you set locking behavior by clicking **Options** (**Tools** menu) or by setting the **RecordLocks** property, when the data comes from an Open Database Connectivity (ODBC) database, the Microsoft Access setting is ignored. All locking for linked ODBC tables, such as Microsoft SQL tables, is determined by the ODBC OLE server.

Choosing a Locking Strategy

To help you decide which locking strategy is best for your particular situation, the following table shows advantages and disadvantages of using pessimistic or optimistic locking.

This strategy	Has these advantages	And these disadvantages
Pessimistic locking (**Edited Record** option)	Simple for the developer. Prevents users from overwriting each other's work. May be less confusing to the user. Works well for small workgroups or where users are not likely to be editing the same record.	Usually locks multiple records; how many depends on the size of the records. When a user is at the end of a table and thus has locked the last page, prevents other users from adding new records. Is not recommended where many users are editing the same records or adding new records at the same time.
Optimistic locking (**No Locks** option)	Simple to use. Allows more than one user to edit the same record at the same time. (In some cases, this may be a disadvantage.) Is less likely to lock other users out of records.	May be confusing to users when there is a write conflict. Users can overwrite each other's edits.

Unless you have a compelling reason to use pessimistic locking, consider an optimistic locking strategy. In most situations, you do not want to prevent users from editing or from adding new records for potentially long periods of time. If you decide to use pessimistic locking in your forms, you may have to teach users to recognize and work with locked records.

With pessimistic locking, users are unable to change a record that is on the same page as a record being edited by another user, as shown in the following illustration.

Locked records are indicated by a circle with a slash.

Category ID	Category Name	Description
1	Beverages	Soft drinks, coffees, teas, beers, and ales
2	Condiments	Sweet and savory sauces, relishes, spreads, and seasoning
3	Confections	Desserts, candies, and sweet breads
4	Dairy Products	Cheeses
5	Grains/Cereals	Breads, crackers, pasta, and cereal
6	Meat/Poultry	Prepared meats
7	Produce	Dried fruit and bean curd
8	Seafood	Seaweed and fish

On the other hand, if you use optimistic locking in your forms, you may have to teach users how to use the **Write Conflict** dialog box, shown in the following illustration.

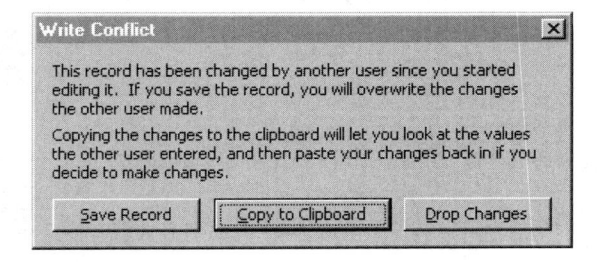

With optimistic locking, users may encounter the **Write Conflict** dialog box when attempting to save a record that has been changed by another user.

Tip If you have set the **RecordSelectors** property of a form to **No**, the circle with a slash does not appear when record locking is pessimistic. Microsoft Access beeps at the user, but users receive no visual cue to explain why they cannot edit the values in the record. No trappable error is generated. Therefore, it is recommended that you leave the **RecordSelectors** property set to **Yes** when you use pessimistic locking with bound forms.

In some situations you may need to use both locking strategies on different forms. For example, in an inventory application you must ensure that the QuantityOnHand column is pessimistically locked, so that sales representatives do not try to post a sale beyond the QuantityOnHand without invoking back-order processing. Conversely, you can use optimistic locking on a vendor address form, as it is unlikely that two change-of-address requests for the same vendor are given to two different users to be posted simultaneously.

Using the Locking Information File

The locking information (LDB) file stores information about any records that are currently locked in the database.

If the locking information file does not exist when the database is opened, the Microsoft Access database engine creates it. It creates one locking information file for every Microsoft Access database file that is opened in shared mode. Microsoft Access gives the file the same name as the database that was opened, but with an .ldb file name extension. For example, Northwind.mdb has an associated locking information file called Northwind.ldb. The locking information file is stored in the same folder as the database. Microsoft Access deletes the LDB file when the database is closed. In a multiuser setting, this occurs when all users have exited the application.

Forcing Microsoft Access to Lock Individual Records

You can force Microsoft Access to lock individual records by creating record sizes that are larger than half a page—that is, larger than 1,024 bytes. This works because Microsoft Access does not begin storing a new record on a partially filled page unless it can fit the entire record on the page. This strategy wastes a lot of disk space and increases network traffic. However, if you decide to use pessimistic locking and absolutely must have record locking, you may want to consider this technique. In order to use this technique, you need to be able to estimate the size of records.

You can estimate the size of records by using the following table and summing the size of each field.

Byte	1 byte
Integer	2 bytes
Long Integer	4 bytes
Single	4 bytes
Double	8 bytes
Currency	8 bytes
AutoNumber	Depends on **FieldSize** property setting: **Long Integer** = 4 bytes **ReplicationID** = 16 bytes

Field data type	Storage size
Yes/No	1 bit
Date/Time	8 bytes
Text	Variable
Memo	14 bytes
OLE Object	14 bytes
Hyperlink	14 bytes

The contents of the Memo, OLE Object, and Hyperlink fields are stored elsewhere in the MDB file, so you need to count only the overhead for their address pointers, as described later in this section. Text columns present the greatest problem for estimating record size because they are variable-length fields. Microsoft Access uses one byte per actual stored character up to the maximum length specified by the **FieldSize** property. Zero-length strings ("") use 1 byte; **Null** values use 0 bytes.

You also have to account for overhead, which includes the following:

- Seven bytes per record for record overhead
- One byte variable-length column overhead for each Text, Memo, OLE Object, and Hyperlink field
- One additional byte for every 256 bytes of the total space occupied by all Text, Memo, OLE Object, and Hyperlink fields
- One byte fixed-column overhead for each Yes/No, Byte, Integer, Long Integer, AutoNumber, Single, Double, Currency, and Date/Time field

Note These numbers are for estimating the record size rather than calculating the exact size.

The easiest way to pad a record so that it exceeds 1,024 bytes is to create one or more dummy text fields in the table with default values that are 255 characters long. For example, if you estimated the record size to be at least 130 bytes, you would calculate the needed dummy fields as follows:

- Bytes you need to pad = (1,025 - 130) = 895 bytes.
- Each whole dummy text field = (255 + 2 bytes overhead) = 257 bytes.
- You need three completely filled dummy fields (257*3 = 771) of 255 xs plus one partially filled dummy field (895 - 771 - 1 overhead byte) of 123 xs.

Do not place these dummy fields on your forms. Whenever a new record is created, Microsoft Access automatically creates a record with the four x-filled dummy fields, which forces it into record-locking mode.

Splitting a Database into a Front-end/Back-end Application

No matter which locking scheme you use, Microsoft Access still puts everything (data, forms, reports, queries, macros, and code) in a single database by default. Performance can suffer considerably using this design, because every time an object (such as a form) is used, it must be sent across the network to the user. In a production setting, where the only thing being changed is the data stored in tables, much of this network traffic is unnecessary.

You can eliminate this unnecessary traffic by splitting the database into a front-end database and a back-end database. Install the *back-end* database, which contains the table data only, on a file server, and store a copy of the *front-end* database, which contains all other objects, on each workstation. From each copy of the front-end database, click **Link Tables** (**File** menu, **Get External Data** submenu) to link the set of tables in the back-end database.

If the database is in Microsoft Access 97 format, you can click **Database Splitter** (**Tools** menu, **Add-Ins** submenu) to split the database and link tables in a single operation.

> **The link to the table on the server keeps breaking**
>
> If you specify the path to a linked table by using a mapped drive letter, the link to the table breaks if another user opens that copy of the front-end database and the network drive is not mapped or is mapped to a different letter on the user's computer.
>
> If your network supports universal naming convention (UNC) format, you can solve this problem by using the UNC path to specify a path to linked tables. Use the following format:
>
> *\\server\share\path\filename*

There are several advantages and disadvantages to splitting a database.

The advantages are:

- Performance is improved, especially user-interface performance.
- You can create temporary tables on each workstation without concern for naming and locking conflicts for temporary objects.
- Applications are easier to update because the table data and application objects are kept separate.

    Changes to the application can be made off-site and merged back into the front-end database without disturbing the table data.

The disadvantages are:

- Microsoft Access ignores referential integrity between local and remote tables.

  Fortunately, Microsoft Access enforces any referential integrity constraints you have established between individual tables in the remote database.

- Microsoft Access hard codes the paths to linked tables. If you move the back-end database, you have to delete and relink all linked tables.

Because Microsoft Access hard codes the paths to linked tables, using linked tables requires extra maintenance. If you move a back-end database with linked tables, you have to delete and relink the tables. Click **Linked Table Manager** (**Tools** menu, **Add-Ins** submenu) to automate this process.

You can also use Visual Basic code to check table links and, if necessary, relink them. To see an example of how to do this, open the Orders sample application that comes with Microsoft Access, open the Startup form in Design view, and then view the event procedure set for the **OnLoad** property of the form. This event procedure calls two functions from the RefreshTableLinks module: the CheckLinks function to see whether links to tables in the Northwind sample database are still working, and, if not, the RelinkTables function to relink tables.

Troubleshooting Other Multiuser Issues

This section covers additional issues you may encounter when sharing a Microsoft Access database among multiple users.

Backup Multiuser Databases

To back up a multiuser database correctly, make sure that you have exclusive access to the database. If you back up a database while others are using it, you risk producing a damaged backup database. If you open a damaged backup database, you may receive a message stating that the database is corrupted. If you repair and compact the database, the data in the database may be truncated.

The only way to ensure the integrity of the backup database is to open a static copy of the database. To do so, you must have exclusive access to all the tables in the database at the same time. After you have exclusive access to the database, you can copy or export the database, and then archive it.

Microsoft Access Locking and Novell NetWare

When you use data from a back-end database located on a server, Microsoft Access uses the locking facilities provided by the server. The defaults in NetWare versions $3.x$ and $4.x$ allow a single workstation to have 500 locks at any given time. This results in a limit of 1 MB of data that Microsoft Access can work with in a single transaction. Because Microsoft Access tries to lock every record involved in either an update or a delete query before carrying out the operation, it is possible to encounter this limit on moderately large databases.

When you use Microsoft Access with a NetWare 3.*x* or 4.*x* server, it is recommended that you increase the number of locks available to avoid encountering the lock limit. To increase the number of locks available, enter the following commands at the file server console or in the Autoexec.ncf file:

set maximum record locks per connection = 10000
set maximum record locks = 200000

The first command specifies the maximum number of locks in any single connection, and the second command specifies the maximum number of locks that the server can keep track of. These values (10,000 and 200,000, respectively) are the maximums that NetWare can accommodate. Microsoft Access can handle a transaction of up to 20 MB of data when you set the maximum record locks per connection to 10,000.

Increasing the Number of Locks in NetWare 3.11

There is an error in NetWare 3.11 that can result in a server *abending* (abnormally ending) if the lock limit is exceeded when Microsoft Access is running certain queries or otherwise requesting a large number of locks. If you are still using NetWare 3.11, it is highly recommended that you download the latest NetWare 3.11 patch file, which is available on CompuServe in the NOVFILES download area. You must load two of the NetWare Loadable Modules (NLMs) from this file, either directly from the file server console or by adding the following commands to the Autoexec.ncf file:

load patchman.nlm

load ttsfix.nlm

This problem is specific to NetWare 3.11 and has been fixed in later versions of NetWare.

Database Replication

Microsoft Access *database replication* is the process of copying a database so that two or more copies can exchange updates of data or objects. This exchange is called *synchronization*. Each copy of the database is called a *replica*, and each replica contains a common set of tables, queries, forms, reports, macros, and modules. Each replica can also contain *local objects* that exist only in that specific replica.

Each replica is part of a *replica set*, which contains the Design Master and the other replicas for a database. The *Design Master* is the only replica where you can make changes to the database design and objects. Replicas that belong to the same replica set can synchronize with one another.

With database replication, you can:

- Share data among offices.

    You can use database replication to create copies of a corporate database to send to each satellite office. Each location enters data into its replica, and all remote replicas are synchronized with the replica at corporate headquarters. An individual replica can maintain local tables that contain information not included in the other replicas in the set.

- Share data among dispersed users.

    New information that is entered into the database while sales representatives are out of the office can be synchronized any time the sales representatives establish an electronic link with the corporate network. As part of their workday routine, sales representatives can dial into the network, synchronize their replicas, and work on the most current version of the database. Because only the incremental changes are transmitted during synchronization, the time and expense of keeping up-to-date information are minimized. By using *partial replicas*, it is also possible to synchronize only certain parts of the data. For more information about partial replicas, see "Replicating Part of a Database" later in this chapter.

- Make server data accessible.

    If a database application does not need to have immediate updates to data, you can use database replication to reduce the network load on your primary server. Introducing a second server with its own copy of the database improves response time. You determine the schedule for synchronizing the replicas, and you can adjust the schedule to meet the changing needs of users. Replication requires less centralized administration of the database while offering greater access to centralized data.

- Distribute application updates.

    When you replicate a database application, you automatically replicate not only the data in its tables, but also the application's objects. If you make changes to the design of the database, the changes are transmitted during the next synchronization exchange; you do not have to distribute complete new versions of the software.

- Back up data.

    At first glance, database replication may appear to be similar to copying a database. However, replication initially makes a complete copy of the database; thereafter it synchronizes the replica's objects with the source objects at regular intervals. This copy can be used to back up data if the original database is destroyed. Furthermore, users of any replica can continue to gain access to the database during the entire backup process.

Although database replication can solve many of the problems inherent in distributed database processing, it is important to recognize the situations in which replication is less than ideal. You may not want to use replication if:

- There are large numbers of record updates at multiple replicas.

    Applications that require frequent updating of existing records in different replicas are likely to have more record conflicts than applications that only insert new records into a database. Record conflicts occur when two changes are made to the same record by users at different locations. Applications with many record conflicts require more time for someone to manually resolve these conflicts.

- Data consistency is critical at all times.

    Applications that rely on information being correct at all times, such as funds transfers, airline reservations, and the tracking of package shipments, usually use a transaction method. Although transactions can be processed within a replica, there is no support for processing transactions across replicas. The information exchanged between replicas during synchronization is the result of the transaction, not the transaction itself.

The flexibility that database replication offers can be illustrated by the development of a simple application. Imagine that a company's field sales staff needs to develop a contact management application to monitor sales and orders. Each sales representative has a laptop computer that can be connected to the company's network.

One approach to building this application is to separate the tables from the other objects in the database. The data resides in tables in a back-end database on a network server, and the queries, forms, reports, macros, and modules reside in a front-end database on each sales representative's computer. When sales representatives want to retrieve or update data, they open and use the front-end database. Because the objects in the front-end database are based on linked tables, changes that sales representatives make to the data using these objects change the data in the back-end database. For more information about this approach to designing database applications, see "Splitting a Database into a Front-end/Back-end Application" earlier in this chapter.

A better way to build this application is to use database replication to create a single database that contains both the data and objects, and then make replicas of the database for each sales representative.

You would begin developing the application by creating a Microsoft Access database as you would for any application. Then you would convert the database to a Design Master and make replicas on each user's computer. Sales representatives update data in the replicas on their computers during the course of a work session, and you synchronize their replicas with the Design Master on the server as needed. You can also create a set of custom forms or reports that is used at only one replica location.

This section addresses the tools you can use to implement this approach to designing database applications.

Implementing Database Replication

You can implement database replication by using:

- Replication commands in Microsoft Access.
- Briefcase replication in Windows 95.
- Replication Manager.
- DAO programming.

The first three replication tools provide an easy-to-use visual interface. You can use DAO to build replication directly into an application's code.

Note If some users of the database need to continue using the database in its original form, make a copy of the database before you implement database replication.

Replication Commands in Microsoft Access

Microsoft Access provides replication menu commands that you can use while working in your databases. By clicking **Replication** (**Tools** menu), you can:

- Create a replica.
- Synchronize your replica with another member of the replica set.
- Resolve synchronization conflicts by using the Conflict Resolver.
- Recover the replica set's Design Master, if necessary.

One of the easiest ways to become familiar with the concepts and procedures associated with database replication is to experiment with the Microsoft Access replication commands. To convert a database to a Design Master and create a replica, open the existing database, click the **Tools** menu, point to **Replication**, and then click **Create Replica**. You can then explore the changes made to the design of the database and the similarities between the replica and the Design Master. Next, make a change to the data in the replica and a change to a table design in the Design Master, and then click **Synchronize Now** (**Tools** menu, **Replication** submenu). You can then open the replica and the Design Master to confirm that the changes appear in the other member of the replica set.

For more information about the changes that are made to the design of a database when you convert it to a Design Master, see "Tracking Changes When a Database Is Replicated" later in this chapter.

Briefcase Replication in Windows 95

Microsoft Windows 95 Briefcase replication is a convenient way to implement replication on a laptop computer.

▶ **To use Briefcase replication**

1. Drag the Microsoft Access database (MDB) file from a shared folder on the corporate network to the My Briefcase icon on your laptop computer's desktop.

    The database file is converted to a Design Master, and a replica is created in your Briefcase.

2. Disconnect your laptop from the network, and make changes to the data in the replica.

3. When you are finished working on the files on the laptop computer, reconnect to the corporate network.

4. Synchronize the changes between the replica on your laptop and the Design Master on the network by double-clicking the My Briefcase icon and clicking **Update All** on the **Briefcase** menu.

During the conversion process, Briefcase gives you the opportunity to make a backup copy of the original database file. The backup copy has the same file name as the original, except that its file name extension is .bak instead of .mdb. It is stored in the same folder as the original database file. Save the backup copy, and use it only in the event that you cannot use a replica to re-create the replica set. For more information about re-creating a replica set, see "Using Replicas Instead of Backups" later in this chapter.

Replication Manager

Replication Manager provides a visual interface for converting databases, making additional replicas, viewing the relationships between replicas, and setting the properties of replicas. Replication Manager is provided only in Microsoft Office 97, Developer Edition. You can use Replication Manager to:

- Manage a large number of replicas.
- Synchronize data over the Internet or an intranet.
- Support laptop users who are not always connected to a network.

    Laptop users can specify a network file location where synchronization information is deposited for later processing.

- Create replicas of more than one database.
- Set schedules for synchronizing replicas.

    You can schedule synchronizations ahead of time so that they can occur unattended at anticipated times. You can also synchronize replicas at any time with a single command.

- Configure synchronizations to send data, receive data, or send and receive data.
- Access additional tools for troubleshooting.

For more information about Replication Manager, see Microsoft Access online Help.

DAO Programming

The DAO programming interface provides methods and properties that you can use to implement several Briefcase replication features in your Visual Basic code. You can use DAO to:

- Convert a database to a Design Master.
- Create and populate additional replicas.
- Create and populate partial replicas.
- Synchronize replicas.
- Get and set specific properties of a replicated database.
- Resolve conflicts and errors.

Although DAO requires programming, it gives you the ability to customize your replication system. Generally, you use DAO under the following circumstances:

- When you need to synchronize replicas when certain events occur

    For example, you may want to trigger synchronization whenever a replica receives updated product pricing information from headquarters.

- When you need to distribute a replicated database to users who have minimal computer expertise

    In this case, you can use DAO to design a simplified replication interface or to make replication completely transparent to users.

- When you want to create a partial replica because you need a replica that contains only part of the data

    For example, to minimize the disk space you use and to maximize performance, you may want to create a replica that contains only a subset of a large amount of data.

For more information about replication with DAO, see Chapter 20, "Using Replication in Your Application," in *Building Applications with Microsoft Access 97*.

Replicating a Database

To make replicas of a database, first convert the database to a Design Master. The Design Master becomes the first replica of the new replica set. As you make additional replicas from the Design Master, they are added to the set. You can have only one Design Master in a replica set. If you want to make changes to the tables, queries, forms, reports, macros, or modules, make the changes in the Design Master. This prevents users at multiple replicas from making conflicting changes to the database's design and objects.

▶ **To convert a database to a Design Master**

- On the **Tools** menu, point to **Replication**, and then click **Create Replica**.

  –or–

- Drag the database file to the My Briefcase icon.

  –or–

- Use DAO in your Visual Basic code.

  For information about using DAO to replicate a database, see "Using DAO to Replicate a Database" in Chapter 20, "Using Replication in Your Application," in *Building Applications with Microsoft Access 97*.

Important If you protect a database with a database password, you cannot synchronize replicas of the database. Before you begin using replication, remove any database password protection from the database. If you established user-level security for the database, this security does not interfere with synchronization. In fact, replicated objects retain the permissions that you give them in the Design Master.

Tracking Changes When a Database Is Replicated

When you convert a database to a Design Master, Microsoft Access makes the following changes to the database:

- Adds new fields to each existing table in the database
- Adds new tables to the database
- Adds new properties to the database
- Changes the behavior of AutoNumber fields

Microsoft Access uses these changes to track modifications to the design and data of the database and to synchronize the database with other replicas in the replica set.

> **Why did my database get so large after I replicated it?**
> The addition of three new fields to your tables increases the size of each record, and the addition of new system tables increases the size of your database. Many of these new tables contain only a few records, but some of the new tables can grow significantly, depending on the frequency of synchronization. To reclaim unused space, compact your database frequently. For more information, see "Compacting a Replicated Database" later in this chapter.

New Fields

When you convert a database to a Design Master, Microsoft Access first examines the existing fields in a table to determine whether any field uses both the **AutoNumber** data type and the Replication ID field size. The Replication ID **AutoNumber** is a 16-byte value that appears in the following format:

{1234AB87-2314-7623-0000012340506801}

If no field uses the data type and field size, Microsoft Access adds the s_GUID field to the table. The s_GUID field stores the Replication ID **AutoNumber** value that uniquely identifies each record. The Replication ID **AutoNumber** value for a specific record is identical across all replicas.

During the conversion process, Microsoft Access also adds the s_Lineage and s_Generation fields to each table in the database. The s_Lineage field contains the value of the **ReplicaID** property of replicas that have updated a record and the last version created by each of the replicas. The s_Generation field stores information about groups of changes. Microsoft Access also adds a field for every Memo and OLE Object field in a table.

Note The s_GUID, s_Lineage, and s_Generation system fields are visible only when the **System Objects** check box on the **View** tab in the **Options** dialog box (**Tools** menu) is selected.

Generally, there is a single field per record that stores information about changes. However, to optimize synchronizations for databases that contain Memo or OLE Object fields (sometimes referred to as BLOBs, or binary large objects), an extra field is associated with each BLOB. If the BLOB is modified, this field value is set to 0 so that the BLOB is sent during the next synchronization. If other fields in the record are modified, but not the BLOB, this field value is not set to 0, and the BLOB is not sent.

This extra field is named Gen_*FieldName*, where *FieldName* is the BLOB field's name (truncated, if necessary). One of these fields is set for each BLOB field.

For more information about the s_GUID, s_Lineage, s_Generation, and Gen_*FieldName* fields, see Microsoft Access online Help.

New Tables

When you convert a database to a Design Master, Microsoft Access adds several new tables to the database. Most of these tables are system tables, which are not normally visible to users and cannot be manipulated by developers. The following table describes a few of the tables that are of the most interest to developers and administrators.

Name	Description
MSysSidetables	Identifies the names of tables that experienced a conflict in the most recent synchronization and the name of the table that contains the conflicting records. MSysSidetables is visible only if a conflict has occurred between the user's replica and another replica in the set.
MSysErrors	Identifies where and why errors occurred during data synchronization.
MSysSchemaProb	Identifies errors that occurred while synchronizing the design of the replica. This table is visible only if a design conflict has occurred between the user's replica and another replica in the set.
MSysExchangeLog	Stores information about synchronizations that have taken place between replicas.

To view these and the other system tables, select the **System Objects** check box on the **View** tab in the **Options** dialog box (**Tools** menu). For more information about these tables, see Microsoft Access online Help.

New Properties

When you convert a database to a Design Master, Microsoft Access adds new properties to it: **ReplicaID**, **ReplicableBool**, and **DesignMasterID**.

The **ReplicaID** property contains the value that uniquely identifies the replica or Design Master. Microsoft Access automatically generates this value when you create a new replica.

During the conversion process, the **ReplicableBool** property is set to **True**, indicating that the database can now be replicated. Once this property is set to **True**, it cannot be changed. If you change the property setting to **False** (or to any value other than **True**), Microsoft Access returns an error message.

You can use the **DesignMasterID** property to make a replica other than the original Design Master the new Design Master. Set this property only in the current Design Master. Under extreme circumstances—for example, the loss of the original Design Master—you can set this property in the current replica. If you set this property in a replica when there is already another Design Master, you may prevent any further synchronization of data.

Caution Never create a second Design Master in a replica set. A second Design Master can result in the loss of data.

For more information about these properties, see Microsoft Access online Help.

Behavior of AutoNumber Fields

When you convert a database to a Design Master, the **NewValues** property for AutoNumber fields in the tables is changed from **Increment** to **Random**. All existing

AutoNumber fields retain their values, but new values for inserted records are random numbers. Random AutoNumber fields are not meaningful because they are not in any particular order, and the highest value is not on the record inserted last. When you open a table with a random AutoNumber field as the primary key, the records appear in the order of ascending random numbers, not in insertion order.

With random AutoNumber fields that have their **FieldSize** property set to **Long Integer**, it is possible for two different records to be assigned the same value, although the probability of this happening is very low. If this happens, updates could be made in incorrect records. To prevent this from happening, consider using the s_GUID field as the primary key. The s_GUID field is an AutoNumber field with its **FieldSize** property set to **ReplicationID** so that it generates a unique 16-byte value called a *globally unique identifier* (GUID) for each newly added record.

Before you convert a database to a Design Master, determine whether any of your applications or users rely on the order and incremental nature of the AutoNumber field. If so, you can use an additional Date/Time field to provide sequential ordering information.

Making Additional Replicas

Although you can make changes to the design of the database only in the Design Master, you can make additional replicas from any replica in the set. In fact, the only way to include new copies of the database in the replica set is to create them from an existing replica. Once you create them, all new replicas become part of the replica set.

All the replicas in a replica set have a unique identity and can communicate and synchronize with one another. Each replica set is independent from all other replica sets, and replicas in different sets cannot communicate or synchronize with each other.

Important Never try to make additional replicas from the original, nonreplicated database. The result would be a new Design Master and replica set, not an additional replica.

When you convert a database to a Design Master by setting its **ReplicableBool** property to **True**, you have only one replica (the Design Master) in the replica set, and you make the second replica from this. Make the second replica, and subsequent replicas, by clicking **Create Replica** (**Tools** menu, **Replication** submenu) in Microsoft Access, or by using the **MakeReplica** method in code. For information about the **MakeReplica** method, see Microsoft Access online Help.

When Microsoft Access creates the new replica, all property settings of the source replica except custom property settings are included in the new replica. You can make subsequent replicas from either the Design Master or another replica in the set.

Microsoft Access locks objects while they are open in Design view or while their data is being updated. When you use the **MakeReplica** method, be sure that the objects you are replicating are not locked. If objects are locked when you make a replica, the **MakeReplica** method fails.

> **Using Replicas Instead of Backups**
>
> With database replication, you do not need to make a separate backup copy of the database. If the Design Master is destroyed, you can recover the data from any one of the replicas in the replica set. However, depending on how frequently you synchronize, a replica may not contain all the data in the Design Master or in other replicas. If you want to be able to recover most of the information in the Design Master, be sure to synchronize frequently.
>
> Although it is possible to back up replicas by using traditional backup methods, you are strongly advised not to back up and restore replicas as you would ordinary files. If you back up and restore the Design Master, you could lose critical information about changes to the design of the database as well as the ability of the Design Master to synchronize with other replicas in the set. If the Design Master is damaged or unusable, do not copy or restore an older version of the Design Master. Instead, make another replica into the Design Master.

Replicating Part of a Database

So far, this section has addressed *full replicas*, in which all records in all replicas of a replica set are synchronized in their entirety. However, you may want to replicate only part of the data. To do this, create *partial replicas*, which contain only a subset of the records in the full replica. With a partial replica, you can set filters and relationships that identify which subset of the records in the full replica you want to synchronize.

By replicating only part of the database, you can restrict access to data. In the case of a sales database, replicating part of a database can help ensure that people in a regional sales office do not view sales data for other regional offices. In addition, sales representatives who carry laptops can filter their data to include only the information that is relevant to their territory. Although you can restrict access to records or filter records when you replicate part of a database, this is not a substitute for a security system.

Replicating part of a database also has benefits for replicating data over local area networks (LANs) and wide area networks (WANs). By applying filters and relationships that restrict which data is replicated, you can reduce the amount of data transferred over a LAN or a WAN. This can reduce network traffic and lower telecommunications costs.

World Wide Web To create a partial replica, you can use DAO code or tools provided through the Microsoft Access Developer Forum. Connect to the Microsoft Access Developer Forum Web site at:

http://www.microsoft.com/accessdev/

For information about using DAO code to create a partial replica, see Microsoft Access online Help, or see "Creating Partial Replicas" in Chapter 20, "Using Replication in Your Application," in *Building Applications with Microsoft Access 97*.

Note You cannot synchronize data between two partial replicas; one of the replicas must be a full replica. Also, when you replicate part of a database, you can set restrictions on which records are replicated, but you cannot indicate which fields are replicated.

Synchronizing Replicas

For database replication to be useful, replicas must communicate with one another to keep up-to-date information. Synchronization is the process of making the design and data in the replicas identical. As changes are made to the existing records in one replica, the changes are communicated to each of the other replicas that has that same record. Similarly, new and deleted records in one replica are communicated to the other replicas in the replica set.

You can synchronize one replica with another by using Microsoft Access commands, the Windows 95 Briefcase, or the **Synchronize** method in Visual Basic code. The method you use corresponds to the method you used to implement database replication.

▶ **To synchronize two replicas using Microsoft Access commands**

- On the **Tools** menu, point to **Replication**, and then click **Synchronize Now**.

If you used the Windows 95 Briefcase to replicate the database, use the following procedure to synchronize replicas.

▶ **To synchronize two replicas using the Windows 95 Briefcase**

1 Double-click the My Briefcase icon on your desktop, and click the database file.

2 On the **Briefcase** menu, click **Update Selection**.

  –or–

  If you want to synchronize all the replicas in the Briefcase, click **Update All**.

For information about synchronizing replicas by using the **Synchronize** method in Visual Basic code, see Microsoft Access online Help.

If you want to prevent users from making changes to the design of a replicated database, do not make the replica on the network server the Design Master. Instead, keep the Design Master at a network location that is accessible only by you. As you make changes to your application, you can synchronize with the replica on the server and rely on it to pass these changes on to other replicas in the replica set.

Tip You can synchronize replicas over the Internet. Before you can synchronize over the Internet, however, you must configure your Internet server for replication. To configure your Internet server, you need Replication Manager, which includes a wizard that guides you through the configuration process. For more information about Replication Manager, see "Replication Manager" earlier in this chapter.

Handling Replication Conflicts and Errors

When using database replication, you may occasionally encounter design errors, synchronization conflicts, or synchronization errors. *Design errors* occur when a design change in the Design Master conflicts with a design change in a replica. The synchronization fails, and the content of different replicas starts to diverge.

Synchronization conflicts occur when users update the same record in two replicas in the replica set and Microsoft Access attempts to synchronize the two versions. The synchronization succeeds, but the changes from only one of the replicas are applied to the other.

Synchronization errors occur when a change to data in one replica cannot be applied to another replica because it would violate a constraint, such as a referential integrity rule. The synchronization succeeds, but the content of replicas is different. For information about integrity rules, see "Synchronization Errors" later in this chapter.

Synchronization errors and design errors are more significant problems than synchronization conflicts because the replicas no longer share a common design or identical data. This section describes the factors that contribute to conflicts and errors, and suggests ways to prevent or resolve them.

Design Errors

When you make changes to the design of a database, Microsoft Access records each change in the MSysSchChange system table. When Microsoft Access applies all the design changes from one replica to another, it applies the changes in the order that the changes occurred in the Design Master. This ensures that all replicas become identical to the Design Master.

A design error most often occurs when you attempt to synchronize design changes with a replica that is opened exclusively. A locking error occurs, and the design changes are not transferred to the replica.

A design error can also occur if you set a primary key on a field in the replica and, before you synchronize this change, a user enters a duplicate value in that field in another replica. When you synchronize with the other replica, Microsoft Access determines that the records do not have unique identifiers and, therefore, the field cannot be used as a primary key.

To identify the cause of an error, you can use the MSysSchemaProb table, which is present only when an error has occurred in updating the design of a replica. The table provides details about the cause of the error, including:

- The action that failed (Create Index, Create Table, and so on).
- The text of the error message.
- The version number of the replica that encountered the problem.
- Context information such as table names and field names.

The MSysSchemaProb table is a local table and is not replicated. The records in the MSysSchemaProb table are automatically deleted when the corresponding design change is successfully applied during synchronization.

To correct design errors, use the MSysSchemaProb table to identify the action that failed, and then manually correct the corresponding object in the replica. Always fix the problem at the replica even if a design change in the Design Master caused the error. For example, to correct a locking error caused by trying to synchronize with a replica that is open exclusively, close the replica and try the synchronization again.

Synchronization Conflicts

When you synchronize replicas, conflict between versions is always possible because the same record may be updated at two different locations. If this happens, Microsoft Access cannot determine which of the two changes should take precedence.

Microsoft Access accepts the changes from one replica and records the rejected changes in a conflict table in the replica whose changes were not accepted. By default, the record with the most changes since the last synchronization has priority. Microsoft Access does not read the content of the data that has changed; instead, it examines the version number of the record. Each time a change is made to the data in a record, the version number increases by one.

For example, a record with no changes has a version number of 0. A change to data increments the version number to 1. A second change to the same data, or a change to different data in the record, increments the version number to 2, and so on. The update with the higher version number takes precedence because Microsoft Access assumes that the replica that changed the most frequently is the correct version. When two replicas give an updated record the same version number, Microsoft Access chooses which update to accept based on the value of the **ReplicaID** property. Because you cannot change the algorithm used to decide which changes are accepted and which are rejected, be prepared to manually resolve the errors in any replica.

Conflict tables derive both their names and fields from the underlying tables. Conflict table names are in the form *table*_conflict, where *table* is the original table name. For example, if the original table name is Customers, the conflict table name is Customers_conflict. Because conflicts are reported only to the replica that originated the rejected update, conflict tables are not replicated.

After synchronizing two replicas, review the database for conflicts and determine whether you need to take any further action. You can determine whether a conflict has occurred for a specific table by looking at the **ConflictTable** property. This property returns the name of the conflict table that contains the database records that conflicted during synchronization. If there is no conflict table, or if the database is read-only or is a replica, the **ConflictTable** property returns a zero-length string ("").

You can then examine the conflicts and work through them record by record, fixing whatever is necessary. For example, you can:

- Manually update the database table with the data from its conflict table.
- Leave the database unchanged and delete the record from the conflict table.
- Develop a custom routine for resolving conflicts where a higher priority is always assigned to changes in one specific replica over another replica.

Microsoft Access automatically notifies you of a synchronization conflict. Click **Resolve Conflicts** (**Tools** menu, **Replication** submenu) to view conflict tables and resolve each conflict manually.

You can substitute a custom routine for the **Resolve Conflicts** command. For information about creating custom code for resolving conflicts, see Microsoft Access online Help.

Synchronization Errors

There are four sources of potential synchronization errors to consider when building your application:

- Table-level validation rules

    Microsoft Access allows you to establish table-level validation rules to restrict the value or type of data entered into a table. However, if you implement a rule without determining whether existing data conforms to the rule, you may encounter a synchronization error in the future. To correct the error, correct the invalid values in the replica that is sending the value. You can avoid the error by synchronizing all replicas in the replica set before you apply a table-level validation rule.

- Duplicate keys

    Duplicate keys can occur when two users of different replicas simultaneously insert a new record and use the same primary key for their respective records, or when a user changes a record's primary key so that it uses the same value as another record. When the replicas are synchronized, the synchronization succeeds, but Microsoft Access records a duplicate key error in the MSysErrors table for each of the records. To correct a duplicate key error, change the value of one of the keys, or delete the duplicate record.

- Referential integrity

    Referential integrity preserves the relationship between tables when you are adding or deleting records. Enforced referential integrity prevents you from adding a record to or deleting a record from a related table if there is no corresponding record in the primary table. In some situations, enforced referential integrity can result in synchronization errors. To reduce referential integrity errors during synchronization, you may want to use the s_GUID field as the primary key in some or all of the replicated tables.

- Record locks

    If a record is locked when Microsoft Access attempts to update it during synchronization, Microsoft Access retries the update several times. If the record remains locked after repeated attempts, the synchronization fails, and Microsoft Access records an error in the MSysErrors system table. Although this type of error is exceedingly rare, it may occur in certain multiuser applications. You can ignore errors caused by locked records, because Microsoft Access retries updating the records during the next synchronization. Because it is unlikely that the same record is locked during the next synchronization, Microsoft Access updates the record and removes the error from the MSysErrors table.

Synchronization errors are recorded in the MSysErrors table and replicated to all replicas in the replica set. This table includes information about the:

- Table involved.
- Record that encountered the errors.
- Replica or replicas where the error was detected.
- Replica that last changed the record.
- Type of operation that failed.
- Reason it failed.

Correct errors as soon as possible, because they indicate that the data in different replicas may be diverging. Be especially careful to correct synchronization errors before you move a database, because the error is recorded against the value of the **ReplicaID** property at the time the error occurred. If the value of the **ReplicaID** property changes, Microsoft Access cannot automatically remove the error records during a subsequent synchronization. If you do not remove the error record, you get an error each time you open the database even if you have corrected the problem.

In many circumstances, errors are self-correcting during the next synchronization. For example, if you attempt to synchronize a record that another user locked, the update fails. Microsoft Access records an error and attempts to reapply the update at a later time. If the subsequent update succeeds, the error record is removed.

As a general rule, always synchronize all replicas in the replica set before manually correcting synchronization errors. Due to the nature of bidirectional synchronizations, it may take more than one synchronization to clear the error record from the MSysErrors table after the error is corrected. However, Microsoft Access should clear all corrected errors from the MSysErrors table after two bidirectional synchronizations.

Compacting a Replicated Database

When you convert a database to a Design Master, Microsoft Access adds three new fields to the tables and adds new system tables to the database. Many of these new tables contain only a few records, but some of the new tables can grow significantly depending on the frequency of synchronization. To reclaim unused space and to help optimize performance, compact a database frequently. In addition, always compact a database before you synchronize.

▶ **To compact a replicated database**

1. Compact the database into the file Db1.mdb. Do not open the file Db1.mdb with Microsoft Access.

   For information about compacting a database, see Microsoft Access online Help.

2. Rename the original (uncompacted) database by giving it a file name with the .bak extension.

   For example, if the original database is named Customers.mdb, rename it Customers.bak.

3. Rename Db1.mdb with the original name of the database.

   For example, rename Db1.mdb Customers.mdb.

Now you can open the original database. Because it has the same path and the same name, the value of its **ReplicaID** property does not change, and it is still recognized as the Design Master.

For more information about compacting databases, see "Compacting a Database" in Chapter 15, "Delivering Your Application," in *Building Applications with Microsoft Access 97*.

Setting Security for Replicated Databases

Replicated databases use the same security model as nonreplicated databases: Users' permissions on the database are determined at the time they start Microsoft Access and log on. It is up to you to make sure the same security information is available at each location where a replica is used. You can do this by making the identical workgroup information file (the file that stores security information) available to users at each location where a replica is used. The default workgroup information file is called System.mdw.

You cannot replicate the workgroup information file, but you can manually copy it to each location. Another way to make the same workgroup information file available to all users is to re-create the entries for users and groups at each location in the local workgroup information file by entering the same user and group names with their associated personal identifiers (PIDs) at each location. Modification to permissions is a design change and can be made only in the Design Master.

There should always be at least one user with Administer permission on the database. For example, a user must have Administer permission on the database to:

- Convert a database to a Design Master.
- Change the setting of the **ReplicableBool** property of an object or make another replica into the Design Master.

    You can change the setting of the **ReplicableBool** property only in the Design Master.

- Make a replica into the Design Master.

By default, Administer permission is granted to the Users group, the Admins group, and the creator of the database.

Designating a New Design Master

The Design Master is the most important replica in a set because it is the only replica where you can make changes to the structure of the database. Under certain circumstances, you may need to make another replica into the Design Master.

For example, you may have the Design Master on your computer, and another member of your development team has a replica on his or her computer. While you are on vacation, you want the other developer to be able to make changes to the database. The following procedure designates a new Design Master by using the **Synchronize Now** command to synchronize the two replicas and set the **DesignMasterID** property of the current Design Master to the value of the other replica's **ReplicaID** property.

▶ **To make a replica into the new Design Master**

1. Make sure that the replica and the current Design Master are not in use elsewhere, and then open the replica that you want to make the new Design Master.
2. On the **Tools** menu, point to **Replication**, and then click **Synchronize Now**.
3. In the **Synchronize With** box, click the current Design Master.
4. Select the **Make '***File name***' the Design Master** check box, and then click **OK**.

The Design Master is a read/write replica. If you make a read-only replica into the Design Master, the new Design Master is read/write, and the old Design Master is made read-only.

If the replica serving as the Design Master is erased or corrupted, you can designate another replica to act as the Design Master. However, remember that you can have only one Design Master at a time. If you decide to make your own replica into the new Design Master for the set, synchronize all the replicas in the replica set before making your replica the new Design Master.

Making a Replicated Database into a Regular Database

After you have converted a database to a Design Master, you cannot convert it back to a regular database. However, if you no longer want to use replication, you can create a new, regular database that contains all of the objects and data in the replicated database without the additional system fields, tables, and properties associated with replication.

▶ **To make a replicated database into a regular database**

1. Create and open a new, blank database in Microsoft Access.
2. On the **File** menu, point to **Get External Data**, and then click **Import**.
3. In the **Import** dialog box, click the replica that contains the objects that you want in the new, regular database, and then click **Import**.
4. In the **Import Objects** dialog box, click the objects (except tables) that you want to import into the new database, and then click **OK**.
5. In the new database, for each table in the replica, create a query that takes all the data in the replica and puts it into tables in the new database.
6. For each table in the new database, create the same indexes and relationships that exist in the replica table.
7. Save the new database.

Visual SourceSafe

Microsoft Visual SourceSafe™ (for use with Microsoft Office 97, Developer Edition only) is a project-oriented version control system for all types of files, including text files, graphics files, binary files, sound files, and video files. You can track changes made to a file from the moment it is created by using Visual SourceSafe, and you can merge changes from two or more different versions of a file into one file that contains them all.

Microsoft Office 97, Developer Edition, provides the Microsoft Access Source Code Control component to integrate Visual SourceSafe functions into the Microsoft Access development environment. However, you must purchase and install Visual SourceSafe in addition to Microsoft Office 97, Developer Edition, to be able to use Visual SourceSafe within Microsoft Access.

A workgroup developing Microsoft Access database applications can use Visual SourceSafe to prevent conflicts and data loss during the development process. Visual SourceSafe includes the following services:

- Prevents accidental deletion of information or the files themselves
- Organizes files into a nearly unlimited hierarchy of projects and subprojects
- Checks files in and out, adding comments to describe what has been done
- Allows two or more users to share files across projects, operating systems, and driver-sharing networks
- Stores any kind of file—text or binary—including Microsoft Office documents, Microsoft Excel worksheets, and Visual Basic, Visual C++, Visual FoxPro, and Microsoft Access files
- Helps in developing applications across operating systems
- Works with modular or object-oriented code
- Checks out files to two or more users at the same time
- Tracks changes users make to files
- Makes older versions of files readily available for bug fixes and other purposes
- Displays differences between two versions of a file
- Tracks date and time of changes to all files in the database
- Creates reports on file or project activity
- Creates journal files, with records of each change to a project
- Controls access to files

    By default, Visual SourceSafe maintains security on projects, so that each new user has either read/write access or read-only access. When the Visual SourceSafe administrator enables security, access rights can be set by project or by user.

For more information about Visual SourceSafe, see the Visual SourceSafe documentation.

CHAPTER 30

Workgroup Features in Microsoft Excel

This chapter explains how to administer features in Microsoft Excel that are designed for sharing workbooks among users in a workgroup. It describes how the various workgroup features of Microsoft Excel work and provides information for supporting them.

In This Chapter
Security Features in Microsoft Excel   855
Shared Workbooks   858
Workbook Merging and Data Consolidation   860
Workgroup Review of Workbooks   862

See Also
- For a summary of new and improved features in Microsoft Excel 97, see Chapter 2, "What's New in Microsoft Office 97."
- For information about supporting workgroups that are running more than one version of Microsoft Excel, see Chapter 22, "Supporting Multiple Versions of Microsoft Office."
- For information about the structure of Microsoft Excel and how its components fit together, see Chapter 36, "Microsoft Excel Architecture."
- For information about designing and implementing Web forms, see Chapter 25, "Web Support in Microsoft Office Applications."

Security Features in Microsoft Excel

As a workgroup administrator, you might initiate or oversee workgroup security practices for protecting Microsoft Excel workbooks. This section describes the options available in Microsoft Excel for protecting workbooks. These options are independent of any additional security measures at the operating system level.

Microsoft Excel 97 incorporates the symmetric encryption routine known as RC4. RC4 is stronger than the encryption routine used in previous versions of Microsoft Excel, known as XOR. Workbooks from previous versions of Microsoft Excel are not as secure as password-protected workbooks in Microsoft Excel 97 format. For more information about Office encryption, see "Security Features in Office" in Chapter 34, "Microsoft Office Architecture."

Note Strong encryption such as RC4 is banned in France. If a user's locale setting in **Regional Settings** on the Control Panel is set to **French (Standard)**, that user is not able to open an Office document that is password protected. Nor can the user save an Office document with RC4 encryption. The user can, however, use XOR encryption by saving an Office document with password protection.

Microsoft Excel supports three levels of workbook file protection. All three are controlled by the author of the workbook, who is the user with read-write access to a workbook. The three levels of workbook protection are:

- File open protection

    Microsoft Excel requires the user to enter a password to open a workbook.

- File modify protection

    Microsoft Excel prompts the user to enter a password to open the workbook read-write. If the user clicks **Read Only** at the prompt, Microsoft Excel opens the workbook read-only.

- Read-only recommended protection

    Microsoft Excel prompts the user to open the workbook read-only. If the user clicks **No** at the prompt, Microsoft Excel opens the workbook read-write, unless the workbook has other password protection.

▶ **To protect a workbook file**

1. On the **File** menu, click **Save As**.
2. Click **Options**.
3. To have Microsoft Excel prompt the user to open the workbook read-only, select the **Read-only recommended** check box.

    –or–

    To require a password to open the workbook, type a password in the **Password to open** box, and then click **OK**.

    –or–

    To require a password to save changes the workbook, type a password in the **Password to modify** box, and then click **OK**.

4. When prompted, type the password again, and then click **OK**.
5. Click **Save**.

Note Because protected workbooks are encrypted, they are not indexed by Find Fast. For more information about document indexing and searching, see Chapter 26, "Finding Microsoft Office Documents on the Network."

In addition to protecting an entire workbook, you can protect specific elements from unauthorized changes. The elements you can protect are:

- Structure of a workbook

    Sheets in a protected workbook cannot be moved, deleted, hidden, unhidden, or renamed, and new sheets cannot be inserted.

- Windows in a workbook

    Windows in a protected workbook cannot be moved, resized, hidden, unhidden, or closed. Windows in a protected workbook are sized and positioned the same way each time the workbook is opened.

- Cells on a sheet

    Contents of protected cells cannot be edited.

- Graphic objects on a sheet

    Protected graphic objects cannot be moved or edited.

- Formulas on a sheet

    Protected formulas cannot be edited.

    Tip You can also hide a formula so that it does not appear in the formula bar but the formula results appear in the cell. On the **Format** menu, click the **Cells** command, and then select the **Hidden** check box on the **Protection** tab. You must then protect the workbook file.

- Scenarios on a sheet

    Definitions of protected scenarios cannot be changed.

- The change history of shared workbooks

    Protected change histories cannot be cleared by the user of a shared workbook or by the user of a copy of a workbook that is to be merged.

▶ **To protect a specific element in a workbook from unauthorized changes**

1 To protect cell contents including formulas, graphic objects, or scenarios, point to **Protection** on the **Tools** menu, and then click **Protect Sheet**.

   –or–

   To protect the workbook structure or windows, point to **Protection** on the **Tools** menu, and then click **Protect Workbook**.

2 Select the check boxes for the elements you want to protect.

3 To prevent others from removing protection from the sheet or workbook, type a password in the **Password** box and click **OK**, and then retype the password in the **Confirm Password** dialog box.

Caution If you or a user in your workgroup assigns password protection to a workbook and then forgets the password, you cannot open the workbook, access its data in another workbook through links, remove protection from the workbook, or recover data from the workbook. Keep a list of your passwords and their corresponding workbook and sheet names in a safe place.

You can protect the change history only if it is not already password protected.

▶ **To protect sharing and change history of a workbook**

1 Point to **Protection** on the **Tools** menu, and then click **Protect Shared Workbook**.

 –or–

 If the workbook is not already shared, click **Protect and Share Workbook**.

2 Select the **Sharing with Track Changes** check box.

3 If you want to require other users to supply a password to turn off the change history or remove the workbook from shared use, type the password in the **Password** box, and then re-enter the password when prompted.

 This option is available only if the workbook is not already shared.

Shared Workbooks

Microsoft Excel allows many users to edit the same workbook simultaneously, or to edit copies of a workbook at different times. In both cases, a user with read-write access to the workbook can share the workbook by clicking **Share Workbook** (**Tools** menu). This section describes *shared workbooks*: multiple users editing the same workbook simultaneously. For information about *workbook merging*—users editing copies of a workbook at different times—see "Workbook Merging and Data Consolidation" later in this chapter.

When a workbook is shared, Microsoft Excel keeps a *change history* of the workbook. The change history records who changes cells, when a change is made, and the previous values of an edited cell.
Shared workbooks have the following characteristics:

- Not all Microsoft Excel commands and features are available.

  For example, you cannot delete a sheet in a shared workbook. For a complete list of limitations when using shared workbooks, see Microsoft Excel online Help.

- Of the commands and features that are available when working with a shared workbook, not all are recorded in the change history.

    For example, formatting changes are allowed in a shared workbook, but not recorded in the change history. For a complete list of actions that are not recorded, see Microsoft Excel online Help.

- History of cell revisions is maintained until the **Track changes** time value on the **Advanced** tab in the **Share Workbook** dialog box (**Tools** menu) expires. The history of revisions older than the **Track changes** time value is lost, but revisions within the **Track changes** time value are kept.

- Turning off workbook sharing clears the entire change history.

    Once cleared, the change history cannot be recovered. To protect the change history, use the **Protect Shared Workbook** command (**Tools** menu, **Protection** submenu). For more information about workbook protection, see "Security Features in Microsoft Excel" earlier in this chapter.

Tip A workbook for which the change history has been enabled grows in size as the change history grows. To conserve disk space, you can enable sharing without enabling the change history. On the **Advanced** tab in the **Share Workbook** dialog box (**Tools** menu), select the **Don't keep change history** option under **Track changes**.

Some common uses of shared workbooks include:

- Sharing a list among several users.

    For example, a shared list could be a customer or parts list or a schedule. In this case, different users might need access to any part of the workbook at any time.

- Consolidating data stored on different worksheets within a single workbook.

    For example, different department managers might maintain their budgets on departmental sheets in a workbook, and a division vice president might consolidate the data onto another sheet in the workbook with the **Consolidate** command (**Data** menu).

- Summarizing data stored on different rows within a single worksheet.

    For example, different department managers might keep track of personnel headcount on specific rows in a worksheet, and a division vice president might summarize the data—apply an outline and subtotals or averages, for example.

Tip Microsoft Excel does not offer the same level of multiuser support as does Microsoft Access. For example, Microsoft Access supports user-level security, but Microsoft Excel does not. If you have more complex needs for data entry, protection, or reporting than Microsoft Excel can manage, consider using Microsoft Access. For information about sharing data between Microsoft Excel and Microsoft Access, see "Sharing Information with Microsoft Access 97" in Chapter 27, "Sharing Information with Microsoft Office Applications."

When two or more users of a shared workbook make conflicting changes (for example, entering different values in the same cell), users can either review the conflicts or automatically save their own changes when they save the workbook. Users set this option for themselves in the **Conflicting changes between users** group on the **Advanced** tab in the **Share Workbook** dialog box (**Tools** menu). If users choose to review changes, they see a dialog box similar to the following when they either save a workbook to which another user has made conflicting changes, or when the **Update changes** time value is met.

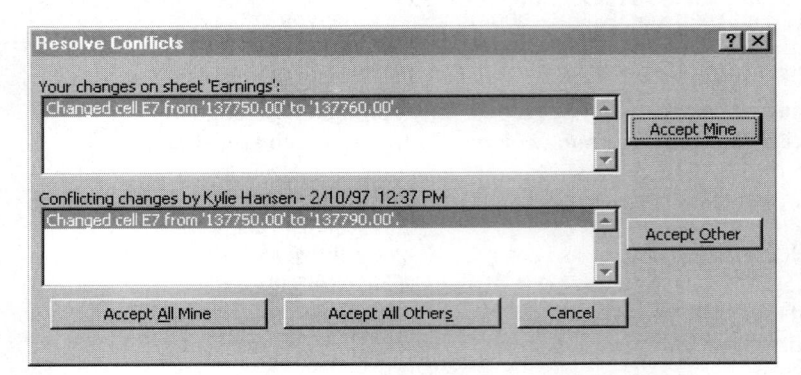

Workbook Merging and Data Consolidation

Workbook merging and data consolidation have similar purposes: in both cases, you start with data from multiple sources and end up with a summary of the data in a single workbook.

Workbook merging combines multiple copies of a single workbook. It is better suited for workbooks in which multiple contributors edit any part of the data at any time, or in which a single user edits different versions of the same workbook on different computers. For example, a mobile user might copy a shared workbook to a laptop computer. While the user is gone, other users can continue to edit the shared workbook. Upon returning, the mobile user can merge changes into the original workbook.

Data consolidation combines multiple workbooks. It is designed for summarizing structured data, such as rolling up departmental budgets into a summary budget for a division.

Merging Workbooks

Merging workbooks is similar to working with shared workbooks, but instead of multiple users editing the same workbook simultaneously, multiple copies of a single workbook are reconciled. As with shared workbooks, merging requires you to turn on the change history with the **Share Workbook** command (**Tools** menu) before making copies and distributing the workbook. To merge workbooks, use the **Merge Workbooks** command (**Tools** menu).

You must turn on the change history in the workbook from the time you create copies of the workbook to the time you merge changes back into the original workbook. Specify the duration of the change history on the **Advanced** tab in the **Share Workbook** dialog box (**Tools** menu). If you do not know how long it will be before you merge changes, set the change history duration to a long period such as 1000 days.

Unless the change history of the workbook is protected, a user can turn it off. If this happens, you cannot automatically merge that user's changes. To protect the change history, use the **Protect Shared Workbook** command (**Tools** menu, **Protection** submenu). For more information about workbook protection, see "Security Features in Microsoft Excel" earlier in this chapter.

Consolidating Data

Consolidating data is similar to merging workbooks, except that it is not necessary to turn on the change history. Use data consolidation when you want to compile repetitive, highly structured data from several subordinate workbooks into one summary workbook.

When you consolidate data on multiple worksheets within one workbook, use consolidation by 3-D references and share or route the workbook. A *3-D reference* includes a cell or range reference, preceded by a range of worksheet names, allowing you to analyze data in the same cell or range of cells on multiple worksheets within a workbook. Use 3-D formulas on the consolidation worksheet to refer to the data sources on the detail worksheets.

If you choose not to use 3-D references, consolidate data by consistent positions on a worksheet, or by the category of data. Whether you use 3-D references or position or category references, start consolidating data by clicking the **Consolidate** command (**Data** menu).

Part 5 Using Microsoft Office Throughout Your Organization

Workgroup Review of Workbooks

Microsoft Excel includes several features that support adding comments to workbooks. If your workgroup has access to e-mail, users can also send or route workbooks to their co-workers.

Tracking Changes and Comments

As with Microsoft Word documents or Microsoft PowerPoint presentations, it is common for many members of a workgroup to revise or annotate a Microsoft Excel workbook.

The commands on the **Track Changes** submenu (**Tools** menu) allow you to record, review, accept, or reject changes to cell values. When you click **Highlight Changes** (**Tools** menu, **Track Changes** submenu), Microsoft Excel turns on both change history (if it was not already on) and workbook sharing. All changes to cell values are recorded and indicated by a small triangle in the upper left corner of changed cells. The triangles are color coded to distinguish among different users. Pointing to such a cell displays the most recent change made to that cell, similar to displaying a ToolTip for a toolbar button.

Marketing	118,125	Kylie, 2/10/97 9:09 AM:		137,781
R&D	80,000	Changed cell C8 from '77,800 ' to '80000.00'.		90,210
Total Wages	315,000			387,000
Insurance	12,670			14,778
Operating Expenses	210,795		141,259	629,769
Net Profit	1,117,005		1,552,491	1,682,931

> ### Viewing the Entire Change History
> The change history box of a cell shows only the most recent change made to the cell. To see all changes in the change history, select the **List changes on a new sheet** check box in the **Highlight Changes** dialog box (**Tools** menu, **Track Changes** submenu). Selecting this option adds a History sheet to the shared workbook that lists all changes recorded in the change history. The list is filtered, so you can easily review all changes that have been made to any cell.

To review the recorded changes, use the **Accept or Reject Changes** command (**Tools** menu, **Track Changes** submenu). This starts a process similar to reviewing revisions in Word: You review each change made to the worksheet, and accept or reject each one.

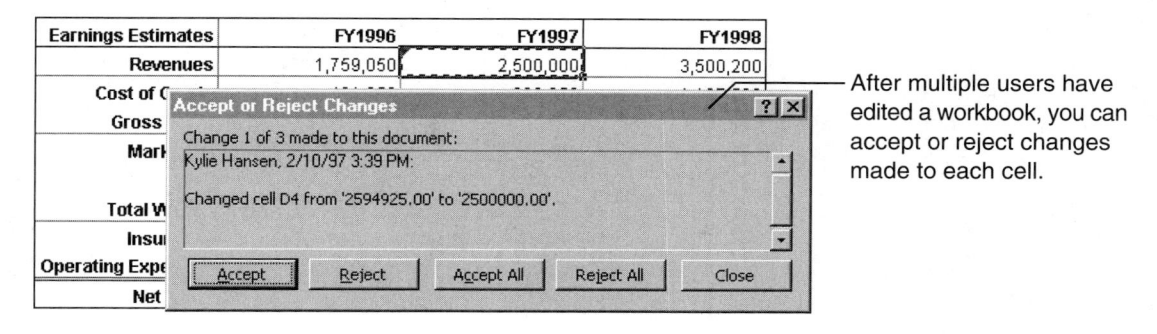

After multiple users have edited a workbook, you can accept or reject changes made to each cell.

You can also record comments for any cell in a workbook. (In previous versions of Microsoft Excel, these were called notes.) To create a comment, click the **Comments** command (**Insert** menu). A cell with a comment has a small red triangle in the upper-right corner. Pointing to the cell displays the cell comment in a box, similar to displaying a ToolTip for a toolbar button.

Routing Workbooks with Electronic Mail

Users in a workgroup who have e-mail capability can review workbooks by routing a them through e-mail, with each recipient adding comments to the workbook. For information about using Office applications with e-mail, see Chapter 28, "Working with Messaging Systems and Connectivity Software."

▶ **To route a workbook to other members of your workgroup**

1. On the **File** menu, point to **Send To**, and then click **Routing Recipient**.
2. If prompted, in the **Profile Name** box select the user profile you want to use.
3. In the **Routing Slip** dialog box, click **Address**, select the recipients, and then click **OK**.
4. In the **Message text** box, type a message, select the **Return when done** check box, and then click **Route**.

   When users in the workgroup receive the workbook, they can insert their own comments. When all routing recipients have reviewed the workbook, it is routed back to you.

Note If you are routing a workbook to a user who has not yet upgraded to Microsoft Excel 97, first save the workbook in a format that the target version of Microsoft Excel can open, such as Microsoft Excel 95 format. For information about sharing workbooks among different versions of Microsoft Excel, see Chapter 12, "Upgrading from Previous Versions of Microsoft Excel."

CHAPTER 31

Workgroup Features in Microsoft Outlook

Microsoft Outlook contains many features that support collaboration within a workgroup. This chapter provides administrators with the information necessary to enable, support, and troubleshoot workgroup features in Outlook.

In This Chapter
Group Scheduling   865
Microsoft Exchange Public Folders   868
Extended Task Management Capabilities with Microsoft Team Manager   873

See Also
- For a summary of new features in Outlook, including built-in workgroup features, see Chapter 2, "What's New in Microsoft Office 97."
- For information about exchanging information between Outlook users and users of other Microsoft mail or scheduling applications, see Chapter 13, "Upgrading to Microsoft Outlook."

Note   Outlook runs only on Windows 95 and Windows NT Workstation version 3.51 or later. Some of the workgroup features described in this chapter also require Microsoft Exchange Server. For more information, see your Microsoft Exchange Server documentation.

Group Scheduling

To implement group scheduling, a workgroup administrator must do the following:

- Set up each user or resource with an electronic mail (e-mail) account on the server
- Have users set the appropriate permissions to share their Calendars with other users

You can also edit the profile script file (Outlook.prf) to create custom profiles for your users. For more information about setting up e-mail accounts, see your Microsoft Exchange Server documentation.

Tools and Utilities The Office Resource Kit Tools and Utilities include information about how to use and customize the default messaging profile used by Outlook and e-mail-enabled Office applications. For more information, see "Outlook 97 Profiles" in Appendix A, "Microsoft Office 97 Resource Kit Tools and Utilities."

Viewing Free/Busy Information in a Workgroup

The most common group scheduling activity is browsing free and busy information to find an available time for a group of users to meet.

Note *Free/busy status* refers to the format displaying the user's time as free, busy, out-of-office, or tentative. This information is published in a common file format on the server. *Free/busy details* include appointment specifics such as subject or meeting location. To see free/busy details, a user must be granted permission to open another user's Calendar.

Outlook users publish their free/busy status using the **Advanced Scheduling** command on the **Calendar** tab in the **Options** dialog box (**Tools** menu). To view other users' unpublished free/busy status, Outlook users must open another user's Calendar (with appropriate permission).

Note Unless noted otherwise, all references to Schedule+ refer to both Schedule+ 95 and Schedule+ 1.0.

For workgroups using a combination of Outlook and Schedule+, Outlook differs slightly from Schedule+ in how it handles unpublished free/busy status. When a Schedule+ user chooses not to publish free/busy status, other Schedule+ users who have at least read permission for that user's schedule can still view the free/busy status in their Meeting Planners. However, when an Outlook user chooses not to publish free/busy status, other Outlook users—even those who have read-only permission—cannot view the user's free/busy status in their Meeting Planners. Schedule+ users cannot see Outlook users' unpublished free/busy status, even if the Outlook Calendar is shared.

> ### Managing Scheduling Data with Microsoft Exchange Server
> For Outlook clients who use Microsoft Exchange Server, free/busy status and free/busy details are stored in a hidden public folder on the server. Within a single site (*intrasite*), this public folder may be replicated to load balance the queries to the free/busy information. When the free/busy folder is replicated, network traffic is reduced, especially when a large number of users are connecting to Microsoft Exchange Server.
>
> You can also replicate the free/busy folder between two Microsoft Exchange Server computers located across a remote link. This reduces the total traffic across the link and improves performance when users read or write remote schedule data.

Scheduling Resources

With Outlook, you can plan schedules not only for workgroup users but also for resources such as conference rooms and AV equipment. This feature makes it easy for everyone in a workgroup to see when resources are available and to reserve the resources in advance. Users can include the resources, along with other attendees, in a meeting request. You can configure each resource account to accept or reject meeting requests automatically, or you can have requests for several resources handled by a single delegate.

To set up a resource on Outlook, first create an e-mail account for each resource, just as you would for a workgroup member. If a delegate is assigned for a resource, you can configure the resource account so that users send meeting requests directly to the delegate.

Unlike Schedule+ resource accounts, Outlook resource accounts cannot be booked directly. To set up automatic booking of Outlook resource accounts, you must configure the resource account so that Outlook automatically responds when meeting requests are delivered to the Inbox. To do this, you must have Outlook running on a computer and logged on to the resource account.

If you want to centralize booking of several resources, you can assign a single delegate to multiple resource accounts and then configure the delegate to respond to meeting requests automatically. All meeting requests sent to the resources are forwarded to the delegate for processing. The advantage to this method is that only one computer is required to handle multiple resources. For example, you can set up a dedicated computer, with Outlook logged on to the delegate account, to handle the booking of several conference rooms at once.

▶ **To assign a delegate to an Outlook resource account**

1 Create an e-mail account with the name of the resource.

   For example, create an e-mail account with the name Conference Room 3/422.

2 Create an e-mail account for the delegate.

   You can create a dedicated delegate account, or you can use an existing user account. For example, you may use a receptionist's e-mail account for booking all conference rooms in a building.

3 Start Outlook and log on to the resource account.

4 On the **Tools** menu, click **Options**, and then click the **Delegates** tab.

5 Click **Add**.

6 In the **Add Users** dialog box, select the delegate user, click **Add**, and then click **OK**.

7 Set the permissions you want the delegate to have, then click OK.

8 On the **Delegates** tab, select the **Send meeting requests and responses only to my delegates, not to me** check box. (This option is not available before you add the delegate.)

   All meeting requests sent to this resource are automatically forwarded to the delegate for processing.

You can also set up the resource account to handle meeting requests automatically.

▶ **To enable automatic booking of resource requests**

1 Start Outlook and log on to the delegate account.

2 On the **Tools** menu, click **Options**, then click the **E-mail** tab.

3 Select the **Process requests and responses on arrival** check box.

4 Click the **Calendar** tab, and then click **Advanced Scheduling**.

5 Under **Processing of meeting requests**, select the check boxes that correspond to the options you want to use.

   Select all three options for complete automatic booking of all meeting requests forwarded to the delegate. If you select only some of these options, you must log on to the delegate account periodically to accept or reject meeting requests.

Microsoft Exchange Public Folders

Note This Outlook feature requires that you use Microsoft Exchange Server mail system.

When you set up Outlook as a workgroup client for Microsoft Exchange Server, you can set up public folders for users to share information. Outlook has built-in Calendar,

Contacts, and Tasks modules that can be customized for workgroups to share details such as company schedules and holidays, employee and customer lists, and project task lists. Public folders can also be set up for users to participate in online conversations, to post information or documents in a bulletin board format, or to collect a list of shared World Wide Web sites.

You can develop custom views and forms for public folders to create custom applications. You can also give public folder users permission to do this. For more information about creating forms for custom applications, see *Building Applications with Microsoft Outlook 97*, published by Microsoft Press and available wherever computer books are sold. For more information about Microsoft Press, see Appendix E, "Other Support References."

The list of available public folders appears in the Outlook Folder List and in the Microsoft Exchange Server Administrator program. Users are not required to know the name or location of the server where public folder data is stored. If they have permission, other Microsoft clients (such as Microsoft Exchange Client) running under different operating systems can also use these public folders.

Setting Up Public Folders

As the workgroup administrator, you use the Microsoft Exchange Server Administrator program and the Outlook client to set up public folders for users in your workgroup. If you grant some or all of the users permission, they can share the task of creating the public folders. If you work in a large organization or expect heavy use of public folders, you might want to create public folder replicas on additional servers to distribute the user load and to set up a replication schedule to keep all public folder information up to date.

Follow these general steps to set up public folders:

1. Determine how the public folders will be used in your organization. Consider the number of users, servers needed, and whether you need to tightly control public folder creation or permit users to share this task.

2. Configure a Microsoft Exchange Server computer to have a public information store.

   The public information store can be on a dedicated public folder server or on a server that also contains a private information store.

3. Use the Administrator program to set up the public folder hierarchy and public folder age and size limits, storage warnings, and access.

4. Use Outlook to create public folders, set permissions levels, and create rules and views for items in the public folders.

5. If necessary, create public folder replicas on additional servers and set up a replication schedule.

Note For more information about how to set up, organize, and maintain public folders and how to set up and maintain public folder replication, see your Microsoft Exchange Server documentation.

Distributing Public Folder Shortcuts to Users

In an organization that has many public folders, it can be awkward for users to navigate to the folders they want to use, especially if the folders are deep in the Folder List hierarchy. To simplify finding a public folder, users can keep frequently used folders in the Public Folders Favorites folder. When you create public folders, you can distribute shortcuts easily by sending a message that contains public folder shortcuts to users who have permission to use them.

▶ **To send public folder shortcuts to users**

1 Create and address a mail message.

   Tip Include the steps of the following procedure in the text of your message.

2 For each public folder for which you want to send a shortcut, drag the public folder from the Folder List to the mail message.

3 Send the message.

Recipients of your mail message must perform the following steps.

▶ **To save a shortcut to a public folder**

1 In the mail message, double-click the public folder shortcut you want to add to the Public Folders Favorites folder.

   The public folder opens in a separate window.

2 On the **File** menu, click **Add to Outlook Bar**.

3 Repeat Steps 1 and 2 for each shortcut you want to add.

Why aren't public folder subfolders available?

When users add a public folder shortcut to the Public Folders Favorites folder, subfolders in that folder are not available when they use the shortcut. To make sure that subfolders are available from shortcuts in the Public Folders Favorites folder, have users create individual shortcuts for each subfolder they want to open from the Public Folders Favorites folder.

Making Public Folders Secure

Depending on the permissions you grant, administrators and users can control access to public folders. Folder access can be controlled at any point in the folder hierarchy. Permissions are grouped into predefined roles, or sets of activities, that can be performed in the folder. For example, the editor role permits users to read, create, edit, and delete any item in the folder, but not to create subfolders.

Hiding Public Folders from Unauthorized Users

By default, users can view the contents of the Public Folders folder and the All Public Folders folder. To keep users from viewing the contents of a public folder or any of its subfolders, you can use the Administrator program to revoke read permission for a user or distribution list. Revoking a user's read permission for a folder prevents the user from opening the folder or any of its subfolders in the Folder List.

▶ **To revoke read permission for a folder or subfolder**

1 In the Administrator window, click **Public Folders** in the Folder List.
2 Double-click the public folder you want to change.
3 Click the **General** tab, and then click **Client Permissions**.
4 Click the name of the user or distribution list for which you want to revoke permissions.

   If you change permissions both for a user and for a distribution list that includes the user, the user permissions take precedence.

5 Clear the **Read Items** check box.

Note A subfolder inherits permissions from the parent folder only when the subfolder is created. If a user adds the subfolder shortcut to the Public Folders Favorites folder before you revoke read permission from the parent folder, the user can continue to use the shortcut to open the subfolder and view its contents. To protect all subfolders in a public folder, you must revoke read permission for the parent folder and each subfolder.

Preventing Unauthorized Delegates from Adding Messages to a Public Folder

When users copy or move messages to a public folder, one of two names can appear in the From field of the posted message: the name of the person who originally sent the message or the name of the person who moved or copied the message. If the name of the person who originally sent the message appears in the From field, it appears as if the message were posted on behalf of the sender, even if the person who moved or copied the message does not have the appropriate delegate access permissions.

▶ **To change the From field setting for a public folder**

1. On the Outlook **View** menu, click **Folder List**.
2. In the Public Folders folder, right-click the public folder for which you want to change the From field setting, and then click **Properties** on the shortcut menu.
3. Click the **Administration** tab.
4. In the **Drag/Drop posting is a** box, click **Forward**.

   The name of the person who originally sent the message appears in the text box of the message, instead of in the From field.

Supporting the Anonymous Exchange of Information

In Outlook, users can send messages or post information anonymously to a public folder. This practice is useful when users want to make a comment or distribute information to a public folder without revealing their identity to other users.

To permit users to exchange information anonymously, you must create an Anonymous account.

▶ **To create an Anonymous account**

1. In the Microsoft Exchange Server Administrator program, create a mailbox with the display name **Anonymous**
2. Give the Windows NT Domain users group (or any other group containing all or some of the Outlook users) Send As permissions on this mailbox.

   The simplest way to give Send As permission to all the users who will send mail through this account is to give permission to the group. Then every user in the group gets the permission automatically.

Once you have created the Anonymous account, users can address messages or post items from Anonymous instead of using their own names.

▶ **To send or post information anonymously**

1. In Outlook, create a message or item to be posted.
2. On the **View** menu, click **From Field**, and then click **From**.
3. In the **Type Name or Select from List** box, enter **Anonymous**, and then click **OK**.
4. Enter recipient names in the **To** and **Cc** boxes.
5. Give the message a subject, type the message text, and then send the message.

Tip To prevent users from sending or posting information anonymously to a public folder, you can limit permissions for the Anonymous account or create a rule for the public folder to reject messages sent from the Anonymous account.

> **How do I know when public folders contain unread messages?**
> Although the name of a private folder appears in bold when the folder contains unread messages, the name of a public folder does not. This may be confusing to users accustomed to working with private folders.
>
> If you want to be notified when a public folder contains unread messages, create a shortcut to the public folder. When the public folder contains unread messages, the name of the public folder shortcut appears in bold.

Extended Task Management Capabilities with Microsoft Team Manager

The Microsoft Team Manager program extends the task management capabilities of Outlook. Team Manager is a team activity manager that makes it possible for a workgroup to assign, track, and consolidate tasks. When Team Manager is used with Outlook, team members use the Tasks folder in Outlook to receive, view, and update team tasks. Outlook also serves as the messaging client through which team members send and receive task information.

You can use Team Manager in your workgroup to extend task management features in Outlook in the following ways:

- Report on the progress of more than one task at a time.

    Managers and team members can send lists of task information to each other.

- Send regular status reports to a manager.

    Team Manager automatically consolidates status information from the entire team in one status report in the manager's team file.

- Permit both the manager and team member to change a task.

    For example, the manager can change the due date for an assigned task, and the team member can accept or reject the change.

- View a read-only team file of tasks to see the status for everyone on the team and to see how individual tasks fit into the team's work.

    This read-only view is also a place for anyone on the team to experiment with schedule changes. For example, a team member can see what effect a different set of dates would have on other team members' tasks, without making permanent changes to the team file.

Setting Up Team Manager

Team Manager has two Setup options. Managers use the manager Setup option, and team members use the team member Setup option. Even though team members track tasks in Outlook, team member Setup is required. Users who function both as managers and as team members must use both Setup options.

When users install Team Manager, they must choose a messaging option. If managers and team members are not all using Outlook as a messaging client, managers can set up a shared folder or directory on the network to send messages to and receive messages from team members. Users who function both as managers and as team members must choose the same messaging option for manager and team member Setup options. If your workgroup needs to switch to another messaging option (for example, if you are switching from network messages to Microsoft Exchange Server with Outlook as a client), users must reinstall Team Manager with the new messaging option.

Note For more information about how to install Team Manager, how to set up a team file, and how to create and update tasks using Team Manager, see your Microsoft Team Manager documentation.

The following commands are added to the Outlook **Tasks** menu when Team Manager is installed using the team member Setup option:

- **Team Manager for team members**

    This command starts the Team Manager for team members utility, so that users can get additional details about team tasks and perform activities such as switching to another team file if they work on tasks for more than one team.

- **Send Updates**

    This command opens the appropriate form to send task update information or a status report to the manager. Task updates integrate with the manager's team task list. A status report is the team member's written account of progress.

- **View Team Status**

    This command opens a read-only version of the team file.

Switching from Schedule+ to Outlook to View Team Tasks

Team Manager can integrate with task lists in either Schedule+ or Outlook. If your workgroup is switching from Schedule+ to Outlook, users must import their Schedule+ files into Outlook to keep team tasks synchronized between Team Manager and Outlook.

When users switch from Schedule+ to Outlook, they may need to set Team Manager to synchronize tasks with Outlook instead of Schedule+.

▶ **To set Team Manager to synchronize with Outlook**

1 On the Outlook **Tasks** menu, click **Team Manager for team members**.
2 In Team Manager, click **Options**.
3 Select the **Keep copies of tasks in** check box, and then click **Outlook** in the box to the right.

Task Priorities

Tasks are prioritized differently in Schedule+, Outlook, and Team Manager.

- Schedule+: Tasks are prioritized from 1 to 9, A to Z, or A1 to Z9. Priority 1 is the highest priority. Priority 3 is the default.
- Outlook: Tasks are prioritized as High, Normal, or Low.
- Team Manager: Tasks are prioritized as Highest, Very High, High, Medium High, Medium, Medium Low, Low, Very Low, and Lowest.

When you import or synchronize tasks between programs, priorities may change. Schedule+ tasks imported into Outlook are prioritized as follows:

- 1 = High
- 5 = Low
- 2–4 and 6–9 = Normal

When Outlook tasks are synchronized with Team Manager, Normal priority tasks appear as Medium priority tasks in Team Manager.

CHAPTER 32

Workgroup Features in Microsoft PowerPoint

This chapter explains how to administer features in Microsoft PowerPoint that are designed for sharing presentations among users in a workgroup. It describes how the various workgroup features of PowerPoint work and provides information for supporting them, including system requirements and troubleshooting tips.

In This Chapter
Security Features in PowerPoint   877
Presentation Conferencing   878
Workgroup Review of Presentations   886
The Pack and Go Wizard   888

See Also
- For a summary of new and improved features in PowerPoint 97, see Chapter 2, "What's New in Microsoft Office 97."
- For information about supporting workgroups that are running more than one version of PowerPoint, see Chapter 22, "Supporting Multiple Versions of Microsoft Office."
- For information about the structure of PowerPoint and how its components fit together, see Chapter 38, "Microsoft PowerPoint Architecture."

Security Features in PowerPoint

PowerPoint has no features for protecting presentations or the content of slides. Instead, use the security features built into the operating system used by your workgroup.

For example, if you administer Windows NT Server version 3.51 or 4.0, you can secure folders and files and configure user access privileges on the server. Users running PowerPoint under Windows NT Workstation version 3.51 or 4.0 can secure folders and files for which they have ownership, and can configure user access privileges if they have permission to do so. Users running PowerPoint on a Windows 95 computer can restrict the way a folder is shared, and can protect files by making them read-only.

For information about using these security features, consult the documentation for your operating system.

Presentation Conferencing

In Windows, presentation conferencing allows a user on one computer to show a slide show on other computers connected over a local area network (LAN) or over the Internet. This section describes how presentation conferencing works, lists system requirements, provides suggestions for troubleshooting, and explains the role of the presenter and the audience members in a presentation conference.

A presentation conference consists of the presenter (or conference owner) and the audience (or conference participants). The following diagram illustrates a presentation conference. Computer A, located in Oregon, is the conference owner and controls the presentation. Computer B in California and Computer C in Ireland are conference participants, or *nodes*, linked to the conference owner.

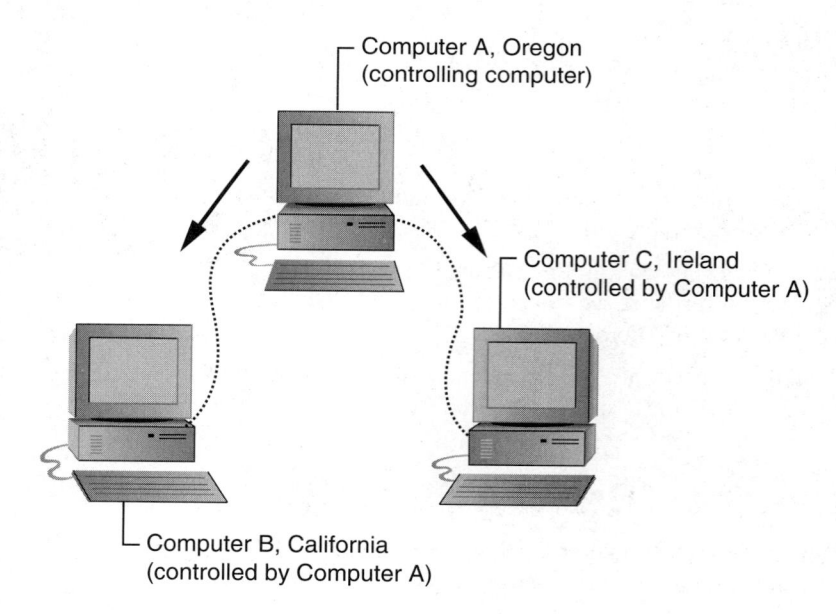

> **Showing a Presentation on Two Linked Computers**
>
> A feature similar to presentation conferencing is the ability to show a presentation on one computer from another computer, connected serially with a null-modem cable. Use the **View On Two Screens** command (**Slide Show** menu) to present slide shows this way.
>
> The advantage to delivering a presentation on two linked machines, rather than connecting a large-screen monitor to the presenter's computer, is that the presenter can use the Stage Manager feature (as in presentation conferencing) without it being visible to the audience. Using the **Stage Manager** toolbar, the presenter can skip to other slides in the show or view the speaker notes. For more information about viewing on two screens, see PowerPoint online Help.

System Requirements

Each computer participating in a presentation conference must have the following:

- PowerPoint 97 or PowerPoint 95 and (if needed) a 97-to-95 converter

    Users with only the PowerPoint Viewer or an earlier version of PowerPoint cannot participate in the conference.

- Windows 95 or Windows NT operating system

    PowerPoint for the Macintosh does not support presentation conferencing.

- File sharing

    For information about file sharing, see your Windows documentation.

- Network connection and correct networking protocol

    Computers communicating over a network must be connected to the same LAN and must have TCP/IP networking protocol installed. Presentation conferences use the Pptconference network port (port number 1711). However, presentation conferences between PowerPoint 97 and PowerPoint 95 users must use the Conference network port (port number 531) to ensure proper compatibility.

Note Presentation conferences over Internet connections cannot be made through a proxy server. The Internet connection must be direct or by modem through an Internet service provider.

Understanding the Conferencing Process

A presentation conference must be set up in advance. Typically, users make a conference call on their telephones to go through the Presentation Conference Wizard together. To start the Presentation Conference Wizard, click **Presentation Conference**

(**Tools** menu). The wizard allows users to identify conference participants and the conference owner; establishes the type of connection for each participant; and allows users to share information for making the connection, such as the computer name or IP address of each participant.

Some of the steps in setting up a conference require advance planning and communication between the presenter and audience members. The following sections explain the details of the conferencing process.

Setting the Type of Connection

Presentation conferences can mix Internet and LAN connections. The conference owner may have an Internet connection to some participants and a LAN connection to others. Each participant chooses either a LAN or Internet connection to the conference owner. For Internet connections, all conference participants (including the presenter) must have an Internet connection active before starting the conference. For LAN connections, conference participants must be connected by TCP/IP protocol.

The following diagram illustrates these connection scenarios.

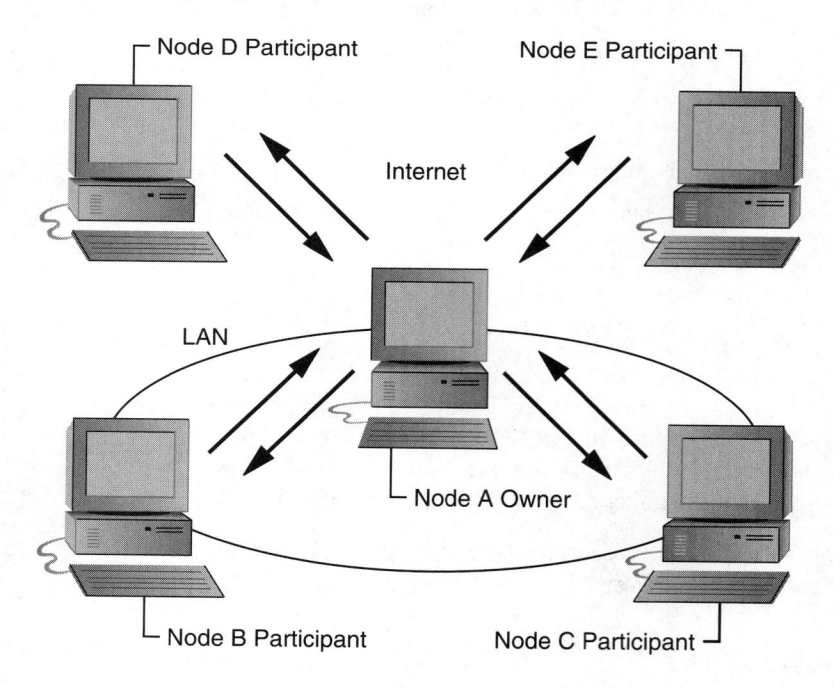

Getting Connection Information

For Internet connections, the presenter must supply the IP address for each Internet audience member. Internet audience members can enter their IP address in the **Connection Details** panel in the Presentation Conference Wizard.

For LAN connections, the presenter must supply the computer name of each audience member. LAN audience members enter their computer name in the **Connection Details** panel of the Presentation Conference Wizard.

Note Presenters can use the **Save List** and **Open List** buttons in the Presentation Conference Wizard to save and reuse lists of audience computer names and IP addresses. These lists, called *conference address lists*, are stored in a CFL file. Presenters can save different address lists for different audience groups.

Starting and Ending the Conference

The presenter can choose whether all participants must join the conference immediately or whether participants may join the conference in-progress.

If all participants must join immediately, all audience members must click **Finish** on the Presentation Conference Wizard before or about the same time as the presenter does. As soon as the presenter clicks **Finish**, PowerPoint connects the presenter's computer to the nodes of all the participants. If a node does not respond (because the user has not yet clicked **Finish**), PowerPoint attempts two or three more times to make the connection. The conference does not begin unless all nodes are connected.

If participants may join the conference in-progress, the conference can begin as long as PowerPoint can connect the presenter's computer to at least one participant node. Once the conference is in progress, the presenter's computer attempts periodically to connect to other nodes.

When the presenter's computer establishes a connection with each audience node, it sends a copy of the presentation to each participant's Windows\Temp folder; the file is named with the standard temporary-file naming scheme. The presentation opens as an untitled presentation on each of the audience nodes.

> **My presentation did not copy successfully to the audience nodes**
> The presentation file cannot be written as a temporary file to an audience members' computer if the computer does not have a valid **SET TEMP** statement in its Autoexec.bat file, or if the folder specified in the **SET TEMP** statement does not exist. Verify that the **SET TEMP** statement exists, and that the specified folder exists.

To end the conference, the presenter clicks the **End Show** button (**Stage Manager** toolbar). PowerPoint terminates communication with the audience nodes.

Understanding the Presenter's Role

For the presenter, a presentation conference appears the same as viewing the presentation in slide show mode. For audience nodes, the presentation is a read-only version of the slide show, although audience members have access to the pen tool for marking slides. The presenter has access to Speaker Notes, Meeting Minder, Slide Meter, and Slide Navigator, but these features are not visible to audience nodes.

The following elements in a presentation are not supported on audience nodes during a presentation conference:

- Objects such as sound or video clips that play when double-clicked play on the presenter's computer, but not on the audience nodes.
- Shared applications, such as Microsoft Graph, do not open on audience nodes.

    For example, if the presenter double-clicks a chart, audience members see a read-only chart. Microsoft Graph runs only on the presenter's computer.

- The component for editing linked and embedded objects does not open on audience nodes.

    For example, if the presenter double-clicks an embedded Microsoft Word table, the table is displayed read-only on the nodes. PowerPoint runs the Word tools necessary for editing the table only on the presenter's computer.

Note Sound effects applied to animation effects and slide transitions are transmitted to audience nodes and play on audience computers, provided the computers are equipped with the necessary hardware and software to play the sounds.

Using the Stage Manager Toolbar

The presenter runs the slide show with the **Stage Manager** toolbar. Buttons on this toolbar allow the presenter to navigate through the presentation by advancing to the next slide, going back to the previous slide, or opening the Slide Navigator to go to any slide in the presentation. Using the toolbar, the presenter can also run Slide Meter to compare presentation timing with pre-recorded rehearsal timing, and can open Meeting Minder to take down minutes and action items.

The **Stage Manager** toolbar also gives the presenter access to the pen tool for marking on the current slide, and a button for erasing all participants' marks. For information about the pen tool, see "Understanding the Audience's Role" later in this chapter. Marks that participants make on the current slide disappear when the presenter goes to another slide.

To pause for an intermission, the presenter can click the **Black Screen** button. Clicking the **End Show** button or closing the **Stage Manager** toolbar ends the presentation.

Using Speaker Notes

The presenter can view speaker notes while delivering the presentation without going to speaker notes view. By right-clicking anywhere on a slide during the slide show, and then clicking **Speaker Notes** on the shortcut menu, the presenter can view and edit notes for the current slide.

Using Meeting Minder

Using Meeting Minder, a presenter can keep meeting minutes and assign action items during the presentation. By right-clicking anywhere on a slide during the slide show, and then clicking **Meeting Minder** on the shortcut menu, the presenter can type minutes on the **Meeting Minutes** tab and action items on the **Action Items** tab in the **Meeting Minder** dialog box.

Action items accumulated during the slide show are placed on a slide that PowerPoint automatically appends to the end of the presentation. Since this slide is created during the slide show, the presenter must send it to the audience members in order for them to see it. The presenter clicks the **Send Slide** button on the **Stage Manager** toolbar to transmit the action items slide to each participant's computer.

> **Did You Know?**
> When PowerPoint appends action items slides to the end of a slide show, it generates a new slide based on the **Number of bullets should not exceed** option on the **Visual Clarity** tab in the **Style Checker Options** dialog box. (To display this dialog box, click **Style Checker** on the **Tools** menu, and then click the **Options** button). This option identifies the maximum number of bullets per slide.
>
> For example, a user can specify that the number of bullets on one slide cannot exceed 6. If the presenter creates 10 action items during a presentation conference, PowerPoint appends 2 slides to the end of the presentation: the first slide contains the first 6 action items, and the second slide contains the remaining 4.

To review the action items, the presenter can distribute them to participants, either as Word documents or as Microsoft Outlook tasks.

▶ **To distribute action items and meeting minutes as a Word document**

1. On the PowerPoint **Tools** menu, click **Meeting Minder**, and then click **Export**.
2. In the **Meeting Minder Export** dialog box, select the **Send meeting minutes and action items to Microsoft Word** check box.
3. Click **Export Now**.

    PowerPoint starts Word and places both the action items and the meeting minutes in a new document.

4. In Word, format the text as desired, and use the **Send To** submenu commands (**File** menu) to send the document to all participants.

Note You must have a messaging system installed on your computer to distribute documents through electronic mail. For information about using Office applications with e-mail, see Chapter 28, "Working with Messaging Systems and Connectivity Software."

If the participants decide to schedule a new meeting, the presenter can click **Schedule** in the **Meeting Minder** dialog box (**Tools** menu) to launch the meeting scheduling feature in Outlook. If Outlook is not installed on the presenter's computer, the **Schedule** command is not available. For information about using Office applications with Outlook see "Sharing Information with Outlook 97" in Chapter 27, "Sharing Information with Microsoft Office Applications."

Understanding the Audience's Role

Audience members cannot control the flow of the slide show; only the presenter can advance from one slide to the next. When the presenter goes to the next slide, that slide is transmitted to the audience nodes.

Audience members can respond to the presentation directly, however, by marking the current slide with the pen tool. To select the pen tool, audience members right-click anywhere in a slide during the slide show and then click **Pen** on the shortcut menu. Audience members can choose their own pen color by pointing to **Pointer Options** on the shortcut menu, clicking **Pen Color**, and then selecting a color. Each mark a participant makes with the pen tool is broadcast to all other participants as soon as the user releases the mouse button.

The conference ends when the presenter ends it, or audience members can leave a conference by right-clicking and then clicking **End Show** on the shortcut menu. At the end of the conference, the presentation remains open on the audience nodes. If audience members close the presentation, the file is not saved on their computers. To save the presentation, they must click **Save As** (**File** menu). If they leave the conference before the presentation is over, PowerPoint prompts them to save the presentation.

Saving a presentation on audience nodes does not save marks made with the pen tool. To save individual slides, along with marks made by participants during a conference, the presenter must send the current slide to audience nodes using the **Send Slide** button (**Stage Manager** toolbar).

> **PowerPoint 95 audience members cannot participate in my presentation conference**
>
> For PowerPoint 95 users to participate in PowerPoint 97 presentation conferences, the conference must be running on the Conference network port (if the conference takes place on a LAN), and the presenter must save the presentation in a format that PowerPoint 95 can read: either the PowerPoint 95 format or the PowerPoint 95 & 97 dual format.
>
> To set the PowerPoint 97 network port to communicate with PowerPoint 95, modify the Windows registry. In the **HKEY_LOCAL_MACHINE\Software \Microsoft\Office\8.0\PowerPoint\DLL Addins\CONFERENCE** subkey, change the value of **ServiceName** to **conference**.
>
> For information about converting PowerPoint 97 presentations to PowerPoint 95 format, see "Sharing Presentations with PowerPoint 95" in Chapter 14, "Upgrading from Previous Versions of Microsoft PowerPoint."

Troubleshooting

If you encounter problems running a presentation conference, determine whether the problem is coming from PowerPoint or from the network connection. You can do this by running the Presentation Conference Wizard and by testing the network connection.

1. Determine whether both the presenter and the audience members can run the Presentation Conference Wizard successfully.

   If they cannot, the problem may not be with the network, but with PowerPoint or the wizard. You may need to reinstall PowerPoint program files from Setup.

2. Determine whether the presenter and audience members can connect to each other's computers outside of PowerPoint—for example, through Windows Explorer. Ask participants to try exchanging files.

   If users cannot connect or exchange files, the problem may not be with PowerPoint, but with the network or with the network configuration on the presenter's or audience members' computers.

> **My workgroup presentation conference failed**
>
> A presentation conference can fail for one of the following reasons:
>
> - The name of an audience computer or the presenter computer is longer than eight characters, contains uppercase characters, contains spaces, or has special characters or symbols ($, @, #, !, ^, &, *, <, >, ?) in the name.
>
>   Change the computer name so that it is eight characters or less and contains no uppercase characters, spaces, or symbols.
>
> - You are running with a third-party TCP/IP protocol stack.
>
>   Use a different TCP/IP protocol stack.
>
> - The presentation is corrupted or damaged.
>
>   Save the presentation in a new file.

Workgroup Review of Presentations

Users in a workgroup can review presentations by routing a presentation through e-mail, with each recipient adding comments to slides. For information about using Office applications with e-mail, see Chapter 28, "Working with Messaging Systems and Connectivity Software."

▶ To review a presentation in a workgroup

1   In slide view, click **Comment** on the **Insert** menu.

    PowerPoint inserts an empty text box on the current slide.

2   Type your comment in the text box.

3   Repeat Steps 1 and 2 for every slide you want to comment on.

4   On the **File** menu, point to **Send To**, and then click **Routing Recipient**.

5   If prompted, select the user profile you want to use in the **Profile Name** box.

6   In the **Add Routing Slip** dialog box, click **Address**, select the recipients, and then click **OK**.

7   In the **Message text** box, type a message, select the **Return when done** check box, and then click **Route**.

    When users in the workgroup receive the presentation, they can insert their own comments. When all routing recipients have reviewed the presentation, it is routed back to you.

Note If you are routing a presentation to a user who has not yet upgraded to PowerPoint 97, first save the presentation in a format that the target version of PowerPoint can open, such as PowerPoint 95 & 97 format. For information about sharing presentations among different versions of PowerPoint, see Chapter 14, "Upgrading from Previous Versions of Microsoft PowerPoint."

Comments are text objects with unique formatting. You can change the default formatting of the object using the **Comment** command (**Format** menu), and you can change the shape of the object by using commands on the **Change AutoShape** submenu (**Draw** menu). Each user in the workgroup can use a different shape or format to differentiate comments, as shown in the following illustration.

- Default format for comments is a yellow rectangular AutoShape.
- Users can choose any AutoShape, color, or font style for their comments.
- When commenting on particular elements on a slide, it's best to use the callout AutoShape.

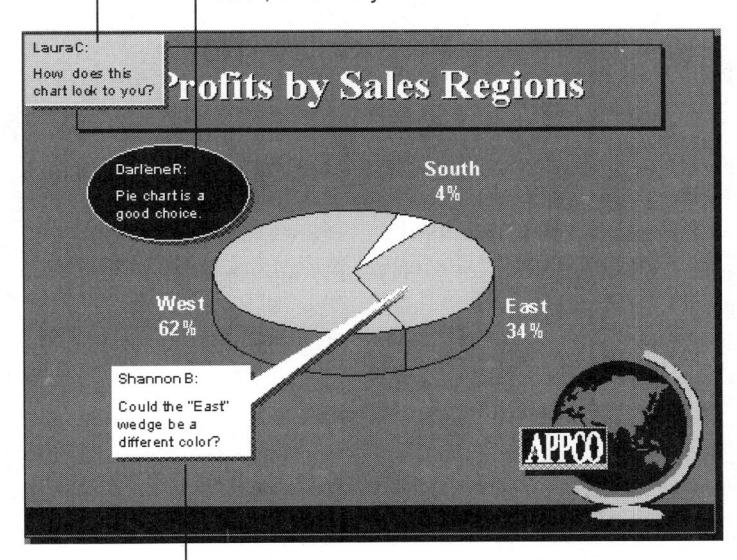

If a slide becomes cluttered with comments, you can use the **Comments** command (**View** menu) to hide them. Clicking **Comments** again on the **View** menu displays the comments. Comments are on the top layer of a slide whenever you display them.

The Pack and Go Wizard

The Pack and Go Wizard packages all the contents of a presentation so that the presentation may be delivered on another computer, such as a laptop. Because the Pack and Go Wizard can pack the PowerPoint Viewer along with the presentation, the destination computer need not have PowerPoint installed on it. To start the Pack and Go Wizard, click **Pack and Go** (**File** menu).

For presentations that contain ActiveX controls or objects that are linked or embedded to the presentation, the corresponding component must be installed on the destination computer for the control or object to run when double-clicked. For example, the Pack and Go Wizard packs Microsoft Graph objects along with the presentation to which they are linked, but it does not pack the Microsoft Graph application. If the destination computer does not have Microsoft Graph installed, the chart is displayed in the presentation read-only.

Packing the Viewer

If the destination computer does not have PowerPoint installed, you must pack the PowerPoint Viewer. The Pack and Go Wizard lets you pack the 32-bit or 16-bit viewer, or both. If the destination computer has PowerPoint installed, you do not need to pack a viewer. If the destination computer runs Windows NT Workstation version 3.51 or 4.0 or Windows 95, then pack the 32-bit viewer. If the destination computer is a Macintosh or runs Windows version 3.1, pack the 16-bit viewer.

Note The 32-bit viewer that comes with PowerPoint 97 is the same as the viewer that came with PowerPoint 95, which is not supported by the Macintosh. Therefore, even though the Macintosh supports 32-bit software, you should pack the 16-bit PowerPoint Viewer if the destination computer is a Macintosh.

The Pack and Go Wizard saves the presentation according to the viewer that is selected in the wizard and the default format for saving presentations specified on the **General** tab of the **Options** dialog box (**Tools** menu).

Tip In Windows 95 and Windows NT Workstation 4.0, you can use a system policy to define the **Save as type** option in the **Save As** dialog box for all PowerPoint users in your workgroup. In the System Policy Editor, set the following policy:

User\PowerPoint\Tools_Options\Save\Default Save

For more information, see "Using Windows System Policies to Customize Office" in Chapter 7, "Customizing and Optimizing Microsoft Office."

Because the PowerPoint Viewer must be able to read the presentation file format, the Pack and Go Wizard may need to pack along converters, depending on the format of the presentation. To determine the file format for saving the presentation and whether to pack along any converters, the Pack and Go Wizard detects which viewer included and what default format for saving presentations is selected, as shown in the following table.

With this viewer	And this default format	The wizard saves in this format	And packs this converter
16-bit	PowerPoint 4.0 or earlier	Default format	None
16-bit	PowerPoint 95 or later	PowerPoint 95 & 97	Pp7trans.dll
32-bit viewer for PowerPoint 95	PowerPoint 4.0 or earlier	Default format	Pp4x32.dll (Windows)
			Pp4x32 (Macintosh)
32-bit viewer for PowerPoint 95	PowerPoint 95 or later	PowerPoint 95 & 97	None
32-bit viewer for PowerPoint 97	PowerPoint 4.0 or earlier	Default format	Pp4x32.dll(Windows)
			Pp4x32 (Macintosh)
32-bit viewer for PowerPoint 97	PowerPoint 95	PowerPoint 95	Pp7x32.dll
32-bit viewer for PowerPoint 97	PowerPoint 97	PowerPoint 97	None

World Wide Web With the updated 32-bit viewer for PowerPoint 97, the Pack and Go Wizard can save the active presentation in the default format specified in the **Options** dialog box (**Tools** menu), regardless of the format of the active presentation. For the latest information about this viewer, connect to the PowerPoint home page at:

http://www.microsoft.com/powerpoint/

For more information about PowerPoint converters and the PowerPoint Viewer, see "Running Multiple Versions of PowerPoint" in Chapter 22, "Supporting Multiple Versions of Microsoft Office."

Tools and Utilities The Office Resource Kit Tools and Utilities include the 16-bit PowerPoint Viewer and a converter that allows PowerPoint 4.0 to read PowerPoint 95 presentations. For more information about installing the viewer or converter, "Conversion Utilities" in Appendix A, "Microsoft Office 97 Resource Kit Tools and Utilities."

Unpacking the Presentation

When you finish the Pack and Go Wizard, it packs up the Pack and Go Setup program, along with all the identified files and links, and stores them in a CAB file. On the destination computer, Pack and Go Setup decompresses the CAB file and writes the necessary PowerPoint entries in the Windows registry or in PowerPnt.ini (depending on the version of Windows), or in the PowerPoint settings file (Macintosh).

If the 16-bit viewer is packed, Pack and Go Setup installs it on the destination computer, and you must run it to open the presentation. If the 32-bit viewer is packed, Pack and Go Setup gives you the option of starting the viewer automatically with the presentation.

Typically, presentations delivered from a laptop are delivered over a large-screen monitor attached to the laptop. If the large-screen monitor has its own CPU with PowerPoint 97 installed, however, you can deliver the presentation from the laptop with the **View On Two Screens** feature (**Slide Show** menu). This feature does not use the PowerPoint Viewer; PowerPoint 97 must be installed on both computers, and the computers must be connected serially by null-modem cable. For more information about viewing a presentation on two screens, see PowerPoint online Help.

CHAPTER 33

Workgroup Features in Microsoft Word

This chapter explains how to administer features in Microsoft Word that are designed for sharing documents among users in a workgroup. It describes the various workgroup features of Word and provides information for supporting them.

In This Chapter
Security Features in Word   891
Workgroup Review of Documents   893

See Also
- For a summary of new and improved features in Word 97, see Chapter 2, "What's New in Microsoft Office 97."
- For information about supporting workgroups that are running more than one version of Word, see Chapter 22, "Supporting Multiple Versions of Microsoft Office."
- For information about the structure of Word and how its components fit together, see Chapter 39, "Microsoft Word Architecture."

Security Features in Word

As a workgroup administrator, you might initiate or oversee workgroup-wide security practices for protecting Word documents. This section describes options available in Word for protecting documents. These options are independent of any additional security measures you put into place at the operating system level.

Word 97 incorporates the symmetric encryption routine known as RC4. RC4 is stronger than the encryption routine used in previous versions of Word, known as Office 4.*x* encryption. Documents from previous versions of Word are not as secure as password-protected documents in Word 97 format. For more information about Office encryption, see "Security Features in Office" in Chapter 34, "Microsoft Office Architecture."

Note Strong encryption such as RC4 is banned in France. If a user's locale setting in the **Regional Settings Properties** dialog box (Control Panel) is set to **French (Standard)**, that user cannot open Office documents that are password protected. Nor can the user save an Office document with RC4 encryption. The user can, however, use Office 4.*x* encryption by saving an Office document with password protection.

Word supports three levels of document protection. All three are controlled by the author of the document, who is the user with read-write access to a document. The three levels of document protection are:

- File open protection

    Word requires the user to enter a password to open a document.

- File modify protection

    Word prompts the user to enter a password to open the document read-write. If the user clicks **Read Only** at the prompt, Word opens the document read-only.

- Read-only recommended protection

    Word prompts the user to open the document read-only. If the user clicks **No** at the prompt, Word opens the document read-write, unless the document has other password protection.

▶ **To protect a document**

1. On the **File** menu, click **Save As**.
2. Click **Options**.
3. To have Word prompt the user to open the document read-only, select the **Read-only recommended** check box.

    –or–

    To require a password to open the document, type a password in the **Password to open** box, and then click **OK**.

    –or–

    To require a password to save changes the document, type a password in the **Password to modify** box, and then click **OK**.

4. When prompted, type the password again, and then click **OK**.
5. Click **Save**.

Note Because protected documents are encrypted, they are not indexed by Find Fast. For more information about document indexing and searching, see Chapter 26, "Finding Microsoft Office Documents on the Network."

In addition to protecting an entire document, you can protect specific elements from unauthorized changes. The elements you can protect are:

- Tracked changes

    Changes made to the document can be neither accepted nor rejected, and change tracking cannot be turned off.

- Comments

    Users can insert comments into the document but cannot change the content of the document.

- Forms or sections

    Users can make changes only in form fields or unprotected sections of a document.

▶ **To protect a specific element in a document from unauthorized changes**

1. On the **Tools** menu, click **Protect Document**.
2. Under **Protect document for**, select the elements you want to protect.
3. To prevent others from removing protection from the document, type a password and click **OK**, and then retype the password in the **Confirm Password** dialog box.

Caution If you or a user in your workgroup assigns password protection to a document and then forgets the password, you cannot open the document, gain access to its data in another document through links, remove protection from the document, or recover data from the document. Keep a list of your passwords and their corresponding document names in a safe place.

Workgroup Review of Documents

Word includes several features that support group review of documents. If your workgroup has access to electronic mail (e-mail), users can also send or route documents to their co-workers.

Many of the features described in this section are available through the **Reviewing** toolbar.

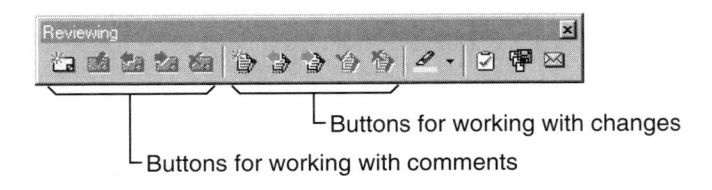

Buttons for working with changes
Buttons for working with comments

To display the **Reviewing** toolbar, click **Toolbars** (**View** menu), and then click **Reviewing**.

Creating a Document with Many Authors

Word provides a number of features that are especially useful when several members of a workgroup jointly write long documents:

- Use master document view (**View** menu) to create a group of subdocuments and compile them into a single long document. On the **View** menu, click **Master Document**.

  When you print the document, Word combines all of the subdocuments into one and automatically numbers pages, lines, and footnotes in sequence. You can generate a table of contents, a table of illustrations, an index, and cross-references for the master document. You can use fields to create captions for illustrations and to number items (such as tables of figures) in series.

- Use templates to ensure that all documents have the same layout and boilerplate text and graphics. On the **Tools** menu, click **Templates and Add-Ins**.

  Templates also allow you to provide customized features, such as additions to toolbars and menus, special key assignments, and macros.

- Use styles to ensure consistent formatting and make it easy to change documents quickly. Use the built-in heading styles in Word to quickly create tables of contents and document outlines. On the **Format** menu, click **Style**.

- Use bookmarks to quickly locate text and create cross-references to other parts of a document. On the **Insert** menu, click **Bookmark**.

- Use AutoText entries to store frequently used text and graphics and quickly insert them into documents without retyping or copying and pasting. On the **Insert** menu, point to **AutoText** and click the entry you want.

- Use document map view to quickly browse a long document and see its outline structure and content side-by-side. On the **View** menu, click **Document Map**.

For more information about using these features, see Word online Help.

The remainder of this section describes other features to use when several members of a workgroup jointly write or review Word documents.

Tracking Changes

The commands on the **Track Changes** submenu (**Tools** menu) allow reviewers to make revisions to a document. The author of the document can then accept or reject these revisions.

Find color-coded changes easily.

Market Analysis

The worldwide market for musical instruments is a very mature, very competitive market. Overall market growth is estimated between 6% and 8% per year, in both units and value. Distribution patterns vary a great deal by ~~customper profile~~ segment, from the mass retail distribution of the low end to the specialized distribution of the high-quality and high-price segments. Encore operates in a narrow part of the market, instruments and equipment sold to professionals ~~musicians~~ who insist on the highest-quality sound. Most of our customers are concert musicians.

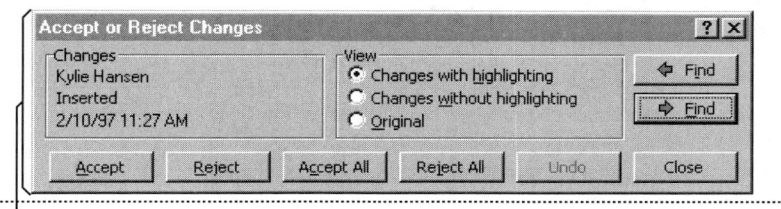

Review, accept, or reject changes through this dialog box.

The author or any reviewer can specify how revisions should appear (for example, whether deleted text should be formatted as strikethrough or hidden) on the **Track Changes** tab in the **Options** dialog box (**Tools** menu).

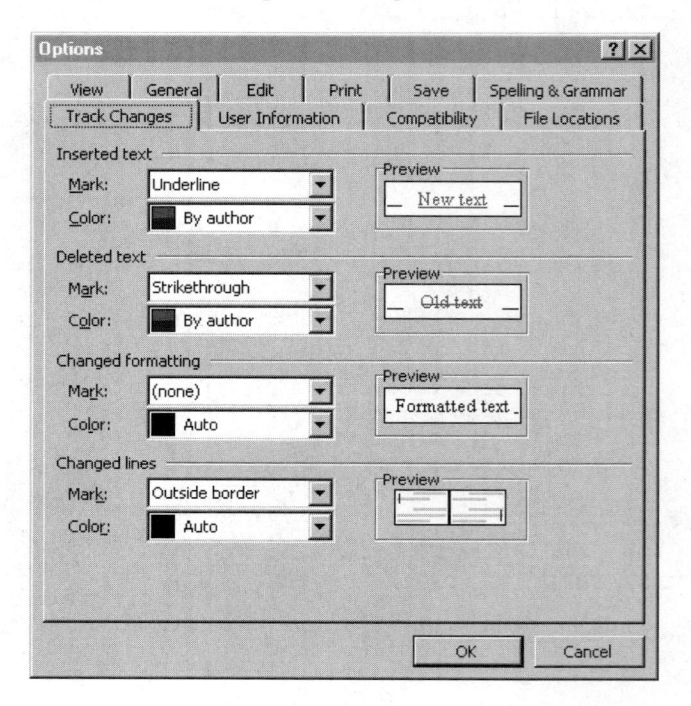

Note In previous versions of Word, the track changes feature was called revision marking.

Commenting on a Document

Comments in a Word document are analogous to reviewer notes written in the margins of a printed document. You insert comments with the **Comment** command (**Insert** menu). Word formats the comment indicator and the preceding word with a light yellow background, so the comment and the text to which it refers are clearly visible. You can also select a range of text before clicking **Comment**, and Word formats all of the selected text with a light yellow background.

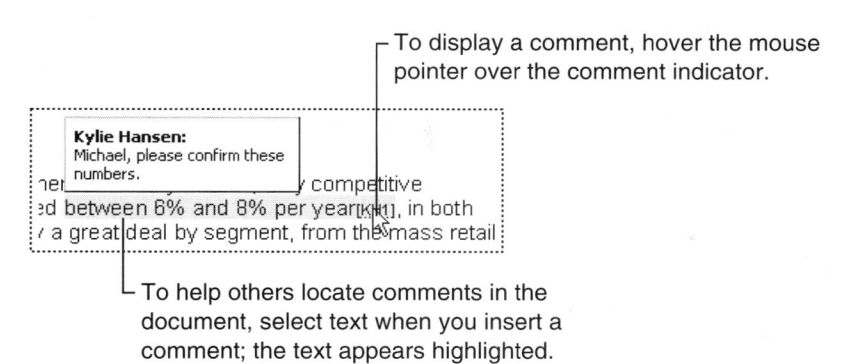

To display a comment, hover the mouse pointer over the comment indicator.

To help others locate comments in the document, select text when you insert a comment; the text appears highlighted.

You can view comments by resting the pointer over text shaded with light yellow, or over a comment indicator in the text. All of the comments appear in the comments pane below the document.

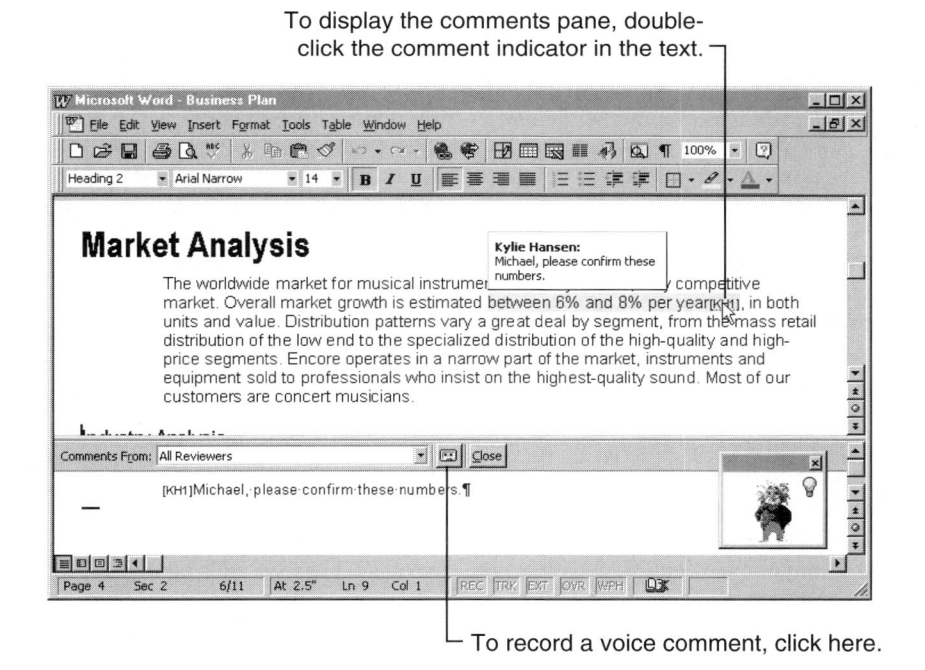

To display the comments pane, double-click the comment indicator in the text.

To record a voice comment, click here.

Tip Comments are especially useful when used with change tracking. When a reviewer makes a change to a document, the reviewer can also insert a comment explaining why the change is necessary.

In addition to entering text comments, users who have computers equipped with sound cards and microphones can insert voice comments. To insert a voice comment, click the **Insert Sound Object** button in the comments pane.

Note In previous versions of Word, comments were called annotations.

Saving and Comparing Different Versions of Documents

Word supports two ways of working with different versions of documents: saving versions of a document in a single file, and comparing differences between different documents.

Saving Document Versions

New in Word 97 is the ability to save multiple versions of a document within a single file. This feature, called *version control*, is available through the **Versions** dialog box (**File** menu). For example, you can use version control to save a version of a document after you write the first draft, save another version after the document is edited, and then save a final version after you have polished the document for publication. All three versions are saved within the document file, but only one version is active at any given time.

Recorded with each version are the name of the author who last saved the version of the document, the date and time it was saved, and any additional comments the author included. In the **Versions** dialog box, you can switch between versions of a document, delete versions, or display a version and then save it as a separate file.

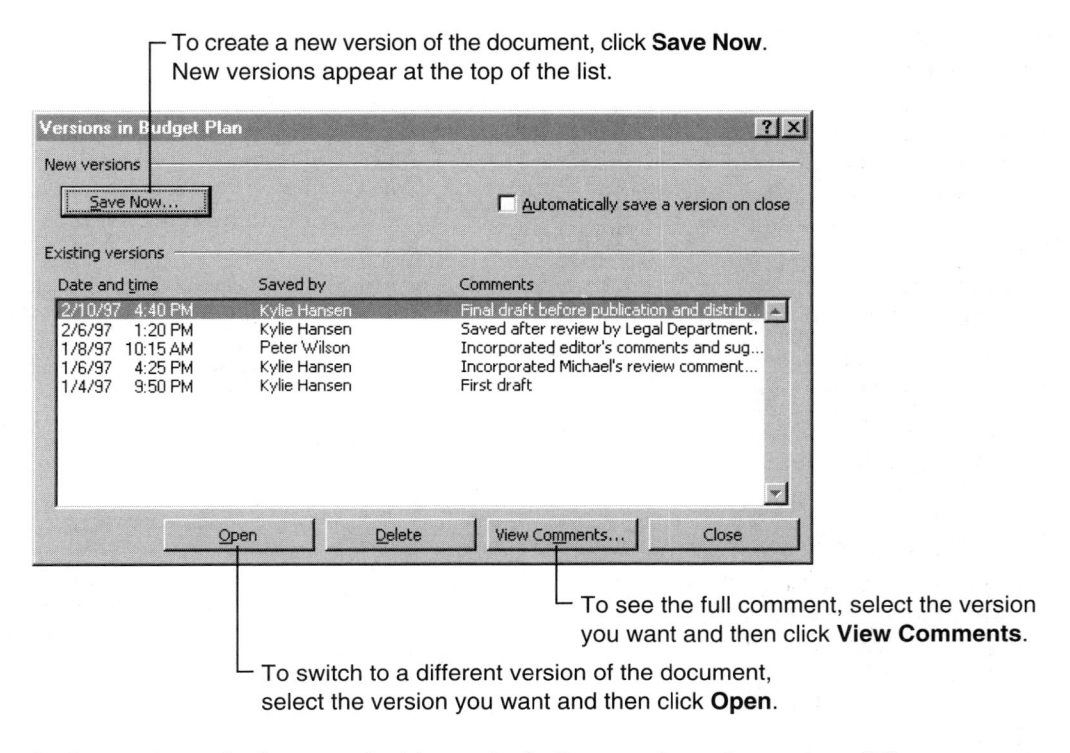

To create a new version of the document, click **Save Now**.
New versions appear at the top of the list.

Versions in Budget Plan

New versions
- Save Now...
- ☐ Automatically save a version on close

Existing versions

Date and time	Saved by	Comments
2/10/97 4:40 PM	Kylie Hansen	Final draft before publication and distrib...
2/6/97 1:20 PM	Kylie Hansen	Saved after review by Legal Department.
1/8/97 10:15 AM	Peter Wilson	Incorporated editor's comments and sug...
1/6/97 4:25 PM	Kylie Hansen	Incorporated Michael's review comment...
1/4/97 9:50 PM	Kylie Hansen	First draft

Open | Delete | View Comments... | Close

To see the full comment, select the version you want and then click **View Comments**.

To switch to a different version of the document, select the version you want and then click **Open**.

Saving versions of a document in this way is similar to saving a document to different file names at different times. For example, you might start with the draft document Mydocument1, save it after editing as Mydocument2, and then save it again before distribution as Mydocument3. Saving multiple versions in the same file is more efficient, however: Word saves only the differences between versions, so less disk space is used, and you can more easily switch between versions. Version control is also a useful tool when you must maintain a clear record, or *audit trail*, of revisions to a document, such as a legal contract.

Comparing Documents

The **Compare Documents** command (**Tools** menu, **Track Changes** submenu) is useful when you want to see the differences between two documents. When you click **Compare Documents**, Word prompts you to select a document to compare with the active document. Word then indicates differences between the two by making revisions to the active document with change marks. You can then review the revisions and accept or reject them.

To compare two documents, open the first document, click **Compare Documents**, and then open the second document.

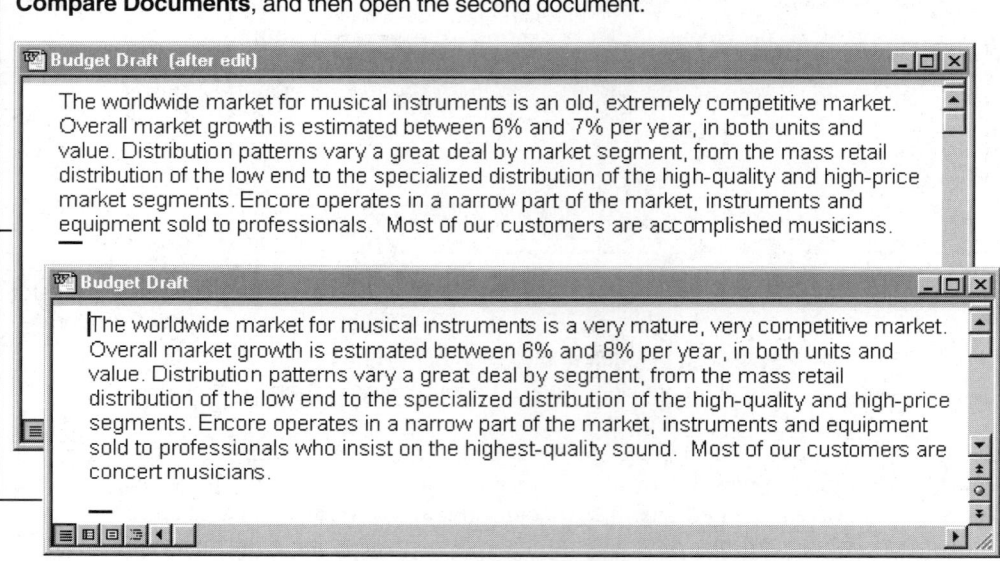

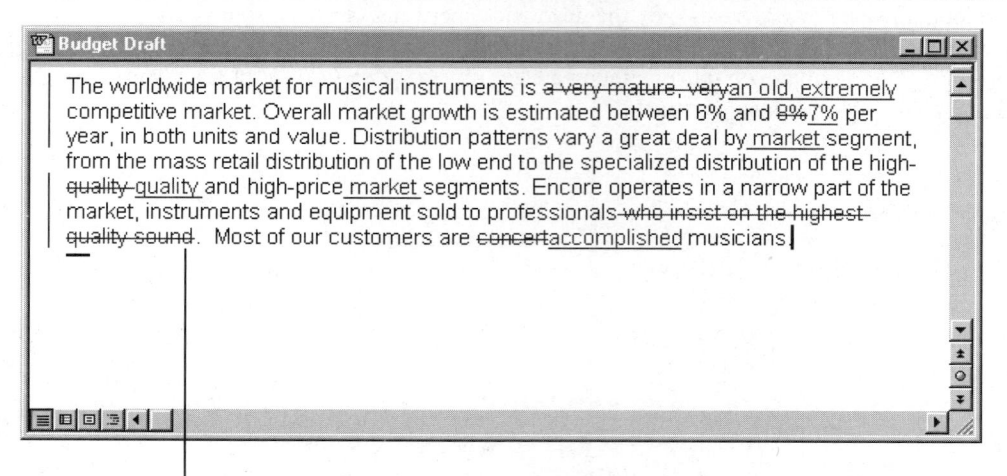

Budget Draft (after edit)

The worldwide market for musical instruments is an old, extremely competitive market. Overall market growth is estimated between 6% and 7% per year, in both units and value. Distribution patterns vary a great deal by market segment, from the mass retail distribution of the low end to the specialized distribution of the high-quality and high-price market segments. Encore operates in a narrow part of the market, instruments and equipment sold to professionals. Most of our customers are accomplished musicians.

Budget Draft

The worldwide market for musical instruments is a very mature, very competitive market. Overall market growth is estimated between 6% and 8% per year, in both units and value. Distribution patterns vary a great deal by segment, from the mass retail distribution of the low end to the specialized distribution of the high-quality and high-price segments. Encore operates in a narrow part of the market, instruments and equipment sold to professionals who insist on the highest-quality sound. Most of our customers are concert musicians.

Budget Draft

The worldwide market for musical instruments is a very mature, very an old, extremely competitive market. Overall market growth is estimated between 6% and 8%7% per year, in both units and value. Distribution patterns vary a great deal by market segment, from the mass retail distribution of the low end to the specialized distribution of the high-quality quality and high-price market segments. Encore operates in a narrow part of the market, instruments and equipment sold to professionals who insist on the highest-quality sound. Most of our customers are concertaccomplished musicians.

After comparing the two documents, Word inserts revisions in the first document to indicate differences between it and the second document.

Unlike version control, comparing documents with the **Compare Documents** command requires two documents to compare. If you used version control and you want to compare two versions of a document in this way, you must first save one of the versions as a separate document. To do so, click **Versions** (**File** menu) to switch to the other version of the document, and then save it with a different file name by clicking **Save As** (**File** menu). You can then use the **Compare Documents** command to compare the two documents.

Merging Documents

With the **Merge Documents** command (**Tools** menu), you can combine tracked changes from several documents into one document. Unlike the **Compare Documents** command (**Tools** menu, **Track Changes** submenu), the merge documents feature requires that you turn on change tracking in order to merge both documents.

Routing Documents with Electronic Mail

Users in a workgroup who have e-mail capability can review documents by routing them through e-mail, with each recipient adding comments to the document. For information about using Office applications with e-mail, see Chapter 28, "Working with Messaging Systems and Connectivity Software."

▶ **To route a document to other members of your workgroup**

1 On the **File** menu, point to **Send To**, and then click **Routing Recipient**.

2 If prompted, select the user profile you want to use in the **Profile Name** box.

3 In the **Routing Slip** dialog box, click **Address**, select the recipients, and then click **OK**.

4 In the **Message text** box, type a message, select the **Return when done** check box, and then click **Route**.

When users in the workgroup receive the document, they can insert their own comments. When all routing recipients have reviewed the document, it is routed back to you.

Note If you are routing a document to a user who has not yet upgraded to Word 97, first save the document in a format that the target version of Word can open (such as Word 95 format), or make sure the recipient has installed the Word 97 file converter. For information about sharing documents among different versions of Word, see Chapter 15, "Upgrading from Previous Versions of Microsoft Word."

PART 6

Microsoft Office Architecture

Contents

Chapter 34 Microsoft Office Architecture 905
Chapter 35 Microsoft Access Architecture 915
Chapter 36 Microsoft Excel Architecture 939
Chapter 37 Microsoft Outlook Architecture 959
Chapter 38 Microsoft PowerPoint Architecture 967
Chapter 39 Microsoft Word Architecture 991

CHAPTER 34

Microsoft Office Architecture

This chapter describes the structure of Microsoft Office 97. It explains how the various component applications in the Office suite work together. An understanding of the architecture of Office can help you take advantage of its features and may help you troubleshoot problems.

In This Chapter
Overview   905
Office Support for Object Linking and Embedding   905
Office Support for ActiveX   906
Security Features in Office   908
Shared Office Components   909

Overview

Office 97 encourages a work style that is centered on information rather than applications. Office allows users to create information and then manipulate it with a suite of software tools. Each of these tools is a standalone application in its own right, but Office integrates their functionality to form a unified work area.

Office Support for Object Linking and Embedding

Object linking and embedding (OLE) is the basis for integration between the Office applications. OLE allows you to insert data from a source document into a client document—cells from a Microsoft Excel workbook into a Microsoft Word document, for example. Data can be either linked or embedded, as follows:

- A *linked* object is a reference to the source and is updated dynamically if the source data is changed. Object linking is analogous to using Dynamic Data Exchange (DDE) in previous versions of Office.
- An *embedded* object is a copy of the source data that can be edited with the tools from the source application; it has no link to the source data.

Object embedding is different from object linking in two key ways:

- The information embedded in the destination document not only consists of a representation of the data (for example, a drawing or a chart) but also includes all of the data that was used to create the object (for example, worksheet values).
- The embedded object is not updated dynamically but can be updated manually by double-clicking the object. Double-clicking activates the object and launches the application that created the object to allow you to update the data.

Documents with embedded objects use more hard disk space than documents with linked objects. This is because embedded objects are copies, whereas linked objects are merely references.

Office Support for ActiveX

ActiveX is an open integration platform that provides developers, users, and World Wide Web developers a fast and easy way to create integrated applications and content for the Internet and intranets. ActiveX is a standard that enables software components to interact with one another in a networked environment, regardless of the language or languages used to create them. Most Web users encounter ActiveX technology in the form of ActiveX controls, ActiveX documents, and ActiveX scripts. Office supports ActiveX controls and ActiveX documents.

> **What's the Difference Between OLE and ActiveX?**
>
> ActiveX and OLE are both based on the Component Object Model (COM), but they provide substantially different services to developers. COM provides the low-level object-binding mechanism that enables objects to communicate with each other. OLE uses COM to provide high-level application services such as linking and embedding, allowing users to create compound documents. ActiveX provides a substantially simpler infrastructure within which controls can be embedded in Web sites or Office documents to respond interactively to events.
>
> Although OLE is optimized for end-user usability and integration of desktop applications, ActiveX is optimized for size and speed. ActiveX also adds a number of important innovations for the Internet (including a 50 percent to 75 percent reduction in size), support for incremental rendering, and asynchronous connections.

World Wide Web For the latest information about ActiveX, connect to the ActiveX Resource Area at:

http://www.microsoft.com/activex/

ActiveX Controls

ActiveX controls, formerly known as OLE controls, are components (or objects) you can insert into Web pages or Office documents to reuse packaged functionality that someone else programmed.

For example, Microsoft Excel 97, Word 97, and Microsoft PowerPoint 97 share powerful new tools for creating custom dialog boxes. Because these applications use the same dialog box tools in the Visual Basic Editor, you have to learn how to create custom dialog boxes in only one way for all three applications, and you can share these dialog boxes across applications.

After you've created a custom dialog box, you can add ActiveX controls to it. You can also place ActiveX controls directly on a document, worksheet, or slide. To determine how the custom dialog box and ActiveX controls respond to user actions—for example, when users click a control or change its value—you write event procedures that run whenever the event occurs.

Just as you can add ActiveX controls to custom dialog boxes, you can add controls directly to a document, sheet, or slide to make it interactive. For example, you might add text boxes, list boxes, option buttons, and other controls to a document to turn it into an online form; you might add a button to a sheet that runs a commonly used macro; or you might add buttons and other controls to slides in a presentation to help users run the slide show.

For more information about creating ActiveX controls in Office 97, see the *Microsoft Office 97/Visual Basic Programmer's Guide*, published by Microsoft Press and available wherever computer books are sold. For more information about Microsoft Press books, see Appendix E, "Other Support Resources."

ActiveX Documents

ActiveX documents allow you to open an application that has its own toolbars and menus available while browsing with either an application that supports ActiveX or a Web browser such as Microsoft Internet Explorer 3.0. This means you can open non-HTML files, such as Microsoft Excel or Word files, using a Web browser that supports ActiveX.

All the Office 97 applications support ActiveX documents, allowing you to seamlessly integrate Office document formats into Web browsers such as Microsoft Internet Explorer 3.0. For more information about integrating Office documents into an intranet, see Chapter 24, "Integrating Microsoft Office with Your Intranet."

Security Features in Office

As a workgroup administrator, you might initiate or oversee workgroup-wide security practices for protecting Office documents. This section describes the password encryption protection offered by the following Office applications:

- Microsoft Access
- Microsoft Excel
- Word

When you read-protect a document in any of these applications, the application calls a shared Office DLL named Mso97.dll to provide the encryption routine. The Office encryption options described here are independent of any additional security measures at the operating system level.

Microsoft Access, Microsoft Excel, and Word incorporate the symmetric encryption routine known as RC4. RC4 is stronger than the encryption routine used in previous versions of most Office applications, known as Office 4.*x* encryption. (Microsoft Access has supported RC4 encryption since version 2.0.) Documents from previous versions of Office are not as secure as password-protected documents in Office 97 format.

Note Strong encryption such as RC4 is banned in France. If a user's locale setting in the **Regional Settings Properties** dialog box (Control Panel) is set to **French (Standard)**, that user cannot open Office documents that are password protected with RC4 encryption. Nor can the user save an Office document with RC4 encryption. The user can, however, use Office 4.*x* encryption when saving an Office 97 document with password protection.

Office password protection does not disable or conflict with Microsoft Exchange Server digital signatures or other security measures provided by the operating system or other programs.

Shared Office Components

This section provides a brief overview of how the Office applications share services and code.

Coordination of Applications

Office coordinates the work of its individual applications such as Microsoft Excel and Word. From a user's point of view, this is apparent in the consistency of the user interface. Menu and command names are standardized, not only in their terminology, but in their order and placement on the screen. If users are already familiar with one Office application, it is easier for them to use the tools of another application.

Shared Application Tools

Individual Office applications share tools such as the Clip Gallery and spelling checker. The following table lists the application tools shared by Office applications, the applications that share them, and their default locations as Office Setup installs them. For a complete listing of these tools, see Appendix D, "List of Installed Components."

This tool	Has this function	Is shared by these applications	And is installed in this location
Clip Gallery	Indexes clip art, pictures, sounds, and movies so you can browse the collection.	Microsoft Access, Microsoft Excel, PowerPoint, Word	Program Files\Common Files\Microsoft Shared\Artgalry
Data Access Objects	Used by custom Visual Basic applications to gain access to external data.	Microsoft Access, Microsoft Excel	Program Files\Common Files\Microsoft Shared\Dao
Equation Editor™	Inserts mathematical symbols and equations into documents.	Microsoft Access, Microsoft Excel, PowerPoint, Word	Program Files\Common Files\Microsoft Shared\Equation

This tool	Has this function	Is shared by these applications	And is installed in this location
Find All Word Forms	Finds and replaces noun forms or verb tenses.	PowerPoint, Word	Program Files\Common Files\Microsoft Shared\Proof
Find Fast	Indexes Office documents for fast retrieval. For more information, see Chapter 26, "Finding Office Documents on the Network."	All Office applications	Program Files\Microsoft Office\Office
Graphics Filters	Convert graphics into file formats that Office applications can use.	All Office applications	Program Files\Common Files\Microsoft Shared\Grphflt
Lotus VIM Mail Support	Allows you to use Lotus Notes version 3.*x*, 4.*x*, or cc:Mail 2.*x* for electronic mail. For more information, see Chapter 28, "Working with Messaging Systems and Connectivity Software."	All Office applications	Windows\System or System32
Microsoft Graph	Creates charts from Microsoft Access, PowerPoint, and Word data.	Microsoft Access, PowerPoint, and Word	Program Files\Microsoft Office\Office
Office Shortcut Bar	Provides application management, including instant access to cross-application Office technology and a starting point for Office components.	All Office applications	Program Files\Microsoft Office\Office
Microsoft Photo Editor	Used to scan, convert, and modify photographic images.	All Office applications	Program Files\Common Files\Microsoft Shared\PhotoEd
Microsoft Query	Helps you retrieve data from external data sources.	Microsoft Access, Microsoft Excel, Word	Program Files\Microsoft Office\Office\Library\Msquery
Microsoft TrueType Fonts	Provides several TrueType fonts.	All Windows applications	Windows\Fonts
MS Info	Gathers system configuration information for troubleshooting purposes.	All Office applications	Program Files\Common Files\Microsoft Shared\MSInfo

This tool	Has this function	Is shared by these applications	And is installed in this location
Organizational Chart	Creates organization charts.	Microsoft Access, Microsoft Excel, PowerPoint, Word	Program Files\Common Files\Microsoft Shared\Orgchart
Office Assistant	Provides Help, tips, and other online assistance.	All Office applications	Program Files\Microsoft Office\Actors
Popular Clipart	Compiles a collection of the popular clips.	All Office applications	Program Files\Microsoft Office\Clipart\Popular
Spelling Checker	Checks the spelling of text in documents. For more information, see "Spelling Checker Dictionary" later in this chapter.	Microsoft Access, Microsoft Excel, PowerPoint, Word	Program Files\Common Files\Microsoft Shared\Proof
Text converters	Convert documents to and from other file formats.	All Office applications	Program Files\Common Files\Microsoft Shared\Textconv

Following are more detailed descriptions of some shared components.

Office Art

Microsoft Excel, PowerPoint, and Word use the same set of drawing tools, called *Office Art*. The Office Art tools, which are accessible through the **Drawing** toolbar, provide hundreds of drawing objects and effects that are common to Microsoft Excel, PowerPoint, and Word. Additionally, each application has extended the Office Art feature set to provide application-specific features such as charting in Microsoft Excel, document backgrounds in Word, and action buttons in PowerPoint.

Spelling Checker Dictionary

The Office applications that implement the spelling checker all share the same dictionary file, Custom.dic. The default path for this file is the Program Files\Common Files\Microsoft Shared\Proof folder. Customizations that users make to the spelling list by running the spelling checker within an application are saved to this file.

It is possible to create a corporate dictionary, although you cannot share this file across a workgroup due to potential sharing violation problems.

▶ **To create a corporate dictionary file**

1. Open the file Custom.dic in a text editor, such as Notepad.
2. Add the words you want the Office applications to evaluate as properly spelled to the Custom.dic file.

    Each word should appear on its own line, and all of the words you add should be in alphabetical order.
3. Save the file and copy it to local workstations.
4. Modify the setting in the following key in each user's Windows registry to point to the location of the corporate Custom.dic file:

    HKEY_LOCAL_MACHINE\SOFTWARE\Microsoft\Shared Tools\Proofing Tools\Custom Dictionaries

Tip In Windows 95 and Windows NT Workstation 4.0, you can use a system policy to specify the path to a custom dictionary for all Word users in your workgroup. In the System Policy Editor, set the following policy:

Computer\Word 97\Spelling Advanced\Custom Dictionaries

For more information, see "Using Windows System Policies to Customize Office" in Chapter 7, "Customizing and Optimizing Microsoft Office."

Microsoft Clip Gallery

The Microsoft Clip Gallery is a repository for all clip art, pictures, sound files, and video clips that you might want to include in an Office document. The media files are not stored in the Clip Gallery; instead, the Clip Gallery stores databases where you can keep track of these files and insert them easily into Office documents. The Clip Gallery user interface makes it easy to import files to the Clip Gallery so that you can add graphics, sounds, and video files of your own. For information about adding files to the Clip Gallery, click **Help** in the Clip Gallery window.

The Clip Gallery stores clip previews, keywords, and category names in Clip Gallery databases (CAG files). You can create a custom Clip Gallery database and distribute it to users or make it available to a workgroup on a shared network drive. For information about Clip Gallery databases and how to distribute custom versions on a network, see "Information for Network Administrators" on the **Contents** tab in Clip Gallery online Help.

The Clip Gallery recognizes certain file formats and media types, and categorizes them as clip art, pictures, sounds, or videos. You can install graphics filters and media devices from independent software vendors so that the Clip Gallery recognizes additional files and allows you to add them to its databases. When you install software from independent vendors, the Setup program for the software registers the filter or device, so that the Clip Gallery recognizes the format and displays the format on the Clip Gallery tabs according to the categories shown in the following table.

This file format	Is displayed on this tab
Vector graphic	**Clip Art**
Raster/bitmap graphic	**Pictures**
Sound, such as WAV and MIDI (Windows) or MacSound and QuickTime (Macintosh)	**Sounds**
Video/movie, such as AVI (Windows) or QuickTime (Macintosh)	**Videos**

Note Compressed pictures lose their compression when inserted from the Clip Gallery into an Office application. This can result in substantially increased document size. For acceptable performance, you should not use the Clip Gallery to insert pictures that are stored in compressed formats, such as GIF, PNG, JPEG, or JFIF format.

Tip In Windows 95 and Windows NT Workstation 4.0, you can use a system policy to make more clip art content available to users. You create new Clip Art Gallery databases (CAG files) and store them on a server. Three policies are included to allow you to divide clip art among one, two, or three files. In the System Policy Editor, set the following policies:

Computer\Clip Art Gallery 3.0\Concurrent Database #1

Computer\Clip Art Gallery 3.0\Concurrent Database #2

Computer\Clip Art Gallery 3.0\Concurrent Database #3

For more information, see "Using Windows System Policies to Customize Office" in Chapter 7, "Customizing and Optimizing Microsoft Office."

Visual Basic for Applications

Office 97 provides developers with a common set of tools, including the Visual Basic for Applications programming language, the Visual Basic Editor, and Microsoft Forms.

All Office applications (including Microsoft Outlook) expose object models, making it possible for developers to control these applications programmatically to create robust custom solutions. In addition, the implementation of each object model is highly consistent, allowing developers to apply their understanding of working with one Office 97 application to working with another.

For more information about creating custom solutions in Office 97, see the *Microsoft Office 97/Visual Basic Programmer's Guide*, published by Microsoft Press and available wherever computer books are sold.

CHAPTER 35

Microsoft Access Architecture

This chapter describes the structure of Microsoft Access 97. It explains how the various components of Microsoft Access work together, and how the application handles changes that users make to those components. An understanding of the architecture of Microsoft Access can help you take advantage of its features and may help you troubleshoot problems.

In This Chapter
How Microsoft Access Is Structured   915
How You Can Customize Microsoft Access   934
How Microsoft Access Resolves Conflicts   936

See Also
- For information about installing Microsoft Access or other Microsoft Office applications, see Chapter 4, "Installing Microsoft Office."
- For information about customizing Microsoft Access to meet the specific needs of your workgroup, see Chapter 7, "Customizing and Optimizing Microsoft Office."

Note Microsoft Access runs on Windows 95 and Windows NT Workstation version 3.51 or later only.

How Microsoft Access Is Structured

Microsoft Access documents are called databases. A Microsoft Access database is a collection of *database objects*: tables, queries, forms, reports, macros, and modules. You can design new objects or open existing ones to work with your database. Unlike many database programs, a Microsoft Access database can contain all of the objects that make up a database application in a single file with the .mdb file name extension. For this reason, a Microsoft Access database file is sometimes called a *database container*.

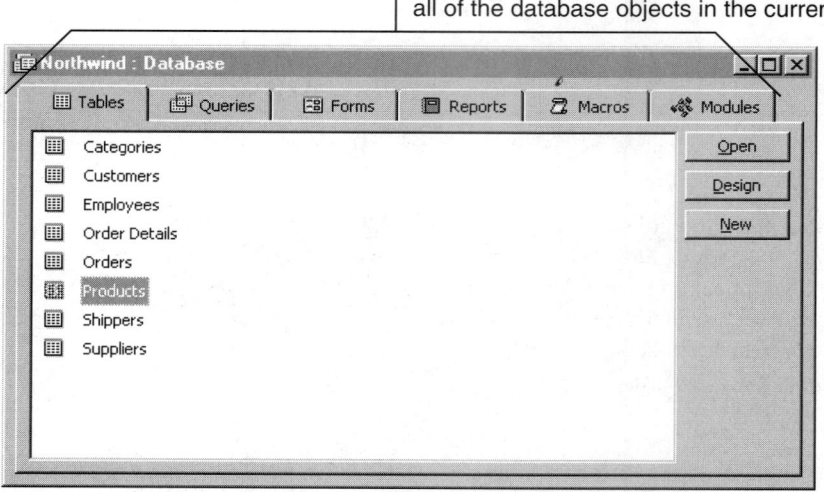

When you open a database, the Database window displays all of the database objects in the current MDB file.

Tables

In Microsoft Access, you store data in *tables*. Tables organize data into columns and rows. Each row in a table is called a *record*. Each column in a record is called a *field*. For example, each record in a Customers table contains information about one customer. Each customer's record contains fields named for each piece of information you want to store about the customer, such as LastName, FirstName, Address, City, State/Province, PostalCode, and Phone. Users can enter and modify data in tables directly or through queries and data-entry forms, which are described later in this section.

Storing Related Data in Separate Tables

You can create a separate table for each topic of data, such as customers, employees, or products. Using a separate table for each topic means that you store that data only once, which makes your database more efficient and reduces data-entry errors. For example, if you store both customer and order information in one table, whenever a customer places an additional order, you have to reenter information about that customer. Not only is this inefficient, but errors can occur when information is reentered. If you keep separate tables for customers and orders, then each customer has only one record—in the Customers table. If you need to update or correct information about a customer, you need to change the data in only one record. This method eliminates redundant entries and reduces data-entry errors.

The process of eliminating redundancy by dividing data into separate related tables is called *normalization*. Microsoft Access provides a wizard called the Table Analyzer Wizard to help you normalize your database. For information about running the Table Analyzer Wizard, see "Optimizing Microsoft Access" in Chapter 7, "Customizing and Optimizing Microsoft Office."

Defining Relationships

To bring the data from multiple tables together for a query, form, or report, you define *relationships* between the tables based on a common piece of information stored in both tables. For example, a Customers table typically contains a CustomerID field whose value uniquely identifies each customer. If the Orders table also has a CustomerID field, then you can define a relationship between the two tables, so that when you enter orders, you can enter a customer's ID number to relate information from the Customers table to that order. Instead of actually typing the CustomerID, you can use a lookup list box, as shown in the Orders form from the Northwind sample database.

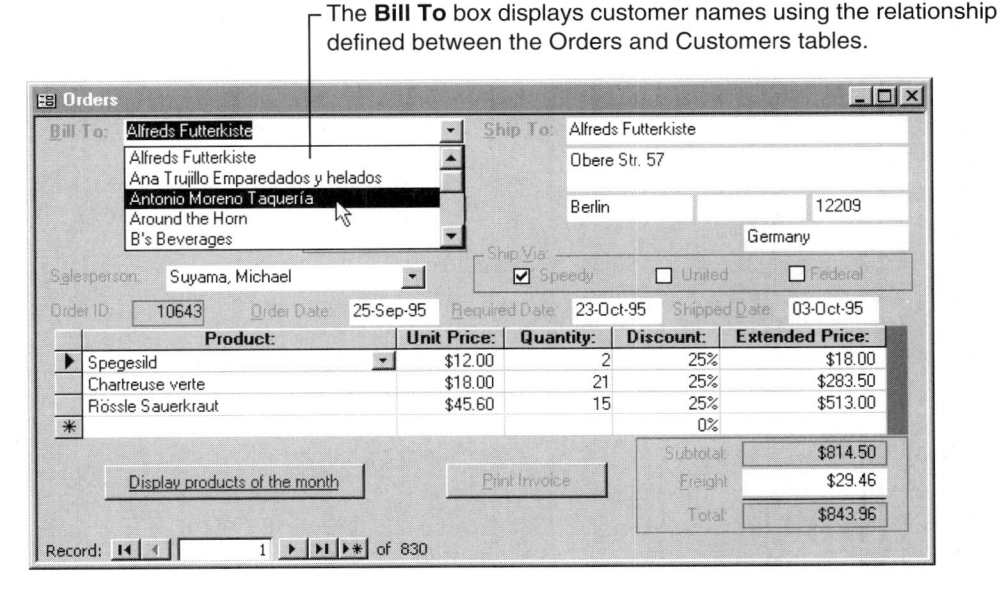

The **Bill To** box displays customer names using the relationship defined between the Orders and Customers tables.

Although the BillTo list displays only the customer's name, picking a customer from the list stores that customer's CustomerID number in the Orders table. The customer's address information that is displayed below the customer's name is not stored in the Orders table. This information is looked up from the Customers table and displayed based on the relationship defined between the CustomerID field in the Customers table and the CustomerID field in the Orders table.

If you need to enter an order for a customer that is not available in the BillTo list, first you open the Customers form and enter a new record for that customer. Then Microsoft Access automatically makes the new customer available in the BillTo lookup list box on the Orders form.

Queries

You use *queries* to view, change, and analyze data in different ways. You can also use them as the source of records for forms and reports. You can create a query either by using a wizard or from scratch in query Design view. In Design view, you specify the data you want to work with by adding the tables or queries that contain the data, and then specifying criteria and other information in the query design grid. In Microsoft Access, you can create many types of queries: select queries, parameter queries, crosstab queries, action queries, and SQL queries. This section describes the types of queries you can use in Microsoft Access.

Select Queries

A select query is the most common type of query. A select query retrieves data from one or more tables based on criteria you specify at design time such as category, range, and Boolean (logical yes/no or true/false) operators. Microsoft Access displays the results on a datasheet where you can update the records (with some restrictions). You can also use a select query to group records and to calculate sums, counts, averages, and other types of totals.

Parameter Queries

When you run a parameter query, it displays a dialog box prompting you for information, such as criteria for retrieving records or a value you want to insert in a field. You can design the query to prompt you for more than one piece of information—for example, you can design it to prompt you for two dates. Microsoft Access can then retrieve all records that fall between those two dates.

Crosstab Queries

A crosstab query displays summarized values (sums, counts, and averages) from one field in a table and groups them by one set of facts listed down the left side of the datasheet and another set of facts listed across the top of the datasheet. You can create a crosstab query either by using the Crosstab Query Wizard or from scratch. You can display crosstab data without creating a crosstab query in your database by using the PivotTable Wizard instead. With a PivotTable, you can change row and column headings on demand to analyze data in different ways.

Action Queries

An action query makes changes to many records in one operation. There are four types of action queries: delete, update, append, and make-table.

Delete Queries

A delete query deletes a group of records from one or more tables. For example, you can use a delete query to remove products that are discontinued or for which there are no orders. With delete queries, you always delete entire records, not just selected fields within records.

Update Queries

An update query makes global changes to a group of records in one or more tables. For example, you can raise prices by 10 percent for all dairy products, or you can raise salaries by 5 percent for the people within a certain job category. With an update query, you can change data in existing tables.

Append Queries

An append query adds a group of records from one or more tables to the end of one or more tables. For example, suppose that you acquire new customers and a database that contains a table of information about those customers. To avoid typing all this information in, you can append it to the Customers table. Append queries are also helpful for:

- Appending fields based on criteria.

    For example, you may want to append only the names and addresses of customers with outstanding orders.

- Appending records when some of the fields in one table do not exist in the other table.

    For example, in the Northwind sample database, the Customers table has 11 fields. Suppose that you want to append records from another table that has fields that match 9 of the 11 fields in the Customers table. An append query appends the data in the matching fields and ignores the others.

Make-Table Queries

A make-table query creates a new table from all or part of the data in one or more tables. Make-table queries are helpful for:

- Creating a table to export to other Microsoft Access databases.

    For example, you may want to create a table that contains several fields from the Employees table, and then export that table to a database used by the personnel department.

- Creating reports that display data from a specified point in time.

  For example, suppose you want to print a report on 15-May-97 that displays the first quarter's sales totals based on the data that was in the underlying tables as of 9:00 A.M. on 1-Apr-97. A report based on a query or an SQL statement extracts the most up-to-date data from the tables (the data as of 15-May-97), rather than the records as of a specific date and time. To preserve the data exactly as it was at 9:00 A.M. on 1-Apr-97, create and run a make-table query at that point in time to retrieve the records you need, and store them in a new table. Then use this table, rather than a query, as the basis for the reports.

- Making a backup copy of a table.
- Creating a history table that contains old records.

  For example, you can create a table that stores all the old orders before deleting them from the current Orders table.

- Improving performance of forms and reports based on multiple-table queries or SQL statements.

  For example, suppose you want to print multiple reports that are based on a five-table query that includes totals. You may be able to speed things up by first creating a make-table query that retrieves the records you need and stores them in one table. Then you can base the reports on this table or specify the table in an SQL statement as the record source for a form or report, so you do not have to rerun the query for each report. However, the data in the table is frozen at the time you run the make-table query.

SQL Queries

An SQL query is a query you create by using an SQL statement. Examples of SQL-specific queries are union queries, pass-through queries, data-definition queries, and subqueries.

Union Queries

A union query combines fields from one or more tables or queries into one field in the query's results. For example, if you have six vendors who send new inventory lists each month, you can combine these lists into one result set by using a union query, and then create a make-table query based on the union query to make a new table.

Pass-through Queries

A pass-through query sends commands directly to Open Database Connectivity (ODBC) data sources, such as Microsoft SQL Server databases, by using commands that are accepted by the server. For example, you can use a pass-through query to retrieve records or change data. You can also use pass-through queries to run *stored procedures* (SQL programs that are stored on the server) and to perform operations that are only available by using server-specific commands.

Data-Definition Queries

A data-definition query uses SQL Data Definition Language (DDL) statements to create, delete, or alter tables and to create indexes. DDL statements can be used only with Microsoft Jet format (MDB) databases. To work with SQL Server tables and indexes, use pass-through queries instead. To work with other non-Microsoft Jet format tables supported by Microsoft Access, use the **Data Access Objects (DAO) Create** methods in Visual Basic for Applications.

Subqueries

A subquery consists of an SQL SELECT statement inside another select query or action query. You can enter these statements in the **Field** row of the query design grid to define a new field, or in the **Criteria** row to define criteria for a field. You can use subqueries to:

- Test for the existence of some result from the subquery (by using the EXISTS or NOT EXISTS reserved words).
- Find any values in the main query that are equal to, greater than, or less than values returned by the subquery (by using the ANY, IN, or ALL reserved words).
- Create subqueries within subqueries (nested subqueries).

Forms

Forms give users a way of entering data into databases, displaying data on the screen, and printing data. For example, database developers can create forms that act as switchboards, using buttons or hyperlinks to navigate to the various objects in a database. Developers can also create forms that are custom dialog boxes that prompt users for the information required to complete operations. Forms can contain text, graphics, data, color, and ActiveX controls (formerly called OLE controls or custom controls). For more information about ActiveX controls, see "Office Support for ActiveX" in Chapter 34, "Microsoft Office Architecture."

To display data on a form from an underlying record source, such as a table or query, set the **RecordSource** property to the name of the table or query. You create a link between a form and its record source by using graphical objects called controls. For more information about controls, see "Controls" later in this chapter. The default appearance of a form is controlled by a form template. For more information, see "Form and Report Templates" later in this chapter.

Reports

A *report* is an effective way to present data from your Microsoft Access database in a printed format. Because you have control over the size and appearance of everything in a report, you can display the information the way you want to see it. The data in a report comes from an underlying table, query, or SQL statement. Other information in the report is stored in the report's design. You create a link between a report and its record source by using graphical objects called controls. For more information about controls, see "Controls" later in this chapter. The default appearance of a report is controlled by a report template. For more information, see "Form and Report Templates" later in this chapter.

Macros

A *macro* is a set of one or more actions that perform a particular operation, such as opening a form or printing a report. You can use macros to automate common tasks. You can run macros directly from the **Macros** tab of the Database window, from another macro or event procedure, or in response to an event that occurs on a form, report, or control.

Modules

Visual Basic code provides another way to automate tasks in a Microsoft Access database application. Visual Basic code is stored in *modules*.

A database can contain two types of modules:

- Standard modules

    Use standard modules to store code you may want to run from anywhere in the application. You can call public procedures in standard modules from expressions, macros, event procedures, or procedures in other standard modules.

- Class modules

    Use class modules to create your own custom objects. The **Sub** and **Function** procedures that you define in a class module become methods of the custom object. The properties you define with the **Property Get**, **Property Let**, and **Property Set** statements become properties of the custom object.

Each form and report in your database can contain an associated form module or report module. Form and report modules are a type of class module, but you cannot save them separately from the form or report that they belong to.

Use a form or report module to contain procedures associated with event properties of the form or report. For example, code associated with a form's **OnOpen** property runs when the form is opened. Procedures-associated event properties are called *event procedures*. A form or report module can also contain procedures that are not triggered by events.

A form or report module is part of the form or report's design. Thus, if you copy a form or report to another database, its module is copied with it; if you delete a form or report, its module is deleted as well. Microsoft Access creates the form or report module automatically when you first add Visual Basic code to the form or report.

Controls

In addition to the database objects discussed in the previous sections, the forms and reports in a Microsoft Access database contain an additional set of objects called *controls*. All the information on a form or report is contained in controls. Controls are objects on a form or report that display data, perform actions, or decorate the form or report. For example, you can use a text box control on a form or report to display data, a command button control on a form to open another form or report, or a line or rectangle control to separate and group other controls to make them more readable.

Microsoft Access includes built-in controls and ActiveX controls, which are all accessible through the toolbox in form Design view or report Design view. Microsoft Access includes the following types of built-in controls: text box, label, option group, option button, check box, toggle button, combo box, list box, command button, image control, bound object frame, unbound object frame, subform/subreport, page break, line, rectangle, and tab control. For information about these controls, see Microsoft Access online Help.

Controls can be bound, unbound, or calculated. A *bound control* is tied to a field in an underlying table or query. You use bound controls to display, enter, and update values from fields in your database. A *calculated control* uses an expression as its source of data. An expression can use data from a field in an underlying table or query of a form or report, or from another control on the form or report. An *unbound control* does not have a data source. You can use unbound controls to display information, lines, rectangles, and pictures.

ActiveX Controls

You can use ActiveX controls to add custom functionality to forms. Microsoft Access 97 includes two ActiveX controls: the Calendar control, and the WebBrowser control. The Calendar control makes it easy to display and update a monthly calendar on a form. You can use the WebBrowser control to display Web pages and other documents in a Microsoft Access form. Before you can add the WebBrowser control to a form, you must have Microsoft Internet Explorer version 3.0 installed. For more information about the WebBrowser control, see Chapter 25, "Web Support in Microsoft Office Applications." Additional ActiveX controls are available in Microsoft Office 97, Developer Edition, and from independent software vendors.

Form and Report Templates

When users create a form or report without using a wizard, Microsoft Access uses a template to define the default characteristics of the form or report. The template determines which sections a form or report has and defines each section's dimensions. The template also contains all the default property settings for the form.

The default templates for forms and reports are named Normal. However, you can use any existing form or report as a template. You specify which template you want to use on the **Forms/Reports** tab in the **Options** dialog box (**Tools** menu). If you specify a template other than Normal, this setting is stored in the Windows registry in the **HKEY_CURRENT_USER\Software\Microsoft\Office\8.0\Access\Settings** key and applies to all new forms or reports that the current user creates. You can import templates (that is, forms or reports to use as templates) to use in your Microsoft Access database, and you can export them to use them in other databases.

Form and report templates define:

- Whether to include a form or report header and footer.
- Whether to include a page header and footer.
- The dimensions (height and width) of the sections.
- Which default properties to use for controls. However, templates do not create controls on new forms or reports.

▶ **To create and specify a form or report template**

1. Create a form or report that includes the formatting and controls you want to use as the basis of your template.
2. On the **File** menu, click **Save**.
3. In the **Save As** dialog box, type a name for your form or report, and click **OK**.
4. On the **Tools** menu, click **Options**, and then click the **Forms/Reports** tab.
5. To specify a form template, type the name of the form in the **Form Template** box.

    –or–

    To specify a report template, enter the name of the report in the **Report Template** box.

Note If you want to use the template in another database, select the form or report in the Database window, and then click **Save As/Export** (**File** menu) to export the form or report. Then open the other database and repeat Step 4.

Library Databases

A library database is a collection of procedures and database objects that you can call from any application. You can use libraries to store routines that you use often, so you do not have to write the same routine for each application you create. You can also use libraries to distribute new features to users.

To use a library database from your Microsoft Access application, you must first establish a link, called a *reference*, from your application to the library. You can establish a reference in the **References** dialog box (**Tools** menu). Library database files have an .mda file name extension.

For more information about creating and using library databases, see Chapter 12, "Using Library Databases and Dynamic-Link Libraries," in *Building Applications with Microsoft Access 97*.

Add-ins

Add-ins are tools written within the Microsoft Access environment that extend the functionality of the basic product. These tools make difficult tasks easier, automate repetitive operations, and add new features. Add-ins can increase productivity by focusing on a single task or function. You can create them to use yourself, to use within your organization, or to distribute along with a database application. You can also purchase add-ins created by independent software developers.

Microsoft Access has three kinds of add-ins: wizards, builders, and menu add-ins. Each type has its own advantages and uses. A *wizard* helps a user create a new table, query, form, report, or control. A *builder* helps a user set properties in Design view. A *menu add-in* is not context-specific and can be used anywhere in Microsoft Access. Wizards and builders are available to the user through the same interface that supports the Microsoft Access wizards and builders. By default, menu add-ins are available through the **Add-Ins** submenu (**Tools** menu). The interface through which an add-in is available is determined by how the add-in is registered when it is installed.

Add-in files are saved like library database files, with the .mda file name extension. Add-in files can also be saved as MDE files. An MDE file has Visual Basic source code removed, and the design of any forms, reports, and modules is secured. MDE files have an .mde file name extension. For more information about MDE files, see Chapter 29, "Workgroup Features in Microsoft Access." Users can add or remove add-ins from Microsoft Access by pointing to **Add-Ins** (**Tools** menu) and then clicking **Add-In Manager**.

For information about creating add-ins in Microsoft Access, see Chapter 17, "Creating Wizards, Builders, and Menu Add-ins," in *Building Applications with Microsoft Access 97*.

Wizards

A wizard handles complex operations. It usually consists of a series of dialog boxes that provide a step-by-step interface to guide the user through the process of creating an object. Wizards usually use forms, graphics, and helpful text to shield the user from the technical intricacies of an operation. Microsoft Access Form and Report Wizards are examples of this type of add-in. These add-ins guide you through creating forms and reports.

Microsoft Access provides direct support for several types of wizards. As a result, the wizards you create are available through the same user interface as the Microsoft

Access wizards. For example, if you create or install a wizard to design a specific type of form, it appears in the same list as the Microsoft Access Form Wizards. The types of wizards that Microsoft Access supports include:

- Control Wizards
- Form Wizards
- Query Wizards
- Report Wizards
- Table Wizards

Builders

A builder is a simpler tool than is a wizard. A builder usually consists of a single dialog box or form that guides the user through the process of setting a property, such as constructing an expression. The Microsoft Access Expression Builder is an example of this type of add-in.

As with wizards, Microsoft Access provides direct support for many types of builders. You can create or install builders for any property, even those that Microsoft Access does not provide builders for. Also, you can install more than one builder for the same property. Additional builders are available to users through the standard builder interface. For example, if one or more builders are already installed for a property, your builder is available from a list of builders. The types of builders that Microsoft Access supports include:

- Property Builders
- Expression Builders

Menu Add-ins

A menu add-in is a general-purpose tool that accomplishes a task that does not fit into the wizard or builder categories. A menu add-in typically operates on multiple objects or on the Microsoft Access application itself. The Add-In Manager is an example of a menu add-in.

Menu add-ins are supported by Microsoft Access through the **Add-Ins** submenu (**Tools** menu). When you install a menu add-in, the command to run it is added to the **Add-Ins** submenu. It is important to understand that menu add-ins are available to the user whenever the **Tools** menu is available. After a menu add-in is installed, you can also add a button or command to run the menu add-in from any toolbar by using the **Customize** dialog box (**View** menu, **Toolbars** submenu). This means that menu add-ins are not context-sensitive like wizards and builders. A wizard is designed to aid the user within a specific context, such as form or query design. A menu add-in is designed to perform a general function that may not fit within the context of the user's current operation.

Several add-ins are included with Microsoft Access. Not all of these add-ins are installed when you choose the Typical installation during Setup. To install the add-ins you need, rerun Setup and click **Add/Remove**; then select the **Wizards** or **Advanced Wizards** option, as described in the following tables. The functionality of an add-in is available to all databases opened with a particular installation of Microsoft Access.

The following table describes the add-ins that are always installed, regardless of the installation option you choose during Setup.

Add-in	File name	Description
Color Builder	An add-in in previous versions; now part of Msaccess.exe	Displays a palette for setting the color values for controls and sections in form and report Design view. Also used to create color property values for customized colors.
Expression Builder	Utility.mda	Creates expressions for macros, queries, and property sheets.
Query Builder	An add-in in previous versions; now part of Msaccess.exe	Creates the correct syntax for a query.
Subform/Subreport Field Linker	An add-in in previous versions; now part of Msaccess.exe	Links fields in a main form and a subform, or in a main report and a subreport.

The following table describes the add-ins included in a Typical installation (or when you select the **Wizards** option under the **Microsoft Access** option) during Setup.

Add-in	File name	Description
AutoForm	Wzmain80.mde	Creates a simple form that displays all fields and records in the selected table or query. Each field appears on a separate line with a label to its left.
AutoReport	Wzmain80.mde	Creates a simple report that displays all fields and records in the selected table or query.
Combo Box Wizard	Wzmain80.mde	Creates a combo box control on a form.
Command Button Wizard	Wzmain80.mde	Creates a command button control on a form.
Crosstab Query Wizard	Wzmain80.mde	Creates a query that summarizes data in a compact, spreadsheet-like format.
Database Wizard	Wzmain80.mde	Creates an entirely new database for a variety of uses based on 1 of 22 models.
Export Text Wizard	Wzlib80.mde	Exports data to a text file.

Add-in	File name	Description
Field Builder	Wzmain80.mde	Sets the properties of a new field by selecting from a list of sample field definitions.
Form Wizard	Wzmain80.mde	Creates a new form.
Import HTML Wizard	Wzlib80.mde	Imports HTML tables and lists from the Internet or an intranet into a Microsoft Access table.
Import Spreadsheet Wizard	Wzlib80.mde	Imports a Microsoft Excel or other spreadsheet into a Microsoft Access table.
Import Text Wizard	Wzlib80.mde	Imports a text file into a Microsoft Access table.
Label Wizard	Wzmain80.mde	Creates mailing labels in standard and custom sizes.
Link HTML Wizard	Wzlib80.mde	Links an HTML table or list on the Internet or an intranet to a Microsoft Access table.
Link Spreadsheet Wizard	Wzlib80.mde	Links spreadsheet data to a Microsoft Access table.
Link Text Wizard	Wzlib80.mde	Links a text file to a Microsoft Access table.
List Box Wizard	Wzmain80.mde	Creates a list box control on a form.
Lookup Wizard	Wzmain80.mde	Creates a lookup column in a table, which displays a list of values the user can choose from.
Microsoft Word Mail Merge Wizard	Wzmain80.mde	Manages mail merge operations by using letters stored in Microsoft Word and addresses stored in Microsoft Access.
Picture Builder	Wzmain80.mde	Creates bitmap images for forms and reports.
PivotTable Wizard	Wzmain80.mde	Places a Microsoft Excel PivotTable on a Microsoft Access form.
Publish to the Web Wizard	Wzmain80.mde	Creates static and/or dynamic HTML documents from your Microsoft Access application to be placed on the Internet or an intranet.
Report Wizard	Wzmain80.mde	Creates a report based on a table or query.
`Simple Query Wizard	Wzmain80.mde	Creates a select query from the fields you pick.

Add-in	File name	Description
Switchboard Manager	Wzmain80.mde	Creates and manages switchboard forms for applications.
Table Wizard	Wzmain80.mde	Creates a new table by selecting from a list of sample table and field definitions.
Web Publishing Wizard	Wpwiz.exe (Installed by running WebPost.exe in the ValuPack\WebPost folder on the Office CD)	Posts HTML documents to an Internet or intranet server. Can be used in conjunction with the Publish to the Web Wizard.

The following table describes the add-ins included in a Custom installation when you select the **Advanced Wizards** option under the **Microsoft Access** option during Setup.

Add-in	File name	Description
Add-In Manager	Wztool80.mde	Installs and uninstalls wizards, builders, and add-ins.
Chart Wizard	Wztool80.mde	Adds a chart to a form or report based on the data in a table or query.
Conflict Resolver	Wzcnf80.mde	Resolves conflicts between replicated databases during synchronization.
Database Splitter Wizard	Wztool80.mde	Splits databases into data and interface portions, so one or more users can have local copies of the interface connected to the data on a server.
Documenter	Wztool80.mde	Prints a report that documents all of the objects in a database.
Find Duplicates Query Wizard	Wztool80.mde	Creates a query that finds records with duplicate field values in a single table or query.
Find Unmatched Query Wizard	Wztool80.mde	Creates a query that finds records in one table that have no related records in another table.
Input Mask Wizard	Wztool80.mde	Creates an input mask for a field you choose in a table.
Linked Table Manager	Wztool80.mde	Manages links to tables in other databases.
Macro to Module Converter	Wztool80.mde	Converts macros to Visual Basic event procedures or modules that perform equivalent actions using Visual Basic code.

Add-in	File name	Description
ODBC Connection String Builder	Wztool80.mde	Creates the correct syntax for a connection to an ODBC database.
Option Group Wizard	Wztool80.mde	Creates a group of option buttons on a form.
Performance Analyzer	Wztool80.mde	Analyzes the efficiency of a database and produces a list of suggestions for improving its performance.
Subform/Subreport Wizard	Wztool80.mde	Creates a new subform or subreport on a form or report.
Table Analyzer Wizard	Wztool80.mde	Takes a table with much duplicate data and splits it into related tables for more efficient storage.
User-Level Security Wizard	Wztool80.mde	Creates a new, encrypted database, with regulated user access, from an existing database.

Workgroup Information Files

A *workgroup information file* is a file that Microsoft Access reads when starting up; it contains information about the users in a workgroup. If user-level security is being used, this information includes users' account names, their passwords, and the groups that they belong to.

Even when user-level security is not being explicitly used, Microsoft Access requires the workgroup information file in order to start up. The reason for this is that user-level security is always activated before Microsoft Access starts running to eliminate the possibility of a security backdoor. Before user-level security is explicitly established, all users are automatically logged on by using the default Admin user account. Once user-level security is established, a user must log on by using a particular account. Each user account can have a password defined that is required when logging on with the account. The default name for the workgroup information file for Microsoft Access 97 is System.mdw.

Note In previous versions of Microsoft Access, user-preference settings specified in the **Options** dialog box (**Tools** menu) are stored in the workgroup information file. In Microsoft Access 97, these settings are stored in the Windows registry in the **HKEY_CURRENT_USER Software\Microsoft\Office\8.0\Access\Settings** key.

For users to share data in a secured workgroup, they must use the Workgroup Administrator to specify a workgroup information file that defines the user and group accounts for the workgroup before they start Microsoft Access. Alternatively, users can specify a workgroup information file by using the **/wrkgrp** command-line option when they start Microsoft Access.

The Workgroup Administrator is a separate application named Wrkgadm.exe that is installed in the Windows\System folder (for Windows 95) or the Windows\System32 folder (for Windows NT Workstation 3.51 and 4.0). Running the Workgroup Administrator specifies the workgroup information file in the Windows registry as the setting for the **SystemDB** value in the **HKEY_LOCAL_MACHINE \SOFTWARE\Microsoft\Office\8.0\Access\Jet\3.5 \Engines** key. Using the **/wrkgrp** command-line option to specify a workgroup information file overrides the value stored in the registry during that program session, but does not change it.

The workgroup information file that a user specifies is the file that Microsoft Access uses every time it starts up, until the user specifies some other file. If a user does not belong to a secure workgroup and has not specified a workgroup information file, Microsoft Access uses the default System.mdw file created when Microsoft Access was installed. The default System.mdw file is located in the Windows\System folder (Windows 95) or the Windows\System32 folder (Windows NT Workstation 3.51 and 4.0).

After users have specified a workgroup information file, they should back up their System.mdw file. If the file somehow becomes corrupted, the user must restore the backup copy, get a new copy from a workgroup administrator (if that is who originally provided the file), or re-create it. Users must have a valid workgroup information file to run Microsoft Access.

For more information about the Microsoft Access user-level security model, see "Security Features in Microsoft Access" in Chapter 29, "Workgroup Features in Microsoft Access."

Microsoft Access and the Microsoft Jet Database Engine

Together, Microsoft Access and the Microsoft Jet database engine form a complete database management system (DBMS). Microsoft Access is responsible for the user interface and all the ways that users view, edit, and manipulate data through forms, queries, reports, and so forth. Microsoft Jet—the data manager component of the DBMS—retrieves data from and stores data in user and system databases.

Microsoft Jet is a relational database engine that handles all database processing for Microsoft Access. Microsoft Jet can also provide data to Open Database Connectivity (ODBC) client applications.

Microsoft Jet is made up of a set of dynamic-link libraries (DLLs):

- Microsoft Jet DLL (Msjet35.dll)

    Msjet35.dll is the main program that evaluates and carries out requests for data. If the request is for *native* data—data stored in the Microsoft Access Database (MDB) format—then Msjet35.dll also handles the reading and writing of the data. If the request involves non-native data, then Msjet35.dll makes calls to either the ODBC Driver Manager DLL (Odbc32.dll) or one of the external installable ISAM DLLs, as explained later in this section.

- Data Access Objects DLL (Dao350.dll)

    Dao350.dll is the Microsoft Jet component that provides a developer interface to Microsoft Jet. Data Access Objects (DAO) includes a rich, high-level set of objects that insulates developers from the physical details of reading and writing records.

- Installable ISAM DLLs

    Microsoft Jet provides access to several external Indexed Sequential Access Method (ISAM) format files by using a series of installable DLL files referred to as *installable ISAMs*. Microsoft Jet supports the external ISAM formats shown in the following table.

ISAM format	Supported by DLL
Xbase (dBASE and FoxPro)	Msxbse35.dll
Paradox	Mspdox35.dll
Lotus	Msltus35.dll
Microsoft Excel	Msexcl35.dll
Microsoft Exchange/Outlook	Msexch35.dll
Text and HTML	Mstext35.dll

    These DLLs handle the reading and writing of data stored in dBASE, FoxPro, Paradox, Lotus, Microsoft Excel, Microsoft Exchange, Microsoft Outlook, fixed-width text, delimited text, and HTML files.

Linked Tables

In general, you store data locally in tables in the database. You can also create links to tables in other Microsoft Access databases, to data in other file formats (such as Microsoft Excel, dBASE, and Paradox), and to ODBC data sources, such as Microsoft SQL Server. These links are stored in the database container and act like native tables. You can use a linked table just as you would use any other table in your Microsoft Access database. For example, you can create forms, reports, and queries that use the external table. Any changes to the table are reflected in the linked database. An icon that represents the linked table appears in the Database window along with icons for the local tables in the database, so you can open the linked table whenever you want to. For more information about linked tables, see "Using External Data in Microsoft Access" in Chapter 17, "Switching to Microsoft Access."

Direct Table Opening

You cannot use the Microsoft Access user interface to open an external table directly. However, you can open external tables directly by using DAO code in Visual Basic. A developer may use this method to get a value quickly from a table that does not need to be accessed very often in the application.

ODBC Connectivity

With Microsoft Jet, users can retrieve data from Open Database Connectivity (ODBC) data sources. The ODBC standard is typically used to connect to server-based database systems. Microsoft Access includes ODBC drivers for Microsoft SQL Server. The ODBC standard can also be used to connect to nonserver databases and spreadsheets.

As with installable ISAM data, Microsoft Access can connect to ODBC data sources by linking or opening tables. Microsoft Access also supports SQL pass-through queries with ODBC data sources, as described earlier in this chapter. The disadvantage of applications that use pass-through queries is that they are not portable. For example, an application written for Microsoft SQL Server fails if it attempts to gain access to an Oracle server, because it contains server-specific commands. Users create SQL pass-through queries by clicking **SQL Specific** on the **Query** menu and then clicking **Pass-Through**.

For an in-depth discussion of Microsoft Jet and its architecture, see the *Microsoft Jet Database Engine Programmer's Guide*, which is published by Microsoft Press and available wherever computer books are sold. For more information about Microsoft Press books, see Appendix E, "Other Support Resources."

> ### Separating the Application from the Data
>
> If you are distributing an application to a number of users, or if the data is located on a server, consider using a back-end database to hold the tables that contain the data and a front-end database to hold the application's other objects. You can then base all objects in the application on linked tables from the back-end database. For an example of this type of architecture, see the Orders sample application (Orders.mdb), installed in the Program Files\Microsoft Office\Office\Samples folder when you choose a Custom installation during Setup. The forms, queries, reports, and other objects are contained in Orders.mdb. The database tables, however, are in the Northwind database (Northwind.mdb).
>
> When you separate the application's data from its objects, you can distribute upgraded queries, forms, reports, macros, and modules in the new version of the front-end database without disturbing the application's data. Similarly, you can exchange one set of data for another or back up the data on the back-end database without affecting the objects in the front-end database. If the data is located on a server, you can reduce the network load and improve performance by having users run the front-end database on their workstations rather than from the server. An additional advantage of separating the data from the rest of the application is that you can upgrade the custom application to future versions of Microsoft Access independently of the shared database tables. This makes it easier for users with different versions of Microsoft Access to use the same data.

How You Can Customize Microsoft Access

Microsoft Access default settings and paths are established when you run the Office Setup program. After Setup, you can customize these settings for a single user, a workgroup, or across an entire organization.

There are several ways to customize the Microsoft Access application:

- Through the **Options** dialog box

  You can customize Microsoft Access in the **Options** dialog box (**Tools** menu). The settings you make here are stored in the Windows registry.

- Through the **Customize** dialog box

  In the **Customize** dialog box (**View** menu, **Toolbars** submenu), you can customize the toolbars, menu bars, and shortcut menus included with Microsoft Access, or you can create your own.

- With an add-in

  For more information about add-ins, see "Add-ins" earlier in this chapter.

These methods of customizing Microsoft Access are described in the following sections. Some of these customizations are stored in the Windows registry, and some are stored in a separate file on the user's system.

User-Defined Options

The settings specified in the **Options** dialog box (**Tools** menu) are saved to the Windows registry, which Microsoft Access reads when it starts up. When two or more users open a shared database on a network, Microsoft Access applies the separate preferences to each user's view of the shared database. For information about Microsoft Access entries in the Windows registry, see Appendix C, "Registry Keys and Values."

Tip In Windows 95 and Windows NT Workstation 4.0, you can use a system policy to define most settings in the **Options** dialog box (**Tools** menu) for all Microsoft Access users in your workgroup. In the System Policy Editor, set the following policy:

User\Access 97\Tools_Options

For more information, see "Using Windows System Policies to Customize Office" in Chapter 7, "Customizing and Optimizing Microsoft Office."

Custom Toolbar, Menu Bar, and Shortcut Menu Settings

In Microsoft Access, you can organize the commands on toolbars, menu bars, and shortcut menus the way you want so you can find and use them quickly. In previous versions of Microsoft Access, toolbars contained only buttons. In Microsoft Access 97, toolbars can contain buttons, menus, or both. This means that menu bars and shortcut menus are now different types of toolbars; therefore, you can customize all three the same way. For example, although the built-in menu bar still appears by default at the top of the screen and contains standard menus such as **File**, **Edit**, and **View**, you can customize it by adding or removing buttons and menus or by moving it to a different location.

In addition to customizing the built-in toolbars, menu bars, and shortcut menus, you can create your own custom toolbars, menu bars, and shortcut menus. To create and customize toolbars, menu bars, and shortcut menus, and to set properties that affect how they look and behave, use the **Customize** dialog box (**View** menu, **Toolbars** submenu). By customizing toolbars, menu bars, and shortcut menus, you can change Microsoft Access to better suit the needs of your workgroup. For example, you can add frequently used commands and dialog box options to toolbars and remove items that users rarely use.

New custom toolbars, menu bars, and shortcut menus are stored in the database file and are available to all users who share the database. If you want to copy custom toolbars and menus from another Microsoft Access database, you can import them.

You cannot import a single toolbar, menu bar, or shortcut menu; you must import all the toolbars, menu bars, and shortcut menus in the database file.

Note Microsoft Access does not import a toolbar, menu bar, or shortcut menu if it has the same name as one in the database you are importing to.

▶ **To import all custom toolbars, menu bars, and shortcut menus from another database**

1 Open the database into which you want to import the custom toolbars, menu bars, and shortcut menus.
2 On the **File** menu, point to **Get External Data**, and then click **Import**.
3 In the **Files of type** box, make sure **Microsoft Access (*.mdb;*.mdw;*.mda)** is selected.
4 In the **Look in** box, select the drive and folder for the Microsoft Access database you want to import from, and then double-click the database.
5 In the **Import Objects** dialog box, click **Options**.
6 Under **Import**, select the **Menus and Toolbars** check box, and then click **OK**.

Customizations made to built-in toolbars, menu bars, and shortcut menus by individual users are stored in the in the Windows registry in the **HKEY_CURRENT_USER\Software\Microsoft\Office\8.0\Access\Settings \CommandBars** key. These customizations cannot be copied to other users.

You can also use Visual Basic code to customize toolbars and menus with the CommandBar object model. To view a form that demonstrates working with the CommandBar object model, open the CommandBarsForm in the Developer Solutions sample application (Solutions.mdb). The Developer Solutions sample application is installed in the Program Files\Microsoft Office\Office\Samples folder when you choose a Custom installation during Setup. For more information about customizing toolbars and menus with Visual Basic, see the *Microsoft Office 97/Visual Basic Programmer's Guide*, published by Microsoft Press and available wherever computer books are sold. For more information about Microsoft Press books, see Appendix E, "Other Support Resources."

How Microsoft Access Resolves Conflicts

Conflicts can occur in Microsoft Access when a database is being replicated or when more than one user attempts to edit the same record in a shared database.

Replication Conflicts

During replication setup—for example, when a user drags a database to the Windows 95 Briefcase—the Jet database engine requests globally unique identifiers

(GUIDs) from the operating system that are associated with each row of data in the Design Master. These GUIDs are then copied into any replica databases. If a row changes in the Design Master or a replica, a counter is incremented for the row. This makes it easy for Microsoft Access to compare the values of rows, detect that a change has been made, and replicate the changed data in other databases. If the same row is changed in more than one database simultaneously, Microsoft Access selects between them based on the following rules:

- Microsoft Access chooses the database that has the highest value for its counter. The row that has changed most often has a higher counter, because the counter is incremented every time a row is changed.
- If both rows have been changed the same number of times (counters are the same on both rows in both databases), Microsoft Access chooses a database randomly, as the replication logic cannot reasonably know which of the two rows has the correct data.

Regardless of how the data is selected, users who submit the data that is not chosen are told by the Conflict Resolver in Microsoft Access that their data was rejected. Users can then resubmit their change or accept the other data.

Locking Conflicts

If record locking is set to **No Locks**, there may be locking conflicts when more than one user attempts to edit or save the same record in a shared database. Users can set record locking on the **Advanced** tab of the **Options** dialog box (**Tools** menu).

The **No Locks** setting allows more than one user to edit a record simultaneously, but the record is locked during the instant when it is being saved. If two users attempt to save changes to the same record, Microsoft Access displays a message to the second user who tries to save the record. This user can then discard the record, copy the record to the Clipboard, or replace the changes made by the other user. By using this last option, it is possible for users to write over one another's changes.

For more information about record locking, see "Multiuser Applications and Locking" in Chapter 29, "Workgroup Features in Microsoft Access."

CHAPTER 36

Microsoft Excel Architecture

This chapter describes the structure of Microsoft Excel. It explains how the various components of Microsoft Excel work together, and how the application handles changes that users make to those components. An understanding of the architecture of Microsoft Excel can help you take advantage of its features and may help you troubleshoot problems.

In This Chapter

How Microsoft Excel Is Structured   939
How You Can Customize Microsoft Excel   951
How Microsoft Excel Resolves Conflicts   956

See Also

- For information about installing Microsoft Excel or other Office applications, see Chapter 4, "Installing Microsoft Office."
- For information about customizing Microsoft Excel to meet the specific needs of your workgroup, see Chapter 7, "Customizing and Optimizing Microsoft Office."

How Microsoft Excel Is Structured

Microsoft Excel documents are called workbooks. A workbook is a collection of worksheets, chart sheets, and Visual Basic for Applications modules. The worksheet is the primary location for storing data in a workbook. Each worksheet can contain cells that store data and formulas, and charts, which present data graphically. Each cell and chart item can have associated formatting, such as fonts, colors, and layout options.

You can save a workbook as a template. A template provides a pattern for creating new workbooks. You can also save workbooks as add-ins, which programmatically add custom features to Microsoft Excel. The following illustration shows how Microsoft Excel components fit together to create a workbook.

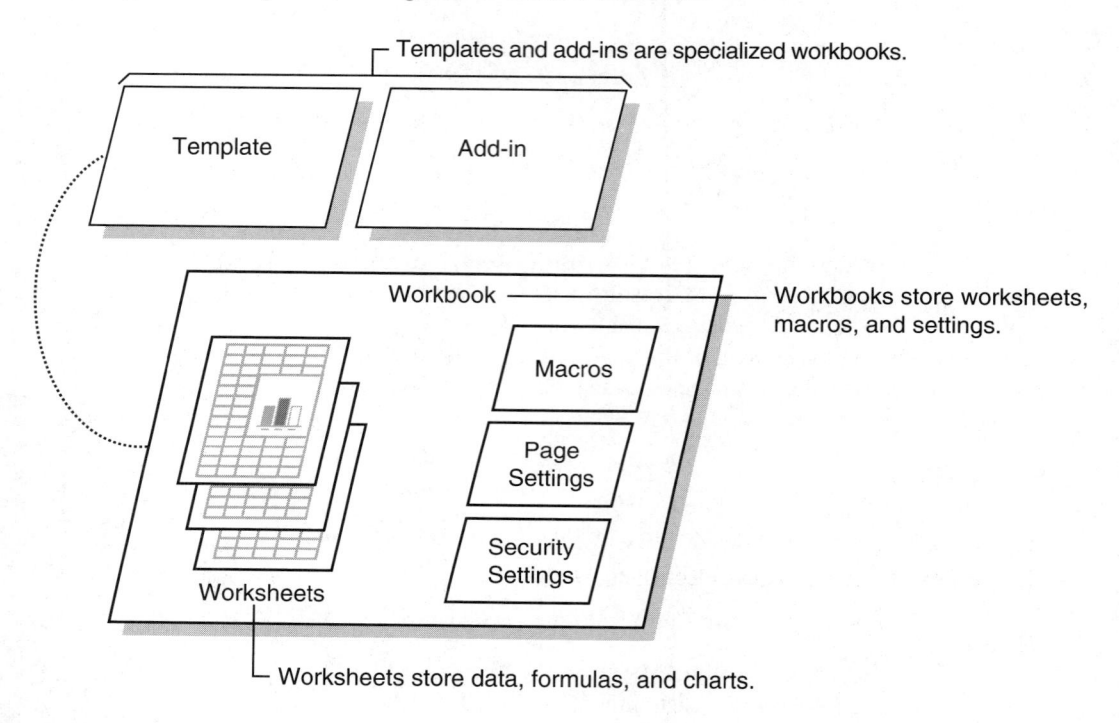

Workbooks

The workbook in Microsoft Excel is analogous to the document in Microsoft Word, or the presentation in Microsoft PowerPoint. The workbook stores data in the Microsoft Excel file format. Microsoft Excel workbook files have the extension .xls (Windows) or the file type Microsoft Excel Document (Macintosh).

The various components of Microsoft Excel, such as cell data and formulas, are stored in the workbook file. Some components, such as cell data and charts, are stored on worksheets in the workbook. Other components, such as macros, book-level security settings, and page settings, are stored in the workbook file but not on worksheets.

Cell Data

Cell data consists of constant values stored in cells and can be either of the following:

- Numeric values, including date, time, currency, percentage, or scientific notation
- Text

The way Microsoft Excel displays numeric values in a cell depends on the number format assigned to a cell. The numeric value displayed may differ from the actual value Microsoft Excel stores, which is with 15 digits of accuracy. By default, Microsoft Excel makes calculations based on the stored value. Such calculation is known as *full precision* calculation. However, you can have Microsoft Excel calculate based on displayed values. To do this, Click **Options** (**Tools** menu), click the **Calculations** tab, and then select **Precision as displayed**.

> **My calculations appear to be inaccurate**
>
> If the results you get from a formula appear to be wrong, it may be due to the difference in precision between displayed and stored values. For example, if two cells each contain the value 1.007, and a formula adds them in a third cell, the result is 2.014. If all three cells are formatted to display two decimal places, Microsoft Excel rounds the values. Using full precision calculation on this formula, the displayed calculation, 1.01+1.01=2.01, appears to be wrong. On the other hand, a calculation on the displayed values, 1.01+1.01=2.02, appears to be correct, but results in a value that is not as precise as a full precision calculation would be.

Calculating with precision as displayed does the following:

- Affects all worksheets in the active workbook.
- Does not affect numbers in the General format, which are always calculated with full precision.
- Slows calculation because Microsoft Excel must round the numbers as it calculates.

Caution Once you switch to calculating on displayed values, Microsoft Excel stores all constant values as their displayed values, and full precision values cannot be restored.

Cell Formulas

Formulas use cell references when performing calculations on your data, and are part of the data that is stored in the workbook. Cell references in a formula can be relative, absolute, or mixed references in any of the following reference styles:

- A1 style
- Row-and-column (R1C1) style
- Name references

Both A1 and row-and-column reference styles refer to data by position. Using these styles, you may experience difficulty with formulas if you reposition or delete cells. One way to avoid this problem is to reference cells by name.

Name References

You can use a name as a reference to a cell, a group of cells, a value, or a formula. Name references can be accessible to an entire workbook or restricted to a worksheet. When a name reference is restricted to a worksheet, it can be repeated on more than one sheet so that it defines related cells on different sheets in the same workbook. A book-level name reference, on the other hand, cannot be repeated on more than one worksheet. Instead, it can be used throughout the workbook to refer to cells on one worksheet. Using book-level names eliminates the need to recreate names for each new worksheet or to type worksheet references in formulas. Sheet-level names override book-level names when used on the sheet where they are defined.

To use book-level name references, you enter the name you want to use in the name box on the formula bar. To use sheet-level name references, however, you must include the name of the sheet when you enter the name, such as Sheet1!Profit.

Tip As an alternative to using name references in formulas, you can often use spreadsheet labels (such as category names you have added to a worksheet) instead. For example, the label of the value at the intersection of a column labeled January and a row labeled Unit Sales is January Unit Sales. For more information about using natural language formulas, see "Intelligent Applications in Microsoft Excel 97" in Chapter 2, "What's New in Microsoft Office 97."

Scenarios

The **Scenarios** command (**Tools** menu) is a tool for creating specialized formulas which pose what-if questions with your data. Scenarios can be sheet-level or book-level.

▶ **To create a scenario**

1. On the **Tools** menu, click **Scenarios**, and then click **Add**.
2. In the **Scenario name** box, type a name for the scenario.
3. In the **Changing Cells** box, enter the references for the cells where you want to store hypothetical data.
4. Under **Protection**, select the options you want, and click **OK**.
5. In the **Scenario Values** dialog box, type the values you want in the changing cells.

Note For the protection options to take effect, you must activate protection for the current sheet. For information about sheet-level security, see "Security Settings" later in this chapter.

You can copy scenarios from other worksheets and other workbooks to the active worksheet. This is known as *merging* scenarios. To merge scenarios among workbooks, all the workbooks must be open.

▶ **To merge scenarios**

1. On the **Tools** menu, click **Scenarios**, and then click **Merge**.
2. In the **Book** box, click a workbook name.
3. In the **Sheet** box, click the names of the worksheets that contain the scenarios you want to merge.

When you merge scenarios, there may be some duplicate names. Best Case and Worst Case, for example, are common scenario names. In such instances, Microsoft Excel appends additional information to the duplicate scenario names, such as creation date, creator name, or an ordinal number.

Cell Formatting and Styles

Styles are collections of format settings for cells. Styles are stored separately from the cell data, which means they can be copied between cells, changed, or deleted, without affecting the data in the cell.

The following table shows the format settings stored in styles.

This format setting	Determines
Number	Decimal places, separator, inclusion of dollar sign, style for displaying negative numbers, and other options for formatting different kinds of numbers such as currency, dates, fractions, and so on.
Alignment	Horizontal and vertical alignment, text orientation, and whether text wraps in the cell.
Font	Font name, style, size, special effects, and color of the text in the cell.
Border	Placement and style of the border of the cell.
Pattern	Shading and color of the cell.
Protection	Whether data in the cell is locked or the formula is hidden. This option does not take effect until you protect the sheet by clicking **Protect Sheet** (**Tools** menu, **Protection** submenu).

Styles are saved in the workbook. If you want to reuse styles in another workbook, you can do either of the following:

- Copy the styles to another workbook.
- Save the workbook as a template.

When you copy the styles to other workbooks, you insert the styles into existing workbooks. When you save the workbook as a template, however, you automatically copy the styles to new workbooks based on this template. For information about creating templates, see "Templates" later in this chapter.

▶ **To copy styles from one workbook to another**

1. Open the source and destination workbooks for the styles you want to copy.
2. On the **Format** menu, click **Style**.
3. Click **Merge**, and select the workbook from which you want to merge styles.

All styles from the source workbook are merged into the destination workbook. If styles in the destination workbook have names that match styles being merged, you are prompted to choose whether or not to overwrite existing styles in the destination workbook.

A style name likely to match in the source and destination workbooks is Normal. All cells in a new workbook are initially formatted with the Normal style. You can change the settings for the Normal style, but the change does not affect new workbooks unless you save the workbook that contains the new Normal style as an autotemplate. For information about autotemplates, see "Autotemplates" later in this chapter.

Tip In Windows 95 and Windows NT Workstation 4.0, you can use a system policy to set the **Standard Font** option on the **General** tab in the **Options** dialog box (**Tools** menu) for all Microsoft Excel users in your workgroup. In the System Policy Editor, set the following policy:

User\Excel 97\Tools_Options\General\Font

For more information, see "Using Windows System Policies to Customize Office" in Chapter 7, "Customizing and Optimizing Microsoft Office."

Charts

You create charts based on a range of selected cells on a worksheet. To create a chart, click **Chart** (**Insert** menu), and follow the instructions in the Chart Wizard. In the **Chart Location** panel, the chart is stored on its own sheet (called a chart sheet) if you select the **As new sheet** option; if you select the **As object in** option, the chart is embedded in a worksheet. Regardless of which type of sheet a chart is stored on, Microsoft Excel stores charts in the workbook file. You can copy charts into other workbooks, and into other Office applications, such as Word documents and PowerPoint presentations.

Charts are linked dynamically to data on a worksheet. This means that changes to the data are updated in the chart, and changes to a data marker on the chart are reflected in the linked data cells. Text on the chart can also be linked to text in worksheet cells. This text appears as titles, data labels, legend entries, and labels for axis tick-marks. Editing text in the worksheet cells affects text in the charts that are linked to the cells. You can edit text directly in charts, but this breaks the link to the cells on the worksheet.

Custom Chart Types

Instead of formatting chart items individually, you can quickly change the look of a chart using a custom chart type. (In previous versions of Microsoft Excel, these were called chart autoformats.) Each custom chart type is based on one of the 14 predefined chart types, and can include a chart subtype, legend, gridline options, data labels, color settings, patterns, and layout. Microsoft Excel includes several built-in custom chart types. You can also create your own custom chart types.

▶ **To create a custom chart type**

1 Select a chart that you want to save as a custom chart type.
2 On the **Chart** menu, click **Chart Type**.
3 On the **Custom Types** tab, click **User-defined**.
4 Click **Add**.
5 In the **Name** box, type a name.

   If you want to add a description, type it in the **Description** box.

Microsoft Excel stores galleries of built-in and user-defined chart types on separate chart sheets in workbooks with reserved file names, as shown in the following tables. Note that the user-defined chart gallery file is created only after a user-defined chart type is created.

Windows chart type	File name and location
Built-in chart gallery	Program Files\Microsoft Office\Office\Xl8galry.xls
User-defined chart gallery	Program Files\Microsoft Office\Office\Xlusrgal.xls

Macintosh chart type	File name and location
Built-in chart gallery	System Folder:Preferences:Excel Chart Gallery (8)
User-defined chart gallery	System Folder:Preferences:Excel Chart User Gallery

To create a unified look, you can build a gallery of custom chart types for your workgroup. For example, you can create a series of custom chart types with a consistent layout and color scheme, perhaps designed to be integrated into a PowerPoint presentation.

▶ **To distribute custom chart types**

- Copy the user-defined chart gallery file Xlusrgal.xls (Windows) or Excel Chart User Gallery (Macintosh) to each user's computer in the location shown in the following table.

Operating system	Folder name and location
Windows	Program Files\Microsoft Office\Office
Macintosh	System Folder:Preferences

Tip In Windows 95 and Windows NT Workstation 4.0, you can use a system policy to specify the path to a standard user-defined chart gallery on a network drive for all Microsoft Excel users in your workgroup. In the System Policy Editor, set the following policy:

User\Excel 97\Miscellaneous\Chart Gallery

For more information, see "Using Windows System Policies to Customize Office" in Chapter 7, "Customizing and Optimizing Microsoft Office."

Macros

Macros are stored in Visual Basic modules in workbooks. Unlike previous versions of Microsoft Excel, Visual Basic modules are not stored on a module or macro sheet. Instead, you view Visual Basic code with the **Visual Basic Editor** command (**Tools** menu, **Macro** submenu). You can distribute macros in the following ways:

- As workbooks

    You can store macros in a workbook. To make the macros available each time Microsoft Excel starts, store the workbook in the startup or alternate startup folder.

- As add-ins

    You can distribute the macros as a standalone, customized version of Microsoft Excel by saving a workbook as an add-in. To automatically open the add-in each time Microsoft Excel starts, store the add-in in the startup or alternate startup folder. For information about startup folders, see "Startup and Alternate Startup Folders," later in this chapter.

Security Settings

You can secure specific sheets or entire workbooks. To configure security settings, including passwords, point to **Protection** (**Tools** menu), and click a command. Security settings are stored in the workbook file. The only way to change them is to open the workbook, modify the security settings, then save the file.

At the sheet level, you can secure items as shown in the following table.

Securing this item	Protects it in this way
Sheet contents	Prevents editing or deleting cells on worksheets, as well as items in chart sheets
Sheet objects	Prevents moving, editing, resizing, or deleting graphic objects on worksheets and embedded charts
Scenarios	Prevents changing the definitions of scenarios

At the workbook level, you can secure items as shown in the following table.

Securing this item	Protects it in this way
Structure	Prevents deleting, moving, hiding, unhiding, renaming, or adding sheets to the workbook
Windows	Prevents moving, resizing, hiding, unhiding, or closing windows in the workbook

Tip   You can get finer levels of protection using Visual Basic properties such as **EnableAutoFilter**, **EnableOutlining**, **EnablePivotTable**, **EnableSelection**, **ScrollArea**, and **EnableResize**. For more information about these properties, see the *Microsoft Office 97/Visual Basic Programmer's Guide*, published by Microsoft Press and available wherever computer books are sold. For more information about Microsoft Press books, see Appendix E, "Other Support Resources."

For more information about security in Microsoft Excel, see "Security Features in Microsoft Excel" in Chapter 30, "Workgroup Features in Microsoft Excel."

Page Settings

Page settings for the layout of the workbook, such as page orientation, margins, and headers and footers, are based on the autotemplate. The page settings in the auto template are initially defined by Microsoft Excel; however, you can modify these settings in the workbook or save them in a template. Once a workbook is created, its page settings are saved in the workbook file; they are not automatically saved back to the template. You modify page settings with the **Page Setup** command (**File** menu).

Templates

A *template* is a special workbook used as a pattern to create new workbooks. Templates have the file extension .xlt (Windows) or the file type Microsoft Excel Document (Macintosh).

To maintain consistency among workbooks, you can create templates for a workgroup. For example, you can create a sales report workbook, save it as a template, and distribute it to a workgroup. When users in the workgroup create weekly sales reports based on the template, Microsoft Excel has a consistent set of menus, macros, and toolbars, and the workbooks have a consistent format.

Settings saved in a template determine the following characteristics of new workbooks based on that template:

- Cell formats
- Custom menus, macros, and toolbars
- Number and type of sheets in a workbook
- Page formats

- Row and column styles
- Text, dates, numbers, formulas, and graphics, such as a company name and logo

When you open a template, Microsoft Excel opens an untitled, unsaved copy of the template that contains all data, formatting, formulas, macros, styles, scenarios, and so forth that are contained in the template. The original template file remains unchanged.

Tip When you create a template linked to external data, Microsoft Excel asks if you want to remove the data before closing and refresh it automatically when the template is opened. Doing this reduces the file size of the template, and can provide additional data security if you require the user to enter a password in order to reconnect to the external data source.

▶ **To create a template**

1. Create a workbook that includes the text, formats, and formulas you want to have in the template.
2. On the **File** menu, click **Save As**.
3. In the **File name** box, enter a file name.
4. In the **Save in** box, select the folder in which to store the template.
5. In the **Save As Type** box, select **Template**.

Storing workbook templates in the startup or alternate startup folder automatically makes the template available when you click **New** (**File** menu). However, this slows the Microsoft Excel startup time. Alternatively, save templates in the Microsoft Office\Templates folder.

Note Although templates in the startup or alternate startup folder are automatically available for creating new workbooks, only the template with the reserved name Book.xlt (Windows) or Workbook (Macintosh) stored in the startup or alternate startup folder is an autotemplate. For more information about autotemplates, see "Autotemplates" later in this chapter.

How Are Word Templates and Microsoft Excel Templates Different?

Unlike Word, Microsoft Excel does not maintain an attachment between workbooks and the templates on which they are based. In both Word and Microsoft Excel, the template works like a read-only document, but in Word, when you create a document, it has at least one template attached to it, and potentially more. In Word, changing a template (redefining a style, for example) can affect all documents to which the template is attached. This is not true in Microsoft Excel. Once a workbook is created from a template, there is no persistent link between the two, and changing one does not affect the other.

Add-ins

You can save workbooks as add-ins. Add-ins compiled from Microsoft Excel workbooks have the file extension .xla (Windows) or the file type Microsoft Excel Document (Macintosh). Once created, add-ins are protected because they cannot be edited.

You can create add-ins to assemble and distribute custom features that, from the user's point of view, act as if they are built into Microsoft Excel. For information about creating, maintaining, and distributing add-ins, see the *Microsoft Office 97/Visual Basic Programmer's Guide*, published by Microsoft Press and available wherever computer books are sold. For more information about Microsoft Press books, see Appendix E, "Other Support Resources."

Note Add-ins can also be written in C. When compiled, these add-ins have the file extension .xll (Windows) or the file type Microsoft Excel Document (Macintosh).

Several add-ins are included with Microsoft Excel. Before you can use an add-in, you must install it by rerunning the Office Setup program, and then load it into Microsoft Excel by clicking the **Add-ins** command (**Tools** menu). The add-in's functionality is then available to all open workbooks and remains loaded in Microsoft Excel until you unload it through the **Add-ins** command (**Tools** menu). You can also load an add-in for just the current Microsoft Excel session by opening the add-in through the **Open** command (**File** menu).

If you choose a Typical installation during Setup, some add-ins are installed and loaded automatically, whereas others are installed only, and must be loaded in Microsoft Excel manually. For information about the components installed for each type of installation, see Appendix D, "List of Installed Components." Except where otherwise indicated, all add-ins are installed in the locations shown in the following table.

Operating system	Add-in location
Windows	Program Files\Microsoft Office\Office\Library
Macintosh	Microsoft Office:Office:Macro Library

The following table describes the add-ins included with Microsoft Excel. Some add-ins require a dynamic-link library (DLL) or compiled C add-in in addition to the add-in file, as indicated in the table.

Add-in	Windows file name	Macintosh file name	Description
Access Links Add-in	Acclink.xla	Not supported	Allows you to use Microsoft Access forms and reports with Microsoft Excel data tables.
Analysis ToolPak	Analys32.xll (Office\Library \Analysis folder)	Analysis ToolPak	Adds financial and engineering functions, and provides tools for performing statistical and engineering analysis.
Analysis ToolPak - VBA	Atpvbaen32.xla	Analysis ToolPak - VBA	Adds Visual Basic functions for the Analysis ToolPak.
AutoSave	Autosave.xla	Auto Save	Saves workbook files automatically.
Conditional Sum Wizard	Sumif.xla	Conditional Sum Wizard	Helps you create formulas to sum selected data in lists.
File Conversion Wizard	Fileconv.xls	File Conversion Wizard	Converts several spreadsheet files to Microsoft Excel format in one step.
Internet Assistant Wizard	Html.xla	Internet Assistant Wizard	Converts Microsoft Excel tables and charts to HTML files.
Lookup Wizard	Lookup.xla	Lookup Wizard	Finds values at the intersection of a row and column based on known values.
Microsoft Query	Xlquery.xla	Xlquery.xla	Retrieves data from external database files and tables using Query. (This add-in is used only when saving files in Microsoft Excel 97 and 5.0/95 format, or for backward compatibility for Visual Basic.)
ODBC	Xlodbc.xla Xlodbc32.dll Xlquery.xla (Office\Library \Msquery folder)	Xlodbc.xla Xlquery.xla (Microsoft Office: Macro Library folder)	Adds worksheet and macro functions for retrieving data from external sources with Microsoft ODBC. (This add-in is included in Microsoft Excel 97 only for backwards compatibility; for programmatic data access, use DAO.)
Report Manager	Reports.xla	Report Manager	Prints reports based on views and scenarios.
Solver Add-in	Solver.xla Solver32.dll Solvsamp.xls (Office\Library \Solver folder)	Solver Add-in (Macro Library: Solver folder)	Calculates solutions to what-if scenarios based on adjustable cells, constraint cells, or cells that must be maximized or minimized.

Add-in	Windows file name	Macintosh file name	Description
Template Utilities	Template Numbering.xls	Not yet available	Contains utilities used by Microsoft Excel templates.
Template Wizard with Data Tracking	Wztemplt.xla	Not yet available	Creates a template to export worksheet data to a database.
Update Add-in Links	Updtlink.xla	Update Add-in Links	Updates links in Microsoft Excel version 4.0 add-ins to directly use Microsoft Excel 97 functionality.
Web Form Wizard	Webform.xla	Web Form Wizard	Helps you create an HTML form based on a Microsoft Excel spreadsheet.

Note To use Query with Microsoft Excel, you must install the Query application, the Query add-in, the drivers for the types of data you want to retrieve, and the necessary ODBC files. To install these files, rerun Setup and click **Add/Remove**; then select the **Data Access** option. For information about using Query with Microsoft Excel, see Chapter 27, "Sharing Information with Microsoft Office Applications."

World Wide Web For the latest information about add-ins for Microsoft Excel for the Macintosh, connect to the Office Resource Kit home page at:

http://www.microsoft.com/office/ork/

How You Can Customize Microsoft Excel

Microsoft Excel default settings and paths are established when you run the Office Setup program. After Setup, you can customize these settings for a single user, a workgroup, or across an entire organization.

There are several ways to customize the Microsoft Excel application:

- Through the **Options** dialog box

    You can customize Microsoft Excel in the **Options** dialog box (**Tools** menu). The settings you make here are stored in the Windows registry.

- With the startup folder

    When Microsoft Excel starts, it opens all workbooks stored in the startup folder, or in the alternate startup folder as specified on the **General** tab in the **Options** dialog box (**Tools** menu).

- With autotemplates

    When Microsoft Excel starts, it opens a new workbook based on your autotemplate. You can specify the default font, formatting, and other options for new workbooks by creating a custom autotemplate.

- With workspace files

    If you want to open a group of workbooks in one step, you can create a workspace file. A workspace file contains information about which workbooks to open, their location, and the size and position of their windows on the screen.

- Through the **Customize** dialog box

    In the **Customize** dialog box (**View** menu, **Toolbars** submenu), you can customize the toolbars, menu bars, and shortcut menus included with Microsoft Excel, or you can create your own.

- With an add-in

    An add-in is a hidden, read-only workbook in which Visual Basic, XLM, or C code has been compiled from a source workbook. For more information about add-ins, see "Add-ins" earlier in this chapter.

These methods of customizing Microsoft Excel are described in the following sections. Some of these customizations are stored in the Windows registry, and some are stored in a separate file on the user's system.

User-Defined Options

The settings specified through the **Options** command (**Tools** menu) are saved to the Windows registry or to various settings files, which Microsoft Excel reads when it starts. When two or more users open a shared workbook on a network, Microsoft Excel applies the separate preferences to each user's view of the shared workbook. For information about Microsoft Excel entries in the Windows registry, see Appendix C, "Registry Keys and Values."

> **Tip** In Windows 95 and Windows NT Workstation 4.0, you can use a system policy to define most settings in the **Options** dialog box (**Tools** menu) for all Microsoft Excel users in your workgroup. In the System Policy Editor, set the following policy:
>
> **User\Excel 97\Tools_Options**

For more information, see "Using Windows System Policies to Customize Office" in Chapter 7, "Customizing and Optimizing Microsoft Office."

Startup and Alternate Startup Folders

When Microsoft Excel starts, it opens all workbooks, charts, and workspace files stored in the startup folder shown in the following table.

Operating system	Startup folder
Windows	Microsoft Office\Office\Xlstart
Macintosh	System Folder:Preferences:Excel Startup Folder (8)

When you click **New** (**File** menu), the workbook templates listed are those stored in the startup folder. If you want to open a workbook automatically when you start Microsoft Excel, move or copy the workbook to the startup folder. This strategy is especially useful if a workgroup is running Microsoft Excel from a shared network drive, and all users are sharing the same startup folder.

Tip A problem that arises in a workgroup using a common startup or alternate startup folder is for the first user to start Microsoft Excel and open the startup workbooks read-write. Subsequent users cannot open the startup documents read-write. Two solutions to this are to make the startup workbooks read-only, or to enable workbook sharing so multiple users can edit the startup workbooks simultaneously. For more information about shared workbooks, see "Shared Workbooks" in Chapter 30, "Workgroup Features in Microsoft Excel."

If you want to start Microsoft Excel with additional workbooks besides those in the startup folder, you can specify an alternate startup folder on the **General** tab in the **Options** dialog box (**Tools** menu). You might want to create an alternate startup folder if Microsoft Excel is installed on individual workstations with individual startup folders.

By specifying a single alternate startup folder on a shared network drive, you have a single folder for maintaining any workbooks, charts, or workspace files you want users to open when they start Microsoft Excel. Or individual users might have personal workbooks and templates they want opened automatically. These could go in the alternate startup folder on a local drive. Microsoft Excel always opens workbooks stored in both the startup and alternate startup folders—not one or the other.

Tip In Windows 95 and Windows NT Workstation 4.0, you can use a system policy to specify an **Alternate startup file location** in the **Options** dialog box (**Tools** menu) for all Microsoft Excel users in your workgroup. In the System Policy Editor, set the following policy:

User\Excel 97\Tools_Options\General\Alternate Startup Folder

For more information, see "Using Windows System Policies to Customize Office" in Chapter 7, "Customizing and Optimizing Microsoft Office."

Autotemplates

If you do not specify a startup workbook, Microsoft Excel opens a new, unsaved workbook when you start Microsoft Excel. This startup workbook is derived from the *autotemplate*, a template that opens automatically because it has a reserved file name, as shown in the following table, and is stored in the startup or alternate startup folder.

Operating system	Autotemplate reserved file name
Windows	Book.xlt
Macintosh	Workbook

You can specify the default font, formatting, and other options for new workbooks by creating a custom autotemplate. For example, you can create an autotemplate that includes customized headers and footers and your company name, or any text, formatting, formulas, and macros that you want to include automatically in new workbooks.

Note Before you customize the autotemplate, it is a good idea to make a backup copy of the original file.

▶ **To create an autotemplate**

1. Create or open the workbook you want to use as the autotemplate.
2. On the **File** menu click **Save As**.
3. In the **Save As Type** box, select **Template**.
4. In the **File name** box, enter **Book.xlt** (Windows) or **Workbook** (Macintosh).
5. In the **Save in** box, select your startup or alternate startup folder.

Workspace Files

If you want to be able to open a group of workbooks in one step, you can create a workspace file. A workspace file contains information about which workbooks to open, their location, and the size and position of their windows on the screen. (The workspace file does not contain the workbooks themselves.)

▶ **To create a workspace file**

1. Open all the workbooks you want to include in the workspace.

   If you plan to distribute the workspace file to other users, make sure that all workbooks referenced by the workspace file are on a shared network drive.

2. Size and position the workbooks as you want them to appear.
3. On the **File** menu click **Save Workspace**.

   The default name Microsoft Excel gives to the workspace file is Resume.xlw (Windows) or Resume (Macintosh). You can rename the file if you want.

If you want the workspace file to open automatically each time users start Microsoft Excel, copy the file to the users' startup or alternate startup folder.

Important The workbook names and folder locations are saved in the workspace file. If the files are moved to another location, Microsoft Excel cannot find them. The best strategy is to save the workspace file and the workbook files it references in the same folder if possible.

Custom Toolbar Settings and Lists

By customizing toolbars and lists, you can change Microsoft Excel to better suit the needs of your workgroup. For example, you can add frequently used commands and dialog box options to toolbars, and remove items users rarely use. You can also customize lists so that users can sort data in a certain order or quickly fill in a series of cells in a particular way.

You can create and maintain lists for custom fill series or sorting order on the **Custom Lists** tab of the **Options** dialog box (**Tools** menu). You can customize toolbars in the following ways:

- By pointing to **Toolbars** (**View** menu) and clicking **Customize**
- By creating a Visual Basic module

When you modify toolbars or create custom lists through the Microsoft Excel user interface, these settings are stored in the file Windows*username*8.xlb where *username* is the user's Windows logon name. Toolbars attached to Visual Basic modules, however, are stored in the workbook file. You can distribute a common set of custom toolbars and custom lists to your workgroup to accomplish specific tasks.

▶ **To share custom toolbars within a workgroup**

1 Create the custom toolbars in a workbook.

2 Save the workbook on a shared network drive.

3 Instruct users to open the file.

   The toolbar settings attached to the workbook are saved to each user's *username*8.xlb file.

Tip In Windows 95 and Windows NT Workstation 4.0, you can use a system policy to specify the path to the custom toolbar settings file on a network drive for all Microsoft Excel users in your workgroup. In the System Policy Editor, set the following policy:

User\Excel 97\Miscellaneous\Personal Toolbars

For more information, see "Using Windows System Policies to Customize Office" in Chapter 7, "Customizing and Optimizing Microsoft Office."

The custom toolbar and lists persist on the user's computer after the user closes or even deletes the workbook. To delete a custom list, you must go to the **Custom Lists** tab in the **Options** dialog box (**Tools** menu).

Tip You can also use Visual Basic code to customize toolbars and menus with the CommandBar object model. For more information about customizing with Visual Basic, see the *Microsoft Office 97/Visual Basic Programmer's Guide*, published by Microsoft Press and available wherever computer books are sold.

How Microsoft Excel Resolves Conflicts

Conflicts can arise in Microsoft Excel when files of the same name reside in the startup and alternate startup folders, or when the user interface has been customized through Visual Basic code.

Startup and Alternate Startup Folders

Microsoft Excel opens files in the startup folder before opening files in the alternate startup folder. If there is a file in the alternate startup folder with a name that matches a file in the startup folder, the file in the alternate startup folder is ignored.

Custom Toolbars

When you open a workbook that has a toolbar attached, the attached toolbar definitions are saved to your custom toolbar file. These definitions persist on your computer after you close or delete the workbook. If custom macros are attached to the toolbar and you try to run a macro from the toolbar after closing or deleting the original workbook, Microsoft Excel displays a message stating that it cannot find the macro. This is because the macro resides in the workbook where the toolbar originated.

If you customize the toolbar, your changes do not affect the original toolbar stored in the original workbook. When you reopen the original workbook, Microsoft Excel uses the copy of the toolbar stored in your custom toolbar file rather than reloading the toolbar stored in the workbook. To generate the original version of the toolbar, delete the customized copy. To do this point to **Toolbars** (**View** menu), click **Customize**, and then select the toolbar and click **Delete**.

Custom Add-ins

If an add-in's source workbook contains a reference to another add-in, make sure that when you distribute the add-in, the referenced add-in is stored on the user's computer where the calling add-in can find it. The best strategy is to always store a referenced add-in in the folder that contains the calling add-in. When you compile a source workbook as an add-in, Microsoft Excel stores a path to the referenced add-in in the calling add-in. If you move the calling add-in to another computer (for example, when you distribute the add-in to other users) and Microsoft Excel cannot find the file in the path, it searches the locations in the following list.

Microsoft Excel for Windows searches the following locations, in this order:

1. Windows\System folder
2. Windows folder
3. The folder that contains the calling add-in
4. The path defined by the Path environment setting (to see the path, type **set** at the command prompt)

For information about creating, maintaining, and distributing add-ins, see the *Microsoft Office 97/Visual Basic Programmer's Guide*, published by Microsoft Press and available wherever computer books are sold.

CHAPTER 37

Microsoft Outlook Architecture

This chapter describes the structure of Microsoft Outlook. It explains how the various components of Outlook work together, and how the application handles changes that users make to those components. An understanding of the architecture of Outlook can help you take advantage of its features and may help you troubleshoot problems.

In This Chapter
How Outlook Is Structured   959
How You Can Customize Outlook   965

See Also
- For a summary of the features in Outlook 97, see Chapter 2, "What's New in Microsoft Office 97."
- For information about installing Outlook or other Office applications, see Chapter 4, "Installing Microsoft Office."

Note   Outlook runs on Windows 95 and Windows NT Workstation version 3.51 or later only.

How Outlook Is Structured

Microsoft Outlook combines information management, electronic mail, and personal and group calendar functions into one application. The building blocks of Outlook are:

- Items

  Outlook categorizes information as one of several *items*. Each item, in turn, consists of a number of *properties*. For example, an e-mail message item consists of properties such as subject, text, and date received.

- Folders

    Outlook stores items in folders, with each folder containing items of a particular type. These item types include Outlook-specific items, such as Journal items, as well as files stored on your computer or on the network.

- Views

    Outlook organizes and displays items in a folder using *views*. Any view can be used with any type of folder, and users can also customize and save views for later use.

The following illustration shows how Outlook components fit together.

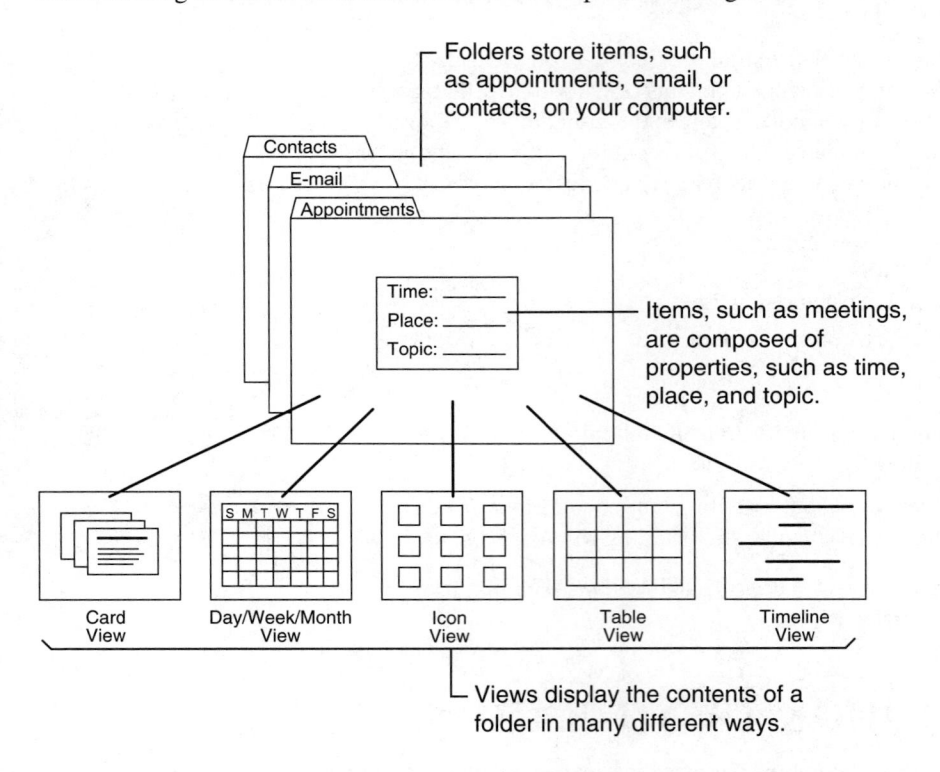

Folders store items, such as appointments, e-mail, or contacts, on your computer.

Items, such as meetings, are composed of properties, such as time, place, and topic.

Card View • Day/Week/Month View • Icon View • Table View • Timeline View

Views display the contents of a folder in many different ways.

As a messaging application, Outlook complies with MAPI, which defines a standard interface between messaging servers and clients. A MAPI *profile* on a your computer defines the MAPI messaging servers, personal folders, and address books that are available to all MAPI applications on that computer. Outlook can connect to any messaging system, folder, and e-mail address book defined in the profile. Outlook even stores nonmail items in the folders defined in the profile.

Outlook can send and receive messages using any e-mail information service defined in the profile, including Microsoft Exchange Server, Microsoft Fax, The MSN online service, and other e-mail applications.

The Outlook Address Book is added to the profile when Outlook is installed. Items in the Outlook Contacts folder that have e-mail address information are automatically added to the Outlook Address Book. Once defined in the profile, the Outlook Address Book is available to all MAPI applications as another address book. For example, a Microsoft Word user can include addresses from the Outlook Address Book when using the Word **Mail Merge** command (**Tools** menu).

Items

Outlook recognizes six Outlook-specific item types, as shown in the following table.

This Outlook item type	Contains this kind of information
Appointment	Appointments, meetings, and events; may be recurring or nonrecurring
Contact	Names, street addresses, e-mail addresses, URLs, phone numbers, FAX numbers, and so forth
Journal	Log of phone calls, e-mail, and so on, with associated date and time information
Mail	E-mail messages
Note	Miscellaneous text
Task	To-do items, including information such as owner, due date, priority, and status

Note Outlook also recognizes files. You can use Outlook to display folders on your hard disk, floppy disks, and network drives.

You can save Outlook items as plain text, as rich text, as Outlook items, or as an Outlook template.

▶ **To save Outlook items**

1. On the **File** menu, click **Save As**.
2. In the **Save in** box, select the folder in which you want to save the file, and type the file name in the **File name** box.

   You must save Outlook template files in the Program Files\Microsoft Office\Templates\Outlook folder. This folder is selected by default if you specify the **Outlook Template** file type in Step 3.

3. Select a file type in the **Save as type** box, and then click **Save**.

When you save Outlook items, choose from the following file types in the **Save as type** box:

- **Text Only**

  Saves only the text of the item. The file can be opened by any text editor, such as Notepad.

- **RTF Text Format**

  Saves the text and formatting in Rich Text Format (RTF), but does not save attachments or embedded objects. The file can be opened by Word or any application that can read RTF format.

- **Message Format**

  Saves the item in Outlook format. The file can be opened by Outlook only, unless the item is an e-mail message.

  Note If the item you save in message format is an e-mail message, the file can be opened by Microsoft Exchange Client. However, if the e-mail message is an Outlook custom form, it is not displayed properly by Microsoft Exchange Client.

- **Outlook Template**

  Saves the item as an Outlook template. You can use this template later to create items of the same type by selecting it with the **Choose Template** command (**Compose** menu).

Folders

Outlook defines special-purpose folders for containing various Outlook item types. Each folder contains one type of item, as shown in the following table.

This Outlook folder	Contains this item type
Calendar	Appointment
Contacts	Contact
Inbox	Mail
Journal	Journal
Notes	Note
Outbox	Mail
Sent Items	Mail
Tasks	Task

Note Outlook uses these folders by default for the corresponding item types listed in the preceding table. However, you can also create additional folders for any of these item types.

Because Outlook performs most of the functions of Explorer in Windows 95 and Windows NT Workstation version 4.0, Outlook can also view folders on your computer and on the network, as well as use additional views to display folder contents.

When connected to Microsoft Exchange Server, an Outlook user can gain access to Microsoft Exchange Server public folders. Public folders are treated fundamentally the same as local folders and they appear in the same folder list as other Outlook folders. There are some unique features of public folders, however, that distinguish them from other Outlook folders:

- You can create a shortcut to a public folder in the Favorites folder under Public Folders.

    This shortcut does not include any subfolders the public folder might contain.

- The folder creator can set specific user access privileges on public folders.

    For example, the folder creator can allow a user to read items in the folder, to post items to the folder, and to modify items the user posts without being able to modify other items in the folder.

- The folder creator can define specific forms to be used with the folder.
- The folder creator can define rules that are applied to items posted in the folder.

    These rules can initiate tasks, such as replying or forwarding automatically, based on certain criteria defined for the item.

For more information about public folders, see your Microsoft Exchange Server documentation.

Views

To display the contents of folders, Outlook provides several types of views. Any of these views can be used with any Outlook folder, providing a great deal of flexibility in displaying folder contents.

This Outlook view type	Contains items in this format
Card	Individual cards, as in a card file
Day/Week/Month	Items arranged as on a calendar, by the day, week, or month
Icon	Items and files represented by individual icons
Table	Grid of rows and columns
Timeline	Horizontal bars indicating chronology and duration

Note The view types in the preceding table are associated with default Outlook folders. For example, mail items appear by default in the Inbox folder in table view. However, you can use any view type with any Outlook folder—for example, you can view mail items in timeline view. You can also use Outlook views with folders on your computer or on the network.

As an example of the flexibility afforded with Outlook views, this section includes illustrations that show the same task data displayed in three different views.

The following illustration shows task data in table view.

Tasks that have not been completed are displayed with regular text.

		Subject	Status	Due Date	% Complete	Categories
		Click here to add a new Task				
✓	✓	~~Outline tools research report~~	~~Completed~~	~~Mon 2/3/97~~	~~100%~~	~~Business~~
✓	✓	~~Draft tools research report~~	~~Completed~~	~~Mon 2/10/97~~	~~100%~~	~~Business~~
✓		Distribute tools research report	Not Started	Fri 2/21/97	0%	Business
✓		Discuss proposal with Yoshi	Not Started	Thu 2/6/97	0%	Business
✓	✓	~~Prepare for annual budget meeting~~	~~Completed~~	~~Wed 2/19/97~~	~~100%~~	~~Business~~
✓	✓	~~Update customer database~~	~~Completed~~	~~Fri 3/28/97~~	~~100%~~	~~Business~~
✓		Review new company handbook	Not Started	None	0%	Business
✓		Plan sales meeting	Not Started	Thu 2/27/97	0%	Business
✓		Call Jean about schedule	Not Started	Wed 2/5/97	0%	Business
✓		Organize files	Not Started	None	0%	Business
✓	✓	~~Write status report~~	~~Completed~~	~~Tue 2/7/97~~	~~100%~~	~~Business~~
✓	✓	~~Write status report~~	~~Completed~~	~~Fri 2/14/97~~	~~100%~~	~~Business~~
✓		Compile meeting notes	Not Started	Tue 2/11/97	0%	Business
✓		Invite Paolo to lunch	Not Started	Mon 2/10/97	0%	Personal
✓		Make dentist appointment	Not Started	Tue 2/4/97	0%	Personal

Completed tasks receive a check mark and are crossed out.

The following illustration shows the same task data in month view.

Team Tasks — February 1997

Mon	Tue	Wed	Thu	Fri	Sat/Sun
January 27	28	29	30	31	February 1 / Get haircut / 2
3 / Outline tools re	4 / Make dentist a	5 / Call Jean about	6 / Discuss propos	7	8 / Buy birthday / 9
10 / Draft tools res / Invite Paolo to	11 / Compile meetir	12	13	14 / Write status re	15 / 16
17	18	19 / Prepare for an	20	21 / Distribute tools	22 / 23
24	25	26	27 / Plan sales mee	28	March 1 / Get haircut / 2

Tasks appear on the calendar on the day they are due.

If there are more tasks than can be displayed, click this icon to open a weekly view.

The following illustration shows the same task data in timeline view.

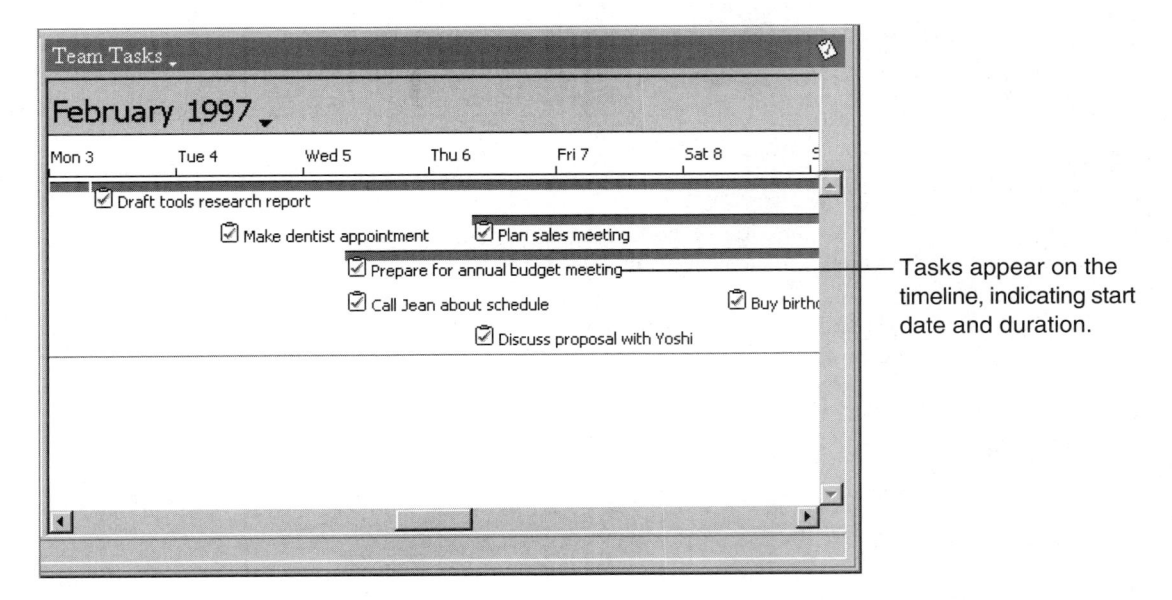

Tasks appear on the timeline, indicating start date and duration.

You can customize each view to display information in a way that best suits your needs. For example, in table view, you can change which items to display in columns, how items are sorted, and whether items are grouped.

When you modify a view, you can save the custom view for the current folder only, or you can save the custom view so that all folders of a single type use your custom view. If you customize a view in a public folder, then you can make that view available to all users of that public folder.

How You Can Customize Outlook

Outlook default settings and paths are established when you run the Office Setup program. After Setup, you can customize these settings for a single user, for a workgroup, or across an entire organization.

There are several ways to customize Outlook:

- Through the **Options** dialog box

    You can customize Outlook in the **Options** dialog box (**Tools** menu). The settings you make here are stored in the Windows registry.

> **Tip** In Windows 95 and Windows NT Workstation 4.0, you can use a system policy to define most settings in the **Options** dialog box (**Tools** menu) for all Outlook users in your workgroup. In the System Policy Editor, set the following policy:
>
> **User\Outlook 97\Tools_Options**
>
> For more information, see "Using Windows System Policies to Customize Office" in Chapter 7, "Customizing and Optimizing Microsoft Office."

- By customizing Outlook views

    You can create custom views for single folders or for all folders of a particular type. Custom views created for a single folder are stored in that folder. Custom views for all folders of a particular type are stored in a hidden folder in the set of personal folders that contains your Inbox. If you create custom views for a public folder, the custom views are stored in the public folder.

▶ **To create a custom view**

1. On the **View** menu, click **Define Views**.
2. To create a new custom view, click **New** and fill out the **Create a New View** dialog box, and then click **OK**.

    –or–

    To customize an existing view, select the view and then click **Modify**.
3. In the **View Summary** dialog box, select the options you want to use, and then click **OK**.

CHAPTER 38

Microsoft PowerPoint Architecture

This chapter describes the structure of Microsoft PowerPoint 97. It explains how the various components of PowerPoint work together, and how the application handles changes that users make to those components. An understanding of the architecture of PowerPoint can help you take advantage of its features and may help you troubleshoot problems.

In This Chapter

How PowerPoint Is Structured   967
How You Can Customize PowerPoint   977
How PowerPoint Resolves Conflicts   989

See Also
- For information about installing PowerPoint or other Office applications, see Chapter 4, "Installing Microsoft Office."
- For information about customizing PowerPoint to meet the specific needs of your workgroup, see Chapter 7, "Customizing and Optimizing Microsoft Office."

How PowerPoint Is Structured

In a PowerPoint presentation, the primary unit for storing objects is the slide. Each slide contains one or more objects, such as title text, a bulleted list, drawing, picture, or chart. Each object on a slide can have associated formatting, such as font settings, color, and animation effects. A presentation consists of a collection of slides.

To give presentations a consistent appearance, PowerPoint uses *masters* and *AutoLayouts*. Masters determine the graphics, layout, and formatting for all the slides in a given presentation. AutoLayouts insert specific content at predefined placeholders on a slide—for example, the title and subtitle on a title slide, or the title and bulleted list on a bulleted list slide. Because AutoLayouts are part of the PowerPoint user interface, you cannot create or modify them. However, you can modify content on slides created from AutoLayouts or change the layout of a slide by modifying the master.

To automate the process of creating a presentation, PowerPoint uses *templates*, which are predefined sets of masters and color schemes. All templates contain a color scheme and a slide master. However, templates can also contain text, clip art, charts, drawings, and other elements. PowerPoint comes with several sample templates. You can also create your own templates or save any presentation as a template.

The following illustration shows how PowerPoint components fit together to create a presentation.

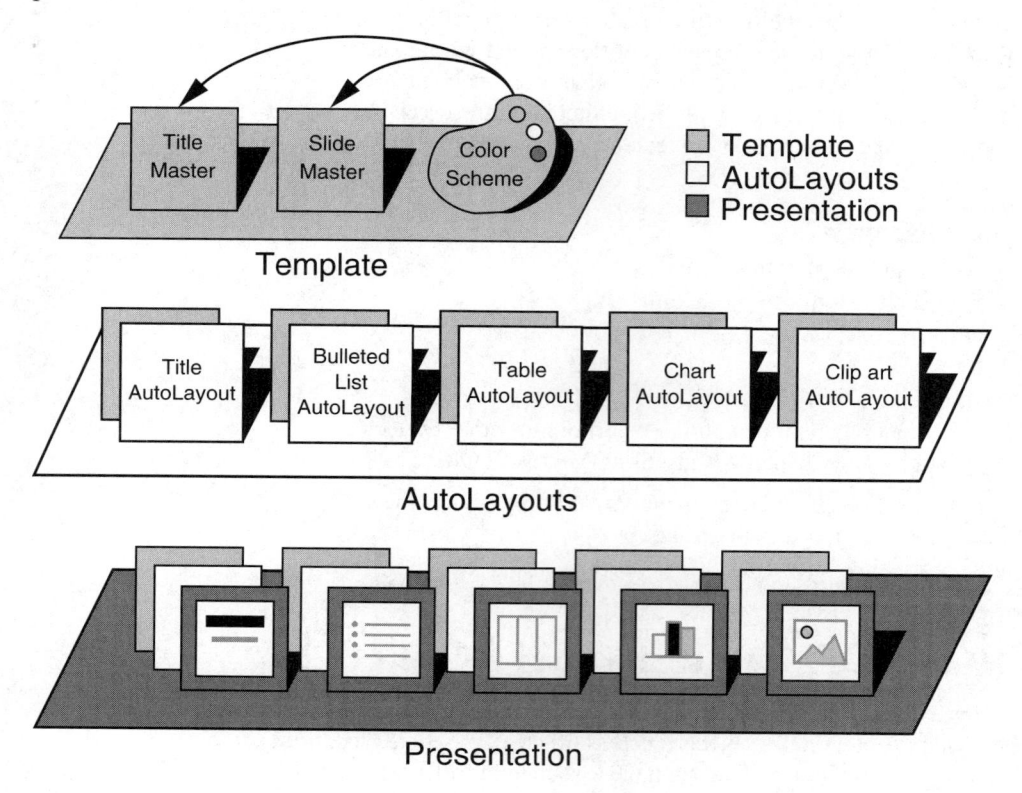

Presentations

A PowerPoint presentation is a collection of slides that share a template and settings for page size and orientation. The presentation file also stores formatting for speaker notes, audience handouts, and color schemes.

Presentations can have two different page-orientation settings: one for slides and another for notes, handouts, and outline pages. These settings apply to all the slides and to all the notes, handouts, and outline pages in a presentation, respectively. For example, a presentation may have all slides in landscape orientation and all notes in portrait orientation.

PowerPoint presentations are stored in a proprietary file format. You can save presentations in other native file formats, too, as shown in the following table.

Save presentations in this file format	When you want to do this
Presentation	Save the file in a format you can open and edit again in PowerPoint 97.
Windows metafile	Use slides as graphics in documents you create with applications other than PowerPoint.
Outline or Rich Text Format	Export the text of the presentation to applications other than PowerPoint.
Content templates	Use the presentation as a template for creating other presentations.
Slide show format	Display the presentation file as a slide show.
PowerPoint add-in	Store only the presentation's Visual Basic for Applications code. For more information about add-ins, see "Add-ins" later in this chapter
PowerPoint 95	Share the presentation with PowerPoint 95 users.
PowerPoint 95 & 97	Share the presentation with PowerPoint 95 users and still maintain a version with all the PowerPoint 97 features.
PowerPoint version 4.0	Share the presentation with PowerPoint 4.0 users.
PowerPoint version 3.0	Share the presentation with PowerPoint 3.0 users.
HTML	Save the presentation as a World Wide Web document.

Note To save presentations as HTML documents, use the **Save as HTML** command (**File** menu) instead of the **Save As** command.

In addition to the native file formats PowerPoint supports, you can install export graphics filters and export modules to save presentations in custom formats. For information about custom export formats, see "Custom Export Formats" later in this chapter. For more information about exporting presentations, see Chapter 20, "Switching to Microsoft PowerPoint."

Slides

Each slide in a PowerPoint presentation stores its own data, including text, drawings, and other objects. Slides also store text in speaker notes, which are visible only in notes page view.

When a new slide is added to a presentation, the appropriate AutoLayout applies the active master and color scheme settings to each object. After the slide is created, however, you can modify objects without affecting other slides in the presentation and without affecting the template, color scheme, or master.

Note Any object listed in the **Insert Object** dialog box (**Insert** menu) can be added to a slide. Double-clicking an object inserted this way opens the appropriate application for editing the object.

Some of the objects stored on slides can also be placed on speaker notes or audience handouts. Most objects can be placed on slides by using the AutoLayout that contains a placeholder for that object. The following sections describe the categories of objects that PowerPoint stores on slides.

Charts

When you insert a chart, PowerPoint runs Microsoft Graph 97. PowerPoint can also copy or import a chart from Microsoft Excel. Data in the chart is stored differently depending on how the chart is inserted onto the slide, as shown in the following table.

If the chart is inserted in this way	Chart data is stored in this location
Created with Microsoft Graph 97 from within PowerPoint	Data is stored on the current slide.
Copied from Microsoft Excel and embedded on the slide	Data is stored on the current slide.
Copied from Microsoft Excel and then linked to the slide	Data is stored in the source Microsoft Excel workbook with a link to the current slide. Changes to Microsoft Excel data are reflected automatically on the slide.
Copied from Microsoft Excel and pasted as a graphic	Data is stored in the source Microsoft Excel workbook with no link to the current slide. The chart on the PowerPoint slide is a static graphic.

Clip Art

Clip art images are installed in the Program Files\Microsoft Office\Clipart folder during Setup. When you insert clip art in a presentation, PowerPoint runs the Microsoft Clip Gallery. You can also add new graphics files to the Clip Gallery. For information about how to add images to the Clip Gallery, see PowerPoint online Help.

Drawings

In PowerPoint 97, you create drawings with Office Art, the drawing layer shared by all the Office applications. Office Art provides graphic effects such as shadows, fills, and 3-D effects. Drawings include AutoShapes, lines, arrows, rectangles, ellipses, WordArt, and text boxes. Unlike text objects that are placed by AutoLayouts, the formatting of text created with Office Art is not constrained by the masters.

> **Did You Know?**
> PowerPoint uses *twips* as its unit of measurement when drawing graphics. A twip is one-twentieth of a point. When a two-point line on a Microsoft Excel chart is pasted as a graphic in PowerPoint, for example, the weight of the line is 40 twips.

Movies

Movies are video clips stored in AVI (Windows) or QuickTime (Macintosh) format, or in a proprietary format if a media control interface driver is installed. To insert a movie onto a slide, use commands on the **Movies and Sounds** submenu or the **Object** command (**Insert** menu). Movie characteristics are described in the following table.

Movies inserted with this	Have these characteristics
Movies and Sounds submenu commands (**Insert** menu)	PowerPoint handles the movie as a native object and plays it directly, allowing limited editing through play options and animation settings. The movie is linked to, rather than embedded in, the slide.
Object command (**Insert** menu)	The movie is a Media Player object. Double-clicking the movie runs Media Player, where you can edit the movie. Movies can be linked or embedded in a slide.

Note Windows users can play QuickTime movies in PowerPoint if they have a QuickTime driver installed.

When you insert movies with commands on the **Movies and Sounds** submenu (**Insert** menu), you can retrieve the movie clip from the Clip Gallery or from a movie file. You can add any movie file to the Clip Gallery. For information about how to add movies to the Clip Gallery, see PowerPoint online Help.

Tip In Windows 95 and Windows NT Workstation 4.0, you can use a system policy to define the default location of video files listed in the **Insert Movie** dialog box for all PowerPoint users in your workgroup. (To display the **Insert Movie** dialog box, click **Movies and Sounds** on the **Insert** menu, and then click **Movie from File**.) In the System Policy Editor, set the following policy:

User\PowerPoint 97\Miscellaneous\Multimedia Directory

For more information, see "Using Windows System Policies to Customize Office" in Chapter 7, "Customizing and Optimizing Microsoft Office."

Pictures

Pictures are image files stored in formats such as JPEG, GIF, and BMP. PowerPoint includes graphics filters for importing image files. These graphics filters are installed during Setup in the Grphflt (Windows) or Graphics Filters (Macintosh) folder.

When you insert pictures with commands on the **Picture** submenu (**Insert** menu), you can retrieve the picture from the Clip Gallery or from a file. You can add any picture to the Clip Gallery. For information about how to add pictures to the Clip Gallery, see PowerPoint online Help.

> **Tip** In Windows 95 and Windows NT Workstation version 4.0, you can use a system policy to define the default location of picture files shown in the **Insert Picture** dialog box for all PowerPoint users in your workgroup. To display the **Insert Picture** dialog box, click **Picture** on the **Insert** menu, and click **From File**. In the Windows System Policy Editor, set the following policy:
>
> **User\PowerPoint 97\Miscellaneous\Picture Directory**
>
> For more information, see "Using Windows System Policies to Customize Office" in Chapter 7, "Customizing and Optimizing Microsoft Office."

Sounds

Sounds are files stored in formats such as WAV and MIDI (Windows) and QuickTime (Macintosh). To insert a sound onto a slide, use commands on the **Movies and Sounds** submenu or the **Object** command (**Insert** menu). Sound characteristics are described in the following table.

Sounds inserted with this	Have these characteristics
Movies and Sounds submenu commands (**Insert** menu)	PowerPoint handles the sound as a native object and plays it directly, allowing limited editing through play options and animation settings. Sound files less than 100K are automatically embedded on the slide; files 100K or larger are linked. Sounds attached to animation effects are embedded regardless of file size.
Object command (**Insert** menu)	A MID file is a Media Player object; a WAV file is a Sound Recorder object. Double-clicking the sound runs Media Player or Sound Recorder, where you can edit the sound. You can link or embed sounds in a slide.

When you insert sounds with commands on the **Movies and Sounds** submenu (**Insert** menu), you can retrieve the sound clip from the Clip Gallery or from a sound file. You can add any sound file to the Clip Gallery. For information about how to add sounds to the Clip Gallery, see PowerPoint online Help.

> **Tip** In Windows 95 and Windows NT Workstation 4.0, you can use a system policy to define the default location of sound files shown in the **Insert Sound** dialog box for all PowerPoint users in your workgroup. (To display the **Insert Sound** dialog box, click **Movies and Sounds** on the **Insert** menu, and click **Sound from File**.) In the System Policy Editor, set the following policy:
>
> **User\PowerPoint 97\Miscellaneous\Multimedia Directory**
>
> For more information, see "Using Windows System Policies to Customize Office" in Chapter 7, "Customizing and Optimizing Microsoft Office."

Text Objects

Text objects use the formatting determined by the master. Text objects can be placed on slides, audience handouts, or speaker notes, as described in the following table.

This text object	Can be placed on these presentation elements
Body text on a note	Notes
Body text on a slide (usually a bulleted list)	Slide
Current date	Slide, handouts, or notes
Footer	Slide, handouts, or notes
Header	Handouts or notes
Page number	Handouts or notes
Slide number	Slide
Subtitle	Slide
Title	Slide

Word Tables

When you insert a Microsoft Word table onto a slide, PowerPoint runs Word, and Word inserts the table on the slide. You can use Word commands to format the table. Word must be installed for you to use this feature.

Slide Masters and Title Masters

Masters determine placement and formatting of text objects, background objects, and background animation effects for every slide in a presentation. When a new slide is added to the presentation, the master elements are copied to the new slide. The placement and formatting of text objects can be changed on individual slides without affecting the master, but to modify background objects and background animation, you must edit the master, which affects all slides in a presentation. To return a modified slide's text objects to the master attributes, select the slide's current AutoLayout in the **Slide Layout** dialog box (**Format** menu), and then click **Reapply**.

PowerPoint presentations can have two masters: the slide master and the title master. All presentations have a slide master, but not necessarily a title master. If a presentation has no title master, you can create one by clicking **New Title Master** (**Insert** menu) in slide master view. The attributes of the new title master are based on those of the slide master.

Either the slide master or the title master is applied to a new slide, depending on the AutoLayout chosen for that slide. With the title slide AutoLayout, the new slide takes on the attributes of the title master. With any other AutoLayout, the new slide takes on the attributes of the slide master. Changes made to the title master affect only slides created from the title slide AutoLayout, and changes made to the slide master affect slides created from all other AutoLayouts.

The following sections describe slide characteristics that are determined by the slide or title master.

Layout

Masters control the position of placeholders for title, text, date, slide number, and footer. By default, all of these elements are included on the master. You may delete any of these elements from the master in master view. Deleted elements can be reinserted by selecting them in the **Master Layout** dialog box (**Format** menu). You can also change the size and position of these elements by modifying them in master view.

Text Styles

You can define the text style for titles, body text, subtitles, date, headers and footers, and slide numbers. Text styles defined on the title master are separate from text styles defined on the slide master, as shown in the following table.

On this master	You can define these text elements
Title	Title, subtitle, title slide date, title slide footer, slide number of title slide
Slide	Slide title, body text, slide date, slide footer, slide number of slide

You can also change an individual slide's text styles by modifying them in slide view.

Backgrounds

Objects that appear on a master provide a background for every slide in a presentation. However, you can change the background of an individual slide. To modify the background fill or hide background objects on an individual slide, select the **Omit background graphics from master** option in the **Background** dialog box (**Format** menu).

Animation Effects

Animation effects applied to objects on a master become part of the background of every slide in the presentation. You can apply additional effects to objects on a slide in slide view, but to edit animation effects on a master, you must go to slide master or title master view. During the slide show, animation on the background is executed before animation on an individual slide.

Handout and Notes Masters

In addition to masters for slides, you can define masters for audience handouts, printed outlines, and speaker notes. These masters control the placement and style of headers, footers, dates, and page numbers. Handout masters and notes masters are stored with the presentation file.

Handout masters allow you to print two, three, or six slides per page. To print handouts, click one of the **Handouts** options in the **Print what** box in the **Print** dialog box (**File** menu). Handout masters also determine the format of printed outlines.

Notes masters place the image of one slide, along with notes relevant to that slide, on each notes page. Besides defining placement and style of headers, footers, dates, and page numbers, notes masters also allow you to choose a format for note text. You can print speaker notes directly from PowerPoint or export them to Word for more formatting options. For information about exporting speaker notes to Word, see "Sharing Information with PowerPoint 97" in Chapter 27, "Sharing Information with Microsoft Office Applications."

Templates

By using a single template for all your presentations, you can quickly create standard presentations with consistent formatting, graphic elements, text, and color schemes. The file format of templates and presentations is the same, but templates are designated by the file extension .pot.

PowerPoint supports two kinds of templates: design templates and content templates. *Design templates* contain a slide master and a color scheme. The design templates that come with PowerPoint also include title masters, and may have more than one color scheme. They are installed in the Presentation Designs folder, and appear on the **Presentation Designs** tab in the **New Presentation** dialog box (**File** menu). When you select a new template for an existing presentation, the **Apply Design** dialog box (**Format** menu) displays the templates stored in the Presentation Designs folder.

Tip In Windows 95 and Windows NT Workstation 4.0, you can use a system policy to define the default location of templates shown in the **Apply Design** dialog box (**Format** menu) for all PowerPoint users in your workgroup. In the System Policy Editor, set the following policy:

User\PowerPoint 97\Miscellaneous\Template Directory

For more information, see "Using Windows System Policies to Customize Office" in Chapter 7, "Customizing and Optimizing Microsoft Office."

Note The Blank Presentation design template, which is the default template for creating new presentations, differs from other PowerPoint design templates; it contains a slide master but no title master.

> ### My custom design templates have no title master
> If you create a custom design template by opening any design template except Blank Presentation, the template includes a slide master and a title master. However, if you create a new design template based on the Blank Presentation template, it includes only a slide master. You can create a title master by clicking **New Title Master** (**Insert** menu) in slide master view. The new title master has the same attributes as the existing slide master.

In addition to color schemes and masters, *content templates* may include a set of slides, each with its own text, graphics, sound clips, charts, organization charts, or other content. These templates can stand alone as presentations, or you can use them to create new presentations. Basing a new presentation on a template that includes slides is similar to opening an existing presentation and saving it with a new name. The new presentation has all the attributes and content of the template.

PowerPoint includes several content templates that are installed during Setup in the Presentations folder. The templates appear on the **Presentations** tab in the **New Presentation** dialog box (**File** menu) or you can choose among them when you run the AutoContent Wizard. For information about the AutoContent Wizard, see "Customizing Templates Used by the AutoContent Wizard" later in this chapter.

A PowerPoint *color scheme* is a set of eight colors used for all the elements on a slide. Design templates include one or more color schemes. Whenever you add objects to a slide, PowerPoint uses the active color scheme to assign colors to the new object. You can choose a different color for the active object, choose a different color scheme for the active slide, change the color scheme for the entire presentation, or create your own color scheme.

Note If you change an element on the slide to a color that is not in the color scheme, and then apply a new color scheme to the slide, the element retains the customized color.

Color schemes apply to speaker notes and audience handouts, as well as to slides. When you modify or create color schemes for notes and handouts, these changes do not affect color schemes for slides. However, when you delete color schemes for notes and handouts, the color schemes are deleted from the presentation file, and are not available for slides.

Color schemes are stored in the presentation file. You can modify or delete existing color schemes or add new color schemes to a presentation without affecting the template on which the presentation is based.

How You Can Customize PowerPoint

PowerPoint default settings and paths are established when you run the Office Setup program. After Setup, you can customize these settings for a single user, a workgroup, or across an entire organization.

There are several ways to customize PowerPoint:

- Through the **Options** dialog box

    You can customize PowerPoint in the **Options** dialog box (**Tools** menu). The settings you select here are stored in the Windows registry.

- With a macro

    A macro, which is written in Visual Basic code, automates one or more tasks.

- With an add-in

    An add-in enhances PowerPoint with new custom features. Add-ins are dynamic-link libraries (DLLs) or Visual Basic code compiled from a source presentation.

- With a custom template

    A custom template can include color schemes and text that helps users create presentations that have a unified look across your organization.

- Through the **Customize** dialog box

    In the **Customize** dialog box (**View** menu, **Toolbars** submenu), you can customize the toolbars, menu bars, and shortcut menus included with PowerPoint, or you can create your own.

- With custom export formats

    You can install your own graphics filters or export modules to export PowerPoint files in formats not supported by PowerPoint.

- With AutoClipArt

    You can customize Clip Gallery keywords so that they map to specific clip art, pictures, sounds, and videos in the Clip Gallery.

- With a custom AutoContent Wizard

    You can customize the user interface of the AutoContent Wizard by modifying the Windows registry settings it uses.

These methods of customizing PowerPoint are described in the following sections. Some of these customizations are stored in the Windows registry, and some are stored in a separate file on the user's system.

User-Defined Options

In PowerPoint (as in all Office applications), you select options for viewing, editing, and saving documents in the **Options** dialog box (**Tools** menu). In Windows 95 and

Windows NT Workstation versions 3.51 or 4.0, these settings are stored in the Windows registry. For information about PowerPoint entries in the Windows registry, see Appendix C, "Registry Keys and Values."

Tip In Windows 95 and Windows NT Workstation 4.0, you can use a system policy to define most settings in the **Options** dialog box (**Tools** menu) for all PowerPoint users in your workgroup. In the System Policy Editor, set the following policy:

Users\PowerPoint 97\Tools_Options

For more information, see "Using Windows System Policies to Customize Office" in Chapter 7, "Customizing and Optimizing Microsoft Office."

Macros

PowerPoint macros are written in Visual Basic. You create macros by recording a series of actions, such as inserting a particular graphic, or by writing macros in Visual Basic code using the Visual Basic Editor (**Tools** menu, **Macro** submenu).

Macros created in a presentation are saved in the presentation file. If the presentation is saved as a template, the macros are saved with the template but are not copied to any other presentations based on that template. If the macro is created in the Visual Basic Editor and the presentation is saved as an add-in, only the Visual Basic code is saved.

Add-ins

Add-ins extend the functionality of PowerPoint—for example, by adding custom menus or commands, loading custom toolbars, or exporting presentations to a particular format. PowerPoint supports two kinds of add-ins: those compiled in Visual Basic code, and those compiled in C. You can obtain add-ins from independent software vendors, or you can write your own.

You generate the Visual Basic code in PowerPoint by creating macros or writing code in the Visual Basic Editor (**Tools** menu, **Macro** submenu) and then saving the presentation as a PowerPoint add-in. For a C add-in, you must write it in C and compile it as a 32-bit DLL. For information about creating add-ins for PowerPoint, see the *Microsoft Office 97/Visual Basic Programmer's Guide*, which is published by Microsoft Press and available wherever computer books are sold. For more information about Microsoft Press books, see Appendix E, "Other Support Resources."

Using Add-ins in PowerPoint

Add-ins can be stored on a user's computer or on the network. To use an add-in, you must be running PowerPoint.

▶ **To make an add-in available**

1 On the **Tools** menu, click **Add-Ins**.
2 In the **Add-Ins** dialog box, click **Add New** and browse the file structure for add-ins.

Once you have identified the add-ins you want, you must load them into PowerPoint.

▶ **To load or unload add-ins for the current PowerPoint session**

- In the **Add-Ins** dialog box, click the add-in you want in the **Available Add-Ins** box, and then click **Load** or **Unload**.

Loading Add-ins Automatically (Windows only)

Add-ins remain available until you exit PowerPoint. However, PowerPoint does not store information about loading add-ins. If you want to load a particular add-in whenever a presentation is opened, you can create a macro in that presentation to load the add-in. In Windows, add-ins can also be registered so that they load automatically when PowerPoint starts.

If you want an add-in to load automatically when PowerPoint starts, change the **AutoLoad** value in the Windows registry key for the add-in to **1**. The following example shows the registry settings for a DLL add-in:

```
[HKEY_LOCAL_MACHINE\Software\Microsoft\Office\8.0\PowerPoint\DLL Addins\MyDLLAddinName]
"AutoLoad"=dword:1
"Path"= "c:\program files\microsoft office\office\Myfeat.dll"
```

For a Visual Basic add-in, you can include code when you write the add-in that loads it automatically. This **Auto_Open** routine is shown in the following example:

```
Sub Auto_Open()
    Dim iIndexPosn As Integer
    iIndexPosn = AddIns.Count
    With AddIns(iIndexPosn)
        .Registered = msoTrue
        .AutoLoad = msoTrue
        .Loaded = msoTrue
    End With
End Sub
```

If you want a Visual Basic add-in to load automatically, but you do not want to edit the Visual Basic code, change the **AutoLoad** value in the Windows registry key for the add-in to **1**. The following example shows the registry settings for a Visual Basic add-in:

```
[HKEY_LOCAL_MACHINE\Software\Microsoft\Office\8.0\PowerPoint\Addins\MyVBAAddinName]
"AutoLoad"=dword:1
"Path"= "c:\program files\microsoft office\office\MyVBAfeat.ppa"
```

> **Using Windows Registry Files To Customize PowerPoint**
>
> In Windows 95 or Windows NT Workstation version 4.0, you can modify existing PowerPoint installations with a Windows registry (REG) file. When you create a custom REG file, you can distribute it to your workgroup. PowerPoint users do not need to rerun Setup to install the customized software.
>
> To create a REG file, start the Registry Editor and modify the values in the registry settings you want. Then, on the **Registry** menu, click **Export Registry File** and click the **Selected branch** option.
>
> To distribute the REG file to all users in your workgroup, send it to them in electronic mail (e-mail). When users double-click the REG file, it overwrites existing settings in the branch of their Windows registry you specified with your new settings.
>
> For more information about working with the Windows registry, see the *Microsoft Windows 95 Resource Kit* or the *Microsoft Windows NT Server 4.0 Resource Kit* and *Microsoft Windows NT Workstation 4.0 Resource Kit*, which are published by Microsoft Press and available wherever computer books are sold.

Caution Be sure that the REG file you distribute includes only the branch of the Windows registry you want to modify. The new settings in the distributed REG file overwrite all entries in that portion of the user's Windows registry.

Custom Templates

Custom templates might include a corporate color scheme, logo, and standard font, as well as standard text, such as a slogan. You can create custom templates for a workgroup and make them available on the network. You can customize the template that PowerPoint opens whenever users create a new presentation. You can also customize templates used by the AutoContent Wizard. This section explains how to customize templates for each of these scenarios.

Customizing Design Templates

To customize a design template, open an existing template, modify it, and save it with a new name.

▶ **To create a custom design template**

1. On the **File** menu, click **Open**.
2. In **Files of type** box, click **Presentation Templates**.

3 In the **Name** box, double-click the template you want to modify.

   PowerPoint design templates are stored in the Presentations Designs folder.

4 In title master view, modify the master for title slides; in slide master view, modify the master for all other slides. You can also modify the masters for notes pages and audience handouts.

5 On the **File** menu, click **Save As**.

6 In the **Save as type** box, click **Presentation Templates**.

7 In the **File name** box, enter a name for the new template.

8 In the **Save in** box, select a folder to store the template, and then click **Save**.

You can store the custom design template in the Presentation Designs folder, or you can store it in some other folder. If you store the custom template on the network, store it in the folder identified on the user's computer as the Workgroup Template location. For more information about Workgroup Template settings, see "Storing Templates" in Chapter 39, "Microsoft Word Architecture."

Customizing the Default Template

You can customize the template that PowerPoint uses for new presentations by replacing Blank Presentation with a custom template. If you create a default template for a workgroup, make sure you copy the template file to each user's Templates folder.

Tip Before you create a custom default template, open the Blank Presentation template and save it with a new name. This preserves the PowerPoint default template as a backup.

▶ **To customize the default template**

1 If you want to make a content template your default template, open and modify a presentation or content template.

   –or–

   If you want to make a design template your default template, open and modify an existing design template.

2 On the **File** menu, click **Save As**.

3 In the **Save as type** box, click **Presentation Templates**.

4 In the **File name** box, type **Blank Presentation**.

5 In the **Save in** box, select the Templates folder, and then click **Save**.

Customizing Templates Used by the AutoContent Wizard

When you start PowerPoint, the quickest way to create a new presentation is to use the AutoContent Wizard. This wizard provides an assortment of content templates, and it steps you through the process of creating a presentation. Content templates in the AutoContent Wizard are listed by category in the **Presentation type** panel. These templates create either standard presentations or online documents that can be read by a Web browser, depending on the output option you select.

You can customize any of the templates included in the AutoContent Wizard.

▶ **To customize a content template for the AutoContent Wizard**

1 On the **File** menu, click **Open**.
2 In **Files of type** box, click **Presentation Templates**.
3 In the **Name** box, double-click the template you want to modify.

    PowerPoint content templates are stored in the Presentations folder.

4 In slide view, modify the text, graphics, and any other objects on the slide.
5 To change the appearance of the content template, modify the masters in title master view or slide master view.
6 On the **File** menu, click **Save** and save the template with the same name.

Naming Convention for AutoContent Wizard Templates

Each type of presentation in the AutoContent Wizard has two templates associated with it: one for standard presentations and one for online documents. If you select the **Presentations, informal meetings, handouts** option on the **Output option** panel in the AutoContent Wizard, then the wizard bases your presentation on the standard presentation template. If you select the **Internet, kiosk** option, the AutoContent Wizard bases your presentation on the online document template.

When you select a presentation type, the AutoContent Wizard determines which content template to use ...

... based on which output option you select.

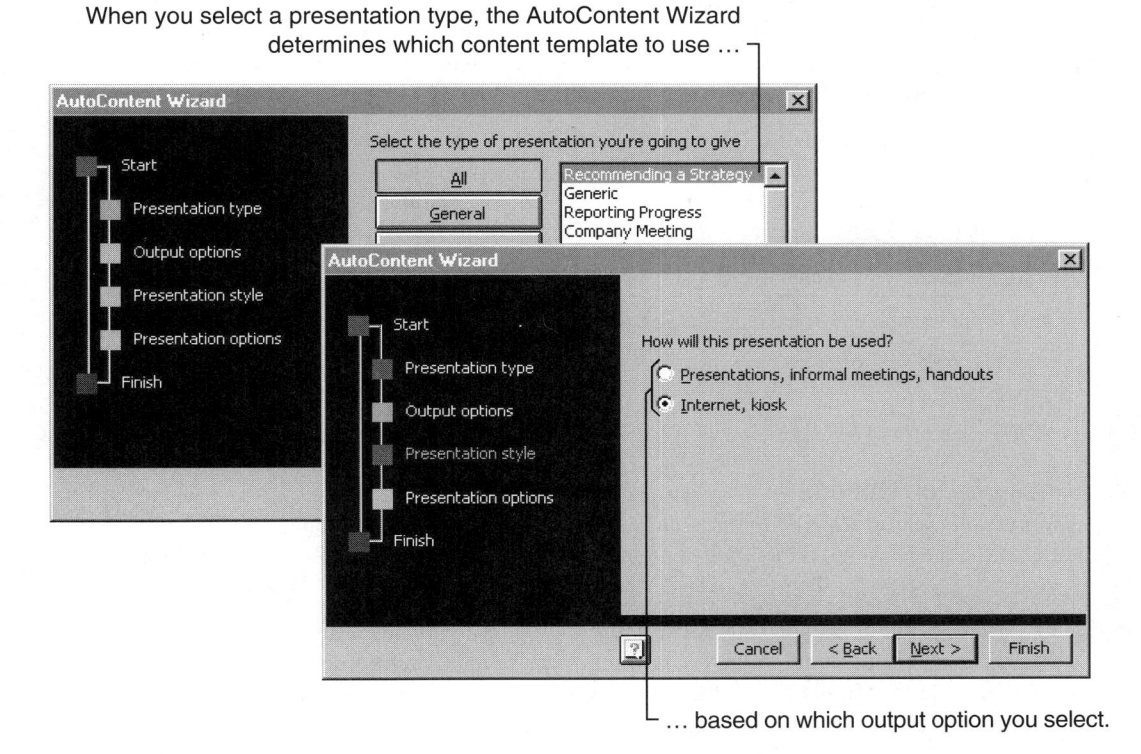

In the Presentations folder, find the template you want to customize according to the following naming convention:

For this kind of template	Open the template with a long file name containing this	Or a short file name containing this
Standard presentation	(Standard) For example, Recommending a Strategy (Standard)	_s For example, Stratg_s
Online document	(Online) For example, Recommending a Strategy (Online)	_o For example, Stratg_o

Note If the templates are stored on a Novell server, they are stored with a short file name, since the NetWare operating system does not support long file names.

Color Schemes for AutoContent Wizard Templates

While you are customizing the template, you can also customize the color schemes used by the AutoContent Wizard. The color scheme is based on the option you select in the **Presentation style** panel of the AutoContent Wizard.

To customize a color scheme used by the AutoContent Wizard, open the content template you want to customize, modify the color scheme, and then save the template with the same name. The following table lists the color schemes associated with each option in the **Presentation style** panel.

To customize this type of output	Modify this color scheme
On-screen presentation	Color scheme with darkest background color
Black and white overheads	Black and white color scheme
Color overheads	Color scheme with the lightest background color
35mm slides	Color scheme with darkest background color

Presentation Options

While you are customizing the template, you can also customize optional items that the AutoContent Wizard includes in the presentation. The available items are based on what you select in the **Presentation options** panel in the AutoContent Wizard.

To customize the items you select with presentation options in the AutoContent Wizard, open the content template you want to customize, modify the master or slide, and then save the template with the same name. The following table associates each presentation option with the item and the type of template to modify.

To customize the item associated with this presentation option	Modify this item	On this type of template
Copyright notice on each page	Footer area on slide and title masters	Online
Date last updated on each page	Date area on slide and title masters	Online
E-mail hyperlink on each page	Number area on slide and title masters	Online
Presentation title	Title area on title master	Standard
Your name	Subtitle area on title master	Standard
Additional information	Subtitle area on title master	Standard

Custom Toolbar Settings

Customize toolbar settings in the **Customize** dialog box (**Tools** menu). For more information about customizing toolbars, see PowerPoint online Help. Custom toolbar settings are stored in the file *username*8.pcb in the Windows folder (Windows), or *username* in the folder where PowerPoint is installed (Macintosh).

Tip In Windows 95 and Windows NT Workstation 4.0, you can use a system policy to define the default value for the location of the custom toolbar settings file for all PowerPoint users in your workgroup. In the System Policy Editor, set the following policy:

User\PowerPoint 97\Miscellaneous\Personal Toolbars

For more information, see "Using Windows System Policies to Customize Office" in Chapter 7, "Customizing and Optimizing Microsoft Office."

Custom Export Formats

You can save either the current slide or the current presentation in any format for which an export graphics filter or export module is installed. Export graphics filters are supplied by independent software vendors, whereas export modules are PowerPoint add-ins you write in Visual Basic. For information about Visual Basic add-ins, see "Add-ins" earlier in this chapter.

You can save slides and presentations in many non-native formats by using the graphics filters that come with PowerPoint. By installing export graphics filters or export modules, however, you can also save slides and presentations in a custom format.

Using Export Graphics Filters

When you install a graphics filter for exporting PowerPoint data to a particular graphics format, the filter is added to the registry (Windows) or to a settings file (Macintosh). When PowerPoint starts, it reads the list of installed filters and includes them in the **Save as type** box in the **Save As** dialog box (**File** menu).

Using Export Modules

An export module is a Visual Basic add-in that registers as an export module in the registry (Windows) or in a settings file (Macintosh). When PowerPoint starts, it reads the list of installed export modules and includes them in the **Save as type** box in the **Save As** dialog box (**File** menu). Formats defined by export modules appear after PowerPoint native formats and before graphics filter formats in the list.

AutoClipArt

When you click **AutoClipArt** (**Tools** menu) in slide view, PowerPoint launches AutoClipArt, a tool that searches the active presentation for words in its list of keywords. From AutoClipArt, you can run Clip Gallery to match keywords found by AutoClipArt with keywords in Clip Gallery, and insert the corresponding clips into the active presentation.

The keyword list in AutoClipArt cannot be modified. However, you can modify the keywords in Clip Gallery, so that the AutoClipArt keywords map to different clips. When you add new clip art, pictures, sounds, or videos to Clip Gallery, you can also add keywords from the AutoClipArt list so that the new clip can be incorporated into presentations through AutoClipArt.

When you modify the Clip Gallery keywords, you create a custom Clip Gallery database, which you can distribute to users or store on the network. When users run AutoClipArt, they can automatically use the custom Clip Gallery, which customizes the way they use AutoClipArt.

For more information about Clip Gallery databases and how to distribute custom databases on a network, see PowerPoint online Help.

Tools and Utilities The Office Resource Kit Tools and Utilities include the list of keywords in AutoClipArt. For information about viewing the AutoClipArt keyword list, see "PowerPoint AutoClipArt Concept List" in Appendix A, "Microsoft Office 97 Resource Kit Tools and Utilities."

Custom AutoContent Wizard Interface

In addition to customizing the templates opened by the AutoContent Wizard, you can also customize the user interface of the AutoContent Wizard so that it opens content templates other than those installed during Setup. For information about customizing templates used by the AutoContent Wizard, see "Customizing Templates Used by the AutoContent Wizard" earlier in this chapter. The following sections explain how to customize the user interface of the AutoContent Wizard.

The user interface of AutoContent Wizard can be customized in two ways:

- The network administrator can customize the user interface for an entire workgroup.
- End-users can add frequently used templates to the list in the **Presentation style** panel.

Administrator Customization of the AutoContent Wizard User Interface (Windows only)

To automate the process of creating presentations using your own content templates, you can customize the user interface of the AutoContent Wizard. In this scenario, clicking **Presentation type** in the AutoContent Wizard displays your labels on the buttons and lists the content templates you specify.

To customize the AutoContent Wizard in this way, modify the self-registration (SRG) files for the AutoContent Wizard; then run Setup and click **Reinstall** to repeat the PowerPoint installation in maintenance mode. Setup reads the settings in the modified SRG files, and then writes those settings to the Windows registry.

Note Unlike system policy files, SRG files can modify Windows registry settings under Windows NT Workstation 3.51, as well as Windows NT Workstation 4.0 and Windows 95. However, SRG files do not modify settings on the Macintosh.

Tip If users have already installed PowerPoint, you can customize the AutoContent Wizard interface by distributing a REG file. For more information about creating and distributing REG files, see "Add-ins" earlier in this chapter.

In the SRG file, you configure the labels of the buttons in the **Presentation type** panel in a heading subkey. The buttons allow you to organize your templates by category. The first button is always labeled **All**, and it displays all topics in the **Presentation type** panel. For all the other buttons you define in a heading subkey, you can define topic names and their corresponding content templates in a topic subkey.

For example, in the following SRG file, the AutoContent Wizard displays **My Category** as the second button. If you click **My Category**, the topics **My First Presentation** and **My Second Presentation** are displayed.

Note The templates associated with these topics are named according to the convention described in "Naming Convention for AutoContent Wizard Templates" earlier in this chapter. That is, the name of the template for creating the standard presentation is My First Presentation (standard), and the name of the template for creating the corresponding online presentation is My First Presentation (online).

The following code sample shows an example of an SRG file that customizes the AutoContent Wizard, as described in the preceding paragraphs.

```
#-------------------------------------------------------------
# Heading 2
#-------------------------------------------------------------
[HKEY_LOCAL_MACHINE\Software\Microsoft\Office\8.0\PowerPoint\AutoContent
Wizard\Heading2]
"Enabled"="dword:1"
"Caption"="reg_sz:&My Category"

[HKEY_LOCAL_MACHINE\Software\Microsoft\Office\8.0\PowerPoint\AutoContent
Wizard\Heading2\Topic1]
"Caption"="reg_sz:My First Presentation"
"OnlineFile"="reg_sz:<product path>\\presentations\\My First Presentation (online).pot"
"StandardFile"="reg_sz:<product path>\\presentations\\My First Presentation (standard).pot"

[HKEY_LOCAL_MACHINE\Software\Microsoft\Office\8.0\PowerPoint\AutoContent
Wizard\Heading2\Topic2]
"Caption"="reg_sz:My Second Presentation"
"OnlineFile"="reg_sz:<product path>\\presentations\\My Second Presentation (online).pot"
"StandardFile"="reg_sz:<product path>\\presentations\\My Second Presentation (standard).pot"
```

The following illustration shows the customized user interface created by this SRG file.

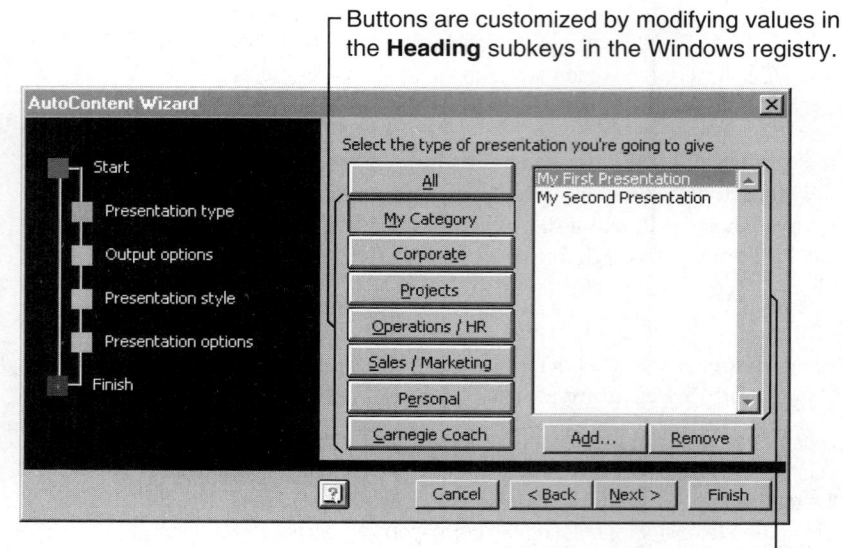

Buttons are customized by modifying values in the **Heading** subkeys in the Windows registry.

List of topics is customized by modifying values in **Topic** subkeys for each heading.

When modifying the SRG files that come with PowerPoint, follow the convention that PowerPoint uses regarding which SRG file is responsible for certain AutoContent Wizard elements. This convention is shown in the following table.

To modify this in the AutoContent Wizard	Modify this	In this SRG file
Button names	Caption data in each Heading subkey	Acminlng or Acminsht
First topic in each category	Data in Topic1 subkey in each Heading subkey	Acminlng or Acminsht
Second topic in each category	Data in Topic2 subkey in each Heading subkey	Actyplng or Actypsht
Third and subsequent topics in each category	Data in Topic3 and subsequent subkeys in each Heading subkey. Create new Topic subkeys as needed.	Acalllng or Acallsht

End-User Customization of the AutoContent Wizard User Interface

End users can customize the AutoContent Wizard so that they have quick access to a list of selected templates.

▶ **To customize the AutoContent Wizard with a list of favorites**

1. In the AutoContent Wizard, click **Presentation type**.
2. Click the button for the category of the presentations you want to add, and then click **Add**.

   All and **Carnegie Coach** are not customizable; if you click these buttons, the **Add** button is not available.

3. In the **Select Presentation Template** dialog box, browse through a folder and select the presentations or templates you want to add, and then click **Open**.

   The AutoContent Wizard adds the files to the list of favorites.

4. Click **Add** and repeat Step 3 to add presentations and templates in other folders.

Adding a file to the list of favorites adds a subkey for that file to the Windows registry under the key **HKEY_LOCAL_MACHINE\SOFTWARE\Microsoft\Office\8.0 \PowerPoint\AutoContent Wizard\Heading**x, where x is a number that stands for the customized category. For example, adding a file to the list of favorites for the **General** button adds a subkey under **\Heading2**. Removing a file from the list removes its subkey from the registry, but does not delete the file.

How PowerPoint Resolves Conflicts

A slide in a presentation has information coming from several sources: templates, masters, and formatting that you have applied to a particular slide. This information follows a hierarchy; at the top are the settings applied to the individual slide. These settings override settings in the master or template. However, you can return a slide to its master settings by reapplying the slide's AutoLayout.

When a new design template is attached to an existing presentation, the master elements in the new design template replace the master elements in the presentation. Changing design templates does not affect the content of a presentation, except for objects that appear as background objects on a master. Design templates do not affect the layout of handout and notes masters.

If you load more than one add-in during a PowerPoint session, all of the loaded add-in elements are available. That is, if one add-in adds a command to the **File** menu and another add-in adds different command to the **File** menu, both commands appear in the **File** menu when both add-ins are loaded.

Note If multiple add-ins affect the same item, the add-in loaded last is used.

> **Why don't the slides in my presentation match the new template?**
>
> You open an existing presentation and apply a new corporate template that includes the company logo and titles in Times New Roman font. Most of the slides in your presentation change their appearance to match the new template, but the logo is missing on one slide, and on another slide the title appears in Arial font instead.
>
> Inconsistencies like these can occur when you have applied custom settings to slides. On the slide that doesn't display the logo, for example, a custom background that hides background objects has been applied. On the slide that formats the title incorrectly, the formatting for title text has been changed to Arial. These modifications to individual slides override the settings in the new design template.
>
> To fix the slide that doesn't display the logo, display the slide in slide view and clear the **Omit background graphics from master** check box in the **Custom Background** dialog box (**Format** menu). To fix the slide that formats the title incorrectly, display the slide in slide view, and then click the **Reapply** button in the **Slide Layout** dialog box (**Format** menu).

CHAPTER 39

Microsoft Word Architecture

This chapter describes the structure of Microsoft Word. It explains how the various components of Word work together, and how the application handles changes that users make to those components. An understanding of the architecture of Word can help you take advantage of its features and may help you troubleshoot problems.

In This Chapter
How Word Is Structured   991
How You Can Customize Word   1006
How Word Resolves Conflicts   1008

See Also
- For information about installing Word or other Office applications, see Chapter 4, "Installing Microsoft Office."
- For information about customizing Word to meet the specific needs of your workgroup, see Chapter 7, "Customizing and Optimizing Microsoft Office."

How Word Is Structured

The architecture of Microsoft Word consists of three layers:

- The Word application
- Templates
- Documents

The application and template layers affect Word documents in different ways. The Word application provides the standard Word menus, commands, and toolbars. Templates serve a dual purpose: they provide a model for creating new documents and also act as a storage container for styles, macros, AutoText entries, and customized

Word commands and toolbar settings. The document file contains the text, graphics, formatting, and settings such as margins and page layout for that particular document.

Like templates, a document can also store macros and customized Word commands and toolbar settings. In previous versions of Word, these components had to be stored in templates, making some tasks more difficult—for example, when one user wanted to share a macro with another user.

The following figure illustrates how the Word components fit together to create a document.

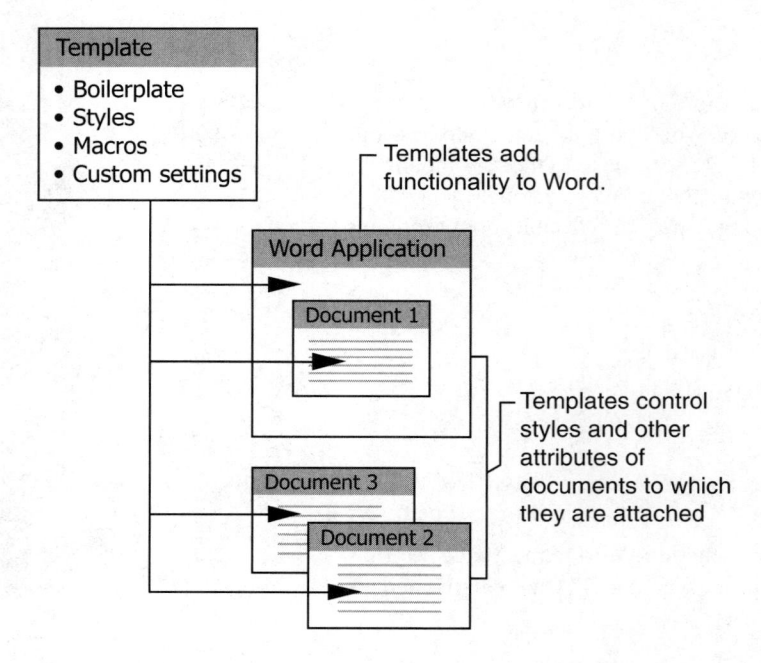

Template
- Boilerplate
- Styles
- Macros
- Custom settings

Templates add functionality to Word.

Word Application

Document 1

Document 3

Document 2

Templates control styles and other attributes of documents to which they are attached

Understanding Templates

The key to understanding Word architecture is understanding how the document, template, and application layers interact. Of the three layers, the template layer has the greatest impact on both the document and the application layers.

Templates can provide the following:

- Customized menus, toolbars, and keyboard assignments that place frequently used commands on the menus and toolbars, remove unused commands from menus and toolbars, and define key combinations to carry out commands and macros.
- Macros to automate complicated and repetitive tasks with a single command.

- Boilerplate text and graphics, such as your company's name and logo, in every document based on that template.
- Standard formatting, such as fonts, styles, margin settings, and page orientation.
- Custom AutoText entries to insert frequently used text and graphics.

Impact of Templates on the Application Layer

You can customize the Word application with templates. Using templates, you can adapt Word menus, toolbars, keyboard assignments, and macros to meet the needs of different types of users or for different types of documents.

For example, you can create a template for new users that includes a toolbar with buttons and menus designed to step them through common tasks. More advanced users, who are familiar with the tasks, do not need the extra guidance and can use a template with toolbar buttons that meet their particular needs.

Impact of Templates on the Document Layer

A template provides a guide or pattern for creating documents. By basing a group of documents on a single template, you or your workgroup can quickly create standard documents, such as letters and memos, with consistent formatting and boilerplate text.

For example, a template for memos can save you time by setting the page margins; inserting the company logo; and providing the text for standard headings, such as Memo, To, and From. With part of the work already done for you, you fill in the additional text.

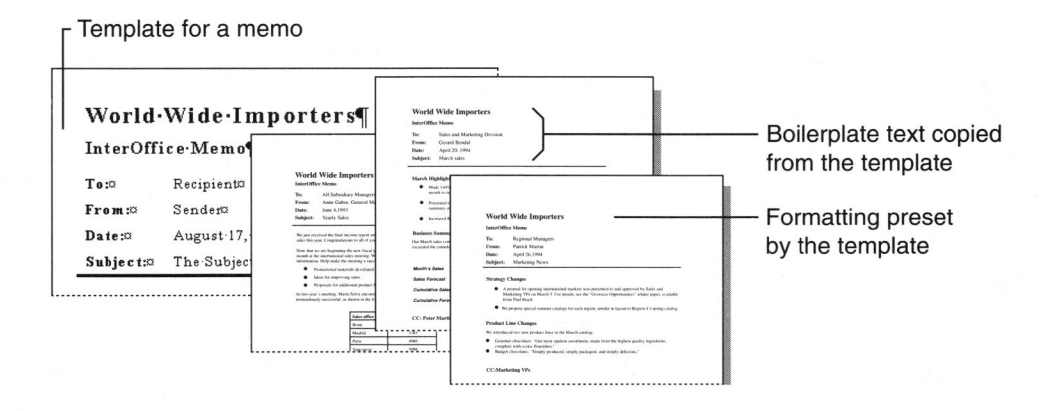

Attaching Templates to Documents

In Word, all documents are based on a template. When you create a new document, it initially has the characteristics of the active template. The templates available for a new document vary according to how you create the new document, as shown in the following table.

If you use this command	These templates are available
On the Word **File** menu, click **New**.	All Word templates and wizards defined in the User and Workgroup templates locations. These locations are specified on the **File Locations** tab in the **Options** dialog box (**Tools** menu).
On the **Office Shortcut Bar** or the Windows **Start** menu (Windows 95 or Windows NT Workstation version 4.0 only), click **New Office Document**.	All Office templates defined in the User and Workgroup templates locations. Word templates appear on the **General**, **Letters & Faxes**, **Other Documents**, and **Web Pages** tabs in the **New Office Document** dialog box.
Click the **New** button on the Word **Standard** toolbar.	The Normal template. The **New** dialog box does not appear.

Unless you select another template when creating a new document, Word uses the Normal template, which is stored in the following location.

Operating system	Normal template location
Windows	Program Files\Microsoft Office\Templates\Normal.dot
Macintosh	Microsoft Office:Microsoft Word:Normal

In addition to the Normal template, Word comes with templates for the most common types of documents, such as letters, memos, reports, and mailing labels. You can use the templates as they are or customize them to meet your needs. You can also create your own templates.

In addition to basing a new document on a template, you can attach a different template to an open document.

▶ **To attach a different template to a document**

1 On the **Tools** menu, click **Templates and Add-Ins**.
2 Click **Attach**, and then select the template you want to attach to the document.

Note When you attach a different template, page settings, such as margins, that are stored in the new template are not applied to the document. For more information, see "Default Page Settings" later in this chapter.

Using Global Templates

Items stored in templates other than the Normal template are available only to documents that are based on that template. Items stored in the Normal template, however, are *global*—that is, they are available to all Word documents. These items include AutoText entries, macros, menu assignments, toolbar button assignments, and keyboard assignments.

Using a template designed for one type of document, such as a fax sheet, you can create document settings and commands specific to that type of document. Other commands and components, such as AutoText entries, that you want available to all documents should be placed in the Normal template or some other global template. By using custom and global templates judiciously, you have a flexible method for creating documents that can be highly customized while adhering to companywide standards of design.

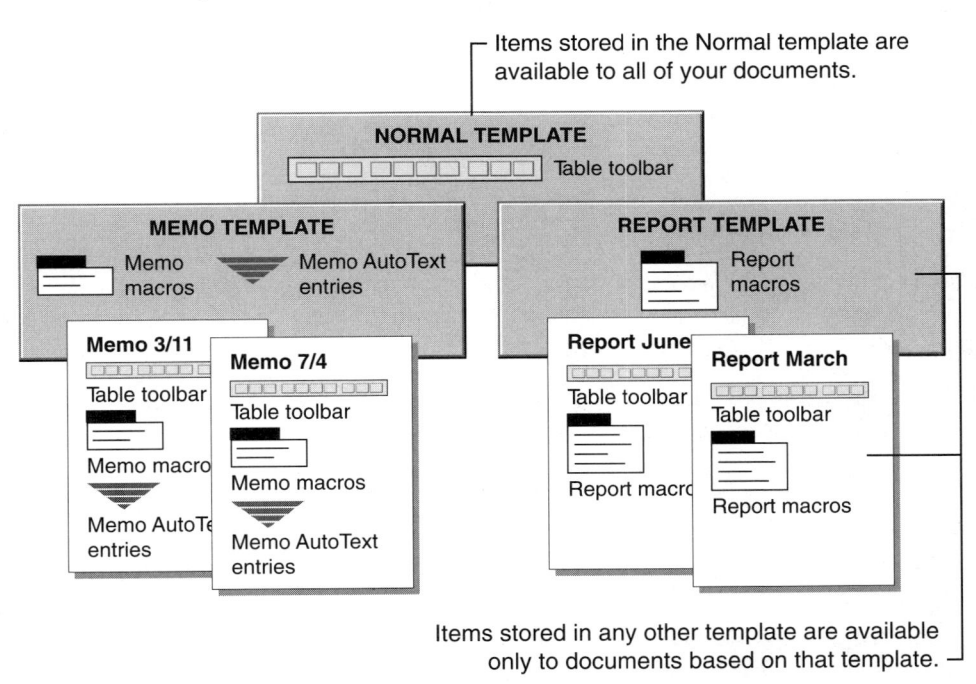

Sometimes you may want to use macros, toolbars, or AutoText entries from a template other than the Normal template in many documents. To make these items available to all open documents, you can open the template as a global template. You can then use the customized settings in all your documents. However, styles in the global template are not applied to your documents; Word continues to use the styles from the template on which the document is based. Customized items in the global template are available for the remainder of the current Word session.

▶ **To open a template as a global template**

1 On the **Tools** menu, click **Templates and Add-Ins**.
2 Under **Global templates and add-ins**, select the check box of the template you want to open globally, or click **Add** to add another template to the list.

Storing Templates

The Office Setup program determines default locations for different kinds of Word components: documents, templates, spelling dictionaries, clip art, and so forth. You can change these default locations.

Note The **User templates** and **Workgroup templates** settings are Office-wide settings. Changing them in Word also changes them for other Office applications that support templates.

▶ **To specify file locations for templates and other Word components**

1 On to **Tools** menu, click **Options**, and then click the **File Locations** tab.
2 Under **File types**, select the Word component for which you want to specify a new file location.
3 Click **Modify**.
4 In the **Folder name** box, enter the new path for the component you selected.

Tip In Windows 95 and Windows NT Workstation 4.0, you can use a system policy to define the default file locations for all Word users in your workgroup. In the System Policy Editor, set the following policy:

User\Word 97\Tools_Options\File Locations

For more information, see "Using Windows System Policies to Customize Office" in Chapter 7, "Customizing and Optimizing Microsoft Office."

When you start Word, the application looks for the Normal template in the following locations, in the order listed:

1. The User templates folder as specified on the **File Locations** tab in the **Options** dialog box (**Tools** menu)
2. The Workgroup templates folder as specified on the **File Locations** tab in the **Options** dialog box (**Tools** menu)
3. The Word folder
4. The current folder

If Word cannot find the Normal template, it uses the standard document and command settings that have been preset by Microsoft. Any AutoText entries, formatted text, AutoCorrect entries, macros, and command settings that you store for global use in the Normal template are not be available until you return the Normal template to one of the default locations and then restart Word.

Note When Word is first installed, there is no Normal template. It is constructed and saved the first time a user exits Word.

Managing User and Workgroup Templates

In a workgroup, there are usually two places where Word templates are stored: the templates folder on each user's hard disk, and on the network.

Templates used by only a few users or that a user may want to customize (such as Normal, because it is always loaded globally) are usually stored in the user's template folder on the hard disk. The location of these templates is determined by the **User templates** setting on the **File Locations** tab in the **Options** dialog box (**Tools** menu). By default, Word stores user templates in the Templates folder.

Templates needed by the entire workgroup or that users do not need to customize are typically stored on a shared network drive. The location of these templates is determined by the **Workgroup templates** setting on the **File Locations** tab in the **Options** dialog box (**Tools** menu). There is no initial default setting for workgroup templates.

When a user creates a new document, templates from both the User and the Workgroup templates folders are listed together in the **New** dialog box (**File** menu).

Don't Reinvent the Wheel

Word 97 includes several templates that you can use as-is or modify to suit your workgroup's needs. The templates included with Word 97 let you quickly create several types of documents, including:

- Fax cover letters
- Memos
- Resumes

To see the full list of templates available, click **New** (**File** menu), and then click the tab that corresponds to the type of document you want.

In addition to the templates that are included with Word 97, Microsoft may create additional templates available for downloading from the Microsoft Web site. For more information, connect to the Office home page at:

http://www.microsoft.com/office/

Locating Word Components

The various components of Word—such as styles, macros, default page settings, AutoText entries, AutoCorrect entries, and custom command settings—are stored in the document and template layers of the three-layer architecture. Some components reside strictly in the document layer, others reside in the template layer, and still others are stored in both the document and the template layers.

Of those components that reside in the template layer, some are always stored with the Normal template or the attached template, while others can be stored in a global template. The following table shows what components are stored in the document and template layers of the Word architecture.

This component	Is stored in this layer of the Word architecture		
	Document file	Normal or other attached template	Global templates
AutoText entries	No	Yes	Yes
Boilerplate text and graphics	Yes Copied to the document when it is created	Yes	No
Custom toolbars, menus, and shortcut keys	No	Yes	Yes
Default page settings	Yes Copied to the document when it is created	Yes	No
Document text and graphics	Yes	No	No
Macros	Yes	Yes	Yes
Styles	Yes Copied to the document when it is created	Yes	No

Tip To copy template styles to a document when it is opened, select the **Automatically update document styles** check box in the **Templates and Add-Ins** dialog box (**Tools** menu).

Note In some cases, macros or custom toolbars, menus, and shortcut keys are stored in the template. However, when you specify them by using the **Customize** dialog box (**Tools** menu), or when you copy them to the document by clicking **Templates and Add-Ins** (**Tools** menu) and then clicking **Organizer**, they are stored in the document.

Did You Know?
AutoCorrect entries that include formatted text are stored in the Normal template. However, plain text AutoCorrect entries are stored in an external file named *.acl in the Windows folder. For more information, see "AutoText Entries" later in this chapter.

Text and Graphics

When you create a document, Word copies all information from the template on which the document is based, including boilerplate text and graphics, to the document. From that point on, the text and graphics are saved with the document file. Any subsequent changes you make to the boilerplate text and graphics in the template do not affect documents previously created from that template.

Styles

When you create a document, Word copies styles from the template on which the document is based. However, no link between template styles and document styles is made. So, if you change the styles in the document, those changes are saved with the document file but not in its attached template. Likewise if you change styles in the template after the document is created, those changes are not automatically reflected in the document. However, you can update the document so that its styles match the styles in its attached template.

▶ **To automatically update the document styles to match the template**

1   On the **Tools** menu, click **Templates and Add-Ins**.
2   Select the **Automatically update document styles** check box.

Each time you open the document, Word copies the styles in the attached template to the document.

Tip   You can also copy a style from another template to the template attached to the document. On the **Format** menu, click **Style**, and then click **Modify**. Select the **Add to Template** check box.

Styles Applied by AutoFormat

The **AutoFormat** command (**Format** menu) analyzes text in a document and applies styles that have been copied to the document. These document styles originally come from the attached template.

If Word cannot find an appropriate style among those in the document, it uses its own built-in styles. These built-in styles allow Word to format body text, headings, bulleted lists, and other text elements. You can customize these built-in styles.

▶ **To customize built-in styles**

1   On the **Format** menu, click **Style**.
2   Under **Styles**, select a style you want to customize.
3   Click **Modify**.
4   Make the changes you want to the style.

Note   If you select the **Add to template** check box in the **Modify Style** dialog box, Word adds the modified style to the template attached to the document. The modified style is available in all documents attached to the template. Otherwise, the style is added to the document only.

The following illustrations show some of the built-in styles you can use to format common text elements.

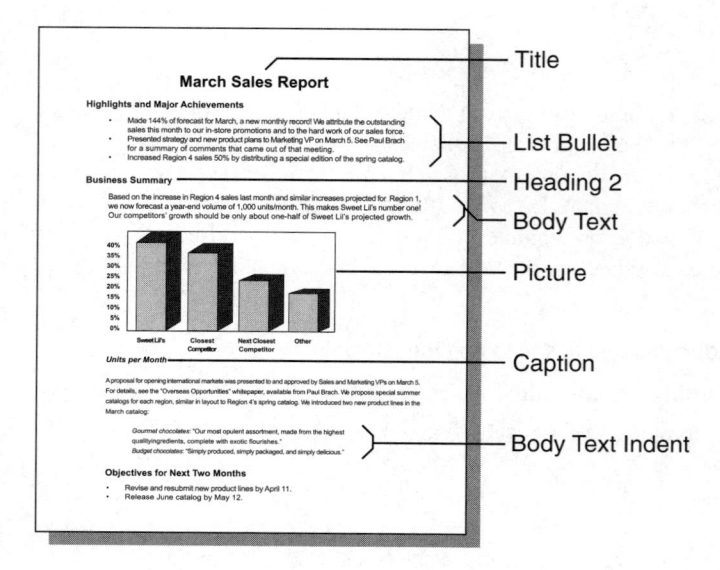

- Title
- List Bullet
- Heading 2
- Body Text
- Picture
- Caption
- Body Text Indent

Style Gallery

You can use the **Style Gallery** command (**Format** menu) to see how the appearance of the document changes according to what template is applied. When you select another template in the Style Gallery, Word does not attach the new template to the active document. Instead, it copies the styles from the selected template to the active document. The template on which the active document is based remains attached to the document. To attach a different template to a document, use the **Templates and Add-Ins** command (**Tools** menu).

When Word copies the styles from the selected template into the active document, the styles in the active document are affected as follows:

- A style from the template that has the same name as a style in the document replaces the style in the document. All paragraphs formatted with that style are changed to reflect the new style definition.
- Template styles that are not in the document are added to the document.
- Styles unique to the document are not affected.

Default Page Settings

Word stores default page settings, such as margins, layout, and paper size, in templates. Each new document based on that template inherits those default settings from the template. All subsequent changes made to the settings that are saved with the document remain with the document; they are not automatically saved back to the template. However, you can save settings from a document to its attached template.

▶ **To save settings from the document to the attached template**

1 On the **File** menu, click **Page Setup**.
2 Click **Default**, and then click **Yes**.

The new default settings are reflected in all subsequent documents created from this template.

AutoText Entries

Word stores AutoText entries in templates. To use an AutoText entry in any Word document, store it in the Normal template or another global template. If you want to make AutoText entries available only in documents of the same type as the active document, store them in the template attached to the active document.

To add or edit AutoText entries in a global template, you must open the template in a non-global mode. This is because global templates cannot be edited.

▶ **To open a global template in non-global mode**

1 On the **File** menu, click **Open**.
2 In the **Files of type** box, select **Document Templates**.
3 Under the **Look in** box, double-click the template you want to open.

Tip To determine whether a template is attached to the document or is global, click **Templates and Add-Ins** (**Tools** menu). The template whose name appears in the **Document template** box is the attached template, and can be edited. The template whose name appears in the **Global templates and add-ins** box is a global template and is read-only.

Macros

Together, macros and templates can be used to create a highly customized version of Word designed to accomplish a particular task or set of tasks. For example, a group of macros and templates could be designed to automate the creation of forms and other documents a company uses.

Word stores macros in templates or documents. When you create a new macro, it is stored by default in the Normal template and is available globally. You can also specify which template a macro should be attached to, or store it in the current document.

To store a new macro in a template other than Normal, either the template or a document attached to the template must be active when you create the macro. If you want to create a new macro in a global template, you must open the template rather than a document attached to it. When attached to a document, global templates are read-only.

You can create macros by writing Visual Basic for Applications code or by recording a series of actions.

▶ **To create a new macro by writing Visual Basic code**

1. On the **Tools** menu, click **Macro**, and then click **Macros**.
2. In the **Macro name** box, enter a name for the macro.
3. In the **Macros in** box, select the template or document in which you want to store the macro, and click **Create**.

    Word opens a new macro in Visual Basic Editor.

▶ **To create a macro by recording a series of actions**

1. On the **Tools** menu, click **Macro**, and then click **Record New Macro**.
2. In the **Macro name** box, enter a name for the macro.
3. In the **Store macro in** box, select the template or document in which you want to store the macro, and click **OK**.

    Word displays the **Stop Recording** toolbar, which you use to pause or end the recording session.

Using the Organizer feature in Word, you can copy macros between documents and templates. Copying macros to documents is especially useful when you want to distribute a document and custom macros throughout your workgroup (through electronic mail, for example), and you want ensure that the document and its macros do not become separated.

▶ **To copy a macro to a document or template**

1. On the **Tools** menu, click **Templates and Add-Ins**.
2. Click **Organizer**, and then click the **Macro Project Items** tab.
3. On the left side of the dialog box, select the document or template that contains the macro you want to copy in the **Macro Project Items available in** box.

    If the document or template you want is not open, click **Close File**. The command switches to **Open File**; click it and then select the file you want.

4 In the **In** *name* box, where *name* is the name of the template or document you selected in Step 3, select the macro name.

5 On the right side of the dialog box, select the document or template into which you want to copy the macro in the **Macro Project Items available in** box.

If the document or template you want is not open, click **Close File**. The command switches to **Open File**; click it and then select the file you want.

6 Click **Copy**.

The macro is copied from the document or template specified on the left side of the dialog box into the document or template specified on the right side of the dialog box.

Custom Toolbars, Menus, and Shortcut Keys

By customizing toolbars, menus, and shortcut keys, you can change Word to better suit the needs of your workgroup. For example, you can add frequently used commands and dialog box options to toolbars and menus, and remove items users rarely use. You can also customize shortcut key assignments by creating the shortcut keys that work best for your organization.

You can save custom toolbars, menus, and shortcut keys in a template or in a document.

Saving in a Template

If you save the custom settings in a template, you can store them in the Normal template, an open template, or the template attached to the active document. To make customized settings available in any document, save the settings in the Normal template or in a template you plan to make global.

Saving in a Document

If you save the custom settings in a document, you can easily distribute the document and custom settings throughout your workgroup (through e-mail, for example). This ensures that the document and its custom settings cannot become separated.

▶ To customize a toolbar

1. On the **Tools** menu, click **Customize**, and then click the **Toolbars** tab.
2. Select the toolbar you want to customize.

   –or–

   To create a new toolbar, click **New**; enter a name for the toolbar and select the template or document in which to store it; and then click **OK**. (The new toolbar appears on your screen.)
3. Click the **Commands** tab, and in the **Categories** box, click the category for the command you want.
4. In the **Commands** box, click the command and drag it onto the toolbar you are customizing.
5. If you have not already done so, select the template or document in which you want to store the custom toolbar in the **Save in** box.

▶ To customize a menu

1. On the **Tools** menu, click **Customize**, and then click the **Commands** tab.
2. On the Word menu bar, click the name of the menu you want to customize.

   –or–

   To create a new menu, click **New Menu** in the **Categories** box; and in the **Commands** box, click **New Menu** and drag it onto the Word menu bar.
3. To change the name of the menu, click **Modify Selection** and enter a name in the **Name** box.
4. To modify the way a command is displayed on the menu, click the command, click **Modify Selection**, and then click one of the options.
5. To add a command to the menu, click a category in the **Categories** box; in the **Commands** box, click the command and drag it onto the menu.
6. To remove a command from the menu, drag the command off the menu.
7. In the **Save in** box, select the template or document in which you want to store the custom menu.

▶ To customize a shortcut key

1. On the **Tools** menu, click **Customize**, and then click **Keyboard** on any tab.
2. In the **Categories** and **Commands** boxes, click the items you want.
3. Click in the **Press new shortcut key** box, and then press the key combination you want to use as a shortcut key.

   In the **Current keys** box you can see the key combination currently assigned to the command.

4   In the **Save changes in** box, select the template or document in which you want to store the custom shortcut key.

As with macros, you can use the Organizer to copy custom toolbars between documents and templates.

▶ **To copy a custom toolbar to a document or template**

1   On the **Tools** menu, click **Templates and Add-Ins**.
2   Click **Organizer**, and then click the **Toolbars** tab.
3   On the left side of the dialog box, select the document or template that contains the toolbar you want to copy in **Toolbars available in** box.

    If the document or template you want is not open, click **Close File**. The command changes to **Open File**; click it and then select the file you want.

4   In the **In** *name* box, where *name* is the name of the template or document you selected in Step 3, select the toolbar name.
5   On the right side of the dialog box, select the document or template into which you want to copy the toolbar in the **Toolbars available in** box.

    If the document or template you want is not open, click **Close File**. The command changes to **Open File**; click it and then select the file you want.

6   Click **Copy**.

    The toolbar is copied from the document or template specified on the left side of the dialog box into the document or template specified on the right side of the dialog box.

AutoCorrect Entries

AutoCorrect entries that use formatted text are stored in the Normal template. These entries have the **Formatted text** option selected on the **AutoCorrect** tab in the **AutoCorrect** dialog box (**Tools** menu). All plain text AutoCorrect entries, however, are stored in an external files named *.acl in the Windows folder. All Office applications share these files. When a new user needs an ACL file, it is copied from Mso97.acl and renamed *username*.acl.

Tip   In Windows 95 and Windows NT Workstation 4.0, you can use a system policy to have all users start with a custom ACL file, which you can store on a shared network drive. Use this policy to point to the custom ACL file. In the System Policy Editor, set the following policy:

Computer\Word 97\Spelling Advanced\Default AutoCorrect File

For more information, see "Using Windows System Policies to Customize Office" in Chapter 7, "Customizing and Optimizing Microsoft Office."

Managing Wizards

From a user perspective, a *wizard* is a fast, easy way to create a document—because the wizard does the work. In Word, wizards are specialized templates with Visual Basic macros. They are designated with a .wiz instead of a .dot extension, and their **Type** property is **Microsoft Word Wizard**, rather than **Microsoft Word Template**. Unlike templates, wizards cannot be modified. The wizards that come with Word all share a common user interface. The key component of the wizard is the macro or set of macros stored within the template. These macros automate the creation of documents.

Word provides wizards to help users create documents such as a fax cover sheet, letter, and resume. Word also includes a wizard to help users create tables. You can create your own wizards to step users through complex tasks specific to your organization. Creating a wizard requires programming in Visual Basic.

For more information about Visual Basic, see the *Microsoft Office 97/Visual Basic Programmer's Guide*, published by Microsoft Press and available wherever computer books are sold.

Creating Add-ins

Add-ins are programs written in the C programming language. They act like custom commands or custom features you can use in Word.

Add-ins place commands on toolbars and menus or assign them to shortcut keys, just as Word macros can. Architecturally, add-ins fit in at the template layer. They modify toolbars, menus, and shortcut keys just as templates do. You can write your own add-ins or obtain them from software vendors.

To use an add-in, you must load it into Word the same way you load global templates. Like a template, the add-in program remains available until you exit Word. If you want to load an add-in automatically each time you start Word, store it in the Word Startup folder. For information about creating your own Word add-ins, see the *Microsoft Office 97/Visual Basic Programmer's Guide*, published by Microsoft Press and available wherever computer books are sold.

How You Can Customize Word

Word default settings and paths are established when you run the Office Setup program. After Setup, you can customize these settings for a single user, a workgroup, or across an entire organization.

There are several ways to customize the Word application:

- Through the **Options** dialog box

  You can customize Word in the **Options** dialog box (**Tools** menu). The settings you make here are stored in the Windows registry.

- Through the **Customize** dialog box

  In the **Customize** dialog box (**View** menu, **Toolbars** submenu), you can customize the toolbars, menu bars, and shortcut menus included with Word, or you can create your own. For more information, see "Custom Toolbars, Menus, and Shortcut Keys" earlier in this chapter.

- With a template

  A template can include customized Word settings and macros, as well as boilerplate text and graphics. For more information about templates, see "Understanding Templates" earlier in this chapter.

- With wizards

  A wizard is special type of template that helps users create specific types of documents. For more information about wizards, see "Managing Wizards" earlier in this chapter.

- With add-ins

  An add-in is a program written in C that adds custom commands and features to Word. For more information about add-ins, see "Creating Add-ins" earlier in this chapter.

- With the Startup folder

  When Word starts, it opens all documents, templates and wizards stored in the **Startup** folder as specified on the **File Locations** tab in the **Options** dialog box (**Tools** menu).

Tip In Windows 95 and Windows NT Workstation 4.0, you can use a system policy to define most settings in the **Options** dialog box (**Tools** menu) for all Word users in your workgroup. In the System Policy Editor, set the following policy:

User\Word 97\Tools_Options

For more information, see "Using Windows System Policies to Customize Office" in Chapter 7, "Customizing and Optimizing Microsoft Office."

How Word Resolves Conflicts

In the discussion of templates earlier in this chapter, you may have noticed that more than one template can affect the working environment of a document. Each document has access to macros, AutoText entries, and custom commands and toolbar settings in the attached template, the Normal template, and any global templates. These templates, as well as add-ins or the Word application itself, may define a macro or setting in a way that differs from the other templates or add-ins associated with the document.

The definition or setting that takes precedence is the one that resides closest to the document. Therefore, Word resolves such conflicts in the following order of priority:

1. Template attached to the active document
2. Normal template
3. Additional global templates
4. Add-ins
5. Application layer

If several global templates have conflicting settings, Word resolves the conflicts in the order in which the templates are listed in the **Templates and Add-Ins** dialog box (**Tools** menu). Templates in the Word Startup folder appear at the top of the list and have a higher priority. Subsequent ranking on the list is determined by alphabetic order.

Appendixes

Contents

Appendix A   Microsoft Office 97 Resource Kit Tools and Utilities   1011

Appendix B   Setup Command-Line Options and File Formats   1045

Appendix C   Registry Keys and Values   1053

Appendix D   List of Installed Components   1081

Appendix E   Other Support Resources   1091

APPENDIX A

Microsoft Office 97 Resource Kit Tools and Utilities

This appendix describes the contents of the Microsoft Office 97 Resource Kit Tools and Utilities CD. Included on the Tools and Utilities CD are a variety of software tools, converters, utilities, and sample files to assist you in supporting users, using Office fully within your organization, and maintaining Office 97 along with previous versions of Office.

In This Appendix
Client Installation Tools   1011
Conversion Utilities   1014
Documentation   1019
General Tools   1027
Tools for Extracting and Copying Files from Office Floppy Disks   1037
World Wide Web and Intranet Tools   1041

Client Installation Tools

Client installation tools include the following:

- Network Installation Wizard, for customizing and automating the installation of Office on a network
- Package definition files (PDFs) for the Microsoft Systems Management Server, which allows you to support client workstations from a remote computer
- System Policy Editor and Office 97 policy templates

For more information about using these tools, see Chapter 6, "Customizing Client Installations" and Chapter 7, "Customizing and Optimizing Microsoft Office."

Appendixes

Network Installation Wizard

The Network Installation Wizard allows you to modify Setup information files to create a customized network installation of Office. If you install Office in batch mode (without user interaction), Setup installs the software using the default values you specify with the Network Installation Wizard. If users install Office in interactive mode, the values you set with the Network Installation Wizard are presented as the default choices during installation.

▶ To install the Network Installation Wizard

1   Insert the Tools and Utilities CD into the appropriate drive.
2   In the Tools\Niw folder, double-click Setupniw.exe and follow the instructions.

For more information about using the Network Installation Wizard, see Chapter 6, "Customizing Client Installations."

Package Definition Files

The sample package definition files (PDFs) can be used by the Microsoft Systems Management Server to install Office or Office applications remotely. Included are the PDFs for Office 97, Standard Edition and Professional Edition, as well as PDFs for Microsoft Access, Microsoft Excel, Microsoft Outlook, Microsoft PowerPoint, and Microsoft Word standalone editions. Also included is the PDF for Clip Gallery, which is located on the Office CD.

▶ To install the Package Definition Files

1   Insert the Tools and Utilities CD into the appropriate drive.
2   Copy the PDF for the application you want to install from the Tools\PDF folder to a network or your hard disk.

The following table shows the PDF that corresponds to each Microsoft application.

This Microsoft application	Uses this PDF
Office 97 Professional	Off97pro.pdf
Office 97 Standard	Off97std.pdf
Word 97	Word97.pdf
Excel 97	Excel97.pdf
PowerPoint 97	Pptsms.pdf
Outlook 97	Outl97.pdf
Access 97	Acc97.pdf
Clip Gallery	Clipart.pdf

Note If you are using load leveling in Microsoft Systems Management Server version 1.2, you must copy two additional files from the Tools\PDF folder on the CD: Ofs97_01.ico and Msapps32.pdf.

For information about using the sample PDFs, see the Readme.doc file in the Tool\PDF folder on the Tools and Utilities CD. This document contains comprehensive information about installing Office 97 using Microsoft Systems Management Server version 1.2.

System Policy Editor and Office 97 Policy Templates

In Windows 95 and Windows NT Workstation version 4.0, you can use the System Policy Editor to configure client computers from a central location by creating a single system policy file that resides on a server. When users log on to the network, client computers use the system policy file to modify local copies of the Windows registry. You can update the system policy file at any time.

The System Policy Editor that comes with Office 97 has been updated from previous versions and is the same as the System Policy Editor provided with the Windows NT Resource Kit. It is recommended that you upgrade your System Policy Editor if you have a previous version. For more information about the System Policy Editor, see the *Microsoft Windows 95 Resource Kit* or the *Microsoft Windows NT Server 4.0 Resource Kit* and *Microsoft Windows NT Workstation 4.0 Resource Kit*.

You can install the System Policy Editor or just the Office 97 policy templates. Because the System Policy Editor is a Windows application, you must install it through Control Panel.

▶ **To install the System Policy Editor and Office 97 policy templates from the Tools and Utilities CD**

1. In Control Panel, double-click the Add/Remove Programs icon.
2. Click the **Windows Setup** tab.
3. Click **Have Disk**.
4. In the **Copy manufacturer's files from** box, type *drive***:\Policy** where *drive* is the drive letter for the Tools and Utilities CD, and then click **OK**.
5. Under **Components**, select the **System Policy Editor** check box to install the System Policy Editor program (Poledit.exe) and related files.
6. Select the **Office 97 Templates for Windows 95** check box to install the Office policy templates for Windows 95.

    –or–

    Select the **Office 97 Templates for Windows NT 4.0** check box to install the Office policy templates for Windows NT Workstation 4.0.
7. Click **Install**.

Appendixes

> **Tip** If the latest System Policy Editor is already installed on your computer, you can copy the Office policy templates from the Policies folder on the Tools and Utilities CD directly to your computer instead of installing them.

The following table lists the Office policy templates included on the Tools and Utilities CD.

Office 97 templates for Windows 95	Office 97 templates for Windows NT 4.0
Off97w95.adm	Off97nt4.adm
Access97.adm	Access97.adm
Outlk97.adm	Outlk97.adm
Query97.adm	Query97.adm

For more information about using system policies with Office 97, see Chapter 7, "Customizing and Optimizing Microsoft Office." For a list of policies that can be set with the Office 97 policy templates, see Appendix C, "Registry Keys and Values."

Conversion Utilities

Conversion utilities convert files from other operating systems, other applications, and other versions of Office so that they are compatible with Office 97.

PowerPoint Converters

PowerPoint 97 can open presentations created in PowerPoint versions 3.0–97 and can save presentations directly in PowerPoint 3.0–97 format. If you are converting many files to PowerPoint 97 format, you can use the PowerPoint 97 batch converter. If your workgroup is running a mixture of versions, PowerPoint 4.0 users can use the PowerPoint 95 converter to read PowerPoint 95 presentations.

For more information about PowerPoint 97 and converters, see "Running Multiple Versions of PowerPoint" in Chapter 22, "Supporting Multiple Versions of Microsoft Office." If you are converting from a previous version of PowerPoint, see Chapter 14, "Upgrading from Previous Versions of Microsoft PowerPoint."

PowerPoint 97 Batch Converter

PowerPoint 97 automatically converts a presentation from a previous version when you open the file and then save it in PowerPoint 97 format. However, converting presentations one at a time can be tedious if your organization is switching to PowerPoint 97 and you have a large number of presentations in PowerPoint 3.0, 4.0, or 95 format. The PowerPoint 97 batch converter can convert a large number of presentations at once to PowerPoint 97 format.

▶ **To install the PowerPoint 97 batch converter for PowerPoint 3.0–95**

1 Insert the Tools and Utilities CD into the appropriate drive.
2 In the PowerPt\BatchCvt folder, double-click Setup.exe and follow the instructions.

For information about how to use the batch converter, see the Readme file in the PowerPt\BatchCvt folder on the Tools and Utilities CD.

PowerPoint 95 Converter for PowerPoint 4.0

If your organization is upgrading gradually to PowerPoint 97, some PowerPoint 95 and PowerPoint 4.0 users may have to share presentations. The PowerPoint 95 converter for PowerPoint 4.0 allows PowerPoint 4.0 users to read PowerPoint 95 presentations. Not all PowerPoint 95 features are fully supported by PowerPoint 4.0.

▶ **To install the PowerPoint 95 converter for PowerPoint 4.0 (Windows only)**

1 Insert the Tools and Utilities CD into the appropriate drive.
2 In the PowerPt\Win4to95 folder, copy Pp7trans.dll to the Powerpnt folder on the computer where PowerPoint 95 is installed.

▶ **To install the PowerPoint 95 converter for PowerPoint 4.0 (Macintosh only)**

1 Insert the Tools and Utilities CD into the appropriate drive.
2 If you have the 68K release of PowerPoint for the Macintosh, copy Pp7trans.hqx from the PowerPt\Mac4to95\68K folder to your computer.

   –or–

   If you have the PowerPC release of PowerPoint for the Macintosh, copy Pp7trans.hqx from the PowerPt\Mac4to95\PowerPC folder to your computer.

3 Decompress Pp7trans.hqx using the utility BinHex 4.0, and then move the decompressed file, Pp7trans, to your PowerPoint folder.

   Note For more information about either of these versions of Pp7trans.hqx, see the Readme file in PowerPt\Mac4to95\68K or PowerPt\Mac4to95\PowerPC.

PowerPoint Viewers

A PowerPoint viewer allows users who do not have PowerPoint installed on their computers to view PowerPoint presentations. The Tools and Utilities CD includes viewers for PowerPoint 95 and 4.0. For more information about PowerPoint viewers, see "Sharing Presentations Across Operating Systems and Versions" in Chapter 22, "Supporting Multiple Versions of Microsoft Office."

PowerPoint Viewer for PowerPoint 95

The viewer for PowerPoint 95 is a standalone, 32-bit executable program that runs only under Windows 95 or the Windows NT operating system. This viewer fully supports and displays all of the PowerPoint 95 slide show effects. The viewer can be freely distributed without any additional license. It opens presentations saved in PowerPoint for Windows 2.0 or later and PowerPoint for the Macintosh 3.0 or later. The viewer supports long file names and automatically configures Netscape Navigator to use this viewer to view PowerPoint presentations on the World Wide Web.

If you are creating presentations in PowerPoint 97, you must first save the presentation in PowerPoint 95 format or in the dual 95 & 97 format before it can be viewed in the viewer for PowerPoint 95. For information about saving presentations in a format compatible with PowerPoint 95, see "Sharing Presentations with PowerPoint 95" in Chapter 14, "Upgrading from Previous Versions of Microsoft PowerPoint."

▶ **To install the viewer for PowerPoint 95**

1. Insert the Tools and Utilities CD into the appropriate drive.
2. In the Powerpt\Viewer95 folder, double-click Pptvw32.exe and follow the instructions.

   –or–

   Copy Pptvw32.exe to a network or your hard disk and run it from there.

PowerPoint Viewer for PowerPoint 4.0

The viewer for PowerPoint 4.0 is a standalone, 16-bit executable program. If you are saving presentations in 3.0 or 4.0 format, or if the presentations are to be viewed on a computer that does not support 32-bit architecture, you must have the 16-bit viewer installed. The 16-bit viewer is installed automatically when you choose a Typical installation during Setup and is also included on the Tools and Utilities CD.

If you are creating presentations in PowerPoint 97 or PowerPoint 95, you must first save the presentation in 4.0 format before it can be viewed in the viewer for PowerPoint 4.0. For information about saving presentations in a format compatible with PowerPoint 4.0, see "Sharing Presentations with PowerPoint 4.0" in Chapter 14, "Upgrading from Previous Versions of Microsoft PowerPoint."

▶ **To install the viewer for PowerPoint 4.0**

1. Insert the Tools and Utilities CD into the appropriate drive.

   In the Powerpt\Viewer40 folder, double-click Vsetup.exe and follow the instructions.

   –or–

   Copy the Powerpt\Viewer40 folder to a network or your hard disk, and run Vsetup.exe from there.

Word Converters

With the help of converters, Word 97 recognizes the file formats of many common word processing, worksheet, and database programs. When you open these types of documents in Word 97, Word 97 automatically converts them to Word 97 format, preserving much of the original content and formatting. You can also save Word 97 documents in other file formats and preserve as much formatting as the other application can support. Likewise, when you open a document from a previous version of Word, Word automatically converts the document to Word 97 format.

For more information about converting other file formats to Word 97, see Chapter 21, "Switching to Microsoft Word." If you are converting from a previous version of Word, see Chapter 15, "Upgrading from Previous Versions of Microsoft Word."

Converter for Word 6.0 or 95

If your organization is upgrading gradually to Word 97, some users may have to share documents with users of Word for Windows 6.0 or 95. The Word 97 converter for Windows allows users of Word for Windows 6.0 or 95 to read Word 97 files. Not all Word 97 features are fully supported by Word 6.0 or 95. For more information, see "Opening Word 97 Documents in Word 6.0 or 95" in Chapter 15, "Upgrading from Previous Versions of Microsoft Word." The document Wrd97cnv.doc, installed with the converter, also describes features that are not supported when a Word 97 document is converted to Word 6.0 or 95 format.

▶ **To install the converter for Word 6.0 or 95**

1 Insert the Tools and Utilities CD into the appropriate drive.

2 In the Word\Convert folder, double-click Wrd97cnv.exe and follow the instructions.

  –or–

  Copy Wrd97cnv.exe to a network or your hard disk and run it from there.

Converter for Word for MS-DOS 3.x–6.0

The Word for MS-DOS 3.x–6.0 converter is a text converter that allows you to open files created in Word for MS-DOS 3.x–6.0 directly in Word 97. You can also save files from Word 97 in Word for MS-DOS 3.x–6.0 format using this converter. All data and formatting created in Word for MS-DOS 3.x–6.0 is fully supported in Word 97. For more information, see "Upgrading from Word 5.x or 6.0 for MS-DOS" in Chapter 15, "Upgrading from Previous Versions of Microsoft Word."

▶ **To install the converter for Word for MS-DOS 3.x–6.0**

1 Insert the Tools and Utilities CD into the appropriate drive.

2 In the Word\Convert folder, copy Doswrd32.cnv to the Program Files\Common Files\Microsoft Shared\Textconv folder on your computer.

If Word is running, you must close and restart it before using the converter.

Converter for DisplayWrite, MultiMate, and RFT-DCA

The Word converter for DisplayWrite, MultiMate, and RFT-DCA is a text converter that converts DisplayWrite and MultiMate documents previously saved in RFT-DCA format to Word 97 format. It also converts any other documents saved in RFT-DCA format to Word 97 format and converts Word 97 files to RFT-DCA format.

▶ **To install the converter for DisplayWrite, MultiMate, and RFT-DCA**

1. Insert the Tools and Utilities CD into the appropriate drive.
2. In the Word\Convert folder, copy Rftdca32.cnv to the Program Files\Common Files\Microsoft Shared\Textconv folder on your computer.

If Word is running, you must close and restart it before using the converter.

Converter for Lotus Ami Pro

The Word converter for Lotus Ami Pro is a text converter that converts documents from Ami Pro versions 3.0, 3.01, and 3.1 to Word 97 format. It also converts Word 97 documents to Ami Pro 3.0, 3.01, and 3.1 formats.

▶ **To install the converter for Lotus Ami Pro**

1. Insert the Tools and Utilities CD into the appropriate drive.
2. In the Word\Convert folder, copy Ami332.cnv to the Program Files\Common Files\Microsoft Shared\Textconv folder on your computer.

If Word is running, you must close and restart it before using the converter.

Converter for Microsoft Windows Write

The Word converter for Windows Write converts documents from Windows Write version 3.0 or 3.1 to Word 97 format. It also converts Word 97 documents to Windows Write 3.0 format.

Tip After converting a Windows Write 3.0 or 3.1 document to Word 97 format and then back again, it may appear that objects were lost in the conversion. If this happens, repaginate the final document in Windows Write; the objects should reappear.

▶ **To install the converter for Windows Write**

1. Insert the Tools and Utilities CD into the appropriate drive.
2. In the Word\Convert folder, copy Write32.cnv to the Program Files\Common Files\Microsoft Shared\Textconv folder on your computer.

If Word is running, you must close and restart it before using the converter.

Conversion Fonts for WordPerfect

Converters for WordPerfect for Windows 5.*x* or 6.*x* documents are installed automatically when you choose the Typical installation during Setup. However, if

WordPerfect 6.x for Windows is not installed on your computer, the WordPerfect 5.x and 6.x converters cannot render the original WordPerfect fonts. In this case, you can install conversion fonts. The converters for WordPerfect map characters from the WordPerfect character sets to the conversion fonts.

The conversion fonts include five TrueType fonts to improve conversion of characters from the WordPerfect 5.x and 6.x character sets. The following table lists WordPerfect character sets and the corresponding fonts.

This WordPerfect character set	Corresponds to this font
Greek	Greek Symbols
Iconic Symbols	Iconic Symbols Extension
Math/Scientific	Math Extension
Multinational	Multinational Extension
Typographic	Typographic Extension

▶ **To install the conversion fonts for WordPerfect**

1 Insert the Tools and Utilities CD into the appropriate drive.
2 In the Word\Fonts folder, copy all the files to the Windows\Fonts or WinNT\Fonts folder on your computer.

Converter for WordStar

The Word converter for WordStar converts documents from WordStar for MS-DOS versions 3.3–7.0 and WordStar for Windows versions 1.0–2.0 to Word 97 format. It also converts Word 97 documents to WordStar 4.0 or 7.0 for MS-DOS format.

▶ **To install the converter for WordStar**

1 Insert the Tools and Utilities CD into the appropriate drive.
2 In the Word\Convert folder, copy Wrdstr32.cnv to the Program Files\Common Files\Microsoft Shared\Textconv folder on your computer.

If Word is running, you must close and restart it before using the converter.

Documentation

Documentation on the Tools and Utilities CD includes the Microsoft Technical Support Help File for Office 97, a comprehensive printer manual, a list of Office files, and other informative documents to aid you in supporting Office 97 users.

Note Unless Word 97 or another application is explicitly specified, you can open and read documents in Word 95. Open and read worksheets in Microsoft Excel 95.

Advanced Documentation

Advanced documentation includes a variety of documents that explain how to alter Office 97 Setup or configuration. The instructions in these documents require knowledge of advanced features, such as the Network Installation Wizard or Setup table file (STF) syntax, and are intended for users familiar with these features.

These advanced documents are described in the following table.

Advanced document	Description
Assistnt.doc	Explains how to install the Office Assistants on users' computers when they run Setup from a network installation point. Requires knowledge of STF syntax.
Bookshlf.doc	Explains how to install Microsoft Bookshelf Basics files manually on a network installation point, and then give users access to these files when they install Office from the network. Requires knowledge of STF syntax.
Clipart.doc	Explains how users can install clip art files on their computers when they run Setup from a network installation point. Requires knowledge of the Network Installation Wizard.
Noutlook.doc	Explains how to prevent users from installing Outlook when they install Office from a network installation point. Requires knowledge of STF syntax.
OSB.doc	Explains how to give users a customized Office Shortcut Bar when they install Office from a network installation point. Requires knowledge of the Network Installation Wizard and the Windows Registry Editor.
StrtMenu.doc	Explains how users who install Office from a network installation point can run Office 97 shortcuts from the **Start** menu by pointing to **Programs** and then pointing to **Microsoft Office**, instead of pointing to **Programs**. Requires knowledge of STF syntax.
Upgrade.doc	Explains how to upgrade multiple users using the same computer from Office 95 to Office 97 if the **Start** menu is included in User Profiles. Requires knowledge of system policies.
Valupack.doc	Explains how to give users a ValuPack folder on their desktop when they install Office from a network installation point. This folder contains the self-extracting executable files that include utilities from the Value Pack on the Office CD. Requires knowledge of the Network Installation Wizard.

▶ **To view the advanced documentation**

1. Insert the Tools and Utilities CD into the appropriate drive.
2. In the Document folder, double-click the document you want to view.

    –or–

    Copy the document to a network or your hard disk and view it from there.

For information about the Network Installation Wizard and STF files, see Chapter 6, "Customizing Client Installations," and Appendix B, "Setup Command-Line Options and File Formats."

Find Fast Stop Word List

The Find Fast utility in Office 97 helps make it easier to find Office documents on local or network drives. Find Fast does this by indexing the words contained in your documents. Some words, such as *and*, *of*, and *or*, occur frequently in most documents. Because these words are of little value as search words, Find Fast does not index them. Words that are not indexed are referred to as *stop words*.

The file Stopword.doc is a complete list of all the stop words for all languages supported by Office. Find Fast uses only the words in your language as stop words. For example, the French word *sur* is in the stop word list but is not considered a stop word when used in a language other than French.

▶ **To view the Find Fast stop word list**

1 Insert the Tools and Utilities CD into the appropriate drive.
2 In the Lists folder, double-click Stopword.doc.

   –or–

   Copy the file to a network or your hard disk, and view it from there.

For more information about Find Fast, see Chapter 26, "Finding Microsoft Office Documents on the Network."

Informational Worksheets

Informational worksheets list items such as all of the files installed by Office 97, all of the registry keys created, all of the font files installed, and so on. These lists assist you by telling you whether a particular key or file on a user's computer is installed by Office.

These informational worksheets are described in the following table.

Informational worksheet	Description
Complete.xls	Lists the files installed when you choose the Custom installation during Setup and select all the files. It also lists the size of each file and the name of the folder where the file is installed.
Fonts.xls	Lists all the font files installed by Office 97. It also lists the name of the folder where the files are installed.
Network.xls	Lists the files installed when you choose the Run from Network Server installation during Setup. It also lists the size of each file and the name of the folder where the file is installed.

Informational worksheet	Description
Regkey.xls	Lists all of the registry keys that are created, changed, or deleted when installing Office 97. This worksheet includes examples of the values to which these keys may be set. These are not default values and may differ depending on the hardware and software configuration of your computer.
Runfrmcd.xls	Lists the files installed when you choose the Run from CD installation during Setup. It also lists the size of each file and the name of the folder where the file is installed.
Typical.xls	Lists the files installed when you choose the Typical installation during Setup. It also lists the size of each file and the name of the folder where the file is installed.
Userlist.xls	Lists each Office 97 file that contains user information, a description of the file, any registry keys or system policies pertaining to the file, and any default values for the registry keys.

▶ **To view the informational worksheets**

1. Insert the Tools and Utilities CD into the appropriate drive.
2. In the Lists folder, double-click the worksheet you want to view.

   –or–

   Copy the worksheet to a network or your hard disk and view it from there.

Microsoft Technical Support Documents

The Microsoft Technical Support documents contain answers to many common questions about installing and configuring Office 97. The articles were produced by Microsoft support engineers and provide information for both users and administrators.

These technical support documents are described in the following table.

Technical support document	Description
Top10.doc	Includes the top 10 issues to consider to ensure a proper Setup of Office 97.
Toolbar.doc	Discusses the Office Shortcut Bar in question-and-answer format.
Binder.doc	Discusses Office Binder in question-and-answer format.
Wiz.doc	Discusses the Upgrade Wizard in question-and-answer format. For more information about the Upgrade Wizard, see Chapter 9, "Troubleshooting Installation."
Niw20.doc	Provides a helpful guide for using the Network Installation Wizard. For more information about the Network Installation Wizard, see Chapter 6, "Customizing Client Installations."

▶ **To view Microsoft Technical Support documents**

1 Insert the Tools and Utilities CD into the appropriate drive.
2 In the Support folder, double-click the support document you want to view.

   −or−

   Copy the document to a network or your hard disk and view it from there.

Microsoft Technical Support Help File

The Microsoft Technical Support Help File contains articles produced by Microsoft support engineers and covers many new features and functionalities in Office 97. The Microsoft Technical Support Help file is a standard Windows Help file.

▶ **To view the Microsoft Technical Support Help file**

1 Insert the Tools and Utilities CD into the appropriate drive.
2 In the Support folder, double-click Ork97.hlp.

   −or−

   Copy the files Ork97.hlp and Ork97.cnt to a network or your hard disk and view the Help file from there.

Office Upgrade Wizard File List

The Upgrade Wizard uses a list of files to determine which files should be deleted when cleaning up your hard disk. OffCln97.txt is a text file containing the list of old Office files for which the Office Upgrade Wizard searches. For more information about the Upgrade Wizard, see "Office Upgrade Wizard" later in this chapter.

▶ **To view the Office Upgrade Wizard file list**

1 Insert the Tools and Utilities CD into the appropriate drive.
2 In the Lists folder, double-click OffCln97.txt.

   −or−

   Copy the file to a network or your hard disk and view it from there.

Appendixes

Outlook Extension Configuration File Document

The Outlook Extension Configuration File (ECF) document describes ECFs and explains how to use them with Outlook. Although Outlook recognizes, loads, and runs extensions that conform to specifications for Microsoft Exchange Client extensions, you can improve the performance of an extension and increase its functionality under Outlook by providing an ECF. Using an ECF, Outlook anticipates the contexts under which the extension needs to be loaded, what commands the extension contributes, the Outlook modules to which the extension applies, and so on. That way, Outlook can delay loading the extension until the extension is needed.

Important You must have a Web browser installed on your computer to view the ECF document.

▶ **To view the ECF document**

1   Insert the Tools and Utilities CD into the appropriate drive.
2   In the Document\Outlook folder, double-click Ecf.htm.

  –or–

  Copy the folder to a network or your hard disk and view the document from there.

PowerPoint AutoClipArt Concept List

The PowerPoint AutoClipArt concept list catalogs the AutoClipArt concepts that PowerPoint stores internally.

These concepts are used by the **AutoClipArt** command (PowerPoint **Tools** menu) to suggest clip art you can add to a presentation based on the text in the presentation. This feature searches the presentation for words that match keywords in the AutoClipArt concept list. If a match is found, AutoClipArt suggests one or more pieces of clip art that correspond to the matching keyword.

▶ **To view the AutoClipArt concept list**

1   Insert the Tools and Utilities CD into the appropriate drive.
2   In the Powerpt\Autoclip folder, double-click Autoclip.txt.

  –or–

  Copy the file to a network or your hard disk and view it from there.

Setup Simulator

The Setup Simulator is a series of HTML pages that mimic the Office Setup program. It includes simulation of these four Setup scenarios:

- Installing Office from the Office CD
- Adding or removing Office components from the Control Panel

- Creating an administrative installation point on a server
- Installing Office over the network from an administrative installation point

The Setup Simulator can help you become familiar with Setup before you install Office in your workgroup. It is especially helpful for network administrators who are helping users with the installation process.

Important You must have a Web browser installed on your computer to view the Setup Simulator.

▶ To run the Setup Simulator

1 Insert the Tools and Utilities CD into the appropriate drive.
2 In the Document\SimSetup folder, double-click Begin.htm.

   –or–

   Copy the Document\SimSetup folder to a network or your hard disk and then run Setup Simulator from there.

Ultimate Printer Manual

The *Ultimate Printer Manual* is a comprehensive manual containing information about every major printer currently available. It includes illustrations of each printer, its interface, error messages, fonts available, and how it handles paper. Also included are a glossary of printing terms, a control code reference index, symbol sets, and so on.

Important You must have a Web browser installed on your computer to view the *Ultimate Printer Manual*.

▶ To install the Ultimate Printer Manual

1 Insert the Tools and Utilities CD into the appropriate drive.
2 Copy the Document\Printers folder from the CD to your hard disk.
3 Double-click Document\Printers\Index.htm.

The *Ultimate Printer Manual* requires approximately 16 MB of disk space. If you do not want to install the *Ultimate Printer Manual*, you can run it from the Tools and Utilities CD.

▶ To run the Ultimate Printer Manual from the Tools and Utilities CD

1 Insert the Tools and Utilities CD into the appropriate drive.
2 In the Document\Printers folder, double-click Index.htm.

Appendixes

Word 97 How-to Documents

The Word 97 how-to documents are examples of some of the most common Word questions answered by Microsoft Technical Support; these examples demonstrate how to accomplish a variety of tasks using Word 97 features. The articles were produced by Microsoft support engineers and provide information of interest to both users and administrators.

These how-to documents are described in the following table.

Word 97 How-to document	Description
Frmfield.doc	Demonstrates how to use form fields. *Form fields* are locations in a document where users enter information.
Headfoot.doc	Demonstrates how to create headers and footers.
Lablgrph.doc	Demonstrates how to put graphics on multiple labels.
Mailmerg.doc	Demonstrates how to use the mail merge feature.
Modiftem.doc	Demonstrates how to create a new template or modify existing templates.
Styles.doc	Demonstrates how to define and use styles.

▶ **To view the Word 97 how-to documents**

1 Insert the Tools and Utilities CD into the appropriate drive.
2 In the Word\Tips folder, double-click the how-to document you want to view.

   –or–

   Copy the document to a network or your hard disk and view it from there.

Visual Basic Win32 API Declarations

The Tools and Utilities CD includes a text file describing Win32 API declarations for Microsoft Visual Basic. For more information about using Win32 API declarations, see "Porting Your 16-bit Office-Based Solutions to 32-bit Office" in Chapter 10, "Upgrading from Previous Versions of Microsoft Office."

▶ **To view the Visual Basic Win32 API declarations document**

1 Insert the Tools and Utilities CD into the appropriate drive.
2 In the Document\Vba folder, double-click Win32api.txt.

   –or–

   Copy the file to a network or your hard disk and view it from there.

General Tools

In the general tools category, the Tools and Utilities CD provides a variety of administrative utilities.

Gallery Location Tools

The gallery location tools allow you to specify where Microsoft Excel and Microsoft Graph look for custom chart gallery files. This tool is useful in organizations that have standardized on a set of chart templates. An administrator can create a custom chart gallery containing custom templates and place the gallery on a server. Users can then run the Microsoft Excel Gallery Location tool or the Graph Gallery Location tool, specifying the server location.

▶ To run the Microsoft Excel Gallery Location tool

1 Insert the Tools and Utilities CD into the appropriate drive.
2 In the Tools\Gallery folder, double-click XLGalLoc.exe.

   –or–

   Copy the file to a network or your hard disk and run it from there.

Note If you run this tool from the network or your hard disk, you must also have the file Vb40032.dll in your Windows\System folder. If you do not have this DLL, copy Tools\Gallery\Vb40032.dll from the Tools and Utilities CD to your Windows\System folder.

▶ To run the Graph Gallery Location tool

1 Insert the Tools and Utilities CD into the appropriate drive.
2 In the Tools\Gallery folder, double-click GrGalLoc.exe.

   –or–

   Copy the file to a network or your hard disk and run it from there.

Note If you run this tool from the network or your hard disk, you must also have the file Vb40032.dll in your Windows\System folder. If you do not have this DLL, copy Tools\Gallery\Vb40032.dll from the Tools and Utilities CD to your Windows\System folder.

Microsoft Excel 97 File Recovery Macro

Sometimes Microsoft Excel 97 is able to open a file but does not work properly with it. This may be caused by corruption in formats, formulas, values, or code. If you can open such a workbook, you can use the Microsoft Excel 97 File Recovery Macro to recreate worksheets, XLM macro sheets, and module sheets in a new workbook.

This macro also creates a log file so that you can see which items caused problems while transferring to the new worksheet. If the File Recovery Macro fails, you can use the last entry in the log file to determine what caused the problem and recreate the workbook without that item. For information about Microsoft Excel macros and add-ins, see Chapter 36, "Microsoft Excel Architecture."

▶ **To install the Microsoft Excel 97 File Recovery Macro**

1. Insert the Tools and Utilities CD into the appropriate drive.
2. In the Excel\Recover folder, copy Cleaner.xla to the Program Files\Microsoft Office\Office\Library folder on your computer.
3. On the Microsoft Excel **Tools** menu, click **Add-Ins**.
4. In the **Add-Ins available** box, click **Corruption Cleaner**.

To use the File Recovery Macro, make the workbook you want to clean the active workbook; then click **Clean Active Workbook** (**Tools** menu). For more information, see Readme.doc in the Excel\Recover folder on the Tools and Utilities CD.

Outlook 97 Profiles

Outlook is a Windows messaging application that requires a Windows messaging profile. Profiles detail user electronic mail (e-mail) settings and services, and are usually configured by double-clicking the Mail and Fax icon in Control Panel.

When a user starts Outlook on a computer without a Windows messaging profile, Outlook automatically creates a profile. Administrators can modify the default profile settings by customizing the Outlook.prf file before installing Outlook, or after installing but before the user starts Outlook for the first time.

For more information about profiles, see the Outlook 97 profiles document on the Tools and Utilities CD.

▶ **To view the Outlook 97 profiles document**

1. Insert the Tools and Utilities CD into the appropriate drive.
2. In the Outlook\Profiles folder, double-click Profiles.doc.

    –or–

    Copy the file to a network or your hard disk and view it from there.

The default profile for Outlook 97, Outlook.prf, creates a profile with Personal Folders and Outlook Address Book. To change the default profile that Outlook creates, replace the Outlook.prf file with an alternative version.

The alternative profiles provided on the Tools and Utilities CD are:

- Exchange.prf

    Creates a profile with Microsoft Exchange Server and Outlook Address Book. To use this profile, you need to know the name of a Microsoft Exchange Server in your organization.

- None.prf

    Causes Outlook to run the Inbox Setup Wizard instead, which allows users to select profile services.

▶ **To install and use the Outlook 97 profiles**

1 Insert the Tools and Utilities CD into the appropriate drive.
2 In the Outlook\Profiles folder, copy Exchange.prf or None.prf to the Windows folder on your computer.
3 If you are using Exchange.prf, open it in a text editor (such as Notepad), find the line HomeServer = in the [Service2] section, and set it to the name of a Microsoft Exchange Server in your organization.
4 In the Windows folder on your computer, delete Outlook.prf.
5 Rename Exchange.prf or None.prf to Outlook.prf.

You can also install an alternative Outlook 97 profile on a network installation point, so that users who install Office from the network can use the new profile.

▶ **To install and use the Outlook 97 profiles on a network installation point**

1 Insert the Tools and Utilities CD into the appropriate drive.
2 In the Outlook\Profiles folder, copy Exchange.prf or None.prf to the Office folder on the network installation point.
3 If you are using Exchange.prf, open it in a text editor (such as Notepad), find the line HomeServer = in the [Service2] section, and set it to the name of a Microsoft Exchange Server in your organization.
4 In the Office folder on the network installation point, delete Outlook.prf.
5 Rename Exchange.prf or None.prf to Outlook.prf.

Appendixes

Outlook 97 Sample Forms

Outlook 97 sample forms include a number of applications created using the Outlook Forms Designer. These applications consist of forms and views. The applications are described in the following table.

Application	Description
Corporate Calendar	Provides a bulletin board for viewing and posting events. Users can post and read about events in the Corporate Calendar using one of five views. These views are editable for fast entry of events.
Employee Handbook	Provides a bulletin board for entering policies and procedures. The sample Policy form identifies a policy or procedure for an organization. A history log tracks changes to a policy. The sample Sub-Section Policy form may be one of several subsections of a policy. The sample ensures that only a few individuals can create policies; most users can only read them.
Office Expense Report	Provides a template for submitting expense reports in the form of a Microsoft Excel worksheet embedded within an Outlook Mail item. Users complete the Expense Report and send it through e-mail.
Help Desk	Manages help requests for the help desk staff. The sample consists of one folder for collecting requests from users and a second folder used by the technicians who handle the requests. A help desk dispatcher can view requests and assign tasks by entering a technician's name in the Technician field on the Help Request form.
Job Candidates	Tracks employment candidates by storing information about them in one location. This sample was created for others to discuss the qualifications of possible candidates. Information stored in Job Candidates includes job history, résumé, position applied for, and status.
Job Postings	Provides a bulletin board for advertising open positions. Users can post and read open positions in the Job Postings public folder. The Job Posting form includes a **Respond** button that opens an e-mail form for sending a résumé to the reporting manager's mailbox.
Knowledgebase	Provides a discussion database for sharing knowledge and information. Users can read and respond by posting information in the Knowledgebase public folder using the Knowledge Discussion form.
Project Management	Tracks projects by storing relevant project information, such as budget, status reports, documents, deliverables, meeting minutes, and tasks. The Project Management sample can be used to track a single project or multiple projects within the same folder.

Application	Description
Office Supplies/ Equipment Requisition	Allows users to order office supplies or equipment using a Microsoft Excel worksheet embedded in an Outlook Post item. Users have the option of sending an e-mail message to the recipient who approves or orders the requested supplies.
Sales Tracking	Tracks clients by storing information about them in one location. Users can keep track of company information, action items, contact records, meeting minutes, and notes from phone conversations. Users can also post responses to any items created.

▶ **To install the Outlook 97 sample forms**

1 Insert the Tools and Utilities CD into the appropriate drive.

2 In the Outlook\Forms folder, copy Forms2.pst to a network or your hard disk.

   The recommended location for the PST files is in the Microsoft Office\Office folder.

▶ **To use the Outlook 97 sample forms**

1 On the Outlook **File** menu, point to **Open Special Folder**, and then click **Personal Folder**.

2 In the **Connect to Personal Folders** box, click **Forms2.pst** in Microsoft Office\Office (or in the folder to which you copied the file).

   A new Outlook window is displayed, containing the Sample Forms 2 folder. This folder contains subfolders that correspond to the sample forms listed in the preceding table. To use one of the sample forms, open the Readme document in the appropriate subfolder. Each Readme contains a detailed description and installation information.

Office 97 Deployment Planner

Chapter 3, "Deployment Guide for Microsoft Office," provides an overview of the primary phases in a typical deployment of Office 97. If you have Microsoft Project, you can use the Office 97 Deployment Planner to help guide you through the process of creating your custom Office 97 installation plan.

Important You must have Microsoft Project installed on your computer to run the Office Deployment Planner.

World Wide Web To download a free trial version of Microsoft Project for Windows 95, connect to the Microsoft project home page at:

http://www.microsoft.com/project/

▶ **To run the Office 97 Deployment Planner**

1. Insert the Tools and Utilities CD into the appropriate drive.
2. In the Deploy folder, double-click Setup.exe.

   –or–

   Copy the Deploy folder to a network or your hard disk and run Setup.exe from there.

   The files are copied to your C:\Deploy folder.
3. In your C:\Deploy folder, double-click Office97.mpt.

If you do not have Microsoft Project, you can view the steps in a worksheet in Microsoft Excel.

Important You must have Microsoft Excel installed on your computer to view the Deployment Planner worksheet.

▶ **To view the Deployment Planner worksheet**

1. Insert the Tools and Utilities CD into the appropriate drive.
2. In the Deploy folder, double-click Setup.exe.

   –or–

   Copy the Deploy folder to a network or your hard disk and run Setup.exe from there.

   The files are copied to your C:\Deploy folder.
3. In your C:\Deploy folder, double-click Office97.xlt.

Office 97 Unbind Utilities

If your workgroup is upgrading gradually to Office 97, some users may have to share the Office 97 Binder with users of previous versions of Office, which cannot read binders created in Office 97. However, when you use the Office 97 Unbind Utilities to separate Office 97 binder files into their component files, the component files can be converted and then opened in Office 95 and Office 4.*x* applications.

▶ **To install and run the Unbind Utilities for Windows**

1. Insert the Tools and Utilities CD into the appropriate drive.
2. In the Tools\Unbind\Windows folder, copy Unbind.exe to a network or your hard disk.
3. To run the utility, double-click Unbind.exe.

▶ **To install and run the Unbind Utilities for the Macintosh**

1. Insert the Tools and Utilities CD into the appropriate drive.
2. In the Tools\Unbind\Mac folder, copy Unbind.hqx to your computer, and then decompress the file using the utility BinHex 4.0.
3. To run the utility, double-click Unbind.

Office Upgrade Wizard

If you install Office 97 on a computer that has a previous version of Office on it, there may be files and registry entries on your hard disk that can be removed. The Upgrade Wizard removes these files and frees space on your hard disk. You can run the utility in one of several modes to remove files that are not needed, remove all the files installed by previous versions of Office, or remove only those files that you specify.

The Office Upgrade Wizard searches only for files that originated from a previous version of Office or an Office application, and removes them only if you indicate that these applications are no longer used on your computer. The files can be removed either through a wizard interface that the end user runs or as an automatic batch process that is fully customizable by the system administrator. You can customize the Upgrade Wizard to remove files and registration entries at your discretion. For more information about the Upgrade Wizard, see Chapter 9, "Troubleshooting Installation."

▶ **To install and run the Upgrade Wizard**

1. Insert the Tools and Utilities CD into the appropriate drive.
2. In the Tools\Upgrader folder, double-click Offcln97.exe and follow the instructions.

   –or–

   Copy the Tools\Upgrader folder to a network or your hard disk and run the wizard from there.

SwitchForms for Outlook

With the SwitchForms utility, you can easily switch between Microsoft Exchange Client and Outlook. Although you can view the same e-mail folders in both applications, each application installs its own forms for composing and reading messages. If you need to run both Microsoft Exchange Client and Outlook on the same system, use SwitchForms to reinstall the correct forms.

The SwitchForms utility is intended for:

- Help desk personnel who support and run both applications.
- Microsoft Exchange Server public folder application designers who need to test their applications under both Microsoft Exchange Client and Outlook.
- Systems professionals who run Microsoft Exchange Client for production use but need to evaluate Outlook.

▶ **To install Outlook SwitchForms**

1 Insert the Tools and Utilities CD into the appropriate drive.
2 Copy the Outlook\Switchfm folder to a network or your hard disk and run SwitchForms from there.

Note SwitchForms requires the form configuration files from Microsoft Exchange Client, which are installed automatically by the Microsoft Exchange Client Setup program. SwitchForms also requires the Outlook 97 form configuration files, which are not installed when you choose a Typical installation during Office Setup. To install these files, rerun Office Setup and click **Add/Remove**. Select the **Outlook** option, and then select the **Visuals for Forms Design** option.

Before you use Outlook SwitchForms, exit from Microsoft Exchange Client or Outlook.

▶ **To use Outlook SwitchForms**

1 In the SwitchFm folder, double-click Regforms.exe.
2 In the **Install forms for** box, select either **Microsoft Exchange Client** or **Microsoft Outlook** to indicate which application you are switching to.
3 In the **Search for form configuration files** box, type the path for the form configuration files.

   You do not need to specify a full path. SwitchForms searches the folder you specify and all of its subfolders. By default, Microsoft Exchange Client form configuration files are installed in C:\Windows\Forms\Configs. Outlook form configuration files are installed in C:\Program files\Microsoft Office\Office\Forms.

You can also automate the use of SwitchForms.

▶ **To use SwitchForms automatically**

- On the **Start** menu, click **Run** and type **regform.exe\exchange** or **regform.exe\outlook**, depending on which application you are switching from.

Note If you have Microsoft Outlook or Microsoft Exchange Client files running on your computer, you may receive errors when you run SwitchForms. To correct this problem, reboot your computer and run SwitchForms again. When SwitchForms has successfully completed, you will receive a message. If you do not receive the message, reboot your computer and run SwitchForms again.

Wipename for Outlook

Outlook keeps a nickname list that is used by the automatic name checking feature in Outlook. The nickname list is automatically generated as you use Outlook. If the nickname list is corrupted, Outlook may not be able to identify recipients, or may send the message to the wrong person. If this happens, you can use the Wipename utility to clean out the nickname list.

Before you run Wipename, exit from Outlook.

▶ **To run Wipename**

1. Insert the Tools and Utilities CD into the appropriate drive.
2. In the Outlook\Wipename folder, double-click Wipename.exe.

   –or–

   Copy the file to a network or your hard disk and run it from there.
3. In the **Clear Outlook97 autonamecheck nickname list from profile** box, select the profile in which you want to clear the nickname list, and then click **OK**.

   Note If you run Wipename.exe from the network or your hard disk, you must also have the files Vb40032.dll in your Windows\System folder. If you do not have these DLLs, copy Vb40032.dll from the Outlook\Wipename folder on the Tools and Utilities CD to your Windows\System folder.

Crystal Reports for Microsoft Outlook 97

Crystal Reports™ for Microsoft Outlook 97 adds report design and viewing capabilities to Outlook 97. This tool has two components: the Crystal Reports Designer, which is used to build, manipulate and format reports; and the Crystal Reports Analyzer, which allows you to view reports created from Outlook data. Together, these two components give Outlook users the ability to:

- Print unique reports using Outlook properties.
- Add graphics to reports, such as pie charts or a company logo.
- Publish simple HTML pages containing Outlook data.
- Use an alternative to the Schedule+ custom printing development environment.
- Create reports with column roll-ups and totals.

Note The Crystal Reports Designer for Microsoft Outlook 97 has a limit of two licenses per organization. For a more information about Crystal Reports, including how to use it, see the documentation included with the software.

▶ **To install the Crystal Reports Designer for Microsoft Outlook 97**

1. Insert the Tools and Utilities CD into the appropriate drive.
2. In the Outlook\Crystal folder, double-click CRWSetup.exe.

–or–

Copy the folder to a network or your hard disk and install the files from there.

▶ **To install the Crystal Reports Analyzer for Microsoft Outlook 97**

1. Insert the Tools and Utilities CD into the appropriate drive.
2. In the Outlook\Crystal folder, double-click CVWSetup.exe.

–or–

Copy the folder to a network or your hard disk and install the files from there.

RegClean Utility

RegClean is a developer's utility that can be used to analyze and correct settings in the Windows registry that can affect your Office applications or the Windows operating system.

In addition to initialization information and performance settings, the Windows registry also includes information that the Office applications and Windows share in a common location in the registry. These shared settings allow separately built components (such as Word and PowerPoint) to work together seamlessly without user interaction. RegClean analyzes and corrects these common settings.

The information stored in the common location in the registry contains cross-references to other registry sections and also to applications and files stored on your hard disk or on the network. Sometimes changes are made to these cross-references or to the settings or files they point to, and the registry is no longer synchronized with Windows or with the Office applications. For example:

- If a file or application is moved or deleted
- If a new version of a component is installed without uninstalling the previous version

In these scenarios, the cross-reference in the registry may appear valid, but the setting or file that is referenced no longer exists.

RegClean verifies that all of these cross-references are valid. If it finds cross-references to files that no longer exist in a particular location, or cross-references to other locations in the registry that do not cross-reference back to that original cross reference, it removes the invalid cross-references.

Note RegClean does not attempt to replace invalid cross-references with valid cross-references elsewhere. Any new settings in the registry must be entered by the installation programs of the applications themselves.

Once the invalid settings are removed, you may notice changes in Windows or in your Office applications: Icons may return to the defaults; items may be removed from the **New** dialog box (**File** menu); or objects may be removed from the **Object** dialog box (**Insert** menu). These icons, items, or objects were probably incorrectly placed. Once they are removed, you can determine what needs to be reinstalled. (For the Office applications, running the application from the **Start** menu restores the correct registry entries.)

RegClean also creates a file in the same folder that contains RegClean.exe or in the Temp folder or Windows\Temp folder. This file, which contains every entry that RegClean removes from your Windows registry, is named Undo *yyyymmdd hhmmss*.reg, where *yyyymmdd* is the current date, and *hhmmss* is the current time. To restore all entries to the registry, double-click the file. Because this file resides on your hard disk, avoid running RegClean from a network folder. For more information, see the Readme.txt file in the Tools\RegClean folder on the Tools and Utilities CD.

▶ **To install and run RegClean**

1 Insert the Tools and Utilities CD into the appropriate drive.
2 In the Tools\Regclean folder, copy RegClean.exe to your hard disk.
3 To run the utility, double-click RegClean.exe.

Tools for Extracting and Copying Files from Office Floppy Disks

The Office 97 floppy disks use a compressed format called Distribution Media Format (DMF) that stores 1.68 MB of data on a standard 3.5-inch double-sided floppy disk. These compressed files are combined into a single large file called a cabinet (CAB) file. Because this reduces the sector gap on the floppy disk, standard tools such as Windows Explorer or the MS-DOS **copy** command do not work for copying files from these disks.

Occasionally, you may want to extract individual files from an Office floppy disk CAB file—for example, if a file is accidentally deleted. To extract individual files from the Office floppy disks, you must use either the Extract or Wextract program, both of which are included on the Tools and Utilities CD.

You can also use Extract to copy the contents of the Office floppy disks to a server, so that users can run Office Setup over the network. For more information about installing Office from floppy disks, see "Installing Office from Floppy Disks" in Chapter 4, "Installing Microsoft Office."

CopyAll and CopyDisk

CopyAll and CopyDisk are MS-DOS batch files you can use to automate the task of copying Office floppy disks. Use Copyall.bat to copy a number of disks; use Copydisk.bat to copy a single disk. CopyAll uses the CopyDisk utility for each disk.

CopyAll

Copyall.bat copies all the CAB files from a DMF floppy disk set to a destination folder. The CAB files are stored in a set of folders named Disk1 through Disk$N$, where N is the number of floppy disks in the disk set. The maximum number of disks handled by this batch file is 50.

The syntax for this command is

CopyAll *path #disks*

where *path* is the path to the destination folder on your hard disk or on a network server, and *#disks* is the number of floppy disks.

For example, to copy the CAB files from a 10-disk set to the X:\Install folder, type:

CopyAll x:\install 10

▶ **To install the CopyAll batch file**

1 Insert the Tools and Utilities CD into the appropriate drive.
2 In the Tools\Extract folder, copy Copydisk.bat and Copyall.bat to your hard disk.

CopyDisk

Copydisk.bat copies a CAB file from a DMF floppy disk to a destination folder. The CAB file is stored in a folder named Disk$N$, where N is the number of the floppy disk in the disk set.

The syntax for this command is:

CopyDisk *path disk#*

where *path* is the path to the destination folder on your hard disk or on a network server, and *disk#* is the floppy disk number.

For example, to copy the CAB file from Disk 4 to the X:\Install folder, type

CopyDisk x:\install 4

▶ **To install the CopyDisk batch file**

1 Insert the Tools and Utilities CD into the appropriate drive.
2 In the Tools\Extract folder, copy Copydisk.bat to your hard disk.

You can also use CopyAll and CopyDisk to copy the contents of the Office floppy disks to a server, so that users can run Office Setup over the network. For more information about installing Office from floppy disks, see "Installing Office from Floppy Disks" in Chapter 4, "Installing Microsoft Office."

▶ **To use CopyAll and CopyDisk to create an Office installation folder on a network server**

1 Create a folder on the server to store the installation files.
2 Insert the Tools and Utilities CD into the appropriate drive.
3 Copy Copyall.bat and Copydisk.bat from the Tools\Extract folder to the folder you created in Step 1.
4 Switch to the folder you created in Step 1, and at the command prompt type

   Copyall *folder #disks*

   where *folder* is the folder you created, and *#disks* is the number of floppy disks to copy.

5 Insert a new disk when CopyAll prompts you.

   A folder named Disks is created, and the contents of the floppy disks are copied to subfolders named Disks\Disk1, Disks\Disk2, and so forth.

6 Make the Disks folder available to users.

   Users can connect to the Disks folder on the server and run Disk1\Setup.exe to install Office. Setup automatically looks in the correct subfolders (Disk2, Disk3, and so on) for the Office files.

Extract Utility

You can use the Extract utility to extract individual files from the Office floppy disks. You can also use Extract to copy the contents of the Office floppy disks to a server, so that users can run Setup over the network.

If you want to use a Windows utility to extract files, see "Wextract Utility" later in this appendix. The Extract program runs under MS-DOS. The syntax for this command is shown in the following examples:

Extract [/y] [/a] [/d | /e] [/l *dir*] *cabinet* [*filename*]
Extract [/y] *source* [*newname*]
Extract [/y] /c *source destination*
Extract /?

At the command prompt, type **Extract** followed by one or more of the command-line options shown in the following table.

Command-line option	Description
cabinet	CAB file (contains two or more files).
filename	Name of the file to extract from the CAB file. You can use wild cards and multiple file names (separated by blanks).
source	Compressed file that is not contained in a CAB file.
destination	Location to which to copy the uncompressed file.
newname	New file name for the extracted file. If you do not supply a new file name, the original file name is used.
/a	Processes all CAB files. Follows CAB chain starting in the first CAB specified.
/c	Copies source file from DMF disk to destination.
/d	Displays CAB file directory. If used with *filename*, it displays the file without extracting it.
/e	Extracts all files.
/l *dir*	Specifies location to store extracted files. (The default is the current directory.)
/y	Overwrites an existing file without prompting.
/?	Displays a list of options.

For example, to list all files in the file Disk1.cab, type

Extract /d a:\disk1.cab

To list all EXE files in Disk1.cab, type

Extract /d a:\disk1.cab *.exe

To extract a file named Any.exe from Disk1.cab and copy it to the current folder, type

Extract A:\Files.cab Any.exe

Note If the file spans more than one disk, Extract prompts you to enter the second disk.

To extract Any.exe from Disk1.cab and copy it to C:\Office, type

Extract A:\Files.cab /l C:\Office Any.exe

▶ **To install Extract**

1 Insert the Tools and Utilities CD into the appropriate drive.
2 In the Tools\Extract folder, copy Extract.exe to your hard disk.

Wextract Utility

You can use Wextract, like the Extract utility described earlier, to extract individual files from a CAB file. Wextract runs on Windows 95 and Windows NT Workstation 3.51 or later. Unlike Extract, however, Wextract cannot copy an entire CAB file from the floppy disk to a folder.

▶ **To install Wextract**

1 Insert the Tools and Utilities CD into the appropriate drive.
2 In the Tools\Extract folder, copy Wextra32.exe (the 32-bit Wextract executable file) and Wextra32.hlp to your hard disk.

▶ **To run Wextract**

1 Double-click Wextra32.exe.
2 On the **File** menu, click **Open Cabinet**.
3 In the **Open** dialog box, select the CAB file on the floppy disk.
4 In the Wextract window, select the file or files you want to extract.
5 On the **Edit** menu, click **Extract**.
6 Enter the destination folder and click **OK**.

Wextract decompresses the selected files and copies them to the destination folder.

World Wide Web and Intranet Tools

Web tools include utilities that improve the compatibility of Office 97 with your organization's intranet or with the Web.

Microsoft Excel 97 Web Connectivity Kit

The Microsoft Excel 97 Web Connectivity Kit was created for Internet and intranet administrators, authors, and Microsoft Excel users. The Kit provides detailed information about using Microsoft Excel 97 with the Internet or an intranet. Topics include hyperlinks, Web queries, and HTML extensions. Hyperlinks allow you to connect directly from a worksheet to a URL. Web queries allow you to copy data from a Web server directly into Microsoft Excel. HTML enhancements give HTML tables Microsoft Excel functionality (such as PivotTables) when you import them into Microsoft Excel.

The Microsoft Excel 97 Web Connectivity Kit consists of the document WebCnKit.doc and associated sample files. Open WebCnKit.doc in Word 97 to view or print it, and then follow the instructions in WebCnKit.doc to use the sample files. To learn about the sample files included in the Web Connectivity Kit, read the appendix in WebCnKit.doc.

Important You must have Microsoft Excel 97 and Microsoft Word 97 installed on your computer to use the Microsoft Excel 97 Web Connectivity Kit.

▶ **To install the Microsoft Excel 97 Web Connectivity Kit**

1 Insert the Tools and Utilities CD into the appropriate drive.
2 In the Tools\Connect folder, copy Webcnkit.exe to a network or your hard disk.
3 Double-click Webcnkit.exe.

Webcnkit.exe is a self-extracting file.

Office MIME Type Information for Netscape Web Servers

If you are using Netscape Web servers, such as the Netscape Commerce and Fast Track Web servers, you may need to edit the Mime.types files on your Web server to include Office file extension mappings. Rather than recording Multipurpose Internet Mail Extensions (MIME) content type and corresponding file extension mappings in the Windows registry, these Web server programs record this information in the Mime.types files. Editing the Mime.types files ensures that Netscape Web servers properly deliver Office documents to Web browsers.

For information about Office MIME types and Netscape Web servers, see "Netscape Web Server Support" in Chapter 24, "Integrating Microsoft Office with Your Intranet."

▶ **To update your Mime.types files**

1 Insert the Tools and Utilities CD into the appropriate drive.
2 In the Tools\Lists folder, open Mime.txt in a text editor (such as Notepad).
3 Using the file searching capabilities of Windows NT Server or some other search method, locate all copies of Mime.types on your Web server.
4 Create a backup of each copy of Mime.types and store the backups in a safe location.
5 Open Mime.types in a text editor (such as Notepad).
6 Paste the content of Mime.txt into Mime.types adjacent to the other file extension mappings.
7 Repeat Steps 5 and 6 for all copies of Mime.types on your Web server.

PowerPoint Animation Player

The PowerPoint Animation Player allows you to view PowerPoint animated Web pages in a Web browser whether or not PowerPoint is installed on your computer. The PowerPoint Animation Player runs under Windows 95 or Windows NT Workstation 3.51 or later.

To view PowerPoint Animation files in your Web browser, you need Microsoft Internet Explorer version 3.0 or Netscape Navigator version 2.0 or later. You can run PowerPoint animation files from Microsoft Internet Explorer version 1.0 or 2.0 and Netscape Navigator version 1.2 or later, but the presentations are displayed full screen and not within the browser window.

▶ **To install the PowerPoint Animation Player**

1. Insert the Tools and Utilities CD into the appropriate drive.
2. In the PowerPt\Player95 folder, double-click Axplayer.exe and follow the instructions.

World Wide Web The PowerPoint Animation Player is also available on the Web. When you save a PowerPoint presentation as an HTML document, a hyperlink to the Animation Player location is automatically saved with the document. When users open the document containing PowerPoint animations on the Web, they can also download the Animation Player. For the latest information, connect to the PowerPoint Animation Player site at:

http://www.microsoft.com/powerpoint/internet/player/

PowerPoint 95 Animation Publisher

The PowerPoint Animation Publisher, an add-in for PowerPoint 95, allows PowerPoint 95 to compress animated PowerPoint presentations before you post them on a server, making downloading and viewing the animations much faster.

For information about saving PowerPoint animations, see "Using Microsoft PowerPoint Animation Player for ActiveX" in Chapter 25, "Web Support in Microsoft Office Applications."

▶ **To install the PowerPoint Animation Publisher**

1. Insert the Tools and Utilities CD into the appropriate drive.
2. In the PowerPt\Player95 folder, double-click Axpub.exe and follow the instructions.

Note In PowerPoint 97, the Animation Publisher functionality is built in, so PowerPoint 97 users do not need to install the Animation Publisher to compress PowerPoint animations. Instead, users click **Save as HTML** (**File** menu) and then click the **Export as PowerPoint Animation** option.

Appendixes

PowerPoint 95 Internet Assistant

The Internet Assistant for PowerPoint 95 is an add-in that provides PowerPoint 95 users with the ability to convert design templates, clip art images, digitized photographs, textures, and formatted text in their PowerPoint slides into rich HTML pages for publishing on the Web. These presentations can be viewed by anyone using one of the popular Web browsers.

Use the Internet Assistant to convert a presentation into a set of HTML documents, ready for publishing on the Web. The Assistant creates two versions of each slide: a text version, which downloads faster and is useful for Web browsers that cannot display graphics; and a graphics version, which maintains the color scheme and appearance of the original presentation. By using interactive settings to define hyperlinks, you can go from one slide to another or to a related Web page. Advanced users can customize the text and graphics template (TLP) files, so that PowerPoint produces HTML pages that match the other Web pages for your organization.

▶ **To install the PowerPoint Internet Assistant**

1 Insert the Tools and Utilities CD into the appropriate drive.
2 In the PowerPt\Intera95 folder, copy Pptia.exe.to your hard disk.
3 Double-click Pptia.exe.

   Pptia.exe is a self-extracting file that copies files to your computer but does not install the Internet Assistant.

4 To install the Internet Assistant, see Readme.txt, which is included in the files copied by Pptia.exe.

Note In PowerPoint 97, the Internet Assistant functionality is built in, so PowerPoint 97 users do not need to install the Internet Assistant to export presentations to HTML. Instead, users click **Save as HTML** (**File** menu) and follow the instructions in the wizard. For more information about saving presentations in HTML, see "Saving Presentations as HTML Documents" in Chapter 25, "Web Support in Microsoft Office Applications."

APPENDIX B

Setup Command-Line Options and File Formats

This appendix describes the technical details of the Setup program for Microsoft Office 97, including the format of the Setup files, command-line options, and general sequence of the Setup process.

In This Appendix
Setup File Formats   1045
Setup Command-Line Options   1047
Setup Process   1051

Note The majority of this appendix assumes that you are running the Windows 95 or Windows NT version 4.0 operating system.

Setup File Formats

Setup files that contain application-specific information control the way Setup installs Office. This section describes the general format of two types of Setup files: the information file (INF) and the Setup table file (STF). These are the files that the Network Installation Wizard modifies. This information is provided to help you understand how Setup works and how you can use the Network Installation Wizard to modify the behavior of Setup.

Caution The behavior of Setup and the successful installation of Office depend on the internal integrity of the Setup files. These files are tab-delimited and rely on positional parameters. Do not modify them directly; instead, use the Network Installation Wizard to customize the Setup process. For more information about using the Network Installation Wizard, see Chapter 6, "Customizing Client Installations."

Setup relies on a set of files that work together to control the installation process for Office. The following table identifies the primary Setup files.

File name	Description
Setup.exe	Primary executable file for Setup
Off97Std.inf (Standard Edition) Off97Pro.inf (Professional Edition)	Disk INF file; provides detailed information about the files to be installed
Admin.inf	Network INF file; used by Setup to run installations in network mode
Off97Std.stf (Standard Edition) Off97Pro.stf (Professional Edition)	STF file; specifies the logic of the installation process
*.dll	Dynamic-link library (DLL) files containing custom procedures
Setup.lst, Setup.ini	Additional information files for Setup

The INF Files

The INF files are text files that contain information about all the Setup files involved in an Office installation. This information includes the following:

- Where a file is located and its default attributes
- Whether a file is to be appended to an existing copy
- Whether a file is to be backed up, renamed, or copied
- Whether a file supports English or another language

There are two INF files:

- The disk INF file, Off97Std.inf (Standard Edition) or Off97Pro.inf (Professional Edition), used in all installation modes except network mode
- The network INF file, Admin.inf, used when the application is installed on a workstation from a network (in network mode).

The STF File

The STF file is the primary tool for configuring Setup to install Office. It specifies the installation process for each installation mode, and determines the nature, sequence, and extent of user input. It determines which options to install, where to install them, and how to respond to current configurations and user input.

The STF file consists of data in a tree-structured table. Setup takes different paths through the tree based on options that the user selects or based on the environment in which Setup is run. For example, Setup takes one path through the tree if it finds a previous version of Office installed, and a different path if it does not.

To eliminate duplicating portions of the table throughout the STF file, a portion of the table may be referenced by multiple paths in the tree. Because Setup carries out each line of the STF file only once no matter how many paths reference it, multiple references to a single line allow Setup to process the STF file more quickly.

The tree structure of the STF file affects the installation process. In particular, there are two effects to be aware of:

- First, because Setup does not know which path it will take through the STF file until the installation begins, Setup cannot precisely predict the amount of disk space required. Setup may display disk space requirements that are slightly higher than the actual space needed.
- Second, if you use the Network Installation Wizard to modify entries in the STF file, you may see duplicate Yes/No questions or **Start** menu items. This is because the Network Installation Wizard displays all the items in the tree even though some items may never be carried out by Setup during installation. For more information about the Network Installation Wizard, see Chapter 6, "Customizing Client Installations."

You can use the **/g** command-line option to generate a log file that keeps track of everything Setup does: what files it copies, where it copies them, what modifications it makes to INI files or the Windows registry, and any errors it encounters. For a description of this Setup command-line option, see "Setup Command-Line Options" in the next section.

Setup Command-Line Options

You can run the Office Setup program from a command line. If you run Setup from a command line, you can add parameters to the command that allow you to specify certain options, such as choosing a Typical installation or creating a network installation log.

▶ **To run Setup from a command line**

1. In Windows 95 or Windows NT Workstation 4.0, click **Start**, and then click **Run**.

    –or–

    In Windows NT Workstation version 3.51, click **Run** on the Program Manager **File** menu.

2. Type the location you are installing from followed by the word **setup**. For example, **a:\setup** or **x:\msoffice\setup**

    If you want to add a command-line option, type it after the command. For example, to run Setup in administrative mode, type **a:\setup /a**

Some command-line options are standalone parameters, while others take an argument, such as a number or file name. Options are not case-sensitive; that is, they can be in uppercase or lowercase. With a few exceptions, you can combine options in the same command line. For example, to run Setup from drive A so that it specifies the user name Laura Callahan, the organization Island Trading, and the log file C:\Tmp\Offlog.txt, you would type the following:

```
a:\setup /n "laura callahan" /o "island trading" /g "c:\tmp\offlog.txt"
```

Command-Line Option Descriptions

The following table shows the command-line options recognized by the Office Setup program.

Command-line option	Description
/a	Creates an administrative installation point. Valid when running from CD only.

/b *number*	Bypasses the **Microsoft Office 97 Setup** dialog box by preselecting the type of installation:
	    1–Typical
	    2–Custom
	    3–Run from CD or Run from Network Server

/c "*number*"	Bypasses the dialog box for entering and validating the 20-character Product ID from the OEM Certificate of Authorization by entering the number you specify.
/f	Specifies that all files be created with an 8-character file name with a 3-character extension, instead of with a long file name.
/g{+} "*file*"	Generates a log file that records details of the Setup process. If **+** is specified, Setup appends new information to the log file instead of overwriting it.
/gc{+} "*file*"	Does the same as /g, except all calls and returns from custom actions are also logged, which can make the log file very large.
/k "*number*"	Bypasses the dialog box for entering and validating the 11-digit key from the CD sticker by entering the number you specify.

Command-line option	Description
/m *number*	Specifies the Microsoft License Pak (MLP) licensing information needed to activate the MLP for floppy disks. Setup does not install any software, but terminates immediately after setting the count at the number you specify.
/n ""	Prompts for a user name to use if no default user name exists in the Windows registry.
/n "*name*"	Specifies the user name to use if no default user name exists in the Windows registry.
/o ""	Prompts for an organization name to use if no default organization name exists in the Windows registry.
/o "*organization*"	Specifies the organization name to use if no default organization exists in the Windows registry.
/q{option}	Specifies the level of user interaction for batch mode installation: **0**–Suppresses all dialog boxes except the final one. Using **0** is the same as using no argument. **1**–Suppresses all dialog boxes, including the final one. **t**–Suppresses all Setup user interface elements.
/qn{option}	Does the same as **/q**, except that the system is not rebooted and **0** is not a valid value. To suppress all dialog boxes except the final one, use **/qn** with no argument.
/r	Reinstalls an application. Use in maintenance mode only.
/s "*folder*"	Overrides the default source (the folder containing Setup.exe or the source specified in the maintenance mode STF file) with the specified folder.
/u{a}	Removes Office. If **a** is specified, shared components are removed without prompting the user; otherwise the user is prompted before removing shared components. Use in maintenance mode only.

Command-line option	Description
/x "*file*"	Creates a network installation log file for tracking the number of installations made from an administrative installation point. This overrides the value, if any, specified in the STF file.
/y	Proceeds normally, including setting registry entries, but does not copy any files to the user's disk. Use this option to restore registry values or to track down processing problems.

Note If you enter any invalid parameter, Setup displays a partial list of valid command-line options.

Following are special considerations when combining options on the same command line:

- The **/a** and **/q** options are mutually exclusive; using both results in a usage error message.
- The **/n** option is ignored if **/a** is used.
- The **/u** and **/r** options are mutually exclusive; using both results in a usage error message.
- The prompt elicited by the **/u** option is suppressed if **/q** is used, and the shared components are not removed.

ERRORLEVEL Values

Under Windows 95, Setup returns one of the following values as the MS-DOS **ERRORLEVEL** value used to control batch file processing.

This ERRORLEVEL value	Indicates this condition
0	Success
1	User quit
2	Parsing Command Line error
3	Default user or organization name error
4	External error
5	Internal error
6	Out of memory
7	Partly installed
8	Restart failed
9	Failed to run Acmesetup.exe

Setup Process

This section describes the process that Setup follows during an installation. Setup performs the following steps in a client installation:

1. Determine whether this is a new or a maintenance mode installation.

   For information about how Setup determines this, see "Determining Maintenance Mode Installation" later in this appendix.

2. If Setup is running from Disk 1 of a floppy disk set, search from drive Z to drive A, and create the Mssetup temporary folder on the first hard disk that has sufficient disk space. If no hard disk is found, create the Mssetup folder in the user's Windows folder.

   If Setup is running from a CD, a hard disk, or a network server, it does not create a temporary folder.

3. Check the STF file for syntax errors.

   If the STF file has been modified, syntax errors may have been introduced.

4. Check for active applications that are potentially disruptive.

   The list of applications that Setup checks is in the **Check Modules** item in the **Header** section of the STF file.

5. Run the STF file according to the branching logic defined in the file, and then perform the following steps:
   - Check for duplicate versions of the application being installed.
   - Prompt the user for input regarding corrections and custom configurations.
   - Determine whether there is adequate space on the hard disk.

6. Copy the files into the system-specified and user-specified folders according to the instructions in the STF and INF files.

   The STF file determines which files or groups of files are copied and their destinations. The INF file specifies the characteristics of each file or group of files in the product, such as size and date. It also specifies instructions to be used when copying the files, such as whether to decompress the file or overwrite the destination file if it already exists.

7. Delete or replace existing files as indicated.

8. Make appropriate changes to the Windows registry and INI files.

9. Remove the Mssetup folder, if one was created.

Appendixes

Determining Maintenance Mode Installation

Setup determines whether an installation is in maintenance mode by looking for an entry in the Windows registry to indicate that Setup has been run before. The entry is under the following key:

HKEY_LOCAL_MACHINE\Software\Microsoft\MS Setup (ACME)\Table Files

The **Name** value in the **Table Files** subkey is the product name and version, and the **Data** value is the path to the STF file. The following is an example of these value entries for Office 97.

Name	**MS Office 97 Professional@v97.0.0.1114(1033)**
Data	**"C:\Program Files\Microsoft Office\Office\Setup\Off97Pro.STF"**

If the **Name** value matches the product name and version of software Setup is attempting to install, Setup runs in maintenance mode using the STF file identified in the **Data** value.

If the **Name** value does not match the product name and version of software Setup is attempting to install, or if Setup cannot find or open the STF file identified in the **Data** value, Setup runs in install mode.

When Setup runs in install mode, it uses the STF file in the folder in which the Setup program (Setup.exe) resides. Setup recognizes the STF file by looking for the 8-character name portion of the Setup program file, with the extension .stf. For example, if Setup.exe has been renamed Newsetup.exe, Setup looks for the STF file Newsetup.stf. If you use the **/t** command-line option to specify a particular STF file, Setup runs in install mode using the STF file you specify.

APPENDIX C

Registry Keys and Values

This appendix describes how to use Windows system policies to modify registry settings used by Microsoft Office 97 applications. With system policies, you can modify registry settings for a large number of users on a network simultaneously. For an overview of Windows system policies and an explanation of how to use the System Policy Editor, see "Using Windows System Policies to Customize Office," in Chapter 7, "Customizing and Optimizing Microsoft Office."

In This Appendix
Installing the System Policy Editor   1053
Using Office 97 System Policies   1055
List of Office 97 System Policies   1068

Note Windows system policies are supported by Windows 95 and Windows NT Workstation version 4.0 only. Office applications store information in the Windows NT Workstation version 3.51 registry in the same way as in Windows 95 and Windows NT Workstation 4.0, but you cannot use system policies to change these settings. The Macintosh operating system does not support system policies.

Installing the System Policy Editor

The Office 97 Resource Kit Tools and Utilities CD includes several policy templates for Office 97. You must install these templates on your system before using them to create system policy files. The following procedure installs the System Policy Editor in your Windows folder, and the Office policy templates in the Windows\Inf subfolder.

Appendixes

▶ **To install the System Policy Editor and Office policy templates from the Tools and Utilities CD**

1. In Control Panel, double-click the Add/Remove Programs icon.
2. Click the **Windows Setup** tab.
3. Click **Have Disk**.
4. In the **Copy manufacturer's files from** box, enter *drive*:**\Policy**, where *drive* is the drive letter for the Tools and Utilities CD, and then click **OK**.
5. Under **Components**, select the **System Policy Editor** check box to install the System Policy Editor program (Poledit.exe) and related files.
6. Select the **Office 97 Templates for Windows 95** check box to install the Office templates for Windows 95.

   –or–

   Select the **Office 97 Templates for Windows NT 4.0** check box to install the Office templates for Windows NT Workstation 4.0.
7. Click **Install**.

World Wide Web If you have Web access, you can also download the System Policy Editor and Office policy templates directly. For more information, connect to the Office Resource Kit home page at:

http://www.microsoft.com/office/ork/

The first time you run the System Policy Editor, it loads the Office 97 template files that you installed.

▶ **To start the System Policy Editor**

1. On the **Start** menu, point to **Programs**, point to **Accessories**, and then point to **System Tools**.
2. Click **System Policy Editor**.

In Windows Explorer, you can also double-click Poledit.exe in the Windows folder to start the System Policy Editor.

Note To create a system policy file for a computer running Windows 95, you must run the System Policy Editor under Windows 95. To create a system policy file for Windows NT Workstation 4.0, you must run the System Policy Editor under Windows NT Workstation 4.0 or Windows NT Server 4.0.

To verify that the template files are loaded in the System Policy Editor, click **Policy Template** on the System Policy Editor **Options** menu. The template files currently loaded are listed in the **Current Policy Template(s)** box, as shown in the following table.

Office 97 templates for Windows 95	Office 97 templates for Windows NT 4.0
Off97w95.adm	Off97nt4.adm
Access97.adm	Access97.adm
Outlk97.adm	Outlk97.adm
Query97.adm	Query97.adm

Note The System Policy Editor includes three Windows template files (Common.adm, Windows.adm, and Winnt.adm). These files do not contain Office policies, but the Windows policies they contain may be useful in managing a workgroup. For more information, see the *Microsoft Windows NT Server 4.0 Resource Kit* and *Microsoft Windows NT Workstation 4.0 Resource Kit.*

Using Office 97 System Policies

The Office 97 policy template files contain system policies that you can use to customize Office applications for your users across a network. This section describes selected system policies that may be of special interest to administrators deploying and maintaining Office 97 in a workgroup or large organization. For the complete list of Office system policies, see "List of Office 97 System Policies" later in this chapter.

Computer Settings

Computer setting policies apply to all users who log on to one computer. If you make the setting to the Default Computer icon, the setting applies to all computers on which these policies are loaded. If you create a new computer icon using the **Add Computer** command (**Edit** menu), then the settings apply only to that computer.

You can view and set computer policies in the System Policy Editor by double-clicking the Default Computer icon or, if you have added a new computer, by double-clicking the new computer icon.

Office 97 Policies

The following computer setting policies appear in the **Office 97** group in the System Policy Editor.

Computer\Office 97\Default Save
This policy sets the prompt text that the Assistant uses when default save is enabled and the user clicks the **Save As** command (**File** menu). The default text is "Other people may not have the latest version of Office, so if you plan to share this file, you should save it in the following format: *format*."

Computer\Office 97\Uninstall
This policy is associated with the registry value **HKEY_LOCAL_MACHINE\SOFTWARE \Microsoft\Windows\CurrentVersion\Uninstall\Office8.0\UninstallString**. The default value

points to the local version of Office Setup and gives it a parameter to find the installed Setup table file (Off97pro.stf or Off97std.stf). If the location moves, you can point to Setup.exe at the new network location. For example, you can set this policy to *newserver\newshare*\Setup.exe.

Note Setting this policy to a new location does not work if any components are run from the server—all Office files must be installed locally. For example, if additional clip art files reside on the server, moving the installation location means users do not have access to the old clip art. To give users access to clip art from the server, you must use the clip art policy described later in this section to point to the new server location.

Computer\Office 97\Assistant\Installed Path
This policy gives the location of the Assistant files (ACT and ACP files). If you move the Assistant files, you can specify the new location of the files with this policy. This location may be a network server. For example, if you want to place all Assistants on a network server, enter that location here, and users will automatically have access to them from the server.

Computer\Office 97\Assistant\Source Path
When a user browses the Assistant Gallery to choose a different Assistant, Office looks for Assistant files in the path specified in the **Computer\Office 97\Assistant\Installed Path** policy. If an ACP file is found, Office uses this as a preview of the Assistant. If the user chooses that Assistant, Office looks in the path specified in this policy for the equivalent ACT file and installs the file on the user's computer. This path defaults to the administrative installation point or the Office CD from which the user installed Office.

If you want to place the Assistant ACT files in another location, such as on a different server, use this policy to change that location.

Microsoft Excel Policies
The following computer setting policy appears in the **Excel 97** group in the System Policy Editor.

Computer\Excel 97\Converters\Excel 9.0 Import Converters
When Microsoft makes import converters available for future versions of Microsoft Excel, place them on your intranet and use this policy to set a URL to the download location.

Outlook 97 Policies
The following computer setting policy appears in the **Outlook 97** group in the System Policy Editor.

Computer\Outlook 97\Use Schedule+
This policy corresponds to the **Use Microsoft Schedule+ 95 as my primary calendar** option on the **Calendar** tab in the **Options** dialog box (**Tools** menu) in Microsoft Outlook. If this policy is set, Outlook uses Schedule+ 95 for calendar operations. In addition, setting this policy disables the option in Outlook so the user cannot override the setting.

Note Schedule+ 95 must be installed to use this policy.

PowerPoint Policies

The following computer setting policy appears in the **PowerPoint 97** group in the System Policy Editor.

Computer\PowerPoint 97\Converters\PowerPoint 9.0 Import Converters

When Microsoft makes import converters available for future versions of PowerPoint, place them on your intranet and use this policy to set a URL to the download location.

Word 97 Policies

The following computer setting policies appears in the **Word 97** group in the System Policy Editor.

Computer\Word 97\Spelling Advanced\Default AutoCorrect File

The default Office AutoCorrect (ACL) file is Mso97.acl. When a new user needs an ACL file, it is copied from Mso97.acl and renamed *Username*.acl. If you want all users to start with a custom ACL file, you can create your own ACL file, save it to a network location, and use this policy to point to it. To create your own ACL file, run Microsoft Word and add entries to the AutoCorrect list with the **AutoCorrect** command (**Tools** menu). These changes are saved in the Windows folder.

Note The new ACL file you create includes all the entries from the default Mso97.acl.

Computer\Word 97\Converters\Word 9.0 Import Converters

When Microsoft makes import converters available for future versions of Word, place them on your intranet and use this policy to set a URL to the download location.

Clip Art Gallery 3.0 Policies

The following computer setting policies appear in the **Clip Art Gallery 3.0** group in the System Policy Editor.

Computer\Clip Art Gallery 3.0\Concurrent Database #1, #2, and #3

These three policies may be used to make more clip art content available to users. You can create new Clip Art Gallery databases (CAG files) and store them on a server. They can contain regular clip art files (WMF); picture files (BMP, GIF, and so on); or multimedia files (AVI or WAV). Three policies are included to allow you to divide clip art among one, two, or three files.

Windows Policies

The following computer setting policy appears in the **Windows** group in the System Policy Editor.

Computer\Windows\Network Install Tab

The **Network Install** tab in the **Add/Remove Programs** dialog box (Control Panel) allows you to distribute software that users can install.

To create the **Network Install** tab, first create an INI file containing a section called `AppInstallList` with a collection of name and value pairs. The user sees the application name listed on the **Network Install** tab, and the value specifies which command installs the software. For example, the following entry adds three new list box items to the **Network Install** tab—**Developer Tools**, **Productivity Tools**, and **Games**:

```
[AppInstallList]
Developer Tools=*\\central\tools\develop\setup.exe
Productivity Tools=*\\central\tools\prod\setup.exe
Games=*\\central\tools\games\setup.exe
```

User Settings

User setting policies apply to all users regardless of the computer to which they log on. If you make the setting to the Default User icon, then the setting applies to all users logged on to computers that load these policies. If you create a new user or group icon using the **Add User** or **Add Group** command (**Edit** menu), then the settings apply only to that user or users in that group, regardless of which computer they log on to.

You can view and set user policies in the System Policy Editor by double-clicking the Default User icon or, if you have added a new user or group, by double-clicking the new user or group icon.

Microsoft on the Web Policies

The user setting policies described in the following sections appear in the **Help_Microsoft on the Web** group in the System Policy Editor. They correspond to commands on the **Microsoft on the Web** submenu (**Help** menu) in the Office applications.

For more information about customizing the commands that appear on the **Microsoft on the Web** submenu, see "Customizing Office Connections to the World Wide Web," in Chapter 7, "Customizing and Optimizing Microsoft Office." The instructions in Chapter 7 describe how to use the Windows Registry Editor to disable commands on this menu and add your own custom commands. You can accomplish the same tasks for multiple users at one time by using the policies described in this section. In addition, you can set a policy that resets the commands on this menu to the default whenever users log on to the network.

Note These three policies should be used one at a time. If you set more than one, only the last policy set takes effect. For example, you might select the **Customize submenu** policy and enter several commands, and then select the **Disable submenu** policy and save the file. In this case, the **Microsoft on the Web** submenu on the user's computer is disabled, not customized.

User*application*\Internet\Help_Microsoft on the Web\Customize submenu

This policy allows you to customize the commands that appear on the **Microsoft on the Web** submenu (**Help** menu) in any Office 97 application. If you open this policy under the **Office 97** group in the System Policy Editor, then you can customize the first set of as many as eight commands displayed on the menu. If you open this policy under an application group (for example, the **Word 97** group), then you can customize the second set of as many as eight commands (the application-specific commands) displayed on the menu. You cannot customize the last command on the menu, which is a hyperlink to the Microsoft home page on the World Wide Web.

When you select the **Customize submenu** policy in the System Policy Editor, the **Settings for Customize submenu** box displays text boxes in which you can enter as many as eight menu commands. Initially, the default commands are displayed. The custom string you enter for each command is identical to the string used in the **Value data** field in the Windows registry. For more information about the format of these commands, see "Customizing Office Connections to the World Wide Web," in Chapter 7, "Customizing and Optimizing Microsoft Office."

Note In this policy, *application* may be **Access 97**, **Excel 97**, **Outlook 97**, **PowerPoint 97**, or **Word 97**.

User*application*\\Internet\\Help_Microsoft on the Web\\Reset Submenu to Original Defaults

This policy deletes all customized commands on the **Microsoft on the Web** submenu, which causes the application to use the default settings. After this policy is set, the **HKEY_CURRENT_USER \\Software\\Microsoft\\Office\\8.0*application*\\WebHelp** registry key still exists, but all of the Command1 to Command8 value entries are deleted. This is equivalent to using the **Customize submenu** policy to set all of the value entries to empty strings.

Note In this policy, *application* may be **Office 97**, **Access 97**, **Excel 97**, **Outlook 97**, **PowerPoint 97**, or **Word 97**.

User*application*\\Internet\\Help_Microsoft on the Web\\Disable Submenu

This policy disables the commands on the **Microsoft on the Web** submenu. If you open this policy under an application group in the System Policy Editor, then the application-specific commands and the separator line are removed. If you also disable the Office-wide commands (by opening this policy under the **Office 97** group), then the default commands are displayed but they are unavailable.

Note In this policy, *application* may be **Office 97**, **Access 97**, **Excel 97**, **Outlook 97**, **PowerPoint 97**, or **Word 97**.

Internet Policies

The following user setting policies affect user access to various resources available on the Internet. These policies appear under several application groups in the System Policy Editor.

User\\Office\\Internet\\FTP Sites\\Add FTP Sites

This policy adds up to 10 FTP sites under the **Look in** box in the **Open** dialog box (**File** menu). When you set this policy in the System Policy Editor, the **Settings for Add FTP Sites** list displays 10 FTP sites. The registry keys associated with these site addresses are **HKEY_CURRENT_USER\\Software\\Microsoft\\Office\\8.0\\Common\\Internet\\FTP Sites\\site_0** through **site_9**. The value name is **Site Name** and its value is **ftp://***address*. There can be more than 10 sites in the list, but the Office template can set only 10 at one time.

To enter an FTP site, you must type **ftp://** in front of the site address. By default, the Office template file enters **ftp://ftp.microsoft.com/** for the first site and enters the **ftp://** prefix for the remaining sites.

Appendixes

Each time the user logs on, Windows adds the sites identified in the policy to the list of sites in the registry if they do not already exist. If you change the sites in the policy, the new sites are added to the registry the next time a user logs on.

Note To remove FTP sites from the user's registry, use the **Delete FTP Sites** policy.

User\Office\Internet\FTP Sites\Delete FTP Sites

This policy is used to remove FTP sites from the **Open** dialog box (**File** menu). The policy can clear only the first 10 sites in the user's registry. If a user has 15 sites, then the first 10 are cleared the first time the user logs on, and the remaining 5 are cleared the second time the user logs on (provided the user has not added more FTP sites in the meantime).

Note If you set both this policy and the **Add FTP Sites** policy, as many as 10 existing sites are deleted from the user's registry before the new sites are added.

User*application*\Internet\Converters\Future File Format Converters

Office applications use the registry value set by this policy to find additional file converters. By setting this policy to an intranet site, for example, you can install new converters on the server as they become available and give users access to them. To define a Web site with this policy, enter the URL.

Note In this policy, *application* may be **Excel 97**, **Outlook 97**, **PowerPoint 97**, or **Word 97**.

This policy is similar to the policy **Computer*application*\Converters*application* 9.0 Converters** described earlier in this chapter, but there are several significant differences. The policy **User*application*\Internet\Converters\Future File Format Converters** addresses any site on the corporate intranet or on the Internet, and Office applications download converters found at the site to the user's hard disk to be used locally.

The policy **Computer*application*\Converters*application* 9.0 Converters** also references a site on the intranet; but instead of copying the converters locally, the Office applications use them over the network. Also, this policy is specific to the future version of Office 9.0. The Web site referenced by policy **User*application*\Internet\Converters\Future File Format Converters** may contain a variety of future file format converters.

User\Internet Explorer 3.0\Options_Navigation

This policy allows you to set the Start Page and Search Pages for Microsoft Internet Explorer 3.0 by entering a URL. The associated registry key is **HKEY_CURRENT_USER\Software\Microsoft\Internet Explorer\Main**, and the value entries are **Start Page** = *URL* and **Search Page** = *URL*.

Office 97 Policies

The following user setting policies affect Office applications in general. These appear under the **Office 97** heading in the System Policy Editor.

User\Office 97\Common\User Templates

This policy defines a path to user templates on a network server or on the hard disk. These templates are added to the list of local templates in the **New** dialog box with tabs for subfolders of the Program Files\Microsoft Office\Templates folder. (The **New** dialog box is displayed when you click **New**

Office Document** on the Windows **Start** menu, or when you click **New** on the **File** menu in any Office application.)

User\Office 97\Common\Workgroup Templates

This policy defines a path to workgroup templates on a network server or on the local hard disk. These templates are merged with local templates in the **New** dialog box with tabs for subfolders of the Program Files\Microsoft Office\Templates folder. (The **New** dialog box is displayed when you click **New Office Document** on the Windows **Start** menu, or when you click **New** on the **File** menu in any Office application.)

User\Office 97\Common\Personal Folder

This policy specifies the location of the My Documents folder by modifying the **Personal** value entry in the key **HKEY_CURRENT_USER\Software\Microsoft\Windows\CurrentVersion\Explorer \User Shell Folders**. Windows propagates the **Personal** value from this key to the subkey **Windows\CurrentVersion\Explorer\Shell Folders**.

On Windows 95, both the **User Shell Folders** subkey and the **Shell Folders** subkey are type REG_SZ (strings). On Windows NT Workstation 4.0, however, the **User Shell Folders** subkey is type REG_EXPAND_SZ (expandable string), which allows it to store environment variables such as **%homedir%**, **%username%**, and **%userprofile%**. When the Windows NT Workstation shell propagates the **Personal** value from **User Shell Folders** to **Shell Folders**, it also expands any environment variables.

For example, if the registry contains:

...\User Shell Folders   Personal = %userprofile%\Personal

This is expanded on Windows NT Workstation 4.0 to:

...\Shell Folders   Personal = c:\winnt\profiles\laurac\Personal

In addition to setting these keys, this policy disables the Personal Folder path for each individual application by deleting the value entries for the following subkeys under **HKEY_CURRENT_USER**. These values are deleted so that applications use the common Office personal folder.

Subkey	Value name
Software\Microsoft\Office\8.0\Excel\Microsoft Excel	DefaultPath
Software\Microsoft\Office\8.0\Access\Settings	Default Database Directory
Software\Microsoft\Office\8.0\PowerPoint\Recent Folder List\Default	@
Software\Microsoft\Office\8.0\Binder	DefaultDirectory
Software\Microsoft\Office\8.0\Word\Options	DOC-PATH

Note The @ symbol for Microsoft PowerPoint means that PowerPoint uses the **Default** value, which has no value name.

By using environment variables in Windows NT Workstation 4.0, the following steps show how to create separate My Documents folders for users on a single network server.

1. Create a folder on a network location and give all users read and write access.

   For example, create the network share *Server*\UserData.

2. Add a home directory to users' profiles.

   For example, map Z: to *Server*\UserData**%username%**.

3. Use this policy to set the personal folder to **%homedir%\%username%**.

   The environment variables **%homedir%** and **%username%** are substituted in the registry as appropriate for each user.

You may want to store user data so the user has separate personal folders for each application. The Office policy templates define only a global personal folder for all Office applications. By modifying the policy template, however, you can create policies for each individual application.

User\Office\Common\Sound
This policy turns Office sounds on or off for all applications.

Microsoft Access Policies

Microsoft Access-specific policies appear under the **Access 97** heading in the System Policy Editor.

Microsoft Access supports Internet settings similar to those supported by the other Office applications. The remaining Microsoft Access policies represent options available in the **Options** dialog box (**Tools** menu).

Note Microsoft Access does not support a default **Save As** format, so there is no corresponding policy.

Microsoft Excel Policies

The following user setting policies are used by Microsoft Excel. These appear under the **Excel 97** heading in the System Policy Editor.

User\Excel 97\Tools_Options\General\Alternate Startup Folder
This policy specifies that the alternate startup folder should be used for default workbook or worksheet templates. If the file Book.xlt is in the alternate startup folder, it is copied when the user clicks the **New** command (**File** menu). Similarly, if the user clicks the **Worksheet** command (**Insert** menu), Microsoft Excel looks for Sheet.xls in the alternate startup folder. You can use these templates to specify such worksheet elements as fonts and page formatting for printing.

User\Excel 97\Tools_Options\Transition\Default Save

This policy is used to set the default format in which to save Microsoft Excel workbooks. Valid formats include the following:

- Microsoft Excel 97 Workbook
- Microsoft Excel 97 & 5.0/95 Workbook
- Microsoft Excel 5.0/95 Workbook
- Microsoft Excel 4.0 Workbook
- Microsoft Excel 4.0 Worksheet
- Microsoft Excel 3.0 Worksheet
- WK4 (1-2-3)
- WK3, FM3 (1-2-3)
- WK3 (1-2-3)
- WK1, FMT (1-2-3)
- WK1, ALL (1-2-3)
- WK1 (1-2-3)
- WKS (1-2-3)
- WQ1 (QuattroPro/DOS)

User\Excel 97\Miscellaneous\Personal Toolbars

Custom toolbar settings are stored in *Username*8.xlb, which is located in the Microsoft Excel folder. Use this policy to change the location for the XLB file. If there is no XLB file in the new location, Microsoft Excel creates one. The location can be a local folder, or you can set it to a folder on a network server.

When you enter the new location, be sure to include the trailing backslash (\) as shown here:

server\share\folder

User\Excel 97\Miscellaneous\Chart Gallery

This policy specifies the path to a custom chart gallery. The file name is Xlusrgal.gra.

Note This policy applies only to Microsoft Excel. The policy **User\Office\Common\Chart Gallery** is a similar policy for other Office applications; that policy uses the file name Grusrgal.gra.

Outlook Policies

The following user setting policies are used by Outlook. These appear under the **Outlook 97** heading in the System Policy Editor.

User\Outlook 97\Tools_Options\E-mail\WordMail
This policy allows you to set WordMail as the electronic mail (e-mail) editor. Valid options are **Always**, **Never**, and **If there is enough RAM**. The third option checks the computer, and if there is 16 MB or more on a Windows 95 operating system or 24 MB or more on a Windows NT operating system, the option is set.

User\Outlook 97\Tools_Options\E-mail\WordMail Template
This policy allows you to specify a path to a WordMail template. This can be a network location.

User\Outlook 97\Tools_Options\Journal\Automatically record these items
You can use this policy to determine which events, such as e-mail or meeting requests, create journal entries.

User\Outlook 97\Tools_Options\Journal\Also record these files
You can use this policy to set which Office applications create journal entries.

User\Outlook 97\Tools_Options\Journal\ Journal Entry Options
This policy allows you to choose whether double-clicking a journal entry opens the entry or opens the associated item (such as a Word document).

User\Outlook 97\Miscellaneous\Disable Forms Designer
This policy allows you to disable the Forms Designer so that the user cannot create or modify custom Outlook forms.

PowerPoint Policies

The following user setting policies are used by PowerPoint. These appear under the **PowerPoint 97** heading in the System Policy Editor.

User\PowerPoint 97\Tools_Options\Save\Default Save
This policy is used to set the default format in which to save PowerPoint presentations. Valid formats include the following:

- Microsoft PowerPoint 3.0
- Microsoft PowerPoint 4.0
- Microsoft PowerPoint 95
- Microsoft PowerPoint 95 & 97
- Microsoft PowerPoint 97

User\PowerPoint 97\Miscellaneous\No Edit Time

This policy allows you to turn off the document property **Total Editing Time**, which appears on the **Statistics** tab in the *Document* **Properties** dialog box (**File** menu). The field is still displayed, but it always shows 0 minutes.

User\PowerPoint 97\Miscellaneous\Multimedia Directory

This policy specifies a location for AVI and WAV files inserted by the **Movie from File** or **Sound from File** commands (**Insert** menu, **Movies and Sounds** submenu). This location may be on a network server. The user cannot set this location in PowerPoint. The default location is the folder in which Office Media was installed (for example, C:\Windows\Media\Office 97). This policy allows you to make additional multimedia content available on the network.

User\PowerPoint 97\Miscellaneous\Picture Directory

This policy specifies a location for clip art files inserted by the **From File** command (**Insert** menu, **Picture** submenu). This location may be on a network server. The user cannot set this location in PowerPoint. The default is the Microsoft Office\Clip Art folder on the user's computer. This policy allows you to make additional multimedia content available on the network.

User\PowerPoint 97\Miscellaneous\Template Directory

This policy specifies a location for template files attached by the **Apply Design** command (**Format** menu). This location may be on a network server. The user cannot set this location in PowerPoint. The default is the Program Files\Microsoft Office\Templates\Presentations Designs folder on the user's computer.

Note The **User\Office 97\Common\User Templates** and **User\Office 97\Common\Workgroup Templates** policies described earlier in this section can also set the PowerPoint template used when the user clicks the **Open** command (**File** menu).

User\PowerPoint 97\Miscellaneous\Personal Toolbars

This policy is similar to the Microsoft Excel policy of the same name described earlier in this section.

Custom toolbar settings are stored in *Username*8.pcb, which is located by default in the Windows folder. Use this policy to change the location for the PCB file. If there is no PCB file in the new location, PowerPoint creates one. The location can be a local folder, or you can set it to a folder on a network server.

Note Unlike the corresponding Microsoft Excel policy, the trailing backslash (\) is not required in the path.

Word Policies

The following user setting policies are used by Word. These appear under the **Word 97** heading in the System Policy Editor.

User\Word 97\Tools_Options\Save\Default Save

This policy is used to set the default format in which to save Word documents. Valid formats include the following:

- Word 97
- Word 6.0/95
- Word 2.x for Windows
- Word 5.0 for Macintosh
- Word 5.1 for Macintosh
- WordPerfect 5.x for Windows
- WordPerfect 5.1 for DOS
- Works 3.0 for Windows
- Works 4.0 for Windows
- HTML Document
- Rich Text Format

User\Word 97\Tools_Options\File Locations

This policy sets the various file locations used by Word and corresponds to options on the **File Locations** tab in the **Options** dialog box (**Tools** menu).

Note Two locations are not specified in this policy. One of these corresponds to the **Template** option on the **File Locations** tab in the **Options** dialog box (**Tools** menu), which is specified in the **User\Office 97\Common** policy (the template path for all Office applications). The other location corresponds to the **User Options** option.

User\Word 97\Tools_AutoFormat\AutoCorrect\Plain Text WordMail Documents

This policy allows you to change the default value of the **Plain text WordMail Documents** option on the **AutoFormat** tab in the **AutoCorrect** dialog box (**Tools** menu). It is selected by default.

Microsoft Query Policies

The following user setting policies are used by Microsoft Query. These appear under the **Query 97** heading in the System Policy Editor.

User\Query 97\File_New\Data Source Folders

You can use this policy to create a list of folders to be displayed in the **Choose Data Source** dialog box. (To display the dialog box, click **New** on the **File** menu.) Files with a .dsn extension are displayed on the **Databases** tab; files with a .dqy extension are displayed on the **Queries** tab.

▶ To add folders to the Choose Data Source dialog box

1. In the System Policy Editor, select the **User\Query 97\File_New\Data Source Folders** policy.
2. In the **Settings for Data Source Folders** box, click **Show**.
3. In the **Show Contents** dialog box, click **Add**.
4. In the **Add Item** dialog box, enter a path (this may be a network location), and then click **OK**.
5. Repeat Steps 3 and 4 for each folder you want to add.

User\Query 97\File_New\Use Wizard

This policy controls the state of the check box in the **Choose Data Source** dialog box. (To display the dialog box, click **New** on the **File** menu.) If the check box is selected, Microsoft Query edits and creates queries using the Query Wizard.

User\Query 97\Edit_Options\Disable Options

This policy disables the **Options** command (**Edit** menu), making the user settings in the **Options** dialog box unavailable.

User\Query 97\Edit_Options\Connection Timeout

This policy sets the **Cancel the connection if not connected within** *number* **seconds** option in the **Options** dialog box (**Edit** menu). In the System Policy Editor, you can set the value for *number*.

User\Query 97\Edit_Options\Limit Records

This policy sets the **Limit number of records returned to** *number* **records** option in the **Options** dialog box (**Edit** menu). In the System Policy Editor, you can set the value for *number*.

User\Query 97\Edit_Options\Auto Disconnect

This policy sets the **Keep connections open until MS Query is closed** option in the **Options** dialog box (**Edit** menu).

User\Query 97\Edit_Options\Disable Edit

This policy sets the **Disable ability to edit query results** option in the **Options** dialog box (**Edit** menu).

User\Query 97\Edit_Options\Table Options\Show Tables

This policy sets the **Tables** option in the **Table Options** dialog box (**Table** menu, **Add Tables** submenu).

User\Query 97\Edit_Options\Table Options\Show Views

This policy sets the **Views** option in the **Table Options** dialog box (**Table** menu, **Add Tables** submenu).

User\Query 97\Edit_Options\Table Options\Show System Tables

This policy sets the **System Tables** option in the **Table Options** dialog box (**Table** menu, **Add Tables** submenu).

User\Query 97\Edit_Options\Table Options\Show Synonyms

This policy sets the **Synonyms** option in the **Table Options** dialog box (**Table** menu, **Add Tables** submenu).

User\Query 97\Records\Automatic Query

This policy sets the **Automatic Query** option on the **Records** menu. When this option is selected (a check mark appears next to the **Automatic Query** command on the menu), then every time you add a field to a query, the query is updated. Clear this option if you have large queries that take a long time to run.

User\ODBC 3.0\Default DSN Folder

This policy allows you to specify a default folder for ODBC file data source names (DSNs). A file DSN specifies a database name, the ODBC used to gain access to the database, and additional connection information and settings. The contents of the specified folder are displayed on the **Databases** tab in the **Choose Data Source** dialog box when you create or edit a query. The default folder created by Setup is C:\Program Files\Common Files\ODBC\Data Sources.

Bookshelf Policies

The following user setting policy is used by Microsoft Bookshelf. This appears under the **Bookshelf** heading in the System Policy Editor.

User\Bookshelf\Location of Bookshelf Content

This policy allows you to enter a path to the location of Bookshelf files. You can change this setting if you want to move Bookshelf to a different server.

List of Office 97 System Policies

This section lists all policies available in the policy template files. The order in this section corresponds to the order in which the policies are defined in the Office policy template files, and closely matches the order in which they appear in the System Policy Editor.

The policies in the templates have been arranged in two sections. Policies grouped under the heading "User Settings" are specific to the user currently logged on to a computer. These policies correspond to **HKEY_CURRENT_USER** keys in the Windows registry. Policies grouped under the heading "Computer Settings" apply to all users running a particular computer. These policies correspond to the **HKEY_LOCAL_MACHINE** keys in the Windows registry.

Under these headings, the policies are grouped by component or (when applicable) by how the corresponding option may be set by the user. For example, all Office 97 Office Assistant policies are grouped together, and all policies that correspond to the **Edit** tab in the **Options** dialog box (Microsoft Excel **Tools** menu) are grouped together.

Policies in the Off97w95.adm Template

Computer Settings

Office 97
    Default Save
        Prompt Text
    Disable Password Caching
    Uninstall
        Command to point Add/Remove to new network install location
    Assistant
        Installed Path
            Location of actor (.act) and preview (.acp) files.
        Source Path
            Location where additional actor (.act) files can be found.

Excel 97
    Microsoft Map
        Map Data
            Directory where map data is stored
        Search Paths
            Directories where shared map data is stored
    Converters
        Excel 9.0 Import Converter
            Path for Excel 9.0 import converter

PowerPoint 97
    Converters
        PowerPoint 9.0 Import Converter
            Path for PowerPoint 9.0 import converter

Word 97
    Spelling Advanced
        Default AutoCorrect File
            Path to default AutoCorrect file for new users
        Custom Dictionaries
            Value Name = 2-10. Value = Dictionary Path
        New Dictionary Locations
            Spelling English (United States)
                Path to MSSP2_EN.LEX
            Spelling English (British)
                Path to MSSP2_EN.LEX
            Spelling English (Australia)
                Path to MSSP2_EN.LEX
            Thesaurus English (United States)
                Path to MSTH_AM.LEX
            Thesaurus English (British)
                Path to MSTH_AM.LEX
            Hyphenation English (United States)
                Path to HY_EN.LEX
            Hyphenation English (British)
                Path to HY_EN.LEX

Appendixes

        Grammar English (United States)
            Path to MSGR_EN.LEX
    Converters
        Word 9.0 Import Converter
            Path for Word 9.0 import converter
            Name of converter:

Clip Art Gallery 3.0
    Concurrent Database #1
        multimedia (.avi and .wav files), or photos (.bmp, .jpg, .gif etc)
    Concurrent Database #2
        multimedia (.avi and .wav files), or photos (.bmp, .jpg, .gif etc)
    Concurrent Database #3
        multimedia (.avi and .wav files), or photos (.bmp, .jpg, .gif etc)

Windows
    Network Install Tab
        Location of INI file with list of network install locations.

User Settings

Office 97
    Common
        Personal Folder
            Path to Personal folder used by all apps
        User Templates
            Path to User Templates folder
        Workgroup Templates
            Path to Workgroup Templates folder
        Sound
        Chart Gallery
            Chart gallery path
    Assistant
        Default State
        Choose File
            Filename of assistant (*.act)
        Position
            Distance from left of screen
            Distance from top of screen
        Options Tab
            Respond to F1 key
            Help with wizards
            Display alerts
            Search for both product and programming help
            Move when in the way
            Guess help topics
            Make sounds
            Using features more effectively
            Using the mouse more effectively
            Keyboard shortcuts
            Only show high priority tips
            Show the Tip of the Day at startup

Internet
    FTP Sites
        Delete FTP Sites
        Add FTP Sites
            Site:
    Web Search
        Internet Lookup Options
            Server Friendly Name
            Server Base URL or UNC
            Index Path
            Template Path
            GIF Path
            Properties
            Protocol
            Sort By
    Help_Microsoft on the Web
        Customize submenu
        Reset submenu to original defaults
        Disable submenu
Tools_Customize
    Options
        Menu Animation
        Large Icons
        Show ToolTips
        Always show shortcut keys
    Office Wizards
Binder Options
    Single Print Job
Visual Basic Editor
    Help_Microsoft on the Web
        Customize submenu
        Reset submenu to original defaults
        Disable submenu

Excel 97
    Tools_Options
        Edit
            Move Enter Direction
                Move selection after Enter
            Fixed Decimal
        General
            Recently Used File List
                Entries on recently used file list
            Default Sheets
                Sheets in new workbook
            Font
                Name,Size
            Alternate Startup Folder
                Alternate startup file location
        Transition
            Default Save
                Save Excel files as:
            Menu Key
                Excel menu or Help key:

Appendixes

> BitFields
> > Options value
> > Options3 value
> > Options5 value
> > Options6 value
> > Options95 value
>
> Microsoft Map
> > Map Matching
> > > *Time Limit (secs)*
> >
> > Sizing Units
> > > *Feature Sizing Units*
> >
> > Compact Legends
> > Auto Correct
>
> Internet
> > Help_Microsoft on the Web
> > > Customize submenu
> > > Reset submenu to original defaults
> > > Disable submenu
> >
> > Converters
> > > Future File Format Converters
> > > > *URL for Converter*
>
> Miscellaneous
> > Personal Toolbars
> > > *Path to roving custom toolbar*
> >
> > Run Query
> > > *Path to saved queries folder*
> >
> > Chart Gallery
> > > *Chart gallery path*

PowerPoint 97
> Tools_Options
> > View
> > > Startup dialog
> > > New slide dialog
> > > Status bar
> > > Vertical ruler
> > > Popup menu on right mouse click
> > > Show popup menu button
> > > End with blank slide
> >
> > General
> > > Recently Used File List
> > > > *Enable recently used file list*
> > > > *Size of recently used file list*
> > >
> > > Macro Virus Protection
> > > Link Sounds File Size
> > > > *Link sounds with file size greater than (Kb):*
> >
> > Edit
> > > Replace straight quotes with smart quotes
> > > Automatic word selection
> > > Use smart cut and paste
> > > Drag-and-Drop text editing
> > > Inserting
> > > Undo
> > > > *Maximum number of undos:*

Print
    Background Printing
Save
    Allow fast saves
    Prompt for file properties
    Full text search information
    AutoRecovery
        Save AutoRecovery info
        AutoRecovery save frequency (min):
    Default Save
        Save PowerPoint files as:
Spelling
    Background spelling
    Hide spelling errors
    Suggest Always
    Ignore words in UPPERCASE
    Ignore words with numbers
Advanced
    Picture
        Render 24-bit bitmaps at highest quality
        Export pictures:

Internet
    Help_Microsoft on the Web
        Customize submenu
        Reset submenu to original defaults
        Disable submenu
    Converters
        Future File Format Converters
            URL for Converter

Miscellaneous
    Personal Toolbars
        Path to roving custom toolbar
    Multimedia Directory
    Template Directory
    Picture Directory
    No Edit Time
        Do not display edit time in document statistics

Word 97
    Tools_Options
        General
            Help for WordPerfect users
            Macro Virus Protection
        Edit
            Picture Editor
                Picture editor:
        Print
            Background Print
        Save
            Default Save
                Save Word files as:
            Background Save

Appendixes

       Spelling & Grammar
          Background Spelling
          Background Grammar
       File Locations
          Clipart Pictures
            Path to Clipart Pictures folder
          AutoRecover Files
            Path to AutoRecover Files folder
          Tools
            Path to folder containing dictionaries, filters and text converters
          Startup
            Path to Startup folder
     Tools_AutoCorrect
       AutoFormat
          Plain Text WordMail Documents
     Internet
       Help_Microsoft on the Web
          Customize submenu
          Reset submenu to original defaults
          Disable submenu
       Converters
          Future File Format Converters
            URL for Converter
     Web Page Authoring
       Bullet Path
       Dialog Bullet Path
       Horizontal Line Path
       Dialog Horizontal Line Path
       Local Content
       Workgroup Content
       Local Page Styles
       Workgroup Page Styles
       Clipart URL
       Template URL
       AutoUpDate
       AutoUpDate Address
     Miscellaneous
       Date Format
          Default date format:
       Time Format
          Default time format:
       No Edit Time

Windows
     Internet Settings
       Proxy Server
       Proxy Override
       Proxy Enable

Internet Explorer 3.0
     Options_Navigation
       Start Page
       Search Page

> **Bookshelf**
> > **Location of Bookshelf Content**
> > **Remove Tools_Look Up Reference menu from Excel**

Policies in the Access97.adm Template

User Settings

Access 97
> **Tools_Options**
> > **View**
> > > **Status Bar**
> > > **Startup Dialog**
> > > **Hidden Objects**
> > > **System Objects**
> > > **Macro Names Column**
> > > **Macro Conditions Column**
> >
> > **General**
> > > **Sort Order**
> > > > *New Database Sort Order*
> > >
> > > **Sound**
> > > **Hyperlink Colors**
> > > > *Already viewed*
> > > > *Not yet viewed*
> > >
> > > **Hyperlink Underline**
> > > **Hyperlink Address**
> > > **Print Margins**
> > > > *Left Margin*
> > > > *Right Margin*
> > > > *Top Margin*
> > > > *Bottom Margin*
> >
> > **Edit/Find**
> > > **Find/Replace**
> > > > *Default Find/Replace Behavior*
> > >
> > > **Record Changes**
> > > **Document Deletions**
> > > **Action Queries**
> >
> > **Datasheet**
> > > **Default Colors**
> > > > *Font*
> > > > *Background*
> > > > *Gridlines*
> > >
> > > **Default Font**
> > > > *Name*
> > > > *Weight*
> > > > *Size*
> > > > *Underline*
> > > > *Italics*
> > >
> > > **Horizontal Gridlines**
> > > **Vertical Gridlines**
> > > **Column Width**
> > > > *Default Column Width*

Appendixes

- **Cell Effect**
  - *Default Cell Effect*
- **Animations**
- **Tables/Queries**
  - **Field Sizes**
    - *Default Text Field Size*
    - *Default Number Field Size*
  - **Field Type**
    - *Default Field Type*
  - **AutoIndex**
    - *AutoIndex on Import/Create*
  - **Show Table Names**
  - **Output All Fields**
  - **Enable AutoJoin**
  - **Run Permissions**
- **Forms/Reports**
  - **Selection Behavior**
  - **Form Template**
  - **Report Template**
  - **Event Procedures**
- **Keyboard**
  - **Move After Enter**
  - **Arrow Key Behavior**
  - **Behavior Entering Field**
  - **Cursor Stop**
- **Module**
  - **Font**
    - *Name*
    - *Size*
  - **Coding Options**
    - *Auto Indent*
    - *Auto Syntax Check*
    - *Break On All Errors*
    - *Require Variable Declaration*
    - *Compile On Demand*
    - *Auto Statement Builder*
    - *Auto Quick Info*
    - *Auto Value Tips*
    - *Tab Width*
  - **Window Options**
    - **Full Module View**
    - **Procedure Separator**
    - **Drag-and-Drop Text Editing**
    - **Debug Window On Top**
    - **Margin Indicator Bar**
- **Advanced**
  - **Default Record Locking**
  - **Ignore DDE Requests**
  - **Enable DDE Refresh**
  - **OLE/DDE Timeout**
    - *OLE/DDE Timeout (sec)*
  - **Update Retries**
    - *Number of Update Retries*

        ODBC Refresh
            ODBC Refresh Interval (sec)
        Refresh Interval
            Refresh Interval (sec)
        Update Retry
            Update Retry Interval (msec)
        Default Open Mode
            Default Open Mode for Databases
Internet
    Help_Microsoft on the Web
        Customize submenu
        Reset submenu to original defaults
        Disable submenu

Policies in the Outlk97.adm Template

Computer Settings

Outlook 97
    Use Schedule+

User Settings

Outlook 97
    Tools_Options
        General
            Warn Before Deleting
            Sychronize Folders
        E-Mail
            Process delivery, read, and recall receipts on arrival
            Process requests and responses on arrival
            Delete receipts and blank meeting responses after processing
        WordMail
            Use WordMail as e-mail editor
        WordMail Template
            Path and file name of WordMail template
        Calendar
            Work Week
            First Day of Week
            First Week of Year
            Working Hours
                Start time:
                End time:
            Appointment defaults
                Duration (min)
                Reminder (min)
            Show Week Numbers
            Use Schedule+
        Tasks/Notes
            Reminder Time
                Reminder time:
            Set Reminders
            Track Tasks
            Send Status Reports

Appendixes

Task color options
Overdue tasks:
Completed tasks:
Work Settings
Hours per day:
Hours per week:
Note Defaults
Color:
Size:
Show time and date

Journal
Automatically record these items
E-mail message
Fax
Meeting cancellation
Meeting request
Meeting response
Task request
Task response
Also record these files
Microsoft Access
Microsoft Office Binder
Microsoft Excel
Microsoft PowerPoint
Microsoft Word
Journal Entry Options
Double-clicking a journal entry:

Reminders
Reminder Options
Display the reminder
Play reminder sound
Sound filename:

Spelling
Suggest Replacements
Check Spelling
Ignore Uppercase
Ignore Numbers
Ignore Original

Internet
Help_Microsoft on the Web
Customize submenu

Reset submenu to original defaults
Disable submenu
Converters
Future File Format Converters
URL for Converter:
Miscellaneous
Disable Forms Designer

Policies in the Query97.adm Template

User Settings

Query 97
    File_New
        Data Source Folders
            Enter paths to data sources
        Use Wizard
    Edit_Options
        Disable Options
        Connection Timeout
            within
        Limit Records
            to
        Auto Disconnect
        Disable Edit
    Table Options
        Show Tables
        Show Views
        Show System Tables
        Show Synonyms
    Records
        Automatic Query

ODBC 3.0
    Default DSN Folder
        Folder where ODBC 3.0 File DSNs are created

APPENDIX D
List of Installed Components

This appendix lists components installed by Microsoft Office Setup when you choose various installation types during Setup.

In This Appendix
Custom and Typical Installations   1081
Run from Network Server Installation   1082
Run from CD Installation   1085

Note The file size values in the tables in this appendix represent the number of bytes used by the files listed. The actual disk space used by these files may differ, depending on the sector size of your disk. For example, a file containing 5,000 bytes might take 16,384 bytes of disk space on a 1-GB disk with 16K sectors, but the same file might take 32,768 bytes of disk space on a 2-GB disk with 32K sectors.

Custom and Typical Installations

When you choose a Typical installation, Setup installs a subset of Office components that includes the most commonly used Office features. To see which components are included in a Typical installation, run Setup and choose a Custom installation. In the check box options displayed by Setup, the components that are selected by default are the components that are installed during a Typical installation.

The following table lists the disk space used in Typical installations and complete installations (Custom installations with all components selected) of Office 97.

This type of Installation	Of this edition of Office 97	Uses this amount of disk space
Typical	Standard Edition	102 MB
Typical	Professional Edition	121 MB
Complete	Standard Edition	167 MB
Complete	Professional Edition	191 MB

Tools and Utilities   The Office Resource Kit Tools and Utilities include complete lists of the files installed during Custom and Typical installations. For more information, see "Informational Worksheets," in Appendix A, "Microsoft Office 97 Resource Kit Tools and Utilities."

Run from Network Server Installation

When you choose a Run from Network Server installation, Setup leaves most Office components on the network server. However, some Office components are copied to your hard disk.

The following table lists the disk space used in Run from Network Server installations of Office 97.

This type of installation	Of this edition of Office 97	Uses this amount of disk space
Run from Network Server	Standard Edition	24 MB
Run from Network Server	Professional Edition	25 MB

The following table lists the components that are installed on your hard disk during a Run from Network Server installation.

This Office component	Is installed in this folder	And has this total file size
Clip Gallery	Program Files\Microsoft Office\Office	357K
Clip Gallery	Windows	1K
Clip Gallery	Windows\System	39K
Data Access	Windows\System	4,542K
E-Mail Information Services	Windows\System	1,148K
File Open Indexer	Windows\System	22K
Fonts	Windows\Fonts	1,952K
Forms	Windows\Forms	77K
Graphics Filters	Windows\System	208K
Help	Windows\Help	36K
Help	Windows\System	378K

Appendix D   List of Installed Components

This Office component	Is installed in this folder	And has this total file size
MAPI	Program Files\Windows Messaging	432K
MAPI	Windows	1K
MAPI	Windows\Forms\Configs	16K
MAPI	Windows\Help	154K
MAPI	Windows\Sysbckup	30K
MAPI	Windows\System	4,406K
Microsoft Access Custom Controls	Windows\System	158K
Microsoft Access Wizards	Windows\System	167K
Microsoft Excel Program Files	Program Files\Microsoft Office\Office	175K
Microsoft Excel Program Files	Windows\System	118K
Microsoft Exchange EFD Runtime	Windows\System	3,518K
Microsoft Exchange Extensions	Windows\System	1,076K
Microsoft Graph	Program Files\Microsoft Office\Office	183K
Microsoft Outlook Program Files	Windows\System	758K
Microsoft Photo Editor	Windows	276K
Microsoft PowerPoint Program Files	Program Files\Microsoft Office\Templates	10K
Microsoft PowerPoint Program Files	Windows\System	163K
Microsoft Word Internet	Program Files\Microsoft Office\Office\HTML	171K
Microsoft Word Internet	Windows\System	92K
Microsoft Word Program Files	Windows\ShellNew	11K
Microsoft Word Program Files	Windows\System	212K
ODBC	Windows\System	451K
Office Binder	Windows\ShellNew	6K
Office Program Files	Program Files\Microsoft Office\Office\Shortcut Bar\Office	1K
Office Program Files	Windows\System	121K
Office Sounds	Windows\Media\Office97	25K
Web Find Fast	Windows	32K
Web Find Fast	Windows\System	114K

Microsoft Office 97 Resource Kit   **1083**

This Office component	Is installed in this folder	And has this total file size
OLE	Windows\System	22K
Proofing Tools	Program Files\Microsoft Office\Office	1K
Proofing Tools	Windows	34K
Setup	Program Files\Microsoft Office\Office\Setup	835K
Setup	Windows\System	182K
Shortcuts	Program Files\Microsoft Office	6K
Shortcuts	Program Files\Microsoft Office\Clipart	1K
Shortcuts	Program Files\Microsoft Office\Clipart\Backgrounds	5K
Shortcuts	Program Files\Microsoft Office\Office\Shortcut Bar\Office	10K
Shortcuts	Program Files\Microsoft Office\Office\WordMail\Favorites	3K
Shortcuts	Program Files\Microsoft Office\Queries	1K
Shortcuts	Program Files\Microsoft Office\Templates\Webpages	1K
Shortcuts	Windows	2K
Shortcuts	Windows\Desktop	1K
Shortcuts	Windows\SendTo	1K
Shortcuts	Windows\Start Menu	1K
Shortcuts	Windows\Start Menu\Programs	4K
Shortcuts	Windows\Start Menu\Programs\StartUp	2K
Templates	Windows\ShellNew	14K
Visual Basic for Applications	Windows\System	1,621K
WordMail	Program Files\Microsoft Office\Office	340K
WordMail	Windows\Forms\Configs	1K

Tools and Utilities   The Office Resource Kit Tools and Utilities include a complete list of the files installed during Run from Network Server installations. For more information, see "Informational Worksheets" in Appendix A, "Microsoft Office 97 Resource Kit Tools and Utilities."

Run from CD Installation

When you choose a Run from CD installation, Setup leaves most Office components on the Office CD. However, some Office components are copied to your hard disk.

The following table lists the disk space used in Run from CD installations of Office 97.

This type of installation	Of this edition of Office 97	Uses this amount of disk space
Run from CD	Standard Edition	51 MB
Run from CD	Professional Edition	61 MB

The following table lists the components that are installed on your hard disk during a Run from CD installation.

This Office component	Is installed into this folder	And has this total file size
Briefcase	Program Files\Microsoft Office\Office	182K
Clip Gallery	Program Files\Common Files\Microsoft Shared\Artgalry	449K
Clip Gallery	Windows	1K
Clip Gallery	Windows\System	39K
Data Access	Program Files\Common Files\Microsoft Shared\DAO	1,454K
Data Access	Windows\System	4,542K
E-Mail Information Services	Windows\System	1,148K
Equation Editor	Program Files\Common Files\Microsoft Shared\Equation	660K
Equation Editor	Windows\Fonts	7K
File Open Indexer	Windows\System	22K
Fonts	Program Files\Common Files\Microsoft Shared\Textconv	8K
Fonts	Windows\Fonts	1,984K
Forms	Program Files\Common Files\Microsoft Shared\VBA	698K
Graphics Filters	Program Files\Common Files\Microsoft Shared\Grphflt	3,332K
Graphics Filters	Windows\System	208K

This Office component	Is installed into this folder	And has this total file size
Help	Program Files\Common Files\Microsoft Shared\Datamap	347K
Help	Program Files\Common Files\Microsoft Shared\Grphflt	31K
Help	Program Files\Common Files\Microsoft Shared\Orgchart	102K
Help	Windows\Help	36K
Help	Windows\System	378K
MAPI	Program Files\Windows Messaging	432K
MAPI	Windows	1K
MAPI	Windows\Forms\Configs	17K
MAPI	Windows\Help	154K
MAPI	Windows\Sysbckup	30K
MAPI	Windows\System	4,406K
Microsoft Access Custom Controls	Windows\System	158K
Microsoft Access Program Files	Program Files\Microsoft Office\Office	15K
Microsoft Access Program Files	Windows\System	68K
Microsoft Access Wizards	Program Files\Microsoft Office\Office	8,428K
Microsoft Access Wizards	Windows\System	167K
Microsoft Excel Main Files	Program Files\Microsoft Office\Office	175K
Microsoft Excel Main Files	Windows\System	118K
Microsoft Exchange EFD Runtime	Windows\System	3,518K
Microsoft Exchange Extensions	Windows\System	1,076K
Microsoft Graph	Program Files\Microsoft Office\Office	183K
Microsoft Info	Program Files\Common Files\Microsoft Shared\MSInfo	518K
Microsoft Map	Program Files\Common Files\Microsoft Shared\Datamap	2,003K

This Office component	Is installed into this folder	And has this total file size
Microsoft Map	Program Files\Common Files\Microsoft Shared\Datamap\Data	2,513K
Microsoft Map	Windows\Fonts	7K
Microsoft Orgranization Chart	Program Files\Common Files\Microsoft Shared\Orgchart	1,394K
Microsoft Outlook Program Files	Windows\System	758K
Microsoft Photo Editor	Program Files\Common Files\Microsoft Shared\PhotoEd	1,611K
Microsoft Photo Editor	Windows	276K
Microsoft PowerPoint Program Files	Program Files\Microsoft Office\Templates	10K
Microsoft PowerPoint Program Files	Windows\Fonts	75K
Microsoft PowerPoint Program Files	Windows\System	163K
Microsoft Word Internet	Program Files\Microsoft Office\Office\HTML	171K
Microsoft Word Internet	Windows\System	92K
Microsoft Word Program Files	Windows\ShellNew	11K
Microsoft Word Program Files	Windows\System	230K
ODBC Direct	Windows\System	451K
Office Binder	Windows\ShellNew	6K
Office Bookshelf	Program Files\Common Files\Microsoft Shared\Reference Titles	157K
Office Program Files	Program Files\Common Files\Microsoft Shared\VBA	476K
Office Program Files	Program Files\Microsoft Office\Office\Shortcut Bar\Office	1K
Office Program Files	Windows\Forms	77K
Office Program Files	Windows\System	121K
Office Sounds	Windows\Media\Office97	25K
Office Templates	Windows\ShellNew	14K
Web Find Fast	Windows	32K
Web Find Fast	Windows\System	114K
OLE	Windows\System	22K

This Office component	Is installed into this folder	And has this total file size
Proofing Tools	Program Files\Common Files\Microsoft Shared\Proof	5,154K
Proofing Tools	Program Files\Microsoft Office\Office	1K
Proofing Tools	Windows	34K
Setup	Program Files\Microsoft Office	1K
Setup	Program Files\Microsoft Office\Office\Setup	797K
Setup	Windows\System	182K
Shortcuts	Program Files\Microsoft Office	5K
Shortcuts	Program Files\Microsoft Office\Clipart	1K
Shortcuts	Program Files\Microsoft Office\Clipart\Backgrounds	3K
Shortcuts	Program Files\Microsoft Office\Office\Shortcut Bar\Office	7K
Shortcuts	Program Files\Microsoft Office\Office\Shortcut Bar\QuickShelf	4K
Shortcuts	Program Files\Microsoft Office\Office\WordMail\Favorites	3K
Shortcuts	Program Files\Microsoft Office\Queries	1K
Shortcuts	Program Files\Microsoft Office\Templates\Webpages	1K
Shortcuts	Windows	2K
Shortcuts	Windows\Desktop	1K
Shortcuts	Windows\Recent	1K
Shortcuts	Windows\SendTo	1K
Shortcuts	Windows\Start Menu	1K
Shortcuts	Windows\Start Menu\Programs	3K
Shortcuts	Windows\Start Menu\Programs\Microsoft Reference	1K

This Office component	Is installed into this folder	And has this total file size
Text Converters	Program Files\Common Files\Microsoft Shared\Textconv	2,770K
Visual Basic for Applications	Program Files\Common Files\Microsoft Shared\VBA	4,694K
Visual Basic for Applications	Windows\System	1,603K
WordMail	Program Files\Microsoft Office\Office	340K

Tools and Utilities   The Office Resource Kit Tools and Utilities include a complete list of the files installed during Run from CD installations. For more information, see "Informational Worksheets" in Appendix A, "Microsoft Office 97 Resource Kit Tools and Utilities."

APPENDIX E
Other Support Resources

This appendix describes resources to help you support your Microsoft Office 97 users. Support is available directly from Microsoft by telephone and through various online services.

In This Appendix
Getting Support from Microsoft   1091
Microsoft on the World Wide Web   1094
Other Microsoft Support Programs   1094
Training and Reference Resources   1099

Getting Support from Microsoft

If you have a question about Office, look first in the Office product documentation (the printed *Getting Results* book and online Help). You can also find updates and technical information in the Readme files that come with Office, and in various online sources, as explained later in this chapter. If you cannot find the answer you need, contact Microsoft Technical Support. Microsoft Technical Support offers high-quality technical support options that allow you to get what you need: the right answers right now.

Note Services and prices may vary outside the United States and Canada. Microsoft Technical Support is subject to current Microsoft pricing, terms, and conditions, and may change without notice.

Primary Support

In the United States, no-charge support from Microsoft support engineers is available through a toll call between 6:00 A.M. and 6:00 P.M. Pacific time, Monday through Friday, excluding holidays.

For technical support with this application	Call this number
Microsoft Access	(206) 635-7050
Microsoft Excel	(206) 635-7070
Microsoft Office	(206) 635-7056
Microsoft Office—Switcher Line (specifically for users switching to Office)	(206) 635-7041
Microsoft Outlook	(206) 635-7031
Microsoft PowerPoint	(206) 635-7145
Microsoft Word	(206) 462-9673

In Canada, support engineers are available through a toll call between 8:00 A.M. and 8:00 P.M. Eastern time, Monday through Friday, excluding holidays. Call (905) 568-3503.

When you call, you should be at your computer and have the appropriate product documentation on hand. Be prepared to give the following information:

- Version number of the Microsoft product that you are using
- Type of hardware that you are using
- Exact wording of any messages that appear on your screen
- Description of what happened and what you were doing when the problem occurred
- Description of how you tried to solve the problem

Outside the United States and Canada, contact Microsoft Product Support Services at the Microsoft subsidiary office that serves your area.

▶ **To get information about Microsoft subsidiary offices outside the United States and Canada**

1. On the **Help** menu in any Office application, click **About** *Office application*.
2. Click **Tech Support**.
3. Follow the instructions on your screen.

Priority Support

Microsoft Technical Support offers priority telephone access to Microsoft support engineers in the United States 24 hours a day, 7 days a week, except holidays. In

Canada, priority support is available from 6:00 A.M. to 12:00 A.M. Eastern time, 7 days a week, excluding holidays. You can choose one of two payment options:

- In the United States, call (900) 555-2020; $55 (U.S.) per incident. Charges appear on your telephone bill. This option is not available in Canada.
- In the United States and Canada, call (800) 936-5500; $55 (U.S.) per incident. These services are billed to your VISA, MasterCard, or American Express card.

Other Support Options

Microsoft Technical Support offers annual fee-based support plans. For information in the United States, contact the Microsoft Technical Support Sales Group at (800) 668-7975 between 6:00 A.M. and 6:00 P.M. Pacific time, Monday through Friday, excluding holidays. In Canada, call (800) 563-9048 between 8:30 A.M. and 6:30 P.M. Eastern time, Monday through Friday, excluding holidays. Technical support is not available through these sales numbers.

Text Telephone

Microsoft text telephone (TT/TDD) services are available for the deaf or hard-of-hearing. In the United States, using a TT/TDD modem, dial (206) 635-4948 between 6:00 A.M. and 6:00 P.M. Pacific time, Monday through Friday, excluding holidays. In Canada, using a TT/TDD modem, dial (905) 568-9641 between 8:00 A.M. and 8:00 P.M. Eastern time, Monday through Friday, excluding holidays.

Microsoft FastTips

For Microsoft FastTips for desktop applications, call (800) 936-4100 on a touch-tone telephone. Receive automated answers to common technical problems, and receive popular articles from the Microsoft KnowledgeBase—all delivered by recording or fax. After you reach FastTips, use the following keys on your touch-tone telephone:

To do this	Press this key on your telephone keypad
Advance to the next message	*
Repeat the current message	7
Return to the beginning of FastTips	#

Microsoft Sales

The Sales telephone number in the United States is (800) 426-9400 between 6:30 A.M. and 5:30 P.M. Pacific time, Monday through Friday, excluding holidays. In Canada, call (800) 563-9048 between 8:00 A.M. and 8:00 P.M. Eastern time, Monday through Friday, excluding holidays. Call this number for information about Microsoft Solution Providers and for Business Value Reports for Office 97 and Windows 95. This is not a technical support number.

Appendixes

Microsoft on the World Wide Web

All of the Microsoft Office applications include menu commands that connect directly to sites on the World Wide Web. These commands appear on the **Microsoft on the Web** submenu (**Help** menu) in each application. If you have Web access, clicking these commands opens your Web browser and connects to the appropriate Web site.

Customizing Microsoft on the Web Commands (Windows only)

As an administrator, you might wish to redirect or disable the Web hyperlinks on the Office application **Help** menus. For example, users might not have access to the Web, or you might prefer to direct them to an internal support page on your intranet. You can do so by customizing settings in the Windows registry.

For more information about customizing or disabling the **Microsoft on the Web** submenu commands, see "Customizing Office Connections to the World Wide Web" in Chapter 7, "Customizing and Optimizing Microsoft Office."

World Wide Web Microsoft Office has a large amount of content on the World Wide Web. Some content that you may find especially useful include the following:

- For more information about Microsoft Office, connect to the Microsoft Office home page at:

    http://www.microsoft.com/office/

- For more information about developing custom solutions with Microsoft Office, connect to the Office Developer Site home page at:

    http://www.microsoft.com/officedev/

Other Microsoft Support Programs

In addition to telephone support, Microsoft offers other resources to help you support your users.

Microsoft Through Online Services

Microsoft support resources are available on several popular online services.

America Online

You can take advantage of the information and tools available through the Microsoft Knowledge Base in America Online.

▶ **To use the Knowledge Base in America Online**

1 On the **Go To** menu, click **Keyword**.
2 In the **Keyword** box, type **microsoft** and then click **Go**.
3 In the **Microsoft Resource Center**, click the **Knowledge Base** button.

MSN, The Microsoft Network

You can access a number of Microsoft forums on MSN™, the Microsoft Network online service. MSN includes the following forums:

- Microsoft Access
- Microsoft Excel
- Microsoft Outlook
- Microsoft PowerPoint
- Microsoft Word
- Microsoft Office
- Microsoft Office Family

These forums are continually updated, so you should consult them for the most up-to-date information about the Office applications.

The Microsoft Knowledge Base

The Knowledge Base is the primary source of product information for Microsoft support engineers and customers. The Knowledge Base contains detailed how-to articles, in addition to answers to technical questions, bug lists, fix lists, and documentation corrections.

Knowledge Base articles are available on CD with a membership in the Microsoft Developer Network (MSDN) or a subscription to Microsoft TechNet. They are also available online from CompuServe (type **go mskb**, or **go mdkb** for the developer Knowledge Base) and the Microsoft Download Service (MSDL).

World Wide Web For more information, connect to the Microsoft Technical Support Knowledge Base home page at:
http://www.microsoft.com/kb/

Microsoft Download Service

The MSDL operates in the same manner as any MS-DOS-based computer bulletin board system (BBS). MSDL contains Application Notes, driver files, and other types of support files you might want to download.

To use MSDL, you must have a modem and a terminal package such as Microsoft Works or Windows 95 HyperTerminal. If you experience difficulty while you are working with the MSDL, try calling a local BBS so you can avoid paying long-distance charges while trying to determine the cause of the problem. Technical support is not available on the MSDL.

MSDL supports 1200, 2400, 9600, and 14,400, baud rates (V.32 and V.42), with 8 data bits, 1 stop bit, and no parity. After you have chosen these settings, you can begin the session as follows.

▶ **To connect to Microsoft Download Service**

1   To reach MSDL, dial (206) 936-6735.
2   Type your full name and the location from which you are calling.
3   At the MSDL Main Menu, type the number of the option you want.

From this menu you can download files, search the file index, view instructions for using MSDL, obtain a Windows driver library update, and obtain other information.

Microsoft Software Library

The Microsoft Software Library (MSL) is a collection of files pertaining to all Microsoft products, including drivers, utilities, Help files, and Application Notes. MSL files are available online from MSN, CompuServe, the Web, and Microsoft Download Service. You can also get the Microsoft Software Library on CD by joining the Microsoft Developer Network (MSDN) or by subscribing to Microsoft TechNet.

Microsoft TechNet

Microsoft TechNet is the comprehensive CD-ROM information resource for evaluating, implementing, and supporting Microsoft business products. A one-year subscription to Microsoft TechNet delivers two CDs every month with over 150,000 pages of up-to-date technical information. The first CD is packed with current technical notes, reviewers' guides, backgrounders, Microsoft product resource kits, the entire Microsoft Knowledge Base, and much more. The second CD contains the Microsoft Software Library with the latest drivers and service packs for Microsoft products.

To subscribe to Microsoft TechNet, see your local authorized reseller or call (800) 344-2121, weekdays, between 6:30 A.M. and 5:30 P.M. Pacific time. For international orders, call (510) 275-0826 (in the U.S.) for contacts in your region.

A one-year single-user subscription to Microsoft TechNet is $299 (U.S.) and $399 (Canada). A server-unlimited users license for TechNet is $699 (U.S.) and $999 (Canada).

World Wide Web For more information about Microsoft Technet, connect to the TechNet home page at:

http://www.microsoft.com/technet/

Microsoft Developer Network

MSDN is the official source from Microsoft for comprehensive programming information, development toolkits, and testing platforms. MSDN delivers all of this through a quarterly subscription, so subscribers can be confident that they're always working with the most up-to-date information and technology.

An MSDN subscription is essential if you are targeting any of the Windows platforms, or you want to get the most out of Microsoft's development products, such as Visual Basic, Visual C++, Visual J++, and Microsoft Access.

To join the Developer Network in the United States and Canada, call (800) 759-5474, 6:30 A.M. to 5:30 P.M. For information about joining the Developer Network in other countries, call (510) 275-0963.

World Wide Web For more information about the Microsoft Developer Network, connect to the Microsoft Developer Network Online home page at:

http://www.microsoft.com/msdn/

Microsoft Solution Providers

Microsoft Solution Providers are independent organizations that provide consulting, integration, development, training, technical support, or other services with Microsoft products. Microsoft equips Solution Providers with information, business development assistance, and tools that help create additional value with Microsoft-based software technology. To locate a Microsoft Solution Provider in your area, or for more information on the Microsoft Solution Provider program in the United States, call Microsoft at (800) SOLPROV (or (800) 765-7768). In Canada, call (800) 563-9048.

World Wide Web For more information about Microsoft Solution Providers, connect to the Solution Providers home page at:

http://www.microsoft.com/msp/

Appendixes

Microsoft Authorized Support Centers

Microsoft Authorized Support Centers (ASCs) are a select group of strategic support providers who offer high quality customized support services for each phase of your system development, including planning, implementing, and maintaining your multivendor environment. Services include:

- On-site support
- Integration and implementation services
- Help desk services
- Hardware support
- Development resources

Choosing an ASC allows you to work with one vendor for all of your technical support and service needs. You can also combine ASC services with your in-house Help desk or the Microsoft support service option that best fits your support needs.

For more information about the ASC program, in the United States call (800) 936-3500 between 6:00 A.M. and 6:00 P.M. Pacific time, Monday through Friday, excluding holidays. In Canada, call (800) 563-9048 between 8:00 A.M. and 8:00 P.M. Eastern time, Monday through Friday, excluding holidays.

World Wide Web For more information about Microsoft Authorized Support Centers, connect to the Service Advantage home page at:

http://www.microsoft.com/syspro/servad/

Microsoft Consulting Services

Microsoft Consulting Services (MCS) provides services that allow corporations, governments, and other institutions worldwide to design and build client-server applications using Microsoft technology. MCS consultants are experienced in designing custom solutions for order entry, payroll, and a variety of other business functions.

For more information, call (800) 426-9400 or the Microsoft Consulting Services office nearest you.

World Wide Web For more information about Microsoft Consulting Services, connect to the Microsoft Consulting Services home page at:

http://www.microsoft.com/msconsult/

Training and Reference Resources

Microsoft offers training services to help you become an expert in Microsoft solutions. These services include the Microsoft Certified Professional Program and Microsoft Technical Education courses. In addition, a large library of books and other training and reference products is available from Microsoft Press.

Microsoft Certified Professional Program

The Microsoft Certified Professional program offers an excellent way to show employers and clients that you have proven knowledge and skills to help them build, implement, and support effective solutions, and that you have the validated expertise to help them get the most out of their technology investment. As a Microsoft Certified Professional, you are recognized and promoted by Microsoft as an expert with the technical skills and knowledge to implement and support solutions with Microsoft products.

To become a Microsoft Certified Professional, you must pass a series of rigorous, standardized certification exams. When you become a Microsoft Certified Professional, you receive benefits including access to technical information, use of the Microsoft Certified Professional logo, and special invitations to Microsoft conferences and technical events.

For more information about the Microsoft Certified Professional program, call Microsoft at (800) 636-7544 in the United States and Canada. In other countries, contact your local Microsoft subsidiary office. Ask for the *Microsoft Education and Certification Roadmap*, an online guide to Microsoft Education and Certification.

World Wide Web For more information about the Microsoft Certified Professional program, connect to the Microsoft Training and Certification home page at:

http://www.microsoft.com/train_cert/

Microsoft Technical Education

Microsoft technical education materials provide computer professionals with the knowledge required to expertly install and support Microsoft solutions. Courses are developed straight from the source—by the Microsoft product and technical support groups. They include in-depth, accurate information and hands-on labs based on real-world experience. Microsoft courses are designed to help you prepare effectively for Microsoft Certified Professional exams.

Microsoft curriculum is available in two forms:

- Instructor-led classes are delivered by Microsoft Certified Trainers at Microsoft Authorized Technical Education Centers (ATECs). As members for the Solution Provider program, the ATECs are independent businesses that have been evaluated as qualified to deliver official Microsoft curriculum.
- Self-paced curriculum materials developed by Microsoft allow you to learn at your convenience. Hands-on lab exercises are included.

For full course descriptions and referral to an ATEC, call (800) SOLPROV (or (800) 765-7768) in the United States and Canada In other countries, contact your local Microsoft subsidiary office. Ask for the *Microsoft Education and Certification Roadmap*, an online guide to Microsoft Education and Certification.

World Wide Web   For more information about Microsoft technical education programs, connect to the Microsoft Training and Certification home page at:

http://www.microsoft.com/train_cert/

Microsoft Press Titles

Following is a list of publications to consult for additional information about Office, the individual Office applications, and the Windows 95 and Windows NT operating systems. These books are published by Microsoft Press and available wherever computer books are sold. In the United States you can place a credit card order directly with Microsoft Press by calling (800) MS PRESS. In Canada, call (800) 667-1115 for direct ordering information. Outside the United States and Canada, fax (206) 936-7329.

World Wide Web   For more information about Microsoft Press, connect to the Microsoft Press home page at:

http://www.microsoft.com/mspress/

Following is information about specific publications you may find useful.

Resource Kits

Microsoft Windows 95 Resource Kit
Microsoft Corporation
Published by Microsoft Press
1376 pages with one CD
ISBN: 1-55615-678-2

This is the complete technical guide to planning for, installing, configuring, and supporting Windows 95 in your organization. It includes details about how to install, configure, and support Windows 95, plus valuable tools, utilities, and accessory software on CD.

Microsoft Windows NT Workstation 4.0 Resource Kit
by Microsoft Corporation
Published by Microsoft Press
One volume and with one CD
ISBN: 1-57231-343-9

This book and CD set provides the in-depth technical information and tools for anyone who uses Windows NT Workstation 4.0, including power users and application developers. Information about installing, configuring, networking, troubleshooting, and optimizing Windows NT Workstation is included, with more than 45 MB of utilities and other valuable software on CD.

Microsoft Windows NT Server 4.0 Resource Kit
by Microsoft Corporation
Published by Microsoft Press
Three volumes and with one CD

This three-volume set provides in-depth technical information and tools that Windows NT Server 4.0 administrators need for installing, configuring, networking, troubleshooting, and optimizing Windows NT Workstation and Windows NT Server 4.0. It contains more than 45 MB of utilities and other valuable software on CD.

Note Single-volume updates to the *Microsoft Windows NT Server 4.0 Resource Kit*, intended for use by those who already have the full three-volume set, are published approximately every six months.

Programming Guides and Technical References

Microsoft Office 97/Visual Basic Programmer's Guide
by Microsoft Corporation
Published by Microsoft Press
704 pages
ISBN: 1-57231-340-4   UPC: 790145134042

This guide teaches those with a grounding in the basics of Visual Basic how to create concise, efficient code with the powerful programming language used in Office 97. The book shows readers how to become more productive with Visual Basic for Applications by customizing and adapting tools for specific needs, including creating custom commands, menus, dialog boxes, messages, and buttons, as well as displaying custom online Help for all these elements.

Microsoft Office 97/Visual Basic Language Reference
by Microsoft Corporation
Published by Microsoft Press
3800 pages in a three volume set
ISBN: 1-57231-339-0   UPC: 790145133908

This reference manual includes core information about Visual Basic and the Visual Basic Editor, as well as reference material about Word Visual Basic for Applications, Microsoft Excel Visual Basic, Microsoft Access Visual Basic, PowerPoint Visual Basic, and DAO. Whether you are customizing Office 97 applications for your own use, creating custom applications for use by others, or writing applications that interact with Office 97, this book is an essential guide.

Microsoft Excel 97 Worksheet Function Reference
by Microsoft Corporation
Published by Microsoft Press
370 pages
ISBN: 1-57231-341-2   UPC: 790145134127

This reference manual provides power users with worksheet functions, which are shortcuts to finding solutions in spreadsheets involving mathematics, statistics, trigonometry, engineering, and accounting.

Building Applications in Microsoft Outlook 97
by Microsoft Corporation
Published by Microsoft Press
450 pages with one CD
ISBN: 1-57231-536-9   UPC: 790145153692

This results-oriented book offers both the nonprogrammer and experienced MIS professional the information, strategies, and sample applications they need to get started building useful workgroup applications and mail-enabled applications almost immediately.

Step by Step Series

The *Step by Step* series of books published by Microsoft Press offers you an easy way to teach yourself to use the Office 97 applications. This series is suitable for new users, as well as those upgrading or switching from competing programs. End-user editions in the series include Microsoft Office integration, Microsoft Access, Microsoft Excel, Microsoft PowerPoint, and Word, among many others.

The Step by Step series includes editions with information about Visual Basic. These editions are described below.

Microsoft Access 97/Visual Basic Step by Step
by Evan Callahan
384 pages with one CD
ISBN: 1-57231-319-6   UPC: 790145131966

Microsoft Excel 97/Visual Basic Step by Step
by Reed Jacobson
384 pages with one CD
ISBN: 1-57231-318-8   UPC: 790145131881

Microsoft Office 97/Visual Basic Step by Step
by David Boctor
384 pages with one CD
ISBN: 1-57231-389-7   UPC: 790145138976

Microsoft Word 97/Visual Basic Step by Step
Michael Halvorson and Chris Kinata
384 pages with one CD
1-57231-388-9 (ISBN)   790145138897 (UPC)

Microsoft White Papers

Microsoft produces white papers and other technical documents about Office 97. These documents provide detailed information about specific aspects of evaluating, using or supporting Office.

The following white papers are available on the Microsoft Web site, the KnowledgeBase, and Microsoft TechNet.

For this information	See this white paper
A list of all the new features in Office 97.	Office 97 Product Enhancements Guide
A description of how IntelliSense and the Office Assistant make it easier for users to get their work done.	Office 97 IntelliSense Whitepaper
A description of how Web functionality has been combined with desktop productivity applications in Office 97.	Office 97 Intranet Whitepaper
A discussion of the workgroup features implemented in Office 97.	Office 97 Workgroup Whitepaper
A discussion of how a large organization can migrate its desktops to Office 97 easily and efficiently.	Migrating to Office 97
Details about the performance testing completed early in the Office 97 development process.	Office 97 Performance Whitepaper
Information about how to use Office 97 to quickly and cost-effectively create line-of-business applications.	Office 97 Solutions Whitepaper

World Wide Web For more information about Microsoft Office white papers and other documents you may find useful, connect to the Microsoft Office 97 Information home page at:

http://www.microsoft.com/office/office97/

Index

32-bit Office, upgrading from 16-Bit Office-Based solutions 236

A

Access Basic, upgrading to Visual Basic for Applications 281–293, 295
accounts
    anonymous, creating for public folders 872
    group, Microsoft Access 97 813
    Outlook 97 resource 868
    user, Microsoft Access 97 813
action buttons, adding to slides 708
Action menu upgrades
    from PowerPoint 3.0 to PowerPoint 97 394
    from PowerPoint 4.0 to PowerPoint 97 380
    from PowerPoint 95 to PowerPoint 97 367
Action queries 919
Active Server Pages (ASP)
    control types 685
    form views 685
    Microsoft HTML Layout control 686
    requirements for using 686
    saving from forms or datasheets 684
ActiveX controls
    defined as technology tool for creating Office solutions 648
    differences from OLE 907
    documents 908
    Microsoft Access databases 923
    Office 97 support 906
    overview 907
    PowerPoint Animation Player 711
    replacing Microsoft Access controls 685
    upgrading from Access Basic to Microsoft Access 97 281
    World Wide Web address for latest information 907
ActiveX documents 650

ActiveX objects, displaying in Microsoft Excel 97 and 5.0/95 format 316
add-in programs
    connecting Microsoft Exchange Client features with Outlook 97 338
    creating from workbooks 949–951
    creating in Word 97 1006
    customizing in PowerPoint 97 978–979
    DLLs 181
    installed always 927
    installed during a Custom installation 929
    installed during a Typical installation 927
    Macintosh location 949
    menus 926
    Microsoft Access, overview 925
    Microsoft Excel 97, listed 950
    Visual Basic 181
    Windows location 949
address books 797
addresses
    referenced by command buttons 674
    referenced by image controls 674
Admin, default user account in Microsoft Access 97 813
administrative installation point
    administrative setup 78
    assigning product identification 90
    client setup 78
    creating 80
    defined 77
    folders 78
    server preparation 79
    updating with new configuration 97
    updating with same configuration 95
Admins, system administrator's group accounts 813
A-functions, Microsoft Excel 97 501
Alias control word 241
All Components network installation option 119
Allways formatting 509
alternate startup folders, Microsoft Excel 97 952

animation
    adding to Web sites 712
    effects on slides 974
    PowerPoint, saving to HTML 711
    PowerPoint, viewing in HTML 711
    settings, new in PowerPoint 27
    templates, overview 27
Animation Player, Microsoft PowerPoint 711
ANSI character set 241
APIs (application programming interface)
    C Declarations, using 250–251
    calling, defined 239
    case sensitivity 240
    Corporate Developer's Guide to Office 95 API issues, referenced 247
    deciding which to call when porting Office-Based Solutions 238
    declarations, Win32 1026
    Declare Statement errors 244
    Declare-Method solution sample 248
    defined 338
    differences between 16-Bit and 32-bit 240–244
    GetVersion 240
    If…Then…Else control structure 244
    interfacing with ANSI character set 241
    interfacing with Unicode character set 241
    locating data on possible call stacks 242
    MyAPICall, possible declarations 242
    name in Win32 SDK documentation 242
    parameter data types 243
    porting Office-Based Solutions 239
    procedure calls 239
    return registers 239
    solution code calling procedure 239
    stacks 239
    using the Alias control word when upgrading to 32-bit Office 241
    Win32 Programmer's Reference 243
    Word solutions upgrading procedure 249
    wrappers 245
Append queries, Microsoft Access 97 919
Apple Help menu upgrades
    from Microsoft Excel 5.0 to Microsoft Excel 97 311
    from PowerPoint 3.0 to PowerPoint 97 395
    from PowerPoint 4.0 to PowerPoint 97 381
    from Word 6.0/95 to Word 97 405
application-specific requirements for installing Microsoft Office 97 75

Arrange menu upgrades, from PowerPoint 3.0 to PowerPoint 97 390
ASCs (Microsoft Authorized Support Centers) 1098
Authorized Academic Training Programs (AATPs) 56
AutoAddress, Microsoft Outlook 97 24
AutoClipArt concept list 1024
AutoCorrect, using for formulas 17
AutoFormat command 999
AutoLayouts, Microsoft PowerPoint 97 967
Automation, defined as technology tool for creating Office solutions 648
AutoName, Microsoft Outlook 97 24
AutoSummary, Microsoft Word 97 28
AutoText entries 1001

B

Balloon Help menu upgrades, from PowerPoint 3.0 to PowerPoint 97 395
bands, Microsoft Access 97 reports 475
binders
    Macintosh, unbinding sections 229
    overview 14
    upgrading from Office 95 229
    Windows 3.1, unbinding sections 229
    Windows 95, unbinding sections 229
    Windows NT, unbinding sections 229
bitness, using to determine appropriate API calls 245
book-level name references, Microsoft Excel 97 942
Briefcase replication, Microsoft Windows 95 837
Browse Saved Hyperlinks form 692
brute force search, Find Fast 720
buffers, used by Microsoft Jet 157
builders 926
built-in autoformats, Microsoft Excel 97 313
built-in templates, Microsoft Excel 97 312
bulletin boards, setting up in Outlook 97 549
buttons *See* toolbars

C

C Declarations 250–251
CAB files, Microsoft Office 97 floppy disk 89
call stacks 239
case sensitivity, API 240

Index

cc:Mail
    bulletin boards, setting up using the Outlook client 549
    folders, importing into Outlook 549
    information service, adding to user profiles in Outlook 97 548
    private mail lists, importing into Outlook 97 550
CD, Microsoft Office 97
    installation (first-time) 86
    installation (subsequent releases) 96
cell tracers 512
cells
    comments, defined 511
    comments, printing 511
    comments, selecting 511
    customizing in Microsoft Excel 97 18
    data, overview 940
    formatting 943
    formulas 941
    merging 18
    name references 942
    ranges, using to create charts 944
    referenced in formulas, illustrated example 18
    references 941
    scenarios for changing formulas 942
    tracers 512
    using to locate formulas not correctly converting to Microsoft Excel 97 511
    workbook, change history 858
    workbook, viewing the entire change history 862
CGI (Common Gateway Interface) protocols 697
change history for Microsoft Excel 97 workbooks 858, 862–863
Change Option button for Microsoft Office 97 installation 86
Chart wizards, Microsoft Excel 97 944
charts
    autoformats, upgraded in Microsoft Excel 97 945
    built-in and user-defined 945
    converting Microsoft Excel data to HTML 693
    custom types, distributing 945
    custom types, Microsoft Excel 97 945
    items, changing colors in Microsoft Excel 97 524
    line, formatting in Microsoft Excel 97 523
    Lotus 1-2-3, using in Microsoft Excel 97 523–525
    Macintosh types 945

charts *(continued)*
    Microsoft Graph 97 970
    PowerPoint 97 970
    updated, as Microsoft Excel 97 intelligence feature 19
    upgrading autoformatting to Microsoft Excel 97 313
    workbooks 944
    xy (scatter), formatting in Microsoft Excel 97 523
class modules 287
cleanup for Microsoft Office 97 installation 203
client computer 56
client setup, interactive 83
client setup, running with modified STF files 130
client/server architecture
    Microsoft Access 97 file server applications 763–767
    overview 762
clip art
    AutoClipArt tool, PowerPoint 97 985
    Gallery 3.0 machine setting properties 1057
    PowerPoint 97 970
Clip Gallery 912
colors, PowerPoint 97 976
combo box performance optimization in Microsoft Access 174
command-line options recognized by the Office 97 Upgrade Wizard 209
commands, adding to the Office package 134
compliance checking for Microsoft Office 97 91–94
computer policies 140
conferencing *See* presentations
control types for Active Server Pages 685
controls, Microsoft Access 97 database *See* ActiveX controls
Conversion Wizard 582
converters
    ACT! 2.0, using to map fields to Outlook 97 551
    additional in Office Resource Kit Tools and Utilities 577
    batch, PowerPoint 97 1014
    confirming which to use in Word 97 581
    default locations 577
    defined 562
    DisplayWrite 1018
    importing presentations to PowerPoint 97 563
    Lotus Ami Pro 1018
    Lotus Organizer 557
    Microsoft Windows Write 1018
    MultiMate 1018

converters *(continued)*
    PowerPoint 95, for PowerPoint 4.0 1015
    PowerPoint 97 1014
    PowerPoint, using to work with other file formats 562
    recognizing various file formats in Word 97 1017
    RFT-DCA 1018
    text, defined 574
    text, included with Word 97 575
    text, locating 577
    utilities, Office 97 1014
    Word 6.0/95 1017
    Word 97 574
    Word for MS-DOS 3.x–6.0 1017
    Word for MS-DOS text 428
    WordPerfect map characters 1018
    WordPerfect, installing before converting documents to Word 97 595
    WordStar 1019
converting
    databases secured with passwords 256
    databases secured with user-level security 256
    databases to Design Master 840
    databases to Microsoft Access from earlier Microsoft Access versions 254–262
    databases, troubleshooting 255
    documents from previous versions of Word *See* upgrading
    documents to Microsoft Excel 97 from other file formats 492
    documents to Word 97 from other file formats 580
    file formats in Microsoft Excel 492
    file formats to Word 97 574–588
    Lotus 1-2-3 worksheets to Microsoft Excel 97 506
    Lotus Freelance presentations to PowerPoint 97 572
    Microsoft Excel charts and data to HTML 693
    Microsoft Excel data to HTML 695
    Microsoft Works files to Microsoft Excel 97 542
    Multiplan files to Microsoft Excel 97 538
    multiple documents to Microsoft Excel 97 493
    multiple documents to Word 97 581
    multiple Harvard Graphics presentations to PowerPoint 97 571
    multiple Lotus 1-2-3 worksheets to Microsoft Excel 97 507
    multiple Lotus Freelance presentations 572
    multiple PowerPoint presentations 567
    multiple WordPerfect documents to Word 97 596

converting *(continued)*
    presentations to PowerPoint 97 from other file formats 566
    presentations to PowerPoint from earlier PowerPoint versions 362
    Quattro Pro for MS-DOS worksheets to Microsoft Excel 97 535
    replicated databases 259
    to Microsoft Access 97 from other databases 460–468
    to Microsoft Excel 97 from Microsoft Excel 4.0 320–327
    to Microsoft Excel 97 from Microsoft Excel 5.0 307–314
    to Microsoft Excel 97 from Microsoft Excel 95 302–306
    to Office 97 from MS-DOS applications 441
    to PowerPoint 97 from Harvard Graphics 570
    to Word 97 from Microsoft Works 3.0/4.0 608–611
    to Word 97 from Word 2.0 414–421
    to Word 97 from Word 5.x for Macintosh 432
    to Word 97 from Word 5.x/6.0 for MS-DOS 426
    to Word 97 from Word 6.0/95 400–407
    to Word 97 from WordPerfect 589–608
    unbound object frame controls to image controls 256
    unbound object frame controls when converting databases 256
    Word 97 styles to Word for MS-DOS 432
    Word documents to HTML 714
    Word for MS-DOS graphics to Word 97 428
    Word for MS-DOS styles to Word 97 428
    WordPerfect 5.x documents to Word 97 599–600
    WordPerfect 6.x documents to Word 97 596–599
    WordPerfect documents to Word 97 594–596
    workbooks from previous versions of Microsoft Excel 302
Corporate Developer's Guide to Office 95 API issues, referenced 247
corporate dictionaries, creating 911
Crosstab queries 918
Crystal Reports, Microsoft Outlook 97 1035
custom autoformats, Microsoft Excel 97 313
custom lists, sharing within workgroups 955
Custom Shows command, Microsoft PowerPoint 97 26
custom templates, Microsoft Excel 97 312
customer support
    annual-fee based support plans 1093
    help options 1093

Index

customer support *(continued)*
    Microsoft Authorized Support Centers (ASCs) 1098
    Microsoft Consulting Services (MCS) 1098
    Microsoft Developer Network 1097
    Microsoft Download Service (MSDL) 1095
    Microsoft FastTips 1093
    Microsoft Knowledge Base 1095
    Microsoft on the Web 1094
    Microsoft Software Library 1096
    Microsoft Solution Providers 1097
    Microsoft TechNet 1096
    Microsoft Technical Support documents 1022
    Microsoft Technical Support Help File 1023
    MSN (Microsoft Network) 1095
    online help services 1094
    overview 1091
    priority 1092
    services for the deaf or hard-of-hearing 1093
    standard technical 1092
    text telephone services 1093
customizing, converted documents in Word 97 582–584

D

DAO
    database replication 839
    methods unsupported for external databases in other formats 749
    object libraries, upgrading from Access Basic to Microsoft Access 97 283
data access applications, running in Microsoft Access 97 487
data matrix commands, Lotus 1-2-3 519
Data menu upgrades
    from Microsoft Excel 4.0 to Microsoft Excel 97 324
    from Microsoft Excel 5.0 to Microsoft Excel 97 310
    from Microsoft Excel 95 to Microsoft Excel 97 305
data regression commands, Lotus 1-2-3 519
Database Wizard 15
databases
    back-end, securing 820
    Briefcase replication 837
    changes made when replicated 840–843
    checked during Office Setup 92
    client/server architecture 762
    compacting 154
    compiling before converting 254
    containers, defined 915

databases *(continued)*
    controls 923
    converting object frame controls to image controls 256
    converting password secured 256
    converting to Design Master 840
    converting to Microsoft Access from earlier versions 254–262
    converting unbound object frame controls to image controls 256
    converting user-level secured 256
    datasheets, defined 457
    Design Master converted, AutoNumber field changes 842
    Design Master converted, new properties 842
    Design Master converted, new tables 841
    documenting 765
    duplicating replicas 843
    enabling 297
    encrypting 810
    external data source troubleshooting 750
    file protection 804
    filter performance optimization 172
    forms, overview 454
    front-end, creating 298
    front-end, securing 820
    GUIDS (globally unique identifiers) 936
    laptop replication 837
    library 924
    linked tables 932
    linked to ODBC tables, converting 261
    macros, overview 454
    Microsoft Access 97, changing or clearing passwords 806
    Microsoft Access 97, defined 452
    Microsoft Access 97, optimizing tips 153–154
    Microsoft Access, sharing with previous Microsoft Access versions 297
    modules, overview 455, 922
    multiuser environments 825–834
    multiuser performance optimization 166
    multiuser, additional issues 833
    multiuser, backing up correctly 833
    naming on network drives 748
    normalization of table data 162
    object format differences in Microsoft Access 97 268, 278
    objects, creating 457
    objects, overview 452

databases *(continued)*
  objects, redesigning 458
  objects, switching between views 458
  open modes 825
  optimizing criteria expressions using Rushmore technology 169–172
  overview 915
  ownership 817
  Paradox, sharing data with Microsoft Access 97 483–486
  partial replication 844
  passwords, setting 805
  Performance analyzing when optimizing Microsoft Access 97 152
  queries, overview 453
  record locking options 826–828
  referencing other databases in MDE files 809
  replica sets, converting 259
  replicas, using instead of backups 844
  replicated, compacting 850
  replicated, making into regular databases 852
  replicated, security 850
  replicated, when not to use 836
  replicating *See* replicated databases
  Replication Manager 838
  reports, overview 454
  reports, previewing and printing 457
  saving as MDE files 178, 806–810
  secured 623
  securing with startup options 804
  securing without sign-on requirement 821
  server 764
  sharing with multiple Microsoft Access versions 623
  splitting advantages and disadvantages, listed 832
  splitting into front-end/back-end applications 832
  splitting, defined 166
  SQL, performance optimization 164
  tables, overview 453
  troubleshooting conversion 255
  user-level security, removing 822
  windows, drag-and-drop features 456
  windows, using to view objects 455
  workgroup information files 256–259, 811
Data-Definition queries 921

dBASE
  catalog differences in Microsoft Access 97 475
  data type conversion 471
  files, importing and linking to Microsoft Access 470
  forms, using in Microsoft Access 97 474
  importing Microsoft Access 97 tables and queries 475
  numeric field types 472
  registry settings in Microsoft Access 97 476
  terms, differences from Microsoft Access 97 terms 469
DBMS (database management system) 931
Debug menu upgrades
  to Microsoft Access 97 from Microsoft Access 2.0 277
  to Microsoft Access 97 from Microsoft Access 95 266
Declare-Method solution sample, Word 97 248
default configurations for the Office 97 Shortcut Bar 234
Delete queries 453, 919
dependency list, Upgrade Wizard 214
dependency variables
  application names, recognized by Office 97 Upgrade Wizard 211
  contained in dependency lists 214
  defined 210
  special purpose keyword descriptions 213
  values 210
deploying
  Microsoft Windows 50
  Office 97, suggested phases 50
  Office 97, using the network 57
Deployment Planner, Microsoft Office 97 1031
Design Master (database replica) 259, 834, 851
Design Outlook Form command 338
Desktop driver for Microsoft Access 97 683
destination folders for Office application files 110
Developer Network News 1097
DisplayWrite, converters for Word 97 1018
DLL add-ins, using for PowerPoint optimization 181
DLLs, recompiling 249
DoCmd objects, Microsoft Access 97 280
document properties
  customizing 639–640
  defined 637

document properties *(continued)*
  entering 638
  Find Fast 733
  prompt, displaying when saving documents 639
  viewing 638
  Web Find Fast 737
documents
  ActiveX 908
  advanced, Microsoft Office 97 1020
  comparing versions 898–901
  converted to Microsoft Excel 97, saving 493
  converted WordPerfect, saving in Word 97 595
  converted, customizing in Word 97 582–584
  converted, line breaks 584
  converted, page breaks 584
  converting from WordPerfect 5.x to Word 97 599–600
  converting from WordPerfect 6.x to Word 97 596–599
  converting from WordPerfect to Word 97 594–596
  converting to Word 97 580–584
  converting to Word 97 from previous Word versions 400
  elements that can be protected 893
  Find Fast, types 724
  font substitution in Word 97 584–586
  hiding properties in public folders 641
  HTML, static 676
  intranet, collaborating in workgroups 654
  Microsoft Excel 97, saving in other file formats 494
  Microsoft Excel, sharing with Quattro Pro for MS-DOS 536
  multiple authors 894
  multiple, converting from WordPerfect to Word 97 595
  multiple, converting to Microsoft Excel 97 493
  multiple, converting to Word 97 581
  not displaying in Open dialog box 581
  opening in Microsoft Excel 97 492–494
  Outlook Extension Configuration File (ECF) 1024
  posting to public folders 799
  PowerPoint, indexes 727
  profiles, Outlook 97 1028
  properties 637–640
  protecting specific areas within 893
  reviewer comments 896
  routing with electronic mail 901

documents *(continued)*
  searching with Find Fast 719
  security levels 892
  sharing with multiple Word versions 635
  symbols and characters troubleshooting 586
  templates 992–997, 1005
  text with layout, not opening properly 612
  text, converting to Microsoft Excel 97 format 494
  tracking changes 895
  troubleshooting conversion to Microsoft Excel 97 493
  types available for indexing 724–726
  Win32 API declarations 1026
  Word 5.x for Macintosh, opening in Word 97 433
  Word 97, attaching templates 994
  Word 97, converted automatically to different formats 579
  Word 97, displaying WordPerfect text 594
  Word 97, how-to 1026
  Word 97, moving between Windows and Macintosh 580
  Word 97, opening in Word 6.0/95 411–414
  Word 97, protecting 892
  Word 97, saving in HTML 714
  Word 97, saving in other file formats 588
  Word 97, saving in Text with Layout format 612–615
  Word 97, saving in Word 2.0 421–425
  Word 97, saving in Word 6.0/95 format 408–411
  Word 97, saving in Word for MS-DOS 429–431
  Word 97, saving in Works for Windows 609
  Word 97, sharing with Word 2.0 421–425
  Word 97, sharing with Word 5.x for the Macintosh 433–434
  Word 97, sharing with Word 6.0/95 407–414
  Word 97, sharing with Word for MS-DOS 429–432
  Word 97, sharing with WordPerfect 5.x 601
  Word 97, sharing with WordPerfect 6.x 599
  Word 97, sharing with Works for Windows 609–611
  Word 97, substituting fonts when converting to other formats 586
  Word 97, template examples illustrated 993
  Word 97, troubleshooting formatting using Reveal Formats 591
  Word for MS-DOS, opening in Word 97 427
  WordPerfect, opening in Word 97 595
  workgroup reviewing 893–901
DoMenuItem Action, Microsoft Access 269

Index

drag-and-drop functionality, Microsoft Access 97 754
Draw menu upgrades
    from PowerPoint 4.0 to PowerPoint 97 379
    from PowerPoint 95 to PowerPoint 97 366
drivers
    Lotus cc:Mail 547
    MAPI-compliant for Outlook, reference for latest information 560
    message stores 560
    Microsoft Access 97, built-in 489
    Microsoft Access 97, ODBC 489
    ODBC, installing 261
DSNs (data source names) 261

E

Edit menu upgrades
    from Microsoft Access 2.0 to Microsoft Access 97 273
    from Microsoft Access 95 to Microsoft Access 97 264
    from Microsoft Excel 4.0 to Microsoft Excel 97 321
    from Microsoft Excel 5.0 to Microsoft Excel 97 308
    from Microsoft Excel 95 to Microsoft Excel 97 303
    from PowerPoint 3.0 to PowerPoint 97 387
    from PowerPoint 4.0 to PowerPoint 97 375
    from PowerPoint 95 to PowerPoint 97 363
    from Word 2.0 to Word 97 416
    from Word 6.0/95 to Word 97 402
electronic mail
    address books 797
    applications, sharing information with WordMail 796
    AutoNameChecking e-mail recipients in Outlook 22
    AutoPreviewing messages in Outlook 22
    capability, installed from Office Setup 794
    commands, using in Office 97 applications 797
    customizing templates 795
    duplicate messages 346
    editor, using WordMail as 338
    forms registry 338
    hyperlink messages 705
    integrating in Office 97 794–798
    Internet Mail 547
    Lotus cc:Mail 547
    messages, composing and viewing in WordMail 795

electronic mail *(continued)*
    Microsoft Access 97, Send command on File menu 797
    Microsoft At Work fax software 547
    Microsoft Exchange Server 547
    Microsoft Mail 547
    MMF (Microsoft Mail message file), moving to hard disk 345
    MMF (Microsoft Mail message file), moving to Outlook 97 personal folder 346
    network resources for mailing 798
    network resources for posting 798
    network resources for routing 798
    operating with the Microsoft network 801
    Outlook 97 resource accounts 868
    Outlook 97 service providers 547
    routing documents 901
    running multiple versions 628–630
    sending messages to Outlook bulletin boards 549
    shortcut keys, supplied by Email.dot template 795
    support workbook merging and data consolidation 860
    templates, setting up in WordMail 795
    WordMail 22, 795
    workbooks, routing 863
    workgroup review of documents 893
enabling process, Microsoft Access 226, 231
encryption for Microsoft Access 97 databases 804, 810
EPS files, supporting in Microsoft Word 97 428
error messages
    API call 239
    API Declare Statement 244
    caused by previously installed Office files 220
    displaying when converting formulas to Microsoft Excel 97 507
    displaying when opening Outlook 97 custom form 342
    Network Installation Wizard 115
    Office Setup 219
    server connection 81
ERRORLEVEL values 1050
errors
    API call 239
    API Declare Statement 244
    caused by special characters in Microsoft Excel 97 528
    exceeding locking limit 834
    MS-DOS based worksheets, auditing 510

errors *(continued)*
  Office 97 setup 219–221
  Word 97, correcting 592
evaluating Microsoft Office 97 53
event procedures 922
explicit permissions 815
export formats, Microsoft PowerPoint 97 985
expressions
  complex, examples 171
  complex, optimizing in Microsoft Access 170
  simple, examples 170
  simple, optimizing in Microsoft Access 169
Extension Configuration File (ECF), using for add-in authoring in Microsoft Outlook 339
Extension Configuration File Format (ECF) document 1024
Extract utility for Microsoft Office 97 floppy disks 1039

F

field mapping
  from ACT! 2.0 to Outlook 97 551
  from Ecco Pro to Outlook 97 553
  from Lotus Organizer to Outlook 97 558
  from Sidekick to Outlook 97 555
  Outlook 97 data files 772
field storage formats, hyperlinks 673
File Conversion Wizard, Microsoft Excel 97 493
file formats
  Allways 509
  changes when upgrading to Microsoft Access 97 268, 278
  Comma Separated Values 546
  common in Word 400
  compressing graphics when optimizing PowerPoint 97 182
  converting from other programs to Word 97 574–588
  differences in Microsoft Excel 97 from earlier versions 312
  EPS, supporting in Microsoft Word 97 428
  export, PowerPoint 97 985
  for saving active worksheets 496
  for saving workbooks 495
  from other source applications, opening in Microsoft Excel 492
  graphics, imported and stored in Word 97 578

file formats *(continued)*
  Impress 509
  INF files 1046
  intermediary, Outlook 97 771
  Lotus 1-2-3 506
  Microsoft Excel 4.0 328–331
  Microsoft Excel 5.0/95 317–320
  Microsoft Excel 97 and 5.0/95 314–317
  Microsoft Excel 97, common with other operating systems 302
  Microsoft PowerPoint 97, pictures 972
  native file formats 563
  Office 97 default 621
  Outlook Extension Configuration File (ECF) document 1024
  PCX, supporting in Microsoft Word 97 428
  PowerPoint 97, for saving presentations 969
  receiving data from Microsoft Access 97 750
  recognized by Clip Gallery 912
  Rich Text Format (RTF) 408, 587
  Setup files for Office 97 1045–1047
  sounds 972
  STF files 1046
  SYLK 538
  Tab Separated Values 546
  text converters available in the Office Resource Kit Tools and Utilities 577
  Text Only 587
  TIFF, supporting in Microsoft Word 97 428
  upgrading to Microsoft Excel 97 492–496
  upgrading to PowerPoint 97 562–570
  using to save Microsoft Works documents 608
  Word 97 graphics filters 578
  Word for MS-DOS graphics 428
  WYSIWYG 509
File menu upgrades
  from Microsoft Access 2.0 to Microsoft Access 97 271
  from Microsoft Access 95 to Microsoft Access 97 263
  from Microsoft Excel 4.0 to Microsoft Excel 97 321
  from Microsoft Excel 5.0 to Microsoft Excel 97 308
  from Microsoft Excel 95 to Microsoft Excel 97 303
  from PowerPoint 3.0 to PowerPoint 97 386
  from PowerPoint 4.0 to PowerPoint 97 374
  from PowerPoint 95 to PowerPoint 97 363
  from Word 2.0 to Word 97 415
  from Word 6.0/95 to Word 97 401
Filter By Form, Microsoft Access 15, 172

Filter By Selection, Microsoft Access 15
Find Fast
    brute force search 720
    differences from Web Find Fast 718–723
    document properties 733
    document searching 732
    document types 724
    excluded file types from indexing 725
    file types not indexed 725
    index files, locating 730
    index search results 720
    index structures 718
    indexer log 728
    indexes, creating and maintaining 729–731
    indexing PowerPoint documents 727
    installation 729
    methods of finding documents 722
    multiple indexes, when to create 730
    Office 95 indexes in Office 97 728
    overview 717
    running startup with switches 731
    searching for documents using index files 719
    specifying file types for indexing 724–726
    stop words 726, 1021
    system requirements 718
    user interface 721
    Windows NT service logon account, changing 741
    words not indexed 726
floppy disk
    CAB files, extracting and decompressing 89
    Office 97 installation (first-time) 88–90
    Office 97 installation (subsequent releases) 96
    product identification 91
folders
    alternate startup, Microsoft Excel 97 952
    anonymous accounts for posting Outlook messages 872
    Browse 121
    bulletins board 549
    cataloging Web sites 706
    cc:Mail, importing into Outlook 549
    Choose Data Source box 1066
    Clip Art 970
    containing Outlook 97 free/busy status information 867

folders *(continued)*
    designed for Outlook and Microsoft Exchange Client users 343
    destination, Office application 111
    identifying in Browse Folders dialog 121
    indexing 730
    item types, Outlook 97 962
    locating easily 870
    maintaining lists of contacts' Web sites 705
    multiple disjointed, included in Web Find Fast indexes 720
    My Documents, creating separate 1062
    My Documents, illustrated example 112
    names used in OPC file commands 214
    Office installation, created from CopyAll/CopyDisk 1039
    Outlook 97, Contacts 961
    Outlook Favorites 963
    package source 132
    public, Microsoft Outlook 97 *See* public folders
    revoking permission access 871
    sample Microsoft Access 97 database 458
    saving Outlook items 961
    setting up for Microsoft Exchange 868
    shortcuts, distributing to users 870
    tasks, Outlook 97 770
    Temporary, removing files when upgrading to Office 97 205
    toolbars 233
    unread messages, identifying 873
    using to hide document properties for documents 641
    Web History 706
font conversion from WordPerfect 1018
fonts
    codes inserted when formatting WordPerfect text 590
    mapping files 586
    modifying font-mapping files 586
    specifying for documents converted to Word 97 584–586
Form and Report Wizard improvements 16
form datasheets
    Microsoft Access 97, opening in Microsoft Excel 97 754
    Microsoft Access 97, opening in Word 752

form datasheets *(continued)*
    Microsoft Access, saving as static HTML
        documents 677
    saving as Active Server Pages (ASP) 684
    saving as IDC/HTX files 679
form views for Active Server Pages (ASP) 685
Format menu upgrades
    from Microsoft Access 2.0 to Microsoft
        Access 97 276
    from Microsoft Excel 4.0 to Microsoft Excel 97 323
    from Microsoft Excel 5.0 to Microsoft Excel 97 310
    from Microsoft Excel 95 to Microsoft Excel 97 305
    from PowerPoint 3.0 to PowerPoint 97 392
    from PowerPoint 4.0 to PowerPoint 97 377
    from PowerPoint 95 to PowerPoint 97 364
    from Word 2.0 to Word 97 417
    from Word 6.0/95 to Word 97 404
formatting
    plain-text 574
    Word 97 text 575
forms
    Design Outlook Form command 338
    Microsoft Access 97, creating 473
    Microsoft Access, overview 921
    Microsoft Exchange Client, upgrading to
        Outlook 97 338
    optimizing Filter By Form performance 172
    Outlook 97, exchanging with Microsoft Exchange
        Client 339
    Outlook 97, storing 342
    performance optimization in Microsoft Access 173
    Post, Outlook 97 341
    registry, using to identify forms for electronic
        mail 338
    standard message, Outlook 97 338, 339
    WordMail 340
forms registry, using to identify forms for electronic
    mail 338
Formula menu upgrades, from Microsoft Excel 4.0 to
    Microsoft Excel 97 322
formulas
    3-D, Microsoft Excel 97 518
    cell references 941
    corresponding with Microsoft Excel 97 from other
        applications 499–501
    Lotus 1-2-3, transitioning to Microsoft Excel 97 499
    Lotus 1-2-3, using in Microsoft Excel 97 512–519
    Microsoft Excel, AutoCorrect 17
    Microsoft Excel, natural language 16

formulas *(continued)*
    nested, Lotus 1-2-3 512
    referencing cells, illustrated example 18
    scenarios 942
    troubleshooting conversion to Microsoft
        Excel 97 511
    workbooks 941
free/busy status, Microsoft Outlook 97 users 866
From field settings, public folders 872
FTP sites, accessing 658
full precision calculation, Microsoft Excel 97 941
Function Wizard, Microsoft Excel 97 768

G

gallery location tools, Microsoft Excel 97 1027
GetVersion APIs 240
global templates 995
glossaries, Word for MS-DOS terms corresponding with
    Word 97 features 426
grammar checking, Word 97 28
graphics
    causes of changed formats in Word 97 580
    created using Word for MS-DOS Capture.com
        utility 428
    disappearing in converted text 580
    files for PowerPoint slides 569
    filters 578–580
    filters, locating in PowerPoint 97 564
    format for PowerPoint presentations 562
    formats for compressing when optimizing
        PowerPoint 97 182
    formats native to PowerPoint 97 564
    formats native to Word 97 578
    PICT, representing ActiveX objects 316
    Portable Network Graphics (PNG) 182
    PowerPoint 97, sharing with previous PowerPoint
        versions 182
    presentation, checked during Office Setup 92
    WMF, representing ActiveX objects 316
    Word 97, displaying in Word for the Macintosh 580
    Word for MS-DOS, converting to Word 97 428
    WordPerfect, importing into Word 97 596
graphics filters
    default locations in PowerPoint 97 564
    defined 562, 574
    exporting data from PowerPoint 97 985

Index

graphics filters *(continued)*
    included with Word 97 578
    installation locations 579
    installing for native Word 97 formats 578
    PowerPoint, importing image files 972
    WordPerfect, installing before converting documents to Word 97 595
graphics formats
    native to PowerPoint 97 564
    not displaying properly 569
    saving PowerPoint 97 presentations 569
group memberships, Microsoft Access 97 258
GUIDS (globally unique identifiers) 936

H

hard disk defragmentation for Microsoft Access 154
hardware and software inventory for Microsoft Office 97 installation 55
Help
    annual-fee based support plans 1093
    Apple menu changes in PowerPoint 97 from version 3.0 395
    Apple menu changes in Word 97 from versions 6.0/95 405
    Apple menu, changes in Microsoft Excel 97 from version 5.0 311
    Corporate Developer's Guide to Office 95 API issues, referenced 247
    information to provide when calling customer support 1092
    locating Microsoft subsidiary offices outside the U.S. and Canada 1092
    Lotus 1-2-3 533–535
    menu changes in Microsoft Access 97 from version 2.0 278
    menu changes in Microsoft Access 97 from version 95 267
    menu changes in Microsoft Excel 97 from version 4.0 326
    menu changes in Microsoft Excel 97 from version 5.0 311
    menu changes in PowerPoint 97 from version 3.0 394
    menu changes in PowerPoint 97 from version 4.0 380
    menu changes in PowerPoint 97 from version 95 367
    menu changes in Word 97 from version 2.0 421

Help *(continued)*
    menu changes in Word 97 from versions 6.0/95 405
    Microsoft Access 97 458
    Microsoft Authorized Support Centers (ASCs) 1098
    Microsoft Consulting Services (MCS) 1098
    Microsoft Developer Network 1097
    Microsoft Download Service (MSDL) 1095
    Microsoft Excel functions 517
    Microsoft FastTips 1093
    Microsoft Knowledge Base 1095
    Microsoft Office 97 Resource Kit 54
    Microsoft Office 97/Visual Basic Programmer's Guide, referenced 327
    Microsoft Office documentation 1019
    Microsoft on the Web 1094
    Microsoft Press publications 1100
    Microsoft Software Library 1096
    Microsoft Solution Providers 1097
    Microsoft Solutions Framework 1098
    Microsoft Support Network 1091
    Microsoft TechNet 1096
    Microsoft Technical Support documents 1022
    Microsoft Technical Support Help File 1023
    Microsoft Windows 95 Resource Kit 53
    Microsoft Windows NT Resource Kit 53
    MSN (Microsoft Network) 1095
    Office 97 Value Pack 546
    Office Assistant 12
    online support services 1094
    Peer Web Services 664
    Personal Web Server 663
    policies, Microsoft on the Web 1058
    priority technical support 1092
    services for the deaf or hard-of-hearing 1093
    technical support numbers 1092
    text telephone services 1093
    training companies supporting Microsoft products 189
    Ultimate Printer Manual 1025
    Web Find Fast administration 740
    Web server 663
    Win32 Programmer's Reference 243
    WordPerfect keyboard commands 605
    WordPerfect step-by-step 605
    WordPerfect, customizing in Word 97 607
    WordPerfect, in Word 97 604–608

Help menu upgrades
    from Microsoft Access 2.0 to Microsoft
        Access 97 278
    from Microsoft Access 95 to Microsoft
        Access 97 267
    from Microsoft Excel 4.0 to Microsoft Excel 97 326
    from Microsoft Excel 5.0 to Microsoft Excel 97 311
    from Microsoft Excel 95 to Microsoft Excel 97 306
    from PowerPoint 3.0 to PowerPoint 97 394
    from PowerPoint 4.0 to PowerPoint 97 380
    from PowerPoint 95 to PowerPoint 97 367
    from Word 2.0 to Word 97 421
    from Word 6.0/95 to Word 97 405
how-to documents, Microsoft Word 97 1026
HTML
    conversion issues for worksheet ranges 695
    converting from Microsoft Excel data and
        charts 693–695
    documents, saving from Microsoft Access
        data 676–688
    documents, when to use for intranet tasks 649
    extension file, Microsoft Access 97 680
    Layout control 686
    placeholders for templates 688
    PowerPoint presentations 710
    query pages, using for Web Find Fast search 742
    Setup Simulator for Office Setup 1024
    static documents 676
    tables, importing or linking data to Microsoft Access
        database 688–691
    tag pairs, defining Microsoft Access tables 689
    templates 687
    Web Find Fast Administration Tool 733, 740
    Word documents 714
hyperlinks
    adding text boxes to forms 671
    adding to PowerPoint slides 707
    addresses, referenced by labels 674
    field storage formatting 673
    intranets 29
    linking to Web pages using URLs 674
    Microsoft applications 669–675
    Office 97 documents 651–653
    storing in Microsoft Access tables 671
    using in electronic mail messages 705
    Visual Basic methods and properties 675
    working from Visual Basic code 675

I

Icon Name Properties dialog box, System Policy
    Editor 141
IDC/HTX files, saving from tables, queries, and form
    datasheets 679
implicit permissions 815
import and export wizards, Microsoft Access 97 15
Impress formatting 509
Indexed Sequential Access Method (ISAM) 746
indexer log, Find Fast 728
indexes
    creating for intranets using Web Find Fast 647
    creating for FrontPage Webs 726
    creating with Find Fast 729–731
    creating with Web Find Fast 736–741
    disabling options 737
    excluded file types 725
    Find Fast indexer log 728
    Find Fast, locating files 730
    limit in Microsoft Access databases 255
    Microsoft Access 97 162
    multiple, when to create 730
    Office 95, upgrading to Office 97 728
    password-protected documents 727
    query pages 738
    security issues 727
    server tables 766
    specifying file types 724–726
    stop words 726
    structure, Find Fast 718
    structure, Web Find Fast 718, 740
INF files
    customizing network installations 106
    modifying for custom installations of Office 107
    running client Setup 130
    specifying for Office 97 installation 110
    updating during Office 97 installation 129
Insert menu upgrades
    from Microsoft Access 2.0 to Microsoft
        Access 97 275
    from Microsoft Access 95 to Microsoft
        Access 97 265
    from Microsoft Excel 5.0 to Microsoft Excel 97 309
    from Microsoft Excel 95 to Microsoft Excel 97 304
    from PowerPoint 3.0 to PowerPoint 97 391
    from PowerPoint 4.0 to PowerPoint 97 376
    from PowerPoint 95 to PowerPoint 97 364

Index

Insert menu upgrades *(continued)*
   from Word 2.0 to Word 97 417
   from Word 6.0/95 to Word 97 403
installation
   add-in programs 927–929
   administrative installation point 77–82
   batch 131
   CAB files, extracting and decompressing 89
   CD, components 1081
   CD, customizing for Office 97 107
   CD, Office 97 (first-time) 86
   CD, Office 97 (subsequent releases) 96
   CopyAll batch files, Office 97 1038
   CopyDisk batch files, Office 97 1039
   Custom, defined 74
   Custom, Office 97 85–86
   electronic mail capability for Office 97 794
   Extract utility, Office 97 1040
   Find Fast 729
   floppy disk, customizing for Office 97 107
   floppy disk, defined 74
   floppy disk, Office 97 (first-time) 88–90
   floppy disk, Office 97 (subsequent releases) 96
   folders for Office 97 1039
   interactive 75, 131
   LAN (Local Area Network) options 448
   local, defined 72
   Maintenance Mode 1052
   methods for Office 97 74
   Microsoft Access Desktop driver 683
   Microsoft Excel 97 File Recovery 1028
   Microsoft Mail 3.x information service 344
   Microsoft Office 97 from floppy disks (first-time) 88–90
   Microsoft Office 97 from floppy disks (subsequent releases) 96
   Microsoft SQL Server Driver 490
   minimal interaction 75
   Network Installation Wizard 1012
   network server, components 1082
   network server, defined 74
   network, customizing for Office 97 106
   Office 97 from CD (subsequent releases) 96
   Office 97 from the network (subsequent releases) 95
   Office 97 network (first-time) 77–86
   Office 97 network (subsequent releases) 95
   Office 97 pilot rollout results 66–67
   Office 97 pilot, planning 63
   Office 97 test version 59–61

installation *(continued)*
   Office 97 test, rolling out to users 68–69
   Office 97 updates with new configuration 96–98
   Office 97 updates with same configuration 94–96
   Office CD, described 74
   Office Upgrade Wizard 1033
   options, additional 86
   options, Office 97 71–77
   options, selecting for shared applications 82
   options, specifying for test client configuration 59
   Outlook 97 profiles 1029
   Outlook 97 sample forms 1031
   Package Definition Files 1012
   Peer Web Services 663
   Personal Web Server 662
   pilot rollout for testing Office 97 62–65
   PowerPoint Animation Player 1043
   PowerPoint Animation Publisher 1043
   PowerPoint converters 1015
   PowerPoint Internet Assistant 1044
   push 63, 75, 131
   RegClean 1037
   scheduling suggestions 447
   shared, defined 72
   special requirements for Office 97 applications 75
   SwitchForms utility for Microsoft Outlook 97 1034
   System Policy Editor 1013
   system policy templates for Office 1053
   tools for Office 97 1011
   troubleshooting Office Setup 219
   troubleshooting problems from previously installed Office files 220
   types for Office 97 74
   types, illustrated 84
   Typical, defined 74
   Ultimate Printer Manual 1025
   Unbind Utilities, Office 97 1032
   uninstalling the test version of Office 97 61
   verifying test version of Office 97 61
   viewers for PowerPoint 4.0 1016
   viewers for PowerPoint 95 1016
   VIM for Office applications 794
   Web Find Fast 735
   Web server 662
   Windows 52
   Word converters 1017
   WordMail 795
   WordPerfect conversion fonts 1019
   WordStar converters 1019

installing
    Office 97 from CD (first-time) 86
    Office 97 from the network (first-time) 77–86
IntelliMouse 32
IntelliSense technology
    Microsoft Access 97 14
    Microsoft Excel 97 16–19
    Microsoft Outlook 97 20–25
    Office Art 13
    Office Assistant 12
    Office Binder 14
    overview 12
    PowerPoint 97 26–27
    toolbars 14
    Word 97 28–29
Internet
    Assistant for PowerPoint 95 1044
    compatibility with Microsoft Access features 666
    connections for PowerPoint presentation
        conferences 880
    Database Connector 680
    documents, opening and saving 658
    FTP sites, accessing 658
    FTP sites, accessing after the initial connection 658
    FTP sites, editing 659
    mail connection 704
    Mail, Post Office Protocol (POP) 547
    Mail, Simple Mail Transfer Protocol 547
    Microsoft Network online service 547
    policies 1059
    protocols in Microsoft Access 674
    protocols in Outlook 705
    publication requirements 662
    receiving data from Microsoft Access 676–688
    tasks performed with Microsoft access features 666
    Webmasters 646
Internet Assistant for Word, reference for latest
    information 579
Internet Assistant Wizard 693
intranets
    ActiveX documents 650
    analyzing data 653
    browsing Office 97 documents 31
    cataloging content using Web Find Fast 647
    compatibility with Microsoft Access features 666

intranets *(continued)*
    content creation from Office 97 applications 653
    creating Office programming solutions 648
    data access 653
    documents, collaborating in workgroups 654
    HTML and Office documents, combining 649
    hyperlinks 29
    indexing content using Web Find Fast 647
    IntelliMouse 32
    locating Office 97 documents 657
    management 646
    managing content with Microsoft FrontPage 646
    merging workgroup document versions into one
        file 655
    Microsoft Access 97, tools available 33–36
    Microsoft Excel 97, tools available 36–39
    Microsoft FrontPage 32
    Microsoft Office 97 29–33
    Microsoft Outlook 97, tools available 39–41
    Outlook 97 overview 656
    overview 646
    overview, as new Office 97 feature 29
    Peer Web Services 660
    Personal Web Server 660
    PowerPoint 97, tools available 41–42
    publication requirements 661
    publishing Web pages 659
    receiving data from Microsoft Access 676–688
    resolving conflicts for workgroup reviews 655
    search features 657
    searching, using Search the Web button on Office
        Web toolbar 653
    security 646
    selecting between HTML and Office documents to
        perform tasks 649
    sharing information with organization members 656
    solutions, customizing 32
    tasks performed with Microsoft access features 666
    TCP/IP (Transmission Control Protocol/Internet
        Protocol) 661
    tools for creation and administration 646–648
    tracking changes for workgroup revisions 655
    using hyperlinks created in Office documents 651
    using shared Microsoft Excel 97 workbooks 654
    Web browsers 650
    Web Find Fast 30
    Web toolbar 30
    Word 97, tools available 42–45

ISAPI (Microsoft Internet Information Server Application Programming Interface) 697
item types for Microsoft Outlook 97 335

J

Jet database engine 931
jobs, Office Package 135
journal, Microsoft Outlook 97 24
JPEG File Interchange format (JFIF) 182

K

keyboard commands
    alternate, Microsoft Excel 97 498
    corresponding with Microsoft Excel 97 from other applications 498
    customizing in Word 97 1004
    Lotus 1-2-3, corresponding with Microsoft Excel 97 504
    Microsoft Access 97, setting 467
    WordPerfect, available in Word 97 605
keys *See* keyboard commands
keywords
    dependency variables, Upgrade Wizard 210
    Visual Basic, supported in Microsoft Access 97 270

L

lab test of Microsoft Office 97 *See* testing
LAN (Local Area Networks)
    installation options for Office 97 448
    presentation conferencing connections 880
Letter Wizard, Microsoft Word 97 28
library databases 924
License Pak, Microsoft Office 97 94
line breaks
    in converted documents 584
    maintaining in text 588
linked tables
    converting along with databases 261
    data source names (DSNs) 261
list box performance optimization in Microsoft Access 174
locking conflicts, avoiding 167
locking information file for stored database records 830
locking Microsoft Access 97 databases
    All Records option 827
    Default Record option 827
    errors in exceeding locking limit 834

locking Microsoft Access 97 databases *(continued)*
    optimistic locking 826
    options available 826
    overview 826
    pessimistic locking 827
    QuantityOnHand column 829
logs, installation 115
Lotus 1-2-3
    auditing converted worksheets 510–512
    charts, using in Microsoft Excel 97 523–525
    commands corresponding with Microsoft Excel 97 504
    Data Distribution command equivalents in Microsoft Excel 97 518
    data matrix command equivalents in Microsoft Excel 97 519
    data regression command equivalents in Microsoft Excel 97 519
    exporting data to Word 97 788
    expressions, evaluation differences from Microsoft Excel 97 500
    features affecting data/formatting of data converted to Word 97 788
    features without Microsoft Excel 97 equivalents 528
    formatting, upgrading to Microsoft Excel 97 508–509
    formulas and functions, transitioning to Microsoft Excel 97 499
    formulas, translating 512
    formulas, using in Microsoft Excel 97 512–519
    functions corresponding with Microsoft Excel 97 513–517
    functions, corresponding to Microsoft Excel A-functions 501
    Graph Options Color commands, equivalents in Microsoft Excel 97 524
    Graph Options Format commands, equivalents in Microsoft Excel 97 523
    Graph Options Grid commands, equivalents in Microsoft Excel 97 524
    Graph Options Scale commands, equivalents in Microsoft Excel 97 524
    Graph Type commands, equivalents in Microsoft Excel 97 524
    Graph View commands, equivalents in Microsoft Excel 97 524
    Help 533–535
    Impress formatting 509

Lotus 1-2-3 *(continued)*
 keyboard commands corresponding with Microsoft Excel 97 504
 line print command equivalents in Microsoft Excel 97 526
 macro interpreters 519
 macros, running in Microsoft Excel 97 519–523
 mathematical operators 518
 multiple worksheets, converting to Microsoft Excel 97 507
 number formatting, corresponding to Microsoft Excel 97 508
 print printer command equivalents in Microsoft Excel 97 526
 printer command equivalents in Microsoft Excel 97 525
 pure functions 517
 questions about upgrading to Microsoft Excel 97 496
 rules, using when calculating formulas and database criteria 500
 System command, accessing through Windows Start menu 510
 task equivalents in Microsoft Excel 97 497
 terms corresponding with Microsoft Excel 97 502–504
 tools available in Microsoft Excel 97 497–506
 underlining, converting to Microsoft Excel 97 509
 WK3 functions 527
 worksheet global default printer command equivalents in Microsoft Excel 97 525
 worksheets, linking to Microsoft Excel 97 530
 worksheets, upgrading to Microsoft Excel 97 506–528
 WYSIWYG formatting 509
Lotus Ami Pro, converters for Microsoft Word 97 1018
Lotus cc:Mail drivers 547
Lotus Freelance
 upgrading to PowerPoint 97 571–572

M

machine setting policies 1055–1057
Macro menu upgrades
 from Microsoft Access 2.0 to Microsoft Access 97 277
 from Microsoft Excel 4.0 to Microsoft Excel 97 326

macros
 actions, defined 454
 changes when upgrading to Microsoft Access 97 269, 279
 creating in Word 97 1001
 defined as Microsoft Access 97 objects 454, 922
 interpreters for Lotus 1-2-3 users 519
 libraries for API Declare Statements 248
 Lotus 1-2-3, running in Microsoft Excel 97 519–523
 Microsoft Access 97, rewriting when DoMenuItem Action is included 269
 Microsoft Access 97, rewriting when SendKeys Action is included 269
 Microsoft Excel File Recovery 1027
 PowerPoint 97 978
 Quattro Pro for MS-DOS, running in Microsoft Excel 97 536
 Word Basic, updating to Visual Basic 406
 workbooks 946
 XLM, upgrading to Visual Basic 327
mail-enabled applications, Microsoft Office 97 793
Maintenance Mode installation 1052
make-table queries 453, 919
masters, Microsoft PowerPoint 97 967
mathematical operators, Lotus 1-2-3 and Microsoft Excel 97 518
MDE files
 creating from databases 806
 replicated databases 809
 saving databases referencing other databases 809
 security 808
MDE files, saving from databases 179
Meeting Minder
 exporting action items and minutes to Word 785
 exporting action items to Outlook 97 778
 presentation conferencing 883
menus
 Action, upgrading to PowerPoint 97 from version 3.0 394
 Action, upgrading to PowerPoint 97 from version 4.0 380
 Action, upgrading to PowerPoint 97 from version 95 367
 Apple Help, upgrading to PowerPoint 97 from version 3.0 395

Index

menus *(continued)*
- Apple Help, upgrading to Word 97 from versions 6.0/95 405
- Arrange, upgrading to PowerPoint 97 from version 3.0 390
- Balloon Help, upgrading to PowerPoint 97 from version 3.0 395
- custom, importing to Microsoft Access from other databases 936
- customizing in Word 97 1004
- Data, upgrading to Microsoft Excel 97 from version 4.0 324
- Data, upgrading to Microsoft Excel 97 from version 5.0 310
- Data, upgrading to Microsoft Excel 97 from version 95 305
- Debug, upgrading to Microsoft Access 97 from version 2.0 277
- Debug, upgrading to Microsoft Access 97 from version 95 266
- Draw, upgrading to PowerPoint 97 from version 4.0 379
- Draw, upgrading to PowerPoint 97 from version 95 366
- Edit, upgrading to Microsoft Access 97 from version 2.0 273
- Edit, upgrading to Microsoft Access 97 from version 95 264
- Edit, upgrading to Microsoft Excel 97 from version 4.0 321
- Edit, upgrading to Microsoft Excel 97 from version 5.0 308
- Edit, upgrading to Microsoft Excel 97 from version 95 303
- Edit, upgrading to PowerPoint 97 from version 3.0 387
- Edit, upgrading to PowerPoint 97 from version 4.0 375
- Edit, upgrading to PowerPoint 97 from version 95 363
- Edit, upgrading to Word 97 from version 2.0 416
- Edit, upgrading to Word 97 from versions 6.0/95 402
- File, upgrading to Microsoft Access 97 from version 2.0 271
- File, upgrading to Microsoft Access 97 from version 95 263
- File, upgrading to Microsoft Excel 97 from version 4.0 321

menus *(continued)*
- File, upgrading to Microsoft Excel 97 from version 5.0 308
- File, upgrading to Microsoft Excel 97 from version 95 303
- File, upgrading to PowerPoint 97 from version 3.0 386
- File, upgrading to PowerPoint 97 from version 4.0 374
- File, upgrading to PowerPoint 97 from version 95 363
- File, upgrading to Word 97 from version 2.0 415
- File, upgrading to Word 97 from versions 6.0/95 401
- Format, upgrading to Microsoft Access 97 from version 2.0 276
- Format, upgrading to Microsoft Excel 97 from version 4.0 323
- Format, upgrading to Microsoft Excel 97 from version 5.0 310
- Format, upgrading to Microsoft Excel 97 from version 95 305
- Format, upgrading to PowerPoint 97 from version 3.0 392
- Format, upgrading to PowerPoint 97 from version 4.0 377
- Format, upgrading to PowerPoint 97 from version 95 364
- Format, upgrading to Word 97 from version 2.0 417
- Format, upgrading to Word 97 from versions 6.0/95 404
- Formula, upgrading to Microsoft Excel 97 from version 4.0 322
- Help, upgrading to Microsoft Access 97 from version 2.0 278
- Help, upgrading to Microsoft Access 97 from version 95 267
- Help, upgrading to Microsoft Excel 97 from version 4.0 326
- Help, upgrading to Microsoft Excel 97 from version 5.0 311
- Help, upgrading to Microsoft Excel 97 from version 95 306
- Help, upgrading to PowerPoint 97 from version 3.0 394
- Help, upgrading to PowerPoint 97 from version 4.0 380
- Help, upgrading to PowerPoint 97 from version 95 367

menus *(continued)*
    Help, upgrading to Word 97 from version 2.0 421
    Help, upgrading to Word 97 from
        versions 6.0/95 405
    Insert, upgrading to Microsoft Access 97 from
        version 2.0 275
    Insert, upgrading to Microsoft Access 97 from
        version 95 265
    Insert, upgrading to Microsoft Excel 97 from
        version 5.0 309
    Insert, upgrading to Microsoft Excel 97 from
        version 95 304
    Insert, upgrading to PowerPoint 97 from
        version 3.0 391
    Insert, upgrading to PowerPoint 97 from
        version 4.0 376
    Insert, upgrading to PowerPoint 97 from
        version 95 364
    Insert, upgrading to Word 97 from version 2.0 417
    Insert, upgrading to Word 97 from
        versions 6.0/95 403
    Macro, upgrading to Microsoft Access 97 from
        version 2.0 277
    Macro, upgrading to Microsoft Excel 97 from
        version 4.0 326
    Microsoft Access 97, upgrades from Microsoft
        Access 2.0 271–278
    Microsoft Access 97, upgrades from Microsoft
        Access 95 263–267
    Microsoft Access, customizing 935
    Microsoft Excel 97, upgrades from Microsoft
        Excel 4.0 321–327
    Microsoft Excel 97, upgrades from Microsoft
        Excel 5.0 307–312
    Microsoft Excel 97, upgrades from Microsoft
        Excel 95 303–306
    new in Microsoft Access 97 270, 294
    Object, upgrading to PowerPoint 97 from
        version 3.0 389
    Options, upgrading to Microsoft Excel 97 from
        version 4.0 325
    PowerPoint 97, upgrading from
        PowerPoint 3.0 386–395
    PowerPoint 97, upgrading from
        PowerPoint 4.0 374–381
    PowerPoint 97, upgrading from
        PowerPoint 95 363–368
    Query, upgrading to Microsoft Access 97 from
        version 2.0 276

menus *(continued)*
    Records, upgrading to Microsoft Access 97 from
        version 2.0 277
    Relationships, upgrading to Microsoft Access 97
        from version 2.0 276
    Run, upgrading to Microsoft Access 97 from
        version 2.0 277
    Run, upgrading to Microsoft Access 97 from
        version 95 265
    Slide Show, upgrading to PowerPoint 97 from
        version 3.0 393
    Slide Show, upgrading to PowerPoint 97 from
        version 4.0 379
    Slide Show, upgrading to PowerPoint 97 from
        version 95 366
    Slide, upgrading to PowerPoint 97 from
        version 3.0 390
    Table, upgrading to Word 97 from version 2.0 420
    Table, upgrading to Word 97 from
        versions 6.0/95 405
    Text, upgrading to PowerPoint 97 from
        version 3.0 389
    Tools, upgrading to Microsoft Access 97 from
        version 2.0 276
    Tools, upgrading to Microsoft Access 97 from
        version 95 266
    Tools, upgrading to Microsoft Excel 97 from
        version 5.0 310
    Tools, upgrading to Microsoft Excel 97 from
        version 95 305
    Tools, upgrading to PowerPoint 97 from
        version 3.0 392
    Tools, upgrading to PowerPoint 97 from
        version 4.0 378
    Tools, upgrading to PowerPoint 97 from
        version 95 365
    Tools, upgrading to Word 97 from version 2.0 418
    Tools, upgrading to Word 97 from
        versions 6.0/95 404
    View, upgrading to Microsoft Access 97 from
        version 2.0 274
    View, upgrading to Microsoft Access 97 from
        version 95 264
    View, upgrading to Microsoft Excel 97 from
        version 5.0 308
    View, upgrading to Microsoft Excel 97 from
        version 95 303
    View, upgrading to PowerPoint 97 from
        version 3.0 388

Index

menus *(continued)*
   View, upgrading to PowerPoint 97 from version 4.0 376
   View, upgrading to PowerPoint 97 from version 95 364
   View, upgrading to Word 97 from version 2.0 416
   View, upgrading to Word 97 from versions 6.0/95 402
   Window, upgrading to Microsoft Access 97 from version 2.0 278
   Window, upgrading to Microsoft Access 97 from version 95 267
   Window, upgrading to Microsoft Excel 97 from version 4.0 326
   Window, upgrading to Microsoft Excel 97 from version 5.0 311
   Window, upgrading to Word 97 from version 2.0 420
   Word 97, upgrades from Word 2.0 415–421
   Word 97, upgrades from Word 6.0/95 401–406
message flags in Outlook 97 23
message forms, Outlook standard 338, 339
message recall, Outlook 97 23
Microsoft Access 97
   add-in programs 925–929
   adding hyperlink text boxes to forms 671
   applications, separating from stored data 934
   back-end databases, securing 820
   banded report designer 475
   Browse Saved Hyperlinks forms 691
   builders 926
   Building Applications with Microsoft Access 97 459
   building the application 465
   changes from Access Basic to Visual Basic for Applications 281–293, 295
   changing option settings 155
   client/server architecture 762
   conflict resolution 936
   contents and index 459
   control types supported for Active Server Pages (ASP) 685
   controls 923
   customizing applications 934
   DAO objects 283
   data access applications, running 487
   data types, saving in HTML 678
   data, making available to the Internet 676
   data, saving as HTML documents 676–688

Microsoft Access 97 *(continued)*
   Database Splitter 166
   database windows 455
   databases defined 915
   databases, compacting 154
   databases, compiling before converting 254
   databases, converting 254–262
   databases, converting to Design Master 840
   databases, defined 452
   databases, documenting 765
   databases, external data source troubleshooting 750
   databases, front-end 298
   databases, linked tables 932
   databases, naming on network drives 748
   databases, objects 452
   databases, open modes 825
   databases, ownership 817
   databases, performance optimization 166
   databases, removing user-level security 822
   databases, replicating 834–852
   databases, sample 458
   databases, saving as MDE files 806
   databases, setting passwords 805
   databases, sharing with previous Microsoft Access 297
   datasheets, opening in Excel 97 754
   datasheets, opening in Word 97 752
   dBASE data type conversion 471
   DBMS (database management system) 931
   deciding when to import or link tables 463
   Design Master 834, 851
   Desktop driver, installing 683
   Developer's Forum, World Wide Web address 763
   displaying World Wide Web pages 691–693
   DoCmd objects, using 280
   documentation available within the application 459
   drag-and-drop functionality 754
   drivers, built-in 489
   drivers, ODBC 489
   enabling process 226, 231
   exporting data to Internet 688–691
   exporting data to various file formats 750
   external data files, exporting to FTP servers 691
   external data sources, importing or linking data 691
   features for working with Internet or intranets 666–668
   field data types 472
   file format changes from Microsoft Access 2.0 278
   file format changes from Microsoft Access 95 268

Microsoft Access 97 *(continued)*
  file protection levels 804
  file server applications, upsizing to client/server applications 763–767
  Filter By Form 15
  Filter By Selection 15
  filter performance optimization 172
  find and replace performance optimization 173
  form and subform performance optimization 173
  form datasheets, saving as static HTML documents 677
  Form Wizard and Report Wizard changes 268
  forms, creating 473
  forms, creating without Form Wizard 269
  forms, opening in Microsoft Excel 97 753
  forms, opening in Word 97 752
  forms, overview 921
  FoxPro data type conversion 479
  FoxPro files, importing and linking 477
  front-end databases, securing 820
  full precision calculation 941
  group memberships, viewing 258
  Help, context-sensitive 459
  HTML extension file (HTX) 680
  hyperlinks 669–675
  imported tables, features available 463
  importing and linking dBASE files 470
  importing data from Internet 688–691
  importing data from other data formats and applications 460
  importing or linking FoxPro files 477
  importing/linking external data sources 746–750
  indexes, defined 162
  IntelliSense technology 14
  Internet Database Connector 680
  Internet protocols 674
  intranet solutions 33–36
  ISAM (Indexed Sequential Access Method) 746
  keyboard options 467
  library databases, referenced 924
  linked tables, managing 833
  linked tables, performance optimization 164
  linked tables, renaming 767
  linking data from other data formats and applications 460
  linking data to Word 97 752
  linking data to Internet 688–691

Microsoft Access 97 *(continued)*
  linking Paradox data 76
  list box and combo box performance optimization 174
  locking conflict avoidance suggestions 167
  locking individual records 830
  locking information file 830
  locking issues with Novell NetWare 833
  locking strategies 828
  Macro Builder 270
  macro changes from Microsoft Access 2.0 279
  macro changes from Microsoft Access 95 269
  macros 922
  Menu Builder 270
  menu command upgrades from Microsoft Access 95 263–267, 271–278
  menus, customizing 935
  menus, new 270, 294
  methods and properties for working with hyperlinks 675
  Microsoft Jet database engine 931
  Microsoft Jet registry settings 155–161
  modules, class and standard 287
  modules, overview 922
  multiple data access applications, running 487
  multiple-field indexes 163
  multiuser database issues 833
  multiuser environments 825–834
  name-mapping queries, creating 764
  new intelligence features 14
  objects, determining which to use 455
  ODBC 746, 759–767
  Office Assistant 459
  optimizing for Office 97 client computers 152–179
  optimizing tips 153–154
  Paradox data type conversion 483
  personal identifers (PID) 813
  PivotTable controls, creating 753
  policies 1062
  programming capabilities 467
  queries 918–921
  queries, creating 472
  queries, exporting to dBASE files 476
  queries, exporting to FoxPro files 480
  queries, exporting to Paradox files 486
  queries, opening in Word 97 752
  queries, saving as static HTML documents 677
  questions about upgrading 254
  RAM (random-access memory) 153

Microsoft Access 97 *(continued)*
  record locking options 826–828
  records, size estimating 830
  recordsets, opening in multiuser environment 826
  referencing hyperlink addresses 675
  referential integrity for table records 463, 466
  refresh interval settings in multiuser environment 825
  registry settings for dBASE 476
  registry settings for FoxPro 480
  registry settings for Paradox 487
  relational database management system 452
  relationships, defining 465
  replication menu commands 837
  report and printing performance optimization 175
  reports, creating without Report Wizard 269
  reports, opening in Microsoft Excel 97 753
  reports, opening in Word 97 752
  reports, overview 921
  reports, saving as static HTML documents 677
  running multiple versions 623–625
  RunPermissions property 823
  Rushmore technology, optimizing criteria expressions 169–172
  screen tips 459
  security features described 803
  security identifiers (SID) 811
  security, user-level 810–824
  Send command for e-mail on the File menu 797
  SendKeys Action or Statement, using 279
  server tables, linking 767
  server tables, triggers 766
  sharing data with Microsoft Excel 97 752
  sharing data with Paradox databases 483–486
  sharing data with Word 97 751
  sharing information with other Office 97 applications 746–767
  shortcut menus, customizing 935
  shortcut menus, new 270, 294
  single file architecture 452
  special installation requirements 76
  SQL database, performance optmization guidelines 164
  startup options, using to protect databases 804
  storing user and group information 811
  table access permissions 748
  table importing and linking tips 462
  table optimization 162
  table server, indexes 766

Microsoft Access 97 *(continued)*
  table-level validation, defining 466
  tables, exporting to dBASE files 475
  tables, exporting to FoxPro files 480
  tables, exporting to Paradox files 486
  tables, exporting to server databases 765
  tables, importing and linking from Paradox 481
  tables, overview 916
  tables, saving as static HTML documents 677
  tables, sharing with Microsoft Access 95 268
  tables, storing hyperlinks 671–674
  tag pairs, interpreting 689
  template changes from Microsoft Access 2.0 279
  template changes from Microsoft Access 95 268
  templates, form and report 923
  terms, differences from dBASE terms 469
  terms, differences from Paradox terms 481
  toolbars, customizing 935
  toolbars, new 270, 294
  training 458
  Unset Database Password, changing or clearing passwords 806
  updating dBASE catalogs 475
  updating dBASE forms 474
  upgrading from dBASE 468–476
  upgrading from FoxPro 476
  upgrading from Microsoft Access 1.x 294
  upgrading from Microsoft Access 2.0 271–294
  upgrading from Microsoft Access 95 262–270
  upgrading from other database management systems 460–468
  upgrading from Paradox 480
  upgrading overview 254
  upsizing tools 763
  user-level security model 811, 812
  User-Level Security Wizard 818
  using the Web toolbar to move between hyperlinks 670
  using Visual SourceSafe 852
  viewers 31
  Visual Basic keywords supported 270
  Visual Basic performance optimization 175–178
  Web sites 459
  Web toolbar 30
  wizards, types 925
  wizards, upgrading from Access Basic 286
  workgroup ID (WID) 813
  workgroup information files, overview 930
  workgroup information files, recreating 258

Index

Microsoft Access 97 *(continued)*
   workgroup information files, using when establishing database security 811
   World Wide Web publishing 33–36
   World Wide Web support 665
Microsoft At Work fax software 547
Microsoft Authorized Support Centers (ASCs) 1098
Microsoft Authorized Technical Education Centers (ATECs) 56
Microsoft Bookshelf, integration with Office 97 applications 790
Microsoft Camcorder 792
Microsoft Certified Professional Program 1099
Microsoft Client for NetWare networks 144
Microsoft Clip Gallery 912
Microsoft Consulting Services (MCS) 1098
Microsoft Developer Network 1097
Microsoft Download Service (MSDL)
   connecting procedure 1096
   hardware and software requirements 1096
   overview 1095
Microsoft Education and Certification Roadmap 1099
Microsoft Excel 97
   add-in types, listed 950
   add-ins, creating from workbooks 949
   advantages and disadvantages of sharing with earlier versions 314
   A-functions 501
   Allways formatting 509
   autotemplates 953
   book-level name references 942
   Bookshelf Basics integration 791
   calculation troubleshooting 941
   cell formatting 943
   cells, customizing 18
   change history for workbooks 858
   chart autoformats 945
   chart format upgrades 313
   chart items, changing colors 524
   chart types, built-in 945
   Chart Wizard 19
   commands corresponding with Lotus 1-2-3 504
   common file formats with other operating systems 302
   conflict resolution 956
   converted documents, saving 493
   converting data and charts to HTML 693–695
   converting workbooks from previous Microsoft Excel versions 302

Microsoft Excel 97 *(continued)*
   custom autoformats 313
   customizing 951–956
   customizing for client computers 179–180
   displaying objects in Microsoft Excel 97 and 5.0/95 format 316
   document conversion from Word 492–494
   documents, saving in other file formats 494
   documents, sharing with Quattro Pro for MS-DOS 536
   expressions, evaluation differences from Lotus 1-2-3 500
   features affecting data/formatting of data converted to Word 97 787
   features without Lotus 1-2-3 equivalents 532
   File Conversion Wizard 493
   file format differences from earlier versions 312
   file formats recognized from other source applications 492
   file formats, upgrading 492–496
   file protection levels 856
   File Recovery macro 1027
   formatting line or xy (scatter) charts 523
   formatting numbers 508
   formulas, troubleshooting conversion 511
   FREQUENCY function 518
   Function Wizard 517, 768
   functions, getting Help 517
   Gallery location tool 1027
   importing text files 494
   IntelliSense technology 16–19
   Internet Assistant wizard 693
   intranet solutions 36–39
   keyboard command alternatives 498
   keyboard commands for Lotus 1-2-3 users 504
   mathematical operators 518
   menu command upgrades from Microsoft Excel 4.0 321–327
   menu command upgrades from Microsoft Excel 5.0 307–312
   menu command upgrades from Microsoft Excel 95 303–306
   Microsoft on the Web submenu, illustrated 146
   new features affecting data/formatting in Microsoft Excel 4.0 328–331
   new features affecting data/formatting in Microsoft Excel 5.0/95 317–320
   new intelligence features 16–19

Index

Microsoft Excel 97 *(continued)*
  Normal style 944
  opening Microsoft Access 97 data 752
  opening worksheets from Lotus 1-2-3 506
  optimizing 180
  PivotTables, creating on Microsoft Access 97 forms 753
  policies 1062
  questions about upgrading 301, 491
  questions about upgrading from version 5.0 307
  questions about upgrading from version 95 302
  Range Finder 18
  RC4, encryption routine 856
  referencing difficulties with Lotus 1-2-3 531
  running Lotus 1-2-3 macros 519
  running multiple versions 626–628
  saving worksheets from Lotus 1-2-3 507
  Scenario Manager 537
  scenarios for creating specific formulas 942
  security features 855–858
  shared workbooks 858–860
  sharing information with other Office 97 applications 768–769
  size optimization 179
  special installation requirements 76
  specifying default formats for workbooks 315, 328
  speed optimization 179
  spreadsheet operations, transitioning from other applications 497–501
  SQL Server 768
  startup folders 952
  styles, saving in workbooks 943
  SYLK files, opening 538
  templates 947
  templates, built-in 312
  templates, custom 312
  terms for Lotus 1-2-3 users 502–504
  toolbars, customizing 955
  tools for Lotus 1-2-3 users 497–506
  Transition Formula Entry 499
  transition formula evaluation 500
  transition navigation keys 498
  Transition tab options, pictured 497
  troubleshooting document conversion 493
  Undo command 19
  updating from Quattro Pro for MS-DOS 535–536
  updating from Quattro Pro for Windows 536
  upgrading from Lotus 1-2-3 496–535
  upgrading from Microsoft Excel 4.0 320–327

Microsoft Excel 97 *(continued)*
  upgrading from Microsoft Excel 5.0 307–314
  upgrading from Microsoft Excel 95 302–306
  upgrading from Microsoft Works 542–543
  upgrading from Multiplan 538–542
  user-defined options, saved in Windows registry 952
  using with Microsoft Query 769
  viewers 31
  Web Connectivity Kit 1041
  Web Form Wizard 696
  Web forms, creating 698
  Web queries 695
  Web toolbar 30
  workbook page settings 947
  workbook security settings 946
  workbooks, file protection procedure 856
  workbooks, merging 860
  workbooks, protecting specific areas 857
  workbooks, saving in 4.0 format 328–331
  workbooks, saving in 5.0/95 format 317–320
  workbooks, saving in Lotus 1-2-3 529–533
  workbooks, saving in Microsoft Excel 97 and 5.0/95 formats 314–317
  workbooks, sharing with Microsoft Excel 4.0 328–331
  workbooks, sharing with Microsoft Excel 5.0/95 314–320
  workgroup review of workbooks 862
  worksheet ranges, converting to HTML tables 695
  worksheets, exporting to Word 97 787
  worksheets, linking to Microsoft Excel 97 530
  workspace files for opening multiple workbooks 954
  World Wide Web publishing 36–39
  XLM macros 327
  XOR encryption routine, upgraded to RC4 856
Microsoft Exchange
  documents, posting to public folders 799
  public folders 868–873
Microsoft FastTips 1093
Microsoft Forms, storing 342
Microsoft FrontPage
  capabilities listed 647
  Editor feature, defined 647
  Explorer feature, defined 647
  indexing Web sites 726
  intranets 32

Index

Microsoft FrontPage *(continued)*
   managing intranets 646
   managing Office documents 647
   security features 647
   Web authoring and management program 646
   World Wide Web home page address 647
Microsoft Graph 97 970
Microsoft HTML Layout control 686
Microsoft IntelliMouse, included with Professional Edition with Bookshelf Basics system requirements 103
Microsoft Jet
   asychronous mode activity 158
   buffers 157
   registry setting adjustments for Microsoft Access 97 155–161
   settings for optimizing Microsoft Access 97 158–161
   synchronous mode activity 158
   threads 156
Microsoft Knowledge Base 1095
Microsoft Mail 547
Microsoft Mail 3.x for Windows
   commands, using in Outlook 97 347
   files, exporting to Outlook 97 345–347
   menus, using in Outlook 97 347
   sharing information with Outlook 97 350–352
Microsoft Mail 3.x, using with Microsoft Office 97 799
Microsoft Network (MSN) 1095
Microsoft Office 97
   ActiveX support 906
   advanced documentation 1020
   applications, deciding which to remove when upgrading 204
   applications, requirements for installation 75
   applications, using electronic mail commands 797
   AutoCorrect (ACL) file, creating 1057
   binders, including from Office 95 229
   Bookshelf Basics 790
   browsing documents 31
   CD and floppy disk installations, customizing 107
   CD installation (first-time) 86
   CD installation (subsequent releases) 96
   CD installation components 1081
   CD, copying contents to a server 87
   CD, ValuPack folder 546
   cleanup process when installing 207
   client installation tools 1011
   client setup, interactive 83

Microsoft Office 97 *(continued)*
   Clip Gallery 912
   compliance checking 91–94
   configuration questions 71
   connecting to Microsoft home pages 146–151
   conversion utilities 1014
   converters for importing and exporting data 547
   CopyAll batch files for copying Office floppy disks 1038
   CopyDisk batch files for copying Office floppy disks 1038
   creating hyperlinks 651–653
   custom installation 85–86
   custom programming solutions for intranets 648
   customer support numbers 1091–1094
   customizing intranet solutions 32
   customizing Microsoft Access 97 for client computers 152–179
   data analysis tools 653
   Deployment Planner 1031
   deployment, overview 50
   deployment, researching server and client configurations 56
   deployment, team tasks 51
   destination folders for application files 110
   distributing to users 447–448
   document properties, using 641
   document types, Find Fast 724
   documentation support for users 1019
   documents, locating on intranets 657
   documents, managed through FrontPage 647
   documents, posting to public folders 799
   documents, when to use for intranet tasks 649
   electronic mail integration 794–798
   evaluation steps 53
   Extract utility for Office floppy disks 1039
   features, selecting when evaluating 58
   file removal warning 207
   file-converter architecture, new 12
   files designed for the client installation process 105
   files, deciding where to install 72–73
   files, selecting which to keep during upgrade 206
   Find Fast 717
   Find Fast stop word list 1021
   floppy disk copy tools 1037
   floppy disk installation (first time) 88–90

Microsoft Office 97 *(continued)*
  floppy disk installation (subsequent releases) 96
  formats for saving documents 621
  Getting Results books 1091
  implementation, planning 54–56
  indexes converted from Office 95 728
  informational spreadsheets 1021
  installation folders created from
    CopyAll/CopyDisk 1039
  installation methods 74
  installation preparation questions 71
  installation types 74
  installation types, illustrated 84
  installation, additional options 86
  installation, scheduling suggestions 447
  installing updates with same configuration 94–96
  integrating with Web browsers 650
  IntelliMouse, included with Professional
    Edition/Bookshelf Basics 103
  IntelliSense technology 12–29
  intranet overview 645
  intranet solutions 29–33
  items, recording in Outlook 97 journals 770
  LAN (Local Area Network) installation options 448
  License Pak 94
  licensing options 94
  local installation overview 73
  machine setting policies 1055
  Mail Recipient command 797
  mail-enabled applications, defined 793
  Maintenance mode installation 1052
  Microsoft Press resource information 1100
  Microsoft Technical Support documents 1022
  Microsoft Technical Support Help File 1023
  migration training overview 186
  MIME type information for Netscape Web
    servers 1042
  MS-DOS applications, steps for upgrading 440
  My Documents folder 112
  network installation (first-time) 77–86
  network installation (subsequent releases) 95
  Network Installation Wizard 108–130, 1012
  network installations, customizing 106
  network server installation 1082
  network .txt files 75
  new features, overview 9
  object embedding and linking differences 906
  Office Art 13, 911

Microsoft Office 97 *(continued)*
  Office Assistant 12
  Office Assistant ACT files, moving 1055
  Office Binder 14
  Office Setup command line options 1047–1050
  Office Setup, installing e-mail capability 794
  Office Upgrade Wizard 1033
  Office Upgrade Wizard file list 1023
  Office Web toolbar 653
  OLE support 905
  online help services 1094
  operating with Lotus Notes Mail and cc:Mail 800
  operating with Lotus Notes/FX 800
  operating with Microsoft Mail 3.x 799
  operating with the Microsoft Exchange Server 798
  Outlook 97 overview 656
  package creation 132–135
  Package Definition Files 1012
  pilot rollout for testing installation *See* pilot rollout
    for Microsoft Office 97
  pilot training 196
  planning an organization's upgrade to 441–443
  planning team, assembling for Office 97
    evaluation 54–56
  policy definitions 139
  post-upgrading tips for getting back to business as
    usual 448
  preparing to distribute to users 90–94
  previous versions, cleaning up when upgrading 203
  product identification 90
  product signatures 91
  products checked when upgrading 92
  products for the Macintosh 104
  Professional Edition system requirements 101
  Professional Edition with Bookshelf Basics system
    requirements 102–103
  promoting for training 196
  purchasing options, referenced 447
  readme files 75
  removing previous versions of Office 201–218
  Replication Manager 838
  reviewing current configuration before
    upgrading 56
  rolling out to users 68–69
  running setup to install 82–86
  sample training programs 194
  secretaries rollout training program 194

Microsoft Office 97 *(continued)*
  security features 908
  setup errors 219–221
  Setup files for Office 97 1045–1047
  Setup process 1051
  Setup program overview 105
  Setup Simulator 1024
  shared installation overview 73
  shared tools between applications 909–911
  Shortcut Bar, default configurations 234
  Shortcut Bar, overview 232
  software administration improvements 9
  spell checking dictionary 911
  Standard Edition system requirements 100
  Starts Here, computer-based training product 189
  storing shared applications 113
  support and maintenance resources 69
  support numbers, training companies 189
  support team preparation for rollout 189
  system policies 137–146
  system policies, installing 1013
  system policies, listed 1068
  System Policy Editor installation 1053
  system policy templates, using 1055
  tasks, adding to Outlook 97 Tasks folder 770
  test client configuration 56–59
  test installation 59–61
  testing applications before installing 444
  tips for using new features 449
  toolbars, adding to the Shortcut Bar 234
  toolbars, overview 14
  Tools and Utilities CD 1013
  tools shared between applications 909
  training and support teams 188–189
  training documentation 195
  training new users 444–445
  training partners 188
  training plan 190–194
  training plan, implementing during rollout 198
  training plan, testing 197
  training tasks for implementation 187
  transition, evaluating success 198
  Ultimate Printer Manual 1025
  Unbind Utilities 1032
  uninstalling the test version 61
  updates, installing with new configuration 96–98
  Upgrade Wizard 218
    See also Office 97 Upgrade Wizard
  upgrading from Office 3.x for Windows 235

Microsoft Office 97 *(continued)*
  upgrading from Office 4.x 230–235
  upgrading from Office 95 226–229
  upgrading from Office Manager for Windows 232–234
  user setting policies 1060
  using ODBC data 762
  Value Pack converters 546
  Visual Basic overview 913
  Web Find Fast 717
  Web tools 1041
  Wextract utility for Office floppy disks 1041
  white papers 1102
  World Wide Web address 1094
  World Wide Web publishing 29–33
Microsoft Office 97 Resource Kit
  chapter contents 5–6
  customer feedback 7
  defined 3
  documentation conventions 7
  documentation defined 54
  Web site address 4
  World Wide Web update information 4
Microsoft Office Manager for Windows, upgrading to Office 97 232–235
Microsoft on the Web
  adding commands 149–151
  commands to connect to the Microsoft Web site 146
  commands, customizing 1094
  disabling application-specific commands 148
  disabling office-wide commands 149
  displaying custom and default commands 150
  getting help for Office 97 1094
  policies 1058
  submenu in Microsoft Excel, illustrated 146
  value data strings for displaying specific commands 151
Microsoft Outlook 97
  adding cc:Mail information service to user profiles 548
  Address Book 961
  anonymous accounts for posting messages 872
  AutoAddress 24
  AutoCreate, using to convert information to various formats 25
  AutoName 24
  AutoNameChecking when sending e-mail 22

Microsoft Outlook 97 *(continued)*
  AutoPreviewing messages 22
  calendar synchronization differences with Schedule+ 359
  cc:Mail bulletin boards, setting up 549
  components illustrated 960
  Contacts folder 961
  converters, ACT! 2.0 551
  Crystal Reports 1035
  custom views 966
  customizing tips 965
  Design Outlook Form command 338
  electronic mail services 547
  enabling booking of resource requests 868
  export file types 546
  Extension Configuration File (ECF), using for add-in installation 338
  Extension Configuration File Format (ECF) document 1024
  Favorites folder 963
  field name mapping 773–781
  files for importing and exporting data 546
  folders 335, 962
  forms, exchanging with Microsoft Exchange Client 339
  forms, sample 1030
  free/busy status 866
  functions, replacing functions from other applications 334
  group scheduling 865–868
  group scheduling management 355, 360
  import file types 546
  imported data file example 772
  importing cc:Mail folders 550
  importing cc:Mail lists 550
  importing ECCO Pro data 553
  importing Lotus Organizer data 557
  importing Sidekick data 555
  IntelliSense technology 20–25
  Internet mail 704
  intranet solutions 39–41
  item types 335, 961
  items, importing and exporting 770–781
  journal folders 770
  journals 24
  machine setting policies 1056

Microsoft Outlook 97 *(continued)*
  MAPI, profiles 960
  mapping fields from ACT! 2.0 551
  mapping fields from ECCO Pro 553
  mapping fields from Sidekick 555
  mapping fields, overview 558
  message flags 23
  message recall 23
  Microsoft Team Manager 873–875
  migrating to Microsoft Exchange Server 350
  MMF (Microsoft Mail message file), importing 346
  new intelligence features 20–25
  nicknames list, maintaining 1035
  Outlook Bar 20
  overview 334–336, 656
  policies 1064
  Post forms 341
  profiles document 1028
  profiles, alternative 1029
  public folders, sharing information with Exchange Server 868
  public folders, sharing with Mail 3.x for Windows 352
  public folders, sharing with Microsoft Exchange Client 342
  questions about upgrading 334
  RegClean utility 1036
  resources, setting up 867
  RTF, turning on for full functionality 548
  saved table views, maintaining 342
  sharing information with Mail 3.x for Windows 350–352
  sharing information with Microsoft Exchange Client 339–343, 629
  sharing information with Microsoft Mail 3.x 629
  sharing information with other Office 97 applications 769–781
  sharing information with Schedule+ 1.0 359, 630
  sharing information with Schedule+ 95 355–356, 629
  standard message form, illustrated 339
  structure 959–965
  SwitchForms 1033
  task data, viewing in various views 963
  task management features, extending 873
  task prioritization 875
  Tasks folder 770
  upgrading folders and views from Microsoft Exchange Client 337

Index

Microsoft Outlook 97 *(continued)*
   upgrading from client/server messaging
      systems 560
   upgrading from ECCO Pro 552
   upgrading from Lotus cc:Mail 548–550
   upgrading from Lotus Organizer 557–560
   upgrading from Mail 3.x for Windows 343–350
   upgrading from Microsoft Exchange
      Client 336–338
   upgrading from Schedule+ 1.0 357–359
   upgrading from Schedule+ 95 352–355
   upgrading from Starfish Sidekick
      Deluxe 95 555–557
   upgrading from Symantec ACT! 2.0 550
   using with PowerPoint 97 777–781
   using WordMail 338
   view switching 24
   view types 963–965
   views 336
   Web Browser 705
   Web History folder 706
   Web site catalog 706
   Wipename 1035
   WordMail 22
   WordMail message conversion to RTF 340
   World Wide Web publishing 39–41
Microsoft PowerPoint 97
   add-in programs, customizing 978–979
   advantages and disadvantages of sharing
      presentations with version 95 369
   Animation Player 711
   Animation Player, installing 1043
   Animation Publisher, installing 1043
   animation, adding to Web sites 712
   animation, saving to HTML 711
   animation, viewing in HTML 711
   AutoClipArt concept list 1024
   AutoClipArt tool 985
   AutoContent Wizard 710
   AutoContent Wizard enhancements 26
   AutoLayouts 967
   automating the presentation creation process 968
   AutoShape differences from version 95 373
   batch converters for earlier PowerPoint
      versions 1014
   Blank Presentations templates 570
   Bookshelf Basics integration 791
   charts 970

Microsoft PowerPoint 97 *(continued)*
   clip art 970, 985
   color schemes 976
   common file formats 362
   conflict resolution 989
   converted slides, editing 570
   converter information on World Wide Web 563
   converters, defined 562
   converters, installing 1014
   converters, using to work with other file
      formats 562
   Custom Shows command 26
   customizing 977–989
   customizing for client computers 180
   determining file formats when converting
      presentations 566
   export formats 985
   features affecting data/formatting in previous
      versions 371–374
   file formats for saving presentations 969
   file formats, converting from other
      programs 562–570
   graphics files 569–570
   graphics filter for importing image files 972
   graphics filters 562, 564
   graphics formats 564
   handouts 975
   hyperlinks, adding to slides 707
   images, displaying with decompression 182
   importing outlines from Word 97 781
   importing Word 97 outlines 790
   IntelliSense technology 26–27
   intranet solutions 41–42
   JPEG File Interchange format (JFIF) 182
   macros 978
   masters 967, 973
   Meeting Minder 785, 883
   Meeting Minder action items, exporting to
      Outlook 97 778
   meetings, scheduling through Outlook 97 777–781
   menu command upgrades from
      PowerPoint 3.0 386–395
   menu command upgrades from
      PowerPoint 4.0 374–381
   menu command upgrades from
      PowerPoint 95 363–368
   Microsoft Graph 97 970
   movies 971

Index

Microsoft PowerPoint 97 *(continued)*
  multimedia performance optimization 183
  native file formats 563
  network connections for presentation conferencing 880
  new intelligence features 26–27
  number of bullets on conference slides 883
  Office Art 970
  opening graphics files as presentations 569
  optimizing 180
  pictures 972
  policies 1064
  Portable Network Graphics (PNG) 182
  PowerPoint Central 712
  Pp8x32.dll converter for backward compatibility 370
  presentation components 968
  Presentation Conference Wizard 879
  presentation conferencing 886
    See also presentations
  presentation conferencing, troubleshooting 885
  presentations, converting from earlier PowerPoint versions 362
  presentations, exporting to Word 97 783
  presentations, moving between Windows and Macintosh 565
  presentations, multislide 570
  presentations, opening multiple 567
  presentations, overview 968
  presentations, saving in HTML 710
  presentations, saving in PowerPoint format 567
  presentations, sharing with PowerPoint 3.0 396
  presentations, sharing with PowerPoint 4.0 382–385
  presentations, sharing with PowerPoint 95 369–374
  presentations, single-slide 570
  questions about upgrading 361, 561
  QuickTime movies 971
  running multiple versions 630–634
  Save as HTML Wizard 710
  saving presentations as RTF files 568
  saving presentations in other file formats 567
  security features 877
  shapes 970
  shared presentations 886
  sharing information with other Office 97 applications 781–786
  Slide Finder 26
  slides 969–973

Microsoft PowerPoint 97 *(continued)*
  slides, inserting graphics files from single-side presentations 570
  slides, saving in graphics files 569
  sounds 972
  special installation requirements 76
  spell checking 27
  Stage Manager toolbar 882
  structure 967
  tables 973
  templates, customizing 980–984
  templates, defined 968
  templates, types 975
  text files, opening as outlines 568
  text objects 973
  toolbars, customizing 984
  transporting presentations (Pack and Go Wizard) 888
  troubleshooting presentation conversions 567
  TrueType font differences from version 4.0 384
  twips 970
  upgrading from Harvard Graphics 570–571
  upgrading from Lotus Freelance 571–572
  upgrading from PowerPoint 3.0 386–395
  upgrading from PowerPoint 4.0 374–381
  upgrading from PowerPoint 95 362–368
  upgrading presentations from other file formats 566
  viewers for version 4.0, installing 1015
  viewers for version 95, installing 1015
  viewers, 16-bit and 32-bit 631
  viewers, defined 31
  viewers, packing 888–889
  Web documents, creating 710
  Web support 707
  Web toolbar 30
  World Wide Web publishing 41–42
  Write-Up 783
Microsoft Press publications for Microsoft Office information 1100
Microsoft Query
  policies 1066
  using with Microsoft Excel 97 769
Microsoft Software Library 1096
Microsoft Solution Providers 1097
Microsoft Support Network 1091
Microsoft Systems Management Server
  installing Office 97 132–135

Microsoft Team Manager
    integrating with task lists in Schedule+ and
       Outlook 97 874
    methods for extending Outlook task capabilities 873
    overview 873
    setting up 874
    task prioritization 875
Microsoft TechNet, overview 1096
Microsoft Technical Education 1099
Microsoft Technical Support documents 1022
Microsoft Technical Support Help File 1023
Microsoft text telephone (TT/TDD) services 1093
Microsoft Visual SourceSafe, using with Microsoft
    Access 97 852
Microsoft Web Browser, using with Microsoft Access
    database application forms 691–693
Microsoft Web Publishing Wizard, Office 97 659
Microsoft Web site, connecting from Microsoft on the
    Web menu item 146
Microsoft Windows
    3.1, unbinding binder sections 229
    95, unbinding binder sections 229
    accessing Lotus 1-2-3 System command 510
    API calls 239
    Application Programming Interface 292
    Briefcase replication 837
    deploying for using Office 97 50
    differences between 16-Bit and 32-bit APIs 240
    features, choosing for installation 51
    installation 52
    local installation overview 73
    registry, changing settings using the SetOption
       method 155
    Resource Kits 53
    shared installation overview 73
    swap files 153
    system policies, computer 140
    system policies, creating 138
    system policies, overview 137
    system policies, understanding 138
    system policies, user 140
    system policies, using 138
    System Policy Editor 51
    Temporary folder 205
    user profiles 52
    virtual memory 180
    wallpaper, when not to display 154
Microsoft Windows *(continued)*
    Windows Disk Defragmenter 154
    Windows NT, unbinding binder sections 229
    Windows Write, converters 1018
Microsoft Word 97
    AutoCorrect entries 1005
    AutoFormat 999
    AutoSummary 28
    Bookshelf Basics integration 791
    built-in styles, customizing 999
    built-in styles, illustrated examples 999
    common file formats 400
    compatibility options, improving with other word
       processors 583
    components 997–1005
    confirming which converters to use 581
    conflict resolution 1008
    Conversion Wizard 582
    converted WordBasic macros 406
    converters for versions 6.0/95 1017
    converters for Word for MS-DOS 3.x–6.0 1017
    converters, described 1017
    converters, DisplayWrite 1018
    converters, Lotus Ami Pro 1018
    converters, Microsoft Windows Write 1018
    converters, MultiMate 1018
    converters, RFT-DCA 1018
    converting documents from previous Word
       versions 400
    converting in plain-text formats 574
    converting multiple WordPerfect documents 595
    customizing converted documents 582–584
    customizing for client computers 184
    customizing methods 1006
    Declare-Method solution sample 248
    displaying WordPerfect step-by-step Help 605
    documents not displaying in Open dialog box 581
    documents, advantages and disadvantages of sharing
       with versions 6.0/95 407
    documents, comparing versions 898
    documents, converting from other file
       formats 580–584
    documents, converting from Word Perfect 594–596
    documents, converting to HTML 714
    documents, exporting to Lotus Notes 790
    documents, moving between Windows and
       Macintosh 580
    documents, opening in Word 6.0/95 411–414
    documents, opening in Word for MS-DOS 427

Index

Microsoft Word 97 *(continued)*
  documents, protecting specific areas within 893
  documents, saving in other file formats 588
  documents, saving in Text with Layout format 612–615
  documents, saving in Word 2.0 421–425
  documents, saving in Word 6.0/95 408–411
  documents, saving in Word for MS-DOS 429–431
  documents, saving in Works for Windows 3.0/4.0 609
  documents, security 892
  documents, sharing with Word 2.0 421–425
  documents, sharing with Word 5.x for the Macintosh 433–434
  documents, sharing with Word 6.0/95 407, 414
  documents, sharing with Word for MS-DOS 429–432
  documents, sharing with WordPerfect 5.x 601
  documents, sharing with WordPerfect 6.x 599
  documents, sharing with Works for Windows 609–611
  documents, substituting fonts when converting to other formats 586
  documents, when converted to different formats 579
  documents, workgroup reviewing 893–901
  features available in WordMail 795
  file formats, converting from other programs 574–588
  font substitution 584–586
  font-mapping files 586
  formatting differences from WordPerfect 590
  formatting information, locating 591
  global templates 995
  grammar checking 28
  graphics filters 574, 578–580
  graphics, converting from Word for MS-DOS 428
  graphics, opened in Word for the Macintosh 580
  how-to documents 1026
  importing from WordPerfect 596
  importing meeting minutes and action items from Meeting Minder 785
  importing PowerPoint 97 presentations 783
  importing worksheets from Lotus 1-2-3 788
  importing worksheets from Microsoft Excel 97 787
  IntelliSense technology 28–29
  intranet solutions 42–45

Microsoft Word 97 *(continued)*
  keyboard shortcuts, customizing 1004
  Letter Wizard 28
  line breaks in converted documents 584
  machine setting policies 1057
  macros, creating 1001
  menu command upgrades 401–406
  menu command upgrades from Word 2.0 415–421
  menus, customizing 1004
  multiple authors of documents 894
  new features affecting data/formatting in Word 2.0 422–425
  new features affecting data/formatting in Word 5.x for the Macintosh 433
  new features affecting data/formatting in Word 6.0/95 409–414
  new features affecting data/formatting in Word for MS-DOS 430–431
  new features affecting data/formatting in WordPerfect 5.x 599–600
  new features affecting data/formatting in WordPerfect 6.x 596–599
  new features affecting data/formatting in Works for Windows 610–612
  new intelligence features 28–29
  Normal template, storing AutoCorrect entries 1005
  opening Microsoft Access 97 data 751
  opening WordPerfect documents 595
  optimizing 184
  outlines, exporting to PowerPoint 97 781, 790
  page breaks in converted documents 584
  page settings, default 1000
  paragraph formatting 590
  personal address books 797
  plain-text files, saving documents as 587
  policies 1066
  printing optimization 184
  protecting documents 892
  questions about upgrading 399, 573
  Redo command 593
  Reveal Formats, using to troubleshoot document formatting 591
  review comments for documents 896
  Reviewing toolbar 893
  running multiple versions 634–636
  saving converted WordPerfect documents 595
  security 891
  sharing information with other Office 97 applications 786

Microsoft Word 97 *(continued)*
  solutions, upgrading to 32-bit 249
  special installation requirements 77
  structure 991
  Style Gallery command 1000
  styles, applying to documents 999–1000
  styles, using in Word for MS-DOS 432
  table drawing tool 29
  template file location 996
  templates 992–997
  templates, differences from Microsoft Excel templates 947
  templates, examples illustrated 993
  templates, user and workgroup 997
  terms and features for Word for MS-DOS users 426
  text and graphics 998
  text converters 574–580
  text selecting differences from WordPerfect 589
  toolbars, customizing 1004
  tools for transitioning WordPerfect users 593
  tracking document changes 895
  troubleshooting file conversion 581
  Undo command 592
  upgrading from Microsoft Works 3.0/4.0 608–611
  upgrading from Word 2.0 414–421
  upgrading from Word 5.x for Macintosh 432
  upgrading from Word 5.x/6.0 for MS-DOS 426
  upgrading from Word 6.0/95 400–407
  upgrading from Word Perfect 589–608
  Web page publishing 713
  Web Page Wizard 714
  Web toolbar 30
  Word for MS-DOS styles, using 428
  Word Mail Merge 752
  WordPerfect blue background/white text, displaying 594
  WordPerfect Help 604–608
  WordPerfect users, transition tips for 589–593
  World Wide Web publishing 42–45
Microsoft Word for MS-DOS
  not opening properly 428
  styles, using in Word 97 428
  terms corresponding with Word 97 features 426
  upgrading to Word 97 426
Microsoft Works
  converted worksheets, saving in Microsoft Excel 97 format 543
  upgrading to Microsoft Excel 97 542–543
  worksheets, opening in Microsoft Excel 97 542

Microsoft Works for Windows
  converting to Word 97 608–611
  documents, saving versions in specific file formats 608
  not listed in Save as Type box 609
  not opening properly 608
migration training for Microsoft Office 97
  budgeting considerations 186
  evaluating success 198
  implementing during rollout 198
  overview 186
  program design 186
  scheduling plan 187
  secretaries rollout 194
  support considerations 186
  task list 187
  training and support teams 188
  training partners 188
  training plan 190
MMF (Microsoft Mail message file)
  moving to hard disk from the post office 345
  moving to Outlook 97 personal folder 346
modules
  class, Microsoft Access 97 287
  Microsoft Access, overview 922
  Microsoft Access, when to use 455
  standard, Microsoft Access 97 287
movies, PowerPoint 97 971
MS-DOS applications
  current configuration, assessing for upgrading to Office 97 441–443
  files, preparing to upgrade to Office 97 446
  steps for upgrading to Office 97 440
  text format 588
  upgrading to Word 97 432
  work environments, reviewing for upgrade to Office 97 442
MultiMate, converters for Word 97 1018
multimedia optimization in PowerPoint 183
Multiplan
  commands corresponding with Microsoft Excel 97 539
  documents, sharing with Microsoft Excel 97 538
  upgrading to Microsoft Excel 97 538–542
multiple data access applications, running in Microsoft Access 97 487
multiple-field indexes 163

multiuser performance optimization for Microsoft Access 166
My Documents folder 112
MyAPICall, possible declarations 242

N

name references for Microsoft Excel 97 cells 942
natural language formulas 16
Netscape Web server
    MIME type information 1042
    supporting in Office 97 648
network .txt files 75
network installation of Office 97
    adding files to the installation process 125
    All Components option 119
    application icons, installing to Program Manager 123
    batch installation 131
    configuring the installation environment 121
    customizing 106
    default folder for documents 112
    destination folders for application files 110
    INF files 110, 129, 130
    installation logs, specifying 115
    interactive installation 131
    Maintenance Mode 1052
    Microsoft Systems Management Server 132–135
    overview 108
    Program Manager items 123
    push installation 131
    registry entries 127
    Setup file formats 1045–1047
    Start Menu items 125
    starting 109
    STF files 110, 130
    storing shared Office applications 113
    types of installation 116–121
    verification troubleshooting 115
    Yes/No questions for Office Setup 121
Network Installation Wizard 108, 1012
networks
    administrative installation point 77–82
    benefits and drawbacks for installing Office 97 448
    deploying Office 97 57
    Developer Network News 1097
    Find Fast 718, 729
    LAN options for installing Office 97 448
    Office CD contents, copying to a server 87

networks *(continued)*
    naming Microsoft Access databases 748
    NetWare 144
    Office installation folders 1039
    Paradox tables 484
    product identification 90
    requirements for linking external tables 748
    requirements for PowerPoint 97 presentation conferencing 879
    server connection error messages 81
    server databases, creating 764
    server preparation for administrative installation 79
    servers, designating for pilot rollout 62
    servers, storing system policy files 139
    Web Find Fast 718
new features in Microsoft Office 97 9

O

Object menu upgrades, from PowerPoint 3.0 to PowerPoint 97 389
ODBC
    Administrator, using to set up data sources 490
    architecture 761
    connecting from IDC files in Microsoft Access 680
    connectivity 933
    data source definition 764
    data source names (DSNs) 261
    data sources, setting up using the Data Source Administrator 490
    drivers, installing 261
    drivers, Microsoft Access 97 489
    functionality 760
    linked data sources, opening in Microsoft Access 97 261
    Microsoft Access 97 746
    overview 759
    system data source, adding when creating Web forms 703
    using with Microsoft Access 97 759
    using with Microsoft Office 97 applications 762
Office 97 Upgrade Wizard
    cleanup process, running 207
    cleanup type, selecting 203
    command line options, customizing 208
    components of Office 97 recognized 202
    creating customized commands 218
    customizing 208

Index

Office 97 Upgrade Wizard *(continued)*
  dependency variables, using to determine Office files to delete 210
  file removal process 207
  file removal warning 207
  OPC file syntax 209
  OPC text file, using for Office file cleanup 207
  overview 201
  selecting applications to remove 205
  selecting files to keep 206
  starting 202
  troubleshooting Office Setup 219
  troubleshooting problems from previously installed Office files 220
Office Art 13, 911
Office Assistant
  ACT files, relocating 1055
  overview 12
  types of assistance available 13
Office Binder 14
Office Setup command line options for Microsoft Office 97 1047–1050
Office Suites, checked during Office Setup 92
Office Upgrade Wizard 1033
OLE
  defined 905
  differences from ActiveX 907
OPC files
  commands section, defined 209
  commands, actions 214
  commands, dependency list 214
  creating customized Office 97 Upgrade Wizard commands 218
  defined 207
  definitions section, defined 209
  dependency variable values 210
  description, as command line option recognized by Office 97 Upgrade Wizard 209
  syntax 209
open modes, Microsoft Access 97, databases 825
optimistic locking
  advantages and disadvantages 828
  defined 826
  No Locks option 826
Options menu upgrades, from Microsoft Excel 4.0 to Microsoft Excel 97 325

outlines
  Word 97, exporting into PowerPoint 97 790
  Word 97, importing into PowerPoint 97 781
outlines, opening in Microsoft PowerPoint 97 568
Outlook Bar, illustrated 20
Outlook Extension Configuration File (ECF) document 1024

P

Pack and Go Wizard, Microsoft PowerPoint 97 888
Package Definition Files 1012
packages
  creating for Office 132
  job schedules 135
  job targets 135
  Office, adding new commands 134
  Office, job creation 135
  Run on Workstation jobs 135
page breaks, in converted Word documents 584
page settings in Word 97 1000
paragraphs, formatting in Word 97 590
parameter data types, API 243
Parameter queries 918
Pass-through queries 920
password-protected databases, converting 256
passwords
  databases, setting 805
  requiring for opening workbooks 856
PCX files, supporting in Microsoft Word 97 428
Peer Web Services
  documentation 664
  installation procedure 663
  installation requirements 661
  online resource information 663
  setting up 660–664
Performance Analyzer
  customizing Microsoft Access 97 databases 152
permissions
  assigning 816
  explicit 815
  implicit 815
  new objects, databases 817
  public folder access, revoking 871
  removing from underlying tables and queries 824

permissions *(continued)*
  revoking 816
  User and Group, using to change ownership of Microsoft Access 97 objects 817
personal address books 797
personal identifiers (PID) 813
personal information management (PIM) products, upgrading to Microsoft Outlook 97 546
Personal Web Server
  documentation 664
  installation procedure 662
  installation requirements 661
  online resource information 663
  setting up 660–664
pessimistic locking
  advantages and disadvantages 828
  defined 827
  QuantityOnHand column 829
pilot rollout for Microsoft Office 97
  automating 63
  budget considerations 67
  defined 62
  final process steps 68
  finalizing 66–67
  goal determination 67
  installation process, planning 63
  network server, designating 62
  performance testing tips 66
  policies and guidelines 67
  process steps 62
  push installation 63
  questions to ask before the final rollout 63
  resources 67
  results 66–67
  scheduling 66
  scripts, creating for test installation 63
  steps for conducting 65
  support plan, developing 64
  surveying areas 66
  tasks for testing teams 62
  tips for installing Office 97 65
  user groups 65
  user training program overview 64
PivotTables, creating in Microsoft Access 97 753
plain-text files
  opening 587
  saving 587
plain-text formats 574

planning team for Microsoft Office 97 implementation 54
policies
  computer 140
  installing 1053
  files, defining default value for Microsoft Excel Save as Type option 315
  files, using to configure client computers 51
  Internet 1059
  machine setting 1055–1057
  Microsoft Access 1062
  Microsoft Bookshelf 1068
  Microsoft Excel 1062
  Microsoft on the Web 1058
  Microsoft Outlook 1064
  Microsoft PowerPoint 1064
  Microsoft Query 1066
  Office 97, available in policy template files 1068
  Office 97, described 1060
  Office 97, installation 1013
  pilot rollout 67
  template files 139
  user 140
  user setting 1058–1068
  Windows system 51
  Windows system, creating 138
  Windows system, overview 137
  Windows system, understanding 138
  Windows system, using 138
  Word 97 1066
Portable Network Graphics (PNG) 182
porting Office-Based Solutions to 32-bit
  API call, defined 239
  API call, procedure 239
  API Declare Statement errors 244
  APIs, deciding which to call 238
  C Declarations, using 250–251
  Declare-Method solution sample 248
  determining if 32-bit applications are running 246–249
  differences between 16-Bit and 32-bit APIs 240–244
  DLL recompiling 249
  overview 236
  scenarios for upgrading 238
  single code bases 244–246
  thunking 249
  Word solutions upgrading procedure 249

Post Office Protocol (POP), Internet Mail 547
PowerPoint Central 712
PowerPoint Viewer 888
Presentation Conference Wizard, Microsoft PowerPoint 879
presentations
    audience member participation in conferences 884
    automating the creation process 968
    components 968
    conferencing 878–886
    conferencing example, illustrated 878
    conferencing process overview 879–881
    conferencing, ending 881
    conferencing, starting 881
    content templates 976
    conversion troubleshooting 567
    converted Harvard Graphics, saving in PowerPoint format 571
    converted Lotus Freelance, saving in PowerPoint format 572
    converted, saving in PowerPoint format 567
    converters, defined 562
    converting to PowerPoint 97 from earlier versions 362
    copying to audience nodes, troubleshooting 881
    distributing meeting minutes through Word 97 884
    elements not supported on audience nodes 882
    exporting to Word 97 783
    file formats 969
    graphics filters, defined 562
    Harvard Graphics, converting to PowerPoint 97 571
    imported to PowerPoint 97 with converters 563
    laptop 890
    Lotus Freelance, opening in PowerPoint 97 572
    Meeting Minder 883
    moving between Windows and Macintosh 565
    multimedia performance optimization 183
    multiple Harvard Graphics, converting 571
    multiple Lotus Freelance, converting 572
    multiple, converting 567
    multislide 570
    network connections 880
    number of bullets on conference slides 883
    opening multiple 567
    overview 968
    page-orientation settings 969
    PowerPoint 97 viewers 888–889
    PowerPoint 97, advantages and disadvantages of sharing with version 95 369

presentations *(continued)*
    PowerPoint 97, saving in 3.0 format 396
    PowerPoint 97, saving in 4.0 format 382–385
    PowerPoint 97, saving in other file formats 567
    PowerPoint 97, saving in PowerPoint 95 and 97 format 369–370
    PowerPoint 97, saving in PowerPoint 95 format 370–374
    PowerPoint Central 712
    PowerPoint, adding to Web sites 711
    PowerPoint, opening from WMF or PICT graphics files 569
    PowerPoint, viewing in HTML 711
    presenter's role in conferences 881
    reusing slides 26
    reviewing in workgroups 886–887
    saving as PowerPoint animation in HTML 711
    saving as RTF files 568
    saving in graphics format 562, 569
    saving in HTML 710
    saving in text format 562
    sharing with multiple PowerPoint versions 631
    showing on two linked computers 879
    single-slide 570
    slide masters 973
    slides 969–973
    speaker notes for conferences 883
    specifying default formats 370, 382, 396, 567
    Stage Manager toolbar 882
    system requirements for conferencing 879
    template changes in PowerPoint 97 368, 381, 395
    text objects 973
    title masters 973
    transporting (Pack and Go Wizard) 888–890
    troubleshooting conferences 885
    TrueType font differences between PowerPoint versions 97 and 4.0 384
    unpacking 889
    upgrading to PowerPoint 97 566
printers
    setup differences between Lotus 1-2-3 and Microsoft Excel 97 525
    Ultimate Printer Manual 1025
private mailing lists, importing into Microsoft Outlook 97 550
procedure calls 239
product identification for Microsoft Office 97 90
profiles for Windows users 52
Program Manager items, installing 123

protocols
    Internet 674
    IPX, connecting for presentation conferencing 880
    TCP/IP, connecting for presentation conferencing 880
public folders
    anonymous accounts for posting Outlook messages 872
    designed for Outlook and Microsoft Exchange Client users 343
    From field setting, changing 872
    hiding document properties for documents 641
    locating easily 870
    Outlook 97 components 963
    Outlook 97, sharing with Mail 3.x for Windows 352
    Outlook 97, sharing with Microsoft Exchange Client 342
    posting documents 799
    revoking permission access 871
    security 871–873
    setting up for Microsoft Exchange 868
    shortcuts, distributing to users 870
    subfolders 870
    unread messages 873
Publish to the Web Wizard, Microsoft Access 687

Q

Quattro Pro for MS-DOS, upgrading to Microsoft Excel 97 535–536
Quattro Pro for Windows
    converted notebooks, saving in Microsoft Excel 97 537
    notebooks, opening in Microsoft Excel 97 536
    upgrading to Microsoft Excel 97 536
queries
    Action 919
    append 453
    creating in Microsoft Access 97 472
    Crosstab 918
    defined as Microsoft Access 97 objects 453
    delete 453
    make-table 453
    merging using the Word Mail Merge Wizard 752
    Microsoft Access 918–921
    Microsoft Access 97, exporting to dBASE files 476
    Microsoft Access 97, exporting to FoxPro files 479
    Microsoft Access 97, exporting to Paradox files 486

queries *(continued)*
    Microsoft Access, saving as static HTML documents 677
    Microsoft Excel 695
    name-mapping, Microsoft Access 97 764
    optimizing Filter By Form performance 172
    pages, linking to Web Find Fast indexes 738
    Parameter 918
    performance optimization 167
    Rushmore technology, optimizing criteria expressions 169–172
    saving as IDC/HTX files 679
    Select 918
    SQL 920
    underlying, securing designs 824
    update 453
Query menu upgrades, to Microsoft Access 97 from Microsoft Access 2.0 276
query pages 738
QuickTime movies, using in Microsoft PowerPoint 97 971

R

RAM (random-access memory), Microsoft Access 153
Range Finder, Microsoft Excel 18
RC4, encryption routine 856
readme files 75
record locking in Microsoft Access 97 830
Records menu upgrades to Microsoft Access 97 from Microsoft Access 2.0 277
Recovery macro for Microsoft Excel 97 files 1027
Redo command, Microsoft Word 97 593
refresh intervals, setting in Microsoft Access 97 multiuser environment 825
RegClean utility for Microsoft Outlook 97 1036
registry entries, adding to Windows registry 127
registry settings 758
relational database management system, Microsoft Access 97 452
Relationships menu upgrades to Microsoft Access 97 from Microsoft Access 2.0 276
relationships, Microsoft Access 97 tables 465
replica sets
    converting 259
    Design Master 259

replicated databases
    compacting 850
    DAO methods and properties 839
    databases, when not to use 836
    design errors 846
    duplicating 843
    error and conflict resolution 846–850
    Globally Unique Identifier (GUID) for new records 843
    implementing 837–839
    laptop replication 837
    local objects 834
    making into regular databases 852
    menu commands 837
    overview 834
    partial 835, 844
    Replication ID AutoNumber 841
    Replication Manager 838
    security 850
    synchronizing 845
    troubleshooting 846–850
    using instead of backups 844
Replication Manager 838
reports
    Crystal, Outlook 97 1035
    database, previewing and printing 457
    defined as Microsoft Access 97 objects 454
    Microsoft Access 97, opening in Microsoft Excel 97 753
    Microsoft Access 97, opening in Word 752
    Microsoft Access, formatting and printing Microsoft Excel 97 data 753
    Microsoft Access, overview 921
    Microsoft Access, saving as static HTML documents 677
    performance optimization in Microsoft Access 175
Resource Kits for Windows 95 or Windows NT 53
return registers 239
Reveal Formats, Microsoft Word 97 591
RFT-DCA, converters for Microsoft Word 97 1018
Rich Text Format (RTF)
    converting documents between Microsoft applications 587
    Minimal 725
    saving Outlook 97 items 962
    saving PowerPoint 97 presentations 568
    turning on in Outlook 97 548
    using to make WordMail messages compatible with other e-mail editors 796

Rich Text Format (RTF) *(continued)*
    Word 97 documents in Word 6.0/95 408
    WordMail message conversion 340
Run menu upgrades
    to Microsoft Access 97 from Microsoft Access 2.0 277
    to Microsoft Access 97 from Microsoft Access 95 265
Run On Workstation jobs 135
RunPermissions property 823
Rushmore technology 169–172

S

Save as HTML Wizard 710
scenarios for porting Office-Based solutions 238
scheduling
    for workgroups in Microsoft Outlook 97 865–868
    pilot training for Office 97 196
Search the Web button, for searching intranets 653
searching for data using Filter By Form 16
searching for data using Filter By Selection 16
secretaries rollout of Microsoft Office 97 194
security
    Admin user account 813
    assigning to databases without sign-on requirement 821
    converting password protected databases 256
    converting user-level protected databases 256
    databases, saving as MDE files 808
    databases, setting passwords 805
    features in Word 891
    front-end/back-end applications 820
    identifiers 811
    index issues 727
    intranets 646
    levels, Microsoft Excel 97 files 856
    Microsoft Access 97 features 803
    Office 97, features 908
    permissions 815–817
    personal identifiers (PID) 813
    protecting PowerPoint 97 features 877
    public folders 871–873
    replicated databases 850
    share-level 811
    specific areas in Word documents 893
    startup options in Microsoft Access 97 804
    user-level in Microsoft Access 97 810–824
    user-level model, Microsoft Access 97 811, 812

Index

security *(continued)*
   User-Level Security Wizard 818, 818–820
   user-level, removing 821
   user-level, using with the RunPermissions
      property 823
   Word documents 892
   workbooks 856, 946
   workgroup information file, Microsoft
      Access 97 811
Select queries 918
SendKeys Action, Microsoft Access 269, 279
server-side scripting 684
Setup program for Microsoft Office 97 105
Setup Simulator 1024
Setup, running to install Microsoft Office 97 82–86
shapes, PowerPoint 97 970
shared workbooks
   characteristics 858
   common uses 859
   overview 858
share-level security 811
Shortcut Bar, Microsoft Office 97
   default configurations 234
   overview 232
shortcut keys *See* keyboard commands
shortcut menus
   custom, importing to Microsoft Access from other
      databases 936
   Microsoft Access, customizing 935
   new in Microsoft Access 97 270, 294
SID (security identifiers) 811
signatures for Microsoft Office 97 product versions 91
Simple Mail Transfer Protocol (SMTP), Internet
   Mail 547
Simple Query Wizard 15
single cabinet files (CAB) 89
single file architecture, Microsoft Access 97 452
Slide Finder, PowerPoint 97 26
slide masters, PowerPoint presentations 973
Slide Show menu upgrades
   from PowerPoint 3.0 to PowerPoint 97 393
   from PowerPoint 4.0 to PowerPoint 97 379
   from PowerPoint 95 to PowerPoint 97 366

slides
   action buttons 708
   action items from presentation conferences 883
   animation effects 974
   audience handouts 975
   background characteristics 974
   content templates 976
   converted, editing 570
   expanding 26
   handout masters 975
   hyperlinks, adding 707
   inserting graphics files from single-slide
      presentations 570
   layout characteristics 974
   menu changes in PowerPoint 97 from
      version 3.0 390
   movies 971
   multislide presentations 570
   naming convention when exported to graphics
      format 569
   notes masters 975
   objects, including 970
   PowerPoint 97 989
   PowerPoint Central presentations 712
   PowerPoint97 969–973
   reusing from existing presentations 26
   saving in graphics format with presentations 569
   Slide Finder 26
   sounds, inserting 972
   summarizing information 26
   tables, inserting from Microsoft Word 97 973
   text style characteristics 974
   workgroup reviewing using unique formatting 887
software administration improvements to Microsoft
   Office 97 9
sounds, PowerPoint 97 972
Speer Software Training, Inc. 185
spell checking dictionary for Microsoft Office 97
   applications 911
spreadsheets
   checked during Office Setup 92
   Deployment Planner, Office 97 1032
   formatting 19
   informational, Office 97 1021
   operations, Microsoft Excel 97 497
   Solutions templates 306
   visual printing 19
SQL databases, performance optimization 164

SQL queries 920
SQL Server, sharing data with Microsoft Excel 97 768
stacks 239
Stage Manager toolbar, presentation conferences 882
standard modules 287
Start menu, Windows 125
startup options to protect applications 804
startup switches for Find Fast troubleshooting 731
Step by Step training materials 442
STF files
    batch mode 120
    configuring the installation environment 121
    customizing network installations 106
    interactive mode 120
    modifying for custom installations of Office 107
    overview 1046
    running client Setup 130
    saving 130
    specifying for Office 97 installation 110
    values, modifying 106
    Yes/No questions for Office Setup 121
Stop word list, Find Fast 1021
Style Gallery, Microsoft Word 97 1000
styles
    applying to Word 97 documents 999–1000
    formatting 943
    Microsoft Excel 97, copying between workbooks 944
    Word 97, customizing 999
    Word 97, illustrated examples 999
    Word 97, using in Word for MS-DOS 432
    Word for MS-DOS, using in Word 97 428
subqueries 921
subscription to Microsoft TechNet 1096
summary information *See* document properties
support *See* customer support
swap files 153
SwitchForms utility for Microsoft Outlook 97 1033
switching *See* converting
SYLK files, opening in Microsoft Excel 97 538
symbols, displaying unexpectedly in documents 586
syntax for OPC files 209–218
system policies
    client computer requirements 144
    computer 140
    files, creating and storing 138
    overview 137
    setting 140–143

system policies *(continued)*
    template files 139
    understanding 138
    user 140
System Policy Editor
    changing Microsoft Access option settings 155
    defining default value for Microsoft Excel Save as Type option 315
    Icon Name Properties dialog box 141
    information, World Wide Web address 1054
    installation 1013
    list of policies 1068
    starting 1054
    user settings 1058
    using to set system policies 141
    Windows 51

T

Table Analyzer Wizard
    defined as Office97 IntelliSense feature 15
    using to normalize table data 162
Table Menu upgrades
    from Word 2.0 to Word 97 420
    from Word 6.0/95 to Word 97 405
tables
    access permissions 748
    added when databases are converted to Design Master 841
    AutoNumber field changes after Design Master conversion 842
    deciding when to import or link to Microsoft Access 97 463
    defined as Microsoft Access 97 objects 453
    drawing in Word 29
    external data source troubleshooting 750
    fields, defined 453
    HTML, importing or linking data 689
    imported, features available in Microsoft Access 97 463
    importing and linking data to Microsoft Access 97 461
    importing to PowerPoint 97 973
    linked in Microsoft Access databases 932
    linked, managing in Microsoft Access 97 833

Index

tables *(continued)*
- linked, performance optimization 163
- linked, renaming 767
- merging using the Word Mail Merge Wizard 752
- Microsoft Access 97, exporting to dBASE files 475
- Microsoft Access 97, exporting to FoxPro files 479
- Microsoft Access 97, exporting to Paradox files 486
- Microsoft Access 97, exporting to server databases 765
- Microsoft Access, normalization 917
- Microsoft Access, overview 916
- Microsoft Access, relationship definition 917
- Microsoft Access, saving as static HTML documents 677
- Microsoft Access, storing hyperlinks 671–674
- optimizing Filter By Form performance 172
- Paradox, exporting or linking to Microsoft Access 97 481
- performance optimization in Microsoft Access 97 162
- records, defined 453
- referential integrity, maintained when adding or deleting records 463
- relationships in Microsoft Access 97 465
- relationships, defining 453
- saving as IDC/HTX files 679
- separated in Microsoft Access, storing related data 916
- server, indexes 766
- server, linking 767
- server, triggers 766
- sharing between Microsoft Access 95 and 97 268
- tips, importing and linking to Microsoft Access 97 462
- underlying, securing designs 824

tag pairs, HTML 689

TCP/IP (Transmission Control Protocol/Internet Protocol), as Web publication requirement 661

templates
- animated, overview 27
- AutoContent wizards 982–984
- autotemplates, Microsoft Excel 97 953
- AutoText entries 1001
- Blank Presentations, PowerPoint 97 570
- changes in PowerPoint 97 368, 381, 395
- changes when upgrading to Microsoft Access 97 268, 279
- content, PowerPoint 97 976
- conversion 582

templates *(continued)*
- creating new documents 994
- customizing for PowerPoint 97 980–984
- defined 947
- differences between Word and Microsoft Excel 947
- electronic mail, setting up 795
- files, defining Office 97 system policies 139
- global 995
- global, opening in non-global mode 1001
- HTML, placeholders 688
- HTML, using to save documents as HTML documents 687
- including text and graphics in documents 998
- keyboard shortcuts, customizing 1004
- macros 1001
- menus, customizing 1004
- Microsoft Access, forms and reports 923
- Microsoft Excel 5.0, locating in Microsoft Excel 97 312
- Microsoft Excel built-in, locating 312
- Microsoft Excel custom, locating 312
- Office policy, installing 1013
- Office, available for Windows 95 1054
- Office, available for Windows NT 4.0 1054
- Outlook 97 files 961
- policy, policies available 1068
- PowerPoint 97 968, 975
- registration, for monitoring final rollouts 67
- Spreadsheet Solutions 306
- storing in Word 97 996
- system policy, installing for Office 1053
- toolbars, customizing 1004
- user 997
- uses in Word 97 992–997
- Word 97 default page settings 1000
- Word 97, AutoCorrect entries 1005
- Word 97, illustrated examples 993
- Word 97, specific file location 996
- WordBasic macros 406
- workbooks 947
- workgroup 997

temporary files, removing when upgrading to Office 97 205

test client configuration for Office 97 evaluation 56–59

testing
- Office 97 applications before installing 444
- Office 97 client configuration 59–61

Index

text
    converters 574–580
    correcting errors in Word 97 592
    editing differences between WordPerfect and Word 97 590–593
    file formats 587
    formatting differences between WordPerfect and Word 97 590–593
    MS-DOS format 588
    plain-text files, opening and saving 587
    selecting, differences between Word Perfect and Word 97 589
    with layout, converting to Word 97 612–615
    with line breaks 588
    WordPerfect, displaying in Word 97 594
text converters
    additional in Office Resource Kit Tools and Utilities 577
    confirming which to use in Word 97 581
    default locations 577
    included with Word 97 575
    locating 577
Text Import Wizard, Microsoft Excel 97 494
Text menu upgrades, from PowerPoint 3.0 to PowerPoint 97 389
text objects, Microsoft PowerPoint 97 973
text, formats native to Word 575
threads, used by Microsoft Jet 156
three-dimensional formulas in Microsoft Excel 97 workbooks 518
thunking 237, 249
TIFF files, supporting in Microsoft Word 97 428
title masters, Microsoft PowerPoint presentations 974
toolbars
    buttons for Office 97 applications or accessories 234
    copying to Word 97 documents or templates 1005
    custom, importing to Microsoft Access from other databases 936
    custom, sharing within workgroups 955
    customizing in PowerPoint 97 984
    customizing in Word 97 1004
    Microsoft Access, customizing 935
    Microsoft Excel 97, customizing 955
    new in Microsoft Access 97 270, 294
    Office 97 Shortcut Bar 233
    Office Web 653

toolbars *(continued)*
    overview 14
    Reviewing, Word 97 893
    Stage Manager, PowerPoint 97 882
    storing in folders 233
tools, Office 97 implementation 54–56
Tools menu upgrades
    from Microsoft Excel 5.0 to Microsoft Excel 97 310
    from Microsoft Excel 95 to Microsoft Excel 97 305
    from PowerPoint 3.0 to PowerPoint 97 392
    from PowerPoint 4.0 to PowerPoint 97 378
    from PowerPoint 95 to PowerPoint 97 365
    from Word 2.0 to Word 97 418
    from Word 6.0/95 to Word 97 404
    from Microsoft Access 2.0 to Microsoft Access 97 276
    from Microsoft Access 95 to Microsoft Access 97 266
training
    assembling for Office 97 188
    Authorized Academic Training Programs (AATPs) 56
    classes for Office 97 migration, overview 444
    companies supporting Microsoft products 189
    evaluating success of Office 97 transition 198
    implementing during Office 97 rollout 198
    Microsoft Access 97 458
    Microsoft Authorized Technical Education Centers (ATECs) 56
    Microsoft Certified Professional Program 1099
    Microsoft Office 97 Starts Here 189
    Microsoft Press publications 1100
    Microsoft Technical Education 1099
    migration 186
    new users for Office 97 444–445
    Office 97, documentation 195
    Office 97, identifying support resources 188
    Office 97, overview 64
    Office 97, plan contents 190
    Office 97, promoting 196
    Office 97, support teams 188–189
    Office 97, task list 187
    Office 97, testing the plan 197
    partners for Office 97 rollout process 188
    pilot Office installation user groups 65
    pilot, Office 97 196
    plan for Office 97 190–194
    plan for Office 97, feedback from end-users 194

Index

training *(continued)*
  plan for Office 97, feedback from information systems personnel 193
  plan for Office 97, feedback from managers 192
  plan for Office 97, feedback from trainers and help desk personnel 193
  plan for Office 97, sample questions for Organization-Wide input 192
  preparing for Office 97 rollout 189
  professional, for Office 97 migration 445
  sample programs 194
  secretaries rollout of Office 97 194
  Speer Software 185
  Step by Step, referenced 442
Transition Formula Entry check box, Microsoft Excel 97 499
triggers, enforcing rules on server tables 766
TrueType fonts, PowerPoint 97 384
twips, PowerPoint 97 970

U

Ultimate Printer Manual 1025
Unbind Utilities, Microsoft Office 97 1032
UNC (Universal Naming Convention) path 80, 114
Undo command
  Microsoft Excel 97 19
  Microsoft Word 97 592
Unicode character set 241
uninstall process, testing for Microsoft Office 97 61
Union queries 920
Unset Database Password, Microsoft Access 97 806
Update queries 453, 919
upgrading
  binders, Office 95 229
  Macintosh users to Outlook 97 345
  MS-DOS users to Outlook 97 345
  scenarios for porting Office-Based solutions 238
  to Outlook 97 from Symantec ACT! 2.0 550
  to 32-bit Office from 16-Bit Office
    See porting Office-Based Solutions to 32-bit
  to Microsoft Access 97 from dBASE 468–476
  to Microsoft Access 97 from FoxPro 476
  to Microsoft Access 97 from Microsoft Access 1.x 294
  to Microsoft Access 97 from Microsoft Access 2.0 270, 294

upgrading *(continued)*
  to Microsoft Access 97 from Microsoft Access 95 262, 271
  to Microsoft Access 97 from other databases 460–468
  to Microsoft Access 97 from Paradox 480
  to Microsoft Excel 97 from Microsoft Excel 4.0 320–327
  to Microsoft Excel 97 from Microsoft Excel 5.0 307–314
  to Microsoft Excel 97 from Microsoft Excel 95 302–306
  to Office 97 from MS-DOS applications 441
  to Office 97 from Office 3.x for Windows 235
  to Office 97 from Office 4.x 230–235
  to Office 97 from Office 95 226–229
  to Office 97 from Office 95 for Windows 232–234
  to Outlook 97 from client/server messaging systems 560
  to Outlook 97 from ECCO Pro 552
  to Outlook 97 from Lotus cc:Mail 548–550
  to Outlook 97 from Lotus Organizer 557–560
  to Outlook 97 from Mail 3.x for Windows 343–350
  to Outlook 97 from Microsoft Exchange Client 336–338
  to Outlook 97 from Schedule+ 1.0 357–359
  to Outlook 97 from Schedule+ 95 352–355
  to Outlook 97 from Starfish Sidekick Deluxe 95 555–557
  to PowerPoint 97 from Harvard Graphics 570–571
  to Word 97 from Word 2.0 414–421
  to Word 97 from Word 5.x for Macintosh 432
  to Word 97 from Word 5.x/6.0 for MS-DOS 426
  to Word 97 from Word 6.0/95 400–407
  WordBasic macros to Visual Basic 406
  XLM macros to Visual Basic 327
Upsizing Wizard, Microsoft Access 97 763
URLs, specifying for Internet connection 674
user policies 140
user setting policies 1058–1068
user-level security
  Admin user account 813
  databases, converting 256
  defined 810
  MDE files 808
  viewing query designs 824
User-Level Security Wizard 818

1146 Microsoft Office 97 Resource Kit

users
  Admin, Microsoft Access 97 813
  anonymous, posting Outlook messages to public folders 872
  changing or clearing passwords for databases 806
  choosing location for installing shared applications 113
  contributing input for the Office 97 training plan 192
  free/busy status in Outlook 97 866
  Office 97, updating with new configuration 97
  Office 97, updating with same configuration 96
  permissions for databases 811
  permissions, explicit and implicit 815
  personal identifiers (PID) 813
  pilot rollout for Office 97 65
  preparing for Office migration training 186
  presentation conference, participation requirements 881
  profiles for Windows 52
  receiving Office rollout 68
  requirements for migrating to Office 97 442
  roles in presentation conferences as audience members 884
  security identifiers (SID) 811
  sharing information with organization members on intranets 656
  surveying for the Office pilot rollout 66
  training to use Office 97 444–445
  upgrading from MS-DOS applications to Office 97 442

V

Value Pack converters, Microsoft Office 97 546
ValuPack folder, Office CD 546
Vendor Independent Messaging (VIM) 548
version control of documents 898–901
View menu upgrades
  from Microsoft Access 2.0 to Microsoft Access 97 274
  from Microsoft Access 95 to Microsoft Access 97 264
  from Microsoft Excel 5.0 to Microsoft Excel 97 308
  from Microsoft Excel 95 to Microsoft Excel 97 303
  from PowerPoint 3.0 to PowerPoint 97 388
  from PowerPoint 4.0 to PowerPoint 97 376
  from PowerPoint 95 to PowerPoint 97 364

View menu upgrades *(continued)*
  from Word 2.0 to Word 97 416
  from Word 6.0/95 to Word 97 402
view switching, Microsoft Outlook 97 24
Viewers
  Microsoft Access 97 31
  Microsoft Excel 97 31
  Microsoft PowerPoint 97 31
  Office 97 31
  packing PowerPoint 97 888
  PowerPoint 4.0, installing 1015
  PowerPoint 95, installing 1015
  PowerPoint 97 631, 888
  World Wide Web location 31
views, Microsoft Outlook 97 336
VIM (Lotus Notes Mail Support), installing for Microsoft Office 97 794
virtual memory
  optimizing 153
  turning on in Windows 95 180
Visual Basic
  add-in programs, optimizing in PowerPoint 97 181
  changes from Access Basic 281–293
  changes when upgrading to Microsoft Access 97 270
  code differences from Access Basic 295
  code, using to create new macros 1002
  DAOs, methods unsupported for external databases 749
  defined as technology tool for creating Office solutions 648
  displaying WordBasic macros converted to Word 97 406
  Editor command, using to view code 946
  methods and properties for hyperlinks 675
  Microsoft Office 97/Visual Basic Programmer's Guide, referenced 327
  modules, Microsoft Access databases 922
  multiple versions of Microsoft Excel 97 626
  overview, as component of Office 97 913
  performance optimization in Microsoft Access 97 175–178
  scoping rules and object naming 289–292
  Win32 API declarations 1026
  working with database objects in Microsoft Access 97 456

W

Web Browser
   controls 691
   integrating with Office 97 documents 650
   Outlook 705
   using PowerPoint Animation Player 711
Web Connectivity Kit, Microsoft Excel 97 1041
Web Find Fast
   administering in Find Fast NT control panel 733
   administering with the Administration Tool 733
   administration tool 740
   administration, Help file 740
   changing the Find Fast NT service logon account 741
   differences from Find Fast 718–723
   disabling indexing options 737
   document location 742
   document properties 737
   index search results 720
   index structures 719, 740
   indexes, creating and maintaining 736–741
   installation 735
   intranet solution 30
   methods of finding documents 722
   overview 717, 733
   phrase searching, enabling 738
   query pages, linking to indexes 738
   searching for documents using index files 720
   searching with HTML query page 742
   system requirements 718
   user interface 721
   Web site administration 741
   with remote administration, requirements 734
   without remote administration, requirements 734
Web Form Wizard 696
Web forms
   client requirements 697
   creating 698–703
   overview 696
   server requirements and capabilities 697
Web Page Wizard 714
Web pages
   cataloging 706
   creating from Microsoft Access 97 forms 666
   creating in Word 97 713
   Peer Web Services 660
   Personal Web Server 660

Web pages *(continued)*
   publishing 659
   searching, using Search the Web button on Office Web toolbar 653
Web servers
   installation procedure 662
   installation requirements 661
   Netscape, MIME type information 1042
   Netscape, supporting 648
   online resource information 663
   publication requirements 661
   setting up 660
Wextract utility for Microsoft Office 97 floppy disks 1041
white papers, Microsoft Office 97 1102
Win32 Programmer's Reference 243
Win32 SDK documentation 242
Win32 API declarations document 1026
Window menu upgrades
   from Microsoft Access 2.0 to Microsoft Access 97 278
   from Microsoft Access 95 to Microsoft Access 97 267
   from Microsoft Excel 4.0 to Microsoft Excel 97 326
   from Microsoft Excel 5.0 to Microsoft Excel 97 311
   from Word 2.0 to Word 97 420
Windows Application Programming Interface 292
Windows Disk Defragmenter 154
Windows machine setting properties 1057
Windows Registry settings 758
Wipename utility for Microsoft Outlook 97 1035
wizards
   AutoContent, PowerPoint 97 26, 710, 982–984, 986–989
   Chart, Microsoft Excel 97 19, 944
   Database, as Office 97 IntelliSense feature 15
   defined 925
   File Conversion, converting documents to Microsoft Excel 97 493
   Form and Report, improvements 16
   Function, Microsoft Excel 97 768
   import and export, as Office 97 IntelliSense feature 15
   Import and Export, Outlook 97 770, 781
   Internet Assistant, Microsoft Excel 97 693
   Letter, Word 97 28
   managing in Word 97 1006

Index

wizards *(continued)*
   Microsoft Access 97, upgrading from Access Basic 286
   Microsoft Access, types 925
   Microsoft Web publishing 659
   Network Installation 108–130
   Office 97 upgrade 202–218
   Office Upgrade 1033
   Pack and Go (transporting PowerPoint presentations) 888
   Presentation Conference, PowerPoint 97 879
   Publish to the Web, Microsoft Access 687
   Save as HTML 710
   Simple Query, as Office 97 IntelliSense feature 15
   Table Analyzer, as Office 97 IntelliSense feature 15
   Table Analyzer, using to normalize tables 162
   Text Import (importing text files to Microsoft Excel 97) 494
   Upsizing, Microsoft Access 97 763
   User-Level Security, Microsoft Access 97 818–820
   Web Form, Microsoft Excel 696
   Web Page, Word 714
   Word Mail Merge 752
WK3 functions, Lotus 1-2-3 527
Word 5.x for the Macintosh
   documents, opening in Word 97 433
   not opening properly 433
   upgrading to Word 97 432
Word for MS-DOS
   graphics created using Capture.com utility 428
   graphics, converting to Word 97 428
   not listed in Save As Type box 429
word processors, checked during Office Setup 92
WordBasic, upgrading macros to Visual Basic 406
WordMail
   disabling for use with Outlook 97 795
   electronic mail templates, setting up 795
   enabling for use with Outlook 97 795
   features available from Word 97 795
   forms, converting messages to RTF 340
   installation 795
   Merge Wizard 752
   messages, composing and viewing 795
   messages, sharing with other applications 796
   Microsoft Outlook 97 feature 338
   network resources for mailing 798
   network resources for posting 798

WordMail *(continued)*
   network resources for routing 798
   overview 795
   personal address books 797
   setting up e-mail templates 795
WordPerfect
   blue background/white text setting in Word 97 document 594
   character sets and corresponding fonts 1019
   conversion fonts 1018
   converted documents, saving in Word 97 595
   converters, installing before converting documents to Word 595
   converting multiple documents to Word 97 595
   converting to Word 97 589–608
   Demos of features 605
   documents, converting to Word 97 594–596
   documents, opening in Word 97 595
   editing differences in Word 97 590–593
   error correction differences in Word 97 592
   formatting differences in Word 97 590–593
   formatting information, locating in Word 97 591
   graphics, importing into Word 97 596
   help available in Word 97 604–608
   Help, customizing in Word 97 607
   keyboard commands available in Word 97 605
   paragraph differences in Word 97 590
   step-by-step Help 605
   text selecting differences in Word 97 589
   tools for transitioning to Word 97 593
   transition tips to using Word 97 589–593
   troubleshooting formatting differences in Word 97 591
WordStar, converters 1019
workbooks
   3-D formulas, Microsoft Excel 97 518
   active, removing from memory 523
   add-in programs 949–951
   autotemplates 953
   book-level name references 942
   cell data, defined 940
   cell references 941
   change history 858, 862–863
   charts and chart types 944
   components illustrated 940
   conflicting revisions, solving 860
   converting to Microsoft Excel 97 from previous Microsoft Excel versions 302

workbooks *(continued)*
   custom toolbars, sharing within workgroups 955
   data consolidation 861
   default formats, specifying 315, 328
   defined 939
   electronic mailing 863
   file protection levels 856
   formatting cells 943
   formulas 941
   history, changing 858, 862–863
   macros 946
   merging 860
   Microsoft Excel 97, erasing active 523
   Microsoft Excel 97, saving in 4.0 format 328–331
   Microsoft Excel 97, saving in 5.0/95 format 317–320
   Microsoft Excel 97, saving in Lotus 1-2-3 529–533
   Microsoft Excel 97, saving in Microsoft Excel 97 and 5.0/95 formats 314–317
   Microsoft Excel 97, saving to other file formats 494–496
   Microsoft Excel 97, sharing with Microsoft Excel 4.0 328–331
   Microsoft Excel 97, sharing with Microsoft Excel 5.0/95 314–320
   multiple, opening simultaneously 954
   name references for cells 942
   Normal style 944
   page settings 947
   protecting files 856
   revisions, accepting and rejecting 862
   scenarios for formulas 942
   scenarios, merging 943
   security 856, 946
   shared 858–860
   sharing and change history, protecting 858
   sharing with multiple versions of Microsoft Excel 626–628
   specific areas, protecting 857
   startup folders 953
   styles, copying from one workbook to another 944
   styles, re-using 943
   templates 947
   viewing the entire change history 862
   workgroup reviewing 862–863
workgroup ID (WID) 813
workgroup information files
   converting user-level protected databases 256–259
   default user and group accounts 813

workgroup information files *(continued)*
   joining from previous Microsoft Access versions 257
   Microsoft Access, overview 930
   recreating from previous Microsoft Access versions 258
   storing user and group information 811
   System.mdw, created by Office Setup 257
   workgroup ID (WID) 813
worksheets
   active, removing from memory 523
   auditing 510–512
   charts 944
   linking between Lotus 1-2-3 and Microsoft Excel 97 530–531
   Lotus 1-2-3, exporting to Word 97 788
   Lotus 1-2-3, opening in Microsoft Excel 97 506
   Lotus 1-2-3, saving in Microsoft Excel 97 507
   Lotus 1-2-3, upgrading to Microsoft Excel 97 506–528
   Microsoft Excel 97, exporting to Word 97 787
   Microsoft Excel 97, saving to other file formats 494–496
   multiple Lotus 1-2-3, converting to Microsoft Excel 97 507
   ranges, converting from Microsoft Excel 97 to HTML 695
   scenarios, merging 943
workspace files, Microsoft Excel 97 954
World Wide Web
   ActiveX Resource area address 907
   address for Microsoft FrontPage home page 647
   address for Microsoft Office home page 1094
   address for Microsoft TechNet information 1096
   intranet publishing solutions in Microsoft Access 97 33–36
   intranet publishing solutions in Microsoft Excel 97 36–39
   intranet publishing solutions in Office 97 29–33
   intranet publishing solutions in Outlook 97 39–41
   intranet publishing solutions in PowerPoint 97 41–42
   intranet publishing solutions in Word 97 42–45
   Microsoft Access Developer's Forum address 763
   Network Installation Wizard information 108
   Office 97 compatibility tools 1041
   Office Resource Kit updates 4
   PowerPoint Animation Player Web site 1043
   PowerPoint home page address 563

World Wide Web *(continued)*
  publishing from Microsoft Access 665–693
  publishing from Microsoft Excel 693–703
  publishing from Outlook 704
  publishing from PowerPoint 707–713
  publishing from Word 713
  System Policy Editor information address 1054
wrappers, API 245
Write-Up, Microsoft PowerPoint 97 783
WYSIWYG formatting 509
WYSIWYG, defined as Word formatting rule 591

X

XLM macros, upgrading to Visual Basic 327
XOR encryption routine, upgraded to RC4 in Microsoft Excel 97 856

Y

Yes/No questions for Microsoft Office 97 Setup 121

IMPORTANT—READ CAREFULLY BEFORE OPENING SOFTWARE PACKET(S). By opening the sealed packet(s) containing the software, you indicate your acceptance of the following Microsoft License Agreement.

MICROSOFT LICENSE AGREEMENT
(Resource Kit Companion Disks)

This is a legal agreement between you (either an individual or an entity) and Microsoft Corporation. By opening the sealed software packet(s) you are agreeing to be bound by the terms of this agreement. If you do not agree to the terms of this agreement, promptly return the unopened software packet(s) and any accompanying written materials to the place you obtained them for a full refund.

MICROSOFT SOFTWARE LICENSE

1. GRANT OF LICENSE. Microsoft grants to you the right to install and use copies of the Microsoft software program included with this book (the "SOFTWARE") on computers you own. The SOFTWARE is in "use" on a computer when it is loaded into temporary memory (i.e., RAM) or installed into permanent memory (e.g., hard disk, CD-ROM, or other storage device) of that computer.

2. COPYRIGHT. The SOFTWARE is owned by Microsoft or its suppliers and is protected by United States copyright laws and international treaty provisions. Therefore, you must treat the SOFTWARE like any other copyrighted material (e.g., a book or musical recording). You may not copy the written materials accompanying the SOFTWARE.

3. OTHER RESTRICTIONS. You may not rent or lease the SOFTWARE, but you may transfer the SOFTWARE and accompanying written materials on a permanent basis provided you retain no copies and the recipient agrees to the terms of this Agreement. Except in cases of a permanent transfer, you may not redistribute any portion of the SOFTWARE without the prior written approval of Microsoft. You may not reverse engineer, decompile, or disassemble the SOFTWARE. If the SOFTWARE is an update or has been updated, any transfer must include the most recent update and all prior versions.

DISCLAIMER OF WARRANTY

The SOFTWARE (including instructions for its use) is provided "AS IS" WITHOUT WARRANTY OF ANY KIND. MICROSOFT FURTHER DISCLAIMS ALL IMPLIED WARRANTIES INCLUDING WITHOUT LIMITATION ANY IMPLIED WARRANTIES OF MERCHANTABILITY OR OF FITNESS FOR A PARTICULAR PURPOSE OR AGAINST INFRINGEMENT. THE ENTIRE RISK ARISING OUT OF THE USE OR PERFORMANCE OF THE SOFTWARE AND DOCUMENTATION REMAINS WITH YOU.

IN NO EVENT SHALL MICROSOFT, ITS AUTHORS, OR ANYONE ELSE INVOLVED IN THE CREATION, PRODUCTION, OR DELIVERY OF THE SOFTWARE BE LIABLE FOR ANY DAMAGES WHATSOEVER (INCLUDING, WITHOUT LIMITATION, DAMAGES FOR LOSS OF BUSINESS PROFITS, BUSINESS INTERRUPTION, LOSS OF BUSINESS INFORMATION, OR OTHER PECUNIARY LOSS) ARISING OUT OF THE USE OF OR INABILITY TO USE THE SOFTWARE OR DOCUMENTATION, EVEN IF MICROSOFT HAS BEEN ADVISED OF THE POSSIBILITY OF SUCH DAMAGES. BECAUSE SOME STATES/COUNTRIES DO NOT ALLOW THE EXCLUSION OR LIMITATION OF LIABILITY FOR CONSEQUENTIAL OR INCIDENTAL DAMAGES, THE ABOVE LIMITATION MAY NOT APPLY TO YOU.

U.S. GOVERNMENT RESTRICTED RIGHTS

The SOFTWARE and documentation are provided with RESTRICTED RIGHTS. Use, duplication, or disclosure by the Government is subject to restrictions as set forth in subparagraph (c)(1)(ii) of The Rights in Technical Data and Computer Software clause at DFARS 252.227-7013 or subparagraphs (c)(1) and (2) of the Commercial Computer Software — Restricted Rights 48 CFR 52.227-19, as applicable. Manufacturer is Microsoft Corporation/One Microsoft Way/Redmond, WA 98052-6399.

If you acquired this product in the United States, this Agreement is governed by the laws of the State of Washington.

Should you have any questions concerning this Agreement, or if you desire to contact Microsoft Press for any reason, please write: Microsoft Press/One Microsoft Way/Redmond, WA 98052-6399.

05/06/96 32100017.DOC

Register Today!

Return this
Microsoft® Office 97 Resource Kit
registration card for
a Microsoft Press® catalog

U.S. and Canada addresses only. Fill in information below and mail postage-free. Please mail only the bottom half of this page.

1-57231-329-3A   **MICROSOFT® OFFICE 97 RESOURCE KIT**   *Owner Registration Card*

_____

NAME

_____

INSTITUTION OR COMPANY NAME

_____

ADDRESS

_____

CITY   STATE   ZIP

Microsoft® Press
Quality Computer Books

For a free catalog of
Microsoft Press® products, call
1-800-MSPRESS

BUSINESS REPLY MAIL
FIRST-CLASS MAIL   PERMIT NO. 53   BOTHELL, WA

POSTAGE WILL BE PAID BY ADDRESSEE

NO POSTAGE
NECESSARY
IF MAILED
IN THE
UNITED STATES

MICROSOFT PRESS REGISTRATION
MICROSOFT® OFFICE 97 RESOURCE KIT
PO BOX 3019
BOTHELL WA 98041-9946